Schondorf

# LABOR RELATIONS LAW IN THE PUBLIC SECTOR

## Cases and Materials

### Second Edition

CONTEMPORARY LEGAL EDUCATION SERIES

# Labor Relations Law in the Public Sector

CASES AND MATERIALS

Second Edition

**HARRY T. EDWARDS**
Professor of Law
University of Michigan

**R. THEODORE CLARK, JR.**
Partner
Seyfarth, Shaw, Fairweather &
Geraldson, Chicago, Illinois

**CHARLES B. CRAVER**
Professor of Law
University of California
Davis

THE BOBBS-MERRILL COMPANY, INC.
PUBLISHERS
INDIANAPOLIS • NEW YORK • CHARLOTTESVILLE, VIRGINIA

# Special Dedication to Russell A. Smith

We dedicate this Second Edition to Russell A. Smith, who participated in the preparation of the First Edition. Russ Smith has significantly influenced the development of labor law during the past three decades. As a distinguished scholar, he has written seminal articles concerning various topics of importance. Anyone even casually acquainted with labor relations law has undoubtedly had occasion to be edified by his articulate and thoughtful style. In addition to his innumerable law review discourses, Russ Smith has substantially contributed to the fundamental understanding of labor law through the compilation of three widely used casebooks: Labor Relations Law; Collective Bargaining and Labor Arbitration; and Labor Relations Law in the Public Sector.

Russ Smith has also made Herculean contributions to labor law through his public service activities. For over twenty-five years he has been a nationally respected labor arbitrator, and he is a past-president of the National Academy of Arbitrators. He served as a public member of the Wage Stabilization Board for Region VI-B from 1951 to 1953. He was Vice-Chairman of the Presidential Railroad Commission from 1960 until 1962, and Chairman of Governor Romney's Advisory Committee on Public Employee Unionism during 1966 and 1967. Since 1954 he has served on the Atomic Energy Labor-Management Relations Panel. He was also an original member of the Florida Public Employees Relation Commission. He has similarly contributed to numerous Bar Association committees and to various other public commissions.

Although Russ Smith has made invaluable contributions to labor law as an exemplary scholar and through his generous public service endeavors, we must note that our lives have been most personally enriched through his work as a law professor at the University of Michigan. All three of us were privileged to have had Russ Smith as a law school mentor. Through his patient but demanding style, he inculcated in his students a quest for excellence. All who have been fortunate to know Russ Smith have been impressed by his soft-spoken modesty and his heart-warming compassion. So many of us have additionally been blessed by his selfless beneficence.

As we publish this Second Edition, we respectfully pay tribute to the person who has so significantly influenced our lives, and the lives of so many others, and we hope that our final product is consistent with the high standard Russ Smith endeavored to establish through his contribution to the First Edition.

*Harry T. Edwards*
*R. Theodore Clark, Jr.*
*Charles B. Craver*

# Preface to Second Edition

The most significant developments in public sector labor relations law since the First Edition pertain to the administrative and judicial explication of the bargaining obligations imposed upon governmental negotiators and to the legal enforcement of collective bargaining agreements. The Second Edition incorporates these major changes and updates all of the other areas. Nonetheless, the basic organizational structure of the book remains largely intact, in the belief that it has proved to constitute a logical and practical arrangement of the material. We plan to continue our practice of publishing an annual supplement, so that the book will be up-to-date at the beginning of each school year.

One important change in coverage should be noted. Since the publication of the First Edition, there has been a veritable explosion in the law affecting equal employment opportunity, most notably under Title VII of the Civil Rights Act of 1964. As a consequence, we have concluded that it is no longer possible to provide adequate treatment of this topic in a book dealing generally with public sector labor relations law. Employment discrimination law is now the focus of several entire casebooks (*e.g.*, A. SMITH, EMPLOYMENT DISCRIMINATION LAW (Bobbs-Merrill 1978)), and many law schools appropriately explore that expansive subject in a separate course. We have thus decided to limit our coverage of employment discrimination to those cases arising under the United States Constitution, *i.e.*, primarily under the Fifth and Fourteenth Amendments. There is no inclusion of material pertaining to Title VII, the Equal Pay Act, Executive Order 11246, or other similar enactments.

This casebook contains more material than would normally be covered in a two or even three hour course. However, we believe that each teacher should have the opportunity for personal selection. One may consider the development of the collective bargaining obligation to be of primary importance, while another may wish to concentrate upon the rights and duties which exist once a bargaining representative has been selected. Both should find ample material to satisfy their pedagogical objectives.

We must finally express our appreciation to those students who served as research assistants during the preparation of this revision: Charles R. Calleros, Deborah E. Driggs, Siona D. Windsor and Lynne Darcy.

*Ann Arbor, Michigan*
*Chicago, Illinois*
*Davis, California*
*June, 1979*

*Harry T. Edwards*
*R. Theodore Clark, Jr.*
*Charles B. Craver*

# Preface to First Edition

Several premises underlie the preparation and offering of the materials contained in this volume. The first is that public sector "unionization" and collective bargaining represent the most important development in "labor relations" since the post-Wagner Act period of the 1930s and 1940s. This significance derives both from the sheer magnitude and success of organizing efforts in the public sector and from its major impacts on the management of governmental affairs and public employees at all levels of government—federal, state and local.

During the past decade, dramatic changes have occurred in the body of relevant public sector law, as was true in the private sector in the earlier era. These changes have both contributed to and resulted from public sector unionization. While labor relations law in the public sector has naturally drawn heavily on private sector precepts and models, it has also involved major departures, in response to numerous problems peculiar to the public sector. These are not only substantive. In contrast with the preemptive "federalization" in the private sector, the most important body of public sector labor relations law is state and local. Thus, there are wide variations, resting on differing judgmental evaluations and determinations of public policy. Indeed, the states have proven to be "laboratories" for socio-political experimentation in the development of the law in this area.

In our judgment, a law school curriculum is incomplete which does not afford students the opportunity to examine in some depth the parameters, important variations and problems of public policy embodied in this area of the law. The traditional law school Labor Law curriculum has given primary attention to the private sector, and the typical Labor Law "casebook" reflects this fact. It is quite apparent now, however, that adequate treatment of both private and public sectors is not feasible in a single volume. Hence a basic objective has been to provide a separate set of teaching materials for use in law schools and in other educational contexts. We have also sought to achieve a kind of approach and treatment of the relevant materials which will be of interest and value to those directly concerned on a working basis with public sector labor relations (lawyers, administrators, officials of labor organizations and public employees).

We have not sought to treat many of the obviously important problems relating to collective bargaining techniques, substantive collective bargaining provisions or the numerous practical aspects of labor relations, except to the extent these matters are affected or influenced by the applicable legal structure or rule. In many of these areas, the law does have significant relevance. But is has not seemed to us to be feasible to attempt to deal fully, in a single volume, with the process of collective bargaining or with the more practical aspects of administering labor agreements. In dealing with collective bargaining, therefore, we concentrate on the legal framework and not on specific techniques of collective negotiations or contract administration.

Although the body of "law" in the public sector is now substantial, it is still in the formative stage. As a consequence, we have sought to supplement the judicial decisions reported herein with numerous excerpts from other publications and with substantial text and note material written by the editors. It is our hope that this textual material, much of which has been written by some of the outstanding scholars and practitioners in the field, will raise significant policy questions for consideration in connection with the proper course of the development of labor relations law in the public sector.

The original footnote numbers from judicial opinions have been retained and bracketed. The editors' footnotes are numbered consecutively within each chapter. For the future, we plan to provide annual softbound supplements so that the work will be up-to-date at the start of each school year.

Our thanks to the following students who served as research assistants during the preparation of this volume: Donald Anderson, Zachary Fasman, Dianne Fraser, and Richard Moon. We are also especially indebted to Miss Patt Alfs and Miss Ruth Iverson, who toiled tirelessly to type the final manuscript.

Mr. Clark wishes to thank his wife, Sandy and children, David, Sarah and Steven; Professor Edwards wishes to thank his wife, Becky and children, Brent and Michelle; and Professor Smith wishes to thank his wife Berta — their patience, faith and encouragement helped to make possible the contribution of each of us.

<table>
<tr><td>Chicago, Illinois</td><td>R. Theodore Clark, Jr.</td></tr>
<tr><td>Ann Arbor, Michigan</td><td>Harry T. Edwards</td></tr>
<tr><td>Ann Arbor, Michigan</td><td>Russell A. Smith</td></tr>
<tr><td>June, 1973</td><td></td></tr>
</table>

# Summary Table of Contents

# Table of Contents

PRELIM

# Table of Cases

Principal cases are those with page references in italics

# Chapter 1

# PUBLIC SECTOR UNIONISM—ORIGINS AND PERSPECTIVES

## A. AN HISTORICAL SURVEY

## 1. GENERALLY

**PROJECT: COLLECTIVE BARGAINING AND POLITICS IN PUBLIC EMPLOYMENT, 19 U.C.L.A. L. Rev. 887, 893-96 (1972)†**

Unionism among government employees began in the 1830's, when mechanics, carpenters and other craftsmen employed by the federal government joined craft unions which already existed to serve those employed by private industry. The natural affinity among skilled craftsmen overcame the differences between public and private employ, and encouraged public employees to join the unions.[1] Within ten years, the embryonic public employee movement began to assert itself, presenting employers across the country with demands for a shorter work day.[2] Private trade unions had already adopted this demand, encouraging their public sector brethren to follow suit.[3] Private sector employers had agreed to a ten hour work day in 1835, and ultimately public employers also acquiesced, not necessarily because they sanctioned union-type activity on the part of their employees, but rather because they competed with private industry for the same workers, and thus had to ensure the availability of their labor supply. Undoubtedly, however, union activities by public employees had some effect in gaining concessions by the government. Moreover, private sector employees, having won their own battle, assisted public employees in applying pressure on local governmental units,[4] and in most cases these combined efforts contributed to the change in policy by the public employers.[5]

While state and local government employees found relative success in union activity, workers in federal employ had less favorable results. Their employers were department heads who were divorced from popular pressure. Moreover, most of the federal artisans and craftsmen were employed by the War and Navy

---

† Copyright © 1972 by The Regents of the University of California. Reprinted by permission.

[1] *See* M. MOSKOW, COLLECTIVE BARGAINING IN PUBLIC EMPLOYMENT 29-30 (1969). . . . According to Moskow, the reasons for the affinity among craftsmen were that they "received the same training, associated socially and moved interchangeably between public and private sector jobs." *Id.*

[2] S. SPERO, GOVERNMENT AS EMPLOYER 77 (1948) [hereinafter cited as SPERO].

[3] *Id.*

[4] In Philadelphia, for example, the ten-hour work day was adopted by the city council after a large demonstration involving privately employed artisans who were joined by a great number of public workers. *See* 6 J.R. COMMONS, DOCUMENTARY HISTORY OF AMERICAN INDUSTRIAL SOCIETY 41-42 (1918).

[5] SPERO, *supra* note 2, at 77. Most strike and pressure activity engaged in during this period was by private sector unions acting on behalf of their government-employed members. Public employees did not have their own union, nor was the right of public employees to organize officially recognized by public officials. Thus, where the ten-hour work day movement was unsuccessful in private industry, the public officials of the same area were able to maintain their own resistance. *Id.*

Departments, which were run by military officers whose jobs were unaffected by public opinion. In the face of unalterable resistance by their employers, the federal workers resorted to the strike; in 1836, workers at the Washington, D.C. Naval Shipyard walked off the job. The strike continued for several weeks without any sign of ending, until finally, as had occurred many times at the local level the previous year, a mass demonstration involving strikers and their comrades from private sector organizations confronted President Jackson. The President yielded, establishing the shorter work day for federal employees.

In succeeding years, public employees maintained their status as secondary characters in the struggles of the labor movement. Any benefits secured by these employees generally resulted from the fact that the private sector labor union in their particular industry had already secured such benefits. Public employees benefitted from the fact that public employers adopted the policy of making pay rates and labor standards conform to those prevailing in private employment in the surrounding area.[6]

Until the 1880's, there were few organizations primarily for public employees; indeed, the trade union movement as a whole was just recovering from the Great Panic of 1873. However, with the return of prosperity, a substantial number of public employee organizations were formed. These organizations, which were called associations, were formed primarily for benevolent purposes, and thus they did not join in the renewed militancy of the labor movement which occurred in the late 1800's.[7] One result of the relatively docile attitude of these associations was that the great labor activities of the two decades preceding the twentieth century, which brought labor in the United States to a position of great importance, occurred virtually without the participation of government workers. Perhaps the alienation of government workers from the mainstream of the labor movement resulted from the fact that militant activity in government employment was not essential, since public employers usually followed private industry job standards; if improvements secured by private sector unions would be granted to public employees without any effort on the part of their own unions, there was virtually no need for a strong, independent bargaining organization.

This situation remained static until well into the twentieth century. However, with the inflationary trend that preceded World War I, state and local government employees began to show an interest in affiliating with the private sector union movement. Significant progress in organizing public employees was stopped, however, in 1919, when the Boston police strike occurred. The great public opposition which resulted from that incident wiped out the progress of

---

[6] *See, e.g.,* Act of July 16, 1862, ch. 184, 12 Stat. 587, *amending* Act of December 21, 1861, ch. 1, § 8, 12 Stat. 330:

> [T]he hours of labor and the rates of wages of the employees in the navy yards shall conform as nearly as is consistent with the public interest with those of private establishments in the immediate vicinity of the respective yards. . . .

This policy of making government employment standards conform with those in private industry was reversed by President Van Buren. Under his direction the foundation was laid for a government employment policy which later became the leader in setting labor standards that were followed by private employers; rather than vice versa. SPERO, *supra* note 2, at 83-84.

[7] . . . "Benevolent" purposes included such goals as the upkeep of morale through association-sponsored social functions. Sometimes associations were formed primarily to take advantage of group insurance benefits. . . . In any event, activity was generally restrained and little, if any, pressure was exerted on public employers by the associations on their members' behalf.

public employee unionization for several years; only in the great labor upsurge of the 1930's did public employees begin to take renewed interest in labor organizations.

In 1936, the American Federation of Labor (AFL) founded the first national union for state and local government employees — the American Federation of State, County and Municipal Employees (AFSCME).[8] At the same time, all types of government employees began joining organizations comprised principally of workers of their own occupation; teachers, firemen and policemen being among the first to organize. But despite these developments unionization in the public sector progressed slowly, and not until the 1960's did organized public employees become a prominent national labor force. . . .

## NOTES

1. Although widescale organization of public employees is a relatively recent phenomenon, some groups of public employees have been organized for decades. For example, the Illinois Supreme Court in Fursman v. Chicago, 278 Ill. 318, 116 N.E. 158 (1917), noted that of the

. . . more than 7,000 teachers employed by the board of education of the city of Chicago . . . more than 3,500 of these teachers have been and are members of the Chicago Teachers' Federation, which is affiliated with a federation of trade unions; that the Chicago Teachers' Federation is a corporation not for profit organized on April 9, 1898 . . .; that in November, 1902, the Chicago Teachers' Federation became and has since continued to be affiliated with the Chicago Federation of Labor; . . . that in 1914 members of the Chicago Teachers' Federation affiliated with the American Federation of Labor. . . .

2. Among the many useful books and articles examining the history of public sector unionism are S. SPERO, GOVERNMENT AS EMPLOYER (1948); Rosenblum & Steinbach, *Federal Employee Labor Relations: From the "Gag Rule" to Executive Order 11491,* 59 Ky. L.J. 833 (1971); Klaus, The Right of Public Employees to Organize — In Theory and in Practice (New York City Dep't of Labor Serial No. L.R. 1, March 1955).

The history of collective bargaining in New York City has been the subject of several books and articles. *See generally* Cook, *Public Employee Bargaining in New York City,* 9 IND. REL. 246 (1970); Russo, *Management's View of the New York City Experience,* in ACAD. POL. SCI. PROC., Vol. 30, at 81 (1970); R. HORTON, MUNICIPAL LABOR RELATIONS IN NEW YORK CITY: LESSONS OF THE LINDSAY-WAGNER YEARS (1973). For a critical review of the latter book by the Executive Director of District Council 37 of the American Federation of the State, County, and Municipal Employees, see Gotbaum, Book Review, THE NEW LEADER, May 14, 1973, at 21.

## REHMUS, LABOR RELATIONS IN THE PUBLIC SECTOR, Paper prepared for the 3rd World Congress, International Industrial Relations Association, London, England (Sept. 3-7, 1973)†

*Scope of Public Employment*

Public service is the most rapidly growing major sector of employment in the United States. In the last 30 years, public employment has tripled. . . .

[8] . . . By this time, the federal service was already well-organized — particularly the Post Office Department. The first national union composed solely of government employees to receive an AFL charter was the National Federation of Post Office Clerks, founded in 1906. Unionism outside the Post Office was also well established with the foundation of the National Federation of Federal Employees in 1917 and, later, the American Federation of Government Employees, chartered by the AFL when the NFFE withdrew from the parent organization in 1935.

† Reprinted by permission of the Institute of Labor and Industrial Relations.

Part of this dramatic increase in public employment can be attributed simply to population growth, necessitating a proportional increase in publicly provided services. More fundamental to growth than simple demographic change, however, have been increases in demand for new services, shifts from private to public provision of certain kinds of service, and advances in technology which have intensified the need for new levels of existing public services. Ever since the Great Depression of the 1930's, United States citizens have expected government to provide more and more service for more and more people. As an example, provision for social welfare services to the poor and those too young and too old to work has created many new public jobs. At state and local levels of government, education, health care, the public highway system and police and fire protection are the largest sources of employment. At the federal level, the government's role in the international arena has steadily increased as the United States has become more and more involved in military assistance and economic aid throughout the world.

This growth of government service has not been steady or equal at all levels of government in the United States federal system. Any consideration of public employment, and public employee labor relations within each, must distinguish between three primary levels of government — federal, state, and local — as well as the large postal and educational subsections of federal and local government. Each level of government has specific areas of administrative authority and service responsibility which are in turn affected by specific constituency demands. Each of these levels of government has its own laws regulating public employer-employee labor relations.

. . . .

### Background of Public Employee Labor Relations

Workers in the industrial private sector in the United States were given the statutory right to organize and bargain collectively in the 1930's. By 1960, approximately 30 percent of all nonagricultural private sector employees were represented by unions. Yet by this same date there was practically no unionization in the public sector other than in the traditionally-organized postal service and in a few other isolated situations.

The reasons for the delay in union organization of employees in the public sector in the United States are complex. In part they stem from certain philosophical ideas long prevalent in the nation. Traditional concepts of sovereignty asserted that government is and should be supreme, hence immune from contravening forces and pressures such as that of collective bargaining. Related to this concept was that of the illegality of delegation of sovereign power. This assertion was that public decision-making could only be done by elected or appointed public officials, whose unilateral and complete discretion was therefore unchallengeable.

More practical considerations also delayed the advent of public employee unionism in the United States. The private sector unions and their international federations were fully occupied in trying to increase the extent of organization in the private sector. They had neither the money nor energy to turn to the public sector until the 1960's. Equally or more importantly, public employees were not generally dissatisfied with their terms and conditions of employment and therefore, except in isolated cases, did not press for collective bargaining rights. Though the wages and salaries of public employees in the United States had traditionally lagged slightly behind comparable private sector salaries, the greater fringe benefits and job security associated with public employment were traditionally thought to be adequate compensation.

By the late 1950's and early 1960's several of these practical considerations which had delayed public employee unionism had disappeared. Moreover, new factors came into play that are difficult to assess as to sequence or relative importance, but in total added to a new militancy. Change increasingly became endemic in American society as more and more groups, including public employees, found it commonplace to challenge the established order. Some public employees were made less secure by organizational and technological changes as government came under pressure to reduce tax increases and therefore turned to devices to increase efficiency and lower unit labor costs. Public employee wages and salaries began to lag further behind those in the unionized private sector as the post-war inflationary spiral continued. The private sector international unions saw the large and growing employment in the non-union public sector as a fertile alternative which might substitute for their failure after 1956 to increase membership steadily in the private sector. Finally, many observers of public employment both in and out of government began strongly and publicly to question the logic behind governmentally-protected collective bargaining in the private sector and government's complete failure to grant similar privileges and protections in the public sector.

By the 1960's these practical challenges to the traditional arguments of sovereignty and illegal delegation of powers came to be seen as overriding in a number of government jurisdictions. The City of New York, the school board of that same city, and the State of Wisconsin gave modified collective bargaining rights to their public employees. Most importantly, in 1962 President Kennedy by executive order gave federal employees a limited version of the rights that private employees had received 30 years before. These seminal breakthroughs in granting some form of bargaining right to public employees led increasingly to similar kinds of state legislation, particularly in the more industrialized states. Today over 30 American states have granted some form of collective bargaining rights to some or all of their public employees. President Nixon in two subsequent executive orders has expanded and clarified the bargaining rights of federal employees. . . .

## NOTE

In recommending that federal employees be affirmatively granted the right to join and participate in employee organizations and to bargain collectively, President Kennedy's Task Force referred to the following statement in ABA Section of Labor Relations Law, REPORT OF COMMITTEE ON LABOR RELATIONS OF GOVERNMENTAL EMPLOYEES 89, 90 (1955):

> A government which imposes upon other employers certain obligations in dealing with their employees may not in good faith refuse to deal with its own public servants on a reasonably similar favorable basis, modified, of course, to meet the exigencies of the public service. It should set the example for industry by being perhaps more considerate than the law requires of private enterprise.

**COMMITTEE ON ECONOMIC DEVELOPMENT, IMPROVING MAN-AGEMENT OF THE PUBLIC WORK FORCE: THE CHALLENGE TO STATE AND LOCAL GOVERNMENT 28-31, 33 (1978)**

### TRENDS IN PUBLIC EMPLOYMENT

From 1955 to 1976, state and local government employment grew at an average annual rate of 4.8 percent, reaching 9,514,463 full-time and 2,654,727 part-time employees in 1976. States and localities now employ more than four times as many people as the federal government and account for 1 in 7 nonagricultural workers in the United States. [See Figures 1 and 2.] This expansion in employment coincided with the growth in budgets and programs. (In contrast, during the same period, the federal government's budget grew substantially, but its employment remained reasonably stable.) State and local purchases of goods and services increased from 8.4 percent of GNP in 1957 to 13.2 percent in 1977. In the early 1970s, that rate of growth slowed; and in 1977, it increased only 1.1 percent in real terms, the smallest annual increase since 1951. This slowdown reflected a combination of declines and slower growth in the demand for some public services, especially primary and secondary education. It also reflected the fact that the growth of state and local revenues also slowed in response to the economic recession of the early to mid-1970s. Although the state-local sector will continue to grow, it is unlikely in the near future to experience the rapid growth characteristic of the 1950s and 1960s. In

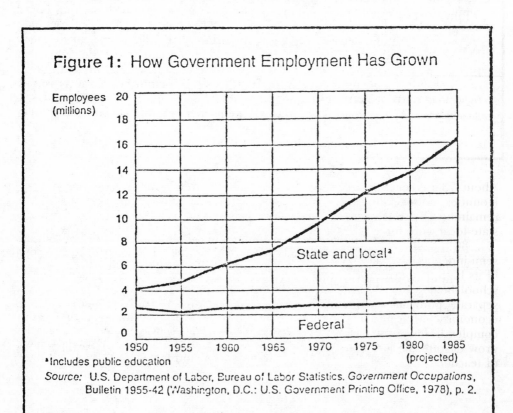

Figure 1: How Government Employment Has Grown

Employees (millions)

[a]Includes public education

Source: U.S. Department of Labor, Bureau of Labor Statistics. *Government Occupations*, Bulletin 1955-42 (Washington, D.C.: U.S. Government Printing Office, 1978), p. 2.

some services, employment levels may actually decline. Nevertheless, the magnitude of employment already attained and the importance of the services provided are themselves significant.

**Figure 2:** Government and Private Employment in the United States, 1957 and 1977 (millions)

| | 1957 | 1977 | Percent Increase |
|---|---|---|---|
| Federal government | 2.2 | 2.7 | 22.7 |
| State and local government | 5.4 | 12.5 | 131.5 |
| Private sector | 45.3 | 66.9 | 47.7 |
| Total nonagricultural employment | 52.9 | 82.1 | 55.2 |

*Note:* Data are for wage and salary workers in nonagricultural establishments.

*Source: Economic Report of the President* (Washington, D.C.: U.S. Government Printing Office, January 1978).

About 73 percent of state and local employees work for local governments (counties, municipalities, townships, school districts, and special districts); the remaining 27 percent work for state governments (see Figure 3). Nearly half the state-local work force is employed in primary, secondary, and higher education . . .; 80 percent of those in education are employed by independent or semi-independent school districts. Thus, education stands apart not only because of its high proportions of expenditure and employment but also because many school boards are elected, levy their own taxes, and consequently constitute separate political-administrative systems with their own characteristics. The economic, political, and employment problems in education are all the more complex because the number of graduates qualified to teach has continued to grow despite the fact that declining student enrollments have required layoffs of teachers.

**Figure 3:** State and Local Government Employment,
by Type of Government, October 1976

| Function | Employees (Full time and Part time) | |
|---|---|---|
| | Number (thousands) | Percent |
| Total | 12,169 | 100.0 |
| State | 3,343 | 27.5 |
| Local | 8,826 | 72.5 |
| County | 1,600 | 13.1 |
| Municipal | 2,442 | 20.1 |
| Township | 401 | 3.3 |
| School districts | 3,985 | 32.5 |
| Special districts | 398 | 3.3 |

*Source:* U.S. Department of Commerce, Bureau of the Census, *Public Employment in 1976* (Washington, D.C.: U.S. Government Printing Office, 1977), p. 3.

The nature of the public work force has been changing along with the nature of the American work force as a whole. Educational levels have increased; larger numbers of women and young people have sought and found gainful employment; consciousness regarding racial and sexual discrimination in employment has been heightened; widespread experience with severe economic deprivation is more remote; the desire for job satisfaction has risen; and the willingness to accept traditional concepts of authority and efficiency has declined. Of course, the magnitude of these changes varies from place to place and among age and educational groups. Nevertheless, their overall impact should not be underestimated. Managers are finding it necessary to rethink traditional notions of supervision and administration.

The state-local government work force has also been rapidly organizing. Between 1968 and 1976, membership in unions and employee associations nearly doubled, from 2.5 million to 4.7 million, or 49.8 percent of full-time workers. (See Figure 4.) The most highly organized professions are teaching and fire fighting, with 69 percent and 72 percent of full-time employees, respectively, belonging to unions or associations. Teachers also represent the largest occupational group of organized public employees; in 1974, the National Education Association had a membership of 1,470,000, and the American Federation of Teachers had a membership of 444,000. (In contrast,

**Figure 4:** State and Local Government Organized Employees, by Function, October 1976 (thousands)

| Function | Number of Full-Time Employees | Percent of All Full-Time Employees per Function | Number of. Organized Full-Time Employees | Percent of All Organized Full-Time Employees per Function |
|---|---|---|---|---|
| Total | 9,514 | 100.0 | 4,737 | 49.8 |
| Education | 4,527 | 47.6 | 2,637 | 58.3 |
| Highways | 542 | 5.7 | 240 | 44.3 |
| Public welfare | 335 | 3.5 | 138 | 41.3 |
| Hospitals | 910 | 9.6 | 360 | 39.5 |
| Police protection | 531 | 5.6 | 288 | 54.3 |
| Fire protection | 210 | 2.2 | 151 | 71.6 |
| Sanitation other than sewerage | 119 | 1.2 | 59 | 49.2 |
| All other functions | 2,341 | 24.6 | 864 | 36.9 |

Source: U.S. Bureau of the Census, *Labor-Management Relations in State and Local Governments: 1976*, State and Local Government Special Studies no. 88 (Washington, D.C.: U.S. Government Printing Office, 1978), p. 9.

approximately 28.3 percent of all workers in nonagricultural establishments belonged to labor organizations in 1976.)[9]

Unionization has brought collective bargaining to government. By 1976, there were bargaining units in 41 state governments and 9,064 local governments, covering a total of 4,353,589 employees, or 46 percent of the full-time state-local work force. Most big-city governments now bargain formally with their employees, although there are important exceptions, such as Chicago. Twenty-eight states have statutes providing for collective bargaining, six prohibit it, and three provide for meet-and-confer relationships. Among those states and localities that do bargain collectively, the laws, procedures, and traditions vary widely.

## ADVISORY COMMISSION ON INTERGOVERNMENTAL RELATIONS, LABOR-MANAGEMENT POLICIES FOR STATE AND LOCAL GOVERNMENT 5-10 (1969)

. . . .

### Public Employee Organizations

. . . .

Most public employee organizations at the State, county, and municipal levels may be divided into three major categories. The professional associations include — among others — employee groups for teachers and school administrators, nurses, and social and welfare workers. The craft unions primarily consist of single occupational groups of employees — while the industrial type of union or association cuts across broad occupational categories in various departments and sometimes in whole governmental jurisdictions.

*Professional Associations.* Professional associations represent a great variety of professional and semi-professional public employees at the State and local levels. All of them, however, are concerned with certification, training, codes of ethics, the right to exclude nonprofessionals from their organization, and the economic and social welfare of their members. Some of them are hardly distinguishable from unions with respect to employer relations and other related activities.

Among the largest is the National Education Association (NEA) with approximately one million members. Public school teachers constitute approximately 85 percent of the total membership of NEA with supervisors, principals, administrators and other school specialists accounting for the

---

[9] U.S. Department of Labor, Bureau of Labor Statistics, "Labor Union and Employee Association Membership, 1976," *News* (Washington, D.C., 1977). The number of organized employees in the private sector increased from 22.0 million in 1968 to 24.4 million in 1974 and actually dropped slightly to 24.0 million in 1976. The proportion of government workers in all labor organizations in the United States increased from 17.5 percent in 1968 to 22.1 percent in 1974. Because the number of federal workers in labor organizations actually declined during those years (from 1.4 million to 1.3 million), these statistics reflect the growth in state and local unionization. *Directory of National Unions and Employee Associations, 1975*, p. 70.

remaining 15 percent. This policy underscores a major difference between the NEA and the American Federation of Teachers, which limits its membership only to classroom teachers. Members of each of the 50 NEA State affiliates and most of the 8,000 local associations include teachers, supervisors, and administrators. At the same time, the State affiliates enjoy a relatively high degree of autonomy in membership policies as well as in other matters.

The NEA in its early history emphasized activities centering on better schools and improved professional status of teachers. It frowned upon any overt activity of State and local affiliates lobbying for higher teachers' salaries and displayed a singular lack of interest in affiliating with the labor movement. Salary discussions and other "bread and butter" concerns were deemed unprofessional and labor unions were considered special interest groups.

In the 1960's the NEA affiliates in large cities across the country began what has since amounted to a complete about-face. Prompted in part by classroom teacher gains of the AFL-CIO American Federation of Teachers in the large urban systems, NEA's doctrine of passive professionalism came under mounting criticism. At its 1961 convention, the Association for the first time called for discussions between local boards of education and the teaching profession for the purpose of achieving common consent on matters of interest to its members. While the word negotiation was not used, the resolution declared that a board of review should be established to resolve differences arising between local affiliates and boards of education. By 1962, however, the NEA began to use the term "professional negotiations" and in that year passed a landmark resolution establishing a system of "professional sanctions." A year later, the NEA issued guidelines for "professional negotiations" in an effort to distinguish its negotiating procedures from the traditional bargaining approaches of the private sector labor movement. Third party intervention in the forms of mediation and fact finding were advocated, but the guidelines opposed the use of a State labor relations or mediation agency to settle disputes, asserting that this mechanism would remove bargaining from "education channels."

The NEA went on record in favor of exclusive recognition in 1965 and issued a revised edition of the guidelines. Until 1967, the Association maintained its traditional disdain for strikes even though prior to that time forms of work stoppages were not uncommon in many local jurisdictions. Professional holidays, for example, were organized in Utah, Oklahoma, and New Jersey during 1964 and 1965. The 1967 NEA convention resolved to support affiliates that strike school systems. Today the Association will provide affiliates with substantial legal and technical services and financial support when strikes occur.

. . . .

Another professional association, the National Association of Social Workers (NASW), was established in 1955 with the merger of several professional groups. As of December 1968, it had an overall membership of slightly over 50,000 including student and private sector worker members. "Bread-and-butter" economic activities are carried on only in a limited way by NASW, but they are a focal point of concern of separate, local social worker unions. The Association, however, has never viewed the latter as a threat to its existence, probably because less than 15 percent of all social welfare workers are unionized. The American Nurses Association is another such professional group with 204,000 members

(1967) or 31 percent of all nurses working in public and private institutions. The ANA is concerned with more than just professional standards. It actively engages in employer discussions and collective bargaining, seeks exclusive recognition, negotiates contracts and agreements, and has, on a few occasions, engaged in walkouts. In the summer of 1968, the ANA removed the clause from its constitution prohibiting strikes.

Another national organization, the Fraternal Order of Police, is independent of labor movement organizations and is the principal professional organization for policemen. FOP does not consider itself a union, although local lodges in some communities engage in collective bargaining, handle grievances and represent the interests of their members to their employer. In general, however, the FOP concentrates on police pension matters and improvement in police working conditions. The Grand Lodge of FOP was organized in 1915 and today claims to have over 620 lodges in 18 States, with a total of 62,600 members.

*Craft-Type Unions.* One of the largest among the craft-type unions is the International Association of Firefighters (IAFF), an affiliate of the AFL-CIO. The organization had its origins in the fraternal and social clubs of the 1880's and today claims that better than 90 percent of the nation's uniformed firemen are enrolled within its membership. In 1935, Association members numbered approximately 26,000. Nearly three decades later, the union claimed 115,000 members. . . . [By 1968] the total came to 131,356. The Association has operated traditionally without written contracts or agreements and adhered loyally to its constitutional ban on strikes. At its 1968 convention, however, the membership removed the fifty-year-old no-strike pledge from its constitution. The union's international president, William Buck, stated:

> . . . certain arbitrary public officials, knowing that we cannot and will not strike — because we voluntarily gave up this right when we were founded — have certainly taken advantage of the professional firefighters across the negotiating table.

Another major public employee "craft" union is the American Federation of Teachers, which affiliated with the old American Federation of Labor in 1919. Their greatest success has been in the large cities . . . with about 80 percent of the Federation's members employed in school systems with an enrollment of 100,000 or more.

Blue collar craft unions also are found frequently at national, State, county and municipal levels. Organization of some of these governmental employees has kept pace with the unionization of the counterpart trades in private industry. International unions active at the State, county, and municipal levels include the International Association of Machinists and Aerospace Workers; International Brotherhood of Teamsters, Chauffeurs, Warehousemen; Service Employees' International Union; United Brotherhood of Carpenters and Joiners of America; United Association of Journeymen and Apprentices of the Plumbing and Pipefitting Industry of the United States and Canada; International Union of Operating Engineers; International Brotherhood of Electrical Workers; International Hod Carriers, Building and Common Laborers' Union; and United Mine Workers. No accurate count, however, is available concerning the number of State and local employees belonging to these craft unions.

. . . .

*Industrial-Type Unions.* The dominant "industrial-type" union at these levels is the American Federation of State, County, and Municipal Employees

(AFSCME), an affiliate of the AFL-CIO. AFSCME traces its ancestry back to 1932 when a small group of Wisconsin State employees formed the Wisconsin State Employees Association and received an AFL charter. A month later, the local had 53 members. Within a year, the organization was exploring the possibility of establishing a national union, but this effort soon generated jurisdictional problems with the American Federation of Government Employees, another AFL affiliate. AFGE's charter from the AFL gave it ill-defined jurisdiction over all government employees, but its organizational activity had been confined almost exclusively to the Federal service. With the emerging threat of a rival national organization, the union's leadership decided to clarify AFGE's position and in 1935 amended its constitution to claim jurisdiction over State and local employees as well as those in the Federal sector.

At that time, the AFL leadership generally was indifferent to the unionization of public employees. Some heads of the older craft unions wanted no part of the public employee field. Yet, the AFL faced another far more difficult problem in 1935: the withdrawal of industrial unions to form the Congress of Industrial Organizations under the leadership of the Mineworker's President, John L. Lewis. The AFL leadership realized that unless the jurisdictional disputes between AFGE and the new organization of State and local employees were resolved, the newly organized CIO might issue a national charter to the ambitious newcomers.

Consequently, the AFL Executive Council promoted an agreement whereby the State and local group would become a semi-autonomous affiliate of AFGE, with its own convention and leadership. In effect, the AFGE would be merely the channel of communication with the parent AFL. The new group then held its first national convention in December 1935 and ratified the agreement. The organization thus formally became the American Federation of State, County, and Municipal Employees, adopted a constitution and elected its own officers.

But the AFGE-AFSCME relationship continued to be competitive. AFGE sought to limit AFSCME organizing to white-collar workers in State and local agencies — a restriction AFSCME would not accept. When AFGE voted in new leadership in 1936, the matter again was placed before the AFL Executive Council, and it finally decided to grant AFSCME independent status.

While the early growth of AFSCME was not impressive, its membership, as of July 1969, had soared to 425,000. It claims — with good reason — to be the fastest growing union in the country. Although two-thirds of its members hold blue collar jobs, its occupational categories range from garbage collectors to zoo keepers, from architects to psychologists, from laborers to lawyers. The Federation's chief aim is to achieve establishment of a system of collective bargaining which produces written agreements. Its basic procedural concerns then center on recognition, bargaining, union security, checkoff, and the use of signed contracts. In recent years, the union's members have not hesitated to strike even in jurisdictions where walk-outs are not permitted. . . .

. . . [AFSCME locals] may represent an entire city or county, or alternatively a particular department, part of a department, or a group of employers in a particular occupational classification which cuts across many departments.

In addition to AFSCME, independent unaffiliated associations of public employees exist in at least 37 State governments and an indeterminate number of local governments. Their membership is drawn from all departments and agencies of these jurisdictions. Nearly all have non-selective enrollment policies and may count as members elected and appointive officials, department heads, supervisors, as well as rank and file workers. At least 14 States have two or more statewide public employee organizations and several associations have local unit affiliates organized on a substate regional basis.

These associations in the past generally have been satisfied with informal recognition by employers, and membership has never been required as a condition of employment. They usually have relied on lobbying to achieve better working conditions and have depended upon civil service procedures rather than on collective negotiations to settle disputes. Their affiliated competitors have frequently referred to them as "company unions."

With the recent passage of public labor-management legislation, however, a good deal of competition has been generated between these independent associations and the affiliated unions, both for membership and exclusive recognition rights. . . . A number of associations at both the State and local levels now are beginning to scrap their traditional passive practices and are adopting a fairly militant stance.

## NOTES

1. The continuing surge in the unionization of public employees is revealed by the rapid growth which many public sector unions and employee organizations have experienced. The membership of six of the major public sector unions and associations as of early 1979 is as follows:

American Federation of Government
    Employees (AFGE) . . . . . . . . . . . . . . . . . . . . . . . . . . . . . . . 260,000
American Federation of State, County and
    Municipal Employees (AFSCME) . . . . . . . . . . . . . . . . . . . . . . . 1,000,000
American Federation of Teachers (AFT) . . . . . . . . . . . . . . . . . . . . . . 500,000
Assembly of Government Employees (AGE) . . . . . . . . . . . . . . . . . . . . 620,000
International Association of
    Fire Fighters (IAFF) . . . . . . . . . . . . . . . . . . . . . . . . . . . . . . 175,000
National Education Association (NEA) . . . . . . . . . . . . . . . . . . . . . . . 1,800,000

Of all the unions in both the private and public sectors that gained 100,000 members or more between 1966 and 1976, the two that showed the greatest percentage increases were the AFT and AFSCME, which registered increases of 257 percent and 167 percent, respectively. U.S. BUREAU OF LABOR STATISTICS, DEP'T OF LABOR, RELEASE NO. 77-771, at 6-7 (Sept. 1977).

2. A survey of union recognition in the federal government released by the United States Civil Service Commission showed that as of November 1977, 58 percent of all executive branch employees (1,197,910) were represented by unions holding exclusive recognition rights. U.S. CIVIL SERV. COMM'N BULL. No. 711-39 (1978), GERR Ref. File 71:201. This is up sharply from the 21 percent of all executive branch employees (excluding postal employees) that were in exclusive bargaining units in 1966, four years after President Kennedy promulgated Executive Order 10988. GERR No. 186, C-1 to C-29 (1967).

At the municipal level, a 1972 Bureau of Labor Statistics study concluded:

Representation of Municipal employees is no longer confined solely to major American cities. In fact, it encompasses a majority of the 2,064 municipalities studied, even towns of 10,000. In total, more than three-fifths of the cities surveyed reported unions and associations within their jurisdictions. . . . These occurred in direct relation to city size. That is, all cities of 1 million or more reported employee organizations, more than 90 percent of cities having populations of one-quarter to 1 million, and over 80 percent of cities of 50,000 to one-quarter million. There was a significant drop in coverage among smaller cities but more than 50 percent noted the presence of organizations. . . .

In the past, efforts to organize were directed toward large cities because of the concentration of workers. In recent years, the focus of organizing drives has shifted toward smaller towns. Aware of successes by unions and associations in large cities, employee associations in smaller towns have pressed for collective bargaining, in addition to their normal fraternal, social, and legislative activities, and have often been successful.

Most cities reporting unions and associations were in the East North Central and Middle Atlantic regions. In both regions, the proportion of cities reporting unions and associations exceeded the national average. This was not unexpected, because these States have strong traditions of unionism in the private sector. However, the highest proportions of cities reporting employee organizations were in New England and the Pacific States, where unions are also common in private industry. California also has a long history of dealing with public employee associations, many of which have now converted to collective bargaining representation. Nelson & Doster, *City Employee Representation and Bargaining Policies*, MONTHLY LAB. REV., November 1972, at 43.

A study jointly prepared by the Department of Commerce and the Department of Labor which was released in 1978 reported that "[t]here were 12,368 State and local governments which engaged in collective negotiations and/or meet and confer discussions with employee organizations as of October 1976 and these governments had 27,418 labor-management agreements with employee organizations in effect as of that time." The report included the following table which provides a summary of the number and percentage of governments with a labor relations policy as of October 1976:

**Governments With a Labor Relations
Policy, by Level and Type of Government**

| Level and type of government | Number of govern- ments | Governments reporting a labor relations policy | |
|---|---|---|---|
| | | Number | Percent |
| Total ........................... | 78,268 | 12,368 | 15.8 |
| State governments ............................ | 50 | 41 | 82.0 |
| Local governments ......................... | 78,218 | 12,327 | 15.8 |
| Counties ................................... | 3,044 | 671 | 22.0 |
| Municipalities ............................. | 18,517 | 2,175 | 11.7 |
| Townships ................................. | 16,991 | 840 | 4.9 |
| Special districts ........................... | 23,885 | 654 | 2.7 |
| School districts ............................ | 15,781 | 7,987 | 50.6 |

U.S. BUREAU OF THE CENSUS, DEP'T OF COMMERCE, & U.S. LABOR-MANAGEMENT SERVICES ADMINISTRATION, STATE AND LOCAL GOVERNMENT SPECIAL STUDIES NO. 88, LABOR-MANAGEMENT RELATIONS IN STATE AND LOCAL GOVERNMENT: 1976, at 1, 2 (1978).

3. For a particularly comprehensive study of public sector unions and associations, see J. STIEBER, PUBLIC EMPLOYEE UNIONISM: STRUCTURE, GROWTH, POLICY (1973). *See generally* U.S. BUREAU OF LABOR STATISTICS, DEP'T OF LABOR, BULL. NO. 1702, MUNICIPAL PUBLIC EMPLOYEE ASSOCIATIONS (1971); Donoian, *The AFGE and the AFSCME: Labor's Hope for the Future?*, 18 LAB. L.J. 727 (1967).

4. For an excellent account of the founding and growth of AFSCME, see L. KRAMER, LABOR'S PARADOX — THE AMERICAN FEDERATION OF STATE, COUNTY, AND MUNICIPAL EMPLOYEES, AFL-CIO (1962). The history of AFGE is traced in J. & L. NEVIN,

AFGE-FEDERAL UNION: THE STORY OF THE AMERICAN FEDERATION OF GOVERNMENT EMPLOYEES (1976).

5. Over the years there has been a fierce and frequently bitter rivalry between the National Education Association (NEA) and the American Federation of Teachers (AFT). For example, in 1966, the President of the NEA categorized the AFT in the following manner:

> The American Federation of Teachers merely serves as a front for organized labor in general, and the Industrial Union Department [of the AFL-CIO] in particular in their drive to unionize white collar workers and professionals in American society. . . .
>
> It is also important that you are aware also of another motivation in this unionizing drive for teachers in particular. This second motivation represents to us one of the most dangerous threats that American education will ever face. . . . [This second motivation] is indoctrination of the pupils and teachers to the labor movement philosophy in order to advance the interests of unionism in this country. BNA WHITE COLLAR REPORT NO. 464, A-4 to A-5 (1966).

In the early 1970's there were signs that the two teacher organizations might merge. At its 1973 convention, the NEA voted in favor of merger talks with the AFT. Subsequently, the AFT executive council stated that it was ready to begin such merger discussions. Although merger discussions took place between October, 1973, and February, 1974, they broke down, primarily on the issue of AFL-CIO membership. As the NEA stated in a press release, "NEA wants teacher unity; AFT wants AFL-CIO membership. The two are not compatible." On the other hand, the AFT blamed the breakoff of discussions on the "unwillingness of the NEA to attempt to work out the problems which separate the two organizations." No merger talks have occurred since 1974 and each organization has since gone its own way. *See generally* M. DONLEY, POWER TO THE TEACHER 141-71 (1976).

Among the many studies of the American Federation of Teachers (AFT) and the National Education Association (NEA) are M. DONLEY, POWER TO THE TEACHER (1976); M. LIEBERMAN & M. MOSKOW, COLLECTIVE NEGOTIATIONS FOR TEACHERS (1966); C. PERRY & W. WILDMAN, THE IMPACT OF NEGOTIATIONS IN PUBLIC EDUCATION: THE EVIDENCE FROM THE SCHOOLS (1970); M. MOSKOW & R. DOHERTY, *United States,* in TEACHER UNIONS AND ASSOCIATIONS 295 (A. Blum ed. 1969). For a critical examination of the AFT, see R. BRAUN, TEACHERS AND POWER (1972). For an excellent article on the development of collective bargaining between the New York City Board of Education and the United Federation of Teachers, see Klaus, *The Evolution of a Collective Bargaining Relationship in Public Education: New York City's Changing Seven-year History,* 67 MICH. L. REV. 1033 (1969).

6. The development of collective bargaining among faculty members at colleges and universities is explored in F. KEMERER & J. BALDRIDGE, UNIONS ON CAMPUS (1975); ACADEMICS AT THE BARGAINING TABLE: EARLY EXPERIENCE (J. Begin ed. 1973); E. DURYEA, R. FISK, & ASSOCIATES, FACULTY UNIONS AND COLLECTIVE BARGAINING (1973); FACULTY BARGAINING IN THE SEVENTIES (T. Tice & G. Holmes eds. 1973); FACULTY POWER: COLLECTIVE BARGAINING ON CAMPUS (T. Tice ed. 1972); *Collective Negotiations in Higher Education: A Symposium,* 1971 WIS. L. REV. 1; Brown, *Professors and Unions: The Faculty Senate: An Effective Alternative to Collective Bargaining in Higher Education,* 12 WM. & MARY L. REV. 252 (1970).

7. In addition to the AFT and the NEA, the American Association of University Professors (AAUP) also seeks to represent college and university faculty members for the purpose of collective bargaining. The AAUP's Statement on Collective Bargaining, GERR No. 478, B-6 to B-7 (1972), states, in relevant part:

> Collective bargaining, in offering a rational and equitable means of distributing resources and of providing recourse for an aggrieved individual, can buttress and complement the sound principles and practices of higher education which the American Association of University Professors has long supported. Where appropriate, therefore, the Association will pursue collective bargaining as a major additional way of realizing its goals in higher education, and it will provide assistance on a selective basis to interested local chapters. . . .

The longstanding programs of the Association are means to achieve a number of basic ends at colleges and universities: the enhancement of academic freedom and tenure; of due process; of sound academic government. Collective bargaining, properly used, is essentially another means to achieve these ends, and at the same time to strengthen the influence of the faculty in the distribution of an institution's economic resources. The implementation of Association-supported principles, reliant upon professional traditions and upon moral suasion, can be effectively supplemented by a collective bargaining agreement and given the force of law.

Commenting on this 1972 statement, the General Secretary of the AAUP, Bertram H. Davis, stated:

The action of the 1972 Annual Meeting did not . . . constitute a total break with the Association's past; it would be inaccurate, however, to state that it was merely another step in an evolution which had begun some seven years earlier. It represented, most particularly, a change in emphasis and attitude, for it was the Association's first decisive affirmation of the view that collective bargaining provides a suitable means to achieve the Association's objectives for higher education. Although there was full recognition that collective bargaining was not the only means to that end and that chapters ought to have complete discretion in deciding whether or not to employ it, there was a clear determination to devote more of the Association's resources to collective bargaining and to give greater assistance, on a selective basis, to chapters seeking exclusive bargaining status. Report of General Secretary Bertram H. Davis to 59th Annual Meeting of AAUP, GERR No. 503, F-1 (1973).

## GOVERNOR'S COMMITTEE ON PUBLIC EMPLOYEE RELATIONS, FINAL REPORT 55-62 (State of New York, March 31, 1966)†

There are at least 8600 governmental employing entities in the State of New York, the employees of which might conceivably desire to exercise the right of association for the purpose of negotiating collectively the terms of their employment and the handling of their grievances. These include 20 State Departments, the State University, 62 cities, 62 counties, 932 towns, 553 villages, 1199 school districts, 53 public authorities, 84 housing authorities, 5540 special districts, an unknown but large number of city departments, and 21 urban renewal agencies. Moreover, many of these entities run special installations (such as hospitals, prisons, etc.), the employees of which have a plausible community of interest in collective representation.

To assume that a single mode of collective participation for the employees of all of these entities can or should be established by state law would exceed the limits of common sense. As a matter of fact, an extensive range of arrangements for that collective participation has developed out of experience in satisfying the interests of not only employees, but also employee organizations, government agency executives and legislative bodies.

It is widely considered, however, that there are basically two models characterizing those arrangements, sometimes referred to as the *Union* model and the *Association* model. . . .

The differences between those two models can be painted with a broad brush. Leaders of particular employee organizations do identify themselves with one or the other model. And when their organizations are competitors with each other for members among the same group of employees, their recruiting appeal

---

† The members of the Committee were George W. Taylor, Chairman, E. Wright Bakke, David L. Cole, John T. Dunlop, and Frederick H. Harbison.

frequently stresses the advantages of the type which they represent. Yet, the problem to which they must adapt their activity in representing public employees is, in many essentials, the same for all employee organizations. It is not surprising, therefore, that over time it becomes harder to distinguish between unions and associations and that each tends to adopt successful practices of the other.

The differences between the two models are normally considered to be related to the following six dimensions:

### A. *The character of the claimed employee-employer unit.*

In the Union model the unit desired is subject to pragmatic determination at the moment, not only in accordance with a community of interests of employees in regard to their sharing of the same conditions of work, the same grievances, the same "boss," the same locality, or the same craft skills, but with regard to a favorable opportunity for organizing them and thus for extending the membership of the organizing union. There is thus a tendency for fragmentized units to appear originally in a number of cases. It is pragmatic opportunity rather than a policy of occupational oriented organizing, however, which predominantly governs their practice.

The unit claimed by those organized on the Association model is also subject to pragmatic organizing strategy considerations, but there is a traditional policy of seeking to represent the employees of more comprehensive units defined by reference to employment in a common-employer unit. . . .

Another dimension of the unit problem has to do with the status level of the members eligible to join the organization. In the Union model supervisors and professional and confidential employees are normally excluded. In the Association model they are normally included.

### B. *Formality of recognition and for what, and for whom.*

The recognition sought ultimately by organizations identified with the Union model is for exclusive representation of all employees of a bargaining unit where the union has been chosen as representative by a majority of the employees. Representation for members only is considered an undesirable second best to be accepted only. until the union has sufficient strength to demand exclusive representation. . . .

The Associations do not differ from the Unions in their predisposition to desire exclusive representation.

The terms of employment about which the two models of organizations negotiate are determined not so much by the policies of the organizations as by the willingness of the executives of the government agencies to negotiate on certain issues. Different executives have different ideas about the scope of issues concerning which they have the discretion to negotiate to a conclusion.

In the case of both Union and Association, however, the kind of representative action for which recognition is sought includes the process of grievance settlement. The expectations of both Associations and Unions concerning what they can negotiate about are limited by the fact that certain terms of employment are mandated by legislative enactment. . . .

Moreover, both the Union and the Association model organizations are subject to the restriction that "nothing in conflict with law and Civil Service rules or benefits" shall be negotiated or made part of a grievance settlement. The tendency of both models, however, is to take the mandated terms as minima, and to negotiate from there. Also, one gets the impression that the Union model organizations stress the amplification of those minima through direct negotiation, and that the Association model organizations have a greater tendency to seek direct legislative modification of the minima.

As experience grows, it is possible that the differences in the two models in regard to the type of recognition sought, for whom, and for what, will be even less significant than in the present. Such predispositions are, after all, not so much a function of what organization leaders want, as a function of what they can expect in view of the possibilities they experience. Those possibilities are constrained by many of the same factors for both of them.

## C. The check off.

Both the Unions and the Associations are interested in and strive to obtain the check off.

## D. Character of participating activity.

The phrase "collective bargaining with management" is frequently used to describe the kind of collective participating activity in which organizations oriented toward the Union model engage. The Association model organization is popularly supposed to accept a more informal type of participation in relations with "management" and to emphasize achievement of results through influencing legislative action. Let us set down several concepts of participating activity in order to see what the reality is at the moment.

1. Discussion of and consultation between the parties followed by ultimately unilateral decision by the executives or the legislative body of the governmental entity involved.
2. Joint study of and negotiation of terms with both parties assuming the desirability of a consensus and mutual agreement.
3. Negotiation of terms on the assumption of the necessity for a joint commitment of the negotiating parties to the terms, but with the necessity to seek approval and the appropriations to implement any agreement from a legislative body.
4. Direct political action before a legislative body in order to acquire statutory confirmation of desired terms.
5. Efforts to obtain a "prevailing rate" arrangement by which legislative authority (and private agreement) is sought to gear wages and benefits to the wages and benefits enjoyed by comparative and relevant groups of employees in private industry.
6. Bargaining with government executives to a mutually acceptable agreement, binding on both parties, both of whom have authoritative discretion to come to such a final and binding agreement, and both of whom have economic power to sustain their veto of any terms to which they do not agree.

A widely-held concept of the two models places the emphasis in the Union model on a demand for the last type of collective participation on the assumption that, in the minds of union leaders, this is the only *real* kind of collective bargaining, as indeed it is considered to be in private industry where the Unions have their longest tradition. The concept of the Association model places the emphasis on the fourth type of collective participation.

These concepts do not correspond with the emphasis which employee organizations actually find it practicable to make in New York State at the present time. Neither is really satisfied with the first type of participation, that is, discussion and consultation before unilateral employer decision. Partly because this is the only kind of collective participation with their "employers" envisioned in public policy proclaimed for State employees and for most local public employees outside of New York City, and partly because of the resistance of public employers to anything but this discussion-and-consultation type participation, many locals both of the Union and the Association type find themselves able to go no further than this. That they go no further arises not from their character or fixed policies, but from the constraints of necessity.

Organizations of both types prefer the second type of negotiations to the first. The second type is distinguished from the first primarily because it involves the assumption that both parties desire to come to a mutually satisfactory consensus.

Practically speaking, the closest approach to "collective bargaining" in the traditional sense that either model of organization can come to in the case of political entities is the third type of collective participation. This, of course, is due to the fact that legislative or Civil Service Commission approval must be obtained for negotiated terms related to those legislatively mandated and in which legislative appropriations must be obtained to implement money terms. Both types of organizations in the public sector can be expected to perfect their strategies and tactics along these lines as long as they are negotiating with the agents of legislatively-governed and tax-supported governmental entities or their subagencies.

The first stage in the "prevailing rate" type of bargaining (type 5) is normally essentially a political process. It involves convincing a legislature to authorize the setting of certain terms of employment for public employees which shall be equitable in relation to terms prevailing for other comparable groups of employees. Once such authorization is given, the succeeding stage consists of convincing whoever is charged with the responsibility for determining what, in fact, the prevailing rate is that certain comparisons are more relevant than others. There is a sense in which this approach to the determination of terms places in the hands of negotiators beyond the organization representing the employees involved the power to determine what the terms for public employees shall be.

This method can be used only by employee organizations representing employees (usually in the "labor" occupations) whose terms are not mandated by Civil Service regulations. In fact, Section 220 of the Labor Law uses this approach. Such employees are usually, but not universally, represented by a union-type organization. The method is thought of, therefore, as characteristic of the union model.

The nearest possibility for the exercise of the kind of collective bargaining envisaged in point 6 is in negotiating with certain Public Authorities (thruway, bridges, transit and publicly-owned utilities), whose governing boards are not only responsible for operating the services but have the authority to meet their needs by revenues from prices charged, from taxes, or from the sale of bonds. The Public Authorities, it should be noted, are the closest approximation to private enterprise which exists in the public sector. Even in these cases, however, such revenues are frequently supplemented by appropriations from the public treasury or are constrained by public policy with respect to the level of prices or taxes which legislatures permit (the New York City Transit Authority is a case in point). The negotiating process must, therefore, be modified to deal with others than the agency in question. Both Unions and Associations have recognized this and have sought political access to those "others."

Neither Unions nor Associations can move, however, to the sixth type of allegedly *real* collective bargaining with the executives of political entities . . . [unless] the public, through the action of its legislatures is ready to delegate to a bargaining "team" composed of the executives of government agencies and the negotiators for employee organizations the virtual determination of its budget, the allocation of public revenues to alternative uses, and the setting of the tax rate necessary to balance that budget. The delegation of those powers is not likely in the foreseeable future. The public, the leaders of employee organizations, and prospective recruits for these organizations would be wise to recognize this and modify their expectations accordingly as to what "collective bargaining" in the public sector can be expected to accomplish unless recognition is given to the practical limitations on public employers to commit themselves unconditionally to a bargain.

The Associations have a long experience in the use of the fourth method, that involving direct political action for terms of employment beneficial to the employees they represent. This mode of collective activity is certainly characteristic of the Association model. Yet, some of the most successful of the employee organizations ... by virtue of their affiliation with the AFL-CIO, are considered to be "unions,". ... The Firefighters and Postal Clerks, are well known for their traditional *primary* utilization of this method.

## E. Type of pressure used.

The concept of "collective bargaining" used to describe the mode of collective participation characterizing the Union model employee organization involves at least two other elements in addition to the kind of activity involved. The first of these elements has to do with the kind of pressure employed to achieve the objective of a joint decision. The Union model pressure is frequently described as economic, and the ultimate actualization of that pressure is the threat of or the actual slowdown or the strike. There is little question that the history and tradition of unions supports this description. The present public insistence by many labor leaders that public as well as private sector employees should not be denied the right to strike gives evidence that their position, at least their strategic public position, is that collective bargaining without the right to apply realistically the strike threat pressure is a contradiction in terms.

The position of Association model organizations on the other hand is widely assumed to have been that economic pressure, including the threat of or an actual strike, is not only illegitimate but irrelevant for organizations of public employees. They are assumed to place greater reliance on political pressure brought upon elected political executives and legislators either in support before a legislative body of proposals mutually agreed to by agency executives and employee representatives or in direct pursuit of legislative action, or in appeals directly to the public.

This differentiation, as indicating traditional emphasis in the two models respectively, is accurate, although association types of organization have employed economic pressure and tactics, and locals of union types of organization have renounced the right to employ the kind of economic power actualized in the strike weapon.

Decision making by executives of government agencies and their calculations of the cost to them of agreement or disagreement on terms desired by employees is often influenced by public or political considerations. Any organization representing public employees knows that from experience. They are also fully aware of the fact that there are normally strata of "employers," including ultimately a legislature, to whom any agreements made with negotiating executives must be referred for approval and financial implementation. They are also aware that sometimes the most dependable process is to work directly for legislation favorable to their members, which legislation will be binding on the government agencies whose employees they represent. It is to be expected that any successful employee organization, whether of the Union or Association type, will understand and utilize the strategy and tactics associated with political activity as a major re-enforcement of, and, on occasion, as a substitute for, the strategy and tactics associated with skill in negotiating with government agency executives.

As both the Union and the Association model organizations adapt their strategies of action and power to the realities of public employment relationships, they may be expected to gear that adaptation to the peculiarities of that type of relationship. . . .

## NOTES

1. The differences between independent employee organizations and employee organizations affiliated with the AFL-CIO are indicated in the following excerpt from the Statement of John R. Doyle, President of the Assembly of Governmental Employees (AGE), in ADVISORY COMMISSION ON INTERGOVERNMENTAL RELATIONS, LABOR-MANAGEMENT POLICIES FOR STATE AND LOCAL GOVERNMENT 123, 124-25 (1969):

AGE, the Assembly of Governmental Employees, is a nationwide federation of independent public employee associations which represents public employees at the federal, state and local jurisdiction levels. AGE works cooperatively with independent public employee organizations in Canada and Puerto Rico.

Founded in 1952, AGE has been growing steadily and currently has a membership of over 500,000 public employees, mostly at the state level. However, recent applications under board consideration are from organizations representing federal, county and city groups. . . .

[T]he question usually comes to mind as to what degree this public employee group differs from others — say those affiliated with the American Federation of Labor-Congress of Industrial Organization.

[T]here are distinct differences and these differences stem from basic philosophies and historical practices. The more obvious differences are these:

1. *Merit System* — The independent associations are extremely strong advocates of the merit system principle. They believe that the selection and promotion of public employees should be based upon demonstrated merit as determined by competitive examination. In this way, the public through the merit system furnishes the manpower to government. In most jurisdictions, the merit system or civil service has been established and is being maintained through the efforts of the independent associations.

Employee organizations affiliated with international unions tend to give "lip service" to civil service. On the one hand, they call for the preservation of the merit principle while on the other they espouse the philosophy of the unions' furnishing the labor force to government through the hiring hall. Their philosophy is diametrically opposed to the essence of the merit system.

2. *Control of Policy* — The internal policies which guide the independent public employee organizations are conceived and executed at the local jurisdictional level. They brook little or no interference from authorities outside their jurisdiction. On the contrary, the union groups' policies are strongly influenced and even dictated by the international councils located outside of the jurisdiction. . . .

. . . .

6. *Tactics* — In representing public employees the independents rely heavily upon possession of the facts and persistent yet dignified persuasion. They believe that impasses can be resolved through mediation and arbitration and contend that adult sophisticated public management and employees should be able to resolve impasses without the pressure of work stoppage through strikes. Those affiliated with

international unions tend to use pressure tactics in the presentation of their requests and generally advocate the threat of strikes at the outset of their presentations or negotiations.

2. The once clear distinction between the union model and the association model has blurred over the past several years. For example, AFSCME is increasingly looking with favor on compulsory arbitration rather than the right to strike as the terminal step in the negotiation process. On the other hand, most independent employee associations that engage in collective bargaining have deleted the no-strike provisions from their constitutions and by-laws and, from time to time, have used the strike weapon. As the Committee on Economic Development (CED) noted:

> The distinctions among traditional trade unions, employee associations, and professional associations have faded in recent years. For example, the National Education Association, whose membership once encompassed school administrators at all levels, has tended to narrow its focus to nonmanagement personnel; principals, superintendents, and state education officials have gravitated toward separate organizations. The merger of the New York State Civil Service Employees Association with AFSCME in 1978 is a further reflection of the blurred distinction between trade unions and employee associations.

## 2. THE RISE AND FALL OF THE SOVEREIGNTY DOCTRINE

### K. HANSLOWE, THE EMERGING LAW OF LABOR RELATIONS IN PUBLIC EMPLOYMENT 11-20 (1967)†

[V]arying policies have grown up at the state and federal levels with respect to the organizing and bargaining rights of public employees and . . . a discernible trend toward enhanced recognition and protection of these rights is now evident. At one time and place or another, however, virtually all aspects of collective bargaining have been deemed incompatible with government employment. Thus, courts have ruled that public employees can be prohibited from joining unions. To the assertion that this interferes with the constitutional right of freedom of association, government has responded that, there being no constitutional right to government employment, it may insist on non-membership as a condition of such employment because of the governmental right and need to maintain operations without interference and interruption. Consequently, it has been ruled that state governments may condition employment on relinquishment of the right to organize, and that no one has a constitutional right to work for the government on his own terms.

Even where public employees are allowed to join unions, this right has often been restricted to organizations not affiliated with the general labor movement. Where not so restricted, affiliation, in any event, must not be with an organization that asserts the right to strike against the government. The reason for the latter restriction is fairly obvious. Strikes of government employees are almost universally deemed to be unlawful. The reasons for the former restriction are thought to be as follows:

(1) Affiliation increases the possibility that conflicting loyalties will arise. For example, it is argued that policemen who are members of a labor federation such as AFL-CIO, or who are members of an international union also representing employees in private industry, cannot be expected to perform in disinterested fashion and with no reservations when called out to eliminate violence on a picket line maintained by their fellow union members.

---

† Reprinted by permission of the New York State School of Industrial and Labor Relations, Cornell University.

(2) Affiliation increases the funds available to public employee organizations and thereby increases their capacity to strike.

(3) Affiliation increases the likelihood of sympathetic strikes by private or public employees to help their fellow union members.

(4) Affiliation with the general labor movement may result in placing too much power in the hands of organized labor. Employees in both sectors might use their respective political and economic power each to enhance the position of the other group at the expense of the rest of society.

The government trend in recent years has been to relax previous restrictions on affiliation. Most jurisdictions which now allow their public employees to organize, also allow them to affiliate with the general labor movement, at least so long as the affiliations are not with organizations asserting the right to strike against the government. More stringent restrictions can still be found in some instances, however, especially with respect to bans on the affiliation of policemen's organizations with other unions.

Other facets of collective bargaining, familiar in the private sector, have been similarly deemed inappropriate in government employment. This is true not only of the strike, but of exclusive recognition of an organization representing a majority of the employees involved, the closed or union shop, the checkoff by the employer of union dues from the employees' wages, and the arbitration of disputes as well. Indeed, the very possibility of *bargaining* with the government has been questioned, and agreements reached between public officials and labor unions have been held invalid as constituting unauthorized abdications of governmental power with respect to conditions of public employment.

These views are reflected in legal opinion. For instance, the attorney general of Florida advised the city manager of Miami that:

> ... no organization, regardless of who it is affiliated with, union or non-union, can tell a political sub-division possessing the attributes of sovereignty, who it can employ, how much it shall pay them, or any other matter or thing relating to its employees. To even countenance such a proposition would be to surrender a portion of the sovereignty that is possessed by every municipal corporation and such a municipality would cease to exist as an organization controlled by its citizens, for after all, government is no more than the individuals that go to make up the same and no one can tell the people how to say, through their duly constituted and elected officials, how the government should be run under such authority and powers as the people themselves give to a public corporation such as a city.[10]

A judicial decision, in 1946, asserted:

> There is an abundance of authority, too numerous for citation, which condemns labor union contracts in the public service. The theory of these decisions is that the giving of a preference [to unions and their members] is against public policy. It is declared that such preferences, in whatever form, involve an illegal delegation of disciplinary authority, or of legislative power, or of the discretion of public officers; that such a contract disables them from performing their duty; that it involves a divided allegiance; that it encourages

---

[10] Florida Attorney General's Opinion, March 21, 1944, reproduced in Rhyne, *Labor Unions and Municipal Employee Law* (Washington: National Institute of Municipal Law Offices, 1946), pp. 252-54.

monopoly; that it defeats competition; that it is detrimental to the public welfare; that it is subversive of the public service; and that it impairs the freedom of the individual to contract for his own services. . . .[11]

At the core of this position is the concept of sovereignty.

. . . In our polity, sovereignty, of course, ultimately reposes in the people but is, out of the practical necessities of circumstance, exercised for them by the constituted state governments and the federal government. It is these governments and their delegates (such as local governments, municipalities, and executive and administrative agencies) which exercise, within constitutional and statutory limitations, the sovereign power to make and enforce law. To the extent that collective bargaining entails joint determination of conditions of employment, such bargaining with the government is seen as unavoidably creating an interference in the sovereign's affairs. Unionization is similarly thought to involve intolerable splitting of the civil servant's loyalty between the government of which he is a part and his union. Furthermore, such practices as exclusive recognition, the closed or union shop, and the checkoff of union dues are thought not only to invite organized interference with the conduct of public business but to involve improper preference for one group at the expense of others in society. The use of arbitrators to resolve disputes is seen to entail an improper abandonment by the sovereign of a portion of his authority. And the strike, needless to say, involving, as it does, concerted coercion of the employer, falls little short of insurrection when the employer is the government.

What this position comes down to is that governmental power includes the power, through law, to fix the terms and conditions of government employment, that this power reposes in the sovereign's hand, that this is a unique power which cannot be given or taken away or shared, and that any organized effort to interfere with this power through a process such as collective bargaining is irreconcilable with the idea of sovereignty and is hence unlawful.

> The [police] commission . . . not only had the power but it was the manifest duty to adopt and enforce the resolution [prohibiting policemen from joining a labor union]. . . . The failure to do so in effect would have amounted to a surrender of power, a dereliction of duty, and a relinquishment of supervision and control over public servants it was their sworn duty to supervise and direct.[12]

This is the orthodox position. We shall see below that in practice it has been widely modified, although not wholly abandoned.

Still another line of analysis must be indicated. What has been said thus far flows from political or legal theory. It can also be argued that the theory is grounded in functional necessity. The sovereign, whether absolute or representative, acts for the entire political entity involved. The functions which the sovereign performs are governmental tasks which need to be discharged on behalf of the whole society. These tasks, whether they be national defense, local security, running an educational system, or whatever, are carried on to further the public weal. Any conduct which interferes with the performance of these tasks is inimical to that weal and is therefore intolerable. Strikes of civil servants clearly

---

[11] Mugford v. Mayor and City Council of Baltimore, opinion Nov. 6, 1944, aff'd, 185 Md. 266, 44 A.2d 745 (1946).

[12] Perez v. Board of Police Commissioners, 78 Cal. App. 2d 638, 651, 178 P.2d 537, 545 (1947).

constitute such interference. So, likewise, to the extent that unionization and collective bargaining may have a tendency to lead to strikes, they can and, indeed, must be outlawed as running counter to the public interest. Thus, the functional necessity of governmental tasks is asserted to combine with the theoretical nature of sovereign power to render collective bargaining on the part of public employees undesirable and unlawful.

## Sovereignty Delimited

So goes the traditional argument. Its difficulty lies in the circumstance that life has a way of running ahead of logic and that history tends to be more complex than political theory. Implicit in the argument is the idea that the sovereign is absolute, all-powerful, and always right. The idea is open to question.

We derive our notions of sovereignty from the English common law which reposed sovereign authority in the king as the fountainhead of law, justice, and government. "The king can do no wrong," wrote Blackstone in his *Commentaries.* This maxim assumed concrete meaning in the context of lawsuits by citizens against the Crown. If the king can indeed do no wrong, the Crown is necessarily immune from suit. Applied to government employment, the Blackstone maxim means that, when the sovereign has fixed the terms of public employment, these are inescapably fair and just, and hence any employee effort to alter them is wrong and runs counter to law.

One difficulty with this is that, insofar as sovereign immunity from suit is concerned, the Blackstone maxim has been misunderstood, and the English kings did not enjoy the absolute immunity commonly thought to be conveyed by the notion that they could "do no wrong." Professor Louis Jaffe writes:

> It is the prevailing view among students of this period that the requirement of consent [to be sued] was not based on a view that the King was above the law. "[T]he king, as the fountain of justice and equity, could not refuse to redress wrongs when petitioned to do so by his subjects." Indeed, it is argued by scholars on what seems adequate evidence that the expression "the King can do no wrong" originally meant precisely the contrary to what it later came to mean. "[I]t meant that the king must not, was not allowed, not entitled to do wrong. . . ." It was on this basis that the King, though not suable in his court . . ., nevertheless endorsed on petitions "let justice be done," thus empowering his courts to proceed.[13]

The petitions referred to were "petitions of right." They were granted when other remedies against the government were unavailable. Thus, legal procedure combined with political theory to delimit sovereign immunity even at its source — the kings of England. By what Professor Jaffe calls a "magnificent irony," these limitations upon sovereign immunity were substantially destroyed in North America when the Colonies, by revoking their allegiance to the Crown, eliminated the king who could "let justice be done."

So it seems that the king was not always absolutely right, and he has, of course, for a long time not been absolute. Absence of absolute power has, in any case, been a dominant characteristic of American government from the start. Yet the doctrine of sovereign immunity has had a sturdy history in American law which, perhaps, helps to explain the reluctance with which American governments have moved in the direction of accepting collective bargaining with their employees.

---

[13] LOUIS LEVENTHAL JAFFE, JUDICIAL CONTROL OF ADMINISTRATIVE ACTION (Boston: Little, Brown & Company, 1965), p. 199. Professor Jaffe's footnotes have been omitted.

....

Mr. Justice Holmes spoke in favor of the immunity of the sovereign:

> A sovereign is exempt from suit, not because of any formal conception or obsolete theory, but on the logical and practical ground that there can be no legal right as against the authority that makes the law on which the right depends.[14]

Nevertheless, the doctrine of sovereignty, in areas other than the labor relations context, as well as in the labor relations field itself, has come to be limited. Indeed, Professor Kenneth Culp Davis has recently written: "Sovereign immunity in state courts is on the run."

The traditional position, for one thing, has been substantially modified by legislative enactments, the effect of which is to "waive" sovereign immunity for certain purposes. A court of claims was established in 1855 to entertain citizens' claims that their private property has been unconstitutionally taken by the federal government for public use without just compensation. Tort claims against the federal government may be asserted under the Federal Tort Claims Act of 1946. Contract claims may be similarly asserted under the Tucker Act of 1948. Several states have legislated in similar vein. . . .

More recently the courts, often without legislative aid, have, in Professor Davis' words, "abolish[ed] large chunks of immunity." According to Professor Davis, thirteen jurisdictions have so acted between 1957 and 1965. Some of the decisions collected by Professor Davis speak in such terms as:

> "[S]overeign immunity" may be a proper subject for discussion by students of mythology but finds no haven or refuge in this Court.[15]

With respect to municipal tort liability, the Supreme Court of Florida made this observation:

> The modern city is in substantial measure a large business institution. . . . To continue to endow this type of organization with sovereign divinity appears to us to predicate the law of the Twentieth Century upon an Eighteenth Century anachronism.[16]

....

One may well ask, therefore, whether conceptions of sovereignty should remain as a barrier to collective bargaining in governmental labor relations. If the "sovereign" government is increasingly assuming ordinary legal responsibility in its relations with its citizens, why should not the same hold true for governmental relations with civil servants?

One point emerges. Whatever immunities the sovereign may possess, there is no barrier to such immunities being delimited. The sovereign power does, indeed, include the power within constitutional limitations to make policy. But does this not include the power to establish, as a matter of public personnel policy, a system of collective bargaining with respect to civil servants. This is, in fact, the position which seems to be emerging. One leading writer has concluded that, while *"the [sovereignty] doctrine is a clear and effective bar to any action on the part of government employees to compel the government to enter*

---

[14] Kawananakoa v. Polyblank, 205 U.S. 349, 353 (1907).
[15] Colorado Racing Commission v. Brush Racing Ass'n, 136 Colo. 279, 284 (1957).
[16] Hargrove v. Town of Cocoa Beach, 96 So. 2d 130, 133 (Fla. 1957).

*involuntarily into any type of collective bargaining relationship, . . . the doctrine does not preclude the enactment of legislation specifically authorizing the government to enter into collective bargaining relationships with its employees."* . . .[17]

## NOTES

1. While the judge in the *Mugford* case quoted by Hanslowe condemned an agreement that gave the union a preferential position which was specifically denied to any other organization, the judge nevertheless stated:

> With the pattern of collective dealing so firmly established in the industrial field, is it reasonable to expect to maintain the fiction of personal relationship between employer and employe in the municipal field among a large number of workers engaged in performing the same tasks as are performed in the industrial field? I think not. To maintain even a semblance of individual contact with a large force of workers would require an increase of supervisory workers, who would still fail to detect and deal grievances and complaints as effectively as an organization of workers would do. The right to organize, and bargain collectively, can be exercised without interference with the exercise of the discretion committed to public officers, without preferment of organization members, without discrimination against others, and without detriment to the public service. Mugford v. Mayor and City Council of Baltimore (Cir. Ct. No. 2, Baltimore City, 1944), *reproduced in* C. RHYNE, LABOR UNIONS AND MUNICIPAL EMPLOYE LAW 166, 168 (1946).

2. In denying public employees many of the rights which their counterparts in the private sector possessed, the courts also relied on the theory that public employees owed extra-loyalty to their governmental employers. The following critique of this "extra-loyalty" theory is contained in Edwards, *The Developing Labor Relations Law in the Public Sector,* 10 DUQUESNE L. REV. 357, 360-61 (1972):

> A close relative of the sovereignty doctrine is the theory that public employees have a commitment to further the programs of government even at a sacrifice of their own interests. . . .
>
> It would seem the extra-loyalty theory is open to the same criticism as the sovereignty theory: it too is vague, conclusory, and not adequately founded in the realities of the modern situation. Based upon an assumed concensus as to the proper role of government in society, it offers no guidance as to what the employee must give up. Further, it puts forth no reason for this sacrifice, save the equation government equals sovereign equals absolute fealty. Such an equation is hardly a viable alternative in our modern society. Indeed, with so many "urgent" demands on the government's admittedly inadequate resources — coupled with the great gains of private sector unions (creating a considerable controversy as to just what the public employee's fair share really is) — it outrages modern notions of industrial democracy to relegate a large segment of the work force to dependence upon the conscience of the government. A degree of self-determinism has become a way of life for the American worker, and nowhere is it more necessary than in the public sector.

## NORWALK TEACHERS' ASSOCIATION v. BOARD OF EDUCATION OF THE CITY OF NORWALK

Connecticut Supreme Court of Errors
138 Conn. 269, 83 A.2d 482 (1951)

JENNINGS, J. This is a suit between the Norwalk Teachers' Association as

---

[17] WILSON R. HART, COLLECTIVE BARGAINING IN THE FEDERAL CIVIL SERVICE (New York: Harper & Row, 1961), p. 44.

plaintiff and the Norwalk board of education as defendant for a declaratory judgment, reserved on the admitted allegations of the complaint for the advice of this court.

The complaint may be summarized as follows: The plaintiff is a voluntary association and an independent labor union to which all but two of the teaching personnel of approximately 300 in the Norwalk school system belong. In April, 1946, there was a dispute between the parties over salary rates. The board of estimate and taxation was also involved. After long negotiations, 230 members of the association rejected the individual contracts of employment tendered them and refused to return to their teaching duties. After further negotiations, in which the governor and the state board of education took part, a contract was entered into between the plaintiff and the defendant, and the teachers returned to their duties. The contract, subject to conditions precedent therein set forth, recognized the plaintiff as the bargaining agent for all of its members, defined working conditions and set up a grievance procedure and salary schedule. Similar contracts were entered into for the succeeding school years, including 1950-51. From September, 1946, to the present, and particularly with reference to the contract for 1950-1951, much doubt and uncertainty have arisen concerning the rights and duties of the respective parties, the interpretation of the contract and the construction of the state statutes relating to schools, education and boards of education. "In addition," the complaint states, "there has been the possibility of strikes, work stoppage or collective refusals to return to work by the teachers through their organization and the possibility of discharges or suspensions by the defendant by reason of difficult personnel relations, all of which tends to disharmony in the operation of the school system and to the ever present possibility that either, or both, the parties may be unwittingly violating statutes by reason of mistaken or erroneous interpretation thereon." The parties agreed that the contract for the school year 1949-1950 would govern their relations for the school year 1950-1951, that they would join in the action, and "that whatever contractual obligations exist will be forthwith modified so soon as they shall have received from the Court judgments and orders declaring their respective rights, privileges, duties and immunities." The specific points of dispute are stated in the questions reserved, printed in the footnote.[1] . . .

---

[1] The plaintiff claimed a declaratory judgment answering and adjudicating the following questions:

"(a) Is it permitted to the plaintiff under our laws to organize itself as a labor union for the purpose of demanding and receiving recognition and collective bargaining?

"(b) Is it permitted to the plaintiff organized as a labor union to demand recognition as such and collective bargaining?

"(c) Is it permissible under Connecticut law for the defendant to recognize the plaintiff for the purpose of collective bargaining?

"(d) Is collective bargaining to establish salaries and working conditions permissible between the plaintiff and the defendant?

"(e) May the plaintiff engage in concerted action such as strike, work stoppage, or collective refusal to enter upon duties?

"(f) Is arbitration a permissible method under Connecticut law to settle or adjust disputes between the plaintiff and the defendant?

"(g) Is mediation a permissible method under Connecticut law to settle or adjust disputes between the plaintiff and the defendant?

"(h) If the answer to the previous questions is yes, are the State's established administrative facilities, such as the State Board of Mediation and Arbitration and the State Labor Relations Board, available, as they are available in industrial disputes, to the plaintiff and the defendant?

"(i) Does the continuing contract law, so-called, create a status of employment within which the plaintiff may claim employment subject to the right to bargain salaries and working conditions?

"(j) Has the plaintiff the right to establish rules, working conditions and grievance resolution procedures by collective bargaining?"

. . . Question (e) will be considered first.

Under our system, the government is established by and run for all of the people, not for the benefit of any person or group. The profit motive, inherent in the principle of free enterprise, is absent. It should be the aim of every employee of the government to do his or her part to make it function as efficiently and economically as possible. The drastic remedy of the organized strike to enforce the demands of unions of government employees is in direct contravention of this principle. It has been so regarded by the heads of the executive departments of the states and the nation. Most of the text writers refer to one or more of the following statements by three of our recent presidents. They are quoted, for example, in 1 Labor Law Journal 612 (May, 1950): "There is no right to strike against public safety by anybody anywhere at any time" (Calvin Coolidge on the Boston police strike). This same strike was characterized by President Wilson as "an intolerable crime against civilization." President Franklin D. Roosevelt said in a letter to the president of the National Federation of Federal Employees on August 16, 1937: "Particularly, I want to emphasize my conviction that militant tactics have no place in the functions of any organization of Government employees. . . . [A] strike of public employees manifests nothing less than an intent on their part to prevent or obstruct the operations of Government until their demands are satisfied. Such action, looking toward the paralysis of Government by those who have sworn to support it, is unthinkable and intolerable." As the author of the article cited says, "The above statement by President Roosevelt, who certainly was no enemy of labor unions, epitomizes the answer to the problem. It seems to be axiomatic."

The commentators, generally, subscribe to this proposition. National Institute of Municipal Law Officers Reports No. 76, 116, 129; 1 Teller, Labor Disputes & Collective Bargaining (1947 Sup.) § 171; 18 N.Y.U.L.Q. Rev. 247; 94 U. of Pa. L. Rev. 427. Notwithstanding this fact, Ziskind was able to publish a well-documented book entitled "One Thousand Strikes of Government Employees," which contains an elaborate bibliography. See also Spero, Government as Employer. This would indicate that the law on the subject is still in the process of development.

Few cases involving the right of unions of government employees to strike to enforce their demands have reached courts of last resort. That right has usually been tested by an application for an injunction forbidding the strike. The right of the governmental body to this relief has been uniformly upheld. It has been put on various grounds: public policy; interference with governmental function; illegal discrimination against the right of any citizen to apply for government employment (where the union sought a closed shop). The following cases do not necessarily turn on the specific right to strike, but the reasoning indicates that, if faced with that question, the court would be compelled to deny that right to public employees. For example, Perez v. Board of Police Commissioners, 78 Cal. App. 2d 638, 178 P.2d 537, held that the board could, by rule, prevent police officers from joining a labor union. If it could do this, it would certainly be upheld in an attempt to enjoin a strike called by the union. . . . [Citations omitted.] The court puts the matter succinctly in the *Miami* case [Miami Water Works Local 654 v. Miami, 157 Fla. 445, 26 S.2d 194 (1946)]: "While strikes are recognized by the statute to be lawful under some circumstances, it would seem that a strike against the city would amount, in effect, to a strike against government itself — a situation difficult to reconcile with all notions of government."

The plaintiff, recognizing the unreasonableness of its claims in the case of such employees as the militia and the judiciary, seeks to place teachers in a class with employees employed by the municipality in its proprietary capacity. No authority is cited in support of this proposition. "A town board of education is an agency of the state in charge of education in the town. . . ." Board of Education of Stamford v. Board of Finance, 127 Conn. 345, 349, 16 A.2d 601. In fulfilling its duties as such an agency, it is acting in a governmental, not a proprietary, capacity. . . .

In the American system, sovereignty is inherent in the people. They can delegate it to a government which they create and operate by law. They can give to that government the power and authority to perform certain duties and furnish certain services. The government so created and empowered must employ people to carry on its task. Those people are agents of the government. They exercise some part of the sovereignty entrusted to it. They occupy a status entirely different from those who carry on a private enterprise. They serve the public welfare and not a private purpose. To say that they can strike is the equivalent of saying that they can deny the authority of government and contravene the public welfare. The answer to question (e) is "No."

Questions (a) and (b) relate to the right of the plaintiff to organize itself as a labor union and to demand recognition and collective bargaining. The right to organize is sometimes accorded by statute or ordinance. See, for example, the Bridgeport ordinance adopted June 17, 1946 (Bridgeport Munic. Reg. [1947] p. 15), discussed in National Institute of Municipal Law Officers Report No. 129, p. 51. The right to organize has also been forbidden by statute or regulation. Perez v. Board of Police Commissioners, 78 Cal. App. 2d 638, 178 P.2d 537. In Connecticut the statutes are silent on the subject. Union organization in industry is now the rule rather than the exception. In the absence of prohibitory statute or regulation, no good reason appears why public employees should not organize as a labor union. Springfield v. Clouse, 356 Mo. 1239, 1246, 206 S.W.2d 539. It is the second part of question (a) that causes difficulty. The question reads: "Is it permitted to the plaintiff under our laws to organize itself as a labor union for the purpose of demanding and receiving recognition and collective bargaining?" The question is phrased in a very peremptory form. The common method of enforcing recognition and collective bargaining is the strike. It appears that this method has already been used by the plaintiff and that the threat of its use again is one of the reasons for the present suit. As has been said, the strike is not a permissible method of enforcing the plaintiff's demands. The answer to questions (a) and (b) is a qualified "Yes." There is no objection to the organization of the plaintiff as a labor union, but if its organization is for the purpose of "demanding" recognition and collective bargaining the demands must be kept within legal bounds. What we have said does not mean that the plaintiff has the right to organize for all of the purposes for which employees in private enterprise may unite, as those are defined in § 7391 of the General Statutes. Nor does it mean that, having organized, it is necessarily protected against unfair labor practices as specified in § 7392 or that it shall be the exclusive bargaining agent for all employees of the unit, as provided in § 7393. It means nothing more than that the plaintiff may organize and bargain collectively for the pay and working conditions which it may be in the power of the board of education to grant.

Questions (c) and (d) in effect ask whether collective bargaining between the plaintiff and the defendant is permissible. The statutes and private acts give broad powers to the defendant with reference to educational matters and school management in Norwalk. If it chooses to negotiate with the plaintiff with regard to the employment, salaries, grievance procedure and working conditions of its members, there is no statute, public or private, which forbids such negotiations. It is a matter of common knowledge that this is the method pursued in most school systems large enough to support a teachers' association in some form. It would seem to make no difference theoretically whether the negotiations are with a committee of the whole association or with individuals or small related groups, so long as any agreement made with the committee is confined to members of the association. If the strike threat is absent and the defendant prefers to handle the matter through negotiation with the plaintiff, no reason exists why it should not do so. The claim of the defendant that this would be an illegal delegation of authority is without merit. The authority is and remains in the board. This statement is not to be construed as approval of the existing contracts attached to the complaint. Their validity is not in issue.

As in the case of questions (a) and (b), (c) and (d) are in too general a form to permit a categorical answer. The qualified "Yes" which we give to them should not be construed as authority to negotiate a contract which involves the surrender of the board's legal discretion, is contrary to law or is otherwise ultra vires. For example, an agreement by the board to hire only union members would clearly be an illegal discrimination. Mugford v. Baltimore, 185 Md. 266, 270, 44 A.2d 745; Rhyne, Labor Unions & Municipal Employe Law, pp. 34, 137, 157. Any salary schedule must be subject to the powers of the board of estimate and taxation. "The salaries of all persons appointed by the board of education . . . shall be as fixed by said board, but the aggregate amount of such salaries . . . shall not exceed the amount determined by the board of estimate and taxation. . . ." 21 Spec. Laws 285, No. 315, § 3; Board of Education of Stamford v. Board of Finance, 127 Conn. 345, 349, 16 A.2d 601. One of the allegations of the complaint is that the solution of the parties' difficulties by the posing of specific issues is not satisfactory. Whether or not this is so, that course will be necessary if this discussion of general principles is an insufficient guide.

Question (f) reads, "Is arbitration a permissible method under Connecticut law to settle or adjust disputes between the plaintiff and the defendant?" The power of a town to enter into an agreement of arbitration was originally denied on the ground that it was an unlawful delegation of authority. Griswold v. North Stonington, 5 Conn. 367, 371. It was later held that not only the amount of damages but liability could be submitted to arbitration. Hine v. Stephens, 33 Conn. 497, 504; Mallory v. Huntington, 64 Conn. 88, 96, 29 A. 245. The principle applies to the parties to the case at bar. If it is borne in mind that arbitration is the result of mutual agreement, there is no reason to deny the power of the defendant to enter voluntarily into a contract to arbitrate a specific dispute. On a proposal for a submission, the defendant would have the opportunity of deciding whether it would arbitrate as to any question within its power. Its power to submit to arbitration would not extend to questions of policy but might extend to questions of liability. Arbitration as a method of settling disputes is growing in importance and, in a proper case, "deserves the enthusiastic support of the courts." International Brotherhood of Teamsters v. Shapiro, 138 Conn. 57, 69, 82 A.2d 345. Agreements to submit all disputes to arbitration, commonly found in ordinary union contracts, are in a different category. If the defendant entered into a general agreement of that kind, it might find itself committed to surrender the broad discretion and responsibility reposed in it by law. For example, it could not commit to an arbitrator the decision of a proceeding to discharge a teacher for cause. So, the matter of certification of teachers is committed to the state board of education. General Statutes §§ 1432, 1433, 1435. The best answer we can give to question (f) is, "Yes, arbitration may be a permissible method as to certain specific, arbitrable disputes."

From what has been said, it is obvious that, within the same limitations, mediation to settle or adjust disputes is not only permissible but desirable. The answer to question (g) is "Yes." The state board of mediation and arbitration and the state labor relations board, however, are set up to handle disputes in private industry and are not available to the plaintiff and defendant for reasons given in the opinion of the attorney general dated July 6, 1948. 25 Conn. Atty. Gen. Rep. 270. This was confirmed as to Norwalk teachers by an opinion dated June 12, 1950, not yet published. See also United States v. United Mine Workers, 330 U.S. 258, 269, 67 S. Ct. 677, 91 L. Ed. 884. The answer to question (h) is "No."

General Statutes, Sup. 1949, § 160a, provides in part: "The contract of employment of a teacher shall be renewed for the following school year unless such teacher has been notified in writing prior to March first of that year that such contract will not be renewed." Question (i) asks whether this law creates "a status of employment within which the plaintiff may claim employment subject to the right to bargain salaries and working conditions?" The meaning of this is not clear and the briefs do not clarify it. It is the type of question that should be related to a specific state of facts. It cannot be answered in vacuo.

As to question (j), the plaintiff has no right to establish rules. As stated above, the right is and remains in the board. . . .

### NOTES

1. For a good review of the case law prior to 1953, see Annot., 31 A.L.R.2d 1142 (1953).
2. The *Norwalk* case at the time of its issuance in 1951 was hailed by public sector unions since the court recognized that collective bargaining was permissible in the public sector. Although the sovereignty doctrine was not utilized to prevent collective bargaining, the court clearly felt that it was pertinent to the various issues presented for decision.
3. The issues which were raised in the *Norwalk* case mirror many of the issues which are explored in subsequent chapters, *e.g.,* the right of public employees to join and form unions, the authority of a public employer to recognize and negotiate with a union, the right to strike, the legality of an agreement to arbitrate disputes, and so forth.
4. The changing judicial attitude concerning the applicability of the sovereignty theory is graphically illustrated by two New York court decisions issued thirteen years apart. In Railway Mail Ass'n v. Murphy, 180 Misc. 868, 44 N.Y.S.2d 601, 607-08 (1943), *rev'd on other grounds,* 326 U.S. 88 (1945), the court stated:

> To tolerate or recognize any combination of Civil Service employees of the Government as a labor organization or union is not only incompatible with the spirit of democracy, but inconsistent with every principle upon which our Government is founded. Nothing is more dangerous to public welfare than to admit that hired servants of the state can dictate to the Government the hours, the wages and conditions under which they will carry on essential services vital to the welfare, safety and security of the citizen. To admit as true that Government employees have power to halt or check the functions of Government, unless their demands are satisfied, is to transfer to them all legislative, executive and judicial power. Nothing would be more ridiculous. . . .
>
> Collective bargaining has no place in government service. The employer is the whole people. It is impossible for administrative officials to bind the Government of the United States or the State of New York by any agreement made between them and representatives of any union. Government officials and employees are governed and guided by laws which must be obeyed and which cannot be abrogated or set aside by an agreement of employees and officials.

Thirteen years later the court in Civil Serv. Forum v. New York City Transit Auth., 3 Misc. 2d 346, 151 N.Y.S.2d 402, 408 (Sup. Ct. 1956), *rev'd on other grounds,* 4 App. Div. 2d 117, 163 N.Y.S.2d 476 (1957), stated:

> The agreement . . . executed with these unions was negotiated for the purpose of protecting the health, safety and vital interests of the people of the City and State of New York and to establish and maintain harmonious and stable labor relations with the unions. In the circumstances it seems clear that these compelling reasons were sufficient to warrant the defendant authority in fostering a peaceful settlement of its prospective labor disputes by entering into the challenged agreement.

5. The full text of President Roosevelt's frequently quoted letter to the President of the National Federation of Federal Employees is reproduced in C. RHYNE, LABOR UNIONS AND MUNICIPAL EMPLOYE LAW 436-37 (1946). This book, by the General Counsel of the National Institute of Municipal Law Officers, contains an invaluable collection of decisions, attorney general's opinions, and other documentation concerning public sector labor relations prior to 1946. For the period from 1946 to 1949, see C. Rhyne, *Labor Unions and Municipal Employee Law — A Supplementary Report,* NAT'L INSTITUTE MUN. L. OFFICER REP. No. 129 (1949).

# B. THE SIMILARITIES AND DIFFERENCES BETWEEN THE PUBLIC AND PRIVATE SECTORS

## 1. GENERALLY

### STATEMENT OF R. SCOTT FOSLER, DIRECTOR OF GOVERNMENT STUDIES, COMMITTEE FOR ECONOMIC DEVELOPMENT

Hearings Before the Subcomm. on the City of the House Comm. on Banking, Finance and Urban Affairs, 95th Cong., 2d Sess., 397-402 (July 26, 1978)

*The Fuzzy Dichotomy: Public and Private Sectors*

Definitions of and distinctions between "business" and "government," or "private sector" and "public sector," are increasingly vague. A business may be anything from a small candy store to a large multinational corporation, and may be involved in manufacturing, services, finance, retailing, transportation, or other diverse pursuits. The nature of a government agency can be equally variable. The Department of Defense is a quite different operation from the Social Security Administration. The sanitation department of New York City is an altogether different operation from the sanitation department of Inglewood, California.

Some private sector organizations that are called businesses may be so heavily regulated or bureaucratic that they tend to behave more like the stereotype of a government agency. Some government institutions, on the other hand, may have an entrepreneurial spirit, independent sources of revenue, and flexibility in administrative structure that tend to resemble what we traditionally think of as a business.

A publicly operated hospital has more in common with a privately operated profit-making hospital than with a publicly operated land fill. The characteristic of being a hospital in this instance is more critical than the characteristic of being a government operation. On the other hand, the public hospital will not necessarily benefit from the management techniques used by a neighborhood camera shop, even though it is a business.

Nor should it be assumed that all businesses are necessarily better managed than government agencies. There has been notable improvement in the quality of public management over the years. For all the criticism of government inefficiency, examples are abundant — at the Federal, state, and local levels — of public institutions that are unusually well run and staffed by highly trained and proficient managers. The city management profession clearly has raised the level of public management in city governments.

It should also be recognized that the scale of operations of state and local governments would rank them among the top corporations in the country in terms of total budget or number of employees. New York City is, of course, in a class by itself, in size if not in other ways. Fairfax County, Virginia, with an annual budget in excess of one-half billion dollars, would rank in the fourth quintile of the Fortune 500 largest industrial corporations. The Community Services Division of the Department of Social and Health Services of the State of Washington would rank about 175th with a budget in excess of $1 billion. Such government operations as these in recent years have attracted top quality personnel whose management ability would compare favorably and perhaps superiorly to that of the nation's top corporations.

Nonetheless, while progress has been made in improving public sector management, it is still safe to say that, in general, government can still learn from business. The question is what can they learn, and under what circumstances?

*Characteristics Common to Business and Government*

To suggest that business possesses expertise that may be applicable to government assumes that there are certain similarities between the two. The key similarities include the following:

First, both business and government are organizations, and hence are subject to principles that seem to be common to all organizations.

Second, both are organizations that presumably have the purpose of producing something of value to others outside of the organization. This distinguishes them, for example, from other organizations whose principal purpose is to produce something of value principally or exclusively to those within the organization, such as most political and social organizations whose essential purpose is to promote the interests of their members.

Third, many business and government organizations are large, both in terms of the numbers of people employed, the size of their budgets, and the amount of capital employed. Principles and techniques for managing large-scale operations are applicable to both in general.

Fourth, many business and government organizations are complex, partly due to their size alone, and partly because of the degree of specialization required for production, the nature of technology employed, the multiplicity and ambiguity of goals, and the corresponding complexity of the environment in which they must function.

Fifth, the nature of the work force employed by both is more or less the same in terms of cultural and social background, education and training, experience, skills, and values.

*Distinctions Between Business and Government*

While the characteristics held in common suggest that there would be substantial opportunity for the application of techniques of management from one to the other, there are also important distinctions between the two which limit that applicability or require a substantial degree of modification.

First, the principal goals of government are politically determined. They consequently tend to be multiple and often ambiguous or intangible goals — even more so than in business. The political goals of government include not only the stated intent of public programs, but also contracts, prestige, power and other such values which are not necessarily related to the presumed "output" of public service organizations.

A second distinction deriving from the first is that in government the measure of output or results is much more cumbersome and less precise than it tends to be in business. Even in those instances where business goals are intangible and in some cases tend to be quite similar to government, business performance is ultimately measurable in terms of the profit and loss statement, whereas government typically does not have so precise a "bottom-line."

A third distinction is in the source of funding. Business revenue derives from sales of the good or service produced, whereas the revenue of most government agencies derives from a budget allocation of taxes collected from the public at large. Businesses and government agencies both have an interest in increasing their revenues, but whereas to do so business must increase the quantity or price of its output (presumably requiring it to be sensitive to consumer tastes and pocketbooks), government agencies can increase the size of their budgets through more skillful competition in the budget process which may require little or no attention to the quantity or quality of its services.

Fourth, government tends to plan and manage on a shorter time perspective than does business. Public policy making is geared as much to the cycle of two or four year elections as to the solving of problems, whereas business decisions have relatively greater flexibility to plan activities according to the time required to meet long-term goals.

A fifth important distinction lies in the structure of employment. Employees in government participate actively in the selection of their employers, i.e., elected officials, in contrast to business where management is selected by means that do not directly involve employees. An elected official, consequently, is in the position of being both the employer of his workers, at the same time that he is their employee in that they are also citizens, taxpayers, and voters. Civil service regulations also limit government management in assigning responsibilities, rewarding performance, and penalizing non-performance.

Finally, government also has fundamental responsibilities for the protection of life and property, the maintenance of order, and the assurance of justice. The government manager works within a complex set of constraints imposed by legislatures and higher levels of governments which presumably are designed to meet a range of public purposes, and which complicate his immediate tasks.

## NOTE

In Holodnak v. Avco Corp., 514 F.2d 285 (2d Cir. 1975), the court held that where nearly all the land, buildings, machinery and equipment of an employer's plant were owned by the federal government and where most of the work done at the plant was defense-related, the links between the employer and the federal government were sufficient to make the employer's action in discharging an employee "state action" and, therefore, actionable under the First and Fourteenth Amendments. The court held that there was such a symbiotic relationship between the employer and the federal government that the federal government in effect became a partner or joint venturer in the enterprise. Would the employees of such an entity be considered federal employees for the purposes of the statutory ban against strikes by federal employees? In United States v. United Mine Workers, 330 U.S. 258 (1947), the Supreme Court held that the employees in coal mines that were seized by the government pursuant to executive order were employees of the United States and that, as a result, the Norris-LaGuardia Anti-Injunction Act was not applicable to a strike by such employees.

**SUMMERS, PUBLIC SECTOR BARGAINING: PROBLEMS OF GOVERNMENTAL DECISIONMAKING, 44 U. Cin. L. Rev. 669, 669-73 (1975)**

## I. The Uniqueness of Public Sector Bargaining

It is a threadbare truism that bargaining in the public sector is different from bargaining in the private sector, but the differences are often described in unhelpful detail, too much like the four blind men describing an elephant. Such descriptions will not help us either to make it work or to keep it under control. We ought, therefore, to describe the differences in more general and fundamental terms. To do that, we must start with the basic question: What, exactly, is unique about public sector bargaining?

There is nothing unique about public employees; they are no different from employees in the private sector. They have the same capacities, the same needs, and the same values; they seek the same advantages and the same gains. Many public sector employees previously have been, and with present trends perhaps even more will again become, private sector employees.

There is nothing unique about the work which public employees perform. The private sector has school teachers, nurses and social workers, as well as secretaries, bookkeepers, janitors, maintenance employees, construction workers, and rubbish collectors. There are private police, private detectives, private armed guards, and even private firefighters. Nor is the work necessarily any more critical because it is performed by public employees. Strikes by parochial school teachers create substantially the same inconvenience as strikes by public school teachers. A strike by janitors in public buildings may create fewer problems than a strike by janitors in private apartment buildings. A disruption in garbage collection may be less serious than a disruption in electric power or telephone service.

The uniqueness of public employment is not in the employees nor in the work performed; the uniqueness is in the special character of the employer. The employer is government; the ones who act on behalf of the employer are public officials; and the ones to whom those officials are answerable are citizens and voters. We have developed a whole structure of constitutional and statutory principles, and a whole culture of political practices and attitudes as to how government is to be conducted, what powers public officials are to exercise, and how they are to be made answerable for their actions. Collective bargaining by public employers must fit within the governmental structure and must function consistently with our governmental processes; the problems of the public employer accommodating its collective bargaining function to government structures and processes is what makes public sector bargaining unique.

To state the difference another way, in private sector bargaining we have never been concerned with how the employer decided on the policy to be brought to the bargaining table. We have been concerned with the union's decisionmaking process, requiring the union to observe minimal democratic standards, but we have not been concerned with the corporation's decisionmaking process. All that the law has required is that the employer send someone to the bargaining table who has authority to speak for and to bind the employer. Who instructs the negotiator, how his instructions are determined, and what his instructions may be is for the corporation to decide. The corporation's decisionmaking process is of no concern in collective bargaining; it is of little concern to the law.

When the employer is government, however, the employer's decisionmaking process becomes of central concern in both legal and political terms. The policies brought to the bargaining table are governmental policies. State constitutions and statutes, city charters and ordinances may prescribe procedures as to how those policies are to be decided, specify what bodies or officials shall make those decisions, and impose limitations on the decisions which can be made.

More specifically, in the private sector, the employer must send someone to the bargaining table with authority to make a binding agreement. In the public sector this may not be legally possible or politically sensible. Wages and other benefits directly affect the budget and the tax rates; but adopting budgets and levying taxes are considered, within our governmental system, fundamental legislative policies to be decided by the legislative body, not by a negotiator at the bargaining table. Dismissal procedures may be subject to constitutional requirements which limit the procedures which can be negotiated. Promotion policies may be governed by civil service principles which are written into the city charter and cannot be eliminated by bargaining. Modifications in state pension plans cannot, in most states, be made binding by negotiators, but must be ratified by the legislature. In the public sector, agreement at the bargaining table may be only an intermediate, not a final, step in the decisionmaking process.

Collective bargaining by a governmental employer is different because governmental decisionmaking is different. The unique problems, and the ones of central concern, focus on how government makes its decision. The unique and interesting legal problems are created by legal limitations on governmental decisionmaking. Beyond the legal problems, however, are the far more important ones of how the governmental decisions in collective bargaining ought to be made. The problems are more in the realm of political science than of labor relations. Our central concern is not, as in the private sector, with what will facilitate bargaining and reaching agreement, but with what are appropriate processes for governmental decisionmaking.

Two cases illustrate this crucial difference between the central questions in public sector and private sector bargaining. In *Madison School District v. Wisconsin Employment Relations Board,*[18] a school teacher at a public meeting of the school board presented a petition urging the board not to agree to a "fair shares" provision in the agreement then being negotiated with the union. The board was charged with a prohibited labor practice for allowing the teacher to speak and for accepting the petition. In the private sector such conduct is barred because it may weaken the union's position as exclusive representative and may interfere with the bargaining process. In the public sector, we must confront the question whether citizens, teachers or otherwise, shall be allowed to make their views known to public officials on public issues. Beyond the constitutional issues of free speech and the right to petition is the judgmental question whether those making governmental decisions should be barred from hearing all views and opinions of all citizens before making decisions. The central concern is not the collective bargaining process but the governmental process.

In *Detroit Police Officers v. City of Detroit,*[19] the voters of the city wrote into the city charter the benefits payable under the police and firemen's pension plan. As a result, those benefits could be changed only by referendum. This, of course, impeded the bargaining process; but that does not end the inquiry in the public

---

[18] 231 N.W.2d 206 (Wis. 1975). [Editors' note: The Supreme Court's decision is at pp. 428-28.]

[19] 214 N.W.2d 803 (1972) 341 Mich. 44. [Editors' note: The text of this decision is at pp. 381-85, *infra.*]

sector. The legal question is whether the collective agreement can override the results of a referendum, but the crucial political question is who should have the final voice in determining the city's pension obligations. When we realize that the pension plan may create a larger long-term obligation than any bond issue, creating a lien of undefined size for an indeterminate period, there are strong arguments for requiring voter approval, even though that impedes bargaining. Again the question is not what will facilitate bargaining, but what is the appropriate way of making the governmental decision. If certain acts may, in some measures, impede bargaining as we have known it in the private sector, that cannot end our inquiry. Our ultimate concern is not to make collective bargaining work, but to make government work. My first and basic proposition, then, is that in public employee bargaining, the fundamental issue to which we should be addressing ourselves is how the decisions of government should be made.

## II. The Political Nature of Public Sector Bargaining

My second and subordinate proposition is that the major decisions made in bargaining with public employees are inescapably political decisions. They are political decisions in at least three senses. First, they involve critical policy choices. The matters debated at the bargaining table and decided by the contract are not simply questions of wages, hours, vacations and pensions. Directly at issue are political questions of the size and allocation of the budget, the tax rates, the level of public services, and the long term obligations of the government. These decisions as to budgets, taxes, services, and debts are political in the second sense that, within our system of government, they are to be made by the political branches of government — by elected officials who are politically responsible to the voters. Indeed, these decisions generally are considered uniquely legislative and not subject to delegation. Finally, these decisions are political in the ultimate sense that those making the decisions will do in the political market what businessmen do in the economic market — maximize their gains and minimize their losses. Politically elected officials in bargaining seek to maximize votes rather than profits.

The major decisions made in public employee bargaining not only are political, but in my view must be, and ought to be, political. The size of the budget, the taxes to be levied, the purposes for which tax money is to be used, the kinds and levels of governmental services to be enjoyed, and the level of indebtedness are issues that should be decided by officials who are politically responsible to those who pay the taxes and seek the services. The notion that we can or should insulate public employee bargaining from the political process either by arbitration or with some magic formula is a delusion of reality and a denigration of democratic government.

# 2. PUBLIC EMPLOYERS — SOME DEFINITIONAL CONSIDERATIONS

In our complex society a seemingly endless variety of legal entities have been established for a wide variety of purposes. Entities such as states, cities and counties are clearly public employers; others such as corporations that are privately owned, financed and operated are clearly private employers. While it is an easy task at the extremes to distinguish a public employer from a private employer, there is a gray area in which the entity has the attributes of both a public employer and a private employer. Courts and the various agencies administering labor relations legislation are not infrequently faced with the threshold question of determining whether an employer is public or private. This determination is important in order to ascertain which statutory provisions, if any, are applicable to a given employer and thus to determine the rights and obligations of the employees and employer. This is particularly significant in those states where public employees are prohibited from striking.

## NLRB v. NATURAL GAS UTILITY DISTRICT OF HAWKINS COUNTY, TENNESSEE

Supreme Court of the United States
402 U.S. 600, 91 S. Ct. 1746, 29 L. Ed. 2d 206 (1971)

MR. JUSTICE BRENNAN delivered the opinion of the Court.

Upon the petition of Plumbers and Steamfitters Local 102, the National Labor Relations Board ordered that a representation election be held among the pipefitters employed by respondent, Natural Gas Utility District of Hawkins County, Tennessee, 167 N.L.R.B. 691 (1967). In the representation proceeding, respondent objected to the Board's jurisdiction on the sole ground that as a "political subdivision" of Tennessee, it was not an "employer" subject to Board jurisdiction under § 2(2) of the National Labor Relations Act, as amended by the Labor Management Relations Act, 1947, 61 Stat. 137, 29 U.S.C. § 152 (2).[1] When the Union won the election and was certified by the Board as bargaining representative of the pipefitters, respondent refused to comply with the Board's certification and recognize and bargain with the Union. An unfair labor practice proceeding resulted and the Board entered a cease-and-desist order against respondent on findings that respondent was in violation of §§ 8(a)(1) and 8(a)(5) of the Act, 29 U.S.C. §§ 158 (a)(1) and 158(a)(5). 170 N.L.R.B. 1409 (1968). Respondent continued its noncompliance and the Board sought enforcement of the order in the Court of Appeals for the Sixth Circuit. Enforcement was refused, the court holding that respondent was a "political subdivision," as contended. 427 F.2d 312 (1970). We granted certiorari, 400 U.S. 990 (1971). We affirm.

The respondent was organized under Tennessee's Utility District Law of 1937, Tenn. Code Ann. §§ 6-2601 to 6-2627 (1955). In First Suburban Water Utility District v. McCanless, 177 Tenn. 128, 146 S.W.2d 948 (1941), the Tennessee Supreme Court held that a utility district organized under this Act was an operation for a state governmental or public purpose. The Court of Appeals held that this decision "was of controlling importance on the question whether the District was a political subdivision of the state" within § 2(2) and "was binding on the Board." 427 F.2d, at 315. The Board, on the other hand, had held that "while such State law declarations and interpretations are given careful consideration . . . , they are not necessarily controlling." 167 N.L.R.B., at 691.

_____

[1] Section 2 (2), 29 U.S.C. § 152(2), provides:

"The term 'employer' includes any person acting as an agent of an employer, directly or indirectly, but shall not include the United States or any wholly owned Government corporation, or any Federal Reserve Bank, or any State or political subdivision thereof, or any corporation or association operating a hospital, if no part of the net earnings inures to the benefit of any private shareholder or individual, or any person subject to the Railway Labor Act, as amended from time to time, or any labor organization (other than when acting as an employer), or anyone acting in the capacity of officer or agent of such labor organization."

We disagree with the Court of Appeals and agree with the Board. Federal, rather than state, law governs the determination, under § 2(2), whether an entity created under state law is a "political subdivision" of the State and therefore not an "employer" subject to the Act.

The Court of Appeals for the Fourth Circuit dealt with this question in NLRB v. Randolph Electric Membership Corp., 343 F.2d 60 (1965), where the Board had determined that Randolph Electric was not a "political subdivision" within § 2(2). We adopt as correct law what was said at 62-63 of the opinion in that case:

"There are, of course, instances in which the application of certain federal statutes may depend on state law. . . .

"But this is controlled by the will of Congress. In the absence of a plain indication to the contrary, however, it is to be assumed when Congress enacts a statute that it does not intend to make its application dependent on state law. Jerome v. United States, 318 U.S. 101, 104 . . . (1943).

"The argument of the electric corporations fails to persuade us that Congress intended the result for which they contend. Furthermore, it ignores the teachings of the Supreme Court as to the congressional purpose in enacting the national labor laws. In National Labor Relations Board v. Hearst Publications, 322 U.S. 111, 123 . . . (1944), the Court dealt with the meaning of the term 'employee' as used in the Wagner Act, saying:

" 'Both the terms and the purposes of the statute, as well as the legislative history, show that Congress had in mind no . . . patchwork plan for securing freedom of employees' organization and of collective bargaining. The Wagner Act is federal legislation, administered by a national agency, intended to solve a national problem on a national scale. . . . Nothing in the statute's background, history, terms or purposes indicates its scope is to be limited by . . . varying local conceptions, either statutory or judicial, or that it is to be administered in accordance with whatever different standards the respective states may see fit to adopt for the disposition of unrelated, local problems.'

"Thus, it is clear that state law is not controlling and that it is to the actual operations and characteristics of [respondents] that we must look in deciding whether there is sufficient support for the Board's conclusion that they are not 'political subdivisions' within the meaning of the National Labor Relations Act."

We turn then to identification of the governing federal law. The term "political subdivision" is not defined in the Act and the Act's legislative history does not disclose that Congress explicitly considered its meaning. The legislative history does reveal, however, that Congress enacted the § 2(2) exemption to except from Board cognizance the labor relations of federal, state, and municipal governments, since governmental employees did not usually enjoy the right to strike.[3] In the light of that purpose, the Board, according to its Brief, p. 11, "has limited the exemption for political subdivisions to entities that are either (1) created directly by the state, so as to constitute departments or administrative arms of the government, or (2) administered by individuals who are responsible to public officials or to the general electorate."

---

[3] See 78 Cong. Rec. 10351 *et seq.;* Hearings on Labor Disputes Act before the House Committee on Labor, 74th Cong., 1st Sess., 179; 93 Cong. Rec. 6441 (Sen. Taft). See also C. Rhyne, Labor Unions and Municipal Employee Law 436-437 (1946); Vogel, What About the Rights of the Public Employee?, 1 Lab. L.J. 604, 612-615 (1950).

The Board's construction of the broad statutory term is, of course, entitled to great respect. Randolph Electric, *supra,* at 62. This case does not however require that we decide whether "the actual operations and characteristics" of an entity must necessarily feature one or the other of the Board's limitations to qualify an entity for the exemption, for we think that it is plain on the face of the Tennessee statute that the Board erred in its reading of it in light of the Board's own test. The Board found that "the Employer in this case is neither created directly by the State, nor administered by State-appointed or elected officials." 167 N.L.R.B., at 691-692 (footnotes omitted). But the Board test is not whether the entity is administered by "State-appointed or elected officials." Rather, alternative (2) of the test is whether the entity is "administered *by individuals who are responsible to public officials* or to the general electorate" (emphasis added), and the Tennessee statute makes crystal clear that respondent is administered by a Board of Commissioners appointed by an elected county judge, and subject to removal proceedings at the instance of the Governor, the county prosecutor, or private citizens. Therefore, in the light of other "actual operations and characteristics" under that administration, the Board's holding that respondent "exists as an essentially private venture, with insufficient identity with or relationship to the State of Tennessee," 167 N.L.R.B., at 691, has no "warrant in the record" and no "reasonable basis in law." NLRB v. Hearst Publications, 322 U.S. 111, 131 (1944).

Respondent is one of nearly 270 utility districts established under the Utility District Law of 1937. Under that statute, Tennessee residents may create districts to provide a wide range of public services such as the furnishing of water, sewers, sewage disposal, police protection, fire protection, garbage collection, street lighting, parks, and recreational facilities as well as the distribution of natural gas. Tenn. Code Ann. § 6-2608 (Supp. 1970). Acting under the statute, 38 owners of real property submitted in 1957 a petition to the county court of Hawkins County requesting the incorporation of a utility district to distribute natural gas within a specified portion of the county. The county judge, after holding a required public hearing and making required findings that the "public convenience and necessity requires the creation of the district," and that "the creation of the district is economically sound and desirable," Tenn. Code Ann. § 6-2604 (Supp. 1970), entered an order establishing the District. The judge's order and findings were appealable to Tennessee's appellate courts by any party "having an interest in the subject-matter." Tenn. Code Ann. § 6-2606 (1955).

To carry out its functions, the District is granted not only all the powers of a private corporation, Tenn. Code Ann. § 6-2610 (1955), but also "all the powers necessary and requisite for the accomplishment of the purpose for which such district is created, capable of being delegated by the legislature." Tenn. Code Ann. § 6-2612 (1955). This delegation includes the power of eminent domain, which the District may exercise even against other governmental entities. Tenn. Code Ann. § 6-2611 (1955). The District is operated on a nonprofit basis, and is declared by the statute to be "a 'municipality' or public corporation in perpetuity under its corporate name and the same shall in that name be a body politic and corporate with power of perpetual succession, but without any power to levy or collect taxes." Tenn. Code Ann. § 6-2607 (Supp. 1970). The property and revenue of the District are exempted from all state, county, and municipal taxes, and the District bonds are similarly exempt from such taxation, except for inheritance, transfer, and estate taxes. Tenn. Code Ann. § 6-2626 (1955).

The District's records are "public records" and as such open for inspection. Tenn. Code Ann. § 6-2615 (Supp. 1970). The District is required to publish its annual statement in a newspaper of general circulation, showing its financial condition, its earnings, and its method of setting rates. Tenn. Code Ann. § 6-2617 (Supp. 1970). The statute requires the District's commissioners to hear any protest to its rates filed within 30 days of publication of the annual statement at a public hearing, and to make and to publish written findings as to the reasonableness of the rates. Tenn. Code Ann. § 6-2618 (1955). The commissioners' determination may be challenged in the county court, under procedures prescribed by the statute. *Ibid.*

The District's commissioners are initially appointed, from among persons nominated in the petition, by the county judge, who is an elected public official. Tenn. Code Ann. § 6-2604 (Supp. 1970). The commissioners serve four-year terms and, contrary to the Board's finding that the State reserves no "power to remove or otherwise discipline those responsible for the Employer's operations," 167 N.L.R.B., at 692, are subject to removal under Tennessee's General Ouster Law, which provides procedures for removing public officials from office for misfeasance or nonfeasance. Tenn. Code Ann. § 8-2701 *et seq.* (1955); First Suburban Water Utility District v. McCanless, 177 Tenn., at 138, 146 S.W.2d, at 952. Proceedings under the law may be initiated by the Governor, the state attorney general, the county prosecutor, or ten citizens. Tenn. Code Ann. §§ 8-2708, 8-2709, 8-2710 (1955). When a vacancy occurs, the county judge appoints a new commissioner if the remaining two commissioners cannot agree upon a replacement. Tenn. Code Ann. § 6-2614 (Supp. 1970). In large counties, all vacancies are filled by popular election. *Ibid.* The commissioners are generally empowered to conduct the District's business. They have the power to subpoena witnesses and to administer oaths in investigating District affairs, Tenn. Code Ann. § 6-2616(5) (1955), and they serve for only nominal compensation. Tenn. Code Ann. § 6-2615 (Supp. 1970). Plainly, commissioners who are beholden to an elected public official for their appointment, and are subject to removal procedures applicable to all public officials, qualify as "individuals who are responsible to public officials or to the general electorate" within the Board's test.

In such circumstances, the Board itself has recognized that authority to exercise the power of eminent domain weighs in favor of finding an entity to be a political subdivision. New Jersey Turnpike Authority, 33 L.R.R.M. 1528 (1954). We have noted that respondent's power of eminent domain may be exercised even against other governmental units. And the District is further given an extremely broad grant of "all the powers necessary and requisite for the accomplishment of the purpose for which such district is created, capable of being delegated by the legislature." Tenn. Code Ann. § 6-2612 (1955). The District's "public records" requirement and the automatic right to a public hearing and written "decision" by the commissioners accorded to all users betoken a state, rather than a private, instrumentality. The commissioners' power of subpoena and their nominal compensation further suggest the public character of the District.

Moreover, a conclusion that the District is a political subdivision finds support in the treatment of the District under other federal laws. Income from its bonds is exempt from federal income tax, as income from an obligation of a "political subdivision" under 26 U.S.C. § 103. Social Security benefits for the District's employees are provided through voluntary rather than mandatory coverage since the District is considered a political subdivision under the Social Security Act. 42 U.S.C. § 418.

Respondent is therefore an entity "administered by individuals [the commissioners] who are responsible to public officials [an elected county judge]" and this together with the other factors mentioned satisfies us that its relationship to the State is such that respondent is a "political subdivision" within the meaning of § 2(2) of the Act. Accordingly, the Court of Appeals' judgment denying enforcement of the Board's order is

*Affirmed.*

[The dissenting opinion of Mr. Justice Stewart is omitted.]

## NOTES

1. In Roza Irrigation Dist. v. State of Washington, 80 Wash. 2d 633, 497 P.2d 166 (1972), the Washington Supreme Court was faced with a question of whether an irrigation district was a "municipal corporation" and thus covered by the Washington public sector collective bargaining statute. In giving the term "municipal corporation" a broad construction, the court stated:

> . . . We find no such restrictive intent expressed in the statute. The service which irrigation district employees render is a vital one in the areas which they serve. It is in the public interest to avoid interruption of irrigation services, just as it is to avoid interruption of services rendered by a city's fire or police department. We are given no plausible reason why the legislature should have chosen to deny such employees the protection of the act or to regard them as private employees, having the right to strike. 497 P.2d at 170.

2. In Nassau Library System, 1 PERB ¶ 399.47 (1968), the New York Public Employment Relations Board held that the library in question was not a "government" or a "public employer" within the meaning of the Taylor Law and that, therefore, it did not have jurisdiction over the employer. The PERB noted that

> It would clearly be improper to apply the term "instrumentality or unit of government" to *any* corporate entity solely on the basis of the state or county aid it receives, the fact that it was established pursuant to a charter by permission of the legislature, or the fact that it performs a public service which is performed by other organs in the public sector as well.

Subsequently the NLRB ruled that it likewise did not have jurisdiction. Nassau Library System, 196 N.L.R.B. 864 (1972). In declining to assert jurisdiction over the Nassau Library System, the Board pointed to the "unique relationship" between the System and the state and county, stating:

> [V]irtually all of the System's operating income is derived either directly or indirectly from the State of New York and Nassau County. In addition, the System's board of trustees is appointed by, and the System itself services, various public libraries. . . .
>
> Moreover, the State of New York has intervened in the past over the System's day-to-day operations. The State of New York also places stringent requirements on the System to see that its plan of service is adequate, that its funds are invested in preapproved securities, and that it complies with state regulations regarding the purchase of books.
>
> For these reasons, we conclude, without deciding the System's status under Section 2(2) of the Act, that it would not effectuate the policies of the Act to assert jurisdiction over the System. Accordingly, we shall dismiss the petition.

In view of these holdings by the New York PERB and the NLRB, where else could a union seeking to represent the System's employees turn? By virtue of these decisions, has a no-man's land been created?

3. For many years the NLRB declined to assert jurisdiction over a private entity where the operations of such a private entity were intimately connected with the statutorily

mandated functions carried out by a governmental entity. In these cases the NLRB held that the private entity shared the public employer's exemption from coverage under the National Labor Relations Act. *See, e.g.,* Camptown Bus Lines, Inc., 226 N.L.R.B. 4 (1976); Roesch Lines, Inc., 224 N.L.R.B. 203 (1976). In National Transportation Inc., 240 NLRB No. 64, 100 L.R.R.M. 1263 (1979), however, the NLRB abandoned its adherence to the "intimate connection" test and asserted jurisdiction over a bus company that provided school bus service to several public school systems. The Board held that the sole test in such cases should be whether the private entity "retains sufficient control over its employees to enable it to engage in meaningful bargaining over conditions of employment with a labor organization."

## MILWAUKEE AUDITORIUM BOARD

Wisconsin Employment Relations Commission
Decision No. 6543 (1963)

The Union petitioned the Board to conduct an election to determine what, if any, representation the operating engineers employed by the Employer desired, pursuant to Section 111.05 of the Wisconsin Employment Peace Act. At the hearing the Employer, by its Counsel, contended that the Employer was a political subdivision of the state within the meaning of Section 111.70 and that therefore any election by the one operating engineer in its employ should be held pursuant to that subsection.

The Employer operates an auditorium and arena for the purpose of providing facilities for public meetings, conventions, expositions, and other purposes of a public nature for which its buildings are suitable. The Employer is in the nature of a joint Employer having two distinct and separate parts. The first is a private corporation and the second is the City of Milwaukee. This form of organization permitted the Employer to acquire some of the necessary capital for the construction of the auditorium. However, the arena was constructed entirely from public funds. The city owns the land and buildings of the Employer and controls the operation of the Employer by virtue of the fact that a majority of the board of trustees of the Employer are city officials. In recent years, the city has acquired portions of the stock of the corporation. However, not all of the corporation stock of the Employer has been transferred to the city since in such event the corporation would be dissolved and the board of trustees would consist of the city officials exclusively.

The Board has held that the fact that a corporation is authorized to disburse public moneys in performing a public purpose and furthermore that it is, by virtue of its organization and statutory limitations, substantially controlled by the State, is not determinative of the question whether such corporation is a state agency or political subdivision of the state.[1] In this same case, the Board looked to the particular language used in the Statute creating the Employer in determining whether such Employer should be deemed a political subdivision of the state. Section 43.44 Wisconsin Statutes provides in part:

"(1) Any city of the first class may establish and maintain public auditoriums and music halls; and may establish, maintain and operate the same jointly, share and share alike, by agreement between the common council of such city and private corporation duly organized for that purpose.

"(2) Such private corporation shall execute to the city a bond, in a sum determined and with sureties approved by said common council, conditioned

---

[1] Milwaukee County War Memorial, Inc., Decision No. 6325, 4/63.

that the said corporation will furnish its share of money as the same shall be required for the purposes specified in subsection (1).

. . . .

"(5) Whenever the city shall have acquired all the stock of such corporation, the said corporation shall ipso facto be dissolved and the title to all its property of whatsoever nature, shall vest in said city; thereupon the auditorium board provided for in section 43.45 shall consist of only the ex officio members specified in said section.

. . . .

"(7) Any such city may build additions to such auditoriums and for the purposes of any such addition, by action of the common council, issue revenue bonds under the provisions of section 66.51 payable exclusively from income and revenues of any such addition and of any auditorium to which it is added which said auditoriums and additions thereto for such purpose are declared a public utility. Said private corporation shall not be required to contribute to any such addition. Any such addition shall be subject in all other respects to the provisions of sections 43.44 to 43.48."

The statutory language recognizes that a portion of the Employer's operation will be carried on by a private corporation operating jointly with the city. Part of the funds necessary to build the auditorium were furnished by the corporation. The corporation elects five members to the eleven member board of trustees which is charged by statute with full and complete control of the Employer. The statute further recognizes that stock in the corporation may be transferred to the city and that the corporation may assume a secondary role in furnishing capital for new buildings for the Employer. Nevertheless, the corporation retains its corporate entity, elects the members of the board of trustees that it is entitled to elect, and shares in the operation of the Employer, share and share alike, until such time as all of the stock of the corporation is transferred to the city. Such being the case, the Employer must be deemed a joint operation between a private corporation and a municipality.

The Petitioner herein petitioned the Board to conduct a representation election in a bargaining unit consisting of one operating engineer employed by the Milwaukee Auditorium Board pursuant to 111.05 of the Wisconsin Statutes. The Employer contends that the election should be conducted pursuant to 111.70(4) (d) of the Wisconsin Statutes since it is a municipal employer and not a private employer subject to the provisions of the Wisconsin Employment Peace Act.

Employes of private employers have greater rights than employes of municipal employers. Section 111.04 grants employes in private industry the right to "engage in collective bargaining through representatives of their own choosing, and to engage in lawful concerted activities, such as strikes, picketing, and bargaining, or other mutual aid or protection," which refers to lawful concerted activities, such as strikes, picketing and boycotts, labor unions traditionally use to induce employers to accede to their demands. Section 111.70(a), while granting the right to representation in collective bargaining, omits the right to engage in concerted activities. Section 111.70(l) prohibits strikes by municipal employes and, in its stead, in Section 111.70 (e) through (g) establishes fact finding procedures for the resolution of disputes. The question here before the Board is not merely an administration matter as to which section of the statutes shall be cited when the Board directs its election, but is determinative of the right of the employe involved to engage in certain concerted activity. The representative of the Petitioning Union indicated his awareness of the basic issue when he stated on the record he sought in this proceeding the right to strike. The Milwaukee Auditorium Board operates the Milwaukee Arena and Auditorium. The operation is controlled by a private corporation established by the Wisconsin Statutes and by representatives of the City of Milwaukee. The private corporation was formed to acquire some of the necessary capital, for the construction of the auditorium. However, the latter building, the Arena, is constructed entirely from municipal funds. The City of Milwaukee has title to the land and buildings and controls the operation by virtue of the fact that a majority of the board of trustees are city officials. Furthermore in recent years the City of Milwaukee has been acquiring portions of the stock of the corporation and eventually all the corporate stock will be transferred to the City of Milwaukee. It appears to the Board that the City of Milwaukee is the senior partner in this organization having the greater control and having made the greater financial contribution and therefore any employes employed by the Milwaukee Auditorium Board are to be deemed municipal employes. Therefore the election shall be conducted pursuant to 111.70(4) (d) of the Wisconsin Statutes.

## NOTE

In Milwaukee County War Memorial Center, Inc., WERC Decision No. 6325 (1963), the Wisconsin Employment Relations Commission held that the war memorial was not a public employer even though (1) eight of the 15 members of the Board of Directors were elected by the Milwaukee County Board, (2) the County retained legal title to the building, and (3) the County made "an annual appropriation to defray the cost of operating the building and auxiliary facilities, less any revenues the Employer receives. . . ."

## C. THE ROLE OF THE FEDERAL GOVERNMENT

## 1. CONSTITUTIONAL CONSIDERATIONS

### NATIONAL LEAGUE OF CITIES v. USERY

Supreme Court of the United States
426 U.S. 833, 96 S. Ct. 2465, 49 L. Ed. 2d 245 (1976)

*overruled Jan '85*

MR. JUSTICE REHNQUIST delivered the opinion for the Court.

Nearly 40 years ago Congress enacted the Fair Labor Standards Act, and required employers covered by the Act to pay their employees a minimum hourly wage and to pay them at one and one-half times their regular rate of pay for hours worked in excess of 40 during a workweek. By this Act covered employers were required to keep certain records to aid in the enforcement of the Act, and to comply with specified child labor standards. This Court unanimously upheld the Act as a valid exercise of congressional authority under the commerce power in United States v. Darby, 312 U. S. 100 (1941), observing:

"Whatever their motive and purpose, regulations of commerce which do not infringe some constitutional prohibition are within the plenary power conferred on Congress by the Commerce Clause." *Id.,* at 115.

The original Fair Labor Standards Act passed in 1938 specifically excluded the States and their political subdivisions from its coverage. In 1974, however, Congress enacted the most recent of a series of broadening amendments to the

Act. By these amendments Congress has extended the minimum wage and maximum hour provisions to almost all public employees employed by the States and by their various political subdivisions. Appellants in these cases include individual cities and States, the National League of Cities, and the National Governors' Conference; they brought an action in the District Court for the District of Columbia which challenged the validity of the 1974 amendments. They asserted in effect that when Congress sought to apply the Fair Labor Standards Act provisions virtually across the board to employees of state and municipal governments it "infringed a constitutional prohibition" running in favor of the States *as States.* The gist of their complaint was not that the conditions of employment of such public employees were beyond the scope of the commerce power had those employees been employed in the private sector, but that the established constitutional doctrine of intergovernmental immunity consistently recognized in a long series of our cases affirmatively prevented the exercise of this authority in the manner which Congress chose in the 1974 Amendments.

I

In a series of amendments beginning in 1961 Congress began to extend the provisions of the Fair Labor Standards Act to some types of public employees. The 1961 amendment to the Act extended its coverage to persons who were employed in "enterprises" engaged in commerce or in the production of goods for commerce. And in 1966, with the amendment of the definition of employers under the Act, the exemption heretofore extended to the States and their political subdivisions was removed with respect to employees of state hospitals, institutions, and schools. We nevertheless sustained the validity of the combined effect of these two amendments in Maryland v. Wirtz, 392 U. S. 183 (1968).

In 1974, Congress again broadened the coverage of the Act. The definition of "employer" in the Act now specifically "includes a public agency," 29 U. S. C. § 203(d). In addition, the critical definition of "enterprises engaged in commerce or in the production of goods for commerce" was expanded to encompass "an activity of a public agency," and goes on to specify that

> "[t]he employees of an enterprise which is a public agency shall for purposes of this subsection be deemed to be employees engaged in commerce, or in the production of goods for commerce, or employees handling, selling, or otherwise working on goods or materials that have been moved in or produced for commerce." 29 U. S. C. § 203(s)(5).

Under the Amendments "[p]ublic agency" is in turn defined as including

> "the Government of the United States; the government of a State or political subdivision thereof; any agency of the United States (including the United States Postal Service and Postal Rate Commission), a State, or a political subdivision of a State; or any interstate governmental agency." 29 U. S. C. § 203(x).

By its 1974 amendments, then, Congress has now entirely removed the exemption previously afforded States and their political subdivisions, substituting only the Act's general exemption for executive, administrative, or professional personnel, 29 U. S. C. § 213(a)(1), which is supplemented by provisions excluding from the Act's coverage those individuals holding public elective office or serving such an officeholder in one of several specific capacities. 29 U. S. C. § 203(e)(2)(C). The Act thus imposes upon almost all public employment the minimum wage and maximum hour requirements previously restricted to employees engaged in interstate commerce. These requirements are essentially identical to those imposed upon private employers, although the Act does attempt to make some provision for public employment relationships which are without counterpart in the private sector, such as those presented by fire protection and law enforcement personnel. See 29 U. S. C. § 207(k).

Challenging these 1974 amendments in the District Court, appellants sought both declaratory and injunctive relief against the amendments' application to them, and a three-judge court was accordingly convened pursuant to 28 U. S. C. § 2282. That court, after hearing argument on the law from the parties, granted appellee Secretary of Labor's motion to dismiss the complaint for failure to state a claim upon which relief might be granted. The District Court stated it was "troubled" by appellants' contentions that the amendments would intrude upon the States' performance of essential governmental functions. The court went on to say that it considered their contentions:

> "substantial and that it may well be that the Supreme Court will feel it appropriate to draw back from the far-reaching implications of [*Maryland v. Wirtz, supra*]; but that is a decision that only the Supreme Court can make; and as a Federal district court we feel obliged to apply the *Wirtz* opinion as it stands."

We noted probable jurisdiction in order to consider the important questions recognized by the District Court. 420 U. S. 906 (1975). We agree with the District Court that the appellants' contentions are substantial. Indeed upon full consideration of the question we have decided that the "far-reaching implications" of *Wirtz* should be overruled, and that the judgment of the District Court must be reversed.

## II

It is established beyond peradventure ~~doubt~~ that the Commerce Clause of Art. I of the Constitution is a grant of plenary authority to Congress. That authority is, in the words of Chief Justice Marshall in *Gibbons v. Ogden,* 9 Wheat. (21 U. S.) 1 (1824), ". . . the power to regulate; that is to prescribe the rule by which commerce is to be governed." *Id.,* at 196.

When considering the validity of asserted applications of this power to wholly private activity, the Court has made it clear that

> "[e]ven activity that is purely intrastate in character may be regulated by Congress, where the activity, combined with like conduct by others similarly situated, affects commerce among the States or with foreign nations." Fry v. United States, 421 U. S. 542, 547 (1975).

Congressional power over areas of private endeavor, even when its exercise may pre-empt express state law determinations contrary to the result which has commended itself to collective wisdom of Congress, has been held to be limited only by the requirement that "the means chosen by [Congress] must be reasonably adapted to the end permitted by the Constitution." Heart of Atlanta Motel, Inc. v. United States, 379 U. S. 241, 262 (1964).

Appellants in no way challenge these decisions establishing the breadth of authority granted Congress under the commerce power. Their contention, on the contrary, is that when Congress seeks to regulate directly the activities of States as public employers, it transgresses an affirmative limitation on the exercise of its power akin to other commerce power affirmative limitations contained in the Constitution. Congressional enactments which may be fully within the grant of legislative authority contained in the Commerce Clause may nonetheless be invalid because found to offend against the right to trial by jury contained in the Sixth Amendment, United States v. Jackson, 390 U. S. 570 (1968), or the Due Process Clause of the Fifth Amendment, Leary v. United States, 395 U. S. 6 (1969). Appellants' essential contention is that the 1974 amendments to the Act, while undoubtedly within the scope of the Commerce Clause, encounter a similar constitutional barrier because they are to be applied directly to the States and subdivisions of States as employers.

This Court has never doubted that there are limits upon the power of Congress to override state sovereignty, even when exercising its otherwise plenary powers to tax or to regulate commerce which are conferred by Art. I of the Constitution. In *Wirtz,* for example, the Court took care to assure the appellants that it had "ample power to prevent . . . 'the utter destruction of the State as a sovereign political entity,' " which they feared. 392 U. S., at 196. Appellee Secretary in this case, both in his brief and upon oral argument, has agreed that our federal system of government imposes definite limits upon the authority of Congress to regulate the activities of the States as States by means of the commerce power. See, *e.g.,* Appellee's Brief, at 30-41; Tr. of Oral Arg. 39-43. In *Fry, supra,* the Court recognized that an express declaration of this limitation is found in the Tenth Amendment:

> "While the Tenth Amendment has been characterized as a 'truism,' stating merely that 'all is retained which has not been surrendered,' United States v. Darby, 312 U. S. 100, 124 (1941), it is not without significance. The Amendment expressly declares the constitutional policy that Congress may not exercise power in a fashion that impairs the States' integrity or their ability to function effectively in a federal system. . . ." 421 U. S., at 547.

In New York v. United States, 326 U. S. 572 (1946), Chief Justice Stone, speaking for four Members of an eight-Member Court in rejecting the proposition that Congress could impose taxes on the States so long as it did so in a nondiscriminatory manner, observed:

> "A State may, like a private individual, own real property and receive income. But in view of our former decisions we could hardly say that a general nondiscriminatory real estate tax (apportioned), or an income tax laid upon citizens and States alike could be constitutionally applied to the State's capitol, its State-house, its public school houses, public parks, or its revenues from taxes or school lands, even though all real property and all income of the citizen is taxed." 326 U. S., at 587-588.

The expressions in these more recent cases trace back to earlier decisions of this Court recognizing the essential role of the States in our federal system of government. Chief Justice Chase, perhaps because of the particular time at which he occupied that office, had occasion more than once to speak for the Court on this point. In Texas v. White, 7 Wall. 700, 725 (1869), he declared that "[t]he Constitution, in all its provisions, looks to an indestructible Union, composed of indestructible States." In Lane County v. Oregon, 7 Wall. 71 (1869), his opinion for the Court said:

> "Both the States and the United States existed before the Constitution. The people, through that instrument, established a more perfect union by

substituting a national government, acting, with ample power, directly upon the citizens, instead of the Confederate government which acted with powers, greatly restricted, only upon the States. But in many Articles of the Constitution the necessary existence of the States, and, within their proper spheres, the independent authority of the States, is distinctly recognized." *Id.,* at 76.

In Metcalf & Eddy v. Mitchell, 269 U. S. 514 (1926), the Court likewise observed that "neither government may destroy the other nor curtail in any substantial manner the exercise of its powers." *Id.,* at 523.

Appellee Secretary argues that the cases in which this Court has upheld sweeping exercises of authority by Congress, even though those exercises pre-empted state regulation of the private sector, have already curtailed the sovereignty of the States quite as much as the 1974 amendments to the Fair Labor Standards Act. We do not agree. It is one thing to recognize the authority of Congress to enact laws regulating individual businesses necessarily subject to the dual sovereignty of the government of the Nation and of the State in which they reside. It is quite another to uphold a similar exercise of congressional authority directed not to private citizens, but to the States as States. We have repeatedly recognized that there are attributes of sovereignty attaching to every state government which may not be impaired by Congress, not because Congress may lack an affirmative grant of legislative authority to reach the matter, but because the Constitution prohibits it from exercising the authority in that manner. In Coyle v. Smith, 221 U. S. 559 (1911), the Court gave this example of such an attribute:

> "The power to locate its own seat of government and to determine when and how it shall be changed from one place to another, and to appropriate its own public funds for that purpose, are essentially and peculiarly state powers. That one of the original thirteen States could now be shorn of such powers by an Act of Congress would not be for a moment entertained." 221 U. S., at 565.

One undoubted attribute of state sovereignty is the States' power to determine the wages which shall be paid to those whom they employ in order to carry out their governmental functions, what hours those persons will work, and what compensation will be provided where these employees may be called upon to work overtime. The question we must resolve in this case, then, is whether these determinations are "functions essential to separate and independent existence," *Coyle v. Smith, supra,* at 580, quoting from *Lane County v. Oregon, supra,* at 76, so that Congress may not abrogate the States' otherwise plenary authority to make them.

In their complaint appellants advanced estimates of substantial costs which will be imposed upon them by the 1974 amendments. Since the District Court dismissed their complaint, we take its well-pleaded allegations as true, although it appears from appellee's submissions in the District Court and in this Court that resolution of the factual disputes as to the effect of the amendments is not critical to our disposition of the case.

Judged solely in terms of increased costs in dollars, these allegations show a significant impact on the functioning of the governmental bodies involved. The Metropolitan Government of Nashville and Davidson County, Tenn., for example, asserted that the Act will increase its costs of providing essential police and fire protection, without any increase in service or in current salary levels, by

$938,000 per year. Cape Girardeau, Mo., estimated that its annual budget for fire protection may have to be increased by anywhere from $250,000 to $400,000 over the current figure of $350,000. The State of Arizona alleged that the annual additional expenditures which will be required if it is to continue to provide essential state services may total $2½ million dollars. The State of California, which must devote significant portions of its budget to fire suppression endeavors, estimated that application of the Act to its employment practices will necessitate an increase in its budget of between $8 million and $16 million.

Increased costs are not, of course, the only adverse effects which compliance with the Act will visit upon state and local governments, and in turn upon the citizens who depend upon those governments. In its complaint in intervention, for example, California asserted that it could not comply with the overtime costs (approximately $750,000 per year) which the Act required to be paid to California Highway Patrol cadets during their academy training program. California reported that it had thus been forced to reduce its academy training program from 2,080 hours to only 960 hours, a compromise undoubtedly of substantial importance to those whose safety and welfare may depend upon the preparedness of the California Highway Patrol.

This type of forced relinquishment of important governmental activities is further reflected in the complaint's allegation that the City of Inglewood, California, has been forced to curtail its affirmative action program for providing employment opportunities for men and women interested in a career in law enforcement. The Inglewood police department has abolished a program for police trainees who split their week between on the job training and the classroom. The city could not abrogate its contractual obligations to these trainees, and it concluded that compliance with the Act in these circumstances was too financially burdensome to permit continuance of the classroom program. The city of Clovis, Cal., has been put to a similar choice regarding an internship program it was running in cooperation with a California State University. According to the complaint, because the interns' compensation brings them within the purview of the Act the city must decide whether to eliminate the program entirely or to substantially reduce its beneficial aspects by doing away with any pay for the interns.

Quite apart from the substantial costs imposed upon the States and their political subdivisions, the Act displaces state policies regarding the manner in which they will structure delivery of those governmental services which their citizens require. The Act, speaking directly to the States *qua* States, requires that they shall pay all but an extremely limited minority of their employees the minimum wage rates currently chosen by Congress. It may well be that as a matter of economic policy it would be desirable that States, just as private employers, comply with these minimum wage requirements. But it cannot be gainsaid that the federal requirement directly supplants the considered policy choices of the States' elected officials and administrators as to how they wish to structure pay scales in state employment. The State might wish to employ persons with little or no training, or those who wish to work on a casual basis, or those who for some other reason do not possess minimum employment requirements, and pay them less than the federally prescribed minimum wage. It may wish to offer part time or summer employment to teenagers at a figure less than the minimum wage, and if unable to do so may decline to offer such employment at all. But the Act would forbid such choices by the States. The only "discretion" left to them under the Act is either to attempt to increase their revenue to meet the additional financial burden imposed upon them by paying congressionally prescribed wages to their existing complement of employees, or to reduce that complement to a number which can be paid the federal minimum wage without increasing revenue.

This dilemma presented by the minimum wage restrictions may seem not immediately different from that faced by private employers, who have long been covered by the Act and who must find ways to increase their gross income if they are to pay higher wages while maintaining current earnings. The difference, however, is that a State is not merely a factor in the "shifting economic arrangements" of the private sector of the economy, Kovacs v. Cooper, 336 U. S. 77, 95 (1949) (Frankfurter, J., concurring), but is itself a coordinate element in the system established by the framers for governing our federal union.

The degree to which the FLSA amendments would interfere with traditional aspects of state sovereignty can be seen even more clearly upon examining the overtime requirements of the Act. The general effect of these provisions is to require the States to pay their employees at premium rates whenever their work exceeds a specified number of hours in a given period. The asserted reason for these provisions is to provide a financial disincentive upon using employees beyond the work period deemed appropriate by Congress. According to appellee,

> "[t]his premium rate can be avoided if the [State] uses other employees to do the overtime work. This, in effect, tends to discourage overtime work and to spread employment, which is the result Congress intended." Appellee's Brief, at 43.

We do not doubt that this may be a salutary result, and that it has a sufficiently rational relationship to commerce to validate the application of the overtime provisions to private employers. But, like the minimum wage provisions, the vice of the Act as sought to be applied here is that it directly penalizes the States for choosing to hire governmental employees on terms different from those which Congress has sought to impose.

This congressionally imposed displacement of state decisions may substantially restructure traditional ways in which the local governments have arranged their affairs. Although at this point many of the actual effects under the proposed Amendments remain a matter of some dispute among the parties, enough can be satisfactorily anticipated for an outline discussion of their general import. The requirement imposing premium rates upon any employment in excess of what Congress has decided is appropriate for a governmental employee's workweek, for example, appears likely to have the effect of coercing the States to structure work periods in some employment areas, such as police and fire protection, in a manner substantially different from practices which have long been commonly accepted among local governments of this Nation. In addition, appellee represents that the Act will require that the premium compensation for overtime worked must be paid in cash, rather than with compensatory time off, unless such compensatory time is taken in the same pay period. Appellee's Supp. Brief, at 9-10; see Dunlop v. New Jersey, 522 F.2d 504 (CA3 1975), *cert. pending,* No. 75-532. This, too, appears likely to be highly disruptive of accepted employment practices in many governmental areas where the demand for a number of employees to perform important jobs for extended periods on short notice can be both unpredictable and critical. Another example of congressional choices displacing those of the States in the area of what are without doubt essential governmental decisions may be found in the practice of using volunteer firemen, a source of manpower crucial to many of our smaller towns' existence. Under the regulations proposed by appellee, whether individuals are indeed "volunteers" rather than "employees" subject to the minimum wage provisions

*Reasons*

of the Act are questions to be decided in the courts. See Appellee's Brief, at 49 and n. 41. It goes without saying that provisions such as these contemplate a significant reduction of traditional volunteer assistance which has been in the past drawn on to complement the operation of many local governmental functions.

Holding

Our examination of the effect of the 1974 amendments, as sought to be extended to the States and their political subdivisions, satisfies us that both the minimum wage and the maximum hour provisions will impermissibly interfere with the integral governmental functions of these bodies. We earlier noted some disagreement between the parties regarding the precise effect the amendments will have in application. We do not believe particularized assessments of actual impact are crucial to resolution of the issue presented, however. For even if we accept appellee's assessments concerning the impact of the amendments, their application will nonetheless significantly alter or displace the States' abilities to structure employer-employee relationships in such areas as fire prevention, police protection, sanitation, public health, and parks and recreation. These activities are typical of those performed by state and local governments in discharging their dual functions of administering the public law and furnishing public services. Indeed, it is functions such as these which governments are created to provide, services such as these which the States have traditionally afforded their citizens. If Congress may withdraw from the States the authority to make those fundamental employment decisions upon which their systems for performance of these functions must rest, we think there would be little left of the States' " 'separate and independent existence.' " *Coyle, supra.* Thus, even if appellants may have overestimated the effect which the Act will have upon their current levels and patterns of governmental activity, the dispositive factor is that

Reasons behind Holding

Congress has attempted to exercise its Commerce Clause authority to prescribe minimum wages and maximum hours to be paid by the States in their capacities as sovereign governments. In so doing, Congress has sought to wield its power in a fashion that would impair the States' "ability to function effectively within a federal system," *Fry, supra,* at 547. This exercise of congressional authority does not comport with the federal system of government embodied in the Constitution. We hold that insofar as the challenged amendments operate to directly displace the States' freedom to structure integral operations in areas of traditional governmental functions, they are not within the authority granted Congress by Art. I, § 8, cl. 3.[17]

### III

One final matter requires our attention. Appellee has vigorously urged that we cannot, consistently with the Court's decisions in *Wirtz, supra,* and *Fry, supra,* rule against him here. It is important to examine this contention so that it will be clear what we hold today, and what we do not.

With regard to *Fry,* we disagree with appellee. There the Court held that the Economic Stabilization Act of 1970 was constitutional as applied to temporarily freeze the wages of state and local government employees. The Court expressly noted that the degree of intrusion upon the protected area of state sovereignty was in that case even less than that worked by the amendments to the FLSA which were before the Court in *Wirtz.* The Court recognized that the Economic

[17] We express no view as to whether different results might obtain if Congress seeks to affect integral operations of state governments by exercising authority granted it under other sections of the Constitution such as the Spending Power, Art. I, § 8, cl. 1, or § 5 of the Fourteenth Amendment.

Stabilization Act was "an emergency measure to counter severe inflation that threatened the national economy." 421 U. S., at 548.

We think our holding today quite consistent with *Fry*. The enactment at issue there was occasioned by an extremely serious problem which endangered the well-being of all the component parts of our federal system and which only collective action by the National Government might forestall. The means selected were carefully drafted so as not to interfere with the States' freedom beyond a very limited, specific period of time. The effect of the across-the-board freeze authorized by that Act, moreover, displaced no state choices as to how governmental operations should be structured nor did it force the States to remake such choices themselves. Instead, it merely required that the wage scales and employment relationships which the States themselves had chosen be maintained during the period of the emergency. Finally, the Economic Stabilization Act operated to reduce the pressures upon state budgets rather than increase them. These factors distinguish the statute in *Fry* from the provisions at issue here. The limits imposed upon the commerce power when Congress seeks to apply it to the States are not so inflexible as to preclude temporary enactments tailored to combat a national emergency. "[A]lthough an emergency may not call into life a power which has never lived, nevertheless emergency may afford a reason for the exertion of a living power already enjoyed." Wilson v. New, 243 U. S. 332, 348 (1917).

With respect to the Court's decision in *Wirtz,* we reach a different conclusion. Both appellee and the District Court thought that decision required rejection of appellants' claims. Appellants, in turn, advance several arguments by which they seek to distinguish the facts before the Court in *Wirtz* from those presented by the 1974 amendments to the Act. There are undoubtedly factual distinctions between the two situations, but in view of the conclusions expressed earlier in this opinion we do not believe the reasoning in *Wirtz* may any longer be regarded as authoritative.

*Wirtz* relied heavily on the Court's decision in United States v. California, 297 U. S. 175 (1936). The opinion quotes the following language from that case:

> " '[We] look to the activities to which the states have traditionally engaged as marking the boundary of the restriction upon the federal taxing power. But there is no such limitation upon the plenary power to regulate commerce. The State can no more deny the power if its exercise has been authorized by Congress than can an individual.' 297 U. S., at 185." 392 U. S., at 198.

But we have reaffirmed today that the States as States stand on a quite different footing than an individual or a corporation when challenging the exercise of Congress' power to regulate commerce. We think the dicta [18] from *United States*

---

[18] The holding of United States v. California, 297 U.S. 175 (1936), as opposed to the language quoted in the text, is quite consistent with our holding today. There California's activity to which the congressional command was directed was not in an area that the States have regarded as integral parts of their governmental activities. It was, on the contrary, the operation of a railroad engaged in "common carriage by rail in interstate commerce . . ." 297 U.S., at 182.

For the same reasons, despite Mr. Justice Brennan's claims to the contrary, the holdings in Parden v. Terminal R. Co., 377 U.S. 184 (1964), and California v. Taylor, 353 U.S. 553 (1957), are likewise unimpaired by our decision today. It also seems appropriate to note that Case v. Bowles, 327 U.S. 92 (1946), has not been overruled as the dissent asserts. Indeed that decision, upon which our Brother heavily relies, has no direct application to the questions we consider today at all. For there the Court sustained an application of the Emergency Price Control Act to a sale of timber by the State of Washington, expressly noting that the "only question is whether the State's power to make the sales *v. California,* simply wrong.[19] Congress may not exercise that power so as to force directly upon the States its choices as to how essential decisions regarding the conduct of integral governmental functions are to be made. We agree that such assertions of power, if unchecked, would indeed, as Mr. Justice Douglas cautioned in his dissent in *Wirtz,* allow "the National Government [to] devour the essentials of state sovereignty," 392 U. S., at 205, and would therefore transgress the bounds of the authority granted Congress under the Commerce Clause. While there are obvious differences between the schools and hospitals involved in *Wirtz,* and the fire and police departments affected here, each provides an integral portion of those governmental services which the States and their political subdivisions have traditionally afforded their citizens.[20] We are therefore persuaded that *Wirtz* must be overruled.

The judgment of the District Court is accordingly reversed and the case is remanded for further proceedings consistent with this opinion.

So ordered.

Mr. Justice Blackmun, concurring.

The Court's opinion and the dissents indicate the importance and significance of this case as it bears upon the relationship between the Federal Government and our States. Although I am not untroubled by certain possible implications of the Court's opinion — some of them suggested by the dissents — I do not read the opinion so despairingly as does my Brother Brennan. In my view, the result with respect to the statute under challenge here is necessarily correct. I may misinterpret the Court's opinion, but it seems to me that it adopts a balancing approach, and does not outlaw federal power in areas such as environmental protection, where the federal interest is demonstrably greater and where state facility compliance with imposed federal standards would be essential. See *ante,* 18-19. With this understanding on my part of the Court's opinion, I join it.

Mr. Justice Brennan, with whom Mr. Justice White and Mr. Justice Marshall join, dissenting.

The Court concedes, as of course it must, that Congress enacted the 1974 amendments pursuant to its exclusive power under Art. I, § 8, cl. 3, of the Constitution "To regulate Commerce . . . among the several States." It must therefore be surprising that my Brethren should choose this Bicentennial year of our independence to repudiate principles governing judicial interpretation of our Constitution settled since the time of Mr. Chief Justice John Marshall,

---

must be in subordination to the power of Congress to fix maximum prices in order to carry on war." 327 U.S., at 102. The Court rejected the State's claim of immunity on the ground that sustaining it would impermissibly "impair a prime purpose of the Federal Government's establishment." *Ibid.* Nothing we say in this opinion addresses the scope of Congress' authority under its war power. Cf. n. 17, *supra.*

[19] Mr. Justice Brennan's dissent leaves no doubt from its discussion, *post,* at 20-22, that in its view Congress may under its commerce power deal with the States as States just as they might deal with private individuals. We venture to say that it is this conclusion, rather than the one we reach, which is in the words of the dissent a "startling restructuring of our federal system . . . ," *post,* at 20. Even the Government, defending the 1974 Amendments in this Court, does not take so extreme a position.

[20] As the denomination "political subdivision" implies, the local governmental units which Congress sought to bring within the Act derive their authority and power from their respective States. Interference with integral governmental services provided by such subordinate arms of a state government is therefore beyond the reach of congressional power under the Commerce Clause just as if such services were provided by the State itself.

discarding his postulate that the Constitution contemplates that restraints upon exercise by Congress of its plenary commerce power lie in the political process and not in the judicial process. For 152 years ago Mr. Chief Justice Marshall enunciated that principle to which, until today, his successors on this Court have been faithful.

> "[T]he power over commerce . . . is vested in Congress as absolutely as it would be in a single government, having in its constitution the same restrictions on the exercise of the power as are found in the constitution of the United States. *The wisdom and the discretion of Congress, their identity with the people, and the influence which their constituents possess at elections, are . . . the sole restraints on which they have relied, to secure them from its abuse. They are the restraints on which the people must often rely solely, in all representative governments.*" Gibbons v. Ogden, 9 Wheat. 1, 197 (1824) (emphasis added).

Only 34 years ago, Wickard v. Filburn, 317 U. S. 111, 120 (1942), reaffirmed that "[a]t the beginning Chief Justice Marshall . . . made emphatic the embracing and penetrating nature of [Congress' commerce] power by warning that effective restraints on its exercise must proceed from political rather than from judicial processes."

My Brethren do not successfully obscure today's patent usurpation of the role reserved for the political process by their purported discovery in the Constitution of a restraint derived from sovereignty of the States on Congress' exercise of the commerce power. . . .

. . . .

My Brethren thus have today manufactured an abstraction without substance, founded neither in the words of the Constitution nor on precedent. An abstraction having such profoundly pernicious consequences is not made less so by characterizing the 1974 amendments as legislation directed against the "States *qua* States." *Ante,* at 13. See *id.,* at 11, 20. Of course, regulations that this Court can say are not regulations of "commerce" cannot stand, Santa Cruz Fruit Packing Co. v. NLRB, 303 U. S. 453, 466 (1938), and in this sense "[t]he Court has ample power to prevent . . . 'the utter destruction of the State as a sovereign political entity.' " Maryland v. Wirtz, 392 U. S. 183, 196 (1968). But my Brethren make no claim that the 1974 amendments are not regulations of "commerce"; rather they overrule *Wirtz* in disagreement with historic principles that *United States v. California, supra,* reaffirmed: "[W]hile the commerce power has limits, valid general regulations of commerce do not cease to be regulations of commerce because a State is involved. If a state is engaging in economic activities that are validly regulated by the federal government when engaged in by private persons, the State too may be forced to conform its activities to federal regulation." 392 U. S., at 196-197. Clearly, therefore, my Brethren are also repudiating the long line of our precedents holding that a judicial finding that Congress has not unreasonably regulated a subject matter of "commerce" brings to an end the judicial role. "Let the end be legitimate, let it be within the scope of the constitution, and all means which are appropriate, which are plainly adapted to that end, which are not prohibited, but consist with the letter and spirit of the constitution, are constitutional." *McCulloch v. Maryland, supra,* at 421.

The reliance of my Brethren upon the Tenth Amendment as "an express declaration of [a state sovereignty] limitation," *ante,* at 8, not only suggests that they overrule governing decisions of this Court that address this question but must astound scholars of the Constitution. For not only early decisions, *Gibbons v. Ogden, supra,* at 196; *McCulloch v. Maryland, supra,* 404-407; and *Martin v. Hunter's Lessee,* 1 Wheat. 304, 324-325 (1816), hold that nothing in the Tenth Amendment constitutes a limitation on congressional exercise of powers delegated by the Constitution to Congress. See F. Frankfurter, The Commerce Power Under Marshall, Taney, and Waite 39-40 (1937). Rather, as the Tenth Amendment's significance was more recently summarized:

> "The amendment states but a truism that all is retained which has not been surrendered. *There is nothing in the history of its adoption to suggest that it was more than declaratory of the relationship between the national and state governments as it had been established by the Constitution before the amendment* or that its purpose was other than to allay fears that the new national government might seek to exercise powers not granted, and that the states might not be able to exercise fully their reserved powers. . . .
>
> "From the beginning and for many years the amendment has been construed as not depriving the national government of authority to resort to all means for the exercise of a granted power which are appropriate and plainly adapted to the permitted end." *United States v. Darby, supra,* at 124 (emphasis added).

. . . .

Today's repudiation of this unbroken line of precedents that firmly reject my Brethren's ill-conceived abstraction can only be regarded as a transparent cover for invalidating a congressional judgment with which they disagree. The only analysis even remotely resembling that adopted today is found in a line of opinions dealing with the Commerce Clause and the Tenth Amendment that ultimately provoked a constitutional crisis for the Court in the 1930's. *E.g.,* Carter v. Carter Coal Co., 298 U. S. 238 (1936); United States v. Butler, 297 U. S. 1 (1936); Hammer v. Dagenhart, 247 U. S. 251 (1918). See Stern, *The Commerce Clause and the National Economy,* 1933-1946, 59 Harv. L. Rev. 645 (1946). We tend to forget that the Court invalidated legislation during the Great Depression, not solely under the Due Process Clause, but also and primarily under the Commerce Clause and the Tenth Amendment. It may have been the eventual abandonment of that overly restrictive construction of the commerce power that spelled defeat for the Court-packing plan, and preserved the integrity of this institution, *id.,* at 682, see, *e.g., United States v. Darby, supra;* Mulford v. Smith, 307 U. S. 38 (1939); NLRB v. Jones & Laughlin Steel Corp., 301 U. S. 1 (1937), but my Brethren today are transparently trying to cut back on that recognition of the scope of the commerce power. My Brethren's approach to this case is not far different from the dissenting opinions in the cases that averted the crisis. . . .

. . . I cannot recall another instance in the Court's history when the reasoning of so many decisions covering so long a span of time has been discarded roughshod. That this is done without any justification not already often advanced and consistently rejected, clearly renders today's decision an *ipse dixit* reflecting nothing but displeasure with a congressional judgment.

. . . .

My Brethren do more than turn aside longstanding constitutional jurisprudence that emphatically rejects today's conclusion. More alarming is the startling restructuring of our federal system, and the role they create therein for the federal judiciary. This Court is simply not at liberty to erect a mirror of its own conception of a desirable governmental structure. If the 1974 amendments have any "vice," *ante,* at 15, my Brother STEVENS is surely right that it represents "merely . . . a policy issue which has been firmly resolved by the branches of government having power to decide such questions." *Post,* at 2. It bears repeating "that effective restraints on . . . exercise [of the Commerce power] must proceed from political rather than from judicial processes." *Wickard v. Filburn, supra,* at 120.

It is unacceptable that the judicial process should be thought superior to the political process in this area. Under the Constitution the judiciary has no role to play beyond finding that Congress has not made an unreasonable legislative judgment respecting what is "commerce." My Brother BLACKMUN suggests that controlling judicial supervision of the relationship between the States and our National Government by use of a balancing approach diminishes the ominous implications of today's decision. Such an approach, however, is a thinly veiled rationalization for judicial supervision of a policy judgment that our system of government reserves to Congress.

. . . .

We are left then with a catastrophic judicial body blow at Congress' power under the Commerce Clause. Even if Congress may nevertheless accomplish its objectives — for example by conditioning grants of federal funds upon compliance with federal minimum wage and overtime standards, *cf.* Oklahoma v. United States Civil Service Comm'n, 330 U. S. 127, 144 (1947) — there is an ominous portent of disruption of our constitutional structure implicit in today's mischievous decision. I dissent.

MR. JUSTICE STEVENS, dissenting.

The Court holds that the Federal Government may not interfere with a sovereign state's inherent right to pay a substandard wage to the janitor at the state capitol. The principle on which the holding rests is difficult to perceive.

The Federal Government may, I believe, require the State to act impartially when it hires or fires the janitor, to withhold taxes from his pay check, to observe safety regulations when he is performing his job, to forbid him from burning too much soft coal in the capitol furnace, from dumping untreated refuse in an adjacent waterway, from overloading a state-owned garbage truck or from driving either the truck or the governor's limousine over 55 miles an hour. Even though these and many other activities of the capitol janitor are activities of the state *qua* state, I have no doubt that they are subject to federal regulation.

I agree that it is unwise for the Federal Government to exercise its power in the ways described in the Court's opinion. For the proposition that regulation of the minimum price of a commodity — even labor — will increase the quantity consumed is not one that I can readily understand. That concern, however, applies with even greater force to the private sector of the economy where the exclusion of the marginally employable does the greatest harm and, in all events, merely reflects my views on a policy issue which has been firmly resolved by the branches of government having power to decide such questions. As far as the complexities of adjusting police and fire departments to this sort of federal control are concerned, I presume that appropriate tailor-made regulations would soon solve their most pressing problems. After all, the interests adversely affected by this legislation are not without political power.

My disagreement with the wisdom of this legislation may not, of course, affect my judgment with respect to its validity. On this issue there is no dissent from the proposition that the Federal Government's power over the labor market is adequate to embrace these employees. Since I am unable to identify a limitation on that federal power that would not also invalidate federal regulation of state activities that I consider unquestionably permissible, I am persuaded that this statute is valid. Accordingly, with respect and a great deal of sympathy for the views expressed by the Court, I dissent from its constitutional holding.

## NOTES

1. On remand from the Supreme Court, the district court entered a judgment declaring "that the minimum wage and overtime compensation provisions of the Fair Labor Standards Act are not constitutionally applicable to the integral operations of the States and their subdivisions in areas of traditional governmental functions." National League of Cities v. Marshall, 429 F. Supp. 703 (D.D.C. 1977). The court also incorporated as part of its judgment two regulations issued by the Secretary of Labor, *i.e.,* 29 CFR, Part 775, §§ 775.2 and 775.3. These regulations provide, *inter alia,* that the Secretary of Labor "will not file suit to enforce the minimum wage and overtime compensation provisions of the FLSA against a State or its political subdivisions unless at least 30 days' notice has first been given that, in the opinion of the Administrator, the activities in question are not integral operations in areas of traditional governmental functions." The regulations further provide that the *National League of Cities* decision applies "only to the minimum wage and overtime compensation provisions of the FLSA" and "do not apply to claims arising under:

(i) The Equal Pay Act of 1963 . . . .
(ii) The Age Discrimination in Employment Act of 1967 . . . .
(iii) The child labor provisions of the Fair Labor Standards Act.
(iv) The protective provisions of Section 15 (a) (3) of the Act, making it unlawful to discriminate against any employee for participating or assisting in FLSA proceedings."

2. Within a week after its decision in *National League of Cities,* the Supreme Court in Fitzpatrick v. Bitzer, 427 U.S. 445, 96 S. Ct. 2666, 49 L.Ed.2d 614 (1976), upheld the constitutionality of the 1972 Amendments to Title VII of the Civil Rights Act which authorize federal courts to award back pay and attorneys' fees against a state. The Court noted that Congress in extending Title VII to public employers was legitimately acting pursuant to Section 5 of the Fourteenth Amendment which grants Congress broad power to enact legislation to enforce the substantive provisions of the Fourteenth Amendment. The *National League of Cities* decision was distinguished on the ground that it involved only the Commerce Clause.

3. Subsequent to the *National League of Cities* decision, numerous courts have held that the Equal Pay Act is applicable to public employers even though it was enacted as an amendment to the Fair Labor Standards Act. For example, the Third Circuit in Usery v. Allegheny County Institution Dist., 544 F.2d 148 (3d Cir. 1976), *cert. denied,* 97 S. Ct. 1582 (1977), held that Congress had the authority under Section 5 of the Fourteenth Amendment to enact the Equal Pay Act. Using the same rationale, the Court in Usery v. Board of Educ. of Salt Lake City, 421 F. Supp. 718 (D. Utah 1976), upheld the constitutionality of the Age Discrimination in Employment Act as it applies to public employers.

In Marshall v. City of Sheboygan, 577 F.2d 1 (7th Cir. 1978), the Seventh Circuit held that "the 1974 extension of the Equal Pay Act to the States and their political subdivisions is a valid exercise of Congress' power under the Commerce Clause, and that the exercise of that power is not prohibited by the Tenth Amendment." The court observed that "[t]he ability to discriminate solely on the basis of sex cannot be considered an attribute of sovereignty necessary to a separate and independent existence." Finally, the court observed "that rather than striking down the 1974 amendments for all purposes, *National League of Cities* is limited and merely gives States and their subdivisions an affirmative defense against actions brought by the Secretary of Labor to enforce minimum wage and overtime provisions against state and local governmental employers." *See generally* Note, *Applying the Equal Pay Act to State and Local Governments: The Effect of National League of Cities v. Usery,* 125 U. PA. L. REV. 665 (1977).

4. In Municipal Government, City of Newark and State, County, and Municipal Workers of America, Local 277, CIO, Case Nos. 47 and 726 (December 23, 1942), reprinted in C. RHYNE, LABOR UNIONS AND MUNICIPAL EMPLOYE LAW 226 (1946), the National War Labor

Board unanimously held that it did not have jurisdiction over labor disputes between state governments, including political subdivisions thereof, and their public employees. In so ruling, the National War Labor Board, in an opinion written by Wayne Morse, stated:

It has never been suggested that the Federal Government has the power to regulate with respect to the wages, working hours, or conditions of employment of those who are engaged in performing services for the states or their political subdivisions. Any action of the National War Labor Board in attempting to regulate such matter by directive order would be beyond its powers and jurisdiction. The employees involved in the instant cases are performing services for political subdivisions of state governments. Any directive order of the National War Labor Board would purport it to regulate the wages, the working hours, or the conditions of employment of state or municipal employees would constitute a clear invasion of the sovereign rights of the political subdivisions of local state government.

Among the labor members who concurred in the foregoing opinion was George Meany, the current president of the AFL-CIO. George W. Taylor, the principal author of the New York Public Sector Collective Bargaining Law, was a public member who likewise concurred in the opinion.

## CITY OF MACON v. MARSHALL

United States District Court, Middle District of Georgia
439 F. Supp. 1209 (1977)

OWENS, District Judge:
Until March 15, 1973, Bibb Transit Company owned and operated a municipally franchised bus transportation system which served the City of Macon. Its drivers and maintenance employees were members of and exclusively represented by Local Division 898 of the Amalgamated Transit Union, AFL-CIO, for collective bargaining purposes.

Following notice that Bibb Transit Company because of monetary losses was ceasing its bus operations, the Mayor and Council of the City of Macon on February 28, 1973, formally approved the city's purchase of Bibb Transit Company's buses and personal property, the rental of the company's Riverside Drive office-maintenance facility, the hiring of those Bibb Transit drivers who desired to make application to the city and the operation of a bus system by the city. Then Mayor Thompson in proposing all of this to the February 28, 1973, meeting of Mayor and Council stated ". . . The City will not become involved with any union."

On March 15 the city began operating its own bus transit system. Except for two drivers physically disqualified and five drivers who were on social security and thus disqualified, all of Bibb Transit Company's drivers and maintenance employees eventually became employees of the City of Macon. From then until now the city has refused to recognize or bargain with the union.

. . . .

On August 23, 1974, the City of Macon applied for a federal grant of $1,020,852 under the congressionally enacted Urban Mass Transportation Act, 49 U.S.C.A. § 1601, *et seq.*, for the stated purpose of making capital improvements to its bus system. In January 1977 the city submitted a second application for a $132,409 operating assistance federal grant under said Act.

The Urban Mass Transportation Act authorizes the Secretary of Transportation to make grants or loans of tremendous sums from the federal treasury — at least TEN BILLION DOLLARS — but specifies that "No financial assistance shall be provided . . . to any State or local public body or agency thereof for the purpose, directly or indirectly, of acquiring any interest in, or purchasing any facilities or other property of, a private mass transportation company, or *for the purpose of constructing, improving, or reconstructing any facilities or other property acquired (after July 9, 1964)* from any such company . . . unless (4) the Secretary of Labor certifies that such assistance complies with the requirements of section 1609(c) of this title." 49 U.S.C. § 1602(e). (emphasis added).

Title 49 U.S.C. § 1609(c) [generally referred to as § 13 (c)] provides:

"(c) It shall be a condition of any assistance under section 1602 of this title that fair and equitable arrangements are made, as determined by the Secretary of Labor, to protect the interests of employees affected by such assistance. *Such protective arrangements shall include,* without being limited to, *such provisions* as may *be necessary for* (1) the preservation of rights, privileges, and benefits (including continuation of pension rights and benefits) under existing collective bargaining agreements or otherwise; (2) *the continuation of collective bargaining rights;* (3) the protection of individual employees against a worsening of their positions with respect to their employment; (4) assurances of employment to employees of acquired mass transportation systems and priority of reemployment of employees terminated or laid off; and (5) paid training or retraining programs. Such arrangements shall include provisions protecting individual employees against a worsening of their positions with respect to their employment which shall in no event provide benefits "less than those established pursuant to section 5(2)(f) of this title. *The contract for the granting of any such assistance shall specify the terms and conditions of the protective arrangements.*" (emphasis added).

. . . .

[The city in its application for federal mass transit assistance maintained that a "collective bargaining contract between the City and a labor union would violate State law." The position of the Department of Labor was summarized in the following paragraph in a letter addressed to the city's mayor from the Assistant Secretary of Labor:

We recognize your position that a collective bargaining arrangement would violate state law. However, we can only reemphasize that the legislative history of the Urban Mass Transportation Act is very clear in stating that existing state or local laws do not create exceptions to the general requirement that assistance under the Act be conditioned on arrangements which, among other things, provide for the continuation of collective bargaining rights.

The union maintained throughout that § 13(c) required full bargaining rights and that none of the suggestions proffered by the city would assure compliance with § 13(c)'s collective bargaining requirements.]

Neither the City of Macon, the Secretary of Labor nor the union deviated from their long-standing positions and opinions, and on September 1, 1977, the city filed its complaint in this court against the Secretary of Labor seeking an order of this court compelling the Secretary of Labor to certify compliance by the City of Macon with Section 13(c).

The parties stipulate that the court has jurisdiction. 28 U.S.C.A. § 1331(a) and § 1361.

. . . .

The Tenth Amendment to the Constitution of the United States, the last of the "Bill of Rights", provides:

"The powers not delegated to the United States by the Constitution, nor prohibited by it to the States, are reserved to the States respectively, or to the people."

In *National League of Cities v. Usery,* 426 U.S. 833, 96 S. Ct. 2465, 49 L. Ed. 2d 245 (1976) the Supreme Court of the United States . . . held that Congress cannot require the States of these United States as employers to comply with the minimum wage laws of the United States because the minimum wage laws "operate to *directly displace* the States' freedom to structure integral operations in areas of traditional governmental functions . . . ." 426 U.S. at 852, 96 S. Ct. at 2474, 49 L. Ed. 2d at 258. (emphasis added). The City of Macon first says that by conditioning grants of federal tax money upon the city affording collective bargaining rights to its employees, the federal government is indirectly requiring Macon to comply with federal labor law concepts and thus violating Georgia's and Macon's sovereignty in the same manner that Congress unconstitutionally attempted to amend the minimum wage laws to include states and their political subdivisions as employers.

Unlike the amendment to the minimum wage laws which included States and political subdivisions as employers under the minimum wage laws and thereby required States and political subdivisions to pay their employees a congressionally determined minimum wage and comply with the many other federal requirements, the Urban Mass Transportation Act does not directly require or command anything of States or their political subdivisions. Neither States nor political subdivisions are compelled to participate in the grand federal scheme created by the Act and thereby receive federal money. The participation is purely at their option. It is because of this that Macon is not now participating — it has elected not to.

While Congress cannot directly command or force a state or municipality to comply with federal wage and hour concepts, it may pursuant to the spending clause of the Constitution fix the terms and conditions upon which money from the United States Treasury will be allotted and disbursed to the States and their political subdivisions. See *Oklahoma v. United States Civil Service Commission,* 330 U.S. 127, 67 S. Ct. 544, 91 L. Ed. 794 (1947), in which the Supreme Court approved a congressionally enacted law which required employees of States applying for and receiving federal highway funds, to comply with the Hatch Political Activity Act, a law of the United States, and further approved the removal by the Civil Service Commission of a member of Oklahoma's State Highway Commission from his office because of violation of the Hatch Act. Also see, *Florida v. Mathews,* 526 F.2d 319 (5th Cir. 1976) in which a regulation of the Secretary of Health, Education, and Welfare governing state programs for licensing administrators of nursing homes which participate in the federal medical assistance program (Medicaid) was found to be reasonably related to the purposes of the enabling legislation passed by Congress and to be non-offensive to the Tenth Amendment.

Paraphrasing *Florida v. Mathews* at 326, the only effect of this Urban Mass Transportation Act is to induce, but not require, the City of Macon to comply with the Urban Mass Transportation Act by doing whatever is necessary to afford its bus drivers and maintenance employees collective bargaining rights in a manner determined by the Secretary of Labor; "this inducement does not infringe upon any power reserved to the state [of Georgia and its political subdivisions] under the Tenth Amendment . . . Once a state [or a municipality] chooses to participate in a federally funded program, it must comply with federal standards.''

## NOTES

1. *See generally* Barnum, *National Public Labor Relations Legislation: The Case of Urban Mass Transit,* 21 LAB. L.J. 168 (1976); Barnum, *From Private to Public: Labor Relations in Urban Transit,* 25 IND. & LAB. REL. REV. 95 (1971); K. JENNINGS, J. SMITH & E. TRAYNHAM, STUDY OF UNIONS, MANAGEMENT RIGHTS, AND THE PUBLIC INTEREST IN MASS TRANSIT, U.S. DEP'T OF TRANSPORTATION (1977).

2. In Division 1287, Amalgamated Transit Union v. Kansas City Area Transp. Auth., 582 F.2d 444 (8th Cir. 1978), *cert. denied,* 99 S. Ct. 872 (1979), the court held that the union could compel the transportation authority to submit a collective bargaining impasse to binding interest arbitration in accordance with the labor protective agreement negotiated pursuant to Section 13(c) of the Urban Mass Transportation Act of 1964. The court held ''that a controversy between a public transit agency and a labor union involving a claim of breach of a § 13(c) agreement is a controversy that arises under the laws of the United States.'' In rejecting the authority's contention that binding interest arbitration would be illegal as an impermissible delegation of authority, the court stated:

> We recognize that under the laws of some states employees of public agencies are not accorded collective bargaining rights nor do they enjoy the benefits of such bargaining, including arbitration. We think, however, that when a state or a combination of states forms a public transit agency for the express purpose of obtaining federal money to enable it to take over the business of a private transit company, and where the agency in order to obtain the money enters into a § 13(c) agreement that calls for interest arbitration, the obligation to arbitrate is binding on the agency, regardless of general state law or policy.

*Accord,* Division 714, Amalgamated Transit Union v. Greater Portland Transit Dist., 589 F.2d 1 (1st Cir. 1978); Division 519, Amalgamated Transit Union v. LaCrosse Mun. Transit Util., 585 F.2d 1340 (7th Cir. 1978). *But see* Division 580, Amalgamated Transit Union v. Central New York Regional Trans. Auth., 95 L.R.R.M. 2643 (N.D.N.Y. 1977), *vacated as moot,* 578 F.2d 29 (2d Cir. 1978).

3. In County of Los Angeles v. Marshall, 442 F. Supp. 1186 (D.D.C. 1977), the court denied a request for a preliminary injunction against enforcement of the 1976 Amendments to the Federal Unemployment Tax Act which require states to extend unemployment compensation benefits to state and local public employees in order to qualify for federal funding. The court distinguished *National League of Cities* on the ground that the extension of the minimum wage and overtime provisions of the FLSA to state and local public employers was mandatory, whereas the requirement that unemployment compensation benefits be provided to state and local public employees ''is at the option of the state.'' The court said that ''Congress has great latitude in fixing the terms upon which its money allotments (and tax credits) may be conditioned.''

## 2. FEDERAL REGULATION OF STATE AND LOCAL GOVERNMENT COLLECTIVE BARGAINING

Starting with the 91st Congress in 1970, bills have been submitted in every session which would make state and local government labor relations subject to federal regulation. Two distinct approaches have been advanced by the principal advocates of federal legislation. First, organizations such as AFSCME have advocated the enactment of comprehensive legislation which would apply to the entire state and local public sector under separate legislation administered by a five-member National Public Employment Relations Commission. Such legislation was introduced as H.R. 7684 in the 92d Congress and as H.R. 8677 and S. 3295 in the 93d Congress. As introduced in the 93d Congress, this legislation would:

1. Authorize supervisory bargaining units.
2. Describe the scope of bargaining broadly to cover "terms and conditions of employment and other matters of mutual concern relating thereto."
3. Provide for compulsory arbitration or strikes as the mechanism for resolving collective bargaining impasses, the choice to be made by the exclusive bargaining representative.
4. Guarantee public employees the right to strike and specifically supersede any inconsistent state laws that prohibit public employee strikes.
5. Override and supersede inconsistent state and local enactments in that the Act would "take precedence over all ordinances, rules and regulations, or other enactments of any State, territory, or other possession of the United States, or any political subdivision thereof."
6. Provide that the Act applies to all state and local jurisdictions unless the five-member National Public Employment Relations Commission determines that a state or local enactment "is substantially equivalent to the system established herein."

On the other hand, H.R. 12532 introduced in the 92d Congress and H.R. 8677 and S. 3294 introduced in the 93d Congress would have brought the entire state and local public sector under the National Labor Relations Act (NLRA). Thus, these latter bills would have removed the exclusion of "any state or political subdivision thereof" from the definition of employers covered by the NLRA.

Hearings on the proposed federal public sector collective bargaining legislation were held in the House of Representatives during the 92d Congress and in the Senate during the 93d Congress. See Hearings on H.R. 12532, H.R. 7684 & H.R. 9324 before the Special Subcomm. on Labor of the House Comm. on Education and Labor, 92d Cong., 2d Sess. (1972); Hearings on S. 3295 & S. 3294 before the Subcomm. on Labor of the Senate Comm. on Labor and Public Welfare, 93d Cong., 2d Sess. (1974). The varying views of some of the principal proponents and opponents of federal legislation governing state and local collective bargaining are set forth below. While the movement towards the enactment of federal legislation was slowed down by the Supreme Court's decision in *National League of Cities,* it is an issue which will be a subject of continuing debate.

## STATEMENT OF JERRY WURF, INTERNATIONAL PRESIDENT, AMERICAN FEDERATION OF STATE, COUNTY, AND MUNICIPAL EMPLOYEES, AFL-CIO

Hearings on H.R. 12532, H.R. 7684, & H.R. 9324
Before the Special Subcomm. on Labor of the House Comm. on Education and Labor, 92d Cong., 2d Sess., 25, 28, 31-32 (1972)

. . . We appear before you this morning in behalf of the over 525,000 public employees who are members of our Union to urge the enactment of Federal legislation dealing with labor relations in state and local government. We are convinced that only through national legislation can public employees be guaranteed full rights to organize and bargain collectively and thereby end unnecessary labor strife in the public sector.

Our views also reflect the concerns and interests of the Coalition of Public Employee Organizations, representing more than two million public employees throughout the nation. This Coalition, formed last March, includes our Union, the National Education Association and the International Association of Fire Fighters, AFL-CIO. The Coalition was established to bring the collective power of public employees to bear on matters of mutual concern.

Over the past several months, our organizations have been working toward a common position on Federal legislation to establish a uniform national labor relations policy in the public sector. We have reached agreement on the substantive provisions of such a bill and the specific legislative recommendations made in behalf of the American Federation of State, County, and Municipal Employees this morning are shared by the other organizations associated with this Coalition. . . .

In the absence of a national uniform labor-management relations policy, labor law in the public sector has developed on a piecemeal, state-by-state, city-by-city basis. State laws are a shameful hodgepodge designed largely to frustrate unionization and collective bargaining.

Inconsistency and confusion best describe the legal setting of labor relations for state and local government employees. Each of the 50 states and the 80,000 units of local government does its own thing. There is no set pattern. The labor programs are regulated by state laws, city ordinances, court decisions, attorneys general opinions, county charters, civil service rules, executive orders, school board policies, and other regulations. . . .

There is clear need for change in public sector labor relations. The choice, in our view, is between continued chaos or Federal legislation.

New state laws are proliferating. Each is different. Most merely add to the confusion and chaos that already exists. Hawaii and Pennsylvania are outstanding exceptions. Although both have provisions with which we disagree, or lack provisions we believe necessary.

The frustrations deriving from the astonishing jungle of state laws, have led our Union to the call for a single, comprehensive Federal law addressing itself to labor relations in the public sector.

There have been enough confrontations. There have been enough studies and experiments. It is time for responsible change.

The problem is national in scope and it requires a national solution.

We need uniformity of law in the public sector, so that a body of law and tradition and practice can be developed. This will only occur under Federal legislation, much like that which governs labor relations in business and industry. We are convinced that the majority of the states are either unwilling or unable to move toward the establishment of rational and reasonable mechanisms.

The needs of public employees do not differ across state lines. They are one and the same throughout the nation. There should be no more difference between the job rights of a public employee in Wisconsin and Virginia than there is between an aerospace worker in California and New York. The labor relations situation of public employees today is different in every city, county, and state — not just between states, but between cities and counties within the same state. There is no more reason to justify fragmentation of labor relations between states and their cities and counties than there is to fragment any other system of dealing with problems on a national level.

We believe it is outrageous to conduct labor relations without a set of uniform rules. We are advocating uniformity of law of this matter for the same reason we advocate government by law rather than by force.

You can say what you want about labor relations in business and industry, but a free society could not get along without the mechanisms that exist there. The mechanisms are firmly established and clearly understood. They have a history of legal precedents applicable to almost every work place in America. Contrast that with the public sector where you can go from one city to the next and find a different mechanism and a different set of precedents and procedures.

Finally, we know what state legislatures have to offer us in the way of labor legislation. We know what the needs are. The two just don't fit and probably never will. We are not turning our backs on the new laws in Hawaii and Pennsylvania. They are good laws, although we have serious points of difference with them. If we continue to rely on state legislation, we will continue to face a crazy quilt-work pattern of law. A national approach is the only answer to meeting them uniformly and fairly. . . .

## STATEMENT OF ALBERT SHANKER, PRESIDENT, AMERICAN FEDERATION OF TEACHERS, AFL-CIO

Hearings on S. 3295 & S. 3294 Before the Subcomm. on Labor of the Senate Comm. on Labor and Public Welfare, 93d Cong., 2d Sess., 281-84 (1974)

This Committee is considering two bills — S. 3294 and S. 3295. These bills provide for Federal regulation of labor relations in the public sector at the state and local level. The AFT firmly believes that the time for such regulation has come.

There has been much activity in recent years toward giving state and local public employees basic recognition rights, and thereby eliminating the need for strikes conducted for the purpose of gaining recognition. In most areas where bargaining rights for public employees exist, they are very limited in comparison to those which exist for private sector workers, both with respect to the bargaining process and with respect to who is covered by the various state public employee bargaining laws.

At present, 13 states still have no provision for recognition of public employees for the purpose of collective bargaining or even "meeting and conferring." As the National Labor Relations Act currently excludes from coverage employees of ". . . any State or political subdivision thereof," there is no framework whatever for the exercise of what the AFT believes is a basic right in a democracy — the right of any worker, in the private or public sector, to have a say in determining the conditions under which he or she must work.

In the 37 remaining states, either by statute or by Executive Order, there is some mechanism by which public employees can be heard but the picture can only be described as imperfect at best and repressive at worst.

1. The coverage of the various state statutes and Executives Orders wanders all over the map. Some states have comprehensive public employee labor relations laws applying to all groups of public employees while others have separate statutes, often granting different degrees of recognition, representation and negotiation rights for different groups of public employees — many even differentiating by location.

2. In some states, groups of public employees can choose through majority vote an organizational spokesman to speak for them but in others, all organizations purporting to represent public employees in any particular unit must be represented at the discussion table.

3. In some states, public employees are only given the right to "meet and confer" with their public employers but there is no requirement on the employer to negotiate in good faith and participate in the kind of give and take which solves

problems. In other states, there is a duty on both parties to engage in good faith negotiations with a host of impasse resolution services provided but if these fail, the public employer can still do whatever it chooses. Only in 7 states is there currently even a qualified right to strike for public employees.

4. In some states (California, Texas, Arizona, South Dakota and most of the Southern States), binding arbitration of grievances of public employees has been held to be illegal while in others the arbitration of grievances has increased stability and lessened strife in public employment.

The AFT believes there is a strong Federal interest in rationalizing this hodgepodge of state public employee labor relations legislation. State and local government is one of the fastest growing sectors in the American economy. . . .

The underlying rationale for the original Wagner Act and the present NLRA is that breakdowns in labor-management relations impede commerce and are contrary to the general welfare of the nation. When these laws were enacted, disruptions of government services due to labor disputes in the public sector were minimal. Over the last 20 years, however, public employees have demanded the same collective bargaining rights as those in the private sector. Clearly, the same rationale applies now in the public sector as first applied 39 years ago in the private sector and for this reason, a Federal statute governing state and local public employee labor relations is a necessity.

Before commenting on the two proposals being considered by the Committee, I want to state in no uncertain terms that the AFT considers the right to strike to be an absolutely basic element in any system of labor relations which has as its aim the granting of employees that fundamental right of having a say in determining the conditions under which they must work through meaningful collective bargaining. When the right to withhold labor is limited then the bargaining loses its meaning because the power of employees is dissipated. With the strike tool, the employer is forced to consider alternatives — does the public value the service enough to indicate meeting the demands; how much of a tax increase is the public willing to assume; is the public willing to do without the service for a time? Without the strike, there is no meaningful pressure on the employer to reach agreement with its employees. At present, none of the state public employee labor relations statutes contains an unlimited right to strike, and as stated, there are only 7 states which grant public employees even a limited right to strike. But, strikes do take place, often in spite of heavy fines and jail sentences.

Any blanket qualifying provision on the right to strike for public employees appearing in any legislative proposal for the Federal regulation of state and local public employee labor relations will be vigorously opposed by the AFT just as we fight that battle on the state and local levels. Furthermore, if a ban against public employee strikes in general is the price of Federal legislation in this area, it is a price that the AFT would not be willing to pay, no matter how otherwise favorable that legislation might be.

Some opponents of public employee strikes suggest compulsory arbitration as a substitute for the right to strike. Let me point out that we have no objection to employers and employee representatives agreeing in advance to submit differences to binding arbitration. But this is arbitration jointly and voluntarily agreed to, not compulsory arbitration which destroys the bargaining process by removing all incentive for compromise. Furthermore, I want to make clear that this discussion is in reference to what is known as interest negotiation — negotiation of a contract. A negotiated grievance procedure with a top step of compulsory binding arbitration as part of a contractual agreement has long been recognized as a legitimate means of resolving disputes during the life of a collective bargaining agreement. But of course, that initial agreement should always be arrived at by a voluntary process or collective bargaining has no meaning.

The two bills before the Committee take two distinctly different approaches to Federal regulation of public sector labor relations at the state and local level. S. 3294, in extending the NLRA to state and local government workers, will bring about a situation in which private and public sector workers and their employers will be subject to the same labor relations laws. S. 3295 establishes a separate legal structure and enforcement apparatus for public employees.

The AFT strongly supports the former approach — S. 3294 — because it reflects a fundamental philosophy which we have been preaching for a long time. That philosophy is that the interests, concerns and problems that public employees have with respect to their jobs are in no basic way different than the interests, concerns and problems of private sector workers. This viewpoint is strengthened by what we believe to be the absolutely absurd situation of the professor of history at New York University having the right to strike, the professor of history at the City University of New York not having the right to strike and the professor of history at the University of Illinois not even allowed to engage in any form of collective negotiation through a recognized representative. This is true not only of professors but of employees of elementary and secondary schools, transit systems, utilities, nursing homes and hospitals to name a few. The fact is that under the present structure of labor relations in the United States, the extent of an employee's right to have a say in the conditions under which he or she must work depends not at all on what he or she does but whom the employer happens to be — public or private sector.

Certainly the co-existence of distinct legislative and administrative bodies in the public sector is a unique aspect of public employment but our experience in collective bargaining convinces us that any special accommodations that are necessary can easily be accomplished within the labor relations framework of the NLRA if public employees are covered. The AFT does not believe there is any justification for the exclusively public employment body of law and structure envisioned in S. 3295.

At its Tenth Constitutional Convention, in October 1973, the AFL-CIO was presented with a clear choice and strongly endorsed the approach embodied in S. 3294 — extending NLRA coverage to state and local public employees. Delegates representing the American Federation of State, County and Municipal Employees did introduce a resolution entitled "Collective Bargaining for Public Employees" which stated in part:

*Resolved,* This convention supports a federal collective bargaining law which gives negotiating equity to public employees, while at the same time taking into account the special problems of collective bargaining in state and local government: the problems of impasse resolution and strikes, the budgetary processes, the relationships between the administrative and the legislative arms of the government.

The AFL-CIO Convention Resolutions Committee rejected the AFSCME resolution and approved a substitute. The substitute resolution which was unanimously adopted by the full convention reads in part:

"Whereas, in many areas of federal and state legislation public employees are still excluded from the full benefits of such legislation, or are frequently discriminated against in separate public employee legislation; therefore be it

"*Resolved,* That the time has come to recognize that public employees are workers who should enjoy the rights and benefits equal to those guaranteed under law to workers in the private sector, and therefore be it further

"*Resolved,* That this convention supports the extension of these rights and benefits — such as the right to collective bargaining, and the right to economic and social insurance legislation — to all public employees through coverage under existing federal, state and local laws."

. . . .

## STATEMENT OF JAMES F. MARSHALL, EXECUTIVE DIRECTOR, ASSEMBLY OF GOVERNMENTAL EMPLOYEES

Hearings on S. 3295 & S. 3294 Before the Subcomm. on Labor of the Senate Comm. on Labor and Public Welfare, 93d Cong., 2d Sess., 338-40 (1974)

Based upon their circumstances, experiences and individual needs the states and political subdivisions have developed a variety of measures to deal with the issue which provide a viable and flexible middle ground to insure public employees equitable treatment, the orderly discharge of public service functions, and the responsible expenditure of public funds. These measures are designed for the public sector and its particular needs. Experience from the tumultuous and sometimes bloody history of private sector labor relations was, of course, reviewed but because of the distinctive nature of public employment there is not and cannot be a blanket adaptation of private sector labor relations to the public sector.

When the 91st Congress passed the Intergovernmental Personnel Act of 1970 (Pub. L. No. 91-648), a Presidential Advisory Council on Intergovernmental Personnel Policy was established. I was fortunate enough to be a Presidential appointee to that Council. In July, 1974 the Supplementary Report to the President and the Congress was issued. In recommendation number 6, the Council stated in part, "that different approaches to public employee-management relations are required in the public and private sectors. These necessary differences and approaches grow out of the very basic and real differences between the two sectors themselves — in character; in structure; and in values." I command this report and its recommendations to your Committee for review, as this study has thoroughly evaluated this point with reasoned study. In reaching this observation the Council in its first recommendation stated that:

"Public sector employee management relations should be conducted within a framework of state law — not Federal law."

AGE sincerely shares this view. First, that there is a distinction between public and private employment. And, secondly, that the variety and experimentation in public employee labor relations adapting to the varied needs through our federated system can produce sound personnel management systems based upon merit principles.

As mentioned above, AGE strongly supports the concept of merit principles in public employment. The private sector generally has no tradition comparable to the application of merit principles in government. The fundamental guarantees of merit principles protect the interest of the public's employee and institutions as well as the public itself. These merit principles can be consistent with collective bargaining, but have to be adapted to the public sector. It cannot, and should not, be made to structure itself around the established precedents and procedures established in the collective bargaining private sector. Both bills before your Committee, we feel, would endanger the protection of merit system principles in non-federal public employment. We fear what actually has happened in a public jurisdiction in Alaska in a contract between the Anchorage Borough School District and the Teamsters Union, when the school desire[s] a bus driver they must go to the "hiring hall" — no merit involved. Public service cannot tolerate such a condition. It is not in the best interest of the public employee, government or the public. Obviously, merit principles are not self executing. Public employee organizations working with public governing bodies must strive to achieve proper implementation. Proper government machinery is necessary. But it is clear from the experience to date that there is no one answer. Effective patterns of public employee labor relations are derived from the successes and failures — but continuing improvement is the by-product. We believe that a stereotyped federal system superimposed on every non-federal employee in this nation is clearly not in the best interest of the public, government or the public employee.

## STATEMENT OF JOHN HANSON, PRESIDENT, NATIONAL PUBLIC EMPLOYER LABOR RELATIONS ASSOCIATION

Hearings on S. 3295 & S. 3294 Before the Subcomm. on Labor of the Senate Comm. on Labor and Public Welfare, 93d Cong., 2d Sess., 360-62 (1974)

The National Public Employer Labor Relations Association is a relatively young professional association, with more than two hundred members who represent state, county and municipal governments in their labor relations. Its membership includes chief negotiators for many of the major cities in the country.

We fully support collective bargaining for the public sector. We believe that the several states should be encouraged to continue to meet their responsibilities in this area by enacting effective legislation that will meet local priorities and establish a firm framework for conducting labor relations at the state and local levels.

We are opposed to the enactment of federal legislation covering public sector collective bargaining at the state and local levels. Because of the vast differences between the several states and their political subdivisions with respect to the manner in which wages, hours and working conditions are established, collective bargaining legislation is not a matter that is susceptible to uniform federal regulation. NPELRA supports the following conclusion of Professors Harry Wellington and Ralph Winter, in a study prepared for the Brookings Institution:

"When an issue is a matter of low federal priority, considerations of federalism dictate that governmental action be left to state or local initiative. One can claim more, however, than that municipal public employee bargaining should have a low priority on any agenda for Congressional action. One can claim that intervention at the national level would be positively harmful. Federal legislation or regulation necessarily tends to a uniform rule. In the case of public employee unionism, uniformity is most undesirable and diversity in rules and structures virtually a necessity." [20]

In examining this question, any objective observer must recognize that there are substantial differences between public sector and private sector collective bargaining. Many of these differences have been identified by either proponents or opponents of the proposed legislation before this Committee. As pointed out by Arvid Anderson, Chairman, Office of Collective Bargaining, New York City,

[20] H. Wellington & R. Winter, *The Unions and The Cities* 52-53 (1971).

in his testimony of October 1, 1974, Congress, itself, in enacting labor relations legislation for the Postal Service, made a major change from private law by the substitution of interest arbitration for the right to strike.

We should like to emphasize two other significant differences which we believe your Committee should keep in mind.

First of all, in the public sector a union has four different methods of influencing, or representing its interest with the public employer as follows:

1. Legislation
2. Pressure on elected officials
3. Campaigning for election of officials who will support the union position, and
4. Collective bargaining

In the private sector there are only two ways of influencing the bargaining process:

1. Legislation
2. Collective bargaining

The result constitutes a significant difference in the union bargaining power between the public and private sector. For example, the public sector bargaining representative is often frustrated by attempts of union representatives, in the midst of bargaining, to deal directly with his elected bosses in an effort to secure benefits not obtained in the process of negotiations. At the same time, this technique places heavy pressure on the elected official.

Secondly, the environment in which local government employees and employers function is different from that in which private sector labor relations is conducted. It is localized geographically. The attitude of the citizens toward public employees varies and thus the framework adopted will also vary.

Then the public official is elected by all the people and is accountable to the general public. The ultimate policy making positions are held by election, not by private appointment. State officials are limited and function under constitutional authority and the local laws and ordinances which vary from state to state.

The impact of Federal legislation is difficult to ascertain. Involved in the process are the state constitution, home rule charters, state civil service laws, tenure laws and the like. Necessarily, attention must be given to federal-state relationships and the impact of labor relations legislation on the separation of the powers doctrine within the states (e.g., when a governor agrees to a contract, what is the obligation of the state legislature? ). These kinds of issues do not exist in the private sector and their consideration and resolution must precede Federal legislation, if it is to contribute to effective government at all levels.

In light of these differences, we are convinced that Federal legislation covering public sector collective bargaining is inappropriate, improper and unnecessary.

Federal legislation is inappropriate because no ideal solution has been achieved. The States are acting to meet the problems as they are seen locally and intimately. The approaches vary but this is not unhealthy. As the Advisory Committee on Intergovernment Relations noted "... experimentation and flexibility are needed, not a standardized, Federal preemptive approach." [21]

The enactment of federal legislation would stifle the experimentation and search for alternative selections that are now going on. The uniformity that would

---

[21] Advisory Commission on Intergovernmental Relations, *Labor-Management Policies for State and Local Government,* 113 (1969).

be an inevitable product of federal legislation would achieve not a solution to the many complex problems faced by state and local governments, but an untoward and premature harnessing of the vital energies of both management and labor that might otherwise make substantial contributions to a new and better system of labor relations.

In reaching this position, we are not, as has been suggested by some advocates of federal legislation, suggesting that any of the states should be encouraged to withhold the basic rights that are necessary to protect employees' freedom of choice and the development of stable labor relations. We are suggesting that these goals can be better achieved by encouraging the states to meet their own local problems.

Federal legislation is improper, because it would contradict the current posture of Congress, which has been to encourage state and local governments to have and exercise greater authority over their own affairs. The development of the latent principle of federalism has been welcomed by the people of all the states, is reflected in the revenue-sharing programs developed by Congress and is supported by the statements of many Senators and Representatives who recommend the desirability of maintaining as much local autonomy as possible.

## ANDERSON,* PROSPECTS FOR NATIONAL PUBLIC SECTOR BARGAINING LAWS, Address prepared for NLRB Tenth Region Labor Management Seminar, Atlanta, Georgia (June 2, 1977)

. . . .

As for my personal view regarding a federal bargaining law, I remain committed to the position of the Association of Labor Mediation Agencies which favors a non-preemptive federal minimum standards law. Such standards would, as a minimum, contain the following:

—Public employees should be granted the right to organize, to join employee organizations, and to bargain with respect to their terms and conditions of employment.

—Standards should be provided for resolution of representation disputes, unit determinations and elections to determine bargaining agents.

—Broadly defined unfair labor practices should be included and should be applicable to both employers and employee organizations.

—At the state or local level a neutral and politically independent administrative agency shall be required to implement the foregoing standards.

—A framework for the resolution for impasses should be mandated, but wide latitude for experimentation should be permitted.

For example, impasse procedures could give the states the right to decide on whether to permit or prohibit strikes, authorize or require binding arbitration of new contracts or merely provide for non-binding fact finding with recommendations.

Under these proposals, if a state or local government chooses to administer and implement its own public employee labor relations statute providing for a system of collective bargaining under the federal minimum standards, it would be permitted to do so without a presumption of federal preemption. Any

---

* Arvid Anderson is the Chairman of the New York City Office of Collective Bargaining.

controversy as to whether a specific provision in a state or local statute was not consistent with the minimum federal standards would be resolved in the federal courts and such proceedings could only be initiated by a federal agency. Thus, the burden of proof of non-compliance with federal minimum standards would fall on the federal agency rather than on the states.

I stress that federal law should not be preemptive because the experience of the administration of the Labor Management Relations Act by the National Labor Relations Board throughout its entire history demonstrates conclusively that a federal administrative agency will, if left to its own discretion, refuse to cede to any competent state authority administration over any phase of its statute. The administrators of the National Labor Relations Board have consistently held the position that those sections of the national act which provide the basis to cede certain administrative authority to states if such state laws or administration are not inconsistent with federal law, that the state statute must be identical with federal law and, thus, in effect, have refused to cede any authority to the states.

I don't think the problem is the language of the statute; it is the lack of willingness of the federal authorities to cede any jurisdiction to state agencies. Thus, states with competent professional administrative agencies in the private sector, such as Wisconsin, New York, Connecticut and Michigan, although they repeatedly tried to obtain the consent of the federal government to assume some responsibility over the administration of private sector labor relations, were unable to complete such agreements.

In June 1975, Betty Southard Murphy, then Chairman of the NLRB, testifying before the House Labor Subcommittee on Labor-Management Relations with regard to proposals to include state and local public employees under the National Labor Relations Act, stated that:

> Our experience has convinced us that the Congressional policy of a national labor law favorably contributes to industrial peace by providing a uniform framework within which management and labor may function. Separate State labor policies would inevitably create jurisdictional problems between and among the States and subject multi-State employers and national labor organizations to a wide variety of inconsistent labor policies and regulations.

She further stated that the question of ceding NLRB jurisdiction "involves a basic policy decision as to whether a uniform national policy should remain paramount or whether there should be some sacrifice in uniformity to permit a degree of cession to state agencies."

A close look at the different union positions on a federal bargaining law makes clear that the "uniformity" they seem to favor does not include a federal preemption of existing tenure, civil service or pension rights which are presently codified in state and local statutes and state constitutions. The unions apparently favor federal preemption of bargaining structures but not of existing employee benefits.

I question the need for total uniformity in a federal bargaining law for state and local government employees. Certainly, the basic right to organize and bargain collectively, and the protection of those rights, should be uniform, but it does not follow that all states or all categories of employees should have the same bargaining structure or method of impasse resolution. Why should not the states decide whether the strike route or binding arbitration, or some combination thereof, is to be an appropriate means of impasse resolution? In other words, everyone need not wear a size 9 shoe.

I also believe that state agencies and local agencies are generally competent and, because of their thorough knowledge of the local scene, are as well or better equipped than a federal agency to administer a public sector labor relations statute. I firmly believe that the right of the states to do so should be protected and that, in the absence of federal judicial restraint, state and local procedures should continue. Total uniformity is not necessary provided there is substantial equivalence in the implementation of a state law to the federal statute. A limitation on federal preemption would permit the freedom of state experimentation which now exists to continue and would encourage additional states to enact bargaining procedures for their state and local employees.

A limitation similar to that which I propose here has worked effectively under the New York State Taylor Law with respect to its relationship to the New York City Collective Bargaining Law. The New York City Law is not identical to the Taylor Law; but it is our belief that its purposes and administration are substantially equivalent to the Taylor Law. Such procedures have worked for the past ten years even though both laws have been amended during that period.

. . . .

## NOTE

The legal and practical ramifications of the possible enactment of federal legislation governing state and local government collective bargaining has been examined in numerous articles and monographs, including Shaller, *The Constitutionality of a Federal Collective Bargaining Statute for State and Local Employees,* 29 LAB. L.J. 594 (1978); Chanin, *Can a Federal Collective Bargaining Statute for Public Employees Meet the Requirements of National League of Cities v. Usery?: A Union Perspective,* 6 J.L. & EDUC. 493 (1977); Weil & Manas, *Can a Federal Collective Bargaining Statute for Public Employees Meet the Requirements of National League of Cities v. Usery?: A Management Perspective,* 6 J.L. & EDUC. 526 (1977); FEDERAL LEGISLATION FOR PUBLIC SECTOR COLLECTIVE BARGAINING (T. Colosi & S. Rynecki eds. 1975); Baird, *National Legislation for Public Employees: "End Run" on the Wagner Act,* 61 ILL. B.J. 410 (1973).

## D. THE IMPACT OF PUBLIC SECTOR UNIONS

### ORR, PUBLIC EMPLOYEE COMPENSATION LEVELS, in PUBLIC EMPLOYEE UNIONS: A STUDY OF THE CRISIS IN PUBLIC SECTOR LABOR RELATIONS 131, 131-33, 139-44 (A. Chickering ed. 1976) †

#### LOOKING BACK

In the job market of the 1950s government or civil service employment was portrayed as a career for somebody content to do routine work and careful to avoid mistakes. The appeal of the calling lay in the elements of predictability, security, and fair if unspectacular compensation. Salaries in the U.S. civil service were somewhat lower than one could earn in a private corporation, but benefit plans — especially retirement and vacations — were much more attractive. And the element of security was indeed present. Through the Eisenhower administrations the federal government had not yet grown used to the giddy pleasures of peacetime deficit finance; and as a consequence an occasional "rif" (reduction in force) was not unknown in some bureaus or agencies. But the civil servant who had been laid off had priority on job openings in other bureaus; and in a job market where many had memories of the 1930s, the civil service exemplified a high degree of freedom from risk.

† Reprinted by permission of the Institute for Contemporary Studies.

Federal employment, while appealing to those among the most talented and highly trained, typified the character of government employment relative to the private alternative. There are, of course, very different kinds of jobs in government, such as police and fire fighting, which embody risk or adventure. But the characteristics of unspectacular compensation with a high degree of security dominated in state and local work as well.

About 1966 the average value of government worker compensation began a steady rise relative to compensation in private employment. Legislation was passed in many states authorizing collective bargaining for government workers; a decade earlier, unions had been formed for federal employees. Increasingly, public employees — including such sensitive job classes as teachers, sanitation workers, firefighters, hospital workers, and police — resorted to the strike. The trend has been an acceleration in the growth of public employee unions and the extension of bargaining rights, with *de facto* threat of strike, into many new locales and many new catagories of government service.

Recent years have seen numerous apparently spectacular wage advances on the part of public employees: street sweepers in San Francisco are earning a comfortably middle-class wage (about $17,000 per annum); gardeners in the same city went on strike, demanding a scale of up to $21,000; professors in New York's City University scored spectacular gains in 1969 when their school temporarily became the salary lodestar of American academe via the bargaining table; and so forth. . . .

. . . .

### MEASURED EFFECTS

The qualitative impact of growing government employment, with increasingly strong commitment to collective bargaining . . ., seems quite clear and unambiguous. Collective bargaining creates incentives and power relationships within the processes of government resource allocation that will likely create important consequences for the size of the governmental labor force, the average workload of government workers (their productivity), and the compensation of government workers relative to private civilian employees.

The modern spirit, however, is to discount or ignore such qualitative analyses unless the indicated effects are significant. Thus, data are processed (usually by linear regression analysis) and judgments rendered on the statistical significance of the relationship or effect in question. The prior questions — How good are the data? How appropriate are the tests to which the data are subjected? — are seldom given thorough attention.

No high-quality data exist to study relative compensation levels in government compared to private employment. The U.S. Department of Commerce, however, does generate data on employment, wages, and compensation in various sectors and industries of the economy, and it is possible from these to make crude comparisons between compensation rates for workers in different industrial sectors and in government.

From Table 1, which presents a biennial summary of the data, we observe the steady growth in state and local employment since 1950, as well as the sharp increase in membership of two important public employee unions, beginning in the late 1950s. From 1952 to 1966, an average full-time government worker's compensation stayed roughly at parity with private wages for equivalent work; during this period government wages occasionally fell as much as 8 percent below the private wage rate, but for most of the period hovered within 3 percentage points of private wages. In the years since 1966 compensation in government employment has risen steadily relative to the private sector until 1973, when the gap had widened to favor government workers by about 10 percent. There is no reason to assume that the 1966-1973 trend has been reversed since that time.

TABLE 1

| Year | Government Employment | | Average Compensation per Full-Time Equivalent Worker | | | Union Membership * |
|------|---------|----------------|------------|---------|-----------|----------------------|
|      | Federal | State/ Local | Government | Private | Ratio G/P | |
| 1950 | 4,117 | 4,285 | 3,181 | 3,145 | 1.011 | N.A. |
| 1952 | 2,583 | 4,522 | 3,437 | 3,626 | .948 | N.A. |
| 1954 | 2,373 | 4,859 | 3,654 | 3,932 | .929 | N.A. |
| 1956 | 2,410 | 5,275 | 4,137 | 4,452 | .929 | N.A. |
| 1958 | 2,405 | 5,892 | 4,661 | 4,709 | .990 | N.A. |
| 1960 | 2,421 | 6,387 | 5,077 | 5,170 | .982 | 280 |
| 1962 | 2,539 | 6,849 | 5,416 | 5,564 | .973 | 326 |
| 1964 | 2,528 | 7,536 | 5,960 | 6,043 | .936 | 374 |
| 1966 | 2,861 | 3,618 | 6,474 | 6.615 | .979 | 481 |
| 1968 | 2,984 | 9,358 | 7,352 | 7,373 | .997 | 659 |
| 1970 | 2,881 | 8,528 | 8,782 | 8,348 | 1.052 | 769 |
| 1972 | 2,795 | 9,237 | 10,502 | 9,519 | 1.103 | 822 |
| 1973 | 2,874 (1974) | 11,784 (1974) | 11,164 | 10,153 | 1.099 | N.A. |

It is important to note certain factual information that Table 1 does not provide. For example, one might argue that government employees on average are better educated or more experienced than their private counterparts, and therefore should expect to earn more. If this is true, compensation differences would be accounted for by federal pay policy, which is committed to pay employees comparably to the private sector — taking training, experience, and skill into account as much as possible. A number of states also try to maintain comparable pay scales.

No good evidence exists on nationwide differences between compensation in private employment and compensation in all categories of government employment — federal, state, and local. We do, however, have an extremely competent and interesting study of pay differences between *federal* government and private employees in an area including the District of Columbia, Maryland, Delaware, and Virginia.

Princeton economist Sharon Smith (1976) analyzed employment-and-wages information on individual households from the censuses of 1960 and 1970. She compared average wages and average earnings (not including fringe benefits) of federal government employees and private employees. Her results are summarized in Table 2.

* Combined American Federation of State, County and Municipal Employees, and American Federation of Government Employees (in thousands).
Sources: *Union Membership and Government Employment: Statistical Abstract of the United States* (various editions); compensation data: U.S. Department of Commerce, Office of Business Economics, *National Income and Product Accounts of the U.S., 1923-65; Survey of Current Business,* July issues 1967-1974.

TABLE 2

|                                      | 1960   | 1970   | % Change |
|--------------------------------------|--------|--------|----------|
| Federal average earnings             | 5,172  | 7,848  | 51.74    |
| Private average earnings             | 3,150  | 4,656  | 47.81    |
| Ratio F/P                            | 1.6419 | 1.6856 |          |
|                                      |        |        |          |
| Federal average wages                | 2.69   | 4.23   | 57.25    |
| Private average wages                | 1.93   | 2.88   | 49.22    |
| Ratio F/P                            | 1.3938 | 1.4688 |          |
|                                      |        |        |          |
| Unaccountable earnings difference    | 65%    | 65%    |          |
| Unaccountable wage difference        | 55%    | 52%    |          |

In 1960 federal earnings were 64.19 percent higher than private; only 35 percent of that difference is accountable by education, experience, family status, race, or other "explanatory variables." The *unaccountable* wage difference thus is 65 percent of 64.19 percent, or about 41 percent. A larger unaccountable difference — about 44 percent — was found for 1970; federal earnings rose more rapidly than private earnings in the intervening decade.

Other analysts have discovered earnings differences between government and private employment. Typically, earnings differentials for state and local employment show up as smaller than for federal employment, and differentials vary from region to region; but the pattern of higher earnings for government workers is clear.

How can the Smith findings reported in Table 2 be reconciled with the aggregate data in Table 1? First, and most obviously, federal employment is more highly paid than employment at other levels of government. Second, private earnings per worker in the Middle Atlantic labor market average in part-time people on a one-for-one basis, while private earnings per full-time equivalent worker nationwide (in the Department of Commerce study) add part-timers together to get full-time equivalents. Earnings comparisons per person that include part-time people will increase estimated wage differentials between public and private employment because of a higher incidence of part-time employment in the private sector than in government.

Whatever the reasons for the indicated differences, the Smith study suggests that a very substantial and quite possibly growing premium is collected by individuals who are fortunate enough to be federal government employees.

. . . .

**CONCLUSION**

Based on various studies to date and on examination of the aggregate data in Table 1, it seems safe to offer the following conclusions:

1. Since the middle 1960s, government employee earnings have grown steadily relative to private employee earnings.
2. These differences are in large part unaccountable in terms of qualifying worker attributes.
3. The growth in these wage differences has been accompanied by an increase in public employee union membership.

Two distinct issues emerge from such data on government vs. private wage differentials. First, there is the issue highlighted in Table 2; do government employees systematically receive greater compensation than they could expect to get in private employment? Sharon Smith's work on this question, and the findings of other analysts, clearly suggest that the answer is yes.

The second question is simultaneously more difficult to answer and more vital. To what extent do the growth of government employee unions and the increasing recourse to collective bargaining forebode that these favorable differentials for government employment will persist or grow? The recent surge in government wages compared to private may mean that the buying of votes through collective bargaining settlements is well underway; or it may mean that "society" wants more government service and is having to pay higher wages to get it; or it may mean that government employment is simply more recession-proof than private employment.

## NOTE

The effect of unionization on the wages of various categories of public employees has been the subject of considerable discussion. In Kasper, *The Effects of Collective Bargaining on Public School Teachers' Salaries,* 24 IND. & LAB. REL. REV. 57, 71 (1970), the author concluded that "collective representation does not seem to have had much, if any, effect on teachers' salaries. . . ." On the other hand, in Hall & Carroll, *The Effect of Teachers' Organizations on Salaries and Class Size,* 26 IND. & LAB. REL. REV. 834, 841 (1973), the authors observed that their "findings strongly indicate that teachers' organizations do indeed increase salaries." *See also* Ashenfelter, *The Effect of Unionization on Wages in the Public Sector: The Case of Fire Fighters,* 24 IND. & LAB. REL. REV. 191 (1971); Hall & Vanderporten, *Unionization, Monopsony Power, and Police Salaries,* 16 IND. REL. 94 (1977) ("Our findings suggest that while police salaries are increased by formal negotiations, the amounts are quite modest"); Ehrenberg, *Municipal Government Structure, Unionization and the Wages of Fire Fighters,* 27 IND. & LAB. REL. REV. 36 (1973).

In Fogel & Lewin, *Wage Determination in the Public Sector,* 27 IND. & LAB. REL. REV. 410, 430 (1974), the authors concluded:

> The available data indicate that public-private pay relationships in the United States can be explained, at least in part, by a combination of two factors: a discretion that public employers must exercise in implementing the prevailing wage rule adopted by most cities and larger government units and the nature of the political forces that affect governmental wage decisions. The result is an occupational pay structure that is more "equalitarian" in the public sector than in private industry, in the sense that public employers tend to pay more than private employers for low-scale and craft jobs and to pay less for top executive jobs.

## REHMUS, LABOR RELATIONS IN THE PUBLIC SECTOR, Paper prepared for the 3rd World Congress, International Industrial Relations Association, London, England (Sept. 3-7, 1973) †

. . . A basic underlying reason for the extension of collective bargaining rights to public sector employees in the United States is the argument that collective bargaining rights which have been mandated by law in the private sector should in equity be given to the government's own employees. This is not to suggest that there are not important differences between private and public employment, however, and that these differences have not created some difficult problems as the private sector bargaining model increasingly pervades the public sector.

---

† Reprinted by permission of the Institute of Labor and Industrial Relations.

Probably the most fundamental of these problems lies in the different purposes of public and private undertakings. The public employer is an artificial creature of the electorate established to minister to the needs and desires of the public and to provide the mechanical and administrative structure to carry on these functions. In a democratic system of government it is elected officials who are normally charged with the control and determination of budget and tax rates, which is the primary way of setting goals and priorities. While extra-parliamentary influences are both inevitable and necessary elements of the democratic process, they should not be allowed to overcome the fact that elected legislative bodies are supposed to be essentially deliberative bodies. If democratic governments are to distinguish between public passions and public interests, legislatures have to be at least partially insulated from group pressures. In a number of major American cities the crisis pressures that result from actual or threatened withdrawal of public employment services has at times usurped the legislature's deliberative process in this most fundamental governmental function of setting goals and priorities.

A second problem lies in the existence of the merit system and civil service in the public sector in the United States. These systems, basically designed to ensure that the selection, retention, and promotion of public employees is based on qualifications and meritorious performance alone, are often considered to be the warp and woof of public employment. To employees, however, merit is sometimes considered a euphemism for favoritism. Public employee organizations therefore attempt to weave into this tight fabric somewhat coarser threads such as strict seniority, across-the-board wage adjustments, and the like. It is a yet-unsettled question whether civil service and the merit system can survive the assault of traditional collective bargaining practices. It is clear that the protection of public employees' right to continued employment, assuming meritorious service, is increasingly being enforced through bargained grievance procedures culminating in binding neutral arbitration rather than through statutory devices such as the tenure system.

A third general problem is that of supervisory unionism. In private industry in the United States the lines of authority and supervision are ordinarily clearly drawn, even in areas of white collar employment. In the public sector, however, the lines between supervisor and employee are far more indistinct. There are several reasons for this. The appellation of supervisor tends to be pushed further down in the organizational hierarchy in public than in private bureaucracies. Where all are dedicated to serving the public, there is a greater community of interest among all employees. In the public service both supervisors and non-supervisors alike are often compensated within an identical and fairly rigid salary payment structure. As a reflection of these facts many existing state collective bargaining laws have not drawn traditional distinctions between supervisors and employees. Hence labor relations boards that implement the state laws have permitted supervisory unionism. In some cases they have required the recognition of supervisory units as components of the same union that organized those who are supervised. Whether conflict of interest is inevitable between the supervisory goals of the organization and the fraternal goals of the union is as yet uncertain. It is clearly a danger, however.

A fourth serious problem in public employee bargaining arises because of the diffusion of decision-making authority which frequently exists in the public sector. Parliamentary systems of government permit a greater unity of legislative and executive authority than is common in United States governmental systems which are more often characterized by division of authority with checks and balances operating between the executive and legislative powers. In federal, state and local governments an agency head may have authority to negotiate only on a portion of the issues which are normally subjects of collective bargaining — other bargainable subjects may be retained within the control of the legislative body or an independent civil service board. Often a chief executive may not have final authority on distribution of funds and can only submit recommendations to the appropriate legislature. May the legislative body repudiate his decisions? Does it have the responsibility to provide the funds to pay for the salary structure which the chief executive has negotiated? Finally, where voter approval of increased millage is necessary to pay for the negotiated increases, local taxpayer revolts and disapproval are increasingly common. What is to be done in these situations? Questions of this kind are extremely difficult within many, though not all, governments in the United States. But the inherent logic of public employee bargaining is leading to considerable centralization of power and to increased executive power vis-a-vis both legislatures and civil service boards.

Related to but distinguishable from the previous problem is one characterized as "end-run" or "double-deck" bargaining. Some public employee unions attempt by lobbying to secure from the state legislature those items which they had failed to obtain or which were traded away at the municipal bargaining table. In many states, civil service organizations have been one of the strongest lobbies in the state legislature. These powers can hardly be taken away from such organizations. But from the municipal government's point of view, freedom to trade cost reductions in one area for contractually bargained new expenditures in another is an essential element of bargaining flexibility and bargaining equality. Where state legislatures mandate wage and fringe bargaining at the municipal level and yet continue to legislate on municipal employee benefits they place local units of government in a Procrustean bed. Public employee bargaining may be desirable and inevitable, but public employees hardly seem entitled to the benefits both of collective bargaining and of traditional protective state laws.

A final problem of collective bargaining in the public sector, one which perhaps receives more attention than it deserves, is that of public employee strikes. Most contemporary discussions of this subject in the United States concern the issue of whether public employees have or should be given the legal right to strike. The fact is, of course, that despite the fact that *de jure* in almost all United States governmental jurisdictions they do not have the right to strike, *de facto* they can and do, often with impunity. Moreover, though it is not commonly recognized, the public employee strike problem exists both in jurisdictions which permit collective bargaining and in those which have not yet granted public employees these rights.

The public employee strike problem is not overwhelming on a national basis. In the last decade such strikes have grown in frequency from approximately one per month to one per day in the whole nation. But strike activity in the public sector is still far below that in the private sector. Public employees involved in work stoppages in recent years represent about 1½ percent of total employment, compared to nearly 4 percent in the private sector. In the most recent year for which data are available, 1970, strike idleness represented 0.08 percent of mandays worked by government employees; for the economy as a whole this figure was 0.28 percent. The average duration of public employee strikes is less than five days for what might be termed "essential" employees; for those in less crucial occupations the average duration is over twice as great. Among teachers, and unlike municipal employees, the absolute number of strikes has declined substantially in the last two years.

Mediation and non-binding neutral recommendations are the most common governmental devices used to help to resolve collective bargaining impasses. While they are effective in the large majority of disputes, they are obviously not a panacea. Where it is deemed that no strike can be permitted, as is almost invariably the decision with police and firemen, compulsory binding arbitration is the most frequently used alternative. . . . The newest, though largely untested, idea in compulsory arbitration is "final offer selection," in which the neutral is given no power to compromise issues in dispute, but must select one or the other of the parties' final offers.

*Conclusion*

The coming of collective bargaining to the public sector is the most significant development in the industrial relations field in the United States in the last thirty years. Its growth has been both rapid and extensive and appears to be continuing. Even now, however, bargaining does not occur in more than half of all governmental jurisdictions in the United States. In many areas where bargaining has begun it is less than ten years old. Hence one must be cautious in making generalizations about the future of public employee labor relations. A few may be put forward tentatively, however.

The coming of unionism to the public sector has provided enough new recruits to the labor movement to reverse the decline in trade union membership which took place during the latter 1950's and early 1960's. Moreover, it is at least possible that as government employees join unions, or convert their traditional professional associations to union-like behavior, that this will change the general blue-collar image of the labor movement in the United States. Private sector trade unionism has never exceeded 30 percent of the non-agricultural workforce and has never had any strong appeal to white collar workers. Organizing successes among white collar and professional employees in the public sector may make unionism acceptable and normal to private sector white collar workers who in the near future, if not already, will represent a majority of employment in private industry. In summary, public employee unionism has halted the decline in trade union size in the United States and may in fact contribute to substantial new growth in the private sector in the next decade or two.

Public employee unionism appears to have contributed to the centralization of governmental decision-making power in the United States, though it is by no means the sole cause of such developments. At the municipal level it is clear that the exigencies of collective bargaining have forced decision-making power toward the chief executive at the expense of municipal legislatures and civil service boards. In the educational field organized teacher pressures along with a number of constitutional decisions are forcing a shift away from the local property tax toward the state-imposed income tax as the primary means of financing public education. Almost inevitably this will mean that many financial decisions will be removed from local school boards and centralized to intermediate or statewide decision-making bodies. At the federal level the movement toward nation-wide bargaining units of federal civil servants may slow or halt efforts toward federal decentralization that were undertaken in the 1960's. In short, public employee unionism appears in many areas to be leading to more centralized decision-making in the United States, similar to the way it has in many other industrialized democracies.

The economic results of public employee bargaining are as yet unclear and controversial. Some authorities believe that public employees have driven their salary and benefit levels far higher than would have been the case in the absence of collective bargaining, and higher than can be justified on the basis of economic equity. Others challenge this assumption. They state that recent increases in public employee compensation are largely reflective of inflationary pressures in the society and the temporary need for public employees to "catch up" with others to whom their wages and salaries should be compared. Quantitative data that would support either argument are still scanty. Public employees in some occupations clearly have fared more favorably in recent years than has the average employee in the private sector. The differences are not large, however, and during 1971 and 1972 increases in both sectors were held down by government wage policies.

As yet, at least, the impact of public employee unionism on governmental decision-making has not been as great as the numerical increase in public union membership and bargaining unit growth might suggest. In the federal sector it is estimated that employees as yet have the right to bargain on perhaps only 25 percent of the subjects that are bargainable in the private sector. Though the scope of bargaining is increasing at the federal level, and is already more extensive at the local and educational levels, it cannot be said with any certainty that the large majority of governmental and public policy decisions are fundamentally different than they would have been in the absence of collective bargaining.

Finally, and most speculatively, it is possible that public employee unionism will bring changes to the whole of the labor relations environment in the United States. As previously noted, white collar and professional organization in the public sector may bring a greater acceptability of white collar unionization in the private sector. If devices such as compulsory arbitration become common and effective for resolving collective bargaining impasses in the public sector, such devices may increasingly be urged for use in the private sector. In general, and with many obvious exceptions, public sector labor relations practices and laws in the United States have thus far been strongly modeled on the private sector structures which had evolved earlier. Over time, experience in the public sector may prove certain procedures and practices, now uncommon or unknown in the private sector, to be useful or effective. It is not at all unlikely that such practices might then become acceptable in the private sector. In sum, the future may well be one of simultaneous changes in both sectors, each tending generally to become more like the other.

## NOTES

1. Collective bargaining in the public sector has been the subject of numerous books and symposia. The following are particularly useful in gaining a broad overview of the issues and problems: H. WELLINGTON & R. WINTER, THE UNIONS AND THE CITIES (1971); PUBLIC WORKERS AND PUBLIC UNIONS (S. Zagoria ed. 1972); LABOR RELATIONS LAW IN THE PUBLIC SECTOR (A. Knapp ed. 1977); PUBLIC EMPLOYEE UNIONS: A STUDY OF THE CRISIS IN PUBLIC SECTOR LABOR RELATIONS (A. Chickering ed. 1976); S. SPERO & J. CAPOZZOLA, THE URBAN COMMUNITY AND ITS UNIONIZED BUREAUCRACIES (1973); P. FEUILLE & T. KOCHAN, PUBLIC SECTOR LABOR RELATIONS: ANALYSIS AND READINGS (1977); M. MOSKOW, J. LOEWENBERG, E. KOZIARA, COLLECTIVE BARGAINING IN PUBLIC EMPLOYMENT (1970); SORRY ... NO GOVERNMENT TODAY: UNIONS VS. CITY HALL (R. Walsh ed. 1969); "Symposium: Labor Relations in the Public Sector," 67 MICH. L. REV. 891 (1969); COLLECTIVE BARGAINING IN THE PUBLIC SERVICE (D. Kruger & C. Schmidt eds. 1969). One of the most concise yet most perceptive discussions of the principal policy issues raised by public sector unionism is D. Bok & J. Dunlop, *Collective Bargaining and the Public Sector*, in LABOR AND THE AMERICAN COMMUNITY 312 (1970). Among the many useful

bibliographies on public sector labor relations are: TANIMOTO, TOPIC CODED TITLES ON PUBLIC EMPLOYEE COLLECTIVE BARGAINING WITH EMPHASIS ON STATE AND LOCAL LEVELS (Univ. of Hawaii Ind. Rel. Center, Occasional Publication No. 130, 5th ed. 1978); PEZDEK, PUBLIC EMPLOYMENT BIBLIOGRAPHY (N.Y. State School of Ind. & Lab. Rel., Bibliography Series No. 11, 1973); PEGNETTER, PUBLIC EMPLOYMENT BIBLIOGRAPHY (N.Y. State School of Ind. & Lab. Rel. 1971); U.S. CIVIL SERVICE COMM'N, EMPLOYEE-MANAGEMENT RELATIONS IN THE PUBLIC SERVICE (Personnel Bibliography Series No. 44, 1972); U.S. DIV. OF PUBLIC EMPLOYEE LABOR RELATIONS, DEP'T OF LABOR, CURRENT REFERENCES AND INFORMATION SERVICES FOR POLICY DECISION-MAKING IN STATE AND LOCAL GOVERNMENT LABOR RELATIONS: A SELECTED BIBLIOGRAPHY (1971).

Another invaluable source of information on public sector collective bargaining are the reports and recommendations of various advisory commissions. *See generally* COMMITTEE ON ECONOMIC DEVELOPMENT, IMPROVING MANAGEMENT OF THE PUBLIC WORK FORCE: THE CHALLENGE TO STATE AND LOCAL GOVERNMENT (1978); ADVISORY COMMISSION ON INTERGOVERNMENTAL RELATIONS, LABOR-MANAGEMENT POLICIES FOR STATE AND LOCAL GOVERNMENT (1969); 1967 EXECUTIVE COMMITTEE, NATIONAL GOVERNORS' CONFERENCE, REPORT OF TASK FORCE ON STATE AND LOCAL GOVERNMENT LABOR RELATIONS (1967), and 1968, 1969 and 1970 Supplements to REPORT OF TASK FORCE ON STATE AND LOCAL GOVERNMENT LABOR RELATIONS; THE COUNCIL OF STATE GOVERNMENTS, STATE-LOCAL EMPLOYEE LABOR RELATIONS (1970); TWENTIETH CENTURY FUND TASK FORCE ON LABOR DISPUTES IN PUBLIC EMPLOYMENT, PICKETS AT CITY HALL (1970). Many of the reports issued by state and local advisory commissions are also useful. For one of the most comprehensive, see FINAL REPORT OF THE ASSEMBLY ADVISORY COUNCIL ON PUBLIC EMPLOYEE RELATIONS, STATE OF CALIFORNIA (March 15, 1973). See also PUBLIC EMPLOYER-EMPLOYEE RELATIONS STUDY COMM'N, REPORT TO THE GOVERNOR AND THE LEGISLATURE (N.J. 1976); GOVERNOR'S ADVISORY COMM'N ON LABOR-MANAGEMENT FOR PUBLIC EMPLOYEES, REPORT AND RECOMMENDATIONS (Ill. 1967). *See generally* Smith, *State and Local Advisory Reports on Public Employment Labor Legislation: A Comparative Analysis,* 67 MICH. L. REV. 891 (1969).

2. The development of collective bargaining among federal employees is comprehensively treated in M. NESBITT, LABOR RELATIONS IN THE FEDERAL GOVERNMENT SERVICE (1976).

# Chapter 2

# THE RIGHT TO JOIN AND FORM UNIONS

## A. CONSTITUTIONAL PROTECTION

### MC LAUGHLIN v. TILENDIS

United States Court of Appeals, Seventh Circuit
398 F.2d 287 (1968)

CUMMINGS, Circuit Judge. This action was brought under Section 1 of the Civil Rights Act of 1871 (42 U.S.C. § 1983) [1] by John Steele and James McLaughlin who had been employed as probationary teachers by Cook County, Illinois, School District No. 149. Each sought damages of $100,000 from the Superintendent of School District No. 149 and the elected members of the Board of Education of that District.

Steele was not offered a second-year teaching contract and McLaughlin was dismissed before the end of his second year of teaching. Steele alleged that he was not rehired and McLaughlin alleged that he was dismissed because of their association with Local 1663 of the American Federation of Teachers, AFL-CIO. Neither teacher had yet achieved tenure.

In two additional Counts, Local 1663 and the parent union, through their officers and on behalf of all their members, sought an injunction requiring the defendants to cease and desist from discriminating against teachers who distribute union materials and solicit union membership.

The District Court granted the defendants' motion to dismiss the complaint, holding that plaintiffs had no First Amendment rights to join or form a labor union, so that there was no jurisdiction under the Civil Rights Act. The District Court's memorandum opinion did not consider the alternative defense presented in the motion that defendants were immune from suit under the Illinois Tort Immunity Act (Ill. Rev. Stats. 1967, Ch. 85, Sec. 2-201). Concluding that the First Amendment confers the right to form and join a labor union, we reverse on the ground that the complaint does state a claim under Section 1983.

It is settled that teachers have the right of free association, and unjustified interference with teachers' associational freedom violates the Due Process clause of the Fourteenth Amendment. Shelton v. Tucker, 364 U.S. 479, 485-487. Public employment may not be subjected to unreasonable conditions, and the assertion of First Amendment rights by teachers will usually not warrant their dismissal. Keyishian v. Board of Regents, 385 U.S. 589, 605-606; Garrity v. New Jersey, 385 U.S. 493, 500; Pickering v. Board of Education, 36 U.S. Law Week 4495. Unless there is some illegal intent, an individual's right to form and join a union is protected by the First Amendment. Thomas v. Collins, 323 U.S. 516, 534; see also Hague v. C.I.O., 307 U.S. 496, 512, 519, 523-524; Griswold v. Connecticut,

---

[1] Section 1983 of Title 42 of the U.S. Code provides:

"Every person who, under color of any statute, ordinance, regulation, custom, or usage, of any State or Territory, subjects, or causes to be subjected, any citizen of the United States or other person within the jurisdiction thereof to the deprivation of any rights, privileges, or immunities secured by the Constitution and laws, shall be liable to the party injured in an action at law, suit in equity, or other proper proceeding for redress."

381 U.S. 479, 483; Stapleton v. Mitchell, 60 F. Supp. 51, 59-60, 61 (D. Kan. 1945; opinion of Circuit Judge Murrah), appeal dismissed, 326 U.S. 690. As stated in N.A.A.C.P. v. Alabama, 357 U.S. 449, 460:

> "It is beyond debate that freedom to engage in association for the advancement of beliefs and ideas is an inseparable aspect of the 'liberty' assured by the Due Process Clause of the Fourteenth Amendment, which embraces freedom of speech."

Even though the individual plaintiffs did not yet have tenure, the Civil Rights Act of 1871 gives them a remedy if their contracts were not renewed because of their exercise of constitutional rights. . . .

Just this month the Supreme Court held that an Illinois teacher was protected by the First Amendment from discharge even though he wrote a partially false letter to a local newspaper in which he criticized the school board's financial policy. Pickering v. Board of Education, 36 U.S. Law Week 4495. There is no showing on this record that plaintiffs' activities impeded "the proper performance of [their] daily duties in the classroom." *Idem* at p. 4498. If teachers can engage in scathing and partially inaccurate public criticism of their school board, surely they can form and take part in associations to further what they consider to be their well-being.

The trial judge was motivated by his conclusion that more than free speech was involved here, stating:

> "The union may decide to engage in strikes, to set up machinery to bargain with the governmental employer, to provide machinery for arbitration, or may seek to establish working conditions. Overriding community interests are involved. The very ability of the governmental entity to function may be affected. The judiciary, and particularly this Court, cannot interfere with the power or discretion of the state in handling these matters."

It is possible of course that at some future time plaintiffs may engage in union-related conduct justifying their dismissal. But the Supreme Court has stated that

> "Those who join an organization but do not share its unlawful purposes and who do not participate in its unlawful activities surely pose no threat, either as citizens or as public employees." Elfbrandt v. Russell, 384 U.S. 11, 17.

Even if this record disclosed that the union was connected with unlawful activity, the bare fact of membership does not justify charging members with their organization's misdeeds. *Idem.* A contrary rule would bite more deeply into associational freedom than is necessary to achieve legitimate state interests, thereby violating the First Amendment.

Illinois has not prohibited membership in a teachers' union, and defendants do not claim that the individual plaintiffs engaged in any illegal strikes or picketing.[3] Moreover, collective bargaining contracts between teachers' unions and school districts are not against the public policy of Illinois. Chicago Education Association v. Chicago Board of Education, 76 Ill. App. 2d 456, 222

---

[3] In Illinois, strikes and certain picketing by public employees are enjoinable. Redding v. Board of Education, 32 Ill. 2d 567, 207 N.E.2d 427 (1965).

N.E.2d 243 (1966). Illinois even permits the automatic deduction of union dues from the salaries of employees of local governmental agencies. Ill. Rev. Stats. 1967, Ch. 85, Sec. 472. These very defendants have not adopted any rule, regulation or resolution forbidding union membership. Accordingly, no paramount public interest of Illinois warranted the limiting of Steele's and McLaughlin's right of association. Of course, at trial defendants may show that these individuals were engaging in unlawful activities or were dismissed for other proper reasons, but on this record we hold that the complaint sufficiently states a justiciable claim under Section 1983. There is nothing anomalous in protecting teachers' rights to join unions. Other employees have long been similarly protected by the National Labor Relations Act. See National Labor Relations Board v. Jones & Laughlin, 301 U.S. 1, 33.

The second ground of defendants' motion to dismiss was that they are protected against suit by the Illinois Tort Immunity Act (Ill. Rev. Stats. 1967, Ch. 85, Sec. 2-201).[4] Under the Supremacy Clause, that statute cannot protect defendants against a cause of action grounded, as here, on a federal statute. Legislators and judges have broad immunity under Section 1983 because in enacting that statute Congress did not intend to overturn their pre-existing defense. Tenney v. Brandhove, 341 U.S. 367, 376; Pierson v. Ray, 386 U.S. 547, 554-555. However, other officials, such as present defendants, retain only a qualified immunity, dependent on good faith action. . . . Even under the Illinois Act, immunity is conditioned upon a showing of good faith (Baum, *Tort Liability of Local Governments and Their Employees: An Introduction to the Illinois Immunity Act,* Ill. Law Forum (1966) 981, 1003-1004), and there has been no hearing on that question. In this Court and in their brief below the defendants also rely on common law immunity, but we rejected a similar contention in Progress Development Corp. v. Mitchell, 286 F.2d 221, 231 (7th Cir. 1961), where it was held that common law immunity did not extend to members of the Deerfield, Illinois, Park Board charged with discriminating against Negroes. Unless they can show good faith action, the reach of that decision extends to the present defendants who are alleged to have discriminatorily discharged Steele and McLaughlin for their union membership. To hold defendants absolutely immune from this type of suit would frustrate the very purpose of Section 1983. Jobson v. Henne, 355 F.2d 129, 133 (2nd Cir. 1966). At best, defendants' qualified immunity in this case means that they can prevail only if they show that plaintiffs were discharged on justifiable grounds. Thus here a successful defense on the merits merges with a successful defense under the qualified immunity doctrine.

Finally in this connection, it should be noted that immunity was *sub silentio* denied to the school officials involved in the *Johnson, Bomar, Smith, Rackley* and *Williams* cases, *supra;* see also Board of Education v. Barnette, 319 U.S. 624, 637-638.

The judgment of the District Court is reversed and the cause is remanded for trial.

---

[4] Sec. 2-201 provides:

"Except as otherwise provided by Statute, a public employee serving in a position involving the determination of policy or the exercise of discretion is not liable for an injury resulting from his act or omission in determining policy when acting in the exercise of such discretion even though abused."

## NOTES

1. Prior to *McLaughlin* the courts had generally upheld regulations or ordinances which prohibited public employees from joining labor organizations. For example, in Perez v. Bd. of Police Comm'rs of the City of Los Angeles, 78 Cal. App. 638, 178 P.2d 537 (1947), the court upheld a regulation prohibiting police officers from becoming members of any organization identified with "any trade association, federation or labor union which admits to membership persons who are not members of the Los Angeles Police Department, or whose membership is not exclusively made up of employees of city of Los Angeles." *Accord*, AFSCME Local 201 v. City of Muskegon, 369 Mich. 384, 120 N.W.2d 197, *cert. denied*, 375 U.S. 833 (1963); King v. Priest, 357 Mo. 68, 206 S.W.2d 547 (1947), *appeal dismissed*, 333 U.S. 852, 68 S. Ct. 736, 92 L.Ed. 1133 (1948).

2. Must a public employee first exhaust whatever state *judicial* remedies may exist before maintaining a suit in federal court under the Civil Rights Act of 1871? The courts have held that "exhaustion of state *judicial* remedies is not a prerequisite to the invocation of federal relief under section 1983 since the cause of action established by that statute is fully supplementary to any remedy, adequate or inadequate, that might exist under state law." Hobbs v. Thompson, 448 F.2d 456 (5th Cir. 1971). *But see* Askew v. Hargrave, 401 U.S. 476 (1971); Egner v. Texas City Independent School District, 338 F. Supp. 931 (S.D. Tex. 1972).

3. Most of the comprehensive state public employee labor relations statutes specifically provide that it is an unfair labor practice for a public employer to discriminate against a public employee because of his union activities. Most of these statutes further establish a public employee relations agency to hear complaints of alleged unfair labor practices and authorize the agency to issue orders remedying any unfair labor practices that are found to exist. Where such a state *administrative* remedy exists, should the employee be required to exhaust this remedy before seeking relief in the federal courts under the Civil Rights Act of 1871? In McNeese v. Board of Education, 373 U.S. 668, 83 S. Ct. 1433, 10 L. Ed. 2d 622 (1963), the Supreme Court held that federal plaintiff need not exhaust state administrative remedies, noting that one of the purposes of the Civil Rights Act was "to provide a remedy in the federal courts supplementary to any remedy any State may have." *Accord,* Houghton v. Shafer, 392 U.S. 639, 88 S. Ct. 2119, 20 L.Ed.2d 1319 (1968); Damico v. California, 389 U.S. 416, 88 S. Ct. 526, 19 L.Ed.2d 647 (1967). *But see* Gibson v. Berryhill, 411 U.S. 564, 93 S. Ct. 1689, 36 L.Ed.2d 488 (1973); Askew v. Hargrave, 401 U.S. 476, 91 S. Ct. 856, 28 L.Ed.2d 196 (1971). The broad negation of the exhaustion doctrine has been critically examined in Comment, *Exhaustion of State Administrative Remedies in Section 1983 Cases,* 41 U. Chi. L. Rev. 537 (1974); Note, *Exhaustion of State Remedies Under the Civil Rights Act,* 68 Colum. L. Rev. 1201 (1968); Note, *Limiting the Section 1983 Action in the Wake of Monroe v. Pape,* 82 Harv. L. Rev. 1486 (1969). For a rebuttal to the latter note, see Comment, *Section 1983 Jurisdiction: A Reply,* 83 Harv. L. Rev. 1352 (1970).

Does the result in *McNeese* make sense in the labor relations context where the public employee's right to join and form unions is affirmatively protected and where the state provides an administrative remedy to protect such right? Should exhaustion be required where such an administrative remedy exists and the inquiry is essentially factual in nature, involving, for example, whether a public employer unlawfully discriminated against the public employee because of his union activities? In Teamsters Local 594 v. City of West Point, 338 F. Supp. 927 (D. Neb. 1972), the court, noting that the Nebraska Court of Industrial Relations had recently been granted authority to hear public sector labor disputes, including charges of discrimination against public employees because of their union activities, stated that it "would be prone toward application of the exhaustion of remedies doctrine. . . ." "[I]n view of the time and cost already expended," however, the court held that "it would be manifestly unjust to apply the doctrine in the instant matter." Similarly, in Michigan City Federation of Teachers, Local No. 399 v. Michigan City Area Schools, 499 F.2d 115 (7th Cir. 1974), the court held that a minority teachers union which brought a section 1983 suit challenging the constitutionality of a school board's grant of exclusive use of certain communication channels to a majority union should first exhaust its state administrative remedy. The court reasoned as follows:

Since the instant case raises an unfair labor practice we hold that the judgment of the district court be vacated and that the cause be remanded with directions that it be held for the purpose of giving the Federation an opportunity to file an unfair labor practice charge with the newly created [Indiana Education Relations] Board. We think it appropriate that the Federation exhaust all available State remedies and the Board have an opportunity to make a determination in the first instance.

The Second Circuit in a long line of cases has held that a plaintiff in a section 1983 case must exhaust speedy and adequate state administrative remedies. *See, e.g.,* Eisen v. Eastman, 421 F.2d 560 (2d Cir. 1969), *cert. denied,* 400 U.S. 841, 91 S. Ct. 82, 27 L.Ed.2d 75 (1970); Blanton v. State University of New York, 489 F.2d 377 (2d Cir. 1973); Perzanowski v. Salvio, 369 F. Supp. 223 (D. Conn. 1974) (a section 1983 "plaintiff cannot turn his back on adequate state administrative remedy and 'rush into a federal forum' "). Several other circuits, however, have specifically rejected the Second Circuit's exhaustion requirement first set forth in *Eisen. See, e.g.,* Simpson v. Weeks, 570 F.2d 240, 242 n.3 (8th Cir. 1978) ("until the Supreme Court changes its position on the exhaustion requirement, we are reluctant to speculate on the advisability of any other rule"); Hochman v. Board of Education of the City of Newark, 534 F.2d 1094 (3d Cir. 1976).

4. If a public employee, whether required to or not, exhausts his state administrative remedy and a decision is issued finding that his right to engage in union activity was not unlawfully interfered with, may the employee subsequently relitigate the same matter in a suit in federal court? Is the determination by the state agency *res judicata?* In Nigosian v. Weiss, 343 F. Supp. 757 (E.D. Mich. 1971), the court held that "[i]t would be improper to accord a determination of the State Labor Mediation Board binding effect where the examiner specifically limited his decision to examination of state, not federal, law." In Ohlan v. City of Montpelier, 100 L.R.R.M. 2975 (D. Vt. 1979), the court held that, while the doctrine of *res judicata* did not bar a terminated police officer's suit under section 1983 contending that he was discharged because of his union activities, the doctrine of collateral estoppel was applicable. The court noted that the Vermont Supreme Court had upheld a decision of the State Labor Relations Board finding that the termination was not because of the officer's union activity and that the claims in both the state court proceeding and the federal court suit were based on the same facts.

5. The Civil Rights Attorney's Fees Award Act of 1976, 42 U.S.C. § 1988 (Supp. 1977), provides that, *inter alia,* in any action under 42 U.S.C. §§ 1981, 1982, 1983, 1985, and 1986 "the court, in its discretion, may allow the prevailing party, other than the United States, a reasonable attorney's fee as part of the costs." In Bond v. Stanton, 555 F.2d 172, 174 (7th Cir. 1977), *cert. denied,* 98 S. Ct. 3146 (1978), the court held that this act was intended by Congress "to apply to actions against state officials in their official capacity" and that the imposition of liability for attorneys' fees on state officials acting in their official capacity was constitutional, notwithstanding the Eleventh Amendment.

6. Since section 1983 does not contain a statute of limitations, the federal courts ordinarily apply the most analogous statute of limitations of the state in which the action arises. *See, e.g.,* O'Sullivan v. Felix, 233 U.S. 318, 34 S. Ct. 596, 58 L.Ed. 980 (1914); Nevels v. Wilson, 423 F.2d 691 (5th Cir. 1970); Carmicle v. Weddle, 555 F.2d 554 (6th Cir. 1977). *See also* Johnson v. Railway Express Agency, Inc., 421 U.S. 454, 95 S. Ct. 1716, 44 L.Ed.2d 295 (1975) (state statute of limitations ordinarily controlling in § 1981 suit). Suppose a state statute provides, as most do, that unfair labor practice charges must be filed within six months from the occurrence of the event giving rise to the allegation. Would this be the most analogous state statute of limitations?

7. If it is determined that a public employee has been unlawfully discharged because of his/her union activities and reinstatement with back pay is ordered, is the public employer liable for the back pay or is this the responsibility of the public official or officials who discharged the employee in question? In Monell v. Dep't of Social Services of City of New York, 98 S. Ct. 2018 (1978), the Supreme Court, reversing Monroe v. Pape, 365 U.S. 167, 81 S. Ct. 473, 5 L.Ed.2d 492 (1961), held that municipalities, including school boards, were "persons" for the purposes of section 1983. While the court held that "a local government may not be sued for an injury inflicted solely by its employees or agents,"

it held that such a government may be sued for monetary, declaratory, and injunctive relief under section 1983 "when execution of a government's policy or custom, whether made by its lawmakers or by those whose edicts or acts may fairly be said to represent official policy, inflicts the injury. . . ."

8. Does a union have standing to bring an action under section 1983 alleging that a public employer interfered with the constitutional right of public employees to join or become members of the union? In Elk Grove Firefighters Local No. 2340 v. Willis, 391 F. Supp. 487 (N.D. Ill. 1975), the court held that a union had standing to sue under section 1983, in both its representative and individual capacity. *Accord,* SEIU v. County of Butler, 306 F. Supp. 1080 (W.D. Pa. 1969). *Contra,* Lontine v. VanCleave, 80 L.R.R.M. 3240 (D. Colo. 1972), *aff'd on other grounds,* 483 F.2d 966 (10th Cir. 1973).

## ATKINS v. CITY OF CHARLOTTE

United States District Court, Western District of North Carolina
296 F. Supp. 1068 (1969)

CRAVEN, Circuit Judge:

This is a civil action brought to obtain a declaratory judgment and injunctive relief declaring unconstitutional and preventing enforcement of Sections 95-97, 95-98 and 95-99 of the General Statutes of North Carolina. We hold G.S. 95-97 unconstitutional on its face. We hold G.S. § 95-98 a valid and constitutional exercise of the legislative authority of the General Assembly of North Carolina. As for G.S. § 95-99, we hold it to be so related to G.S. § 95-97 that it cannot survive the invalidation of that section. . . .

[T]he court finds the facts to be as follows:

### FACTS

The statutes sought to be invalidated are these:

N.C.G.S. § 95-97: . . . [Prohibits any employee employed by any governmental unit engaged full-time in law enforcement or fire protection activity from being or becoming a member of any labor organization or aiding or assisting any labor organization] which is, or may become, a part of or affiliated in any way with any national or international labor union, federation, or organization, and which has as its purpose or one of its purposes, collective bargaining. . . .

N.C.G.S. § 95-98: . . . [Any agreement or contract between any unit or government and any labor organization] is hereby declared to be against the public policy of the State, illegal, unlawful, void and of no effect.

N.C.G.S. § 95-99: . . . [Violations of §§ 95-97 and 95-98 are misdemeanors] punishable in the discretion of the court.

All of the plaintiffs are members of the Charlotte Fire Department, and the gist of the complaint is that the statutes are overbroad and prohibit constitutionally guaranteed rights of the plaintiffs in violation of the First Amendment and the Due Process and Equal Protection Clauses of the Fourteenth Amendment to the Constitution of the United States. Specifically, plaintiffs want to become dues paying members of a Local which would become affiliated with International Association of Fire Fighters, the intervenor. Affidavits of some 400 fire fighters of the Charlotte Fire Department have been put into evidence to the effect that, if allowed to do so by law, affiants would join the Union.

The City of Charlotte is a municipal corporation which operates and maintains the Charlotte Fire Department pursuant to the City Charter. The Chief of the Department is appointed by the City Council and is accountable to the Council for the faithful performance of his duties. He is responsible for the discipline and efficiency of the Department and for carrying out all orders, rules and regulations approved by the Council. He is also responsible for approving all promotions of members in the Department subject to the approval of the Civil Service Board.

The Department has approximately 438 employees, consisting of the Chief, two assistant chiefs, 14 deputy chiefs, 60 fire captains, and 56 fire lieutenants, with the remainder being fire fighters, inspectors, fire alarm personnel and office personnel. The plaintiffs consist of deputy chiefs, captains, lieutenants and fire fighters and range in service with the department from two to 40 years.

For many years prior to the enactment in 1959 of the North Carolina General Statutes complained of, the International Association of Fire Fighters operated or maintained a union made up of Charlotte Fire Department members and designated as Local 660, an affiliate of the International Association of Fire Fighters. A number of Fire Department members paid dues to that organization which was engaged in collective bargaining activity. Further, the City checked off dues for union membership.

During 1959, the North Carolina Legislature enacted General Statutes §§ 95-97 through 95-99. Following the enactment of these statutes, Local 660 terminated its affiliation with the International Association of Fire Fighters and became, or took the name, Charlotte Fire Fighters Association. This organization continued the activities and representations very much as had been the practice with Local 660. The Fire Fighters Association continued to negotiate with the City and to represent the Charlotte firemen with respect to wages, grievances, and other conditions of employment, and the City continued its recognition of the association and permitted dues check-off. This practice continued from 1959 until 1962. On January 29, 1962, the City Council received and approved a report compiled by the City Manager. One of the recommendations of this report as it was approved established as a condition of continued employment in the Fire Department non-membership in the Fire Fighters Association or in any successor thereto. The City Council approved this report after having been advised by the City Attorney that the Fire Fighters Association was not illegal per se under the statutes complained of, but that the association and its recognition by the City was in violation of public policies of the State. Sometime after this action on the part of the City Council, the Fire Fighters Association terminated its activities and the City discontinued its recognition and dues check-off. A grievance procedure was established to allow individual employees to process grievances, but no provisions were made for group grievance procedure or for collective bargaining with respect to grievances, wages, and conditions of employment.

During March of 1967, members of the Charlotte Fire Department, the plaintiffs herein, organized the Charlotte Firemen's Assembly. This organization has as its purpose collective bargaining with the City of Charlotte with respect to wages, grievances, hours of employment and other conditions of employment. It would like to become a local affiliate of intervenor but is prevented by the statutes. The Firemen's Assembly has not been recognized by the City as a representative of firemen. . . .

## THE CONSTITUTIONAL QUESTION AND THE REMEDY

We think N.C.G.S. § 95-97 is void on its face as an abridgment of freedom of association protected by the First and Fourteenth Amendments of the

Constitution of the United States. The flaw in it is an intolerable "overbreadth" unnecessary to the protection of valid state interests. Cf. United States v. Robel, 389 U.S. 258, 88 S. Ct. 419, 19 L. Ed. 2d 508 (1967). The Supreme Court of the United States has accorded "freedom of association" full status as an aspect of liberty protected by the Due Process Clause of the Fourteenth Amendment and by the rights of free speech and peaceful assembly explicitly set out in the First Amendment. In NAACP v. Alabama ex rel. Patterson, the Court said:

> "It is beyond debate that freedom to engage in association for the advancement of beliefs and ideas is an inseparable aspect of the 'liberty' assured by the Due Process Clause of the Fourteenth Amendment, which embraces freedom of speech. [Citations omitted.] Of course, it is immaterial whether the beliefs sought to be advanced by association pertain to political, *economic,* religious or cultural matters, and state action which may have the effect of curtailing the freedom to associate is subject to the closest scrutiny." 357 U.S. 449, 460-461, 78 S. Ct. 1163, 1171, 2 L. Ed. 2d 1488, 1498-1499 (1958). (Emphasis ours.)

The Court had previously noted the close connection between the freedoms of speech and assembly. In DeJonge v. Oregon, 299 U.S. 353, 364, 57 S. Ct. 255, 81 L. Ed. 278, 283-284 (1937), the Court held that the right of peaceable assembly is a right cognate to those of free speech and free press and equally fundamental. It was said that the right is one that cannot be denied without violating fundamental principles of liberty and justice which lie at the base of all civil and political institutions. The Court made a careful distinction between the proper exercise of legislative power to protect against abuse of the right of assembly and legislative infringement per se of that right, holding that the latter is not permissible. Especially pertinent to the problem confronting us is the following:

> "[C]onsistently with the Federal Constitution, peaceable assembly for lawful discussion cannot be made a crime. The holding of meetings for peaceable political action cannot be proscribed. Those who assist in the conduct of such meetings cannot be branded as criminals on that score. The question, if the rights of free speech and peaceable assembly are to be preserved, is not *as to the auspices under which the meeting is held* but as to its purpose...." DeJonge v. Oregon, 299 U.S. 353, 365, 57 S. Ct. 255, 260, 81 L. Ed. 278, 284 (1937). (Emphasis ours.)

We would make the same distinction here. It matters not, we think, whether the firemen of the City of Charlotte meet under the auspices of the intervenor, a national labor union, but whether their proposed concerted action, if any, endangers valid state interests. We think there is no valid state interest in denying firemen the right to organize a labor union — whether local or national in scope. It is beyond argument that a single individual cannot negotiate on an equal basis with an employer who hires hundreds of people. Recognition of this fact of life is the basis of labor-management relations in this country. Charlotte concedes in its brief that the right of public employees to join labor unions is becoming increasingly recognized (with the exception of firemen and policemen) and even admits that collective bargaining might be beneficial in many situations in the case of municipal firemen. But Charlotte insists that the State has a valid interest in forbidding membership in a labor union to firemen. It is said that fire departments are quasi-military in structure, and that such a structure is necessary because individual firemen must be ready to respond instantly and without question to orders of a superior, and that such military discipline may well mean the difference between saving human life and property, and failure. The extension of this argument is, of course, that affiliation with a national labor union might eventuate in a strike against the public interest which could not be tolerated, and the very existence of which would imperil lives and property in the City of Charlotte. This is the only state interest that can be validly asserted for N.C.G.S. § 95-97. The thought of fires raging out of control in Charlotte while firemen, out on strike, Neroicly watch the flames, is frightening. We do not question the power of the State to deal with such a contingency. We do question the overbreadth of G.S. § 95-97, which quite unnecessarily, in our opinion, goes far beyond the valid state interest that is suggested to us, and strikes down indiscriminately the right of association in a labor union — even one whose policy is opposed to strikes.

Since the only valid state interest suggested by defendants in support of the constitutionality of G.S. § 95-97 is the quite legitimate fear that fire protection for the people of Charlotte might be disrupted by violence or by strike, it seems quite clear that the statute must be invalidated for "overbreadth."

The Supreme Court "has repeatedly held that a governmental purpose to control or prevent activities constitutionally subject to state regulation may not be achieved by means which sweep unnecessarily broadly and thereby invade the area of protected freedoms." NAACP v. Alabama ex rel. Flowers, 377 U.S. 288, at 307, 84 S. Ct. 1302, at 1314, 12 L. Ed. 2d 325, at 338 (1964).

Again, "even though the governmental purpose be legitimate and substantial, that purpose cannot be pursued by means that broadly stifle fundamental personal liberties when the end can be more narrowly achieved." Shelton v. Tucker, 364 U.S. 479, 488, 81 S. Ct. 247, 256, 5 L. Ed. 2d 231, 237 (1960). As previously indicated, the plaintiffs and intervenor do not question the power of the State to prohibit strikes against the public interest.

What we have said thus far supports our ultimate conclusion: that the firemen of the City of Charlotte are granted the right of free association by the First and Fourteenth Amendments of the United States Constitution; that that right of association includes the right to form and join a labor union — whether local or national; that membership in such a labor organization will confer upon the firemen no immunity from proper state regulation to protect valid state interests which are, in this case, the protection of property and life from destruction by fire. We think such a conclusion flows inevitably from the enunciations of the United States Supreme Court set out above. Our decision is consistent with that of the Seventh Circuit according the same right to teachers. McLaughlin v. Tilendis, 398 F.2d 287 (7th Cir. 1968). We do not think the *McLaughlin* decision is distinguishable on the asserted ground that the State in that case had not undertaken to prohibit membership in a teachers' labor union. The court's recitation that there was no such state legislation went to the question of whether there was a valid state interest. It held that there was no such state interest, and that the right of a teacher to join a labor union rested upon the First Amendment to the United States Constitution. In our case, we hold that the valid state interest may be served by more narrowly drawn legislation so as not to infringe the First Amendment.

We find nothing unconstitutional in G.S. § 95-98. It simply voids contracts between units of government within North Carolina and labor unions and expresses the public policy of North Carolina to be against such collective bargaining contracts. There is nothing in the United States Constitution which entitles one to have a contract with another who does not want it. It is but a step further to hold that the state may lawfully forbid such contracts with its instrumentalities. The solution, if there be one, from the viewpoint of the firemen, is that labor unions may someday persuade state government of the asserted value of collective bargaining agreements, but this is a political matter and does not yield to judicial solution. The right to a collective bargaining agreement, so firmly entrenched in American labor-management relations, rests upon national legislation and not upon the federal Constitution. The State is within the powers reserved to it to refuse to enter into such agreements and so to declare by statute. . . .

Finally, we are asked to enjoin the defendants from enforcing these statutes now adjudged to be unconstitutional, *viz.,* N.C.G.S. § 95-97 and § 95-99. We decline to do so. There has not been the slightest intimation that our decision adjudging these statutes invalid will be ignored by the City of Charlotte or by any of the other defendants. If our decision should be thought wrong, we may properly assume it will be appealed — not ignored. There is no evidence that the solicitor of the district has sought indictments against any firemen or that he intends doing so. We adhere to the philosophy of federalism and think it unseeming that a federal court should issue its injunctive process against state or local officers except in situations of the most compelling necessity. Entry of a declaratory judgment decreeing G.S. § 95-97 and § 95-99 invalid because in violation of the First and Fourteenth Amendments of the United States Constitution seems to us, on the facts of this case, a fully sufficient remedy.

Declaratory judgment granted. Injunction denied.

Addendum:

The Eighth Circuit has decided that public employees have a right, grounded in the Constitution, to join a labor union, in the absence of a "paramount public interest of the State of Nebraska or the City of North Platte [which] warranted limiting the plaintiffs' right to freedom of association." *See* American Federation of State, County, and Municipal Employees v. Woodward, 406 F.2d 137 (8th Cir. Jan. 17, 1969) (Jan. 28, 1969).

## NOTES

1. The *Atkins* case is noted in 55 Va. L. Rev. 1151 (1969).

2. In Alabama Labor Council v. Frazier, 81 L.R.R.M. 2155 (Ala. Cir. Ct., Madison County, 1972), the court held unconstitutional a state act that provided any public employee who joined or participated in the activities of a labor union lost all rights "afforded him under the state merit system, employment rights, re-employment rights, and other rights, benefits or privileges which he enjoys as a result of his public employment." Ala. Code tit. 55, § 317(2) (1958).

3. A three-judge federal district court in Melton v. City of Atlanta, 324 F. Supp. 315 (N.D. Ga. 1971), held unconstitutional a Georgia statute that made it a misdemeanor for a policeman to join or belong to a labor union. The court stated:

. . . we are faced with the problem of weighing the plaintiffs' interests in the First Amendment rights and the defendants' interest in securing and having an impartial police force. While the statutes here undoubtedly tend toward securing the desired impartiality, their practical effect in that direction would not appear so efficacious or certain as to offset or outweigh the obvious impairment in plaintiffs' First Amendment rights. This is particularly true where, as we are informed by plaintiffs, the FOP [Fraternal Order of Police] has no members outside the Atlanta Police Department, and no affiliation with any organizations other than the national FOP. We accept these assurances in ruling as we do.

In Lontine v. VanCleave, 80 L.R.R.M. 3240 (D. Colo. 1972), *aff'd,* 483 F.2d 966 (10th Cir. 1973), the court in an action under the Civil Rights Act of 1871 ordered the reinstatement of a deputy sheriff who had been suspended because he "refused to indicate whether he would disaffiliate with the union." The court observed that the plaintiff has "a constitutional right to join a union and may not be discharged from employment for joining or continuing membership in a union, absent a showing of compelling state interest." *See generally* Juris & Hutchinson, *The Legal Status of Municipal Police Employee Organizations,* 23 IND. & LAB. REL. REV. 352 (1970); Hilligan, *Police Employee Organizations: Past Developments and Present Problems,* 24 LAB. L.J. 288 (1973).

The New Jersey Act states that unless "established practice, prior agreement, or special circumstances dictate the contrary, no policeman shall have the right to join an employee organization that admits employees other than policemen to membership." N.J. STAT. ANN. § 34:13A-5.3 (Supp. 1968). Is this provision constitutional? Are there any legitimate reasons for restricting the kind of labor organization that police officers can join? In ABA PROJECT ON STANDARDS FOR CRIMINAL JUSTICE, THE URBAN POLICE FUNCTION 171 (Tentative Draft, March 1972), the Advisory Committee on the Police Function made the following recommendations:

> The need to preserve local control over law enforcement and over the resolution of law enforcement policy issues requires that law enforcement policy not be influenced by a national police union.
> The maintenance of police in a position of objectivity in engaging in conflict resolution requires that police not belong to a union which also has non-police members who may become party to a labor dispute.

*See also* Illinois Governor's Advisory Commission on Labor-Management Policy For Public Employees 14 (March 1967).

Executive Order 11491, adopting the NLRA approach, provides that no unit shall "be established if it includes . . . any guard together with any other employees." Section 10(b) (3). Is this provision constitutional? In terms of a constitutional challenge, is there any difference between this provision and the provision contained in the New Jersey Act?

## ELK GROVE FIREFIGHTERS' LOCAL 2340 v. WILLIS

United States District Court, Northern District of Illinois
400 F. Supp. 1097 (1975)
*Aff'd,* 539 F.2d 714 (7th Cir. 1976) (unpublished order)

DECKER, District Judge.

This case is brought by two unions: the International Association of Firefighters, AFL-CIO and its local affiliate, Elk Grove Firefighters' Local No. 2340, against certain officials of the Village of Elk Grove. The Village officials have forbidden captains and lieutenants of the Elk Grove fire department to belong to any union which also has as members rank and file firefighters. The plaintiff unions, which had as members both firefighters and officers of the Elk Grove fire department at the time the Village officials promulgated this policy, claim that this policy infringes the First Amendment freedom of association of the officers. They bring this action under 42 U.S.C. § 1983, seeking a declaration that any employee of the Elk Grove fire department, regardless of rank, can join them, an injunction against any further interference with membership of any firefighter or officer in plaintiff unions and damages for union dues lost because of the defendant officials' actions.

Defendants have now answered and both sides have moved for summary judgment. Plaintiffs ask for judgment on the pleadings and defendants have supported their motion with the affidavit of Allen Hulett, Fire Chief of Elk Grove Village.

Neither motion is to be granted, of course, unless there is no genuine issue as to any material fact and the moving party is entitled to judgment as a matter of law. F.R.Civ.P. 56(c). All parties agree that there is no genuine issue as to any material fact. The question on these motions is whether, as a matter of law, the Village officials' prohibition of membership by captains and lieutenants in plaintiff unions on the grounds that the unions also represent rank and file firefighters infringes the First Amendment rights of the officers. For the reasons set forth below, this court finds that the prohibition is constitutionally valid.

I.

There can be no doubt that First Amendment rights are affected by the actions of the Village officials. Whatever doubts there may once have been, it is now uncontrovertible that the First Amendment's freedom of association extends to economic associations such as unions. Thomas v. Collins, 323 U.S. 516, 531, 65 S.Ct. 315, 89 L.Ed. 430 (1945). Nor is there any doubt that public employees as well as private enjoy First Amendment protection of their union associations. McLaughlin v. Tilendis, 398 F.2d 287 (7th Cir. 1968); Am. Fed. of State, Co., & Mun. Emp. v. Woodward, 406 F.2d 137 (8th Cir. 1969). Public employees do not waive their constitutional rights by virtue of their status as public employees. Elfbrandt v. Russell, 384 U.S. 11, 86 S.Ct. 1238, 16 L.Ed.2d 321 (1966); Keyishian v. Board of Regents, 385 U.S. 589, 87 S.Ct. 675, 17 L.Ed.2d 629 (1967).

Broad as the protections of the First Amendment are, however, they are not without limit. See Civil Serv. Comm'n v. National Ass'n of Letter Carriers, 413 U.S. 548, 93 S.Ct. 2880, 37 L.Ed.2d 796 (1973), and Broadrick v. Oklahoma, 413 U.S. 601, 93 S.Ct. 2908, 37 L.Ed.2d 830 (1973), upholding severe restrictions on the partisan political activities of federal and state governmental employees on the grounds that the restrictions are necessary to insure an efficient civil service dedicated to public rather than partisan ends. *See also* Clark v. Holmes, 474 F.2d 928 (7th Cir. 1972), discussing the limits on the freedom of a teacher at a public university to teach as he likes.

The determination of what limits may constitutionally be put on the First Amendment activities of public employees requires a balancing of the public interest asserted as justification for the limitation against the interests of the individuals or groups whose rights are being curtailed. Where the state seeks to limit First Amendment freedoms it must show (1) that a substantial, legitimate state interest (2) will in fact be served, and (3) that the limit imposed on First Amendment activities is the least drastic restriction of constitutional rights which will accomplish the state's pupose. Shelton v. Tucker, 364 U.S. 479, 81 S.Ct. 247, 5 L.Ed.2d 231 (1960).

II.

The interest asserted by the Village officials in this case is the need for a disciplined, efficient fire department. They claim that the lieutenants and captains are supervisory personnel for whom membership in a union which exists for the purpose of representing rank and file firefighters, whom the officers are supposed to supervise, concerning wages, hours and conditions of employment would present a conflict of interest. This, it is argued, would impair the efficiency of the fire department which plays a crucial role in safeguarding the lives and property of the citizens of Elk Grove Village.

Clearly, an efficient fire department is a legitimate and substantial state interest. *Civil Serv. Comm'n v. National Ass'n of Letter Carriers, supra,* and *Broadrick v. Oklahoma, supra,* establish that the efficiency of public employees generally is a legitimate and substantial governmental interest. This interest is particularly strong with respect to firefighters because of the need for them to act quickly and effectively to prevent grievous loss of life and property.

The question of whether the restrictions at issue in this case will sufficiently further this governmental interest to warrant limitation of First Amendment rights might be a difficult one but for some recent legislation and case law on precisely the issue of the impact of joint rank and file — supervisor unions on efficiency and discipline. Section 14(a) of the Labor Management Relations Act (LMRA), 29 U.S.C. § 164(a), provides that no employer subject to that Act can be compelled under any law, federal, state, or local, to deal with supervisors as members of collective bargaining units. This provision, added by the Taft-Hartley Amendments of 1947, reflects a strong congressional judgment that supervisor membership in unions is inimical to efficiency. See Beasley v. Food Fair of North Carolina, 416 U.S. 653, 658-662, 94 S.Ct. 2023, 40 L.Ed.2d 443 (1974). The LMRA is inapplicable to public employers, but § 14(a) represents a considered congressional judgment of which this court takes notice.

The validity of this judgment in First Amendment considerations was implicitly recognized by the Supreme Court in *Beasley, supra,* where the Court reversed, on the basis of § 14(a), a state court judgment against an employer who had fired a supervisor for union membership. The judgment was based on the North Carolina right-to-work law, which creates a cause of action in damages for any person discharged for union activities. The Court held that § 14(a) served to free all employers subject to the LMRA from any liability for discharges of supervisors for union activities. Although the Court did not explicitly consider First Amendment issues in *Beasley,* its decision recognized industrial efficiency and discipline as a substantial interest which is furthered by restrictions on supervisory unionization. While § 14(a) does not apply to public employers such as Elk Grove Village, that section is subject to the strictures of the First Amendment insofar as it overrides state laws which protect the organizational rights of supervisors.[2]

The New York Court of Appeals found the rationale of § 14 (a) constitutionally applicable to public employers in Shelofsky v. Helsby, 32 N.Y.2d 54, 343 N.Y.S.2d 98, 295 N.E.2d 774 (1973), *appeal dismissed,* 414 U.S. 804, 94 S.Ct. 60, 38 L.Ed2d 41 (1973). *Shelofsky* considered a First Amendment challenge to a section of the New York Civil Service Law which forbids "managerial" public employees to belong to any union which also represents lower echelon public employees. The court upheld the statute, saying:

"The exclusion of supervisory personnel from collective bargaining rights enjoyed by employees is not a new concept. [Citation omitted.] In 1947, the Taft-Hartley Act (Labor Management Relations Act) amended the National

---

[2] See Railway Employees Department v. Hanson, 351 U.S. 225, 232, 76 S.Ct. 714, 718, 100 L.Ed. 1112 (1956), which held that union shop contracts entered into pursuant to § 2, Eleventh of the Railway Labor Act, 45 U.S.C. § 152, Eleventh, which made such agreements legal notwithstanding any state right to work laws which might otherwise preclude them, were, for constitutional purposes, governmental action. "If private rights are being invaded, it is by force of an agreement made pursuant to federal law which expressly declares that state law is superseded. [Citation omitted.] . . . The enactment of the federal statute authorizing union shop agreements is the governmental action on which the Constitution operates, though it takes a private agreement to invoke the federal sanction."

Labor Relations Act in part to exclude 'supervisors' from collective bargaining rights enjoyed by private employees generally.... The objective of the Taft-Hartley Act, held permissible in [NLRB v. Budd Mfg. Co., 169 F.2d 571, 578 (6th Cir. 1958)], was to assure the employer of a loyal and efficient cadre of supervisors and managers independent from the rank and file. [Citation omitted.] That objective is equally applicable to the State, as an employer." 32 N.Y.2d at 59-60, 343 N.Y.S.2d at 101, 295 N.E.2d at 775.

The treatment of § 14(a) of the LMRA in *Beasley* and of the New York Civil Service Law in *Shelofsky,* both of which held that limitations of supervisory union activity is a legitimate means of achieving the important governmental goal of an efficient, effective work force, public or private, is applicable to this case. There appears to be no controversy that the lieutenants and captains are supervisors. The duties and responsibilities of the supervisory officers are detailed in the uncontroverted affidavit of Fire Chief Allen Hulett, which states as follows:

"1.  That I am the Chief of the Fire Department of the Village of Elk Grove Village and have held said position since January 1, 1969....

"2.  That as of April 15, 1975, the Fire Department of the Village of Elk Grove Village consists of one Chief, three Captains, 15 Lieutenants, 53 Fire Fighters, and one engineer. There are also six civilians who serve in the Fire Department as well. (sic)

"3.  That each of the three Captains is in charge of one shift, and pursuant to the Rules and Regulations of the Fire Department, is 'held strictly responsible for discipline, conduct and efficiency of all members of the department during the entire shift.'

"4.  That each of the lieutenants supervises a company and, pursuant to the Rules and Regulations of the Fire Department, is responsible 'for the efficient operation of the company,' is charged with the responsibility to 'preserve the discipline of his company and instruct the members in their duties,' and 'in the absence of a superior officer, exercise[s] the same duties and [has] the same powers as devolve upon the Captain.'

"5.  That on May 14, 1974, I issued an officer's general order directing that Captains and Lieutenants would serve in the capacity of Acting Chief of the Fire Department of the Village of Elk Grove Village in the absence of the Chief.

"6.  That when Captains or Lieutenants serve in the capacity of Acting Chief of the Department they have all the duties and responsibilities that I would have as Chief of the Fire Department of the Village of Elk Grove Village.

"7.  That Captains and Lieutenants are responsible for making written performance evaluations of the Fire Fighters under their supervision...."

These duties present precisely the conflict of interests which the limits on supervisory unionization are designed to avoid. Lieutenants and captains are hired as agents of the Village to supervise, discipline and evaluate the rank and file firefighters. "Management, like labor, must have faithful agents." Beasley, 416 U.S. at 660, 94 S.Ct. at 2027. To permit the officers to join and become subject to the discipline of a union in which they are outnumbered by firefighters by greater than a three-to-one ratio could deprive the Village of the undivided loyalty of the officers to which it is entitled. Cf. Florida Power & Light v. IBEW, 417 U.S. 790, 805-813, 94 S.Ct. 2737, 41 L.Ed.2d 477 (1974).

As one example of the sort of conflict likely to arise, an officer, as Acting Chief, could be in a position to order the firemen to work overtime. The union could be taking a position in opposition to involuntary overtime. An officer who is a member of the union would be caught in a clash between his duty as Acting Chief to make the firefighters work the overtime he deems necessary for effective fire protection for the Village and his duty as a union member to pursue the union's ends. Either way he acts he will breach his duty to the Village or to the union. It is to avoid such conflicts that supervisory unionization may be curtailed.

Plaintiff unions dispute that any legitimate interest is served by the Village policy at issue here, asserting that this is a "pure membership" case, the policy being analogous to one prohibiting common membership in the Elks. This is a rather disingenuous argument. Plaintiffs themselves allege in their complaint that,

"... Local No. 2340 has been organized and exists for the purpose of representing its membership in connection with their hours, wages and working conditions." (Complaint, ¶ 3.)

In light of the purpose of the union, it is improbable in the extreme that the sorts of conflicts which the prohibition on common membership prevents would not arise were membership unrestricted. The decisions of the Village officials which affect the working conditions of the firefighters, an issue with which the union is admittedly concerned, can only be implemented through the officers which the unions seek to bring into their ranks. Practically the only circumstance in which a conflict of interest would fail to arise would be if there were no conflict between the Village officials and the Firefighters Union over an aspect of working conditions, a rather unlikely eventuality.

The Village cannot be told to wait and see whether any conflict develops in fact. The creation of a common union composed of rank and file firefighters and their superior officers poses a sufficiently serious threat of ineffective supervision based upon divided loyalties to warrant preventive action.

Finally, there can be no doubt that the actions of the defendant Elk Grove Village officials are the least restrictive means of effecting the substantial, legitimate governmental purpose of an efficient fire department. As discussed above, surveillance by the officials from above to prevent less than complete supervisor loyalty would be impracticable and ineffective. Given that there must be some sort of limitation on the associational rights of the fire lieutenants and captains, the rule promulgated by the defendants is as narrow as possible. The officers are not precluded from forming or joining a union which does not represent rank and file firemen. In this respect the rule is less stringent than the complete prohibition of supervisory union membership allowed in the private sector by § 14(a) of the LMRA. The *only* union closed to the officers is one which also represents rank and file firefighters whom it is the officers' duty to supervise. The limitation on union activity is clearly and precisely drawn to achieve the Village officials' legitimate ends. It is not overbroad or vague. Compare Police Officers' Guild, National Union of Police Officers, AFL-CIO v. Washington, 369 F.Supp. 543, 550-553 (D.D.C. 1973); Melton v. City of Altanta, 324 F.Supp. 315 (N.D. Ga. 1971); and Atkins v. City of Charlotte, 296 F.Supp. 1068 (W.D.N.C. 1969), all striking down blanket proscriptions on police and firefighter union activity on overbreadth and vagueness grounds.

In sum, though the actions of the defendants have undeniably trenched on an area generally protected by the First Amendment's guarantee of freedom of association, the restrictions at issue here effectively serve a legitimate and substantial public interest by an unambiguous policy narrowly drawn to achieve that end. In such circumstances this limitation of freedom of association is not repugnant to the First Amendment.

Therefore, plaintiffs' motion for summary judgment is denied; defendants' motion for summary judgment is granted, and the cause is dismissed.

## NOTES

1. In Local 2263, IAFF v. City of Tupelo, 439 F. Supp. 1224 (N.D. Miss. 1977), the court upheld the constitutionality of resolutions adopted by a city prohibiting shift captains and station captains "from belonging to a labor organization having in its membership rank and file firefighters employed by the Tupelo Fire Department." In its lengthy decision, the court said that it "accept[ed] the rationale of the well-reasoned opinion of the District Court in *Elk Grove Fire Fighters Local No. 2340 v. Willis . . . .*" The court further observed that the policy judgment contained in the Taft-Hartley Act "that supervisory membership in rank and file unions is inimical to efficiency" was relevant even though that Act is not applicable to public employers. The court thus noted that it was "persuaded that the judgment of Congress affords a reliable guide for our determination of balancing the interests of the City of Tupelo in seeking to maintain an efficient fire department with the constitutionally protected interest of union members." Similarly, a Missouri court in Germann v. City of Kansas City, Mo., 1979-80 PBC ¶ 36,463 (1978) (Mo. Ct. App. 1978), upheld the constitutionality of an ordinance adopted by Kansas City which provides that supervisors are "forbidden to join or maintain membership or engage in activities of any labor organization which admits to membership, or is affiliated directed or indirectly with an organization which admits to membership, non-supervisory employees who work under the direction of such supervisors, or otherwise are engaged in the type of work performed by such non-supervisory employees."

2. In Norbeck v. Davenport Community School Dist., 545 F.2d 63 (1976), *cert. denied,* 431 U.S. 917, 97 S. Ct. 2179, 53 L.Ed. 2d 227 (1977), the Eighth Circuit held that a school district did not violate a high school principal's constitutional rights when it refused to renew his contract because, *inter alia,* he served as the chief negotiator for the union representing the district's teachers. The court stated:

> "We conclude, under the existing factual circumstances, that the interest asserted by the school board in efficient school administration is paramount to the right of a school principal to bargain collectively for classroom teachers who he was hired to supervise, discipline and evaluate. A school board is properly concerned over conflicts relating to the maintenance of discipline and co-worker harmony. More importantly, the board members were properly concerned with whether the close working relationship among a principal, superintendent and school board was threatened by Norbeck's role as chief negotiator for the DEA."

3. In Jones v. North Carolina Prisoners' Labor Union, 97 S. Ct. 2532 (1977), the Supreme Court held, *inter alia,* that prison regulations that prohibited inmates from soliciting other inmates for membership in a prisoners' labor union or from conducting union meetings did not violate either the First or Fourteenth Amendment. After noting that "numerous associational rights are necessarily curtailed by the realities of confinement," the Court held that such associational rights "may be curtailed whenever the institution's officials, in the exercise of their informed discretion, reasonably conclude that such associations, whether through group meetings or otherwise, possess the likelihood of disruption to prison order or stability, or otherwise interfere with the legitimate penological objectives of the prison environment."

# TEACHERS' LOCAL 2032 v. MEMPHIS BOARD OF EDUCATION

United States Court of Appeals, Sixth Circuit
534 F.2d 699 (1976)

WEICK, Circuit Judge:

The principal issue in this appeal is whether the Board of Education violated the constitutional rights of a rival labor union by refusing to extend to it the same rights and privileges previously granted by the Board to another organization of its professional employees, which organization it had duly recognized as representing all of its employees for collective bargaining purposes. The rival union represented fewer than three hundred of the employees. The duly recognized bargaining agent represented more than two-thirds of the fifty-four hundred employees of the Board; nevertheless the rival union made demand upon the Board to extend to it the same rights and privileges, and upon the Board's rejection of the demand it filed the present suit in the District Court.

The plaintiffs in the case are the Memphis American Federation of Teachers (MAFT) and two members of that organization individually and on behalf of a class, seeking to establish their constitutional entitlement to certain rights and privileges previously granted by the Board to Memphis Education Association (MEA). MAFT sought declaratory and injunctive relief.

MAFT is an affiliate of the American Federation of Teachers, a national labor organization. MEA is an organization of professional employees of the Memphis City School System. It is possible to be a member of both organizations.

The parties stipulated the relevant facts. In 1970 the Board of Education recognized MEA as the authorized representative of all professional personnel in the Memphis City Schools. Such recognition was contingent upon MEA's continuing ability to substantiate that it represented two-thirds of the approximately fifty-four hundred professional employees in the Memphis Schools. At the time of the suit MEA's membership was well in excess of the two-thirds requirement and approximated 90% of the professional employees. MAFT's membership numbered fewer than three hundred professional employees.

In recognizing MEA as the exclusive representative of all professional personnel in the Memphis schools, the Board granted to it certain privileges. Those privileges included the use of the school bulletin boards, payroll deduction of union membership dues, use of school facilities for meetings without charge, and use of interschool and intraschool delivery ("mail") services, including faculty mailboxes.

. . . [T]he District Judge held that MAFT was unable to demonstrate any substantive abridgement of its First Amendment rights. However, the District Judge agreed with MAFT that the Board policy created a classification which violated its rights under the Equal Protection Clause of the Fourteenth Amendment. The District Judge ordered the Board to submit an amended policy statement with regard to the use of school bulletin boards and mail service, use of school facilities for meetings, access to schools by persons not assigned to those schools, leave policy, payroll deduction of union dues, and the right to make announcements at faculty meetings. The amended policy statement ordered by the District Judge provided that the above-mentioned privileges would be granted equally not only to MAFT but also to all other bona fide organizations which claimed membership in excess of 225 and which may make application to the Superintendent. The Court, however, did not require that MAFT be accorded equal recognition with MEA for purposes of conferring or negotiating with the

Board over the terms and conditions of employment of its members.

The Board appealed. We reverse.

. . . .

We are faced, first, with the issue of whether First Amendment rights of MAFT were violated by the Board of Education's decision denying to it the privileges granted to MEA, in the public schools.

[A]bove all else, the First Amendment means that government has no power to restrict expression because of its message, its ideas, its subject matter, or its content. Police Dep't of Chicago v. Mosley, 408 U.S. 92, 95 (1972). This language was quoted in Hudgens v. NLRB, 424 U.S. 507, 91 LRRM 2489, 2494 (44 LW 4281, 4285, March 3, 1976).

The grant of exclusive privileges by the Board to MEA did not involve the Board in regulating either the content or the subject matter of speech in its schools. The Board neither censored nor promoted a particular point of view. MEA was granted privileges because it was the recognized collective bargaining representative of well over two-thirds of the professional employees in the Memphis City Schools, and not because the Board attempted to regulate the content of the message conveyed to those professional employees. The exclusive privileges granted to MEA did not in any way impair the independent rights of other groups of teachers to exercise their First Amendment rights in the context of the school setting.

In the absence of any attempt by the Board to restrict the content or subject matter of speech in its schools, we agree with the holding of the District Judge that no substantive abridgement of First Amendment rights has been established by MAFT. Federation of Del. Teachers v. De La Warr Bd. of Educ., 335 F.Supp. 385 (D. Del. 1971); Local 858, A.F.T. v. School Dist. No. 1, 314 F.Supp. 1069 (D. Colo. 1970).

Second, we consider whether the grant of special privileges to MEA, because of its status as representative of more than two-thirds of the professional employees in the Memphis schools, was violative of MAFT's rights under the Equal Protection Clause of the Constitution. For purposes of Equal Protection analysis it is clear that when fundamental rights or suspect classes are involved the state classification must be supported by a compelling state interest. San Antonio Bd. of Educ. v. Rodriguez, 411 U.S. 1, 16-17 (1973). In Rodriguez, however, the compelling interest test was rejected.

Designation of MEA as authorized representative of the professional employees in the Memphis school system and the concomitant grant of certain privileges involved no such fundamental right and did not involve a suspect class. Therefore, we examine the preferred position of MEA by inquiring whether the classification was rationally related to achieving a valid state objective (the "rational basis test").

It is clear that the goal of labor peace and stability was promoted by the Board's recognizing and attempting to deal with the organization which more than two-thirds of the Board's professional employees had chosen to join. Furthermore, by granting to MEA certain privileges the Board was able to accommodate the large number of its employees who were members of MEA without placing an undue strain on its facilities. Board policy served only to recognize the realities of labor relations in the Memphis school system. We agree that the preferred status of MEA was rationally related to the valid state objective of ensuring labor stability.

. . . .

The District Judge did not make clear the nature of the test he applied in determining the propriety of the Board's classification. It appears to us that the District Judge may have invoked the compelling state interest test. As we have previously stated, no fundamental rights were infringed by the Board granting special privileges to MEA, and no suspect classifications were involved; it was inappropriate to apply to the Board's action anything other than the rational basis test. The District Judge erred to the extent that he ruled that the Board's classification was not rationally related to promoting labor stability.

The content of the First Amendment rights of teachers in the school setting is not in question in this appeal. We hold that the grant of exclusive privileges to MEA by the Memphis Board of Education violated no First Amendment rights, and that the grant of those privileges survives rational basis scrutiny under the Equal Protection Clause. Federation of Del. Teachers v. De La Warr Bd. of Educ., *supra;* Local 858, A.F.T. v. School Dist. No. 1, *supra.* In each of these cases the Court held that, even applying the strict compelling interest test, the grant of exclusive privileges to an employee organization survived constitutional attack.

In our opinion the holding of the District Court constitutes an unwarranted incursion into the rights and practices of public employees in bargaining collectively with their employer.

. . . .

## SMITH v. ARKANSAS STATE HIGHWAY EMPLOYEES, LOCAL 1315

Supreme Court of the United States
U.S.     , 99 S. Ct. 1826,     L. Ed.     (1979)

PER CURIAM: — In grievance proceedings initiated by employees of the Arkansas State Highway Department, the State Highway Commission will not consider a grievance unless the employee submits his written complaint directly to the designated employer representative. The District Court for the Eastern District of Arkansas found that this procedure denied the union representing the employees the ability to submit effective grievances on their behalf and therefore violated the First Amendment. The United States Court of Appeals for the Eighth Circuit affirmed.[1] We disagree with these holdings; finding no constitutional violation in the actions of the Commission or its individual members, we grant certiorari and reverse the judgment of the Court of Appeals.

*Holding*

The First Amendment protects the right of an individual to speak freely, to advocate ideas, to associate with others, and to petition his government for redress of grievances. And it protects the right of associations to engage in advocacy on behalf of their members. NAACP v. Button, 371 U.S. 415; Eastern Railroad Presidents Conf. v. Noerr Motor Freight Inc., 365 U.S. 127. The Government is prohibited from infringing upon these guarantees either by a

---

[1] This suit was brought by the Arkansas State Highway Employees, Local 1315 and eight of its individual members, after the Commission refused to consider grievances submitted by the union on behalf of two of its members. The facts in these two cases are not in dispute:

"[E]ach employee sent a letter to Local 1315, explaining the nature of their grievance and requesting the union to process the grievance on their behalf. In each case the union forwarded the employee's letter stating that it represented the employees and decided to set up a meeting. The employer's representative did not respond to the union's letter. Thereafter each employee filed a written complaint directly with the employer representative. Local 1315 represented each employee at subsequent meetings with the employer representative." Arkansas State Highway Employees, Local 1315 v. Smith, 99 LRRM 3168 (CA8 1978), Pet. App., at 2.

The individual Commissioners of the Arkansas State Highway Commission and the Director of the State Highway Department were named as defendants, and are the petitioners in this Court.

*Facts*

general prohibition against certain forms of advocacy, NAACP v. Button, supra, or by imposing sanctions for the expression of particular views it opposes, e.g., Brandenburg v. Ohio, 395 U.S. 444, Garrison v. Louisiana, 379 U.S. 64.

But the First Amendment is not a substitute for the national labor relations laws. As the Court of Appeals for the Seventh Circuit recognized in Hanover Township Federation of Teachers, Local 1954 v. Hanover Community School Corporation, 457 F.2d 456 (1972), the fact that procedures followed by a public employer in bypassing the union and dealing directly with its members might well be unfair labor practices were federal statutory law applicable hardly establishes that such procedures violate the Constitution. The First Amendment right to associate and to advocate "provides no guarantee that a speech will persuade or that advocacy will be effective." Id., at 461. The public employee surely can associate and speak freely and petition openly, and he is protected by the First Amendment from retaliation for doing so. See Pickering v. Board of Education, 391 U.S. 563, 574-575; Shelton v. Tucker, 364 U.S. 479. But the First Amendment does not impose any affirmative obligation on the government to listen, to respond or, in this context, to recognize the association and bargain with it.[2]

In the case before us, there is no claim that the Highway Commission has prohibited its employees from joining together in a union, or from persuading others to do so, or from advocating any particular ideas. There is, in short, no claim of retaliation or discrimination proscribed by the First Amendment. Rather, the complaint of the union and its members is simply that the Commission refuses to consider or act upon grievances when filed by the union rather than by the employee directly.

Were public employers such as the Commission subject to the same labor laws applicable to private employers, this refusal might well constitute an unfair labor practice. We may assume that it would, and further, that it tends to impair or undermine — if only slightly [3] — the effectiveness of the union in representing the economic interests of its members. Cf. Hanover Township, supra.

But this type of "impairment" is not one that the Constitution prohibits. Far from taking steps to prohibit or discourage union membership or association, all that the Commission has done in its challenged conduct is simply to ignore the union. That it is free to do.

The judgment of the Court of Appeals is therefore reversed.

Mr. Justice POWELL took no part in the consideration or decision of this case.

[The dissenting opinion of MR. JUSTICE MARSHALL is omitted.]

# B. STATUTORY PROTECTION

Virtually all of the public sector collective bargaining statutes set forth the rights of public employees. This statutory statement frequently parallels the

---

[2] See Hanover Township Federation of Teachers, Local 1954 v. Hanover Community School Corporation, 457 F.2d 456, 461 (CA7 1972), quoting Indianapolis Education Assn. v. Lewallen, 72 LRRM 2071, 2072 (CA7 1969) ("there is no constitutional duty to bargain collectively with an exclusive bargaining agent").

[3] The union does represent its members at all meetings with employer representatives subsequent to the filing of a written grievance. See n. 1, supra. The "impairment" is thus limited to the requirement that written complaints, to be considered, must initially be submitted directly to the employer representative by the employee. There appears to be no bar, however, on the employee securing any form of advice from his union, or from anyone else. Cf. United Mine Workers v. Illinois State Bar Association, 389 U.S. 217; Brotherhood of Railroad Trainmen v. Virginia, 377 U.S. 1.

statement of the rights of employees in section 7 of the National Labor Relations Act, as amended. For example, the Pennsylvania statute, PA. STAT. ANN. tit. 43, § 1101.401 (1970), provides that:

> It shall be lawful for public employes to organize, form, join or assist in employe organizations or to engage in lawful concerted activities for the purpose of collective bargaining or other mutual aid and protection or to bargain collectively through representatives of their own free choice and such employes shall also have the right to refrain from any or all such activities, except as may be required pursuant to a maintenance of membership provision in a collective bargaining agreement.

Most of the comprehensive statutes, again adopting the NLRA model, specify unfair labor practices by both public employers and employee organizations. Thus, these comprehensive statutes generally provide that it is an unfair labor practice (sometimes referred to as an "improper practice" or "prohibited practice") for a public employer to

(1) interfere with, restrain or coerce public employees in the exercise of their enumerated rights;

(2) dominate or interfere with the formation or administration of an employee organization;

(3) discriminate in regard to hire or tenure of employment or any term or condition of employment to encourage or discourage membership in any employee organization;

(4) discharge or otherwise discriminate against an employee because he has filed charges or given testimony under the act; and

(5) refuse to bargain in good faith with the duly designated bargaining agent.

Similarly, these statutes also provide, with some exceptions, that it is an unfair labor practice for an employee organization to

(1) restrain or coerce employees in the exercise of their enumerated rights;

(2) cause or attempt to cause an employer to interfere with, restrain or coerce employees in the exercise of their enumerated rights;

(3) restrain or coerce employers in the selection of their representatives for the purposes of collective bargaining or the adjustment of grievances; and

(4) refuse to bargain in good faith.

Some of the comprehensive statutes, however, contain broader proscriptions than those set forth in the NLRA. For example, the following unfair labor practices are specified in some of the laws for *both* public employers and unions:

(1) refusing or failing to participate in good faith in statutory impasse procedures: United States, California (teachers), Connecticut (teachers), Hawaii, Iowa, Kansas, Massachusetts, Oregon, Pennsylvania, and Tennessee (teachers);

(2) violating any rules and regulations issued to regulate the conduct of representation elections: Connecticut (municipal and state employees), Minnesota, and Pennsylvania;

(3) refusing to comply with any provision in the act: United States, Hawaii, Indiana (teachers), New Hampshire, and Oregon;

(4) violating the terms of a collective bargaining agreement: Hawaii, New

Hampshire, Oregon, and Wisconsin (municipal and state employees);

(5) refusing to comply with or accept an arbitration award: Connecticut (municipal employees), Minnesota, Oregon, Pennsylvania, and Wisconsin (municipal and state employees); and

(6) discriminating on basis of race, color, religion, sex, handicap or national origin: District of Columbia, Nevada, and Vermont (municipal employees).

Among the additional union unfair labor practices specified in some of the laws are the following:

(1) instigating a strike or other concerted refusal to work: District of Columbia, Florida, Iowa, Maine (state and municipal employees), Minnesota, New Hampshire, Vermont (state employees), and Wisconsin (state employees);

(2) secondary boycotts: Iowa, Minnesota, Pennsylvania, and Vermont (municipal employees);

(3) jurisdictional strikes: Iowa, Minnesota, and Pennsylvania;

(4) causing or attempting to cause a public employer to pay for services not performed or which are not needed or required by a public employer: Minnesota and Vermont (municipal employees);

(5) hindering or interfering with an employee's work performance or productivity: United States and New Mexico;

(6) coercing or intimidating a supervisor working at the same trade or profession as employees to induce him to become a member of or act in concert with the employee organization of which employees are members: Wisconsin (state employees);

(7) soliciting or advocating support from students for an employee organization's activities: Connecticut (teachers) and Florida;

(8) endorsing candidates, spending income for partisan or political purposes, or advocating or opposing elections of candidates for public office: Kansas;

(9) using agency shop fees for contributions to political candidates or parties at state or local levels: Montana; and

(10) communicating during negotiations with officials other than those designated to represent the public employer concerning employment relations: Oregon.

Additional employer unfair labor practices included in various laws are the following:

(1) lockouts: Iowa, Kansas and New Hampshire;

(2) denying an employee organization the rights accompanying certification or recognition: Iowa and Kansas;

(3) blacklisting: Maine (municipal and state employees) and Minnesota;

(4) communicating directly with bargaining unit employees during negotiations concerning employment matters, except where related to work performance: Oregon;

(5) refusing to appropriate sufficient funds to implement a written collective bargaining agreement: Vermont (municipal employees); and

(6) refusing to provide an exclusive representative, upon request, all information pertaining to a public employer's budget: Minnesota.

The determination of whether an unfair labor practice has occurred is generally left to a public employment relations agency. If the agency finds that the person named in the complaint has engaged in or is engaging in an unfair labor practice, the agency is generally empowered, as the Pennsylvania Act provides, to "cause to be served on such person an order requiring such person to cease and desist from such unfair practice, and to take such reasonable affirmative action, including reinstatement of employes, discharged in violation of Article XII of this act, with or without back pay, as will effectuate the policies of this act." PA. STAT. ANN. tit. 43, § 1101.1303 (1970).

*Statute of Limitations.* The statute of limitations for filing an unfair labor practice charge is typically six months, the same as under the NLRA; however, several laws or ordinances specify a shorter period. The New Mexico State Personnel Board regulations and the District of Columbia Personnel Manual provide that unfair labor practice charges must be filed within 30 and 60 days, respectively, of the alleged offense. N.M. State Personnel Bd., § 17(a)(2); D.C. Personnel Manual, Ch. 25, § a, Item 18(c). Both the Iowa statute and the Tennessee law covering teachers have a 90-day period for filing charges. Iowa Code Ann., § 11(1) (West); Tenn. Code Ann. tit. 49, § 9(c).

## NOTES

1. Should the complaining party have the burden of prosecuting an unfair labor practice charge before a public employment relations agency? The contrasting approaches under the NLRA and under several of the comprehensive public sector statutes is discussed in 1967 EXECUTIVE COMMITTEE, NATIONAL GOVERNOR'S CONFERENCE, REPORT OF TASK FORCE ON STATE AND LOCAL GOVERNMENT LABOR RELATIONS 15 (1967):

In the administration of the unfair labor practice provisions of their statutes, the states have tended *not* to follow the National Labor Management Relations Act. The federal act originally conferred responsibility for investigating, prosecuting, and determining the merits of charges of unfair practices to the National Labor Relations Board. This led to the accusation that the board was both prosecutor and judge. Later the judicial functions were administratively separated from the investigatory and prosecuting functions. This softened the accusation but did not totally eliminate it. To avoid this functional conflict, the state laws in Wisconsin and Michigan have restricted the board's function to hearing and deciding a charge, and leaving to the complaining party the responsibility of raising the issue at the outset and also of making a valid case in support of the charge. The Illinois Commission reviewed these procedural questions and concluded that it was basically sound to limit the board's function to deciding charges even though this practice might in some instances place a burden on an individual employee. At the same time, it also warned the board against holding formal hearings on trivial charges.

Under Executive Order 11491, a charging party had the responsibility of prosecuting an unfair labor practice charge. However, under the Federal Service Labor Management and Employee Relations Law which was enacted as part of the Civil Service Reform Act of 1978, the position of General Counsel has been created and the General Counsel is given the authority to "investigate alleged unfair labor practices" and to "file and prosecute complaints. . . ." Civil Service Reform Act of 1978, Pub. L. No. 95-454, 92 Stat. 1111, codified at 5 U.S.C. § 7104(f)(3)(A)8(B).

2. Although attorney's fees and costs are typically not recoverable, the Florida law provides that the Commission's order in an unfair labor practice case "may award to the prevailing party all or part of the costs of litigation and reasonable attorney's fees and expert witness fees, whenever the commission determines that such an award is appropriate." Fla. Stat. Ann. § 447.503(4)(c) (West). In City of Venice, 4 FPER ¶ 4107 (Fla. PERC 1978), the Florida PERC held that attorney's fees should only be awarded where there is "something special about the circumstances from which the case arose or something distinguishing about the manner in which the case is litigated."

3. As noted above, most of the comprehensive statutes protect the right of public

employees to bargain collectively and specifically provide that it is an unfair labor practice for an employer to refuse to bargain collectively. This area is discussed in detail in Chapter IV.

4. Section 14(b) of the NLRA permits the states to enact right-to-work legislation, 29 U.S.C. § 164(b) (1970), and at present twenty states have enacted right-to-work laws.[1] The general purpose of most of these laws is to make it illegal to condition employment on membership *or* non-membership in a labor organization. Although right-to-work laws have been vehemently attacked by organized labor, public sector unions have occasionally relied on such laws to support their contention that public employees have the right to join labor organizations of their own choosing. For example, in Levasseur v. Wheeldon, 79 S.D. 442, 112 N.W.2d 894 (1964), a resolution adopted by a municipality which prohibited fire, police, and health department employees from becoming members of any labor organization whose membership was not exclusively confined to employees of the municipality was held to contravene the "right-to-work" provision in the state's constitution. The court held that the "constitutional amendment does not exclude public employment and that membership among city employees cannot be banned by municipal legislation or rule." *Accord,* Potts v. Hay, 229 Ark. 830, 318 S.W.2d 826 (1958); Beverly v. City of Dallas, 292 S.W.2d 172 (Tex. Civ. App. 1956). *Contra,* Keeble v. City of Alcoa, 204 Tenn. 286, 319 S.W. 2d 249 (1958).

# 1. INTERFERENCE, RESTRAINT AND COERCION

## CHARLESTON NAVAL SHIPYARD

Assistant Secretary for Labor-Management Relations
A/SLMR No. 1 (1970)

. . . The complaints in the instant cases filed by the Charleston Metal Trades Council (herein called the Union) against the Charleston Naval Shipyard (herein called the Shipyard) alleged violations of Sections 19(a)(1) and 20 of Executive Order 11491 based on the Shipyard's notice of February 18 and its subsequent memoranda of March 16 and 27, 1970. The Union contends that the notice and memoranda effectively coerced, restrained, and intimidated employees in the exercise of their rights assured under Executive Order 11491. The Shipyard, on the other hand, defends its conduct in issuing the above-mentioned directives on the basis that it was merely acting in accordance with outstanding instructions of the Civil Service Commission which provide, in part, that during the period subsequent to the filing of a valid challenge requiring a redetermination of exclusive status, an "agency should not authorize the use of agency facilities to either the incumbent exclusive or the challenging organization(s) to conduct membership or election campaigns." [4] In this respect, the Shipyard contends that the Assistant Secretary of Labor is without authority to find that a directive, regulation, order or policy issued by the Civil Service Commission, Department of Defense, or any other "higher authority" over the Shipyard is invalid because such a determination would violate Sections 4(b) and 25(a) of the Order.

---

[1] Alabama, Arizona, Arkansas, Florida, Georgia, Iowa, Kansas, Louisiana, Mississippi, Nebraska, Nevada, North Carolina, North Dakota, South Carolina, South Dakota, Tennessee, Texas, Utah, Virginia, and Wyoming.

[4] Federal Personnel Manual Letter 711-6 also provides in part, that "There shall be no restriction at any time on the right of employees to freedom of normal person-to-person communication at the workplace provided there is no interference with the work of the agency. Employees may engage in oral solicitation of employee organization membership during nonwork periods on agency premises."

The Hearing Examiner concluded that the directives governing union electioneering activities promulgated by the Shipyard [5] interfered with, restrained, or coerced employees in the rights assured by Executive Order 11491 since such rules infringed on the employees' right under Section 1 of the Order to "assist a labor organization."

In reaching his recommendation, the Hearing Examiner relied on precedent developed under the National Labor Relations Act. He reasoned that in view of the similarity of language between Sections 7 and 8(a)(1) of the Act and Sections 1 and 19(a)(1) of the Order, that "the decisions under the statute dealing with employee rights in solicitation and in distribution of literature are applicable under the Order (footnote omitted)." The Hearing Examiner also rejected the Shipyard's contention that in issuing the disputed regulations it was acting under a legal obligation to follow the directives of the Civil Service Commission and the Department of Defense. In this regard he stated that rights of employees established under the Executive Order "are not diminished by erroneous rulings of the Civil Service Commission or the Department of Defense."

There is no indication in the reports and recommendations which preceded Executive Orders 10988 and 11491 that the experience gained in the private sector under the National Labor Relations Act would necessarily be the controlling precedent in the administration of labor-management relations in the Federal sector. Thus, many of the provisions of Executive Order 10988 constituted clear attempts to take into account situations peculiar to Federal sector labor-management relations. Moreover, in 1969, when it was determined that improvements in the Federal labor-management relations program were warranted, it was made clear by the Study Committee that the proposed changes dealt only with deficiencies found to exist under Executive Order 10988, and there was no intention to adopt some other model for Federal labor-management relations.

Based on the foregoing, it is my belief that decisions issued under the Labor-Management Relations Act, as amended, are not controlling under Executive Order 11491. I will, however, take into account the experience gained in the private sector under the Labor-Management Relations Act, as amended, policies and practices in other jurisdictions, and those rules developed in the Federal sector under the prior Executive Order. Accordingly, I reject the reasoning of the Hearing Examiner in the instant case insofar as he implies that all of the rules and decisions under the Labor-Management Relations Act, as amended, would constitute binding precedent on the Assistant Secretary with

---

[5] The Shipyard's notice of February 18, 1970, provided, in pertinent part, that:

a. Neither the currently recognized Charleston Metal Trades Council nor the challenging National Association of Governmental Employees shall conduct any type of electioneering on Naval Base premises until campaign procedures are established. Prohibited actions include:

(1) Posting or distribution on Naval Base premises of any poster, bulletin or other material which relates to the challenge;
(2) Meetings on Naval Base premises for the purpose of electioneering or campaigning;
(3) Solicitation of authorization revocations by the challenged union on Naval Base premises;
(4) Solicitation of further authorizations by the challenging union on Naval Base premises.

b. The prohibitions stated in paragraph 3a above, apply equally to employees and non-employee representatives of the organizations involved. . . .

The Shipyard's memorandum of March 16, 1970, as amplified on March 27, 1970, placed certain restrictions on the Union's stewards with respect to the time allowed for their conducting of union business. The March 16 memorandum also stated, in part, that "Electioneering or campaigning at this time is prohibited."

respect to the implementation of his responsibilities under Executive Order 11491.

Also, I reject the Shipyard's assertion that I am without authority to determine whether directives or policy guidance issued by the Civil Service Commission, Department of Defense or any other agency are violative of the Order when those directives or policies are asserted by the activity as a defense to allegedly violative conduct. Both the Study Committee's Report and Recommendations and the Order itself clearly indicate the role which the Assistant Secretary was intended to play in the processing of unfair labor practice complaints under the Order. Thus, the Study Committee's Report and Recommendations stated that the lack of a third party process in resolving unfair labor practice charges was a serious deficiency under the prior Federal Labor-Management program. To rectify this deficiency, it was recommended that the Assistant Secretary of Labor-Management Relations be authorized to issue decisions to agencies and labor organizations subject to a limited right of appeal to the Federal Labor Relations Council. The Study Committee stated that as the Assistant Secretary issues decisions a body of precedent would be developed from which interested parties could draw guidance. The recommendations of the Study Committee culminated in Section 6(a)(4) of the Order which provides, in part, that the Assistant Secretary of Labor for Labor-Management Relations shall ". . . decide complaints of alleged unfair labor practices and alleged violations of the standards of conduct for labor organizations." Hence, neither the Study Committee's Report and Recommendations nor the Order itself require that in processing unfair labor practices complaints I am bound to accept as determinative those directives or policies of the Civil Service Commission, the Department of Defense or any other agency which in my view contravene the purposes of the Order.

Accordingly, I reject the Shipyard's contention that I am without authority to find a violation in the instant case because its conduct was based on directives issued by the Civil Service Commission and the Department of Defense.

As did Executive Order 10988, Executive Order 11491 guarantees to employees of the Federal Government the right "to form, join and assist" a labor organization "without fear of penalty or reprisal." Section 19(a)(1) of Executive Order 11491 states that "Agency management shall not interfere with, restrain or coerce employees in the exercise of the rights assured by this Order." That provision raises the basic issue to be resolved herein, i.e. — were the Shipyard's attempts to control employee electioneering on its premises, as evidenced by its February 18 notice to employees and its subsequent memoranda of March 16 and 27, in derogation of expressly guaranteed employee rights under Executive Order 11491? [11]

In attempting to resolve this issue, I have carefully reviewed the policy and practice developed in the Federal sector under Executive Order 10988 pursuant to the Civil Service Commission's Personnel Manual Letter 711-6. As noted above, such policy and practice was adopted to cover a particular period prior to the execution of an election agreement when a valid and timely challenge had been filed with respect to an incumbent labor organization's exclusive representative status. During this period, agencies were counseled not to authorize the use of their facilities to either the incumbent exclusive

---

[11] As noted in footnote 2 of the Hearing Examiner's Report and Recommendations, the subject cases involve only the rights of employees and not the rights of non-employee union representatives.

representative or the challenging organization for the purpose of conducting membership or election campaigns.[12]

The Civil Service Commission contended that this procedure represents "the most reasonable approach we have discovered to achieving among the contending unions the requisite fairness or equality of opportunity which alone can guarantee a genuinely free and representative election."

The Shipyard and the Department of Defense offered further justification for the Civil Service Commission policy on the grounds that the Government, as an employer, is "more neutral" in these matters than private employers and that there exists a substantial past practice under this policy which, if changed, would result in instability in Federal labor-management relations.[14]

The basic rules governing employee solicitation and distribution were established by the Supreme Court in Le Tourneau Co. of Georgia v. NLRB, 324 U.S. 793 (1945) and Republic Aviation Corp. v. NLRB, 324 U.S. 793 (1945). The Court held that the enforcement of no-distribution and no-solicitation rules against employees during their non-working time was unlawful except where there were unusual circumstances present.

In the instant cases there is no evidence to establish that employee solicitation activity with respect to the forthcoming election or their distribution of campaign literature had the effect or would have had the effect of creating a safety hazard or interfering with work production or the maintenance of discipline in the Shipyard. Moreover, the argument that a moratorium on electioneering prevents the incumbent from exercising its natural advantage over the challenger is likewise unpersuasive since equality also can be maintained by granting full communication rights to both unions. A prohibition on any reasonable form of solicitation or election campaigning, works not only to the detriment of unit employees who may seek to become informed, but also to the detriment of the challenging union, which, unlike the incumbent, has not enjoyed the advantage of a prior relationship among the unit employees. I conclude, therefore, that the purposes sought to be achieved by the operation of the Shipyard's rules are neither attained, nor do they justify limiting the employees' right established under Executive Order 11491 "to assist a labor organization."

Accordingly, in the absence of any evidence of special circumstances which would have warranted the Shipyard's limiting or banning employee solicitation during nonwork time and the distribution of campaign materials on its premises during employee nonwork time and in nonwork areas, I find that the Shipyard's notice of February 18, 1970, and its subsequent memoranda of March 16 and

---

[12] As noted above in footnote 4 and as distinguished from the Shipyard's directives herein, normal employee "person-to-person communication at the workplace" was permitted under Federal Personnel Manual Letter 711-6 and employees were allowed to "engage in oral solicitation of employee organization membership during non-work periods on agency premises."

[14] In its exceptions to the Hearing Examiner's Report and Recommendations, the Department of Defense contended, among other things, that to the extent the Shipyard's notice of February 18, 1970, attempted to restrict the solicitation rights of individual employees it was too broad since Section 11 of Federal Personnel Manual Letter 711-6 made it clear that nothing therein was intended to interfere with freedom of normal person-to-person communication at the work place which does not disrupt work operations. The Department of Defense further asserted that a valid and meaningful distinction should be made between such constitutionally protected communication on the one hand, and, on the other, participation in organized electioneering activities on behalf of a union on activity premises during a period before mutually agreed upon rules for such electioneering have been adopted.

27, 1970,[15] interfered with employee rights assured under Executive Order 11491 and were therefore violative of Section 19(a)(1) of the Order.[17]

## Conclusion

The promulgating and maintaining a rule which prohibits employees from engaging in solicitation on behalf of the Union or any other labor organization during nonwork time and from distributing literature for the Union of any other labor organization on Activity premises in nonwork areas during nonwork time, the Shipyard has violated Section 19(a)(1) of the Executive Order....

## NOTES

1. Can a public employer prohibit solicitation and distribution of union materials on its premises by *nonemployees?* Under the NLRA, the courts and the NLRB have made a distinction between the rights of employees and the rights of nonemployees. The leading NLRB decision concerning the legality of an employer's no-solicitation and no-distribution rules is Stoddard-Quirk Mfg. Co., 138 N.L.R.B. 615 (1962). In NLRB v. Babcock & Wilcox Co., 351 U.S. 105, 76 S. Ct. 679, 100 L. Ed. 975 (1956), the Court stated:

> ... an employer may validly post his property against nonemployee distribution of union literature if reasonable efforts by the union through other available channels of communication will enable it to reach the employees with its message and if the employer's notice or order does not discriminate against the union by allowing other distribution.

Should the same distinction be made in the public sector where public property rather than private property is involved?

2. Occasionally an employee organization's right of access, as well as the limitations on such right, are spelled out in considerable detail in the applicable law. For example, the Tennessee Education Professional Negotiations Act specifically provides that it is unlawful for a board of education to

> ... refuse to permit a professional employees' organization to have access at reasonable times to areas in which professional employees work, to use institutional bulletin boards, mailboxes, or other communication media, or to use institutional facilities at reasonable times for the purpose of meeting concerned with the exercise of the rights guaranteed by this act: Provided, that if a representative has been selected or designated pursuant to the provisions of this act, a board of education may deny such access and/or usage to any professional employees' organization other than the representative until such time as a lawful challenge to the majority status of the representative is sustained pursuant to this act....

---

[15] As noted above, the Shipyard's memoranda of March 16 and 27, 1970, placed certain restrictions on the Union's stewards with respect to their handling of union business at the facility. Under these restrictions, before being granted time off to carry out their responsibilities to the unit employees, stewards were required to specify to management representatives the type of union business to be conducted and, unless such business was included on a list of 18 permissible activities, excused time would be denied. The Shipyard admitted that the desire to limit electioneering activities was one of the reasons for issuance of these memoranda. Although, under Article VI, Section 5 of the parties' agreement, stewards must first obtain oral permission from their supervisor when they desire to leave their work area to transact appropriate union business during work hours, insofar as the Shipyard's March 16 and 27 memoranda constituted a broad restriction against electioneering by stewards during their nonwork time, they violated Section 19(a)(1) of the Order.

[17] The fact that the Government, as an employer, must remain neutral during an election campaign was not considered to require a contrary result. Thus, standing alone, this factor would not warrant a curtailment of *employee* rights under the Order.

TENN. CODE ANN. tit. 49, § 9(a)(4) (1978).

3. Even though an employee's right to join and form a union is affirmatively protected by statute or executive order, are there any legitimate restrictions which an employer can place on such activity? In Department of Transportation, Federal Aviation Admin., FLRC No. 72A-1 (1973), the Federal Labor Relations Council held that the teacher-student relationship between instructors and new employees justified greater restrictions on union activity than those which may be placed on other employees. The FLRC stated:

> It is a generally-felt belief that instructors have suasion over their students, even if they do not "supervise" the students. Students inherently feel pressure to "please" instructors and to be deferential to their desires. This is particularly significant in the circumstances of this case where students are often in attendance at the academy and away from their normal workplaces for extended periods of time. If the student is "solicited" by the instructor — for example, is asked to sign a union authorization card or membership application or to tender an initiation fee, this places undue pressure upon the student to respond affirmatively, notwithstanding the sophisticated judgment that the instructor is neither a management official nor a supervisor. Further, such action on the part of an instructor places agency management in an equally untenable position. The agency must insure the efficiency of its employees and the administration of a total labor relations program. It is required to insure that undue pressures do not distort true employee choices or the viability of the representation process or impair the efficiency of agency operations.

The FLRC held, however, that it was an unfair labor practice for the agency to ban instructors from wearing union buttons:

> There is a great difference between actively soliciting in behalf of a labor organization and merely wearing a union membership button, particularly in the facts of the instant case where the buttons at issue are described as "unobtrusive membership pins bearing no campaign propaganda." We see no reasonable potential for employee coercion or adverse impact on the operation of the facility resulting from instructors wearing union membership buttons. While a balancing of competing rights and obligations justifies permitting the agency to restrict the right of instructors to solicit students in behalf of a labor organization, the same kinds of considerations do not exist — certainly, at least, not to a comparable degree — when the restriction goes to the very personal act of wearing a union membership button.

4. The statutory proscription against interfering with, restraining, or coercing an employee in the exercise of his rights to join or form a union and to engage in collective bargaining has been held to cover numerous matters:

(a) *Surveillance.* An employer's surveillance of union activities constitutes illegal interference, restraint and coercion. For example, in Green Lake County, Decision No. 6061 (Wis. ERC 1962), the Wisconsin Employment Relations Commission held that it was illegal for an employer to spy on a union meeting for the purpose of determining who attended. In City of Midland, 1971 MERC Lab. Op. 1129 Mich., the Michigan Commission held that "[t]he representation of a city government in the bargaining process does not include infiltration and subversion of the union's strategy meetings." *See also,* Pennsylvania Game Commission, 657 GERR B-8 (Pa. PLRB 1976).

(b) *Interrogation.* An employer's action in interrogating or questioning employees about their union activities, about whether they have signed union cards, about how they intend to vote in a representation election, etc., constitutes illegal interference. *See* Baraga County Memorial Hospital, 1969 MERC Lab. Op. 6 (Mich.); Wisconsin Council of County and Municipal Employees, Case No. 17768 MP-345 (Wis. ERC 1977); Jess Parrish Memorial Hospital, 4 FPER ¶ 4007 (Fla. PERC 1977).

(c) *Promise of benefit or threat of reprisal.* The granting or withholding of benefits for the purpose of influencing employees with respect to union activity constitutes illegal interference, restraint, and coercion. As the Supreme Court stated in NLRB

v. Exchange Parts Co., 375 U.S. 405, 84 S. Ct. 457, 11 L. Ed. 2d 435 (1964):

We think the Court of Appeals was mistaken in concluding that the conferral of employee benefits while a representation election is pending, for the purpose of inducing employees to vote against the union, does not "interfere with" the protected right to organize.

. . . The danger inherent in well-timed increases in benefits is the suggestion of a fist inside the velvet glove. Employees are not likely to miss the inference that the source of benefits now conferred is also the source from which future benefits must flow and which may dry up if it is not obliged. The danger may be diminished if, as in this case, the benefits are conferred permanently and unconditionally. But the absence of conditions or threats pertaining to the particular benefits conferred would be of controlling significance only if it could be presumed that no question of additional benefits or renegotiation of existing benefits would arise in the future; and, of course, no such presumption is tenable.

. . . Other unlawful conduct may often be an indication of the motive behind a grant of benefits while an election is pending, and to that extent it is relevant to the legality of the grant; but when as here the motive is otherwise established, an employer is not free to violate § 8(a)(1) by conferring benefits simply because it refrains from other, more obvious violations. We cannot agree with the Court of Appeals that enforcement of the Board's order will have the "ironic" result of "discouraging benefits for labor." 304 F.2d, at 376. The beneficence of an employer is likely to be ephemeral if prompted by a threat of unionization which is subsequently removed. Insulating the right of collective organization from calculated good will of this sort deprives employees of little that has lasting value.

In addition to the actual conferral or withdrawal of benefits, employer statements which contain promises of benefit or threats of reprisal constitute unlawful interference, restraint, and coercion. *See, e.g.,* City of Marysville, 1970 MERC Lab. Op. 458 (Mich.).

5. A wide variety of activities have been held to constitute "protected concerted activity" and therefore covered by statutes making it an unfair labor practice for a public employer to interfere with or discriminate against employees because of their involvement in such activities. Examples:

(a) peaceful picketing on employees' own time, City of Fitchburg, Case No. MUPL-72 (Mass. LRC 1975);

(b) communicating with newspaper reporter about matter of concern to fellow employees, City of Venice, 4 FPER ¶ 4059 (Fla. PERC 1978);

(c) publishing newspaper ad authorized by union questioning adequacy of fire protection following layoffs in fire department, Town of Johnson, Case No. ULP-3236 (R.I. SLRB 1975); and

(d) union petition to fire chief and city officials expressing lack of confidence in fire captain and requesting his termination, City of Dunedin, 4 FPER ¶ 4258 (Fla. PERC 1978).

The various commissions and boards, however, have distinguished between activities which involve a single employee as opposed to activities which benefit or involve two or more employees. For example, the Florida PERC in City of Hollywood, 4 FPER ¶ 4131 (Fla. PERC 1978), noted that "[w]here an employee engages in activities for his benefit alone, his action is not *concerted* protected activity." (Emphasis in original.)

## SOCIAL WORKERS' UNION, LOCAL 535 v. ALAMEDA COUNTY WELFARE DEP'T

California Supreme Court
113 Cal. Rptr. 461, 521 P.2d 453 (1974)

TOBRINER, Justice:

In this case we must determine whether a public employee may be disciplined for declining to attend, without his union representative, a meeting with his supervisor concerning the employee's alleged misuse of a county car at a union rally. The Alameda County Welfare Department (Department) ordered three-day suspensions for seven employees after the employees declined to attend such a meeting from which their union representative had been excluded. The employees, and their union, Social Workers Union, Local 535, SEIU, AFL-CIO (union), then sought a writ of mandate to compel the Department to set aside the suspensions, but the superior court denied the writ, concluding that the relevant statutory provisions granted the employees no right to the presence of a union representative at such a meeting with their employer. The union and the individual employees appeal from that adverse judgment.

For the reasons discussed below, we have concluded that a public employee's statutory right to effective union representation (Gov. Code, § 3500 et seq.) includes a right to have a union representative accompany him to a meeting with his employer when the employee reasonably anticipates that such meeting may involve union activities and when the employee reasonably fears that adverse action may result from such a meeting because of union-related conduct. In the instant case we find that the public employees could reasonably anticipate that the meetings, set up by their employer to investigate their transportation to a union rally protesting the employer's conduct, might result in disciplinary action related to their union activity. Thus, we believe such employees were justified in insisting that their union representative be permitted to attend the meeting and were not subject to sanction for such insistence. Accordingly, we reverse the judgment as to those employees who properly exhausted their administrative remedies.

The essential facts underlying this litigation are not at issue. On May 14, 1969, the union sponsored a noon hour rally at the Alameda County Administration Building to protest, as described by the union, the failure of the County of Alameda to "meet and confer in good faith" with the union concerning subjects within the scope of representation allowable under the statute. (Gov. Code, § 3505.) An investigation undertaken by county administrators indicated that certain county vehicles were observed at the union rally; further examination of county garage records and "employee day sheets" suggested that some of the employees using these vehicles did not have official business at the administration building during the time in question. The responsible county supervisor testified at the administrative proceeding that, based on these revelations, "circumstantially it appeared" that a misuse of county property had occurred. In July 1969, some 30 employees were ordered to attend individual meetings with the chief assistant welfare director or his deputy concerning the employees' possible misuse of county vehicles to attend the May 14, 1969, union rally.

A dispute soon arose over the right of the employees to be accompanied to these meetings by their union representative. After the chief assistant welfare director made clear that the union representative would not be permitted to attend, 23 employees acquiesced in the supervisor's demand that they appear alone before him or his assistant. Based solely on these meetings, the assistant supervisor transmitted a report on the matter to the welfare director including recommendations as to discipline.

The seven employees involved in the instant case, however, declined to meet with the chief assistant welfare director or his deputy to discuss the alleged misuse of county vehicles in connection with a union rally without a union representative. All seven individuals were ultimately suspended for three days for insubordination in refusing to attend the interview without a union representative. Thereafter, the employees and their union commenced the instant proceeding, challenging the validity of the suspensions.

After reviewing the facts outlined above, the superior court concluded that "no law, ordinance, rule or regulation authorizes or requires the presence of union representatives at such interview." "Such interview," in the language of the findings of the court, consisted of a confrontation by the county with workers upon the issue "whether or not the vehicles were in the area because the employees had departmental business in the vicinity, or, in the alternative, whether the vehicles were used for the transportation of the employees to and from the demonstration." On the basis of its conclusion, the court denied the requested writ of mandate.

We shall explain why we have concluded that, contrary to the conclusion of the trial court, the subject matter of the employer's investigation in the instant case fell within the penumbra of the protected rights of the employees and justified the employees' claim to a right of union representation. Since the investigation touched upon the statutorily guaranteed associational rights of the employees, and since the employees could reasonably fear that the investigation might lead to disciplinary penalties for such union participation, we hold that the employee could properly demand the presence of a union representative at such an interview.

The Meyers-Milias-Brown Act, the controlling statutory structure in this field, is built upon the recognition of the rights of association and representation of the public employee. Government Code section 3500 guarantees public employees "the right . . . to join organizations of their own choice and be represented by such organizations in their employment relationships with public agencies." After many years of indecision as to the organizational rights of public employees, the Legislature finally accorded them this basic right of association which, obviously, embraces that most vital aspect of unionism: the right of attendance at a union meeting or rally. Thus, section 3502 provides that "public employees shall have the right to form, join, and *participate in the activities of employee organizations* of their own choosing for the purpose of representation on all matters of employer-employee relations." (Emphasis added.)

Two sections of the code specifically protect public employees against interference or intimidation by public agencies in the exercise of the employees' right of association. Thus, section 3506 provides: "Public agencies . . . shall not interfere with, intimidate, restrain, coerce or discriminate against public employees because of their exercise of their rights under Section 3502." Section 3508 reiterates this principle: "The right of employees to form, join and participate in the activities of employee organizations shall not be restricted by a public agency on any grounds other than those set forth in this section." And, in recent years, numerous cases have enforced these prohibitions against a variety of employer conduct which impinged upon or threatened employees because of their union affiliations or activities. . . .

In addition to ensuring a public employee's right to engage in a wide range of union-related activities without fear of sanction, the Meyers-Milias-Brown Act defines the *scope* of the employee's right to union representation in language that is broad and generous.

Section 3503 establishes the right of recognized employee unions directly to represent their members in "employment relations with public agencies." This right to representation reaches "*all* matters of employer-employee relations" (Gov. Code, § 3502; emphasis added) and encompasses "but [is] not limited to, wages, hours, and other terms and conditions of employment" (Gov. Code, § 3504).

The narrow question presented in the instant case is whether this broadly defined right of representation attaches to an employer-conducted interview which an employee reasonably anticipates may involve his union activities and reasonably fears may ultimately lead to disciplinary action because of such union-related conduct. For the reasons discussed hereafter, we hold that the right of union representation does apply under these circumstances.

Over the lengthy history of governmental regulation of employee-management relations, the inherent threat to union activism posed by employer interrogation has been well documented. Scores of judicial decisions, on both the state and federal levels, attest to the potentially coercive and intimidating effect of employer inquiries into an individual employee's union activities. . . . Even when an employer presents an entirely "innocent" motive for such a questioning session, because of the normal tension between management and union and the interview's connection with union matters, the questioned employee is likely to view the employer's inquiries as directed at or arising out of his union activity, and the employee will frequently, and understandably, assume that such questioning sessions can be avoided in the future by curtailing his participation in union activities.

In light of the inherently coercive nature of such questioning sessions, numerous cases have imposed limitations on the employer's right to carry out such investigation into union activity generally . . . and, in particular, have found improper coercive inquiries directed at an employee's attendance at union meetings or rallies. . . .

In the instant case, of course, the employer possessed what appears to be a legitimate reason for inquiring into its employee's method of transportation to the union rally, and the union does not contend that the employer's questioning session, in itself, was improper or discriminatory. (Cf. Blue Flash Express, Inc. (1954) 109 NLRB 591, 34 LRRM 1384.) Nevertheless, such an interview, touching as it did upon the employee's participation in a union activity, contained the inherent potential for intimidation and coercion noted above and, in our view, justified the employee's request for the presence of a union representative under the applicable, broad statutory provisions.

Recognition of the right to union representation in this setting is vital for several reasons. First, from the point of view of the questioned employee, the presence of a union representative will help assure the employee that he will not be penalized for his union activities and will tend to reduce the potentially coercive atmosphere of the employer-directed interview. Second, the union itself, of course, has a considerable interest in assuring that no sanctions, blatant or subtle, are meted out by the employer on account of an individual member's participation in union affairs. Finally, the union and its members have an additional, more generalized interest in guaranteeing that the employer does not adopt any new employment policies which, in application, tend to discriminate against union members or their activities. Thus, for example, in the instant case a union representative present at the interview might have protested an attempt by the employer to discriminatorily resurrect a generally unenforced rule concerning the noon hour use of county cars simply because of a connection here with union activities.

In light of these considerations, we now hold that a public employee's right to union representation under section 3504 attaches to an employer-employee interview which an employee reasonably fears may investigate and sanction his union-related activities.

The respondent county suggests, however, that the recognition of an employee's right to union representation under the circumstances of the instant case is inconsistent with several recent federal decisions interpreting similar "right to representation" provisions of the federal Labor Management Relations Act (29 U.S.C. §§ 157, 158(a), 158(d)). Although we agree with respondent's suggestion that the interpretation of the analogous provisions of the federal act is relevant to our present decision, as we shall explain, we find nothing in the recent federal cases which conflict with the conclusion we have reached above.

Federal labor relation legislation has, of course, frequently been the prototype for California labor enactments, and, accordingly, in the past we have often looked to federal law for guidance in interpreting state provisions whose language parallels that of the federal statutes. . . . Unquestionably, in defining the scope of representation in section 3504, the Legislature relied heavily upon the analogous sections of the federal Labor Management Relations Act: as one commentator has noted: "[t]he phrase 'wages, hours and other terms and conditions of employment' [of section 3504] is taken verbatim from the LMRA, where it has been given a generous interpretation, including anything that might affect an employee in his employment relationship." (Grodin, Public Employee Bargaining in California: The Meyers-Milias-Brown Act in the Courts (1972), 23 Hastings L. J. 719, 749; fns. omitted.) Professor Grodin additionally observes, however, that "[t]he phrasing of the first part of section 3504 [i.e., 'including *but not limited to*'] suggests the scope of representation under the [Meyers-Milias-Brown] Act is even more broad" than under the federal statute (id.); thus, while the federal authorities undoubtedly provide a useful starting point in interpreting the scope of our state provision, they do not necessarily establish the limits of California public employees' representational rights.

In the instant case, however, we need not probe the area in which the state provision extends the right of representation beyond federal law, because the two recent federal decisions relied on by the county to support its position that no representational right attached in the instant case are clearly distinguishable from the instant matter. In N.L.R.B. v. Quality Manufacturing Co. (4th Cir. 1973) F.2d     , 83 LRRM 2817 and Mobil Oil Corp. v. N.L.R.B. (7th Cir. 1973) F.2d     , 83 LRRM 2823, the respective Circuit Courts of Appeals refused to enforce a National Labor Relations Board rule which recognized the right of an employee to have a union representative present at *any* employer-employee interview when the employee reasonably anticipated that disciplinary action might result from the interview.[13]

Neither Quality Manufacturing nor Mobil Oil are applicable to the instant case, however, for in neither decision did the employer-employee interview arise under circumstances in which the employee could reasonably fear that the questioning would relate to his union activities. Indeed the Mobil Oil court was careful to note explicitly that the circumstances before it did not involve such potential interrogation of union activities, emphasizing that "this is not a case in which there is any danger that the questioning was actually motivated by a desire to

---

[13] The National Labor Relations Board adopted its interpretation of the scope of the federal act's "right to representation" provision in a recent en banc decision. (See Weingarten Inc. & Retail Clerks Union, Local Union No. 445, Retail Clerks International Association AFL-CIO, March 16, 1973, 202 NLRB No. 69, 82 LRRM 1559 (en banc) [1973 C.C.H. N.L.R.B. ¶ 25, 151].) Although the two recent judicial decisions cited above did not concur in the agency's interpretation of the federal act, to date the board has not acquiesced in the judicial rulings, and thus the cited cases are only authoritative precedent in the circuits from which they arose. Accordingly, the state of the federal law in this area remains unsettled.

impair the employee's right to organize, to detect union activity, or in any way to influence collective bargaining negotiations." (— F.2d at p. —, 83 LRRM at p. 2825; see Dobbs Houses, Inc. (1964) 145 NLRB 1565, 1571, 55 LRRM 1218.)

In sum, the employer's investigation here did not constitute a normal interview with regard to employment matters but, instead, an inquiry that focused upon the employee's conduct regarding the use of county cars in connection with a union rally. The very lifeblood of the union is its meetings and rallies; without them, the union expires. An inquiry into this subject matter, with its overtones of discipline of union members who attended the rally, could only create fear on the part of those subject to the process and lead them to urge the reasonable request that a union representative be present to assist them.

The judgment of the superior court is affirmed with respect to appellants Doyle, Pofscher and Chan. With respect to the remaining appellants the judgment is reversed and the cause remanded to the superior court for proceedings consistent with this opinion.

Wright, Chief Justice, and Mosk, Burke, Sullivan, and Clark, Justices, concur.

[The dissenting opinion of Justice McComb is omitted.]

# NOTES

1. Is the right to union representation enunciated by the court in *Alameda County* limited to employer-conducted interviews which relate to an employee's union activities? Should it be? If not, why?

2. In NLRB v. Weingarten, Inc., 420 U.S. 251, 95 S. Ct. 959 (1975), the Court sustained the position of the NLRB that it is an unfair labor practice for an employer to deny an employee's request that a union representative be present at an investigatory interview which the employee reasonably believes might result in disciplinary action. The Court observed that (1) "the right arises only in situations where the employee requests representation," (2) "the employee's right to request representation as a condition of participation in an interview is limited to situations where the employee reasonably believes the investigation will result in disciplinary action," (3) "the employer has no obligation to justify his refusal to allow union representation, and despite refusal, the employer is free to carry on his inquiry without interviewing the employee," and (4) "the employer has no duty to bargain with any union representative who may be permitted to attend the investigatory interview." *Accord,* International Ladies' Garment Workers' Union v. Quality Mfg. Co., 420 U.S. 276, 95 S. Ct. 972 (1975).

3. In Regents of the University of Michigan, 1977 MERC Lab. Op. 496 (Mich. 1977), the Michigan Commission adopted the *Weingarten* doctrine. Similarly, in Duval County School Board, 4 FPER ¶ 4154 (Fla. PERC 1978), the Florida Commission adopted *Weingarten,* but added an additional exception for emergency situations "in which (1) the employer must conduct a prompt investigation in order to resolve an existing or eminent problem, (2) a union representative is not readily available, and (3) delay in conducting the interview may reasonably be expected to jeopardize some significant interest of the employer." In East Brunswick Board of Education, 5 NJPER ¶ 10061 (N.J. PERC 1979), the Hearing Examiner held that under the *Weingarten* principle, the right to union representation only attaches where the meeting is initiated by the employer and that there is no right to such representation where the meeting initiated at the request of the employee.

4. Although a union's failure to fairly represent all employees is not typically specified as an unfair labor practice, the various commissions have generally held that a union's failure to fairly represent all unit employees is an unfair labor practice. For example, in AFSCME Local 1633, 4 FPER ¶ 4168 (Fla. PERC 1978), the Florida Commission held that the privilege of exclusive representation granted by the Florida law "required the correlative duty of fair representation to all unit employees" and that "any default in the

performance of [the duty of fair representation] constitutes infringement of [the rights granted to employees under the Act] and is therefore enforceable as an unfair labor practice." In Auburn Administrators Association, 11 PERB ¶ 3086 (N.Y. 1978), the New York PERB held that it was an unfair labor practice for a union to tell a non-member that it would not represent him in negotiations because of his non-member status. The New York PERB ruled that "[a]n aspect of an employee organization's duty to represent all unit employees fairly without regard to membership is that it may not coerce employees into joining by implying that it will not honor that duty faithfully as to them."

## 2. EMPLOYER DISCRIMINATION

### MUSKEGO-NORWAY CONSOLIDATED SCHOOLS v. WERB

Wisconsin Supreme Court
35 Wis.2d 540, 151 N.W.2d 617 (1967)

...In 1960 the Muskego-Norway Education Association (MNEA), an organization composed of practically 100 percent of all teaching and administrative personnel in the employ of the school district, was organized. The MNEA is affiliated with the Wisconsin Education Association (WEA), which renders assistance to local affiliates in regard to their representation of teachers in conferences and negotiations concerning salaries and other conditions of employment.

This controversy concerns certain activities in the school district during the period from 1960 through early 1964. On the one hand is a group of teachers employed by the district who in May, 1964, complained of violations of sec. 111.70, Stats., on the part of the school board and certain of its supervisory personnel. These teachers alleged that the school district . . . discouraged labor activity on the part of the teachers by its failure to renew the teaching contract of Carston C. Koeller because of his labor activities on behalf of the MNEA.

On the other hand are the school district; Robert J. Kreuser, superintendent of schools; Jack C. Refling, high school principal; Paul J. Ussel, assistant principal; and Charles A. Ladd, coordinator of instruction.

Certain facts in this involved dispute are uncontroverted and best be set forth here. Other pertinent facts, some controverted, are detailed in the opinion. . . .

Carston Koeller, a first-year teacher in the district, was elected chairman of a reorganized and enlarged MNEA welfare committee for the 1963-1964 year. (He remained chairman at all times pertinent herein.) In September of 1963 the committee began operations by requesting salary information from Superintendent Kreuser. When this information was not forthcoming, the committee obtained it by circulating questionnaires to the teachers. The MNEA also began sending representatives to board meetings. Largely through Koeller's efforts, this information was tabulated prior to mid-January, 1964, and proposals for the year 1964-1965 were formulated. The committee worked hard and held as many as 26 meetings. Its proposals, which were very comprehensive and were approved by the MNEA membership, were presented to the personnel committee of the school board. The proposals dealt with matters of teacher salaries, insurance, personal and sabbatical leaves, class size and load, job security, teacher qualifications, and other matters supporting said proposals including various tables and graphs.

The personnel committee took these proposals under advisement. The personnel committee met again with MNEA representatives and questioned the accuracy of these proposals and whether they represented the wishes of a majority of the teachers. Further questionnaires were circulated and modified proposals were submitted (as approved by the MNEA membership). The report and proposals were submitted to the board meeting on March 2, 1964. What transpired at that meeting and subsequently will be described later in the statement of facts.

Paralleling in importance the development of the MNEA as an effective representative of the teachers are the activities of the chairman of its welfare committee, Carston Koeller, both educational and as a leader in the MNEA. Mr. Koeller was hired by the school district in 1962 following three years of teaching experience in the air force and one year at Belleville, Wisconsin. Mr. Koeller taught five classes of general mathematics, a subject taken by students deficient in mathematics and incapable of comprehending algebra. These students were also slower learners in other subjects as well. In 1963, at the end of Koeller's first year of teaching, a report was filed by the then principal, Donald Helstad, listing him in the bottom quarter of the faculty in teaching ability, although this did not necessarily mean he was a poor teacher. Helstad advised that Koeller had shown as much progress as any other high school teacher at the time and Helstad unqualifiedly recommended that Koeller he rehired for the year 1963-1964. Koeller was retained. Subsequently, Koeller engaged in a number of activities related to his duties as a teacher rather than to his extracurricular duties with the MNEA.

1. On October 2, 1963, Koeller mailed to six parents a statement asking them to sign a request to give Mr. Koeller permission to use whatever physical means was necessary in order to enforce discipline. On October 7th the new principal, Refling, held a conference with Koeller informing him he was not to determine a course of discipline contrary to established school procedures. At this conference, Koeller's difficulty in handling students in study hall was also discussed. (Koeller had placed a female student in a large unlighted closet as a disciplinary procedure.)

2. On October 14th Koeller suggested in writing to a committee of teachers established to create procedures for disciplining study halls that enforcement of discipline could be implemented by "tweak or pull an ear, rap on head, pull hunk of hair or sit in front closet with door shut."

3. In the fall of 1963, football players were excused from their seventh-hour classes on the day of the game. On October 22d Koeller sent a note to Principal Refling, objecting to this practice. Koeller was then called into a conference with Ussel and Refling, in which conference Koeller's disagreement with school policies and his lack of judgment in handling student situations were discussed. Koeller then appealed by letter directly to Mr. Guhr (school board president) but was told to go through the normal grievance procedures. No further action was taken on this matter except that on October 28th Refling sent Koeller a letter warning him about insubordination.

4. On December 2, 1963, following a visit to Koeller's classroom, coordinator of instruction Ladd made the following comments and suggestions for improving inadequacies in Koeller's teaching techniques: (a) More student "involvement," (b) "less teacher talk," (c) the elicitation of "clear, confident responses" from students, (d) personal supervision of assignments, (e) various approaches to various students, and (f) permitting students to make their own evaluations. Koeller visited an experienced mathematics teacher from a Racine school and his class, and thereafter Ladd noticed that Koeller's teaching techniques improved.

5. On December 10, 1963, as a layman, Koeller wrote the state department of public instruction, concerning state aids formulas and the financial condition

of the Muskego-Norway district. In this letter Koeller complained of inadequate facilities in the district.

6. On January 28, 1964, Koeller scheduled a meeting of the National Honor Society which conflicted with the meeting of the high school P. T. A. Koeller was given oral confirmation from Ussel but school policy required a written approval. A memo from the principal chastized Koeller for failing to obtain the approval of the principal, and Koeller circulated the memo.

7. On February 5, 1964, Koeller sent a student to the office with a note indicating he had suspended the student for three days. Koeller was told that the administration decided whether suspensions were in order. Koeller then publicly challenged the position of the administration in the MNEA newsletter, quoting from the private memo he had received from the administration. In the newsletter, Koeller maintained he had the right to suspend students for disciplinary reasons. Koeller was called into conference with the principal, where he was advised he was skating on "thin ice" in utilizing the MNEA newsletter to vent a private grievance.

8. On February 18th Koeller read the memo received in regard to the scheduling problem to the National Honor Society students and announced that this was the reason for resigning as adviser from the group. Koeller then sent Kreuser a note explaining his reasons for resigning and charging that Kreuser had exhibited vindictiveness toward him. Koeller subsequently withdrew this statement.

9. Koeller's record as a teacher includes having 43 disciplinary referrals to Principal Refling, while the 49 other teachers on the faculty had a total of 150 disciplinary referrals.

There is a dispute about what transpired at the March 2, 1964, meeting of the board. In addition to the salary-and-working-conditions proposals of the MNEA during executive session the board also considered whether to rehire Koeller. Kreuser denied that he made any recommendations at that session against renewing Koeller's contract. He denied that the subject was even discussed. Yet board member Vogel recalled that Kreuser had advised him on March 3d that Kreuser had made this recommendation at the meeting the previous night. Between March 2 and March 9, 1964, a summary of Koeller's activities was prepared and, upon the recommendation of Kreuser, at another executive session on March 9, 1964, the school board formally determined not to offer Koeller a teacher's contract for 1964-1965. On March 11, 1964, conditions of employment were again announced at a general teachers' meeting. No prior notice of action taken on its proposals was received by the MNEA.

On March 12, 1964, Koeller was called to Kreuser's office and given a notice that his contract would not be renewed. Kreuser read from a sheet of paper a number of reasons for the dismissal, but he did not give Koeller a copy of the list of the reasons even though Koeller requested one. Kreuser also advised Koeller that a successful contest of the discharge was unlikely, because all statutory requirements had been met. Further, Kreuser advised Koeller that such an appeal would be professional suicide because Koeller needed Kreuser's signature to obtain a life-time teaching certificate.

A dispute exists as to whether or not Kreuser first offered to give Koeller a recommendation for another job if Koeller would resign. Koeller's testimony indicates this is true while the testimony of Kreuser and Refling is that Koeller was only offered the opportunity to resign. Nonetheless, Koeller refused to resign and was then handed a prepared notice of termination, the letter stating that the action was "deemed advisable in view of actions and conduct on your part which have previously been discussed with you."

After a full hearing on the complaints, the WERB found:

"29. That the primary motivation of Kreuser's recommendation to the School Board not to renew Koeller's teaching contract for the 1964-1965 school year was not based on any shortcomings Koeller may have had as a teacher, nor upon his differences with certain policies with the School Board, but rather upon Koeller's activity and efforts on behalf of the MNEA Welfare Committee as the collective bargaining representative of the majority of the professional teaching personnel in the employ of the School District; that the discriminatory refusal of the School Board to renew Koeller's teaching contract and the recommendations with respect thereto made by Superintendent Kreuser and other supervisory employes of the School District, interfered, restrained and coerced not only Koeller, but also the remaining teachers in the employ of the School District in the exercise of their right to engage in lawful concerted activities."

And it reached the following conclusion of law:

"2. That Muskego-Norway Consolidated Schools Joint School District No. 9, Town of Muskego, Waukesha County, and Town of Norway, Racine County, by its School Board, by refusing and failing to renew Carston C. Koeller's teaching contract for the year 1964-1965 upon the recommendation of Kreuser, Refling, Ussel and Ladd, discriminated against him in regard to the conditions of his employment, for the purpose of discouraging membership in and activities on behalf on the Muskego-Norway Education Association and, thereby, has committed, and is committing, prohibited practices, within the meaning of Section 111.70 (3) (a)1 and 2 of the Wisconsin Statutes."

. . . .

The WERB ordered the school district . . . to offer Koeller his former position without prejudice, to pay Koeller any damages he may have suffered and to post a notice to all teachers notifying them of the actions taken and future policy to be followed by the district.

A petition for review of the WERB's order was filed under ch. 227, Stats. Thereafter, judgment was entered setting aside the order of the WERB. On the merits the trial court found that the finding of the WERB that the school board's primary motivation for firing Koeller was his labor activities was based on speculation and conjecture. . . . Further, the trial court ruled that there had been no proof of any relationship between the the school board and the administrators. The WERB has appealed.

WILKIE, J. Four issues are raised on this appeal:

*First,* is the authority of school boards under secs. 40.40 and 40.41, Stats., subject to the limitations of sec. 111.70?

. . . .

*Third,* is the WERB finding that the refusal of respondents to renew Koeller's contract was prompted by his labor activities supported by substantial evidence?

*Fourth,* must the WERB make an express finding that Kreuser, Refling, Ladd and Ussel were agents of the Muskego-Norway school board in order to impute their actions to the board in deciding whether unfair labor practices were committed?

*Relation of Secs. 40.40, 40.41 and 40.45 and Sec. 111.70, Stats.*

One of the principal premises for the trial court's decision was that secs. 40.40 and 40.41, Stats., require the school board to contract individually with each teacher each year. . . .

The provisions of sec. 111.70, Stats., apply to the authority of school districts to the same extent as the authority of other municipal governing bodies. Sec. 111.70 was enacted after secs. 40.40 and 40.41 and is presumed to have been enacted with a full knowledge of preexisting statutes. Construction of statutes should be done in a way which harmonizes the whole system of law of which they are a part, and any conflict should be reconciled if possible.
. . .

Respondents . . . contend that secs. 40.40 and 40.41, Stats., permit the school board to refuse to rehire on any ground or for no reason at all. Assuming this to be true, secs. 40.40 and 40.41 can be modified by subsequent statutes which forbid refusing to rehire a teacher for a particular reason. For example, a school board may not refuse to rehire a teacher because of his race, nationality or political or religious affiliations. Modification of statutes is a question of legislative policy. In 1959 the legislature enacted sec. 111.70 (3) (a), which prohibits municipal employers, including school districts, from:

"1. Interfering with, restraining or coercing any municipal employe in the exercise of the rights provided in sub. (2).
"2. Encouraging or discouraging membership in any labor organization, employe agency, committee, association or representation plan by discrimination in regard to hiring, tenure or other terms or conditions of employment."

This also restricts the reasons a teacher can be refused reemployment. A school board may not terminate a teacher's contract because the teacher has been engaging in labor activities.

## Scope of Judicial Review

The second and third issues concern whether crucial findings of the WERB are supported by credible evidence. This makes it necessary to state the standard of judicial review of the findings of the WERB. It is well established that under sec. 227.20 (1) (d), Stats., judicial review of the WERB findings is to determine whether or not the questioned finding is supported "by substantial evidence in view of the entire record." This court has held that the key to the application of this standard is to determine what is meant by "substantial evidence."[10]

In *Copland* this court quoted from an article by E. Blythe Stason [11] as follows:

" '[T]he term "substantial evidence" should be construed to confer finality upon an administrative decision on the facts when, upon an examination of the entire record, the evidence, including the inferences therefrom, is found to be such that a reasonable man, acting reasonably, *might* have reached the decision; but, on the other hand, if a reasonable man, acting reasonably, *could not* have reached the decision from the evidence and its inferences then the decision is not supported by substantial evidence and it should be set aside.' "

Moreover, in *Copland* we reiterated that " 'substantial evidence' is 'such

---

[10] Copland v. Department of Taxation (1962), 16 Wis. (2d) 543, 554, 114 N.W.(2d) 858.
[11] "Substantial Evidence" in Administrative Law, 89 University of Pennsylvania Law Review (1941), 1026, 1038.

relevant evidence as a *reasonable mind* might accept as adequate to support a conclusion.' (Emphasis supplied.)" [13] In *Copland* we declared that the test of reasonableness "is implicit in the statutory words 'substantial evidence,'" and that the "[u]se of the statutory words 'in view of the entire record as submitted' strongly suggests that the test of reasonableness is to be applied to the evidence as a whole, not merely to that part which tends to support the agency's findings."

. . . .

## Termination of Employment for Labor Activities

The WERB found that the primary motivation for the refusal of the school board to renew Koeller's contract was because of his activities and efforts on behalf of the MNEA welfare committee. The WERB concluded that the school board discriminated against Koeller in regard to the conditions of his employment for the purpose of discouraging membership in and activities on behalf of the MNEA and was thereby committing a prohibited practice under sec. 111.70 (3) (a), Stats.

A major premise in the trial court's argument for reversing the WERB's determination in this respect is that if a valid reason for discharging an employee exists, this is a sufficient basis for holding that the employee was not dismissed for union activities. The trial court quotes *Wisconsin Labor Relations Board v. Fred Rueping Leather Co.* as follows:

". . . When a valid reason as heretofore defined is found to be present, it is relatively difficult and may be impossible to more than guess which reason motivated the discharge. The board could find discrimination here only by finding that the assigned reason for the discharge of Assaf was false because if it was not, the evidence is in such state that a finding of discrimination would be pure conjecture. Furthermore, we have some misgivings whether, if a valid and sufficient reason for discharge exists, the real or motivating reason has any materiality whatever, unless it can be shown that in other cases where similar grounds for discharge of nonunion men existed, no such action was taken." [16]

In other words, if there was good reason for terminating Koeller's employment because of teaching deficiencies and his differences of teaching philosophy with the school board and the supervisory personnel, it would not matter whether the contract was not renewed for his labor activities. But this is not the law. In *Rueping* there was no speculation as to what the real reason for the discharge was. Moreover, the law concerning discharge for labor activities has changed since 1938. In N.L.R.B. v. Great Eastern Color Lithographic Corp.[17] the federal courts [sic] stated:

"The issue before us is not, of course, whether or not there existed grounds for discharge of these employees apart from their union activities. *The fact that the employer had ample reason for discharging them is of no moment. It was*

---

[13] Copland v. Department of Taxation, *supra,* footnote 10, at page 554, quoting from Gateway City Transfer Co. v. Public Service Comm. (1948), 253 Wis. 397, 405, 406, 34 N.W.(2d) 238; and Consolidated Edison Co. v. National Labor Relations Board (1938), 305 U.S. 197, 59 Sup. Ct. 206, 83 L. Ed. 126.

[16] (1938), 228 Wis. 473, 499, 279 N.W. 673, 684.

[17] (2d Cir. 1962), 309 F.2d 352, 355.

*free to discharge them for any reason good or bad, so long as it did not discharge them for their union activity.* And even though the discharges may have been based upon other reasons as well, if the employer were partly motivated by union activity, the discharges were violative of the Act." (Emphasis added.)

Several other federal cases are in accord. Although these cases all involve a construction of unfair labor practices under the Wagner Act, the case of *St. Joseph's Hospital v. Wisconsin Employment Relations Board* adopts their legal conclusion that an employee may not be fired when one of the motivating factors is his union activities, no matter how many other valid reasons exist for firing him.

The trial court opined that the WERB reached finding of fact No. 29 "purely upon conjecture." It concluded that there was ample reason for the school board's actions for Koeller's deficiencies as a teacher and his philosophical differences with the individual respondents on school matters.

But in this court's judicial review we are not required to agree in every detail with the WERB as to its findings, conclusions and order. We must affirm its findings if they are supported by substantial evidence in view of the entire record. Sec. 227.20 (2), Stats., requires that upon such review due weight shall be accorded the experience, technical competence, and specialized knowledge of the agency involved. In short, this means the court must make some deference to the expertise of the agency.

In *St. Joseph's Hospital v. Wisconsin Employment Relations Board* the WERB found that the discharge of an employee was primarily because of her union activities. The court discussed the scope of review of this finding as follows:

"Finding 20 is a finding of ultimate fact and is of necessity based upon inferences from other testimony before the board. Such inferences may not be based upon conjecture but must be drawn from established facts which logically support them. The drawing of inferences from other facts in the record is a function of the board and the weight to be given to those facts is for the board to determine. International Union v. Wisconsin E.R. Board, 258 Wis. 481, 46 N.W. (2d) 185. Such findings, when made, cannot be disturbed by a court unless they are unsupported by substantial evidence in view of the entire record submitted."

The board is the judge of the credibility of the witnesses and the reviewing court is not to substitute its judgment for the judgment of the board.

In essence, in the instant case we must decide whether the WERB's crucial findings, conclusions and order are based on inferences reasonably drawn on the entire record or whether they are the result of conjecture on the part of the WERB.

On the whole record we conclude that WERB's finding No. 29 is supported by substantial evidence and reasonable inferences drawn therefrom in view of the entire record, that the failure to renew Koeller's teaching contract was motivated by his activities as chairman of the welfare committee of MNEA and not on any shortcomings Koeller may have had as a teacher nor upon his differences with certain policies of the school board and the respondent supervisory personnel.

The WERB's finding No. 29 is the logical final determination as to the motivation behind the failure to renew Koeller's contract following the stepped-up labor activities of the welfare committee in which Koeller had such a major part and the difficulties [he] had in assembling and presenting proposals on salaries and working conditions to Kreuser and the school board.

The WERB placed heavy emphasis on the timing and manner of the dismissal. Although there was dispute about it the WERB could reasonably find that the first recommendation of Koeller's nonrenewal was made at the executive session of the school board on March 2, 1964, immediately following the very meeting when the MNEA proposals for 1964-1965 were submitted to the school board for the first time and were discussed; that at that time no written reasons were given for the dismissal; that on March 9, 1964, a summary of reasons having been prepared since March 2d, the school board acted formally to terminate Koeller's services; that Koeller was not notified of this action until March 12, 1964, the day after the school teachers were called together and told of the school board's determinations about salaries and working conditions for the year 1964-1965 (there having been no negotiations about the MNEA proposals).

In a memorandum accompanying its findings of fact, conclusions of law and order the WERB discussed its reasons for concluding that the respondents were motivated by Koeller's labor activities in ending his employment. The WERB also thoroughly discussed and rejected the other reasons that were alleged to have motivated the respondents relating to the shortcomings of Koeller as a teacher and his disagreement with certain policies established by the school board.

The WERB carefully considered each one of the reasons compiled in the summary prepared by supervisory personnel prior to the school board's final action on March 9th as to why Koeller's contract should not be renewed. The WERB's analysis is summed up as follows:

"It seems incredible to us that the Superintendent could be sincere in the gravity of complaints made against Koeller and at the same time offer to recommend him to another position. We believe this to be a gross act of intimidation."

The WERB concluded:

". . . in light of the entire record, we do not find that Koeller's competence as a teacher or disciplinarian motivated the determination not to extend his teaching contract.

"We have therefore concluded that the Respondent School District refused Koeller a contract in order to discourage membership and collective bargaining activities on behalf of the Welfare Committee of the MNEA."

In any event, it may be assumed arguendo that the school board would have been warranted in terminating Koeller's services on these grounds if the motivation for the action were not connected with his labor activities. Yet the WERB could reasonably find, as it did, that the motivation for failing to renew Koeller's contract was his activities in the MNEA and on behalf of his fellow teachers' welfare.

*Agency*

The WERB specifically found that Kreuser, Refling, Ussel, and Ladd were supervisory personnel in the employ of the Muskego-Norway school district. The WERB considered the actions of these supervisory personnel in determining whether unfair labor practices had been committed by the school board and the school district. The trial court ruled that there was nothing in the findings of the WERB or in the evidence to establish that these supervisory personnel were agents of the Muskego-Norway school board. Therefore, ruled the trial court, actions of the supervisory personnel could not be attributed to the board in determining whether unfair labor practices had been committed, and only actions by school board members could be considered.

The trial court's ruling places form over substance. Where the WERB expressly found that Kreuser, Refling, Ussel, and Ladd were "supervisory personnel in the employ of said School District," such employment is sufficient to constitute an agency relationship. The employment policies of the school district are implemented through the actions of the supervisory personnel. Under the trial court's ruling, the school board could tacitly engage in unfair labor practices through actions by the supervisory personnel, and the employees discriminated against would have no effective recourse. Such a technical interpretation — as made by the trial court — of the findings of the WERB deprives sec. 111.70 (3), Stats., of any real substance.

*By the Court.* — Judgment reversed.

HANSEN, J., took no part.

[The dissenting opinion of BEILFUSS, J., is omitted.]

## NOTES

1. Suppose there is evidence that the reason for an employee's termination was because of his or her union activities *and* one or more legitimate grounds. In Columbia County Board of Public Instruction v. PERC,——So.2d——, 4 FPER ¶ 4032 (Fla. Dist. Ct. App. 1977), the court enunciated the following test:

When there is proof before PERC that an impermissible motive was one of two or more factors in the employer's decision to terminate, the burden necessarily falls on the employer to adduce evidence that it would have reached the same decision without consideration of the protected activity. The United States Supreme Court recently adopted a similar rule for assessing the significance of an employee's First Amendment activity in a discharge decision. Mount Healthy City School District v. Doyle, 429 U.S. 274, 97 S. Ct. 568, 50 L.Ed.2d 471 (1977).

In *Mount Healthy,* a teacher was terminated because of (1) his statement to a radio station, and (2) his use of obscene gestures to students. In reversing the district court's holding that the teacher had to be reinstated since the teacher's exercise of his First Amendment rights played a part in his termination (*i.e.,* his statement to the radio station), the Court unanimously stated:

A rule of causation which focuses solely on whether protected conduct played a part, "substantial" or otherwise, in a decision not to rehire, could place an employee in a better position as a result of the exercise of constitutionally protected conduct than he would have occupied had he done nothing. The difficulty with the rule enunciated by the District Court is that it would require reinstatement in cases where a dramatic and perhaps abrasive incident is inevitably on the minds of those responsible for the decision to rehire, and does indeed play a part in that decision—even if the same decision would have been reached had the incident not occurred. The constitutional principle at stake is sufficiently vindicated if such an employee is placed in no worse a position than if he had not engaged in the conduct. A borderline or marginal candidate should not have the employment question resolved against him because of constitutionally protected conduct. But that same candidate ought not to be able, by engaging in such conduct, to prevent his employer from assessing his performance record and reaching a decision not to rehire on the basis of that record, simply because the protected conduct makes the employer more certain of the correctness of its decision.

. . . .

Initially, in this case, the burden was properly placed upon respondent to show that his conduct was constitutionally protected, and that this conduct was a "substantial factor"—or to put it in other words, that it was a "motivating factor" in the Board's decision not to rehire him. Respondent having carried that burden, however, the District Court should have gone on to determine whether the Board had shown by a

preponderance of the evidence that it would have reached the same decision as to
respondent's reemployment even in the absence of the protected conduct. 97 S. Ct. at
575, 576.

Would the Wisconsin Supreme Court have reached the same result in the principal case
if it had applied the rule enunciated by the Supreme Court in *Mount Healthy?*

2. In City of New Berlin, WERC Decision No. 7293 (1966), the Wisconsin Employment
Relations Commission in holding that an employee's termination was not motivated
because of union activities, stated:

> The most that Complainant can assert under the circumstances is that his selection
> for termination was arbitrary; but if the reason for discharge is not for an unlawful
> purpose prescribed [sic] by Section 111.70 (3) (a), this Board has no jurisdiction to
> remedy mere arbitrary action. . . .

*Accord,* Westport Transport Dist., Case No. MPP-3447 (Conn. SBLR 1977) (Board has
no jurisdiction to decide whether discharge is too severe in absence of proof action was
motivated by employee's union or protected activities).

3. The precedents established in the private sector under the National Labor Relations
Act have been repeatedly referred to by the various state boards and state courts, especially
where there is a parallel or analogous statutory provision involved. As the Connecticut
Supreme Court of Errors noted in Town of Windsor v. Windsor Police Dep't Employees
Ass'n, Inc. 154 Conn. 530, 227 A.2d 65 (1967), ". . . the judicial interpretation frequently
accorded the federal act is of great assistance and persuasive force in the interpretation
of our own act."

4. Normally a labor relations agency conducts an investigation to determine whether
an unfair labor practice charge has any merit. If the agency dismisses the charge, to what
extent can the individual seek judicial review of such a determination? Under the National
Labor Relations Act, the courts have uniformly held that the exercise of discretion by the
NLRB General Counsel in dismissing an unfair labor practice charge is not subject to
judicial review. *See, e.g.,* United Electric Contractors Ass'n v. Ordman, 366 F.2d 766 (2d
Cir. 1966) (per curiam), *cert. denied,* 385 U.S. 1026 (1967); Hourihan v. NLRB, 201 F.2d
187 (D.C. Cir. 1952), *cert. denied,* 345 U.S. 930 (1953).

## MIDDLESEX COUNTY ENGINEERING DEPARTMENT
## MASSACHUSETTS LABOR RELATIONS COMMISSION
### CASE NO. MUP-472 (1973)

[During an election campaign involving the seats of two of the three Middlesex
County Commissioners, two "reform" candidates, Tsongos and Ralph, promised
to reduce the size of the engineering department which had grown from 25-30
employees in 1962 to approximately 125 in 1972. After the reform candidates
had pledged to reduce the size of the engineering department, a union organizing
meeting was held and by September, 1972, approximately 90% of the
engineering department employees had signed union authorization cards. In
September a seven member union organizing committee was elected and the
names of the members were announced in mid-November. Tsongos and Ralph
were successful in defeating the two incumbent commissioners in the primary
election and were elected in the general election in November 1972. On
December 1, 1972, a petition was filed by the American Federation of State,
County and Municipal Employees (AFSCME) for certification of a bargaining unit
consisting of the employees in the engineering department. The petition was held
in abeyance pending the outcome of the instant proceeding.

After Tsongos and Ralph took their positions as county commissioners on
January 3, 1972, Commissioner Tsongos requested certain employees in the
engineering department to draw up lists of 50 employees that they would
recommend be retained. Data from the six lists that were received was compiled

by the staff aides for the two new commissioners. Based on these compilations, 46 employees were terminated on January 26, 1973. Of the seven-member union organizing committee, three were terminated (including the Chairman, Gino Porreca) and four were retained.

A prohibited practice charge was filed on February 27, 1973, alleging that the county commissioners interfered with and restrained

employees from the formation, organization and creation of an employee organization by terminating the employment, summarily, of all employees having been designated as members of the Negotiating Committee to represent the Engineering Department and others active in the formation and organization of the employee organization.

Following an investigation, the Massachusetts Labor Relations Commission on March 29, 1973, issued a complaint alleging "that all forty-six (46) employees involved were active in the formation of an employee organization" and that their "dismissal was an interference and restraint on the formation of said employee organization."

At the hearing the chairman of the local union organizing committee, Gino Porreca, characterized four of the six individuals who submitted lists as "anti-union," and that the remaining two "were friendly." This same witness testified that he was in charge of patronage for the two defeated commissioners and knew that employees came into the department under the sponsorship of a commissioner. He further testified that he was aware of the pledge made by Tsongos and Ralph to reduce the size of the engineering department.]

The Petitioner [Gino Porreca] avers that he and others were discharged for joining, assisting, and participating in lawful union activity. The Municipal Employer denies this, and says all were discharged in accordance with procedures for reducing the overall size of the Middlesex County Engineering Department.

. . . .

The question raised in the instant case is whether certain employees of the County Government of Middlesex County were discriminatorily terminated because of their activity on behalf of a labor organization. When a Municipal Employer violates individual rights guaranteed by *General Laws Chapter 149, Section 178 L* by terminating the employment of individuals for having engaged in protected activity, it is the responsibility of the Labor Relations Commission to remedy that violation and make whole the injured party by ordering his reinstatement, . . . and, in appropriate cases, awarding back pay. . . . Where, however, such motive is not established, this Commission will not substitute its judgment for the legitimate authority of the Employer. . . .

We begin, then, from the premise that, where an improper motive is not shown, the Commission cannot question the personnel policies and practices of a Municipal Employer. This rationale applies equally whether the employee is discharged, suspended or laid off. *Cf. McNeil v. Mayor and City Council of Peabody,* 297 Mass. 499 (1937), where the Court held that the purpose of the Civil Service legislation was to "protect public employees from partisan political control. . . . But it was not designed to prevent a city from undertaking in good faith a reorganization of a political department in order to promote effectiveness and economy."

The Seventh Circuit Court of Appeals stated the matter succinctly in interpreting sections 8 (a) (1) and (3), National Labor Relations Act, which General Laws Chapter 149, section 178 (L) closely parallels:

"The mere coincidence of the layoffs with the union activity, without more, is not substantially indicative of a discriminatory motive." *Beaver Valley*

*Canning Co. v. N.L.R.B.,* 332 F.2d 429 (7th Cir. 1964).

The burden is on the charging party to demonstrate by direct testimony or fair inference that the layoffs were improperly motivated. *N.L.R.B. v. Whitin Machine Works,* 264 F.2d 383 (1st Cir. 1953). The New York P.E.R.B. has similarly held "the charging party had to initially establish by a preponderance of the credible evidence that the respondent . . . was unlawfully motivated. It had to establish respondent's anti-charging party animus." *General School District No. 3, Town of Huntington and Babylon, Suffolk County and Half Hills Teachers Ass'n, Inc.,* 5 PERB ¶ 4515 (1972).

We find the reasoning of these and similar cases persuasive. To find a violation of General Laws Chapter 149 section 178 (L) the record must reveal more evidence from which the implication of discriminatory intent may fairly be drawn.

We note in this regard that the so-called "reform" slate had announced its intention of reducing staff size prior to the commencement of any union activity and that reduction of staff size was a major plank in the "reformers'" campaign platform. We therefore find that the decision to layoff was not discriminatively motivated, and unless we are to conclude that the layoff was carried out in a discriminatory manner, there was no violation of the Act.

The record does not support such a conclusion. Although three members of the union steering committee were laid off, four were retained. In the total staff reduction, the percentage of pro-union employees laid off does not appear to be disproportionate. The record does not disclose any substantial anti-union animus on the part of either the selection committee or the Commissioners. Mr. Porreca testified to his "feelings" that several members of the rating panel were against the union. Others, however, were in favor. At least one member of the panel had signed an authorization card. There is no credible evidence that any member of the rating panel was selected because of his anti-union bias, or that anti-union motives influenced the evaluations. Rather, the testimony indicates that if the members of the rating panel were influenced by any factor other than the ability of employees to perform their jobs, that factor was political partisanship. Such a claim, while not free from legal complexity, is potentially within the jurisdiction of this Commission.

Non-tenured public employees do not forfeit First and Fourteenth Amendment rights by the mere act of accepting such employment. While it has been held that a non-tenured public employee has no constitutionally protected right to his continued employment, *Bailey v. Richardson,* 182 F.2d 46 (D.C. Cir. 1950), *aff'd per curiam,* 341 U.S. 918 (1950), recent federal decisions indicate that such employees may not be discharged solely because of the exercise of First Amendment rights to freedom of speech and association. *Wiesmann v. Updegraff,* 348 U.S. 183 (1952); *Pickering v. Board of Education,* 391 U.S. 563; *Perry v. Sindermann,* 400 U.S. 593 (1972), and cases cited therein. Recently courts have been faced with the issue of whether a political partisan may be discharged from a non-tenured public position solely on the basis of past or present political affiliations. The circuits have divided on the issue. . . . *

. . . .

While the Labor Relations Commission is not, strictly speaking, empowered to decide constitutional questions, public employee labor relations is often inextricably intertwined with the political process. This Commission has

---

* Editors' Note: In *Elrod v. Burns, infra* p. 858, the Supreme Court held that public employees in non-policymaking positions could not be terminated solely because of their political affiliations.

recognized, for example, that the right of access to the press is a necessary and proper tool of both labor organizations and employers, in attempting to persuade and inform the public of their respective positions. See *Quincy School Committee and National Association of Government Employees,* MUPL-18 (4/25/72). We might, at some point, have to determine whether certain activity, such as petitioning a legislative body for passage or defeat of a measure, or even political activity on behalf of certain candidates constitutes protected activity within the meaning of the Statutes we are empowered to interpret and enforce. We refrain from further consideration of arguably constitutional questions, however, since we are satisfied that, on the record in this case, they are not properly raised. Despite being given every opportunity to do so, neither party herein has argued that the discharges were in any way politically motivated. That the parties could mutually agree on this point strains our credulity, but the charging parties are bound by their testimony on the record specifically denying that the discharges were purely political in the pejorative sense.

. . . .

Since it has been determined previously that the layoff of the employees involved was not related to their belated organizational efforts on behalf of a union, the complaint should be, and hereby is, DISMISSED.

## NOTE

*Accord,* City of Philadelphia and Register of Wills, Case No. R-7189-E (Pa. PLRB 1977) (termination of employees for political reasons did not violate act where not motivated by anti-union animus).

## TOWN OF DEDHAM v. LABOR RELATIONS COMMISSION

Supreme Judicial Court of Massachusetts
365 Mass. 392, 312 N.E.2d 548 (1974)

KAPLAN, Justice.

We face again the problem of meshing the new labor rights guaranteed to public employees with earlier provisions of law. On the present appeal we have to deal with an accommodation between the statute empowering the Labor Relations Commission to rectify alleged interference by municipal employers with the protected mutual-aid activities of their employees, and the older statute establishing the Civil Service Commission as a guard against arbitrary disciplining of classified employees by their public employers. The field is dynamic. . . .

1. *Facts.* On September 9, 1970, Warren W. Vaughan, a Dedham firefighter, one of the interveners-appellants herein, engaged in a "heated conversation" with the deputy chief of the fire department, James Hall, at the Dedham fire station. On September 14 the chief of department, John L. O'Brien, one of the appellees, notified Vaughan that commencing that day he was suspended for five days with loss of pay for "insubordination" toward a superior officer arising out of the incident with Deputy Chief Hall.

On September 23 Vaughan requested a hearing before a member of the Civil Service Commission pursuant to G.L. c. 31, § 43(e), as to whether the suspension was for "just cause." A week later, on September 30, Vaughan filed a complaint with the Labor Relations Commission charging a prohibited labor practice on the part of the appellees town of Dedham and its fire chief within the meaning of c. 149, § 178L(1), in that they had violated his protected rights under

§ 178H(1) to engage in activities on behalf of the firefighters for mutual aid free from interference, restraint, or coercion.

A Civil Service Commissioner held a hearing on October 20 attended by Vaughan and counsel, and on January 13, 1971, the Civil Service Commission notified the fire chief that the suspension was justified but that the penalty should be reduced to a two-day suspension with loss of pay. The present record on appeal does not indicate what issues were considered, nor are any particular findings set out. Meanwhile the Labor Relations Commission, after investigation by its agents, issued its formal complaint on November 5, 1970, against the town and fire chief. At a hearing on January 5, 1971, before a Labor Relations Commissioner, the town and fire chief moved to dismiss the complaint on the ground that the commission lacked jurisdiction of the subject matter. The motion was not allowed. Testimony was taken and recorded, and the following facts as to the September 9 incident appeared, embodied in the "Findings of Fact and Decision" of the commission, made part of its "Decision and Order" contained in the record on appeal.

Vaughan was a member of the executive board and past president of Local 1735, Dedham Firefighters Association. He was off duty on September 9, when he got into the "heated conversation" with Deputy Chief Hall in the presence of another firefighter. The subject was the duties to be performed by firefighters on holidays (such as Labor Day just passed). Vaughan objected to the men's being assigned window washing and similar chores and said this was in violation of the practice of "holiday routine" by which the men were to be excused certain maintenance jobs. Deputy Chief Hall refused to discuss this issue on the ground that "Vaughan was not running the Department." Vaughan told the deputy chief that he was going to bring the matter up at the next union meeting. He advised the men not to do work on holidays in the future beyond the "holiday routine." He then left the fire station.

On evidence going beyond the immediate incident, the Labor Relations Commission also found that Vaughan had an excellent record as a firefighter. In processing grievances and negotiating on labor matters over the previous two years, he had had many heated discussions with the fire chief. Examining the circumstances surrounding the fire chief's decision to suspend Vaughan, the commission found that the chief had ordered the suspension for other than disciplinary reasons. It may be added that the commission found there had in fact been a right to a "holiday routine" which had become vested by practice over a period of years despite "rules and regulations" promulgated by the fire chief.

On the whole case, the commission concluded that the formal complaint it had issued was supported by the testimony. Accordingly, it issued its order in two parts: first, that the appellees, town of Dedham and its fire chief, cease and desist from interfering with their employees in the exercise of their protected rights under the statute; second, that they take affirmative action to "reinstate" Vaughan and make him whole by payment of the withheld salary, make available on request the records as to back pay, post a notice announcing their intention to comply with the directions to cease and desist and to reinstate, and notify the commission as to steps taken to comply with the order.

The appellees petitioned the Superior Court under the State Administrative Procedure Act, G.L. c. 30A, § 14, for review of the decision and order of the Labor Relations Commission. Although the pleader recited all plausible grounds of review listed in § 14(8), the two distinctive grounds that appear pertinent were lack of jurisdiction of the Labor Relations Commission, and lack of substantial evidence to support the decision. The judge of the Superior Court held for the appellees on the first ground, ruling that the matter was beyond the jurisdiction of the Labor Relations Commission and "fell exclusively within the jurisdiction of the Civil Service Commission" under c. 31, § 43; thus the appellees' motion to dismiss should have been allowed, and the commission's prohibited practice complaint was now to be dismissed. The judge rested essentially on c. 149, § 178N, which states that "[n]othing in sections one hundred and seventy-eight F to one hundred and seventy-eight M, inclusive [the sections of c. 149 setting forth the rights and duties of municipal employees, and the relevant responsibilities of the Labor Relations Commission], shall diminish the authority and power of the civil service commission, or any retirement board or personnel board established by law, nor shall anything in said sections constitute a grant of the right to strike to employees of any municipal employer." The judge did not reach the question of substantial evidence. Appeal from the final decree was claimed by the Labor Relations Commission and the interveners, Vaughan and Local 1735.

2. *Statutes.* Until 1958, public employees in the Commonwealth, as in most States, had virtually none of the rights that had been widely guaranteed since the nineteen thirties to employees in private business to organize and bargain collectively and to be protected in the associated activities of asserting and negotiating grievances. Classified public employees were indeed entitled to the benefits of a civil service system, designed, according to the "merit principle," to bring nonpartisanship and rationality into the processes of hiring, promotion, transfer, and discipline. These employees were protected against arbitrary punishment, the usual issues being whether the charges made by the public authority as grounds for dismissals or suspensions — neglect of duty, incompetency, insubordination, venality, or the like — could be supported in fact. The question whether the charges were being used by the employers as excuses or masks for interference with the employees' rights to organize, present grievances, and so forth, had no particular place in proceedings before the Civil Service Commission because the rights themselves had not received recognition by law.

The civil service statute to this day does not in terms reflect labor rights of this character. Dismissal or suspension may be exacted only for "just cause," see G.L. c. 31, § 43, a formula that is not less than seventy years old. The pattern of the procedure now is that the employee receives written notice from the "appointing authority" of the reason for its action, whereupon the employee may request a hearing by that authority; if the decision is unfavorable, he may request a hearing before a member of the Civil Service Commission, who reports his findings to the commission, which acts to affirm, reverse, or modify. From an adverse determination, the employee may petition for review by a District Court (or the Municipal Court of the City of Boston), with the appointing authority and the commission named as respondents. § 45.

Turning to the origin of the labor statute, the traditional hostility to organizational rights on the part of public employees gradually diminished in the postwar period, and in 1958 Massachusetts was among the first States to take steps — but they were quite ineffectual steps — to afford a measure of recognition to those rights. See St.1958, c. 460, adding G.L. c. 149, § 178D. The Presidential Executive Order of 1962 (No. 10988, 5 U.S.C.A. § 7301 at 300 [1967], replaced by No. 11491 [1969], as amended, 3 C.F.R. 262 [1973]) granting rights of collective bargaining to Federal employees added to the respectability and impetus of the movement, and by 1965 there had been much growth of unionization among public employees. 1971 Ann.Surv. of Mass.Law, §§ 6.1, 6.2.

Legislation of 1964 and 1965 provided a fairly comprehensive code of collective bargaining law, both substantive and procedural, for the benefit of State and municipal employees, and it is this code which applied at the time of the events in suit and with which we are here concerned. St. 1964, c. 637, adding c. 149, § 178F. St. 1965, c. 763, adding c. 149, §§ 178G-178N.

All municipal employees are embraced in the 1965 code, "whether or not in the classified service of the municipal employer," except elected officials and certain others. § 178G. Passing over the rather elaborate provisions directed to the process of collective bargaining itself (§§ 178I-178K), § 178H(1) states the basic rights of employees to self-organization and to engage in the various ancillary concerted activities. By § 178L, first paragraph, municipal employers are prohibited from interfering with those guaranteed rights (subdivision [1]), and from committing certain acts more particularly enumerated, such as "refusing to discuss grievances with the representatives of an employee organization recognized or designated as the exclusive representative in an appropriate unit" (subdivision [5]). Certain prohibitions are also laid on employee organizations (second paragraph). When complaint is made to the Labor Relations Commission that a prohibited practice has been committed, the commission may dismiss, or order a hearing, or an investigation to be followed by hearing, which may be conducted before the commission itself or by a member of the commission. The proceeding is then in the name of the commission against the allegedly offending municipal employer, employee, or other person, who may appear to defend; others, including the original complainant, may be admitted as interveners. A transcript of the testimony is taken. There is a right of review from the Commissioner to the commission, which may receive further testimony. If, on all the proof, the commission finds that a prohibited practice has occurred, it makes findings of fact and issues an order against the offender to cease and desist and to take such affirmative action as will comply with the provisions of § 178L, including an order for "reinstatement with or without back pay of an employee discharged or discriminated against" in violation of the first paragraph. Review of an order of the commission, available to any party aggrieved, may be had by petition to the Superior Court under the State Administrative Procedure Act, c. 30A, § 14. Section 178N contains the saving clause, quoted above, relating to the Civil Service Commission and other agencies. (As noted, material changes are brought into the scheme by legislation effective July 1, 1974.)

3. *Discussion.* The Legislature's attempt to solve the whole problem of the interrelation of the labor statute with the civil service law by the general saving clause of § 178N "invites litigation," as we said of a similar facile effort in Mathewson v. Contributory Retirement Appeal Bd., 335 Mass. 610, 614, 141 N.E.2d 522 (1957). As elsewhere in the field of labor law, "it ... [becomes] the task of the courts to accommodate, to reconcile the older statutes with the more recent ones." Boys Mkts., Inc. v. Retail Clerks Union, Local 770, 398 U.S. 235, 251, 90 S.Ct. 1583, 1593, 26 L.Ed.2d 199 (1970).

The judge below read § 178N to mean that upon a complaint by a municipal civil service employee under c. 31, § 43, that there was not just cause for his suspension (or dismissal) on the ground of alleged "insubordination," the matter was to be handled exclusively by the Civil Service Commission and the Labor Relations Commission was wholly excluded and without jurisdiction to take any action; just as such a case would be handled solely by the Civil Service Commission before the creation of the Labor Relations Commission, so, according to the judge, it must be handled now.

This seems to us not a reasonable accommodation. Neither § 178N nor any other statutory provision purports to confer "exclusive" jurisdiction on either commission. Such routing of cases involving municipal employees under civil service solely through the Civil Service Commission, while cases of municipal employees not under civil service alleging prohibited practices could move only through the Labor Relations Commission, would result in distortions and disregard of enacted law that would call in question any supposed legislative purpose to create that kind of dual system.

If the Civil Service Commission were to administer in such cases only the substantive law which it has historically fashioned under the title of "just cause," and no recourse could be had there or before the Labor Relations Commission to the new labor statute in its material aspects, then a plain perversion of the legislative purpose would occur and a gulf would be created between the treatment of classified and nonclassified municipal employees that could not be justified in policy or logic. The opinion below does not disavow this result.

But if it be suggested that the Civil Service Commission should attempt in those cases to apply the labor law as well, with the Labor Relations Commission wholly excluded — a suggestion made by the appellees in their brief, although with little elaboration — then there would still be a plain defiance of the definitional clause of § 178G, already quoted, joining together classified and nonclassified employees for the purposes, procedural and substantive, of the labor statute.

Employees of both classes (and their employers as well) are entitled to the specialized services of the Labor Relations Commission in the administration of the labor rights, and to the related adjective arrangements. Considering the indissoluble linkage of the character of a tribunal, its procedure, and the substantive law that it enforces, it seems clear that the parties before the Civil Service Commission would not — and in the nature of things could not — secure from that body alone substantive rights equivalent to those assigned by the statute for enforcement to the other commission. So the idea of using the Civil Service Commission to act as a substitute for the Labor Relations Commission in cases involving employees in the civil service would turn out to be quite unsatisfactory. It must, after all, have been a prime legislative purpose in creating the Labor Relations Commission to promote uniformity rather than disuniformity of interpretation and application of the labor law. In this light we need hardly point out that "cease and desist" and "affirmative" remedies, not only available but required in certain cases under the labor statute, could in no event attach to determinations by the Civil Service Commission, and that the nature and course of judicial review of orders of the Civil Service Commission depart from those prescribed for review of orders of the Labor Relations Commission.

In our view, the statutes can be read "so as to constitute a harmonious whole" (Mathewson v. Contributory Retirement Appeal Bd., *supra,* 335 Mass. at 614, 141 N.E.2d at 525) by attributing to the Legislature certain commonsense general purposes. There was a legislative design to introduce new substantive law as to the rights of municipal employees which must in ultimate effect impinge on the traditional "just cause" formula. The Civil Service Commission was to remain concerned with the functions and with protection of the interests with which it had long been associated, while the Labor Relations Commission was to be engaged in the new tasks and protection of the new interests. But neither agency should be oblivious of the actions of the other. It could follow that some marginal litigious events — relatively few in comparison with the bulk — might have to be handled by both agencies. With mutual restraint, aided by cooperation of those representing employees and employers, the two agencies could reach a fair adjustment, and the precept of § 178N would be reasonably satisfied.[18]

Preliminarily we observe that it was open to the Legislature in writing the new law to prescribe, as a ground for examining, and in proper cases overturning disciplinary action by a municipal employer (as well as for securing independent relief against it), that it had engaged in a prohibited practice. This the Legislature did by means of §§ 178H and 178L. Though the new law can be thought of as amending or affecting the civil service law, with its traditional reading of "just cause," it did not exceed legislative power, or in itself qualify the policy of § 178N. . . .

Nor is § 178N abused when functional lines are respected within reason in the conduct of particular dismissal or suspension cases. The present case was evidently conducted on all sides without forethought as to the optimum procedure to be used, but the functional idea may still be followed to a solution. Although the charge before the Civil Service Commission was "insubordination," it was not improbable that the question of anti-union bias might come up in the unfolding of the facts as possibly qualifying or negating the charge. The record, however, does not disclose that the question did come up; if it did, there is no indication of what attention it actually received. In this situation, it would be strange indeed to say that the Labor Relations Commission lacked "jurisdiction" to proceed with an inquiry into anti-union bias upon a complaint before it charging a prohibited practice. This consideration is enough to dispose of the present appeal.

We think we should go on to say that, had the Civil Service Commission examined into the motivation of the suspension as a phase of the question whether the employee was in fact insubordinate, and had it ruled against the employee, then the Labor Relations Commission, in comity, could properly take the ruling of the other agency into account as support for a determination to dismiss the employee's concurrent complaint charging a prohibited practice. But the Labor Relations Commission would not be deprived of "jurisdiction," and if not satisfied that the question of anti-union bias had been sufficiently explored, could decline to dismiss, issue its own complaint, and proceed to prosecute and later grant relief which might comprehend "reinstatement" and more.[20]

Whether the Labor Relations Commission, acting within its "jurisdiction" in the present case, reached the right decision in substance, can be tested when the cause is remanded to the Superior Court and the employers' petition for review under the State Administrative Procedure Act is proceeded with there. If the employers succeed, the suspension stands, and no offence is given to § 178N. It is very unlikely that there can be any such offence if the employers fail and the employee's suspension is wiped out by an order for "reinstatement." This follows from two added considerations. An employer's commission of a prohibited practice usually, if not always, so far pervades and dominates a case as to call for revoking the discipline ordered by the employer even if the employee could

---

[18] To make anything turn on whether one agency has some priority in time over the other would be without support in the statutes and might encourage regrettable competitive races between the agencies.

[20] Analogy can be found in the attitude of deference that may be taken by the National Labor Relations Board toward certain arbitral decisions, although it does not yield ultimate jurisdiction. See The Developing Labor Law, 488-495 (A.B.A., Section of Labor Relations Law, ed. Morris, 1971); Yourga Trucking, Inc., 197 N.L.R.B. No. 130, 80 L.R.R.M. 1498 (1972). Cf. n. 23 below.

otherwise be properly called insubordinate (and other relief, negative and affirmative, would then also be in order). The "insubordination" that was found is not negated but may be taken to be outweighed. Second, the Labor Relations Commission operates on a basis different from that of the Civil Service Commission. The latter agency vindicates a private right of the complaining employee (although of course the right is given in part to serve a public purpose). The former agency, although stirred to action by a private complaint, acts when it chooses to do so in its own name as a public prosecutor to test a public right, with the possible remedy not limited to the grievance of the particular employee.[22]

In retrospect, considering the apparent seriousness with which the prohibited practice charge was here being pressed, one imagines that it would have been advantageous to hold the civil service proceeding in abeyance by consent or otherwise while the Labor Relations Commission acted. A finding of prohibited practice against the municipal employer would likely have ended the matter (subject to review in the Superior Court on the employer's petition); a finding by the commission for the employer on that charge (or reversal of a contrary finding on review) would leave the employee with his § 43 route to protest that he was not "insubordinate."

We have, of course, been speaking of the rare cases with potentialities of conflict between the agencies. The much larger number will fall to one or the other as a matter of routine. In the present situation, indeed, the employee might well have applied only to the Labor Relations Commission. On a favorable decision there, he would be reinstated, and this would not interfere in any way with the Civil Service Commission, which would not have been applied to. Otherwise the suspension would stand.

While some awkwardness must be felt in those few cases where a single episode may be twice examined at the administrative level, there is in fact considerable precedent for giving the employee more than one string to his bow. Thus in the recent case of Alexander v. Gardner-Denver Co., 415 U.S. 36, 94 S.Ct. 1011, 39 L.Ed.2d 147 the Supreme Court held that the employee could maintain an action under Title VII of the Civil Rights Act of 1964, 42 U.S.C. § 2000e et seq. (1970), for a discharge based on alleged racial discrimination, although he had failed in a previous arbitration under the collective bargaining agreement with his employer where he (with his union) had charged the same wrongful discrimination. Justice Powell observed that "legislative enactments in this area have long evinced a general intent to accord parallel or overlapping remedies against discrimination." Id. at 47, 94 S.Ct. at 1019. Where our statutes allow alternative remedies or avenues of relief there is perhaps less anomaly, because as we have seen the interests protected are not the same, and in the one case it is the individual, in the other an agency of the Commonwealth, that seeks vindication of the interest.[23]

---

[22] This difference in the operations of the agencies is among the reasons why an employee's application to either agency should not be considered an "election" against or a "waiver" of resort to the other. So also it is immaterial that the employee here did not attempt judicial review of the determination of the Civil Service Commission (which, according to the judge below, the employee thought to be a futile course). See n. 23 below.

[23] Justice Powell's opinion in the *Alexander* case will be found rich in suggestion about the nonapplicability of "election" and "waiver" (415 U.S. at 49-54, 94 S.Ct. 1011 (1974) [42 U.S.L. Week at 4218-4219] and about a court's possible deference to or acceptance of findings made by the arbitrator (415 U.S. at 55-60, 94 S.Ct. 1011 (1974) [42 U.S.L. Week at 4220-4221]).

4. *Conclusion.* The decree appealed from, dismissing the proceeding before the Labor Relations Commission for lack of jurisdiction, is reversed, and the cause is remanded to the Superior Court for further proceedings consistent with this opinion.

## NOTES

1. In Hinfey v. Matawan Regional Board of Education, 77 N.J. 514, — A.2d — (1978), the New Jersey Supreme Court held that where concurrent administrative jurisdiction exists, it is the responsibility of both agencies to make a comparative analysis of their respective statutes and determine which agency is best equipped to resolve a particular dispute.

2. The New Hampshire Public Employee Bargaining Law provides that "[t]he board shall have primary jurisdiction of all violations . . ., but no complaints may be filed with the board for violation of [the equivalent of §§ 8(a)(3) and (4) of the NLRA] until the complainant has exhausted the administrative remedies provided by statutes other than this chapter." N.H. Rev. Stat. Ann. § 273-A:6 (1976).

# Chapter 3

# ESTABLISHMENT OF THE COLLECTIVE BARGAINING RELATIONSHIP

## A. QUALIFICATION OF THE PROPOSED BARGAINING REPRESENTATIVE

Most of the state labor relations acts provide that labor organizations can file representation petitions seeking to represent employees in an appropriate unit. A preliminary question is occasionally raised as to whether a given organization or group constitutes a "labor organization" or "employee organization" within the meaning of the act. Many of the acts contain the definition of labor organization that is set forth in section 2(5) of the National Labor Relations Act:

> The term "labor organization" means any organization of any kind, or any agency or employee representation committee or plan, in which employees participate and which exists for the purpose, *in whole or in part,* of dealing with employers concerning grievances, labor disputes, wages, rates of pay, hours of employment, or conditions of work. 29 U.S.C. § 152(5) (1970) (emphasis added).

This definition has been given an expansive interpretation. Thus, an organization that has as one of its purposes negotiations with an employer is a labor organization even though it has no written constitution or by-laws, its officers do not serve for a specified period of time, and it is funded by voluntary contributions. Yale University, 184 N.L.R.B. 860 (1970). Moreover, the Supreme Court has held that an organization that deals with an employer concerning grievances is a labor organization within the meaning of the act, even though it does not negotiate collective agreements with the employer in the usual sense. NLRB v. Cabot Carbon Co., 360 U.S. 203 (1959). Social clubs and "flower" committees have also been held to be labor organizations if they serve as the medium for the presentation of employee recommendations and grievances to the employer. NLRB v. Precision Castings Co., 130 F.2d 639 (6th Cir. 1942).

Where the state act's definition of the term "labor organization" parallels the definition found in the National Labor Relations Act, the term has likewise been interpreted liberally. For example, in Wayne County Board of Supervisors, 1965-1966 MERC Lab. Op. 320 (Mich.), the Michigan Employment Relations Commission held that a bar association was a labor organization even though its by-laws did not list collective bargaining as one of the purposes of the organization. And in Wayne State University, 1969 MERC Lab. Op. 670 (Mich.), the MERC held that an organization composed entirely of students was a "labor organization," rejecting the contention that such an organization "would not have the permanence, experience, or strength necessary to constitute" a labor organization within the meaning of the Michigan Act.

In contrast to the NLRA-type definition, the New York Taylor Law, as well as several other state statutes, defines the term "labor organization" or "employee organization" to mean "an organization of any kind having as its primary purpose the improvement of terms and conditions of public employees. . . ." N.Y. Civ. Serv. Law § 201(5) (McKinney Supp. 1971). In view of this definition, it was contended that an organization whose membership included both public employees and private employees was not an "employee organization." The New

York PERB refused to accept this interpretation. City of Ogdensburg, 1 PERB ¶ 414 (N.Y. 1968). Joseph Crowley, a member of the New York PERB, explained the Board's position as follows:

> In those situations where the employee organization does admit to membership both public and private employees, it has been held that if the public employee members of the organization select their own negotiating committee and, without participation by private sector members, ratify negotiation agreements, the organization is an employee organization within the meaning of section 201(5). The reasoning of the Board is that the public employees who are responsible for the conduct of the negotiations would, therefore, not be submerged in an organizational structure dominated by private sector employees. Hence, where the independence of action of public employee members involved is protected, such organizations have been found to be within the purview of section 201(5) of the Law.

Crowley, *The Resolution of Representation Status Disputes Under the Taylor Law,* 37 FORDHAM L. REV. 517, 529-30 (1969).

In State of New York (State University of New York), 2 PERB ¶ 3070 (N.Y. 1969), the New York PERB held that a faculty senate was an "employee organization" for purposes of the Taylor Law, agreeing with the following conclusion of its director of representation (2 PERB ¶ 2010):

> The record makes it clear that the senate, in its role as faculty governor, has represented the faculty position with regard to economic goals as well as a number of matters of educational concern, such as admissions policies, faculty hiring, promotion and tenure procedures, curriculum, and class size. It is equally clear that many of these matters would constitute, to some degree, negotiable terms and conditions of faculty employment. Moreover, the "purpose" clause of the senate's constitution was revised in late 1968 to specifically mandate the senate to work to improve the terms and conditions of employment of all members of the professional staff. Clearly then, there is no basis in fact for finding that the senate's "primary purpose" is other than the improvement of terms and conditions of employment. Therefore, I find that the senate satisfies the statutory definition of an "employee organization."

## CONNECTICUT STATE BOARD OF LABOR RELATIONS, TWENTY-FIRST ANNUAL REPORT 8-9 (1967)

The Act defines this term ["employee organization"] as meaning "any lawful association, labor organization, federation or council having as a primary purpose the improvement of wages, hours and other conditions of employment among employees of municipal employers." . . .

In two cases where employee associations met this primary purpose requirement, they were challenged on the ground that supervisors, excluded from the unit by the Act, were active members and officers of the association. The Board, following decisions by the federal courts, the National Labor Relations Board, and the New York State Labor Relations Board, ruled that such membership rendered the organization ineligible to be a bargaining representative of municipal employees under the Act. Such membership "inevitably conflicts with the policy of the Act 'to insulate employees' jobs from their organizational rights.' " Local 636, United Association of Journeymen, etc. v. NLRB, 287 F.2d 354, 362 (D.C. Cir. 1961). Therefore the Board concluded:

"These decisions did not, of course, involve thé Connecticut statute which we must construe and administer. They were, however, made under statutes which were similar to ours in forbidding domination or interference by the employer in the associations which are to represent the employees. And we find the federal and New York decisions persuasive that the policies underlying this prohibition are violated when supervisory personnel excluded from the bargaining unit are allowed to become active voting members of the association; and more clearly violated when such supervisors became officers of the association.

"The next question is whether an association which permits such supervisors to be active members or officers is a 'lawful association' within Section 1(3) of our Act. The giving of such permission is not made a prohibited practice on the part of an employee organization under Section 4(b) of the Act, nor is it unlawful in the sense that it will subject the association to criminal penalties, but this is not, we feel, dispositive of the question. We believe that the legislature used the words 'lawful association' in this connection to mean broadly an association which is so constituted and organized that it is fully capable of serving the law's policy to have a disinterested and independent bargaining representative for employee units which want representation. And we find that an association which acquiesces in or permits voting membership or office-holding by supervisors excluded from the bargaining unit is thereby acquiescing in a practice which is prohibited because it tends to subvert the policies of the Act and render the association incapable of fulfilling the law's policies. This prevents it from being a 'lawful association' within the meaning and purposes of this provision." City of Stamford (Public Works Department), Dec. No. 682, April 1, 1966; City of Hartford, Dec. No. 681, April 6, 1966.

## CITY OF MILWAUKEE

Wisconsin Employment Relations Commission
Decision No. 6960 (1964)

### Effect of Supervisory Employes as Members of Employe Organization

The Board is confronted herein with a problem as to whether it should permit an employe organization to be on a ballot in an election proceeding which organization has a substantial number of supervisors among its membership. In *Joint School District No. 1 of the City of West Allis, etc.*,[5] the Board stated:

"The fact that supervisory personnel are members of, or any hold office in, any labor organization subject to the provision of Section 111.70 may raise a suspicion, but does not in itself establish domination or interference with the organization by the Municipal Employer employing such supervisory personnel. The number of supervisors among the members of the organization and the ratio of supervisors to other members are factors to be evaluated in each case. Likewise, the office held by supervisors and the extent to which they formulate the bargaining policy and programs of their labor organizations will also be scrutinized in each case."

In said case the issue of participation by supervisors, as members, in a labor organization was raised in a prohibitive practice proceeding before the Board and not in a representation case. The function of the Board in a representation

---

[5] Decision No. 6544.

proceeding is to determine whether or not a question of representation exists, to take evidence with respect to the appropriate collective bargaining unit and with respect to the employes eligible to participate in the election if one is ordered by the Board. It is now our opinion that the Board should not, in a representation proceeding, question the internal affairs of an organization, which the Board is satisfied exists for the purpose of representing municipal employes in conferences and negotiations with municipal employers on matters pertaining to wages, hours and conditions of employment. Therefore, in a representation proceeding, we do not believe that we should impose conditions on any organization seeking to represent municipal employes, which conditions would limit the right of such organizations to establish rules for the acquisition, retention and rejection of membership. To do so in a representation proceeding would impinge on the voluntary nature of such organizations. If the rules of such an organization permit supervisors to membership and/or exclude classes of employes from membership, the employes involved have a right to refuse to become members thereof, and if said organization is seeking to represent the employes in an election proceeding before this Board, the employes can vote to reject such organization as their collective bargaining representative. If it can be established, in a prohibitive practice proceeding, that any labor organization which has been selected as the collective bargaining representative of municipal employes in an election conducted by the Board, that the rules and regulations of such an organization interfere with the rights of employes under Section 111.70 or that supervisory employes have dominated that organization and thus interfered with the rights granted to the employes, we will, among other remedies, set aside the certification.

We have held that supervisory employes should be barred from the collective bargaining unit since we do not consider them to be employes within the meaning of Section 111.70. Since supervisors are not employes within the meaning of the Statute then they should not participate in the activities of an employe organization concerned with wages, hours and conditions of employment.

As noted previously herein, the inclusion of supervisors in the same bargaining unit with employes would create a conflict of interest since supervisors are agents of the municipal employer. Where supervisory employes are members of the rank and file employe organization, the fact that they are not included in the appropriate collective bargaining unit would not eliminate the possible conflict of interest above noted. Supervisors who are members of an employe organization, with rights and privileges extended to employe members, could exercise a voice and vote in the administration and in the deliberations of the affairs of that employe organization. Their membership in the employe organization would permit them to run for office, to nominate candidates for office, to vote on candidates for office, to act on committees meeting in conferences and negotiations with the municipal employer on questions concerning hours, wages and conditions of employment and to vote and participate in such matters. By such membership they could actively exercise an interest in conflict with that of the employes and thereby dominate or interfere with the internal affairs of the employe organization. The active participation by supervisory employes in the affairs of an employe organization could result in impeding and defeating the primary purpose of the employe organization — that of representing municipal employes in conferences and negotiations concerning their wages, hours and conditions of employment. Since supervisors are the agents of the municipal employer, a municipal employer, by permitting supervisory employes to participate actively, in any manner similar to that described above, in the affairs of an organization representing employes for the purposes set forth in Section 111.70, could, in the proper proceedings, be found to have committed prohibitive practices by interfering, restraining and coercing its employes in the exercise of their rights granted to them under the law. As previously noted in this case, the president of the Association and two members of its Board of Directors have been found to be supervisors by the Board. Whether the activities of supervisors as members of a labor organization constitute prohibitive practices under Section 111.70 will be determined by the Board in formal complaint proceedings before the Board and by the facts established in each case.

### Effect of Limiting Membership to Certain Employes

As noted above, during the hearings in the matter, a question arose as to whether or not the Board would consider the Association as a qualified labor organization under Section 111.70 since it admitted to membership only registered engineers and architects, or those who had obtained a degree in their respective fields. The Board has found the unit appropriate here not only to include certain classifications of engineers and architects, but also the Engineering Technician IV, V and VI classifications, the incumbents of which, although not degreed or registered, are performing duties identical to various degreed or registered employes employed in the engineering and architectural classifications.

Section 111.70(2) confers upon municipal employes the right to affiliate with employe organizations of their own choosing. In our view this provision does not limit employe organizations from adopting reasonable rules for the acquisition, retention or rejection of membership. As noted above, we have indicated that we will not, in a representation proceeding, prescribe or review the rules governing the internal affairs of labor organizations representing municipal employes and, therefore, the fact that the Association's constitution and by-laws do not provide membership for non-degreed or non-registered employes does not affect the right of the Association to appear on the ballot in this election proceeding. Any labor organization selected by a majority of employes in an appropriate collective bargaining unit has the duty and obligation to represent all of the employes in the bargaining unit with equal vigor, whether members of the organization or not. If any labor organization certified by the Board as the exclusive bargaining representative for employes in an appropriate unit fails in that duty and obligation, the Board can, in a proper proceeding, vacate its certification and eliminate the right of such organization to continue as the exclusive collective bargaining representative of said employes. . . .

### NOTES

1. The New York PERB in State of New York (State University of New York), 2 PERB ¶ 3070 (N.Y. 1969), held that questions of employer domination should be handled in a prohibited practice proceeding "separate and apart from a representation proceeding."

2. The NLRB considers the effect of supervisory membership on labor organization status in representation proceedings. *See, e.g.,* International Paper Co., 172 N.L.R.B. 933 (1968).

## TOWN OF HUNTINGTON

New York Public Employment Relations Board
1 PERB ¶ 399.96 (1968)

This is an appeal from part of a decision by the Director of Representation in this proceeding dated October 11, 1968.

The Director in his decision determined the units he deemed to be appropriate; however, he stayed further proceedings to certification on the ground that one of the intervenors, Local 342, Long Island Public Service Employees, United Marine Division, National Maritime Union, AFL-CIO (NMU), the appellant herein, has a charge pending against it, alleging a violation of § 210.1 of the Public Employees' Fair Employment Act (Act).

Appellant appeals from this portion of the Director's decision staying the representation proceedings.

This representation proceeding was commenced by the filing of a petition on May 24, 1968. Appellant intervened in this proceeding.

While this proceeding was pending, the Counsel to this Board filed a charge alleging that appellant violated § 210.1 of the Act [2] in that "it caused, instigated, encouraged, condoned and engaged in a strike by certain employes of the Town of Huntington."

The Director reasoned that if this were sustained it ". . . may cause the Board to look behind the NMU's no strike affirmation and conclude that it was a sham." The Director concluded that, "In that event, the NMU would not be permitted to participate in any further proceedings leading to certification." The Director therefore stayed this representation proceeding pending a decision on the charge of violation of § 210.1.

The thrust of appellant's contention on this appeal is that this Board and *a fortiori* the Director of Representation lack the power to deny an employee organization participation in representation proceedings on this ground, or even to inquire into the good faith of an employee organization in making the "no strike" affirmation required by § 207.3(b) of the Act.

We modify the decision of the director insofar as he stayed the proceedings herein and direct him to proceed with the certification process in accordance with § 201.6 of the Rules of Procedure of this Board. However, we do, for the reasons set forth below, reserve the right to inquire, upon reasonable grounds, into the good faith of the "no strike" affirmation made by any employee organization prior to its being certified.

The Legislature, in enacting the Act, granted to public employees in this state rights which are unparalleled in this nation — the right to form, join and participate in any employee organization; the right to be represented by employee organizations to negotiate terms and conditions of employment. The Legislature provided procedures for the resolution of disputes concerning representation status. The obvious purpose of these procedures was not only to provide a reasonable and peaceful means of resolving disputes between competing employee organizations but also to assure public employees that they may select employee organizations of their own choosing.

---

[2] § 210.1. "No public employee or employee organization shall engage in a strike, and no employee organization shall cause, instigate, encourage or condone a strike."

However, the Legislature, not unmindful that strikes by public employees are prohibited, provided that this Board may not certify an employee organization until such organization has provided an affirmation that it does not assert the right to strike against any government.

What was the purpose of this legislative mandate? The appellant in its brief sets forth a most adequate answer. Appellant states, "The affirmation is simply a formal renunciation of the right to strike or to assist or participate in a strike against a public employer." If this be the purpose of this legislative requirement, and we would concur, then a formal renunciation of the right to strike would seem to require that the entity making such a renunciation has a sense of purpose to act in accord with such a renunciation and to strive to observe the affirmation. Clearly the Legislature did not intend that such affirmation be simply a meaningless recitation or an affirmation without substance or obligation. Simply put, no one would attribute to the Legislature that its enactment in whole or in part was designed to be an exercise in futility. Rather, logic requires us to assume that the Legislature intended this affirmation to be precisely as characterized by appellant, a "formal renunciation of the right to strike."

Consider a situation where an employee organization would make such an affirmation at a time when the same organization was engaged in a strike. To say in such circumstances that this Board should accept such affirmation without question would be such an adherence to form in disregard of substance as to constitute a classic absurdity. Similarly, it would appear to be incumbent upon this Board to make an inquiry in a situation where such affirmation or "formal renunciation" is repudiated soon after it is made and before certification.

Appellant argues in support of its contention that this Board lacks power to so inquire, and to deny certification as a result of such inquiry would constitute a penalty beyond that provided in § 210.3(f) of the Act, *i.e.,* forfeiture of dues deduction privileges.

In advancing this contention, appellant fails to give effect to the statutory scheme. The statute requires that recognition or certification of an employee organization be conditioned upon an affirmation made in good faith that the organization does not assert the right to strike against any government. A determination by this Board that an employee organization is not qualified for certification by reason of its failure to make such an affirmation in good faith is therefore administrative and not penal.

Appellant is an employee organization which is neither recognized nor certified. Rather, appellant is an employee organization seeking to be certified and a requisite to certification is the making of the affirmation referred to above. For the reasons stated, such an affirmation must be made in good faith, and if there are present facts and circumstances which place the good faith of the affirmation in question, this Board has not only the power but the obligation to make an inquiry and to take such affirmative action as is necessary, including the withholding of certification in order to effectuate the purposes and provisions of the Act.

Accordingly, the stay granted by the Director is vacated and the certification proceedings shall proceed subject to the right of inquiry asserted herein.

## NOTES

1. The constitutionality of the Taylor Law's requirement that an employee organization must affirm that it does not assert the right to strike before it can be certified as a collective bargaining representative was upheld by the New York Appellate Division in Rogoff v.

Anderson, 34 App. Div. 2d 154, 310 N.Y.S.2d 174 (1970), *aff'd*, 28 N.Y.2d 880, 271 N.E.2d 553, 322 N.Y.S.2d 718, *appeal dismissed for want of a substantial federal question,* 404 U.S. 805 (1971). The union argued "that the requirement for an affirmation that Respondent does not assert the right to strike is a violation of Respondent's right of free speech under the Federal and State Constitutions," relying on the decision in National Association of Letter Carriers v. Blount, 305 F. Supp. 546 (D.D.C. 1969), *appeal dismissed,* 400 U.S. 801 (1970), in which the court struck down as unconstitutional a statutory provision that made it illegal for federal employees to belong to employee organizations that asserted the right to strike. In distinguishing this case, the court held the problem "was not job acquisition for retention, but certification with its attendant benefits." As a result, the court held that "the condition imposed is reasonable for the benefits conferred, and is reasonably calculated to achieve the ultimate desired end." The court further observed that it did not construe the statutory requirement as an infringement "upon the exercise of rights protected by the First Amendment."

2. The Georgia Fire Fighters Bargaining Law provides that a municipal employer shall recognize the organization selected by a majority of the fire fighters in a given fire department if "said organization does not advocate striking and has a 'no-strike' clause in its Constitution and By-laws. . . ." GA. CODE ANN., ch. 54-13, § 54-1305 (Supp. 1972). The Nevada statute provides that a local government employer may only recognize an employee organization that has affirmatively pledged "in writing not to strike against the local government employer under any circumstances." NEV. REV. STAT. § 288.160 (1971). Are either or both of these requirements unconstitutional? In determining the constitutionality of prohibiting the granting of recognition to an employee organization that advocates striking, would it make any difference if the jobs of the employees in question are essential to the safety and health of the public?

# B. EXISTENCE OF QUESTION CONCERNING REPRESENTATION

## 1. SHOWING OF INTEREST

A condition precedent to invoking the representation procedures under most of the public sector collective bargaining statutes is a showing by the union or employee organization that it has substantial support among the employees in the bargaining unit petitioned for. The purpose of such a requirement is "to avoid needless dissipation of P.E.R.B.'s resources on frivolous representation claims." Civil Service Employees Ass'n v. Helsby, 63 Misc. 2d 403, 312 N.Y.2d 386 (Sup. Ct. 1970), *aff'd,* 35 App. Div. 2d 655, 314 N.Y.S.2d 159 (1971). Most of the statutes incorporate the long standing NLRB rule that the union or employee organization must affirmatively demonstrate that it has the support of at least 30 percent of the employees in the unit claimed to be appropriate. Although there are some statutory variations, this showing of interest is usually made by submitting membership cards or dues checkoff authorizations to the labor relations agency. These cards or authorizations are then checked against a list of employees submitted by the employer. Following the private sector precedent, the determination of whether the employee organization has submitted the requisite showing of interest has been held to be an administrative matter that is within the discretion of the agency to determine and is not a matter that can be litigated. Civil Service Employees Ass'n v. Helsby, *supra;* Union Free School Dist. No. 21, 1 PERB ¶ 405 (N.Y. PERB 1968); Defense Supply Agency, Boston, Mass., A/SLMR No. 34 (1971); South Redford School Dist., 1965-1966 MERC Lab. Op. 160 (Mich.). Several PERBs have promulgated rules to this effect. For example, Section 95.17 of the Rules of the Pennsylvania Labor Relations Board provides that the administrative determination of the showing of interest "shall not be subject to collateral attack at any hearing."

Unlike other statutory schemes, the Florida law provides that "[a]ny employee, employers, or employee organization having sufficient reason to believe any of the employees' signatures were obtained by collusion, coercion, intimidation or misrepresentation, or are otherwise invalid shall be given a reasonable opportunity to verify and challenge signatures appearing on the petition." Fla. Stat. § 447.307(2) (1977). In School Board of Marion County v. PERC, 334 So. 2d 582 (Fla. S. Ct. 1976), the Florida Supreme Court interpreted this provision "to mean that a public employer's good faith allegation of one of the grounds enumerated in the statute is sufficient to require the Commission to give access to the authorization cards, and that the Commission is not authorized to review or test the employer's judgment or assertions at that stage of the proceedings."

## WAUWATOSA BOARD OF EDUCATION

Wisconsin Employment Relations Commission
Decision No. 8300-A, aff'd, 1 PBC ¶ 10,303
(Wis. Cir. Ct. 1968)

. . . Under the pertinent statutory provisions a question of representation must exist as a condition precedent to the processing of a petition for an election among employes. The Commission has not required any showing of interest to be demonstrated by any petitioner with respect to the processing of election petitions filed pursuant to the Wisconsin Employment Peace Act or the Municipal Employer-Employe Labor Relations Act. The Commission has considered the filing of the petition, whether it be to certify or decertify a representative, as a good-faith claim that the employes desire to be represented or not to be represented. This policy has been applied in initial and subsequent elections on the basis of our experience that the overwhelming number of petitions have been filed in good faith with the expectation of obtaining the results prompting the petition. . . .

The establishment of a policy which would now require labor organizations seeking representation to present a showing of interest or to require that an employer establish a good faith doubt that the employes desire to continue their representation by an incumbent union, requires a consideration of the rights of employes to select or change their bargaining representative, with the interest of preserving stability in existing collective bargaining relationships. We have considered the above-discussed factors in order to balance and achieve these objectives when confronted with issues involving the timely filing of petitions for elections.

Although the Commission has not in the past processed a substantial number of petitions which have not been filed in good faith, the results of recent elections seeking a change in the present representative status indicate that an increasing number of petitions have been filed where there was little likelihood of success by the petitioner. The processing of such election petitions has resulted in no change in the bargaining relationship and has had an adverse impact upon such existing relationship, in that such processing has interrupted and delayed negotiations, thus affecting the stability of the collective bargaining relationship. Such unwarranted delays create problems especially in municipal employment with respect to the effect of budgetary deadlines and other special deadlines which may be imposed by statute, and in both the private and public employment where such delays create additional issues for bargaining, such as effective dates of agreements, as well as their retroactive application.

The Commission concludes that there is now sufficient reason requiring parties requesting elections seeking a change in representation or the rejection of the present representative to furnish the Commission with objective data raising the question concerning representation before it will conduct such an election, which if otherwise held, might delay and frustrate the relationship between the recognized or certified labor organization and the employer. . . .

Accordingly, where there is an existing collective bargaining relationship resulting from a good faith voluntary recognition of the labor organization, or where the labor organization has been certified in an election conducted by this agency, an organization filing a petition for an election among the employes involved at the time of filing must administratively demonstrate that at least 30 percent of the employes in the claimed appropriate collective bargaining unit desire the petitioning organization to represent them for the purposes of collective bargaining. Where the petition is filed by an employe or employes seeking to terminate the representative status of the incumbent labor organization, the petitioning employe or employes must administratively demonstrate to this agency at the time of filing that at least 30 percent of the employes in the requested bargaining unit desire to terminate the representative status of the union. An employer petitioning for an election in an existing unit must demonstrate to this agency at the hearing, by objective considerations, that it has reasonable cause to believe that the incumbent organization has lost its majority status since its certification or the date of voluntary recognition. This objective evidence must not have been obtained by the employer through prohibited means. . . .

## NOTES

1. Is there a valid question concerning representation if the employee organization does not request the public employer to grant recognition prior to filing a representation petition? Following the long established policy of the NLRB, the Wisconsin Employment Relations Commission has held that the filing of a representation petition is sufficient to raise a question concerning representation. Thus, in Village of Brown Deer, WERC Decision No. 6650 (Wis. ERC 1964), the Wisconsin Commission stated:

> Our experience in administering Section 111.70 indicates that the Municipal Employer has a different mode of operation which makes it exceedingly difficult, at best, for it to respond with any dispatch to a demand for recognition by a Union. The private employer can recognize or decline to recognize a Union after a decision by the individual owner of the business or after conferences among members of the management. On the other hand, the Municipal Employer must decide upon its action through legislative process, which is often slow and drawn out and which lends itself more to inaction than action. During this same period, disputes concerning the terms and conditions of employment and the representative status of the Union would be aggravated by the Union's and the employes' suspicion that the Municipal Employer might be using the time to undermine its organization. Such delays are eliminated through the unhampered use of the Board's election machinery. . . .

> [W]e have encouraged Municipal Employers to extend voluntary recognition to a Union where they are satisfied that the Union is the representative of the majority of the employes in the unit. Indeed, where the Union believes the Municipal Employer will recognize its claim of representation and enters into conferences and negotiations with the employe representative, such action is entirely in keeping with the voluntary nature of the collective bargaining process. However, the fact that the Union may choose to seek voluntary recognition does not mean that it must make known its claim to the Municipal Employer before filing an election petition with the Board.

2. Many of the public sector statutes specifically provide that a decertification petition must be supported by a 30 percent showing of interest.

3. Where a given statute specifically authorizes employees to file a decertification petition but makes no provision for an employer to do so, may an employer nevertheless file a petition challenging the continued majority status of the collective bargaining representative? May an employer test the union's majority status by refusing to bargain with the union and assert as its defense that the union no longer represents a majority of the employees in the appropriate bargaining unit? See PLRB v. Houtzdale Municipal Authority, Case No. PERA-C-5692-W, GERR No. 638, B-17 (Pa. PLRB 1976) (unfair labor practice for employer to refuse to bargain based on doubt as to union's majority status; proper course of action is for employer to file a decertification petition).

4. The NLRB, like the WERC, has held that an employer may file a petition challenging a union's majority status if it can establish that it has a good faith doubt based on objective considerations that the union has lost its majority status. United States Gypsum Co., 157 N.L.R.B. 652 (1966). In Lloyd McKee Motors, Inc., 170 N.L.R.B. 1278, 1278-79 (1968), the Board stated:

> . . . Respondent had engaged in protracted bargaining for a 5-month period over the single issue of the apprentice program followed by absolutely no communication from the Union or the mediator during the final 6 weeks. There had been several changes in the makeup of the union negotiating committee and what appeared to Respondent to be a loss of majority on the part of the Union. The Union failed to fill the post of steward, and there had been a considerable turnover of employees within the unit. In addition, McKee had asked the supervisors to make an "assessment" of the Union's strength, and, thereafter, McKee received various "opinion" reports from the supervisors which were to the effect that the Union had lost its majority status. Finally, on May 21, McKee asked Cook, the Union's vice president and chief employee negotiator, if he had heard from Jones, and Cook replied that he had not seen Jones since the meeting of April 14.
>
> While these factors may not, in and of themselves, establish as a fact a loss of majority, we are of the opinion that taken in their totality they present an objective basis which could furnish reasonable grounds for Respondent to believe in good faith that the Union had lost its majority status. . . .

The NLRB has further held that the determination as to whether the employer has presented sufficient objective considerations is an administrative matter and cannot be litigated. United States Gypsum Co., 161 N.L.R.B. 601 (1966).

5. The Nevada statute is unique in that it expressly provides that a public employer may withdraw recognition if the employee organization "ceases to be supported by a majority of the local government employees in the negotiating unit for which it is recognized." NEV. REV. STAT. § 288.160(3) (c) (1971). The employee organization may appeal, however, to the Local Government Employee-Management Relations Board. The Board is given the authority to direct an election if it "in good faith doubts whether any employee organization is supported by a majority of the local government employees in a particular negotiating unit." NEV. REV. STAT. § 288.160(4) (1971).

# 2. EFFECT OF AN EXISTING AGREEMENT (CONTRACT BAR DOCTRINE)

## TOWN OF MANCHESTER

Connecticut State Board of Labor Relations
Decision No. 813 (1968)

The Municipal Employees' Group, Inc., on March 7, 1968, petitioned for an election in a unit consisting of salaried employees. The employees in this unit are presently represented by the Intervenor, Local 991, of Council #4, American

Federation of State, County and Municipal Employees, AFL-CIO, and are covered by a collective agreement between the Intervenor and the Municipal Employer. That Agreement is due to expire January 1, 1969.

The Intervenor objects to the petition on the ground that an election is barred by the present contract and that a petition filed ten months prior to the termination of the contract is premature. We agree and order the petition dismissed. However, because our past decisions have raised some questions as to the operation of the contract bar principle in the field of municipal employment and when a petition will be considered to be timely filed, we feel it appropriate to provide as much clarification as our evolving experience presently permits.

We start with the basic statutory premise that employees have a right to bargain through representatives of their own choosing. That freedom of choice includes the freedom to change their mind as to which, if any, employee organization they want to represent them. At the same time, the purpose of choosing a representative is for collective bargaining, and that purpose cannot be realized unless there is some stability of representation. The employees must be permitted periodically to reconsider their choice, but this ought to be done at a time when it will not disrupt the bargaining process any more than necessary. To that end, the National Labor Relations Board developed the contract bar rule which this Board has generally followed. The least disruptive time for a change of representative is at the end of the contract term. Therefore, the appropriate time for a petition for an election is in that period prior to the end of the contract when a change in the bargaining representative can be most smoothly effectuated with the least disruption of the bargaining process.

The National Labor Relations Board evolved a set of subsidiary rules governing the timeliness of a petition prior to the end of the contract. See Leedom, *Industrial Stability and Freedom of Choice,* in COLLECTIVE BARGAINING AND THE LAW (1959), p. 63; Reed Roller Bit Co., 72 N.L.R.B. 927 (1947). Petitions filed more than 150 days prior to the end of the contract would not be accepted because the holding of an election would leave the incumbent union as a lame duck in administering the old contract. Also, petitions filed less than 60 days prior to the end of the contract would not be accepted so that the parties would have the last 60 days of bargaining undisrupted by any doubts as to the union's status in election proceedings. To these rules governing the timeliness of a petition, the NLRB added a third rule that a petition would not be barred by the negotiation of a new contract prior to the end of the time for filing a petition. Deluxe Metal Furniture Co., 121 N.L.R.B. 995 (1958). For example, if the contract were to expire on December 31, a petition filed on October 30 would not be barred by a new contract made prior to that date. The challenging union could not be blocked by the incumbent union's premature renewal of the contract. Later the NLRB modified these time limits to require filing not more than 90 days or less than 60 days prior to the end of the contract. Leonard Wholesale Meats, Inc., 136 N.L.R.B. 1000 (1962).

These rules were developed by the National Labor Relations Board for collective bargaining in the private sector. Although we have never adopted the rigid time limits set down by the NLRB, we believe that the principles they are built upon are sound and that the time spans indicated are generally appropriate in the sphere for which they were designed. That is, for collective bargaining in the private sector.

Collective bargaining in the public sector raises different considerations. Experience during the last two years has suggested that the bargaining process in public employment is often more protracted than in private employment. This means that bargaining for a new contract may begin longer in advance of the end of the contract term. If there is to be a change of the bargaining representative, that change can be most smoothly made at the time when contract negotiations would normally begin. Therefore, a petition filed somewhat more than 90 days prior to the end of the contract would be at an appropriate time. Our experience is too limited to now fix limits with certainty, but we are presently persuaded that a petition filed as much as four months prior to the end of that contract should not be considered premature.

Collective bargaining in the public sector often requires quite different time limits for filing petitions for another reason. Collective agreements are often timed to expire at the end of the fiscal year. In that case, the parties usually contemplate that negotiations for a new contract will be held while the budget is being prepared so that when the budget is presented and adopted, it will reflect the costs of the new collective agreement.

Where the collective bargaining process is thus coordinated with the budget-making processes, the normal time for beginning negotiations may be as much as five or six months before the end of the contract term. This time is considered necessary to complete negotiations, get the results of the negotiations reflected in the budget and have the budget adopted before the end of the fiscal year. A petition filed for a change of representatives at the time when negotiations for a new contract normally begin cannot be considered to be premature. On the contrary, it might well be considered to be at the most appropriate time. It would avoid having negotiations disrupted in mid-course by a change of bargaining representatives. For this reason, we ordered an election in the *Greenwich* case (Case No. ME-1631, April 17, 1968), even though the collective agreement still had several months to run.

We are not prepared at this time to establish any rigid time limit in such cases, for our experience is yet too limited to say with any assurance how long a time may be required. Nor do we know in practical terms what difficulties the incumbent union may have in administering the remainder of the existing contract. For the present, we will follow the general guide that a petition filed within a month prior to the time when negotiations will normally begin will be considered timely. We consider it preferable that when negotiations normally begin, everyone will know who are the proper negotiators.

In this case, the contract is not scheduled to coordinate with the fiscal year, but is to expire on January 1, 1969. The parties have testified that, as in private employment, negotiations would normally begin about three months prior to the end of the contract. To hold an election in May could mean that the incumbent union could continue to administer the contract for seven or eight months in a lame duck status. Such problems should and can be avoided. The appropriate time for a petition to be filed in this case is after the first of September. This will permit the question of representation to be resolved in time for negotiations to take their regular course. A petition filed any earlier than the first of September will, in this case, be considered premature.

The petitioner here need have no fear that it will be barred by a new contract made before it files a new petition. If a petition is filed at any time between September 1, and November 1, then a new agreement made prior to the filing of the petition will not constitute a bar to an election.

The petition is hereby dismissed.

# NOTES

1. Who administers an existing agreement if a rival union decertifies the incumbent union prior to the expiration date of the agreement? The Wisconsin Employment Relations Commission in City of Milwaukee, Decision No. 8622 (Wis. ERC 1968), held that if a rival union unseats an incumbent union prior to the expiration of the agreement, the rival union administers the agreement for the balance of its term. *Accord,* Old Orchard Beach Police Dep't, CCH LAB. LAW REP., 3 STATE LAWS ¶ 49,999C.44 (Me. PELRB 1974). In State of New York, 5 PERB ¶ 3060 (N.Y. 1972), GERR No. 489, B-10 (1973), *aff'd sub nom.,* Police Benevolent Ass'n v. Osterman, 73 Misc. 2d 184, 340 N.Y.S.2d 291 (Sup. Ct. 1973), the New York PERB held that the successor organization administers the agreement "until a new agreement can be negotiated effective upon the start of a new fiscal year of the employer or the expiration of the old agreement, whichever is sooner." On the other hand, the Connecticut State Board of Labor Relations in City of Norwich, Decision No. 804 (1968), held that

> . . . even though an election is held prior to the termination date of the contract, it is for determining the status of the bargaining agent after the termination of the contract. During the remainder of the contract term, the Union retains its right to recognition and its authority to represent the employees, regardless of the outcome of the election.

Under the NLRA if an incumbent union is decertified, it loses its status as the bargaining agent and it has no right to administer the agreement for the balance of its term. *See* Modine Mfg. Co. v. Grand Lodge Int'l Ass'n of Machinists, 216 F.2d 326 (6th Cir. 1954); Farmbest, Inc., 154 N.L.R.B. 1421 (1965), *enforced as modified,* 370 F.2d 1015 (8th Cir. 1967). The Supreme Court in NLRB v. Burns Int'l Security Services, Inc., 406 U.S. 272, 92 S. Ct. 1571, 1580 n.8 (1972), held that "[w]hen the union which has signed a collective-bargaining contract is decertified, the succeeding union certified by the Board is not bound by the prior contract, need not administer it, and may demand negotiations for a new contract, even if the terms of the old contract has not yet expired." What are the advantages and disadvantages of each approach? Which approach is more likely to promote labor relations stability?

2. Not infrequently the period of time within which a representation petition may be filed where there is an existing collective bargaining agreement is specifically set forth in the applicable statute. For example, section 967(2) of the Maine Municipal Public Employees Labor Relations Act provides that "[w]here there is a valid collective bargaining agreement in effect, no question concerning unit or representation may be raised except during the period not more than 90 nor less than 60 days prior to the expiration date of the agreement." ME. REV. STAT. ANN. tit. 26, § 967(2) (Supp. 1972). The Hawaii statute contains a similar provision. HAWAII REV. STAT. § 89-7 (Supp. 1971). In other instances the contract bar rules are set forth in rules and regulations promulgated by the agency administering the act. For the applicable contract bar rules under Executive Order 11491, see section 202.3 of the rules promulgated by the Assistant Secretary of Labor, 29 C.F.R. § 202.3 (1978).

3. Normally, a representation petition is timely if it is filed after the expiration date of a collective bargaining agreement. Suppose, however, that prior to the expiration date the parties had reached agreement on all but one issue and had agreed to submit that issue to binding arbitration. Would a representation petition filed by a rival union be timely if it was filed after the termination date of the agreement but prior to the receipt of the arbitrator's award that would resolve the one remaining issue in negotiations between the employer and the incumbent union? In City of Norwich, Decision No. 804 (Conn. SLRB 1968), the Connecticut State Board of Labor Relations stated:

> [T]he agreement to submit the principal issue in dispute to binding arbitration creates a contractual relationship between the Union and the employer which bars an election, and if that arbitration leads directly to the concluding of a collective agreement, an election is barred until the termination of that collective agreement. The purpose of the contract bar is to promote stability in collective bargaining

relations. The arbitration agreement substantially settles the parties' relation and removes the uncertainty and instability of unsettled negotiations. To open the question of representation during the time required for arbitration to crystalize into a completed contract would be to disrupt this peaceful method of resolving disputes. Uncertainty as to the union's status would undermine or distort the arbitration and open the award to a kind of collateral attack. . . .

Would the same considerations be applicable if the parties had agreed to submit the unresolved issues to non-binding fact finding as opposed to binding arbitration? Would it make any difference if non-binding fact finding was legislatively mandated? *See* City of Appleton, Decision No. 7423 (Wis. ERC 1966).

## CITY OF GRAND RAPIDS (HEALTH DEPARTMENT)

Michigan Employment Relations Commission
1968 MERC Lab. Op. 194

. . . On July 11, 1967, MNA [Michigan Nurses Association] petitioned the Board for a representation election in a unit defined as:

"All registered nurses employed by the Health Department of the City of Grand Rapids."

AFSCME and the City oppose this petition on the grounds that . . . there existed as of July 11, 1967, a collective bargaining agreement sufficient under section 14 of PERA to bar the Board from conducting any election. . . .

The 1966 contract contained an expiration date of June 30, 1967. In March, 1967, AFSCME and the City commenced negotiations for a new agreement. Since no new agreement had yet been reached as of June 28, 1967, the parties extended the 1966 agreement to July 7, 1967. On July 5, 1967, the City Commission adopted Ordinance No. 67-43, a general salary ordinance which set pay ranges for the various classifications of work. On July 7, the City Manager completed negotiations with AFSCME and reached an oral agreement on salaries and all other working conditions. This oral agreement called for certain salary increases beyond those just provided in Ordinance No. 67-43 of July 5, 1967. The City Commission followed through by adopting Ordinance No. 67-44, on July 11, 1967, upping salaries to the level orally agreed to on July 7, 1967 by the City Manager and AFSCME. Also on July 11, a two page "letter of agreement" was signed by the City Manager and AFSCME officials, agreeing that the old 1966 Contract would remain in effect until May 31, 1968, with several specific modifications, including the substance of Salary Ordinance 67-43 as amended by 67-44. Other modifications affected the grievance procedure, compensatory time off, pay for work out of classification, vacation pay, number of holidays, hospitalizations, life insurance, safety committee, uniforms, tool allowance, and a parking facilities study committee. The MNA's election petition, as noted earlier, was filed with the Board on July 11, 1967, the same date as the "letter of agreement" and Ordinance No. 67-44. The election petition was not served upon the City and AFSCME until several days later. Section 14 of PERA provides in pertinent part:

"*No election shall be directed* in any bargaining unit or subdivision thereof *where there is in force and effect a valid collective bargaining agreement* which was not prematurely extended and which is of fixed duration. . . ." (emphasis added)

The ultimate issue is whether there was in force and effect as of July 11, 1967,

a valid collective bargaining agreement between the City and AFSCME. What
existed as of that date was a written agreement between the City Manager and
AFSCME, covering all areas of wages and working conditions, coupled with City
Commission ordinances confirming the salary portion of the City Manager's
agreement. The ordinances were silent as to the several other contract
modifications agreed to in the "letter of agreement," except for the following
relevant provision of Ordinance No. 67-43:

> "Section 21. The City Manager shall make rules not in conflict with Civil
> Service provisions, *and subject to the approval of the City Commission,* on
> the subjects of sick leave, annual leave (vacation), military leave, leave
> without pay, holidays, working hours, and other personnel matters. *Until
> such rules are approved existing resolutions and rules on such subjects shall
> remain in full force and effect."* (emphasis added)

It is clear from the above that the several non-salary modifications agreed to
by the City Manager were to be of no effect until the City Commission approved
them. There is no evidence that the City Commission ever formally approved
these modifications to which the City Manager had agreed. Accordingly, it is
concluded that the only collective bargaining agreement "in force and effect"
(Section 14 of PERA) as of the date the election petition was filed was the
agreement on a salary schedule.[1] The City Manager patently lacked power to
bind the City or its City Commission to terms for a new contract. While he was
authorized by a 1965 Commission action to "represent" the City in union
matters, the Commission never pretended to delegate to him the power to
legislate wages and working conditions without the Commission's ratification of
any agreement reached by him at the bargaining table. Inasmuch as the "letter
of agreement" was legally unenforceable without Commission approval taken at
a Commission meeting, it is found that no "collective bargaining agreement" was
"in force and effect" as of July 11, 1967, except for the salary agreement which
was adopted by Commission Ordinances Nos. 67-43 and 67-44.

As a general rule the Board will follow a policy of treating as a section 14 bar
only such agreements of public employers as have been rendered legally
enforceable by virtue of having been duly enacted, adopted or approved by the
competent governing body, e.g., city council or commission, board of education,
or county board of supervisors. However, it is apparent that the unavoidable
delay [3] between tentative agreement by negotiators at the bargaining table and
the convening of an official meeting of the legislative body encourages disruptive
rival union activity and consequent raids if the the tentative agreement does not
serve to bar an election. This is so because it encourages dissident groups of
employees to make capital out of their asserted ability to negotiate an even better
contract. Such a situation discourages reasonable settlements and responsible
representation. Accordingly, in the interest of striking a balance between
employee freedom of choice and stability of existing bargaining relationships, the

---

[1] The Charter of the City of Grand Rapids, Title V, vests all City legislative and administrative
powers in the City Commission (sec. 1(a)); provides that no monies shall be paid out except in
pursuance of appropriations approved by the City Commission (sec. 20); and provides that the City
Commission shall fix by ordinance the salary or rate of compensation of all officers and employees
of the City (sec. 35).

[3] Administrative notice is taken of the fact that the majority of such local legislative bodies, are
composed of citizens who have other occupations, serve on a voluntary basis, and are unable to meet
on a continuous basis because of other commitments.

Board announces the following policy which will be applied in implementing PERA section 14 for all petitions filed after the date of this order:

> A complete written collective bargaining agreement made between and executed by, authorized representatives of a public employer and the exclusive bargaining agent of its employees will, for a period of up to thirty days thereafter, bar a rival union election petition or a decertification petition pending subsequent action on the agreement by the legislative body. A petition filed within the thirty day period will not be dismissed if the legislative body meets and votes to reject the proposed agreement or takes no action within the thirty day period. If the legislative body approves the collective bargaining agreement negotiated by its representative within the thirty day period, the petition will be dismissed.

The determinative issue in this case is whether the salary agreement (the only agreement approved by the governing City Commission *at any time*) was sufficient *in scope* to constitute the type of agreement contemplated by section 14 as barring an election.[4] This question must be answered in the negative, consistent with the holding in School District No. 61, Berrien County-Buchanan Public Schools, 1967 Labor Opinions, 518, 520 wherein we stated:

> "The National Labor Relations Board consistently refuses to treat an agreement as a bar to an election petition unless it contains substantial terms and conditions of employment deemed sufficient to stabilize the bargaining relationship. A contract limited to wages only or to one or several insubstantial provisions is not recognized as a bar. Appalachian Shale Products Co., 121 NLRB 1160. We have adopted the NLRB rule. South Redford School District MLMB R65 J-184, 1966 Labor Opinions 160; Sterling Township, MLMB R65 H-20, 1966 Labor Opinions 9. Accordingly, the agreement of June 20, 1966, being limited to a wage schedule, is not a bar, under section 14 of PERA, to the conduct of an election at this time."

Accordingly, it is concluded that no section 14 bar exists to the direction of an election. . . .

## NOTES

1. The NLRB has held that "[w]here ratification is a condition precedent to contractual validity by express contractual provision, the contract will be ineffectual as a bar unless it is ratified prior to the filing of the petition. . . ." Appalachian Shale Products Co., 121 N.L.R.B. 1160 (1958). The New Jersey Public Employment Relations Commission adopted a similar policy in Camden County Welfare Board, Decision No. 65 (N.J. PERC 1972).

2. The Michigan Employment Relations Commission, following the uniform practice of the NLRB, has ruled that "a contract to act as a bar to an election must embrace a unit that is appropriate to the extent that the unit is one neither prohibited by PERA nor contrary to Board policy." Kent County Road Commission, 1969 MERC Lab. Op. 34 (Mich.).

3. Does a contract that does not include any wage or fringe benefit provisions constitute a bar to a representation proceeding? The New York City Office of Collective Bargaining has held that a contract that "contains substantial non-economic provisions" was sufficient to be a bar since the wages and fringe benefits were mandated by the state's "prevailing

---

[4] It is unnecessary to apply the 30 day rule, announced above, in reaching a decision in the instant case, since the record contains no evidence that the City Commission *ever* met and approved a complete collective bargaining agreement.

rate" law and bargaining was prohibited on subjects covered by the law. Teamsters Local Union 237, Decision No. 11-71, GERR No. 396, B-7 (N.Y.C. OCB 1971).

4. In West India Mfg. & Serv. Co., 195 N.L.R.B. No. 203, 79 L.R.R.M. 1619 (1972), the NLRB held that an employer and a union caught in mid-negotiations by the wage-price freeze ordered by President Nixon in August 1971 were entitled to an additional 60-day period during which they were insulated from an election petition filed by a rival union.

5. Does the inclusion of an illegal union security clause remove the contract as a bar to an election? In the private sector, the NLRB has uniformly held that a contract which contains a union-security clause or a checkoff clause which is illegal on its face or has been determined to be illegal in an unfair labor practice proceeding does not bar a representation election. Paragon Products Corp., 134 N.L.R.B. 662 (1961); Gary Steel Supply Co., 144 N.L.R.B. 470 (1963). What are the advantages and disadvantages of adopting this policy in the public sector?

6. Does an agreement that is conditioned upon the appropriation of funds by another public body operate as a bar prior to the time the condition is met? In Camden County Welfare Board, Decision No. 65 (N.J. PERC 1972), the New Jersey PERC stated:

> . . . The incorporation of two conditions regarding funds for salary increases in no way detracts from the substance of the agreement. It simply represents the most that a public employer could do under the circumstances at that time. A collective negotiations agreement in public employment frequently requires a later appropriation of funds after execution of the agreement in order to implement it. Even if that subsequent appropriation is not made an express condition in the contract, it is nevertheless a fundamental condition which is incorporated by necessary implication. Many, probably most, public employers are not self-appropriators; they are dependent for funds upon a political mechanism outside of their direct control. The conditions involved here are of that kind; the contract does not contain a condition, the fulfillment of which is reserved to one of the parties. The parties struck a bargain, the funding of which was necessarily conditioned by the Board's limitations. The expression of these conditions in their agreement merely recognizes a fact of political life. Under the circumstances, we conclude that the execution date of their written agreement, January 13, 1971, should control for purposes of applying the contract bar rule. . . .

## 3. ELECTION, CERTIFICATION AND RECOGNITION BARS

*Election Bars.* In order to balance the right of employees freely to decide whether they wish to be represented with the desirability of providing some degree of finality to the results of an election, most public sector collective bargaining statutes provide for a one-year election bar. Section 23.40.100(c) of the Alaska statute, which parallels section 9(c) (3) of the NLRA, is typical: "An election may not be held in a bargaining unit or in a subdivision of a bargaining unit if a valid election has been held within the preceding 12 months." ALASKA STAT. tit. 23, ch. 40, § 23.40.100(c) (1972). There are some variations, however. The Los Angeles ordinance states that "At least six months shall lapse following an election without a majority representative being chosen before a petition for certification may be filed covering the same group of employees." Los Angeles, Cal., Admin. Code, div. 4, ch. 8, § 4.822(c) (6) (1971). On the other hand, Section 213.1 of the rules promulgated by the Indiana Education Employment Relations Board provides that "no election shall be conducted until at least 24 months after a previous election." An election bar, however, does not prohibit the holding of a runoff election or a second election if the first election has been set aside on the basis of objections filed by a party to the election or has otherwise been ruled invalid.

Under the NLRA the period of time within which another election is barred is computed from the date of the election, not the date on which the results of the election are certified. Bendix Corp., Automation & Measurement Div., 179 N.L.R.B. 140 (1969). *Accord,* Holland Bd. of Public Works, 1968 MERC Lab. Op. 853 (Mich.). While an election in a broad bargaining unit bars an election in a smaller bargaining unit for the specified period of time, an election in a smaller unit does not bar an election in a broader unit. For example, if a group of craft employees were included in a broad overall unit, a subsequent election limited to the craft employees would be barred for the specified period. *See* Vickers, Inc., 124 N.L.R.B. 1051 (1959). On the other hand, if an election were held in a unit limited to craft employees, it would not bar an election in a larger bargaining unit that included the craft employees, even though the specified period of time had not elapsed. *See* Thiokol Chemical Co., 123 N.L.R.B. 888 (1959). Would the same results be required under the Los Angeles ordinance quoted above?

Suppose a valid election is held on June 1 in which Union A fails to poll a majority of the votes cast. Suppose further that within three months thereafter Union B obtains authorization cards from a substantial majority of the same employees that voted in the June 1 election. Does the employer, knowing Union B represents a majority of its employees, commit an unfair labor practice if it refuses to recognize Union B where the act bars the holding of an election if a valid election has been held within the twelve preceding months? Would it be necessary to show that the employer has engaged in unfair labor practices aimed at dissipating the union's majority support? *See* Conren, Inc. v. NLRB, 368 F.2d 173 (7th Cir. 1966), *cert. denied,* 386 U.S. 974 (1967), *noted* 80 HARV. L. REV. 1805 (1967).

*Certification Bars.* Several public sector collective bargaining statutes expressly provide that no question concerning representation can be raised during a designated period of time from the date of the employee organization's certification as the collective bargaining representative. A one-year period is typically specified. The Delaware, Maryland, and Tennessee teachers' statutes are exceptions; they provide that the designation or certification of an exclusive representative shall be for a minimum period of two years. DEL. CODE tit. 14, § 4006(c) (1977); MD. ANN. CODE, art. 77, §§ 6-406(A) & 6-507(A) (1978); TENN. CODE ANN. tit. 49, § 4(c) (1978). Under the NLRA there is a conclusive presumption that a union, in the absence of unusual circumstances, continues to represent a majority of the employees during the year following certification and no question concerning representation can be raised during the certification year. Brooks v. NLRB, 348 U.S. 96 (1954). The Michigan Employment Relations Commission has adopted a similar policy. Sunshine Hospital, 1968 MERC Lab. Op. 440 (Mich.); City of Bay City, 1967 MERC Lab. Op. 155. One of the underlying premises is that "a union should be given ample time for carrying out its mandate on behalf of its members, and should not be under exigent pressure to produce hothouse results or be turned out." Brooks v. NLRB, *supra.*

In Kenosha Board of Education, WERC Decision No. 8031 (Wis. ERC 1967), a local affiliate of the American Federation of Teachers filed a representation petition seeking to represent the District's teachers. In opposing the petition, the Kenosha Education Association, the incumbent bargaining representative, urged, *inter alia,* "that the Board adopt a rule to the effect that where the Board has previously certified an organization as the exclusive bargaining representative of employes in an appropriate unit, the second election should not be conducted within two years of the date of the certification of the results of the first election, and further, that said two-year certification bar rule be extended at two-year intervals." With respect to this contention, the WERC stated:

The Board has seriously considered whether it should adopt a two-year certification bar rule. That is to say, whether the Board should not conduct a second election in a period earlier than two years from the certification of the results of a previous election. In such consideration we must weigh the right of the employes to select or change their bargaining representative with the interest of preserving the stability of the established collective bargaining relationship. The problem is aggravated as a result of the fact that collective bargaining agreements in public employment, and especially those involving teachers, are not coextensive in time with budgetary considerations. Because of its statutory budgetary deadline and because of the nature of teacher employment, the School Board herein normally commences bargaining in May of each year for terms and conditions of employment for the following school year. It therefore becomes a necessity that if the employes are to select a new collective bargaining representative, said representative should be given a reasonable time to negotiate the collective bargaining agreement. If the ordinary contract bar rules were to apply, the election would not be held during the term of an existing agreement, and the selected collective bargaining representative, therefore, normally would not have a reasonable period of time to negotiate a collective bargaining agreement to succeed the existing agreement.

No rule with respect to certification bar is being established because the history of employment relations in municipal employment has not been such as to require such a rule at the present time, and because that history is not sufficiently developed to indicate a pattern of similar conditions. The conditions to be regulated are still too vaguely defined, and the Board prefers to wait until it is sufficiently certain that its rule, once adopted, will not be eroded by exceptions. Each case will be reviewed and determined on its own facts in order to balance the objective of employe choice with the objective of a stable bargaining relationship.

In determining how the two objectives will best be balanced and achieved, the Board will be influenced by various factors such as (1) the presence or absence of a current agreement; (2) the presence or absence of current and active negotiations for an agreement and how long such negotiations have been in progress; (3) the budgetary deadlines imposed upon the parties; (4) the special deadlines imposed by statute, such as the case with respect to teachers' personal contracts; (5) whether the current bargaining agent was certified or recognized; (6) the period of time since the current bargaining agent was certified or recognized; and (7) the employment relations history involved.

What effect would a finding that an employer had not bargained in good faith have on the computation of the certification year? In City of Norwich, Decision No. 804 (Conn. SBLR 1968), the Connecticut State Board of Labor Relations stated:

There remains the question whether the petition in this case should be barred by the Municipal Employer's past prohibited labor practices in refusing to fulfill its statutory obligation to bargain collectively. In a number of cases under the National Labor Relations Act, it has been held that where a union's majority was dissipated after an employer has engaged in unfair labor practices, particularly the refusal to bargain collectively, the Union is entitled to recognition for a reasonable period even though it has lost its majority support. For example, in Franks Bros. v. NLRB, 321 U.S. 702 (1944) the Supreme Court held that even though the union had lost its majority the employer should be compelled to continue bargaining with it for a reasonable period. The underlying principle expressed by the Court was that the union was entitled to a period of recognition and stability in order to demonstrate to the employees its capacity to represent them and to obtain benefits on their behalf. *See also* NLRB v. Warren Co. Inc., 350 U.S. 107 (1955); NLRB v. John S. Swift Co., 302 F.2d 342 (7th Cir. 1962); Irving Air Chute Co. v. NLRB, 350 F.2d 176 (2nd Cir. 1965).

We subscribe to this general principle. The employees can have no freedom of choice between whether they will engage in collective bargaining or not if the employer's refusal to bargain has prevented them from experiencing collective bargaining. We will not entertain a petition for an election where the employer's unfair labor practices have undermined the union's majority before it has had an opportunity to demonstrate its capabilities of representing the employees in collective bargaining.

*Recognition Bars.* Under many public sector bargaining statutes an employer may voluntarily grant recognition to an employee organization if it represents a majority of the employees in an appropriate unit. Should such a voluntary grant of recognition likewise constitute a bar to a representation petition filed by a rival organization? The NLRB has held that voluntary recognition bars a representation election "for a reasonable period." Keller Plastics Eastern, Inc., 157 N.L.R.B. 583 (1969). The so-called "reasonable period" is determined on a case-by-case basis and is frequently much less than one year from the date recognition was granted. *Compare* Universal Gear Service Corp., 157 N.L.R.B. 1169 (1969) (two month period not reasonable), *with* Brennan's Cadillac, Inc., 231 N.L.R.B. 225 (1977) (three month period reasonable). What reasons, if any, are there for establishing different periods of unchallenged representation depending on whether the union is certified or voluntarily recognized by the employer? Should the same policy be adopted in the public sector?

## 4. EFFECT OF AFL-CIO INTERNAL DISPUTES PLAN

The purpose of the AFL-CIO Internal Disputes Plan as set forth in Article XX of the AFL-CIO Constitution is to prevent member unions from raiding the jurisdiction of other member unions. Article XX provides that if a member union feels that another member union is invading its jurisdiction, it can file a complaint and have the complaint heard by the Internal Disputes Tribunal. Article XX provides that the decision of the impartial tribunal is binding on member unions. The NLRB, however, has uniformly refused to dismiss a representation petition on the basis that an appeal to the AFL-CIO Internal Disputes Plan is being made or the petitioner has been found to be in violation of Article XX. In S.G. Adams Co., 115 N.L.R.B. 1012, 1013 n.1 (1956), the Board stated:

> [T]he pendency of proceedings before an intra-union tribunal for adjudication of representation questions does not affect the duty of the Board to resolve such questions.... Nor is the fact that the filing of a representation petition violates a union constitutional provision sufficient ground under Board policy for dismissing the petition. The Board has frequently held that it will not concern itself with the internal regulations of a labor organization.

*Accord,* Weather Vane Outerware Corp., 233 N.L.R.B. No. 67 (1977).

That the same approach may be adopted in the public sector is indicated by the decision of the New York City Office of Collective Bargaining in Local Union No. 3, IBEW and the City of New York, Decision No. 36-69, GERR No. 305, B-4 (N.Y.C. OCB 1969), wherein the New York City OCB stated:

> Although Article XX may constitute a binding contract between affiliates of the AFL-CIO, it is not binding on third parties. In the State of New York, public employees have the statutory right to bargain collectively through representatives of their own choosing. . . . That statutory right manifestly is paramount to the contract between AFL-CIO affiliates, and must be recognized and effectuated by this Board.

The New York City OCB further noted that "the paramount right of the employees to select a bargaining representative cannot and should not be stultified by the fact that a rival union had represented employees in the past." *Accord,* Elizabeth Bd. of Educ., Docket No. RO-792 (N.J. PERC 1974). *But see* Sevey v. AFSCME, 48 Cal. App. 3d 64, 89 L.R.R.M. 3049 (1975) (umpire's award in Article XX proceeding upheld despite potential conflict with employees' right to choose a bargaining representative).

# C. DETERMINATION OF THE APPROPRIATE BARGAINING UNIT

## 1. INTRODUCTION

### PRASOW, PRINCIPLES OF UNIT DETERMINATION — CONCEPT AND PROBLEMS, IN PERSPECTIVE IN PUBLIC EMPLOYEE NEGOTIATION 61-62 (Public Employee Relations Library Special Issue, 1969) †

Unit determination has a considerable impact on the interested parties, which consist of four groups: employees, the employee organization, the public employer, and the public.

*Employees* prefer the unit which provides the maximum pressure to achieve their economic objectives. Where special skills are involved, they desire tight, compact, small units which preserve their bargaining power in terms of numbers and skill. Also, the smaller unit gives more weight to each vote.

*Employee organizations* are quite pragmatic in their approach to the unit question. Their first interest is in organization. They seek that unit which strengthens or ratifies the extent of employee organization. A major problem in unit determination arises when there are two or more rival organizations, each seeking recognition for some or all employees. The older and more established organization generally has more members and prefers a broader unit to offset the strength of the rival organization. The newer organization will insist on a narrow unit because its strength is concentrated in that area.

Rival employee organizations occasionally take opposing sides on two different unit questions. One will argue for a narrow unit in the first situation and a wide unit in the second. Exactly the opposite position is taken by the rival organization. There are internal, political, economic, and technological reasons for such apparent contradictions.

In state and local government, management's interest in unit formation is influenced by several factors. Public managers are subject to inevitable political pressures, from below as well as from above. They must be sensitive and responsive to the views of higher officials, legislative or administrative, who have

---

† Reprinted by permission of the International Personnel Management Association.

the ultimate decision-making power. Public managers in state and local government are often reluctant to take a firm stand on the boundaries of the bargaining unit. They may have mixed feelings on whether to include or exclude such categories as supervisors or professional personnel.

Public executives are properly concerned with efficiency in operations, stability of the work force, and administrative convenience. Accordingly they may prefer the all-inclusive unit to avoid the rivalry resulting from fragmentation of employees into competing units. Public management may sometimes press for a wider unit in order to prevent a particular organization from winning an election. In other situations, a unit is sought which favors a more cooperative employee organization.

Public management has a major stake in unit determination because it can significantly affect administrative functioning. For example, the larger the number of units, the greater the tendency, usually, of organizations to multiply. Certain kinds of unit determinations may preclude equitable treatment for *all* employees. The formation of units can be reflected in the quality of work performed. Administrators and public officials are expected to insure that service is rendered promptly, efficiently, and economically.

*The Public Interest*

We come now to "the public," the fourth and last, but not the least interested party in unit determination. It is altogether impossible to define this term precisely because the public is so diffuse, so heterogeneous and such a conglomerate assortment of individual and group interests.

We are never quite sure what the public interest really is. It is certainly not in the public interest for teachers to strike. Neither is it in the public interest for local officials to maintain an intransigent attitude in the face of reasonable teacher demands.

However, there are some aspects of the public interest which can be stated affirmatively: First, the public does not want any deterioration in the quality of the service rendered. There is an interest in maintaining harmonious relations in public employment. But the greatest concern is over the possibility of a disruption or stoppage of the service. The public has a right to expect uninterrupted service, but public employees also have the right to obtain effective representation. Both rights are legitimate. The difficulty arises when they conflict and are headed on a collision course. . . .

**SHAW AND CLARK, DETERMINATION OF APPROPRIATE BARGAINING UNITS IN THE PUBLIC SECTOR: LEGAL AND PRACTICAL PROBLEMS, 51 Ore. L. Rev. 152, 152-54, 157-58 (1971) †**

Determination of the appropriate bargaining unit in the public sector is of fundamental importance. It is both a prerequisite to negotiations and a vital factor in their structure and outcome. The more bargaining units public management deals with, the greater the chance that competing unions will be able to whipsaw the employer. Moreover, a multiplicity of bargaining units makes if difficult, if not impossible, to maintain some semblance of uniformity in benefits and working conditions. Unfortunately, in many states and localities bargaining units have been established without consideration of the effect such units will have on negotiations or on the subsequent administration of an agreement. The resulting crazy-quilt pattern of representation has unduly complicated the collective bargaining process in the public sector. . . .

## The Legal Framework

*State Legislation.* In states which do not have applicable legislation, the determination of the appropriate bargaining unit is made by the parties. With increasing frequency, however, the determination of whether a unit is appropriate, in the absence of voluntary agreement by the parties, is made by a public employee relations board. Wisconsin, in 1959, was the first state to enact a comprehensive statute concerning collective bargaining by public employees. Since then there has been a virtual onslaught of legislation. More than thirty states have enacted legislation covering some or all categories of public employees. Various criteria have been suggested for determining the appropriate bargaining unit; [1] the following considerations are most frequently mentioned: (1) whether the employees concerned have a clear and identifiable community of interest; (2) whether the proposed unit will result in effective dealings and efficiency of operations; and (3) whether the employees have a history of representation. Generally the extent of organization may not be a controlling consideration.

Recently, there has been a distinct trend toward prescribing criteria explicitly designed to avoid fragmented bargaining units. The Pennsylvania Act, for example, provides that the board, in determining the appropriate bargaining unit, must take into consideration the effects of over-fragmentation and the existence of an identifiable community of interest. It further requires the board to consider "that when the Commonwealth is the employer, it will be bargaining on a statewide basis unless the issues involve working conditions peculiar to a given governmental locale." Similarly, the Kansas Act directs the public employee relations board to consider "the effects of overfragmentation and the splintering of a work organization."

Hawaii has gone one step further; it has legislatively established statewide bargaining units. Thus, there are separate units for supervisory and nonsupervisory employees in blue-collar positions. The same is true for white-collar groups. There are separate units for teachers, for faculty of the University of Hawaii and the community college system, and for employees of the university and community college system other than faculty. Optional appropriate bargaining units are designated for registered nurses, nonprofessional hospital and institutional workers, firemen, policemen, and professional and scientific employees other than nurses.

On both the state and national level, statutory criteria necessarily determine the framework within which decisions of the various public employee relations boards can be made. The Wisconsin and New York statutes illustrate how the statutory framework affects bargaining unit determinations. . . .

*Occupational Group Statutes.* The Wisconsin and New York statutes are comprehensive in that they (1) cover all categories of employees, (2) provide a method for resolving questions concerning representation, and (3) establish a public employee relations board to administer the act. It should be noted, however, that there are numerous statutes that apply to only one occupational

---

[1] Most of the statutes covering specific occupational groups such as firefighters, policemen or teachers specifically set forth the boundaries of the collective bargaining unit. . . .

group, such as firefighters, policemen, or teachers. In contrast to the general criteria for determining the appropriate unit set forth in the comprehensive statutes, the occupational group statutes prescribe the boundaries of the bargaining unit. Furthermore, these statutorily prescribed bargaining units usually include supervisory and managerial personnel.[2]

The . . . Georgia, Idaho, Rhode Island, and Wyoming statutes [provide] that the organization selected by the majority of the firefighters shall be the sole and exclusive bargaining agent for *all* the classified members of the fire department.

## NOTES

1. Section 23.40.090 of the Alaska Public Employment Act specifically provides that "bargaining units shall be as large as is reasonable and unnecessary fragmenting shall be avoided." ALASKA STAT. tit. 23, ch. 40, § 20.40.090 (1972).

2. The Nevada statute provides that where a local government employer has recognized one or more employee organizations, the employer is to determine the appropriate bargaining unit, after consultation with the employee organization or organizations, pursuant to the criteria set forth in the statute. If an employee organization disagrees with the unit determination, it may appeal to the PERB which is directed to apply "the same criterion" as the government employer. NEV. REV. STAT. § 288.170 (2) (1971).

3. In states where public employers have the authority to engage in collective bargaining in the absence of applicable legislation, the employer has wide discretion in establishing bargaining units, both in terms of their breadth and in terms of categories of employees who are to be included in or excluded from bargaining units. Thus, a public employer in this situation can normally condition its willingness to engage in collective bargaining upon the establishment of bargaining units that it deems appropriate. For example, in FOP v. City of Dayton, 99 L.R.R.M. 2276 (May 16, 1978), the Ohio Court of Appeals upheld a city ordinance which excluded supervisory employees from inclusion in any bargaining units recognized by the city. The Fraternal Order of Police (FOP) and the International Association of Fire Fighters (IAFF) challenged the constitutionality and legality of this ordinance since it had the effect of excluding sergeants, lieutenants and captains from the police bargaining unit and lieutenants, captains and district chiefs from the fire fighters bargaining unit. In upholding the supervisory exclusion, the Ohio Court of Appeals stated:

> There is no provision in the Ohio Constitution or Statute that requires the City of Dayton to bargain collectively with its employees through their representatives FOP and IAFF. Since the city is not required to bargain collectively with its employees it may refrain from doing so or it may set conditions under which it elects to do so. If the employees' bargaining unit chooses not to comply with those conditions, the alternative is no agreement to bargain. The City of Dayton has not violated any constitutional provisions in barring supervisory employees from the bargaining units.

*See also* Tobin v. Cook County Hosp. Comm'n, 99 L.R.R.M. 3234 (Ill. App. Ct. 1978) (in absence of legislation, public employer is "empowered to determine the parameters of a bargaining unit of its employees"); Chicago High School Assistant Principals Ass'n v. Bd. of Educ., 5 Ill. App. 3d 672, 284 N.E.2d 14 (1972).

In some instances where the parties have been unable to reach agreement on the appropriate bargaining unit, they have submitted the question to a mutually selected arbitrator. *See, e.g.,* Rochester Board of Education, 52 Lab. Arb. 1062 (Arb. Jean

---

[2] The Statutes covering firefighters are a prime example. Occasionally, individual units are prescribed within a comprehensive act. The Michigan Act, for example, provides that ". . . in any fire department, or any department in whole or part engaged in, or having the responsibilities of, fire fighting, no person subordinate to a fire commission, safety director, or other similar administrative agency shall be deemed to be a supervisor." MICH. COMP. LAWS ANN. § 423.213 (1967).

McKelvey, 1969). *See generally* Rehmus, *Arbitration of Representation and Bargaining Unit Questions in Public Employment Disputes,* in NATIONAL ACADEMY OF ARBITRATORS, THE ARBITRATOR, THE NLRB, AND THE COURTS, PROCEEDINGS OF THE TWENTIETH ANNUAL MEETING 251 (1967).

**ROCK, THE APPROPRIATE UNIT QUESTION IN THE PUBLIC SERVICE: THE PROBLEM OF PROLIFERATION, 67 Mich. L. Rev. 1001, 1001-08 (1969) †**

## I. Introduction

It is becoming increasingly clear that of the numerous problems which complicate the practice of collective bargaining in the public sector, none is more important than the appropriate unit question. In the public sector as well as in private industry, determination of the size and composition of the bargaining unit at the initial stages of organization and recognition can be decisive of the question of which employee organization will achieve majority recognition, or whether any organization will win recognition. Save for the employee organization which limits its jurisdiction along narrow lines such as the craft practiced by its members, the normal tendency may be to request initially a unit whose boundaries coincide with the spread of the organization's membership or estimated strength. The public employer, on the other hand, may seek to recognize a unit in which the no-union votes will be in the majority, or a favored employee organization will have predominant strength; or the employer may simply seek to avoid undue proliferation of bargaining units.

The problem in the public sector, however, is of far greater depth than the initial victory-or-defeat aspect of recognition. In the private sector, it is clear that the scope and nature of the unit found to be appropriate for bargaining has acted as an important determinant of the union's basic economic strength — that is, its bargaining over bread-and-butter economic issues. In the public sector, it seems clear that the scope and nature of the unit found to be appropriate will also affect the range of subjects which can be negotiated meaningfully, the role played in the process by the separate branches of government, the likelihood of peaceful resolution of disputes, order versus chaos in bargaining, and ultimately, perhaps, the success of the whole idea of collective bargaining for public employees.

Although the appropriate unit question has received much attention in the private sector during the past thirty years, it has not received the same attention for public sector employees until recently. The purpose of this Article is to focus on certain distinguishing aspects of both the problem and the experience in the public sector, and to discuss a possible approach or philosophy for the future. The primary concern here is undue proliferation of units among the large pool of blue-collar and white-collar employees in the public service.

## II. Past Tendencies and Patterns

Traditionally, the public employer and union have given little thought to the appropriateness of a unit that requested recognition. More often than not, in the years prior to the enactment of definitive rules for recognition of public employees, a union requesting and receiving some form of recognition was

---

† Reprinted by permission of The Michigan Law Review Association.

considered the spokesman for its members — in whatever job classifications, functional departments, or physical locations they happened to be. This lenient approach was facilitated by (and perhaps had its start in) the fact that "recognition" frequently carried no legal consequences beyond the ability to appear before legislative or executive bodies hearing budgetary requests or the power to lobby with key political figures. Even when recognition was followed by a procedure similar to bargaining — including in some instances an embodiment of the bargain in a written agreement or memorandum — little if any consideration was given to the appropriateness of the unit being dealt with. Apart from the obvious problems stemming from the failure to grant "exclusive bargaining rights" to these early public employee units and from the inattention to the matter of excluding supervisors from the units representing those whom they supervise, a groundwork was laid for the creation of illogical unit lines. All too frequently the result was a proliferation of bargaining units. The task of changing this ill-conceived basis has often proved troublesome in the current period of rule-oriented bargaining.

Nor has the enactment of rules in the past ten years invariably led to a different pattern. For example, under New York City's Executive Order 49, issued by Mayor Wagner in the late fifties, certificates of recognition were granted for over 200 separate units, some containing as few as two employees. The proportion of units to number of member-employees found in New York City is perhaps exceeded only in Detroit, where some seventy-eight separate units have come into existence. At the federal level, marked proliferation of units has also characterized the pattern of recognition under Executive Order No. 10,988; a similar tendency seems inherent in a number of recently enacted state legislative standards for unit determination.

Notwithstanding this rather pessimistic summary, the past ten years have clearly been the decisive decade for all aspects of public sector bargaining, and this is particularly true for the specific rules regarding unit determination. A major example of this development occurred in 1962 with President Kennedy's promulgation of Executive Order No. 10,988. In this document, which was originally regarded as the federal employee's Magna Carta of labor relations, the following general standards are specified for appropriate unit determination when "exclusive" recognition is sought by a majority organization:

> Units may be established on any plant or installation, craft, functional or other basis which will ensure a clear and identifiable community of interest among the employees concerned, but no unit shall be established solely on the basis of the extent to which employees in the proposed unit have organized.

Another section of the Order also provides for "formal" recognition in a "unit as defined by the agency" when an employee organization has ten percent of the employees as members, and no other organization holds exclusive representation rights. Finally, another section provides for "informal" recognition when the employee organization does not qualify for exclusive or formal recognition, without regard to whether other employee organizations hold one of the other forms of recognition in the same unit.

Regardless of whether this three-sided format was justified under the state of recognition and bargaining then prevalent in the federal service, there can be little question that the system was calculated to encourage representational footholds on a mass scale within small units. And, it did result in proliferation of units, albeit on a reduced scale, as informal or formal recognition often led to exclusive recognition. Emphasis on the "community of interest" standard in the administration of Executive Order No. 10,988, and the use in some instances of the National Labor Relations Board's technique of the "*Globe* election" — a procedure in which the members of a homogeneous occupational group are allowed to vote on separate recognition for their own unit, as opposed to a rival organization's request that they be included in a larger unit — have undoubtedly contributed further to widespread fragmentation of units in federal employment.

At the state and local levels, virtually all of the significant legislation passed since 1960 has spelled out standards of some type for unit determination. In many instances these state enactments made possible further proliferation by adding to the existing illogical patterns of recognition new units made possible through espousal of the federal "community of interest" standard and its converse, separate units for groups having "conflicting interests"; by providing for *Globe*-type elections or similar approaches designed to facilitate small unit separation; and, in the states of Delaware and Minnesota, by permitting the government agency to rely on the extent of employee organization. Notwithstanding the fact that some of the state laws embody specific standards used by the National Labor Relations Board for the private sector, observers familiar with bargaining conditions in both sectors have contended that the degree of fragmentation in some of the states exceeds that of the private sector.

Clearly, at both state and federal levels the standards place a high premium on the subjective judgment of the decision-making body or individual, and results are also shaped to a high degree by the happenstance of the petitioning organization's requested unit at the time of the petition. Particularly when there is no rival organizational claim for a larger unit — which is often the case — the over-all effect has been to encourage recognition of the smaller unit. Even if a union succeeds in winning recognition in a large unit, employees in that unit are generally not required to become members of the union. The relative lack of union security clauses in the collective bargaining agreements of the public service assures that, to a degree unparalleled in the private sector, dissident small-unit groups are able to maintain their separate identities and to prolong the battle for break-off from the larger group's exclusive bargaining agent.

### III. The Case for and Against the Small Unit

It cannot be assumed automatically that the pattern of many small units is wrong. A single craft, classification, department, or installation which would otherwise constitute a small minority if included in a larger unit can argue with some justification that its specialized interests and needs may be subordinated to the wishes of the larger unit's majority. Moreover, the smaller unit which performs a particularly essential function may also be capable of striking a better bargain for itself when left to do its own negotiating.

"Community of interest" is more than a catch phrase. It not only points up that like-situated employees will better understand their own problems and press their unique needs, but it also recognizes the instinct of exclusiveness which causes employees to *want* to form their own organization rather than become a part of a larger organization in which they may feel themselves strangers. The desire to possess such "freedom of choice" or "self-determination" should, it can be argued, receive greater weight for public employees, because they are "public," than for those in the private sector.

There is nothing inherently wrong in permitting an employee organization to gain a foothold in a smaller unit, if the employees in that unit select it; and, if the union is effective in the small unit, it may grow and achieve recognition in other separate units or in a single large unit. This consideration may be particularly significant in the early period after the promulgation of legislation or executive orders encompassing a vast group of employees whose right to representation had not previously been formally legitimized. It is frequently easier for unions to secure employees' allegiance in smaller, distinctive groups than in larger, heterogeneous ones.

At the same time, there are important considerations which, it seems, point toward a unique long-range need for larger units in the public sector. The special problems of unit determination in the public sector were most clearly recognized legislatively in 1967 in New York's Taylor Law, which included, in addition to the common standards of community of interest and necessity to promote the public welfare, the further requirement that in defining an appropriate unit the following standard should be taken into consideration: "the officials of government at the level of the unit shall have the power to agree, or to make effective recommendations to other administrative authority or the legislative body with respect to, the terms and conditions of employment upon which the employees desire to negotiate. . . ." The latter clause clearly reflects awareness of the fact that the employer-negotiator in the public service frequently has only limited authority, and that this condition will affect the scope of bargaining. As pointed out by the New York Governor's Committee on Public Employee Relations, the picture in the public sector is fundamentally different from that in the private sector. In private business, the authority to bargain on all of the normally bargainable matters is present or can be delegated, no matter what the size or make-up of the bargaining unit. By contrast, in the public service the necessary authority may not be delegable to lower-level functional units; legal requirements and tradition often call for uniformity of certain working conditions for like categories of employees throughout the governmental entity, regardless of bargaining unit categorization; and, even at the top of the particular level of government involved, authority is normally divided at least three ways — among the executive branch, the legislative branch, and a civil service commission.

Inherent in the previously quoted section of the Taylor Law, therefore, is the necessity that some consideration be given to the nature of the subject matter sought to be bargained upon in seeking to arrive at the appropriateness of a unit. This provision of the Taylor Law also recognizes that the subject matter of bargaining must normally be limited by the scope of the "employer's" authority to make agreements or effective recommendations, and a likely consequence is that the smaller the unit decided upon, the more restricted the scope of the bargaining by that unit will be.

Apart from this inhibiting effect on the bargaining experience, an approach which permits or favors small units makes it very difficult to resolve other institutional complications which arise in bargaining in the public service. The New York Governor's Committee, in both its 1966 Report and its 1968 Report, pointed out the unique importance of completing a negotiation with public employees in time to incorporate the agreement's financial essence in the budget of the governmental unit — which, by law, generally must be submitted to the legislature by a specified date. However, many of the annual bargaining sessions in the public sector today are extraordinarily prolonged, starting with direct negotiation, followed by resort to mediation and the frequently used machinery of fact-finding or impasse panels. After all of this there may be further extensive dealings with upper-echelon individuals or groups in the executive and legislative branches. Thus, the sheer weight of the process [3] may lead to its breakdown if the trend toward proliferation of bargaining units in numerous jurisdictions continues unabated. It is noteworthy that in the City of Philadelphia [4] — which is frequently cited as an example of well-established, peaceful, and effective bargaining at the municipal level — all employees except policemen and firemen have been represented by a single unit for most of the last two decades. Even with only a single unit and without use of impasse resolution machinery, however, the experience in Philadelphia has been marked by many instances of abnormally prolonged annual negotiations. The Philadelphia experience also demonstrates the need to establish detailed liaison between the executive branch, the legislative branch, and the civil service commission during the course of an annual bargaining program in order to minimize the chaotic effects of overlapping authority on the government side.

While it is possible that a city the size of Philadelphia might also have had a history of successful labor relations in the public sector under a pattern which broke down the public employee bargaining group into a small number of separate units, there is little question that the success could not have been achieved under the patterns of excessive fragmentation found elsewhere. In any event, the existence of the single large unit clearly contributed significantly to that city's ability to surmount effectively the institutional obstacles complicating public sector bargaining. Moreover, proliferation can and does breed excessive competition among rival organizations. One consequence of this may be a high incidence of breakdowns in peaceful bargaining. To be sure, competition in bargaining is to some extent unavoidable; this condition is not necessarily undesirable socially, and will continue to characterize the experience in private and public sector alike, regardless of the size of units involved. Nevertheless, there is hardly a permanent justification for permitting what appears to be a greater proliferation of bargaining units in the public sector than that now prevailing in the private sector. The institutional factors discussed above add a unique dimension to the task of achieving peaceful and successful bargaining in the public sector. Because of this, and because of the likelihood that proliferation will result in an increased number of breakdowns in the bargaining process, larger units must become the accepted norm in the public sector. . . .

●

## NOTE

For other useful discussions, see UNIT DETERMINATION, RECOGNITION, AND REPRESENTATION ELECTIONS IN PUBLIC AGENCIES, PROCEEDINGS OF A CONFERENCE ON PUBLIC SECTOR LABOR MANAGEMENT RELATIONS, 1971 (Univ. of Calif. Institute of Ind. Rel. 1972); Mack, *Public Sector Collective Bargaining: Diffusion of Managerial Structure and Fragmentation of Bargaining Units,* 2 FLA. ST. L. REV. 281 (1974); H. WELLINGTON & R. WINTER, THE UNIONS AND THE CITIES 97-114 (1971); Anderson, *Selection and Certification of Representatives in Public Employment,* in N.Y.U. TWENTIETH ANNUAL CONFERENCE ON LABOR 277 (1967); Thompson, *Unit Determination in Public Employment,* PUBLIC EMPLOYEE RELATIONS REPORTS, No. 1 (N.Y. State School of Industrial and Labor Relations, 1968); Sullivan, *Appropriate Unit Determinations in Public Employee Collective Bargaining,* 19 MERCER L. REV. 402 (1968); Lahne, *Unit*

---

[3] For example, a February 27, 1968, report by an impasse panel for the unit of Detroit police officers recommended a procedure for future bargaining. The essential steps which the panel proposed were to extend over a period of nine months in a particular year. *Excerpts from Detroit Police Panel Report,* GOV'T EMPLOYEE REL. REP. [*hereinafter* GERR] No. 235, at D-1, D-10 (March 11, 1968).

[4] The author was the labor relations adviser to the City of Philadelphia between 1952 and 1962.

*Determinations in the Federal Service,* in N.Y.U. TWENTY-FIRST ANNUAL CONFERENCE ON LABOR 469 (1969); Newman, *Major Problems in Public Sector Bargaining Units,* in N.Y.U. TWENTY-THIRD ANNUAL CONFERENCE ON LABOR 373 (1971). The NLRB's unit policies in the private sector are thoroughly explored in J. ABODEELY, THE NLRB AND THE APPROPRIATE BARGAINING UNIT (1971).

## 2. CRITERIA CONSIDERED

### CONNECTICUT STATE BOARD OF LABOR RELATIONS, TWENTY-FIRST ANNUAL REPORT 1-3 (1967)

Questions concerning the unit and the related questions concerning the supervisory level at which membership in a unit is to be cut off obviously involve competing legitimate interests. The municipal employer, for example, often wants the broadest possible unit for reasons of administrative simplicity and convenience. Some employee organizations also want wide units because of their own traditions and institutional patterns. Other employee organizations have different and narrower traditions and practices, sometimes stemming from those of the old-line trade or craft unions. And some groups, heretofore unorganized or loosely organized, have their own traditions and special communities of interest. The Legislature itself has resolved these conflicts by providing specific guides in the case of uniformed and investigatory members of the police and fire departments, and in the case of professional employees. Even these guides have presented some problems of interpretation. Beyond them the Legislature has charged the Board with the difficult and often delicate task of balancing these competing interests under the broad injunction to insure to employees "the fullest freedom in exercising their rights" under the Act, and "to insure a clear and identifiable community of interest among employees" included in a unit. The Commission which drafted the Act stated that it did "subscribe to the view that the units should be the broadest possible which will reflect a community of interest and at the same time will respect the special interests of certain groups of employees." REPORT OF THE INTERIM COMMISSION TO STUDY COLLECTIVE BARGAINING BY MUNICIPALITIES (1965), p. 15 (hereinafter *Report*).

In attempting to implement this broad legislative mandate, the Board has given attention to the following factors in cases where one or more of them were made to appear:

1. *Agreements by the parties.* The Commission's Report indicates that the framers of the Act believed that questions of this nature should be governed by agreement of the parties where agreement can be had. *Report,* page 15. There has been such agreement in a majority of cases processed by the Agent during the reporting period, upon at least some aspects of the case. The Board has adopted the policy of approving such agreements unless the resulting unit clearly contravenes the policy of the Act, and this has not occurred in practice.

2. *The similarity (or dissimilarity) of work and working conditions.* This includes any aspects of the work which would tend to create a community of interest, or the reverse, and covers a great variety of matters. Whether the work is clerical or manual (white collar or blue collar); whether there is common supervision; whether the work is performed in a single location, are examples of the sort of things the Board will look for and try to weigh. Obviously these considerations may sometimes pull in opposite directions. Employees in the same department may, for instance, perform different kinds of work, and work classifications often cut across department lines. This was the case in Greenwich, Dec. No. 692, June 7, 1966.

3. *The convenience of the municipal employer* in the light of its personnel and other relevant policies and practices. Thus in the Town of Greenwich the Board declined to carve a unit out of blue collar workers in the Public Works Department alone, when the Town showed that this would disrupt its policy of uniform treatment for all employees in the work classifications involved, many of whom were in other departments, and where there appeared to be no countervailing consideration. See also City of Bridgeport, Dec. No. 677, February 21, 1966.

4. *Past bargaining history, if any.* The Board has given weight to the municipal employer's past practices and patterns of negotiation and recognition where there have been any. It is true that these would have antedated the Act, and are not legally binding on the parties. Nevertheless they have some tendency to show what the parties themselves have considered appropriate and feasible and what they are used to. And the patterns are likely to reflect any traditions that have evolved in the municipal service. Patterns worked out in other cities and towns, where they have attained a measure of consistency, seem entitled to some consideration in determining what is appropriate (though less than the municipal employer's own practices). They may be compared roughly to the customs of an industry which have often been given similar consideration. Even the employee organization's overall pattern (in this country), where there is one, seems entitled to some weight, since it has at least a slight tendency on pragmatic grounds to show something about feasibility and about the kind of unit which the organization can effectively represent.

5. *The desires of the members of a group* to be associated together for bargaining purposes. . . .

6. *The Commission's admonition to keep the unit as broad as possible,* where that is consistent with the need for community of interest, and respect for legitimate special interests. . . .

The above discussion should indicate something of the complexity and difficulty of the Board's task. It should be quite apparent that many of the above considerations overlap, and many work at cross-purposes with each other. The problems and practices of the 169 cities and towns of the State vary infinitely, and the extent to which each of the factors listed above appears is not the same in any two of them. . . . For this reason there is great variety among the size and the kinds of units found appropriate in the cases decided by the Board during the reporting period. Just as the Commission "concluded that it would be impossible to lay down any hard and fast rules for the determination by the Board of appropriate units," . . . so the Board has refrained from applying rules which would put a strait-jacket on the types of units it would find appropriate. Rather it has sought to determine the problems in each municipality by applying to them the broad principles which the Act lays down, and by weighing the factors which the Board believes to be relevant to those principles in each individual case.

## CITY OF APPLETON

Wisconsin Employment Relations Commission
Decision No. 7423 (1966)

Local 73, AFSCME, hereinafter referred to as the Petitioner, petitioned the Board to conduct an election among employes of the City of Appleton, employed in the Sewerage Division of the Department of Public Works, to determine what representation, if any, the employes therein desired for the purposes of collective bargaining, pursuant to Section 111.70 of the Wisconsin Statutes. At the hearing, Teamsters Local 563, hereinafter referred to as the Intervenor, was permitted to intervene on the basis of its claim to be the recognized representative for all hourly-paid employes employed in the Department of Public Works.

The Intervenor would have the Board dismiss the petition on two grounds, (1) that the unit sought by the Petitioner is inappropriate, and (2) that the petition was untimely filed.

### Appropriateness of Unit

The Department of Public Works consists of five separate divisions, Street, Sanitation, Sewerage, Maintenance and Engineering. There are approximately 120 employes in the Department of Public Works, and 18 are employed in the Sewerage Division. The Intervenor, up until at least the date of the filing of the petition, September 27, 1965, has been recognized as the collective bargaining representative of all hourly-paid employes in the first four divisions. The Engineering Division consists of professional engineers and clericals.

While the Intervenor claims that it has been recognized as the representative of the employes in the Department of Public Works and that such a Department is an appropriate unit, it should be noted that the clerical employes in the Engineering Department have not been included as part of that departmental-wide unit.

The Sewerage Division is physically and functionally located separate and distinct from the remainder of the functions and divisions of the Municipal Employer. Its employes primarily carry out their functions at the Sewage Disposal Plant. It has its own Superintendent, who is in charge of the entire Division, and the employes in said Division are not subject to the supervision of any other agent or officer of the Municipal Employer. The employes perform duties which, except for the Laborer I and II classifications, of which there are four positions, are distinct from the duties performed by employes of the Municipal Employer employed in other divisions or departments. There are very few temporary transfers either to or from the Sewerage Division.

The Board's function with respect to the establishment of an appropriate collective bargaining unit of municipal employes is governed by the following statutory provisions:

"Section 111.70(4) (d). *Collective Bargaining Units.* Whenever a question arises between a municipal employer and a labor union as to whether the union represents the employes of the employer, either the union or the municipality may petition the board to conduct an election among said employes to determine whether they desire to be represented by a labor organization. Proceedings in representation cases shall be in accordance with ss. 111.02(6) and 111.05 insofar as applicable, except that where the board finds that a proposed unit includes a craft the board shall exclude such craft from the unit. The board shall not order an election among employes in a craft unit except on separate petition initiating representation proceedings in such craft unit."

"Section 111.02(6). The term 'collective bargaining unit' shall mean all of the employes of one employer . . ., except that where a majority of such employes engaged in a single craft, division, department or plant shall have voted by secret ballot as provided in Section 111.05(2) to constitute such group a separate bargaining unit they shall be so considered, . . . ."

"Section 111.05(2). Whenever a question arises concerning the determination of a collective bargaining unit as defined in Section 111.02(6), it shall be determined by secret ballot, and the board, upon request, shall cause the ballot to be taken in such manner as to show separately the wishes of the employes in any craft, division, department or plant as to the determination of the collective bargaining unit."

Whenever a petition for an election is filed with the Board, and wherein the petitioner requests an election among certain employes not constituting all of the employes of the employer, the Board has no power, except if the employes constitute a single craft, to determine what constitutes an appropriate collective bargaining unit. It does determine whether the group of employes set out as being an appropriate bargaining unit does in fact constitute a separate craft, division, department or plant. The employes involved, if they do constitute a separate division, department, or plant, are given the opportunity to determine for themselves whether they desire to constitute a separate collective bargaining unit.

The Intervenor contends that the statutes should be interpreted to give weight to past bargaining history to determine whether a non-craft group should be permitted to establish itself as a separate unit, whether for the purpose of decertification or for substituting another union for its current bargaining agent. It emphasizes the bargaining history between the Intervenor and the Municipal Employer, and argues that the unit established through bargaining history should not be disturbed.

The bargaining and negotiations in the past have been conducted by the City's Personnel Committee for all of the employes in the Department of Public Works, with the City Personnel Committee consulting with and receiving the advice of the Director of Public Works. The wage increases, fringe benefits and work rules negotiated for the Department of Public Works have been applied to all the employes in the Department and, in some instances, on a City-wide basis. The recommendations made by the Sewerage Division Superintendent with respect to promotions, tranfers, discipline and individual wage adjustments, are subject to the approval of the Director of Public Works, and are not made independently by the Superintendent of the Sewage Disposal Plant.

The Intervenor would have the Board establish an appropriate collective bargaining unit on criteria considered by the National Labor Relations Board in establishing appropriate units under the federal labor law. The National Labor Relations Board considers the following factors:

(1) Duties, skills and working conditions of the employes.

(2) History of collective bargaining.

(3) Extent of union organization among the employes.

(4) Desires of the employes where one or two units may be equally appropriate.

Similarly, in recently adopted labor laws applying to public employes, the Connecticut State Board of Labor Relations and the Michigan Labor Mediation Board determine appropriate collective bargaining units with due consideration to "... a clear and identifiable community of interest to employes concerned...."

However, the criteria established in the Wisconsin Employment Peace Act, as quoted above, do not permit the Board to rely on the bargaining history as grounds for denying elections among employes in a separate division to determine for themselves whether they desire to constitute a unit separate and apart from the other employes of the municipal employer.

The Board has also today issued a Direction of Elections in a case involving the City of Kenosha. Another local of the Teamsters filed a petition with the Board requesting the Board to conduct an election among employes in the Waste Division of the Department of Public Works. In that proceeding, another local of the AFSCME has been historically recognized as the representative of all civil service employes of that community, with the exception of uniformed employes. In the instant proceeding, the intervening Teamster's local objects to the fragmentation of an existing unit. In the City of Kenosha case, the petitioning Teamster's local would fragmentize the existing unit. The Intervenor AFSCME Local in the City of Kenosha case would retain the overall unit and opposes fragmentation of an existing unit, while in the instant proceeding, the petitioning AFSCME Local would fragmentize the existing unit. The position of the parties in said two proceedings are inconsistent and demonstrate the problems faced by the Board in establishing units as required by the Statute. Fragmentizing of larger units of employes may result in requiring a municipal employer to engage in conferences and negotiations with more than one labor organization representing the same general category of employes on wages, hours and working conditions of its employes, may encourage needless rivalry among labor organizations, and may disturb an existing legitimate relationship and tend to delay the collective bargaining process. However, these factors must be weighed against the rights of the employes, where they constitute a separate department or division, to determine for themselves whether they desire to constitute a separate appropriate collective bargaining unit and, further, what representation, if any, they desire for the purposes of conferences and negotiations with their municipal employer. It is interesting to note that there has been an insignificant number of cases where the Board has observed fragmentation of bargaining units, in accordance with the statutory requirements, among employes of private employers. Apparently, the employes, labor organizations and employers alike, at least in private employment, have recognized that an effective collective bargaining relationship is best maintained in the absence of fragmentizing an over-all collective bargaining unit. This observation is not intended to apply to those smaller units consisting of craft employes or employes with specialized skills. . . .

The Board, therefore, is today issuing a Direction of Elections wherein the employes in the Sewerage Division will be given an opportunity to determine for themselves whether they desire to constitute a collective bargaining unit separate and apart from other employes of the Municipal Employer, and what, if any, representation they desire for the purposes of conferences and negotiations with the Municipal Employer on questions of wages, hours and conditions of employment.

The results of the unit vote will be tabulated first, and if there is no question that the required number of employes vote in favor of the separate unit, then the ballots with respect to the selection of the bargaining representative will be tallied. However, if the result of the vote on the unit determination does not establish a separate unit, the Board agent conducting the elections will immediately impound the ballots on the question of representation and the results thereof will not be determined. . . .

## NOTES

1. Chairman Morris Slavney of the Wisconsin Employment Relations Commission made the following comments with respect to the statutory provisions referred to in the principal case:

> [S]uch requirements with regard to the establishment of bargaining units have
> resulted in an overfragmentation of bargaining units in municipal employment in
> Wisconsin. For example, the City of Milwaukee has over 20 separate bargaining units.
> In the City of Appleton, somewhere in the neighborhood of 60,000 population, both
> AFSCME and Teamsters were engaged in organizational efforts among clerical
> employees in some six departments of the city hall. As a result of the statutory
> provision granting employees in each department an opportunity to establish
> separate units, the City of Appleton ended up with six units of stenographers and
> clericals in six departments. The Teamsters represented three of the departmental
> units while AFSCME was certified as the representative in the remaining three
> departments. You can imagine the frustration of management in having to bargain
> with two unions, who are forever competing with each other, for the same
> classification of employees under the same civil service system. Slavney,
> *Representation and Bargaining Unit Issues,* in DISPUTE SETTLEMENT IN THE PUBLIC
> SECTOR 35, 49-50 (T. Gilroy ed. 1972).

The Wisconsin Municipal Employment Law was subsequently revised to broaden the
discretion of the WERC in determining appropriate bargaining units, while at the same
time mandating it to avoid excessive fragmentation. WIS. STAT. ANN. § 111.70(4) (d)
(Supp. 1972) now provides, in relevant part, that:

> The commission shall determine the appropriate bargaining unit for the purpose
> of collective bargaining and shall whenever possible avoid fragmentation by
> maintaining as few units as practicable in keeping with the size of the total municipal
> work force. In making such a determination, the commission may decide whether,
> in a particular case, the employees in the same or several departments, divisions,
> institutions, crafts, professions or other occupational groupings constitute a unit.
> Before making its determination, the commission may provide an opportunity for the
> employees concerned to determine, by secret ballot, whether or not they desire to
> be established as a separate collective bargaining unit. . . .

2. Community of interest among the employees in the unit petitioned for is one of the
most important determinants of whether the unit is appropriate. The Michigan
Employment Relations Commission in City of Warren, 1966 MERC Lab. Op. 25, 28
(Mich.), noted that

> Community of interest is determined by a number of factors and criteria, some
> of which are as follows: similarity of duties, skills and working conditions, job
> classifications, employee benefits, the amount of interchange or transfer of
> employees, the integration of the employer's physical operations, the centralization
> of administrative and managerial functions, the degree of central control of
> operations, including labor relations, promotional ladders used by employees,
> supervisory hierarchy, and common supervision.

Even if the employees in the unit petitioned for have an established community of interest,
the unit may not necessarily constitute an appropriate bargaining unit. In Kelly Air Force
Base, GERR No. 228, at Unit Arbitrations 1 (1968), the arbitrator conceded that there
was a community of interest in the proposed unit; nevertheless, he held that "where that
homogeneous group is only part of a larger essentially homogeneous group, sharing
essentially the same common employment interests, a smaller group may not be found
to be an appropriate unit."

3. What is the unit status of employees who are hired under the Comprehensive
Employment and Training Act (CETA)? This question has been frequently litigated and,
for the most part, the various PERBs and PERCs have included CETA employees in
bargaining units. For example, in Erie County Area Vocational-Technical School, 9 PPER
¶ 9275 (Pa. PLRB 1978), the Pennsylvania Board held that "CETA employes who perform
the same duties, work the same hours and enjoy the same benefits as non-CETA employes
may be included in the same unit with non-CETA employes. . . ." In this case the
Pennsylvania Board rejected "the Employer's contention that CETA employes enjoy no
reasonable expectancy of continued employment and have no identifiable community of

interest with non-CETA employes." *Accord,* City of Three Rivers, 1977 MERC Lab. Op. 213 (Mich.); Passaic County Board of Freeholders, 4 NJPER ¶ 4006 (N.J. PERC 1977). Following enactment of the 1978 amendments to CETA, the Florida PERC, however, held that while CETA participants were public employees under the Florida Act they should be excluded from bargaining units with non-CETA employees. Hillsborough County Board of County Commissioners, 5 FPER ¶ 10019 (Fla. PERC 1979). Pointing to the existence of the $10,000 salary maximum for CETA participants and the prohibition against employer supplementation of CETA salaries, as well as the new requirement that no CETA participant may receive federally funded wages for more than 78 weeks in a five-year period, the Florida Commission stated:

> Since the Commission concludes now, based upon the CETA Amendments of 1978 and the record in the instant case, currently employed Board CETA employees do not possess a reasonable expectation of continued employment and that certain statutorily-defined elements of community of interest between regular and CETA Board employees will no longer be in existence, the Commission recedes from its decision to include blue-collar CETA employees in the defined unit herein.

In Mon Valley United Health Services, Inc., 238 N.L.R.B. No. 129, 99 L.R.R.M. 1332 (1978), the NLRB, reversing prior decisions, ruled that federal Manpower training employees should be included in bargaining units. The Board reasoned as follows:

> . . . assimilation of the unemployed and underemployed into the Nation's work force is a fundamental aim of Manpower programs in general. We see no useful purpose served by excluding such employees from the question of bargaining unit representation, particularly in light of the substantial work interests they shared with other unit employees. . . .

4. Are prisoners in state correctional institutions entitled to representation for the purposes of collective bargaining? In Prisoners' Labor Union v. Helsby, 44 A.D.2d 708, 354 N.Y.S.2d 694 (1974), the court sustained PERB's dismissal of representation petitions filed by prisoners' labor unions seeking to represent inmates, noting that "[i]f there be merit in petitioners' claims of a right to organize and bargain collectively, it is for the Legislature so to determine." The Massachusetts Labor Relations Commission ruled in Commonwealth of Massachusetts Dep't of Corrections and Walpole Chapter of the Nat'l Prisoners' Reform Ass'n, GERR No. 532, B-1 (1973), that prisoners were not state employees for the purposes of the state collective bargaining law. *Accord,* Salah v. PLRB, 95 L.R.R.M. 2731 (Pa. Ct. C.P. 1977). *But see* State of Michigan Dep't of Corrections, GERR No. 552, B-13 (1974), where the MERC dismissed a representation petition filed by a group of prisoners on the ground that it had no jurisdiction over state agencies, but nevertheless observed that there was a sufficient employer-employee relationship to warrant collective bargaining for prisoners.

In two states — Delaware and Hawaii — prison inmates are specifically excluded from coverage under the public sector bargaining law. DEL. CODE tit. 13, § 1301(b) (1977); HAW. REV. STAT. § 89-6(c) (1976).


## STATE OF NEW YORK

New York Public Employment Relations Board
1 PERB ¶ 399.85 (1968), *aff'd per curiam sub nom.* Civil Service Employees
Ass'n v. Helsby, 32 App. Div. 2d 131, 300 N.Y.S.2d 424, *aff'd per curiam,*
25 N.Y.2d 842, 250 N.E.2d 731, 303 N.Y.S.2d 690 (1969)

On November 15, 1967, the State of New York, herein referred to as the employer, recognized the Civil Service Employees Association, Inc., herein referred to as CSEA, as negotiating representative of employees in a general unit made up of all State employees other than professional members of the State University of New York and members of the State Police. Timely petitions contesting the designation of the general unit and the recognition of CSEA were filed by many organizations, all of which proposed one or more negotiating units alternative to the unit designated by the employer.

## The Petitioners and the Units They Claim

New York State Employees Council 50, American Federation of State, County and Municipal Employees, AFL-CIO, herein referred to as Council 50, directly and through several of its affiliated locals, seeks the following units:

1. All correction officers, correction youth camp officers and correction hospital officers in the Department of Correction, excluding all supervisors and all other persons.

This identical unit is claimed by another of the petitioners, Local 456 of the International Brotherhood of Teamsters, Chauffeurs, Warehousemen and Helpers of America, herein referred to as IBT.

2. All employees in the Psychiatric Attendant Series, including psychiatric attendant, psychiatric senior attendant, psychiatric staff attendant, psychiatric supervising attendant, psychiatric head attendant, psychiatric chief supervising attendant and all (T.B.) titles in this series.

3. All nonsupervisory employees in the Rehabilitation Counselor Series in the Department of Education, including counselors and senior counselors. There are a few rehabilitation counselors in the Department of Social Services and Mental Hygiene and in the State University. Council 50 takes no position on whether these rehabilitation counselors should also be included in the proposed unit.

4. All clerical employees of the Department of Labor proper.

5. All professional and technical employees of the Department of Labor proper, excluding managerial and confidential employees, nurses, attorneys and safety inspectors.

6. All professional and technical employees of the Division of Employment, excluding managerial and confidential employees, nurses and attorneys.

7. All clerical employees of the Division of Employment.

8. All nonsupervisory office and clerical employees of the State Insurance Fund.

9. All nonsupervisory professional and technical employees of the State Insurance Fund, excluding field service, confidential and managerial employees, nurses and attorneys.

10. All supervising professional and technical employees of the State Insurance Fund, excluding field service, confidential and managerial employees, nurses and attorneys.

11. All investigators of the Workmen's Compensation Board, Grade 12 through Grade 20.

12. All hearing officers of the Workmen's Compensation Board, Grade 14, and all those calendar clerks who are assigned to the Workmen's Compensation Board Referees' Bureau.

13. All assistant workmen's compensation examiners, Grade 8.

Local 30D, International Union of Operating Engineers, AFL-CIO, herein referred to as Operating Engineers, seeks a unit of:

14. Nonsupervisory employees in the power plants and related skilled trade shops.

The Safety Officers Benevolent Association, herein referred to as SOBA, seeks to represent:

15. All nonsupervisory safety officers. SOBA leaves to the discretion of this Board whether all nonsupervisory safety officers should be included in a single unit or whether there should be separate units for those employees

in the Department of Mental Hygiene, Department of Correction, and the State University, respectively. It takes no position with respect to the inclusion or exclusion from the proposed unit or units of safety officers, if any, in the Department of Health.

Local 381 of the Building Service Employees International Union, AFL-CIO, herein referred to as BSEIU, seeks two units consisting, respectively, of:

16. Lifeguards employed by Long Island State Park Commission.

17. Seasonal patrolmen employed by Long Island State Park Commission.

District 15, International Association of Machinists and Aerospace Workers, AFL-CIO, herein referred to as IAM, seeks a unit of:

18. Long Island State Park Police, Grade 14 and Grade 16.

The Police Conference of New York, Inc., through two of its affiliates, seeks units of:

19. Niagara State Park Police, excluding the captain and lieutenants.

20. All Capital Buildings Police.

The Correction Officers Association claims a unit of:

21. All correction officers and their supervisors, excluding the deputy warden and correction deputy superintendent.

Local 223 of the Building Service Employees International Union, AFL-CIO, seeks a unit of:

22. Inspectors in the Division of Industrial Safety Service of the Department of Labor, excluding chief inspectors.

The Association of New York State Civil Service Attorneys, Inc., seeks a unit of:

23. Lawyers holding competitive class positions in the attorney series of titles for which permission to practice law in the State of New York is a mandatory requirement, and persons holding training-level positions whether or not admitted to practice law in New York State. It would exclude lawyers who hold competitive class positions as counsel to a department or agency.

The New York State Nurses Association seeks a unit consisting of:

24. All registered professional nurses and every person lawfully authorized by permit to practice as a registered professional nurse in nursing service or in nursing education. The proposed unit would include persons on the faculty of the State University and, therefore, not within the general unit designated by the employer.

The American Physical Therapy Association claims a unit of:

25. All physical therapists. This unit would include physical therapists employed on the faculty of the State University and, therefore, not within the general unit designated by the employer.

Petitions were also filed by SOBA for a unit of nonsupervisory narcotics security assistants in the Department of Mental Hygiene, by the New York State Council of Carpenters, AFL-CIO, for a unit comprising all carpenters; and by Local 200 of the Building Service Employees International Union, AFL-CIO, for a unit consisting of all nonsupervisory employees of the Syracuse State School. Each of these petitions was withdrawn, as was a petition of the Police Conference, Inc., on behalf of a unit of police officers of the Palisades Interstate Park Commission.

Council 50 and BSEIU both filed timely petitions to decertify CSEA as the negotiating representative of employees in the general unit, on the ground that the general unit is inappropriate for the purpose of collective negotiations.
. . . .

[The Board denied a motion to disqualify the CSEA on the ground that it was not a labor organization within the meaning of the act. The Board granted motions disqualifying the American Physical Therapy Association and the Association of New York State Civil Service Attorneys, Inc., on this basis.]

### Unit Determination of Director of Representation

With respect to the unit claims of the petitioners, the Director of Representation gave full consideration to the evidence produced and to the arguments made. He found that the employees within the general unit did not share a community of interest in that the range of their work assignments and of the training required for the performance of such assignments was inordinately broad. On the other hand, he found that, in the language of the employer:

> none [of the petitioners] has related its unit to a meaningful pattern of collective negotiation. Each would leave the State with a jumble of mixed vertical and horizontal units. They would leave it to the State to bring order out of the chaos they had created.

We agree with this analysis of the Director of Representation.

The employees concerned in this representation dispute are employed in over 3,700 job classifications, categorized in some 90 occupational groupings. These job classifications far surpass in diversity and number those usually found in public or private employment. These classifications run the gamut from Aircraft Pilot to Wild Life Trapper.

The enormity of this diversity of occupations and the great range in the qualifications requisite for employment in these occupations would preclude effective and meaningful representation in collective negotiations if all such employees were included in a single unit. The occupational differences found here give rise to different interests and concerns in terms and conditions of employment. This, in turn, would give rise to such conflicts of interest as to outweigh those factors indicating a community of interest.

Thus, the implementation of the rights granted by the Act to all public employees mandates a finding that a single unit would be inappropriate.

On the other hand, to grant the type of narrow occupational fragmentation requested by the petitioners would lead to unwarranted and unnecessary administrative difficulties. Indeed, as the State contends, it might well lead to the disintegration of the State's current labor relations structure.

Having rejected the unit designated by the employer and those proposed by petitioners, the Director of Representation decided that there should be six negotiating units, as follows:

> Operational Services Unit, Inspection and Security Services Unit, Health Services and Support Unit, Administrative Services Unit, Professional, Scientific and Technical Services Unit, and a unit of seasonal employees of the Long Island State Park Commission.

Excluded from all units are all other seasonal and part-time employees inasmuch as there is not sufficient evidence in the record to determine their proper unit placement, and persons claimed to be managerial or confidential employees by the employer. With respect to the latter group, the Director stated that further proceedings would be necessary to develop criteria to be utilized in categorizing an employee as managerial or confidential and to determine the desirability and practicality of their inclusion in the negotiating structure of State employees.

Both the employer and CSEA have contended on this appeal that the decision of the Director constitutes error, in that the units found in his decision do not coincide with any of the units petitioned for in this proceeding. Thus, a most basic question presented on this appeal is whether this Board, in a representation proceeding, may devise a unit that it deems to be most appropriate although such a unit is not sought by any of the parties.

We are convinced that this question must be answered in the affirmative. The statutory grant of authority to this Board to resolve disputes concerning representation status mandates this Board to define appropriate units and does not restrict its power simply to the approval or disapproval of units sought by a party or parties to the proceeding. Even apart from such clear statutory intent, the logic of the situation compels the same conclusion. If the Board's power herein were so restricted, a representation dispute might be interminable, in that it would continue until a party to the proceeding petitioned for a unit which the Board found to be appropriate in the light of statutory criteria. Such a restrictive interpretation of the Act would delay unduly participation by public employees in the determination of their terms and conditions of employment. It is for this reason that the Director of Representation has, in many proceedings, devised negotiating units which were not sought by any of the parties.

We believe that the statutory criteria that "the unit shall be compatible with the joint responsibilities of the public employer and public employees to serve the public" (Civil Service Law, § 207(c)) requires us to designate negotiating units which provide the employer with a comprehensive and coherent pattern for collective negotiations. Moreover, we believe that this statutory standard requires the designation of as small a number of units as possible consistent with the overriding requirement that the employees be permitted to form organizations of their own choosing to represent them in a meaningful and effective manner. It is our conviction that the approach of the Director of Representation in designating a limited number of negotiating units, each consisting of families of occupations, is reasonably designed to achieve this goal.

In evaluating the specific units determined to be appropriate by the Director of Representation, we defer consideration of the unit for the seasonal employees of the Long Island State Park Commission. The unit itself and the questions it raises regarding seasonal employees in parks and elsewhere throughout the State are separable from problems involving the other State employees. Further, these problems are not ripe for resolution as the seasonal employees of the Long Island State Park Commission are not presently on the State payroll and will not be until the advent of summer.

We find the following five units to be appropriate:

1. Operational Services Unit:

This unit is similar to that determined to be appropriate by the Director of Representation except that we delete those occupations associated with institutions and related to the preparation and distribution of food, and to personal and domestic services. For the reasons discussed below, these occupations are placed in Unit 3.

2. Security Services Unit:

This unit is a contraction of the Inspection and Security Services Unit determined to be appropriate by the Director of Representation in that we delete all inspectors, investigators and examiners from that unit. The unit now comprises all occupations involving the protection of persons and property; the enforcement of laws, codes, rules and regulations concerned with vehicle and highway safety; and the security aspects of correctional institutions. Inspectional services cover a broad range or occupations which are distinct from security services and cannot be properly allocated to the same unit. The inspectors, investigators and examiners who have been deleted from this unit have been placed in Units 4 and 5.

3. Institutional Services Unit:

This unit is an expansion of the Health Services and Support Unit determined to be appropriate by the Director of Representation in that the unit now includes those occupations associated with institutions and related to the preparation and distribution of food and to personal and domestic services. We find that working conditions in institutions are significantly different from working conditions elsewhere. Accordingly, we conclude that employees engaged in these occupations — which are unique to institutions — have a greater community of interest with their fellow institutional employees than with operational services employees.

4. Administrative Services Unit:

This unit is similar to the unit determined to be appropriate by the Director of Representation except that it also includes certain inspectors, investigators and examiners who were deleted from Unit 2. All inspectors, investigators and examiners are placed in this unit unless their responsibilities are of a professional, scientific or technical nature.

5. Professional, Scientific and Technical Services Unit:

This unit is similar to that determined to be appropriate by the Director of Representation except that it includes inspectors, investigators and examiners, the nature of whose responsibilities are of a technical, professional or scientific nature.

The implementation of these units in this representation proceeding requires a determination as to those eligible for inclusion in each unit. In making this determination, we must consider these as yet unanswered questions —

First — A determination as to which job titles shall be included in each unit. We feel that the delineation of the units heretofore made provides sufficient specificity to allocate the majority of job titles to their respective units. However, there may be a question with respect to some job titles as to which unit they belong.

Second — In his decision, the Director included in each unit those responsible for the supervision of the activities of that unit. It is our policy not to exclude all supervisors arbitrarily from a rank-and-file unit. Rather, supervisors have been excluded when there was a showing that their supervisory duties and obligations were of such a nature to give rise to such a conflict of interest as to preclude their inclusion in the same unit with rank-and-file. Thus, a determination must be made as to what supervisors will be excluded from any unit and the disposition of those excluded.

Third — The dimensions of the exclusion of managerial and confidential employees.

We believe that these specific questions of eligibility and exclusion can be resolved most expeditiously in the following manner: This Board shall prepare a list of job titles to be placed in each unit. This list shall include the Board's disposition of the supervision question. A second list prepared by the Board will indicate those excluded as managerial or confidential. Within seven days after these lists have been submitted to the parties, a conference will be scheduled by the Board, at which time the Board will consider and rule on any objections of the parties to such lists. . . .

## NOTES

1. Following the trend toward broad statewide units, the Maine Labor Relations Board in Council 74, AFSCME, GERR No. 682, E-1 (Me. LRB 1976), established seven statewide bargaining units: (1) administrative services, (2) professional and technical services, (3) institutional services, (4) law enforcement, public safety and regulatory services (non-police), (5) state police services, (6) operations maintenance and support services, and (7) supervisory personnel services. The Board in its decision made a special reference to the expert testimony that was presented concerning the experience in New York and Massachusetts with broad bargaining units at the state level.

2. In State of Iowa and Iowa AFSCME Council 61, 734 GERR 10 (Iowa PERB 1977), the Iowa PERB held that a unit of approximately 7,000 technical employees constituted an appropriate unit. In holding that the broad unit that included classifications ranging from airplane pilots to seed analysts was appropriate, the Iowa PERB held that the statutory phrase "principles of efficient administration of government" required it to establish "the smallest number of bargaining units consistent with meaningful and effective representation of the employees so involved." In so ruling, the Iowa PERB held that a separate unit of licensed practical nurses (LPNs) was not appropriate in view of their community of interest with other health care classifications also included in the technical unit, as well as the need to avoid unnecessary fragmentation.

3. In establishing appropriate bargaining units, is it necessary that the agency establish the *most* appropriate unit as distinguished from *an* appropriate unit? In the private sector the NLRB has uniformly held that the unit petitioned for does not have to be the most appropriate unit. In Morand Brothers Beverage Co., 91 N.L.R.B. 409, 418 (1950), the Board stated that "there is nothing in the statute which requires that the unit of bargaining be the *only* appropriate unit, or the *ultimate* unit or the *most* appropriate unit; the Act requires only that the unit be appropriate. It must be appropriate to insure to employees, *in every case,* 'the fullest freedom in exercising the rights guaranteed by this Act.' " Although similar rulings have been made by several state labor relations boards, there are at least two noteworthy exceptions. In the principal case the New York PERB held that the statutory criteria mandated the establishment of the most appropriate bargaining unit. The Michigan Employment Relations Commission (MERC) has adopted a position somewhere between the NLRB approach and the New York PERB approach. Thus, the MERC has stated that in making unit determinations it is guided by the following standard set forth by the Michigan Supreme Court in Hotel Olds v. State Labor Mediation Board, 333 Mich. 382, 387, 53 N.W.2d 302, 304 (1952): "In designating bargaining units as appropriate, a primary objective of the Commission is to constitute the largest unit which in the circumstances of the particular case is most compatible with the effectuation of the purposes of the law and to include in a single unit all common interests." Relying on the *Hotel Olds* decision, the MERC held in City of Charlevoix, 1970 MERC Lab. Op. 404 (Mich.), that a city-wide bargaining unit that included fire and police personnel was appropriate since "the larger overall unit is more in keeping with the policy of the State than separate departmental units, especially in a municipality where only a small number of employees are employed." On the other hand, in Regents of the University of Michigan, 1971 MERC Lab. Op. 337 (Mich.), the MERC stated that "[t]he statute does not require that only the 'ultimate unit' can be certified. There may be smaller groupings within the employment of a single employer which are appropriate for collective bargaining. . . ." The California Educational Employment Relations Board has likewise eschewed adopting either the "most" or "an" appropriate unit standard. Antioch Unified School Dist., Decision No. 37 (Cal. EERB 1977).

4. The Kansas Public Employee Relations Board in Ft. Hays Kansas State College, Case No. 1 (1972), GERR No. 487, B-3 (1973), stated that it "would allow public employees at each unit of higher education to organize on individual institutional units." The Kansas Board stated:

> Each institution, the Board feels, is a separate distinct operating entity with a complex relationship already existing between the public employees and the administration therein. The principles of efficient administration will be maintained inasmuch as the evidence before this Board indicates that most problems concerning

conditions of employment with university employees have been handled on a local basis; *i.e.*, between the local university administration and the employee. Evidence before this Board also indicates that a distinct "community of interest" is enjoyed by employees at the individual institutions. Particularly, it was expressed that the workers with similar occupations at KU Medical Center and at Kansas University were working under different environments with different benefits in some cases. Contrasted with this, the employees at each institution had a common base in their working conditions and the evidence indicated a similarity of problems at each institution that is not evident between employees of separate institutions.

... The difficulties of employees organizing over a great distance (*i.e.*, the distance between Wichita and Ft. Hays) when considered in light of the fact that each institution has operated as a separate identity, made the unit determinations on an individual institutional basis seem most logical. The Board did not view the problems of overfragmentation and splintering of a work force as automatically requiring a statewide unit in every case, but that each case must be reviewed on its own merit, thus our decision of the individual institutional units.

## STATE OF FLORIDA

Florida Public Employees Relations Comm'n
Case No. 8H-R3 (June 17, 1976)

MACK, Chairman, and FILIPOWICZ and GITOMER, Commissioners:

The State of Florida, filed a Petition on March 4, 1976 pursuant to §§ 120.54(b) (4) and 447.201(1), Fla. Stat. (1975) requesting the Commission to establish bargaining units for state employees by rule. In its petition, the State, through the Department of Administration, proposed that four statewide occupational units be established by rule in addition to the two units that have already been approved through the consent election process.

The Commission held a hearing on April 8, 1976 to consider the wisdom and propriety of adopting unit configurations for state employees through rulemaking. . . .

The only questions which the Commission addressed at the April 8 hearing were the feasibility and legality of unit determination by rule. These issues were considered by the Massachusetts Labor Relations Commission at length in their decision of March 3, 1975, wherein a minimum of ten statewide occupationally based units were established for employees of the Commonwealth of Massachusetts. The Massachusetts Commission was faced with a crazy quilt of units that had been established under a statute granting to state employees limited collective bargaining rights in geographically determined single agency units. Under a comprehensive collective bargaining act, the Massachusetts Commissioner of Administration was delegated the duty of representing the Commonwealth of Massachusetts as the employer for collective bargaining purposes of all commonwealth employees. The Massachusetts Labor Relations Commission, following a petition by the Commonwealth to consolidate large numbers of pre-existing units, determined that establishing the configuration of a small number of units for these employees by rule was both wise and economical. Thereafter, following extensive public hearings, that Commission's Rules and Regulations were amended to provide minimum standards against which any petition for Commonwealth employees would be measured.

Florida, of course, had no formal collective bargaining structure for state employees prior to the passage of Chapter 74-100, Laws of Florida (§§ 447.201-.609, Fla. Stat. (1975)), hereinafter the Act. During the year and a half of experience under the Act, numerous petitions have been filed by organizations seeking to represent state employees. Of these petitions a significant number have been dismissed for proposing units which, we have found, do not comport with the standards established in § 447.307(4) of the Act and § 8H-3.31 of the Commission's Rules and Regulations. In the process of petition and dismissal, bargaining elections have been delayed by the absence of precedent in Florida public employee relations law and by the multifarious units that can legitimately be proposed for employees of the state. Thus, when the State of Florida proposed rulemaking as a means to expedite the weighty policy questions involving unit determinations for state employees, we were ready to listen to all those who wished to appear and argue the pros and cons of the State's petition.

The Administrative Procedure Act, Chapter 120, Florida Statutes, and other statutes under which this Commission operates provide us with two methods of devising rules and orders: quasi-legislative rulemaking and case by case adjudication. Rule-making is required for the promulgation of "... agency statement[s] of general applicability that [implement], interpret, or prescribe law policy. ..." Fla. Stat. § 120.52(13) (1975). Ad hoc adjudication, on the other hand, determines the statutory rights of particular parties to a particular controversy or legal question.

Before any administrative agency may adopt rules and regulations, it is required by statute to give notice of its proposed action, with a statement of the purpose and effect of the proposed rule, a summary of the rule, and a reference to the statutory authority for the particular proposed rule.[1] Fla. Stat. § 120.54(1) (1975). By law, we are required to "give affected persons an opportunity to present evidence and argument on all issues under consideration appropriate to inform [us] of their contention," Fla. Stat. § 120.54(2) (1975), if an affected person timely requests such opportunity.[2]

In short, rulemaking provides the opportunity for an agency to receive and consider the arguments, positions and evidence presented by all parties affected by a policy decision before it decides questions that affect broad classes of persons. Since the Commission must give notice that rulemaking is under consideration and must further summarize its proposed action, those who would be affected by our decision are given the opportunity to:

"effectively advance their own policy by mobilizing their sources of information and experience and making them available to the Commission." Memorandum, "Why Establish Units By Rule Making Rather Than The Case-By-Case Method?" [3]

---

[1] Section 447.207 (1) of the Act provides:

After public hearing, the commission shall adopt, promulgate, amend or rescind such rules and regulations as it deems necessary and administratively feasible to carry out the provisions of this part.

In addition, § 447.307 (4) (h) of the Act establishes for the determination of appropriate collective bargaining units "[s]uch other factors and policies as the commission may prescribe by regulations or by its decisions."

[2] See Note, "The Use of Agency Rule Making," 54 Iowa L. Rev. 1086, 1097, 1098 (1969):

"An agency may consider and decide many broad policy issues in adjudicatory proceedings ... (but) formulating these broad policies in an adjudication eliminates or defers the participation of many parties who ultimately are affected by the decision. Making these same decisions in a rulemaking proceeding gives all interested parties notice and a chance to participate in the agency decisions."

[3] Memorandum, "Why Establish Units By Rule Making Rather Than The Case-By-Case Method?" (Mass. Lab. Rel. Comm'n, Nov. 13, 1974.)

In rulemaking we may be provided the opinions of many interested and concerned parties; in adjudication our field of inquiry is limited to only those parties and those questions directly at issue in a particular case. Thus, the advantages of rulemaking hearings flow to the organizations and employees involved as well as to the state and to this Commission.

Many commentators on the administrative process have expressed doubts on the desirability of case by case adjudication of issues that result in broad policy decisions.[4] They would suggest, as an alternative to ad hoc decision making on policy matters by an administrative agency, the quasi-legislative rule-making procedure wherein the data and theories upon which policies may rest are subject to public scrutiny and review before the interests of individual parties are affected.

As the Massachusetts Commission recognized, certainly rulemaking provides an expeditious alternative to case by case adjudication.[5] "Clearly enunciated and properly drawn rules should reduce litigation by authoritatively advising affected parties what general types of units will or will not be deemed appropriate." [6]

While the National Labor Relations Board (NLRB) has chosen the adjudicatory method for the promulgation and amendment of substantive rules of law, it does so through the exercise of its own "informed discretion." [7] And indeed, when compared to the short time required for unit determinations under the NLRB's jurisdiction and the publication system available for dissemination of decisions, the rulemaking process is indeed cumbersome. However, the time heretofore required for unit determinations under our statute, the part-time nature of this Commission, and the difficulties encountered in providing our decisions to all potentially affected parties make rulemaking in the context of unit determinations for state employees expeditious, economical, and administratively feasible.

While certain questions have been raised as to our authority to promulgate specific standards for units for state employees, we conclude that both the Act

---

[4] H. Friendly, "The Federal Administrative Agencies," 146-147 (1962); I. K. Davis, "Administrative Law Treatise," § 6.13 (1965); Recommendations of Section of Labor Relations Law, American Bar Association, 42 LRRM 513 (1958); Peck, "The Atrophied Rule Making Powers of the National Labor Relations Board," 70 Yale L.J. 729 (1961); Shapiro, "The Choice of Rule Making or Adjudication in the Development of Administrative Policy," 76 Harv. L. Rev. 921, 942 (1965); Bernstein, "The NLRB's Adjudication-Rule Making Dilemma Under the Administrative Procedures Act," 79 Yale L.J. 571 (1970); Kahn, "The NLRB and Higher Education: The Failure of Policy Making Through Adjudication," 22 UCLA L. Rev. 63 (1973); Silverman, "The Case for the National Labor Relations Board's Use of Rule Making in Asserting Jurisdiction," Labor L.J. at 607 (October 1974); NLRB v. Wyman Gordon Co., 394 U.S. 759 (1969); NLRB v. Textron, Inc., 416 U.S. 267 (1974).

[5] Memorandum, "Why Establish Units by Rule Making Rather Than by The Case-By-Case Method? " (Mass. Lab. Rel. Comm'n November 13, 1974.)

[6] Id. at 7.

*[7] NLRB v. Textron, Inc., 416 U.S. 267, 294 (1974); NLRB v. Wyman Gordon Co., 394 U.S. 759 (1969). Indeed, the United States Supreme Court recognized

that rulemaking would provide the Board with a forum for soliciting the informed views of those affected in industry and labor before embarking on a new course. But surely the Board has the discretion to decide that the adjudicative procedures in this case may also produce the relevant information necessary to mature and fair consideration of the issues. NLRB v. Textron, Inc., supra at 295.

and Florida administrative law grant the power which we have chosen to exercise. Adopting general unit configurations for state employees as standards against which petitions are measured is a policy decision which § 447.307(4) (h) of the Act specifically states may be promulgated by rule *or* decision. In addition, we have set forth above the factors which lead us to the conclusion that these standards are "necessary and administratively feasible to carry out the provisions of this part." Thus, we conclude that the Legislature has delegated to us the authority under which we propose to act.

Accordingly the Commission has determined to grant the petition of the State of Florida to institute rulemaking proceedings to determine the general type and kind of units which are appropriate for state employees under the Act.

Commissioner Stouffer dissents on the grounds that, in his opinion, the Commission has only the authority to determine the appropriateness or inappropriateness of particular bargaining units as they are proposed by petition. Commissioner Rose dissents only as to the wisdom of proceeding by rulemaking at this time.

# NOTES

1. Following a hearing on the State's petition for adoption of a rule establishing six statewide bargaining units, the Florida Commission in State of Florida, 2 FPER 166 (Fla. PERC 1976), adopted a rule establishing the following seven statewide bargaining units: (1) administrative and clerical services, (2) operational services, (3) human or institutional services, (4) health care professionals, (5) all other professionals, (6) law enforcement employees, (7) supervisory employees. Rather than including all professional employees in one unit, the Commission included all health care professional employees in one unit and all other professional employees in a separate unit. For a review of the establishment of bargaining units at the state level in Florida, see McHugh, "The Florida Experience in Public Employee Collective Bargaining, 1974-1978: Bellwether for the South," 6 FLA. ST. U. L. REV. 263, 302-06 (1978).

2. Are there any limits on how broad bargaining units should be in the public sector? That the law of diminishing returns may be applicable is indicated in the following remarks of Clyde Summers:

> City employment spans an exceedingly wide range of skills, from the professionally trained engineer and health officer to the unskilled janitor and park attendant. The work and working conditions of city employees vary so greatly that their interests may be better represented by separately chosen unions and their different problems may be better worked out in separate negotiations. A single union can, and commonly does, represent employees with varied and even competing interests. In fact, one function a union serves is to reconcile and compromise those interests by its internal processes. However, diverse interests within the union create internal tensions. If the diversity is too great the resulting tensions may be more than the union can manage. These tensions are then manifested at the bargaining table by the union making an array of demands designed to placate every group in the union. Bargaining becomes protracted and if the union is unable to resolve differences by its internal processes, it may be unable to work out compromises at the bargaining table or accept what might otherwise be considered a reasonable package. Thus, while multiple bargaining units add to the employer's negotiating burden, that cost may be less than negotiating with a conglomerate union which is trying to represent greater diversity than its internal processes can reconcile. Moreover, if bargaining reaches an impasse, the consequences will be less disruptive if only one group of employees is involved than if all employees are involved.

Summers, "Public Employee Bargaining: A Political Perspective," 83 YALE L.J. 1156, 1190 (1974).

## STATE OF NEW JERSEY

New Jersey Public Employment Relations Commission
Decision No. 68, GERR No. 457, E-1 (1972)

The above-captioned cases raise questions concerning the representation of various groups of professional employees [2] employed by the State of New Jersey. Hearings were conducted on each of the petitions and thereafter Hearing Officers made the following recommendations. In Case No. R-111 *ad hoc* Hearing Officer Joseph McCabe recommended that separate state-wide units of supervisory and non-supervisory Registered Nurses be found appropriate. No exceptions were timely filed to that recommendation. In Case No. RO-196, wherein Petitioner sought certification in a unit of all Social Workers and Social Worker trainees employed by the Bureau of Childrens Services, Hearing Officer Martin Pachman recommended dismissal of that petition on two grounds.

First, since not all social workers in state classified service were included, the unit sought, being less than state-wide in scope, failed to meet the minimum standards set forth by the Commission in its earlier disposition of other state cases.[3] Second, even if that state-wide standard were not a requirement, the exclusion of other social workers located in hospitals, training schools, etc., who share the same characteristics of employment is not consistent with any reasonable definition of community of interest. In Case No. RO-230, wherein Petitioner sought certification in a unit of all Rehabilitation Counselors, their supervisors, aides and trainees employed by the Department of Labor and Industry, the same Hearing Officer recommended dismissal of that petition essentially because the unit, even though state-wide as to the titles sought, would exclude employees with similar duties, skills, functions, goals and job qualifications and thus there was a community of interest which extended beyond those titles which that Petitioner sought to represent. Neither of the two Petitioners involved in these recommendations filed exceptions to the proposed dismissals of their petitions. The Employer took exception to certain observations made by the Hearing Officer which were not material to his recommendations above, but which were relied on to support his suggested resolution of the larger question of appropriate unit or units for professional employees of the State. Finally, in Cases Nos. RO-164 and RO-208, which, by virtue of certain amendments, amount to a single petition for a unit of all professional, non-supervisory, educational employees in the Departments of Education and Institutions and Agencies, Hearing Officer Jeffrey B. Tener recommended that a unit of all professional, educational employees be found appropriate. This is a modification of Petitioner's unit, principally in that it also includes a small number of employees in the Department of Higher Education.[4] The Employer filed exceptions to a variety of the Hearing Officer's findings and conclusions as well as to his ultimate recommendation on unit.

Following submission of all Hearing Officers' Reports and exceptions thereto, a three member panel of the Commission heard oral argument on the positions

---

[2] In most instances the parties do not contest the use of the term "professional" in describing the employees involved. For purposes of this decision, there is an assumption, but no determination, that such description is appropriate.

[3] State of New Jersey (Neuro-Psychiatric Institute, et al), P. E. R. C. No. 50.

[4] The unit does not contemplate inclusion of the teaching faculties found within the Department of Higher Education, most of whom are already represented.

of the parties in these consolidated cases. The Commission has considered the record, briefs, Hearing Officer's Report and Recommendations, exceptions and oral argument in each of these cases and makes the following dispositions.

The cases will be discussed as one since the bases for disposition are the same in each. The Commission is not persuaded that the above units where recommended as appropriate for collective negotiations be found so. There are two interrelated reasons for this conclusion, the statute's policy and the community of interest of the employees concerned.

It was the Legislature's express determination that Ch. 303 be enacted to promote permanent employer-employee peace and the health, welfare, comfort and safety of the people of the State. N.J.S.A. 34:13A-2. As the Supreme Court later observed, "The nature of the appropriate negotiating unit is a most significant factor in the production and maintenance of harmony and peace in public employment relations." [5]

Against this background the statute provides that the negotiating unit ". . . shall be defined with due regard for the community of interest among the employees concerned . . ." N.J.S.A. 34:13A-5.3. Community of interest is an accepted term of art and the statute does not attempt to define it. There are several guidelines, however, only one of which is relevant here, namely, that in deciding which unit is appropriate for collective negotiations, the Commission may not include professional employees in the same unit with non-professional employees unless a majority of the former vote for inclusion. N.J.S.A. 34:13A-6(d).

When the Commission last examined the question of unit involving State employees, it concluded, with respect to the employees in question there, that to be appropriate the scope of the unit must be state-wide. Expressed and implied in that conclusion was an assessment that the strength and significance of the factors cited — in brief, a high degree of centralization of authority in the top echelon of State government and a general uniformity of major terms and conditions of employment for State employees — required a finding that the first distinctive level of common interest among employees extended state-wide and that this was the minimum level for meaningful negotiation of terms and conditions of employment. The Commission recognized but refused to give controlling weight to the variety of lesser but more particularized points of common employee interest known to exist in a specific institution or department. Admittedly, a reasonably persuasive case was made for establishing units at the institution or department level by highlighting local differences in conditions and duties, but on balance the factors demonstrating a broader community of interest were considered more compelling. Conceivably, the Commission could have stopped at that point and relied on the factors cited to conclude, as one organization urged, that not only was this the first level of common interest, but that this was the only set of interests to be recognized in determining the unit question, meaning that there would be only one unit for all State employees. Instead, the Commission relied on that set of facts only to establish the base or scope of the unit. It then found, in agreement with the principal parties, that it was appropriate to fashion a unit, statewide in scope, to encompass all employees sharing a broad occupational objective or description. That is, it found an additional mutuality of employee interest arising from the kind of work performed, not expressed in terms of specific job titles or functions, but in terms of the nature of the service provided. As a result of that proceeding, the following three units of nonprofessional, nonsupervisory employees were established:

---

[5] Board of Education of the Town of West Orange v. Wilton, 57 N.J. 404, 424 (1971).

Health, Care and Rehabilitation Services; Operations, Maintenance and Services; and Craft.

The Commission is now asked to find appropriate several units whose composition would conform to certain individual professions. To do so would require the Commission to recognize as controlling the common attributes and bonds which distinguish a particular profession, be it teaching, nursing, counseling, etc., and find therein the necessary regard for community of interest. The Commission views that concept in much broader perspective in these cases. Community of interest is, as the writers have said, an elusive concept. While it is purposely vague and undefined, a considerable number of factors has been identified as useful indicators. But in given cases some factors are emphasized over others, with still others regarded as insignificant; in other fact settings the weight given the same indicators may be substantially altered. It is essentially a question of weighing the facts in each case and deciding what will best serve the statutory policy.

For example, no one would dispute that registered nurses share an identity simply by virtue of their common background and qualifications required for licensure and by virtue of their common goal to provide care of various kinds to those in medical need. Yet, it is obvious that these professional characteristics do not necessarily create an exclusive community of interest. The statute, which generally provides little insight, does contemplate that there may, in fact, be an identity of interest between professionals and nonprofessionals. In that event it requires a majority vote by professionals for inclusion with nonprofessionals, thereby recognizing the professional interest. But material to this discussion is the recognition that such interest is not so unique that it must be insulated.[6] A fortiori, the lines between professional disciplines are not necessarily natural barriers. The goal of providing medical care is common to nurses but it is equally common to medical doctors, clinical psychiatrists and psychologists. True, the particular skills, functions and qualifications of these groups differ, but the same observation may be made of the shop teacher at Bordentown Youth Correction Institution, the teacher of the deaf at Marie Katzenbach and the curriculum consultant for elementary education, all of whom are sought to be included in the educational unit. Given the policy considerations of this statute, the Commission believes that the characteristics of a particular profession should not be the determinant in establishing units for negotiations. If community of interest is equated with and limited to such characteristics, the stability and harmony which this Act was designed to promote are in jeopardy. Potentially, every recognized professional group would be segregated, presenting the Employer with multiplicity of units and the likelihood of attendant problems of competing demands, whipsawing, and continuous negotiations which, disregarding the Employer's inconvenience, are not judged to be in the public interest. Fragmentation to that degree cannot be justified on the ground that individual professional interests are so unique that they cannot be adequately represented in concert with others, especially in the absence of a determination that matters of a professional concern are in every instance negotiable as terms and conditions of employment. At this point in the statute's development the Commission is inclined to believe that the purposes of the Act will be better served if, when

---

[6] A graphic example from recent private sector experience is found in Barnes-Hind Pharmaceuticals, 183 N.L.R.B. No. 38 where the Board found it would be appropriate to group professional scientists in the same unit with non-professional technicians and employees such as glassware washer and animal caretaker.

dealing with professional employees, the individual distinctions among the professions not be regarded as controlling, but rather the more elementary fact that they are simply professionals and on that basis alone to be distinguished from other groups of employees. This approach would parallel that taken in the case of craft employees where individual craft lines were not observed and the unit was established simply on the basis of a general craft distinction.

The Commission is not unmindful of the fact that several organizations were interested in representing all craft employees in one unit, whereas here the organizations concerned seek representation along the lines of separate professions. We consider the right to organize and be represented, not as an absolute right, but as one that is qualified by the statute's policy and purpose and by the requirement that the exercise of the right be channeled through units appropriate for negotiations. Moreover the Commission takes note of the fact that units already exist at state level containing substantial diversity of function and ranging in size up to 7,500 employees.

The Commission concludes for the reasons above that each of the petitions be and are hereby dismissed.

## NOTES

1. The New Jersey Commission's decision that a statewide unit of professional employees is appropriate was affirmed by the New Jersey Supreme Court in State of New Jersey v. Professional Ass'n of New Jersey Dep't of Educ., 64 N.J. 231, 315 A.2d 1 (1974). The court, in relevant part, stated:

> The contention of the petitioning organizations that designation of a statewide unit of professional employees ignores the statutory criterion of "due regard" for the "community of interest" of the employees concerned cannot be sustained. What is called for on the part of the Commission is "due regard for," not exclusive reliance upon such community of interest. We have shown above that the interests of the employer and of the public at large are also relevant factors. In any event, we conceive the State is not unreasonable in arguing that there is a common interest and character in relation to professional employees, as such, with respect to their status, training and functions, as well as with respect to their fairly common expectations concerning the range of compensation and working conditions negotiable on their behalf, in contradistinction to other groupings of employees. . . .
>
> As to the suggestion that in a general professional employees unit, the special problems and interests of the registered nurses will be submerged and inadequately dealt with by the common representative, this is always a problem where discrete categories are placed in a common negotiating unit. It must be assumed, however, except where shown to the contrary in a particular case, that the common representative will perform its duty fairly in respect of all within the unit and exercise its good faith judgment as to when or whether different characteristics within the group warrant different demands. See Steele v. Louisville & Nashville R. R. Co., 323 U.S. 192, 203, 204, 89 L.Ed. 173, 183, 184, 15 LRRM 708 (1944).

2. Although the New York Taylor Law does not specifically provide that professional employees are entitled to separate units, the New York PERB has allowed professional employees to form their own units, primarily on the basis of their substantially different community of interest from that of nonprofessional employees. Chemung County, 1 PERB ¶ 415 (1968); New York State Thruway, 1 PERB ¶ 423 (1968). In New York State, 1 PERB ¶ 424 (1968), the New York PERB placed all of the state's professional employees, e.g., doctors, lawyers, accountants, and economists, in one unit. A member of the New York PERB, Joseph Crowley, commented as follows concerning this decision:

> Though the disciplines differed, the interest in the maintenance of professional

standards and status would provide a common bond. Further experience is necessary to determine whether this grouping of professions may preclude effective and meaningful negotiations. The desire to avoid unwarranted fragmentation appears to dictate this approach. Fragmentation should be granted only where the evidence to support it is clear and convincing. . . . Crowley, *The Resolution of Representation Status Disputes Under the Taylor Law,* 37 FORDHAM L. REV. 517, 526 (1969).

3. Section 9(b) (3) of the NLRA provides that

> . . . the Board shall not (1) decide that any unit is appropriate [for the purposes of collective bargaining] if such unit includes both professional employees and employees who are not professional employees unless a majority of such professional employees vote for inclusion in such unit. . . . 29 U.S.C. § 159(b) (3) (1970).

A premise underlying this provision is that professional employees should not be automatically included in bargaining units with nonprofessional employees against their wishes since they usually have distinct professional standards, different working conditions, and are frequently paid on a different basis than nonprofessional employees. In order to differentiate professional employees from nonprofessional employees, Congress defined the term "professional employee" as follows:

> (a) any employee engaged in work (i) predominantly intellectual and varied in character as opposed to routine mental, manual, mechanical, or physical work; (ii) involving the consistent exercise of discretion and judgment in its performance; (iii) of such a character that the output produced or the result accomplished cannot be standardized in relation to a given period of time; and (iv) requiring knowledge of an advanced type in a field of science or learning customarily acquired by a prolonged course of specialized intellectual instruction and study in an institution of higher learning or a hospital, as distinguished from a general academic education or from an apprenticeship or from training in the performance of routine mental, manual or physical processes; or
>
> (b) any employee, who (i) has completed the courses of specialized intellectual instruction and study described in clause (iv) of paragraph (a), and (ii) is performing related work under the supervision of a professional person to qualify himself to become a professional employee as defined in paragraph (a). 29 U.S.C. § 152(12) (1970).

4. One of the reasons advanced for allowing professional employees to establish separate bargaining units in the private sector is that they would constitute in many instances only a small minority of the bargaining unit if they were included with nonprofessionals. This consideration may not be as valid in the public sector. The Illinois Study Commission, for example, noted that "there are public agencies in which the nonprofessionals are a small portion of the total, and they should not automatically be blanketed in with a larger professional group that did not reflect their interests." Based on this finding, the Illinois Study Commission recommended that *both* "[p]rofessional and nonprofessional employees should be given the opportunity to decide whether they want to be included in the same unit if that issue is raised by either group." ILLINOIS GOVERNOR'S ADVISORY COMMISSION ON LABOR-MANAGEMENT FOR PUBLIC EMPLOYEES, REPORT AND RECOMMENDATIONS 20 (Mar. 1967). Incorporating this approach, the Florida law provides that "no unit shall be established or approved for purposes of collective bargaining which includes both professional and non-professional employees unless a majority of each group votes for inclusion in such unit." Fla. Stat. § 447.307(3) (h) (1977). The Connecticut Board accomplished the same result by decision in Clifford W. Beers Guidance Clinic, Decision No. 1104 (Conn. SBLR 1972).

5. One of the current policies of government employers is to encourage job advancement of racial minorities. The Report of the Fortieth American Assembly on Collective Bargaining in American Government included the following recommendation:

> As an increasing number of Americans obtain access to the rights inherent in a free society, there is a particular responsibility placed on public employers and public

unions. Both unions and public employers have an affirmative obligation to effectuate a change in the racial composition of government's work forces so that the number of minority employees on all levels more adequately reflects the racial balance of residents in the governmental unit. Unions have an affirmative obligation to the full extent of their bargaining capabilities to press employers to hire or promote minorities and to eliminate artificial, non-job related barriers which impede minority employment. Employers have the same obligation to remove such barriers and to withdraw or deny recognition from a union which impedes affirmative action. . . .

None of this will be easy, but public employers and public unions as the beneficiaries of tax revenues derived from the population have a particular responsibility to act on these matters. They may have to revise or overcome collective bargaining agreements if exclusive rights for unions block necessary changes in the work force. . . .

REPORT OF THE FORTIETH AMERICAN ASSEMBLY, COLLECTIVE BARGAINING IN AMERICAN GOVERNMENT 7 (1971). What effect does the establishment of separate bargaining units for professional and nonprofessional employees have on job mobility? Consider, for example, the various categories of jobs related to nursing, *i.e.,* registered nurses, licensed practical nurses, and nurses' aides. If each of these three groups is allowed to form its own separate bargaining unit, it is quite possible that artificial barriers would be created in terms of advancement from a nurses' aide to a licensed practical nurse and finally to a registered nurse. This suggests that it might be necessary to review the usual statutory provision, borrowed from the private sector, which provides that professional employees may not be included in the same bargaining unit with nonprofessional employees unless they affirmatively vote to be included in such a unit. Perhaps some discretion should be given to the agency on a case-by-case basis to determine whether the appropriate unit should include both professional and nonprofessional employees. *See* State of Alaska, Alaska State Labor Relations Agency Decision No. 1, GERR No. 492, G-1 (1973) (combined unit of technical, professional and clerical employees held appropriate since "the interests of these groups are intertwined and the distinctions between them are often blurred"); Detroit Bd. of Educ. and Michigan Nurses Association, 1969 MERC Lab. Op. 229 (professional employees have no statutory right to separation from nonprofessional employees and may be included in same bargaining unit).

## MICHIGAN STATE UNIVERSITY

Michigan Employment Relations Commission
1971 MERC Lab. Op. 82

[The University College Chapter — MSU District of the Michigan Association for Higher Education filed a petition seeking an election among certain employees of Michigan State University. The American Association of University Professors — MSU Chapter was allowed to intervene on the basis of a sufficient showing of interest.]

The Employer herein is a public employer within the meaning of PERA, and both the Petitioner and the Intervenor are labor organizations within the meaning of PERA.

Michigan State University, an institution of higher learning established under Article VIII, Section 5, of the Michigan Constitution of 1963, is composed of approximately fifteen colleges. The . . . University employs approximately two thousand persons in its teaching faculty from the rank of instructor and up. The unit sought in the petition is composed of approximately two hundred and twenty teaching personnel including all academic rankings from instructor, associate professor, through full professor. While the Petitioner contends that this unit is appropriate, the Employer and the Intervenor take the position that only a university-wide unit of teaching personnel would be appropriate for collective bargaining.

The nature of this case is such that there is minimal dispute over the factual situation. The relationship of University College to the University in terms of administrative structure is comparable to that of the other colleges or schools making up the University. The petitioned for unit includes teaching personnel in all of the academic ranks as does every other college. The range of teaching duties and other obligations, counseling, research and related activities, required and expected of the faculty of University College is comparable, if not identical, with those of faculty members of all the other colleges and schools. The employment relationships of the individual faculty member with the University is uniform throughout all the colleges. The general salary scale and the enjoyment of various employment benefits are uniform throughout the University.

The Petitioner introduced evidence by which it proposed to delineate University College and its faculty as a separate entity within the University with sufficient separate identity to warrant the finding of a unit limited to its faculty. The University catalog and other publications identify the College within the structure of Michigan State University as a separate college. As is the case with each of the other fifteen colleges, it has its own dean. It has two major responsibilities. It offers four courses which are required as a condition of graduation of substantially all students. It also enrolls and is responsible for the academic progress of substantially all freshmen and sophomores in the University. In addition to the four basic courses, which are embodied in four departments, the College maintains a noninstructional department which provides testing services within the college and for other colleges of the University. Virtually all of the students in the University College courses, therefore, are freshmen or sophomores and, it is not unfair to say, that their unique problems and needs form the primary concern of the college. It is one of the few colleges in the University which does not grant a degree.

The Petitioner presented evidence of the separate activities of the University College faculty. The University College faculty has promulgated a set of bylaws which govern its internal procedures. However, it should be noted that these bylaws refer primarily to intra-college matters and are authorized and controlled by the bylaws of the University. Its faculty periodically conducts meetings. It publishes a newsletter written by and distributed to its own faculty. It also publishes the "University College Quarterly," a journal related to the scholarly concerns of the faculty.

The University College faculty participate in a variety of university-wide committees and councils made up of elected or appointed representatives of the various colleges and schools. These committees and councils govern the broad spectrum of academic and internal activities of the University. The broadest based of these is the Academic Senate. All members of the University faculty are members of the Academic Senate of Michigan State University which is made up of all tenured faculty. University College elects representatives to the Academic Council of the University and its faculty are among the appointed Council members. Its faculty participates fully in all faculty standing committees. These standing committees relate in their activities to aspects of the University's functioning in which University College stands on equal footing with the other colleges and schools. Among these committees are the University Curriculum Committee, University Educational Policies Committee, University Faculty Affairs Committee, University Faculty Tenure Committee, and other committees reflecting the multiple concerns and activities of a large university.

With reference to faculty appointments, University College personnel are employed primarily within the College. Dual appointments, that is, an appointment of an individual to different colleges simultaneously, constitute a small percentage of the total appointments within the entire University and a slightly larger percentage of the faculty of this College. More common, although not involving University College, is the joint administration of a department by two or more colleges. This also involves a relatively small percentage of the total faculty.

Testimony of an administrative officer of the University emphasized the centralized control of vital aspects of University academic and personnel activities. As is implicit in the titles of several of the standing committees listed above, significant areas are within the purview of university-wide committees. The University Tenure Committee has jurisdiction over all faculty. Major curriculum decisions must be approved by a university-wide committee. Non-academic administrative control is uniform throughout the University. In matters such as appointments, promotions or tenure, recommendations originate with the department head or dean of the college involved but are then channeled through the office of the Provost and ultimately to the President and Board of Trustees. Recruiting is conducted by the individual department although ultimate approval must come from the central office of the University. Higher ranking appointments involve a personal interview by the office of the Provost, the highest academic officer of the University.

The budget of the University is prepared centrally and allocated by the Legislature to the University rather than to individual schools. The dean prepares the budget request for his school. After the final budget is returned to him, he has certain freedom, with approval of the Provost, to make adjustments. Some members of the University College faculty are involved in the Office of Evaluation Services of the College. These sixteen persons provide technical advice and assistance to other professors and departments in a variety of testing and evaluation procedures. They teach part-time either in University College or in other colleges in the University.

## Analysis and Conclusions of Law

The picture painted by this record is one of dual levels of administrative authority within a large university. It reflects significant departmental freedom in many areas, although centralized authority and control is retained. Thus, there is substantial recognition of the competence of each department to find and recommend persons for hire based on their status as scholars and competence as teachers. Generally, recommendations of departmental faculty, approved by the individual dean, are followed by the University. Similarly, in granting tenure, the collegial decisions of each department are generally respected by the central administration. Within each school and within individual departments the chairman or dean is the direct and effective supervisor in terms of immediate day-to-day employment relations. However, policy decisions and administrative control are allocated, as appropriate, between various committees and the central administration.

The petitioner would now have us find a separate bargaining unit made up of one school composed of five departments. Our prior decisions have expressed the essential elements of evidence of an appropriate bargaining unit. The record must show that the sought-for unit has inherent cohesiveness, that is, an internal community of interest among the employees in the proposed unit, and a cleavage between the community of interest of those employees and all other employees of the employer. City of Warren, 1966 MERC Lab. Op. 225; 61 LRRM 1206; Wayne State University Board of Governors, 1969 MERC Lab. Op. 670. It is clear from this record that the employees in the proposed unit share a community of interest among themselves. They perform basically the same duties under the same conditions and under separate supervision. They are employed in a subdivision of the Employer which is nominally distinguished and, to a limited extent, administratively separate, from the balance of the employing institution.

We must search the record with substantial diligence, however, to discover factors that will create a cognizable line of demarcation between the employees in the proposed unit and the balance of the faculty. They perform the same function. The separate supervision of the College, to the extent that is shown by the record, is not sufficient to support a separate unit finding. City of Warren, *supra.* The intra-college activities, such as the journal and bylaws, do not significantly affect the community of interest question. No geographical or physical separation of this faculty school is reflected in the record. It is not contended that the professional or academic character of the petitioned for group is sufficiently distinguishable from the overall faculty as to constitute a basis for a separate finding. Although the College is primarily concerned with teaching freshmen and sophomores, there are at least three other colleges in the University which admit and conduct courses for lower classmen.

Accordingly, on the facts on this record, we find that the unit sought does not constitute an appropriate unit for collective bargaining and we will order the petition dismissed. Wayne State University, Board of Governors, 1969 MERC Lab. Op. 670; Grand Rapids Board of Education, 1966 MERC Lab. Op. 241.

## NOTES

1. At the university level, the various labor relations agencies have differed on whether a single department or college within a university constitutes an appropriate unit and on whether the appropriate unit may be limited to one campus of a multi-campus university. In the private sector, the NLRB has ruled that one college within a university may, in appropriate circumstances, constitute a separate appropriate bargaining unit. For example, in Fordham University, 193 N.L.R.B. 134 (1971), the Board held that the faculty of the Fordham Law School constituted a separate appropriate unit, based on a finding that they possessed a community of interest separate and apart from the balance of the university. In University of Pittsburgh, 7 PPER 21 (Pa. PLRB 1976), the Pennsylvania Board held that the medical, dental, and law school faculty constituted separate appropriate bargaining units in that "all Doctors, Dentists, and Lawyers are Doctors, Dentists, and Lawyers before they are teachers and their communities of interest are separate and apart from all other areas of the university if only by virtue of their much higher income." *Accord,* Temple University, 3 PPER 209 (Pa. PLRB 1973). *But see* Coggins v. PERB, 1977-78 PBC ¶ 36,416 (Kans. Ct. App. 1978) (not arbitrary for Kansas Board to include law faculty in campus-wide bargaining unit).

2. In State of New York (State University of New York), 2 PERB ¶ 3070 (1969), *aff'd sub nom.,* Wakshull v. Helsby, 35 App. Div. 2d 183, 315 N.Y.S.2d 371 (1970), the New York PERB held that a university-wide faculty bargaining unit was appropriate. In so ruling, the PERB affirmed its Director of Representation who held that "the concomitant differences among the campuses do not establish such conflicts of interest between their respective professions as to warrant geographic fragmentation." *Accord,* Minnesota State College Bd. v. PERB, 303 Minn. 453, 228 N.W.2d 551 (1974) (PERB erred in not finding appropriate a statewide unit of faculty employed at seven state colleges); State of New Jersey, Docket Nos. RO-210 and RO-221 (N.J. PERC 1972), GERR No. 484, F-1 (1973) (statewide unit of faculties at six state colleges held appropriate). On the other hand, in

AAUP v. University of Nebraska, 198 Neb. 243, 253 N.W.2d 1 (1977), the Nebraska Supreme Court affirmed a decision of the Nebraska Court of Industrial Relations establishing separate bargaining units for the faculty of the University of Nebraska at Lincoln (UN-L) and the faculty of the University of Nebraska at Omaha (UN-O). The court observed that "the UN-L faculty has a separate community of interest, separate from the faculty of UN-O, which warrants a separate unit." The court also affirmed the decision of the Nebraska Court of Industrial Relations that the faculty at the University's College of Law and the faculty at the College of Dentistry had a sufficient separate community of interest to warrant separate bargaining units. *See generally* McHugh, *Collective Bargaining with Professionals in Higher Education: Problems in Unit Determinations,* 1971 WIS. L. REV. 55.

3. With respect to elementary and/or secondary school districts, the state boards have uniformly denied requests for bargaining units on less than a system-wide basis. *See, e.g.,* Joint School Dist. No. 8 (City of Madison), Decision No. 6746 (Wis. WERC 1964); Grand Rapids Bd. Educ., 1966 MERC Lab. Op. 241 (Mich.).

4. The various state agencies have split on whether part-time faculty members should be included in faculty units. In University of Massachusetts, Case Nos. SCR 2079, 2082 (Mass. LRB 1976), part-time faculty were included in a faculty unit if "they . . . taught one course for three consecutive semesters." In Los Rios Community College Dist., Decision No. 18 (Cal. EERB 1977), part-time faculty were included if they "taught the equivalent of three or more semesters during the last six semesters inclusive." On the other hand, the NLRB in New York University, 205 N.L.R.B. 4 (1973) held "that part-time faculty do not share a community of interest with full-time faculty and, therefore, should not be included in the same bargaining unit." *See also* Eastern Michigan University v. AAUP, 84 L.R.R.M. 2079 (Mich. Ct. App. 1973), where the court reversed a MERC decision which included lecturers in a faculty bargaining unit.

5. In establishing teacher bargaining units the question of whether "fringe" personnel such as counselors, nurses, psychologists, social workers, and the like, should be included in or excluded from the bargaining unit is frequently raised. In Janesville Board of Education, Decision No. 6678 (Wis. WERC 1964), the WERC set forth the following standard:

> Where there are issues with respect to the eligibles in an appropriate collective bargaining unit, the Board will usually include as eligible in a unit consisting of regular full-time certificated teaching personnel those certificated teachers who are regularly employed on a part-time basis and those who, although not directly engaged in normal classroom teaching, work directly with students or with teachers, other than in a supervisory capacity, in support of the education program.

Applying this standard, the WERC has included the following categories of personnel in teacher bargaining units: social workers and psychometrists, La Crosse City Public School Dist. Joint No. 5, Decision No. 7347 (Wis. WERC 1965); psychologists, counselors and guidance personnel, reading teachers, and physical and occupational therapists, Joint City School Dist. No. 1, Decision No. 6677 (Wis. WERC 1964).

# 3. SEVERANCE PETITIONS

## SHAW AND CLARK, DETERMINATION OF APPROPRIATE BARGAINING UNITS IN THE PUBLIC SECTOR: LEGAL AND PRACTICAL PROBLEMS, 51 ORE. L. REV. 152, 167-68 (1971)†

### Standards for Processing Severance Petitions

Where broad units are established there are occasionally requests to sever certain employees. Typically, a severance petition is limited to a subgroup of employees who claim to have special interests which entitle them to be separately

---

† Reprinted by permission. Copyright © 1971 by University of Oregon.

represented. Under the NLRA, a severance petition will be denied unless it is established that the employees petitioned for constitute "a functionally distinct group with special interests sufficiently distinguishable from those of the Employer's other employees to warrant severing them from the overall unit." [6]

The Assistant Secretary of Labor has adopted a similar approach to severance petitions under Executive Order 11,491. Where an established, effective and fair bargaining relationship exists, severance will not be found appropriate except in "unusual circumstances." [7] Applying this formula, the Assistant Secretary has denied virtually every severance request. The same approach was followed by the New Jersey Public Employee Relations Commission in denying a request by a group of nurses to be severed from a larger school unit, and by the Michigan Commission in denying a petition by a group of community college instructors to be severed from an established unit composed of both elementary and secondary teachers and community college instructors.

Recently, the former chairman of the National Labor Relations Board, Frank W. McCulloch, denied a request to sever a group of licensed practical nurses (LPNs) from an overall unit of nonprofessional employees at the Baltimore City Hospital. After stating that an "established structure for bargaining . . . should be altered or upset only for clear and compelling reasons," McCulloch cogently set forth the reasons why severance petitions should not ordinarily be granted in the public sector:

> To split off the LPNs . . . would result in three separate bargaining representatives for employees who make up the patient care teams. The possibilities for confusion and conflict in developing uniform and efficient working conditions on the job would be considerably enhanced. It is common experience that "whip-sawing" and service interruptions tend to occur more frequently where public agency employees are represented in a multiplicity of bargaining units.
>
> Of course tensions can arise within as well as between bargaining units. But the bargaining representative in seeking to achieve a harmony or working balance among the interests of various groups within the inclusive unit is one more buffer against dislocations of public service. [8]

## NOTE

The Federal Labor Relations Council has upheld the Assistant Secretary's so-called *Davisville* rule in which he held that "where the evidence showed that an established, effective and fair collective bargaining relationship is in existence, a separate unit carved out of the existing unit will not be found to be appropriate except in unusual

---

[6] Kalamazoo Paper Box Corp., 136 N.L.R.B. 134, 139 (1962). The Board set forth the following considerations for determining whether a substantial difference in interests and working conditions exists: ". . . a difference in method of wages or compensation; different hours of work; different employment benefits; separate supervision; the degree of dissimilar qualifications, training, and skills; differences in job functions . . . the infrequency or lack of integration with the work functions of other employees or interchange with them; and the history of bargaining."

[7] United States Naval Construction Battalion, Davisville, R.I., A/SLMR No. 8 (1971).

[8] Baltimore City Hosp., 56 L.A. 197, 202-03 (McCulloch, 1971).

circumstances." [9] Department of the Navy, Naval Air Station, Corpus Christi, Texas, FLRC No. 72A-24 (1973).

# D. UNIT STATUS OF CERTAIN CATEGORIES OF EMPLOYEES

## 1. SUPERVISORS

**HAYFORD AND SINICROPI, BARGAINING RIGHTS STATUS OF PUBLIC SECTOR SUPERVISORS, 15 Ind. Rel. 44, 59-61 (1976) †**

. . . .

The bargaining rights status of public sector supervisors is far from being settled. While it is clear that a federal employment experience has paralleled that of the private sector, several state legislatures and/or administrative agencies have chosen a more expansive approach, which has taken two principal forms.

The first approach is reflected by Wisconsin, Oregon, and Connecticut which have chosen to exclude only bona fide supervisors from the coverage of their public employee collective bargaining laws. This has been accomplished by the application of a rigorous test of the statutory definition of "supervisor." Thus, many individuals with supervisory titles are not held to be supervisors for statutory purposes. This policy is founded upon the often cited contention that many public employees in supervisory positions are not really managers. As a rule these "less than bona fide supervisors" are placed in the same bargaining units with rank-and-file employees.

The second view is exemplified by the actions of five states: Hawaii, Minnesota, New York, Massachusetts, and Michigan. They have elected to grant full bargaining rights protection to all supervisory employees. The policy makers in these states apparently do not see any conflict of interest (between the supervisors' role as a member of management and their participation in collective bargaining with management) when bona fide supervisors are allowed to bargain collectively. In these jurisdictions bona fide supervisors are placed in autonomous bargaining units, while less than bona fide supervisors are included in rank-and-file units. This approach is analogous to the final position adopted by the National Labor Relations Board prior to enactment of the Taft-Hartley amendments.

Several factors have contributed to the divergent direction taken by the states vis-à-vis the private sector and the federal government. Perhaps foremost among them is the desires of the supervisors themselves. In several jurisdictions public sector supervisors have demonstrated a strong desire to be included in the bargaining process. This desire is manifested in elections and unit determination petitions and also was no doubt felt through lobbying activities when much of the legislation was developed. This activity, coupled with the questionable managerial status of many supervisors in public employment, has undoubtedly weighed heavily upon the decisions of the various state legislatures and administrative agencies.

The early stage of development of public sector collective bargaining must also be considered a critical factor. In many public sector bargaining relationships the major emphasis has yet to shift from contract negotiation to contract

---

[9] United States Naval Construction Battalion, Davisville, R.I., A/SLMR No. 8 (1971).

† Reprinted by permission.

administration. In the private sector, the grievance procedure is well institutionalized, and the supervisor's key role in contract administration is widely recognized. Since successful contract administration has not yet become the focus of the labor relations programs in the majority of public sector jurisdictions, the role of the supervisor in those labor relations structures has not been clearly delineated. Therefore, the role ambivalence felt by public sector supervisors has not yet emerged as a major concern which their superiors have considered in depth.

The diversity that presently exists in the statutory treatment of supervisors is not likely to persist. The major reason for this observation is the strong possibility that some form of national public employee collective bargaining legislation will be enacted in the immediate future. It appears likely that such national legislation will incorporate the private sector approach to supervisory bargaining rights. This conclusion is based upon three primary factors: the well established policy position of the federal government which essentially excludes all supervisors from any form of bargaining rights protection, the pervasive effect of the private sector treatment of supervisors, and the disruptive effect that a continuing expansion of supervisory bargaining rights in public employment will have upon private sector labor relations.

If national public employee legislation is enacted, it is reasonable to assume that the influence of the executive branch of the federal government would be considerable. The position of the executive branch on the supervisory bargaining rights issue is clear from the discussion here. The language of Executive Order 11838 gives no indication of a change in that policy.

A national public employee collective bargaining statute granting bargaining rights protection to supervisors would inevitably result in a demand by private sector supervisors for similar treatment. There is no evidence to suggest that Congress would be willing to amend the Taft-Hartley Act in such a manner. The disruptive effect of such an act upon the relatively stable collective bargaining structure in the private sector would be of such a magnitude as to make it politically infeasible. The convergence of private and public sector collective bargaining is clear. Because of the factors discussed here, it seems highly probable that, if national public employee collective bargaining legislation is enacted, supervisory bargaining rights is one area in which the private sector treatment will prevail.

Notwithstanding the persuasive arguments that all but the top echelon of public employees should be allowed to bargain collectively and the lack of negative reports from those jurisdictions pursuing such a policy, it is our feeling that an effective statutory structure must provide that true bona fide supervisors be excluded from statutory bargaining rights protection. The heart of a viable labor relations structure lies in effective contract administration. It is a widely accepted fact that in mature bargaining relationships, the key person in day-to-day contract administration is the front line supervisor. The formidable problems inherent in weakening that first line of management-labor communication and cooperation by allowing such individuals to bargain collectively are apparent.

Because there are many individuals in public employment with supervisory titles who do not have consequential management responsibilities or authority, the authors advocate a statutory and interpretative policy that requires substantial proof of "bona fide" supervisory status before an individual is excluded from bargaining rights protection. The policy and practice of the Wisconsin Employment Relations Commission best exemplify this approach.

The authors have advanced the view that only supervisors who possess consequential managerial responsibilities and authority should be excluded from bargaining rights protection. If such a policy is adopted by public employers, many factors which have prompted public sector supervisors to seek statutory bargaining rights protection will diminish in importance. The emergence of this type of labor relations structure should contribute greatly to the achievement of stability and maturity in public sector labor management relations.

## NOTES

1. In recommending that bona fide supervisory employees be excluded from public sector collective bargaining units, the Committee on Economic Development (CED) stated:

> The structure of bargaining units can also have an impact on the effectiveness of middle management and supervisory personnel. In order to assure strong management direction and to have the ability to administer negotiated contracts, bona fide supervisory personnel should be considered part of management, dealt with as management and encouraged to think of themselves as management. In the event of a strike or other job action, it is especially important that supervisory personnel be clearly allied with management so that they can be counted on to help provide a minimum level of essential services. We believe that supervisory personnel should be considered part of management and consequently should not be included in bargaining units. In those instances in which supervisory personnel do have bargaining rights, they should not be included in the same bargaining unit or belong to the same organization as nonsupervisory personnel. Committee on Economic Development, IMPROVING MANAGEMENT OF THE PUBLIC WORK FORCE: THE CHALLENGE TO STATE AND LOCAL GOVERNMENT 68-69 (1978).

For a similar recommendation, as well as a good discussion of the policy issues involved, see ADVISORY COMMISSION ON INTERGOVERNMENTAL RELATIONS, LABOR-MANAGEMENT POLICIES FOR STATE AND LOCAL GOVERNMENT 95-96 (1970).

2. Among the many articles examining the status of supervisory personnel in the public sector are Rains, *Collective Bargaining in the Public Sector and the Need for Exclusion of Supervisory Personnel,* 23 LAB. L.J. 275 (1972); Bers, *The Status of Managerial, Supervisory and Confidential Employees in Government Employment Relations,* A Report sponsored by the New York State Public Employment Relations Board (January 1970).

## CITY OF WAUSAU

Wisconsin Employment Relations Commission
Decision No. 6276 (1963)

At the hearing the parties stipulated to the description of the collective bargaining unit as being all the employes of the Municipal Employer employed in the Board of Public Works, which consists of the Engineering, Sanitation, Electrical, Public Works and Inspection departments. However an issue exists with respect to whether individuals employed as supervisors should be included as eligibles in the unit.

The Municipal Employer contends that only those employes excluded from the term "municipal employe" as defined in Section 111.70 can be excluded from the unit. It argues that supervisory employes have a right to engage in concerted activity and to be represented for the purposes of collective bargaining since that right is given to "employes," and that therefore no basis exists for their exclusion from the eligibles in the bargaining unit.

The Union, on the other hand, takes the position that the Board should apply the same principles and rules that it applies in determining eligibles in elections conducted by the Board among employes of non-public employers pursuant to Section 111.05 of the Wisconsin Employment Peace Act.

Section 111.70(1)(b) defines the term "municipal employe" as follows:

". . . any employe of a municipal employer except city and village policemen, sheriff's deputies and county traffic officers."

A municipal employer performs its functions and services through elected and appointed officials and by employes hired by the municipal employer through its administrative and managerial officials and employes. Broadly, any individual receiving compensation for services performed by him on behalf of the municipal employer, with the exception of those services performed under contract, can be said to be an employe of the municipal employer. Such application could encompass the mayor, city manager, alderman and department heads. A municipal employer as such is a corporate being. Governmental units, including municipal employers, are managed by persons who, among their duties, may represent the municipal employer in its relationship to employes thereof who are performing services and who have no connection with any managerial function. As in private industry, the managerial function of the municipal employer is not normally performed by any single individual. The usual chain of command originates with the mayor or city manager, and is channeled to various committees, boards, department heads, and through various supervisory personnel in the various departments. Managerial and supervisory functions are performed in the interest of the municipality as an employer. The representative of the municipal employer has the responsibility and authority connected with the municipal employer's operation and presumably perform their duties in what is the best interest of the municipality as the employer. Their inclusion in a collective bargaining unit consisting of employes whom they supervise is inconsistent with their obligation to the performance of their supervisory function on behalf of the municipal employer. Should supervisors be included in the same bargaining unit with employes they supervise said individuals would be in a position either to prefer the interest of employes over that of the municipal employer or to prefer the interest of the municipal employer as the agents thereof over that of the employes.

Supervisors are generally responsible for the direction of the work force, the maintenance of discipline and the processing of routine grievances. We do not believe that supervisors can properly carry out such responsibilities if they were included in the bargaining unit.

The rights conferred upon municipal employes under Section 111.70(2) to form and join labor organizations of their own choosing and the right to engage in conferences and negotiations with their municipal employer on the questions of wages, hours, and conditions of employment could be seriously impaired, if not nullified, if the agents of the municipal employer, with whom the representatives of the employes could be expected to negotiate, were included in the employes bargaining unit. To permit supervisory personnel to participate in the election of the representative of the employes he supervises would constitute an interference with their rights as provided in Section 111.70, for it may very well be possible that the ballots of supervisors, if permitted to vote, would affect the results of the representation election. If supervisors were not excluded from bargaining units, then presumably chief executive officers of a municipal employer could be included in the same bargaining unit as other employes. We believe such an interpretation would be clearly at variance with the statutory intent, for who would then be the statutory representative of the municipal employer with whom the municipal employes have a right to confer and negotiate?

Section 111.70(4)(d) provides:

"(d) *Collective bargaining units.* Whenever a question arises between a municipal employer and a labor union as to whether the union represents the employes of the employer, either the union or the municipality may petition the board to conduct an election among said employes to determine whether they desire to be represented by a labor organization. Proceedings in representation cases shall be in accordance with ss. 111.02(6) and 111.05 insofar as applicable, except that where the board finds that a proposed unit includes a craft the board shall exclude such craft from the unit. The board shall not order an election among employes in a craft unit except on separate petition initiating representation proceedings in such craft unit."

The legislature by making reference to the election provision in the Wisconsin Employment Peace Act has granted the Board the power to utilize procedures there provided which are not inconsistent with the substantive provisions of Section 111.70. The Board's determination to exclude supervisory personnel from collective bargaining units of public employes is consistent with the policy applied by the Board in elections conducted under Section 111.05 of the Wisconsin Employment Peace Act.

The Board therefore has and will continue to exclude managerial and supervisory personnel from collective bargaining units on the basis that they are agents of the municipal employer in the performance of the "employer" function. . . .

## NOTES

1. Unlike the employer in the principal case, employers generally argue for the exclusion of individuals whom they consider to be supervisors. Why do you think the city in the instant case sought to include supervisors in the bargaining unit? Sometimes the reason is the employer's belief that the individuals in question are likely to vote against union representation and therefore tip the vote in the employer's favor. Is such a short-range consideration valid from an employer's standpoint? Consider the following comments of Wellington and Winter:

Municipalities are frequently not well organized for collective bargaining and never will be if they cannot create positions with effective responsibility for the administration of collective agreements. Such positions must necessarily be filled by persons who identify with, and are part of, management, not by those who are unionized, whether or not the union is exclusively supervisory. Nor can such responsibilities be carried out by persons who are members, much less officers, of the other party to the contract, as might occur when supervisors are in a unit with regular employees. Indeed, the creation of such positions and the delegation of supervisory power are likely to constitute a principal change in municipal structure as a consequence of collective bargaining. The law should not discourage this trend by permitting the holders of these positions to organize or be in units with nonsupervisory employees. H. WELLINGTON & R. WINTER, THE UNIONS AND THE CITIES 114 (1971).

2. Under the National Labor Relations Act as initially enacted in 1935, there was no specific exclusion of supervisors from the definition of the term "employee." In interpreting the Act the National Labor Relations Board vacillated with respect to whether supervisory employees were entitled to organize and have representation petitions processed. *Compare* Godchaux Sugars, Inc., 44 N.L.R.B. 874 (1942) (supervisory employees may organize in an affilated union), *with* Maryland Drydock Co., 49 N.L.R.B. 733 (1943) (unit of supervisory employees was not appropriate). In Packard Motor Car Co. v. NLRB, 330 U.S. 485, 67 S. Ct. 789, 91 L. Ed. 1040 (1947), the Supreme Court

upheld the authority of the Board to establish bargaining units for supervisory employees. In rejecting the various policy arguments that were proffered as to why supervisory employees should not be allowed to organize, the Court noted that "[t]hey concern the wisdom of the legislation; they cannot alter the meaning of otherwise plain provisions."

When Congress amended the National Labor Relations Act in 1947, it specifically excluded supervisors from the definition of the term "employee" and defined the term "supervisor" to mean

> . . . any individual having authority, in the interest of the employer, to hire, transfer, suspend, lay off, recall, promote, discharge, assign, reward, or discipline other employees, or responsibly to direct them, or to adjust their grievances, or effectively to recommend such action, if in connection with the foregoing the exercise of such authority is not of a merely routine or clerical nature, but requires the use of independent judgment. 29 U.S.C. § 152(11) (1970).

The reasons why Congress excluded supervisors from coverage under the NLRA are indicated in the following excerpt from the relevant House Report:

> *Management, like labor, must have faithful agents.* — If we are to produce goods competitively and in such large quantities that many can buy them at low cost, then, just as there are people on labor's side to say what workers want and have a right to expect, there must be in management and loyal to it persons not subject to influence or control of unions. . . .
>
> . . . What the bill does is to say what the law always has said until the Labor Board, in the exercise of what it modestly calls its "expertness," changed the law: That no one, whether employer or employee, need have as his agent one who is obligated to those on the other side, or one whom, for *any* reason, he does not trust. 1 Legislative History of the Labor-Management Relations Act 307, 308 (1948).

*See generally* Daykin, *Legal Meaning of "Supervisor" Under the Taft-Hartley Act,* 13 LAB. L.J. 130 (1963).

## HILLSDALE COMMUNITY SCHOOLS

Michigan Employment Relations Commission
1968 MERC Lab. Op. 859, *aff'd,* 24 Mich. App. 36,
179 N.W.2d 661 (1970)

The instant case arose when the Hillsdale Community Schools Principals and Supervisory Association (PSA), a labor organization under the Act, sought an election in a proposed bargaining unit:

> "High School, junior high, and elementary school principals, curriculum coordinator, reading coordinator, ESEA coordinator, cooperative education coordinator, head librarian, and physical education director; excluding: teachers, superintendent, assistant superintendent, business manager and all non-certificated employees."

The Hillsdale Education Association (HEA) is a labor organization which is recognized by the School District as exclusive bargaining agent for the District's non-supervisory certificated teachers.

The School District opposes the petition on the grounds that: (1) supervisors and executives have no rights to collective bargaining under PERA; (2) assuming, arguendo, that PERA allows such rights to principals and other supervisors, this Board should deny such rights as a matter of public policy; (3) the proposed unit is inappropriate because it contains six staff specialists who are supervised by seven principals, also included in the unit; and (4) PSA may not be certified as exclusive representative of principals and teachers' supervisors, since it is affiliated with the state organization (MEA) which is the parent organization of many teacher organizations, including the organization of teachers in the petitioner's District.

We now turn to the discussion of the issues individually.

## 1. The unit of supervisors.

The Trial Examiner, in his Report, rejected the School District's position on this issue, consistent with our decision in Saginaw County Road Commission, 1967 Labor Opinions 196. During oral argument, the School District and certain amici curiae prayed that we reverse Saginaw and hold that supervisory employees are excluded from statutory coverage.

We have studied the briefs and arguments urging reversal of our position, but we are not persuaded that the *Saginaw* decision is contrary to proper construction of PERA.

Our duty as described in Section 13 of PERA is to:

". . . decide in each case, in order to insure *public employees* the full benefit of their right to self organization, to collective bargaining and otherwise to effectuate the policies of this act, *the unit appropriate for the purposes of collective bargaining as provided in Section 9e of Act No. 176* (Labor Mediation Act) . . . ." (Emphasis supplied)

From this section, the argument is made that "employees," as used in 9e, specifically excludes executives and supervisors; that is, "employees" as used in Section 9e is defined in Section 2(e) of LMA.[3] However, this argument ignores the use of "public employee" in Section 13 of PERA. "Public employee" is defined in Section 2 of PERA and not in Section 2(e) of LMA. PERA, Section 2, does not exclude supervisors or executives from the provisions of PERA as does its counterpart in LMA.

Section 9e is incorporated into PERA only for standards of unit determination and to provide a prohibition against supervisors and executives being included in the same unit with employees they supervise. There is no prohibition against supervisory units except by virtue of LMA's Section 2(e), which is not included by specific mention in PERA.

The School District maintains that our interpretation of the statutes ignores the canon of construction that statutes which have the same general purpose should be read *in para materia* as constituting one law, especially where there is specific reference from one statute to the other. The purpose of this canon of statutory construction is to avoid a strict construction of one statute which defeats the main purpose of another statute or statutes relating to the same subject.

However, this construction of two statutes dealing with the general subject of labor relations is subject to being made more specific by other canons of construction. *Expressio unius est exclusio alterius* restricts the effect of a statute to the area specifically mentioned, *i.e.,* public employment relations. *E pressum facit cessare tacitum* means that "when the law designates the actors none others can come upon the stage." PERA is restricted to public employees, which term is defined in the Act.

We affirm our *Saginaw* decision and adopt the Trial Examiner's Findings of Fact and Conclusions of Law on this issue.[7]

---

[3] The customary basis for prohibition of supervisory units is found in the definition of employee, which excludes supervisors. If supervisors are not employees, they cannot avail themselves of the provisions of the Act.

[7] We find no merit to the contention that the principals in the instant case are distinguishable from the traffic director supervisor in *Saginaw* because principals have a policy function. This argument is a *non sequitur* if supervisors are not excluded from the definition of employee. We note

## 2. Public Policy.

The School District devotes a substantial portion of its brief to urging the adoption of a policy that supervisors should not be allowed rights under PERA. Our *Saginaw* decision was based on statutory construction, not policy. The School District's argument is that "(t)he policy as well as the letter of the law is a guide to decision."

We recognize this Board's responsibility as guardian of public policy discussed in National Labor Relations Board v. Atkins & Company, 331 U.S. 398 (1947). While there are certain areas of policy to be considered in every matter, this policy should not be used to frustrate the intent of the Legislature as we interpret it. Thus, it would be inconsistent for us to find supervisory status encompassed within the definition of "public employees," and then deny that status because we believed that the policy should be to the contrary.

We do note that competent authorities have expressed the opinion that supervisory personnel in the public sector have characteristics which differ from supervisors in private employment.[9] These differences, far from disqualifying public employment supervisors from representation, make a stronger case for allowing supervisors separate bargaining units, particularly when they are not excluded from the definition of "employee." [10]

There is a common interest among school boards, superintendents, principals and teachers to provide "a superior education for the nation's youth." All of those parties work professionally toward the same goal. . . .

## 3. Appropriate Unit.

The Trial Examiner found that the petitioned for unit was appropriate although it contained purported principal supervision of the staff specialists. We affirm the Trial Examiner's Findings that the nature of the supervision was not sufficient to invoke the prohibition against supervisors being included in units with those employees they supervise.

---

that the New York State Public Employment Relations Board has included principals and assistant principals in bargaining units, stating that: "Principals act merely as conduits rather than as decision makers." Board of Education, Union Free School District and Depew Teachers Organization, Inc., 255 GERR C-2 (1968). Similarly, see Metropolitan Transit Authority, 48 L.R.R.M. 1296 (Mass. Labor Relations Board, 1961). We also dismiss the argument concerning Governor Romney's veto of HB 3388, which bill would have amended PERA to allow the inclusion of police supervisors in the bargaining unit with patrolmen. The issue raised by the bill was solely the inclusion, or exclusion, of police supervisors in the same unit with the rank and file. Police supervisors had, on the enactment of PERA, the privilege to engage in concerted activities, including the choice of an exclusive bargaining representative in a designated unit.

[9] See, for example, Slavney, "The Public Employee — How Shall He Be Represented in Collective Negotiations?" Governor Rockefeller's Conference on Public Employment Relations, 269 GERR E-1 (1968). Mr. Slavney observes at p. E-4: "I think most of us here would admit that supervisors in public employment are for the most part different than supervisors in the private sector, not only in the concept of employer loyalty but also in the performance of identifiable supervisory functions. Under a civil service system, the authority supervisors might have with regard to the hire, transfer, suspension, layoff, recall and promotion is subject to more stringent review than in private employment. Further, in civil service, employees performing normal supervisory duties have the same rights and protections as do rank and file employees with respect to tenure, job security and civil service grievance procedures, and normally their salary increments and increases have a distinct relationship to increments and increases granted to non-supervisory personnel. These factors tend to create a community of interest with employees supervised rather than with management." *See also*, New York Public Library, 69-1 ARB ¶ 8067 (Yagoda, 1968).

[10] Metropolitan New York Nursing Home Association, 60 L.R.R.M. 1281 (N.Y. State Labor Relations Board, 1965).

The evidence reveals that the supervision is mere routine direction not requiring the exercise of independent judgment. . . .

Regarding the unit in question, we find a community of interest between the staff specialists and the principals. There are similarities in administrative duties, professional skills and working conditions. Additionally, we agree with the Trial Examiner's conclusion that the staff specialists' distinct community of interest is insufficient to separate them from the principals.

Thus, we find the petitioned for unit appropriate for collective bargaining purposes under PERA.

### 4. MEA domination of PSA.

The School District argues here that the parent organization (MEA), exercises an overwhelming degree of control over its affiliates, particularly respecting collective bargaining policy. Also, it is alleged that it is impossible for PSA to be truly independent within the MEA organizational framework. Where both the principals' and teachers' organizations are MEA affiliates, the School District maintains that there is a conflict of interest where principals are the first step in the grievance procedure. Hence, if the MEA exercises such a degree of control over its affiliates, it will control the initial stage of the grievance procedure. The Trial Examiner agreed with the School District's contentions.

Perhaps this situation may arise, but it is speculative. We are charged with the duty to protect the organizational rights of *all* public employees. Where, as here, principals are public employees, we should not restrict their free exercise of Sec. 9 rights, which includes the selection of a collective bargaining representative. City of Escanaba, 1966 Labor Opinions 451. The petitioning organization must, however, proceed with the normal proof establishing itself as a labor organization within the terms of the Act.

Similarly, there is no more basis for restricting the choice of bargaining agent to one not representing the rank and file employees here, than there is in restricting that choice respecting craft, technical, or professional employee units. Just as professional, craft, and technical employees are not restricted in their choice of bargaining representative, supervisory employees should also not be so restricted.

We agree with the principals [sic] enunciated by the New York State Labor Relations Board: [14]

> "We also have noted that the 'conflict of loyalties,' allegedly resulting from the selection of the same representative by supervisory or protection employees and by rank and file employees, is a misnomer; that it arises, if at all, from the employees' fundamental right of association which exists independent of statute; that the denial of all rights under the Act to one of the two groups of employees provides no solution; and that any problems which arise can and should be adjusted and resolved in the collective bargaining process, when, and if, that eventuality occurs."
>
> . . . .

Before this position is interpreted as allowing the organization of "vice presidents" mentioned in the *Packard* [15] case, we note that there is a level at which organization must end. That level consists of "executive" employees, and

---

[14] Yonkers Raceway, Inc., 63 L.R.R.M. 1098, 1100 (N.Y. State Labor Relations Bd., 1966).

[15] Packard Motor Car Company v. NLRB, 330 U.S. 485 (1947). The briefs of some amici curiae noted the comment by Mr. Justice Jackson.

is limited to those employees who formulate, determine and effectuate management policies.[17]

The application of this exclusion is not necessary in this case because there is no evidence that the employees in the proposed unit act in any other manner than as resource people in collective bargaining or as conduits for labor relations policy established without their participation. We do not consider that employees who serve the employer at the first step of the grievance procedure are within the executive category by reason of that responsibility. Thus, we do not feel that our determination impinges upon management's right to have trusted personnel act in its behalf in formulating, determining and effectuating policies and in collective bargaining. . . .

## NOTES

1. In contrast to the principal case, the Nebraska Supreme Court in Nebraska Ass'n of Public Employees v. Nebraska Game and Parks Comm'n, 247 N.W.2d 449, 94 L.R.R.M. 2428 (Neb. S. Ct. 1976), held that supervisory and managerial employees could not be represented by the same union that represented rank and file employees, reasoning as follows:

> To permit supervisory personnel to retain the same bargaining agent as the employees' union would be tantamount to permitting them to enter the same bargaining unit and such agent could, and doubtless would, manipulate its efforts jointly in behalf of each. We hold that supervisory or managerial personnel may not enter into a bargaining unit with rank and file employees and may not retain the same bargaining agent.

2. The California Educational Employment Relations Act permits employees in management or confidential positions to be represented for meet and confer purposes only by an employee organization "whose membership is composed entirely of employees designated as holding such positions, in his employment relationship with the public school employer. . . ." CAL. EDUC. CODE § 3543.4.

3. A number of commentators have supported the view that supervisory employees should have the right to be represented for the purposes of collective bargaining. *See, e.g.,* White, *Rights and Responsibilities in Municipal Collective Bargaining,* 22 ARB. J. (n.s.) 31, 32 (1967); Schmidt, *The Question of the Recognition of Principal and Other Supervisory Units in Public Education Collective Bargaining,* 19 LAB. L.J. 283 (1968).

4. In City of Detroit, Dep't of Parks and Recreation, 1969 MERC Lab. Op. 661, the MERC noted that it "does not intend to mechanically apply private employment supervisory concepts to public employment situations," observing:

> Frequently, under governmental employment, by its very nature and history, numerous promotional steps exist in a department or agency in order to provide upward mobility and increased compensation, and each upward step means that the lower classification is in a sense subservient to the higher. Therefore, a series of leader-type steps are instituted, each of which exercises a certain degree of authority over lower classifications without necessarily possessing actual supervisory authority in a labor relations context and as such authority normally exists in private industrial employment where the lines of demarcation between employee and supervisor are often much clearer. Thus, the "responsibility to direct" guideline of Section 2(11) of the Federal Labor Management Relations Act is not necessarily a viable criteria in determining supervisory status under PERA.

5. Where a civil service commission has the authority to hire and fire employees and to determine which employee is to be promoted, what effect, if any, does this have on the determination of supervisory status? In Wauwatosa Board of Education, Decision No.

---

[17] The executive designation is basically synonymous with managerial employees as defined in Ford Motor Co., 66 N.L.R.B. 1317, 17 L.R.R.M. 394 (1946), and as applied in Quincy City Hospital, 60 L.R.R.M. 1244 (Mass. Labor Relations Comm., 1965).

6219-D (Wis. ERC 1967), the Wisconsin Employment Relations Commission made the following observation:

> Because certain conditions of employment are governed by civil service rules and regulations, the employees in the positions in question have limited authority with respect to hiring and promotion and discharge of employees. However, they can make recommendations with respect thereto. The lack of such authority, however, will not preclude the Commission from making a supervisory determination.

6. The various labor relations agencies have had considerable difficulty in deciding whether department chairpersons should be considered "supervisors" and therefore excluded from faculty or teacher bargaining units or considered "employees" and included in such units. *Compare* University of Pittsburgh, 7 PPER 21 (Pa. PLRB 1976) (department chairpersons held supervisors), *with* Tamaqua Area School District, 7 PPER 253 (Pa. PLRB 1976) (department heads held not supervisors). The NLRB has likewise struggled with the question of whether department chairpersons are "supervisors." *Compare* Fordham Univ., 193 N.L.R.B. 134 (1971) (held not supervisors), *with* Syracuse Univ., 204 N.L.R.B. 641 (1973) (held supervisors). *See generally* Comment, *The Bargaining Unit Status of Academic Department Chairmen,* 40 U. CHI. L. REV. 442 (1973).

7. The unit status of supervisory officers in fire fighter bargaining units has generated considerable litigation over the years. Public employers typically seek to exclude lieutenants, captains, battalion chiefs, etc., from fire fighter bargaining units, while the International Association of Fire Fighters or the employee organization representing fire fighters seeks their inclusion. *Compare* United States Naval Weapons Center, China Lake, California, A/SLMR No. 297 (1973), *on remand from* FLRC No. 72 A-11 (1973) (fire captains excluded as supervisors), and St. Louis County Fire Fighters Ass'n v. City of University City, Case No. 76-018 (Mo. SBM 1977) (fire captains excluded as supervisors), *with* City of Davenport v. PERB, 264 N.W.2d 307, 98 L.R.R.M. 2582 (Ia. S. Ct. 1978) (captains and lieutenants included in bargaining unit), and Professional Fire Fighters Ass'n, Local 446 v. City of Aberdeen, 99 L.R.R.M. 3038 (S.D. S. Ct.) (captains and lieutenants included in fire fighter bargaining unit). *See generally* Wheeler, *Officers in Municipal Fire Departments,* 28 LAB. L.J. 721 (1977).

## 2. MANAGERIAL EMPLOYEES

Many of the public sector statutes exclude managerial employees from the definition of the term "employee." The definition of the term "managerial employee" varies, but it usually refers to persons who are involved in formulating, determining or effectuating policies on behalf of the public employer. A number of labor relations agencies have excluded managerial employees even though the applicable statute in question does not contain such a specific exclusion. The Michigan Employment Relations Commission, for example, in City of Detroit and Governmental Accountants and Analysts Ass'n, 1969 MERC Lab. Op. 187, excluded them on the ground that they are creators of policy and thus should not be included in bargaining units. The NLRB has likewise determined, as a matter of policy, that managerial employees should be excluded. *See* J. ABODEELY, THE NLRB AND THE APPROPRIATE BARGAINING UNIT 209-10 (1971).

### STATE OF NEW YORK

New York Public Employment Relations Board
5 PERB ¶ 3001 (1972)

On September 21, 1971 the State of New York filed a timely application pursuant to CSL § 201.7, as amended,[1] seeking to have this Board designate as managerial or confidential certain employees of the State of New York in specified job titles. . . .

*Discussion*

## I. *Authority of PERB*

One of the points made by the State is that,

"The initial and primary fact in the determination of whether a position or person should be designated as managerial or confidential is the opinion of the public employer. Only the employer can accurately judge its needs. Accordingly, when the over-all position of the employer appears to be reasonable, the employer's judgment should be supported by this Board unless for particular positions the employer's judgment is not supported by substantial evidence."

In support of this proposition, the State argues that a managerial employee is defined as one who formulates policy or "may reasonably be required on behalf of the public employer" to exercise certain specified labor relations functions. According to the State, the words, "may reasonably be required on behalf of the public employer," express a legislative intent that this Board should adopt the employer's analysis of what it may reasonably require unless the employer has been arbitrary.

We do not read the quoted language of the statute as creating a presumption in favor of an employer's judgment concerning the employees whom it may reasonably require to conduct its labor relations responsibilities; we understand it as providing a criterion which PERB must observe in making its determination. While an employer's opinion as to the designation of employees as management or confidential is entitled to serious consideration, nevertheless, this Board's determination is not limited simply to a review of the opinion of the employer and of the reasons supporting such opinion. Rather, the determination is based upon the application of the statutory criteria to all the evidence offered by the parties.

The respective responsibilities of PERB and the public employer are set forth in the Taylor Law (CSL § 201.7), which provides for the exclusion of "persons who may reasonably be designated from time to time as managerial or confidential upon application of the public employer to the appropriate board. . . ." It is the function of the public employer to apply; it is the responsibility of the Board to determine. . . .

## II. *Managerial and Confidential Employees Before the 1971 Amendment of the Taylor Law*

Even before the enactment of Chapters 503 and 504 of the Laws of 1971, there

---

[1] CSL § 201.7 provides: "The term 'public employee' . . . shall not include . . . persons who may reasonably be designated from time to time as managerial or confidential upon application of the public employer to the appropriate board in accordance with procedures established pursuant to section two hundred five or two hundred twelve of this article, which procedures shall provide that any such designations made during a period of unchallenged representation pursuant to subdivision two of section two hundred eight of this chapter shall only become effective upon the termination of such period of unchallenged representation. Employees may be designated as managerial only if they are persons (a) who formulate policy or (b) who may reasonably be required on behalf of the public employer to assist directly in the preparation for and conduct of collective negotiations or to have a major role in the administration of agreements or in personnel administration provided that such role is not of a routine or clerical nature and requires the exercise of independent judgment. Employees may be designated as confidential only if they are persons who assist and act in a confidential capacity to managerial employees described in clause (b)."

was a concept of managerial and confidential employment under the Taylor Law. This concept derived from the Report of the Taylor Committee. Although the Taylor Law did not expressly exclude persons who were managerial or confidential, the Office of Collective Bargaining of the City of New York interpreted the Taylor Law to require such an exclusion. This Board did not have occasion to rule on whether managerial and confidential employees were covered by the Taylor Law, but it did find that they could not be in the same units as rank-and-file employees because of the conflict of interest between them, and no separate unit of managerial and confidential employees had ever been designated by PERB.

## IV. *Comparison of Statutory Definition with Prior PERB Definition*

The definition used by this Board to exclude persons from the five units established in 1968 was that a person is managerial or confidential if he:

"Formulates or determines State or agency policy (e.g., department and agency heads and their deputies); or

"Directs the work of an agency or a major subdivision thereof with considerable discretion in determining the methods, means and personnel by which State or agency policy is to be carried out (e.g., institution heads, administrative directors); or

"Is so closely related to or involved with the activities noted above as to present a potential conflict of interest or clash of loyalties in matters concerning employer-employee relationships (e.g., staff agents, confidential assistants), or in a geographically separated location is responsible for representing the State's position in dealing with a significant number of employees."

The first two paragraphs of the above-quoted PERB definition were intended by this Board to delineate persons who might be deemed "managerial." The two criteria set forth in those paragraphs were clearly not limited to labor relations functions or responsibilities, but were intended to cover all activities that might be deemed "managerial," such as the formulation and determination of State, agency or institutional policy. The Legislature, however, in defining "managerial" in the same broad sense simply said "persons . . . who formulate policy."

## A. *Criterion One — Formulation of policy.*

This criterion is but one of four criteria established by the Legislature for designating persons as managerial. The other three criteria are limited to labor relations functions or responsibilities of the public employer. Thus, it would appear to have been the intent of the Legislature that persons who formulate policy may be designated managerial even though they do not exercise a labor relations function.

We will first discuss the "policy" criterion and later the other three criteria. It would appear desirable to first consider the term "policy." Policy is defined in a general sense as "a definite course or method of action selected from among alternatives and in the light of given conditions to guide and determine present and future decisions." [10] In government, policy would thus be the development of the particular objectives of a government or agency thereof in the fulfillment of its mission and the methods, means and extent of achieving such objectives.

---

[10] Webster's Seventh New Collegiate Dictionary.

The term "formulate" as used in the frame of reference of "managerial" would appear to include not only a person who has the authority or responsibility to select among options and to put a proposed policy into effect, but also a person who participates with regularity in the essential process which results in a policy proposal and the decision to put such a proposal into effect. It would not appear to include a person who simply drafts language for the statement of policy without meaningful participation in the decisional process, nor would it include one who simply engaged in research or the collection of data necessary for the development of a policy proposal.

We conclude that this legislative criterion is similar in scope and meaning to the earlier one stated by this Board, namely, one who "formulates or determines State or agency policy."

## B. *Criterion Two — Involvement in collective negotiations.*

The remaining three criteria for designating an employee as managerial all specifically relate to the labor relations functions of the employee. The first of these is that the employee "may reasonably be required on behalf of the public employer to assist directly in the preparation for and conduct of collective negotiations." This part of the definition is an addition to the criteria set forth in our decision In the Matter of the State of New York, 1 PERB ¶ 399.85 (1968), although many of the persons to whom it is applicable were designated as managerial under other criteria then used and now restated. We interpret this criterion to include those who may reasonably be required to be directly involved in the preparation and formulation of the employer's proposals or positions in collective negotiations. We do not think that the Legislature intended, however, that if an employer consulted with supervisory personnel on the implication or feasibility of negotiation proposals that such supervisory personnel should be deemed managerial. Admittedly, such supervisory personnel would be assisting in the preparation for collective negotiations, but such assistance without participation in the actual conduct of negotiations would not satisfy the statutory criterion. Moreover, we take the phrase "to assist directly" to mean direct involvement or participation in the preparation for collective negotiations so as to be part of the decision-making process therein. Similarly, with respect to "conduct of collective negotiations," there must be direct involvement or participation in the negotiating process, and simply being present at the negotiations as an observer or other non-participatory role would not suffice. The largest group of persons not previously designated as managerial, but encompassed by this part of the definition, are persons holding positions in newly created titles specifically related to the preparation for and conduct of collective negotiations. Examples of these are Labor-Management Relations Officers and Employee Relations Representatives.

## C. *Criterion Three—Administration of agreements.*

The third criterion is that a person is managerial if he has "a major role in the administration of agreements . . . provided that such role is not of a routine or clerical nature and requires the exercise of independent judgment." The administration of an agreement involves basically two functions: (1) observance of the terms of the agreement and (2) interpretation of the agreement both within and without the grievance procedures of the contract. The observance of the terms of the agreement is largely a routine and ministerial function. Undoubtedly many supervisory employees have a responsibility to insure that terms and conditions of an agreement are adhered to, but this responsibility does not usually require "the exercise of independent judgment." There will be occasions where the implementation of an agreement will necessitate a change in a government's procedures or methods of operation. The person or persons who effect such implementation and change do exercise independent judgment and would have a "major role" in the administration of an agreement. Such a person is one the Legislature sought to exclude by this criterion.

Many supervisors are involved in grievance procedures. It does not appear, however, that supervisors who participate in first step grievances exercise independent judgment. Rather, such participation generally conforms to policy established at a higher level.

The interpretation of an agreement involving State agency or institution policy involving employee relations would constitute a "major role" in the administration of an agreement, and would require the exercise of independent judgment.

D. *Criterion Four — Personnel administration.*

The final criterion for defining managerial employees is that they "have a major role . . . in personnel administration, provided that such role is not of a routine or clerical nature and requires the exercise of independent judgment." Many of the persons so defined were previously excluded under the old definition because they were "so closely related to or involved with the activities [of those who formulate policy or direct the work of major subdivisions] as to present a potential conflict of interest or clash of loyalties in matters concerning employer-employee relationships." To some extent, this final criterion is a compression of our prior definition. Some persons were previously excluded from the five units because their relationship to personnel administration was very close, even though it was of a routine or clerical nature. In any event, they are not managerial employees under the new statutory definition. Examples of these are the staff of the health services unit of the Department of Civil Service. . . .

# 3. CONFIDENTIAL EMPLOYEES

## SHAW AND CLARK, DETERMINATION OF APPROPRIATE BARGAINING UNITS IN THE PUBLIC SECTOR: LEGAL AND PRACTICAL PROBLEMS, 51 Ore. L. Rev. 152, 171 (1971)†

Another common exclusion from bargaining units is confidential employees. Although the breadth of this exclusion varies from state to state, the term "confidential employees" usually refers to "employees who assist and act in a confidential capacity to persons who formulate, determine, and evaluate management policies in the field of labor relations." The rationale for excluding confidential employees from larger bargaining units in the private sector was to separate those employees "who, in the normal performance of their duties may obtain advance information of the Company's position with regard to contract negotiations, the disposition of grievances, or other labor relations matters."

In some states, including Oregon, confidential employees are specifically excluded from bargaining units. In other states, such as Connecticut and Michigan, confidential employees have been excluded from bargaining units on a case-by-case basis by the public employee labor relations board. For example, the Michigan Employment Relations Commission has adopted the following rule:

[W]e are of the opinion that the "confidential" employees rule should be

---

† Reprinted by permission. Copyright © 1971 by University of Oregon.

applied cautiously. Only those employees whose work is closely related to that of supervisory employees and involves matters which should be held in confidence should be excluded from a bargaining unit with nonsupervisory employees. . . .[10]

Applying this rule, the MERC has held that the secretary to a public employer's negotiator, and the secretary to a director of budget, finance, and accounting were confidential employees. On the other hand, persons who from time to time may have access to confidential information are not necessarily confidential employees. Similar decisions have been issued by other public employee relations boards.

# NOTES

1. In PLRB v. Altoona Area School District, 389 A.2d 553 (Pa. S. Ct. 1978), the Pennsylvania Supreme Court upheld the test utilized by the PLRB to determine confidential employee status, *i.e.,* "whether or not the employe acts in a confidential capacity to a person who formulates, determines or effectuates management policies in the field of labor relations." After finding that the considerations underlying the exclusion of confidential employees under the NLRA were identical to the Pennsylvania statutory exclusion of confidential employees, the court held that the PLRB properly considered NLRB precedent in "formulat[ing] a workable definition of that term as it appears in the Pennsylvania statute."

2. In New Hampshire University System v. State of New Hampshire, 369 A.2d 1139 (N.H. S. Ct. 1977), the court, after essentially adopting the NLRB standards for determining confidential status, held that department chairpersons were not confidential employees since the recommendations they made concerning tenure and promotions did "not constitute confidential interaction between department chairmen and the administration on labor relations matters."

3. The NLRB's exclusion of confidential employees from bargaining units is thoroughly explored in Note, *Confidential Employees and the National Labor Relations Act,* 29 WASH. & LEE L. REV. 350 (1972).

4. The Florida statute defines confidential employees as "persons who act in a confidential capacity to assist or aid managerial employees as defined in [the Act]." Fla. Stat. § 447.203(5) (1977). In Palm Beach County School Board v. PERC, 99 L.R.R.M. 3035 (Fla. Dist. Ct. App. 1978), the court held "that the personal secretary of a managerial employee such as a school principal is, by definition, 'one who aids or assists a managerial employee in confidential matters.' " In setting aside a PERC order, the court held that the statute "does not require a 'nexus' between the confidential matters and the particular managerial duties of the principal listed in [the statutory definition of a managerial employee]," *i.e.,* the confidential aid or assistance does not have to necessarily relate to those duties and responsibilities deemed managerial in nature under the Florida act.

5. The Federal Labor-Management and Employees Relations Law provides that no unit shall be determined to be appropriate if it includes confidential employees or employees "engaged in personnel work in other than a purely clerical capacity." 5 U.S.C. § 7112(b)(2) & (3) (1978). The term "confidential employee" is defined to mean "an employee who acts in a confidential capacity with respect to an individual who formulates or effectuates management policies in the field of labor-management relations." 5 U.S.C. § 7103 (13) (1978). How does this definition differ from the definition construed by the Florida court in the *Palm Beach County School Board* case discussed in the note immediately above?

6. Are city attorneys who furnish legal opinions to various municipal agencies and in such capacity participate in negotiations between such agencies and the unions that represent their employees confidential employees? In City of Milwaukee, Decision No. 8100 (Wis. ERC 1967), *aff'd,* 43 Wis. 2d 596, 168 N.W.2d 809 (1969), the WERC stated:

---

[10] Benton Harbor Bd. of Educ., 1967 MERC Lab. Op. 743, 746.

Although the Assistant City Attorneys do act in a confidential capacity with respect to the determination and implementation of management policies in the field of labor relations, the information available to these attorneys is not directly related to the relationship between the City and their representative. Employees who have access to confidential labor relations information of other employers, unrelated to the relationship between the employer and the employees included in the unit in question, does not mean that such employees should be excluded from one unit because they are "confidential employees."

The WERC did find, however, that the assistant city attorney who represented the city in negotiations and was regularly assigned to furnish legal assistance to the office of the city's labor negotiator should be excluded from the unit. The WERC noted that the individual in question "cannot possibly serve both parties" and that "his relationship with the office of the Labor Negotiator is too intimate to permit him to be included in the unit."

# 4. TEACHING ASSISTANTS AND STUDENTS

## REGENTS OF THE UNIVERSITY OF MICHIGAN v. MERC

Michigan Supreme Court
— Mich. —, 204 N.W.2d 218 (1973)

SWAINSON, J. In 1966, a group of interns, residents and post-doctoral fellows connected with the University of Michigan Hospital and its affiliates organized the University of Michigan Interns-Residents Association (hereinunder referred to as the Association). The Association attempted to bargain with the University Hospital Administrators concerning the compensation of interns and residents. The University asserted its right to unilaterally determine such compensation. On March 19, 1970 the Association filed a written request that the Regents of the University of Michigan recognize it as the bargaining representative of the interns, residents and post-doctoral fellows serving at the University Hospital and its affiliates. The Regents denied this request on or about March 31, 1970.

The Association then filed a petition for representation with the Michigan Employment Relations Commission (hereinafter referred to as MERC) on April 19, 1970. . . .

On March 16, 1971·a majority of the members of the commission issued a decision holding:

1. That the Association is a labor organization within the meaning of the Michigan Public Employees Relations Act (hereinafter referred to as PERA).

2. That the University of Michigan is a public employer subject to the provisions of PERA and thus the commission has jurisdiction of the matter.

3. That the members of the Association are public employees under the provisions of PERA.

4. The employment relationship between the parties is not a casual one as that term is used to designate exclusions from a bargaining unit.

The majority of the commission further ordered that an election be held and defined the appropriate bargaining unit. One member of the commission held in a dissent that interns and residents are post-graduate students whose activities are primarily educational and are not employees in the traditional sense.

The Regents applied for leave to appeal in the Court of Appeals and such was granted on June 9, 1971. The Court of Appeals denied the Regents' motion to stay the representation election and MERC conducted such an election. Of the 419 individuals who cast votes, 296 voted for representation, 115 voted against, and four ballots were challenged. The Association soon after the election requested that negotiations be instituted, but the Regents refused on the theory that the matter was still pending in court. The Court of Appeals on June 24, 1971 issued an order staying all proceedings until a final decision of that Court.

On January 21, 1972 the majority of the Court of Appeals reversed the findings of the MERC and held as a matter of law that interns, residents, and post-doctoral fellows cannot be characterized as employees. 38 Mich. App. 55. Judge McGregor in dissent held that the members of the Association could be both students and public employees. 38 Mich. App. 66. We granted leave to appeal. 387 Mich. 773. . . .

The key contention of the respondent, concurred in by a majority of the Court of Appeals, that to hold the members of the Association are employees would contravene Article VIII, section 5 of the 1963 Constitution.* This constitutional provision has its roots in Article XIII, section 6-8 of the 1850 Constitution. The desires of the framers of the 1850 and subsequent constitutions to provide autonomy to the Board of Regents in the educational sphere have been protected by our Court for over a century.

This concern for the educational process to be controlled by the Regents does not and cannot mean that they are exempt from all the laws of the state. When the University of Michigan was founded in the 19th Century it was comparatively easy to isolate the University and keep it free from outside interference. The complexities of modern times make this impossible. Problems concerning the disputes between employees and public employers were not given full constitutional recognition until the 1963 Constitution. The people, through the passage of Article IV, section 48 of the 1963 Constitution have deemed the resolution of public employee disputes a matter of public policy. This Court must attempt to harmonize the various constitutional provisions and give meaning to all of them. . . .

We agree with the reasoning of the Court of Appeals in Branum v. Board of Regents of University of Michigan, 5 Mich. App. 134 (1966). The issue in that case was whether the Legislature could waive governmental immunity for the University of Michigan because it was a constitutional corporation. The Court of Appeals stated (pp. 138-139):

"In spite of its independence, the board of regents remains a part of the government of the State of Michigan.

. . . .

"It is the opinion of this Court that the legislature can validly exercise its police power for the welfare of the people of this State, and a constitutional corporation such as the board of regents of the University of Michigan can lawfully be affected thereby. The University of Michigan is an independent branch of the government of the State of Michigan, but it is not an island.

---

* "The regents of the University of Michigan and their successors in office shall constitute a body corporate known as the Regents of the University of Michigan; the trustees of Michigan State University and their successors in office shall constitute a body corporate known as the Board of Trustees of Michigan State University; the governors of Wayne State University and their successors in office shall constitute a body corporate known as the Board of Governors of Wayne State University. Each board shall have general supervision of its institution and the control and direction of all expenditures from the institution's funds. Each board shall, as often as necessary, elect a president of the institution under its supervision. He shall be principal executive officer of the institution, be ex-officio a member of the board without the right to vote and preside at meetings of the board. The board of each institution shall consist of eight members who shall hold office for terms of eight years and who shall be elected as provided by law. The governor shall fill board vacancies by appointment. Each appointee shall hold office until a successor has been nominated and elected as provided by law." [Eds.]

Within the confines of the operation and the allocation of funds of the University, it is supreme. Without these confines, however, there is no reason to allow the regents to use their independence to thwart the clearly established public policy of the people of Michigan."

Thus, we believe that the two sections of the 1963 Constitution can be harmonized. We hold that interns, residents and post-doctoral fellows may be employees and have rights to organize under the provisions of PERA without infringing on the constitutional autonomy of the Board of Regents. However, as the Court of Appeals pointed out in Regents of the University of Michigan v. Labor Mediation Board, 18 Mich. App. 485 (1969), pp. 490-491:

"While recognizing that the plaintiff is a public employer and the employees in question are public employees, we also recognize that this plaintiff, because of the provisions of Const. 1963, art. 8, § 5, is a unique public employer. Its powers, duties and responsibilities are derived from the constitution as distinguished from other public employers whose authority is derivative from enactments of the legislature."

Because of the unique nature of the University of Michigan, above referred to, the scope of bargaining by the Association may be limited if the subject matter falls clearly within the educational sphere. Some conditions of employment may not be subject to collective bargaining because those particular facets of employment would interfere with the autonomy of the Regents.

For example, the Association clearly can bargain with the Regents on the salary that their members receive since it is not within the educational sphere. While normally employees can bargain to discontinue a certain aspect of a particular job, the Association does not have the same latitude as other public employees. For example, interns could not negotiate working in the pathology department because they found such work distasteful. If the administrators of medical schools felt that a certain number of hours devoted to pathology was necessary to the education of the intern, our Court would not interfere since this does fall within the autonomy of the Regents under Article VIII, section 5. Numerous other issues may arise which fall between these two extremes and they will have to be decided on a case by case basis. Our Court will not, as it has not in the past, shirk its duty to protect the autonomy of the Regents in the educational sphere. Thus, we hold that it does not violate Article VIII, section 5 of the 1963 Constitution if the members of the Association are held to be public employees.

The Regents further contend that interns and residents are not employees as that term is used in the PERA. However, as we stated in the *Eastern Michigan* case, *supra,* (p. 566) concerning the scope of the PERA:

" 'Public employment' is clearly intended to apply to employment or service in all governmental activity, whether carried on by the state or by townships, cities, counties, commissions, boards or other governmental instrumentalities. *It is the entire public sector of employment as distinguished from private employment.* The public policy of this state as to labor relations in public employment is for legislative determination." [Emphasis added.]

The only exception is for the classified civil service. No exception is made for people who have a dual status of students and employees. If the Legislature had intended to exclude students/employees from the operation of PERA, they could have written such an exception into the law. However, as noted above, the only exception is for the classified civil service. We thus hold that members of the

Association are employees within the meaning of the PERA.

Finally, we must determine whether the findings by the Michigan Employment Relations Commission that members of the Association are employees is supported by competent, material and substantial evidence on the record. We hold that it is.

There is ample evidence to support the findings of the Commission that the members of the Association are employees. For example, they have a portion of their compensation withheld for the purposes of federal income tax, state income tax, and social security coverage (75a, 149a, 513a, 524a). As Judge McGregor pointed out in his dissent in the Court below, 38 Mich. App. 55 (p. 67):

> Doctors are not eligible for the Internal Revenue Code § 117 exclusion of income for fellowships and education stipend. See Woddail v. Commissioner of Internal Revenue. 321 F.2d 721, (CA 10, 1963).

The interns, residents and post-doctoral fellows receive fringe benefits available only to regular University of Michigan employees through use of the identification cards which are issued to them by the University. (517-518a). This includes partial payment of Blue Cross-Blue Shield coverage, identical to coverage offered to other regular University employees. (91a, 143a, 508-509a). The University furnishes the W-2 forms required by the Internal Revenue Service for all employees. (510-512a). The compensation is paid by University checks drawn from a University account. (65a, 103a, 138a).

All interns and residents are required as a condition of employment to sign a loyalty oath required by Michigan law to be signed by all public employees. (422a, 601a). The interns and residents spend over three-quarters of their time providing patient care services (72-3a, 106a, 120-1a) for which the University is compensated. (33a-4a). In particular, they are entrusted with many responsibilities that medical students are not. These include:

1. Writing of prescriptions without the required approval of a senior person. (46a, 60a, 74a, 200a, 399a).

2. Taking full charge and responsibility for the running of an outpatient clinic. (100-101a, 397a).

3. Admitting and discharging patients. (121-2a, 130a, 375-6a, 397a, 461a).

4. Performing operations and surgical techniques on actual patients under minimal or no supervision. (201a, 376a, 398a).

Moreover, Dr. John A. Gronvall testified that the principal duty and responsibility of interns and residents is to diagnose and prescribe a patient care program and put it into effect. (203-4a). We agree with counsel for the Association that this is far more indicative of an employee (i.e. — in this case a doctor) than a student.

The Regents point out other evidence from the record that would indicate that interns, residents and post-doctoral fellows are students. All internship and residency programs at the University of Michigan are fully approved by the Council of Medical Education of the AMA. The stipend that interns and residents receive is unlike a salary because it has no relation to the number of hours an individual works or the duties they perform. All interns are not licensed to practice medicine. The Regents also relied on the testimony given at the hearing by several doctors which demonstrates that the medical education is different from other professions and graduate school educations. Medical education begins to include patient care responsibilities in the third year of medical school. The type of patient care responsibility given to an intern and resident is part of a continuing medical education and not evidence that an intern or resident is primarily an employee.

We do not regard these categories as mutually exclusive. Interns, residents and post-doctoral fellows are both students and employees. The fact that they are continually acquiring new skills does not detract from the findings of the MERC that they may organize as employees under the provisions of PERA. Members of all professions continue their learning throughout their careers. For example, fledgling lawyers employed by a law firm spend a great deal of time acquiring new skills, yet no one would contend that they are not employees of the law firm. The Regents contend vigorously that the MERC was incorrect in its findings that interns, residents and post-doctoral fellows are employees and contend that they are primarily students. However, since at this point we are dealing with a question of fact, under section 106d of the Administrative Procedures Act, we cannot, pursuant to said section, overturn the findings of the MERC unless they are not supported by competent, material, and substantial evidence on the record. We hold that the findings of the MERC that interns, residents and post-doctoral fellows are employees are supported by competent, material, and substantial evidence on the whole record.

The judgment of the Court of Appeals is reversed and the decision of the MERC is affirmed. No costs, a public question being involved.

## NOTES

1. In Cedars-Sinai Medical Center, 223 N.L.R.B. No. 57, 91 L.R.R.M. 1398 (1976), the NLRB in a 3-2 decision held that interns and residents were not employees covered by the National Labor Relations Act on the basis of the Board's conclusion that they were "primarily students." However, in Physicians National House Staff Ass'n v. Murphy, 100 L.R.R.M. 3055 (D.C. Cir. 1979), the Court of Appeals for the District of Columbia held that the legislative history demonstrated an affirmative intent to consider house staff as employees within the meaning of the NLRA and that this legislative intent could "not be contravened by administrative fiat."

2. The Pennsylvania Supreme Court in Philadelphia Ass'n of Interns & Residents v. Albert Einstein Medical Center, 92 L.R.R.M. 3410 (1976), held, that hospital interns, residents, and clinical fellows were not public employees covered by the Pennsylvania PERA since the primary thrust of their hospital affiliation was to continue their medical education rather than to provide services as normal wage earners. The court observed that the purpose of the Act was to provide "for stability accounted for by a continuous employer-employee relationship" and that "[t]he interns, residents, and fellows had no such interest." On the other hand, in House Officers Ass'n v. Univ. of Nebraska Medical Center, 198 Neb. 697, 225 N.W.2d 258 (1977), the Nebraska Supreme Court held that residents and interns were employees covered by the Nebraska public sector collective bargaining law. The court said it found "nothing in the stated purpose of the act that would indicate the Legislature intended that persons who were students but also employees of the University of Nebraska should be exempted from the provisions of the Act." In rejecting the university's reliance on the NLRB's Cedars-Sinai decision, the court noted that "[t]he great weight of authority in state courts has come to a contrary decision. . . ."

3. In Iron Mountain Area Public Schools, 1972 MERC Lab. Op. 35 (Mich.), the MERC held that high school students working in office clerical or custodial jobs under a federally financed work-study program did not have a sufficient community of interest with the regular full-time employees to be included in the unit since there was no expectation that they would continue their employment beyond graduation.

4. The NLRB has held that graduate students who serve as teaching assistants "are primarily students and do not share a sufficient community of interest with faculty members to warrant their inclusion in . . . [a faculty bargaining] unit." College of Pharmaceutical Sciences, 197 N.L.R.B. 959 (1972); Adelphi University, 195 N.L.R.B. 639 (1972). In Cornell Univ., 202 N.L.R.B. 290 (1973), the NLRB excluded students from a unit of full-time employees, noting that "for the great majority of student employees, since

they have no expectation of remaining permanently in their present jobs, their employment is incidental to their academic objectives."

# E. SELECTION OF THE COLLECTIVE BARGAINING REPRESENTATIVE

## 1. SECRET BALLOT ELECTION

Most of the comprehensive public sector collective bargaining statutes provide, as the Alaska statute does, that "[i]f the labor relations agency finds that there is a question of representation, it shall direct an election by secret ballot to determine whether or by which organization the employees desire to be represented and shall certify the results of the election." ALAS. STAT. tit. 23, ch. 40, § 23.40.100(b) (1972). Adopting the practice under the NLRA, Executive Order 11491 and most of the state acts further provide that an employee organization is to be certified if it receives a majority of the votes *cast* in the election. In other words, if there are 100 employees in the unit and 80 employees vote in the election, only 41 votes favoring representation would be needed for certification, even though this would not constitute a majority of the employees in the unit. There are some exceptions, however. For example, Section 10 of the Indiana law covering certificated school employees provides that "[c]ertification as the exclusive representative shall . . . be granted only to a school employee organization that has been selected, in a secret ballot election, by a majority of all of the employees in an appropriate unit as their representative." INDIANA CODE tit. 20, art. 7.5, § 10 (1971).

In addition to conducting secret ballot elections, the various labor relations agencies are frequently called upon to decide who is eligible to vote in such elections. Employees who are not on the active payroll because of illness, vacation, leave of absence and those who are on layoff but have a reasonable expectation of being recalled are generally considered eligible to vote in representation elections. Occasionally this is specifically spelled out in the applicable statute or ordinance. For instance, the Los Angeles ordinance provides that employees who did not work in the period immediately prior to the election "because of illness, vacation or authorized leaves of absence" are entitled to vote. Probationary employees are considered eligible voters since they share a community of interest with other employees in the unit and have a reasonable expectation of becoming permanent employees. *See* Taylor County, Highway Dep't, Decision No. 8178 (Wis. ERC 1967); Department of Navy, Navy Exchange, Mayport, Florida, A/SLMR No. 24 (1971).

## 2. CARD CHECK OR OTHER MEANS

Several of the comprehensive public sector collective bargaining statutes provide that the labor relations agency has the authority to ascertain whether the employees desire to be represented by methods other than conducting a secret ballot election. For example, section 207 of the New York Taylor Law gives the PERB the authority to resolve questions concerning representation "on the basis of dues deduction authorization and other evidences or, if necessary, by conducting an election." N.Y. CIV. SERV. LAW § 207 (McKinney Supp. 1971). The Connecticut statute provides that the State Board of Labor Relations has the authority to either direct a secret ballot election, or "use any other suitable method to determine whether and by which employee organization the employees desire to be represented . . . ." Conn. Gen. Stat. Ann. § 7-471(1)(B) (1972). This latter provision is very similar to the language in the National Labor Relations Act as originally enacted in 1935. When Congress amended the NLRA in 1947, the phrase "any other suitable method" was deleted.

## UNION FREE SCHOOL DISTRICT NO. 6

New York Public Employment Relations Board
1 PERB ¶ 399.01 (1968)

[The Amityville Federation of Teachers filed a petition seeking to decertify the Amityville Teachers Association. At a conference the parties entered into a consent agreement which set forth the appropriate bargaining unit.]

The consent agreement further provides that an election will be held unless the employee organizations who are parties thereto submit to the Director of Representation (hereinafter called the Director) of the Board within seven days from the execution date of the agreement "dues deduction authorizations and other evidences" sufficient to satisfy the requirements of Section 201.6 (h) (1) of the Rules for certification without an election. The significance and meaning of this Section was carefully explained to all parties by the trial examiner prior to their entering into the consent agreement.

On December 13, 1967, the petitioner submitted to the Board 83 "authorization and designation" cards. These cards contained the following information: the name of the employee, the date of signing, the school involved, the position of the employee, the school district, and the home address and telephone number of the employee. The following statement is also included above the signature of the employee:

> I hereby designate and authorize the American Federation of Teachers as my exclusive agent and representative for the purpose of collective negotiations with respect to the terms and conditions of employment, the negotiation of collective agreements, and the administration of grievances arising thereunder.

On December 18, 1967, the Director approved the aforesaid consent agreement.

By letter dated December 20, 1967, the intervenor, pursuant to the consent agreement, submitted to the Director 155 "cards" containing the following information: the name of the individual employee and his position, the school involved, the date of execution, and the following statement:

> This is to certify that as a paid member of the Amityville Teachers Association, I hereby designate and authorize the ATA as my exclusive representative for collective negotiations under the New York Public Employees' Fair Employment Act.

The Rules elaborately detail the circumstances under which an employee organization may be certified without an election. If an employee organization can demonstrate by "dues deduction authorizations and other evidences" that a sufficient proportion of the employees in the appropriate unit have designated it as the negotiating agent, it will be certified as long as a substantial proportion of the employees in the unit have not authorized a competing employee organization to represent them by executing dues deduction authorizations and other evidences. The Rules specifically define "dues deduction authorizations and other evidences" as membership in an employee organization in addition to proof that such membership is for purposes of representation in collective negotiations. Further, the Rules specify (a) the minimum proportion of employees in the negotiating unit which must support an employee organization by dues deduction authorizations and other evidences for that organization to be certified without an election, and (b) the minimum proportion of employees in the negotiating unit which must support a competing organization by dues deduction authorizations and other evidences to prevent certification without an election. The following illustration, taken from Section 201.6 (h) (1) of the Rules, is pertinent:

| Column I (Percentage necessary to be certified without an election) | Column II (Percentage necessary to prevent certification without an election) |
|---|---|
| 55 | 10 |
| 60 | 15 |
| 65 | 20 |
| 70 | 25 |

In the instant case, while petitioner's submission of cards is sufficient to constitute a showing of interest, and did indeed satisfy the applicable 10% showing of interest requirement, it is clear from the above that they do not satisfy the requirements of certification without an election, nor do they block the certification of the intervenor without an election, since evidence of membership is lacking.

On the other hand, the cards submitted by the intervenor satisfy the requirements for certification without an election in that they specify the two necessary ingredients: (1) membership, and (2) proof that such membership is for purposes of representation in collective negotiations.[7] Since these cards were executed by 55% of the employees in the unit agreed to in the consent agreement (this percentage has been computed without taking into consideration the twenty employees who signed cards on behalf of both competing employee organizations) and since the petitioner has not submitted any "dues deduction authorizations and other evidences," the Board finds that the Amityville Teachers Association is entitled to be certified as the exclusive negotiating agent for the employees in the unit specified in the consent agreement.

## NOTES

1. The Idaho Fire Fighters Bargaining Law provides that

> The organization selected by the majority of the Fire Fighters in any city, county, fire district or political subdivision shall be recognized as the sole and exclusive bargaining agent for all of the members of the Fire Department, unless and until recognition of said bargaining agent is withdrawn by a vote of the majority of the Fire Fighters of such department. IDAHO CODE § 44-1803 (Supp. 1971).

The Georgia and Wyoming Fire Fighter bargaining laws contain substantially similar provisions. Under such a provision, may an employer require that the petitioning organization demonstrate that it, in fact, has been selected by a majority of the members

---

[7] These ingredients might conveniently be referred to as "membership plus."

of a given fire department? May an employer, for example, condition the grant of recognition upon the holding of a secret ballot election? Under a similar provision in the Oklahoma law prior to its amendment, the Oklahoma Attorney General ruled that a city had no right to establish the standards and procedures for the selection of a bargaining agent. Okla. Op. Att'y Gen. No. 71-420 (Dec. 29, 1971).

2. In Bowman v. Hackensack Hospital Association, 116 N.J. Super. 260, 282 A.2d 48 (1971), the New Jersey Superior Court rejected an employer's contention that a bargaining order should not be entered until an election was held to determine the union's majority status. The court noted that there were relatively few employees in the bargaining unit and that the union's majority status had been established by the pro-union trial testimony of a substantial majority of the unit members.

# 3. POST-ELECTION OBJECTIONS TO REPRESENTATION ELECTION

## BRANCH COUNTY ROAD COMMISSION

Michigan Employment Relations Commission
1969 MERC Lab. Op. 247

[At an employee meeting three days before a scheduled representation election employees were informed that the Branch County Road Commission had previously decided to give the employees a 25 cents per hour wage increase but that it could not do so because the Teamsters had filed a petition for an election. The employees were also told that if the Teamsters did not win the election the Commission would bargain with the Employees Association (which did not participate in the election) and agree to a three-year contract with a cost-of-living provision, a benefit which the employees had not previously enjoyed. When the Teamsters lost the election, it filed objections to the election based on the foregoing conduct.]

These circumstances establish that the intent and purpose of the Road Commission and its agents in holding the meeting, was to discourage the employees from voting for representation by the Teamsters union, and in addition was showing favoritism towards another organization that was not participating in the election.

We agree with the statement of the National Labor Relations Board, in the Baltimore Catering Company, 148 N.L.R.B. 970, wherein that Board stated:

"Although the granting of benefits during the relevant period preceding an election is not necessarily cause for setting aside an election, the Board has set aside elections where it appears that the granting of the benefits at that particular time was calculated to influence the employees in their choice of a bargaining representative. In the absence of evidence demonstrating that the timing of the announcement of changes and benefits was governed by factors other than the pendency of the election, the Board will regard interference with employee freedom of choice as the motivating factor. The burden of establishing a justifiable motive remains with the employer. The fact that the employees may have known about or otherwise anticipated the increase in wages is not necessarily controlling. The crucial determination is whether the benefits were conferred for the purpose of influencing the employees in their choice of bargaining representatives and were of a type reasonably calculated to have that effect."

Accordingly, we hereby sustain the Objections to Elections discussed above, and direct an Election Officer of the Board to conduct a new election according to the attached Direction of Second Election, to determine whether the employees in the unit desire to be represented by Teamsters, State, County and Municipal Workers, Local 214, or no labor organization.

## NOTES

1. There is a continuing debate concerning the extent to which a public employer should be allowed to state its views on unionization to employees prior to a representation election. The MERC has adopted the NLRA private sector standard, i.e., an employer is permitted to state its views as long as such expressions of opinion do not contain any threat of reprisal or promise of benefit. The Report of the Fortieth American Assembly on Collective Bargaining in American Government recommended a similar approach, stating:

> Public employers at all levels of government should have the right to be active or passive in the face of a union organizing campaign. This right to free speech should not permit coercive conduct or dismissals of union adherents.

REPORT OF THE FORTIETH AMERICAN ASSEMBLY, COLLECTIVE BARGAINING IN AMERICAN GOVERNMENT 5 (1971). At the other extreme is the approach adopted by the federal government under Executive Order 11491, whereby the federal government, as an employer, maintains "a position of neutrality as far as union representation of its employees is concerned, and Government officials do not mount 'vote no' campaigns." Hampton, *Federal Labor-Management Relations: A Program in Evolution*, 21 CATHOLIC U.L. REV. 493, 502 (1972). *See* Vandenberg Air Force Base, A/SLMR No. 349 (1974) (election set aside where management did not maintain neutral posture). A position somewhere between these two approaches was recommended by the Federal Reserve System Labor Relations Panel. Thus, in Federal Reserve Bank of San Francisco, Panel Report and Decision (July 19, 1971), GERR No. 413, A-6 (1971), the Panel, chaired by William E. Simkin, recommended that there be "greater restraint" by the various federal reserve banks in asserting their views on unionization than the NLRB would require of employers in the private sector.

2. In Oregon Employee Ass'n v. Dep't of Commerce, 98 L.R.R.M. 3076 (Ore. Ct. App. 1978), the court affirmed an order of the Oregon Employment Relations Board holding that a state agency was not prohibited "from using state time and funds to campaign against a labor organization in a representation election." The court quoted with approval the ERB's statement that " '[w]ithin the bounds of fair comment, and reasonable and timely opportunity to answer charges leveled, both sides may be heard.' "

## KENT COUNTY ROAD COMMISSION

Michigan Employment Relations Commission
1969 MERC Lab. Op. 314

[Following an election in which the Teamsters defeated the Kent County Road Commission Employees Association by a vote of 127 to 117, the Kent County Road Commission and the Kent County Road Commission Employees Association filed objections to conduct affecting the results of the election.]

The Kent County Road Commission Employees Association made the following objections:

. . . .

"C. That Teamsters Local 214, did engage in material representation, involving substantial departure from the truth, just prior to the election ordered herein in the form of hand-bills and oral representations at a time which prevented this Petitioner from making an effective reply, said misrepresentations were designed and could be reasonably expected to have a significant impact on said election."

. . . .

The main thrust of Objection C by the Kent County Road Commission Employees Association is that the Teamsters engaged in material misrepresentation. The alleged misrepresentations are that in a handbill distributed by the Teamsters by mail on or about February 6, 1969, and again on February 9, 1969, stated that if the Teamsters were the bargaining agent there would be: "no more staggering hours — to avoid paying overtime," and that there would be "no more reprimands that the Commission is the final judge (we want a grievance procedure with arbitration)" and "no more kangaroo courts — full steward representation and grievance procedure."

An additional matter objected to was a statement contained in a letter mailed to the employees' homes by the Teamsters on or about February 6th or 7th wherein it was stated:

"Another fact must be carefully considered — if the Association commits by accident or voluntarily any unlawful act, the employer will sue the Association and all its employees. Under the Teamsters' contract, the Teamsters Union will stand completely liable and you and your family cannot be sued."

The last statement objected to in the Teamster literature was the statement that the Teamsters' Pension Plan would be available to the employees of the Road Commission.

The National Labor Relations Board has considered various types of campaign misrepresentations for years. We are in agreement with the view taken by the National Labor Relations Board in Hollywood Ceramics Co. Inc., 140 N.L.R.B. 221. In that case the National Labor Relations Board stated:

"We believe that an election should be set aside only where there has been a misrepresentation or other similar campaign trickery, which involves a substantial departure from the truth, at a time which prevents the other party or parties from making an effective reply, so that the misrepresentation, whether deliberate or not, may reasonably be expected to have a significant impact on the election. However, the mere fact that a message is inartistically or vaguely worded and subject to different interpretations will not suffice to establish such misrepresentation as would lead us to set the election aside. Such ambiguities, like extravagant promises, derogatory statements about the other party, and minor distortions of some facts, frequently occur in communication between persons. But even where a misrepresentation is shown to have been substantial, the Board may still refuse to set aside the election if it finds upon consideration of all the circumstances that the statement would not be likely to have had a real impact on the election. For example, the misrepresentation might have occurred in connection with an unimportant matter so that it could only have had a de minimis effect. Or, it could have been so extreme as to put the employees on notice of its lack of truth under the particular circumstances so that they could not reasonably have relied on the assertion. Or, the Board may find that the employees possess independent knowledge with which to evaluate the statements."

We are, however, of the opinion, that the Teamsters, in their campaign literature which was specifically directed to the wives of the employees of the

Road Commission in the unit, exceeded the permissible bounds of election propaganda, allowed by the *Hollywood Ceramics* case. The statements that the Employer will sue the Association and all its employees because of any accidental or voluntarily unlawful act, is an outright falsehood. The untruth of the statement, when accompanied with the taint of threat inherently contained therein, can [sic] have prevented a fair election. The National Labor Relations Board stated in United Aircraft Corporation, 31 L.R.R.M. 1437:

> "Although the Board has traditionally declared its intention not to censor or police pre-election propaganda by parties to elections, it has imposed some limits on free campaigning which, when transgressed, require corrective action. Thus, exaggerations, inaccuracies, partial truths, name-calling, and falsehoods, while not condoned, may be excused as legitimate propaganda, provided they are not 'so misleading' as to prevent the exercise of a free choice by the employees in the selection of their bargaining representative. Propaganda of this sort, the Board has said, will not be censored or policed if it remains within 'bounds,' and in this connection the question to be decided is 'one of degree.' In sum, the ultimate consideration is whether the challenged propaganda has lowered the standards of campaigning to the point where it may be said that the uninhibited desires of the employees cannot be determined in an election."

As indicated above, we are of the opinion that what has occurred here, has prevented the employees from exercising their uninhibited desires in selection of a bargaining agent. . . .

### Order and Direction of Election

It is ordered that an Election Officer of the Board, shall conduct a new election. . . .

### NOTES

1. The NLRB in a split 3-2 decision in Shopping Kart Food Market, Inc., 228 N.L.R.B. 1311 (1977), abandoned its *Hollywood Ceramics* standard for reviewing alleged misrepresentations in representation elections. The majority stated that henceforth it would "no longer set elections aside on the basis of misleading campaign statements," but would continue the Board's "policy of overseeing other campaign conduct which interferes with employee free choice outside the area of misrepresentations which have been objectionable only under the *Hollywood Ceramics* rule." In overruling *Hollywood Ceramics,* the majority relied, in significant part, on the results of an empirical study of NLRB elections reported in J. GETMAN, S. GOLDBERG, & J. HERMAN, UNION REPRESENTATION ELECTIONS: LAW & REALITY (1976).

A little over a year later, following a change in Board membership, the NLRB in General Knit of California, Inc., 239 N.L.R.B. No. 101, 99 L.R.R.M. 1687 (1978), overruled *Shopping Kart* and readopted the *Hollywood Ceramics* rule. The three-member Board majority stated:

> In addition to acting as a deterrent to deceitful campaign trickery, the existence of the Hollywood Ceramics standard has provided a means of redress for a party who doubts the validity of the election results because of prejudicial campaigning by the prevailing side. The parties' access to the Board for review further legitimatizes the integrity of the electoral process. And, because of its deterrent effect, the Hollywood Ceramics standard has been well accepted by the courts and by the parties who have used our election procedure.

2. In City of Ft. Lauderdale, 4 FPER ¶ 4167 (Fla. PERC 1978), the Florida Commission, citing the NLRB's decision in *Shopping Kart,* abandoned its past reliance on the *Hollywood Ceramics* test in determining the propriety of campaign propaganda. Relying in part on the free speech proviso in the Florida Act, the Florida Commission stated:

> ... the employees' free choice of collective bargaining representation is better enhanced through competition of ideas than by Commission regulation. The Commission's experience with objections alleging material misrepresentation has indicated that it is both unwise and undesirable for the agency to involve itself too directly in evaluating the wisdom of campaign tactics and propaganda. Judging the probable effect of an alleged misrepresentation on an election, after the fact, is simply too speculative to outweigh the competing policies encouraging free speech and finality of election results, unless the alleged misrepresentation contravenes a statutory policy . . . .

The Florida Commission also noted that the application of the *Hollywood Ceramics* test "has resulted in more harm than benefit in effectuating the employees' free choice for or against collective bargaining representation," as well as "encouraged frivolous objections by losing parties, created unconscionable delays and finalizing election results, and spawned numerous unwarranted appeals of certification orders."

3. The District of Columbia Board of Labor Relations in Metropolitan Police Department of the District of Columbia, Decision No. 20 (D.C. BLR 1978), used the *Hollywood Ceramics* standard in setting aside an election based on a union's "serious and material misrepresentation." In this case, the District of Columbia Board specifically refused to adopt the *Shopping Kart* standard.

4. In a few jurisdictions rules have been promulgated setting forth the type and kind of conduct that would be sufficient to set aside an election. For example, Rule 5.4(3) of the Rules and Regulations of the Iowa PERB reads as follows:

> The following types of activity, if conducted during the period beginning with the filing of an election petition with the board and ending at the conclusion of the election, and if determined by the board that such activity could have affected the results of the election, shall be considered to be objectionable conduct sufficient to invalidate the results of an election:
>
> a. Electioneering within three hundred feet or within sound of the polling place established by the board during the conduct of the election;
>
> b. Misstatements of material facts by any party to the election or their representative without sufficient time for the adversely affected party to adequately respond;
>
> c. Any misuse of board documents, including an indication that the board endorses any particular choice appearing on the ballot;
>
> d. Campaign speeches to assembled groups of employees during working hours within the twenty-four-hour period before the election;
>
> e. Any polling of employees by a public employer which relates to the employees' preference for or against a bargaining representative;
>
> f. Commission of a prohibited practice;
>
> g. Any other misconduct or other circumstance which prevents employees from freely expressing their preferences in the election.

5. The NLRB in Excelsior Underwear Inc., 156 N.L.R.B. 1236 (1966), held that an employer is required to furnish a petitioning union, as well as any other employee organizations on the ballot, with the names and addresses of all eligible voters within a specified time period prior to the election and that an employer's failure to provide the names and addresses of its employees constitutes a valid ground for setting aside an election. The so-called *Excelsior* rule was upheld by the Supreme Court in NLRB v. Wyman-Gordon Co., 394 U.S. 759, 89 S. Ct. 1426, 22 L. Ed. 2d 709 (1969). *Accord,* City of Quincy, Case No. MCR-1311 (Mass. LRC 1974). The state boards or commissions in Connecticut, Iowa, Maine, Michigan, South Dakota, and Washington have incorporated similar policies in their rules and regulations. In PLRB v. Upper Darby Township, Case

No. C-3935-E (Pa. PLRB 1974), the Pennsylvania Board held it was an unfair labor practice for an employer to refuse to provide the names and addresses of all eligible voters.

## WISCONSIN EMPLOYMENT RELATIONS COMMISSION v. CITY OF EVANSVILLE

Wisconsin Supreme Court
69 Wis. 2d 140, 230 N.W.2d 688 (1975)

[Teamster Local 579 on October 16, 1969 informed the mayor and city clerk of the City of Evansville that the union represented a majority of the city's blue collar employees in three separate departments. Four days later the union filed a petition for an election with the Wisconsin Employment Relations Commission (WERC). At that time the union had signed authorization cards from all but one of the employees involved and all but two of the employees had paid the union initiation fee. In the election conducted on December 9, 1969, the union lost in one department and the votes in the remaining two departments were impounded. Subsequently the union filed objections to the election alleging that the city and its officers had committed prohibited practices during the pre-election period. Following a hearing, an examiner for the WERC found that the city committed prohibited practices by (1) threatening a loss of benefits if the union won, (2) promising future benefits if the union lost, (3) interrogating an employee about his union affiliation, and (4) threatening to subcontract work and eliminate jobs if employees voted for the union. To remedy these violations, the examiner, *inter alia,* ordered the city to recognize the union as the exclusive representative. On March 15, 1971, the WERC adopted the examiner's findings, conclusions and orders. The circuit court affirmed the WERC's orders on November 3, 1972, and the city appealed.]

HEFFERNAN, J.

On this appeal the city contends that it committed no prohibited practices. This raises the question of whether the evidence of record is sufficient to support the findings of the commission that the acts of the city constituted practices prohibited by the statutes. The quantum of evidence sufficient to support the findings and conclusions of the commission in this proceeding, a circuit court action for an enforcement order, is set forth in sec. 111.07 (7), Stats. 1969. That standard of review is that: "The findings of fact made by the commission, if supported by credible and competent evidence in the record, shall be conclusive."

. . . .

The WERC based its findings and conclusions that the city had indulged in prohibited practices of a threatening and coercive nature on the basis of three incidents. The first was a letter signed by the mayor and the aldermen which was sent to each employee and was published in the Evansville newspaper on November 27, 1969. The most significant paragraph of that letter stated:

"We wonder if the city employees are cognizant of the fact that if they voted to accept the union, all fringe benefits now being paid by the city, would cease and the only pay they would receive, would be their base pay. Any fringe benefits gained there-after, would have to be bargained for. If a union were to be accepted, it is conceivable that many new problems and hardships would be created not only on the city, but on the employees as well. Some examples might be the installation of time clocks, regulated coffee breaks, and the possible loss of certain freedoms that the employees now enjoy. In essence, a demarcation line would be drawn, with the salary or white-collar workers and supervisors on one side and the hourly employees on the other."

The examiner found that statement threatened a loss of benefits and was a violation of sec. 111.70 (3) (a) 1, Stats. 1969. . . .

On the other hand, the city referred to the second and twelfth paragraphs of the same letter as evidence that it had no intent to interfere with the employees' right to organize.

Paragraph 2 stated:

"The City cannot prevent their employees from petitioning for union representation, and it is not our intent to do so, nor is it our intent to degrade unions."

Paragraph 12 stated:

"Lastly, there shall be no animosity shown or reprimand given to any employee who has taken an active part in trying to procure Union services."

The examiner's memorandum concluded that the specific threat of loss of benefits and other privileges encompassed in the fifth paragraph outweighed the "pious platitudes" and "benign generalities" that appeared in paragraphs 2 and 12.

The Wisconsin Employment Relations Commission, in its review of the examiner's findings, concluded that the statement appearing in paragraph 5 of the letter was coercive and unlawful, both in the context of the letter itself and in the context of other activities of the municipal employer.

On appeal to this court, the city acknowledges that the references in paragraph 5 to a more regimented employment relationship under the union, and particularly the statement that all benefits would cease if union representation was accepted, while incorrect, were merely innocent misstatements of the law and that the letter was intended to be informative and not coercive.

The city also argues that the union had ample opportunity prior to the election to correct any misstatements which appeared in the letter published on November 27, 1969.

While there are instances when an innocent misstatement of fact may be harmless or the union may have the burden of correcting a misstatement, the situation here does not constitute an instance of that kind. A misrepresentation, though innocent, may be sufficient to cause an election to be set aside. *Hollywood Ceramics Co., Inc., and United Brick and Clay Workers of America, AFL-CIO* (1962), 140 NLRB 221. The *Hollywood Ceramics Case* also stated that a misrepresentation could be the basis for setting aside an election if it were made so shortly before the election that the other party does not have an opportunity for reply. The city, therefore, argues that the *Hollywood Ceramics Case* stands for the proposition that the union could have corrected the city's misstatement and its failure to do so was a waiver of the misrepresentation.

While the *Hollywood Ceramics Case* stands for the proposition that the injured party may have a duty to correct a harm that is caused by a misstatement alone, the misstatement here was not merely a misstatement of fact but was coupled with phraseology which the examiner and the WERC could correctly conclude constituted a threat. Here, the WERC specifically concluded that the city's unlawful and coercive statements were not waived as mere factual misstatements even though the union might have attempted to counter them with a correct statement of the facts and law prior to the election.

The fifth paragraph of the letter was more than a misstatement. It was a threat that "if they voted to accept the union, all fringe benefits now being paid by the city, would cease."

The city has cited a number of cases in which misstatements were found to be noncoercive. However, the effect of a misstatement is to be subjectively determined on a case-to-case basis. In *NLRB v. Gissel Packing Co.* (1969), 395 U. S. 575, 619, 89 Sup. Ct. 1918, 23 L. Ed. 2d 547, Mr. Chief Justice WARREN, speaking for the court, said that it was the national board's duty to focus on the question: " '[W]hat did the speaker intend and the listener understand?' (A. Cox, Law and the National Labor Policy 44 (1960))." The United States Supreme Court stated that the coercive impact of statements was initially a question to be decided by the administrative board and that, in review, the court must recognize "the Board's competence in the first instance to judge the impact of utterances made in the context of the employer-employee relationship." *Gissel, supra,* page 620.

. . . .

We conclude that the evidence was sufficient to support the findings and conclusion of the WERC that the statement embraced in paragraph 5 of the November 27, 1969, letter constituted a threat. We also agree with the WERC and its examiner that the "benign generalities" which the city has cited to show that it had no animosity toward the union were insufficient to overcome the specific threats of paragraph 5.

. . . .

The WERC also concluded that a coercive conversation took place between an employee of the Water and Light Department and his supervisor sometime near the end of November in 1969. The employee testified:

"Well, he asked me if I belonged to the Union and I asked him if it made any difference and he said 'You might just as well tell me because if you don't I'll find out anyway.' So, I said 'I do. I belong to the Union.' "

This conversation took place in the presence of two other employees. The WERC concluded that this conversation was not only threatening to the particular employee but was probably threatening to his fellow workers. The city contends, however, that the supervisor in question had no history of an antiunion animus, that the incident was an isolated one, and no reprisals were threatened or taken against the employee. The National Labor Relations Board, upon whose authority the WERC relied in the instant case, has, however, concluded in *Struksnes Construction Co., Inc., and International Union of Operating Engineers, Local No. 49, AFL-CIO* (1967), 165 NLRB 1062, 1063, that the polling of employees in respect to union membership would be considered a restraint upon the employees' right to organize and would be considered coercive unless the following safeguards were observed:

"(1) the purpose of the poll is to determine the truth of a union's claim of majority, (2) this purpose is communicated to the employees, (3) assurances against reprisal are given, (4) the employees are polled by secret ballot, and (5) the employer has not engaged in unfair labor practices or otherwise created a coercive atmosphere."

We agree with the WERC's conclusion that the city met none of the criteria of *Struksnes.* Under that rationale, the conversation with an employee of the Water and Light Department in the presence of other employees constituted a violation of sec. 111.70 (3) (a) 1, Stats. 1969. There is sufficient evidence to support that finding.

In addition, during the last week of November, 1969, the director of the Department of Public Works called a meeting of his department's employees. One of the employees testified that the director said:

"... if the Union got in, why, that really didn't necessarily give us any job protection. He said that if the City wanted to, they could contract the garbage out and they could contract the snowplowing out and, therefore, these jobs could be eliminated."

The Director of Public Works admitted that he had talked to the employees and stated he did not think the union would be beneficial to them. He denied, however, any statement that the jobs would be eliminated by subcontracting garbage pickups or snow-removal work. The WERC resolved this conflict of testimony in favor of the employee and concluded, on the basis of the evidence:

". . . that the threat of subcontracting unit work was just one more example of Respondent's attempt to undermine the Union's majority status."

. . . .

The WERC's finding is supported by the evidence; and, in the context of the case and in the exercise of its expertise, it could properly conclude that the statement was threatening and was a violation of sec. 111.70 (3) (a) 1, Stats. 1969.

In view of these findings of prohibited conduct, the examiner ordered, and the WERC affirmed, an order directing the city to recognize the union, even though no election results were tabulated that showed a union victory.

. . . .

The question remains, however, whether the language of sec. 111.07 (4), Stats. 1969, authorizes the commission to direct the city to recognize the union. Such power is given to the WERC under the language of that statute which provides, in respect to an offending party, that the WERC "require him to take such affirmative action . . . as the commission deems proper."

*Folding Furniture Works v. Wisconsin Labor Relations Board* (1939), 232 Wis. 170, 181, 285 N. W. 851, 286 N. W. 875, said, "affirmative action" was limited "to what is considered by the board reasonably necessary to 'effectuate the policies' of the act."

More recently, that portion of sec. 111.07 (4), Stats. 1969, was interpreted in *Libby, McNeill & Libby v. WERC* (1970), 48 Wis. 2d 272, 286, 179 N. W. 2d 805, wherein we stated an order of the WERC "should be affirmed unless the respondent can show that the order has no tendency to effectuate the purposes of the Employment Peace Act."

While the reference in *Libby* is to the purposes of the Employment Peace Act, which appear in sec. 111.01, Stats., those purposes are identical with the policy purpose of sec. 111.70 (2), the Municipal Employment statute, wherein it is declared that municipal employees shall have the right to affiliate with labor organizations "of their own choosing" and the right to be represented by labor organizations "of their own choice."

The order, which directs the municipal employer to recognize the union, under the circumstances here effectuates the policy of the municipal employment statutes.

In the instant case, the recognition order gave effect to the wishes expressed almost unanimously prior to the campaign of threats and coercion undertaken by the municipal employer. The order here effectuated the employees' freedom of choice, which became impossible in the climate created by the employer — a climate that the WERC found tainted any possible election results. The effectuation of this fundamental policy of labor law was discussed in *Gissel, supra,* in which the United States Supreme Court recognized the necessity of recognition orders to assure the implementation of the employees' freedom of choice. It further pointed out the appropriateness of such affirmative action. The court said:

"If the Board could enter only a cease-and-desist order and direct an election or a rerun, it would in effect be rewarding the employer and allowing him 'to profit from [his] own wrongful refusal to bargain,' *Franks Bros., supra,* at 704, while at the same time severely curtailing the employees' right freely to determine whether they desire a representative. The employer could continue to delay or disrupt the election processes and put off indefinitely his obligation to bargain; and any election held under these circumstances would not be likely to demonstrate the employees' true, undistorted desires." (Brackets in *Gissel*) (Pp. 610, 611)

The court added:

"If an employer has succeeded in undermining a union's strength and destroying the laboratory conditions necessary for a fair election, he may see no need to violate a cease-and-desist order by further unlawful activity. The damage will have been done, and perhaps the only fair way to effectuate employee rights is to re-establish the conditions as they existed before the employer's unlawful campaign. There is, after all, nothing permanent in a bargaining order, and if, after the effects of the employer's acts have worn off, the employees clearly desire to disavow the union, they can do so by filing a representation petition." (Pp. 612, 613)

The latter paragraph well states the manner in which a recognition order effectuates the purpose of the labor law, and its rationale is applicable to the fundamental public policy of sec. 111.70, Stats. 1969. It also points out the appropriateness of a recognition order, rather than the mere issuance of a cease-and-desist order, which can in no way re-establish the conditions which existed prior to the employer's contamination of the election atmosphere.

It should be pointed out additionally that the recognition order utilized by the WERC is particularly appropriate to preserve municipal employees' freedom of choice. If the Wisconsin Employment Relations Commission did not have the power to order union recognition under circumstances such as those in the instant case, employees of municipalities, who under sec. 111.70 (4) (l), Stats. 1969, do not have the right to strike, would be defenseless and without any meaningful remedy against an employer who followed a course of threats and coercion. As *Gissel* points out, the issuance of a cease-and-desist order would be insufficient to recoup the employees' freedom of choice. Rather, it would, as the consequence of an employer's own prior misconduct, make it possible for him to avoid union recognition.

In the instant case, of course, the status quo which the union recognition order seeks to maintain is that existing prior to the election, when all but one member of the employee group wished to be represented by the union. The city indeed correctly points out the infirmities of conferring union recognition on the basis of authorization cards that have been circulated by union organizers prior to the submission of the petition for an election. We do not conclude that authorization cards are foolproof. They probably are not, and in some instances the method of securing the cards may be coercive. Nevertheless, a test of the validity of those authorization cards has been effectively interdicted by the employer, who now contends they should not be considered evidence of employee choice. This problem, too, was considered by the United States Supreme Court in *Gissel,* wherein it said that the superiority of determining the will of the employees through the election process does not render authorization cards useless in all circumstances, because "where an employer engages in conduct disruptive of the election process, cards may be the most effective — perhaps the only — way of assuring employee choice." (P. 602)

Although, as we have concluded, the affirmative action taken by the commission in ordering union recognition is of the type contemplated by sec.

111.07 (4), Stats. 1969, the city argues on this appeal that another section of the statutes, 111.70 (4) (d), provides for the election process "to determine whether they desire to be represented by a labor organization."

The city argues that this is the exclusive method by which the WERC can exercise any authority to recognize a union and that, had the WERC the power to recognize a union on the basis of authorization cards alone, the legislature would have specifically granted that option.

There is no doubt that sec. 111.70 (4) (d), Stats. 1969, confers the right upon the municipality to have the representation question determined by an election. However, we have pointed out above that sec. 111.07 (4), which we held to be applicable to prohibited practices within the municipal labor field, provides that the rights, immunities, privileges, or remedies of an offending party may be suspended for not more than one year; and affirmative action, including the recognition of the union, may be required.

While the case relied upon by the city, *Sales & Service Union, Local 1348 v. Gimbel Brothers Department Store* (1942), WERC Dec. No. 366, is undoubtedly correct in that the commission does not have the power to certify bargaining representatives on the basis of authorization cards alone, the situation there was concerned with an original petition and did not involve the rectification of harm done by an employer's commission of prohibited practices, which the commission here concluded would vitiate the better normal practice, a free and open election.

The union recognition in the instant case arises out of the powers conferred on the WERC to remedy the employer's commission of prohibited practices. The WERC does not have that authority as a matter of original determination to recognize a union on the basis of cards alone. While an election held under laboratory conditions is most likely to result in a vote that represents the free and uncoerced choice of the employees, when an employer has destroyed the opportunity for such free choice, a recognition order, in the commission's discretion, may be the only method available to reasonably achieve the goal of determining or implementing the employees' choice.

Nor are we persuaded by the city's reliance on sec. 111.70 (3) (a) 3, Stats. 1969. It argues that, under that section, it is only a prohibited practice to refuse to bargain with a representative certified after an election has been held. It argues, therefore, that, whether the union has been recognized or not, it cannot be the bargaining representative. This, of course, is a problem that has not yet arisen; but it is apparent that, in any event, the recognition given to the union in this case has in fact resulted from a situation created by the employer that prevented certification by election under the terms of sec. 111.70 (4) (d). Carried to an absurdity, an employer could avoid effective unionization by committing prohibited practices that would preclude fair elections. It would appear that the remedial action which the WERC was authorized to undertake by a recognition order effectuates the purposes of the act and obviates the absurd situation which the city raises as a future dilemma.

The city also points to a revision of the statute which came in 1971. Prior to the laws of that year, there was no specific duty imposed upon a municipal employer to bargain with the representative of a majority of its employees. That duty was imposed by sec. 111.70 (3) (a) 4, Stats. 1971. That statute also provides that:

"An employer shall not be deemed to have refused to bargain until an election has been held and the results thereof certified to the employer by the commission."

We conclude, on the basis of the rationale stated above, that by the procedure adopted here, the WERC has exercised its powers authorized by statute to certify a union under circumstances where a fair election could not be held. The legal effect of the recognition order is the equivalent of the certification of the union following an election. Under sec. 111.70 (3) (a) 4 of the statutes of 1971, the recognition order, by operation of law, has become a bargaining order.

Although we have, in conjunction with the legality of the order, also discussed reasons why the recognition order is an appropriate remedy, the city argues that there was no evidence or indication that the violations could not be completely and effectively remedied by a less extreme form of relief. It argues that a recognition order is never appropriate unless the employer has destroyed all possibility of a free and secret election. That position has been rejected by the supreme court in *Gissel,* where it said the use of a bargaining order may be appropriate if the practices indulged in "nonetheless still have the tendency to undermine majority strength and impede the election processes" (p. 614), even though it cannot be said that there is no possibility of a valid election.

This lesser showing, *Gissel* emphasized, is particularly appropriate when there is evidence that at a time prior to the commission of the prohibited practices the union had a clear majority.

Additionally, the city argues that the WERC has the subjective duty of analyzing the particular violations and has the duty of explaining why a recognition order is appropriate in the instant case. The city correctly cites several United States Court of Appeals cases which have refused to enforce NLRB bargaining orders in the absence of a board analysis of the factual situation demonstrating subjectively why the order was warranted.

. . . .

In the instant case, the examiner painstakingly discussed the effect of each prohibited practice and its relationship to the bargaining order. Those findings and conclusions of the examiner were expressly approved by the commission, and hence the policy of *General Stencil* was satisfied.

The analysis of the examiner complied with requirements of *Gissel,* wherein the court stated, at pages 614 and 615, that a recognition order should issue:

"If the Board finds that the possibility of erasing the effects of past practices and of ensuring a fair election (or a fair rerun) by the use of traditional remedies, though present, is slight and that employee sentiment once expressed through cards would, on balance, be better protected by a bargaining order . . . ."

After discussing the facts, the examiner stated:

"Viewed in this light, the Examiner finds that the possibility of eradicating the effects of past prohibited practices through the possible direction of a Commission directed election, although present, is at best marginal and that the overwhelming employe sentiment as expressed through the Union authorization cards could better be protected by ordering Respondent to recognize Complainant Union."

In its separate conclusions, after referring to the findings of the examiner, the WERC stated:

"To require the employes to cast a ballot to determine their bargaining representative after the unlawful acts committed by the Municipal Employer, would permit the Municipal Employer to take advantage of its own unlawful activities."

In the instant case, although it would have been preferable for the commission itself to have given additional detailed explanation of the appropriateness of the remedy in respect to each violation, our review of the record shows that each act of the city constituted a prohibited practice that undermined the possibility of a fair election.

A remand to the WERC could result in only a superfluous reanalysis of prohibited practices that clearly impaired the possibility of a reasonably free and fair election.

The examiner's conclusion, as incorporated in the WERC's order, that a new election would only marginally have the opportunity to protect the rights of the majority, is sufficient, when considered with the acts of the employer, to justify the appropriateness of the order.

The city persistently argues that the acts of the employer were not of a nature to warrant the drastic remedy of a recognition order. In *Libby, McNeill & Libby v. WERC* (1970), 48 Wis. 2d 272, 287, 179 N. W. 2d 805, this court stated:

" '. . . It is an established principle that a Board order "should stand unless it can be shown that the order is a patent attempt to achieve ends other than those which can fairly be said to effectuate the policies of the Act." ' "

It is the obligation of the court to defer to the commission in its selection of a remedial order. Where, as in this case, it cannot be said that the recognition order is a patent attempt to achieve ends other than those contemplated by the Municipal Employment Relations Act, and it is otherwise within the legal authority of the commission, and the findings upon which it is based are supported by sufficient evidence, it will not be set aside by this court.

. . . .

We accordingly conclude that there is sufficient evidence to support the WERC's findings and conclusions that the acts of the city constituted prohibited practices. We conclude that, under the statutes, the WERC has the authority to order recognition of the union as the employees' exclusive representative and that the invocation of that authority was appropriate under the circumstances. . . .

# F. JUDICIAL REVIEW OF REPRESENTATION PROCEEDINGS

## LINCOLN COUNTY MEMORIAL HOSPITAL v. MISSOURI STATE BOARD OF MEDIATION

Missouri Court of Appeals, Kansas City District
549 S.W.2d 665, 95 L.R.R.M. 3110 (1977)

WASSERSTROM, JUDGE.

Lincoln County Memorial Hospital appealed under Section 105.525 (all statutory references herein being referred to RSMo 1969 unless otherwise noted) from a determination by the Missouri State Board of Mediation that all registered nurses of the Hospital, with one exception, constituted an appropriate unit for collective bargaining. From an affirmance by the circuit court of the Board's determination, the Hospital again appeals to this court.

. . . .

On the present appeal, the Hospital assigns six points of error, the most serious of which complains of the inclusion in the bargaining unit of the nine registered nurses whom the Hospital insists are supervisors or managerial personnel. However, none of the errors assigned by the Hospital can be reached on this appeal unless this court has proper jurisdiction. That in turn depends on whether the Board's determination of the appropriate bargaining unit constitutes an appealable order. If it does not, then the circuit court lacks jurisdiction of the subject matter. *National Ass'n of Women's and Children's Apparel Salesmen, Inc. v. F. T. C.,* 479 F.2d 139, 144, footnote 9 (5th Cir. 1973); *Bd. of Tr. of Mem. Hosp. of Fremont County v. N. L. R. B.,* 523 F.2d 845 (10th Cir. 1975); *State Board of Registration for Healing Arts v. Masters,* 512 S.W.2d 150, 1. c. 159 (Mo.App.1974).

And the want of jurisdiction by the circuit court would in turn deprive this court of the power to make any decision on the merits. *Shepler v. Shepler,* 348 S.W.2d 607, 609 (Mo.App.1961); *Allen v. State Department of Public Health and Welfare,* 479 S.W.2d 183, 186 (Mo.App.1972); *Swetnam v. U. S. By-Products Corp.,* 510 S.W.2d 829, 831 (Mo.App.1974). Even though this jurisdictional issue has not been raised by the parties, it is the duty of this court to consider the problem sua sponte. . . .

The question of whether an appeal lies from an administrative determination of the appropriate bargaining unit, prior to determination of majority representative status, is not answered by the wording of § 105.525, which is ambiguous in this regard.[1] The same question has given rise to much litigation in other jurisdictions, with conflicting results. The rule followed uniformly in the federal courts under the National Labor Relations Act is that such an administrative determination is only interlocutory and is not separately appealable. Except in extraordinary situations, the aggrieved party must await the completion of the administrative process by an election certification and an order compelling the employer to enter into collective bargaining. This result is reached partially on the basis of the statutory language granting the right of appeal, contained in 29 U.S.C.A. § 160. However, these decisions, more importantly for our purposes, rest also in part upon grounds of public policy. Thus in a leading case, *American Federation of Labor v. N. L. R. B.,* 308 U.S. 401, 1. c. 409, 60 S.Ct. 300, 304, 84 L.Ed. 347 (1940) the Supreme Court discussed and relied upon Congressional history to show a legislative purpose to eliminate delay which had occurred under the previous federal law (Public Resolution 44) and which had permitted judicial review at the stage of the determination of the appropriate bargaining unit. In this connection, the Supreme Court quoted the committee report as follows:

" 'Weaknesses in Existing Law. . . . (6) *Obstacles to elections.* — Under Public Resolution 44, any attempt by the Government to conduct an election of representatives may be contested ab initio in the courts, although such election is in reality merely a preliminary determination of fact. This means that the Government can be delayed indefinitely before it takes the first step toward industrial peace. After almost a year not a single case, in which a company has chosen to contest an election order of the Board, has reached decision in any circuit court of appeals.' Sen.Rep. No. 573, Committee on Education and Labor, 74th Cong., 1st Sess., pp. 5, 6.

"After referring to the procedure for review under Public Resolution 44, the House Committee declared: 'The weakness of this procedure is that

---

[1] Section 105.525 grants right of appeal as follows: "Issues with respect to appropriateness of bargaining units and majority representative status shall be resolved by the state board of mediation. In the event that the appropriate administrative body or any of the bargaining units shall be aggrieved by the decision of the state board of mediation, an appeal may be had to the circuit court of the county where the administrative body is located or in the circuit court of Cole County. . . ." § 536.100 and Rule 100.03, governing judicial review of administrative rulings in contested cases generally, provide that the review be of "a final decision." The decisions from other jurisdictions hereinafter referred to generally address the question of whether determination of the appropriate bargaining unit, taken alone, constitutes "a final decision" of the administrative agency.

under the provision for review of election orders employers have a means of holding up the election for months by an application to the circuit court of appeals. . . . At the present time 10 cases for review of the Board's election orders are pending in circuit court of appeals. Only three have been argued and none have been decided.' House Rep. No. 1147, Committee on Labor, 74th Cong., 1st Sess., p. 6."

So also, in another leading case, *Boire v. Greyhound Corporation,* 376 U.S. 473, 1. c. 477-478, 84 S.Ct. 894, 1. c. 897, 11 L.Ed.2d 849 (1964), the Supreme Court made the following observations concerning the public policy involved:

"That this indirect method of obtaining judicial review imposes significant delays upon attempts to challenge the validity of Board orders in certification proceedings is obvious. But it is equally obvious that Congress explicitly intended to impose precisely such delays. At the time of the original passage of the National Labor Relations Act in 1935, the House Report clearly delineated the congressional policy judgment which underlay the restriction of judicial review to that provided for in § 9(d):

'When an employee organization has built up its membership to a point where it is entitled to be recognized as the representative of the employees for collective bargaining, and the employer refuses to accord such recognition, the union, unless an election can promptly be held to determine the choice of representation, runs the risk of impairment of strength by attrition and delay while the case is dragging on through the courts, or else is forced to call a strike to achieve recognition by its own economic power. Such strikes have been called when election orders of the National Labor Relations Board have been held up by court review.' "

The same policy of furthering labor peace by not permitting delays in elections is reiterated in *Bd. of Tr. of Mem. Hosp. of Fremont County v. N. L. R. B., supra,* and in *Bishop v. N. L. R. B.,* 502 F.2d 1024, 1027 (5th Cir. 1974).

A number of state courts in the application of state labor relations statutes have followed the above federal rule. *City Manager of Medford v. State Labor Relations Commission,* 353 Mass. 519, 233 N.E.2d 310 (1968); *Worcester I. T. I. Instructors Ass'n v. Labor Relations Commission,* 357 Mass. 118, 256 N.E.2d 287 (1970); *Harrison v. Labor Relations Commission,* 363 Mass. 548, 296 N.E.2d 196 (1973); *Jordan Marsh Co. v. Labor Relations Commission,* 312 Mass. 597, 45 N.E.2d 925 (1942); *Town of Windsor v. Windsor Police Department Employees Ass'n,* 154 Conn. 530, 227 A.2d 65 (1967); *Southeast Furniture Co. v. Industrial Commission,* 100 Utah 154, 111 P.2d 153 (1941); *McGee v. Local No. 682,* 70 R.I. 200, 38 A.2d 303 (1944); *Klamath County v. Laborers Int'l Union of N. A., Local No. 915,* 534 P.2d 1169 (Or.App.1975). The opinion last cited typically holds:

"Since (1) the designation of an appropriate bargaining unit is but one step in the process of certifying a bargaining agent with whom the employer is obligated to bargain, (2) several other actions by PERB are necessary to complete the process, and (3) the designation could be of no effect if the employes [sic] vote for no representation, we hold that the designation of an appropriate bargaining unit is not a 'final order' as the term is used in ORS 183.480."

On the other hand, New York, Minnesota and New Jersey have declined to follow the above approach and instead hold that the administrative determination of the appropriate bargaining unit does constitute a final order which is subject to immediate and separate judicial review. The leading case so holding is *Civil Service Employees Association v. Helsby,* 31 A.D.2d 325, 297 N.Y.S.2d 813 (1969), aff'd by a sharply divided vote of the New York Court of Appeals, 24 N.Y.2d 993, 302 N.Y.S.2d 822, 250 N.E.2d 230 (1969). Other cases following the lead of that case are: *Wakshull v. Helsby,* 35 A.D.2d 183, 315 N.Y.S.2d 371 (1970); *Minnesota State College Board v. Public Employment Relations Board,* 228 N.W.2d 551 (Minn.1975); *County of Gloucester v. Public Employment Relations Commission,* 107 N.J.Super. 150, 257 A.2d 712, 714 (1969). See also the *Pennsylvania Labor Relations Act,* 43 P.S. § 211.9, applied in *Pennsylvania Labor Relations Board v. Butz,* 411 Pa. 360, 192 A.2d 707 (1963).

In determining which of these opposing views should be adopted in Missouri, the most persuasive factor is the public policy reflected in the United States Congressional debates. The potential for calculated stalling of collective bargaining by dilatory tactics, which led Congress to eliminate separate judicial review of the determination of an appropriate bargaining unit, is well illustrated in this very case. By the time this opinion is handed down, it will be more than two years since the Association filed its petition before the Board and there still has not been any certification of a bargaining representative, much less the commencement of any negotiations between the parties. Such a long frustration of the employees' right of collective bargaining is simply unfair. Moreover, the Missouri General Assembly, like the Federal Congress and the legislatures of many other states, has concluded that collective bargaining by public employees serves the public interest by being conducive to peaceful employment relationships in the public sector. Achievement of this public policy requires expeditious completion of the administrative process, and this can best be done by adoption of the federal rule requiring that the entire administrative process be terminated before judicial review can become operative.

The adoption of this rule will also harmonize with the general principle prevailing in this state as to what constitutes an appealable order. Only one which disposes of all the issues qualifies. *Spires v. Edgar,* 513 S.W.2d 372 (Mo. banc 1974); *P. I. C. Leasing, Inc. v. Roy A. Scheperle Construction Co., Inc., supra; Laclede Gas Co. v. Solon Gershman, Inc.,* 539 S.W.2d 574 (Mo.App.1976). The reason for this principle is expedition of judicial business so that one appeal will cover all aspects of a case, rather than to permit successive piecemeal appeals. The same principle should apply, and with even more reason, in this labor relation situation.

Indeed, the adoption of this rule causes even less difficulty in Missouri than in the federal arena and in states having statutes closely patterned after the federal labor relations statute. The federal statute contains prohibition against unfair labor practices and judicial review of all representation questions is postponed until such time as the administrative board issues an unfair labor practice order. Then all questions between the parties, including the determination of the appropriate bargaining unit, are reviewed as part of the unfair labor practice case. The Missouri statute, § 105.500 et seq., contains no provision dealing with unfair labor practices and the entire administrative procedures are completed just as soon as the Board of Mediation has held an election and certifies the collective bargaining representative. Judicial review can therefore appropriately begin in Missouri at that time, a point which is much earlier than is permissible under the federal and similar state legislation.

Adoption of the federal rule does not foreclose the possibility that in a very unusual case, judicial review might be appropriate even before the holding of an election. The federal courts and the courts of the state following the federal rule do permit such exceptions in extraordinary circumstances. *Boire v. Greyhound Corporation, supra; Jordan Marsh Co. v. Labor Relations Commission, supra; Bays v. Miller,* 524 F.2d 631 (9th Cir. 1975). The adoption of the federal rule will therefore leave ample flexibility for special situations.

. . . .

## NOTES

1. Assume that Union A and Union B are vying for the right to represent the employees of a public employer and that Union A loses the election and subsequently files timely objections to the election alleging that Union B engaged in illegal pre-election conduct that affected the outcome of the election. Assume further that the PERB overrules the objections and certifies Union B as the exclusive bargaining representative of the employees. On the basis of the federal rule referred to in the principal case, could Union A obtain judicial review of the PERB decision overruling its objections?

2. In Indiana Education Employment Relations Board v. Benton Community School Corporation, 95 L.R.R.M. 3084 (Ind. S. Ct. 1977), the Indiana Supreme Court held that the Indiana Public Employees Collective Bargaining Act was unconstitutional because it precluded "judicial review of unit determinations and certification of exclusive bargaining representatives. . . ."

## CIVIL SERVICE EMPLOYEES ASSOCIATION v. HELSBY

New York Supreme Court, Appellate Division
31 App. Div. 2d 325, 297 N.Y.S.2d 813, *aff'd per curiam,*
24 N.Y.2d 993, 250 N.E.2d 230, 302 N.Y.S.2d 822 (1969)

STALEY, JR., J. This is an appeal from a judgment of the Supreme Court at Special Term, entered in Albany County on January 9, 1969, which dismissed a petition in a proceeding under article 78 of the CPLR to review a determination of the Public Employment Relations Board in a representation status dispute, and denied an application to vacate an order issued by such board temporarily restraining the State Negotiating Committee from continuing negotiations with the Civil Service Employees Association pending final certification of representation status.

Following the enactment of the Public Employees' Fair Employment Act (Civil Service Law, art. 14; L. 1967, ch. 392, also known as the Taylor Law), the State Negotiating Committee determined that it would negotiate collectively with three units of State employees and recognized the Civil Service Employees Association to negotiate on behalf of employees of one such unit commonly called the general unit. Employee organizations opposed to the association filed petitions with the Public Employment Relations Board contesting both the establishment of the general unit and the recognition of the association. The board issued an order on November 30, 1967 restraining exclusive negotiations between the State Negotiating Committee and the association until the representation status dispute initiated by the filing of such petitions was resolved, which order was vacated in a prior proceeding in which the statute was construed as "conferring of power on the public employer to recognize and negotiate with employee organizations, untrammeled by representation dispute proceedings until they have been resolved by the Board through certifications of appropriate bargaining units and employee organizations." (Matter of Civil Serv. Employees Assn. v. Helsby, 21 N.Y.2d 541, 548.)

Following extensive hearings upon the petitions filed by the employee organizations opposed to the association, the board, on November 27, 1968, handed down its decision which rejected the general unit designated by the State Negotiating Committee and found five separate units to be appropriate. The question of which job titles should be included in each unit and the ascertainment of the employers' choice of employee organizations as their representatives were reserved pending further proceedings before the board. The association promptly commenced the present proceeding to review such determination by petition and order to show cause issued November 27, 1968. Before service of the petition and order to show cause was effected, the board issued an order, also dated November 27, 1968, in which it ordered the State Negotiating Committee and the association to refrain from conducting further negotiations until the representation status dispute was resolved through certifications of employee organizations for employees in each of the five units.

Respondents moved to dismiss the petition upon the ground that the determination sought to be reviewed is not final within the meaning of subdivision 1 of CPLR 7801, which motion was granted. Special Term also denied the association's application, apparently made upon the argument of the motion to dismiss its petition, for judgment vacating the order restraining negotiations between the State Negotiating Committee and the association.

The first issue raised on this appeal is whether the board's determination is subject to judicial review under article 78 of the CPLR. CPLR 7801 provides that article 78 "shall not be used to challenge a determination which is not final or can be adequately reviewed by appeal to a court or some other body or officer." It is this exception upon which the board relies to defer judicial review.

The board in its decision concluded that in a representative proceeding it was empowered to devise a unit that it deemed most appropriate, although such a unit was not specifically sought by any of the parties. It further held that the general unit designated by the employer was not appropriate and approved five separate units as appropriate. The board contends that its determination is not final and, therefore, the association is not, at this time, free to question the appropriateness of the units it has devised.

The pertinent provisions of the Taylor Law to the issues involved on this appeal read as follows:

"§ 205. Public employment relations board. . . . 5. In addition to the powers and functions provided in other sections of this article, the board shall have the following powers and functions . . . (f) To conduct studies of problems involved in representation and negotiation, including, but not limited to . . . (ii) the problems of unit determination. . . .

"§ 207. Determination of representation status. For purposes of resolving disputes concerning representation status, pursuant to section two hundred five or two hundred six of this article, the board or government, as the case may be, shall

"1. define the appropriate employer-employee negotiating units taking into account the following standards:

"(a) the definition of the unit shall correspond to a community of interest among the employees to be included in the unit;

"(b) the officials of government at the level of the unit shall have the power to agree, or to make effective recommendations to other administrative authority or the legislative body with respect to, the terms and conditions of employment upon which the employees desire to negotiate; and

"(c) the unit shall be compatible with the joint responsibilities of the public employer and public employees to serve the public."

It should be noted that subdivision 1 of section 207 of the Civil Service Law provides for the determination of the negotiating unit, while subdivisions 2 and 3 provide for the implementation of the unit for the purpose of certification.

Nothing in the Taylor Law or the CPLR makes the certification of an employee organization a prerequisite to judicial review of the determination establishing separate negotiating units. If that determination is final as to the rights of the parties, with respect to the matter involved, it should be reviewable. The units deemed to be appropriate by the board are as final now as they will be upon certification. The matter involved in this proceeding is the propriety of the recognition of the association as a negotiating representative for the employees of the general unit, as contrasted with the board's determination that the general unit should be divided into five separate negotiating units. The determination mandated by subdivision 1 of section 207 of the Civil Service Law having been accomplished, the procedure provided by statute to implement that determination cannot alter the original determination. Whatever organization may ultimately be certified to represent the employees involved cannot affect the determination with respect to the structure of the five units.

The argument that the determination of the board establishing the five negotiating units should be reviewed only after certification as provided by subdivision 3 of section 207 of the Civil Service Law is contrary to prompt disposition of a dispute where a party is aggrieved as of the moment of the determination.

Judicial review at this time may avoid costly and time-consuming intermediate procedures. There would be no economy in deferring the question of the correctness of the board's determination until after all the proceedings required to ascertain and establish the employee representative for the five proposed units, should the courts ultimately decide that the five units established were not appropriate. Resolution of the issues in this proceeding at the earliest possible moment is in the best interest of the State and its employees. Unless there is some statutory prohibition, there is no reason to defer judicial review. As the Court of Appeals said of a comparable situation in Long Is. Coll. Hosp. v. Catherwood (23 N.Y.2d 20, 36): "A decision that the validity of the board's certification cannot be tested in the court until time-consuming mediation, fact-finding and compulsory arbitration proceedings have been exhausted can only serve to delay a prompt determination of the representation issue — a delay which is not in the interest of the public, the nonprofitmaking hospitals or the unions, since unresolved representation issues may cause the very strife which the 1963 amendments were enacted to prevent."

We are here required to construe a unique statutory scheme, one that has as its main purpose the promotion of harmonious and cooperative relationships between government and its employees to protect the public by assuring at all times the orderly and uninterrupted operations and functions of government. Certainly such a statute should be construed with the liberality needed to carry out its public benefit purposes and, therefore, the determination involved should be afforded prompt and effective judicial review.

The board's decision finally and irrevocably rejected the bargaining unit designated by the State Negotiating Committee and determined appropriate alternate units. Such determination is in no sense interlocutory or merely an intermediate procedural ruling incident to the administrative process (cf. Matter of Carville v. Allen, 13 A.D.2d 866), but instead as to such matters it is final and thus reviewable under article 78. . . .

## NOTES

1. *Accord,* AAUP v. University of Nebraska, 198 Neb. 243, 253 N.W.2d 1 (1977) (". . . an order establishing bargaining units is a final order . . . , and a party may appeal therefrom prior to the holding of elections").

2. In New Hampshire Dep't of Revenue Adm. v. PELRB, 380 A.2d 1085 (N.H. S. Ct. 1977), the court held that a bargaining unit determination was not an appealable final order. In holding "that final certification of representative capacity is the proper order to appeal," the court reasoned that until that time "no one's legal rights have been affected." *Accord,* Panama City v. PERC, 333 So.2d 470 (Fla. Ct. App. 1976) (certification following election constitutes final agency action from which petition for review of bargaining unit determination can be filed).

3. The California Educational Employment Relations Act provides that "[n]o employer or employee organization shall have the right to judicial review of a unit determination except: (1) when the board in response to a petition from the employer or employee organization, agrees that the case is one of special importance and joins in the request for such review; or (2) when the issue is raised as a defense to an unfair labor practice complaint." CAL. EDUC. CODE § 3542(a).

# Chapter 4

# THE OBLIGATION AND DUTY TO BARGAIN

## A. THE OBLIGATION TO BARGAIN COLLECTIVELY

## 1. CONSTITUTIONAL CONSIDERATIONS

### BEAUBOEUF v. DELGADO COLLEGE

United States District Court,
Eastern District of Louisiana
303 F. Supp. 861 (1969),
*aff'd per curiam,* 428 F.2d 470 (5th Cir. 1970)

RUBIN, District Judge:

. . . .

[The American Federation of Teachers, AFL-CIO, Local 1130] . . . sought recognition as the exclusive collective bargaining agent of the faculty. The Board of Advisors recommended its recognition, but the Board of Managers refused to enter into collective bargaining negotiations with the Union. However, the Union has appeared to represent its members in presenting grievances, and Delgado's president and other administrative officials have met with the Union's representatives to discuss any matters of concern whenever requested to do so. Delgado's policy has been to recognize the Union as a responsible body, representing its members, but to refuse to bargain collectively with it as an exclusive bargaining agent.

. . . .

The Union seeks an injunction compelling Delgado to bargain collectively with it as the exclusive representative of Delgado's teachers. It contends that Delgado is an agency of the City of New Orleans, that the City has bargained with other labor unions representing other municipal employees, and hence that the Union is denied equal protection of the law by Delgado's refusal to bargain with it.

Louisiana prohibits public employees from striking. LSA-R.S. 23:822, 23:861, 23:862. But Louisiana law, as interpreted by its Attorney General, neither commands municipal corporations to, nor prohibits them from, bargaining collectively with unions representing groups of municipal employees. . . .

Delgado College is an agency of the City of New Orleans. . . .

Delgado College is administered by a Board of Managers composed of sixteen members. It is not a part of the Orleans Parish School system, and its affairs are not subject to the control of the Orleans Parish School Board. The primary fiscal support of the college is provided by the State of Louisiana. The school derives additional operational revenue from federal grants, tuition charges, and minor amounts from other sources.

Although the Union alleges that it has been denied equal protection because the City has bargained with its public employees through their respective labor unions but has arbitrarily refused to bargain with it, the evidence proves only that representatives of the City are meeting with representatives of the Teamsters Union with a view to framing a collective bargaining agreement covering sanitation workers for submission to the City Council; that the Sewerage and Water Board has entered into a collective bargaining contract with the American Federation of State, County and Municipal Employees, AFL-CIO; and that the City has negotiated labor problems with the Fire Fighters Union. These facts fall

243

short of proving a pattern of recognition of other unions by the City, nor do they prove any sort of discrimination against the Union.

The prohibitory commandment of the Fourteenth Amendment forbids the states to "deny to any person within its jurisdiction the equal protection of the laws." This is not the philosophical assertion of the Declaration of Independence that all men are created equal; it is a mandate that the law must in terms deal equally with all to whom it applies, and it must treat like subjects in like manner. Equal Protection further requires that the executive authorities who apply the law treat all citizens in the same manner. "Though the law itself be fair on its face, and impartial in appearance, yet if it is applied and administered by public authority with an evil eye and an unequal hand, so as practically to make unjust and illegal discrimination between persons in similar circumstances, material to their rights, the denial of equal justice is still within the prohibition of the constitution. . . ." Yick Wo v. Hopkins, 1886, 118 U.S. 356, 374, 6 S.Ct. 1064, 1073, 30 L.Ed. 220.

But Equal Protection is not a Procrustes bed for either legislature or executive. "Under our constitutional system the States in determining the reach and scope of particular legislation need not provide 'abstract symmetry.' Patsone v. Pennsylvania, 232 U.S. 138, 144, 34 S.Ct. 281, 282, 58 L.Ed. 539." Skinner v. Oklahoma ex rel. Williamson, 1942, 316 U.S. 535, 539-540, 62 S.Ct. 1110, 1112, 86 L.Ed. 1655. "The Constitution does not require things which are different in fact or opinion to be treated in law as though they were the same." Tigner v. Texas, 1940, 310 U.S. 141, 147, 60 S.Ct. 879, 882, 84 L.Ed. 1124. And even in the enforcement of criminal statutes "the conscious exercise of some selectivity in enforcement is not in itself a federal constitutional violation," provided "the selection [is not] deliberately based upon an unjustifiable standard such as race, religion, or other arbitrary classification." Oyler v. Boles, 1962, 368 U.S. 448, 456, 82 S.Ct. 501, 506, 7 L.Ed.2d 446.

When a government official grants rights to some and denies them to others, this may constitute a denial of equal protection. But the executive branch is entitled no less than the legislature to reasonable discretion in handling its affairs and to a range of experiment in determining its course. Here no "intentional or purposeful discrimination" has been shown, Snowden v. Hughes, 1944, 321 U.S. 1, 8, 64 S.Ct. 397, 401, 88 L.Ed. 497. Nor have "conspicuously artificial lines" been established. Skinner v. Oklahoma ex rel. Williamson, 1942, 316 U.S. 535, 542, 62 S.Ct. 1110, 1114, 86 L.Ed. 1655.

Schoolteachers have been legislatively classified differently from other public employees in many ways. They have generally been accorded more favorable treatment, with respect to such matters as guarantee of tenure, security against discharge, opportunity for leave, and provision for advancement. Public education is a basic function of American state and local government, and the teachers to whom this task is imparted have rightly been considered deserving of special consideration.

It is therefore not unreasonable and hence not unconstitutional for a legislature to exclude public school teachers from a public employees' labor relations act, which gives other state employees the right to bargain collectively. Minneapolis Fed. of Teachers, Local 59 v. Obermeyer, 1966, 275 Minn. 347, 147 N.W.2d 358. It would appear that equal latitude may be exercised by executive officials in determining whether they should bargain collectively with school teachers as well as with various other classes of public employees. This is particularly true when public officials are presented with a demand that one union be recognized as exclusive bargaining agent for *all* teachers, whether or not the teachers are union members. . . .

Control of the terms and conditions of school teachers' public employment through collective bargaining raises practical problems. Budget deadlines exist that do not confront private industry. There are financial limitations not soluble by the expedient of raising prices, which may be used by a private employer, or of raising charges, which may be pursued by those public agencies that exact a charge for their services [such as by the Sewerage and Water Board]. Defining "conditions of employment" for a teacher may involve matters of educational policy imparted by law for decision to an administrative board. And these public officials may think that public sovereignty is more important in matters of education than in connection with other municipal problems.

A responsible legislature or executive might well decide that to bargain collectively with unions representing school teachers is in the public interest. Conceivably, a public body might bargain so universally with unions representing other employees that the denial of the right of union representation to teachers might be considered a denial of equal protection. But no anti-union bias has been shown. Delgado has merely refused to bargain collectively with a union representing some (but not all) of its teachers. This is not a denial of equal protection of the laws.

Therefore judgment will be entered rejecting the demand for a mandatory injunction.

## NOTES

1. *Accord,* Confederation of Police v. City of Chicago, 529 F.2d 89 (7th Cir.), *vacated on other grounds,* 427 U.S. 902, 96 S. Ct. 3186, 49 L.Ed.2d 1196 (1976) (denial of collective bargaining rights to police officers not denial of equal protection even though non-academic employees of city board of education possessed such rights since board of education not comparable to police department for equal protection purposes).

2. The courts have uniformly held that it is not a violation of the First Amendment for a public employer to refuse to engage in collective bargaining with a bargaining representative chosen by the employees of the public employer. In Alaniz v. City of San Antonio, 80 L.R.R.M. 2983 (W.D. Tex. 1971), a three-judge federal court rejected the contention that the right to engage in collective bargaining is protected by the First Amendment, reasoning as follows:

... While it is now clear that public employees have a constitutionally protected right to self-organization, this right has never been extended to include collective bargaining through a recognized group representative. The private employee's right to such concerted activity, now "fundamental" under national legislative policy in the private arena, is not guaranteed to public employees such as plaintiffs, either by national legislation or the constitution. The State [of Texas], in declaring its policy against bargaining-agent recognition and collective bargaining contracts in its dealing with public employees, is not interfering with any constitutionally protective [sic] rights of plaintiffs.

*Accord,* Hanover Township Fed'n of Teachers v. Hanover Community School Corp., 457 F.2d 456 (7th Cir. 1972); Winston-Salem/Forsyth County Unit, N.C. Ass'n of Education v. Phillips, 381 F. Supp. 644 (M.D.N.C. 1974); Newport News Fire Fighters Ass'n, Local 794 v. City of Newport News, 339 F. Supp. 13 (E.D. Va. 1972); Adkins v. City of Charlotte, 296 F. Supp. 1068 (W.D.N.C. 1969); Gary Teachers Union, Local 4 v. School City of Gary, 427 Ind. App. 211, 284 N.E.2d 108 (1972). *But see* School Committee of the Town of Westerly v. Westerly Teachers Ass'n, 111 R.I. 96, 299 A.2d 441 (1973) (dissenting opinion).

In Indianapolis Educ. Ass'n v. Lewallen, 72 L.R.R.M. 2071 (7th Cir. 1969), a school board entered into an agreement with a teachers' association in which the board agreed that it would recognize the association as the exclusive bargaining representative for a unit of teachers and would bargain in good faith with the association if the association received a majority of the votes cast in a representation election. Although the association received approximately 95 percent of the votes, it alleged that the school board thereafter refused to bargain in good faith and that this refusal violated the First and Fourteenth Amendments. The court rejected this contention, stating:

> The gravamen of the complaint goes to the failure on the part of the defendants-appellants to bargain collectively in good faith. But there is no constitutional duty to bargain collectively with an exclusive bargaining agent. Such duty, when imposed, is imposed by statute. The refusal of the defendants-appellants to bargain in good faith does not equal a constitutional violation of plaintiffs-appellees' positive rights of association, free speech, petition, equal protection, or due process. Nor does the fact that the agreement to collectively bargain may be enforceable against a state elevate a contractual right to a constitutional right.

## O'BRIEN v. LEIDINGER

United States District Court, Eastern District of Virginia
452 F. Supp. 720 (1978)

MERHIGE, District Judge.

Plaintiffs, members of Teamsters Local Union # 592 ("Union"), are employed as police officers by the City of Richmond, Virginia ("City"). Plaintiffs bring this action against the City Manager and members of the City Council, who are sued individually and in their official capacities, alleging that the defendants' refusal to enter into good faith discussions with the Union concerning police officers' wages, hours, and working conditions violates plaintiffs' rights guaranteed by the First, Ninth, and Fourteenth Amendments of the United States Constitution. Jurisdiction is alleged under the Constitution, *see Bivens v. Six Unknown Named Agents of the Federal Bureau of Narcotics,* 403 U.S. 388, 91 S.Ct. 1999, 29 L.Ed.2d 619 (1971), and pursuant to 28 U.S.C. §§ 1331, 1343. The matter has been tried on the merits and is ripe for disposition.

Absent express statutory authority, local governments in Virginia are prohibited by state law from recognizing a labor organization as the exclusive representative of a group of public employees, and hence from negotiating collective bargaining contracts with such organizations. *Commonwealth v. County Board of Arlington County,* 217 Va. 558, 232 S.E.2d 30 (1977).

The Attorney General of Virginia has made it clear that municipalities may, however, legally enter into "discussions" concerning wages, hours, and working conditions with representatives of public employee organizations. In short, while the City may not confer *exclusive* bargaining rights upon a particular union or organization, so that a vote of a majority of employees on a contract would bind dissenters, the City may, if it so chooses, discuss employment matters with representatives chosen by its employees. *See, e. g., Commonwealth v. County Board of Arlington County, supra; Newport News Firefighters Ass'n. v. City of Newport News,* 339 F.Supp. 13, 17 (E.D.Va.1972).

Plaintiffs allege that the City has discussed the terms and conditions of employment with labor organizations representing other groups of similarly situated employees, while refusing to discuss such matters with certain of the plaintiffs in their capacities as representatives of Teamsters Local # 592, in violation of each plaintiff's right to equal protection of the laws. Additionally, plaintiffs assert that the City's refusal to meet with Teamster representatives who are not employees of the City, but whom plaintiffs have chosen to be their spokesmen, abridges plaintiffs' First Amendment rights of free speech and association. The Court will address each of these issues seriatum.

## Equal Protection

For the plaintiffs to establish an equal protection violation the Court must be satisfied, by a preponderance of the evidence, that (1) the City has entered into discussions concerning the employment relationship with representatives of other groups of similarly situated public employees, while refusing to do the same with representatives of plaintiffs' Union, and (2) there exists no rational reason for this disparate treatment.

The City states that it has followed a policy whereby it has been willing to "discuss working conditions, including wages and hours, with individual employees or with organizations which they form, so long as these are not unions." The Court concludes that this policy has not been followed. Despite assertions to the contrary, the evidence discloses and the Court finds as a fact that the defendants have discussed the terms and conditions of employment with agents, *qua* agents, of unions and other employee organizations not objectionable to the City, while refusing to engage in similar discussions with agents of the plaintiffs' Union.

The evidence reveals that, for several years, both prior and subsequent to July, 1974, the City, through its authorized personnel, has discussed such topics as wages, hours, pensions, holidays, and other fringe benefits with persons it knew to be, and dealt with as, agents of the Richmond Firefighters Association Local #995, the Fraternal Order of Police, and the Solid Waste Bureau Employees Committee. Defendants contend that the City adopted a new policy in July, 1974, and thereafter refused to recognize persons as union agents for purposes of such discussions. While that policy may have been adopted, the Court finds from the evidence that defendants did not adhere to such policy and in fact continued to deal with union agents as representatives of their respective organizations.

It is undisputed that defendants have steadfastly refused to discuss employment matters with certain of the plaintiffs in their capacities as representatives of the remaining plaintiffs and approximately four hundred other City police officers who are members of Teamsters Local # 592. Defendants have offered no explanation whatever for this disparate treatment.[3] While equal protection is satisfied if there exists a rational basis for the City's refusal to engage in "discussions" with plaintiffs' chosen representatives, plaintiffs are not bound to speculate as to possible explanations and refute each one. Rather, defendants have the burden of offering an explanation for their conduct. Since defendants have not met this burden, the Court must conclude that defendants have violated plaintiffs' constitutional right of equal protection by refusing to discuss the terms and conditions of employment with certain of the plaintiffs (all of whom are City employees) as representatives of those police officers who affiliate with the Teamsters Union, while engaging in such discussions with agents of other employee labor organizations.

Defendants' refusal to meet with Teamster bargaining agents who are *not* City employees ("outside" agents) raises a wholly separate question. The Equal

---

[3] In particular, the City has offered no explanation for its willingness to discuss such topics as wages and benefits with agents of the Fraternal Order of Police, which represents police officers who are members of the FOP, but not with plaintiffs, who represent police officers who belong to the Teamsters.

Protection clause requires only that groups of similarly situated persons be treated equally. The evidence discloses that the City has met with union representatives who were themselves employees of the City ("inside" agents), but not with outside union agents. Therefore, while defendants have an equal protection duty to meet with plaintiffs' inside agents, defendants have no duty under *that* constitutional provision to meet with plaintiffs' outside representatives. Such is not the case, however, under the First Amendment.

### First Amendment

Plaintiffs appropriately claim that once they are accorded the right to choose a union representative, whether by voluntary action of the City or by Court order, the First Amendment guarantees them the right to select *any* representative they wish, whether or not that person be a City employee. Since different constitutional provisions provide different rights, it is entirely logical that the First Amendment may grant plaintiffs rights quite apart from the rights secured by the Equal Protection Clause.

The first inquiry the Court must address under a First Amendment analysis is whether the First Amendment protects plaintiffs' interest in selecting the spokesman of their choice to advocate on their behalf in discussions with the appropriate officials of the City. If the First Amendment's protection applies, the Court must then balance the plaintiffs' interests against the City's competing interests to determine whether the City's refusal to meet with non-employee representatives of the Union impermissibly infringes upon plaintiffs' constitutionally protected rights. *Pickering v. Board of Education,* 391 U.S. 563, 88 S.Ct. 1731, 20 L.Ed.2d 811 (1968).

It is clear that the First Amendment not only protects the right of an individual to associate with other like-minded persons to advance common goals, but also guarantees the derivative [4] right of an association to advocate on behalf of its members. *Runyon v. McCrary,* 427 U.S. 160, 96 S.Ct. 2586, 49 L.Ed.2d 415 (1976); *Buckley v. Valeo,* 424 U.S. 1, 96 S.Ct. 612, 46 L.Ed.2d 659 (1976); *Eastern Railroad Presidents Conference v. Noerr Motor Freight,* 365 U.S. 127, 81 S.Ct. 523, 5 L.Ed.2d 464 (1976); *NAACP v. Alabama,* 357 U.S. 449, 78 S.Ct. 1163, 2 L.Ed.2d 1488 (1958). This protection extends to economic as well as political associations and specifically encompasses the right to unionize. *Thomas v. Collins,* 323 U.S. 516, 65 S.Ct. 315, 89 L.Ed. 430 (1945). Moreover, it is clear that public employees enjoy many of the same rights as other workers to advance their common interests through unionization. *AFSCME v. Woodward,* 406 F.2d 137 (8th Cir. 1969); *McLaughlin v. Tilendis,* 398 F.2d 287 (7th Cir. 1968); *Melton v. City of Atlanta,* 324 F.Supp. 315 (N.D.Ga.1971) (three judge court); *Atkins v. City of Charlotte,* 296 F.Supp. 1068 (W.D.N.C.1969) (three judge court) (Craven, J.).

The right to associate for common goals encompasses the right to advocate effectively in pursuit of such goals. *Buckley v. Valeo, supra; Eastern Presidents Railroad Conference v. Noerr Motor Freight, supra.* "[The] right [of association] is protected because it promotes and may well be essential to the '[e]ffective advocacy of both public and private points of view, particularly controversial

---

[4] Associations such as unions derive their First Amendment right from the rights of their members. Thus, when a union's right to speak is abridged, its members' rights of association and speech are abridged as well.

ones' . . . that the First Amendment is designed to foster." *Runyon v. McCrary,* 427 U.S. at 175, 96 S.Ct. at 2597, 49 L.Ed.2d — (citation omitted). The right to advocate would be hollow indeed if the state, rather than the association's members, could select the group's advocate. For example, the City could not limit the right of the Union to advocate on behalf of its members in a public forum by restricting the eligible speakers to persons employed by the City. *Cf. City of Madison Joint School District v. Wisconsin Employment Relations Commission,* 429 U.S. 167, 97 S.Ct. 421, 50 L.Ed.2d 376 (1976) (First Amendment rights of non-union teachers violated by defendant's order limiting right to speak at open meetings of the Board of Education, on matters involving the employment relationship, to persons selected by the Teachers Union); *Williams v. Rhodes,* 393 U.S. 23, 89 S.Ct. 5, 21 L.Ed.2d 24 (1968) (voters' First Amendment right to associate with the candidate of their choice unconstitutionally abridged by state law that effectively limits ballot position to persons endorsed by one of the two major political parties).

The City argues, however, that the First Amendment's protection is not applicable in the instant case because plaintiffs' right to speak through their Union derives not from the existence of a public forum, but solely from defendants' equal protection violation, and the extent of that violation necessarily delimits the extent of the remedy the Court may impose.

While superficially appealing, defendants' argument must be rejected. The City is a public body, bound in *all* its official actions — including those in its role as employer — by the commands of the First Amendment. Defendants contend that the First Amendment's protection cannot be invoked to extend the limited right created by virtue of the Equal Protection violation. But the First Amendment's protection is often triggered by the government's voluntary actions. *See, e. g., Elrod v. Burns,* 427 U.S. 347, 96 S.Ct. 2673, 49 L.Ed.2d 547 (1976) (while government has no duty to employ its citizens, once it chooses to do so it cannot grant or deny such employment because of a citizen's affiliation with a particular political party); *Perry v. Sindermann,* 408 U.S. 593, 92 S.Ct. 2694, 33 L.Ed.2d 570 (1972) (while state college has no duty to renew non-tenured professor's contract of employment, it cannot predicate its refusal to do so on the professor's exercise of First Amendment rights); *Sherbert v. Verner,* 374 U.S. 398, 83 S.Ct. 1790, 10 L.Ed.2d 965 (1963) (while state has no duty to provide unemployment benefits, it may not cut off such benefits on the basis of a citizen's exercise of her religious faith); *Hannegan v. Esquire, Inc.,* 327 U.S. 146, 66 S.Ct. 456, 90 L.Ed. 586 (1946) (although government need not establish postal service, once it does, it may not condition grant of mailing permit on promise that certain ideas not be disseminated). *See generally* Van Alstyne, *The Demise of the Right-Privilege Distinction in Constitutional Law,* 81 Harv.L.Rev. 1439 (1968); Note, *Unconstitutional Conditions,* 73 Harv.L.Rev. 1595 (1960). Thus, once plaintiffs are accorded the right to advocate through union representatives in employment discussions with the City, whether by voluntary action of the City or by Court order to redress an equal protection violation, the First Amendment necessarily defines what limits, if any, the City may permissibly place on that right.[5]

---

[5] The City suggests that even if plaintiffs have a right to speak through any union representative they select, the City has no duty to listen to such a representative. This attempted distinction misconceives the very nature of the jurisprudential concept of rights and duties. Whenever there exists a *right* in any person, there also exists a correlative *duty* in some other person or persons not to abridge or interfere with the exercise of that right. Hohfeld, *Some Fundamental Legal Conceptions*

"The prohibition on encroachment of First Amendment protections is not an absolute. Restraints are permitted for appropriate reasons." *Elrod v. Burns,* 427 U.S. at 360, 96 S.Ct. at 2683. It remains, then, to determine whether defendants' refusal to meet with non-employee representatives of plaintiffs' Union *impermissibly* burdens plaintiffs' right of association.

In *Pickering v. Board of Education,* 391 U.S. at 568, 88 S.Ct. at 1734, the Supreme Court stated:

> [I]t cannot be gainsaid that the State has interests as an employer in regulating the speech of its employees that differ significantly from those it possesses in connection with regulation of the speech of the citizenry in general. The problem in any case is to arrive at a balance between the interests of the [employee] . . . and the interests of the State, as an employer, in promoting the efficiency of the public services it performs through its employees.

Thus, it has been held that the government may regulate the speech of its employees in furtherance of the goals of their employment. *See, e. g., Civil Service Commission v. National Association of Letter Carriers,* 413 U.S. 548, 93 S.Ct. 2880, 37 L.Ed.2d 796 (1973) (upholding restrictions on partisan political activities of federal employees); *Broadrick v. Oklahoma,* 413 U.S. 601, 93 S.Ct. 2908, 37 L.Ed.2d 830 (1973) (same as to state employees). It follows that defendants may not restrict plaintiffs' choice of representative to employees of the City without satisfying the Court that the reasons for such a rule justify the consequential encroachment upon plaintiffs' constitutional liberties.

Defendants suggest two reasons why they prefer to discuss employment matters with police representatives who are themselves employed by the City, rather than with outside union agents. Defendants assert that discussions between employer and employees promote a harmonious employment relationship, while discussions with professional union representatives encourage strife and discord. Further, defendants contend that direct discussions with their employees are more efficient in finding mutually acceptable solutions to grievances.

Plaintiffs counter that the City's refusal to meet with their chosen union representatives severely restricts their freedom of speech. They explain that none of their local union members is experienced or skilled in presenting employee grievances or discussing employment matters on behalf of union members. Additionally, plaintiffs assert that a non-employee representative would be less subject to intimidation and harassment by City officials and thus would more aggressively represent the policemen's interests in discussions with the City.

The Court has no doubt that the City's articulated interests are legitimate and worthwhile. A public employer, as any employer, reasonably is concerned with maintaining open lines of communication between management and labor. However, to justify its policy of meeting only with police representatives who are City employees, the City must demonstrate that that policy directly furthers its

---

*as Applied in Judicial Reasoning,* 23 Yale L.J. 16 (1930). As Justice Harlan has stated, "the right to have one's voice heard and one's views considered by the appropriate governmental authority is at the core of the right of political association." *Williams v. Rhodes,* 393 U.S. 23, 41, 89 S.Ct. 5, 16, 21 L.Ed.2d 24 (1968) (concurring opinion). Thus, if plaintiffs have a right to be represented by an agent of their choosing in discussions with the City, they also have the right to have their views, expressed by their agent, heard by the City. In defendants' terms, the City, acting through defendants, would have a "duty to listen" to the plaintiffs' representative, correlative to and inseparable from the plaintiffs' right to speak through that representative.

legitimate interests and is reasonably necessary to those ends. *See, e. g., Tygrett v. Washington,* 177 U.S.App.D.C. 355, 543 F.2d 840 (1974); *Elk Grove Firefighters Local v. Willis,* 400 F.Supp. 1097 (N.D.Ill.1975).

It must be remembered that the issue before the Court is not whether police unions per se are beneficial or harmful, but rather whether the City's refusal to deal with outside union representatives is justifiable in light of its equal protection obligation to discuss employment matters at least with "inside" representatives of the Teamsters local. The Court is not convinced that the City's action in this regard closely promotes its avowed interests. Upon consideration of all factors suggested by the parties, the Court concludes that, on balance, the plaintiffs' interest in effective advocacy of their views outweighs the City's allegedly competing interests.

. . . .

## NOTES

1. In Kenai Peninsula Borough School Dist. v. Kenai Peninsula Borough School Dist. Classified Ass'n, 1979-80 PBC ¶ 36,512 (Alaska S. Ct. 1979), it was conceded that the right of non-certificated employees to engage in collective bargaining arose solely out of a labor relations policy adopted by the district. The policy stipulated that the district would not negotiate with any individual who was not a district employee or with any employee organization that was affiliated with any state or national labor union. In holding that the district could not grant these employees the right to bargain collectively and "simultaneously decree whom the employees may send to the bargaining table as their representative, and with whom they may affiliate to effectuate this right under the [district's] policy," the Alaska Supreme Court stated:

> We can find no sound basis for distinguishing an employee's freedom in affiliation from the right to freely choose his or her representative at the bargaining table. . . .
>
> . . . .
>
> . . . A government may not confer a statutory right or benefit and withdraw it when the beneficiary exercises a constitutional prerogative. Neither may [it] confer a right and condition it unconstitutionally in the same breath. . . .
>
> The District is thus left with the task of persuading us that the interest embodied in the labor policy's restrictions outweigh the value of the associational freedoms impinged. . . .
>
> The essence of the District's asserted interest is that it needs to exercise prospective control over the vigor with which its non-certificated employees will be represented at the bargaining table. . . . To construe the School District's interest here as so paramount as to override the fundamental right to freely choose one's representatives, would render the latter right illusory, for it is difficult to imagine a context in which public employees could then successfully assert it.

*But cf.* Arnett v. Kennedy, 416 U.S. 134, 94 S. Ct. 1633, 40 L.Ed.2d 15 (1974) (plurality opinion of Mr. Justice Rehnquist).

2. Review the decision of the Supreme Court in Smith v. Arkansas State Highway Employees Local 1315, *supra,* pp. 103-04. Are the holdings of the court in the principal case on the First Amendment question and the court in the *Kenai Peninsula* case noted immediately above consistent with the Supreme Court's decision in *Smith?*

*without equal protection issue, no 1st A. issue would arise*

## 2. AUTHORITY OF PUBLIC EMPLOYERS TO BARGAIN IN THE ABSENCE OF LEGISLATION

### INTERNATIONAL UNION OF OPERATING ENGINEERS, LOCAL 321
v.
### WATER WORKS BOARD OF THE CITY OF BIRMINGHAM

Alabama Supreme Court
276 Ala. 462, 163 So. 2d 619 (1964)

SIMPSON, Justice. The question presented by this appeal is res integra in this jurisdiction, viz.: Can a public agency in Alabama bargain with and enter into an enforceable collective agreement with a labor organization concerning the wages, hours, and conditions of employment of its employees in the absence of express constitutional or statutory authorization to do so? Appellant has represented the employees of appellee for some thirty years, during which period a series of twelve collective contracts were executed between the parties. (There is no question of union membership, per se, involved on this appeal.)

The lower court, in a declaratory judgment action, ruled, inter alia, that such a contract was ultra vires and unenforceable and therefore the relief sought by appellant (union) was denied.

This Court has been favored with excellent and exhaustive briefs from both appellant and appellee and also from amicus curiae which present every conceivable facet of arguments, citing numerous cases from other jurisdictions where the question has arisen.

Concededly, appellee, as the Water Works Board of the City of Birmingham, is a public agency and its employees are public employees. . . .

It appears from the cases cited to us in brief, and our research also reveals, that the strongest current of opinion from the highest courts of states where the question has been presented has ruled that a public agency has no legal authority to bargain or contract with a labor union in the absence of express statutory authority. Appellant argues to the contrary and asks us to adopt a rule that would permit such contracts or agreements where there is no statutory prohibition against collective bargaining.

The Supreme Court of Florida in Miami Water Works Local No. 654 v. City of Miami, 157 Fla. 445, 26 So. 2d 194, 165 A.L.R. 967 (where the Union sought a declaratory judgment that the city might bargain with it) held, and we think correctly so, that the City was under no obligation to bargain with the Union and stated:

"The City of Miami is a governmental entity created by the state. It derives its powers and jurisdiction from the sovereign authority. It is limited to the exercise of such powers as are expressly granted to it by the state, or as are necessarily and fairly implied in or incident to the powers expressly granted. . . . It is a public institution designed to promote the common interests of the inhabitants in their organized capacity as a local government. Its objects are governmental, not commercial. . . . It has no authority to enter into negotiations with the labor union, or any other organized group, concerning hours, wages, or conditions of employment. . . ."

The Florida Court of Appeals (1963) in the case of Dade County v. Amalgamated Association of Street Electric Railway and Motor Coach Employees of America, 157 So. 2d 176, held in part:

"'Unless clearly authorized to do so by the enactment of legislation, the plaintiffs would not be authorized and are not now authorized to enter into collective bargaining agreements, within the labor relations meaning of the term, with the defendants. . . .

" 'The courts have said that as a general rule collective bargaining has no place in government service. The employer is the whole people. This is a government of law, not men. For the courts to hold otherwise than as I have just explained would be to sanction control of governmental functions not by laws but by men. Such policy, if followed to its logical conclusion, would inevitably lead to chaos.' "

The Supreme Court of Colorado in Fellows v. LaTronica, Colo., 377 P.2d 547, held that an action to compel the city to arbitrate a claim for vacation pay for city firemen under a collective agreement should be dismissed because the City had no authority to enter into such a contract with the union in the first instance.

The Maryland Court of Appeals, in Mugford v. Mayor and City Council of Baltimore, 185 Md. 266, 44 A.2d 745, 162 A.L.R. 1101 (affirming the lower court) in an action by a taxpayer to enjoin enforcement of and to have declared invalid a collective agreement between the City and Union, held that the City did not have the power to "delegate its governing power to any agency" and that such a contract was void.

See also Nutter v. City of Santa Monica, 74 Cal. App. 2d 292, 168 P.2d 741; City of Los Angeles v. Los Angeles Building and Construction Trades Council, 94 Cal. App. 2d 36, 210 P.2d 305; City of Springfield v. Clouse, 356 Mo. 1239, 206 S.W.2d 539; City of Alcoa v. International Brotherhood of Electrical Workers, 203 Tenn. 12, 308 S.W.2d 476; Weakley County Municipal Electric System v. Vick, 43 Tenn. App. 524, 309 S.W.2d 792; International Longshoremen's Assn., etc. v. Georgia Ports Authority, 217 Ga. 712, 124 S.E.2d 733, cert. den., 370 U.S. 922, 82 S. Ct. 1561, 8 L. Ed. 2d 503, all of which are in accord.

The rule stated by the annotator in 31 A.L.R.2d 1142 at page 1170 seems to be the rule of the majority, and supported by well reasoned cases:

"Public employers cannot abdicate or bargain away their continuing legislative discretion and are therefore not authorized to enter into collective bargaining agreements with public employee labor unions. Constitutional and statutory provisions granting the right to private industry to bargain collectively do not confer such right on public employers and employees."

The opinions of the Alabama Attorneys General are likewise without conflict to the effect that state, county, and municipal agencies of this State are without legal authority to negotiate or to enter into collective bargaining agreements with labor unions. . . . In the April 10, 1941 opinion of the Attorney General of Alabama, . . . it appears that the President of the County Board of Revenue of Gadsden, Alabama presented an inquiry to the Attorney General as to whether or not said Board of Revenue "may legally enter into a contract or agreement with a labor organization . . . as a bargaining agent for county employees with respect to hours of employment, wages, etc." The opinion of the Attorney General was as follows:

"It is my opinion that your inquiry must be answered negatively.
"In reaching this conclusion, I have not failed to recognize the fact that the county employees have a legitimate interest in collective action for the purpose of improving their economic and social situation wherever change is needed. I think it cannot be seriously questioned by anyone that beneficial results to

society, as well as to employees individually and as a class, have come from an assertion of the collective economic force of employees. The beneficial results of cooperative action on the part of labor generally is apparent. But the question raised by your inquiry does not involve the power or authority of the employee class. Solely presented is the right of a county, a mere political subdivision of the State (First National Bank v. Jackson County, 227 Ala. 448, 150 So. 690; Pickens County v. Williams, 229 Ala. 250, 156 So. 548; Moore v. Walker County, 236 Ala. 688, 185 So. 175) — an agency of limited jurisdiction having only those powers expressly authorized by statute or necessarily implied therefrom (Corning v. Patton, 236 Ala. 354, 182 So. 39) — to enter into a contract, the ultimate effect of which might be to remove the control of the government from the people as a whole, acting through their duly constituted officials.

"I have found no specific authorization for such a contract, nor has there come to my attention a provision of law from which the right to enter such an agreement might be necessarily implied. . . .

> "Thomas S. Lawson,
> "Attorney General"

Thus the public agencies of Alabama have long been advised, without conflict, that matters of wages, hours, and conditions of employment never have been, and cannot become, a matter of collective bargaining and contract in the absence of constitutional or statutory authority and of course such administrative rulings having been in force and effect for many years, are highly persuasive authority of the correctness of the rule. State v. Southern Electric Generating Co., 274 Ala. 668, 151 So. 2d 216; Haden v. McCarty, 275 Ala. 76, 152 So. 2d 141. Such administrative construction is neither binding on the State nor its agencies nor on the court. Therefore, the use of the word "bound" in the last paragraph of the opinion in State v. Southern Electric Generating Co., supra, was not intended to impinge upon the longstanding rule hereinabove adverted to. A clearer statement of what was there intended is that where an administrative construction by proper officials is fair and reasonable and has been followed for the prescriptive period of twenty years or longer, the courts are not disposed to alter that construction merely because the highest officials may have changed their minds about the matter under consideration.

On a thorough canvass of the pertinent authorities and a careful study of the entire case, despite the cogent arguments of learned counsel for appellants and amicus curiae, we are constrained to hold that the trial court ruled correctly.

Affirmed.

LIVINGSTON, C.J., and MERRILL and HARWOOD, JJ., concur.

## NOTES

1. *Accord,* Wichita Public Schools Employees Union, Local No. 513 v. Smith, 194 Kan. 2, 397 P.2d 357 (1964); State of Delaware v. AFSCME, Local 1726, 81 L.R.R.M. 2836 (Del. Ch., New Castle County, 1972) (dictum) ("The prevailing rule at common law is that, absent such a statute, public employees are not entitled to collective bargaining and public employers are without power to enter into such agreements").

In Virginia v. Arlington County Bd., 232 S.E.2d 30, 94 L.R.R.M. 2291 (1977), the Virginia Supreme Court was faced with the question of whether a local governing body or school board, in the absence of express statutory authority, could recognize a union as the exclusive representative of a group of public employees and negotiate and enter into a binding collective bargaining agreement. In holding that public employers in the

State of Virginia did not have such authority, the court stated:

> For this court to imply the power here sought, we would be required to find that because local governmental boards possess the power to enter into contracts and to hire employees and fix the terms and conditions of their employment, the boards also possess the authority to bargain collectively with labor organizations. But if the power cannot be found in this source, the boards in the present case then would have us find that, nonetheless, they possess the power to bargain collectively because they have discretionary authority to select any reasonable method of exercising a power expressly granted but silent upon its mode or manner of execution.
>
> We cannot make either finding. To imply the contended for authority would constitute the creation of a power that does not exist or, at least, the expansion of an existing power beyond rational limits. To sanction the method of exercising authority which the boards have selected in this case, even giving the selection the benefit of any doubt, would result in an unreasonable and strained application of the doctrine of implied powers. To approve the actions taken in this case would ignore the lack of any support for the proposition that collective bargaining by the boards is necessary to promote the public interest. And, finally but not least important, to imply the power asserted by the boards would be contrary to legislative intent.
>
> . . . .
>
> We are faced in this case with overwhelming indications of legislative intent concerning the concept of collective bargaining in the public sector. For this court to declare that the boards have the power to bargain collectively, when even the wisdom of incorporating the concept into the general law of the Commonwealth is the subject of controversial public and political debate, would constitute judicial legislation, with all the adverse connotations that term generates. Conscious of the respective roles of the General Assembly and the judiciary, we decline to intrude upon what the Attorney General succinctly describes as a "singularly political question."

2. The court in the principal case discussed both a public employer's authority to bargain *and* to enter into an enforceable collective bargaining agreement. Is there any legal distinction between an employer's authority to bargain and its authority to execute a binding contract?

3. Should the *capacity* in which the government employer acts, rather than the *fact* of government employment, be determinative of a public employee's collective bargaining rights? In several cases courts have held that employees of a government agency performing a proprietary function are entitled to collective bargaining rights similar to private sector employees. Civil Service Forum v. New York City Transit Authority, 4 App. Div. 2d 117, 163 N.Y.S.2d 476 (1957); Local 266, IBEW v. Salt River Project Agricultural Improvement & Power Dist., 78 Ariz. 30, 275 P.2d 393 (1954); Christie v. Port of Olympia, 27 Wash. 2d 534, 179 P.2d 294 (1947). Most courts, however, have rejected the proprietary/governmental dichotomy, citing one or more of the following reasons: (a) it is unfair to discriminate among employees in this fashion; (b) the proprietary/governmental distinction is too hard to apply in practice; (c) state law makes no such distinction, indicating the legislative intent that all public employees are subject to the same rules; and (d) even when a government agency is performing a proprietary function, this function becomes no less public than the agency's governmental functions. *See* Nutter v. City of Santa Monica, 74 Cal. App. 2d 292, 168 P.2d 741 (1946); City of Alcoa v. IBEW Local 760, 203 Tenn. 12, 308 S.W.2d 476 (1957); Weakley County Municipal Elec. Sys. v. Vick, 309 S.W.2d 792 (Tenn. S. Ct. 1958); Miami Waterworks Local 654 v. City of Miami, 157 Fla. 445, 26 So.2d 194 (1946).

4. Over the years there have been numerous opinions issued by state attorneys general with respect to the obligation and legal right of public employers to bargain collectively, or to enter into collective bargaining agreements, as well as their obligations and duties under public sector collective bargaining statutes. In most states, it is one of the duties of a state attorney general to issue opinions to the Governor and the heads of the various executive agencies. For example, the Illinois statute provides that the attorney general is

"to consult with and advise the Governor and other state officials, and give, when requested, written opinions upon all legal or constitutional questions relating to the duties of such officers respectively." ILL. ANN. STAT. ch. 14, § 14 (1963). The Illinois courts, in accord with the overwhelming weight of authority, have held that opinions rendered by the Attorney General are persuasive, but are not binding upon the court. In City of Champaign v. Hill, 29 Ill. App. 2d 429, 173 N.E.2d 839, 846 (1961), the Illinois Appellate Court stated that opinions of the State Attorney General ". . . are the legal opinions of the chief law officer of the State of Illinois on the precise question before this Court, and will be accorded considerable weight." See Scott, The Role of Attorney General's Opinions in Illinois, 67 NW. U.L. REV. 643 (1972); Larson, The Importance and Value of Attorney General Opinions, 41 IOWA L. REV. 351 (1956).

## LITTLETON EDUCATION ASSOCIATION v. ARAPAHOE COUNTY SCHOOL DISTRICT NO. 6

Supreme Court of Colorado
— Colo. —, 553 P.2d 793 (1976)

DAY, Justice.

This appeal involves a determination of the validity of a collective bargaining agreement between defendant-appellee school board of Arapahoe County school district No. 6 (the board) and plaintiff-appellant Littleton Education Association (LEA). . . .

We do not adopt the court's ruling that, absent legislative authority, the board has no power to enter into collective bargaining agreements.

. . . .

Collective bargaining negotiations entered into on a voluntary basis have resulted in agreements in 38 of the state's 181 school districts. In 1975 these contracts affected approximately 21,896 teachers in the state public school system.

In arguing for affirmance of the trial court's determination of the per se invalidity of such agreements, the board argues that this court's ruling in Fellows v. LaTronica, 151 Colo. 300, 377 P.2d 547 (1962), is controlling. In Fellows a municipal fireman claimed the city of Pueblo was required by a collective bargaining agreement to submit his dispute concerning vacation and sick leave to binding arbitration. The court held that the contract between the city and the labor union representing the firemen constituted an unlawful delegation of legislative responsibility by the municipality.

Upon reconsideration of the collective bargaining issue in light of subsequent case law, we now make it clear that Fellows should not be considered as per se invalidation of collective bargaining agreements in the public sector even though there is no express statutory authorization for the practice. See Rockey v. School District #11, 32 Colo.App. 203, 508 P.2d 796 (1973). Rather, Fellows should be limited to the holding on its facts: a public employer cannot be compelled to arbitrate disputes arising from collective bargaining agreements. This view is reflected in some of the dictum in the decision:

> ". . . A proper exercise of the legislative function might well involve consultation and negotiation with spokesmen for public employees, but the ultimate responsibility rests with the legislative body and, under the record here presented, that responsibility cannot be contracted away. For a complete annotation on the question see 31 A.L.R. (2d) 1142."

Also this view was elaborated upon in the specially concurring opinion of the present Chief Justice:

"That public employees may organize in unions and may designate a representative to present their views as to terms and conditions of employment to the body charged with the duty of setting such terms and conditions if the body chooses to hear them seems now to be generally accepted. Agreements reached between the negotiating parties may be translated into effect by proper legislative action, providing such agreements do not conflict with constitutional, charter or statutory provisions."

It is to be noted that *Fellows* did not address the question of the bargained-for agreement itself. And we also point out that the subject agreement did not provide for binding arbitration on the points of disagreement when the negotiations broke down as involved in *Greeley Police Union v. City Council of Greeley,* Colo., 553 P.2d 790. On the contrary, only the services of an impartial fact finder are provided for. The agreement specifically states that the fact finder's report ". . . shall be advisory only . . ." If the parties are still at an impasse after the advisory report of a fact finder, the agreement provides that ". . . the Board has the authority *to make the final decision and determination on all unresolved issues,* without further negotiation." (Emphasis added.)

The defect in the board's position that the subject agreement constitutes an unlawful delegation of authority and places control of a school system in the hands of an employee organization reflects a basic misperception of the negotiations process. Negotiations between an employer and an employee organization entered into voluntarily, as in this case, do not require the employer to agree with the proposals submitted by employees. Rather, the *ultimate* decisions regarding employment terms and conditions remain exclusively with the board. While the employees' influence is permitted and felt, the control of decision-making has not been abrogated or delegated.

Furthermore, school boards in this state are empowered with the general authority to contract. Section 22-32-101, C.R.S. 1973. Section 22-32-109(1)(f), C.R.S. 1973, indicates that school boards may contract for the purpose of performing their specific duty:

"To employ all personnel required to maintain the operations and carry out the educational program of the district, and to fix and order paid their compensation;"

Also, the district boards may, under section 22-32-110(1)(k), C.R.S. 1973, enter into a contract for the purpose of exercising their specific power:

"To adopt written policies, rules, and regulations, not inconsistent with law, which may relate to the efficiency, in-service training, professional growth, safety, official conduct, and welfare of the employees, or any classification thereof, of the district. . . ."

In *Chicago Division v. Board of Education,* 76 Ill.App.2d 456, 222 N.E.2d 243 (1966), the court held that a school board does not require legislative authority to enter into a collective bargaining agreement and that such an agreement is not against public policy.

In *Louisiana Teachers' Association v. New Orleans Parish School Board,* 303 So.2d 564 (La.App.1974), *cert. denied,* 305 So.2d 541 (La.S.Ct.1975), a school board was held empowered to engage in collective bargaining in the absence of express legislative authority to do so. The court stated:

"The Board has the statutory authority to determine the number of teachers to be employed, to select such teachers, to hire them and to fix their salaries, as well as to determine the number and location of schools. [Citation omitted] The Board is further authorized to make rules and regulations for its own government, not inconsistent with law or with the regulations of the Louisiana State Board of Education.

"We hold that a school board, incidental to its statutory duties above enumerated, has the power and authority to collectively bargain with an agent selected by the employees, if the Board determines in its discretion that implementation of collective bargaining will more effectively and efficiently accomplish its objectives and purposes. In our opinion the Board can select reasonable means to carry out its duties and responsibilities incidental to the sound development of employer-employee relations, as long as the means selected are not prohibited by law or against public policy."

See also *Gary Teachers Union Local No. 4 v. School City of Gary,* 152 Ind.App. 591, 284 N.E.2d 108 (1972); and *Dayton Classroom Teachers v. Dayton Board of Education,* 41 Ohio St.2d 127, 323 N.E.2d 714 (1975).

As one commentator has noted:

"If a public employer has the authority to execute individual employment contracts and is interested in efficiency and administrative simplicity, those individual contracts will contain standardized terms. Once one realizes that contracts negotiated for the same kind of work — office clerical, for example — are subject to standardization, it becomes apparent that a general power to contract can fairly encompass powers to confer exclusive recognition and execute collective bargaining contracts. A collective bargaining contract is essentially a master contract which sets the terms and conditions of employment for individual employees without requiring formal negotiation of these matters with each employee. If a public employer can standardize individual contracts of employment, it should also be able to utilize the more efficient master contract negotiated with an employee representative to achieve the same result. To say that standardized individual contracts are permissible, but a master contract is not, is to exalt form over substance." Dole, *State & Local Public Employee Collective Bargaining in the Absence of Specific Legislative Authority,* 54 Iowa L. Rev. 539 (1969).

In determining that a school board's participation in collective bargaining is not *per se* an unlawful delegation of its authority, we are cognizant of the fact that agreements reached pursuant to such procedures, in the absence of specific statutes to the contrary, must not conflict with existing statutes concerning the governance of the state school system.

We do not say, absent a statute so requiring, a school board can be compelled to enter into collective bargaining.

. . . .

## NOTES

1. *Accord,* Weest v. Indianapolis Bd. of School Comm'rs, 320 N.E.2d 748, 88 L.R.R.M. 2208 (Ind. Ct. App. 1974).

2. In Board of Regents v. Packinghouse, Food & Allied Workers, Local 1258, 175 N.W.2d 110, 73 L.R.R.M. 2529 (Iowa S. Ct. 1970), the Iowa Supreme Court held that a public employer, in the absence of specific legislative authorization, "has the power and authority to meet with representatives of an employee's union to discuss wages, working conditions and grievances if it so desires." The court held, however, that a public

employer, in the absence of specific legislative authorization, does not have the authority "to agree to exclusive representation, depriving other employees of the right to be represented by a group of their choosing or an individual the right to represent himself."

## 3. LEGAL AUTHORIZATION

Increasingly the right of public employees to bargain collectively is established and protected by legislation, executive orders, or municipal ordinances. The right of federal employees to bargain collectively was initially authorized in 1962 by Executive Order 10988. In 1969, Executive Order 10988 was reissued and modified by Executive Order 11491. In 1978, the provisions of Executive Order 11491 were, to a very significant extent, codified as Title VII of the Civil Service Reform Act of 1978.* 5 U.S.C. § 7101 *et seq.* (1978). The approximately 750,000 postal employees who were formerly covered by Executive Orders 10988 and 11491 are now covered by the labor relations provisions of the Postal Reorganization Act* which incorporates most of the provisions of the National Labor Relations Act, as amended.*

Wisconsin in 1959 was the first state to enact legislation authorizing collective bargaining for public employees. Since then, well over half the states have enacted legislation permitting collective bargaining by some or all categories of public employees. The following is a summary of the legislation enacted to date:

Twenty-seven states have enacted reasonably comprehensive statutes of general applicability: Alaska (all public employees), California (substantially all public employees; three statutes),* Connecticut (all municipal employees, teachers, and state employees; three statutes), Delaware (all public employees), Florida (all public employees), Hawaii (all public employees),* Iowa (all public employees),* Kansas (all public employees; local option as to coverage), Maine (all municipal and state employees; several statutes), Massachusetts (all public employees; two statutes), Michigan (all public employees except classified state employees), Minnesota (all public employees), Missouri (all public employees except policemen and teachers), Montana (all public employees), Nebraska (all municipal and state employees), Nevada (all local government employees including teachers), New Hampshire (classified state employees and non-academic university employees), New Jersey (all public employees), New York (all public employees),* North Dakota (all public employees), Oregon (all public employees), Pennsylvania (all public employees, including fire fighters and police officers; two statutes),* Rhode Island (all public employees; five statutes), South Dakota (all public employees), Vermont (all public employees; three statutes), Washington (all state and local government employees), Wisconsin (all state and municipal employees including teachers; two statutes).*

Fifteen states have enacted separate statutes granting teachers the right to bargain collectively: Alaska, California,* Connecticut, Delaware, Idaho, Indiana, Kansas, Maryland, Nebraska, North Dakota, Oklahoma, Rhode Island, Tennessee, Vermont, Washington.

Eleven states have enacted collective bargaining laws covering fire fighters

---

*Included in Statutory Appendix.

and/or police officers: Alabama (fire fighters), Georgia (fire fighters), Idaho (fire fighters), Kentucky (both, but only covers Louisville and Jefferson County), New Hampshire (police officers), Oklahoma (both), Pennsylvania (both), Rhode Island (both; two statutes), South Dakota (both), Texas (both), Wyoming (fire fighters).

Several states have also enacted collective bargaining legislation that is limited to transit authorities, port authorities, or other special districts.

In addition to the numerous states laws referred to above, a number of municipalities in states that do not have collective bargaining legislation have passed charter provisions or enacted ordinances granting their employees the right to bargain collectively. Phoenix, Arizona, Baltimore, Maryland, and Washington, D.C., are three prominent examples.

## NOTES

1. Whereas some states such as New York and Hawaii have one law which covers all public employees, other states such as California and Rhode Island have numerous statutory enactments covering various categories of public employees.

Most advisory commissions have recommended the enactment of one comprehensive statute rather than separate statutes for different categories of public employees. The Advisory Commission on Intergovernmental Relations in its Report "endorse[d] the single law approach," noting that "the State statute should deal with all occupational categories of public employees" since "separate statutory treatment of certain types of public employees is incompatible with the need for a smoothly-functioning labor-management relations process in the public sector." ADVISORY COMM'N ON INTERGOVERNMENTAL RELATIONS, LABOR-MANAGEMENT POLICIES FOR STATE AND LOCAL GOVERNMENT 103-04 (1969). The Rhode Island Study Commission recommended that the state's five public sector collective bargaining laws be encompassed in one comprehensive law. In Discussion and Recommendations for Changing Public Employee Legislation in Rhode Island, GERR No. 498, E-1, E-2 (1973), the following critique was made of the state's existing patchwork of laws:

> There is little question that the evolution of public sector legislation within the
> · state was accomplished without any real consideration as to the totality of the impact
> of all of the legislation. We have in the state five collective bargaining laws each
> relating to a specific type of public employee, i.e., teachers, police, firefighters,
> municipal employees and state employees. Each of these laws was framed only with
> reference to that particular class of employee. The major deficiency in this individual
> approach is that the impact of the bargains ultimately made draws upon common tax
> revenues and crosses administrative lines and if the laws are not considered together
> the administration of the acts as well as the requirements for dispute resolution are
> also inevitably handled independently. It is only incidental that the total economic
> and organizational impact is ever effectively understood. *In a word, we have
> over-legislated* and this "over legislation" in itself (since it has not taken into
> consideration the total system of impacts) has and will continue to have a serious,
> detrimental effect upon the collective bargaining process and the decisions made
> thereby.

2. If a municipality, in the absence of applicable state legislation, enacts an ordinance establishing bargaining rights for its employees, can the ordinance be challenged on preemption grounds, i.e., that collective bargaining legislation is a matter of statewide concern and can only be enacted by the state legislature? Would it make any difference if the municipality had home rule powers? In Louisville Fire Fighters v. Burke, 75 L.R.R.M. 2001 (Ky. Cir. Ct., Jefferson County, 1970), the court upheld the power of the City of Louisville to enact a collective bargaining ordinance. The court noted, *inter alia,* "that the Legislature meant to and did confer home rule upon the City of Louisville except where specifically denied by statute." *But see* Midwest Employers Council v. City of Omaha, 131 N.W.2d 609 (Neb. 1964), where the court held that the City of Omaha did

not have authority to enact a fair employment practices ordinance since "the power relating to labor relations and practices, and civil rights lies in the state, and such matters are of statewide concern and not of local concern nor municipal government concern."

3. Several of the state public sector bargaining laws permit local governmental jurisdictions to adopt their own procedures. The New York Law, for example, provides that provisions and procedures enacted by a local government, with certain exceptions, are applicable if the New York PERB has determined "that such provisions and procedures and the continuing implementation thereof are substantially equivalent to the provisions and procedures set forth . . . with respect to the state. . . ." N.Y. CIVIL SERV. LAW § 212 (McKinney, 1972). With respect to New York City, however, the Act provides that the PERB is not required to make such a determination, but rather may file suit for declaratory judgment alleging that the provisions and procedures are not substantially equivalent. The Kansas Act requires that local provisions and procedures be "reasonably equivalent" rather than "substantially equivalent." KAN. STAT. ANN. § 75-4334 (Supp. 1972). What is the difference between "reasonably equivalent" and "substantially equivalent"? *See* Statement of Arvid Anderson, pp. 73-75, *supra.*

4. In a number of cases employee organizations and unions have contended that labor relations statutes that do not specifically cover public employers are nevertheless applicable to the public sector. The courts, however, have uniformly rejected this contention. For example, in Westly v. Board of City Comm'rs of Salt Lake City, — P.2d —, 97 L.R.R.M. 2580 (Utah S. Ct. 1978), the court stated that "[i]n the absence of explicit legislative language, statutes governing labor relations between employers and employees apply only to private industry and not to the sovereign or its political subdivisions." *Accord,* Retail Clerks Local 187 v. University of Wyoming, 531 P.2d 884 (Wyo. S. Ct. 1975); Local 283, IBEW v. Robison, 91 Idaho 445, 423 P.2d 999 (1967).

## ADVISORY COMMISSION ON INTERGOVERNMENTAL RELATIONS, LABOR-MANAGEMENT POLICIES FOR STATE AND LOCAL GOVERNMENT 100-02 (1969)

Existing legislation which deals comprehensively with public employer-employee relations takes one of two basic forms: collective negotiation or meet and confer. Great interstate differences, of course, exist in the treatment accorded public employees under either approach. Both types of statute may deal extensively, or sketchily, with the rights of employees, the strike question, and coverage by level of government or occupation. But meet and confer laws generally are less comprehensive than those governing collective negotiations. In particular, they usually treat more superficially the questions of representation, administrative machinery, dispute settlement, and unfair practices. Moreover, they usually accord a different status — a superior one — to the public employer vis-a-vis employee organizations.

While both systems involve continuing communication between the employer and employee representatives, under collective negotiations both parties meet more as equals. The employee organization's position is protected by statutory provisions relating to organization rights, unfair practices, third party intervention in disputes, and binding agreements. The labor and management negotiators hopefully will arrive at a mutually binding agreement which is a byproduct of bilateral decisions. If they reach an impasse, the law generally sets forth a range of procedures to be followed, including such third-party assistance as mediation, fact-finding, and arbitration. The strike ban and the practical difficulties in making agreements binding, however, sometimes produce a system that is much less than bilateral.

Under a meet and confer system, the outcome of public employer-employee discussions depends more on management's determinations than on bilateral decisions by "equals." In some jurisdictions, the public employer may be under statutory obligation to "endeavor" to reach agreement or to "meet and confer in good faith" with an employee organization. If an agreement is reached, it is put into writing, but it normally does not become binding on the employer until such time as the legislative body takes appropriate action with executive concurrence. In other jurisdictions, the meet and confer system does not go this far, since management retains the exclusive right to act when and how it chooses concerning procedures for entering into discussions with employee organizations. Most meet and confer laws also give the employer the final "say" in the adoption and application of rules for employee organization recognition and of methods for settling disputes and handling grievances. Legislative criteria relating to these matters usually are lacking.

Fourteen States have enacted mandatory collective negotiations laws, while two have passed legislation permitting management to negotiate with unions and associations. Five States have meet and confer statutes under which the public employer is required to discuss the terms and conditions of employment with employee organizations and authorized to enter into non-binding memoranda of understanding with such representatives. In the absence of an express statutory authorization or laws to the contrary, other jurisdictions have conferred or negotiated with their employees on a *de facto* basis. Finally, a few States and some local governments have flatly refused to engage in either negotiations or discussions with employee organizations.

A major reason for these wide differences in practice is lack of consensus on the relationship between governmental sovereignty and the public labor-management dialogue. While some jurisdictions continue to cling to traditional interpretations of this doctrine, others are seeking to adapt it to, or as some would argue, move it ahead of contemporary conditions. A related issue is the belief of some public employers that they, as well as their employees, have certain "rights" which should not be surrendered or abridged through entering into a negotiating relationship with unions and associations. Some phrase this argument in terms of the multiple responsibilities falling upon anyone assuming the tough assignment of political executive at this point in time, and the corresponding duty of the public employer to balance the conflicting demands and pressures swirling around him.

. . . .

At this point in time, the crying need in a majority of situations is for a general statute that balances management rights against employee needs, recognizes the crucial and undeniable differences between public and private employment, and establishes labor-management relationships in which the public-at-large and their elected representatives have confidence.

The Commission believes that legislation embodying the essentials of a meet and confer in good faith system constitutes this kind of statute. "Meet and confer in good faith," as we view it, means the obligation of both the public employer and an employee organization to meet at reasonable times, to exchange openly and without fear information, views, and proposals, and to strive to reach agreement on matters relating to wages, hours, and such other terms and conditions of employment as fall within the statutorily defined scope of the discussion. The resulting memorandum of understanding is submitted to a jurisdiction's governing body, and it becomes effective when the necessary implementary actions have been agreed to and acted on by pertinent executive and legislative officials.

To a greater degree than collective negotiations, the meet and confer approach is protective of public management's discretion. To a greater extent, it seeks a reconciliation with the merit system since agreements reached through the discussional process and actions taken as an implementary follow-up cannot contravene any existing civil service statute. To a far greater degree than collective negotiations, it is candid and squarely confronts the reality that a governmental representative cannot commit his jurisdiction to a binding agreement or contract, and that only through ratifying and implementing legislation and executive orders can such an agreement be effected. To a greater extent, it avoids detailed, statutorily prescribed procedures applicable to all situations, and this lack of specificity in some degree and in some areas permits greater flexibility and adaptability in actual implementation. To a much greater degree, it recognizes — indeed, is rooted in — the vital differences existing between private and public employment, and does not make the mistake of relying heavily on the National Labor Relations Act as a blueprint for action in the public service.

"In good faith" has a number of important connotations as it applies to the meet and confer process. It obligates the governmental employer and a recognized employee organization to approach the discussion table with an open mind. It underscores the fact that such meetings should be held at mutually agreeable and convenient times. It recognizes that a sincere effort should be made by both parties to reach agreement on all matters falling properly within the discussion's purview. It signifies that both sides will be represented by duly authorized spokesmen prepared to confer on all such matters. It means that reasonable time off will be granted to appropriate agents of a recognized employee organization. It calls for a free exchange to the other party, on request, of non-confidential data pertinent to any issues under discussion. It implies a joint effort in drafting a non-binding memorandum of understanding setting forth all agreed upon recommendations for submission to the jurisdiction's appropriate governing officials. It charges the governmental agent to strive to achieve acceptance and implementation of these recommendations by such officials. It affirms that failure to reach agreement or to make concessions does not constitute bad faith when real differences of opinion exist. It requires both parties to be receptive to mediation if *bona fide* differences of opinion produce an impasse. Finally, it means that the State public labor-management relations law should list as an unfair practice failure to meet and confer in good faith, thereby providing a basis for legal recourse.

These special obligations convert the system into something broader and more balanced than the usual "meet and confer" setup, but still something less than the glittering and often unfulfilled promises of a collective bargaining statute.

## EDWARDS, AN OVERVIEW OF THE "MEET AND CONFER" STATES — WHERE ARE WE GOING?, Law Quadrangle Notes, Vol. 16, Winter 1972, at 10-15†

. . . .

As a theme for my speech, my first inclination was to share with you my strong opposition to the "meet and confer" bargaining model in the public sector and to suggest to you that "meet and confer" should be conceived as nothing more than an interim measure to bridge the gap between no collective bargaining and full collective bargaining rights for public employees. Most critics of the "meet and confer" model argue that it forces a union to engage in "collective begging"

† Reprinted by permission of the University of Michigan Law School.

in place of collective bargaining in the public sector. While this criticism is not wholly without justification, it surely is too simplistic to afford a realistic appraisal of the "meet and confer" bargaining model. So while I am still inclined to reject the "meet and confer" approach as obsolete, I nevertheless feel that public sector labor questions are too complex to be disposed of by reference to one's subjective inclinations.

Before I launch into an appraisal of "meet and confer" legislation, it may be helpful to attempt to define what is meant by the "meet and confer" approach, particularly in contrast to the "collective negotiations" approach presently recognized in the private sector. The glossary in the *Government Employee Relations Report* defines "meet and confer negotiations" as a —

> "Term for process of negotiating terms and conditions of employment intended to emphasize the differences between public and private employment conditions. Negotiations under 'meet and confer' laws usually imply discussions leading to unilateral adoption of policy by legislative body rather than written contract, and take place with multiple employee representatives rather than an exclusive bargaining agent."

I think this definition fairly describes what was originally intended by the "meet and confer" standard of bargaining. Implicit in this *pure* meet and confer approach is the assumption that the private sector bargaining model is overly permissive and therefore not applicable in the public sector. In other words, it is argued that public employers — who are by definition political souls — should retain broad managerial discretion in the operation of a governmental agency, subject only to the recall of the electorate pursuant to the lawfully designed political process. Thus, under the pure "meet and confer" bargaining model, the outcome of any public employer-employee discussions will depend more on management's determinations than on bilateral decisions by "equals" at the bargaining table.

On the other hand, in the private sector the parties meet as equals at the bargaining table and are free to discuss all matters concerning wages, hours, and conditions of employment. Except for "illegal" terms, there really is no statutorily created class of subjects which are not deemed to be bargainable. The only distinction of consequence in the private sector is between those "mandatory" items which may be negotiated to a point of impasse and those merely "permissible" subjects which may not be insisted upon. Since the NLRB has tended to construe "mandatory" subjects liberally, the result has been that when the parties face each other across a private sector bargaining table, they are in effect free to discuss virtually all matters which touch on the employment relationship.

It is generally assumed that most states which have passed statutes dealing with public sector labor relations problems have opted for the private sector "collective negotiations" model over the "meet and confer" approach. Upon close study of the applicable state legislation, however, it can be seen that this statement is somewhat of an overstatement and at best misleading. Actually it is true that most states have rejected the pure "meet and confer" bargaining model as it has been here defined, but by the same token, most states also rejected the traditional private sector "collective negotiations" approach. So, in practice, what we have really seen is the adoption by most states of either a "*modified* meet and confer" statute (which is more liberal than the traditional model) or a "*modified* collective negotiations" statute (which is more restrictive than its private sector counterpart). For this reason alone, it is often difficult to distinguish between "meet and confer" and "collective negotiations" as viable working concepts in the public sector. . . .

Most critics of "meet and confer" have argued that any bargaining structure which presumes to relegate the employees' representative to the status of a "conferee" or "discussant," rather than a negotiator, is patently deficient. But this criticism rests on the assumption that the bargaining process is *in fact* different under a "meet and confer" as opposed to a "collective negotiations" model. I would suggest, however, that, based upon the recent history of collective bargaining experiences which we have witnessed in the public sector in the United States, there is little to support the notion that there is any wide-spread difference in tactic or technique in the bargaining processes under these two models. Notwithstanding the statutory terminology used, unions in the public sector have pressed for the same type of demands and with the same vigor under both statutory bargaining models.

Furthermore, and with all due respect to the recent Supreme Court pronouncement that public employees do not have a constitutional right to strike, there has developed a *de facto* right to strike among public employees in this country — the threat or exercise of which appears to be no less effective than the legalized right enjoyed by employees in the private sector.

I would maintain, then, that in practice there has been no measurable difference in the *bargaining process* as seen in those states which have opted for "meet and confer" versus those states which have enacted statutes following the more traditional "collective negotiations" approach in the public sector. Indeed, many of the states which have passed "meet and confer" statutes have so distorted the pure "meet and confer" bargaining model that it is no longer accurate to say that the parties governed by some of these statutes do not meet as "equals" at the bargaining table.

At last count, I was able to identify ten states which have enacted some form of "meet and confer" legislation covering various groups of government employees: California, Idaho, Kansas, Minnesota, Missouri, Montana, Oregon, South Dakota, Maine, and Alabama.

With the exception of the Missouri and Alabama laws, . . . none of these so-called "meet and confer" states has passed a statute which embodies what I have labelled the *pure* "meet and confer" bargaining approach. . . . The Supreme Court of Missouri, in Missey v. City of Cabool, 441 S.W.2d 35, 41 (1969), ruled that the Missouri Statute did

> ". . . not purport to give to public employees the right of collective bargaining guaranteed to employees in private industry. . . . The act does not constitute a delegation . . . to the union of the legislative power of the public body, and therefore . . . the prior discretion in the legislative body to adopt, modify or reject outright the results of the discussions is untouched. . . . The act provides only a procedure for communication between the organization selected by public employees and their employer without requiring adoption of any agreement reached."

. . . .

Thus, it is plain that at least . . . in Missouri, the parties do not meet as equals at the bargaining table. But the matter surely has not been so clearly resolved in other "meet and confer" states.

The other jurisdictions mentioned almost uniformly define the "meet and confer" obligation as

". . . the process whereby the representatives of a public agency and representatives of recognized employee organizations have the mutual obligation to meet and confer in order to exchange freely information, opinions and proposals to endeavor to reach agreement on conditions of employment."

The last-quoted definition is found in the Kansas statute and it is noteworthy that the law requires bargaining with an eye toward reaching an agreement. This clearly is at variance with the pure "meet and confer" model, which in theory does not require the employer to agree.

Other "meet and confer" statutes are even more explicit on this point. For example, the Montana statute makes it an unfair labor practice for a government employer to refuse to "meet, confer, or negotiate in good faith." The duty to "meet and confer in good faith" was proposed by the report of the Advisory Commission on Intergovernmental Relations published in March 1970. In its report, the Commission opted for a "modified meet and confer" approach; that is, one requiring meeting and conferring in "good faith." . . .

It is noteworthy that the ACIR recommendations, which have been followed by many of the states adopting "meet and confer" statutes, include the suggestion that the parties may be required to bargain in "good faith" to a point of impasse. Surely, if this is a part of the definition of "meet and confer" then the *bargaining process* is arguably not much different from what is seen in states which have followed the "collective negotiations" approach in dealing with public sector labor problems.

The marked distinction between the ACIR "modified meet and confer" approach, and the traditional "collective negotiations" approach, is the ACIR suggestion that the result of bargaining should be "a non-binding memorandum of understanding setting forth all agreed upon recommendations for submission to the jurisdiction's appropriate governing officials." This is essentially the approach taken by the California Meyers-Milias-Brown Act, which sets forth a modest scheme for local government collective bargaining.

But the required adoption of a *conditional agreement* at the conclusion of bargaining does not really distinguish the "modified meet and confer" states from some of the states which have followed the "collective negotiations" model. For example, under the New York Taylor Act it is provided that any labor agreement between a public employer and a union must include, "in type not smaller than the largest type used elsewhere in the agreement," the following clause:

"It is agreed . . . that any provision of this agreement requiring legislative action to permit its implementation by amendment of law or by providing the additional funds therefore, shall not become effective until the appropriate legislative body has given approval."

Thus, even in New York, which has enacted one of the most comprehensive "collective negotiations" statutes governing public sector labor relations, the end product of bargaining may be nothing more than a *conditional* agreement. . . .

. . . I am persuaded that there is no compelling evidence to demonstrate that the parties do not meet as "equals" under existing "meet and confer" bargaining statutes. It is true that, under the *pure* "meet and confer" model . . . the employee representative may be reduced to a role of "collective begger" rather than a collective bargainer. But most "meet and confer" states have adopted the *modified* ACIR design which substantially enhances the role of the employees' agent at the bargaining table. On this score then, it can be concluded that, excluding those few states which rely on outmoded notions of "sovereign authority," the *bargaining process* — as distinguished from the problem of the scope of permissible bargaining — is very similar under existing "meet and confer" and "collective negotiations" statutes. . . .

In conclusion, and in partial answer to the question posed by my speech topic, I would suggest to you that the term "meet and confer" is a misnomer in public sector labor relations. Excluding the two or three statutes, such as . . . the one in Missouri, I would argue that the actual differences between the "meet and confer" and "collective negotiations" approaches have been grossly overstated. This is so because less than a handful of states have adopted what I have called the *pure* "meet and confer" bargaining model. As a consequence, the bargaining process and the techniques used to seek to reach an agreement are very similar in both those states which have followed and rejected "meet and confer." I think that we sometimes see a greater sophistication at the bargaining table in the states where a comprehensive and comprehensible state statutory scheme has been enacted, but this sophistication is not a necessary by-product of having public sector bargaining governed by a "collective negotiations" versus a modified "meet and confer" statute. Indeed, in Illinois, which has *no* state statutory scheme to regulate public sector bargaining, many highly sophisticated bargaining relationships have nevertheless developed.

My prognostications:

(1) . . . I am inclined to think that the *pure* "meet and confer" approach to bargaining is obsolete and will pass with time. Labor leaders probably will not tolerate, for too much longer, any bargaining system which is founded on the worn-weary notion of sovereign-authority.

(2) "Meet and confer" will soon pass from the lexicon of labor relations terminology. To the extent that "meet and confer" suggests that the parties do not meet as "equals" at the bargaining table, it is a bad term; and to the extent that it suggests that there is a meaningful distinction between "meet and confer" and "collective negotiations," it is a misleading term. . . .

I think we can excuse the present chaotic state of affairs of labor relations in the public sector by reference to the statement once made by Justice Holmes that: "The life of the law has not been logic; it has been experience."

For those states which have yet to deal with the problem of public sector labor relations, and for those states still wallowing in obsolete notions of sovereign authority under the guise of "meet and confer," I would quote Justice Stewart's admonition in the recent *Boys Markets* case, to the effect that —

> "Wisdom too often never comes, and so one ought not to reject it merely because it comes late."

## NOTE

The interpretation and application of the Meyers-Milias-Brown Act is exhaustively explored in Grodin, *Public Employee Bargaining in California: The Meyers-Milias-Brown Act in the Courts,* 23 HASTINGS L.J. 719 (1972).

# 4. THE PRINCIPLE OF EXCLUSIVE REPRESENTATION

## LULLO v. FIRE FIGHTERS, LOCAL 1066

Supreme Court of New Jersey
55 N.J. 409, 262 A.2d 681 (1970)

FRANCIS, J. In this action plaintiffs Lullo and Wood, individually and as officers of the plaintiff Firemen's Mutual Benevolent Association of New Jersey, Branch No. 1, attacked the constitutionality of L. 1968, c. 303, known as "New Jersey Employer-Employee Relations Act." N.J.S.A. 34:13A-1 *et seq.* The challenge was two pronged. One was directed at section 7 (N.J.S.A. 34:13A-5.3) of the Act which provides that the representative duly elected by a majority of the public employees in an appropriate unit shall be *the exclusive representative* of all employees in the unit. The other challenged the portion of section 7 which authorizes such representative and the employer in the appropriate unit involved to engage in *collective negotiations* concerning the terms and conditions of their employment. It was alleged that in these two respects section 7 is repugnant to Article I, paragraph 19 of the *New Jersey Constitution* of 1947. The trial court sustained the Act, and this Court certified the ensuing appeal while it was awaiting hearing in the Appellate Division.

Since 1895 the Firemen's Mutual Benevolent Association (FMBA), Branch No. 1, has been an incorporated association of this State. Its membership has always been made up of Jersey City firemen who desired to join. It is not a labor organization in the usual sense and has never held itself out as a negotiating agent for all the firemen of the City. However, on a purely voluntary basis it has interceded for and spoken on behalf of its members with the proper City representatives in matters affecting salaries, working conditions and grievances.

After L. 1968, c. 303, became effective, the New Jersey Public Employment Relations Commission (PERC) which was created by the Act, acceded to a request of defendant International Association of Fire Fighters, Local 1066 (IAF), a labor organization, and ordered an election to determine if those firemen eligible to vote wished to be represented by IAF for purposes of collective negotiation with Jersey City. N.J.S.A. 34:13A-5.2, 5.3, 6. Notice of the time and place of the election and a sample ballot were given to the firemen. As stated in the ballot the question to be voted upon was:

> Do you desire to be represented for purposes of collective bargaining by International Association of Fire Fighters, Local 1066? . . .

Plaintiffs were notified of the election but declined to participate because of their view that L. 1968, c. 303 is unconstitutional. Instead they instituted this action in the Superior Court, Chancery Division, seeking a declaration of the statute's invalidity and a temporary and permanent injunction against holding the election. The trial judge declined a temporary restraint and directed that the election be held, the result not to be certified until disposition of the court proceeding. See N.J.S.A. 34:13A-11; PERC Rule 19:11-19(g). The election was held and 417 of the 430 eligible firemen voted; 399 voted for representation by IAF, 17 voted against such representation, and one vote was not counted. Thereafter the trial court heard the attack on the statute, and as already indicated sustained its constitutionality.

I

*The Exclusive Representation Issue*

The right of employees in private and public employment to organize and to deal with their employers was dealt with in general terms in Article I, paragraph 19 of the 1947 *Constitution.* It provides:

> Persons in private employment shall have the right to organize and bargain collectively. Persons in public employment shall have the right to organize, present to and make known to the State, or any of its political subdivisions or agencies, their grievances and proposals through representatives of their own choosing.

... In general language it grants and secures to employees in the private and public sectors certain basic rights. At the same time, it recognizes and clearly projects a difference as between private and public employees in the quality and substance of the rights thus elevated to constitutional stature. Obviously, as Delaware River & Bay Auth. v. International Org., etc., 45 N.J. 138, 145 (1965) suggests, employees in private employment were endowed in broad terms with the right to organize and bargain collectively. However, public employees were invested inviolably in significantly narrower terms with the right to organize, present and make known to their public employers their grievances and proposals through representatives of their own choosing. But it is important to note that the delegates made no effort to detail or to prescribe the nature or scope of the representation or the authority of the representative to act for the employees whether their employment was in the public or private sector. The decision as to whether there should be a single representative to speak exclusively for all the employees, or multiple representatives to speak for different groups of employees or whether an individual employee should have the right to represent himself in all dealings with his employer, or whether all three forms of representation should be authorized, was left to the Legislature.

This Court declared in Board of Ed., Borough of Union Beach v. N.J.E.A., 53 N.J. 29, 44-45 (1968) that the purpose of Article I, paragraph 19 was to secure the specified rights of employees in private and public employment against legislative erosion or denial. It reveals no intention to deprive the Legislature of the power to grant to public employees a further right designed to implement or effectuate those rights secured by Article I, paragraph 19, or to grant more expansive relevant rights which do not conflict with that article. *Id.,* at 45. ...

In 1966 the Legislature, noting that Article I, paragraph 19 of the *Constitution* "explicitly distinguishes between persons in private employment and persons in public employment with respect to the constitutional right to bargain collectively," created a commission to study the need for establishing an effective procedure for considering the grievances of public employees. L. 1966, c. 170. A number of other states have created similar study groups. See Smith, "State and Local Advisory Reports on Public Employment Labor Legislation: A Comparative Analysis," 67 Mich. L. Rev. 891 (1969). The New Jersey Commission Report [1] which was filed on January 9, 1968 asserted broadly that "the public interest requires that public employers and public employees be provided with an effective procedure for the mutual resolution of disputes involving terms and conditions of employment." It recommended "legislation

---

[1] Final Report to the Governor and the Legislature of the Public and School Employees' Grievance Procedure Study Commission, 1.

setting forth a procedure that is fully compatible with and complementary to existing Civil Service systems and present laws and regulations governing personnel matters in public employment at all governmental levels in New Jersey.". . .

Under the heading "Administrative Procedures," the Report contains a strong recommendation respecting a primary problem in the present case. It says:

> a. When a majority of employees in a given negotiating group or unit indicate by secret election a preference for a specific representative organization, no other organization should be designated, certified, or recognized for the purpose of collective negotiations. (Report, p. 2).

In a later portion of the Report setting forth the recommendations in greater detail, the following appears at the end of the above paragraph and as a continuation thereof:

> . . . but this should not preclude an employee's right to process grievances individually. (Report, p. 22, par. c).

On the subject of exclusive representation by a representative duly elected by public employees in an appropriate unit, the Commission observed:

> Multiplicity of organizations claiming or possessing representation rights for the same group or unit of employees has long been regarded as undesirable. Multiple representation of employees encourages rivalries among employee groups and severely handicaps private and public employers in the development of effective negotiations and stable relationships.

> Expert witnesses and representatives of interested employer and employee groups appearing before the Commission were almost unanimous in their opposition to multiple representation within any employee negotiating unit. . . . The New Jersey Department of Civil Service, in its presentation to the Commission, accepted this viewpoint and advocated restriction of multiple bargaining following the pattern of the federal executive order. . . . (Report, p. 15).

In preparing the article in 67 Michigan Law Review, supra, Professor Smith surveyed similar reports of special advisory groups of other states. In discussing them he said:

> It was generally agreed that public sector labor legislation should embrace the principle of exclusive recognition of the union or organization selected by the majority of employees in a defined bargaining unit. 67 Mich. L. Rev. at 897.

Chapter 303, L. 1968, was adopted in response to the New Jersey Commission Report and incorporated most of its recommendations. The controversy now before us centers around section 7 of Chapter 303. N.J.S.A. 34:13A-5.3. It provides among other things:

> Representatives designated or selected by public employees for the purposes of collective negotiation by the majority of the employees in a unit appropriate for such purposes or by the majority of the employees voting in an election conducted by the commission as authorized by this act *shall be the exclusive representatives for collective negotiation concerning the terms and conditions of employment of the employees in such unit.* Nothing herein shall be construed to prevent any official from meeting with an employee organization for the purpose of hearing the views and requests of its members in such unit so long as (a) the majority representative is informed of the meeting; (b) any changes or modifications in terms and conditions of employment are made only

through negotiation with the majority representative; and (c) a minority organization shall not present or process grievances. Nothing herein shall be construed to deny to any individual employee his rights under Civil Service laws or regulations. When no majority representative has been selected as the bargaining agent for the unit of which an individual employee is a part, he may present his own grievance either personally or through an appropriate representative or an organization of which he is a member and have such grievance adjusted.

A majority representative of public employees in an appropriate unit shall be entitled to act for and to negotiate agreements covering all employees in the unit and shall be responsible for representing the interests of all such employees without discrimination and without regard to employee organization membership. Proposed new rules or modifications of existing rules governing working conditions shall be negotiated with the majority representative before they are established. In addition, the majority representative and designated representatives of the public employer shall meet at reasonable times and negotiate in good faith with respect to grievances and terms and conditions of employment.

When an agreement is reached on the terms and conditions of employment, it shall be embodied in writing and signed by the authorized representatives of the public employer and the majority representative.

Public employers shall negotiate written policies setting forth grievance procedures by means of which their employees or representatives of employees may appeal the interpretation, application or violation of policies, agreements, and administrative decisions affecting them, provided that such grievance procedures shall be included in any agreement entered into between the public employer and the representative organization. Such grievance procedures may provide for binding arbitration as a means for resolving disputes. (Emphasis added.)

Plaintiffs allege that this section which constitutes IAF the exclusive representative of all the employees in the unit for collective bargaining negotiation concerning their terms and conditions of employment violates Article I, paragraph 19 of the *Constitution.* In support of the contention they point to the language of paragraph 19 which gives "persons" in public employment the right to organize, present to and make known to their public employers their grievances and proposals "through representatives of their own choosing." Then they seize upon the pluralistic significance of "persons" and urge that the language authorizes any "person" in public employment to present *his* grievances and proposals through a representative of his own choosing. Thus they say that each public employee has been vested with the basic right to present his proposals and grievances to the employer through his individually chosen representative, and that this right, being entrenched in the organic charter, is beyond the power of the Legislature to qualify or dilute. Consequently they claim that section 7 of the statute is invalid because it undertakes to place effectuation of this right exclusively in the hands of a representative elected by a majority of an individual's fellow employees in the designated unit, even though the individual did not vote with the majority or does not belong to the organization selected as the representative.

We cannot accept such a narrow view of the constitutional purpose. It seems obvious to us that the very general language of Article I, paragraph 19 was oriented toward collectivity. The purpose was to secure to employees collectively in the various employer divisions and agencies of government the right to get together — to organize — and to select representatives to present their (*i.e.,* all employees in all divisions and agencies) proposals and grievances. The use of the plural form — "representatives" — signifies an awareness that there would be many different organizations involved and that they would represent many different groups or units of employees in many separate divisions or agencies of government. It is not reasonable to say that the delegates to the Constitutional Convention, many of whom were described as well informed in the field of labor relations, intended the broad language they employed in paragraph 19 to prevent the Legislature from establishing a commonly known means of giving potency and practical effect to the guaranteed right to organize. Delaware River & Bay Auth. v. International Org., etc., supra, 45 N.J., at 144. Surely it could not have been the purpose of such knowledgeable men to give constitutional sanction to the scene of each employee or group of employees in a public agency presenting proposals and grievances through a substantial number of different representatives. Such delegates would have known that "multiplicity of organizations claiming or possessing representation rights for the same group or unit of employees has long been regarded as undesirable. Multiple representation of employees encourages rivalries among employee groups and severely handicaps private and public employers in the development of effective negotiations and stable relationships." Report, supra, at 15.

It cannot be overlooked that the delegates to the Convention realized that the particular aspect of labor relations in the public employment sector was being drawn into a New Jersey Constitution for the first time. They were in virgin territory and although they wished to ensconce certain basic guarantees in the charter, obviously they felt the need to phrase them in most general terms and leave to legislative judgment their implementation and augmentation, and particularly the decision as to whether there should be a single representative for all employees, or multiple representation or individual self-representation.

When Chapter 303, L. 1968, was under consideration by the Legislature, experience on a vast scale in the private employment sector on the national scene had demonstrated that just and harmonious labor relations for both employer and employee are best achieved when the employees' cause is in the hands of an exclusive representative freely and fairly chosen by a majority of the employees in an appropriate unit.

It seems hardly necessary to explain this principle of majority representation in light of the common acceptance of that principle as an integral part of our democratic form of government. Moreover, that principle of representation was adopted by the National War Labor Board during World War II and likewise was embodied in the Railway Labor Act. See 2 *Teller, Labor Disputes and Collective Bargaining,* § 243, p. 688 (1940). As far back as 1903 the pertinency of the principle in industrial relations was spoken of as beyond dispute. In Wabash Railroad v. Hannahan, 121 F. 563, 571 (E.D. Mo. 1903) the court said:

> The will of the individual must consent to yield to the will of the majority, or no organization either of society into government, capital into combination, or labor into coalition can ever be effected. The individual must yield in order that the many may receive a greater benefit. The right of labor to organize for lawful purposes and by organic agreement to subject the individual members to rules, regulations, and conduct prescribed by the majority is no longer an open question in the jurisprudence of this country.

In 1935 when the National Labor Relations Act was adopted to regulate employer-employee relations in the private employment sector, section 7 thereof, 29 U.S.C.A. § 157, provided:

> Employees shall have the right to self-organization, to form, join, or assist labor organizations, to bargain collectively through representatives of their own choosing. . . .

In the 35-year history of the Act the phrase "representatives of their own choosing" has become a phrase of art, designed to convey the intention that the employees' selection of a bargaining representative should be an uncoerced and free choice. . . . It has never been deemed to be inconsistent with the grant of exclusive representation in section 9(a), 29 U.S.C.A. § 159(a), which says:

> Representatives designated or selected for the purpose of collective bargaining by the majority of the employees in a unit appropriate for such purposes, shall be the exclusive representatives of all the employees in such unit. . . . (Emphasis added.)

This meaning of the phrase and the absence of any indication or ruling by the courts that it was inconsistent with the existence of the exclusive representation concept in section 9(a) obviously did not escape the attention of the framers of the 1947 *New Jersey Constitution*. Thus in using the phrase in paragraph 19 of Article I, it is reasonable to assume that their intention was to assure that the choice of a representative in the public sector would be uncoerced and free. Knowing, as they must have, that the language "representatives of their own choosing" had always been considered consistent with exclusive representation in the federal statutory scheme, they could not have intended, as plaintiffs argue here, to exclude such representation in the future simply by using the words "representatives of their own choosing" in the *Constitution*.

When we pass on to an examination of L. 1968, c. 303, attention is drawn immediately to the almost identical language of its section 7 and that of section 9(a) supra, of the Labor Management Relations Act. Since, as we have noted above, there is no conflict between section 7 and 9(a) (29 U.S.C.A. § 157, 159(a)) of the federal statute it would seem to follow logically that Article I, paragraph 19 of the *Constitution* and section 7 of our 1968 Act are likewise harmonious and may stand together.

A wide-ranging consideration of the problem makes it particularly noteworthy that both section 9(a) of the federal act and our section 7 speak of "representatives designated or selected . . . by the majority of the employees in a unit appropriate for such purposes"; also that both say that representatives "shall be the exclusive representatives" of all the employees in the appropriate unit. The parallelism is not merely coincidental. It is obvious from the Report that the New Jersey Study Commission was conscious of the federal legislation, its mandate for exclusive recognition of the bargaining representative chosen by a majority of the employees involved, the need for such a mandate, the accepted consistency between its sections 7 and 9(a), 29 U.S.C.A. §§ 157, 159(a), and the satisfactory experience resulting from its application on the national scene in the private employment sector. Manifestly such knowledge was responsible for the Commission's disparagement of multiple representation of employees in the appropriate unit and its recommendations of exclusivity for the representative freely and fairly chosen by the majority of such employees. See Smith, supra, 67 Mich. L. Rev., at 897-98, 901. Adoption by the Legislature of the federal act's language establishing the exclusive representation of the elected representative demonstrates acceptance of the Commission's recommendation in that regard.

Further, for purposes of judicial interpretation in a context such as is presented to us here, such legislative approval brings to the fore the well known tenet of statutory construction that the experience and the adjudications under the copied act were probably accepted as an intended guide for the administration of the later act. See 2 *Sutherland, Statutory Construction* (3d ed. 1943) § 5209, p. 551....

The labor union movement was born of the realization that a single employee had no substantial economic strength. He had little leverage beyond the sale of his own efforts to aid him in obtaining fair wages, hours of work and working conditions.... Realization by individual employees that their reasonable expectations were common to their fellow workers turned them toward organization to strengthen and further that community of interest. The concept that in union there is strength and a means of achieving an equitable balance of bargaining power with employers flourished in this country. Ultimately it found legislative acceptance of monumental proportions in the 1935 National Labor Relations Act and its subsequent revisions. It is undisputed the major purpose of Congress in enacting that legislation was to bring about such a balance in private employment.

However, the major aim could not be accomplished if numerous individual employees wished to represent themselves or groups of employees chose different unions or organizations for the purpose. Such absence of solidarity and diffusion of collective strength would promote rivalries, would serve disparate rather than uniform overall objectives, and in many situations would frustrate the employees' community interests. See *Chamberlain, Labor* 179 (1958). Obviously parity of bargaining power between employers and employees could not be reached in such a framework. So the democratic principle of majority control was introduced on the national scene, and the representative freely chosen by a majority of the employees in an appropriate unit to represent their collective interests in bargaining with the employer was given the exclusive right to do so. 29 U.S.C.A. § 159(a). Thus this policy was built on the premise that by pooling their economic strength and acting through a single representative freely chosen by the majority, the employees in such a unit achieve the most effective means of bargaining with an employer respecting conditions of employment. N.L.R.B. v. Allis-Chalmers Mfg. Co., 388 U.S. 175, 87 S. Ct. 2001, 18 L. Ed. 2d 1123 (1967); Medo Photo Supply Corp. v. N.L.R.B., 321 U.S. 678, 684, 64 S. Ct. 830, 88 L. Ed. 1007, 1011 (1944); J.I. Case Co. v. N.L.R.B., 321 U.S. 332, 338, 64 S. Ct. 576, 88 L. Ed. 762, 768 (1944). Experience in the private employment sector has established that investment of the bargaining representative of the majority with the exclusive right to represent all the employees in the unit is a sound and salutary prerequisite to effective bargaining. Beyond doubt such exclusivity — the majority rule concept — is now at the core of our national labor policy. N.L.R.B. v. Allis-Chalmers Mfg. Co., supra, 388 U.S. at 180, 87 S. Ct. 2001.

Application of the majority rule concept strengthens the right of the individual employee to obtain fair and equitable terms of employment. It brings the collective strength of all the employees in the unit to the negotiating table and thus enhances the chances of effectuating their community purposes and serving the welfare of the group. The employee who votes against the representative chosen by the majority or who exercises his privilege not to join the organization of the representative suffers no constitutional infringement of his basic freedom of contract right because of the exclusivity principle. Freedom of contract is a qualified, and not an absolute right. There is no absolute freedom to do as one wills or to contract as one chooses.

It follows from what has been said that in the private employment sector the individual employee's right to organize and to bargain collectively has been implemented and made truly meaningful by the legislative mandate for exclusive representation. The exclusivity concept carries with it an equally heavy responsibility toward dissident employees in the unit as for employee-members of the representative organization. Although the representative has the sole right to negotiate and consummate a contract respecting the terms and conditions of employment and the processing of grievances for all employees in the unit, the right to do so must always be exercised with complete good faith, with honesty of purpose and without unfair discrimination against a dissident employee or group of employees. This is true not only in the negotiating of the employer-employee agreement but in its administration as well. N.L.R.B. v. Allis-Chalmers Mfg. Co., supra, 388 U.S. at 180-181, 87 S. Ct. 2001; Vaca v. Sipes, 386 U.S. 171, 177, 87 S. Ct. 903, 17 L. Ed. 2d 842 (1967). When the collective bargaining agreement has been made, it becomes the code of the plant and in policing it the union cannot trample upon the rights of a non-member minority. All must be treated fairly and evenly, particularly with respect to employment of procedures established therein to adjust and settle individual grievances. Vaca v. Sipes, supra; Donnelly v. United Fruit Co., 40 N.J. 61, 76, 80 (1963); Wellington, "Union Democracy and Fair Representation: Federal Responsibility in a Federal System," 67 Yale L.J. 1327 (1958) . . . .

Undoubtedly the delegates to the 1947 Constitutional Convention were aware of the exclusivity doctrine which was at the heart of the national employer-employee labor relations policy in the private employment sector. The broad general language they used in drafting Article I, paragraph 19, particularly the portion referring to public employment reveals no express or implied intention to control or regulate, approve or disapprove the rule of majority representation. The Commission plainly was familiar with it and its successful operation as a means of stabilizing industrial relations in the private sector. For that reason the Report opposed multiple representation of public employees for purposes of negotiating with their employer. It is significant that the Legislature agreed and in adopting section 7 of L. 1968, c. 303, used almost the identical language of the federal act, 29 U.S.C.A. § 159(a) in mandating that the representative selected by the majority of the employees in an appropriate unit for purposes of collective negotiation shall be the exclusive representative of all the employees for that purpose.

The legislative aim in writing section 7 was to aid, not to hinder, public employees in their relationship with their employers. The purpose was to discourage rivalries among individual employees and employee groups and to avoid the diffusion of negotiating strength which results from multiple representation. On the positive side the Legislature was seeking through the medium of the collective agreement to supersede separate agreements with employees and to substitute a single compact with terms which reflect the strength, negotiating power and welfare of the group. The benefits and advantages of the collective agreement are then open to every employee in the unit whether or not he is a member of the representative organization chosen by the majority of his fellow workers. He can be certain also that in negotiating with the employer the representative is obliged to be conscious of the statutory obligation to serve and protect the interests of all the employees, majority and minority, equally and without hostility or discrimination. And he can rest secure in the knowledge that so long as the union or other organization assumes to act as the statutory representative, it cannot lawfully refuse to perform or neglect to perform fully and in complete good faith the duty, which is inseparable from the power of exclusive representation, to represent the entire membership of the employees in the unit. The obligations of the exclusive representative as they have been described herein evolved largely from experience in administering section 9(a) of the National Labor Relations Act, 29 U.S.C.A. § 159(a). The absence of any express specifications of the obligations by Congress made it necessary for the courts to define them. The New Jersey Legislature accepted the judicial exposition of the exclusive representative's duty to all employees in the appropriate unit, and made it part of L. 1968, c. 303, N.J.S.A. 34:13A-5.3. . . .

The above considerations lead us to the conviction that the creation in section 7 of an exclusive representative under the conditions stated therein is not repugnant to Article I, paragraph 19 of the *Constitution.* Fairly construed in light of the history of employer-employee relations, the section enhances, implements and effectuates the right secured public employees to organize, present and to make known to their public employers their grievances and proposals through representatives of their own choosing. . . .

## NOTES

1. In Dade County Classroom Teachers Ass'n Inc. v. Ryan, 225 So. 2d 903 (Fla. 1969), the Florida Supreme Court held that a Florida constitutional provision which provides that "[t]he right of employees, by and through a labor organization, to bargain collectively shall not be denied or abridged" and a statute which substantially restated the constitutional provision were applicable to public employees. The court held that the statute precludes a labor organization from acting as the sole bargaining agent for all the employees in a given unit, noting that "a labor organization can represent all those [employees] who are members of the organization or who freely and expressly give their consent for that organization to act as their collective bargaining agent." Accordingly, a collective bargaining agreement, as well as the grievance procedure set forth therein, was held to apply only to those teachers who specifically consented to be bound by it. Subsequently, the Florida Legislature enacted a comprehensive public sector collective bargaining law that specifically provides for exclusive representation by a sole collective bargaining representative. FLA. STAT. § 447.201 *et seq.* (1977). *See also,* Note 2, p. 258, *supra.*

2. Obviously, an exclusive bargaining representative is entitled to certain rights and privileges not granted to minority organizations. Yet, it may be claimed that the grant of some privileges to a majority union results in an unfair discrimination against minority unions and an effective denial of freedom of association to employees. Should this be a matter of concern for a state legislature? Since the principles of majority rule and exclusive representation are well-established in the private sector, are there any legitimate reasons for rejecting these principles in the public sector? *See generally* Comment, *The Privilege of Exclusive Recognition and Minority Union Rights in Public Employment,* 55 CORNELL L. REV. 1004 (1970); pp. 101-03, *supra.*

## B. SCOPE OF BARGAINING

## 1. PUBLIC POLICY CONSIDERATIONS

### H. WELLINGTON AND R. WINTER, THE UNIONS AND THE CITIES 21-30 (1971)†

*The Public Sector Model: Nonmonetary Issues*

---

† Reprinted by permission. Copyright © 1971 by The Brookings Institution, Washington, D.C.

In the private sector, unions have pushed to expand the scope of bargaining in response to the desires of their members for a variety of new benefits (pension rights, supplementary unemployment payments, merit increases). These benefits generally impose a monetary cost on the employer. And because employers are restrained by the market, an expanded bargaining agenda means that, if a union negotiates an agreement over more subjects, it generally trades off more of less for less of more.

From the consumer's point of view this in turn means that the price of the product he purchases is not significantly related to the scope of bargaining. And since unions rarely bargain about the nature of the product produced, the consumer can be relatively indifferent as to how many or how few subjects are covered in any collective agreement. Nor need the consumer be concerned about union demands that would not impose a financial cost on the employer, for example, the design of a grievance procedure. While such demands are not subject to the same kind of trade-off as are financial demands, they are unlikely, if granted, to have any impact on the consumer. Their effect is on the quality of life of the parties to the agreement.

In the public sector the cluster of problems that surround the scope of bargaining are much more troublesome than they are in the private sector. The problems have several dimensions.

First, the trade-off between subjects of bargaining in the public sector is less of a protection to the consumer (public) than it is in the private. Where political leaders view the costs of union demands as essentially budgetary, a trade-off can occur. Thus, a demand for higher teacher salaries and a demand for reduced class size may be treated as part of one package. But where a demand, although it has a budgetary effect, is viewed as involving essentially political costs, trade-offs are more difficult. Our paradigmatic mayor, for example, may be under great pressure to make a large monetary settlement with a teachers' union whether or not it is joined to demands for special training programs for disadvantaged children. Interest groups tend to exert pressure against union demands only when they are directly affected. Otherwise, they are apt to join that large constituency (the general public) that wants to avoid labor trouble. Trade-offs can occur only when several demands are resisted by roughly the same groups. Thus, pure budgetary demands can be traded off when they are opposed by taxpayers. But when the identity of the resisting group changes with each demand, political leaders may find it expedient to strike a balance on each issue individually, rather than as part of a total package, by measuring the political power of each interest group involved against the political power of the constituency pressing for labor peace. To put it another way, as important as financial factors are to a mayor, political factors may be even more important. The market allows the businessman no such discretionary choice.

Where a union demand — such as increasing the disciplinary power of teachers — does not have budgetary consequences, some trade-offs may occur. Granting the demand will impose a political cost on the mayor because it may anger another interest group. But because the resisting group may change with each issue, each issue is apt to be treated individually and not as a part of a total package. And this may not protect the public. Differing from the private sector, nonmonetary demands of public sector unions do have effects that go beyond the parties to the agreement. All of us have a stake in how school children are disciplined. Expansion of the subjects of bargaining in the public sector, therefore, may increase the total quantum of union power in the political process.

Second, public employees do not generally produce a product. They perform a service. The way in which a service is performed may become a subject of bargaining. As a result, the nature of that service may be changed. Some of these services — police protection, teaching, health care — involve questions that are politically, socially, or ideologically sensitive. In part this is because government is involved and alternatives to governmentally provided services are relatively dear. In part, government is involved because of society's perception about the nature of the service and society's need for it. This suggests that decisions affecting the nature of a governmentally provided service are much more likely to be challenged and are more urgent than generally is the case with services that are offered privately.

Third, some of the services government provides are performed by professionals — teachers, social workers, and so forth — who are keenly interested in the underlying philosophy that informs their work. To them, theirs is not merely a job to be done for a salary. They may be educators or other "change agents" of society. And this may mean that these employees are concerned with more than incrementally altering a governmental service or its method of delivery. They may be advocates of bold departures that will radically transform the service itself.

The issue is not a threshold one of whether professional public employees should participate in decisions about the nature of the services they provide. Any properly run governmental agency should be interested in, and heavily reliant upon, the judgment of its professional staff. The issue rather is the method of that participation.

Conclusions about this issue as well as the larger issue of a full transplant of collective bargaining to the public sector may be facilitated by addressing some aspects of the governmental decision-making process — particularly at the municipal level — and the impact of collective bargaining on that process.

### Public Employee Unions and the Political Process

Although the market does not discipline the union in the public sector to the extent that it does in the private, the municipal employment paradigm, nevertheless, would seem to be consistent with what Robert A. Dahl has called the " 'normal' American political process," which is "one in which there is a high probability that an active and legitimate group in the population can make itself heard effectively at some crucial stage in the process of decision," for the union may be seen as little more than an "active and legitimate group in the population." With elections in the background to perform, as Mr. Dahl notes, "the critical role . . . in maximizing political equality and popular sovereignty," all seems well, at least theoretically, with collective bargaining and public employment.

But there is trouble even in the house of theory if collective bargaining in the public sector means what it does in the private. The trouble is that if unions are able to withhold labor — to strike — as well as to employ the usual methods of political pressure, they may possess a disproportionate share of effective power in the process of decision. Collective bargaining would then be so effective a pressure as to skew the results of the " 'normal' American political process."

One should straightway make plain that the strike issue is not simply the importance of public services as contrasted with services or products produced in the private sector. This is only part of the issue, and in the past the partial truth has beclouded analysis. The services performed by a private transit authority are neither less nor more important to the public than those that would be performed if the transit authority were owned by a municipality. A railroad or a dock strike may be more damaging to a community than "job action" by police. This is not to say that governmental services are not important. They are, both because the demand for them is inelastic and because their disruption may seriously injure a city's economy and occasionally impair the physical welfare of its citizens. Nevertheless, the importance of governmental services is only a necessary part of, rather than a complete answer to, the question: Why be more concerned about strikes in public employment than in private?

The answer to the question is simply that, because strikes in public employment disrupt important services, a large part of a mayor's political constituency will, in many cases, press for a quick end to the strike with little concern for the cost of settlement. This is particularly so where the cost of settlement is borne by a different and larger political constituency, the citizens of the state or nation. Since interest groups other than public employees, with conflicting claims on municipal government, do not, as a general proposition, have anything approaching the effectiveness of the strike — or at least cannot maintain that relative degree of power over the long run — they may be put at a significant competitive disadvantage in the political process.

The private sector strike is designed to exert economic pressure on the employer by depriving him of revenues. The public employee strike is fundamentally different: its sole purpose is to exert political pressure on municipal officials. They are deprived, not of revenues but of the political support of those who are inconvenienced by a disruption of municipal services. But precisely because the private strike is an economic weapon, it is disciplined by the market and the benefit/unemployment trade-off that imposes. And because the public employee strike is a political weapon, it is subject only to the restraints imposed by the political process and they are on the whole less limiting and less disciplinary than those of the market. If this is the case, it must be said that the political process will be radically altered by wholesale importation of the strike weapon. And because of the deceptive simplicity of the analogy to collective bargaining in the private sector, the alteration may take place without anyone realizing what has happened.

Nor is it an answer that, in some municipalities, interest groups other than unions now have a disproportionate share of political power. This is inescapably true, and we do not condone that situation. Indeed, we would be among the first to advocate reform. However, reform cannot be accomplished by giving another interest group disproportionate power, for the losers would be the weakest groups in the community. In most municipalities, the weakest groups are composed of citizens who many believe are most in need of more power.

Therefore, while the purpose and effect of strikes by public employees may seem in the beginning designed merely to establish collective bargaining or to "catch up" with wages and fringe benefits in the private sector, in the long run strikes may become too effective a means for redistributing income; so effective, indeed, that one might see them as an institutionalized means of obtaining and maintaining a subsidy for union members.

As is often the case when one generalizes, this picture may be considered overdrawn. In order to refine analysis, it will be helpful to distinguish between strikes that occur over monetary issues and strikes involving nonmonetary issues. The generalized picture sketched above is mainly concerned with the former. Because there is usually no substitute for governmental services, the citizen-consumer faced with a strike of teachers, or garbage men, or social workers is likely to be seriously inconvenienced. This in turn places enormous pressure on the mayor, who is apt to find it difficult to look to the long-run balance sheet of the municipality. Most citizens are directly affected by a strike of sanitation workers. Few, however, can decipher a municipal budget or trace the relationship between today's labor settlement and next year's increase in the mill rate. Thus, in the typical case the impact of a settlement is less visible — or can more often be concealed — than the impact of a disruption of services. Moreover, the cost of settlement may fall upon a constituency much larger — the whole state or nation — than that represented by the mayor. And revenue sharing schemes that involve unrestricted funds may further lessen public resistance to generous settlements. It follows that the mayor usually will look to the electorate that is clamoring for a settlement, and in these circumstances the union's fear of a long strike, a major check on its power in the private sector, is not a consideration.[1] In the face of all of these factors other interest groups with priorities different from the union's are apt to be much less successful in their pursuit of scarce tax dollars than is the union with power to withhold services.[2]

With respect to strikes over some nonmonetary issues — decentralization of the governance of schools might be an example — the intensity of concern on the part of well-organized interest groups opposed to the union's position would support the mayor in his resistance to union demands. But even here, if the union rank and file back their leadership, pressures for settlement from the general public, which may be largely indifferent as to the underlying issue, might in time become irresistible.[3]

The strike and its threat, moreover, exacerbate the problems associated with the scope of bargaining in public employment. This seems clear if one attends in slightly more detail to techniques of municipal decision making.

Few students of our cities would object to Herbert Kaufman's observation that:

> Decisions of the municipal government emanate from no single source, but from many centers; conflicts and clashes are referred to no single authority, but are settled at many levels and at many points in the system: no single group can guarantee the success of any proposal it supports, the defeat of every idea it objects to. Not even the central governmental organs of the city — the Mayor, the Board of Estimate, the Council — individually or in combination, even approach mastery in this sense.

> Each separate decision center consists of a cluster of interested contestants, with a "core group" in the middle, invested by the rules with the formal

---

[1] Contrast the situation in the private sector: ". . . management cannot normally win the short strike. Management can only win the long strike. Also management frequently tends, in fact, to win the long strike. As a strike lengthens, it commonly bears more heavily on the union and the employees than on management. Strike relief is no substitute for a job. Even regular strike benefits, which few unions can afford, and which usually exhaust the union treasury quite rapidly (with some exceptions), are no substitute for a job." E. Livernash, *"The Relation of Power to the Structure and Process of Collective Bargaining,"* 6 JOURNAL OF LAW & ECONOMICS 10, 15 (October 1963).

[2] A vivid example was provided by an experience in New Jersey. After a twelve-hour strike by Newark firefighters on July 11, 1969, state urban aid funds, originally authorized for helping the poor, were diverted to salary increases for firemen and police. See *New York Times,* Aug. 7, 1969, p. 25. Moreover, government decision makers other than the mayor (for example, the governor) may have interests different from those of the mayor, interests that manifest themselves in pressures for settlement.

[3] Consider also the effect of such strikes on the fabric of society. See, for example, M. MAYER, THE TEACHER STRIKE: NEW YORK, 1968 (Harper and Row, 1969).

authority to legitimize decisions (that is to promulgate them in binding form) and a constellation of related "satellite groups" seeking to influence the authoritative issuances of the core group.

Nor would many disagree with Nelson W. Polsby when, in discussing community decision making that is concerned with an alternative to a "current state of affairs," he argues that the alternative "must be politically palatable and relatively easy to accomplish; otherwise great amounts of influence have to be brought to bear with great skill and efficiency in order to secure its adoption."

It seems probable that such potential subjects of bargaining as school decentralization and a civilian police review board are, where they do not exist, alternatives to the "current state of affairs," which are not "politically palatable and relatively easy to accomplish." If a teachers' union or a police union were to bargain with the municipal employer over these questions, and were able to use the strike to insist that the proposals not be adopted, how much "skill and efficiency" on the part of the proposals' advocates would be necessary to effect a change? And, to put the shoe on the other foot, if a teachers' union were to insist through collective bargaining (with the strike or its threat) upon major changes in school curriculum, would not that union have to be considerably less skillful and efficient in the normal political process than other advocates of community change? The point is that with respect to some subjects, collective bargaining may be too powerful a lever on municipal decision making, too effective a technique for changing or preventing the change of one small but important part of the "current state of affairs."

Unfortunately, in this area the problem is not merely the strike threat and the strike. In a system where impasse procedures involving third parties are established in order to reduce work stoppages — and this is common in those states that have passed public employment bargaining statutes — third party intervention must be partly responsive to union demands. If the scope of bargaining is open-ended, the neutral party, to be effective, will have to work out accommodations that inevitably advance some of the union's claims some of the time. And the neutral, with his eyes fixed on achieving a settlement, can hardly be concerned with balancing all the items on the community agenda or reflecting the interests of all relevant groups.

### The Theory Summarized

Collective bargaining in public employment, then, seems distinguishable from that in the private sector. To begin with, it imposes on society more than a potential misallocation of resources through restrictions on economic output, the principal cost imposed by private-sector unions. Collective bargaining by public employees and the political process cannot be separated. The costs of such bargaining, therefore, cannot be fully measured without taking into account the impact on the allocation of political power in the typical municipality. If one assumes, as here, that municipal political processes should be structured to ensure "a high probability that an active and legitimate group in the population can make itself heard effectively at some crucial stage in the process of decision," then the issue is how powerful unions will be in the typical municipal political process if a full transplant of collective bargaining is carried out.

The conclusion is that such a transplant would, in many cases, institutionalize the power of public employee unions in a way that would leave competing groups in the political process at a permanent and substantial disadvantage.

## NOTES

1. The Advisory Commission on Intergovernmental Relations recommended that certain "management rights" be removed from the scope of bargaining. The Commission stated:

> Commission believes statutory description of management rights is necessary if well defined parameters to discussions are to be established. In a democratic political system, dealings between public employers and public employee organizations — whether they are called negotiations or discussions — must necessarily be limited by legislatively determined policies and goals. This may involve merely a restatement of basic management prerogatives and civil service precepts. Listing such rights in law eliminates many of the headaches of administrative elaboration and some of the cross pressures generated by ambiguities. Wages, hours, and other terms and conditions of employment, however, are left for the conference table. Hence, the framework for a meaningful dialogue remains intact. ADVISORY COMMISSION ON INTERGOVERNMENTAL RELATIONS, LABOR-MANAGEMENT POLICIES FOR STATE AND LOCAL GOVERNMENT 102-03 (1969).

The Committee on Economic Development similarly recommended that "[i]n enacting or revising public-sector collective bargaining legislation, states should identify the topics subject to bargaining and should also stipulate those management prerogatives not subject to bargaining." COMMITTEE ON ECONOMIC DEVELOPMENT, IMPROVING MANAGEMENT OF THE PUBLIC WORK FORCE 76-77 (1978).

On the other hand, the California Assembly Advisory Council chaired by Benjamin Aaron stated that it did "not see any compelling distinction between the public and private sector that would justify the inclusion of management-rights clauses in public employee relations statutes." FINAL REPORT OF THE ASSEMBLY ADVISORY COUNCIL ON PUBLIC EMPLOYEE RELATIONS 139 (Cal. 1973).

2. Should the determination of whether public employees are allowed to strike have any bearing on the scope of bargaining? Bok and Dunlop answered affirmatively:

> [T]he scope of bargaining will be influenced by the procedures adopted to resolve impasses in negotiations. If public employees are permitted to strike, the range of bargainable topics presumably should be closely confined. The exercise of economic pressure through disruption of public services is too haphazard a way of deciding significant issues affecting the public, such as institution of a police review board, decentralization of administrative services, and initiation or discontinuation of a specific government facility. This is especially true in the public sector, where decisions are much less restricted by competition and related market pressures. If disputes are settled by the more reasoned process of fact finding or arbitration, on the other hand, the scope of negotiation may be somewhat broader, although there will still be many important matters excluded from bargaining on the ground either that they should be within the province of management or that they seem more suited to resolution through the political process. Finally, a system that does not provide for strikes or arbitration, but reserves final power in a legislative body to settle bargaining disputes, can appropriately entrust a broad range of subjects to the bargaining process. D. BOK & J. DUNLOP, LABOR AND THE AMERICAN COMMUNITY 327 (1970).

## WOLLETT, THE BARGAINING PROCESS IN THE PUBLIC SECTOR: WHAT IS BARGAINABLE?, 51 Ore. L. Rev. 177, 177-82 (1971)†

Bargainability is a subject which seems to have a peculiar fascination for the National Labor Relations Board, and for lawyers, law professors, law students, directors of industrial relations, union representatives, and other persons in the labor relations business. A vast body of jurisprudence dealing with what the

---

† Reprinted by permission. Copyright © 1971 by University of Oregon.

parties *must* bargain about, what they *may* bargain about, and what they *cannot* bargain about has developed in the last 30 years.

Predictably, as collective bargaining has come to public employment, the same concern has been demonstrated. For example, Professors Wellington and Winter have recently argued that collective bargaining is too powerful a lever on governmental decision-making and too effective a technique for changing or maintaining public policies to allow it to run unchecked. Therefore, the subject matter which is negotiable should be more sharply circumscribed in the public sector than in the private sector.

My thesis is that the vast literature concerning the scope of bargaining is much ado about nothing and that the preoccupation with this subject is mischievous as well as mistaken. Many practitioners will regard this as a glossing over of a fundamental issue, as an oversimplification, and as a blithe ignoring of vital matters.

The case for my thesis lies in the attitude which one brings to the bargaining table. If the negotiator conceives his function to be one of establishing immutable principles, winning points and outscoring the adversary, massaging his client's ego, or building a reputation as a protagonist of ordered government and managerial sovereignty, the issue of what is bargainable is fertile ground. If, on the other hand, he approaches the table in a spirit of meeting problems rather than avoiding them, and of trying to find ways to reach agreement rather than identifying obstacles which make a negotiated settlement impossible, I submit that the question of scope of bargaining becomes of little significance.

During my eight years of law practice in New York City, exclusively on the management side in the private sector, I cannot recall a single instance when my colleagues and I refused, on behalf of our client, to bargain about *anything* in the sense of refusing to discuss it on its merits. If we perceived that the proposal reflected a problem of genuine concern to the employees, we were willing to talk about it. In focusing on the facts, it often turned out that the problem was more fanciful than real, or that it could be more appropriately handled outside the context of periodic crisis bargaining, that it made no sense from either party's point of view to deal with it as a fixed provision of a collective agreement, that it could be dealt with without invading interests in respect to which management felt it must retain the power to act unilaterally, or that it could be traded off. In my experience, this approach to scope of bargaining questions is both realistic and constructive. If one is willing to be imaginative in dealing with a proposal and is motivated by a desire to reach a negotiated settlement, an acceptable accommodation can generally be reached. If one is unwilling to consider new proposals, conflict is a certainty and exacerbation of the dispute a likelihood.

Although some union proposals represent institutional imperatives, most of them (in the public sector as well as in the private sector) are manifestations of the ambitions, fears, and frustrations of the employees represented. For purposes of this discussion, union proposals may be categorized into three groups. The first group contains those proposals which are psychological and political. These wash out in the bargaining process not because they are nonnegotiable but because they are frivolous, and for management to react to them by asserting that they invade prerogatives or sovereignty would be gratuitous and counter-productive. The second group includes those proposals which arguably intrude into policy matters usually thought to be within the sole control of management, which, while seriously made, are subject to trade-offs for improvements in wages, hours, and working conditions.[4] The third group

---

[4] This subject is, of course, academic unless the aggressive party, usually the union, has enough bargaining power to compel trade-offs.

consists of proposals which arguably intrude into managerial prerogatives or governmental sovereignty, which are seriously made and which are not readily tradable. The proposals in the last category do present problems, but they are not usually insoluble if they are dealt with on their merits rather than avoided on conceptualistic grounds.

The fourth set of negotiations between the New York City School Board and the United Federation of Teachers provides an excellent example of how problems encompassed in the third category above can be resolved. The fourth set of negotiations involved in part a proposal by the union that the collective bargaining agreement provide for the removal of disruptive children from regular classrooms. The parties had great difficulty with this issue because it involved educational policy as well as conditions of work, but the result of their negotiations was an acceptable compromise which preserved management's basic concern by agreeing that the procedures would be embodied in a "Special Circular" of the School Board which would be *appended to,* but would not be *a part of,* the collective bargaining agreement.

The Wellington-Winter thesis is based on two assumptions: (1) that public employee unions aspire to take over the responsibility for the management of governmental enterprises, and (2) that they have the power to do so. Both assumptions are, in my judgment, unsound. The scope of bargaining is partly a function of relative bargaining power, and most employee organizations in the public sector lack the power to force bargaining (or to force agreement) over such matters as operational efficiency, educational policy, and other matters which relate to the so-called "mission" of the enterprise.

Most public employee unions, even those which are professional in nature, do not think of collective bargaining primarily as a vehicle for social change. They do not have ambitions to take over the responsibility for running the agency. Specific aspirations will vary, of course, according to the skills and traditions of the occupational group involved. For example, teachers as a group tend to be interested in social change; and some agreements resulting from teacher-school board bargaining have worked changes in educational programming. But it is not true, at least in my experience, that teachers use collective bargaining primarily as an instrumentality for promoting social change. Public employees, including those whose responsibilities and skills are professional or quasi-professional, think of collective bargaining primarily as a vehicle for protecting and advancing their interests as an employed occupational group.

The key word is "interests." If classes are large, teachers will express their concern at the bargaining table because the size of the class creates problems affecting their working conditions. The same is true of disruptive children and student disciplinary problems. If school facilities are inadequate or poorly designed, teachers will manifest their concerns at the bargaining table, not because they want to take over the schools, but because they are frustrated by their working milieu.

It is fashionable to argue that teachers must be held "accountable" for what students can or cannot do, what they learn or do not learn. The criteria for accountability and how these criteria apply are not clear, but student performance on achievement tests appears to be a major factor. Presumably, the teacher will be rewarded with merit salary increases or penalized with decreases or perhaps dismissal once the system of academic due process (i.e., tenure) has been "decimated." Given this threatening circumstance, one can expect teachers to have an expansive view of their occupational interests. At the bargaining table, they can be expected to demand authority over those areas for which they are held accountable. If they are to be held accountable for the behavior of their colleagues, they will want a voice in recruiting; if their accountability is to be determined by tests, they will want a voice in determining what those tests are and who applies them. Clearly they will want a voice over what is taught and how it is taught. Class size and procedures for handling the disruptive child will be more important than ever.

An argument frequently made in support of a limited scope of bargaining is that third-party intervenors (i.e., mediators, fact-finders, arbitrators) will, absent such constraints, invade the business of government itself. The contention is that even though an organization lacks the power to make a credible strike threat, it may be able to gain its ends by enlisting the support of an outsider.

This argument is unpersuasive. First, mediators or fact-finders who make recommendations in respect to matters regarded by management as being in the area of prerogatives or sovereignty will not be taken very seriously by the public employer unless the employee organization has sufficient bargaining power to enforce those recommendations. Thus a mediator or a fact-finder will not be able to force incursions into the prerogatives of management or government which the organization could not achieve on its own.

The situation is different when the arbitrator has the authority to bind the parties. However, the concern still seems more fanciful than real. To illustrate, what is an arbitrator likely to do in a typical situation where the parties have bargained on a package basis and a multiplicity of issues remain unresolved (for example, wages, holidays, shift premiums, overtime, transfer procedures, work rules, or seniority in general employee units; class size, student discipline, or curricular reform in education; or civilian review boards for police)? He will be inclined to deal solely with those issues with which he feels comfortable because these are acceptable criteria, ducking other issues in respect to which he feels uncomfortable, if not incompetent. It would be a rare arbitrator presumptuous enough to make a binding determination on class size, student discipline, curriculum reform, or the existence of a civilian police review board.

Law professors and management negotiators are not the only persons who are "uptight" about the scope of collective bargaining in public employment. Many legislative bodies suffer from the same syndrome.

The Nevada statute governing public employee bargaining specifies that a local government employer need not negotiate over its right to direct its employees, to hire, to promote, to classify, transfer, assign, retain, suspend, demote, discharge, or take disciplinary action against an employee, to relieve any employee from duty because of lack of work or for any other legitimate reason, to maintain the efficiency of its governmental operations, to determine the methods, means, and personnel by which its operations are to be conducted, and to take whatever actions may be necessary to carry out its responsibilities in emergency situations. . . .

The Hawaiian statute goes even further. It makes it *illegal* for an employer and a labor organization to agree to any proposal which interferes with the right of a public employer to direct its employees, to determine qualifications, standards for work, the nature and content of examinations, to hire, to promote, transfer, assign, and retain employees in positions; to suspend, demote, discharge, or take other disciplinary action against its employees for proper cause; to relieve an employee from duty because of lack of work or other legitimate reasons; to maintain the efficiency of government operations; and to determine methods, means and personnel by which the employer's operations are to be conducted.

Even the most imaginative negotiators will have their work cut out for them under this language. Can they agree to a standard job security clause, to a provision requiring posting and bidding on promotions, to an article which makes seniority a controlling factor in lay-off and recall?

Such laws, which encourage or require public employers to avoid problems rather than deal with them, are mischievous because they produce strife and frustration rather than understanding and peaceful accommodation of conflicts between government and its employees. In the public sector, as well as the private, what is bargained about, as well as what the terms of the bargain are, should be a function of the bargaining process, not of abstract concerns over sovereignty or responsiveness to misconceived legislative constraints.

**SUMMERS, PUBLIC EMPLOYEE BARGAINING: A POLITICAL PERSPECTIVE, 83 Yale L. Rev. 1156, 1192-97 (1969) †**

  . . . .

## C.  *Subjects for Bargaining*

Collective bargaining in the public sector, from the perspective of this inquiry, is a specially structured political process for making certain governmental decisions. The primary justification for this special process is that it gives the employees increased political effectiveness to help balance the massed political resistance of taxpayers and users of public services. One consequence of public employee bargaining is at least partial preclusion of public discussion of those subjects being bargained. And the effect of an agreement is to foreclose any change in matters agreed upon during the term of the agreement. Because it constitutes something of a derogation from traditional democratic principles, collective bargaining should be limited to those areas in which public employees do indeed encounter massed resistance. In other areas, disputes by public employees should be resolved through the customary channels of political decisionmaking.

Borrowing concepts of bargainable subjects from the private sector can be misleading for two reasons. First, in the private sector collective bargaining is the only instrument through which employees can have any effective voice in determining the terms and conditions of employment. One purpose of the duty to bargain is to provide employees a measure of industrial democracy; that duty, therefore, appropriately extends to all subjects which directly relate to their employment. In the public sector employees already have, as citizens, a voice in decisionmaking through customary political channels. The purpose of collective bargaining is to give them, as employees, a larger voice than the ordinary citizen. Therefore, the duty to bargain should extend only to those decisions where that larger voice is appropriate.

Second, in defining bargainable subjects in the private sector, the government is establishing boundaries for the dealings between private parties. In the public sector, however, government is establishing structures and procedures for making its own decisions. In the private sector the parties may agree at the bargaining table to expand the subjects of bargaining, but a public employee union and a public official do not have the same freedom to agree that certain decisions should be removed from the ordinary political processes and be

† Reprinted by permission of The Yale Law Journal Company, Inc.

decided by them in a special forum. The private employer's prerogatives are his to share as he sees fit, but the citizen's right to participate in governmental decisions cannot be bargained away by any public official.

In legal terms the principal question in the private sector is what the *mandatory* subjects of bargaining are, *i.e.,* what decisions the employer *must* share with his employees. The principal question in the public sector is what the *permissible* subjects of bargaining are, *i.e.,* what decisions *may* be made through the specially structured political process.

The special political structure and procedure of collective bargaining is particularly appropriate for decisions where the employees' interests in increased wages and reduced work load run counter to the combined interests of taxpayers and users of public services. Therefore, decisions as to wages, insurance, pensions, sick leave, length of work week, overtime pay, vacations, and holidays should be considered proper subjects for bargaining. Collective bargaining, however, lacks the same claim of appropriateness for decisions where budgetary or level of service considerations are not dominant and where the political alignment of taxpayers and users against employees does not occur.

For example, a decision concerning the content of the school curriculum does not centrally involve salary levels or work loads of teachers on the one hand, or the size of the budget or the level of service on the other. Rather, the decision requires a choice of the kinds of services to be provided within the limitations of the funds available.[5] On such an issue there is no reason to assume that the teachers' views can be summarized by a single voice, nor is there reason to believe that taxpayers, parents, or users of other services have any unified position. Two-sided bargaining on such issues misrepresents both the range of views and the alignment of interests which should be considered in making the decision.

Furthermore, channeling discussion into closed bargaining sessions inhibits a full airing of viewpoints, for it precludes equal consideration of differing professional judgments of teachers and of differing judgments and concerns of parents, students, and other interested citizens. Even if all of these views are presented at the bargaining table, the decision is made by public representatives whose primary charge is to protect the public purse. Thus the decision is not made solely on the merits of the issue, but as part of a package which results from trading off unrelated items. Because of its structure and function, collective bargaining does not provide an appropriate political process for making such decisions.

To say that curriculum content is not a proper subject of bargaining does not mean that teachers have no legitimate interest in that subject or that they should not participate in curriculum decisions. It means only that the bargaining table is the wrong forum and the collective agreement is the wrong instrument.

---

[5] Collective bargaining on such matters as the content of the curriculum, the number of speech therapists, the choice of textbooks, and grading standards has been justified on the ground that teachers, as professionals, should have a greater voice in these decisions than politically sensitive lay boards of education and bureaucratic minded administrators, and that bargaining insulates decisionmaking from the pressures of the unenlightened populace. *See* Wollett, *The Coming Revolution in Public School Management,* 67 MICH. L. REV. 1017 (1969). The assumption is that on all of these matters professional judgments should prevail over public choice. This assumption may be subject to question on several levels. *See* Goldstein, *supra* note 4. Undoubtedly, there are decisions which should be left to professional judgment, but submitting them to collective bargaining is a clumsy, inadequate, and even dangerous way of achieving that. Bargaining is a political process responding to political forces and leaves teachers vulnerable on some matters which should be beyond reach of local majorities.

Because of the teachers' special interests and competence, the school board can properly be authorized, or even required, to consult with them before making a decision. But no organization should purport to act as an exclusive representative; the discussions should not be closed; and the decision should not be bargained for or solidified as an agreement. In addition, all of the ordinary political processes should remain open for individuals or groups of teachers to make their views known to the politically responsible officials and thus to influence the decision.[6]

This analysis, which restricts collective bargaining to subjects that substantially implicate budgetary issues, provides some guide for separating bargainable and nonbargainable subjects in the public sector. Yet it cannot provide a clear boundary line.

If teachers demand reduction in class size or policemen demand minimum manning of patrols, the interests of the employees may coincide with the interests of users of the particular service; the clear confrontation created by wage demands does not then exist. However, there remains the opposition of taxpayers and users of other services. Granting the union demands would almost certainly require increased appropriations for the schools or the police department. Even some parents may prefer that any increase in the school budget be spent to improve other aspects of the educational program. The configuration of political interest groups remains sufficiently similar to make the collective bargaining structure appropriate for resolving such issues.

Collective bargaining might initially seem inappropriate for subjects such as seniority, promotions, work assignments, and discipline, which do not directly affect budget allocation. But union demands on these subjects are commonly resisted on the grounds that they reduce efficiency and efficiency is an interest shared by both taxpayers and users of public services.

If the union's demands do not in fact affect efficiency, then the dispute is simply one between the employees in the bargaining unit and their supervisors, department heads, or personnel department. Such disputes do not involve the public's interest but rather concern the relative roles of opposing interest groups within the government in determining the terms and conditions of employment. These competing interests are represented at the two-sided bargaining table; the proper parties are on each side of the table. The structure and procedure seem quite appropriate for reconciling their interests and working out the rules to govern their relationships.

Demands by policemen for disciplinary procedures which effectively foreclose use of a public review board further illustrate the need to examine each subject to determine whether it should be decided within the special political process of collective bargaining. In making such a demand the union probably represents the consensus of the employees and can thus properly speak with a single voice. However, such a demand has no identifiable budget cost; those interested in more police protection are more likely to support than oppose the demand. Hence there is not the combined opposition which typified resolution of

---

[6] A wide variety of procedures can be developed to ensure that teachers participate in these decisions without depriving any interested group of an opportunity to be heard. Representatives of the union and other teacher groups can meet with the school board for full discussion of the problem. Committees can be elected by the affected teachers wholly outside the union framework. School faculties may discuss and make recommendations. And school boards can hold open public meetings at which teachers and their various spokesmen may present their views just as spokesmen for parents, students, and other groups do.

budgetary and level of service issues. Nor is there the opposition of supervisors which characterizes internal management and personnel issues, for the chief of police and the police commissioners who sit on the employer's side of the bargaining table find the prospect of a public review board equally frightening. Those who favor a public review board are those who fear that policemen will act abusively or unlawfully and that their superiors will not take appropriate disciplinary action. The interests of this group are not represented at the bargaining table. Collective bargaining thus does not provide an appropriate political process for full discussion of the issue or for weighing and reconciling the competing interests.*

Again, the conclusion that this subject should be nonbargainable does not mean that policemen have no legitimate interest in whether their conduct should be subject to public review. They certainly have a right to participate in that decision, but only through the ordinary avenues of the political process which are equally open to all competing views and interest groups.

## C. PERRY AND W. WILDMAN, THE IMPACT OF NEGOTIATIONS IN PUBLIC EDUCATION: THE EVIDENCE FROM THE SCHOOLS 165-71 (1970) †

The effect of collective bargaining is to grant to employees a greater measure of control over the decisions of management. A question does exist, however, as to the range of such decisions over which this control can or should be extended. On what kinds of issues have teachers sought to exercise influence through collective bargaining?

At a pragmatic level, this question centers on the scope of bargaining and the definition of the appropriate subject matter for collective bargaining. The issue, at this level, is whether collective bargaining shall be limited to "wages, hours, and conditions of employment" or shall extend to "anything that affects the working life of the teacher" and "all matters which affect the quality of the educational program."

On a more basic level, the question involves the extent to which collective bargaining will alter the distribution of lay and professional control over basic educational policy. This has been raised by one union leader in the following terms:

> The coming of age of the teaching profession, through collective bargaining, forces us to meet, head-on, the critical problem of the respective roles of teachers and civic and parent groups in the system of public education. . . . It is inconceivable that laymen will insist on keeping the educational process out of the control of educators, any more than they would think of depriving doctors, lawyers and theologians of the ultimate control of their respective professions. Lay groups will have to recognize and accept the realities of the new world of collective bargaining by teachers in the educational system. By definition, bargaining means codetermination, together with Boards of Education, and not unilateral decisions.

Boards of education have generally taken quite the opposite position. In the words of one board member:

> It is the belief of our scheme of public education that the objectives of the school system, the basic emphasis on the teaching effort, the goals to be

---

† Reprinted by permission of Charles A. Jones Publishing Company, Worthington, Ohio.

achieved, shall be determined by the community itself, and not by the professionals. . . . I do not believe that this philosophy is altered, or modified by the fact that a Board of Education has entered into a collective bargaining agreement with an organization which represents the teachers in that system.

Collective bargaining in the private sector has not raised a comparable issue. Despite perennial concern over management prerogatives in the face of an expanding scope of bargaining, unions have generally been more than willing to leave the basic direction of the enterprise to management. To do otherwise would require the organization to compromise its adversary role and assume responsibility for management decisions. Except in crisis situations, unions have not been willing or able to make this change in role.

It is not yet wholly clear what the experience will be in public education. The extension of collective bargaining beyond its traditional scope — salaries, benefits, a narrow range of employment conditions, and protection of individual rights in the day-to-day application of the agreement — requires two things. First, teachers must enjoy the expertise required to set policy and be able to achieve a consensus on policy issues. Second, the teacher organization must be willing to accept responsibility as well as authority in policy areas. It remains to be seen whether these conditions can be met within the adversary framework of collective bargaining, or whether they will require some other decision-making structure.

### The Definition Problem

First, it should be noted that it is exceedingly difficult to distinguish between "educational policy" and "salaries and working conditions" where teacher bargaining is concerned. For instance, it is generally accepted that salary schedule and teacher benefits are "bargainable" if anything is. However, if raising teacher salaries in a district as a result of bargaining forces a budget reallocation of sums set aside for textbooks, hiring of additional professional personnel, building maintenance, or even new school construction, a decision on school district "policy" is clearly involved and may, indeed, be discussed as such, although all that is ostensibly under consideration is the salary schedule.

Or, take for example the problem of teacher transfers. Transfer rules and procedures have long been considered, in both private and public employment, as falling clearly within any reasonable definition of "working conditions." Yet, in our major cities, where schools in lower socio-economic areas have a grossly disproportionate share of the system's inexperienced teachers who are minimally qualified in terms of training and advanced degrees, the problem of fairly and equitably balancing teaching staffs, and thus curtailing the right of transfer by seniority, has become, for large city boards, a "policy" issue of great significance.

Examples of this kind pointing up the difficulty of distinguishing between "policy" and "working conditions" can be cited endlessly. Similarly, no really satisfying distinction can be made between "policy" matters and many so-called "professional" issues. For instance, basic decisions concerning many aspects of curriculum, methodology, or textbook selection are clearly at one and the same time both "policy" questions for the board or the administration and "professional" concerns of the teaching staff. However, despite overlap and untidiness, it is necessary and possible for purposes of analysis and discussion to establish a rough, somewhat arbitrary category of "policy" and "professional" issues.

It is, of course, true that in many school systems in this country, teachers, through one medium or another, have exercised significant influence over numerous policy and professional questions long before the advent of formal collective negotiation relationships. However, our focus here is the extent to which collective negotiations in the schools has been used as a vehicle for gaining a greater measure of teacher control over or participation in decisions in these areas.

## Overall Impact

Investigations indicate that, as yet, the direct impact of collective negotiations on the board's freedom to set basic policy and on administrative discretion to implement that policy and decide questions involving school or system-wide "professional" judgment is not as great as might be assumed.

The evidence from the districts studied by the authors — a survey of substantive collective negotiation agreements from around the country, and awareness of the reality behind many seemingly significant contract clauses — has led to the conclusion that there are few cases where negotiations have actually forced a significant shift in basic school district policy on a reluctant, unwilling board, and few examples of a board being blocked from initiating action or change on a basic policy matter solely as a result of teacher power exercised through the negotiation process.[7] Also, administrative discretion in areas calling for significant exercise of professional judgment, while curbed or modified in certain instances, has rarely been radically altered.

It should be remembered, though, that collective negotiations in education is a quite recent and immature phenomenon, and it must be recognized that there is evidence that the potential clearly exists for the power generated by negotiations to bring about significant changes in the distribution of authority among boards, administrators, and teacher organizations with respect to "policy" and "professional" matters.

As yet, there are relatively few instances where specific, substantive issues which might be considered in the policy or "professional" realm have become the focus of pointed conflict at the bargaining table.[8] However, while bargaining over specific, tangible issues of policy or professional judgment may be rare as yet, bargaining is being used as a vehicle for establishing procedures and structures for interaction assuring teachers a voice in so-called policy and

---

[7] As has been pointed out previously in this book, teacher power exercised in negotiations on salary and other cost items has resulted in significant reassessment of budget priorities and forced boards to make reallocations with definite policy consequences, at least in the short run. The present focus here, however, is on the impact of negotiations in policy areas not directly budget related.

[8] There are exceptions, of course, and dramatic ones at that. The most recent significant instance of a "policy" question providing bargaining table conflict occurred in the fall of 1967 between the New York City Board of Education and the United Federation of Teachers. A key teacher demand in New York was for the extension to more inner city schools of the expensive "saturation services" More Effective Schools program. The board, which had judged that the additional outlay for the MES program had not been justified by the results and that extra sums might better be spent on alternative compensatory educational activities, argued that the issue was clearly an educational policy matter, not appropriate for resolution through collective bargaining. Ultimately, the issue was compromised by establishment of a committee which included parent and community representatives. This important confrontation took place well after the authors' work in the New York system was completed; thus, a thorough investigation of this issue is not a part of this research.

It should be noted here, too, that in several cities besides New York, the AFT has induced boards in negotiations to allot funds for compensatory experiments similar in nature to the New York More Effective Schools program. Also, of course, the fall and early winter of 1968 saw the teachers in New York City striking the system three separate times in the struggle over decentralization and community control. The community control dispute in New York is most complex and of a magnitude which seems to threaten destruction or wholesale restructuring of the system; in the authors' judgment, an escalation of basic conflict is involved which far transcends the "normal" negotiating process. In the final chapter of this book, there will be a brief discussion concerning the anticipated impact of teacher power on attempts to effectively decentralize large city systems.

"professional" matters outside and independent of the process of negotiations over the collective agreement.[9] For instance, a number of contracts have provided for committees to be established for a wide variety of research — deliberative and decision-making purposes embracing subjects such as curriculum, methodology, textbook selection, promotion to the principalship, screening and recommendations of candidates for openings at any level in the system (including the superintendency), methods of achieving pupil and teacher integration in the system, pupil discipline, and many more. In some instances the establishment of committees for such purposes has constituted a dramatic departure from past practice. In other cases, the functioning reality behind the exciting contract clause may be anything but impressive. Also, in some cases, clauses which seem to represent significant inroads on a board's traditional, unilateral discretion over "policy" are actually not a source of conflict in negotiations; indeed, in some instances what may appear to be "revolutionary" commitments are actually encouraged by the administration and the board.

Some boards of education have agreed to clauses in collective agreements calling for mutual agreement between board and teacher organization before adoption and installation of innovative programs which might force modification of fixed class size, programming, or assignment provisions in the agreement. In one district studied, the administration rationale for accepting such a clause was to the effect that "we haven't given anything up, because if the teachers aren't in favor of a new program, it wouldn't succeed and there wouldn't be any sense in trying it out anyway." Reflecting on the need or desirability in some circumstances for administration to exercise innovative leadership, and given what is known of frequent resistance to change in large organizations (especially, perhaps, schools) one might find this justification less than satisfying. However, in none of the systems studied had new programs or innovations been proposed which might have made such a clause the focal point of conflict or dispute between a school administration and teacher organization.

In a somewhat related vein, boards have agreed to general clauses committing them to negotiate any new "policies" and/or "policy changes" which might "affect" professional personnel before adoption or implementation of same. Here again, while one can note from the board and administration point of view the loss of flexibility potentially inherent in such a clause, no issues had yet arisen in any of the districts studied which became the subject of dispute under such an agreement.

## REHMUS, CONSTRAINTS ON LOCAL GOVERNMENTS IN PUBLIC EMPLOYEE BARGAINING, 67 Mich. L. Rev. 919, 921-28 (1969) †

### II. Financial Limitations on Local Governmental Units

Three major sources of revenue are available for financing government: taxes

---

[9] A distinction should be recognized at this point between "teacher" in a system and the organization representing teachers in the system. Particularly in systems where the exclusive representative organization has far from all of the teachers enrolled, the board and the administration may evidence much desire to assure a continuing voice for teachers who are not in the majority organization, especially with regard to issues involving subject matter expertise and professional judgment generally. On the other hand the right to appoint teachers to any and all committees or councils in a school (particularly those which have been established by contract) regardless of the subject to be considered has important organizational security and prestige implications for the exclusive representative. Thus, the stage may be set in bargaining for significant conflict over an important issue.

† Reprinted by permission of The Michigan Law Review Association.

on sales, on income, and on property. Of these, the property tax is the workhorse of local government; it accounts for ninety per cent of local tax revenues in the United States. Local governments in Michigan — municipalities, counties, and school districts — have no authority to levy sales taxes, and the development of city income taxes is just beginning.[10] Thus, Michiganders have traditionally relied heavily on the property tax not only to finance city and village governments, but also to support townships, counties, and school districts. In many areas, three or four local governing units, not to mention special district authorities, all depend upon the same overburdened property tax base. Nevertheless, the state legislature, jealous of its own tax sources and protective of its citizens, has not permitted much change in local taxing structure. The new Michigan Constitution adopted in 1963 theoretically delegated broad taxing powers to home rule charter cities. Despite this, the state legislature has reserved most nonproperty taxes to itself and has prohibited municipalities from levying such taxes without specific legislative authorization. Moreover, Michigan, like most states, limits the total amount of millage that can be levied upon property without specific authorization from the voters.[11] The specific constitutional limit in Michigan upon a city council's unrestricted taxing power is eighteen mills, and another fifteen mills must be divided among township boards, county supervisors, and school boards.

Even those cities that desire to tax themselves more heavily often find that the legislature forces them to beg for the privilege. States that permit cities to levy income taxes frequently place limitations upon the amounts that can be obtained through this resource. It is common to find statutes which restrict municipalities to a flat rate rather than a progressive income tax, limit the percentage of residents' income which they can tax, and place even more severe limitations upon the percentage of commuters' incomes which they can reach. Michigan, for example, limits city income taxes to a flat rate of one per cent and the tax on commuters' incomes to half that amount. Moreover, state legislatures commonly allow voters a veto over new city income taxes, a privilege seldom if ever accorded for similar state levies. Under the uniform Michigan city income tax law, the imposition of city income taxes is subject to a protest referendum. In order for city councils to obtain an affirmative vote in these referendum elections, they must often promise the voters major property tax reductions. Thus, the amount of new money generated is limited, and much of the purpose of the new taxes is defeated. Related to this, the Michigan Constitution prohibits cities from issuing general obligation bonds without an affirmative vote of property owners. Consequently, many cities, rather than attempting to get the voters to approve capital bonds, squeeze capital improvements out of their operating millage and further limit the resources available for short-run operational flexibility.

These constitutional and legislative constraints upon the taxing powers of home rule charter cities are sometimes aggravated by the cities themselves. Some cities have in their original charters limited the total operating millage which they can levy administratively to an amount lower than the state-imposed twenty-mill

---

[10] At the present time, fewer than 200 cities in the United States levy an income tax, but growth of this form of taxation will undoubtedly expand rapidly.

[11] MICH. CONST. art. 9, § 6. Pennsylvania is an important exception. It is alone among the states whose public employees are strongly organized and which permit local governing bodies to levy unlimited property taxes without specific voter authorization.

maximum. This handicaps them further in generating the funds necessary to meet employee demands.

In summary, a state-imposed obligation upon local governments to negotiate wages and fringe benefits inevitably entails increased budget expenditures for employee compensation. If the state simultaneously maintains existing limitations upon the unilateral taxing power of local governments, the situation often becomes intolerable. Local government administrators are helplessly caught between employee compensation demands, public unwillingness to vote for increased operating millage levied on property, and the state legislature's reluctance to allow local governments the freedom to impose income, sales, or excise taxes.

An example which highlights the problem recently occurred in Detroit. Following both a "ticket-writing strike" and a "blue flu" epidemic among police officers, the disputants finally referred the issue of police salaries to a neutral three-member panel for recommendations. The panel found that police officers' salaries should be substantially increased. Money to pay the recommended increases could be found on an emergency basis within Detroit's current operating budget, but beyond the first year, the panel concluded:

> the City of Detroit urgently needs new taxing authority which can be granted only by the State Legislature. ... Detroit is in serious financial trouble, and we join others who have suggested that the State Legislature raise the authorized level of the municipal income tax, to restore the authority to levy local excise taxes, and to revise the 2 percent restriction on property tax levies.[12]

The problem of financial straight-jacketing in the face of collective bargaining pressure is equally serious for school districts. Collective bargaining for Michigan public school teachers appears to have produced annual pay increases averaging ten to twenty per cent higher than those which the teachers would otherwise have received. Over all, the salaries of Michigan teachers have increased by about one third in the last three years. Most, if not all, of these increases were long overdue, but they resulted in severe pressure on school district budgets. In the 1966-1967 academic year, the first full year of teacher bargaining under the 1965 Act, these increases in teacher compensation were paid for largely from minor economies and from new revenues. Among the new revenue sources were increases in state aid, imposition of previously authorized millage, and growth in assessed valuation. In the second full year of collective bargaining, however, school districts began to use less desirable sources of funds to pay the wage increases demanded by organized teachers. Administrators generated new sources of funds through liquidation of operating reserves and contingency funds, transfer of millage from building and site reserves to operating accounts, and substantial program cutbacks. Most important — and despite the fact that Michigan law is generally construed to forbid school districts from deficit financing — a quarter of the school districts studied in one survey showed a deficit by the end of fiscal 1968.

The financial constraints on local governments constitute the most serious

---

[12] Detroit Police Dispute Panel, Findings and Recommendations on Unresolved "Economic" and Other Issues 32-33 (Feb. 27, 1968, unpublished mimeo).

problem they face in coping with public employee collective bargaining. However, public officials must contend with at least three other problems which, although related to financing, are not as severe as the shortage of funds per se. The first problem is that of coordinating the budget-making process with collective bargaining. An acute aspect of this problem is the difficulty which local governmental units face in meeting budget deadlines, particularly when the state legislature itself imposes the deadline. The collective bargaining process often entails months of negotiations, mediation, and fact-finding or arbitration; it does not respect time limits. Yet budgets must be filed under the law, and this requires local officials to make preliminary estimates. As a result, municipalities may often feel constrained to take rigid positions based upon estimates which were submitted to the legislature before bargaining is completed. A second aspect of the coordination problem arises after budget submission deadlines have been passed: the issue then is whether negotiated pay increases should apply prospectively from the date of the agreement or retroactively from the beginning of the budget period. Finally, it may be difficult to synchronize legislative decisions concerning the amount of funds to be allocated to local governmental units with local governmental responsibilities in the bargaining process. For instance, teacher bargaining for the 1967-1968 school year in Michigan proved exceptionally difficult because the state legislature failed to act on the school aid formula until August 1967. Consequently, spring and summer bargaining in many school districts dragged on beyond budget submission deadlines because school administrators were unable to predict how much state funding would be available to help them meet teacher demands. The state legislature avoided this problem the following year by acting on the school aid formula in April, well before budget deadlines. Perhaps as a result, a smaller number of bargaining impasses occurred during teacher negotiations for the 1968-1969 school year. This problem of coordinating the budget-making process with collective bargaining is more an irritating than an insurmountable obstacle. The difficulties can be minimized by using open-ended budgets, resorting to short-term internal and external borrowing, allowing more time for bargaining before budget deadlines, and negotiating collective bargaining contracts for longer terms than are currently settled upon.

A second complication of collective bargaining in the public sector results from the tradition that public budgets and accounts are not secret documents. In the private sector the employer may under most circumstances refuse to disclose his profit and loss figures, but the public employer is forced to open his books to all interested persons. As a result, any operating reserves or contingency funds that may be available simply become targets for the employees to shoot at. Prudent management — whether in business or in public administration — ordinarily requires the retention of some operating reserves. It is not reprehensible for a public administrator to maintain a reserve account to pay operating costs in periods before tax money becomes available or to provide for unforeseen contingencies. In practice, however, even if cities and school districts have not had to resort to deficit financing in order to meet collective bargaining demands, the retention of operating reserves has proved almost impossible. Many cities and most school districts in Michigan, their reserves depleted to satisfy the bargaining demands of employees, are now operating on little better than a year-to-year cash basis. In jurisdictions where reserves remain, this result has often been accomplished by padding various budget items — a recurrent practice but hardly one to be encouraged.

A third anomaly of collective bargaining in the public sector is that the union can often invade the management decision-making structure. Particularly in public school and junior college districts, organized teacher groups have succeeded in electing their members, relatives, or sympathizers to school and governing boards. Under these circumstances it is often impossible for the management decision-making group to hide its bargaining strategy and tactics from employees. Democratic government does allow almost anyone to run for office, but this tactic may make collective bargaining a farce.

### III. Other State-Imposed Constraints on Collective Bargaining

State legislatures have imposed many limitations upon the authority of local governmental units to manage their own personnel systems. One of the most common limitations is the statutory or de facto requirement that home rule cities establish a civil service and merit system for recruitment and promotion of personnel. This requirement, although beneficial in its thrust and general impact upon city government, operates to reduce substantially the flexibility of local governmental units at the collective bargaining table. State legislatures have seldom given enough thought to the problems that may be encountered when they impose a collective bargaining requirement covering "terms and conditions of employment" upon an existing merit structure.

The civil service concept ordinarily contemplates the establishment of a nonpartisan board or commission at the local or state level with rulemaking authority to assure adherence to the merit principle. In practice, merit systems have over the years grown to encompass many aspects of employee relations and personnel management other than recruitment, classification, and promotion. These new areas of concern include the handling of grievances, employee training, salary administration, safety, morale, and attendance control programs — the very subjects that most employee organizations regard as appropriate for bargaining. If an independent civil service commission has authority over bargainable matters, then perhaps bargaining responsibilities should lie with the commission. But as it is, authority to bargain is usually vested in the chief executive officer of the local government unit. If he has the duty to bargain over the terms and conditions of employment while authority over many personnel matters remains with an independent commission, the scope of negotiations will be unduly restricted.

This problem is not insoluble. If the principle of collective bargaining by local governments is to be effectuated, all nonmerit functions should be transferred from the civil service commission to a personnel department under the chief executive officer of each local unit. In practice, however, such a transfer of authority has seldom been made. In Massachusetts, for example, the state collective bargaining law for public employees specifically states that it shall not "diminish the authority and power of the civil service commission, or any retirement or personnel board established by law. . . ." The Wisconsin public employment relations statute excludes from the mandatory scope of bargaining a large range of matters established by law or governed by civil service. In practice, in localities where public employee collective bargaining is fully developed, informal bargaining arrangements to deal with these problems are already appearing.[13] At the very least, any state considering collective bargaining

---

[13] For example, Michigan's Wayne County has created special labor boards with the power to negotiate collective agreements with employees. The labor board for a negotiation is composed of a representative of the county Civil Service Board, a representative of the county Board of Supervisors, and a representative from the particular administrative unit involved (such as the county Highway Department).

legislation for public employees should carefully analyze its personnel system in order to minimize the potential conflict between bargaining relationships, existing merit systems, and the rules promulgated by civil service boards and commissions.

State legislatures contemplating collective bargaining in the public sector should also ensure that they have not imposed undue restrictions upon the permissible scope of bargaining. Some years ago the Michigan legislature imposed upon its municipalities a fifty-six-hour maximum duty week for firemen. This law not only raised municipal fire protection costs substantially, but also eliminated from the scope of bargaining one of the major subjects which should have been left there. In Pennsylvania, the state legislature prohibited combined police-fire departments, another potentially bargainable subject. Laws of this kind place many local governments, particularly smaller communities, in a Procrustean bed. These municipalities are obligated to bargain over wages and hours, yet uniform state laws fundamentally weaken their negotiating position by creating mandatory high-cost requirements without the freedom to trade cost reductions in one area for new expenditures in another.

State legislatures have also limited the negotiating flexibility of school boards. For example, the Attorney General of Michigan has recently ruled that under existing law boards of education lack statutory authority to award severance pay, to pay for any unused portion of sick leave at the end of a school year or upon termination of employment, or to reimburse teachers' tuition for college credit courses beyond the baccalaureate degree. Under the Michigan collective bargaining statute, school boards had assumed prior to the Attorney General's ruling that they were obligated to bargain on all of these subjects, and concessions had in fact been made on many. Probably a majority of existing teacher collective bargaining agreements in Michigan call for one or more of these payments that have now been declared to be unlawful. The attempt of school boards to negotiate such benefits back out of existing contracts is likely to engender bitter conflict. A new grant of authority to make the disputed payments would seem to be a preferable alternative. . . .

## NOTE

Among the many useful articles examining the scope of bargaining in the public sector are SCOPE OF PUBLIC-SECTOR BARGAINING (W. Gershenfeld, J. Loewenberg, & B. Ingster eds. 1977); Clark, *The Scope of the Duty to Bargain in Public Employment,* in LABOR RELATIONS LAW IN THE PUBLIC SECTOR 81 (A. Knapp ed. 1977); Sackman, *Redefining the Scope of Bargaining in Public Employment,* 19 B.C.L. REV. 155 (1977); Sabghir, *The Scope of Bargaining in Public Sector Collective Bargaining,* A Report sponsored by the New York State Employment Relations Board (October 1970); U.S. DEP'T OF LABOR, SCOPE OF BARGAINING IN THE PUBLIC SECTOR — CONCEPTS AND PROBLEMS (1972); Edwards, *The Emerging Duty to Bargain in the Public Sector,* 71 MICH. L. REV. 885 (1973); Kilberg, *Appropriate Subjects for Bargaining in Local Government Labor Relations,* 30 MD. L. REV. 179 (1970); Gerhart, *The Scope of Bargaining in Local Government Negotiations,* 20 LAB. L.J. 545 (1969); Blair, *State Legislative Control Over the Conditions of Public Employment: Defining the Scope of Collective Bargaining for State and Municipal Employees,* 26 VAND. L. REV. 1 (1973); Vial, *The Scope of Bargaining Controversy: Substantive Issues vs. Procedural Hangups,* CALIFORNIA PUBLIC EMPLOYEE RELATIONS No. 15, at 4 (Nov. 1972).

## 2. WAGES, HOURS AND WORKING CONDITIONS — WHAT IS NEGOTIABLE?

### WESTWOOD COMMUNITY SCHOOLS

Michigan Employment Relations Commission
1972 MERC Lab. Op. 313

[The Westwood Education Association (Association) filed an unfair labor practice charge against the Westwood Community Schools (Employer) alleging, *inter alia,* that the Employer violated Section 10(a) and (e) of the Michigan Public Employment Relations Act (PERA) by refusing to negotiate with the Association over the beginning and ending dates of the school term and by unilaterally establishing said dates. The Trial Examiner ruled "that there is no obligation on the Employer to bargain in regard to the opening of school and that subject is a voluntary subject of bargaining." The Association filed a timely exception to the Trial Examiner's recommendation that this portion of the Association's unfair labor practice charge be dismissed.]

The issue of whether the opening date of the school term is a mandatory subject of bargaining is one of first impression for this Commission. We have never definitively established a list of subjects which lie within the scope of bargaining, nor does PERA define such subjects. Section 15 of the statute provides that the collective bargaining duty of the Employer is "... to meet at reasonable times and confer in good faith with respect to wages, hours and other terms and conditions of employment...." Disputes involving bargainable subjects have been resolved on a case by case basis. City of Detroit, Police Department, 1971 MERC Lab. Op. 237, 241.

This ad hoc method of determination has, however, embraced the traditional private sector distinctions between mandatory, non-mandatory and illegal subjects of bargaining. Bullock Creek School District, 1969 MERC Lab. Op. 497, 504; City of Detroit, Police Department, *supra;* Coleman Community Schools, 1970 MERC Lab. Op. 813. While we have made no extensive analysis of these categories of bargaining proposals, we have held that the words "... other terms and conditions of employment ..." from Section 15 of PERA mean "those items which *affect* employees after they have become employees." City of Detroit, Police Department, *supra* at 249 (emphasis added).

The traditional classification of bargaining proposals was enunciated in the leading United States Supreme Court case, National Labor Relations Board v. Wooster Division of Borg-Warner, 356 U.S. 342, 42 L.R.R.M. 2034 (1958). Here, the employer insisted that its collective bargaining contract with some of its employees contain a ballot clause calling for a pre-strike secret vote of the employees as to the employer's last offer, and a recognition clause which excluded as a party to the contract the International Union which had been certified by the NLRB as the employees' exclusive bargaining agent and substituted for it the agent's uncertified local affiliate. The NLRB found that the employer's insistence upon either of such clauses amounted to an unlawful refusal to bargain. Borg-Warner Corporation, 113 N.L.R.B. 1288, 36 L.R.R.M. 1439 (1955). The Sixth Circuit of the United States Court of Appeals upheld the Labor Board's finding as to the recognition clause, but reversed on the ballot clause issue. NLRB v. Wooster Division of Borg-Warner, 236 F.2d 898, 38 L.R.R.M. 2660 (6th Cir., 1956). In reversing the Court of Appeals' decision as to the latter issue, the Supreme Court sustained the Labor Board's opinion.

The Court held that both the ballot clause and the recognition clause are not mandatory subjects of bargaining; thus, the employer could not insist upon contractual inclusion of these subjects. It reached this result by reading together Sections 8(a) (5) and 8(d) of the National Labor Relations Act. The former makes it an unfair labor practice for an employer to "refuse to bargain collectively with the representatives of his employees." National Labor Relations Act, 29 U.S.C. § 158(a) (5). The latter defines collective bargaining as the

"... performance of the mutual obligation of the employer and the representative of the employees to meet at reasonable times and confer in good faith with respect to wages, hours and other terms and conditions of employment . . . but such obligation does not compel either party to agree to a proposal or require the making of a concession." *Id.,* 29 U.S.C. § 158(d).[3]

The court found that the duty to bargain is limited to the subjects (mandatory) "wages, hours and other terms and conditions of employment," and that neither party is legally obligated to yield. "As to other matters (non-mandatory), however, each party is free to bargain or not to bargain, and to agree or not to agree." 356 U.S. at 349, 42 L.R.R.M. at 2036. The Court explicitly held that ". . . (I)t is lawful to insist upon matters within the scope of mandatory bargaining and unlawful to insist upon matters without. . . ." *Id.,* 42 L.R.R.M. at 2037.

Thus, the teaching of *Borg-Warner,* is that the employer cannot take unilateral action with regard to a mandatory subject of bargaining where there has been no bargaining. But the parties do not have to agree. In the absence of agreement, the employer may act unilaterally. NLRB v. American National Insurance Co., 343 U.S. 395, 30 L.R.R.M. 2147 (1952). Under *Borg-Warner,* the employer may act without bargaining as to non-mandatory subjects of bargaining.

The elusive question that continually plagues courts, administrative tribunals and practitioners focuses on the phrase "other terms and conditions of employment." No satisfactory answer has been formulated to resolve this problem; *Borg-Warner* provides little help.

The Supreme Court again dealt with this issue in Fibreboard Paper Products Corp. v. NLRB, 379 U.S. 203, 57 L.R.R.M. 2609 (1964). The Court held that an employer is required to bargain over the contracting out of bargaining unit work, within the limits of the evidence in that case. This decision has not been universally acclaimed; indeed, it has generated substantial criticism. M. Bernstein, "The NLRB's Adjudication — Rule Making Dilemma under the Administrative Procedure Act," 79 Yale L.J. 571, 580 (1970). However, the tests established in *Fibreboard* for the determination of a mandatory subject of bargaining are helpful. Summers, "Labor Law in the Supreme Court," 1964 Term, 75 Yale L.J. 59, 60 (1965). The Court noted that industrial practices in this country are a factor in determining a statutory subject of bargaining. The majority in *Fibreboard* held that bargaining is compelled to promote one of the primary purposes of the National Labor Relations Act, viz., ". . . the peaceful settlement of industrial disputes by subjecting labor-management controversies to the mediatory influence of negotiation. . . ." 379 U.S. at 211, 57 L.R.R.M. at 2612. From this premise flow two tests: (1) Is the subject of such vital concern to both labor and management that it is likely to lead to controversy and industrial conflict? And (2) is collective bargaining appropriate for resolving such issues?

The most recent decision by the Court dealing with this issue reaffirmed the *Fibreboard* test. Chemical Workers v. Pittsburgh Plate Glass Co., 40 U.S.L.W.

---

[3] The PERA analogues to these provisions can be found at Sections 10(e) and 15 of the Act.

4043, 78 L.R.R.M. 2974 (U.S., Dec. 7, 1971). In holding that benefits of retired employees are not within the mandatory rule the Court said, ". . . in each case the question is . . . whether it (the subject) vitally affects the terms and conditions of their (bargaining unit employees) employment." *Id.,* at 4050, 78 L.R.R.M. at 2982. However, the Court carefully pointed out in footnote No. 19 that the effect on the employer's freedom to conduct business must also be considered. *Id.*

This caveat specifically refers to Mr. Justice Stewart's concurring opinion in *Fibreboard,* wherein he argued that the majority's interpretation of the equivocal phrase "conditions of employment" ". . . seems to imply that any issue which may reasonably divide an employer and his employees must be the subject of compulsory collective bargaining." 379 U.S. at 221, 57 L.R.R.M. at 2616. After concluding that the term "conditions of employment" offers no workable guide, the opinion intuitively distinguished between ". . . managerial decisions which lie at the core of entrepreneurial control . . . and (those) not in themselves primarily about conditions of employment." *Id.* at 223, 57 L.R.R.M. at 2617. Those decisions which are fundamental to the basic direction of a corporate enterprise should not be subject to compulsory bargaining. *Id.*

The instant case presents the challenge the Court faced in *Fibreboard.* The Employer argues that establishment of the opening day of school is a management function not subject to mandatory bargaining. The Education Association responds that the Employer's unilateral act affected a vital employee interest. We agree with the Association that the careful planning of summer interlude activities, e.g., advanced study, supplementary employment, travel and vacation, causes the teachers to have a substantial interest in the opening date of school. Thus, the classic confrontation between management rights and employee interests is created. This conflict can be appropriately reconciled by balancing the interests involved.

In this process, we are confined by the doctrine of illegal delegation of power which commands that certain discretionary decisions be made solely by a designated official rather than through the collective bargaining process. Wellington and Winter, "The Limits of Collective Bargaining in Public Employment," 78 Yale L.J. 1107, 1109 (1969). In the instant case, neither the Michigan Statutes nor the regulations of the State Department of Education interfere with a holding that the school calendar is a subject which must be bargained. With respect to the opening of school, the Michigan law provides only that the school year of all school districts shall commence on the first day of July. MCLA 340.353. State law also requires that every school district shall determine the length of the school term, but that the length of the term shall be a minimum of 180 days. MCLA 340.575, as amended. Since these rules are silent as to establishing the opening day of school, we find that there are no delegation problems created by submitting the school calendar to bargaining.

The rather substantial interest which the school teachers have in planning their summer activities outweigh any claim of interference with the right to manage the school district.

We agree with the holding of the Wisconsin Supreme Court, which has said, in affirming a Wisconsin Employment Relations Commission decision, that the school calendar (including the opening day of school) has a direct and intimate relationship to the salaries and working conditions of the teachers. City of Madison v. Wisconsin Employment Relations Board, 37 Wis. 2d 43, 155 N.W.2d 78, 65 L.R.R.M. 2488 (1967). In accord with that decision is Norfolk Education Association v. South District of Norfolk, Nebraska Court of Industrial Relations, Case No. 40, October 6, 1971, 430 GERR B-7 (December 6, 1971).

Since a Michigan school district has already been required to bargain collectively with respect to certain aspects of the school calendar, e.g., holiday and vacation dates (Reese Public School District, 1967 MERC Lab. Op. 489), requiring the employer to bargain about the beginning and terminating dates of the school term does not impair significantly its right to manage. Nor are we impressed by the argument that bargaining with the teachers over the school calendar would foreclose bargaining on this subject with other school district employees. Other subjects of bargaining affect more than one bargaining unit. Bargaining over such subjects as fringe benefits, holidays, hours and the work day, vacations and wages, as well as the school calendar, would be facilitated by joint or coalition bargaining. Furthermore, the order to bargain does not command that there be agreement; we only order that the parties bargain in good faith about this subject.

A balancing approach to bargaining may be more suited to the realities of the public sector than the dichotomized scheme — mandatory and non-mandatory — used in the private sector. The Supreme Court in *Fibreboard* argued that this private sector concept was necessary to preserve a primary purpose of the National Labor Relations Act — industrial peace. The Court argued that labor disputes should be peacefully settled by subjecting the controversies to the "mediatory influence of negotiation." This scheme prohibits the use of economic weapons to compel agreement to discuss non-mandatory subjects of bargaining but strikes are permissible once the point of impasse concerning mandatory subjects of bargaining is reached. Economic force is illegal in the public sector in Michigan as PERA prohibits strikes by public employees. In Michigan, in the public sector, economic battle is to be replaced by invocation of the impasse resolution procedures of mediation and fact finding.

An expansion of the subjects about which the public employer ought to bargain, unlike the private sector, should not result in a corresponding increase in the use of economic force to resolve impasses. In the absence of legal public sector strikes, our only proper concern in the area of subjects of bargaining is whether the employer's management functions are being unduly restrained. All bargaining has some limiting effect on an employer.

Therefore, we will not order bargaining in those cases where the subjects are demonstrably within the core of entrepreneurial control. Although such subjects may affect interests of employees, we do not believe that such interests outweigh the right to manage.

In reversing the Trial Examiner on this issue, we hold that the opening and terminating days of the school term are subjects about which the employer must bargain. However, we apply this decision prospectively, and we hold that the Employer did not commit an unfair labor practice in its unilateral setting of the opening day of school. . . .

Chairman Howlett, dissenting: . . .

The opening (and, indeed, the closing) date for the school year is a function which should be within the province of the school board. It is a power which should not be delegated, even to the extent of bargaining.

While Michigan statutes do not specifically vest this power in boards of education, it flows logically from MCLA 340.353 (Mich. Stat. Ann. 15.3353) which specifies that the school year of all school districts commences on the 1st day of July, and the requirement of MCLA 340.575 (Mich. Stat. Ann. 15.3375) that the length of the term shall be a minimum of 180 days. Within these two specifications, the school board should determine when the schools open and the period within which the 180 days (or more, at the option of the school board) shall be held.

It is urged that the opening day of school (as well as the calendar) has a direct and intimate relationship to the salaries and working conditions of the teachers. The majority opinion notes the contention of the Association "that the careful planning of summer activities, e.g., advance study, supplementary employment, travel and vacation causes the teachers to have a substantial interest in the opening date of school." And, the parents of children have summer interlude activities which cause them to have a substantial interest in the opening day of school. The parents are not — and should not be — part of the bargaining process. Under the school law, the members of the school board are elected to represent the citizens of the district, including the parents. The parents' interest in the opening date of school is equal, if not paramount, to that of the teachers. This interest of the citizens of the district, including the parents, is not, however, within the sphere of collective bargaining. Their rights are in the political (using the word in its broad sense) arena. The legislative body — the school board — should make the decision of the period that school will be in session for all citizens of the district.

The majority notes that the United States Supreme Court, in Allied Chemical and Alkali Workers v. Pittsburgh Plate Glass Co., — U.S. —, 92 S. Ct. 383, 78 L.R.R.M. 2974 (1971), said that ". . . in each case the question is . . . whether it (the subject) vitally affects the terms and conditions of their (bargaining unit employees) *employment*." (Emphasis supplied.)

Here I depart from the rationale of the majority. Is the opening date of school a term or condition of *employment*? While teachers may be considered employees for some purposes from the date they are required by law to notify the school board that they will return for the next school year (MCLA 38.83, Mich. Stat. Ann. 15.1983), or, in the case of non-tenured teachers, have signed a contract, teachers' active employment does not start until the day they are required to report at the beginning of the school year.

We have held, as the majority opinion notes, that bargaining is required with respect to holiday and vacation dates (Reese Public School District, 1967 MERC Lab. Op. 489). These are working conditions within the period of employment. Actual employment does not start until teachers report to work. There is no term or condition of employment prior to the *start* of employment. This is consistent with our decision in City of Detroit, Police Department, 1971 MERC Lab. Op. 237, that recruitment standards (before employment begins) are not included with "other terms and conditions of employment," as that phrase is used in Section 15 of PERA.[1]

Perhaps the nearest parallel in the private sector is the right of management to determine when an establishment shall be opened for the manufacture of the product produced or performing of the service offered, by the employer.

## NOTES

1. *Accord*, Edmonds Education Ass'n v. Edmonds School Dist. No. 15, Decision No. 207-EDUC (Wash. PERC 1977).

2. The Maine Municipal Employees Labor Relations Act provides for negotiations over wages, hours, and working conditions, but specifically excludes "educational policies"

---

[1] Teachers are often paid over the 12 months of the year. This is, in most instances, at the choice of the teacher. However, the teacher is paid for services *performed* from the day school opens until the day school closes.

from the scope of mandatory negotiations. ME. REV. STAT. ch. 9-A, tit. 26, § 965(1)(c) (1975). In City of Biddeford v. Biddeford Teachers Association, 304 A.2d 387 (Me. Sup. Jud. Ct. 1973), the court held that the scheduling and length of school vacations and the setting of the beginning and ending dates for the school year were "matters of 'educational policies' and, as such, non-negotiable and beyond the scope of binding arbitration." After noting that this issue involved "a substantial intermixing of judgments transcending teacher interests and embracing important interests of the general citizenry," the court observed that in establishing a calendar it is necessary to take into account "the plans and interests of families, the need to arrange for the presence of all non-teaching personnel who function while students are in attendance at school and the interests and concerns of all other parts of the community related to, or affected by, the times when students will be in attendance at school or on vacation." Accord, Burlington County Faculty Ass'n v. Burlington County College, 64 N.J. 10, 311 A.2d 733 (1973) (although "calendar undoubtedly has some practical effect on the faculty's employment arrangements . . ., it is not a subject of mandatory negotiation"). See also West Hartford Education Ass'n v. DeCourcy, 162 Conn. 566, 295 A.2d 526 (1972), in which the court held that since the scope of bargaining under the Connecticut Teachers Act was limited to "salaries and other conditions of employment" and did not include "hours," the legislature intended to exclude such matters as length of the school day and school calendar from the scope of mandatory negotiations.

3. The scope of bargaining in the private sector and role of the NLRB has been the subject of extended discussion. Among the many excellent articles are Cox & Dunlop, *Regulation of Collective Bargaining by the National Labor Relations Board*, 63 HARV. L. REV. 389 (1950); Cox, *The Duty to Bargain in Good Faith*, 71 HARV. L. REV. 1401 (1958).

4. The *Borg-Warner* distinction between mandatory, permissive, and illegal subjects of bargaining has been utilized by several state labor relations agencies. See, e.g., Town of Danvers, Case Nos. MUP-2292 and 2299 (Mass. LRC 1977); Town of Stratford, Decision No. 1069 (Conn. SLRB 1972).

5. The determination of whether a given subject is mandatory or permissive has legal significance in at least five respects. *First,* while a party can propose a permissive subject of bargaining, it is generally an unfair labor practice for that party to insist on negotiations over a permissive subject to the point of impasse. Conversely, it is perfectly legal for the other party to refuse to negotiate over a permissive subject. In a few states like Pennsylvania an employer is required, upon request, to meet and confer but not negotiate on policy matters affecting wages, hours and terms and conditions of employment.

*Second,* if a permissive subject is incorporated in a collective bargaining agreement, there is normally no obligation to negotiate over its deletion in a succeeding agreement. Thus, several PERBs have held that a permissive subject may be removed from a succeeding agreement upon the request of either party without any further obligation to negotiate over the subject. See, e.g., City of Troy, 10 PERB ¶ 3015 (N.Y. 1977); Town of Maplewood, 4 NJPER 258 (N.J. PERC 1978).

*Third,* a public employer may not take unilateral action without first giving the union notice and an opportunity to negotiate to impasse over a mandatory subject of bargaining. This limitation on a public employer's right to take unilateral action does not, however, normally exist during the term of a collective bargaining agreement where the employer has specifically or implicitly retained the right to take the action in question. See pp. 405-10, *infra.*

*Fourth,* a public employer may take unilateral action on a permissive subject without any prior notice or bargaining with the union. Nevertheless, the employer may be required to negotiate over the *impact* of the action. See City of New York and MEBA, District No. 1, pp. 333-35, *infra.*

*Fifth,* the determination of whether a given topic is mandatory or permissive affects what items can be submitted for resolution pursuant to a statutory impasse procedure. Under most impasse procedures, the fact finder or arbitrator, in the absence of mutual agreement, does not have the authority to make a recommendation or decision on permissive subjects of bargaining. In other words, if a party seeks to submit a permissive subject to an arbitrator, the other party can normally oppose consideration of this issue by the arbitrator on the ground that it is not a mandatory subject of bargaining.

6. While most public sector statutes define the scope of bargaining in general terms
*(e.g.,* wages, hours and other terms and conditions of employment), there are a few
noteworthy exceptions. For example, the California Rodda Act covering certificated and
classified educational personnel specifically sets forth what is negotiable and provides that
all matters not specifically enumerated as mandatory subjects of bargaining "are reserved
to the public school employer and may not be a subject of meeting and negotiating. . . ."
CAL. GOV'T CODE, § 3543.2 (West 1975). In this situation, the legal subjects of bargaining
are coterminous with the mandatory subjects set forth in the Act; there are not permissive
subjects. Unless specifically enumerated, a subject that might be considered as a
permissive subject in other jurisdictions is an illegal subject under the Rodda Act in that
a school board is legally prohibited from meeting and negotiating over such
non-mandatory subjects.

7. Both the National Education Association and the American Federation of Teachers
have asserted that the scope of negotiations in education should be virtually unlimited.
The National Education Association in 1965 stated:

   A professional group has responsibilities beyond self-interest, including a
   responsibility for the general welfare of the school system. Teachers and other members
   of the professional staff have an interest in the conditions which attract and retain a
   superior teaching force, in the in-service training programs, in class size, in the selection
   of textbooks and in other matters which go far beyond those which would be included
   in a narrow definition of working conditions. Negotiations should include all matters
   which affect the quality of the educational system. NATIONAL EDUCATION ASSOCIATION,
   GUIDELINES FOR PROFESSIONAL NEGOTIATIONS 21-22 (1965).

The past president of the American Federation of Teachers, Charles Cogen, stated that
"class size, number of classes taught, curriculum, hiring standards, textbooks and supplies,
extra curricular activities — in fact anything having to do with the operation of the school
— is a matter for professional concern and should thus be subject to collective
bargaining." Cogen, *Collective Negotiations in Public Education,* in SORRY . . . No
GOVERNMENT TODAY 141, 148 (R. Walsh ed. 1969).

8. Following the lead of the United States Supreme Court in Fibreboard Paper Products
Corp. v. NLRB, 379 U.S. 203, 85 S. Ct. 398, 13 L.Ed.2d 233 (1964), most state courts
and boards have held that contracting out is a mandatory subject of bargaining if it affects
bargaining unit employees. *See, e.g.,* Van Buren Public Schools, 1973 MERC Lab. Op.
714 (Mich.), *aff'd,* 61 Mich. App. 6, 232 N.W.2d 278 (1975); Southington Board of
Education, Decision No. 1221 (Conn. SLRB 1974); PLRB v. Sto-Rox School Board, 9
PPER ¶ 9065 (Pa. LRB 1978); Saratoga Springs School District, 11 PERB ¶ 3037 (N.Y.
1978); State of Rhode Island (Univ. of R.I.), Case No. EE-1899 (R.I. SLRB 1973);
Metropolitan Utilities District Employee Ass'n v. Metropolitan Utilities District, Case No.
59 (Neb. CIR 1972); Township of Little Egg Harbor, 2 NJPER 5 (N.J. PERC 1976);
Teamsters Local 2 v. Board of Cty. Comm'rs, ULP Case No. 4-76 (Mont. PBA 1976);
Unified School District of Racine County v. WERC, 81 Wis. 2d 89, 259 N.W.2d 724 (1977).
On the other hand, the Federal Labor Relations Council in Tidewater, Virginia Federal
Employees Metal Trades Council, Case No. 71A-56 (1973), held that a proposal
concerning contracting out was not negotiable since Section 12(b) (5) of Executive Order
11491 "requires agency management to reserve on a continuing basis the right to decide
what methods, means, and personnel will be utilized to accomplish its work." In rejecting
the union's reliance on private sector precedent, the FLRC stated that "the special public
policy considerations relevant to Federal Government contracting are so substantial as
to warrant rejection of private sector experience and law as controlling on the subject."
The FLRC did note, however, that "proposals to establish procedures which management
would observe leading to the exercise of the retained management rights under 12(b) (5)
would be negotiable to the extent they do not interfere with the exercise of the rights
themselves." *Accord,* AFSCME District Council 37 and City of New York, Decision No.
B-1-74 (N.Y.C. OCB 1974) (right to subcontract "would clearly be within the city's
reserved management rights," but "it is equally clear that the practical impact of the
decision to subcontract on the terms and conditions of employment of the affected
employees must be bargained over").

9. In Allied Chemical & Alkali Workers Local 1 v. Pittsburgh Plate Glass Co., 404 U.S. 157, 92 S. Ct. 383, 30 L. Ed. 2d 341 (1971), the Supreme Court held that retirees were not "employees" within the meaning of the National Labor Relations Act and that therefore an employer was not mandatorily required to negotiate over a union's proposal that the pension benefits for retirees be increased. The New York City Office of Collective Bargaining in District Council 37, AFSCME and City of New York, NYC OCB Decision No. B-21-72 (1972), held that the City's collective bargaining law should be construed similarly. Accordingly, it held that retired city employees could not appropriately be included in a unit with active employees for the purposes of collective bargaining and that a union could not bargain on behalf of retired city employees for contributions to the health and welfare fund. *Accord,* Troy Uniformed Firefighters Ass'n and City of Troy, 9 PERB ¶ 3015 (N.Y. 1977).

While pensions and retirement benefits are normally considered mandatory subjects of bargaining, several states have enacted legislation which specifically prohibits or restricts the negotiation of pensions or retirement benefits. For example, the New York Taylor Law was amended to specifically exclude from the scope of negotiations "any benefits provided by or to be provided by a public retirement system, or payments to a fund or insurer to provide an income for retirees, or payment to retirees or their beneficiaries." The New York Law further provides that "[n]o retirements benefits shall be negotiated pursuant to this article, and any benefits so negotiated shall be void." NEW YORK CIVIL SERVICE LAW § 201(4) (McKinney Supp. 1978). Similarly, the Hawaii Law excludes from the scope of negotiations "retirement benefits." HAWAII REV. STAT. § 89-9(c) (Supp. 1978). In Hawaii Fire Fighters Ass'n, Local 1463, Decision No. 65 (Hawaii PERB 1975), the Hawaii Board held that the legislature did not intend this exclusion to be narrowly construed and that, therefore, the entire retirement system was excluded from negotiations and not just the amount of benefits to be paid.


### RIDGEFIELD PARK EDUCATION ASSOCIATION v. RIDGEFIELD PARK BOARD OF EDUCATION

Supreme Court of New Jersey
78 N.J. 144, 393 A.2d 278 (1978)

PASHMAN, J.

At issue herein is whether the 1974 amendments to the New Jersey Employer-Employee Relations Act, *L.* 1968, *c.* 303, as amended by *L.* 1974, *c.* 123, *N.J.S.A.* 34:13A-1 *et seq.* (the Act), created a class of permissively negotiable matters which, while not qualifying as mandatorily negotiable terms and conditions of employment, are nevertheless negotiable on a voluntary basis. The Public Employment Relations Commission (PERC) has concluded that such permissive category indeed exists. . . . PERC has also determined that disputes involving provisions of collectively negotiated agreements covering permissive matters may be resolved by binding arbitration if the matter is otherwise arbitrable, as is the case with those covering mandatorily negotiable matters. . . . The public employer herein contends that with respect to the issue of negotiability there are but two types of subjects — those as to which collective negotiation is mandatory and those as to which it is unlawful. The former category is comprised of those subjects which pertain to the terms and conditions of public employment while the latter includes all other subjects. It claims that any provision of a negotiated agreement which concerns subjects in the latter category is *ultra vires* and thus unenforceable.

The facts of this case are not in dispute. The collective agreement between plaintiff Association, the majority representative of the Board's teaching employees, and the defendant Board, which ran until July 1, 1977, defined a grievance as follows:

The term "grievance," means a complaint by an employee, group of employees, or the Association, that, as to him, there has been an inequitable, improper, or unjust application, interpretation, or violation of a policy, agreement, or administrative decision.

The contract provided for binding arbitration as the terminal step in the grievance process:

In the event the aggrieved party is dissatisfied with the determination of the Board he shall have the right to request arbitration pursuant to rules and regulations established by the Public Employment Relations Commission under the provisions of Chapter 303, Public Laws of 1968. The findings of the arbitrator shall be binding on all parties.

The collective agreement included a provision governing the subject of teacher transfers and reassignments.

### ARTICLE XIV—*Voluntary and Involuntary Transfers and Reassignments—*

A. Employees who desire a change in grade and/or subject assignment or who desire to transfer to another building may file a written statement(s) of such desire with the superintendent. Such statement(s) shall include the grade and/or subject to which the employee desires to be assigned and the school or schools to which he desires to be transferred, in order of preference.

As soon as practicable, and in no case later than June 1, the superintendent shall post in each school and deliver to the Association a system-wide schedule showing the names of all employees who have been reassigned or transferred and the nature of such reassignment or transfer.

B. In the determination of requests for voluntary reassignments and/or transfers, the wishes of the individual employee shall be honored, upon the recommendation of the superintendent and approval of the Board, to the extent that the transfer or reassignment does not conflict with the instructional requirements and best interests of the school system.

C. Notice of an involuntary transfer or reassignment shall be given to the employee as far in advance as practicable. In the case of teachers, except in an emergency situation, notice shall be given not later than April 30.

During the 1975-1976 and 1976-1977 school years certain teachers were involuntarily reassigned to teach courses or grades which they did not wish to teach, were refused a desired transfer to a different school, or were involuntarily transferred to another school. The Association filed grievances on behalf of these teachers. The Board denied all of them. The Association then sought to have these grievances resolved by binding arbitration, pursuant to the contractual arbitration clause. See *ante* at 280. The Board contended that the grievances pertained to matters outside the legal scope of negotiations, and hence were not arbitrable.

The Association instituted this action under *N.J.S.A.* 2A:24-1 and 3 seeking an order from the Chancery Division compelling the Board to submit the grievances involving transfers and reassignments to binding arbitration. The Board made a cross-application for an order enjoining the arbitrations. In the proceedings before the Chancery Judge, the Board admitted that it had a contractual duty to arbitrate the disputes herein, but submitted that the real issue was the legality of arbitrating these matters. The Board's request that the case be transferred to PERC for a decision on the negotiability of the issues involved in the grievances was denied. On March 4, 1977 the Chancery Division rendered an oral opinion adverse to the Board. On March 22, 1977 the Chancery Judge issued a judgment and order that the parties proceed to arbitration.

On March 2, 1977 the Board had filed a Petition for Scope-of-Negotiations Determination with PERC pursuant to *N.J.S.A.* 34:13A-5.4(d). It sought an order from PERC enjoining arbitration on both an interim basis and on a permanent basis. The interim request was denied in an interlocutory decision on April 5, 1977. PERC No. 77-45, 3 *NJPER* 150. This denial was based on PERC's determination that its decisions in *In re Bridgewater-Raritan Regional Bd. of Ed., supra,* and *In re Bd. of Ed. of City of Trenton, supra,* mandated a conclusion that the matters in issue, though permissive and not mandatorily negotiable, would be arbitrable if otherwise within the contractual arbitration clause.

Meanwhile, the Board obtained a temporary stay of the enforcement of the Chancery judgment in order to enable it to apply for a stay from the Appellate Division. On April 20, 1977 a single judge of the Appellate Division denied the motion for a stay. However, arbitration had not commenced as of July 7, 1977, when a full panel of the Appellate Division granted the Board's motion for a stay.

PERC gave the matter a full hearing and issued its scope determination on August 17, 1977. PERC No. 78-9, 3 *NJPER* 319 (1977). PERC reaffirmed its earlier holding in *In re Bridgewater-Raritan Bd. of Ed., supra,* 3 *NJPER* at 25, that in enacting *L.*1974, *c.* 123, the Legislature reacted to the restrictiveness the standards enunciated by this Court in *Dunellen Bd. of Ed. v. Dunellen Ed. Ass'n,* 64 *N.J.* 17, 311 *A.2d* 737 (1973), concerning negotiability and arbitrability in the public sector. PERC observed that the critical factor in the Court's *Dunellen* holding was the *L.*1968, *c.* 303 version of *N.J.S.A.* 34:13A-8.1, which provided, in effect, that negotiated agreements could not "annul or modify any statute or statutes of this State." Thus, great significance was ascribed to *L.*1974, *c.* 123, § 6, which amended that statute effectively to provide that no negotiated agreement could "annul or modify any *pension* statute or statutes of this State." PERC also cited pertinent language from the 1974 amendments to *N.J.S.A.* 34:13A-5.3, which establishes the primacy of the negotiated grievance procedures in dispute resolution:

> Notwithstanding any procedures for the resolution of disputes, controversies or grievances established by any other statute, grievance procedures established by agreement between the public employer and the representative organization *shall be utilized* for any dispute covered by the terms of such agreement. (emphasis added)

PERC concluded that one of the purposes of *L.*1974, *c.* 123 was to expand the scope of arbitrable issues. So long as no specific statutes are violated and no overriding public policy contravened, PERC was of the opinion that both negotiation and arbitration of permissive matters are acceptable. In support of this view, PERC cited *In re Bd. of Ed. of City of Trenton, supra,* 2 *NJPER* at 352, where it had found that involuntary employee transfers were not precluded from negotiation by statute and were thus a permissible subject of negotiation, and *In re Bd. of Ed. of the Borough of Verona,* PERC No. 77-42, 3 *NJPER* 80 (1977), where it had found that a Board's decision to replace a teacher's non-teaching duty period with a classroom teaching period was also a permissibly negotiable subject. PERC held that the disputes herein were permissively negotiable and thus arbitrable if otherwise arbitrable under the agreement. 3 *NJPER* at 320-321.

The Board filed a motion for direct certification on July 18, 1977. On July 27,

1977 the Association appealed to this Court to vacate the interlocutory stay issued by the Appellate Division. In the alternative the Association requested direct certification. We directly certified this case while it was pending unheard in the Appellate Division, 75 *N.J.* 584, 384 *A.2d* 815 (1977).

I

Before we address the merits, some guidelines regarding proper procedure in these cases should be set. Under our existing legislative scheme it may be necessary to go to both PERC and the Superior Court in order to completely resolve a disagreement concerning the arbitrability of a particular dispute. When one party claims that a given dispute is arbitrable under the contract and the other party resists arbitration, the party desiring arbitration should seek an order from the Superior Court compelling arbitration. See *N.J.S.A.* 2A:24-1 *et seq.* Where the trial judge determines that the real controversy is not one of contractual arbitrability, but rather concerns the propriety of the parties negotiating and agreeing on the item in dispute, he should refrain from passing on the merits of that issue.

PERC has primary jurisdiction to make a determination on the merits of the question of whether the subject matter of a particular dispute is within the scope of collective negotiations. *N.J.S.A.* 34:13A-5.4(d). . . . However, the reach of this decision is limited. PERC discussed this point in *In re Hillside Bd. of Ed.*, PERC No. 76-11, 1 *NJPER* 55, 57 (1975):

> The Commission is addressing the abstract issue: is the subject matter in dispute within the scope of collective negotiations. Whether that subject is within the arbitration clause of the agreement, whether the facts are as alleged by the grievant, whether the contract provides a defense for the employer's alleged action, or even whether there is a valid arbitration clause in the agreement, or any other question which might be raised is not to be determined by the Commission in a scope proceeding. Those are questions appropriate for determination by an arbitrator and/or the courts.

Of course, where the existence of a contractual obligation to arbitrate is not contested, the parties need only go to PERC for a ruling on whether the subject matter of the dispute whose grievability is contested is within the scope of collective negotiations. PERC can then afford complete relief. If PERC concludes that the dispute is within the legal scope of negotiability and agreement between the employer and employees, the matter may proceed to arbitration. Where PERC concludes that a particular dispute is not within the scope of collective negotiations, and thus not arbitrable, it must issue an injunction permanently restraining arbitration. *See Bd. of Ed. of Englewood v. Englewood Teachers,* 135 *N.J. Super.* 120, 124, 342 *A.2d* 866 (App.Div. 1975). Moreover, we agree with the decision in *Bd. of Ed. of Englewood v. Englewood Teachers, supra,* that PERC is empowered to order that arbitration proceedings be suspended during the pendency of a scope-of-negotiations proceeding. Where necessary, PERC may go to the Appellate Division to seek an appropriate order to compel compliance with its orders in scope proceedings. *N.J.S.A.* 34:13A-5.4(f). Where a party disagrees with PERC's determination on the scope question, an appeal to the Appellate Division is expressly authorized. *N.J.S.A.* 34:13A-5.4(d).

We agree with PERC that contract interpretation is a question for judicial resolution. Thus, where a party resists an attempt to have a dispute arbitrated, it may go to the Superior Court for a ruling on the issue of its contractual obligation to arbitrate. However, the issue of contractual arbitrability may not be reached if the threshold issue of whether the subject matter of the grievance is within the scope of collective negotiations is contested. In that event, a ruling on that issue must be obtained from PERC. Thus, the preferable procedure in the instant case would have been for PERC to have rendered its scope determination before the issue of contractual arbitrability was addressed. Where an item is within the scope of collective negotiations, and a court determines that the agreement contains a valid arbitration clause, the matter must proceed to arbitration.

The arbitrator's function is to comply with the authority the parties have given him in the agreement. Assuming that the item is a proper subject of arbitration under the agreement, the arbitrator will reach the merits and render an award. If the losing party is unwilling to abide by the award, the prevailing party may seek to have the award confirmed by the Superior Court. *See N.J.S.A.* 2A:24-7; *Amal. Transit Wkrs. Local 540 v. Mercer Cty. Impr. Authority,* 76 *N.J.* 245, 386 *A.2d* 1290 (1978).

Thus, PERC, the Superior Court and the arbitrator have distinct functions under our present scheme. To avoid needless procedural delays, we commend these guidelines to the bar.

## II

By way of preliminary observation, we note that PERC was correct in concluding that under the test set forth in *Dunellen Ed. Assn. v. Dunellen Bd. of Ed.,* 64 *N.J.* 17, 25, 311 *A.2d* 737 (1973) and *Englewood Bd. of Ed. v. Englewood Teachers Ass'n,* 64 *N.J.* 1, 7, 311 *A.2d* 729 (1973), and today reaffirmed in *State v. State Supervisory Employees Ass'n, supra,* 78 *N.J.* at 67, 393 *A.2d* at 233, teacher transfers and reassignments are not mandatorily negotiable terms and conditions of employment. That test defined negotiable terms and conditions of employment as those matters which intimately and directly affect the work and welfare of public employees and on which negotiated agreement would not significantly interfere with the exercise of inherent management prerogatives pertaining to the determination of governmental policy. *State v. State Supervisory Employees Ass'n, supra,* 78 *N.J.* at 67, 393 *A.2d* at 233. The selection of the school in which a teacher works or the grade and subjects which he teaches undoubtedly have an appreciable effect on his welfare. However, even assuming that this effect could be considered direct and intimate, we find that this aspect of the transfer decision is insignificant in comparison to its relationship to the Board's managerial duty to deploy personnel in the manner which it considers most likely to promote the overall goal of providing all students with a thorough and efficient education. Thus, we find that the issue of teacher transfers is one on which negotiated agreement would significantly interfere with a public employer's discharge of inherent managerial responsibilities. Accordingly, it is not a matter as to which collective negotiation is mandatory.

## III

To bolster its conclusion that *L.*1974, *c.* 123 contemplated an expansion of negotiation into a permissive category of items, PERC makes several arguments. First, it points out that in passing *L.*1974, *c.* 124, enacted on the same day as Chapter 123, which created a Public Employer-Employee Relations Study Commission, the Legislature implicitly assumed that there were already three categories of negotiating subjects. That statute directs the Commission, *inter alia*, to study

> Whether or not it is necessary and desirable either to define the phrase "terms and conditions of employment" as used in section 7 of the 1968 act [*N.J.S.A.* 34:13A-5.3] *and, in so doing, specify what subjects are mandatory, voluntary or illegal within the scope of bargaining or of grievance arbitration,* or to require that procedural guidelines be established for determining the same. [*L.*1974, *c.* 124, § 3(c) (emphasis added)]

We do not accord the great degree of significance to this legislative action that PERC does. The mandate of the Study Commission was not necessarily limited to examining the law as it existed. Moreover, it is abundantly clear that a proposal to study and suggest changes is not given the same close scrutiny by legislators as is one which has the force of law. Thus, even legislators vehemently opposed to permissive negotiation may have voted in favor of setting up the Study Commission. Finally, the Legislature was well aware of the fact that we had held in *Burlington Cty. Fac. Assoc. v. Bd. of Trustees, supra,* that no expansive view of negotiations would be implied from ambiguous legislation. We specifically required "clear and distinct phraseology" for a change of such magnitude.

PERC also alludes to *L.*1977, *c.* 85, *N.J.S.A.* 34:13A-14 to 21, which provides for compulsory and binding "interest" arbitration of impasses in contract negotiations between local, county and state governments and policemen and firemen. That statute expressly contemplates a permissive category of negotiation:

*legis. here recog- nizes a permissive category*

> Factfinding shall be limited to those issues that are within the required scope of negotiations unless the parties to the factfinding agree to factfinding on permissive subjects of negotiation. [*N.J.S.A.* 34:13A-16b]

> Arbitration shall be limited to those subjects that are within the required scope of collective negotiations, except that the parties may agree to submit to arbitration one or more permissive subjects of negotiation. [*N.J.S.A.* 34:13A-16f(4)]

Of course, this enactment is not now before us. Neither is it of great importance to our interpretation of *L.*1974, *c.* 123. It represents a specific decision on the part of the Legislature to authorize permissive negotiations with respect to police and firemen. Moreover, if it were so clear that *L.*1974, *c.* 123 had created such a permissive area, we doubt that the Legislature would have had to provide carefully for a permissive category in *L.*1977, *c.* 85. This recent statute covering a small percentage of all public employees may not be accorded dispositive effect in interpreting a more general statute passed three years earlier. We intimate no view as to the validity of the authorization for binding arbitration of "permissive subjects of negotiation" in *N.J.S.A.* 34:13A-16f(4).

PERC also cites federal precedents under the Labor Management Relations Act, 29 *U.S.C.* § 141 *et seq.* Illustrative of these cases is *NLRB v. Wooster Div. of Borg-Warner Corp.,* 356 *U.S.* 342, 349, 78 *S.Ct.* 718, 2 *L.Ed.2d* 823, 828 (1958), where the United States Supreme Court held that under 29 *U.S.C.* § 158(a)(5) and § 158(d), collective bargaining was mandatory only as to terms and conditions of employment. As to other matters, each party was "free to bargain or not to bargain, and to agree to or not to agree." Of course, *Borg-Warner* dealt with the private sphere, and is therefore inapposite here.[2]

---

[2] In *Galloway Tp. Bd. of Ed. v. Galloway Tp. Ass'n of Ed. Secretaries,* 78 *N.J.* 1, 393 *A.2d* 218 (1978), we held that since the unfair practice provisions of *N.J.S.A.* 34:13A-5.4 closely parallel those

In *Lullo v. Intern. Assoc. of Fire Fighters,* 55 *N.J.* 409, 436-441, 262 *A.2d* 681 (1970), we pointed out the significant differences between *N.J.S.A.* 34:13A-5.3 which grants a right to "collective negotiations" and 29 *U.S.C.* § 157 which grants a right to "collective bargaining."

> It is crystal clear that in using the term "collective negotiations" the Legislature intended to recognize inherent limitations on the bargaining power of public employer and employee.... And undoubtedly they were conscious also that public agencies, departments, etc., cannot abdicate or bargain away their continuing legislative or executive obligations or discretion. Consequently, absent some further changes in pertinent statutes public employers may not be able to make binding contractual commitments relating to certain subjects.... Finally, it signified an effort to make public employers and employees realize that the process of collective bargaining as understood in the private employment sector cannot be transplanted into the public service. [55 *N.J.* at 440, 262 *A.2d* at 697]

Thus, federal precedents concerning the scope of collective bargaining in the private sector are of little value in determining the permissible scope of negotiability in public employment labor relations in New Jersey.

It is also contended that *N.J.S.A.* 34:13A-5.3, as amended by *L.*1974, *c.* 123, § 4, see *ante* at 282, which mandates that grievance procedures negotiated by the parties supersede any mechanisms for the resolution of disputes provided by any statute, indicates that a category of permissively negotiable matters is now contemplated by the Act. PERC placed particular emphasis on the fact that the Legislature used the words "disputes and controversies" in the amended version of *N.J.S.A.* 34:13A-5.3, since they are the very words found in *N.J.S.A.* 18A:6-9 which gives the Commissioner of Education jurisdiction to resolve disagreements arising under the education laws. PERC contends that *Dunellen, supra,* 64 *N.J.* at 30-31, 311 *A.2d* 737, relied upon these words in *N.J.S.A.* 18A:6-9 to distinguish those matters which could be arbitrated from those matters which could not. Thus, the 1974 amendment is viewed by PERC as modifying the narrow scope of arbitration permitted by the Act which we found in *Dunellen.* *(leg is intent to incl. a broad area of barg subjects)*

PERC errs in two respects. First, standing alone, *N.J.S.A.* 34:13A-5.3 is ineffective as a vehicle for expanding the permissible scope of arbitration. To be arbitrable, a matter must qualify as one on which the parties may negotiate. A matter which is not legally negotiable in the first place cannot be arbitrable. We have today held that the scope of grievability mandated by *N.J.S.A.* 34:13A-5.3 is limited to matters which affect the terms and conditions of public employment as that concept has been defined in our cases. *Tp. of West Windsor v. PERC,* 78 *N.J.* 98, 393 *A.2d* 255 (1978). Thus, only insofar as *N.J.S.A.* 34:13A-8.1 is viewed as increasing the legal scope of collective negotiation may *N.J.S.A.* 34:13A-5.3 be viewed as expanding the permissible coverage of contractual procedures for the resolution of grievances. Second, PERC and the Association both err in concluding that the *Dunellen* Trilogy was wholly based on statutory considerations. While our decisions in *Dunellen* and its companion cases were primarily based on the statutory language of *L.*1968, *c.* 303 and the legislative intent underlying that enactment, we were not oblivious to more fundamental, constitutionally-rooted considerations of policy. As we observed in *Dunellen:*

---

of the Labor Management Relations Act, 29 U.S.C. § 158 and § 160, the federal precedents should guide our interpretation of this State act. However, this is not true with respect to scope of negotiability. We wish to specifically caution PERC and the Appellate Division of the limited relevance of private sector precedents with respect to scope-of-negotiations determinations.

*[T]he Legislature,* in adopting the very general terms of *L.*1968, *c.* 303, *did not contemplate that the local boards of education would or could* abdicate their management responsibilities for the local educational policies or that the State educational authorities would or could abdicate their management responsibilities for the State educational policies. . . .

[64 *N.J.* at 25, 311 *A.2d* at 741 (emphasis added)]
Moreover, full application of PERC's view that everything which in any way affects the terms and conditions of public employment is negotiable at the option of the parties, unless such negotiation on a given topic is precluded by a specific statute, would be inconsistent with a successor statute in the education area. The Legislature has determined that community involvement in educational decisions, insuring some democratic control over such matters, is a significant part of a thorough and efficient system of education in this state. In passing the Public School Education Act of 1975, *L.*1975, *c.* 212, now codified as *N.J.S.A. 18A:7A-1 et seq.,* it gave that assumption the force of law:

(a) The Legislature finds and declares that:
. . .
(5) In order to encourage citizen involvement in educational matters, New Jersey should provide for free public schools in a manner which guarantees and encourages local participation consistent with the goal of a thorough and efficient system serving all of the children of the State:
(6) A thorough and efficient system of education includes local school districts in which decisions pertaining to the hiring and dismissal of personnel, the curriculum of the schools, the establishment of district budgets, and other essentially local questions are made democratically with a maximum of citizen involvement and self-determination and are consistent with Statewide goals, guidelines and standards; . . .
[*N.J.S.A.* 18A:7A-2]
Literal application of PERC's interpretation of *L.*1974, *c.* 123 would result in the emasculation of the intent of this later act. There would be little room for community involvement if agreements concerning educational policy matters could be negotiated behind closed doors and disputes concerning that agreement settled by an arbitrator who lacks public accountability. We simply find insufficient evidence of a legislative intent to permit this result to justify interpreting *N.J.S.A.* 34:13A-5.3 and 8.1 in the manner suggested by PERC.

Our holding herein is that *L.*1974, *c.* 123 did not clearly indicate a legislative intent to create a permissive category of negotiations. Thus, we reaffirm our holding in *Dunellen* that there are but two categories of subjects in public employment negotiation — mandatorily negotiable terms and conditions of employment and non-negotiable matters of governmental policy. Since the subject of teacher transfers is not within the scope of mandatory negotiability, the Board acted in excess of its authority in agreeing to a provision of its collective agreement with the Association which would limit its managerial prerogatives on the subject. Accordingly, the contractual provision purporting to do so is invalid and may not be enforced against the Board in any arbitration proceeding. While a policy such as that expressed in the relevant contractual provision may be a salutary one, adherence to that policy is not something to which the Board could obligate itself in a collective agreement providing for binding arbitration.

## IV

We are hesitant to find the existence of a permissive category of negotiable matters in public employment labor relations to be implicit in the amended act because such a classification might create serious problems in our democratic system. These potential difficulties should be carefully considered by the Legislature before taking any action expressly to authorize permissive negotiability with respect to all public employees. It is quite clear from our reading of the legislative history of *L.*1974, *c.* 123 that the lawmakers did not purport to sanction the delegation of governmental policy decisions on every matter in any way touching upon the terms and conditions of public employment to the sphere of collective negotiation. We deem it appropriate for this Court to comment on these difficult questions concerning the permissibility of delegating governmental powers to private groups or of entrusting the formulation of governmental policy to an arena where the democratic voice of the electorate cannot be heard.

In *Tp. of West Windsor v. PERC,* 78 *N.J.* 98, 393 *A.2d* 255 (1978), we indicated that public employees' special access to government applies only where the government is acting in the capacity of an employer, and not where it is acting in its capacity as public policymaker. A private employer may bargain away as much or as little of its managerial control as it likes. *Tp. of West Windsor, supra.* However, the very foundation of representative democracy would be endangered if decisions on significant matters of governmental policy were left to the process of collective negotiation, where citizen participation is precluded. This Court would be most reluctant to sanction collective agreement on matters which are essentially managerial in nature, because the true managers are the people. Our democratic system demands that governmental bodies retain their accountability to the citizenry.

Our concern is with the very function of government. Both state and federal doctrines of substantive due process prohibit delegations of governmental policymaking power to private groups where a serious potential for self-serving action is created thereby. . . . To be constitutionally sustainable, a delegation must be narrowly limited, reasonable, and surrounded with stringent safeguards to protect against the possibility of arbitrary or self-serving action detrimental to third parties or the public good generally.

. . . .

Since teachers possess substantial expertise in the education area, negotiations between teachers' associations and boards of education present a situation where an agreement which effectively determines governmental policy on various issues is especially likely. The impropriety of permitting such educational policy matters to be determined in the forum of collective negotiation — just as if they pertained to the terms and conditions of employment — is every bit as strong as it is in other areas of public employment. The interests of teachers do not always coincide with the interests of the students on many important matters of educational policy. Teachers' associations, like any employee organizations, have as their primary responsibility the advancement of the interests of their members. Arbitrators, to whom the resolution of grievances under collective agreements is generally entrusted, are concerned primarily with contractual rights and remedies. Of the relevant actors at the local level, only school boards have a primary responsibility to the public at large, as they have been delegated the responsibility of ensuring that all children receive a thorough and efficient education. These boards are responsible to the local electorate, as well as to the State, and may not make difficult educational policy decisions in a forum from which the public is excluded. Moreover, a multi-year contract covering policy matters would freeze the *status quo* and prevent a school board from making a flexible, creative response to changed circumstances, which might well preclude its acting in the best interests of the students.

The Legislature is of course free to exercise its judgment in determining whether or not a permissive category of negotiation is sound policy. We wish merely to point out that careful consideration of the limits which our democratic system places on delegation of government powers is called for before any such action is taken. On the other hand, we are in no way prejudging the constitutionality of the concept of permissive negotiation *per se.*

We hold that the enactment of *L.*1974, *c.* 123, §§ 4 and 6, *N.J.S.A.* 34:13A-5.3 and 8.1, did not have the effect of creating a new category of negotiating subjects in public employment labor relations comprised of matters negotiable at the option of the parties even though primarily concerned with governmental policy. PERC's scope-of-negotiations determination requiring that the Ridgefield Park Board of Education submit the propriety of teacher transfers and reassignments to binding arbitration is disapproved. In view of the foregoing, the Chancery Division order that the parties proceed to arbitration is reversed and arbitration is permanently enjoined.

CONFORD, P. J. A. D. (temporarily assigned), concurring and dissenting.

I concur in the Court's judgment in this case that arbitration be permanently enjoined. But I do not reach that conclusion by the Court's rationale — *i. e.,* that there is no legal category of permissively negotiable items in public employment relations but only the mandatorily negotiable category of "terms and conditions" of employment. I agree with the Public Employment Relations Commission (PERC) that the Legislature has by *L.*1974, *c.* 123 and *L.*1977, *c.* 85 manifested its recognition of a class of permissive as well as of mandatory items for labor negotiation and with PERC's implementation by regulations of that understanding in the exercise of its scope-of-negotations jurisdiction under *L.*1974, *c.* 123 (*N.J.S.A.* 34:13A-5.4d.).

Practical recognition of negotiations in the permissive area has become a fact of life in the course of actual negotiations of collective agreements throughout the State in recent years and the validity thereof has been adjudicated in several leading jurisdictions beyond our borders. Today's holding by the Court is therefore a backward step in the heretofore progressive development of public sector labor law in this State which will not conduce toward the legislative policy of promoting peace and stability in public employment relations.

However, I enter one qualification to my agreement with PERC's view as to this matter, and this will explain my concurrence in the Court's injunction against arbitration of the dispute in this case. Although, for reasons I shall presently set forth, a public employer may at its option choose to negotiate a permissive item, *i. e.,* one which involves inherent managerial policy but also impacts appreciably upon the welfare of employees, it may not agree to binding arbitration of a dispute with respect to a negotiated item if so doing would transfer the making of an inherent managerial decision from a governmental official to an arbitrator. . . .

## NOTES

1. In Oakland County Sheriff's Dep't, 1968 MERC Lab. Op. 1, the Michigan Employment Relations Commission held "that binding arbitration of grievances concerning the interpretation and enforcement of a collective bargaining agreement was

a mandatory subject of bargaining...." *Accord,* Local 1226, AFSCME v. City of Rhinelander, 35 Wis. 2d 209, 151 N.W.2d 30 (1967); City of Auburn v. Nash, 34 App. Div. 2d 345, 312 N.Y.S.2d 700 (1970); Rockland Professional Fire Fighters Ass'n v. City of Rockland, 261 A.2d 418 (Me. 1970); Central City Educ. Ass'n v. School Dist. of Central City, Neb. Ct. of Ind. Rel. Case No. 35 (1971).

2. Several statutes expressly provide that the parties may negotiate over a grievance procedure with binding arbitration as the terminal step. The Hawaii Act, for example, provides that the parties may include in their labor agreement a provision "setting forth a grievance procedure culminating in a final and binding decision, to be invoked in the event of any dispute concerning the interpretation or application of a written agreement." HAWAII REV. STAT. § 89-11(a) (Supp. 1972). The Iowa, New Hampshire, Washington, and Wisconsin statutes covering state employees and the Kansas, Oregon, and Vermont statutes covering teachers contain similar provisions. Executive Order 11491 is somewhat broader in that it provides that "[n]egotiated procedures may provide for the arbitration of employee grievances *and* of disputes over the interpretation or application of existing agreements." E.O. 11491, § 14(a). In United States Kirk Army Hospital, Aberdeen, Md., FLRC No. 70A-11 (1971), however, the Federal Labor Relations Council held "that the arbitration of union disputes over the 'interpretation or application' of 'any policy, regulation, or practice' within the employer's discretion . . . is violative of sections 13 and 14 of the Order and is not negotiable."

A number of states mandate the inclusion of a provision providing for the binding arbitration of disputes concerning the interpretation and application of the agreement. The Minnesota statute is illustrative: "All contracts shall include a grievance procedure which shall provide compulsory arbitration of grievances." MINN. STAT. ANN. ch. 179, § 179.70(1) (Supp. 1973). The Minnesota Act provides that if the agreement does not contain such a procedure the parties are subject to the grievance procedure promulgated by the Director of the Bureau of Mediation Services. The Florida act contains a similar provision. The New Jersey act requires public employers to negotiate grievance procedures which "may provide for binding arbitration as a means for resolving disputes." N. J. STAT. ANN. ch. 34:13A, § 5.3 (1977).

3. Would a proposal by one party that any unresolved issues in the negotiations for a successor agreement be submitted to binding arbitration be a mandatory subject of bargaining? A permissive subject of bargaining? An illegal subject of bargaining? *See* State Employees Ass'n of N.H. v. Mills, 344 A.2d 6, 90 L.R.R.M. 2571 (N.H. S. Ct. 1975) (impasse arbitration held non-negotiable). Would it make any difference if the applicable statute provides, as the Pennsylvania act does, that nothing in the act "shall prevent the parties from submitting impasses to voluntary interest arbitration . . . ." PA. STAT. ANN. tit. 43, § 1101.804 (1970). *See* PLRB v. Richland Education Ass'n, Case Nos. PERA-C-3477-C et al., 542 GERR B-7 (Pa. LRB 1974) (proposal for voluntary interest arbitration permissive subject of negotiations; neither party is required to negotiate over such a proposal). Under the National Labor Relations Act, the NLRB and the courts have uniformly held that interest arbitration is a non-mandatory subject of bargaining. *See, e.g.,* Massachusetts Nurses Ass'n, 225 N.L.R.B. 678 (1976), *aff'd,* 557 F.2d 894 (1st Cir. 1977); NLRB v. Sheet Metal Workers, Local 38, 98 L.R.R.M. 2147 (2d Cir. 1978).

4. In a number of instances state attorneys general have issued opinions concerning the scope of bargaining under a public sector collective bargaining law, even though a labor relations agency has been established under such legislation. *See, e.g.,* Pa. Op. Att'y Gen. No. 133 (1972) (whether full wages or reduced wages must be paid if schools close before end of school year concerns wages, hours and other conditions of employment and therefore negotiable). Should an attorney general abstain from issuing an opinion where the same question is within the jurisdiction of a state public employment relations board? If the state public employment relations board and the attorney general issue conflicting decisions on the same question, which decision prevails in the absence of applicable court precedent? *See generally* Note 4, p. 255, *supra.*

5. Following the lead of the federal government in Executive Orders 10988 and 11491, several states have also limited the scope of bargaining by enumerating certain management rights or prerogatives. New Hampshire, for example, provides that

The State retains the exclusive right through its department heads and appointing authorities, subject to the provisions of law and the personnel regulations (a) to direct and supervise employees, (b) to appoint, promote, discharge, transfer or demote employees, (c) to lay off unnecessary employees, (d) to maintain the efficiency of government operations, (e) to determine the means, methods and personnel by which operations are to be conducted, and (f) to take whatever actions are necessary to carry out the mission of the agency or department in situations of emergency. N.H. REV. STAT. ANN. ch. 98-C, § 98-C:7.

Hawaii, Kansas, and Nevada have similar provisions. The Minnesota Act provides that

A public employer is not required to meet and negotiate on matters of inherent managerial policy, which include, but are not limited to, such areas of discretion or policy as the functions and programs of the employer, its overall budget, utilization of technology, the organizational structure and selection and direction and number of personnel. MINN. STAT. ANN. ch. 179, § 179.66(1) (Supp. 1972).

The Pennsylvania Act contains a nearly identical provision. Vermont (for state employees) and California (for local government employees) have also exempted to a lesser extent certain management prerogatives from the scope of negotiations. Thus, the California Act provides "that the scope of representation shall not include consideration of the merits, necessities, or organization of any service or activity provided by law or executive order." CAL. GOV'T CODE § 3504 (West Supp. 1971).

Numerous questions have arisen concerning the scope of bargaining under state statutes that include a statement of management prerogatives since most of these statutes also provide that the parties are required to negotiate in good faith over wages, hours and other terms and conditions of employment. The basic problem is to what extent are items which would otherwise be considered "wages, hours and other terms and conditions of employment" removed from the mandatory area of bargaining by a statutory statement of management rights. This problem is addressed in both the *Washoe* and *State College Area School District* cases which follow.

## WASHOE COUNTY SCHOOL DISTRICT AND WASHOE COUNTY TEACHERS ASSOCIATION

Nevada Local Government Employee-Management Relations Board
Item #3 (1971), *aff'd*, 90 Nev. 442, 530 P.2d 114 (1974)

When Chapter 288, the Local Government Employee Relations Act, was enacted in 1969, valuable rights both on the part of the local government employees and the local government employer were relinquished in order to provide a more harmonious labor-management relationship on the local government level. NRS 288.180 declared strikes on the part of public employees to be illegal. NRS 288.150, Subsection 1, imposed upon the local government employer the duty of good faith negotiation with employee organizations on matters concerning wages, hours, and conditions of employment. However, NRS 288.150, Subsection 2, recognizes that the local government employer still maintains what is referred to as management prerogative, i.e. the responsibility under appropriate situations to direct its employees; hire, promote, suspend, or terminate employees; maintain efficiency of its governmental operations; and to otherwise proceed to do such things, without reference to negotiation or any negotiated agreement which, if not done, would seriously infringe upon the local government employer's duty to the taxpayers and to the public.

Although it has been urged upon this Board by the counsel for the Washoe County School District that the provisions of Subsection 2 limit the areas of negotiability on matters relating to wages, hours, and conditions of employment if said matters also involve any items in Subsection 2, the Board rejects this view as untenable.

It is presumed the Legislature in enacting Chapter 288 did not enact a nullity. Under the school district's interpretation of the relationship between NRS 288.150, Subsection 1, and NRS 288.150, Subsection 2, any matter, including the very question of wage scale, involves management prerogative; and consequently, under said view would not be negotiable.

The Board does not believe that the Legislature so intended such an interpretation. Public employees by this Act have been denied perhaps their most valuable right — the right to strike. On the other hand, the local government employer has retained the right to define and recognize particular bargaining units, the right to exercise its management prerogatives without reference to negotiation or any prior negotiated agreement.

It is the opinion of the Board, therefore, that any matter significantly related to wages, hours, and working conditions is negotiable, whether or not said matters also relate to questions of management prerogative; and it is the duty of the local government employer to proceed and negotiate said items.

## FINDINGS OF FACT

Based upon the evidence introduced, the Board makes the following findings of fact:

*Class Size:* Class size is significantly related to wages, hours, and working conditions inasmuch as student density directly affects a teacher's workload including the required hours of preparation and post-class evaluation; affects the teacher's control and discipline problems; affects the teacher's teaching and communication techniques; and affects the total amount of work required for a fixed compensation.

*Article F. Professional Improvement:* The professional improvement of a teacher is significantly related to working conditions since it directly affects his career opportunities within his profession as well as his ability to more effectively produce meritorious results in the classroom. However, no evidence has been presented to show that the determination of standards of the quality of education for a school district is so significantly related to wages, hours, and working conditions as to abrogate management prerogatives of the local government employer.

*Article J. Student Discipline:* The matter of student discipline is significantly related to a teacher's working conditions since the requirements for discipline at any given time usually demand a priority of the teacher's attention. The degree of control and discipline required in a classroom affects the demands on a teacher's ability to effectively teach the class.

*Article K. School Calendar:* The selection of those days that a teacher must work in a given school year is significantly related to the teacher's working conditions and the amount of work the teacher is expected to perform for a fixed compensation.

*Article N. Teacher Performance:* The evaluation of a teacher's performance is significantly related to wages and working conditions inasmuch as the evaluation affects transfer, retention, promotion and the compensation scale.

*Article P. Special Student Program:* The evidence produced in this hearing showed that management prerogatives predominate the entire subject matter as existing in Washoe County in that the Washoe County School District has provided a method and specialized staff to fulfill the sensitive responsibility of the school district to individual families in making determinations of which children are to be labeled special education cases. The evidence showed that the School District had relieved the teachers of this responsibility and there was insufficient evidence produced by the Teachers Association to demonstrate that the Association's proposal would significantly affect or alter the teacher's working conditions.

*Article S. Differentiated Staffing:* Any plan of differentiated staffing which categorizes teachers on the basis of competency, experience, responsibilities and other factors, affects wages, hours, and working conditions of individual teachers relative to their peers.

*Article W. Teacher Load:* Where a teacher works, the amount of work done, and the kind of work done is a part of a teacher's working conditions. The remuneration for overtime for extra work assignments is a matter of wages and hours.

*Article X. Instructional Supplies:* The amount, type, quality, and availability of instructional supplies affects the ability of a teacher to discharge his job properly and is significantly related to the teacher's working conditions and, in some cases, hours.

## CONCLUSIONS OF LAW

. . . .

[The Board held that all of the foregoing subjects were negotiable except for Article F on Professional Improvement which the Board held was "non-negotiable only in relation to the determination of the quality of education. . . ."]

## NOTES

1. In affirming the Commission's decision in the principal case, the Nevada Supreme Court stated:

> It is not conceivable that the legislature would give its extensive time and attention to study, draft, meet, hear, discuss and pass this important piece of legislation were it not to serve a useful purpose. For this court to hold that any item even though remotely relevant to management policy is beyond the pale of negotiation defeats the purpose of the legislation. Many matters involved in a teacher's work day bear somewhat on management policy and at the same time are inextricably linked to wages, hours and conditions of employment. What the legislature gave was not intended to immediately be taken away.

Washoe County Teachers Ass'n v. Washoe County School Dist., 90 Nev. 442, 530 P.2d 114 (1974).

Subsequent to this decision, the Nevada statute was amended to limit the scope of negotiations to 20 enumerated items and to specifically provide that the management prerogatives reserved to a local government employer without negotiation "are not within the scope of mandatory bargaining." NEV. REV. STAT. § 288.150 (1976). Class size, student discipline, and school calendar are not among the enumerated mandatory subjects of bargaining.

2. Utilizing an approach similar to that of the Nevada Commission in *Washoe,* the Rhode Island Supreme Court in Barrington School Committee v. Rhode Island SLRB, 388 A.2d 1369 (R.I. S. Ct. 1978), held that the elimination of certain departmental chairmanships was a mandatory subject of bargaining. The court reasoned as follows:

> While we postulate no general rule, in the circumstance here we conclude that the abolition of the 12 department chairmanships is not completely a matter of educational policy but is an appropriate matter for negotiating or bargaining

concerning the effect on the individual teachers involved. In addition, to require the committee to bargain about the matter at issue would not in our opinion significantly abridge its freedom to manage and control the school system. We do not mean that the union should be able to dictate to the committee on matters strictly within the province of management. What we do say is that when, as here, the problem involved concerns both a question of management and a term or condition of employment, it is the duty of the committee to negotiate with the teachers involved.

## PENNSYLVANIA LABOR RELATIONS BD. v. STATE COLLEGE AREA SCHOOL DIST.

Supreme Court of Pennsylvania
337 A.2d 262 (1975)

NIX, J.

The subject of this appeal is the relatively recent enactment of the Public Employe Relations Act. The dispute centers upon the tension evoked between what the legislature has specifically made bargainable and what the legislature has also specifically allowed management to reserve to its unilateral decision-making. In this instance we are required to interpret section 701 and determine its scope in light of sections 702 and 703.

[The State College Area Education Association (Association) filed an unfair labor practice charge with the Pennsylvania Labor Relations Board alleging that the Board of School Directors of State College Area School District (School District) refused to bargain with respect to 23 different items. Subsequently, the Association withdrew its allegations with respect to two of these items. The Board found five of the items were mandatory subjects of bargaining and the remaining 16 were not negotiable. Both parties appealed and the Commonwealth Court affirmed an order of the Court of Common Pleas holding that all 21 items concerned inherent managerial policy and that, therefore, the School District was not required to negotiate over any of them. The 21 disputed items, as set forth in the opinion of the Commonwealth Court, were as follows:

1. The availability of proper and adequate classroom instructional printed material;
2. The provision for time during the school day for team planning of required innovative programs;
3. The timely notice of teaching assignment for the coming year;
4. Providing separate desks and lockable drawer space for each teacher in the district;
5. Providing cafeteria for teachers in the senior high school;
6. Eliminating the requirement that teachers perform nonteaching duties such as but not limited to hall duty, bus duty, lunch duty, study hall, and parking lot duties;
7. Eliminating the requirement that teachers teach or supervise two consecutive periods in two different buildings;
8. Eliminating the requirement that teachers substitute for other teachers during planning periods and teaching in noncertificated subject areas;
9. Eliminating the requirement that teachers chaperone athletic activities;
10. Eliminating the requirement that teachers unpack, store, check or otherwise handle supplies;
11. Providing that there shall be one night each week free for Association meetings;
12. Providing that a teacher will, without prior notice, have free access to his personnel file;

13. Permitting a teacher to leave the building any time during the school day unless he has a teaching assignment;

14. Providing special teachers with preparation time equal to that provided for other staff members;

15. Provision for maximum class sizes;

16. Provision that the Association will be consulted in determining the school calendar;

17. Provision that school will officially close at noon of the last day of classes for Thanksgiving, Christmas, Spring and Summer vacation;

18. Provision that at least one-half of the time requested for staff meetings be held during the school day;

. . . .

20. A provision that the present Tuesday afternoon conference with parents be abolished and teachers hold conferences with parents by appointment at a mutually convenient time;

21. Provision that secondary teachers not be required to teach more than 25 periods per week and have at least one planning period per day; and

22. A provision that elementary teachers shall have one period or fifteen minutes per day for planning purposes.]

It is argued that the absence of precedent interpreting the relatively new Act 195 in this area and the similarity of language between section 701, now under consideration, and section 8(d) of the National Labor Relations Act, 29 U.S.C. 158(d), would suggest that the National Labor Relations Board's cases and federal decisions interpreting section 8(d) should provide compelling authority for the resolution of the current dispute. Since NLRB v. Wooster Division of Borg-Warner Corp., 356 U.S. 342 (1958), private employers are required to bargain only with respect to those matters which directly relate to "wages, hours and working conditions." Other matters of mutual concern may be discussed if both parties agree. When a subject under discussion is not mandatory a strike or lockout may not be used to compel negotiation or agreement. Allied Chemical & Alkali Workers of America v. Pittsburgh Plate Glass Co., 404 U.S. 157 (1971); Fibreboard Paper Products Corp. v. NLRB, 379 U.S. 203 (1964). While this basic dichotomy has been followed under Act 195, it does not necessarily follow that federal precedent relating to private employment is particularly helpful in resolving the difficulties arising in the public sector.

Although these decisions may provide some guidance, we are mindful of the distinctions that necessarily must exist between legislation primarily directed to the private sector and that for public employes. The distinction between the public and private sector cannot be minimized. Employers in the private sector are motivated by the profit to be returned from the enterprise whereas public employers are custodians of public funds and mandated to perform governmental functions as economically and effectively as possible. The employer in the private sector is constrained only by investors who are most concerned with the return for their investment whereas the public employer must adhere to the statutory enactments which control the operation of the enterprise. We emphasize that we are not suggesting that the experience gained in the private sector is of no value here, rather we are stressing that analogies have limited application and the experiences gained in the private employment sector will not necessarily provide an infallible basis for a monolithic model for public employment.

We also recognize the wisdom of refraining from attempting to fashion broad and general rules that would serve as a panacea. The obviously wiser course is to resolve disputes on a case-by-case basis until we develop, through experience in the area, a sound basis for developing overall principles.

Guided by these preliminary observations, we will now proceed to consider the sections in question and determine their applicability to the items at issue. Section 701 provides:

> "Collective bargaining is the performance of the mutual obligation of the public employer and the representative of the public employes to meet at reasonable times and confer in good faith with respect to wages, hours and other terms and conditions of employment, or the negotiation of an agreement or any question arising thereunder and the execution of a written contract incorporating any agreement reached but such obligation does not compel either party to agree to a proposal or require the making of a concession."

That the right to collective bargaining as to "wages, hours and other terms and conditions of employment" is not unlimited, is made clear by the two succeeding sections. Section 702 states:

> "Public employers shall not be required to bargain over matters of inherent managerial policy, which shall include but shall not be limited to such areas of discretion or policy as the functions and programs of the public employer, standards of services, its overall budget, utilization of technology, the organizational structure and selection and direction of personnel. Public employers, however, shall be required to meet and discuss on policy matters affecting wages, hours and terms and conditions of employment as well as the impact thereon upon request by public employe representatives."

Section 703 states:

> "The parties to the collective bargaining process shall not effect or implement a provision in a collective bargaining agreement if the implementation of that provision would be in violation of, or inconsistent with, or in conflict with any statute or statutes enacted by the General Assembly of the Commonwealth of Pennsylvania or the provisions of municipal home rule charters."

The conflict in the Commonwealth Court centered upon the extent the legislature intended to limit the scope of negotiation made mandatory under section 701 by its inclusion of sections 702 and 703 within this act. The majority of that court concluded that any item of wages, hours, and other terms and conditions of employment affecting policy determinations or the impairment of other performance of the duties and responsibilities imposed upon public employers by statute are not bargainable. Pa. L. R. B. v. State College Area School District, 9 Pa. Commonwealth Ct. 229, 306 A.2d 404 (1973). Judge Kramer, in a dissent joined by two other members of the court, took a different view. Judge Kramer wrote:

> "My reading of the statute (Act 195) leads me to find a legislative intent to provide for good faith collective bargaining wherever the teachers' employment rights are directly affected by 'wages, hours and other terms and conditions of employment.' " *Id.* at 247, 304 A.2d at 414-415 (dissenting opinion).

Where provisions of a statute appear to be ambiguous or inconsistent, the intention of the legislature may be determined by examining the occasion, reason or necessity for the law. Thus, we should look to the circumstances that existed at the time of the enactment and determine the mischief sought to be remedied or the object to be obtained in its passage. . . . Prior to the passage of Act 195 the prior law prohibited all strikes by public employes and did not require collective bargaining by public employers. The chaotic climate that resulted from this obviously intolerable situation occasioned the creation of a Governor's Commission to Revise the Public Employe Law of Pennsylvania. This commission, which is commonly referred to as the Hickman Commission, issued a report recommending the repeal of the then existing law and the passage of new law which would permit the right of all public employes to bargain collectively. In recommending this change the commission suggested the need for collective bargaining to restore harmony in the public sector and to eliminate the numerous illegal strikes and the widespread labor unrest.

"The 1947 Act does not require public employers to bargain collectively with their employes. This has led to an almost complete breakdown in communication where the public employer has not chosen to recognize the right of its employes to bargain collectively. In our judgment, this inability to bargain collectively has created more ill will and led to more friction and strikes than any other single cause."

The declaration of policy contained in Act 195, section 101 clearly establishes that the legislature concurred with the commission's belief that the right to collective bargaining was necessary to promote orderly and constructive relationships between public employers and employees.

In this setting we are forced to conclude that the legislature at the time of the passage of Act 195 fully recognized that the right of collective bargaining was crucial to any attempt to restore harmony in the public sector. It would be absurd to suggest that the legislature deliberately intended to meet this pressing need by providing an illusory right of collective bargaining. . . .

## II.

Section 702, when read in conjunction with section 701, requires us to distinguish between the area of managerial prerogative and the areas of vital concern to employees. The Commonwealth Court's premise that any interpretation of sections 701 and 702 must recognize the dominance of a legislature intention to preserve the traditional concept of inherent managerial policy emasculates section 701 and thwarts the fulfillment of the legislative policy sought to be achieved by the passage of the Act. Further, such a view ignores the fact that the acceptance of the Hickman Commission's recommendation and the passage of Act 195 was a repudiation of the traditional concept of the sanctity of managerial prerogatives in the public sector. The introduction of a concept of mandatory collective bargaining, regardless of how narrowly the scope of negotiation is defined, necessarily represents an encroachment upon the former autonomous position of management. Further, the Hickman Commission's recognition of the need for collective bargaining to produce stability in the public sector argues against an inference that they intended their recommendation to be construed as suggesting something less than a viable bargaining process in the public sector.

The necessity for qualifications to adjust private sector concepts to meet the needs of the public sector does not justify the conclusion that the qualifications should be interpreted in a manner that would strip the bargaining provision of any meaning. We recognize the principle that a statute is never presumed to deprive the State of any prerogative or right unless the intention to do so is clearly manifest. . . . However, the passage of Act 195, in our view, expresses a manifest intention to create a sufficiently vital collective bargaining process capable of meeting the need to restore harmony within the public sector. . . .

The majority in the Commonwealth Court and some of the briefs filed in this Court attempt to equate the preservation of the inherent managerial policy as synonymous with the public interest and the concern of the employes as a private interest. Proceeding from this premise it is asserted that the private interest must give way before the public good. This reasoning is offered to provide the basis for their premise, the dominance of the legislative intention to preserve managerial prerogatives. This argument fails to perceive that the true public interest is the effective and efficient operation of public employment and that collective bargaining as well as managerial prerogatives are only significant insofar as they further this objective. In view of the recognized importance of a meaningful system of collective bargaining in maintaining harmony and order in the public sector an interpretation of section 702 that would virtually eclipse the legislative intent expressed in section 701 would render a real disservice to the true public interest.

A determination of the interrelationship between sections 701 and 702 calls upon us to strike a balance wherein those matters relating directly to "wages, hours and other terms and conditions of employment" are made mandatory subjects of bargaining and reserving to management those areas that the public sector necessarily requires to be managerial functions. In striking this balance the paramount concern must be the public interest in providing for the effective and efficient performance of the public service in question. The Supreme Court of Kansas was recently required to consider this problem. National Education Ass'n of Shawnee Mission, Inc. v. Board of Education of Shawnee Mission Unified School District No. 512, 212 Kan. 741, 512 P.2d 426 (1973). In that decision the Court was confronted with a dispute between a teachers' association and the board of education. In resolving questions relating to the scope of negotiations provided under their statute they recognized that "terms and conditions" which were negotiable under the terms of the statute as something more than minimal economic terms of wages and hours, but something less than the basic educational policies of the board of education. That Court suggested that the courts of that jurisdiction should resolve these issues on a case-by-case basis. As has been indicated, we also agree with the wisdom of this approach at this time. Further, the Kansas Court suggested:

> "The key, as we see it, is how direct the impact of an issue is on the well-being of the individual teacher, as opposed to its effect on the operation of the school system as a whole." *Id.* at ——, 512 P.2d at 435.

We believe that the suggested test is helpful in attempting to strike the balance between sections 701 and 702 of our statute. We recognize that in many instances the line will be difficult to draw, however, if we remain ever mindful that our paramount concern in this area is the public interest, no situation will be insoluble.

Thus we hold that where an item of dispute is a matter of fundamental concern to the employes' interest in wages, hours and other terms and conditions of employment, it is not removed as a matter subject to good faith bargaining under section 701 simply because it may touch upon basic policy. It is the duty of the Board in the first instance and the courts thereafter to determine whether the impact of the issue on the interest of the employe in wages, hours and terms and conditions of employment outweighs its probable effect on the basic policy of the system as a whole. If it is determined that the matter is one of inherent managerial policy but does affect wages, hours and terms and conditions of employment, the public employer shall be required to meet and discuss such subjects upon request by the public employe's representative pursuant to section 702.

## III.

The relationship between sections 701 and 703 is particularly significant in a highly regulated area such as public education. Article 3, Section 14 of the Pennsylvania Constitution provides:

"The General Assembly shall provide for the maintenance and support of a thorough and efficient system of public education to serve the needs of the Commonwealth."

Under the Public School Code of 1949, the General Assembly provided a comprehensive system to meet the educational needs of the citizens of this Commonwealth. In so doing, school districts were created as an agency of the State charged with the responsibility of administering the educational program within its assigned territory.... To enable the school districts to discharge this constitutional mandate, the General Assembly vested in the school districts the necessary powers. Public School Code of 1949, *supra,* § 2-211. The majority of the Commonwealth Court reasoned that the duties and prerogatives imposed upon and granted to school boards under the Public School Code of 1949, and other pieces of legislation could not be the subject of collective bargaining under the terms of section 703. We cannot agree.

The mere fact that a particular subject matter may be covered by legislation does not remove it from collective bargaining under section 701 if it bears on the question of wages, hours and conditions of employment. We believe that section 703 only prevents the agreement to and implementation of any term which would be in violation of or inconsistent with any statutory directive.

The distinction between this view and that expressed by the majority of the Commonwealth Court (as we understand it) is best illustrated by an example. Under section 1142 of the Public School Code, a minimum salary scale is set forth. Section 1151 provides that school boards may pay salaries in excess of the minimum salary. Framing the issue in accordance with the formulation suggested by the majority in the Commonwealth Court, section 1142 created a duty not to pay below the minimum scale and section 1151 granted the employer the prerogative to pay more than the minimum rate. Clearly, the parties are precluded from agreeing to a rate lower than the minimum scale but even though the statute vested in the public employer the prerogative to pay a higher rate, to do so as a result of collective bargaining is not "in violation of, or inconsistent with, or in conflict with" the statute in question. The mere fact that the General Assembly granted the prerogative to the employer does not exclude the possibility that the decision to exercise that prerogative was influenced by the collective bargaining process.

The fallacy in the view expressed by the Commonwealth Court's majority is the failure to perceive the distinction between the "inherent managerial prerogative" concept as set forth in 702 and the thrust of section 703. The purpose of section 703 was not to further define "inherent managerial policy" but to recognize that Act 195 did not affect the continuing vitality of existing law at the time of that Act's passage. Thus, the fact that a prerogative was statutorily recognized under section 1151 does not mandate that it be included within the "inherent managerial policy" concept of section 702. That determination rests solely on the considerations suggested in our discussion under Part II of this Opinion. Section 703 merely prevents a term of a collective bargaining agreement from being in violation of existing law. Cf. Board of Education, City of Englewood Teachers Ass'n, 64 N.J. 1, 311 A.2d 729 (1973); Board of Education of Union Free School District #3 v. Associated Teachers of Huntington, Inc., 30 N.Y.2d 122, 282 N.E.2d 109 (1972); Joint School District #8 v. Wisconsin Employment Relations Board, 37 Wis.2d 483, 155 N.W.2d 78 (1967). If however the General Assembly mandates a particular responsibility to be discharged by the board and the board alone, then the matter is removed from bargaining under section 701 even if it has direct impact upon "wages, hours and other terms or conditions of employment." The removal from collective bargaining results not because it necessarily falls within the purview of section 702 (in fact it may clearly be within the scope of section 701), but rather because to do otherwise would be in direct violation of a statutory mandate and thus excluded under section 703. . . .

We therefore conclude that items bargainable under section 701 are only excluded under section 703 where other applicable statutory provisions explicitly and definitively prohibit the public employer from making an agreement as to that specific term or condition of employment.

### IV.

The areas of bargaining that are in issue in this lawsuit provide a wide spectrum of concern. It is, however, clear that there has been significant disagreement as to the principles to be applied in determining the applicability of section 701. As noted by Judge Kramer, the wording of many of the items in issue is ambiguous and difficult to categorize in accordance with the principles set forth herein. It is clear that many of the items were framed in terms of the objective sought to be obtained as opposed to the issue sought to be negotiated. We assume the reason for the artless framing of the issues was as a result of the general confusion which prevailed in the area. We also believe that the Pennsylvania Labor Relations Board should have an opportunity to again re-assess the respective positions of the parties in light of the principles set forth herein.

We therefore remand the cause to the Pennsylvania Labor Relations Board for further proceedings consistent herewith, granting leave to each party to modify and amend their position as they may wish.

### CONCURRING OPINION

POMEROY, J.,

. . . .

As to the main thrust of the Court's opinion, that Act No. 195 should be so construed as to afford a viable framework for meaningful collective bargaining in the public sector, I am in complete agreement, for this is necessary to accomplishment of the public policy announced by the legislature. I also agree that this requires a balancing approach, and that in striking the balances undue emphasis must not be placed on either Sec. 702 or Sec. 703 of the Act, lest the innovative provision of Sec. 701 be lost in the shuffle. Thus, as the Court's opinion states, an item of dispute must not be removed from the orbit of bargaining under Sec. 701 "simply because it may touch upon basic policy." I have difficulty, however, with the Court's statement that the Board is to "determine whether the impact of the issue on the interest of the employee in wages, hours and terms and conditions of employment outweighs its probable effect on the basic policy of the system as a whole." Opinion of the Court, ante at ——, for I fear that in application this directive may prove no more lucid than the words of the Act of which we strive to give meaning. I am not sure how one identifies the "interest" of the employee in wages, hours and conditions of employment, determines the "impact" of a particular issue upon such an interest, or weighs that impact against "probable effect on the basic policy of the system as a whole." I venture to suggest that the governing test might preferably be formulated as follows:

> As to each item of potential dispute, (i.e., the items put forward in a request for bargaining) the factors to be balanced in determining the susceptibility of an item to collective bargaining are the probable effects of the granting or refusal of the item upon (a) the individual performance by the teachers of their duties as such, and upon (b) the school board's overall operation of an educational system within its district. If the effect of the granting or denial of a request would be more direct, immediate and substantial upon the teachers' individual performance of their duties than it would be upon the school board's overall operation of an educational system, the item should be considered negotiable. On the other hand, if the effect would bear more directly, immediately and substantially upon the school board's overall operation of an educational system, the opposite result should obtain — i.e., the item should be considered non-negotiable. Such balancing, of course, should be made with due regard for those areas of discretion or policy which by the terms of Sec. 702 are expressly included within the phrase "inherent managerial policy."

. . . .

MR. CHIEF JUSTICE JONES joins in this opinion.
[The dissenting opinion of EAGEN, J., is omitted.]

## NOTES

1. In accord with the decision in the principal case, an increasing number of boards and courts are utilizing a balancing test to determine whether a given subject is mandatory or permissive. For example, in Sutherlin Education Ass'n v. Sutherlin School Dist. No. 130, 25 Or. App. 85, 548 P.2d 208 (1976), the Oregon Court of Appeals stated that "the appropriate test to be applied in determining whether a proposed subject is a 'condition of employment' and therefore a mandatory subject of bargaining is to balance the element of educational policy involved against the effect that the subject has on a teacher's employment." Other decisions in which courts have adopted a balancing standard to resolve negotiability disputes include Beloit Education Ass'n v. WERC, 73 Wis. 2d 43, 242 N.W.2d 231 (1976), and City of Biddeford v. Biddeford Teachers' Ass'n, 304 A.2d 387, 83 L.R.R.M. 2098 (Me. S. Ct. 1973). See generally Clark, The Scope of the Duty to Bargain in Public Employment, in LABOR RELATIONS LAW IN THE PUBLIC SECTOR 81 (A. Knapp ed. 1977).

In adopting the balancing test to resolve negotiability disputes, the New Jersey PERC in Ridgefield Park Board of Education, 3 NJPER 303 (1977), rejected the union's contention "that a 'significant relation' standard should be applied by the commission in rendering scope of negotiations determinations." After noting that "[t]his standard categorizes a specific issue as a required subject of collective negotiations if it is significantly related to wages, hours, and other terms and conditions of employment," the New Jersey PERC stated:

> . . . The Commission in its scope determinations has not adopted the approach that a given subject is mandatorily negotiable if it is significantly related to wages, hours and other terms and conditions of employment. We have decided that this "significant relation" standard is inadequate because it does not properly recognize the competing interests at stake where there is an overlap between conditions of employment on the one hand and management prerogatives on the other. By focusing on only one half of this overlap situation, this standard would give undue, if not exclusive, weight to terms and conditions of employment.
>
> Instead, the Commission has applied a balancing test in determining whether a particular subject is a mandatory or permissive subject for collective negotiations. This pragmatic test openly acknowledges that there may be an overlap between terms and conditions of employment and certain management prerogatives which requires a careful consideration of the competing interests at issue. . . .

Citing the New Jersey Commission's decision in *Ridgefield Park,* the New York PERB in City of New Rochelle, 10 PERB ¶ 3078 (1977), stated that " [b]alancing tests are appropriate in deciding whether or not a matter is a mandatory subject of negotiations. . . ." *See also* Department of Army Corps of Engineers, FLRC No. 71A-46 (1972) (". . . determinations as to negotiability . . . require consideration and balancing of all the factors involved, including the well-being of the employees . . .").

2. In the principal case, the Pennsylvania Supreme Court adopted the balancing test set forth by the Kansas Supreme Court in National Education Ass'n of Shawnee Mission, Inc. v. Board of Education of Shawnee Mission Unified School Dist. No. 512, 212 Kan. 741, 512 P.2d 426 (1973). Utilizing this test, the Kansas Supreme Court in *Shawnee Mission* held that in addition to wages and other economic matters, negotiations were required over "such things as probationary period, transfers, teacher appraisal procedure, disciplinary procedure, resignations and termination of contracts." On the other hand, the court held that negotiations were not required over "curriculum and materials, payroll mechanics, certification, class size and the use of paraprofessionals, the use and duties of substitute teachers, and teachers' ethics and academic freedom."

3. Assuming a balancing test is utilized to determine whether a given item is a mandatory subject of bargaining, how should the following items be classified:

1. Institution of a civilian review board for police officers. *Compare* Berkeley Police Ass'n v. City of Berkeley, 76 Cal. App. 3d 931, —P. 2d— (1977) (managerial decision outside scope of negotiation), *with* Pontiac Police Officers Ass'n v. City of Pontiac, 397 Mich. 674, 246 N.W.2d 831 (1976) (mandatory subject of negotiations).
2. Decentralization of a school system.
3. Type of weapons and/or bullets issued to police officers.
4. Assignment of police officers to shifts on basis of seniority.
5. Student discipline.
6. Quality of patient care and the type and kind of medical equipment provided.
7. Promotions based on seniority.
8. Number of police officers assigned to a squad car.
9. Determination of a school or college curriculum.
10. Conditions under which police officer may use deadly force. *See* San Jose Officers Ass'n v. City of San Jose, 1977-78 PBC ¶ 36,250 (Cal. App. Ct. 1978).

What arguments could be made for and against mandatory negotiations of each of the foregoing items? Would it make any difference if compulsory interest arbitration is the terminal step of the statutory impasse procedure? *See* Pontiac Police Officers Ass'n v. City of Pontiac, 397 Mich. 674, 246 N.W.2d 831 (1976) (compulsory arbitration statute does "not affect the analysis of what constitutes mandatory subjects for collective bargaining under the 'other terms and conditions' language").

4. Contrast the Hawaii Act which specifically provides that "[t]he employer and the exclusive representative shall not agree to any proposal which would be inconsistent with merit principles . . . or which would interfere with the rights of a public employer to . . .," HAWAII REV. STAT. § 89-9(d) (Supp. 1971), with the Pennsylvania Act which provides that "[p]ublic employers shall not be required to bargain over matters of inherent managerial policy, which shall include but shall not be limited to such areas of discretion or policy as . . ." PA. STAT. ANN. tit. 43, § 1101.702 (Supp. 1972). Whereas the parties are prohibited from bargaining over certain subjects by virtue of the Hawaii Act, the Pennsylvania Act only provides that the employer is not required to negotiate over certain matters. In other words, while the Pennsylvania Act specifically provides that certain matters are not *mandatory* subjects of bargaining, such matters may nevertheless be *permissible* subjects of negotiations, *i.e.,* the employer could voluntarily negotiate over such matters and include any agreements reached in a written labor contract.

## WEST IRONDEQUOIT BOARD OF EDUCATION

New York Public Employment Relations Board
4 PERB ¶ 3070, *aff'd on rehearing,* 4 PERB ¶ 3089 (1971),
*aff'd,* 35 N.Y.2d 46, 315 N.E.2d 775, 358 N.Y.S.2d 720 (1974)

The West Irondequoit Teachers Association (charging party) filed an improper practice charge against the West Irondequoit Board of Education (employer) alleging that the employer violated Section 209-a.1 (d) of the Public Employees' Fair Employment Act by refusing to negotiate on two issues.

The parties submitted the case to the hearing officer on stipulated facts. In summary, the charging party is the recognized negotiating representative for all of the full-time and part-time certificated personnel excluding some job titles which are immaterial herein.

During negotiations for the 1970-71 academic year, the charging party submitted a proposal entitled "Class Size and Teaching Load." [1]

In response to the charging party's proposal, the employer submitted its own proposal.[2]

---

[1] "Class Size and Teaching Load."
The pertinent provisions are: "B. Maximum Class Size:
(Definition: The number of pupils for whom a teacher is responsible during a single period in a single day.)
1. The class size of the kindergarten shall be 20 pupils.
2. The class size of the first grade in the elementary schools shall be 20 pupils.
3. The class size of the second-fourth grades in the elementary schools shall be 25 pupils.
4. The class size of the fifth-sixth grades and vocal music classes in the middle schools shall be 25 pupils. . . . [The proposal also specified class sizes for other grades.]
Classes that increase beyond the *maximum* must be agreed upon by the teacher and the building principal involved. Any disagreement over such an exception shall be subject to the procedure set forth in the Grievance Procedure." (emphasis in original)
[2] The pertinent provisions of respondent's proposal on "Class Size" are as follows:
D.1. Basic Understandings.
a. One key to effective learning is the quantity and quality of interrelations between and among pupils and teachers.
b. Excessive class size or teacher load may affect the emotional or mental well-being of the teachers.
c. A number of factors, such as available space, degrees of difficulty of the subject or grade level, the methodology utilized, the particular strengths of the teachers, and the individual characteristics of pupils must be considered by administrators when arranging classes and teacher assignments.
2. Agreements.
The Board and the Association agree that:
a. The relationships between effective learning and class size and teacher load shall be subject to continued examination by the parties, in order to determine optimal classroom conditions for pupils.

The charging party also submitted to the employer a proposal entitled "Promotional Policy."

The respondent in May 1970 informed the charging party that it would not negotiate with respect to numerical limitations of class size (hereinafter referred to as class size) or on promotional policy in that both subject matters involved nondelegable duties and responsibilities of the employer.

The charging party has contended that class size is a term and condition of employment and inasmuch as the negotiations on class size do not contravene any law, it is a mandatory subject of negotiations. Further, the charging party argued that since the employer in its counter-proposal stated that excessive class size may affect the emotional or mental well-being of a teacher, the employer had conceded that class size is a term and condition of employment.

The hearing officer stated that, in resolving this matter, we must weigh the duty of government officials to make decisions affecting the entire electorate against the statutory obligation of public employers to negotiate on subjects directly affecting the terms and conditions of employment.

The hearing officer further found that class size does have a major impact on a teacher's working conditions and that class size is not an expression of a primary policy goal of the basic direction of government. The hearing officer concluded that class size is a term and condition of employment and, as such, is a mandatory subject of negotiation.[4]

The issue before this Board raised in this proceeding is a most serious one because of the effect such decisions will have upon school negotiations throughout the State.

In the *New Rochelle* case [5] this Board stated that the determination as to the manner and means by which education service is rendered and the extent of such service is the duty and obligation of the public employer. A public employer should not be required to delegate this responsibility. The decisions of a public employer as to the carrying out of its mission — a decision to eliminate or curtail a service — are not decisions that a public employer should be compelled to negotiate with its employees.

Specifically in the *New Rochelle* case we held that budgetary cuts with concomitant job eliminations were not mandatory subjects of negotiations. Underlying this determination was the concept that basic decisions as to public policy should not be made in the isolation of a negotiation table, but rather should be made by those having the direct and sole responsibility therefor, and whose actions in this regard are subject to review in the electoral process. It would appear that class size is also a basic element of education policy. This follows our decision in the *New Rochelle* case. In that case, the budgetary decisions involved the elimination of a substantial number of teacher positions. These eliminations affected class size.

---

b. Administrative flexibility in arranging class sizes and teacher loads shall be maintained in order to allow for program diversity and innovation, and to allow for arrangements among teachers which are equitable. The district's administrators shall consider the guidelines established by the NYSTA Special Committee on the Duties of Teachers as optimal conditions in their planning for the 1971-72 school year.

[4] This conclusion of the hearing officer was reached prior to this Board's decision in City School District of the City of New Rochelle v. New Rochelle Federation of Teachers, 4 PERB ¶ 4-3060, 3704.

[5] See Footnote 4, *supra*.

While we state that such decisions may be determined unilaterally by a public employer, nevertheless the employer is obligated to negotiate with the representative of its public employees on the impact of such decisions on terms and conditions of employment. Clearly such negotiations on the impact of decisions will have an effect on the allocation of resources. Nevertheless, impact is a matter for negotiations. Thus, it is not the thrust of this decision that an employer is not required to negotiate on subjects which affect the allocation of resources because salaries clearly have such an effect; rather, the thrust of this decision and the decision in the *New Rochelle* case is that basic policy decisions as to the implementation of a mission of an agency of government are not mandatory subjects of negotiations.[6]

It should be noted that the line of demarcation between a basic policy decision and the impact on terms and conditions of employment may not always be clear. For example, a policy decision as to class size may have an impact on teaching load. At first look, class size and teaching load may seem the same, but as we see them, they are not. The first represents a determination by the public employer as to an educational policy made in the light of its resources and other needs of its constituency. This decision may have an impact on hours of work and the number of teaching periods which are clearly mandatory subjects of negotiations.

Further, we would make clear that this decision does not prohibit negotiations on class size. A *fortiori,* neither does it preclude a public employer, such as a school board, from consulting with teacher organizations in making basic decisions as to educational policies; rather this should be encouraged so as to take advantage of the teachers' professional expertise.

WE, THEREFORE, modify the decision of the hearing officer and hold that class size is a policy decision of government and thus is not a mandatory subject of negotiations. As to that portion of the charge dealing with negotiation on promotional policy, we agree with the distinction and decision of the hearing officer and affirm and adopt the recommendations of the hearing officer.

Thus, we find that promotional policy for job titles outside the negotiating units, as well as the determination of qualifications for promotion into positions within the negotiating unit, are not terms and conditions of employment and, therefore, are not mandatory subjects of negotiations.

The employer is therefore

ORDERED to negotiate upon the request of the charging party with respect to promotional policy relating to job titles within the negotiating unit; in all other respects, the charge herein is dismissed.

## NOTES

1. Contrast the decision in the principal case with the decision of the Nevada Commission in *Washoe, supra,* p. 316. Does the inclusion of a statutory management prerogatives clause make any difference in scope of bargaining determinations? What effect, if any, should the absence of a statutory reservation of management prerogatives have?

In Fire Fighters Union, Local 1186 v. City of Vallejo, 12 Cal. 3d 608, 526 P.2d 971, 116 Cal. Rptr. 507 (1973), the California Supreme Court was faced with the question of determining the scope of negotiations under a city charter which provided for negotiations

---

[6] However, the impact which such decisions have on the terms and conditions of employment is a mandatory subject of negotiation.

on "wages, hours, and working conditions," but excluded from negotiations "matters involving the merits, necessity, or organization of any service or activity provided by law." Concerning the effect of this latter exclusion on the mandatory scope of negotiations, the California Supreme Court stated:

> Although the NLRA does not contain specific wording comparable to the "merits, necessity or organization" terminology in the city charter and the state act, the underlying fear that generated this language — that is, that wages, hours and working conditions could be expanded beyond reasonable boundaries to deprive an employer of his legitimate management prerogatives — lies imbedded in the federal precedents under the NLRA. As a review of federal case law in this field demonstrates, the trepidation that the union would extend its province into matters that should properly remain in the hands of employers has been incorporated into the interpretation of the scope of "wages, hours and terms and conditions of employment." Thus, because the federal decisions effectively reflect the same interests as those that prompted the inclusion of the "merits, necessity or organization" bargaining limitation in the charter provision and state act, the federal precedents provide reliable if analogous authority on the issue.

2. Did the New York PERB hold that the decisions with respect to class size or promotional policy are not conditions of employment? In *New Rochelle,* a decision referred to in the principal case, the New York Board noted that a proposed budgetary cut that would have resulted in the termination of 140 positions "[o]bviously ... does effect 'conditions of employment'. . . . However, it does not follow that every decision of a public employer which may affect job security is a mandatory subject of negotiations." City School Dist. of the City of New Rochelle, 4 PERB ¶ 3060 (1971).

3. The Oregon Public Employment Relations Board in Springfield Educ. Ass'n v. Springfield School Dist. No. 19, Case No. C-278, GERR No. 618, B-12 (1975), *aff'd in relevant part,* 24 Or. App. 751, 547 P.2d 647 (1976), held that class size was not a mandatory subject of bargaining. After noting that "[c]lass size can have a broad impact on the economics of school administration," the Oregon PERB noted:

> Class size is beyond the control of even the school board. It is determined by the number and size of available buildings and by changes in socio-economic patterns. A local school board has a duty to provide educational services to all students, actual and potential. Class size is at best a permissive subject for bargaining.

The Oregon PERB also held that curriculum development, school year calendar, teacher evaluation, use of teacher aides, and selection of substitute teachers were permissive rather than mandatory subjects of bargaining. On the other hand, the Oregon PERB held that the following were mandatory subjects of bargaining: teacher transfers (excluding criteria for transfers), access to school facilities, bulletin boards, unpaid leaves of absence, teacher reference library, teaching supplies, teaching hours (excluding number of pupil contacts), preparation time, academic and personal freedom, and compensation for bargaining unit members who have additional duties such as department chairpersons.

4. Other decisions holding that class size is not a mandatory subject of bargaining include Beloit Education Ass'n v. WERC, 73 Wis.2d 43, 242 N.W.2d 231 (1976); City of Biddeford v. Biddeford Teachers Ass'n, 304 A.2d 387 (Me. Sup. Jud. Ct. 1973); Seward Education Ass'n v. School Dist. of Seward, 188 Neb. 772, 199 N.W.2d 752 (1972); Kenai Peninsula District v. Kenai Peninsula Education Ass'n, 557 P.2d 416, 97 L.R.R.M. 2153 (Alaska S. Ct. 1977); Aberdeen Education Ass'n v. Aberdeen Bd. of Education, 215 N.W.2d 837 (S.D. S. Ct. 1974); Rutgers, The State University, 2 NJPER 13 (N.J. PERC 1977). *Contra,* West Hartford Education Ass'n v. DeCourcy, 162 Conn. 566, 295 A.2d 526 (1972).

5. What has been the impact of negotiations, either *de jure* or *de facto,* over class size? In Hall and Carroll, *The Effect of Teachers' Organizations on Salaries and Class Size,* 26 IND. & LAB. REL. REV. 834, 840 (1973), the authors concluded:

> [I]t appears that teachers' organizations are associated with a larger student-teacher

ratio. This lends support to the common allegation that school boards are offering teachers higher salaries in exchange for larger classes and that these offers are being accepted. Certainly, there is nothing to suggest that teachers' organizations have had any success in reducing the number of pupils per classroom. . . .

*See generally* C. PERRY & W. WILDMAN, THE IMPACT OF NEGOTIATIONS IN PUBLIC EDUCATION: THE EVIDENCE FROM THE SCHOOLS (1970).

6.  In Board of Higher Educ. of New York City, 7 PERB ¶ 3028 (1974), the New York PERB held that student membership on a faculty evaluation committee is not a mandatory subject of bargaining. The New York PERB stated "that the composition of committees that evaluate employees is not a term or condition of the employees being evaluated." In hesitating to allow college teachers to shut out non-faculty members, the Board noted that policy questions about a university's responsibilities

> . . . often involved issues of social concern to many groups within the community other than the public employer's administrative apparatus and its employees. It would be a perversion of collective negotiations to impose it as a technique for resolving such dispute and thus disenfranchising other interested groups.

Member Joseph Crowley dissented, rejecting what he regarded as the majority's overreliance on transposing an industrial model of collective bargaining into an academic setting. He noted that appointment and promotion matters have traditionally been matters for mandatory negotiation.

7.  In the absence of a specific statutory reservation of the employer's right to establish minimum manning, the courts and boards are divided over whether minimum manning proposals, especially with respect to fire and police departments, are mandatory or permissive subjects of bargaining. Cases holding that minimum manning is a mandatory subject of bargaining include Town of Narragansett v. IAFF Local 1589, 97 L.R.R.M. 2582 (R.I. S. Ct. 1977); City of Alpena v. Alpena Fire Fighters Association Local 623, 56 Mich. App. 568, 224 N.W.2d 672 (1974); Fire Fighters Union, Local 1186 v. City of Vallejo, 12 Cal. 3d 608, 526 P.2d 971, 116 Cal. Rptr. 507 (1974). Cases holding that minimum manning is not a mandatory subject of bargaining include International Association of Fire Fighters v. Helsby, 399 N.Y.S.2d 334, 97 L.R.R.M. 2297 (N.Y. App. Div. 1977); City of West St. Paul v. IAFF Local 1059, 93 L.R.R.M. 2797 (Minn. Dist. Ct. 1976); Cinnaminson Township, 4 NJPER 310 (N.J. PERC 1978) (". . . the size of the police force, either in total or a particular crew size, relates to questions of manning requirements which is a permissive subject for negotiations"); City of New Rochelle, 10 PERB ¶ 3078 (N.Y. 1977), *aff'd sub nom.* City of New Rochelle v. Crowley, 61 App. Div. 2d 1031, 403 N.Y.S.2d 100 (1978). In these latter jurisdictions where minimum manning has been held to be a non-mandatory subject of bargaining, it has generally been held that the employer is obligated to negotiate over the impact of manning on safety. For example, in City of Newburgh, 10 PERB ¶ 3001 (N.Y. 1977), the New York PERB, after finding that a minimum manning proposal was not a mandatory subject of bargaining, stated:

> As we found here and in other cases, the general subject of safety as a means of protecting employees beyond the normal hazards inherent in their work is a mandatory item of negotiation. Hence, the presence of a general safety clause in the collective bargaining agreement should provide a basis for testing the safety guarantee in individual fact situations which may arise during the life of the agreement by presentation of disputes in such specific situations for resolution through the grievance procedure.

8.  The Supreme Court has held that the public employer, in the absence of a statutory bar, can require public employees, as a condition of employment, to establish and maintain residency within the employer's boundaries. McCarthy v. Philadelphia Civil Service Comm'n, 424 U.S. 645, 96 U.S. 1154, 47 L.Ed.2d 366 (1976). Most of the state courts and boards have held, however, that the establishment of residency requirements is a mandatory subject of bargaining. *See, e.g.,* Detroit Police Officers Ass'n v. City of Detroit, 391 Mich. 44, 214 N.W.2d 803 (1974); Boston School Committee, 3 MLC 1603 (Mass.

LRC 1977); PLRB v. School District of the City of Erie, PPER ¶ 9123 (Pa. LRB 1978); City of Buffalo, 9 PERB ¶ 3015 (N.Y. 1976); City of Brookfield v. WERC, 1 PBC ¶ 10,279 (Wis. Cir. Ct. 1974). *See generally* Hayford & Gurkee, *Residency Requirements in Local Government Employment: The Impact of the Public Employer's Duty to Bargain,* 29 Lab. L.J. 343 (1978). Would it make any difference if the residency requirement is only a condition of initial employment and is not a continuing condition of employment after being hired? In Detroit Federation of Teachers, Local 231 v. Board of Education, 237 N.W.2d 238, 92 L.R.R.M. 2121 (Mich. Ct. App. 1975), the court held that a residency requirement which is only a condition of initial hire is not a mandatory subject of bargaining. *Accord,* City of Buffalo, *supra.* Occasionally the subject of residency is specifically dealt with in a state act. For example, the Maine public sector bargaining law provides that "[i]f a municipality engages in collective bargaining . . . , then it shall not enact any ordinance which requires employees to reside within the boundaries of the municipality as a condition of employment." The Maine act further provides that "[a] collective bargaining agreement may, however, include a residency requirement for persons not yet employed at the time the agreement becomes effective." Me. Rev. Stat., ch. 491, tit. 30, § 2152-A (1978).

## CITY OF NEW YORK AND MEBA, DISTRICT NO. 1

New York City Office of Collective Bargaining
Decision No. B-3-75 (1975)

[After the expiration of a collective bargaining agreement between the City of New York and the Marine Engineers Beneficial Association, District No. 1 (MEBA or Union), the Union initiated impasse proceedings. Subsequently, the city filed a petition alleging, *inter alia,* that Article II concerning job security in the parties' prior agreement was not a mandatory subject of bargaining and that this topic could not be raised before the impasse panel over the city's objection. While the OCB denied the City's motion to stay the impasse panel proceedings pending a determination of the negotiability of the disputed items, the OCB issued an interim order providing that in the absence of "the consent of both parties, the panel may not hear arguments on or make any determination on matters the bargainability of which has been challenged by the City until such time as the Board rules." Article II, entitled "Job Security," reads as follows:

> During the term of this agreement, the Employer will attempt to retain all per annum employees who hold positions by permanent appointment. If curtailment because of a reduced number of runs becomes necessary, the Employer will make every effort to re-employ such Employees in vacancies or to replace persons who have provisional appointments to positions for which such Employees are eligible, at the rates and working conditions prevailing in the department in which such Employees are re-employed. However, no such curtailment shall become effective without prior discussion with the Union.]

The City's claim of non-bargainability is based upon its position that the issue of job security is a management right covered specifically by Section 1173-4.3(b) of the NYCCBL. Under that section, the Employer has the right to "relieve its employees from duties because of lack of work or for other legitimate reasons" as well as the right to determine standards of services to be offered, to maintain efficiency of government operations and to maintain complete control and discretion of over its organization and the technology of performing its work.

The City also argues that the Board has previously held (in B-4-71 and B-1-70) that layoffs are a managerial right. Thus, the City is not obligated to negotiate a contract provision committing itself to "attempt to retain employees." The City further contends that terms and conditions of laid off employees who replace provisional employees are either covered by the Civil Service system or a contract covering the position into which the re-employed employee is returning.

The Union asserts that the Job Security provision challenged by the City is identical with a provision in the Agreement between the City and Local 333, United Marine Division, National Maritime Union, covering unlicensed ferry crew members employed in the same department. The Union alleges that the City's attempt to have this article of the prior agreement declared non-mandatory is based on discriminatory motivation of the City designed to interfere with employee rights and to discredit the Union.

Section 1173-4.3b of the NYCCBL specifically gives the City the right "to relieve its employees from duty because of lack of work or for other legitimate reasons." Where the employer is authorized by law to lay off employees for lack of work, that authority is not diminished by requiring the employer to negotiate a pledge that he will attempt not to lay off per annum permanent employees.

A second element of the Union's Job Security demand provides that the employer attempt to re-employ permanent per annum employees if vacancies occur. As we noted in Decision No. B-4-71 *(Assoc. of Building Inspectors and HDA)*, however, the rights of competitive civil service employees with respect to Job Security are governed and protected by Civil Service Law.

. . . .

The Union urges that the Job Security clause it seeks is supported by the United States Supreme Court's decision in *Fibreboard Paper Products Corp. v. NLRB*, 379 U.S. 203 (1964). That decision, however, dealt only with the narrow issue of private sector subcontracting under certain circumstances, and Chief Justice Warren, writing for the Court, noted that the *Fibreboard* holding was limited to "the facts of this case."

Clearly, the *Fibreboard* decision was based on a factual situation quite different from that in the instant matter, and it promulgated a narrow rule requiring bargaining in those circumstances where an employer, through subcontracting, replaces his own employees with others who will perform the same work under the same conditions, but for less money. Moreover, *Fibreboard* applies to the private sector and does not establish a precedent applicable to the matter before this Board.

In *City School District of New Rochelle v. New Rochelle Federation of Teachers, Local 280, AFL-CIO,* 4 PERB 3060 (1971), the Public Employment Relations Board determined that a managerial decision to approve budgetary cuts resulting in reduction of work force is a non-mandatory bargaining subject.

. . . .

PERB concluded that although a decision to layoff workers necessarily affects working conditions, the employer is obligated to negotiate only the impact of its managerial decision.

This brings us to the third element of the instant Job Security demand, which would require discussion with the Union prior to effectuation of any layoffs. Insofar as we interpret this language to mean a demand for information and notification prior to implementation of a managerial decision to lay off, this requirement would not abridge a public employer's right to curtail or eliminate a service and would be a mandatory subject of bargaining. Under Section 1173-4.3b, the employer may unilaterally decide to relieve employees, but a Union demand for notice and discussion of imminent layoffs prior to their implementation relates directly to the Union's statutory right to negotiate on questions of the impact of managerial decisions on employees' working conditions.

. . . .

In the instant case and with particular regard to the management prerogative to effect layoffs for lack of work, we find and herein decide that practical impact on those laid off or to be laid off is implicit in any exercise of that prerogative; and that wherever the employer exercises this particular power, a practical impact will be deemed to have occurred and to have been established.

Because practical impact is held herein to be implicit in any exercise by management of its prerogative to lay off, we further hold and enunciate as a rule in this Decision, that the Union need not wait until employees are, in fact, laid off before it exercises its right to negotiate the impact of management's decision. With respect to those issues over which the employer has discretion to act, and which relate to the practical impact of a managerial decision to lay off employees, the City is obligated to bargain immediately.

That aspect of the Union's Job Security demand which seeks to achieve re-employment rights falls within the area governed by Sections 80 and 81 of the Civil Service Law; it, therefore, is not a mandatory subject of bargaining to the extent that it would conflict with the cited sections of the Civil Service Law. Those issues, however, which fall within the practical impact of a managerial decision to lay off employees and which do not infringe Civil Service Law or § 1173-4.3b of the NYCCBL are mandatory subjects of bargaining. Notice and prior discussion of an intent to lay off employees is such an issue.

We do not hold herein that a per se practical impact flows from every exercise of a managerial prerogative. In certain situations, the impact of a management decision on working conditions, specifically job security, may be only slight or indirect and may involve questions of fact requiring hearings or other procedures to establish the facts. In the latter circumstance and in other circumstances, such as that underlying our Decision B-9-68, management's action may be so directly related to the mission of the agency that even if practical impact is alleged and subsequently determined by this Board to exist, management should first have the opportunity to act unilaterally to alleviate the impact.

In the instant decision, we determine only that a management decision to lay off employees will result per se in a practical impact and that this impact is immediately bargainable. Therefore, a union demand in collective negotiations for a contract provision that provides for impact-related procedures, such as notice and discussion, in the event the employer decides to relieve employees, is a mandatory subject.

Having decided this case differently than Decision B-9-68 with respect to practical impact, the Board thereby makes known its intention to determine other scope of bargaining disputes involving alleged practical impact on a case-by-case basis.

. . . .

## NOTES

1. As indicated in the principal case, the New York City Collective Bargaining Law, which is included in the Statutory Appendix, contains a fairly lengthy enumeration of management rights and provides that "[d]ecisions of the city or any other public employer on those matters are not within the scope of bargaining." The New York law further provides, however, that "questions concerning the practical impact that decisions on [management prerogatives] have on employees, such as questions of workload or

manning, are within the scope of collective bargaining." N.Y. CITY ADMIN. CODE, ch. 54, § 1173-4.3(b). The New York City Office of Collective Bargaining has held that the following items are embraced within the City's management prerogatives and therefore not negotiable: determination of whether to grant merit increases, City of New York and Civil Service Ass'n, Decision No. B-9-69 (7/18/69); job content and shift hours, City of New York and District Council 37, AFSCME, Decision No. B-4-69 (6/12/69); starting and finishing times of each tour of duty, City of New York and PBA, Decision No. B-24-75 (9/18/75); creation of new positions, District Council 37, AFSCME and City of New York, Decision No. B-3-69 (6/2/69). On the other hand, the OCB has held that the following matters are mandatory subjects of negotiations: procedures and criteria used to determine eligibility for merit increases, City of New York and Civil Service Ass'n, Decision No. B-9-69 (7/18/69); seniority and examination eligibility, City of New York and District Council 37, AFSCME, Decision No. B-4-69 (6/12/69); free parking facilities, availability of office supplies, educational leave, legal counsel for employees in court on official business, and theft and damage funds, City of New York and Social Service Employees Union, Decision No. B-11-68 (1/8/69); paid time off for the conduct of labor-management relations, City of New York and MEBA, District No. 1, Decision No. B-3-75 (2/6/75).

2. Should evidence that other parties have included the disputed subject in agreements or that the parties' prior agreement, as in the principal case, contains the disputed item be a relevant factor in determining whether a given subject falls within the mandatory scope of negotiations? The Connecticut Supreme Court in West Hartford Education Ass'n v. DeCourcy, 162 Conn. 566, 295 A.2d 526 (1972), held that "the history and custom of the industry in collective bargaining" is a factor which "must [be] consider[ed] in order to determine if an item falls within the scope of negotiability." On the other hand, in Town of Maplewood, Decision No. 78-89 (N.J. PERC 1978), the New Jersey Commission stated, "The fact that a permissive subject of negotiations is included in a contract does not elevate that subject to mandatory status in negotiations for a successor agreement." Accord, Town of Ipswich v. IAFF, Local 1913, Docket No. 4296 (Mass. Super. Ct. 1977) ("Bargaining and agreeing on a permissive subject do not make the subject a mandatory subject of future bargaining"). See also Allied Chemical & Alkali Workers v. Pittsburgh Plate Glass Co., 404 U.S. 157, 92 S. Ct. 383, 30 L.Ed.2d 341 (1971) (industry practices are not "determinative" and they "cannot change the law"); U.S. Kirk Army Hospital, FLRC No. 70A-11 (1971) ("although other contracts may have included such provisions, as claimed by the union, this circumstance cannot alter the express language and intent of the Order [concerning negotiability] and is without controlling significance in this case"); City of Troy, 10 PERB ¶ 3105 (N.Y. 1977) ("... agreement on a non-mandatory subject of negotiations does not obligate either party to negotiate over a demand to extend the agreement to a successor contract").

## CITY OF NEW YORK

New York Public Employment Relations Board
10 PERB ¶ 3003 (1977)

. . . .

Prior collectively negotiated agreements between the City and the PBA [Patrolmen's Benevolent Association of the City of New York] and between the City and the three intervenors* had expired on June 30, 1974. Those agreements and the City's agreement with COBA contained "parity" clauses. Typical of them is the City-USA parity clause, which provides:

"[I]t is expressly understood and agreed that should, at any time during the term of the Agreement, the City of New York, or any Mayoral Agency or instrumentality thereof, be or become, directly or indirectly, a party to any agreement or obligation (in any way resulting from the collective bargaining process) negotiated, consummated, executed, or awarded, in whole or in part, with respect to comparable employees [there follows formula language which

---

* Uniformed Sanitationmen's Association, Local 831 [USA], The Uniformed Firefighters Association, Local 94, International Association of Firefighters, AFL-CIO [UFA], and the Correction Officers Benevolent Association [COBA].

encompasses, among others, employees in the negotiating unit represented by PBA] where such agreement or obligation is as to such term or condition, in any respect, on balance, more favorable to the employees participant therein than any of the terms and conditions hereof, then such more favorable term or condition shall be extended to the Uniformed Sanitationmen's Association at its option."

This agreement on "parity" did not become public information until October 23, 1974, the day on which the USA contract was filed with New York City's Office of Collective Bargaining, but there had been rumors indicating that such a clause had been included in the agreement prior thereto.

As part of the negotiations process between the City and PBA under the New York City Collective Bargaining Law, on December 9, 1974 a hearing was held before the City's Board of Collective Bargaining to determine whether the parties were at impasse, during which the City referred to the "parity" clauses. Thereafter the unresolved issues, which included the salary dispute, were submitted to an impasse panel under § 1173-7.0(c) of that law. That impasse panel held fourteen days of hearings between January 21 and February 19, 1975. During the course of these hearings, the City argued that its financial ability to pay for the PBA demands was impaired by reason of the "parity" clauses. For example, on February 13, 1975, the City argued that:

"It [the parity clause] is vitally pertinent to the outcome of this proceeding. ... The fact is that ... as long as it stands in the contract, the Panel is obliged to consider as a further impact what will be the consequence of meeting the demands of PBA ... which puts the City in the untenable position of being obliged to deal not only with a demand such as we have before us now but to bear the burden which might flow if their demand was met favorably by the Panel." The City introduced evidence that the "parity" clauses would cost it about triple the amount that it would have to pay employees represented by PBA for each dollar in excess of the UFA/USA formula.

The hearing officer concluded that, by using the "parity" agreements as a basis for resisting PBA demands, the City refused to negotiate in good faith with PBA. He further concluded that the City violated its duty to negotiate in good faith with PBA when it agreed to the "parity" clauses. These conclusions are contested by the City and by USA. The exceptions of the City and USA also argue that the charge was not timely, that the issue has become moot, and that the Board lacks jurisdiction to consider the validity of the contracts entered into between the City and the intervenors. USA also raises procedural objections to the conduct of the hearing which, in substance, constitute a protest to the failure of the hearing officer to dismiss the charge.

### Discussion

Having reviewed the record, heard oral argument, and read the extensive and thorough briefs, we confirm the hearing officer's findings of fact and his conclusion of law that a "parity" clause is a prohibited subject of negotiations.

In *Matter of the City of Albany (Firefighters),* 7 PERB Paragraph 3079, we determined that a demand for "parity" is not a mandatory subject of negotiation.

We said (at page 3146) that the parties demanding "parity" were, in effect, seeking "to be silent partners in negotiations between the employer and employees in another negotiating unit" and that "an agreement of this type between the City and other employee organizations would improperly inhibit negotiations between the City and another employee organization representing employees in a different unit." The New York City Board of Collective Bargaining has also dealt with the negotiability of demands for "parity." It reached this issue in *Matter of Uniformed Fire Officers Association,* B-14-72, and in *Matter of Lieutenants' Benevolent Association,* B-10-75, and determined that "parity/differential clauses establishing fixed pay relationships with other titles which must be maintained throughout the life of a contract are incompatible with sound bargaining principles. . . ." The issue before us in the instant case goes beyond our holding in the *Albany* case; we are now asked to determine whether a demand for "parity" is not only a non-mandatory, but is also a prohibited, subject of negotiation. The opinion of the Board of Collective Bargaining in B-10-75 contains an illuminating discussion of the arguments that were presented to it in B-14-72, saying:

"In that case the City maintained that parity clause advanced by the Uniformed Firefighters Association seeking equality in the wage levels of Firefighters and Patrolmen, and a clause advanced by the Uniformed Fire Officers Association establishing and maintaining a 3.0 to 3.9 wage relationship between the Firefighters and Fire Officers were 'prohibited, or at least, permissive subjects of bargaining.' The City maintained in that case that a parity or differential clause, if agreed to by the City, would constitute an improper labor practice because it would interfere with the bargaining rights of employees in the benchmark title who were represented by a different union, not a party to the parity agreement; would require the City to make automatic and unilateral changes in terms and conditions of employment; and would involve the City in assisting the contracting union to limit, control or otherwise adversely affect the bargaining in the unit of benchmark employees."

The arguments of the City in B-14-72 are supportive of our reasoning in this case. So is a recent decision of the Connecticut Supreme Court in *Local 1219, International Association of Firefighters v. Connecticut Labor Relations Board,* 171 Conn. 342 (1976), 93 LRRM 2098. In that decision, the Connecticut Supreme Court confirmed a determination of the defendant Board that a "parity" clause of an agreement between the Borough of Naugatuck and Local 1219 was void and unenforceable notwithstanding an arbitration award that would have commanded adherence to that award. The Connecticut court noted with approval that,

"[T]he Board concluded that the mere presence and necessary operation of the clause would inevitably interfere with, restrain and coerce the police union in future negotiations with the City. . . ." It reasoned that the "parity" clause thwarted the duty of the contracting parties to refrain from interfering with, coercing or restraining the negotiating rights of employees in a second negotiating unit.

. . . .

We recognized in our *Albany* decision, *supra,* that,

"[s]ettlements often follow established patterns, historical relationships, as well as cost of living indices. In negotiations, parties appropriately develop demands that reflect an awareness of such patterns and relationships. This is not inappropriate." A similar distinction between "parity" and "pattern" bargaining was noted in the cited OCB decisions. Indeed, CSL § 209.9(c) (v) a. indicates that where interest arbitration is used to resolve negotiations deadlocks, the arbitration panel should consider a "comparison of the wages, hours and conditions of employment of the employees involved in the arbitration proceeding with the wages, hours, and conditions of employment of other employees performing similar services or requiring similar skills under similar working conditions. . . . ," but CSL § 209.4(c)(v)b. also requires such an arbitration panel to consider, "The financial ability of the public employer to pay."

In this case, the City, by entering into "parity" agreements, has diminished its financial ability to grant benefits to employees represented by PBA beyond the formulas contained in the agreements negotiated with the intervenors. In brief, the "parity" agreement inhibits the public employer from evaluating or negotiating over PBA demands on their merits, but, requires it to view PBA demands in the light of the "parity" agreement. Inevitably this interferes with the negotiation rights of PBA. In *Sperry Rand Corp. v. NLRB,* 492 F2d 63 (1974), the Second Circuit said (at p. 70):

"Even though in an interdependent economy the wages of one group of workers potentially might affect the wages of all other workers, an employer generally cannot bargain with a union over the wages that the union will negotiate with other employers [citation and footnote omitted]." Similarly, a union cannot bargain with an employer over the wages that the employer will negotiate with other unions absent evidence that other employees' wages vitally affect terms and conditions of employment. In our judgment, the "parity" clause has this effect.

. . . .

Finally, we reject the contention advanced in the exceptions that this Board lacks jurisdiction or authority to declare a "parity" clause to be a prohibited subject of negotiations absent some explicit statutory declaration or indication that it is an impermissible subject.

Admittedly, there is no expressed limitation on the scope of negotiations in the Public Employees' Fair Employment Act. However, this Board, in interpreting the act, has found some limitations and restrictions on the scope of negotiations. The Court of Appeals has endorsed the concept that this Board has the power to supervise the negotiating process — not to the extent of compelling the inclusion of a substantive subject in the negotiated agreement — but to the extent of finding that a subject, such as class size, is not a mandatory subject of negotiation, *West Irondequoit Teachers Association v. Helsby,* 42 AD 2d 808, affirmed 35 NY 2d 46 (1974). This finding was made and approved by the Court even in the absence of any statute stating that the specific subject — class size — is not a mandatory subject.

The issue in the instant case does go beyond the class size decision; the determination there was that there was no duty to negotiate over the demand; here the determination is that a demand is a prohibited subject of negotiation. This Board has, in a prior decision, determined that the subject of an agency shop is a prohibited subject, *Matter of Monroe-Woodbury Teachers Association,* 3 PERB paragraph 3104 (1970), confirmed *Farrigan v. Helsby,* 42 AD 2d 265 (1973). This decision, which was based upon implicit rather than explicit statutory authority, was confirmed in court. Further, the Court of Appeals has stated that this Board has been delegated the power to resolve disputes arising out of negotiations and inherent in this delegation is the power to interpret and construe the statutory scheme, *West Irondequoit Teachers v. Helsby, supra.*

A "parity" clause is not expressly prohibited by statute, but an analysis of its effect indicates that it is implicitly prohibited by reason of its inhibiting effect upon related collective negotiations. Under a "parity" clause, an employer agrees with one employee organization representing one group of municipal employees, not only upon the terms and conditions of employment, economic or otherwise, under which its constituents will be employed, but also agrees that any higher wage or any other more favorable term and condition agreed upon in subsequent negotiations with another employee organization representing another group of municipal employees, shall be granted to the employees represented by the first organization. Such an agreement seriously inhibits the second employee organization in its negotiations with the employer. For example, assume that the first organization sought other benefits in lieu of a substantial increase in wages and, having obtained such other benefits, settled for a three percent wage increase and that the cost of such benefits and the wage increase represented to the employer an overall increase of labor costs for that unit of six percent. Now, assume that a second employee organization comes to the negotiating table and its constituents are interested only in a wage increase of six percent and would eschew the other benefits granted to the first organization. Absent the "parity" clause, the employer would consider the demand solely on the merits and could accede to the wage demands, for it would be in accord with the overall cost increase of six percent. However, because of the "parity" clause, the employer will, of necessity, consider the demand of the second employee organization, not on its merits, but upon the impact that the grant of such demand would have in increasing the cost of the prior negotiated contract. Obviously the negotiation opportunities of the second organization are constricted by the agreement of the first. Moreover, as we said before, the first organization, having achieved its negotiation goal, does, by reason of the "parity" clause, seek to participate as a silent partner in the second employee organization's negotiations.

Clearly, in the grant of rights to public employees in Civil Service Law sections 202 and 204.2, the intent of the Legislature was that public employees have the right to be represented by an employee organization of their choosing and to have such representative negotiate about their terms and conditions of employment. The statute contemplates that their negotiation representative should be able to seek improvements in whatever terms and conditions of employment that are a matter of concern to them, to determine their negotiating priorities and not to be limited, curtailed or foreclosed by the terms that another employee organization has negotiated. To permit a "parity" clause, therefore, would diminish the legislative grant of rights, if not make them illusory, and thus would contravene the letter and intent of CSL sections 202 and 204.2.

The result reached herein is not contrary to the decision of the Court of Appeals in *Board of Education of Town of Huntington v. Associated Teachers of Huntington*, 30 NY 2d 122 (1972). In subsequent decisions the Court of Appeals clarified its holding to the effect that the scope of negotiations is limited by plain and clear prohibitions in statutory or decisional law and by public policy "whether derived from, and whether explicit or implicit in statute or decisional law, or in neither." *Syracuse Teachers Association v. Board of Education*, 35 NY 2d 743 (1974) and *Matter of Susquehanna Valley School District*, 37 NY 2d 614, 616-7 (1975).

We conclude that bargaining for, or the agreement to, such a "parity" clause effectively precludes the meaningful implementation of grant of negotiating rights to public employees and thus contravenes the statutory scheme.

For these reasons, we conclude a "parity" clause to be a prohibited subject of negotiation. . . .

IDA KLAUS, dissenting:

The Board has now declared, as a matter of its own basic decisional law, that a "parity" clause is a prohibited subject of negotiation and, hence, unenforceable. It has found further that reliance on such clause in the course of negotiations with another organization representing a different unit contravenes the good-faith bargaining requirement of the Act. I cannot agree with either conclusion.

The "parity" provision here in question was negotiated in each instance as part of an overall agreement of definite duration as to wages, hours and working conditions. The clause undertakes to grant to the employees in the units covered by the agreement the benefits of more favorable terms that may thereafter during the life of that agreement be reached with other organizations for similar categories of employees in other units.

Both the hearing officer and the Board have found that the clause was not deliberately devised by either side for the purpose of depriving employees represented by PBA of their rights under the Act. Nor has it been found that the intent of the City and each of the signatories to the basic agreements was to impose upon the PBA unit through the mechanism of the "parity" clause the terms of their basic agreements. Rather, the majority's conclusion is that the clause "is implicitly prohibited by reason of its inhibiting effect upon related collective negotiations."

In my view, this Board is without authority to declare such clause to be illegal *per se,* and thus to be outlawed as a subject of negotiation.

The Court of Appeals has now established and clarified through progressive decisions the guiding principles which govern the legally allowable scope of negotiations under the Act. Those decisions reflect a clear disposition toward an expansive view of the reach of the basic collective negotiation policy of the Act. . . .

A provision in a collective agreement negotiated by a public employer is valid if it constitutes a "term or condition" as defined by the Act, unless other applicable statutory or decisional law prohibits its making. While the prohibition is not to be deemed to exist only where a particular subject is "explicitly and definitively" proscribed, it must nevertheless be "plain and clear," *Huntington, supra,* as clarified by *Syracuse Teachers, supra.* It may derive from "objectively demonstrable" public policy as expressed in "imperative" provisions of other applicable laws. *Union Free School District, Town of Cheektowaga v. Nyquist,* 38 N.Y. 2d 137 (1975) and *Cohoes City School District v. Cohoes Teachers Ass'n,* 42 N.Y. 2d 774, December 2, 1976.

The "parity" clause here in question covers only the terms and conditions of employment of the employees in the unit for which it was negotiated. It is not prohibited by any plain and clear provisions of the Act itself, or of applicable external statute, or of decisional law or public policy derived from the conflicting and paramount imperative provisions of other law. Yet this Board has condemned the clause as a clearly and plainly prohibited subject of bargaining because it believes its presence in an agreement to be so pernicious as to deprive employees of their basic rights under the Act. I find that this analysis has no solid basis in the record and that it is subject to question on relevant grounds of established practice and countervailing opinion.

Historically, "parity" at least as to basic wages, between police and fire forces has been the established pattern in New York City for three quarters of a century. A fixed wage relationship as between those uniformed forces and sanitation workers has been in effect for some eight years. At various times, one force or the other has sought and obtained "parity" clauses in its collective bargaining agreements either by direct negotiation or through third-party intervention. In 1970, for example, the PBA (the charging party here) sought and obtained enforcement in the courts of a so-called "vertical-parity" clause, establishing a fixed ratio between the salaries of patrolmen and sergeants it had included in a collective bargaining agreement for patrolmen. *PBA v. City of New York,* 76 LRRM 3087 (1971), and *PBA v. City of New York,* 78 LRRM 2747 (1971) (neither decision officially reported), on remand from 27 N.Y. 2d 410 (1971).

Looking at the way in which the "me-too" kind of clause involved in this case has functioned in the conduct of collective bargaining in New York City, it would not, it seems to me, be unrealistic to observe that its inclusion may well have a beneficial effect on the bargaining relationship of the parties. Recourse to such clause may reasonably serve to promote the early resolution of bargaining disputes and the timely conclusion of an agreement by affording the necessary assurance to the contracting union that it will not risk less favorable treatment by an early settlement as against those in other units who may play for the competitive advantage of a long wait-and-see policy. Thus the strains and uncertainties of a protracted hiatus between contracts, and their inevitable threat to labor peace and the conduct of the governmental function, may well be avoided by the mechanism of the "parity" clause.

Agencies administering other public employment relations statutes in two other states have found "parity" clauses not to be improper subjects of collective bargaining agreements. *West Allis Professional Policemen's Ass'n. v. City of West Allis,* Decision #12706 (May 1974) of the Wisconsin Employment Relations Commission; *City of Detroit and Detroit Police Officers,* Case No. C72 A-1, decided by the Michigan Employment Relations Commission December 29, 1972.

In the private sector, the National Labor Relations Board, in what appears to be its sole decision on this point, has found that a reverse type of "parity" provision (i.e., one favoring the employer if lesser benefits are reached elsewhere) demanded by an employer and adamantly insisted upon by him in the course of negotiations with a union representing his employees was a proper subject of collective bargaining. It held that the clause was therefore not in itself illegal and that the insistence did not constitute a bad-faith refusal to bargain. The Board characterized the employer's demand as "not an effort to impose wages and working conditions on other employers or employees in other bargaining units" but as "designed only to assure that this Employer could be relieved of any disadvantage that it might otherwise suffer if the Union subsequently negotiated more favorable wage and benefit levels with other employers." *Dolly Madison Industries, Inc.,* 182 N.L.R.B. 1037 (1970).

In light of such countervailing considerations, it would be difficult to conclude that the clause in dispute is so unquestionably in conflict with the Act or with other law as to establish beyond doubt its "plain and clear" illegality.

I cannot join the majority's position that its authority to ban as illegal a particular term or condition of employment properly derives from its general power to supervise the negotiating process. To be sure, the decision as to what kinds of substantive subjects (e.g. class size) are encompassed within the broad category of "terms and conditions" as to which the parties must negotiate is a function left to the expert competence of this Board to develop under the scheme of the Act. That role does not, however, embrace authority to outlaw a particular subject not prohibited by the Act or other appropriate law. Nor does the Board's confirmed authority to find an agency-shop provision to be prohibited support its claim of similar authority as to the type of clause here in question. The

Appellate Division held that the agency shop "is made illegal by clear and definite statutory mandates" and by a "crystal clear" showing of legislative intent in the improper practice provisions of the Act expressly prohibiting employer discriminatory conduct of the kind practiced under an agency shop. *Farrigan v. Helsby,* 42 A.D. 2d 265 (1973). The proper practice provision prohibiting in general terms a refusal to bargain in good faith expresses no such "crystal clear" intent to ban the making of a "parity" clause.

I must conclude that in banning the "parity" clause, the Board is imposing upon the parties a public policy of the bargaining table not specified or defined by the statute or other applicable law and is thereby regulating those very substantive terms of wages, hours and working conditions which the Act has left to the parties to delineate for themselves. I find no indication that the Legislature put it to this Board to define such public policy *through its processes.* If a public policy is to be devised here, I believe that it should be declared by the Legislature. Until the Legislature moves to that point, I do not see how the Board can do so on its own.

Finally, as to the finding that the City violated the Act in its reliance upon the clause in negotiations with the PBA, the Board is inferring a lack of good faith solely and simply from the City's reference to the clause at the bargaining table and from its forceful reliance upon it as one of several arguments it put forward to the arbitration panel to support its bargaining position as to the extent of the wage increase it was willing to grant.

It is to be assumed that, but for its prohibition of the clause, the Board would not have found such bargaining strategy and advocacy to constitute bad-faith bargaining. As I do not agree with the prohibition, I cannot accept the bad-faith condemnation.

I would dismiss the complaint.

## NOTES

1. In Niagara Wheatfield Administrators Association v. Wheatfield Central School District, 44 N.Y.2d 68, — N.E.2d — (1978), the New York Court of Appeals held that a provision which required the salaries of school administrators be tied to the salaries of teachers was not illegal or otherwise unenforceable as against public policy. The court noted that a similar tie-in provision had been "statutorily required until 1971." Does this decision conflict with the holding in the principal case?

2. In City of Yonkers, 10 PERB ¶ 3048 (1978), the New York PERB drew a distinction between the type of parity agreement it held illegal in the principal case and a "favored nations" clause. The favored nations clause in *Yonkers* provided that the fire fighters union could reopen negotiations if the wages and benefits negotiated for other bargaining units exceeded those included in the fire fighters' agreement. The New York PERB affirmed the hearing officer's determination that the favored nations clause was not a prohibited parity clause on the ground that the reopening occurs only at the union's option, is not automatic, and even if reopened, "there would be no automatic increase."

3. The Pennsylvania Labor Relations Board in PLRB v. Commonwealth of Pa., 9 PPER ¶ 9084 (1978), held that the Commonwealth committed an unfair labor practice when it entered into a "parity agreement" which provided that the contracting union would receive the same benefits as another union with whom the Commonwealth was currently negotiating. The Pennsylvania PLRB stated that "parity agreements necessarily affect subsequent negotiations, impermissibly bringing another party to the bargaining table, and thereby interfere with good faith negotiations between the employer and the union not protected by the parity agreement." *Accord,* Town of Methuen, Case No. MUP-507, 545 GERR B-17 (Mass. LRC 1974); City of Plainfield, 4 NJPER 255 (N.J. PERC 1978).

4. In West Allis Professional Policemen's Ass'n v. City of West Allis, Decision No. 12706

(1974), the Wisconsin Employment Relations Commission held that it was not an unfair labor practice for the city to agree to pay fire fighters the same as police and to grant them any additional increases that the police union might negotiate. In rejecting the police union's contention that the parity clause in the fire fighters' agreement restrained and interfered with its statutory right to bargain collectively, the WERC stated:

> Such [parity] agreements are not rare or limited to police and fire settlements and do, as the [police union] urges, affect the calculations of a municipal employer in its subsequent negotiations with other labor organizations. However, even in the absence of such agreements, employers ... calculate the effects of proposed settlements upon their relations with other groups of employees. ... This is a "fact of life" in collective bargaining. The [police union] recognizes this, but distinguishes the present case on the basis of the existence of a formal agreement. ... We hold that this distinction is artificial and not to be adopted herein. ...
>
> The parity agreement does not place an absolute "ceiling" on settlements with the [police union]. It adds to the cost of higher settlements. The normal, unformalized considerations of employers, on the other hand, are very compelling, not only because of cost considerations, but because of very significant tactical considerations that an employer dealing with a number of unions must make respecting the relative positions of such unions. We would indeed be unrealistic and excessively legalistic if we attempted to minimize or eliminate these considerations. We would be engaging in unwarranted conclusions if we held agreements reflecting such considerations to be contrary to the duty to bargain in good faith. ...

5. In Lewiston Fire Fighters Ass'n, Local 785 v. City of Lewiston, 354 A.2d 154, 92 L.R.R.M. 2029 (Me. Sup. Jud. Ct. 1976), the court held that a charter provision which required the city to pay fire fighters wages that were "no less" than those paid to police officers was impliedly repealed by the enactment of the Maine public sector collective bargaining law. The court held that the procedures established by the Maine act "for determining the configuration of the unit whose wages will be determined by collective bargaining between its elected representatives and the employer are evaded by the parity pay provision which at the bargaining table, necessarily interjects the interests of the Lewiston Firefighters into the unit created to represent the Lewiston Police."

6. Can a public employer legally agree to a contractual provision whereby the wages for the employees in the bargaining unit are tied to the wages of a comparable group of public employees employed by *another* public employer? *Compare* Voigt v. Bowen, 53 App. Div. 2d 277, 385 N.Y.S.2d 600 (N.Y. App. Div. 1976) (contract which granted city police officers parity with county police officers held invalid as violation of New York Taylor Law and public policy), *with* Kugler v. Yocum, 69 Cal.2d 371, — P.2d — (1968) (ordinance providing that salaries for city fire fighters would be no less than average wage for fire fighters employed by two other public bodies upheld).

7. Would a union's demand that a negotiated wage increase be made retroactive be a mandatory subject of negotiation? The Wisconsin Employment Relations Commission in Racine County, WERC Decision No. 10917-B (1972), held that "[t]he retroactive application of matters relating to wages, hours and conditions of employment ... are proper subjects of collective bargaining under the Act." *Accord,* Town of Groton, Decision No. 806 (Conn. SLRB 1968); Allegheny County, Case No. PERA-C-2443-W, GERR No. 517, B-13 (Pa. LRB 1973).

Many state constitutions include prohibitions against the payment of extra compensation after the services or work have been performed. For example, Article XI, Section 10 of the California Constitution reads as follows:

> A local government body may not grant extra compensation or extra allowance to a public officer, public employee, or contractor after service has been rendered or a contract has been entered into and performed in whole or in part, or pay a claim under an agreement without authority of law.

In San Joaquin County Employees Ass'n v. County of San Joaquin, 39 Cal. App. 3d 83, 86 L.R.R.M. 2942 (1974), the court held that the foregoing constitutional prohibition did not prohibit a public employer from providing in a salary ordinance or by appropriate agreement for retroactive pay increases. *Accord,* Christie v. Port of Olympia, 27 Wash. 2d 534, 179 P.2d 294 (1947).

## 3. EFFECT OF CIVIL SERVICE LAWS

The origins of civil service systems can be traced to passage of the Pendleton Act of 1883. This Act was viewed as the *modus operandi* for protecting federal employees from the spoils system. The core concept underlying the Act and other civil service legislation is that public employees should be selected and retained solely on merit. But over the years these systems have expanded to cover many matters not essential to implementation of the merit principle.

In many respects the development of civil service systems paralleled the growth of collective bargaining in the private sector. George Shultz observed: "Civil service regulations set forth the law of the public workplace. The governing charter in the private sphere is normally the collective bargaining agreement." GERR No. 319, F-2 (1969). In fact, for many years unions representing public employees staunchly supported the strengthening of civil service systems. The American Federation of State, County and Municipal Employees (AFSCME) was founded in 1934 in Wisconsin in order to lobby against proposed legislation that would have gutted that state's civil service system. *See generally* L. KRAMER, LABOR'S PARADOX 27-38 (1962). As late as its 1960 convention AFSCME's official position was to "stimulate the growth and extension of civil service and to improve existing merit systems." Proceedings, AFSCME, 12th Int'l Convention, Philadelphia, April 25-29, 1960, p. 341. Increasingly over the past 15 years, however, AFSCME and other unions representing public employees have come to view civil service as an arm of management. More and more they are demanding that matters covered by civil service be made negotiable. The obvious conflict between civil service and collective bargaining has resulted in numerous problems concerning the scope of negotiations.

**1967 EXECUTIVE COMMITTEE, NATIONAL GOVERNORS' CONFERENCE, REPORT OF TASK FORCE ON STATE AND LOCAL GOVERNMENT LABOR RELATIONS 18-19 (1967)†**

A critical issue for many governments is how the merit principle can be preserved and how collective bargaining can be accommodated within the merit system.

Because the two terms, "merit principle" and "merit system" are frequently confused, they should be defined. The merit principle is the concept that public employees should be selected and retained solely on the basis of merit. Political, religious, or racial considerations should play no part in such employment practices as selection, promotion, wages, career progression, assignment, and discharge. The merit principle was originally conceived to minimize the effect of patronage on the efficiency of government operations.

The merit system (or civil service system) is a public employment procedure designed to implement the merit principle. The procedure varies from place to place, but it commonly involves the establishment of a board (civil service commission) with rule-making authority to insure adherence to the merit principle. The essential elements of a merit system are: an impartial recruiting, examining and selecting program; position classification plans based on duties

---

† Reprinted by permission of the International Personnel Management Association.

and responsibilities; promotion on merit; protection against arbitrary disciplinary action.

In practice, many merit systems over the years have come to encompass other aspects of employee relations and personnel management not essentially related to the merit principle. These aspects include the handling of grievances, labor-management relations, employee training, salary administration, safety, morale, and attendance control programs.

In discussing the implications of collective bargaining for the merit system, consideration should be given to the determination of those procedures necessary to the merit principle as compared to procedural aspects of personnel management. Most public administration experts agree that merit system rules on examination, placement and promotion are indispensable to the merit principle and should therefore not be subject to collective bargaining. Many would like to extend the list of exemptions.

Most employee organizations regard every aspect of work as subject to bargaining. They want a voice in all areas that may affect the lives of their members. These areas include position classification, compensation, grievance procedures, discipline, discharge, layoff, and other subjects.

Care should be exercised not to restrict collective bargaining so unreasonably as to nullify the values of the process. Experience has shown that employee organizations denied reasonable scope in bargaining — particularly over the matter of wages — resort to lobbying and political pressure. They attempt a quasi-negotiation of sorts with the group that sets salaries, whether it is a civil service commission or a legislative body.

To the extent that a civil service commission has authority over personnel administration beyond the merit principle, the introduction of collective bargaining raises other problems. One problem is that if an independent civil service commission has authority over bargainable matters, then bargaining responsibility must lie with the commission rather than with the executive department. Conversely, if full authority over personnel matters is vested in an independent commission which is not the bargaining agent, then the scope of negotiation is unduly restricted. In Michigan, for example, a constitutional provision gives the independent commission full authority over salaries, wages, and other conditions of work for state employees.

A possible solution to these problems would be to transfer non-merit functions from a civil service commission to a personnel department under the chief executive. Negotiators would thus have full authority to conclude an agreement. In Canada, a new law gives the Treasury Board, as management's bargaining representative, responsibility for pay, classification, and conditions of employment. The Public Service Commission (formerly the Civil Service Commission) retains authority over examinations, promotions, staffings, and career development of Canadian federal employees.

## Attitudes Toward the Civil Service Commission

In this connection it is pertinent to examine how the role of the civil service commission is perceived by different groups. Some public administrators look upon the civil service commission as an arm of management. Others view it as an impartial third party that protects employees from patronage or from excessively arbitrary management.

Unions generally regard the commissioners, who in their eyes represent management, as adversaries. They do not believe that a commission is an impartial third party. Rather, they feel that the duties of the commission should be confined to recruitment, hiring, and the prevention of patronage. Union leaders have asserted that if their unions are to achieve a full, mature relationship with public employers through collective bargaining, they must be free to negotiate on all matters.

Independent associations tend to take a less hostile position. They speak of "working with" civil service commissions, but they also want a share in decision-making and a change in the traditionally paternalistic method of administration.

Employee organizations often contend that bargaining will have an influence on agencies that are not covered by a merit system or those whose system is weak and does not preserve the merit principle. It is argued that strong employee groups can act as an effective counter to patronage and bring pressure to bear for efficient, impartial administration. Others argue that strong employee organizations may actually reinforce a patronage system.

Legislation in the United States for public employee collective bargaining has attempted in different ways to protect the merit principle and fit collective bargaining into the existing merit system structure. . . .

## NOTES

1. In recommending that federal employees be given the right to organize and bargain collectively, President Kennedy's Task Force, headed by then Secretary of Labor Arthur Goldberg, stated:

> The principle of entrance into the career service on the basis of open competition, selection on merit and fitness, and advancement on the same basis, together with the full range of principles and practices that make up the Civil Service system govern the essential character of each individual's employment. Collective dealing cannot vary these principles. It must operate within their framework.

*1961 Task Force Report on Employee-Management Cooperation in the Federal Service,* in LABOR-MANAGEMENT RELATIONS IN THE PUBLIC SERVICE, Pt. 1, at 14 (H. Roberts ed. 1968).

Whereas Executive Order 11491 provided that an agreement between an agency and a labor organization was subject to "existing or future laws in the regulations of appropriate authorities, including policies set forth in the Federal Personnel Manual" (E.O. 11491, § 12(a)), the Federal Service Labor-Management and Employee Relations Law which was enacted as part of Title VII of the Civil Service Reform Act of 1978 provides that "the duty to bargain in good faith shall, to the extent not inconsistent with any federal law or any Government-wide rule or regulation, extend to matters which are the subject of any rule or regulation only if the rule or regulation is not a Government-wide rule or regulation." 5 U.S.C. § 7117(a) (1).

2. The extent of potential conflict between the civil service laws and collective bargaining agreements is illustrated by the growing popularity of civil service systems. In 1955, only 23 states had civil service laws covering approximately 65 percent of full-time state employees. H. KAPLAN, THE LAW OF CIVIL SERVICE 24, 25 (1958). In 1970, 84 percent of the cities, 83 percent of the counties, and 96 percent of the states in a National Civil Service League survey reported adoption of some form of merit system. Approximately 80 percent of all public employees are now covered by merit systems. National Civil Service League, *Survey of Current Personnel Systems in State and Local Governments,* GOOD GOVERNMENT 1-28 (Spring 1970). For an excellent treatise on civil service law, *see* R. VAUGHN, PRINCIPLES OF CIVIL SERVICE LAW (1976).

3. Among the many articles examining the relationship between collective bargaining and civil service are Lewin & Horton, *The Impact of Collective Bargaining on the Merit*

*System in Government,* 30 Arb. J. 199 (1975); Comment, *The Civil Service — Collective Bargaining Conflict in the Public Sector: Attempts at Reconciliation,* 38 U. Chi. L. Rev. 826 (1971); Stanley, *What are Unions Doing to Merit Systems?,* 31 Public Personnel Rev. 109 (1970); Camp & Lomax, *Bilateralism and the Merit Principle,* Public Administration Rev., Vol. 28, at 132-34 (March/April 1968); Morse, *Shall We Bargain Away the Merit System,* 24 Public Personnel Rev. 239 (1963); U.S. Dep't of Labor, Collective Bargaining in Public Employment and the Merit System (1972).

## HELBURN AND BENNETT, PUBLIC EMPLOYEE BARGAINING AND THE MERIT PRINCIPLE, 23 Lab. L.J. 618, 623-26 (1972)†

Discussion below includes the laws of 20 states which afford general coverage to at least one major category of public employees, state, county, and/or municipal.[14] In general, the laws may be classified into two broad categories with respect to the accommodation of polar views of merit systems: (1).—11 states with legal provisions related to the problem; and (2).—10 states with no related provisions.[15]

### Accommodation Provisions

The 11 state laws which have provisions bearing on the accommodation problem basically attempt to resolve the conflict by excluding certain matters from the scope of negotiations. This exclusion takes three general forms: (1).— blanket exclusion of all matters covered by law; (2).—specific exclusion of matters covered by merit system laws and regulations; and (3).—selective exclusion only of certain merit-related items.

The statutes of New Hampshire, Vermont, and Pennsylvania exemplify the blanket exclusion approach. The New Hampshire and Pennsylvania laws do not specifically mention the merit system, but appear to limit bargaining to matters not covered by merit system laws. Vermont law includes the blanket exclusion plus the stipulation that bargaining law should not be construed to contravene the spirit and intent of the merit principle. However, since these laws fail to adequately clarify the relationship between merit systems and collective bargaining, they provide little guidance for a viable approach to the problem of accommodation.

The laws of California, Massachusetts, Rhode Island, and Washington, and the Wisconsin law covering state employees only are of the specific exclusion type. The California statute provides that:

> Nothing contained herein shall be deemed to supersede the provisions of existing state law and the charters, ordinances and rules of local public agencies which establish and regulate a merit or civil service system or which provide for other methods of administering employer-employee relations.

The Wisconsin law for state employees is even more specific:

---

† This material appeared originally in the October 1972 issue of *Labor Law Journal,* published and copyrighted 1972 by Commerce Clearing House, Inc., Chicago and is reproduced with permission.

[14] The states include California, Connecticut, Delaware, Hawaii, Maine, Massachusetts, Michigan, Minnesota, Missouri, Nevada, New Hampshire, New Jersey, New York, Oregon, Pennsylvania, Rhode Island, South Dakota, Vermont, Washington, and Wisconsin. Joel Seidman has made a general analysis of the public employee labor relations laws of the 16 states which he considers to have the most advanced and comprehensive statutes. Included were all the above except California, Missouri, Nevada, and New Hampshire. See "State Legislation on Collective Bargaining by Public Employees," Labor Law Journal, XXII (January, 1971), pp. 13-22.

[15] Because two sets of Wisconsin laws were considered, the states appear to add to 21. One Wisconsin law was placed in each of the two major groups.

Nothing herein shall require the employer to bargain in relation to statutory and rule provided prerogatives of promotion, layoff, position classification, compensation and fringe benefits, examinations, discipline, merit salary determination policy, and other actions provided for by law and rules governing civil service.

Rhode Island law exempts from bargaining only those matters exclusively reserved for merit systems by law or regulation. The Massachusetts and Washington statutes are least specific of this group, merely exempting matters delegated to civil service and personnel boards. Wellington and Winter note that the Washington statute appears "to subordinate collective bargaining provisions to civil service rules and regulations. However, there is some uncertainty among local officials . . . as to which statute takes precedence."

## Problems in Definition

While all of these specific exclusion laws provide to some extent a basic framework for accommodation, there still exist problems in defining the merit system-bargaining relationship and in establishing a reasonable scope of bargaining. Merely excluding merit system matters from the scope of bargaining does not necessarily bring about the proper relationship between the merit principle and bargaining, especially if the merit systems involved have authority over personnel matters not essentially related to the merit principle.

Generally the selective exclusion laws manage to avoid this pitfall. By extending bargaining to all matters not deemed essential to the merit principle, they provide a reasonably broad scope of bargaining and at the same time apparently maintain a viable merit system. The statutes of Hawaii, Connecticut, and Maine are in this category.

All three laws remove the appointment and promotion functions from the scope of bargaining, with the Connecticut law providing that:

Nothing herein shall diminish the authority and power of any municipal civil service commission, personnel board, personnel agency or its agents established by statute, charter or special act to conduct and grade merit examinations and to rate candidates in order of their relative excellence from which the appointments or promotions may be made to positions in the competitive division of the classified service of the municipal employer served by such civil service commission or personnel board. The conduct and grading of merit examinations, the rating of candidates and the establishment of lists from such examinations and the appointments from such lists and any provisions of any municipal charter concerning political activity of municipal employees shall not be subject to collective bargaining.

The above law is affected, however, by a previous subsection:

Where there is a conflict between any agreement reached by a municipal employer and an employee organization and approved in accordance with the provisions of [this act] on matters appropriate to collective bargaining, as defined in this act, and any charter, special act, ordinance, rules or regulations adopted by the municipal employer or its agents such as a personnel board or civil service commission . . . the terms of such agreement shall prevail."

The Connecticut, as well as the Maine, law permits bargaining over personnel movements other than appointment and promotion, indicating that at least in these states the protection of all personnel movements is not deemed essential to the merit principle. While the Hawaii law does not specifically exclude all personnel movements from bargaining, it does stipulate that agreements cannot contain provisions inconsistent with [the] merit principle. However, "merit principles" are not defined.

Despite problems in specifying the items essential to the merit principle, the above laws confront the problem of accommodation. Unfortunately this is not true of those state laws which have no provisions pertaining to the accommodation of collective bargaining and the merit principle.

The public employee labor relations statutes of Delaware, Michigan, Minnesota, Missouri, Nevada,* ... New York, Oregon, and South Dakota, and the municipal employee law of Wisconsin contain no provisions dealing with accommodation. Although the Oregon bargaining statute does not deal with the problem, the state's civil service law attempts to achieve accommodation by redesignating the state Civil Service Board as the Public Employee Relations Board with the authority to interpret and administer the bargaining statutes. The Board is to make rulings which will preserve the merit principle.

In Michigan, the lack of provisions has resulted in legal conflict between collective bargaining and local merit systems. Since the Michigan Public Employee Relations Act does not specifically exempt the various aspects of merit systems from the scope of bargaining, both the Wayne County and Macomb County Circuit Courts have held that agreements reached through collective bargaining guaranteed by the bargaining statute supersede the provisions of the state civil service law when the two conflict. The Michigan experience suggests a great need for legislation clarifying the relationship between merit systems and public employee bargaining if the merit principle is to be preserved.

## NOTE

The California Assembly Advisory Council on Public Employee Relations made the following recommendations concerning the accommodation between civil service and collective bargaining:

> ... We prefer ... the approach adopted by the State of Connecticut in respect to municipal labor relations, according to which the terms of a negotiated agreement prevail over conflicting laws and regulations, including civil service systems, if the appropriate legislative body approves the agreement. We believe that this approach can be adopted to all public jurisdictions, not only municipal agencies. ... [W]e believe a provision should be included in our proposed statute, stating that whenever there is a conflict between any agreement reached by a public employer and an employee organization on matters appropriate to collective bargaining, which is approved in accordance with the provisions of the proposed statute, the terms of such agreement shall prevail over any conflicting statute, charter provision, ordinance, resolution, or regulations adopted by a public employer or its authorized agents.
>
> We also believe that such a provision will minimize the necessity of going to court to resolve negotiability issues involving conflicts with other laws, and that it will, at the same time, enhance the authority of the [Public Employees Relations] Board to deal with impasses over the scope of bargaining. Finally, by leaving the initiative to the parties themselves and exercising the scope of bargaining into areas presently covered by other laws, we believe that active publics will be able to exercise a greater

---

* Editors' Note: While the Nevada Act does not have a specific provision with respect to civil service, NEV. REV. STAT. § 288.150(3) provides that "[t]hose subject matters which are not within the scope of mandatory bargaining and which are reserved to the local government employer without negotiation include: (a) The right to hire, direct, assign or transfer an employee, but excluding the right to assign or transfer an employee as a form of discipline. ..." What effect would a provision such as this have on resolving whether the terms of a collective bargaining agreement superseded inconsistent civil service rules and regulations?

influence than before in shaping the future of bilateral relationships in the public sector.

ASSEMBLY ADVISORY COUNCIL ON PUBLIC EMPLOYEE RELATIONS, FINAL REPORT 175-76 (Cal. 1973).

## CIVIL SERVICE COMMISSION v. WAYNE COUNTY BOARD OF SUPERVISORS

Michigan Supreme Court
384 Mich. 363, 184 N.W.2d 201 (1971)

PER CURIAM: — Two admittedly conflicting statutes compete in litigious depth for jurisdiction over the process of collective bargaining by Wayne county employees with their employer (or employers). As two courts already have come to know in painful and dissentient succession (see Wayne County Civil Service Comm. v. Wayne County Bd. of Supervisors, 22 Mich. App. 287), the competition presents that most difficult of all appellate problems; the ascertainment of legislative intent when there is no evidentiary or other reasonably authoritative guide to pertinent meaning or purpose of the legislators. For such difficulty Cardozo has provided our first and most dependable range light (The Nature of the Judicial Process, pp. 14, 15, published 1921):

> "Interpretation is often spoken of as if it were nothing but the search and the discovery of a meaning which, however obscure and latent, had nonetheless a real and ascertainable pre-existence in the legislator's mind. The process is, indeed, that at times, but it is often something more. The ascertainment of intention may be the least of a judge's troubles in ascribing meaning to a statute. 'The fact is,' says Gray in his lectures on the 'Nature and Sources of the Law,' 'that the difficulties of so-called interpretation arise when the legislature has had no meaning at all; when the question which is raised on the statute never occurred to it; when what the judges have to do is, not to determine what the legislature did mean on a point which was present to its mind, *but to guess what it would have intended on a point not present to its mind, if the point had been present."* (emphasis presently supplied).

The first of these competing statutes (1941 PA 370; MCLA 38.401 et seq; 1948 CL 38.401 et seq; MSA 5.119[1]), stated and now states expressly its purpose. Section 1 thereof reads, in full:

> "Section 1. Civil service act; purpose. The purpose of this act is to guarantee to all citizens a fair and equal opportunity for public service; to establish conditions of service which will attract officers and employees of character and capacity, and to increase the efficiency of the county governmental departments, commissions, boards and agencies, by the improvement of methods of personnel administration."

The second of these statutes (1965 PA 379; MCLA 423.201 et seq; MSA 17.455[1]), correspondingly stated and now states the legislative purpose; this time by a redesigned title of that which previously was known as the Hutchinson Act of 1947 (No. 336). The new title:

"An act to prohibit strikes by certain public employees; to provide review from disciplinary action with respect thereto; to provide for the mediation of grievances and the holding of elections; to declare and protect the rights and privileges of public employees; and to prescribe means of enforcement and penalties for the violation of the provisions of this act."

(We insert here a significant farce. It is that there is no hint in this new title or, for that matter, in any of the sections of the act of 1965, of legislative thought that the prohibition of strikes by public employees, effected by legislatively authorized collective bargaining and administratively enforced mediation, might conflict in whole or in part with the authority vested, by the act of 1941, in an established county civil service commission. Thus the issue of 1965 legislative intent, vis-a-vis the act of 1941, was deposited in Wayne county as a first class vexer.)

A majority of 3 judges of the circuit court concluded that "the employer of all county employees is the county of Wayne and that the board of supervisors is the legally constituted body authorized to act for and on behalf of the county as the public employer."

. . . .

On application for rehearing the majority stood by its first ruling after having noted that, as against the "complex and apparently contradictory statutes that have been adopted," it would be better to hurry on its way the inevitable appeal "in the public interest." The opinion on rehearing concluded, appropriately by this bullet pass of the male deer:

> "The slightest modification at this time would unduly prolong and delay conclusive and complete decision by the High Court. This would hopefully put to rest once and forever the turbulence so clearly existent within the county and between county agencies. Should such a decision fail in this respect, it is for the legislature to act promptly and with dispatch."

On appeal a majority of the assigned panel of the Court of Appeals ruled that plaintiff Wayne County Civil Service Commission is possessed of statutory power to classify positions in the county employment service and to submit uniform pay plans for the standardization of salaries; but does not have exclusive control over such classification and standardization, since all such must be approved by the county board of supervisors. To its reasoning the panel, having finally made a judgment, added this declaration of heartfelt relief (p. 299):

> "While this is not the simplest solution to the difficult problem with which we are faced, and though it may even tend to confuse and complicate the area of collective bargaining within Wayne county, it is the only plausible solution under the confines of the present statutory law."

This Court granted leave (383 Mich. 782) to settle if possible what was regularly termed below a "chaos of legislation."

The plaintiff Civil Service Commission contends that act 370 has made it the exclusive bargaining agent for all employees of the county of Wayne, subject only "to concurrence of the board of supervisors on salaries and wages," and that it is entitled to a judicial declaration that "collective bargaining shall be conducted by the Civil Service Commission for all County employees and in accordance with the requirements of act 370."

The defendant County Board of Supervisors, searching the involved statutes in somewhat greater depth, contends that:

> "3. Act 379, to the extent that it places rates of pay, hours of work and other conditions of employment of public employees, including employees of Wayne county, into the area of collective bargaining supersedes *pro tanto* those provisions or parts of Act 370 dealing with the same subject matters."

. . . .

Having arrayed these contentions for scrutiny, our ensuing views doubtless will be understood better by an outset declaration of specific decision. We disagree with the stated position of the plaintiff Civil Service Commission. We agree with what in our view is the generally dispositive contention of the defendant Wayne County Board of Supervisors.

*First:* To read the act of 1941, carefully in conjunction with the act of 1965, is to understand the judicial difficulty. The earlier act was conceived and enacted immediately after the people had adopted the civil service amendment of 1940, effective January 1, 1941 for State employment (Const. 1908, art. 6, § 22). Designed as that act was for adoption by counties having a *population of 300,000 or more,* the measure strove in applicable terms to provide the same rights for employees of such counties, and the same betterment of public service in such counties, as the people had just approved hopefully with respect to the State service. In neither instance could collective bargaining by public employees have been in the minds of the people, or of the legislators. The thought of strikes by public employees was unheard of. The right of collective bargaining, applicable at the time to private employment, was then in comparative infancy and portended no suggestion that it ever might enter the realm of *public* employment.

However, the act of 1941 brought within its purposefully inclusive as well as exclusive purview "all positions not specifically included by this act in the unclassified service." (§ 10[b]). Then by section 27, headed "Scope," it provided that *all* of its declared aims should apply to the employees of *all* boards, commissions and departments of each statute-adopting county. So, upon adoption of the act by Wayne county, there came into being a Wayne county civil service commission, the authority of which in important if not exclusive part extended to control of the relation of public employer and public employee within the county.

The view taken here of these separate statutes is that they cannot be harmonized, as in *pari materia* or otherwise. The attempts and counter-attempts made below do not prove that premise. In the course of our review of the act of 1965, the conviction grows that it did not occur to the legislators that the manifestly well thought out provisions of the act would both encroach upon and impair, to some extent, the previously assigned authority and duty of a civil service commission operating under the act of 1941, and that serious trouble might arise on account of that fact.

The drafting and enacting legislature of 1965, as with this equally mortal Court on occasion when it endorses an opinion of public moment, did not foresee what since has come to pass. It did not include that needed exclusory clause or proviso, as Judge Fitzgerald noted (22 Mich. App. 287, 294), and therefore left no specific evidence of intent either way. In the words of Cardozo, we are left to *guess* what the 1965 legislature would have done had the point come to its attention, and our *guess* is that it would have advised all established county civil service commissions as we now do by today's judgment.

This is not to say that the act of 1965 repeals outright the act of 1941. Respecting as always our long since declared and regularly maintained rule that repeals by implication are not favored, and that it is only when the two measures in view are so incompatible that both or all cannot fully stand, we can only find that this is a striking instance for application of that rule which, back in 1877, was written into the Court's opinion of Breitung v. Lindauer, 37 Mich. 217, 233 (1887): "The rule is that the latter act operates *to the extent of the repugnancy,* as a repeal of the first, or, if the two acts are not in express terms repugnant, yet if the latter *covers the whole subject of the first,* and contains new provisions showing that it was intended as a substitute, it will operate as a repeal."

Note the emphasis supplied by the writer of Breitung; Justice Marston for himself and Justices Cooley, Campbell and Graves. We stress it anew and hold that the act of 1965 operates, *"to the extent of the repugnancy,"* as a partial repeal of the act of 1941; but no more than that. In short shrift this means that the purposed thrust of the act of 1965, that of prohibiting strikes by public employees and providing collective bargaining, negotiation and enforced mediation of labor disputes arising out of public employment coming within the scope of the act, must be implemented and administered exclusively as provided therein. Hence, the original authority and duty of the plaintiff civil service commission was diminished *pro tanto* by the act of 1965, to the extent of free administration of the latter according to its tenor. . . .

To summarize and restrict:

1. Our instant rulings are limited to

(a) Determination that the plaintiff Civil Service Commission has no lawful part in the administration, directly or indirectly, of the act of 1965. . . .

## NOTES

1. Subsequent to the principal case, the Michigan Supreme Court affirmed the general terms of its holding in Sloan v. Warren Civil Service Comm'n, 386 Mich. 437, 192 N.W.2d 499 (1971). At least one major arbitration award in Michigan has also upheld the precedence of the collective bargaining agreement. In AFSCME Local 1390 and City of Lansing, GERR No. 411, B-2 (1971), Arbitrator Alan Walt sustained the grievances of three employees who contended that pay increases were withheld in violation of the collective bargaining agreement. The arbitrator held that the city's past practice of granting or withholding pay raises according to merit was superseded by the contract which called for automatic wage progressions based on seniority. The city's personnel rules, embodying the merit increase concept, were held not to have been negotiated or incorporated by reference in agreement.

The rule in the principal case, however, does not apply to employees in the state classified civil service. The 1963 Michigan Constitution states that "[t]he legislature may enact laws providing for the resolution of disputes concerning public employees, except in the state classified civil service." Mich. Const. art. 4, § 48. The Constitution grants to the State Civil Service Commission the power to "regulate all conditions of employment in the classified service." Mich. Const. art. 11, § 5. In Welfare Employees Union v. Michigan Civil Service Comm'n, 28 Mich. App. 343, 184 N.W.2d 247 (1970), the Michigan Court of Appeals held that these Constitutional provisions exempted the petitioning employees from the coverage of the Public Employment Relations Act and that the Civil Service Commission was not required to bargain about the effect on working conditions of a reorganization plan in the State Department of Social Services. The union, the court held, would have to pursue its grievances according to rules established by the Civil Service Commission. Subsequently, the Michigan Civil Service Commission adopted an Employee Relations Policy which provides for the "designation of exclusive representatives for the purpose of negotiating on a meet and confer basis." For the full text of the Employee Relations Policy, *see* 732 GERR 39 (10-31-77).

2. In AFSCME v. County of Lancaster, 200 Neb. 301, 263 N.W.2d 471 (1978), the court had to determine what effect, if any, a civil service act passed *after* the public sector collective bargaining law had on the scope of bargaining under the bargaining law. The court held that with respect to such things as hours of work, vacations, wages, transfers, and layoff and recall, "[t]here is nothing in the civil service act which prohibited the county board from bargaining with its employees in regard to these topics." The court noted that there were other matters on which the union presented proposals

. . . which were controlled by the civil service act to some extent, such as promotions, discipline, grievance procedure, nondiscrimination, and termination. To the extent that the civil service act contains specific and mandatory provisions relating to such matters, the county board is not free to bargain. As an example, the act provides all appointments and promotions shall be based on merit and fitness. The county board has no power or authority to bargain or agree that any appointment or promotion shall be based upon anything other than merit and fitness except as provided in the act.

## STATE EMPLOYEES' ASSOCIATION OF NEW HAMPSHIRE v. PELRB

New Hampshire Supreme Court
100 L.R.R.M. 2484 (1978)

PER CURIAM: — This is an appeal under RSA 273-A:14 from a declaratory judgment of the Public Employee Labor Relations Board (PELRB) rendered pursuant to RSA 541-A:8 and Rule 8.1 of the Rules and Regulations of the PELRB upon a joint petition filed by the State Negotiating Committee (SNC) and the State Employees' Association (SEA). The PELRB found that certain collective bargaining contract proposals presented by the SEA to the SNC during the 1976-77 negotiations were not bargainable subjects under New Hampshire's collective bargaining statute, RSA ch. 273-A.

Laws 1975, ch. 490, now RSA ch. 273-A, established a State policy of "foster(ing) harmonious and cooperative relations between public employers and their employees and (of protecting) the public by encouraging the orderly and uninterrupted operation of government." Laws 1975, 490:1. To this end RSA 273-A:9 states: "Cost items and terms and conditions of employment affecting State employees generally *shall* be negotiated by the State . . ." (Emphasis added.) This section, along with RSA 273-A:3, which requires that the State negotiate in "good faith," delineates the scope of the State's obligation and authority to bargain. That obligation, as well as that authority, is limited by only two exceptions, the "managerial policy" exception included within the definitions of the phrase "terms and conditions of employment," RSA 273-A:1 XI, and the "merit system" exception contained in RSA 273-A:3 III. These limitations follow in full:

(RSA 273-A:1) XI 'Terms and conditions of employment' means wages, hours and other conditions of employment other than *managerial policy* within the exclusive prerogatives of the public employer, or confided exclusively to the public employer by statute or regulations adopted pursuant to statute. The phrase 'managerial policy within the exclusive prerogative of the public employer' shall be construed to include but shall not be limited to the function, programs and methods of the public employer, including, the use of technology, the public employer's organizational structure, and the selection, direction and number of its personnel, so as to continue public control of governmental functions. (Emphasis added.)

(RSA 273-A:3) III. Matters regarding the policies and practice of any *merit system* established by statute, charter or ordinance relating to recruitment, examination, appointment and advancement under conditions of political neutrality and based upon principles of merit and competence shall not be subjects of bargaining under the provisions of this chapter. Nothing herein shall be construed to diminish the authority of the state personnel commission or any board or agency established by statute, charter or ordinance to conduct and grade merit examinations from which appointments or promotions may be made. (Emphasis added.)

The present action was commenced by a joint petition filed with the PELRB by the SNC, a committee constituted under RSA 273-A:9 to engage in labor negotiations on behalf of the State as employer, and the SEA, then the sole representative of State employees in labor negotiations. The two petitioners sought a definitive ruling with respect to the State's obligation to bargain certain proposals presented by the SEA. Those proposals deal with the following: (1) employee classification; (2) contracting out of bargaining unit work; (3) employee promotion, transfer and layoff, and seniority rights; (4) employee training and education; (5) employee discipline and involuntary separation; and (6) wage and salary administration.

A hearing was held before the PELRB on February 4, 1977, and on February 24, 1977, the PELRB ruled that many of the contract proposals were nonnegotiable because they were either "managerial policy within the exclusive prerogative of the public employer," or already covered by the rules published by the personnel commission pursuant to RSA ch. 98. The SEA requested and received a rehearing, following which the original ruling was reaffirmed. The matter is now before this court to determine whether the PELRB erred in its interpretation of RSA ch. 273-A.

In 1950, the legislature enacted Laws 1950, ch. 9 (RSA 98), which established for the first time in New Hampshire a State "merit system" for public employment, and created a department of personnel and a personnel commission with duties including the "recruitment, appointment, compensation, promotion, transfer, layoff, removal, and discipline of state employees." RSA 98:3. That statute requires the commission to "(m)ake such rules and regulations . . . as it shall deem necessary or proper to carry out its purposes." RSA 98:8 III. Subject to the approval of the commission and the Governor and Council, the director can "prescribe . . . rules for the classification, compensation, recruitment, selection, appointment, promotion, demotion, transfer, discipline, removal and lay-off of employees, . . . (and) for attendance, holidays, leaves of absence, merit rating and the hearing of appeals from employees." RSA 98:13 X. The 1975 statute (RSA ch. 273-A), however, includes no direct reference to chapter 98.

In the interim from 1950 to the present, the personnel commission promulgated a multitude of rules and regulations under chapter 98 pertaining to nearly every facet of public employment. The dilemma which faced the PELRB, and indeed which now faces this court, is how to read the two statutes together.

The PELRB resolved the problem in the following fashion:

> The Personnel Commission Law and the rules which are promulgated under it, comprise the "Merit System" for hiring, pay, classification and promotion in New Hampshire, as is reflected in RSA 98:18 and other provisions of the statute designed to separate classified state services from politics.
>
> . . .
>
> The Board cannot find that the Legislature intended to repeal, alter or make bargainable any of the provisions of RSA 98 or the rules published by the Personnel Commission. Specific reference is made in RSA 273-A to the merit system which was law at the time and known to the Legislature when RSA 273-A was passed. *The parties are prohibited by law from bargaining over items specifically covered by that system.* (Emphasis added.)

The PELRB ruling went on to define the managerial policy exception as follows: "The Legislature did not wish to allow governmental direction to be bargained away; which means among other things *what* the government is to do, *how* it is to do it, and *who* is to perform it (following the personnel commission rules). Such matters are not bargainable." (Emphasis in original.)

Turning to the specific contract proposals, the PELRB ruled that proposals relating to subcontracting out of work are nonnegotiable, that certain proposals relating to employee training and education are negotiable, but that proposals concerning leaves of absence, time off and State-established training programs are not negotiable. It also ruled that proposals concerning employee discipline and removal, classification, promotion, transfer, layoff, seniority, and wage and salary administration, other than "wages themselves," are not negotiable.

The SEA contends that the PELRB's broad interpretations of the managerial policy and merit system exceptions effects an unduly restrictive interpretation upon the intended scope of collective bargaining under RSA ch. 273-A. We agree with this contention only in a qualified sense. The PELRB is "vested . . . with primary authority to define the terms of (RSA ch. 273-A)." State Employees' Ass'n v. Bd. of Trustees, 118 N. H. —, —, 388 A.2d 203, 204, 99 LRRM 2437 (1978); N. H. Dept. of Revenue Admin. v. Public Employee Labor Relations Board, 117 N. H. —, 380 A.2d 1085, 97 LRRM 2095 (1977). Overall statutory interpretation, on the other hand, is ultimately a matter of law within the province of this court. See Kalloch v. Bd. of Trustees, 116 N. H. 443, 362 A.2d 201 (1976); Kinchla v. Baumner, 114 N. H. 818, 330 A.2d 112 (1974).

We cannot agree with the PELRB that in enacting RSA ch. 273-A:3 III, the legislature intended to exempt from the State's bargaining obligation all matters covered by personnel commission rules. Even the SNC admits that certain commission rules deal with aspects of public employment that are indisputably proper subjects of bargaining and are in fact currently bargained with the consent of both the SNC and the SEA. These subjects include overtime, legal holidays, annual and sick leave, maternity leave, and other such matters. The merit system exception excludes only "matters regarding the policies and practice of any merit system;" it does not exclude everything that the personnel commission has passed upon. Nor does the other exception, the managerial policy exception embodied in RSA 273-A:1 XI, require such broad deference to the personnel rules; that exception excludes from negotiation "managerial policy within the exclusive prerogative of the public employer, or confided exclusively to the public employer by statute or regulations adopted pursuant to statutes." Id. The mere existence of a commission rule does not *ipso facto* bring the subject of that rule within this provision. Only that part of the subject which deals with managerial policy within the sole prerogative of the employer, or managerial policy which by statute or regulation is confided to the sole prerogative of the employer is excluded from negotiation.

RSA ch. 273-A and RSA ch. 98 must be read together as a cohesive whole. State v. Woodman, 114 N. H. 497, 323 A.2d 921 (1974). When this is done it appears clear that the personnel commission's role has been modified, at least to some extent. The PELRB was correct in our view, however, in not extending the provisions of RSA ch. 273-A beyond that which clearly was intended. At stake in public collective bargaining is the continued operation of State government. Therefore, we hold that the PELRB properly gave a broad definition of "managerial policy within the exclusive prerogative of the public employer." RSA 273-A:1 XI. For that reason we do not adopt an "impact test;" fairness in collective bargaining in the public sector is adequately assured by the provisions of RSA ch. 273-A as we have interpreted them. Whatever the desirability of that test in the private sector, we consider it a matter more appropriately left to the legislature in dealing with employment relations of government.

In sum, we hold that the PELRB erred to the extent that it ruled that none "of the provisions of RSA 98 or the rules published by the Personnel

Commission" are bargainable. Notwithstanding that error, we hold that the PELRB was correct in giving broad meaning to the term "managerial policy." We hold that the board's rulings on the specific proposals before it are supported under the principles of this decision. The PELRB should in the future decide as a matter of fact which contract proposals are proper subjects of negotiation. In doing so, however, we caution that body not to construe the merit system exception quite so broadly.

*Appeal dismissed.*

## NOTE

In Laborers' International Union, Local 1029 v. State of Delaware, 310 A.2d 664 (Del. Ch. Ct. 1973), *aff'd per curiam,* 314 A.2d 919 (Del. S. Ct. 1974), the court resolved a conflict between the scope of bargaining and the state merit system in favor of the state merit system. The court noted that "where there is uncertainty as to areas where the General Assembly has indicated a clear intention to deny collective bargaining, any doubt should be resolved in favor of the merit system." The court noted that its "decision should not be taken to indicate a negative attitude . . . towards the rights of public employees," but rather should be viewed as "an attempt to reconcile conflicts inherent in a public employment program which contemplates both merit system protection as well as collective bargaining for state employees."

## LOS ANGELES COUNTY CIVIL SERVICE COMMISSION v. SUPERIOR COURT

California Supreme Court
588 P.2d 249, 100 L.R.R.M. 2854 (1978)

NEWMAN, JUSTICE: — In this case we must reconcile two sections of the Meyers-Milias-Brown Act (MMBA). Section 3500 declares that the MMBA shall not supersede local charters, ordinances, and rules that establish civil service systems or other methods of administering employer-employee relations.[2] Section 3505 requires governing bodies of local agencies or their properly designated representatives to meet and confer as to conditions of employment with representatives of employee organizations.

Since we conclude that the Legislature did not intend to exempt counties with civil service systems from the meet-and-confer requirement, we also consider the

---

[2] Section 3500 provides:

"It is the purpose of this chapter to promote full communication between public employers and their employees by providing a reasonable method of resolving disputes regarding wages, hours, and other terms and conditions of employment between public employers and public employee organizations. It is also the purpose of this chapter to promote the improvement of personnel management and employer-employee relations within the various public agencies in the State of California by providing a uniform basis for recognizing the right of public employees to join organizations of their own choice and be represented by such organizations in their employment relationships with public agencies. Nothing contained herein shall be deemed to supersede the provisions of existing state law and the charters, ordinances, and rules of local public agencies which establish and regulate a merit or civil service system or which provide for other methods of administering employer-employee relations nor is it intended that this chapter be binding upon those public agencies which provide procedures for the administration of employer-employee relations in accordance with the provisions of this chapter. This chapter is intended, instead, to strengthen merit, civil service and other methods of administering employer-employee relations through the establishment of uniform and orderly methods of communication between employees and the public agencies by which they are employed."

constitutionality of requiring chartered counties and cities to comply with the MMBA. We rule that the meet-and-confer requirement is not inconsistent with a charter provision that requires a civil service commission to hold public hearings before amending its rules. Therefore requiring Los Angeles County to meet and confer with employee unions before amending its civil service rules does not, we hold, offend the home-rule provisions of the California Constitution.

Article IX of the Los Angeles County Charter provides for the civil service. The civil service commission, created by section 30 of the charter, shall "prescribe, amend and enforce rules for the classified service, which shall have the force and effect of law. . . ." (Charter § 34.) Those rules are to provide: "For layoffs or for mandatory reductions in lieu of layoff . . . for reasons of economy or lack of work" (§ 34(18)); "For transfer from one position to a similar position in the same class and grade and for reinstatement within one year of persons who without fault or delinquency on their part are separated from the service or reduced" (§ 34(10)); "For the discharge or reduction in rank or compensation after appointment or promotion is complete . . ." (§ 34(13)); and "For the adoption and amendment of rules only after public notice and hearing" (§ 34(16)).

In February and March 1976 the commission held hearings concerning amendments to its rules governing layoffs and grade reductions in lieu of layoff. It sent notice of the hearings to several employee unions, but union representatives attended under protest. They claimed that section 3505 of the MMBA required the commission to meet and confer before amending the rules, which the commission refused to do.

Without waiving the asserted right to meet and confer the union representatives expressed their views at the hearings. They supported layoffs based on straight seniority. County management preferred reducing in grade higher ranked employees to displace lower-ranked (though possibly more senior) employees. Displaced employees would be laid off. After the hearings the commission adopted amendments supporting management's position.

In April 1976 the unions petitioned the superior court for a writ of mandate to compel the commission to set aside the amended rules and to meet and confer before adopting any rules regarding layoffs or reductions in lieu of layoff. The court issued the writ. In this proceeding we consider the propriety of the lower court's action.

The commission maintains that, because of the nonpreemption language in section 3500, it should not be required to comply with provisions of the MMBA that interfere with its administration of employer-employee relations. Further it asserts that, under article XI, sections 3 and 4 of the California Constitution, the Legislature does not have authority to require bargaining over matters governed by the county charter that, except for the charter, would be within the scope of representation under the MNBA.[6]

---

[6] Article XI, section 3(a) provides: "For its own government, a county or city may adopt a charter by majority vote of its electors voting on the question. . . . County charters adopted pursuant to this section shall supersede any existing charter and all laws inconsistent therewith. The provisions of a charter are the law of the State and have the force and effect of legislative enactments."

Section 4(g) provides: "Whenever any county has framed and adopted a charter, and the same shall have been approved by the Legislature as herein provided, the general laws adopted by the Legislature in pursuance of Section 1 (b) of this article, shall, as to such county, be superseded by said charter as to matters for which, under this section it is competent to make provision in such charter, and for which provision is made therein, except as herein otherwise expressly provided."

### The meaning of "meet and confer"

At the outset we note that a meet-and-confer session amounts to much more than the public hearing authorized by the Los Angeles County Charter. Section 3505 of the MMBA requires governing bodies or their representatives to "meet and confer [with employee representatives] in good faith regarding wages, hours, and other terms and conditions of employment" and to "consider fully" such employee presentations. Section 3505.1 provides that, if the representatives successfully reach an agreement, they shall jointly prepare a nonbinding memorandum of understanding.

The meet-and-confer requirement means that "a public agency, or such representatives as it may designate, and representatives of recognized employee organizations, shall have the mutual obligation personally to meet and confer promptly upon request by either party and continue for a reasonable period of time in order to exchange freely information, opinions, and proposals, and to endeavor to reach agreement on matters within the scope of representation prior to the adoption by the public agency of its final budget for the ensuing year" (§ 3505). Thus a public agency must meet with employee representatives (1) promptly on request; (2) personally; (3) for a reasonable period of time; (4) to exchange information freely; and (5) to try to agree on matters within the scope of representation. Though the process is not binding, it requires that the parties seriously "attempt to resolve differences and reach a common ground." (Placentia Fire Fighters v. City of Placentia (1976) 57 Cal.App.3d 9, 25, 92 LRRM 3373.) The public agency must fully consider union presentations; it is not at liberty to grant only a perfunctory review of written suggestions submitted by a union.

In contrast the character of a public hearing may vary according to "the subject of the hearing, the nature of the board or person holding the hearing and nature of the board or person to be heard." (Silver Burdett Co. v. State Board of Education (1940) 36 Cal.App.2d 714, 718.) It may be only "the opportunity to present statements, arguments, or contentions in writing, with or without opportunity to present the same orally." (§ 11425; see also Davis, Administrative Law (6th ed. 1977) pp. 241-247, 272.) As Justice Kaus pointed out in the Court of Appeal opinion vacated by our hearing this case, "a public hearing by a legislative body is often nothing but an order to show cause why tentatively predetermined action should not be taken."

### Are counties with civil service systems exempt from the MMBA's meet-and-confer requirement?

According to its section 3500 the MMBA has two purposes: (1) to promote full communication between public employers and employees; (2) to improve personnel management and employer-employee relations within the various public agencies. Those purposes are to be achieved by establishing methods for resolving disputes over employment conditions and for recognizing the right of public employees to organize and be represented by employee organizations. Section 3500 states, however: "Nothing contained herein shall be deemed to supersede the provisions of existing state law and the charters, ordinances, and rules of local public agencies which establish and regulate a merit or civil service system or which provide for other methods of administering employer-employee relations ...." Those words, the commission asserts, exempt it from the meet-and-confer requirement.[8]

The meaning of those words was discussed in Huntington Beach Police Officers' Assn. v. City of Huntington Beach (1976) 58 Cal.App.3d 492, 500-503, 92 LRRM 2996, and in Los Angeles County Firefighters Local 1014 v. City of Monrovia (1972) 24 Cal.App.3d 289, 294-295, 80 LRRM 2648. Those cases recognize that section 3500 reserves to local agencies the right to pass ordinances and promulgate regulations consistent with the purposes of the MMBA. To extend a broader insulation from MMBA's requirements would allow local rules to undercut the minimum rights that the MMBA guarantees. (See Grodin, Public Employee Bargaining in California: The Meyers-Milias-Brown Act in the Courts (1972) 23 Hastings L.J. 719, 724.)

The commission suggests that civil service rules carve out a particular area in employee-employer relations that should remain untouched by the meet-and-confer requirement. It maintains that, since Huntington and Monrovia, supra, dealt with general regulations and not civil service rules, they are distinguishable. The danger of undermining employee rights, though, is equally apparent if civil service commissions may freely and without negotiation alter the content of their rules.

The MMBA's stated purpose to guarantee full communication between employers and employees can hardly be met if the commission is not required directly to address employee concerns — concerns that frequently, of course, will be consistent with merit system principles. To carve out for the commission a unilateral authority over civil service rules would place an unjustifiable burden on public employees' right to representation. On the other hand, guaranteeing public employees an opportunity to have their views seriously considered (with the possibility that a nonbinding agreement will be adopted) serves employees' interests without destroying the commission's merit objectives.

Section 3505 extends to all matters "regarding wages, hours, and other terms and conditions of employment." Rules delineating how layoffs will be made clearly fall within the "conditions of employment" phrase of the section. Though section 3504 would permit the commission to consider "the merits, necessity, or organization of any service or activity" without meeting with employee representatives, that exception does not exempt the present rules from the meet-and-confer requirement. As we noted in Fire Fighters Union v. City of Vallejo (1974) 12 Cal.3d 608, 621-622, 87 LRRM 2453, cases under the National Labor Relations Act — persuasive precedents in interpreting the MMBA — indicate that, though an employer has the right unilaterally to decide that a layoff is necessary, he must bargain about such matters as the timing of the layoffs and the number and identity of employees affected. (NLRB v. United Nuclear Corp. (10th Cir. 1967) 381 F.2d 972, 66 LRRM 2101.)

The commission also asserts that it is not a public agency within the meaning of section 3501(c) and that it is therefore exempt from the section 3505

---

[8] After the sentence relied on by the commission, the following sentence appears in section 3500: "This chapter is intended, instead, to strengthen merit, civil service and other methods of administering employer-employee relations through the establishment of uniform and orderly methods of communication between employees and the public agencies by which they are employed." The commission does not adequately explain how this sentence would be interpreted if we were to adopt the view that section 3500 exempts counties with civil service systems from the meet-and-confer requirement. On its face the sentence expresses a legislative view that civil service systems will be strengthened through addition of the communication methods established by the MMBA.

meet-and-confer requirement. Section 3501(c) defines public agencies to include all governmental subdivisions, city or county, whether chartered or not "[e]xcept as otherwise provided." Section 3505 imposes the duty to meet and confer on the governing bodies of all public agencies and on such commissions or "other representatives as may be properly designated by law." Because we have ruled above that the nonpreemption language in section 3500 does not exempt counties with civil service systems from the MMBA's requirements, section 3501(c)'s "[e]xcept as otherwise provided" clause does not apply. The commission fits within section 3505 as a representative designated by the county charter to administer rules for the classified service.

The commission contends that, under the charter, the board of supervisors rather than the commission administers salaries and benefits and that the commission therefore is left with little to bargain with in the meet-and-confer process. (See charter § 11(1).) We believe that Los Angeles County's decision to divide decision-making authority in labor matters does not affect bargaining over the content of layoff rules. As Justice Kaus' opinion noted, the commission's poor bargaining position may be reason for reallocating governmental functions but does not excuse noncompliance with section 3505.

Finally the commission argues that a failure to adopt rules tentatively agreed on in the meet-and-confer session would subject it to charges of bad faith. Nothing in the MMBA precludes the commission from altering its rules after the charter-mandated hearing to accommodate more persuasive or previously unexpressed views.[10] A bad faith attack must be supported by specific facts, not simply conclusory statements. (Cf. Placentia Fire Fighters v. City of Placentia, supra, 57 Cal.App.3d at pp. 25-27.)

### Constitutionality of the meet-and-confer requirement in chartered counties

We have concluded that the MMBA requires the commission to meet and confer regarding its layoff rules. The commission argues that such a requirement violates the home-rule provisions for charter counties contained in article XI, section 3(a) of the California Constitution, which provides in part: "County charters adopted pursuant to this section shall supersede any existing charter and all laws inconsistent therewith." Further, section 4(g) states: "Whenever any county has framed and adopted a charter . . . the general laws adopted by the Legislature in pursuance of Section 1(b) of this article, shall, as to such county, be superseded by said charter as to matters for which, under this section it is competent to make provision in such charter . . . ." Section 1(b) authorizes the governing body of each county to provide for the number, compensation, tenure, and appointment of employees.

When applicable, those provisions nullify state laws inconsistent with county charters. The commission asserts (1) that to require it to bargain with employee unions irreconcilably conflicts with the charter requirement that it hold a public hearing before amending its rules, and (2) that its unique status as an independent administrator of the merit system would be seriously threatened by requiring it to bargain.

We conclude that the meet-and-confer requirement can coexist with the

---

[10] This case illustrates the kind of views that could be expressed at the hearing by employees not speaking for a union. As we have noted, a group of such employees convinced the commission to add a provision permitting employees whose pay would be greatly decreased by a proposed grade reduction to elect to be laid off instead.

charter-mandated hearing.[12] We see no reason why the commission's integrity as a neutral administrator of the merit system would be jeopardized by its participating in bargaining sessions with union and management representatives.

The fact that the commission must give notice of what it proposes to do and afford interested parties a chance to be heard does not mean that it must approach the hearing without even a tentative view of what it will do after everyone there has had her or his say. The complexity of matters before rulemaking bodies often does not permit their acting only on input received at a hearing. (California Optometric Assn. v. Lackner (1976) 60 Cal.App.3d 500, 508.) We can see no inherent conflict between tentative understandings reached at a meet-and-confer session and an objectively conducted public hearing.

The commission's fear that meet-and-confer sessions will compromise its neutral status appears unfounded. The unions' suggestion that layoffs be based on seniority appears no less objective than management's view that layoffs should be based on employee grade. The commission's commendable concern for impartiality will be served by a fair application of whichever standard ultimately is adopted. The civil service system's goal of eliminating arbitrary decisions surely can coexist with a good-faith bargaining process.

## Conclusion

In sum, we hold that MMBA section 3505 does apply to the layoff rules, that it does govern the commission, and that the meet-and-confer requirement is not satisfied simply by convening the charter-mandated public hearing. The MMBA requires that the commission meet and confer directly with employee representatives.

Further we hold that a meet-and-confer session and a public hearing can coexist and that unions do not relinquish their right to a serious bargaining session merely because they express their views at a hearing. To diminish that right would impair the vitality of the MMBA. We see no constitutional barrier to requiring the county here to meet and confer with employee representatives before amending civil service rules that govern layoff procedures.

The superior court's writ compelling the commission to set aside the amendments and to meet and confer with the unions before adopting rules on layoffs and mandatory reductions in lieu of layoff was properly granted. The commission's petition for our writ is denied.

## STATE OF NEW JERSEY v. STATE SUPERVISORY EMPLOYEES ASSOCIATION

New Jersey Supreme Court
98 L.R.R.M. 3267 (1978)

PASHMAN, JUSTICE: — These cases involve the question of the permissible scope of collective negotiations concerning the terms and conditions of public

---

[12] Because we hold that the requirements for a meet-and-confer session and a public hearing do not conflict, we need not decide here if it would be constitutional for the Legislature to require a chartered city or county to comply with a labor law that conflicts with its charter. We note, however, that Professional Fire Fighters, Inc. v. City of Los Angeles (1963) 60 Cal.2d 276, 53 LRRM 2431, expressly held that labor relations is an area of statewide concern in which the Legislature can pass laws to be applied in chartered cities. While that case was decided before the 1970 revision of article XI of the California Constitution, Huntington Beach Police Officers' Assn. v. City of Huntington Beach, supra, 58 Cal.App.3d 492, 92 LRRM 2996, was decided after the revision. Huntington Beach adopts the reasoning of Professional Fire Fighters, Inc.

employment in this State. At issue is the correctness of the decisions of the Public Employment Relations Commission (PERC) in two scope-of-negotiations determinations rendered pursuant to the New Jersey Employer-Employee Relations Act, L. 1968, c. 303, as amended by L. 1974, c. 123, N.J.S.A. 34:13A-1 et seq. (the Act). Because of the public importance of these questions, both appeals were directly certified by this Court and have also been consolidated. The real point of dispute is the question of the extent, if any, to which the 1974 amendment to N.J.S.A. 34:13A-8.1, L. 1974, c. 123, § 6, expanded the scope of collective negotiation. In short, we must determine whether the amendment signaled an intent by the Legislature to permit negotiation and agreement to supplant Civil Service statutes and regulations. N.J.S.A. 11:1-1 et seq.; N.J.A.C. 4:1-1 et seq. We must also determine whether negotiation of any of the proposals made by the employee organizations is precluded by N.J.Const. (1947), Art. VII, § 1, par. 2, as being inimical to the merit and fitness principles which govern the hiring and promotion of public employees pursuant to that constitutional provision.

. . . .

The fundamental dispute before PERC centered around the various interpretations to be given to the amendments to the Act contained in L. 1974, c. 123, particularly N.J.S.A. 34:13A-8.1. In the original Act, L. 1968, c. 303, this section effectively limited the scope of collective negotiations by clearly stating that no provision of the Act could "annul or modify any statute or statutes of this State." In Dunellen Bd. of Ed. v. Dunellen Ed. Ass'n, 64 N.J. 17, 31, 85 LRRM 2131 (1973), we held that the Legislature's use of this strong qualifying language "clearly precluded any expansive approach" to the negotiability of the terms and conditions of public employment. The 1974 amendment to that section, L. 1974, c. 123, § 6, changed the wording of N.J.S.A. 34:13A-8.1 to its present form, "nor shall any provision hereof annul or modify any pension statute or statutes of this State."

. . . .

There are three schools of thought concerning the significance of the addition of the word pension to N.J.S.A. 34:13A-8.1. Each proposed interpretation will be discussed in detail.

## A

PERC's view, and that of the State Supervisory Employees Association, is that while proposals concerning terms and conditions of employment are mandatorily negotiable, the parties may agree only to contractual terms which are within the minima and maxima set by specific statutes. PERC refuses to sanction negotiation of subjects on which the parties' agreement might contravene a specific statute, noting that "[t]he courts have held that when the literal reading of a statute such as the amendment to N.J.S.A. 34:13A-8.1 leads to an absurd result, . . . a reasonable construction consistent with its underlying purposes is presumed." Local 195, supra, 3 NJPER at 121. PERC concluded that such a construction would impliedly repeal a number of statutes which set maxima and minima or absolutes concerning terms and conditions of public employment. PERC is not willing to permit public employers to agree to any terms which would contravene a specific statutory imperative. PERC has decided that the scope of negotiations under N.J.S.A. 34:13A-8.1 is not that expansive and that it is effectively limited by the lawful authority of the public employer to determine or recommend employment policy. Moreover, PERC conceives its role to be that of harmonizing the Employer-Employee Relations Act with the Civil Service statutes in such a way that each scheme suffers minimal disruption.

The case of In re Byram Tp. Bd. of Ed., 152 N.J. Super. 12, 96 LRRM 3059 (App. Div. 1977), . . . provides a useful example of how this approach works in practice. One matter determined to be mandatorily negotiable was a proposal by the employee organization therein that special area teachers have no more than three hours of contact with pupils per day. The court agreed with PERC's conclusion that this proposal dealt with teacher work loads, which is a term and condition of employment. 152 N.J.Super. at 26. However, the court hastened to add that ". . . with respect to area teachers, the proposal is not to be construed as reducing the total daily employment time of such teachers below four clock hours, the minimum required by N.J.A.C. 6:3-1.13 for full employment of teachers." Id.[3] Thus, if the contract called for a daily schedule of three clock hours of student-teacher interaction, at least one clock hour more of education related duties would be required if these area teachers desired to be recognized as and reimbursed as full time teachers.

The advantage to this approach is that where terms and conditions of public employment are set by specific statutes, the somewhat odd spectacle of some state employee groups having different rules governing their employment from other similar groups would be avoided. Presumably, if the Legislature intended varied terms and conditions of employment for different employee groups to exist, it would not have enacted specific statutes nor permitted the Civil Service Commission to promulgate specific regulations which apply on a statewide basis. Moreover, repeals by implication have always been disfavored in this state. When the Legislature intends to drastically alter a prior law or policy, it must do so by a deliberate expression rather than by implication. Delaware River and Bay Auth. v. Intl. Org., etc., 45 N.J. 138, 148, 59 LRRM 2845 (1965); see Laboda v. Clark Tp., 40 N.J. 424, 435 (1963) citing Henninger v. Bd. of Chosen Freeholders of Bergen Cty., 3 N.J. 68, 71 (1949); Guff v. Hunt, 6 N.J. 600, 606 (1951). An expansive view of negotiability would effectively limit the applicability of these statutes to those instances where public employer and employees did not set any contrary terms and conditions of employment in a collective agreement, or did not cover a particular matter at all therein. PERC rejects this view.

## B

The State contends that L. 1974, c. 123 had no effect whatsoever on the Dunellen trilogy. Much is made of Justice Jacobs' comment in Burlington Cty. Col. Fac. Assoc. v. Bd. of Trustees, 64 N.J. 10, 16, 84 LRRM 2857 (1973) that educational policy matters would not be negotiable unless the Legislature expressed such a desire in "clear and distinct phraseology." The State contends that the 1974 amendments did not define terms and conditions of employment and did not specify that an enlarged sphere of negotiations was contemplated. The lack of anything even approaching "clear and distinct phraseology" is also cited as evidence that the Legislature agreed with Dunellen on the issue of what is negotiable. The State ascribes little significance to the addition of the word "pension" in N.J.S.A. 34:13A-8.1. That action is interpreted to mean that while

---

[3] N.J.A.C. 6:3-1.13 is bottomed upon N.J.S.A. 18A:29-6 to 29-16, and reads as follows:
Full-time employment of teachers

The period of time in each day required for full-time employment shall be the number of hours prescribed by the local board of education, but shall not be less than four clock hours.

the Legislature could not agree on anything else, there was a consensus that pension statutes were not proper subjects of negotiation. As to all other matters, there was no agreement, meaning that by its inaction the Legislature acquiesced in the Dunellen decision. Cf. Lemke v. Bailey, 41 N.J. 295, 301 (1963); Egan v. Erie R. Co., 29 N.J. 243, 250 (1959); Asbury Park Press v. City of Asbury Park, 19 N.J. 183, 190 (1955).

This construction has the advantage of simplicity. In adopting it, we would be holding that L. 1974, c. 123 meant essentially nothing. However, the vote in the Assembly on the amendment to delete the addition of the word "pension" to N.J.S.A. 34:13A-8.1 was 35-35. It is unlikely that the legislators would be so divided over a meaningless change. Moreover, carried to its logical extreme, the State's position would render most terms and conditions of employment non-negotiable. For example, a literal application of N.J.S.A. 11:5-1(f) would all but emasculate the Employer-Employee Relations Act. That section directs the Civil Service Commission to

> Establish procedures for maintaining adequate employer-employee relations, and for the orderly consideration of disputes, grievances, complaints and proposals relating to the employer-employee relationship, in the classified service of the State; and make investigations, conduct hearings and make rulings with respect thereto. Such rulings shall not be interpreted to compel or require the expenditure of moneys which are not available or the incurring of obligations not otherwise authorized by law.

We cannot accept the proposition that the Legislature went through the trouble of establishing PERC through L. 1968, c. 303 and then decided that a general statute such as N.J.S.A. 11-5.1(f) would automatically preclude the negotiability of all items within its scope. If that were the case, there would be no need for PERC or for collective negotiations concerning the terms and conditions of employment in the classified State service. Attributing such an intent to the Legislature is at best unrealistic.

Finally, we reject the State's argument that N.J. Const. (1947), Art. VII, § 1, par. 2, see ante at —, (slip opinion at 4) precludes negotiation and agreement concerning the matters brought out in these cases. The State submits that this provision was intended to render the whole Civil Service scheme a part of this constitutional command. Rather than according that paragraph such sweeping scope, we prefer to interpret it in a more literal fashion so that it provides that appointments and promotions must be based on merit and fitness. So long as terms and conditions of reemployment and layoffs are not at odds with merit and fitness, we discern no constitutional obstacle to giving effect to appropriate provisions of collectively negotiated agreements.

## C

The most expansive interpretation of the effect of L. 1974, c. 123 is that offered by Locals 195 and 518. They assert that, as to terms and conditions of employment, the legislative intent was to preclude only negotiation concerning matters covered by pension statutes; in their view everything else is negotiable. They contend that the Legislature was responding to our holding in Dunellen, supra, see ante at — (slip opinion at 4) that the 1968 version of N.J.S.A. 34:13A-8.1 "clearly precluded an expansive approach" to negotiation. The transcript of the May 7, 1974 hearing of the joint committee of the Legislature is cited in support of this construction. At that hearing the labor relations counsel for the New Jersey State League of Municipalities indicated to Senator Greenberg that S.1087 would effectively overrule Dunellen. Also noted is the accompanying statement to the final effort to amend S.1087 by removing the word "pension." The Locals have concluded that all parties knew the implication of the insertion of the word pension at the time of the vote, and that this Court should thus give effect to the literal language of the statute as amended.

This approach is the most faithful to the literal text of the amendment. It also represents the most radical departure from the earlier scheme. One might reasonably believe that had the Legislature determined to permit specific Civil Service statutes to be contravened by collective negotiation, it would have said so with greater clarity.

If adopted, this approach would give wide sway to collective negotiations. While the employees could press for greater rights in one area than are presently permitted by statute, the State would be free to demand concessions concerning some of the rights presently guaranteed employees by statute in exchange. This system would most nearly approximate collective bargaining in the private sector.

The most significant problem with this interpretation is that it would permit total diversity in the terms and conditions of employment for each public employee negotiating unit in the State. Matters now governed by specific statute would be regulated only by the negotiated agreement of the public employer and the majority representative. Civil Service statutes and regulations could be abrogated entirely if the parties so agreed. Areas where state-wide uniformity has been deemed a necessity would simply break down into a mass of confusion.

## D

The 1974 amendment to N.J.S.A. 34:13A-8.1 is ambiguous and the legislative intent is less than clear. However, of the three possible interpretations of the amendment, we find that PERC's approach comports most closely to the intention of the Legislature. If the insertion of the word pension in N.J.S.A. 34:13A-8.1 was not of considerable significance, the reason for the protracted struggle in the Legislature would be difficult to fathom. Yet, the expansive interpretation called for by Local 195 and Local 518 would signal a revolutionary change in government direction. While we do not doubt that the Legislature has the power to ordain that collective negotiations may contravene specific as well as general statutes, we will await the "clear and distinct phraseology" which we called for in Burlington, supra, 64 N.J. at 16, before so interpreting the amended Act.

Initially, we note our agreement with PERC that negotiated agreement with respect to matters beyond the lawful authority of the public employer is impermissible. A binding agreement concerning matters whose regulation the Legislature has chosen to place outside the control of a public employer would not be within the employer's power. A public employer may not agree to a contractual provision which purports to bind the administrative discretion of the Civil Service Commission. Furthermore, we affirm PERC's determination that specific statutes or regulations which expressly set particular terms and conditions of employment, as defined in Dunellen, for public employees may not be contravened by negotiated agreement. For that reason, negotiation over matters so set by statutes or regulations is not permissible. We use the word "set" to refer to statutory or regulatory provisions which speak in the imperative and leave nothing to the discretion of the public employer. All such statutes and regulations which are applicable to the employees who comprise a particular unit are effectively incorporated by reference as terms of any collective agreement covering that unit.

Yet, the 1974 amendment to N.J.S.A. 34:13A-8.1 was not an empty gesture. Under Dunellen, terms and conditions of public employment whose regulation was entrusted to the Civil Service Commission by general statutes were not negotiable even though the Commission had not promulgated any rule governing a particular matter. Under the amended version of N.J.S.A. 34:13A-8.1, such a general statute will not preclude mandatory negotiation over particular terms and conditions of employment as to which the Civil Service Commission could have but has not enacted preemptive regulations. There are many areas in which the Commission has not sought to comprehensively regulate the terms and conditions of public employment. The Legislature has determined that collective negotiation concerning such nonregulated terms and conditions of public employment should be mandatory and any negotiated agreement thereon valid. It must be emphasized, however, that the adoption of any specific *statute* or *regulation* setting or controlling a particular term or condition of employment will preempt any inconsistent provision of a negotiated agreement governing that previously unregulated matter. In short, the parties must negotiate upon and are free to agree to proposals governing any terms and conditions of public employment which have not been set, and thus preempted, by specific statutes or regulations.

It is implicit in the foregoing that statutes or regulations concerning terms and conditions of public employment which do not speak in the imperative, but rather permit a public employer to exercise a certain measure of discretion, have only a limited preemptive effect on collective negotiation and agreement. Thus, where a statute or regulation mandates a minimum level of rights or benefits for public employees but does not bar the public employer from choosing to afford them greater protection, proposals by the employees to obtain that greater protection in a negotiated agreement are mandatorily negotiable. A contractual provision affording the employees rights or benefits in excess of that required by statute or regulation is valid and enforceable. However, where a statute or regulation sets a maximum level of rights or benefits for employees on a particular term and condition of employment, no proposal to affect that maximum is negotiable nor would any contractual provision purporting to do so be enforceable [7] where a statute sets both a maximum and a minimum level of employee rights or benefits, mandatory negotiation is required concerning any proposal for a level of protection fitting between and including such maximum and minimum.

Our holding is consistent with the current understanding and actual practices of those involved in the public employment relations field. If the subject matter is covered by a specific Civil Service regulation and the parties are dissatisfied,

---

[7] In referring to those statutes which contain maxima, we are speaking, for example, of enactments providing that employees may receive "up to" or "not to exceed" a given level of benefits. An example is N.J.S.A. 11:13-2, which provides that where service ratings are used to determine layoffs, seniority credits, not to exceed ten points, may be added to the ratings.

Our reference to statutes containing minimum employee rights or benefits relates, for example, to those enactments which provide that employees receive "at least" or "not less than" a certain level of benefits. An example is N.J.S.A. 11:26D-1, post at — (slip opinion at 41), which provides a notice of "at least 45 days" be given to an employee in the classified Civil Service before he may be subject to layoff.

Mandatory or imperative statutes ordinarily are those enactments which set up a particular scheme which "shall" be handled as directed. An example of such a statute is N.J.S.A. 18A:28-5(b), which provides that teachers "shall be under tenure during good behavior and efficiency and they shall not be dismissed . . . after employment in such district or by such board for . . . three consecutive academic years, together with employment at the beginning of the next succeeding academic year," except for specifically enumerated reasons.

their recourse is to seek a modification of such regulation through the administrative process. Indeed, they may even petition the Legislature where a particular term and condition of employment is controlled by a statute with which they disagree. As a practical matter, Civil Service could be made aware of the course of negotiations so that the parties may anticipate whether its approval of a desired change in regulations could ever be obtained. This would promote labor peace by focusing the concerns of employers and employees on matters as to which they have the power to act.

Our holding permitting negotiation concerning matters not covered by a specific statute does not apply to pension statutes. The Legislature has determined that the entire subject matter of public employee pensions is to be insulated from negotiated agreement which would contravene or supplement its comprehensive regulation of that area. Public employees and employee representatives may neither negotiate nor agree upon any proposal which would affect the sacrosanct subject of employee pensions.

. . . .

[The balance of the court's decision dealing with the negotiability of specific contract proposals based on the foregoing guidelines is omitted.]

## NOTE

One of the primary features of the conflict between collective bargaining and the civil service is the philosophical difference between the seniority principle, characteristic of labor contracts, and the merit principle embodied in civil service legislation. Consider the distinction between the merit *principle* and the merit *system*. Should public employers and unions be allowed to substitute seniority provisions for competitive examinations and merit pay raises? In New York, the Supreme Court for Erie County held, in Kenmore Club, Police Benevolent Ass'n v. Civil Service Commission, 61 Misc. 2d 685, 307 N.Y.S.2d 63 (Sup. Ct. 1969) and in Selover v. Civil Service Comm'n, 61 Misc. 2d 688, 307 N.Y.S.2d 66 (Sup. Ct. 1969), that the petitioning unions, notwithstanding contract provisions, had no right to orders cancelling or regulating the preparation, conduct or rating of competitive examinations. The court said:

> The authority of municipal civil service commissions to prescribe certain minimum qualifications in a promotional examination as here is authority granted by the Civil Service Law. The above agreement although arising from the Taylor Act can take no precedence under the above-mentioned provisions of the Civil Service Law. The Civil Service Law gives to the municipal commission the right to prescribe minimum training and experience qualifications for promotional examinations. No agreement between a municipal corporation and its employees although basically sanctioned by the Taylor Act has any precedence and makes no claim to any precedence over the Civil Service Law.

*Accord,* Civil Service Employees Ass'n, Local 860 v. Town of Harrison, 407 N.Y.S.2d 627, 99 L.R.R.M. 2742 (App. Div. 1978).

## 4. EFFECT OF OTHER STATUTORY PROVISIONS

**HANSLOWE & OBERER, DETERMINING THE SCOPE OF NEGOTI- ATIONS UNDER PUBLIC EMPLOYMENT RELATIONS STATUTES (1971), A Special Report Prepared for the New York Public Employment Relations Board**

### *1. General Problem*

The general problem examined herein is the relationship of the Taylor Law and of PERB to other laws of the State of New York and to the agencies which administer them, with regard to the determination of the scope of negotiations under the Taylor Law — i.e., the subjects as to which there is a duty to negotiate.

A question within the foregoing question is: What impact, if any, does the Taylor Law have on the pre-existing authority of public employers to determine "terms and conditions of employment" of their employees? In other words is the scope of negotiations under the Taylor Law coterminous with or greater than the scope of the unilateral power held by the particular public employer under pre-existing law, as declared by the Constitution, Legislature, courts, State Comptroller, Attorney General, etc.?

### 2. A Hypothetical Case: PERB vs. the Comptroller as to Local Government Conditions of Employment

Employee Organization, duly certified representative of certain professional employees, presents to School Board, the public employer, a list of negotiating demands which includes the following item: "Payment of accrued sick leave to the estate of a deceased employee."

School Board refuses to discuss the above item on the ground that inclusion of such a provision in the collective agreement would be illegal, citing 23 Op. State Compt. 649 (1967, #67-735) and Article VIII, § 1 of the State Constitution, prohibiting government entities, including school districts, from giving gifts.

Employee Organization files a charge with PERB under Section 209-a.1 (d), alleging that the above-described action of the School Board constitutes a refusal to negotiate concerning "terms and conditions of employment."

What should PERB do?

Under the 1969 amendments it is clearly PERB's responsibility to determine whether or not the alleged improper practice occurred. Section 205.5, as amended, provides:

> In addition to its powers and functions provided in other sections of this article, the board shall have the following powers and functions: . . . (d) To establish procedures for the prevention of improper employer and employee organization practices as provided in section two hundred nine-a of this article. . . . The board shall exercise exclusive nondelegable jurisdiction of the powers granted to it by this paragraph. . . .

PERB must, therefore, determine whether the unused sick leave demand falls within the scope of "terms and conditions of employment," within the meaning of the Taylor Law.

Concerning the relationship of the above-cited opinion of the State Comptroller to this determination, PERB has three courses of action available: PERB might accept the opinion of the Comptroller as conclusive of the matter and dismiss the charge; PERB might ignore the opinion of the Comptroller as irrelevant; PERB might take into account the opinion of the Comptroller, giving it, however, only such weight as, in the judgment of PERB, its persuasive force merits.

The third course of action is patently the proper one. The decision as to the scope of negotiability is PERB's in the first instance. The first two options — abandonment of decision to the Comptroller and ignoring the opinion of the Comptroller — have little to commend them. As to the first, the Comptroller has no mandate under the law to resolve such questions; his opinions with respect to such local government expenditures are admitted by himself to be "informal and advisory" only. . . . As to the second, the Comptroller has, by arrogation or otherwise, been in the business of advising local governments as to their powers under a broad body of law for a substantial period of time; in the process he has accumulated considerable experience concerning the legal framework within which local governments of the State of New York operate. For PERB to ignore completely this source of potential guidance would seem unwise.

The burden of demarcating those subjects which are within the scope of the statutory criterion "terms and conditions of employment" is initially PERB's, not merely because PERB has been designated by the State Legislature to make such determinations in the first instance, but because the vitality of the administrative process lies in the development and application of expertise in specially difficult areas of government regulation. The definition of the scope of negotiations under the Taylor Law is such an area.

One way of validating the foregoing position is to consider the matter of judicial review. However the decision as to the scope of negotiability under the Taylor Law is made in the first instance, it is subject to review in the courts. Such review is dependent upon the quality of the record made below and the sophistication of the trial tribunal with regard to the questions before it. Employment relations, as several decades of experience in the private sector demonstrate, is a complex and delicate area in which the adequacy of judicial review is particularly dependent upon the quality of the proceedings, record, and judgment below.

It is instructive to note, in the foregoing regard, that Comptroller opinions are typically rendered on the basis of a mere exchange of letters, without the sharpening of issues through pleadings, the presentation of evidence, confrontation and cross examination of witnesses, oral or written argument. Proceedings before PERB, on the contrary, under sections 209-a and 205.5 (d), entail all of these aids to administrative adjudication and judicial review.

Turning now to the merits of the hypothetical case posed, namely, whether the issue of "payment of accrued sick leave to the estate of a deceased employee" is within the statutory mandate of "terms and conditions of employment," the problems presented to PERB are the following: (1) whether the demand concerning the treatment of accrued sick leave is a term or condition of employment, and (2) whether Article VIII, § 1 of the State Constitution and/or some other state constitutional or legislative provision takes the matter out of the scope of negotiability. The answer to the first question would seem quite clearly to be yes. The real question for the purposes of this memorandum is the second. As to this, PERB must determine, within the limiting context of all relevant constitutional and statutory provisions (i.e., all relevant "law"), whether, as a matter of sound employment relations in the public sector, including such a subject within the scope of negotiability makes sense.

Stated more clearly perhaps, in cases such as the hypothetical one posed, PERB has two questions potentially before it: (1) whether the particular subject should be deemed, as a matter of sound public employment relations, to be within "terms and conditions of employment," (2) whether, even if it should be so deemed, the particular subject has been withheld or withdrawn from negotiability by the operation of some competing provision of law. Where the answer to the second question is unclear by reason of ambiguity in the competing law, the question of negotiability should be decided by PERB on the basis of sound public employment relations.

Whatever the determination of PERB, that determination is of course reviewable in the courts pursuant to Section 210.4 of the Taylor Law....

### 4. The Relationship of PERB to Other Competing Agencies

What has been said of the Comptroller is dispositive of PERB's relationship with other potentially competing agencies of state government. Whatever the competing agency, the question of negotiability is to be answered by PERB in the first instance. In the process of answering the question, PERB should take into account all pertinent constitutional and statutory provisions; its consideration should not be confined to the Taylor Law alone. Neither the Taylor Law nor PERB exists in a void. (Cf., e.g., Southern Steamship Co. v. NLRB, 316 U.S. 31, 47 (1942) ("... the Board has not been commissioned to effectuate the policies of the Labor Relations Act so single-mindedly that it may wholly ignore other and equally important Congressional objectives. Frequently the entire scope of Congressional purpose calls for careful accommodation of one statutory scheme to another, and it is not too much to demand of an administrative body that it undertake this accommodation without excessive emphasis upon its immediate task."); American News Co., 55 NLRB 1302 (1944).

In addition to taking into account other constitutional and statutory provisions, PERB should consider the decisions of tribunals competent to interpret those constitutional and statutory provisions. The weight which PERB gives to any aspect of the foregoing array of law (constitutional, statutory, decisional) should depend on PERB's own interpretation of such of that law as it deems relevant. PERB's interpretation would, of course, be oriented to sound public employment relations as perceived through its own expertise. While PERB cannot and should not ignore clear mandates from the Constitution, the Legislature, or the Court of Appeals, it should deem itself free in the absence of such mandates to exercise its own best judgment, understanding of course that its decisions are themselves subject to judicial review. It would be obviously wasteful for PERB to determine questions of negotiability in the context of the Taylor Law alone, leaving to the reviewing courts in the first instance the questions of the relevance and force of competing law. Such an approach would deny to the reviewing courts the benefit of PERB's developing expertise with respect to the implications of such competing law for sound public employment relations (which is to say, sound public policy in a public employment context) in the State of New York.

Applying the foregoing principles to a concrete case, the decision of the Supreme Court of Nassau County in the *Central High School District No. 3* case (72 LRRM 2858, 305 N.Y.S.2d 724, November, 1969) — to the effect that an arbitration award, granting a sum of money to a deceased employee's estate in lieu of unused sick leave, was unenforceable by reason of the unconstitutional gift provision — should be accorded no more weight by PERB than the persuasive force of the court's reasoning merits. Without repeating again all of the considerations leading to this conclusion, it would seem quite incongruous for important questions of public employment relations to be resolved without any participation in the decisional process by the agency specially constituted by the Legislature to superintend such matters.

### 5. The Relationship of Scope of Negotiations to the Unit Problem

A somewhat different variety of scope of negotiations question confronts PERB in the following type of situation: where the subject sought to be negotiated is quite clearly within the statutory scope, "terms and conditions of employment," but is not within the authority of management at the unit level. An example of this type of subject is annuities and pensions under the State Employees' Retirement System. (Retirement and Social Security Law, Article 2.) This system applies not only to state employees but also to the employees of "participating" municipalities and other local government entities. The State Comptroller is declared by § 11 of the Retirement and Social Security Law to be the "administrative head" of the Retirement System, with the express power, among others, to adopt and amend "rules and regulations for the administration and transaction of the business of the retirement system. . . ."

Without delving more deeply into the Retirement and Social Security Law, it may be seen that two sets of potential questions for PERB as to scope of negotiations are presented thereunder. The first set of questions has to do with negotiations in *state* employment; the second set has to do with negotiations in *local* employment.

As to the *state* negotiations, a tug-of-war seems possible between the Office of Employee Relations, on the one hand, and the State Comptroller, on the other. With whom, it may be asked, do state employees have the right to negotiate concerning those aspects of the pension program which the Legislature has expressly placed in the discretionary control of the Comptroller. Those aspects may be said to be (1) not negotiable except with the Comptroller himself (is the Comptroller a "public employer" with regard to employees not employed in the Department of Audit and Control?), (2) negotiable only if the Comptroller *chooses* to negotiate concerning the exercise of his discretionary authority, (3) negotiable only to the extent that the state employer (Office of Employee Relations?) and the employee organization involved may agree upon joint recommendations to be made to the Comptroller and/or to the Legislature.

A possible legislative resolution of the foregoing type of problem may be foreshadowed by a very recent amendment to § 8 of the State Finance Law. The duties of the Comptroller with regard to a related matter have been modified as follows in subdivision 16 thereof:

> Notwithstanding any inconsistent provision of law, no change shall be made in the rate or eligibility standards for state employees' travel, meals, lodging, and other expenses for which the state makes payment (either in advance or by reimbursement), without the approval of the director of employee relations.

As to negotiations over pensions involving *local* governments participating in the State Retirement System, the only practical effect of such would be to produce joint proposals to be presented in the form of requests to the Comptroller and/or the State Legislature. This is an instance of a larger question which will confront PERB in several different contexts. The question is whether PERB should require a particular public employer to negotiate with regard to a subject as to which the employer has no control *except* the power to make recommendations. This question is dealt with in the ensuing section.

### 6. Subjects of Negotiation: Mandatory, Permissible, Illegal?

The subjects of bargaining in the private sector have been trichotomized into mandatory, permissible, and illegal. Mandatory subjects are those which fall within the meaning of "wages, hours, and other terms and conditions of employment" (National Labor Relations Act, Section 8(d)); as to these, the proposing party may bargain to impasse, and the other party has a duty to bargain in response. Permissible subjects are those not within "wages, hours, and other terms and conditions of employment," but not illegal; as to these, the proponent may propose, but not insist upon, and the other party need not, but may, bargain; if agreement is reached on a permissible subject, that agreement is an enforceable part of the contract. Illegal subjects are those which, even if agreed upon, are unenforceable; of course there is no duty to bargain over such a subject. (See generally, sections 8(a)(5), 8(b)(3), 9(a), and 8(d) of the National Labor Relations Act, and NLRB v. Wooster Division of Borg-Warner Corporation, 356 U.S. 342 (1958).)

The situation in public employment is sufficiently different as to impugn the relevance of the trichotomy. The *terminology* may, however, be helpful for purposes of analysis. Assuming a subject to be clearly within "terms and conditions of employment" and at the same time not within the authority of management at the level of the unit, should PERB enforce a duty to negotiate at that level? To put it otherwise, should such a subject be treated as mandatory, permissible, or illegal — i.e., should negotiation be required, permitted, prohibited?

The real choice would seem to lie between the mandatory and permissible approaches; little purpose would be served in *prohibiting* negotiations on such a subject. Even where public management at the level of the unit is without authority to control subject X, it would ordinarily have authority to agree with the employee organization involved to make a joint recommendation to the appropriate higher echelon of authority as to the desired disposition of subject X. Accordingly, subjects found to be within the statutory language "terms and conditions of employment" but not within the authority of management at the unit level might, nonetheless, be treated as mandatory subjects and negotiations over them therefore required. A difficulty with this approach is that it might tend to clutter up negotiations with a laundry list of demands for joint importuning of distant and perhaps intractable holders of pertinent powers. On the other hand, a good deal of negotiations in the public sector concerning the most central of subjects is conducted by "public employers" who lack authority to resolve finally those issues. Examples of this are (1) a dependent school board negotiating teacher salaries and (2) the State Office of Employee Relations negotiating state employee salaries; in the case of the first, the pertinent authority resides in the city council; in the second, it resides in the State Legislature.

Perhaps guidance toward a middle course between the mandatory and permissible approaches is offered by Section 207.1(b) of the Taylor Law when it speaks of "*effective* recommendations." Subjects which the particular employer does not control but as to which he has the power to make *effective* recommendations might be treated as mandatory subjects. On the other hand, subjects as to which the employer could make only *ineffective* recommendations might be treated as permissible subjects only.

### 7. The Impact of the Taylor Law on the Pre-Existing Authority of Public Employers

The array of positions with regard to the effect of the enactment of the Taylor Law on the pre-existing authority of public employers to confer benefits on their employees ranges from the response of the Comptroller at the right extreme, "nil," to a hypothetical position at the left extreme to the effect that the Taylor Law impliedly repeals all prior inconsistent legislation and judicial and administrative rulings. . . .

The Comptroller's position, "a fundamental premise which underlies every

Opinion of the State Comptroller, concerning situations involving Article 14, of the Civil Service Law (known as the Taylor Law)" (see Comptroller's Memorandum of Law in the *Town of Huntington* case, page 4), was stated in 23 Op. State Compt. 316, 318-19 (1967, #67-378):

> The new statutory provisions [the Taylor Law] do not in any way enlarge the legal benefits which public employers may confer on their employees nor has there been any expansion of the authority of such public employers in regard to these benefits. Therefore, it will be necessary for us to consider in order each of the employee demands herein to determine whether, irrespective of collective bargaining, this school district may legally comply with the same.

We disagree with the position thus taken by the Comptroller (and also with the position at the opposite extreme of the spectrum). At least two pertinent changes, both, in our judgment, rather basic, have been produced by the Taylor Law. The effect of these two changes is potentially to expand the scope of negotiations beyond the scope of pre-Taylor *exercise* of employer power. The first change is that a new public agency, PERB, has been created and empowered by the Legislature to deal with and decide issues of public employment relations in the State of New York — issues previously presided over (to the extent they were presided over at all) by other agencies. To the extent that those other agencies lacked authority or occasion to render final decisions on questions of employer power presently falling within the purview of PERB, such questions are still open. This means that the only questions of employer power definitively answered at the time of this writing are those questions which have heretofore been unambiguously resolved by the Constitution of the State of New York, the State Legislature, or the Court of Appeals. Opinions of the State Comptroller, and even decisions of lower state courts never challenged in the ultimate through appellate review to the Court of Appeals, establish no controlling precedents.

A second basic change in the public policy of the State of New York occasioned by the enactment of the Taylor Law is the introduction into public employment relations of the whole new concept of resolving employer-employee disagreements through the institution of collective negotiations. We concede that matters unambiguously resolved by the State Constitution, by statutory enactment, or by Court of Appeals interpretation of either of the foregoing are not affected by the passage of the Taylor Law. Where ambiguity exists, however, or where the source of the competing "law" is of a lower order than Constitution, Legislature, Court of Appeals — i.e., in the gray area of public employer authority over "terms and conditions of employment" — strong reason exists for concluding that the legislative intent was to have such gray-area problems resolved through the process of collective negotiations. Indeed, the Taylor Law declares it to be the public policy of the State of New York to resolve disputes between public employees and public employers by that process. (Section 200) . . . .

## NOTE

Oberer and Hanslowe suggested that a PERB should (1) determine whether a given subject is within the "terms and conditions of employment," and, if it is, (2) determine whether such subject should nevertheless be "withheld or withdrawn from negotiability by the operation of some competing provision of law." Is there or should there be any difference in the scope of judicial review with respect to these two determinations? Should the scope of judicial review be greater with respect to the second determination?

## CITY OF BROOKFIELD v. WERC

Wisconsin Supreme Court
275 N.W.2d 723 (1979)

COFFEY, Justice.

This is an appeal of a July 16, 1976 judgment that reversed an April 16, 1975 order of the Wisconsin Employment Relations Commission (hereinafter WERC). The appellant, WERC, ordered the respondent, City of Brookfield (hereinafter Brookfield) to reinstate and reimburse five city firefighters laid off due to a decrease in the funds allocated to the fire department by the city budget. The ordered remedy was based upon the WERC's finding that Brookfield in the 1973 bargaining agreement had violated its duty to collectively bargain when it refused to negotiate the decision to lay off the five firefighters or the effects of the lay off decision, contrary to sec. 111.70(1)(d), Stats. The circuit court reversed the WERC order and found that Brookfield was not required to negotiate the lay off decision; the WERC conclusion in regard to the duty to bargain the effects of the lay off decision was affirmed and is not at issue in this appeal.

. . . .

Thus, the two issues presented are:

1. Whether an economically motivated decision to lay off five firefighters as a means to implement a fire department budget reduction is a mandatory subject of collective bargaining pursuant to sec. 111.70(1)(d), Stats., of the Municipal Employment Relations Act?

2. Is the commission's order providing remedies for the respondent's failure to collectively bargain in violation of sec. 111.70(1)(d), Stats., reasonable and appropriate under the circumstances?

This appeal challenges a municipality's decision to lay off five union firefighters due to a cut in the department budget. Local 2051 (firefighter's union) maintains that budget related lay offs are a mandatory subject of bargaining pursuant to sec. 111.70(1)(d), Stats., as a matter affecting wages, hours and conditions of employment. The city of Brookfield contends that the layoff decision is a management prerogative by virtue of its municipal powers vested in ch. 62, Stats. Consequently, this case will be decided upon the statutory interpretation the WERC gave to sec. 111.70(1)(d) and ch. 62, Stats., and whether it was appropriate in the particular fact situation.

In dealing with this subject the court must determine which reviewing standards used to interpret sec. 111.70(1)(d) are appropriate herein. In *Unified School District of Racine County v. WERC*, 81 Wis.2d 89, 259 N.W.2d 724 (1977) the court discussed the standard of review applicable to WERC decisions dealing with mandatory bargaining and stated:

> Because the case raised 'very nearly questions of first impression,' this court held that it was 'not bound' by the Commission's interpretation of the statute, although the Commission's decision would have 'great bearing' on the court's decision, and would be accorded 'due weight.' *Beloit Education Asso., supra,* at 68, 242 N.W.2d 231. As in the *Beloit* case, because of the limited experience of the Commission with the questions presented, and their strictly legal nature, it is appropriate for this court to reach an independent determination of the intent and meaning of the statute, giving due weight to the decision of the Commission." *Id.* at 93, 259 N.W.2d at 727.

Thus, in this problem area the court finds it necessary to undertake an independent judicial inquiry into the proper construction of sec. 111.70(1)(d) and its impact on the exercise of municipal powers enumerated in ch. 62. A question of interpretation confronts this court to determine whether or not the commission's competence or expertise extends beyond ch. 111. This court in *Glendale Professional Policemen's Assoc. v. Glendale,* 83 Wis.2d 90, 264 N.W.2d 594 (1978) dealt with the harmonizing of sec. 111.70(1)(d) Stats., and sec. 62.13, Stats., as to whether a promotion of a police officer within the department was enforceable through the collective bargaining agreement. This court answered the question regarding the commission's expertise in the following language:

> "In the typical case, the application of sec. 111.70-77, Stats., to a particular labor dispute requires the expertise of the Commission, the agency primarily charged with administering it. Here the question does not concern the application of a labor statute but the Commission's power to enforce it in the first instance in the light of another state statute. This issue, for relationship between two state statutes, is within the special competence of the courts rather than the Commission, and therefore this court need not give great weight to the arbitrator's determination of the issue." *Id.* at 100-01, 264 N.W.2d at 600.

We are persuaded by the *Glendale* reasoning that the WERC should not be accorded the authority to interpret the appropriate statutory construction to ch. 62. The general charter law for cities as recited in ch. 62 deals solely with the powers and privileges of municipalities to promote the general welfare, peace, good order and prosperity of its inhabitants. These objectives are accomplished by the enactment of charter and general ordinances dealing with finance, public works, zoning, safety and building codes, annexations, etc. Thus, the exclusive grant of authority to municipalities in ch. 62 is far afield from the powers and limitations in the area of labor relations as enumerated in secs. 111.70-77. Accordingly, a question of a strictly legal nature is presented. This court in *Whitefish Bay v. WERB,* 34 Wis.2d 432, 149 N.W.2d 662 (1967) eloquently pointed out the limitations on the interpretation of statutes by an administrative agency and the agency's void of legal expertise and knowledge when it stated:

> " 'In view of this poverty of administrative experience and of the recent passage of the statute giving rise to this strictly legal question of jurisdiction, perhaps the court ought to examine it afresh as a question of law not especially involving administrative expertise. For such a question the court feels free to substitute its own judgment for that of the administrative agency.' Citing *Pabst v. Department of Taxation* (1963), 19 Wis.2d 313, 323, 120 N.W.2d 77." *Id.* at 444-45, 149 N.W.2d at 669.

This case is an instance where the circuit court, now with this court's approval, is placing a limitation on the attempt of the WERC to expand its scope of authority beyond the limits of the legislative enactment contained in ch. 111. In like situations, WERC's statutory interpretations beyond the field of labor law will not be entitled to persuasive or substantial weight.

Sec. 111.70(1)(d) is controlling upon the duty to collectively bargain between a municipality and its public employees, and reads:

> " 'Collective bargaining' means the performance of the mutual obligation of a municipal employer, through its officers and agents, and the

representatives of its employes, to meet and confer at reasonable times, in good faith, with respect to wages, hours and conditions of employment with the intention of reaching an agreement, or to resolve questions arising under such an agreement. The duty to bargain, however, does not compel either party to agree to a proposal or require the making of a concession. Collective bargaining includes the reduction of any agreement reached to a written and signed document. The employer shall not be required to bargain on subjects reserved to management and direction of the governmental unit except insofar as the manner of exercise of such functions affects the wages, hours and conditions of employment of the employes. In creating this subchapter the legislature recognizes that the public employer must exercise its powers and responsibilities to act for the government and good order of the municipality, its commercial benefit and the health, safety and welfare of the public to assure orderly operations and functions within its jurisdiction, subject to those rights secured to public employes by the constitutions of this state and of the United States and by this subchapter."

As stated in sec. 111.70(1)(d) a mandatory subject of bargaining is a matter which affects "wages, hours and conditions of employment." The statute also provides for a public sector "management rights" clause guaranteeing as a management prerogative the exercise of municipal powers and responsibilities in promoting the health, safety and welfare for its citizens. Unless the bargaining topic affects "wages, hours and conditions of employment" a municipality is not compelled to collectively bargain but may choose to if not expressly prohibited by legislative delegation. Obviously, it is not the intent of the legislature to permit the elasticity of the phrase "bargaining topics affecting wages, hours and conditions of employment" to be stretched with each and every labor question.

In *Beloit Education Asso. v. WERC, supra,* 73 Wis.2d at 54, 242 N.W.2d 231, the court held that a mandatory subject of bargaining was distinguished from a permissive subject of bargaining if the topic "primarily" or "fundamentally" related to wages, hours and conditions of employment, now known as the "primary relation test." The primary relation test reflects substantial change in public sector labor law. Prior to the *Beloit* case, mandatory and permissive subjects were delineated in the private sector "change of direction" test. This rule of law was adopted by the court in 1970 wherein *Libby, McNeil & Libby v. WERC, supra,* recited ". . . most management decisions which change the direction of the corporate enterprise, involving a change in capital investment, are not bargainable." *Id.* 48 Wis.2d at 282, 179 N.W.2d at 811. In *Unified School Dist. No. 1 of Racine v. WERC, supra,* 81 Wis.2d at 96, 259 N.W.2d 724, it was reasoned that the primary relation test rather than the change of direction standard better encompassed the inherent differences between public and private sector bargaining. *See* Weisberger, *The Appropriate Scope of Mandatory Bargaining in the Public Section: The Continuing Controversy and the Wisconsin Experience,* 1977 Wis.L.Rev. 685, 694-99. The *Racine County* decision emphasized that:

> "[I]n the public sector, the principal limit on the scope of collective bargaining is concern for the integrity of political processes." *Unified School Dist. No. 1 of Racine County v. WERC, supra* at 96, 259 N.W.2d at 730.

We hold that economically motivated lay offs of public employees resulting from budgetary restraints is a matter primarily related to the exercise of municipal powers and responsibilities and the integrity of the political processes of municipal government. The citizens of a community have a vital interest in the continued fiscally responsible operation of its municipal services. Thus, it is imperative that we strike a balance between public employees' bargaining rights and protecting the public health and safety of our citizens within the framework of the political and legislative process.

Ch. 62, Stats., which enumerates legislatively delegated municipal powers and obligations mandates this result and recites in its relevant portions:

"(5) POWERS. Except as elsewhere in the statutes specifically provided, the council shall have the management and control of the city property, finances, highways, navigable waters, and the public service, *and shall have power to act for the government and good order of the city, for its commercial benefit, and for the health, safety, and welfare of the public,* and may carry out its powers by license, regulation, suppression, borrowing of money, *tax levy,* appropriation, fine, imprisonment, confiscation and other necessary or convenient means. The powers hereby conferred shall be in addition to all other grants, *and shall be limited only by express language."* Sec. 62.11, Stats. (emphasis supplied).

"(5m) DISMISSALS AND REEMPLOYMENT. (a) When it *becomes necessary, because of need for economy, lack of work or funds,* or for other just causes, *to reduce the number of subordinates,* the emergency, special, temporary, part-time, or provisional subordinates, if any, shall be dismissed first, and thereafter subordinates shall be dismissed in the order of the shortest length of service in the department, provided that, in cities where a record of service rating has been established prior to January 1, 1933, for the said subordinates, the emergency, special, temporary, part-time provisional subordinates, if any, shall be dismissed first, and thereafter subordinates shall be dismissed in the order of the least efficient as shown by the said service rating." Sec. 62.13(5m)(a), Stats. (emphasis supplied).

This court has held that sec. 111.70 should be harmonized with existing statutes when possible, inasmuch as sec. 111.70 "is presumed to have been enacted with full knowledge of the pre-existing statutes and that construction should give each section force and effect." *Glendale Professional Policemen's Assoc. v. Glendale, supra,* citing *Muskego-Norway C.S.T.S.D. No. 9 v. WERB,* 35 Wis.2d 540, 556, 151 N.W.2d 617 (1967). In fulfilling the exclusive judicial role of interpreting and harmonizing diverse statutes as ch. 62 and 111.70(1)(d), we adhere when possible to the express legislative policy stated in sec. 62.04, Stats.:

"INTENT AND CONSTRUCTION . . . . For the purpose of giving the cities the largest measure of self-government compatible with the constitution and general law, it is hereby declared that sections 62.01 to 62.26, inclusive, *shall be liberally construed in favor of the rights, powers, and privileges of cities to promote the general welfare, peace, good order and prosperity of such cities and the inhabitants thereof."* (emphasis supplied.)

Ch. 62 requires that the city of Brookfield and other municipalities possess the power to decide when a lay off is necessary in order to secure the policy objectives of the community's citizenry as spoken through the actions of its duly elected representatives. The residents of Brookfield through their elected representatives on the city council requested city budget reductions. Unquestionably, fewer firefighters will reduce the level and quality of services provided, but this is a policy decision by a community favoring a lower municipal tax base. Ch. 62 does not expressly prohibit the topic of economically motivated lay offs from becoming a permissive subject of collective bargaining, but the decision to discuss the topic at a bargaining table is a choice to be made by the electorate as expressed through its designated representatives and department heads.

This court's concern for the maintenance of the municipalities' political processes was forcefully stated in *Unified School Dist. No. 1 of Racine County v. WERC, supra* 81 Wis.2d at 99-100, 259 N.W.2d at 730.

> "As a public body composed of elected officials, a school board is vested with governmental powers and has a responsibility to act for the public welfare. The United States Supreme Court recognized this responsibility in *Hortonville Jt. School Dist. No. 1 v. Hortonville Ed. Asso.,* 426 U.S. 482, 495, 496, 96 S.Ct. 2308, 49 L.Ed.2d 1 (1976).

. . . .

The court recognizes that unions, such as Local 2051, are not powerless in their ability to formulate and influence the direction of public policy decisions. As demonstrated in this case, unions can and do attend public budget meetings and can and do lobby with legislative bodies and organize and motivate the general public regarding the union's position. The distribution of informational fliers, newsletters and media releases as well as the solicitation of prominent and influential speakers are but a few of the ways in which unions can and do have a significant impact on the political processes. Local 2051 exerted acceptable political pressures upon the Brookfield City Council to halt the lay offs resulting from the budget cut. To decide the issue to be a mandatory subject of bargaining would destroy the equal balance of power that insures the collective bargaining rights of the union and protects the rights of the general public to determine the quality and level of municipal services they consider vital. The legislature has made it clear that a budgetary lay off decision is not a subject of mandatory bargaining. If it were, the right of the public to voice its opinion would be restricted as to matters fundamentally relating to the community's safety, general welfare and budgetary management.

While not at issue in this case, we add that the trial court correctly determined that the issue as to the effects of the lay offs was a mandatory subject of bargaining. A reduction in the total work force caused by the economically motivated lay offs will affect the number of employees assigned to a particular shift and thus alter their individual fire fighting responsibilities. Therefore, there is a primary relation between the impact of the lay off decision and the working conditions of the remaining unit employees. Brookfield, after initially refusing to discuss the issue, made an offer to do so on January 15, 1973. We view with disfavor Local 2051's refusal to bargain the effect of the lay offs unless the five firefighters were returned to work and reimbursed for lost time.

In reaching our decision, we deem it important that the Brookfield City Council made the specific decision that the budget cuts would be implemented by personnel lay offs pursuant to its powers. Our decision does not reinstate the WERC ordered remedy of re-employment for the five laid off firefighters and reimbursement of back wages. Therefore, we do not reach the second issue of whether the award was reasonable and appropriate under the circumstances.

Judgment affirmed.

## NOTES

1. In Glendale Professional Policemen's Ass'n v. City of Glendale, 83 Wis. 2d 90, 264 N.W.2d 594 (1978), the Wisconsin Supreme Court was faced with the question of whether a promotion clause in a collective bargaining agreement covering police officers was valid in view of a statutory requirement that all subordinates within a police department be appointed by the police chief. In holding that the promotion clause was a mandatory subject of bargaining and therefore enforceable, the court noted that "[s]pecific contract provisions authorized by MERA must ... be harmonized with the preexisting statutory scheme." In this regard, the court observed that "[a] requirement that the chief promote the most senior qualified applicant merely restricts the discretion that would otherwise exist." The court did note, however, that the clause in question did not require the chief "to promote an unqualified person or a person determined solely by the union."

2. In Board of Regents, State University System, 4 FPER ¶ 4319 (Fla. PERC 1978), the Florida Commission held that group health insurance was a prohibited subject of bargaining for the university system since it was specifically covered by state law. In so ruling, the Commission stated:

> ... It recognizes that the law has never required a party to do that which has been rendered impossible by statute. ... Requiring the parties to bargain over a subject, knowing in advance that the product of such bargaining cannot lawfully be implemented, would be elevating form over substance. This the Commission will not do.

## DETROIT POLICE OFFICERS ASSOCIATION v. CITY OF DETROIT

Supreme Court of Michigan
319 Mich. 44, 214 N.W.2d 803 (1974)

SWAINSON, Justice.

In 1965, the Legislature passed 1965 P.A. 379 which amended the Public Employment Relations Act (PERA) to allow public employees to select a collective bargaining representative and to enter into collective bargaining negotiations with their public employer. Pursuant to the newly amended PERA the Detroit Police Officers Association (DPOA) gained recognition as the exclusive collective bargaining agent for a unit of Detroit patrolmen and policewomen in January of 1966. Shortly thereafter, extensive collective bargaining negotiations proceeded between the City of Detroit (City) and the DPOA.

The collective bargaining negotiations continued until 1968 without resolving several areas of disagreement. The DPOA in July of 1968 filed an unfair labor practices charge with the Labor Mediation Board, later redesignated the Michigan Employment Relations Commission, (MERC) alleging that the City had refused to bargain in good faith on key issues. A hearing was held and MERC issued a Decision and Order on March 18, 1971 addressing the issues raised by the DPOA. City of Detroit, Police Department, 6 MERC Lab. Op. 237 (1971). The conclusions of MERC on the issues relevant to today's appeal can be summarized as follows:

. . . .

3. The City erroneously refused to bargain on changes in the police retirement plan when it initiated and conducted a voter referendum to amend the City Charter provisions controlling the police retirement plan. MERC ordered, on this issue, "that the City of Detroit shall not require as a condition to any agreement reached regarding retirement provisions for police officers that [such agreement] be approved by a vote of the electorate."

. . . .

[The issue is as follows:]

Does the City have a duty under PERA to bargain in good faith with the DPOA on the subject of police retirement plan changes where retirement provisions are a part of the City Charter and amendable only by a popular vote of the electorate?

. . . .

. . . We summarily find that MERC was correct in holding that changes in the police retirement plan are mandatory subjects of bargaining. Our primary inquiry, then, must be to determine if the incorporation of the retirement provisions into the City Charter obviates the duty under PERA to bargain in good faith over a mandatory subject of bargaining. Secondarily, we must determine if the City committed an unfair labor practice in 1968 by unilaterally submitting a retirement plan amendment to the electorate and thereby foreclosing bargaining.

To briefly answer the City's argument that retirement provisions are not a mandatory subject of bargaining, we cite the leading federal case of Inland Steel Co. v. NLRB, 77 NLRB 1; 21 LRRM 1310, enforced 170 F.2d 247 (CA 7, 1948), cert. den., 336 U.S. 960, 69 S.Ct. 887, 93 L.Ed. 1112 (1949), which has firmly established that pension and retirement provisions are mandatory subjects of bargaining under the NLRA. We see no reason to deviate from this well-reasoned and long-established federal precedent in interpreting PERA. As we have discussed above, the scope of bargaining under PERA is patterned after that found under the NLRA. Consequently, we deem that the Legislature intended the courts to view the federal labor case law as persuasive precedent.

Turning to our primary inquiry in this second issue, we are confronted with what was accurately described in Wayne County Civil Service Commission v. Board of Supervisors, 384 Mich. 363, 367, 184 N.W.2d 201, 202 (1971), as ". . . that most difficult of all appellant problems; the ascertainment of legislative intent where there is no evidentiary or other reasonably authoritative guide to pertinent meaning or purpose of the legislators." On the one hand the Legislature has adopted PERA which, as we have explained above, foreseeably placed retirement plan issues on the collective bargaining table. On the other hand, it has allowed cities under the Home Rule Cities Act to incorporate the substance of their retirement plans into their city charters and to make those plans amendable only by a popular vote.

A statutory conflict would result if we were to accept the arguments of all parties to this appeal. The City argues that its present retirement plan was placed in the City Charter pursuant to the authority of M.C.L.A. §§ 117.4i, 117.4j; M.S.A. §§ 5.2082, 5.2083, of the Home Rule Cities Act; furthermore, that under the Act the City may not change any aspect of the retirement plan without first seeking voter approval. The DPOA and MERC argue that sections 11 and 15 of PERA require uninhibited collective bargaining between the employees' representative and the public employer; and, if voter approval is required to effect a change in a mandatory subject of bargaining, the collective bargaining process would be impeded. If the positions of all parties were accepted, we would face direct conflict between that which the City contends the Legislature intended under the Home Rule Cities Act and that which MERC and the DPOA contend that the Legislature intended under PERA and we would be required to determine which state statute should prevail and which would be impliedly repealed.

After closely examining the statutes, however, we find that no such conflict in state law is present and that the statutes can be reconciled and a purpose found to be served by each. While we agree with the DPOA and MERC that PERA contemplates open negotiations between the parties unless controlled by a specific state law, we disagree with the contentions of the City that the Home Rule Cities Act requires voter approval for changes in the substantive details of the retirement plan.

The Home Rule Cities Act was originally enacted in 1909 (P.A. 279) under authority of the Constitution of 1908. The Act has been modified by various amendments over the years, but it has continued to reflect the position now expressed in Const.1963, art. 7, § 22 that Michigan is a strong home rule state with basic local authority. The Home Rule Cities Act itself appropriately contains very little substance that the cities must include in their governing document — the city charter. In essential part the Act is enabling legislation that permits the cities to mold local government to the needs of the local populous.

Retirement plans are a "permissible charter provision" adoptable under the broad grant of authority bound in M.C.L.A. §§ 117.4i and 117.4j; M.S.A. §§ 5.2082 and 5.2083 of the Home Rule Cities Act. Nowhere in the Home Rule Cities Act is there a requirement that the charter contain more than a general grant and outline of authority to a city government to implement and maintain a retirement plan. When the City placed the complete detail of its police retirement plan into the City Charter it went beyond the requirement of state law as set forth in the Home Rule Cities Act.

The distinction between incorporating the general outline of the retirement plan and incorporating the total detail of such a plan into the City Charter controls our present analysis. The Home Rule Cities Act, a state law, requires only that the charter grant to the city government the authority to institute and maintain a retirement plan. The substantive details of a retirement plan, such as those now a part of the Detroit City Charter, are contractual and charter provisions only and do not rise to the stature of a state law requirement as the City would have us hold. Accordingly since the substantive details of the retirement plan may be classified only as contractual or charter provisions, they are subject to the duty to bargain found in PERA — a state law. Such an outcome comports with M.C.L.A. § 117.36; M.S.A. § 5.2116 of the Home Rule Cities Act which states:

> "No provision of any city charter shall conflict with or contravene the provisions of any general law of the state."

See also, Geftos v. Lincoln Park, 39 Mich. App. 644, 654, 198 N.W.2d 169 (1972); Local Union No. 876, International Brotherhood of Electrical Workers v. State Labor Mediation Board, *supra.*

To summarize, the Home Rule Cities Act does not require that the substantive terms of pension plans be voter approved. In this important respect it does not conflict with PERA. The Home Rule Cities Act and PERA can be easily harmonized by reading the Home Rule Cities Act to empower a city to set up the procedures for its pension plan in the charter and to leave the substantive terms of the plan to collective negotiation. We therefore follow the most basic tenet of statutory construction and construe these two independent acts of the Legislature to be consistent with each other.

This statutory analysis fits well with the will of the voters of the City of Detroit as expressed through their adoption of a new City Charter on November 6, 1973 to become effective July 1, 1974. Under Article 11 of the new City Charter only the broad outline of the "retirement plan" is included in the charter with the substantive terms and changes in the plan left to city ordinance. We quote in part from Article 11:

"11-101(1) The city shall provide, by ordinance, for the establishment and maintenance of retirement plan coverage for city employees.

. . . .

"11-102 The retirement plans of the City existing when this charter takes effect, including the existing governing bodies for administering the plan, the benefit schedules for those plans, and the terms for accruing rights to and receiving benefits under those plans shall, in all respects, continue in existence exactly as before until changed by ordinance in accordance with this article."

This change in the method for dealing with police retirement plans is more than coincidental. The commentary accompanying Article 11 expresses the view that this more flexible system of retirement plan change was proposed to meet the requirements of collective bargaining. We quote:

"The detail contained in chapters 5, 6 and 7 of title 9 of the present charter, dealing with the City's retirement systems, has been eliminated from the new charter.

"The security of City employees' accrued rights and benefits is in no way dependent upon detailed language in the charter. The employees' best protection is article 9, section 24 of the 1963 Michigan constitution . . . .

"Thus, the new charter, despite the great reduction in the number of words used, makes no change in the existing rights of active and retired City employees. It does, however, permit the benefit schedules of retirement plans to be changed by ordinance, thereby creating a more flexible system for implementing any agreement concerning retirement benefits resulting from the City's legal obligation to bargain collectively with its employees."

The Detroit electorate, in effect, adopted the new City Charter with the intention of facilitating the collective bargaining process.

Before leaving this portion of the retirement issues, we desire to comment upon Const.1963, art. 9, § 24 which states in part:

"The accrued financial benefits of each pension plan and retirement system of the state and its political subdivisions shall be a contractual obligation thereof and shall not be diminished or impaired thereby.

"Financial benefits arising on account of service rendered in each fiscal year shall be funded during that year and such funding shall not be used for financing unfunded accrued liabilities."

With this paramount law of the state as a protection, those already covered by a pension plan are assured that their benefits will not be diminished by future collective bargaining agreements.

Although we agree with MERC that the City had the duty to bargain over changes in the police retirement plan, we will not grant enforcement of the MERC order to bargain. See p. 807, *supra.* Prior to today's opinion there has been no clear statement by this Court regarding the scope of the duty to bargain under

PERA. Under today's holding and the mandate of the City's voters as expressed in Article 11 of the new City Charter, the City will be required to bargain over prospective changes in the police retirement and pension plan. We find this to be an equitable result.

## NOTES

1. In Pontiac Police Officers Ass'n v. City of Pontiac, 94 L.R.R.M. 2175 (1976), the Michigan Supreme Court held that even though a city charter provided for a civilian review board to handle citizen complaints with respect to police officers, the subject of a civilian review board is a mandatory subject of bargaining and "that a public employer's collective bargaining obligation prevails over a conflicting 'permissible charter provision.' "

2. Are the various public sector labor relations acts applicable to both the executive and legislative branches of government? This question was recently raised in a case before the Pennsylvania Labor Relations Board in which the City of Pittsburgh was alleged to have committed an unfair labor practice by subcontracting the work of five meter collectors. PLRB v. City of Pittsburgh, PLRB Case No. PERA-C-1488-W, GERR No. 521, at B-5 (1973). Although the Board held that the subcontracting of work which affects bargaining unit employees is a mandatory subject of bargaining, the Board nevertheless held that the unilateral action of the City Council did not violate Act 195. The Board stated:

> The Act consistently indicates and the legislature, it would appear, intended a separation between the executive and legislative branches of the public employer in the operation and application of the act. Unstated, but existing by the very nature of state government, the act exists and remains in existence at the sufferance of the legislature. Certainly an act which is a creature of the legislature cannot restrict or limit legislative discretion in matters of budget, services offered, or services withheld. The act can and does regulate the relationship between the executive branch of government and the states' employees. . . .
>
> The foregoing can only lead to the conclusion that where the executive and legislative branches of the government (whether state or any subdivision thereof) are separate entities, the legislative branch in its considerations and application of its legislative duties cannot be bound by the application of Act 195 which regulates the conduct of the public employer acting in its executive capacity. Thus, the charge of a violation under Section 1201 (a) (5), refusing to bargain cannot be sustained against the employer, the City of Pittsburgh.

Can the decision of the PLRB be squared with the decision of the Michigan Supreme Court in the principal case?

3. In providing financial assistance to state and local governments Congress frequently specifies certain conditions which must be met as a condition precedent to receiving such assistance. For example, in authorizing the Surgeon General to "make grants to State, health or mental health authorities to assist the States in establishing and maintaining adequate public health services . . . ," Congress stipulated that a state must submit a plan which must, *inter alia,*

> Provide such methods of administration (including methods relating to the establishment and maintenance of personnel standards on a merit basis, except that the Surgeon General shall exercise no authority with respect to the selection, tenure of office, and compensation of any individual employed in accordance with such methods) as are found by the Surgeon General to be necessary for the proper and efficient operation of the plan.

42 U.S.C. § 246 (d) (2) (F) (1970). To what extent does such a statutory provision affect the scope of bargaining?

The Urban Mass Transportation Act of 1964 provides for grants to states and local agencies for the purpose, among others, of acquiring privately-operated transit facilities.

As a condition precedent to receiving such a grant, however, the Act requires that there be "fair and equitable arrangements . . . , as determined by the Secretary of Labor, to protect the interest of employees affected by such assistance." Among the protective arrangements which must be provided for is "the continuation of collective bargaining rights." Urban Mass Transportation Act § 13 (c), 49 U.S.C. § 1609 (c) (1972). What effect, if any, does this statutory provision have on the interpretation or application of a public sector bargaining statute which provides for a narrower scope of bargaining than that allowed under the National Labor Relations Act? Would the state act apply? *See* Regional Transp. Dist., Inc. v. Local Div. 282 of Amalgamated Transit Union, 316 N.Y.S.2d 325, 64 Misc. 2d 865 (Sup. Ct. 1970). *See generally* pp. 61-64, *supra*.

4. In ADVISORY COMMISSION ON INTERGOVERNMENTAL RELATIONS, LABOR-MANAGEMENT POLICIES FOR STATE AND LOCAL GOVERNMENT 111 (1969), the following recommendation is made:

> Having assessed [the] various facets of present and potential federal mandating and recognizing that further intervention is quite possible, the Commission adopts the general position that Congress should refrain from any additional mandating of requirements related to the working conditions of State and local employees or the authority of these governments to deal with their personnel in whatever fashion they see fit.

## C. ELEMENTS OF GOOD FAITH BARGAINING

## 1. GENERALLY

### WEST HARTFORD EDUCATION ASSOCIATION v. DECOURCY

Connecticut Supreme Court
162 Conn. 566, 295 A.2d 526 (1972)

RYAN, Associate Justice: . . . Since [the court has ruled that class size, teacher load, the assignment to and compensation for extracurricular activities, and the submission of grievances to binding arbitration were mandatory subjects of bargaining], the parties ask us to decide whether or not the board violated its duty to negotiate with the plaintiff by: (i) Not making counter-proposals on those topics, or (ii) taking the position that such matters be reserved for unilateral decision by the board, or (iii) taking the position that such matters be included in the "board prerogatives" clause of the contract.

Section 10-153d requires the board to "confer in good faith with respect to salaries and other conditions of employment, or the negotiation of an agreement, or any question arising thereunder and the execution of a written contract incorporating any agreement reached if requested by either party, but such obligation shall not compel either party to agree to a proposal or require the making of a concession." This language is almost identical to the corresponding portion of the National Labor Relations Act.

The duty to negotiate in good faith generally has been defined as an obligation to participate actively in deliberations so as to indicate a present intention to find a basis for agreement. N.L.R.B. v. Montgomery Ward & Co., 133 F.2d 676, 686 (9th Cir.). Not only must the employer have an open mind and a sincere desire to reach an agreement but a sincere effort must be made to reach a common ground. Ibid.

This duty does not require an employer to agree to a proposal or require the making of a concession. The National Labor Relations Board has interpreted this provision as freeing an employer from any duty to make counterproposals in the form of concessions, so that the failure to make counterproposals is not a per se violation of the act, but must be tested against the usual standard of good faith. N.L.R.B. v. Arkansas Rice Growers Assn., 400 F.2d 565, 571 (8th Cir.). The answer to question (b)(i) is "No." The board of education does not violate its duty to negotiate by refusing to make counterproposals on the mandatory subjects listed in question (a) as long as it is negotiating in good faith.

Questions (b)(ii) and (b)(iii) should be discussed together. Question (b)(ii) is somewhat vague because there are insufficient facts contained in the stipulation to indicate what is meant by reserving matters for the "unilateral action of the board." If the conduct of the board amounted to a complete refusal to negotiate with the teachers' representatives on mandatory subjects of bargaining, such conduct would, of course, constitute a violation of its statutory duty to negotiate. On the other hand, the board's insistence on a broad "board prerogatives clause," or as it is referred to in nonpublic labor relations cases, a "management rights clause," would not constitute a per se violation of § 10-153d. In N.L.R.B. v. American National Ins. Co., 343 U.S. 395, 72 S. Ct. 824, 96 L. Ed. 1027, the Supreme Court of the United States held that employer-bargaining for a clause under which management retains the exclusive right to control what certain conditions of employment will be does not amount to conduct which constitutes refusal to bargain per se, nor does it alone demonstrate a lack of good faith. In effect, the court was saying that this type of provision is itself a condition of employment, and a mandatory subject of collective bargaining. Long Lake Lumber Co., 185 N.L.R.B., No. 65, 74 L.R.R.M. 1116.

"While it is well established that an employer's insistence upon a management rights clause does not itself violate ... [the act], the nature of the employer's proposals on management's rights ... are material factors in assessing its motivations in approaching negotiations." Stuart Radiator Core Mfg. Co., 173 N.L.R.B., No. 27, 69 L.R.R.M. 1243. Thus, if the employer insisted on retaining for himself absolute unilateral control over wages, hours and other conditions of employment in effect requiring the union to waive practically all of its statutory rights his good faith is suspect. Stuart Radiator Core Mfg. Co., supra; I.T.T. Corporation, Henze Valve Service Division, 166 N.L.R.B. No. 65, 65 L.R.R.M. 1654; East Texas Steel Castings, 154 N.L.R.B., No. 94, 60 L.R.R.M. 1097; "M" System, Inc., 129 N.L.R.B., No. 64, 47 L.R.R.M. 1017; Dixie Corporation, 105 N.L.R.B., No. 49, 32 L.R.R.M. 1259. Where the subject of a dispute is a mandatory bargaining point adamant insistence on a bargaining position is not necessarily a refusal to bargain in good faith. N.L.R.B. v. Wooster Division, Borg-Warner Corporation, 356 U.S. 342, 349, 78 S. Ct. 718, 2 L. Ed. 2d 823. To determine the question of good faith the totality of the parties' conduct throughout the negotiations must be considered. N.L.R.B. v. Alva Allen Industries, Inc., 369 F.2d 310, 321 (8th Cir.); New Canaan v. Connecticut State Board of Labor Relations, 160 Conn. 285, 293, 278 A.2d 761.

Questions (b)(ii) and (b)(iii) cannot be answered categorically.

## Question (c)

The issue in this question is the extent to which the school board may communicate with its teachers about salaries and other conditions of employment while collective bargaining negotiations are being conducted. Section 10-153d makes it unlawful for the board to interfere with, restrain or coerce employees in the exercise of their rights under the Teacher Negotiation Act. A similar prohibition appears in the National Labor Relations Act, 29 U.S.C. § 158(a)(1) which makes it an unfair labor practice to interfere with, restrain or coerce employees who seek to pursue their rights under that act. Thus, we can again turn to cases arising under the federal act for guidance.

The National Labor Relations Act makes it an employer's duty to bargain collectively with the chosen representatives of his employees, and since this obligation is exclusive, it exacts the negative duty to treat with no other. Medo Photo Supply Corporation v. N.L.R.B., 321 U.S. 678, 64 S. Ct. 830, 88 L. Ed. 1007; International Ladies' Garment Workers' Union v. N.L.R.B., 108 U.S. App. D.C. 68, 280 F.2d 616, aff'd, 366 U.S. 731, 81 S. Ct. 1603, 6 L. Ed. 2d 762. After a duly authorized collective bargaining representative has been selected, the employer cannot negotiate wages or other terms of employment with individual workers. Medo Photo Supply Corporation v. N.L.R.B., supra, 321 U.S. 684, 64 S. Ct. 830; N.L.R.B. v. United States Sonics Corporation, 312 F.2d 610 (1st Cir.). Thus, an employer interferes with his employees' right to bargain collectively in violation of 29 U.S.C. § 158(a)(1) when he treats directly with employees and grants them a wage increase in return for their promise to repudiate the union which they have designated as their representative. N.L.R.B. v. Katz, 369 U.S. 736, 92 S. Ct. 1107, 8 L. Ed. 2d 230. The statutory obligation thus imposed is to deal with the employees through the union rather than dealing with the union through the employees. Attempts to bypass the representative may be considered evidence of bad faith in the duty to bargain. The conduct proscribed in the *Medo* case was direct negotiation with the employees and bypassing the union. The act does not prohibit an employer from communicating in noncoercive terms with his employees while collective negotiations are in progress. Proctor & Gamble Mfg. Co., 160 N.L.R.B., No. 36, 62 L.R.R.M. 1617. The element of negotiation is critical. Another crucial factor in these cases is whether or not the communication is designed to undermine and denigrate the union. Flambeau Plastics Corporation v. N.L.R.B., 401 F.2d 128 (7th Cir.), cert. denied, 393 U.S. 1019, 89 S. Ct. 625, 21 L. Ed. 2d 563.

The question in the present case is whether the defendant Richter was engaging in direct negotiation with teachers offering something in return for a consideration, dealing with them in a manner calculated to subvert the union, or merely communicating with them without interfering, restraining or coercing them.

The first situation occurred in March, 1969, while negotiations between the parties were continuing. During that month the defendant board proposed a new work year, vacation schedule and salary schedule for department chairmen, coordinating teachers and subject area specialists. The program involved a substantially different length of work day, length of work year and a salary schedule for the personnel involved, and was to take effect July 1, 1969. Before this program was presented to the plaintiff association the defendant Richter called special meetings on March 5 and 6, 1969, and discussed the plan directly with the staff members who would be affected.

It is proper for an employer to discuss his proposals with his employees and to defend his position. Tobasco Prestressed Concrete Co., 177 N.L.R.B., No. 101, 71 L.R.R.M. 1565. Moreover, it is permissible for an employer to discuss certain items with his employees before he presents them to the union. In Little Rock Downtowner, Inc., 168 N.L.R.B., No. 107, 66 L.R.R.M. 1267, an employer had discussed with two employees the possibility of giving them additional duties and additional compensation before any proposal had been made at the bargaining table. The board found that the communication was for the purpose of exchanging ideas and did not constitute negotiation or a violation of the act where the employees understood that the matter would be determined between the employer and the union at the bargaining table.

The law as to attempts to negotiate with employees for the purpose of bypassing or denigrating the union is clear. On this very limited stipulation of facts, however, we cannot conclude that communicating to these special employees some of the details of a new program was unlawful. There is nothing to indicate that the defendant Richter was engaged in negotiations with the teachers nor that this was an attempt to bypass or subvert the union. The proposed new program was discussed later at the bargaining table with the union.

The plaintiff next alleges that the defendant board violated § 10-153d by communicating directly with the teachers concerning the "resource teacher program." On February 13, 1970, during negotiations, the board proposed that the teaching staff be differentiated into two groups, one working more days and more hours per day than heretofore and the other group continuing to work the same days and hours as in the past. This became known as the "extended plan" or "resource teacher program." Despite failure to reach accord on the working conditions of this plan, the board adopted a resolution resolving to implement the program and directing the superintendent to solicit the advice of the plaintiff association and of individual teachers in order to develop a tentative guide for this position. On April 6, 1970, the defendant Richter, acting as superintendent and with the knowledge and assent of the defendant board, informed the entire teaching staff of the West Hartford school system of the adoption of said resolution by distributing copies of it in the Staff Bulletin.

The defendants contend that this conduct on the part of the board and the defendant Richter did not violate the law because the board was merely implementing a policy decision to employ certain personnel as resource teachers. The decision to create a new type of position is a matter which goes to the heart of educational policy. It is true that the salary and working conditions of the resource teachers were mandatory subjects of negotiation, and these matters were actually being negotiated between the plaintiff and the defendants. The adoption of the resolution in question and the communication of this to the teachers and to the plaintiff association did not involve direct negotiations with employees on mandatory subjects of negotiation nor can it be construed as an attempt to bypass the union.

The answer to question (c) is "No."

## Question (d)

The final question presented in this case involves the legality of the board of education's unilateral implementation of their contract proposals after the parties had failed to reach agreement on them. The particular proposals which the board put into effect were those dealing with the salary and working conditions of department chairmen, coordinating teachers and subject area specialists for the school year 1969-70. Contrary to the claims of the plaintiff the stipulated facts do not indicate that the proposals involving the extended program or resource teacher program, first made on February 13, 1970, were "implemented." We have no occasion, therefore, to discuss the subject under question (d).

The duty to bargain under the National Labor Relations Act is similar to the duty to negotiate that is created by our Teacher Negotiation Act. A breach of this duty in the federal area is deemed a refusal to bargain and an unfair labor practice under § 158(a)(5). It is a fundamental tenet of the federal labor law that an employer who unilaterally changes wages and other working conditions which are under negotiation commits a § 158(a)(5) unfair labor practice. N.L.R.B. v. Katz, 369 U.S. 736, 743, 82 S. Ct. 1107, 8 L. Ed. 2d 230. The employer who engages in such conduct circumvents his duty to deal exclusively with the union and is refusing to bargain in fact with the employee organization. Id., 743, 82 S. Ct. 1107.

The defendants contend that there was a legally cognizable impasse in negotiations over these topics such that it had the right to put its plans into operation. There is no acid test for determining whether or not an impasse exists. N.L.R.B. v. Tex-Tan, Inc., 318 F.2d 472 (5th Cir.), describes it as a state of facts in which the parties, despite the best of faith, are simply deadlocked. In most cases, the National Labor Relations Board and the courts have looked at the fact pattern for certain indicia of impasse. Have the parties stopped talking? How many bargaining sessions were held? Have the positions become solidified and the parties intransigent? Was a mediator called in? See American Ship Building Co. v. N.L.R.B., 380 U.S. 300, 85 S. Ct. 955, 13 L. Ed. 2d 855; 44 Tex. L. Rev. 769. Here, although the stipulated facts reveal that the parties had negotiated but were unable to agree on the topics in question, we note that both sides remained at the bargaining table and continued to negotiate on a wide range of topics. Neither party expressed a desire to terminate these discussions. Moreover, the record indicates that mediation was not requested until after the board had suggested implementation of its proposals. It would appear that at this point the parties believed that a continuation of discussions might be fruitful. On this limited statement of facts, we cannot conclude that the parties were "simply deadlocked." Newspaper Drivers & Handlers', Local No. 372 v. N.L.R.B., 404 F.2d 1159 (6th Cir.).

The defendants, however, claim that impasse may exist with reference to a particular issue, and, even though the parties are still negotiating about other topics, the deadlock on the individual issue permits the board to implement its last proposal thereon. This claim is inaccurate. The relevant federal cases deal with the situation where the inability to resolve one or two key issues creates a general impasse, and, despite agreement or willingness to talk about other subjects, it is apparent that further negotiations would not produce a broad meeting of the minds. American Federation of Television & Radio Artists v. N.L.R.B., 129 U.S. App. D.C. 399, 395 F.2d 622; Dallas General Drivers, Local No. 745 v. N.L.R.B., 122 U.S. App. D.C. 417, 355 F.2d 842; N.L.R.B. v. Intercoastal Terminal, Inc., 286 F.2d 954 (5th Cir.). "It cannot be doubted that a deadlock on one critical issue can create as impassable a situation as an inability to agree on several or all issues." American Federation of Television & Radio Artists v. N.L.R.B., supra, 395 F.2d 627 n.13. Some bargaining may go on even though the parties are unable to agree on many topics. But, only if the deadlock on the critical issue demonstrates that there is no realistic possibility that further discussions would be fruitful in bringing the parties together generally on salaries and other conditions of employment, can we conclude that there is an impasse.

Even though an impasse had not been reached, however, it does not follow on the facts in the present case that the defendants were in violation of the statute. While N.L.R.B. v. Katz, supra, holds "that an employer's unilateral change in conditions of employment under negotiation is . . . a violation of § 8(a)(5)," because it is circumvention of the duty to negotiate, the court did, however, note that circumstances might justify unilateral employer action. The language of the court, 369 U.S. on page 745, 82 S. Ct. on page 1113, is significant: "Of course there is no resemblance between the situation wherein an employer, after notice and consultation, 'unilaterally' institutes a wage increase identical with one which the union has rejected as too low. See National Labor Relations Board v. Bradley Washfountain Co., 192 F.2d 144, 150-152 [7th Cir.]; National Labor Relations

Board v. Landis Tool Co., 193 F.2d 279 [3d Cir.]." In the *Bradley Washfountain* case, the employer, before an impasse had been reached, after notice and consultation with the union, unilaterally instituted a wage increase identical to the one which the union had rejected as too low, it was held that the employer did not violate the statute.

In the case at bar the defendant board, in March, 1969, proposed a new work year, vacation schedule and salary schedule for department chairmen, coordinating teachers and subject area specialists involving changes in work day, work year and salary schedules. During April, 1969, the parties negotiated but were unable to agree as to the salary and conditions of employment for these positions and neither party offered further proposals on these subjects. In May and June, 1969, the defendant Richter with the approval of the board hired teachers to fill these positions on the basis of the salary schedule and conditions of employment originally proposed by the board but rejected by the plaintiff. During the 1969-70 school year the persons hired to fill these positions performed duties on the basis of the conditions of employment originally proposed, and received salaries based on the salary schedule originally proposed but on which the parties had been unable to agree in their negotiations. A letter appointing the department head of the high school informed the appointee as follows: "Your salary rate cannot be determined precisely until the salary schedule is finally negotiated with the W.H.E.A. I suspect, however, that you may already know the approximate range in which it will fall and that you are informed as to how you will be placed within that range. For your information, this formula is enclosed." A letter from this department head to the superintendent acknowledged receipt of a check for initial services as a department head and informed the superintendent that the employee was cashing the check "with the express understanding and stipulation that it is received on account as part payment and that it does not necessarily constitute my total compensation for my services in the West Hartford schools for the initial pay period of the 1969-70 school year." On these facts it is clear that the defendants did not "interfere, restrain or coerce employees in derogation" of their rights under the statute. There was no attempt to bypass or denigrate the union. We recognize the fact that the terms of the board's proposal embraced not only subjects which are clearly matters of board policy but mandatory subjects of negotiation as well. Our statutes have given the boards of education a clear mandate to "maintain . . . good public elementary and secondary schools." § 10-220. It was not the intention of the legislature to permit progress in education to be halted until agreement is reached with the union. . . .

## NOTES

1. To what extent, if any, may an employer communicate with his employees concerning the negotiations while negotiations are in progress? In General Electric Co., 150 N.L.R.B. 192 (1964), *enf'd*, 418 F.2d 736 (2d Cir. 1969), *cert. denied*, 397 U.S. 965 (1970), the NLRB held that an employer's communications program, in conjunction with its take it or leave it approach to bargaining, constituted bad faith bargaining. In so ruling, the NLRB stated:

> It is not consistent with . . . [the obligation to bargain in good faith] for an employer to mount a campaign, as Respondent did, both before and during negotiations, for the purposes of disparaging and discrediting the statutory representative in the eyes of its employee constituents, to seek to persuade the employees to exert pressure on the representative to submit to the will of the employer, and to create the

impression that the employer rather than the union is the true protector of the employees' interest. As the Trial Examiner phrased it, the employer's statutory obligation is to deal with the employees through the union, and not with the union through the employees.

The NLRB, however, has held that it is permissible for an employer to communicate its position on the various issues in negotiations as long as the purpose of such communications does not undermine the union's role as the collective bargaining representative of the employees. Proctor & Gamble Mfg. Co., 160 N.L.R.B. 334, 339-41 (1966). In Grand Haven Bd. of Educ., 1973 MERC Lab. Op. 1 (Mich.) the MERC held that an employer did not commit an unfair labor practice when it communicated to bargaining unit employees the offer it had previously presented to the union where such communication was not coercive and did not contain threats or offers of benefit. *Accord,* Town of Sharon, Case No. MUP-275 (Mass. LRC 1972); Ogdensburg City School Dist., 11 PERB ¶ 4667 (N.Y. 1978). On the other hand, in PLRB v. Northern Bedford School Dist., 7 PPER 194 (Pa. PERB 1976), the Pennsylvania Board held that a school board committed an unfair labor practice by disseminating to employees minutes of bargaining sessions which were attached to the employer's bargaining position. The Pennsylvania Commission reasoned as follows:

> To afford public employees the full benefit and protection of the collective bargaining rights guaranteed to them by the Act, it is necessary to insulate them from any efforts by the public employer, direct or indirect, to undercut the authority of the employees' duly selected representative, or fragment the unity of the bargaining unit. Any such action by the public employer is considered to be an unfair labor practice.

*See also* Reno Police Protective Ass'n v. City of Reno, Item No. 52 (Nev. LGE-MRB 1976) (placing misleading newspaper advertisement held violation of employer's duty to bargain in good faith).

2. Does a party commit an unfair labor practice by submitting to the terminal step of a statutory impasse proceeding which was not previously discussed at the bargaining table? In Police Local 798, AFSCME and Town of Enfield, Case No. MEPP 3872 & 3946, 723 GERR 22 (Conn. SBLR 1977), the Connecticut Board, after noting that the statutory scheme "contemplates collective bargaining as the normal and preferred way to resolve labor-management differences" and that binding arbitration is provided as "a last resort when all else fails," stated:

> Any practice that would tend to reduce the chances for resolution through bargaining would therefore work against the grand plan of the Act and if a party were free to raise in arbitration a claim that he had not proposed in bargaining, he might be tempted to. withhold claims from bargaining whenever he expected a more favorable resolution of them in arbitration. Such a result would, we believe, run counter to the policies of the Act. If it is shown that a party withheld a claim from collective bargaining with the intent to present it for the first time in arbitration we should probably hold that this constituted a refusal to bargain in good faith.

In this particular case, however, the Connecticut Board held that the issue presented was outside its jurisdiction in that it should be presented to the Board of Mediation and Arbitration for decision. *See also* Sunnyside Valley Irrigation Dist., Decision No. 314 (Wash. PERC 1977) (union's action in increasing demands and adding new demands violated its duty to bargain in good faith).

3. In State of New Jersey and Council of New Jersey State College Locals, Decision No. 79, 628 GERR 13-22 (N.J. PERC 1975), the New Jersey PERC held that "[a]n adamant position that limits wage proposals to existing levels is not necessarily a failure to negotiate in good faith." The New Jersey PERC further stated:

> Good faith collective negotiations do not require one party to adopt the position of the other; they only require a willingness to negotiate the issue with an open mind and a desire to reach an agreement. The fact that the two parties approach

negotiations with different priorities does not mean that either side is not negotiating in good faith.

*Accord,* PLRB v. Commonwealth of Pennsylvania and State Liquor Control Bd., 367 A.2d 738, 94 L.R.R.M. 2346 (Pa. Commw. Ct. 1977).

## INTERNATIONAL ASSOCIATION OF FIREFIGHTERS
## v. CITY OF HOMESTEAD

Florida Circuit Court, Eleventh Judicial Court
Case No. 72-9285 (1973), *aff'd,* 291 So. 2d 38
(Fla. Ct. App. 1974)

JUDGE GROSSMAN: . . .

### I. *Factual Background of This Litigation*

Plaintiff, Local No. 2010 of the International Association of Firefighters, is a labor organization representing a majority of the persons employed as firefighters by the Defendant, City of Homestead. In January, 1971, Plaintiff sent to the City Manager and the City Councilmen of the City of Homestead a letter seeking recognition as collective bargaining agent for the firefighter employees of the City of Homestead. Subsequently, recognition was granted by the City Council and thereafter the council designated Homestead City Manager, Olaf R. Pearson, as the City's bargaining representative. Negotiations between Pearson and Plaintiff commenced with the mutual understanding that any agreement reached between the parties would be subject to the approval of the City Council.

In November, 1971, after more than 50 hours of negotiations, the City Manager and the Plaintiff reached accord on a collective bargaining agreement. This agreement with the recommendations of the City Manager attached was submitted to the Homestead City Council for its approval. The council met with representatives of Plaintiff on January 10th, 1972 for that purpose. At this meeting, however, the City Council proceeded to renegotiate the contract from the beginning and, in fact, changed every provision of the contract brought up before the meeting terminated. Among the changes made, the Council altered the "bargaining unit" clause (which had been agreed to by City Manager Pearson and Plaintiff) by excluding certain members of the Union from the contract's coverage, and proposed that the entire negotiated wage provisions be stricken from the contract and in substitution therefor these wages unilaterally established by the City Council in their budget hearings of the year before be inserted in the contract. In addition, notwithstanding the fact that the City had recognized the Plaintiff and had bargained with their representatives, the Council directed the City Attorney to write an opinion concerning the city's duty to further recognize and bargain with the Plaintiff.

In response to these actions of the City Council, Plaintiff's representatives walked out of the meeting, and on January 27th, 1972, sent a letter to the City Manager invoking the arbitration provisions of the Firefighters Collective Bargaining Act. However, Defendant City failed to respond to said letter except by passing an Ordinance (No. 72-01-4) designed to supersede the Firefighters Collective Bargaining Law.

. . . .

This action was brought by Plaintiffs to enforce their constitutional right to bargain collectively and to bring the City once again to the bargaining table.

## II. *Issues Before This Court*

This litigation presents several issues to the Court for decision. First, the Court must determine whether the City has performed its obligation of negotiating in good faith with its employees under Article I, Section 6 of the Florida Constitution. Second, the Court must determine if the Firefighters Collective Bargaining Law establishes collective bargaining guidelines in support of the Constitutional obligation and, if so, the respective duties of the parties thereunder. . . .

## III. *The City Did Not Meet Its Duty to Bargain in Good Faith*

Article I, Section 6 of the Constitution of the State of Florida grants public employees the right of collective bargaining. The Florida Supreme Court and the Circuit Courts of this State have on several occasions held that this Section imposes a duty upon the public employer to negotiate in good faith with their employees through an organization such as Plaintiff Union.

This Court finds that the practices followed by the Defendant City in this case did not constitute good faith collective bargaining. The defendant's conduct in attempting to renegotiate the entire contract after the lengthy negotiations between the Union and the City Manager, indicates that the bargaining between the City Manager and the Union was only surface bargaining and not a good faith effort by the City to reach agreement with Plaintiff Union. This change in the ground rules after the lengthy contract negotiations were completed demonstrates that the City Manager's function was not to negotiate with the Union on behalf of the City, but rather *to induce the Union to compromise some of its demands in the belief that they were reaching an agreement and then present these compromises to the City Council where further concessions from the Union were to be demanded.* The refusal of the City to show any confidence in the preliminary agreement reached by its City Manager (its appointed negotiator) and its attempt to renegotiate the entire agreement and gain further concessions from the Union on almost every provision of the preliminary agreement, is not good faith bargaining and does not fulfill the duty imposed by the Florida Constitution. . . . a proper case for the award of punitive damages; this is especially so since the compensatory damages awarded for actual losses to the persons deprived by his conduct are small and difficult to ascertain. The denial of a constitutional right, however, even without any accompanying financial loss, is reprehensible. It is the duty of the Court to protect the constitutional rights of our citizens and to punish those who deliberately subvert these rights. To that end, the Court hereby declares that Councilman Rhodes is a violator of the constitutional rights of the citizens of this State and reprimand him for his unlawful activities which are unbecoming to any American citizen and are even more unworthy in one who purports to be a public servant. There is no higher duty in one who serves in government than obedience to the law. When an elected official acts as Councilman Rhodes has acted, in deliberate violation of his oath of office (that is, to support the Constitutions of this State and of the nation), he sets a shameful and humiliating example of lawlessness.

Since this is the first instance of judicial action upon one of the many recalcitrant public employers who wish to purposely ignore the new collective bargaining mandates of Article I, Section 6 of our State's Constitution this Court will, in addition to the foregoing reprimand, only impose $1.00 as punitive damages upon Councilman Rhodes. Such judgment should, however, be a warning and an indication of the intent of this Court to compel obedience to our laws and to the Constitution of this State in the future, by whatever means may be required. . . .

## NOTES

1. Does a PERB have the authority to issue a "make-whole" order where it finds that an employer has failed to bargain in good faith? In IUE v. NLRB (Tiidee Products), 426 F.2d 1243 (D.C. Cir.), *cert. denied,* 400 U.S. 950 (1970), the Court of Appeals for the District of Columbia held that where an employer's refusal to bargain constituted "a clear and flagrant violation" of the NLRA, a cease-and-desist order was not sufficient. The court noted "that damages can be awarded on an assessment of the contract terms that would have been in effect if the law had been complied with even though the law-violating employer has not yet entered into the contract." On remand, however, the Board declined to issue a "make-whole" remedy, reasoning as follows:

> We have carefully considered the Union's request for a make-whole remedy in light of the record herein and have decided that it is not practicable. The Union suggests that we determine what the parties "*would* have agreed to" in 1967 and thereafter on the basis of a record which contains only a proposed collective-bargaining agreement submitted by the Union to Respondent on December 18, 1967; a chart comparing the wages then paid by Respondent for certain job classifications with those paid by other employers in comparable industries in the Dayton area who were then under contract with the Union; testimonial evidence of employee wage rates as of the date of the hearing herein and a list thereof as of May 25, 1970; certain testimony about the time required to negotiate a first contract; and several charts and tables depicting nationwide changes in wages and benefits since 1967. We know of no way by which the Board could ascertain with even approximate accuracy from the above what the parties "*would* have agreed to" if they had bargained in good faith. Inevitably, the Board would have to decide from the above what the parties "*should* have agreed to." And this, the court stated, the Board must not do.

Tiidee Products, Inc., 194 N.L.R.B. 1234 (1972). Nevertheless, the Board devised certain "alternative remedies . . . [to] undo some of the baneful effects pointed out by the court as having resulted from Respondent's 'clear and flagrant violation of the law.' " The Board thus ordered the employer to (1) mail copies of the notice to employees to all employees in the unit, (2) give the union reasonable access to the employer's bulletin boards during the period of contract negotiations, and (3) reimburse the union and the NLRB for litigation costs and expenses.

In Duval Teachers United v. Duval County School Bd., 3 FPER 96 (Fla. PERC 1977), the Florida PERC held that a school board's flagrant violations of its bargaining obligations under the Florida Act required the issuance of an extraordinary remedy. The Florida PERC stated:

> Due to the flagrant nature of respondent's violation, and length of time during which the employees were deprived of an opportunity to reach an agreement (over a year since the union's request to bargain on March 16, 1976), an extraordinary remedy is required. The Commission will therefore require the respondent to bargain in good faith not only as to wages, hours, and terms and conditions of employment for the future, but also to bargain in good faith with respect to the monetary benefits sought by the employee representative for the employees since March 16, 1976.

2. Does an employer have an obligation to bargain in good faith following the issuance of a fact finder's recommendations? The MERC in City of Dearborn, 1972 MERC Lab. Op. 749, responded affirmatively, stating:

> Statutory fact finding may be invoked only after the parties have bargained and a genuine impasse has occurred. Although the duty to bargain does not mean that

parties must engage in futile bargaining in the face of a genuine impasse, changed circumstances may develop, and therefore require compliance with the bargaining requirement. . . . Even though there may be a strike, the duty to bargain may not necessarily be suspended. . . . Just as a strike may create conditions in which the parties would be more willing to make concessions to compromise the matters in difference, the fact finder's recommendations may enlighten or persuade them of the reasonableness or unreasonableness of their bargaining position. The fact finder's report, thus, is the functional equivalent of a strike and may change the factual situation regarding "the negotiation of an agreement, or any question arising thereunder." MCLA 423, 215; MSA 17.455(15). It must be given the same serious consideration as the initial bargaining proposals. Therefore, there is an affirmative obligation to bargain in good faith about the substantive recommendations of the report of a statutory fact finder.

*Accord,* East Hartford Educ. Ass'n v. East Hartford Bd. of Educ., 30 Conn. Supp. 63, 299 A.2d 554 (Conn. Super. Ct. 1972).

The MERC further held that "the duty to bargain requires that the employer make a reasonable effort in some direction to close the differences with the union." Does this mean that the employer in order to meet its obligation to bargain in good faith must modify its position on some of the issues? If so, would this be consistent with the statutory provision that the duty to bargain "does not compel either party to agree to a proposal or require the making of a concession"? Would an employer meet its obligation to bargain in good faith if it stated in detail its reasons for rejecting the fact finder's recommendations? In Lamphere School District, 1978 MERC Lab. Op. 194 (Mich.), the Michigan Commission stated that "[w]here a party in good faith intends to resolve its differences with its bargaining adversary, although not accepting the fact finder's recommendations, there is no bad-faith refusal to bargain."

3. In Sanilac County Road Comm'n, 1969 MERC Lab. Op. 461, the MERC held that an employer's sincere, but mistaken, belief that a given proposal was illegal does not constitute a valid defense to an unfair labor practice charge.

## 2. SELECTION AND AUTHORITY OF THE PARTIES' REPRESENTATIVES

### CITY OF SAGINAW

Michigan Employment Relations Commission
1969 MERC Lab. Op. 293

Trial Examiner Joseph Bixler: The charge in this matter was filed by the Charging Party on November 19, 1968. The charge alleges a violation of Section 10(e) of PERA, and reads as follows:

"At meetings between parties hereto, conducted January 9, 15, February 15, and October 30, 1968, the City agreed to a 'modified agency shop' in return for several concessions made by the Union. The City representative later repudiated his agreement and contended that he did not have authority to bind the City and refuse[d] to submit Union proposal to City Council. The City is, therefore, guilty of refusing to bargain in good faith in that they:
1. Did not provide a Negotiator that had authority to negotiate.
2. Repudiated a previously agreed provision.
3. Refused and failed to submit Union proposals to City Commission."

## The Facts

The parties in 1966, began negotiating on a collective bargaining contract. During the years of 1967 and 1968, various economic matters were agreed upon and put into effect. The non-economic portions of the contract, however, were not completed during either of these years.

In January, 1968, the parties were at a standstill, and a Mediator of the State Labor Mediation Board was called in, and tentative agreement was finally reached on all of the non-economic matters of the contract in May, of 1968. Among the various matters tentatively agreed upon between the parties was a "modified agency shop." The parties then went to economic matters and an agreement was reached which was rejected by the membership of the Charging Party. Final economic agreement was reached in July, of 1968.

On September 10, 1968, the following agency shop provision was agreed upon:

> "Requirements of Union membership.
> All employees *covered by this agreement who are members of the Union at the time this agreement is ratified or who hereafter become members thereof during the term of this agreement must as a condition of continued employment retain their membership in the Union for the duration of this agreement.* New employees covered by this agreement who fail to acquire or maintain membership in the Union shall be required, as a condition of employment beginning on the 91st day following the beginning of such employment or the date of the signing of this agreement, whichever is later, to pay to the Union each month a service charge as a contribution towards the administration of this agreement and the representative of such employee. The service charge for the first month shall be an amount equal to the Union's regular and usual initiation fee and monthly dues and for each month thereafter, an amount equal to the regular and usual monthly dues."
> (Emphasis added)

Apparently, after the last bargaining meeting, by agreement of the parties, the City of Saginaw undertook to type up the final agreement. The Charging Party received its copy of the final draft of the agreement in September, 1968. The City negotiators explained that the reason that it took so long to type up the agreement was because they were engaged in negotiations with other Unions.

After the final draft of the agreement had been checked through by the Charging Party, it was then ready for submission to the City Council. In mid-October, 1968 Jack Houk, the head of the City's Personnel Department and the chief negotiator for the City, informed the Charging Party that they had presented another contract to the Council for approval involving the Registered Nurses in the City hospital, and that the Council had rejected the union security provisions of the nurses contract which were similar to the one contained in the contract involving the unit represented by the Charging Party. Houk informed the Charging Party that he did not think there was any sense in submitting the contract reached by the Charging Party and the City's negotiators to the Council as long as it contained the union security provisions. Houk further informed the representatives of the Charging Party that as the City Council in all likelihood would not accept the union security provision, the Charging Party could take back those concessions that had been given by the Charging Party in exchange for the union security clause, and that he, Houk, was prepared to negotiate something else in exchange for the Charging Party relinquishing the union security clause.

This proposition by Houk was rejected by the Charging Party. Sometime during the month of November or December, 1968, the agreement that had been reached between the City's negotiators and the Charging Party was submitted to the Council, and the union security clause was rejected by the Council by a five to two vote.

On January 2, 1969, Houk met again with the Charging Party's representatives. Houk again offered to give back the management rights clause and the no strike clause of the proposed agreement that had been given to the City in return for agreement on agency shop. This was again rejected by the Charging Party.

### Conclusion and Recommendation

The main thrust of the charge as filed by the Charging Party is that the bargaining representative of the City did not have sufficient authority to commit the City to matters agreed upon at the bargaining table. It is urged that because the bargaining representative of the City agreed to the union security clause as set forth above, that the City was thereby committed and the Council had no right to refuse to agree to this clause. A similar argument was made to the Board by the Charging Party in City of Saginaw,1967 Labor Opinions, 465. In that case, the Trial Examiner stated:

> Obviously, the negotiating team must receive instructions from the governing body and submit oral or written reports to it, if its concessions and tentative commitments are to be meaningful, that it need not, and probably cannot, be vested with final authority to bind the public employer, since that would seem to involve an illegal delegation of the lawmaking power of the City Council. People vs. Sell, 310 Michigan, 305, 17 NW2d 193 (1945); C. F. Millard vs. Guy, 334 Michigan, 649.

I agree that as indicated by the Trial Examiner in the earlier *Saginaw* case cited above, the requirement that the governing body be present at the bargaining table would be far too burdensome in public employment. I am also of the opinion that if a governmental body gave its negotiator absolute right to make a labor agreement it would be improperly delegating the legislative function as indicated in the *Saginaw* case. The undersigned however, does find that, as stated in the *City of Saginaw* decision by the Trial Examiner, the bargaining representative of a governmental body is under an obligation to keep that governmental body advised as to the progress of negotiations. Further, in those cases where, as here, the governmental body has taken the position that it will not agree on principle to some contractual provision within the range of mandatory bargaining, that the bargaining agent be informed of this fact, and that at the request of the bargaining agent, the governmental body itself will meet at the negotiating table to discuss the rejected subject matter.

In the case at hand, the undersigned is of the opinion that the Charging Party had no opportunity to bargain in regard to union security in the form of agency shop, a mandatory subject of bargaining. Oakland County Sheriff's Department & Oakland County Board of Supervisors, 1968 Labor Opinions 1. This deprivation of the bargaining right of the Charging Party does not arise from the rejection of union security, but from the City negotiators removal of the subject from the bargaining table without affording the bargaining agent the opportunity to bargain or discuss the subject matter with those making the rejection.

The Charging Party should have requested bargaining on union security with the City Council, and that body would under these circumstances, have been obligated to bargain on the subject.

Under the circumstances evidenced by this record I do not believe, however, that a bargaining order should be granted. My reasons for so concluding are that: (1) The union did not request bargaining on the matter of "agency shop" with the city Council after they were notified of the rejection of such a contract provision. (2) The clause contained in the proposed agreement negotiated by the Charging Party and the City negotiators and presented to the City Council, is one not permitted by PERA.

[The Trial Examiner's decision was adopted by the MERC in the absence of exceptions.]

## NOTES

1. Does the principal case stand for the proposition that a public employer (city council, board of education, etc.) has to negotiate with the union on each and every proposal within the mandatory area of negotiations which its designated representative has rejected at the bargaining table? If so, does the ruling in the instant case undermine the right of the employer to designate its representative for the purposes of collective bargaining? Suppose a union agrees to a proposal but later seeks to withdraw it on the basis that the membership would never accept it. Would the employer then have the right, upon making a request, "to bargain or discuss the subject with those making the rejection," *i.e.*, the rank-and-file?

2. A year after the decision in *City of Saginaw*, the MERC in City of Detroit, Bd. of Fire Comm'rs, 1970 MERC Lab. Op. 953, 957, stated:

> It is not required that Municipal Councils, Commissions and Boards bargain directly with the representatives of their employees. This may be done by administrative employees or other agents who are clothed with authority to participate in effective collective bargaining but reserving final approval to the governing body. Such is common practice in the private sector, and it is effective and workable.

Does this statement conflict with the holding in *City of Saginaw?*

3. The Wyoming Fire Fighter Bargaining Law provides that a city, town, or county is required to negotiate in good faith through its corporate authorities with the bargaining agent chosen by a majority of the firefighters. The law defines the term "corporate authorities" to "mean the council, commission or other proper officials of any city, town, or county, whose duty or duties it is to establish wages, salaries, rates of pay, working conditions, and other conditions of employment of firefighters." WYO. STAT. § 27-265(b). In Nation v. State of Wyoming ex rel. Fire Fighters Local 279, 518 P.2d 931, 86 L.R.R.M. 2574 (Wyo. S. Ct. 1974), the mayor appointed the personnel director, the city treasurer, the assistant city attorney, and the fire chief as the city's representatives for negotiations with the fire fighters local. In upholding the union's contention that these individuals were not "corporate authorities" within the meaning of the Wyoming Act, the Wyoming Supreme Court held that the corporate authorities were required to negotiate in person with the representatives of the fire fighters union and that the corporate authorities could not be represented through agents.

4. The Tennessee Education Professional Negotiations Act appears to preclude either party from using outside representatives for the purposes of negotiations. Thus, Section 3(e) provides:

> . . . The term "negotiator" means that person or persons selected by the board of education and the professional employees' organization to do the negotiating. The board may select the superintendent, any member of the board, or fulltime system-wide employees as prescribed in Section 6. The professional employees' organization may select from among those who are members of the organization. 1978 TENN. PUB. ACTS, ch. 570, § 3(e).

Are these restrictions on who may sit as the parties' representatives at the bargaining table constitutional? *See* Kenai Peninsula Borough School Dist. v. Kenai Peninsula Borough School Dist. Classification Ass'n, 1979-80 PBC ¶ 36,512 (Alaska S. Ct. 1979), discussed at p. 251, *supra*.

5. Most commentators have recommended that the ultimate policy-making body, whether it be a school board, city council or board of county commissioners, should not directly participate in collective bargaining. As one commentator observed,

> The problems arising from the delegation of bargaining to staff personnel are far outweighed by greater proficiency, objectivity and continuity. Elected officials are rarely trained in personnel matters. . . . Further, elected officials offer no guarantee of continuity for future bargaining sessions.

Mulcahy, *A Municipality's Rights and Responsibilities Under the Wisconsin Municipal Labor Law*, 49 MARQ. L. REV. 512, 515 (1966). Herbert Haber, the former Director of Labor Relations for New York City, made the following comments concerning the need for establishing a separate labor relations function in the public sector:

> [D]ealing with the unions is a full-time job requiring professional help. Anyone who has authority over a given agency is well-advised to secure full-time professional help or regular professional consultations, whatever he can manage. In running a large scale public operation, he has innumerable responsibilities of which only one small part is dealing with the union. The union, on the other hand, devotes its full time to representing its members and can therefore concentrate on the specifics of each individual matter. Professional assistance from people who can work exclusively on collective bargaining problems is a must for dealing effectively with the unions.

Haber, *The Relevance of Private Sector Experience to Public Sector Collective Bargaining*, in Proceedings of a Conference held by the Institute of Management and Labor Relations, The State University of New Jersey, May 23, 1968, p. 7.

6. May either party refuse to negotiate with the other party because it objects to the presence of one or more members of the other party's negotiating team? In City of Superior, Decision No. 8325 (Wis. ERC 1967), the Wisconsin Employment Relations Commission stated:

> Personal differences arising between the representatives of the parties engaged in negotiations with respect to wages, hours and working conditions of municipal employes do not constitute a valid reason for refusing to bargain in good faith. Both municipal employers and representatives of their employes have the right to designate whomever they choose to represent them at the bargaining table. To allow either or both parties to refuse to bargain with each other because of alleged or actual conflicts between their representatives would be contrary to the intent and purpose of Section 111.70. . . .

In Fort Jackson Laundry Facility, A/SLMR Decision No. 242 (1972), the Assistant Secretary of Labor held that with respect to formal discussions under Section 10(e) of Executive Order 11491, "The right to choose its representatives at such discussions must be left to the discretion of the exclusive bargaining representative and not to the whim of management." *Accord*, United States Postal Service (Tampa, Florida), 202 N.L.R.B. No. 823 (1973); City of Reno, Item #86 (Nev. LGE-MRB 1978).

7. In most jurisdictions it is an unfair labor practice for a managerial or supervisory employee who is excluded from the bargaining unit to be a member of the union's bargaining team. *But see* Commonwealth of Pennsylvania v. PLRB, 100 L.R.R.M. 2930 (Pa. Commw. Ct. 1979) (participation by first level supervisors as members of rank and file bargaining team not improper under Pennsylvania Act). On the other hand, would it similarly be improper for an employer to have a bargaining unit employee sitting on its bargaining team? In Department of Health, Education and Welfare, Office of the Secretary, A/SLMR No. 701 (1976), the Assistant Secretary of Labor for Labor-Management Relations held that Executive Order 11491 did not preclude an

agency from selecting a bargaining unit employee to participate on the agency's bargaining team. Accordingly, the Assistant Secretary held that an exclusive bargaining representative committed an unfair labor practice "by refusing to negotiate because a bargaining unit employee was serving as a member of the management negotiating team."

8. The NLRB has held that a union can include on its bargaining team "observers" from other unions representing an employer's employees. General Electric Co., 173 N.L.R.B. 253 (1968), enf'd as modified, 412 F.2d 512 (2d Cir. 1969). This tactic, commonly referred to as coordinated bargaining, is discussed in Comment, *Coordinated — Coalition Bargaining: Theory, Legality, Practice and Economic Effects*, 55 MINN. L. REV. 599 (1971). What are the advantages and disadvantages of coordinated bargaining in the public sector? *Cf.* City of Reno, Item #86 (Nev. LGE-MRB 1978) (union could select one bargaining team to represent several bargaining units). Would the same legal principles be applicable to a public employer if it sought to include a taxpayer's representative or a representative of another public employer on its bargaining team?

# 3. DUTY TO SUPPLY INFORMATION

## SAGINAW TOWNSHIP BOARD OF EDUCATION

Michigan Employment Relations Commission
1970 MERC Lab. Op. 127

... The Charging Party [Saginaw Township Education Association] takes exceptions to the Trial Examiner's decision that the Respondent [Saginaw Township Board of Education] did not violate the Act by its refusal to submit to the union certain information requested. The information is set forth as:

1. Audited financial statements for the fiscal year ending June 30, 1967, including the general fund balance sheet;
2. The proposed budget for the ensuing fiscal year;
3. A list of the teachers who had left the school system; and
4. A list of the new teachers who had been hired for the 1967-68 school year.

The Trial Examiner held that all requests by the Charging Party for information must be set forth in writing.

The Employer in its cross-exceptions contends that it had a right to insist that demands for information by the Charging Party be specific written requests for information so that the Respondent could properly evaluate each request and therefore be able to give an answer to the Charging Party.

The National Labor Relations Board and federal courts have, over a period of many years, wrestled with the subject of the employer's duty to submit information to the bargaining agent. It is clear that there is a duty on the employer to furnish relevant data and information to the bargaining agents of its employees. Whitin Machinery Works, 108 N.L.R.B. 1537, 34 L.R.R.M. 1251 (1954), enf'd 217 F.2d 593; General Controls, 88 N.L.R.B. 1341, 25 L.R.R.M. 1475 (1950); International Telephone & Telegraph Corporation v. N.L.R.B., 62 L.R.R.M. 1339, enf'd in part, 65 L.R.R.M. 3002 (1967); National Labor Relations Board v. Item Company, 108 N.L.R.B. 1634, 34 L.R.R.M. 1255, enf'd, 220 F.2d 956 (5th Cir., 1955); Aluminum Ore Co., 39 N.L.R.B. 1286, 10 L.R.R.M. 49, enf'd 131 F.2d 485, 11 L.R.R.M. 693 (7th Cir., 1942).

In the above cases, the National Labor Relations Board and the courts have laid down the general rule that an employer is required on request to furnish a union with sufficient data with respect to wage rates, job classifications and other allied matters to permit the union to:

1. Bargain understandingly;
2. Police the administration of the contract; and
3. Prepare for coming negotiations.

A union is not required to show the purpose of their requested data unless the data appears to be clearly irrelevant. The data should also be reasonably available from the employer's records. General Controls, *supra;* Oliver Corporation, 162 N.L.R.B. No. 68, 64 L.R.R.M. 1092 (1967); KCMO Broadcasting, 145 N.L.R.B. 550, 55 L.R.R.M. 1001 (1963).

The federal courts and the NLRB have held that unions need not place their request for relevant information in writing. In the International Telephone & Telegraph Corporation, *supra,* decision, the employer had suggested that the union incorporate its request for information in a letter to the company so that the employer could give it to its counsel for review. The letter was submitted by the union after unfair labor practice charges had been filed. The NLRB held that the company had unlawfully refused to give the union the requested information. The NLRB's order was eventually enforced by the U.S. Court of Appeals for the Third Circuit, which held as follows:

"We have considered the petitioner's argument that the union's failure to put its request for information in writing until after the unfair labor practice charges had been filed shows that the earlier oral requests for such data were not made in good faith and were merely 'to set the company up' for an unfair labor practice charge. This argument is without merit. *No rule requires that requests for information be in writing."* (Emphasis added)

While the above cases deal with private employees, it is clear that in the field of public employment much of the information is in the public domain. Records of public employers such as school boards, in the absence of specific statutes, do not enjoy immunity from public scrutiny. Any citizen or taxpayer may review the public records of a school board. The statutes involving the Board of Education deal specifically with this matter.

Section 562 of the School Code of 1955, M.S.A. Section 15.5362, provides, among other things, as follows:

"All records of the board shall be public records subject to inspection under Section 750.492 of the Compiled Laws of 1948 (CL 48, Section 350.562)."

Section 750.492, as referred to above, reads as follows:

"Any officer having the custody of any county, city or township records of this state who shall when requested fail or neglect to furnish proper and reasonable facilities for the inspection and examination of records and files in his office and for making memoranda of transcripts therefrom during the usual business hours which shall not be less than four (4) hours per day, to any person having occasion to make examination of them for any lawful purpose, shall be guilty of a misdemeanor, punishable by imprisonment in a county jail of not more than one (1) year or by a fine of not more than five hundred ($500) dollars."

It is accordingly clear that the Charging Party was entitled to receive the information requested above. We reject Respondent's cross-exceptions that the Employer is entitled to evaluate each request for information. The duty to request and supply information is part and parcel of the fundamental duty to bargain. This duty is not an additional negotiable subject matter of the bargaining process. The employer cannot make the subject of bargaining the submission of relevant data needed by a labor organization. Washtenaw Community College and Washtenaw College Education Association, 1968 MERC L. Op. 956.

The employer would also impose the condition that the Union must have no reasonable way to obtain the information except from the employer's records. We reject this contention for the reasons set forth above. Whitin Machinery Works, *supra;* Aluminum Ore Co., *supra;* Curtiss-Wright Corporation v. National Labor Relations Board, 59 L.R.R.M. 2433, 347 F.2d 61 (3rd Cir., 1965); J.I. Case Company v. National Labor Relations Board, 253 F.2d 149 (7th Cir., 1958).

We also reject the Employer's proposed criteria for the additional reasons that the information requested is in the public domain, and there should be an obligation on the part of a labor organization to seek alternative methods of obtaining the information prior to the request made to the employer. Alternative sources of information could require the Charging Party to use secondhand data which would impede rather than expedite intelligent bargaining.

There was no showing in this case that any of the information was available for public inspection in a public location. When information is accessible to the public, we have held that a public employer is not required to furnish it. Washtenaw Community College and Washtenaw College Education Association, *supra....*

## NOTES

1. *Accord,* Timberlane Regional Education Ass'n v. Crompton, 88 L.R.R.M. 3095 (N.H. S. Ct. 1974) (school board ordered to provide teachers association with names and addresses of all employees, including substitutes employed during strike, in order to permit association to review credentials of substitutes, etc.); Community Mental Health Center of Beaver County, 8 PPER 114 (Pa. LRB 1977). *But see* Doolin v. Board of Cooperative Educational Services, Second Supervisory Dist. of Suffolk Cty., 1977-78 PBC ¶ 36,392 (N.Y. App. Div. 1978) (union not entitled to comparative analysis of school district salaries, class size, etc. which was designed to assist the participating districts in negotiations).

2. The failure to provide relevant information in *timely* fashion is also considered to be an unfair labor practice. Westwood Community Schools, 1972 MERC Lab. Op. 313; Kohler Co., 128 N.L.R.B. 1062, 1074 (1960), *aff'd in relevant part,* 300 F.2d 699, *cert. denied,* 370 U.S. 911 (1962).

3. The Supreme Court in NLRB v. Truitt Mfg. Co., 351 U.S. 149 (1956), held that the employer committed an unfair labor practice under the NLRA when it failed, upon request, to supply financial data in support of its claim that it could not afford to pay higher wages. In so ruling, the Court stated:

We think that in determining whether the obligation of good faith bargaining has been met, the Board has a right to consider an employer's refusal to give information about its financial status. While Congress did not compel agreement between employer and bargaining representatives, it did require collective bargaining in the hope that agreements would result. Section 204(a)(1) of the Act admonishes both employers and employees to "exert every reasonable effort to make and maintain agreements concerning rates of pay, hours, and working conditions...." In their effort to reach an agreement here, both the union and the company treated the company's ability to pay increased wages as highly relevant. The ability of an employer to increase wages without injury to his business is a commonly considered factor in wage negotiations. Claims for increased wages have sometimes been abandoned because of an employer's unsatisfactory business condition; employees have even voted to accept wage decreases because of such conditions.

Good-faith bargaining necessarily requires that claims made by either bargainer should be honest claims. This is true about an asserted inability to pay an increase in wages. If such an argument is important enough to present in the give and take of bargaining, it is important enough to require some sort of proof of its accuracy. And it would certainly not be farfetched for a trier of fact to reach the conclusion that bargaining lacks good faith when an employer mechanically repeats a claim of inability to pay without making the slightest effort to substantiate the claim. Such has been the holding of the Labor Board since shortly after the passage of the Wagner Act. In *Pioneer Pearl Button Co.,* decided in 1936, where the employer's representative relied on the company's asserted "poor financial condition," the Board said: "He did no more than take refuge in the assertion that the respondent's financial condition was poor; he refused either to prove his statement, or to permit independent verification. This is not collective bargaining." 1 N.L.R.B. 837, 842-843. This was the position of the Board when the Taft-Hartley Act was passed in 1947 and has been its position ever since. We agree with the Board that a refusal to attempt to substantiate a claim of inability to pay increased wages may support the finding of a failure to bargain in good faith.

*Accord,* Sergeant Bluff-Luton Community School Dist., Case No. 984 (Iowa PERB 1977); Macomb County Community College, 1972 MERC Lab. Op. 775 (Mich.) (union's right to financial information dependent on employer's claim of inability to pay).

4. Does an employer's obligation to provide relevant information to a union extend to a request for information concerning a grievance which is being processed in accordance with the contractual grievance procedure? In NLRB v. Acme Indus. Co., 385 U.S. 432, 87 S. Ct. 565, 17 L. Ed. 2d 495 (1967), the Court answered this question affirmatively, stating that the "duty to bargain unquestionably extends beyond the period of contract negotiations and applies to labor-management relations during the term of an agreement." *Accord,* Commonwealth of Mass., Dep't of Public Works, Case No. SUP-20 (Mass. LRC 1972); Joint School Dist. No. 9, Merton School, Decision No. 15155-D (Wis. ERC 1978) (unfair labor practice to refuse to provide tapes of disciplinary meetings where requested in order to process grievance).

5. An employer is not required to supply the information in the same form requested as long as it is submitted in a manner which is not unreasonably burdensome to interpret. Sergeant Bluff-Luton Community School Dist., Case No. 984 (Iowa PERB 1977); Westinghouse Electric Corp., 129 N.L.R.B. 850 (1960); McLean-Arkansas Lumber Co., 109 N.L.R.B. 1022 (1954).

6. In Detroit Edison Co. v. NLRB, 100 L.R.R.M. 2728 (S. Ct. 1979), the Supreme Court held that the NLRB abused its discretion in ordering an employer to provide a union, upon request, with the questions used on an aptitude test battery, as well as the answer sheets. The Court held that the company's interest in maintaining the confidentiality of this information outweighed the union's interest in obtaining it. The Court noted that "[a] union's bare assertion that it needs information to process a grievance does not automatically oblige the employer to supply all the information in the manner requested." In rejecting the NLRB's contention that the confidentiality of the information requested would be adequately protected, the Court stated:

> ... The restrictions barring the Union from taking any action that might cause the test to fall into the hands of employees who have taken or are likely to take them are only as effective as the sanctions available to enforce them. In this instance, there is substantial doubt whether the Union would be subject to a contempt citation were it to ignore the restrictions. . . . Moreover, the Union clearly would not be accountable in either contempt or unfair labor practice proceedings for the most realistic vice inherent in the Board's remedy — the danger of inadvertent leaks.

The Court also held that the company could require an employee's consent before releasing an employee's test score to the union "[i]n the light of the sensitive nature of testing information" and "the minimal burden that compliance with the Company's offer would have placed on the Union."

In sharp contrast to the Supreme Court's decision in *Detroit Edison,* the Minnesota Supreme Court in Operating Eng'rs Local 49 v. City of Minneapolis, 305 Minn. 364, 233 N.W.2d 748 (1975), after noting that "the duty to meet and negotiate in good faith includes the obligation to provide information which is necessary to intelligent functioning in the bargaining process," held that an employee organization that was challenging the validity of a civil service examination is entitled to access to "the questions and the answer key to the civil service examination." The court noted "that the public interest in protecting the confidentiality of civil service examinations can be adequately served if respondent is directed to refrain from disclosing the requested information to applicants who will take this examination in the future."

7. Articles examining an employer's duty to furnish information under the NLRA include Cox, *The Duty to Bargain in Good Faith,* 71 HARV. L. REV. 1401 (1958); Huston, *Furnishing Information as an Element of Employer's Good Faith Bargaining,* 35 U. DET. L.J. 471 (1958); Miller, *Employer's Duty to Furnish Economic Data to Unions — Revisited,* 17 LAB. L.J. 272 (1966).

## 4. UNILATERAL ACTION

Once a union has been duly designated as the collective bargaining representative for a given group of employees, the employer is thereafter obligated to negotiate and bargain in good faith with the union with respect to matters that are negotiable. Concomitant with this obligation is the requirement that an employer refrain from taking unilateral action with respect to matters that are subject to negotiation without first offering to negotiate with the union. Thus, in NLRB v. Katz, 369 U.S. 736, 82 S. Ct. 1107, 8 L. Ed. 2d 230 (1962), the Court stated:

The duty "to bargain collectively" enjoined by § 8(a) (5) is defined by § 8(d) as the duty to "meet . . . and confer in good faith with respect to wages, hours, and other terms and conditions of employment." Clearly, the duty thus defined may be violated without a general failure of subjective good faith; for there is no occasion to consider the issue of good faith if a party has refused even to negotiate *in fact* — "to meet . . . and confer" — about any of the mandatory subjects. A refusal to negotiate *in fact* as to any subject which is within § 8(d), and about which the union seeks to negotiate, violates § 8(a) (5) though the employer has every desire to reach agreement with the union upon an overall collective agreement and earnestly and in all good faith bargains to that end. We hold that an employer's unilateral change in conditions of employment under negotiation is similarly a violation under § 8(a)(5), for it is a circumvention of the duty to negotiate which frustrates the objectives of § 8(a)(5) much as does a flat refusal.

. . . Unilateral action by an employer without prior discussion with the union does amount to a refusal to negotiate about the affected conditions of employment under negotiation, and must of necessity obstruct bargaining, contrary to the congressional policy. It will often disclose an unwillingness to agree with the union. It will rarely be justified by any reason of substance. It follows that the board may hold such unilateral action to be an unfair labor practice in violation of § 8(a) (5), without also finding the employer guilty of over-all subjective bad faith. While we do not foreclose the possibility that there may be circumstances under which the Board could or should accept as excusing or justifying unilateral action, no such case is presented here.

Citing *Katz,* the Connecticut State Board of Labor Relations in Town of Stratford, Decision No. 1069 (1972), observed that "[i]t is well recognized that unilateral employer action upon a matter which is the subject of current collective bargaining between the parties constitutes a failure and refusal to bargain in good faith upon the issue in question." *Accord,* Borough of Naugatuck, Conn. State

Bd. of Lab. Rel. Decision No. 769 (1967) (unilateral adoption of a new classification plan while negotiations were in progress). *See generally* West Hartford Educ. Ass'n v. DeCourcy, *supra* pp. 386-91.

## BOARD OF COOPERATIVE EDUCATIONAL SERVICES OF ROCKLAND COUNTY v. NEW YORK STATE PERB

Court of Appeals of New York
41 N.Y.2d 753, 363 N.E.2d 1174 (1977)

COOKE, Judge.

We hold that, after the expiration of an employment agreement, it is not a violation of a public employer's duty to negotiate in good faith to discontinue during the negotiations for a new agreement the payment of automatic annual salary increments, however, long standing the practice of paying such increments may have been. Accordingly, it was error for the Public Employment Relations Board (PERB) to order the petitioner in this proceeding to negotiate in good faith because of its failure to pay increments after expiration of an employment agreement.

This labor dispute arose between the Board of Cooperative Educational Services of Rockland County (BOCES), a public employer, and the BOCES Staff Council (the Staff Council), the recognized negotiating representative of instructional employees of BOCES. Since 1968, the parties have been signatories to a series of four agreements, the most recent of which covered the period from July 1, 1972 to June 30, 1974. A progression of automatic step increments for employees in the unit has been provided for in each of these agreements. In addition, in prior years, when a contract between the parties had expired, even if a successor agreement had not yet been reached, BOCES paid the automatic step increments to returning unit employees.

In March, 1974, the Staff Council advised BOCES that it wished to negotiate a successor contract to the 1972-1974 agreements. Prior to the commencement of negotiations, on June 19, 1974, BOCES adopted a resolution which provided that pending the execution of a new agreement or September 1, 1974, whichever came earlier, the provisions of the agreement expiring June 30, 1974 would be recognized, including salary and salary rates in effect on June 30, 1974, for the period herein contemplated. Pursuant to this resolution, which was subsequently extended, BOCES maintained the salaries at the rate in effect on June 30, 1974 during negotiations for the successor agreement, but refused to pay the step increments to returning unit employees. Because of this refusal, the Staff Council filed with PERB an improper practice charge against BOCES alleging that the latter had unilaterally withdrawn a previously enjoyed benefit — automatic salary increments — while a successor agreement was being negotiated, in violation of section 209-a (subd. 1, par. [d]) of the Civil Service Law (the Public Employees' Fair Employment Act).

At the hearing, BOCES raised an affirmative defense that the right to the salary increments was extinguished when the most recent agreement expired on June 30, 1974. This argument was rejected by the hearing officer, who reasoned that the duty of an employer to maintain the *status quo* during the course of negotiations is not directly concerned with whether or not contractual obligations survive a contract's expiration. Authority for this reasoning was based on PERB's decision in *Matter of Triborough Bridge & Tunnel Auth. (District Council 37 & Local 1396)* (5 PERB 3064 [1972]). In that decision, PERB held that it is a violation of a public employer's duty to negotiate in good faith for it to alter, unilaterally during negotiations, terms and conditions of employment which include a long-standing and continued practice of providing annual salary increments, even though the agreement under which such increments were negotiated has expired. The hearing officer, applying this decision, commonly referred to as the "Triborough Doctrine", found that BOCES had violated its duty to negotiate in good faith and recommended that it be ordered to negotiate in good faith, such order contemplating that it would cease and desist from refusing to pay the increments and would forthwith pay such increments retroactive to the commencement of the 1974-1975 school year.

Thereafter, PERB indorsed the reasoning of the hearing officer and his conclusions of law. It also reasserted the validity of the Triborough "doctrine" or proposition and further noted that it makes no difference under said proposition whether or not the practice of paying increments was ever embodied in an agreement. In addition, while recognizing that it could not compel BOCES to pay the increments, it rejected BOCES' request that it limit its order to a direction that BOCES negotiate in good faith. PERB's order, therefore, stated in relevant part: "we order respondent to negotiate in good faith, such order contemplating that respondent will cease and desist from refusing to pay increments to those of its employees entitled to increments under the recently expired agreement and that it will forthwith pay to such employees increments retroactive to the commencement of the 1974-75 school year".

BOCES thereafter commenced an article 78 proceeding seeking to annul and vacate PERB's order. . . .

. . . [W]e granted leave . . in order to consider PERB'S so-called "Triborough Doctrine". At the outset, it should be noted that the Federal cases involving the private sector relied on by the Staff Council and PERB are not dispositive. That there are problems peculiar to public employers is manifested by the number of cases before this court concerning the financial difficulties of these employers. In addition to financial pressures, other factors enter in the budgetary considerations of such employers (see, e.g., L. 1976, ch. 132, commonly known as the Stavisky-Goodman bill). Perhaps for this reason, the Legislature provided with respect to improper labor practices that "fundamental distinctions between private and public employment shall be recognized, and no body of federal or state law applicable wholly or in part to private employment, shall be regarded as binding or controlling precedent" (Civil Service Law, § 209-a, subd. 3). So mindful, we turn to a consideration of "Triborough".

It has been held that the Triborough proposition is unnecessary where the unilateral conduct of an employer in refusing to grant agreed upon increments occurs before the bargaining agreement expires, because in that instance the evidence of failure to negotiate in good faith is manifested by the failure to live up to the terms of the existing contract. . . . The proposition, however, is sought to be applied in circumstances where the contract has expired because, it is said, an unilateral failure to pay increments under the expired contract also manifests a lack of good faith. While such a principle may apply where an employer alters unilaterally during negotiations other terms and conditions of employment, it should not apply where the employer maintains the salaries in effect at the expiration of the contract but does not pay increments.

The reasons for not giving effect in these circumstances to the so-called "Triborough Doctrine" should be apparent. Involving a delicate balance between fiscal and other responsibilities, its perpetuation is fraught with problems, equitable and economic in nature. As a reward and by encouraging the retention of experienced personnel in public positions, the concept of increments based on continuance in service, properly exercised, is creditable for the public entity and the citizenry are better served, and time losses suffered because of training periods and inefficiency in performance are likely to be reduced. The concept of continual successive annual increments, however, is tied into either constantly burgeoning growth and prosperity on the part of the public employer, or the territory served by it, or a continuing general inflationary spiral, without admeasurement either of the growth or inflation and without consideration of several other relevant good faith factors such as comparative compensation, the condition of the public fisc and a myriad of localized strengths and difficulties. In thriving periods the increment of the past may not squeeze the public purse, nor may it on the other hand be even fair to employees, but in times of escalating costs and diminishing tax bases, many public employers simply may not be able in good faith to continue to pay automatic increments to their employees.

PERB's counsel takes the position that applying "Triborough", so as, in effect, to require the payment during negotiations of salary increments under an expired contract, does not lock the employees into a guaranteed gain position. Rather, it is argued, payment of such increments merely preserves the existing relationship until different conditions are established through collective bargaining which may include the entire abolition of the incremental structure. Such arguments, though superficially appealing, are not convincing. They are based on the erroneous assumption that it is the "existing relationship" which is being preserved, when, in reality, such payments extend or change the relationship established by the parties. In times either of inflation or depression, employees, quite naturally, will be reluctant to accept abolition of automatic increments which they have been receiving. To the extent that it provides that such increments must be paid even after expiration of contract, the proposition gives an edge and makes negotiation of that point that much more difficult.

To say that the *status quo* must be maintained during negotiations is one thing; to say that the *status quo* includes a change and means automatic increases in salary is another. The matter of increments can be negotiated and, if it is agreed that such increments can and should be paid, provision can be made for payment retroactively. The inherent fallacy of PERB's reasoning is that it seeks to make automatic increments a matter of right, without regard to the particular facts and circumstances, by establishing a rule that failure by a public employer to continue such increments during negotiations is a violation of the duty to negotiate in good faith. No such principle appears in the statute, nor should one exist by administrative fiat. Therefore, without expressing complete disapproval of the "Triborough Doctrine", we hold that it was error for PERB to determine that BOCES had violated its duty to negotiate in good faith solely because of its failure to pay increments after the expiration of an employment agreement.

Accordingly, the judgment of the Appellate Division should be modified, without costs, by annulling and vacating PERB's determination in its entirety, and, as so modified, affirmed.

BREITEL, C.J., and JASEN, GABRIELLI, JONES, WACHTLER and FUCHSBERG, J.J., concur.

## NOTES

1. *Accord,* Warren Consolidated Schools, 1975 MERC Lab. Op. 129 (Mich.) (salary grids providing for wages based on years of employment and education expire with contract and there is no obligation to move employees on the salary grid after contract expires).

2. In Ledyard Bd. of Educ., Decision No. 1564 (Conn. St. Bd. Lab. Rel. Aug. 15, 1977), the Connecticut SBLR held that a school board committed an unfair labor practice when it unilaterally withheld payment of vertical salary increments, even though the contract which provided for the increments had expired. The Connecticut SBLR held that "[r]egular annual salary increments payable under existing policies or practice constitute an existing condition of employment whether or not the increment was mandated by contract, and a discontinuance of such policy or practice constitutes a change in existing wages and conditions of employment." *Accord,* Hudson County Bd. of Chosen Freeholders, 4 NJPER 39 (N.J. PERC 1978).

3. In Pinellas County Police Benevolent Ass'n v. City of St. Petersburg, 3 FPER 205 (Fla. PERC 1977), the Florida PERC held that under Florida law a fact finding proceeding "is held after impasse" and that "during that time, continued negotiations between the parties are encouraged." The Florida PERC held that an "employer is not statutorily authorized to take unilateral action until it acts as the legislative body at the conclusion of the impasse resolution procedures. To this extent, the Act goes beyond the provisions of the NLRA." Accordingly, the Florida PERC held that a

...public employer has a duty to maintain the *status quo* with regard to the expired agreement. This *"status quo"* requires the employer to maintain the terms and conditions of the expired contract in the same state that the terms existed on the expiration date of the agreement.

With respect to merit increases and step increases, the Florida PERC stated:

Under this rationale, a public employer is only under a duty to maintain the salary levels that existed at the agreement's expiration date. If the expired agreement provided for a step increase in salary for each employee on his anniversary date, the employer is not required to provide those steps which occur during the hiatus between the expired agreement and the Section 447.403 legislative action for the ratification of a new agreement. Those increases, during the hiatus, were beyond the contemplation of the public employer when it executed and ratified the agreement for a specific period of time.

4. In U.S. Army Corps of Engineers, Philadelphia District A/SLMR No. 673 (June 23, 1976), the question presented was whether an agency could make a unilateral change with respect to a negotiable item after reaching impasse but before conclusion of the impasse procedure specified in Executive Order 11491 if utilization of that procedure was requested by the exclusive bargaining representative. The Assistant Secretary of Labor responded as follows:

[S]hould one of the parties involved in an impasse exercise the option available under Section 17 of the Order and request the services of the [Federal Services Impasse] Panel, I believe that it will effectuate the purposes of the Order to require that the parties must, in the absence of an overriding exigency, maintain the *status quo* and permit the processes of the Panel to run its course before a unilateral change in terms or conditions of employment can be effectuated.

5. In Vermont State Employees Ass'n v. State of Vermont, 92 L.R.R.M. 2309 (1976), the Vermont Supreme Court held that the Vermont Employee Labor Relations Board exceeded its jurisdiction in ordering that overtime pay for State employees as provided for in an expired collective bargaining agreement be restored pending either a new agreement or the reaching of a bona fide impasse in negotiations.

6. In City of Jackson, 1977 MERC Lab. Op. 1018 (Mich.), the Michigan Commission held that a contractual provision which provided for cost of living adjustments did not survive the contract and that, as a result, an employer did not take improper unilateral action in discontinuing payment of cost of living adjustments after the expiration of the contract. The Administrative Law Judge, whose decision was affirmed by the Commission, held that the cost of living adjustment was "a future contingency undertaken only during the contract term and not an obligation that the employer was required to continue indefinitely after the contract expired." Accordingly, he held that "the refusal of the

Respondent to pay additional cost of living accruing [after the termination of the agreement] was not a unilateral change in working conditions that required bargaining to impasse with the Charging Party before discontinuance."

7. In State of New York and AFSCME Council 82, Case No. U-0984 (Feb. 4, 1974), GERR No. 569, C-6, the New York PERB held that the Governor's signing of a bill prohibiting negotiations on retirement benefits is legislative action and not subject to challenge before the Board. In thus dismissing an unfair practice charge filed by AFSCME alleging that the Governor's action interfered with the collective bargaining process, PERB upheld its hearing officer who stated:

> In reaching this conclusion, a distinction must be drawn between the Governor's constitutional role in the lawmaking process and his executive and/or delegated role in the proper implementation of legislation. . . . Only his proprietary actions in the latter role may be reviewed by this Board. . . .

Since the Governor's role in signing law was legislative in nature, the hearing officer concluded that "it must then follow that the Governor's constitutional mandate to approve or veto legislative bills cannot be abrogated by statute and certainly not by an administrative decision of this tribunal."
*See also,* Oregon State Employees Ass'n. v. State of Oregon, Case No. C-6-75 (Ore. PERB 1975) (Governor's budget recommendation not an unlawful refusal to bargain in good faith).

# 5. EFFECT OF BUDGETARY PROCESS

### D. STANLEY, MANAGING LOCAL GOVERNMENT UNDER UNION PRESSURE 112, 115-19 (1972)†

Local government employee unions have added new stresses to the already difficult financial situation of these governments but have not basically altered the budget and finance processes. Department heads still prepare preliminary estimates of expenditures. Budget and finance officers organize and adjust the requests of department heads and estimate available revenues. Chief executives make "final" decisions on the budget to be submitted to the legislative body, and the latter holds hearings, approves the budget, and sets tax rates. All this is familiar. What the unions have done is to assume a greatly strengthened and highly visible role in decisions that ultimately have a major impact on the size of the budget. Their political and emotional effect is heightened by the fact that the larger local governments are generally either in or approaching a condition of financial crisis. . . .

In [the] nineteen localities [studied], as in most fair-sized local governments, budget preparation begins about six months before the start of the new fiscal year when the budget office sends to the various department heads instructions on the format and schedule to be followed in preparing estimates. Departments may or may not be told how rigorously to economize or what programs to emphasize as they look ahead. Generally using the current budget figures as a base, department heads make their estimates, often in consultation with a member of the budget staff. Where it is feasible they use workload figures, past and estimated, to back up their calculations — numbers of fires, miles of streets, cubic yards of rubbish. The department heads do not consult unions at this time and are influenced by union pressures only to the extent that previous union-sponsored changes in work rules or pay provisions have changed the expense outlook. Meanwhile the budget office (or the finance staff if it is a separate organization) is estimating expected revenues. Then both revenue and

---

† Reprinted by permission. Copyright © 1972 by the Brookings Institution, Washington, D.C.

expenditure sheets go to the chief executive, who, aided by the budget and finance staff, must trim the expense estimates, or plan to seek extra revenues, or both, in order to balance his budget before it goes to the legislative body.[16]

In the days before unions acquired collective bargaining rights, this budget process readily accommodated changes in pay and benefits. Modifications were proposed by the personnel office or civil service commission, approved by the budget office and chief executive, and ultimately enacted by the legislative body. They were kept within anticipated financial resources and were usually timed to begin at the start of the next fiscal year. In the present era of collective bargaining, even though most of the budget process is unrelated to union activities, the schedule has become less controllable for three reasons. First, the bargaining process is time-consuming. Second, unions may adopt a strategy that calls for bargaining to reach a climax at the time the legislative body is considering the budget. Third, the results of bargaining may require new financing measures involving further legislation locally, or a referendum, or action by the state legislature. However, in situations where there is a multi-year union agreement, without pay reopener provisions, such problems are spaced out and therefore less troublesome.

Cities in New York State (including, among those studied, Binghamton and Buffalo but not New York City) are expected to be kept on schedule by the Taylor Law, which provides that negotiations, including mediation and fact finding, must be concluded sixteen [sic] days before the budget is submitted to the local legislative body.[17] Despite the law, Buffalo ran late in 1968. That city's charter requires the mayor to submit the budget to the council by May 1 for adoption by June 1. However, when the 1968 union negotiations (the first under the law) had not been completed by June 1, the city had to include a lump-sum "salary adjustment fund" in the budget to cover the estimated costs of the union settlements.

Several of the cities and counties in other states try to complete bargaining before legislative body starts work on the budget. Hartford has been successful thus far in concluding negotiations well before the budget is closed, even though state law permits bargaining to run on beyond that time. The city aims to finish bargaining by January 1 and to pass the budget in February; the fiscal year begins April 1. Still another method was found in Detroit, where pay discussions are part of the budget process and separate from union negotiations on other matters. Pay settlements there are not included in agreements, but are recommended by the mayor to the common council along with the budget.

Two governments, Dade County and Philadelphia, bargain while the legislative body has the budget under review but before it completes action.

In a still later category are cities and counties where bargaining continues even after the budget is adopted. This means that if the budget does not contain enough funds to finance the agreement, additional revenues must be obtained. Boston, Dayton, New Castle County, and New York have all been in the position of concluding agreements after the budget has been decided. Boston lacks a fixed schedule for both budget submissions and bargaining. Although the fiscal year

---

[16] For a concise, sophisticated summary of local government budgeting, see John P. Crecine, *A Computer Simulation Model of Municipal Budgeting*, MANAGEMENT SCIENCE, Vol. 13 (July 1967), pp. 786-815.

[17] New York, Public Employees' Fair Employment Act of 1967, sec. 209, as amended, March 4, 1969. Section 212 of the law exempts New York City from this requirement.

there begins in January, departmental estimates trickle in until April, when a supplementary budget request based on bargaining settlements is submitted to the city council. The tax rate is set the following July. New York City's scores of agreements are concluded at different times of the year (usually January or July) and vary in their duration; hence it is virtually impossible to budget realistically for bargaining settlements. Budgeting and bargaining have become two very separate operations.

Turning to the four governments that do not have general collective bargaining, in Los Angeles County, New Orleans, and San Francisco the personnel authorities recommend salaries and benefits for consideration by the legislative bodies before budgets are adopted. St. Louis has found it necessary in the past to consider the salary demands of the unions after the budget is adopted. However, tentative agreement has now been reached between the city and four unions to conduct annual negotiating sessions *before* the budget is drafted.

Reconciling the budget schedule with the bargaining schedule is an annual problem where the agreements are for one year only. Elsewhere these coordination problems have to be faced only in the years when agreements are up for renewal.

### What Timing Is Best?

Financial management is obviously more efficient when negotiations are finished before the budget goes to the legislature. Under such circumstances the executive branch has considered the unions' demands along with other spending needs and with estimated revenues, reconciled any problems, and prepared a budget package that is fully ready for legislative action. This is hard to achieve for reasons already stated: slow bargaining, union strategies, and authorization of supplementary financing. The experience of the governments studied here suggests that bargaining results can feasibly go to the legislative body *after* it has begun work on the budget. It is even possible for bargaining to be completed after the budget has been approved by the legislature. In either event the budget process becomes more protracted, less businesslike, and less controllable from a management standpoint. The city council may have to enact supplementary appropriations and new revenue measures after the start of the new fiscal period.

Several of the governments studied have adapted themselves to these difficulties. The problems perhaps would be lessened if elected officials, citizens' groups, and the news media brought pressure for timely conclusion of bargaining. The union members too would like to have their uncertainties ended sooner — but not at the cost of lower settlements. It seems inevitable on the whole that rigid bargaining schedules to meet budget deadlines will be viewed with more nostalgia than respect. Delayed and revised budgets are inconvenient and stressful for executives and staffs and are more difficult for citizens to understand, but they can be expected to continue, and local governments will make the necessary adaptations.

### Reserves For Settlements

Representatives of all the cities and counties, regardless of their budget schedules, were asked if they budgeted any "cushions" (contingency funds) or if they "hid" any money to pay for union settlements that were higher than they had anticipated. A majority of the governments studied answered in the negative. Buffalo, Hartford, Milwaukee, and New Castle County all reported that they use contingency funds for this purpose. One other county and three cities, whose identity will not be disclosed, candidly said that they "hid" money in the estimates for various departments. The former method (use of an earmarked fund) is risky.

It may become a "sitting duck" for legislators who want to eliminate it or use it for another purpose; or it may become a target for bargaining demands — unions may ask for the total amount and more too. Cincinnati operates under another method, financing settlements out of an "income tax permanent improvement fund," which receives income tax revenues that exceed estimates. The city manager commits part of the fund to capital improvement projects, but it is difficult for the unions to find out how much is uncommitted, thus giving the city some bargaining leeway.

## NOTES

1. The impact of bargaining on the budgetary process and on public finance is explored in Hayes, *Collective Bargaining and the Budget Director,* in PUBLIC WORKERS AND PUBLIC UNIONS 89 (S. Zagoria ed. 1972).

2. Concerning the impact of bargaining on municipal pay plans, Kenneth O. Warner, then Executive Director of the Public Personnel Association, stated:

> The traditional approach to pay plans may have to be tossed out the window. With bargaining there is a good chance that the tidy, systematic, integrated pay plan — designed to give equitable treatment to all employees in a given jurisdiction — will undergo considerable change. The 64-dollar question is how do you maintain fairness and equity when many unions bargain for wages in several different units of an organization. It should be noted that union representatives argue that anything would be an improvement over what now exists. The reason: Pay administration is not really scientific.

Warner, *Financial Implications of Employee Bargaining in the Public Service,* in SORRY . . . NO GOVERNMENT TODAY 189, 197 (R. Walsh ed. 1969).

3. Several of the comprehensive public sector collective bargaining statutes contain impasse procedures which are specifically geared to the budget submission date and contemplate that collective bargaining will be concluded prior to said date. Suppose a union is recognized or certified as a bargaining representative subsequent to the budget submission date and the union requests that the public employer negotiate over wages and fringe benefits for the year covered by the budget. If the public employer refused to negotiate on the grounds that the budget submission date had already passed, would it be committing an unfair labor practice? In Ligonier Valley School Dist., Case No. PERA-C-1542-W (September 29, 1972), the Pennsylvania Labor Relations Board held that an employer had a duty to bargain even though the budget submission date had passed. *Cf.* Town of New Canaan, Decision No. 828 (Conn. SLRB 1968).

In Garden City Educators' Ass'n v. Vance, 100 L.R.R.M. 2536 (Kan. S. Ct. 1978), the court held that negotiations could not be halted prior to exhaustion of the impasse resolution procedures even though this would extend beyond the employer's budget submission date. Although the court recognized that "the issue of salary is the most often disputed item in negotiations," it noted "that redistribution of monies along line items is a common practice in school districts" and that "[t]o the extent of the flexibility of the budget, the issue of salaries of teachers continues to be a negotiable item." This decision should be contrasted with the decision of the Supreme Court of Iowa in City of Des Moines v. PERB, —N.W.— (Iowa S. Ct. 1979), in which the court held that the budget submission date for Iowa's political subdivisions constitutes the termination date for all mandated statutory impasse procedures. In giving considerable deference to the statutory budget submission date, the court stated:

> A construction of the Act which failed to recognize the certified budget submission date as a mandatory cutoff for impasse procedures would be inimical to the purpose of the Act. Such a construction would make it impossible for a political subdivision to deal effectively with its duty to formulate a budget and carry out its provisions. The year-round bargaining which could result would only detract from the effective and orderly delivery of governmental services by political subdivisions.

# 6. DUTY TO EXECUTE AN AGREEMENT

## CITY OF SAGINAW

Michigan Employment Relations Commission
1967 MERC Lab. Op. 465

Trial Examiner James McCormick: I . . . am unable to conclude that the City's announced unwillingness to enter into a signed bilateral labor contract is a breach of the bargaining duty as spelled out in Section 15 of PERA. It is true that, under federal law, the refusal of either party to labor negotiations to enter into a signed contract covering agreements reached constitutes an unlawful failure to bargain in good faith. H.J. Heinz Company v. N.L.R.B. 311 U.S. 514, 7 L.R.R.M. 291 (1941); National Labor Relations Act, as amended, sec. 8(d). As stated by National Labor Relations Board Solicitor William Feldesman in a speech reported in the October 31, 1966, Labor Relations Reporter, 53 L.R.R. 186:

"Of course the labor contract has always been regarded as the hoped-for product of collective bargaining, as it brings to the industrial community concerned a charter of voluntarily made law and palpably evidences labor relations stability."

Professor Archibald Cox (Cases on Labor Law, p. 2) refers to the basic labor relations statutes as the "constitution" of industrial self-government and views the written collective bargaining agreements as the "statutory law" of the employer-employee relationship. It can be seen from such an analogy how important the written contract is to effective collective bargaining in private enterprise. Local governmental bodies, however, must conduct business in a way appropriate to the making of a proper official record. They may act by ordinance, resolution, motion or order. Fordham, *Local Government Law*, p. 403. (In Michigan practice an ordinance ordinarily prescribes a permanent rule for the conduct of government, while a resolution is of a special or temporary character.) Kalamazoo Municipal Utilities Assn. v. City of Kalamazoo, 345 Mich. 318, 76 N.W.2d 1 (1956). Modifications in wages, hours and working conditions have generally been effected by adoption of a resolution approving changes in the governmental body's personnel "plan" or "policy." Even where such action has followed upon, and represented the fruit of, consultation with a union, the resolution of the City Council or other legislative body has not reflected that fact, but has appeared to be a unilateral act.

One of the problems created by incorporating collective bargaining agreements into ordinances or resolutions is the fact that these are subject to being modified or repealed by the body that enacted or adopted them. City of Saginaw v. Consumers Power Co., 213 Mich. 460, 182 N.W. 146 (1921). Imagine the situation which would exist if a private employer could modify or repeal its contracts at will. Enforcement of an ordinance or resolution against the public employer also presents legal difficulties.

In any event, the Michigan legislature has specified in Section 15 of the PERA that the "execution of a written contract, ordinance or resolution incorporating any agreement reached if requested by either party" satisfies the bargaining duty. While the language is ambiguous, the more reasonable interpretation is that any of these three ways of evidencing or memorializing the verbal understanding is sufficient, and that either party may lawfully hold out for its preferred way, not being obliged to sign a bilateral written contract if it prefers an ordinance or resolution.

It may be, however, that an ordinance or resolution which represents and incorporates a final meeting of minds on a collective bargaining agreement results in contractual rights in both employees and public employer, and is, in fact, a contract, even though it is, in another sense, the free and unilateral decree of a duly-empowered governing body. In Dodge v. Board of Education of Chicago, 302 U.S. 74, 58 S. Ct. 98 (1937) the issue was whether a statute providing for pensions for retired teachers created a contract with the teachers, the obligations of which could not be impaired by a later statute decreasing the annuities. The Court recognized that a state may enter into contracts with citizens, the obligation of which the legislature cannot impair by subsequent enactment, but said "On the other hand, an act merely fixing salaries of officers creates no contract in their favor, and the compensation named may be altered at the will of the legislature. . . . The presumption is that such a law is not intended to create private contractual or vested rights, but merely declares a policy to be pursued until the legislature shall ordain otherwise. He who asserts the creation of a contract with the state in such a case has the burden of overcoming the presumption." It would appear that where an ordinance or resolution "incorporates" a collective bargaining "agreement," following extensive "negotiations," any presumption against the creation of contractual rights could be rebutted. In either event, the peculiar language used in Section 15 of the PERA precludes the finding of a violation in the City's anticipatory refusal to enter into a written contract.

[The Trial Examiner's decision was adopted by the MERC.]

## NOTES

1. If the parties reach agreement on a substantial number of issues in negotiations but are nevertheless at impasse on a number of other issues, is the employer obligated to reduce to writing and execute an agreement on those issues on which the parties have reached agreement? In Local 1363, International Association of Fire Fighters v. DiPrete, 103 R.I. 592, 239 A.2d 716 (1968), the union, relying on a statutory provision which imposed on employers "the duty to cause any agreement resulting from negotiations to be reduced to a written contract," alleged that the statute required "that whatever matters may have been agreed upon, even though less than all in issue, shall be embodied in a formal writing which, upon execution, will become the collective bargaining agreement governing the working conditions of the Cranston firefighters." The Rhode Island Supreme Court, noting that the word "agreement" "presumes that the parties have arrived at a mutual understanding on all of the matters in negotiation," held that there was no obligation on the city to execute an incomplete collective bargaining agreement.

2. Where a union is certified as the exclusive bargaining representative for a unit of public employees, can the union limit a ratification vote on a proposed collective bargaining agreement to its members only and exclude non-members from participating? In Daigle v. Jefferson Parish School Board, 345 So.2d 583 (La. App. Ct. 1977), the court held that there was no statutory law or constitutional provision which granted employees an absolute right to vote for or against ratification of a collective bargaining agreement and that a policy adopted by a union which permitted only members to vote on ratification was reasonable and rational. *Accord,* Wald v. Civil Service Employees Ass'n, 72 Misc. 2d 723, 340 N.Y.S.2d 451 (S. Ct., Nassau Cty., 1973). *Contra,* National Education Ass'n of Shawnee Mission, Inc. v. Board of Education of Shawnee Mission Unified School Dist. No. 512, 212 Kan. 741, 512 P.2d 426 (1973) (". . . ratification is required by a majority of the entire negotiating unit, not just of the negotiating organization"). *See also* City of Detroit, 1978 MERC Lab. Op. 519 (Mich.) (no exceptions filed to ALJ opinion that membership

ratification is not required by the Michigan Act). In City of Reno, Item #86 (Nev. LGE-MRB 1978), the Nevada Board held that "the means, methods, and procedures whereby an employee organization ratifies its collective bargaining agreement with an employer are internal concerns of the organization into which the employer may have no input." The Nevada Board further stated that "[e]fforts by an employer to attempt to dictate the contract ratification procedure utilized by an employee organization would clearly be an interference in the internal administration of an employee organization."

3. Is a collective bargaining agreement which extends beyond the contracting officials' term of office binding on their successors? In AFSCME Dist. Council No. 33 v. Philadelphia, 83 Pa. D. & C. 537 (C.P. 1952), the court held that a collective bargaining agreement was binding on a successive administration. *Accord,* Malone v. Court of Common Pleas of Cuyahoga County, 594 GERR B-6 (Ohio App. Ct. 1974). *But see* City of Springfield v. Clouse, 356 Mo. 1239, 206 S.W.2d 539 (1947) (". . . of course, no legislature could bind itself or its successor to make or continue any legislative act").

# 7. EFFECT OF ILLEGAL CONCERTED ACTIVITY

## WARREN EDUCATION ASSOCIATION

Michigan Employment Relations Commission
1977 MERC Lab. Op. 818

On December 29, 1976, this Commission issued its Decision and Order in the above-entitled matter, holding that a strike by public employees does not constitute a per se refusal to bargain in good faith violative of Section 10(3)(c) of the Public Employment Relations Act (PERA), 1965 PA 379, as amended by 1973 PA 25, MCLA 423.210; MSA 17.455(10). In so ruling, the Commission adopted the reasoning set forth in *Warren Education Association,* 1975 MERC Lab Op 76, in which the Commission adopted the findings of the Administrative Law Judge but ruled that Respondent's work stoppage on October 8, 1973, did not violate Section 10(3)(c) of the Act. This Commission order was vacated and remanded by the Court of Appeals on other grounds.[2] Thereafter, Charging Party filed a motion requesting oral argument and seeking reconsideration of the Commission decision issued December 29, 1976.

In its brief in support of the motion for reconsideration, Charging Party has withdrawn its exception to the Administrative Law Judge's determination that the Union's refusal to agree in writing to items no longer in dispute is not a refusal to bargain in good faith. Charging Party has confined its argument to the issue of whether a strike by a labor organization during the course of bargaining is a per se refusal to bargain in good faith violative of PERA; and, alternatively, whether for purposes of the instant proceeding the Union refused to bargain in good faith based upon the totality of its conduct at and away from the bargaining table. In his Decision and Recommended Order, the Administrative Law Judge found that the strike of October 8, 1973, and concomitant threat to strike violated Respondent's duty to bargain in good faith mandated by Section 10(3)(c) of PERA. The Administrative Law Judge reasoned that in enacting PERA the legislature did not contemplate public employers bargaining under the duress of a work stoppage. To permit a labor organization to bring to the bargaining table pressure through its strike activity would conflict with the policy and the purposes of PERA. Similarly, Charging Party contends that a strike is by

---

[2] Warren Consolidated Schools v. MERC, 67 Mich App 58, 240 NW2d 265, 92 LRRM 3051 (1976).

definition inconsistent with good faith bargaining; hence, a work stoppage held violative of Section 2 of PERA constitutes a per se refusal to bargain in good faith under the Act.

Charging Party urges this Commission to exercise its discretion to reverse our earlier ruling in *Montrose Community Schools,* 1975 MERC Lab Op 38, and to fashion an unfair labor practice in this matter consistent with the legislative intent to prohibit strikes. Initially, we reject Charging Party's contention that the Union escapes accountability for an unlawful work stoppage in that Section 6 of PERA provides a discipline procedure only for individual employees. The attempt to dichotomize the Association and its teacher members was expressly rejected by the Michigan Supreme Court in *Lamphere Schools v Federation of Teachers,* 400 Mich 104, 252 NW2d 818, 95 LRRM 2279 (1977). The Court rejected the notion that PERA, and specifically the Section 6 remedies, in effect applies only to public employees individually but not their collective bargaining agents. Moreover, the Court acknowledged: "The utilization of Section 6 remedies results in a significant sanction against the Federation, as an organization consisting of its public employee members." As such, the argument that a strike authorized by a union must be violative of Section 10(3)(c) because Section 6 applies only to individuals must fail.

Charging Party would have this Commission ignore the results of two Court of Appeals decisions addressing the issue of whether a strike is a refusal to bargain in good faith. In *Lamphere School District v Lamphere Federation of Teachers,* 67 Mich App 485, 241 NW2d 257, 92 LRRM 3182 (1976), *aff'g* 1975 MERC Lab Op 555; *lv to app den,* 396 Mich 842 (1972), the Court of Appeals determined that a strike need not indicate failure to bargain in good faith and accordingly affirmed a Commission refusal to accept as binding a party's stipulation that a teacher strike constituted an unfair labor practice. While the Court determined that the stipulation was properly set aside, it further concluded that the school district should have full opportunity to prove its refusal to bargain allegation and remanded to MERC the determination of whether a strike may be evidentiary of bad faith bargaining.

In its decision the Court excerpted from the Court of Appeals decision in *Detroit Board of Education v Detroit Federation of Teachers,* 55 Mich App 499, 503, 223 NW2d 23, 25, 88 LRRM 2389 (1974). In determining that the Circuit Court had subject matter jurisdiction to enjoin the teachers' strike, the Court of Appeals rejected the Union's argument that a strike is an unfair labor practice, vesting in MERC exclusive jurisdiction. In so holding, the Court of Appeals acknowledged the possibility that a union could both bargain in good faith and still strike. We find these Court of Appeals decisions instructive and supportive of our prior ruling in *Montrose Community Schools, supra.* Charging Party likewise discounts the Court of Appeals rationale in *Detroit Board of Education, supra,* as mere dicta having no authoritative or precedential value. It is clear from a review of the briefs filed in this matter by Charging Party, Respondent, and *amici curiae* that the appellate decision which most directly addresses the issue of whether a strike constitutes a per se refusal to bargain is Presiding Judge Gillis' decision in *Lamphere School District v Lamphere Federation of Teachers,* at 67 Mich App 485 — a decision which Charging Party fails to discuss or distinguish.

As noted by the Court of Appeals in *Detroit Board of Education v Federation of Teachers, supra,* the term "strike" is conspicuously absent from the list of statutory unfair labor practices delineated in Section 10 of PERA.[5] Nonetheless,

---

[5] Some jurisdictions expressly designate strike activity a prohibited or unfair labor practice. *See* e. g., *Florida Stat Ann,* § 447.501(2)(e); *Kansas Stat Ann,* §75-4333(c)(5); *Maine Rev Stat Ann,* tit.

Charging Party contends that Section 16 of PERA authorizes the Commission to adjudicate and remedy unfair labor practices; and, since no section of the Act explicitly excludes strike activity from the scope of unfair labor practices, the Commission should effectuate legislative intent by recognizing a strike as an unfair labor practice. The force of this argument is diminished in light of the 1973 legislative amendments to PERA, which, while delineating union unfair labor practices and vesting in MERC jurisdiction to adjudicate charges against employee organizations, nonetheless failed to include work stoppage in the enumerated unfair labor practices. The significance of the legislature's failure to categorize a strike as an unfair labor practice stems from the high incidence of strike activity which characterized public sector labor relations at the time the amendments were enacted. Section 16 of PERA does not parallel Section 23(2) of the Labor Relations and Mediation Act (LRMA), which expressly authorizes MERC to remedy, as an unfair labor practice, an unauthorized or illegal strike. Moreover, we must conclude that the legislature was not unmindful when it amended PERA of the Michigan Supreme Court decision in *Holland School District,* ... wherein the Court injected traditional prerequisites for obtaining injunctive relief into equity proceedings which involve public sector work stoppages.

In its brief on reconsideration and at oral argument, Charging Party places a strong emphasis on the applicability of the Administrative Law Judge's decision in *Genesee Intermediate School District,* 1970 MERC Lab Op 261, to the issues in the instant matter. Charging Party even goes so far as to contend that when the legislature amended PERA in 1973 it somehow acknowledged the *Genesee* decision as the authoritative analysis for the proposition that an unlawful strike constitutes a refusal to bargain within the meaning of the amended statute. It is difficult for this Commission to conjecture that the legislature when it amended PERA in 1973 had in mind a decision of an Administrative Law Judge, to which no exceptions were filed with this Commission, and not a decision of this State's highest court requiring public employers to prove more than the mere existence of a strike to obtain injunctive relief.

Assuming arguendo that the legislature did contemplate application of the *Genesee* decision by this Commission to strike activity, we nonetheless conclude that the *Genesee* case is not dispositive of the issues in this matter. As *Genesee Intermediate School District* involves a Decision and Recommended Order of the Administrative Law Judge to which no exceptions were taken, the case's limited precedential value must be noted. More importantly, a careful reading of the Administrative Law Judge's Decision and Recommended Order discloses that he construed PERA's strike prohibition as the basis for prohibiting *offensive* lockouts. Nowhere has this Commission determined that a lockout per se constitutes a refusal to bargain in good faith. As such, this Commission has not been faced with the issue of whether a "bargaining" lockout vis-a-vis an economically-justified lockout is a refusal to bargain in good faith; nor has this Commission flatly recognized that in all bargaining disputes strikes and lockouts are equivalent weapons, as contended in Charging Party's brief. Based upon the foregoing, we reaffirm that portion of our ruling in *Montrose Community Schools,* 1975 MERC Lab Op 38, which holds that a public sector work stoppage does not constitute ipso facto a refusal to bargain violative of Section 10 of PERA.

26, Ch. 9-A, § 964(2)(c)(3); *Minnesota Stat Ann,* § 179.68(3)(11); *New Hampshire Rev Stat Ann,* § 273-A:5(II)(e); *Pennsylvania Stat Ann,* tit. 43 § 43, § 1201(b)(6)(7); *Vermont Stat Ann,* tit. 3, Ch. 27, § 962(5); *Wisconsin Stat Ann,* § 111.84(2)(e).

This ruling of law leaves unresolved the determination of whether Respondent refused to bargain in good faith based upon its total course of conduct surroundings negotiations as developed in the record below. We must address this factual issue and modify our December 29, 1976, Decision and Order based upon our recent ruling in *Kalamazoo Public Schools,* 1977 MERC Lab Op 771. Therein we held that conduct away from the bargaining table can constitute such gross interference with employee rights as to render a sham bargaining table conduct which otherwise appears legitimate. Accordingly, we now hold that while a public sector strike does not constitute a per se refusal to bargain, such strike activity can be evidentiary of bad faith bargaining. This holding challenges that portion of our decision in *Montrose Community Schools* wherein we stated, "We are in agreement with the conclusions and reasoning in *Insurance Agents* and will henceforth limit our inquiry as to 10(3)(c) violations to the actual conduct of the Union with regard to meeting and conferring with the Employer."

In the case at hand, the evidence demonstrates that Respondent's at-the-table conduct fulfilled its obligation to bargain in good faith. We are left with the issue of whether Respondent's conduct away from the bargaining table can amount to a repudiation of that apparent good faith. In the case of an employer, we have held that conduct away from the table can lead to the conclusion that bargaining table conduct is superficial, a sham to cover an underlying intent to undermine the union's representative status and bargaining strength, thus violating the employer's 10(3)(c) obligation. *Kalamazoo Public Schools, supra.* The precise issue remaining here is whether a union's total course of conduct away from the table can lead to a related violation; namely, that the union does not desire agreement except on its own unilaterally-imposed terms.

In briefest summary, Respondent's actions here which Charging Party contends should evidence such a violation are the following:

1. The setting of a strike deadline, including a whole series of well-publicized plans and activities designed to persuade the Board and the community that a strike would take place if agreement was not reached by the deadline date.

2. Refusal to accept the Employer's proffer that the parties seek the recommendation of a neutral factfinder.

3. A written statement that Respondent, once the strike began, would not "initiate negotiations" until Charging Party's proposals for change in the previous collective bargaining agreement were withdrawn.

4. The strike itself, which began on the date which Respondent had set as the deadline.

A decision on whether these acts violate the good faith bargaining obligation set forth in 10(3)(c) requires analysis of the principles underlying the statute (PERA) which this Commission is required to enforce. PERA's language in many respects is akine [sic] to the National Labor Relations Act, and the Supreme Court of Michigan has approved this Commission's use of federal precedents in construing parties' obligations under the Act. *Detroit Police Officers Association v City of Detroit,* 391 Mich 44, 214 NW2d 803, 85 LRRM 2536 (1974). It was on this basis that the Commission in *Montrose Community Schools* relied on the decision of the U.S. Supreme Court in *NLRB v Insurance Agents Union,* 361 US 477, 80 S Ct 419, 4 L Ed 2d 454, 45 LRRM 2704 (1960), that unprotected and even illegal activity away from the bargaining table does not constitute a refusal to bargain in good faith.

But PERA is not identical with NLRA in every respect. One of the most important differences is that PERA declares the strike illegal. Under MERC's administration of PERA the parties are instead provided alternatives to the strike, enabling them to press each other for changes in unacceptable positions when a temporary impasse develops. Initially in negotiations, PERA, like NLRA, requires both parties to bargain in good faith in an effort to reach agreement. If these efforts prove unavailing, neutral and professional mediation services are provided under both statutes to assist the parties in their search for peaceful agreement. But if no agreement is reached during mediation, as will inevitably occur in some situations, parties may invoke factfinding procedures, in contrast to the NLRA, rather than strike.

It is unnecessary here to describe in detail the theory and practice of factfinding. Neither is it necessary that we consider whether factfinding is always adequate to force changes in positions leading to voluntary agreement. It is sufficient to note that the legislature of the State of Michigan has determined that either party, or the Commission on its own motion, may institute the factfinding process as a pressure device alternative to the strike.

During the course of negotiations in the instant proceeding, well prior to the strike, Charging Party suggested to Respondent that they seek factfinding recommendations on the outstanding issues. Respondent refused, initially on the basis that in past years Charging Party had not always accepted the recommendations of factfinders. Subsequently, Respondent stated that it would accept factfinding only if the results thereof were agreed upon by both parties to be binding upon them. Neither of these counterproposals provide an adequate defense for the failure of Respondent to seek a factfinder's recommendation as the legislature provided.[15] Respondent here did not exhaust, much less indicate a willingness to utilize, the legal remedies set forth in the statute for impasse resolution.[16] Rather, Respondent was more inclined to resort to a work stoppage than to employ available statutory impasse resolution mechanisms.

Based upon the foregoing, we conclude that Respondent's totality of conduct constituted a refusal to bargain in good faith. Specifically, we find that Respondent's rejection of proffered recourse to factfinding, the strike and strike-related activity are evidentiary in determining whether the duty to bargain has been breached.

In light of the circumstances as a whole, including Respondent's conduct away from the table and its circumvention of impasse resolving procedures contemplated by the legislature, we further find that Respondent's action amounted to a refusal to bargain in good faith.

To the extent that the foregoing conflicts with that portion of our decision in *Montrose Community Schools, supra,* regarding the use of economic pressure away from the bargaining table, that rationale is hereby overruled.

Any bargaining dispute involving a total course of conduct alleged to violate the obligation to bargain in good faith must be evaluated in light of its own facts and circumstances. On the record here, Respondent violated its good faith bargaining obligation under 10(3)(c).

---

[15] Charging Party's failure to accept recommendations in the past repudiated no obligation upon it, nor predicted what the result might have been had the parties gone to the factfinding prior to the strike in the instant dispute. Moreover, "binding factfinding," as counterproposed by Respondent, is not the impasse resolution procedure which the legislature provided. Such a counter offer, therefore, does not constitute a satisfactory fulfillment of Respondent's obligation to use the legislative alternatives available.

[16] The parties ultimately did settle the dispute following court-ordered bargaining and resort to factfinding.

## NOTES

1. In City of New Haven, Decision No. 1555 (Conn. St. Bd. Lab. Rel. July 5, 1977), the Connecticut SBLR held that a union's boycott of extra duty assignments constituted prohibited economic coercion and that the use of such coercion constituted a refusal to bargain in good faith. After concluding that "the Legislature did not intend in MERA to have both good faith bargaining and economic pressure devices 'exist side by side' as means available to obtain bargaining objectives," the Connecticut Board stated:

> Before the labor statutes the employer was free to change conditions of employment unless that freedom had been restricted by contract. If it is a prohibited practice to introduce economic coercion into bargaining by unilaterally changing these conditions it is hard to see why the Union should be free to resort unilaterally to measures of self-help that exert a similar kind of extraneous coercion on the bargaining process.

2. The Los Angeles County Employee Relations Commission in County of Los Angeles and Los Angeles County Employees Association, SEIU, Local 660 AFL-CIO (August 25, 1972), held that a sick-out was not a refusal to bargain in violation of the Los Angeles County Collective Bargaining Ordinance. The Commission stated that it was unprepared to hold that the union had unlawfully refused to bargain when its conduct stemmed directly from the County's unlawful refusal to negotiate over a matter which the Commission had earlier held to be negotiable.

3. The WERC in City of Portage, Decision No. 8378 (1968), in response to the city's assertion that a work stoppage constituted a defense to a prohibited practice charge, noted that it did "not apply the unclean hands' doctrine as a defense to prohibited practices . . . ." However, in City of Milwaukee (Department of Public Works), Dec. No. 6575B (Dec. 12, 1963), the WERC held:

> The fact finding procedure set forth in the statute is designed to give representatives of municipal employes an opportunity to persuade the municipal employer and the public of the merits of their particular requests with reference to the wages, hours and working conditions of municipal employes. As administrators of this statute we do not believe that labor organizations, who ignore these considerations by engaging in a strike, should at the same time be entitled to the benefits of fact finding or other rights granted to them by statute. The Board as a general policy and in the absence of good cause shown will decline to process any fact finding petition filed by a labor organization which is engaged in a strike.

4. In Saginaw Township Bd. of Education, 1970 MERC Lab. Op. 127, the Michigan Commission in a split decision held that a union's illegal strike did not relieve an employer from the obligation to negotiate during the duration of the strike.

5. In Cherry Hill Board of Education, 4 NJPER 462 (N.J. PERC 1978), the New Jersey Commission held that a board of education "was within its rights to schedule the makeup day without negotiating with the teachers" where this was necessary due to illegal teacher strike. The New Jersey Commission, however, held that it was an unfair labor practice for the employer to unilaterally reduce teachers' pay by refusing to pay teachers who struck for days of work that were rescheduled.

6. The National Labor Relations Board has held "that it is a defense to a charge of employer bad faith [bargaining], that the union was not itself in good faith." Roadhome Constr. Corp., 170 N.L.R.B. 91 (1968). In Times Publishing Co., 72 N.L.R.B. 676, 682-83 (1947), the NLRB reasoned as follows:

> . . . The test of good faith in bargaining that the Act requires of an employer is not a rigid but a fluctuating one, and is dependent in part upon how a reasonable man might be expected to react to the bargaining attitude displayed by those across the table. It follows that . . . a union's refusal to bargain in good faith may remove the possibility of negotiation and thus preclude the existence of a situation in which the employer's own good faith can be tested. If it cannot be tested, its absence can hardly be found.

Is this statement consistent with the holding of the majority in the principal case?

# D. THE DUTY TO BARGAIN DURING THE TERM OF A COLLECTIVE BARGAINING AGREEMENT

## CITY OF MILWAUKEE

Wisconsin Employment Relations Commission
WERC Decision No. 8505 (1968)

[A union alleged that an employer violated the Wisconsin Municipal Employment Act when it unilaterally made certain revisions in the duties of several employees during the term of the parties' agreement. The employer asserted that it was under no obligation to bargain with the union before taking the action on the ground that the management rights clause in the agreement gave it the right to revise the duties in question.]

In private employment labor relations an employer is under a continual duty to bargain with the representative of the majority of its employes despite the existence of a collective bargaining agreement, except where such collective bargaining representative, in the agreement, surrenders its right to insist upon bargaining on certain conditions of employment by agreeing to permit the employer to make unilateral determinations in that regard. There is no provision in Section 111.70 of the Wisconsin Statutes which prevents the representative of municipal employes from making such an agreement with the municipal employer involved.

We recognize and agree with the rule that a waiver of the right to bargain on a mandatory subject of bargaining will not be readily inferred, and that a waiver of such a statutory right, in order to be recognized, must be "clear and unmistakable." We conclude that the "management rights" clause in question here specifically provides, "thoroughly and unmistakably," that the Municipal Employer has the authority, during the term of the agreement, to unilaterally make revisions in duties of employes in order to increase the efficiency of the particular operation involved. . . .

## NOTES

1. The NLRB has ruled "that an employer's duty to give a union prior notice and an opportunity to bargain normally arises where the employer proposes to take action which will effect some change in existing employment terms or conditions within the range of mandatory bargaining." Westinghouse Electric Corp., 150 N.L.R.B. 1574 (1955). If the applicable collective bargaining agreement, however, gives the employer the right to take the action in question, then the employer can act unilaterally without bargaining with the union. See, e.g., Ador Corp., 155 N.L.R.B. 1658 (1965). Finally, the NLRB has consistently held that an employer, in the absence of mutual agreement, cannot modify a condition of employment which is set forth in an agreement during the term of the agreement even though it has given the union advance notice and an opportunity to bargain over the proposed modification. In this regard, the NLRB relies on Section 8(d) of the NLRA which provides "[t]hat where there is in effect a collective-bargaining contract . . . , the duty to bargain collectively shall also mean that no party to such contract shall terminate or modify such contract. . . ." For example, in Standard Oil Co., 174 N.L.R.B. 177 (1969), the NLRB held that an employer violated Section 8(d) when it unilaterally increased certain wage rates during the term of the parties' agreement without obtaining the union's consent. The Board observed that the employer "was not free . . . to modify the unexpired

agreement over the Union's objections, but was obligated to maintain in effect all preexisting contractual commitments for the contract term."

2. Not infrequently the parties' collective bargaining agreement incorporates a broad waiver clause which provides, among other things, that each party voluntarily and unqualifiedly waives the right to bargain collectively with respect to any subject referred to or covered by the agreement or with respect to any subject not specifically referred to or covered by the agreement, even though said subject may not have been within the knowledge or contemplation of either or both of the parties at the time they negotiated the agreement. In Keystone School Dist., 9 PPER ¶ 9058 (Pa. LRB 1978), the Pennsylvania Board held that such a waiver clause constituted a waiver of a union's right to negotiate over matters not covered by the agreement. Thus, the Pennsylvania Board held that a public employer did not commit an unfair labor practice when it unilaterally imposed a residency requirement. The PLRB stated:

> While residency was never discussed in any pre-contract negotiations, the "waiver" clause specifically applies to those subjects wholly omitted from the agreement "irrespective of whether said subject was mentioned or discussed during the negotiations preceding the execution of the agreement." Therefore, by virtue of the express provisions of the contract it was not improper for Respondent to unilaterally impose this requirement.
>
> . . . .
>
> . . . Waiver or zipper clauses such as the one at issue herein have broad and far-reaching consequences and may impact heavily on issues that the parties have not specifically addressed. However, such clauses do demonstrate that the parties have satisfied their bargaining obligation and for the life of the present agreement authorize actions such as is complained of herein.

Accord, Waynesboro Area School Board, 9 PPER ¶ 9066 (Pa. LRB 1978). But see New Paltz Central School Dist., 11 PERB ¶ 3057 (N.Y. 1978) (zipper clause did not waive union's right to negotiate over agency shop clause during the term of contract).

3. The effect of a negotiated grievance and arbitration procedure on an employer's obligation to bargain during the term of a collective bargaining agreement is covered at pp. 732-L, infra.

# E. PUBLIC SECTOR COLLECTIVE BARGAINING AND THE PUBLIC'S RIGHT TO KNOW

## CITY OF MADISON, JT. SCHOOL DIST. NO. 8 v. WERC

Supreme Court of the United States
429 U.S. 167, 97 S. Ct. 421, 50 L.Ed.2d 376 (1976)

MR. CHIEF JUSTICE BURGER delivered the opinion of the Court.

The question presented on this appeal from the Supreme Court of Wisconsin is whether a State may constitutionally require that an elected Board of Education prohibit teachers, other than union representatives, to speak at open meetings, at which public participation is permitted, if such speech is addressed to the subject of pending collective-bargaining negotiations.

The Madison Board of Education and Madison Teachers, Inc. (MTI), a labor union, were parties to a collective-bargaining agreement during the calendar year of 1971. In January 1971 negotiations commenced for renewal of the agreement and MTI submitted a number of proposals. One among them called for the inclusion of a so-called "fair-share" clause, which would require all teachers, whether members of MTI or not, to pay union dues to defray the costs of collective bargaining. Wisconsin law expressly permits inclusion of "fair share" provisions in municipal employee collective-bargaining agreements. Wis. Stat. § 111.70(2) (1973). Another proposal presented by the union was a provision for binding arbitration of teacher dismissals. Both of these provisions were resisted by the school board. The negotiations dead-locked in November 1971 with a number of issues still unresolved, among them "fair share" and arbitration.

During the same month, two teachers, Holmquist and Reed, who were members of the bargaining unit, but not members of the union, mailed a letter to all teachers in the district expressing opposition to the "fair share" proposal.[2] Two hundred teachers replied, most commenting favorably on Holmquist and Reed's position. Thereupon a petition was drafted calling for a one year delay in the implementation of "fair share" while the proposal was more closely analyzed by an impartial committee.[3] The petition was circulated to all teachers in the district on December 6, 1971. Holmquist and Reed intended to present the results of their petition effort to the school board and to MTI at the school board's public meeting that same evening.

Because of the stalemate in the negotiations, MTI arranged to have pickets present at the school board meeting. In addition, 300 to 400 teachers attended in support of the union's position. During a portion of the meeting devoted to expression of opinion by the public, the president of MTI took the floor and spoke on the subject of the ongoing negotiations. He concluded his remarks by presenting to the board a petition signed by 1,300 — 1,400 teachers calling for

---

[2] The text of the letter was as follows:
"Dear Fellow Madisonian Educator,
                    "E. C.—O. L. O. G. Y.
"*Educator's Choice—Obligatory Leadership Or Grievance by You*
                    "SAVE FREEDOM OF CHOICE
"A Closed Shop (agency shop) Removes This Freedom
"1. Does an organization which represents the best interests of teachers and pupils NEED mandatory membership deductions?
"2. Need relationships between administrators and teachers be further strained by LEGALLY providing for mandatory adversary camps?
"3. Should minority voices be mandatorily SILENCED?
"4. Could elimination of outside dissent produce NONRESPONSIVENESS to change?
"5. And . . .
    isn't this lack of FREEDOM OF CHOICE undemocratic?
    "*SUPPORT FREEDOM OF CHOICE—OPPOSE AGENCY SHOP*
"I wish to maintain freedom of choice:
    "I oppose agency shop on principle
    "I oppose agency shop and would sign a petition stating so          _____
    "I oppose agency shop and would work actively to main-
    tain freedom of choice                                             _____
"Let us hear from YOU.
    "Al Holmquist /s/                    E. C.—O. L. O. G. Y.
    Al Holmquist                         P.O. Box 5184
    Ralph Reed /s/                       Madison, WI 53705
    Ralph Reed
    Teacher co-chairmen"
[3] The text of the petition was as follows:
"To: Madison Board of Education
        Madison Teachers, Incorporated
"We the undersigned ask that the fair-share proposal (agency shop) being negotiated by Madison Teachers, Incorporated and the Madison Board of Education be deferred this year. We propose the following:
"1) The fair-share concept being negotiated be thoroughly studied by an impartial committee composed of representatives from all concerned groups.
"2) The findings of this study be made public.
"3) This impartial committee will ballot (written) all persons affected by the contract agreement for their opinion on the fair-share proposal.
"4) The results of this written ballot be made public."

the expeditious resolution of the negotiations. Holmquist was next given the floor, after John Matthews, the business representative of MTI, unsuccessfully attempted to dissuade him from speaking. Matthews had also spoken to a member of the school board before the meeting and requested that the board refuse to permit Holmquist to speak. Holmquist stated that he represented "an informal committee of 72 teachers in 49 schools" and that he desired to inform the Board of Education, as he had already informed the union, of the results of an informal survey concerning the "fair share" clause. He then read the petition which had been circulated to the teachers in the district that morning and stated that in the 31 schools from which reports had been received, 53% of the teachers had already signed the petition.

Holmquist stated that neither side had adequately addressed the issue of "fair share" and that teachers were confused about the meaning of the proposal. He concluded by saying: "Due to this confusion, we wish to take no stand on the proposal itself, but ask only that all alternatives be presented clearly to all teachers and more importantly to the general public to whom we are all responsible. We ask simply for communication, not confrontation." The sole response from the school board was a question by the president inquiring whether Holmquist intended to present the board with the petition. Holmquist answered that he would. Holmquist's presentation had lasted approximately two and one-half minutes.

Later that evening, the board met in executive session and voted a proposal acceding to all of the union's demands with the exception of "fair share." During a negotiating session the following morning, MTI accepted the proposal and a contract was signed on December 14, 1976.

(1)

In January 1972 MTI filed a complaint with the Wisconsin Employment Relations Commission (WERC) claiming that the Board had committed a prohibited labor practice by permitting Holmquist to speak at the December 6 meeting. MTI claimed that in so doing the board had engaged in negotiations with a member of the bargaining unit other than the exclusive collective-bargaining representative, in violation of Wis. Stat. § 111.70(3)(a)1, 4. Following a hearing the Commission concluded that the board was guilty of the prohibited labor practice and ordered that it "immediately cease and desist from permitting employees, other than representatives of Madison Teachers, Inc., to appear and speak at meetings of the Board of Education, on matters subject to collective bargaining between it and Madison Teachers, Inc." The Commission's action was affirmed by the Circuit Court of Dane County.

The Supreme Court of Wisconsin affirmed. The court recognized that both the Federal and State Constitutions protect freedom of speech and the right to petition the government, but noted that these rights may be abridged in the face of "a clear and present danger that [the speech] will bring about the substantive evils that [the legislature] has a right to prevent." 69 Wis.2d, at 211, 231 N.W.2d at 212, citing *Schenck v. United States,* 249 U.S. 47, 39 S.Ct. 247, 63 L.Ed. 470 (1919). The court held that abridgment of the speech in this case was justified in order "to avoid the dangers attendant upon relative chaos in labor-management relations." 69 Wis.2d, at 212, 231 N.W.2d at 213.

(2)

The Wisconsin court perceived "clear and present danger" based upon its conclusion that Holmquist's speech before the school board constituted "negotiation" with the board. Permitting such "negotiation," the court reasoned, would undermine the bargaining exclusivity guaranteed the majority union under Wis. Stat. § 111.70(3)(a)4. From that premise it concluded that teachers' First Amendment rights could be limited. Assuming, *arguendo,* that such a "danger" might in some circumstances justify some limitation of First Amendment rights, we are unable to read this record as presenting such danger as would justify curtailing speech.

The Wisconsin Supreme Court's conclusion that Holmquist's terse statement during the public meeting constituted negotiation with the board was based upon its adoption of the lower court's determination that, "[e]ven though Holmquist's statement superficially appears to be merely a 'position statement,' the court deems from the total circumstances that it constituted 'negotiating.' " This cryptic conclusion seems to ignore the ancient wisdom that calling a thing by a name does not make it so. Holmquist did not seek to bargain or offer to enter into any bargain with the board, nor does it appear that he was authorized by any other teachers to enter into any agreement on their behalf. Although his views were not consistent with those of MTI, communicating such views to the employer could not change the fact that MTI alone was authorized to negotiate and to enter into a contract with the board.

Moreover, the school board meeting at which Holmquist was permitted to speak was open to the public. He addressed the school board not merely as one of its employees but also as a concerned citizen, seeking to express his views on an important decision of his government. We have held that teachers may not be "compelled to relinquish the First Amendment rights they would otherwise enjoy as citizens to comment on matters of public interest in connection with the operation of the public school in which they work." *Pickering v. Board of Education,* 391 U.S. 562, 568, 88 S.Ct. 1731, 1734, 20 L.Ed.2d 811 (1968). . . . Where the State has opened a forum for direct citizen involvement, it is difficult to find justification for excluding teachers who make up the overwhelming proportion of school employees and are most vitally concerned with the proceedings. It is conceded that any citizen could have presented precisely the same points and provided the board with the same information as did Holmquist.

Regardless of the extent to which true contract negotiations between a public body and its employees may be regulated — an issue we need not consider at this time — the participation in public discussion of public business cannot be confined to one category of interested individuals. To permit one side of a debatable public question to have a monopoly in expressing its views to the government is the antithesis of constitutional guarantees. Whatever its duties as an employer, when the board sits in public meetings to conduct public business and hear the views of citizens, it may not be required to discriminate between speakers on the basis of their employment, or the content of their speech. *See Police Department v. Mosley,* 408 U.S. 92, 96, 92 S.Ct. 2286, 2290, 33 L.Ed.2d 212 (1972).

(3)

The Employment Relations Commission's order was not limited to a determination that a prohibited labor practice had taken place in the past; it also restrains future conduct. By prohibiting the school board from "permitting employees to appear and speak at meetings of the Board of Education" the order constitutes an indirect, but effective, prohibition on persons such as Holmquist from communicating with their government. The order would have a substantial impact upon virtually all communication between teachers and the school board. The order prohibits speech by teachers "on matters subject to collective bargaining." As the dissenting opinion below noted, however, there is virtually no subject concerning the operation of the school system that could not also be characterized as a potential subject of collective bargaining. Teachers not only constitute the overwhelming bulk of employees of the school system, but they are the very core of that system; restraining teachers' expressions to the board on matters involving the operation of the schools would seriously impair the board's ability to govern the district. . . .

MR. JUSTICE BRENNAN with whom MR. JUSTICE MARSHALL joins, concurring in the judgment.

By stating that "the extent to which true contract negotiations may be regulated [is] an issue we need not consider at this time," *ante,* at 426, the Court's opinion treats as open a question the answer to which I think is abundantly clear. Wisconsin has adopted, as unquestionably the State constitutionally may adopt, a statutory policy that authorizes public bodies to accord exclusive recognition to representatives for collective bargaining chosen by the majority of an appropriate unit of employees. In that circumstance the First Amendment plainly does not forbid Wisconsin from limiting attendance at a collective-bargaining session to school board and union bargaining representatives and denying Holmquist the right to attend and speak at the session. That proposition is implicit in the words of Mr. Justice Holmes, that the "Constitution does not require all public acts to be done in town meeting or an assembly of the whole." *Bi-Metallic Investment Co. v. State Board of Equalization,* 239 U.S. 441, 445, 36 S.Ct. 141, 142, 60 L.Ed. 372 (1915). Certainly in the context of Wisconsin's adoption of the exclusivity principle as a matter of state policy governing relations between state bodies and unions of their employees, "There must be a limit to individual argument in such matters if government is to go on." *Ibid.* For the First Amendment does not command "that people who want to [voice] their views have a constitutional right to do so whenever and however and wherever they please." *Adderley v. Florida,* 385 U.S. 39, 48, 87 S.Ct. 242, 246, 17 L.Ed.2d 149 (1966). For example, this Court's "own conferences [and] the meetings of other official bodies gathered in executive session" may be closed to the public without implicating any constitutional rights whatever. *Branzburg v. Hayes,* 408 U.S. 665, 684, 92 S.Ct. 2646, 2658, 33 L.Ed.2d 626 (1972). Thus, the Wisconsin Supreme Court was correct in stating that there is nothing unconstitutional about legislation commanding that in closed-bargaining sessions a government body may admit, hear the views of, and respond to only the designated representatives of a union selected by the majority of its employees.

But the First Amendment plays a crucially different role when, as here, a government body has either by its own decision or under statutory command, determined to open its decisionmaking processes to public view and participation. In such case, the state body has created a public forum dedicated to the expression of views by the general public. "Once a forum is opened up to assembly or speaking by some groups, government may not prohibit others from assemblying or speaking on the basis of what they intend to say. Selective exclusions from a public forum may not be based on content alone, and may not be justified by reference to content alone." *Police Department of Chicago v. Mosley,* 408 U.S. 92, 96, 92 S.Ct. 2286, 2290, 33 L.Ed.2d 212 (1972). The order sustained by the Wisconsin Supreme Court obviously contravenes that principle. Although there was a complete absence of any evidence that Holmquist's speech was part of a course of conduct in aid of an unfair labor practice by the Board, the order commands that the Board "shall immediately cease and desist from permitting employees other than [union] representatives . . . to appear and speak at [Board] meetings, on matters subject to collective bargaining. . . ." Obedience to that order requires that the Board, regardless of any other circumstances, not allow Holmquist or other citizens to speak at a meeting required by Wis.Stat. § 66.77 to be open and dedicated to expressions of views by citizens generally on such subjects, even though they conform with all procedural rules, even though the subject upon which they wish to speak may be addressed by union representatives, and even though they are part of the "public" to which the forum is otherwise open. The order is therefore wholly void. The State could no more prevent Holmquist from speaking at this public forum than it could prevent him from publishing the same views in a newspaper or proclaiming them from a soapbox.

I therefore agree that the judgment of the Wisconsin Supreme Court be reversed.

[The concurring opinion of MR. JUSTICE STEWART is omitted.]

## NEW YORK PUBLIC EMPLOYMENT RELATIONS BOARD, SURVEY ON DISCLOSURE DURING PUBLIC SECTOR NEGOTIATIONS, GERR No. 463, D-2 to D-6 (1972)

### Introduction

On January 3, 1972, Governor Rockefeller requested that the Public Employment Relations Board give top priority to the problem of public disclosure following negotiations with public employee groups.

For some time the problem of disclosure at various stages of the negotiating process had been discussed by PERB with the parties, the media, and knowledgeable people in the labor relations field. To completely encompass this field, PERB's analysis of the question was broadened beyond the Governor's request to include all stages of the negotiating process. Opinions on disclosure throughout the process were solicited from the media, mediators and fact-finders, and recognized industrial and labor relations experts. In addition, a questionnaire soliciting information on what actually occurred with respect to disclosure during the course of negotiations and their opinions was sent to the parties in impasse situations in which the fact-finding report and recommendations had not been acted upon within 10 days.

For purposes of structuring the analysis, the negotiating process was broken into the following stages:

1. Negotiations prior to third-party assistance.
2. During the course of mediation.
3. During the course of fact-finding.
4. After the fact-finder has rendered his report and recommendations but before agreement.
5. After agreement has been reached but prior to employee ratification.
6. After agreement has been reached but prior to enactment of legislation required to implement the agreement.

In addition to the above points, the respondents also were requested to recommend whether disclosure should be mandated by statute.

A full discussion of the issue follows PERB's Recommendations.

### Recommendations

On the basis of the inquiry and responses from the affected parties and others, PERB recommends that:

*No amendments to the Taylor Law are required with respect to disclosure of agreements negotiated between public employers and employee groups.*

1. Legislation regarding disclosure is unnecessary because:

(a) Inquiry indicates that the basic details of most such agreements are made public either when agreement is reached or after ratification by the employee groups.

(b) If the negotiations reach the fact-finding stages, the fact-finding report and recommendations are made public by PERB five days after receipt by the parties as required by law. Often the parties themselves release the substance of the report within the five-day period. Subsequent negotiations, if any, take place within the framework of the fact-finder's report.

(c) If a legislative hearing is required, the law mandates a *public* hearing.

(d) In almost all instances the agreement is made available to the public by the employer, and sometimes by the employee organization. Normally, the contract is also available from PERB on request.

(e) A substantial part of all memoranda of agreement, including the fiscal aspects, requires legislative implementation. Public sector labor agreements appear to receive essentially the same amount of disclosure as do other government matters.

2. Legislation regarding disclosure is *undesirable* because:

(a) It would deny governments necessary flexibility. Given the diversity of negotiating situations among the 1,100 public employers and 2,500 negotiating units (varying from three-man police departments to units with 30,000 or more employees), it would be difficult to devise legislation which would fit this wide variety of situations.

(b) It subverts the authority of elected officials.

Negotiations under the Taylor Law are, in theory at least, between the Chief Executive and the employee organization on behalf of the public and as the public's agent. The Chief Executive is authorized to pursue his policies, and by entering into the contracts to obligate the government to carry out those policies. If disclosure of an agreement of the Chief Executive is not designed to induce renunciation or modification of that agreement, it is meaningless, adding nothing but costs and delay to ordinary disclosure requirements. If disclosure contemplates renunciation or modification of the agreement, it subverts the authority of the Chief Executive and imperils the negotiation process.

This analysis suggests one caveat. Most employee organizations require disclosure of their agreements to — and ratification by — their members. The possibility of the agreement of labor officials being renounced by their constituency is no less troublesome than the possibility of the agreement of a Chief Executive being renounced under pressure from his constituency. A case could be made for giving to the constituency of the Chief Executive an opportunity to be informed of an agreement before it is executed by the Chief Executive if the employee organization reserves to its members the right of ratification. We would not mandate such disclosure by law but recognize that under such circumstances, the government might choose to disclose the terms of the proposed agreement before executing it.

## Discussion

### The Study

In making his request of PERB to study the question of disclosure, the Governor said:

> "The public has a right to know the full details of agreements reached with public employee groups. More often than not, these agreements involve large sums of public funds. At the same time every effort should be made to avoid interference with the collective negotiating process.
>
> "I have, therefore, called upon the State Public Employment Relations Board to make specific recommendations on this subject, including any necessary amendments to the Taylor Law."

As noted earlier in this report, PERB expanded the inquiry to include disclosure at various stages of negotiations. Among those queried were the parties to actual impasses, media representatives and recognized labor relations experts. A discussion of the responses received from each group follows:

### Media Responses

In discussions with representatives of the Public Employment Relations Board from time to time throughout the years, representatives of the media have generally taken a strong position that much, if not all, of the negotiating process should be "public." However, responses from media representatives were generally somewhat more conservative.

The following is a representative response:

> "While there is one element of even public sector bargaining which concededly should be private — that is, the bargaining session itself (to assure the maximum opportunity for fruitful discussion and expeditious reaching of agreement), it is in the public interest that full and prompt public disclosure be made, presumably by a PERB spokesman, on the following points as they develop:
>
> "1. The issues.
>
> "2. The points of difference, including the sums of public money involved.
>
> "3. Progress or lack of progress in the negotiations.
>
> "4. The basis of agreement, including the amount of public money involved."

Another respondent stated:

> "We agree wholeheartedly with the Governor's position that the public has a right to know the full details of agreements reached with public employee groups.
>
> "We also feel that since public money is involved, there should be disclosure from the start of negotiations of what the employees are asking and what the employer is offering. . . ."

Another respondent, a distinguished long-time observer of the labor relations scene, said in part:

"The notion that disclosure interferes with the bargaining process has little validity in my experience. There might be something to be said for it if unions in the public sector clothe their bargainers with full power to conclude an agreement. Then, it could be argued that both sides ought to go in prepared to put their best offers on the table, confident that a final deal can be made.

"But desirable as such a procedure would be in narrow terms of the efficacy of bargaining, it has distinct flaws in a period of institutional upheaval when union leaders are hard pressed to hold their members in line even when the contracts are superb in every respect. Rank and file ratification is a fact of life and must be reckoned with in unions that were once the acme of conservatism.

"By the same token, taxpayers will have every right to rebel if they keep finding themselves stuck with a *fait accompli* that pushes up cost while necessitating reductions in service. Such rebellion is even more likely where the basic issues of public policy affecting schools, hospitals or other vital agencies are determined by union and public management with no direct voice for the neighborhood or other affected groups. Whatever embarrassments disclosing may create, they are vastly preferable in a democracy to shutting the public away from knowledge of things that the community has committed itself to until after the commitment is irrevocable."

The essence of the media response would appear to be that there should be disclosure with respect to the opening position of the parties, limited disclosure during the course of negotiations with periodic progress reports dealing with how far apart the parties are or how near they are, but not necessarily with substance, and full disclosure once agreement has been reached.

## Clientele Responses

### Public Employers

The responses summarized below are those received from representatives of organizations representing public employers, e.g., Conference of Mayors, N.Y.S. School Boards Association, etc. Answers received from public employers as such are summarized in a later section dealing with questionnaire responses as previously indicated.

There appears to be substantial consensus among public employer representatives that there should be no disclosure until the fact-finder has rendered his report and recommendations. If no third-party assistance is required or if third-party assistance is confined to mediation, there appears to be agreement that disclosure should not take place until the parties have ratified the contract. Response to the specific questions are summarized below:

1. During the course of negotiations without third-party assistance.

Employer representatives felt that the least possible disclosure should be made during the normal course of negotiations. The situation should be kept flexible. When either side makes public pronouncements of its position, it must then answer to its constituents for any deviation from the stated position. This has the effect of prolonging the negotiations and defeats the normal give-and-take which should be available to the negotiating teams.

2. During the course of mediation.

Mediation is an extension of the negotiating process with a third party present in an informal procedure. The considerations discussed under Question 1 were held to apply to Question 2.

3. During the course of fact-finding.

Fact-finding is a more formalized procedure for impasse resolution. However, none of the public employer representatives advocated making the fact-finding proceeding public or for disclosure of the positions of the parties during fact-finding.

4. After the fact-finder has rendered his report and recommendations but before agreement.

Section 209.3(c) provides that a fact-finding report and recommendations shall be made public within five days of its transmission to the parties. Thus, at this point, some disclosure is mandated in that the fact-finding report in some manner is reported to the public. (See section on questionnaire responses below.) Representatives of public employers generally felt that public pressures have little effect upon employee groups. All the respondents agreed that the public does have a right to know prior to the legislative hearing. The opinion was expressed that if agreement had not been reached at this point, it would be difficult to predict when agreement would be reached. Therefore, the public employer, at least, should be free to make such disclosure as he sees fit at the time the fact-finder's report becomes public.

Section 209.3(e) provides that if either party does not accept the fact-finder's recommendations in whole or in part, the chief executive officer shall, within ten days after receipt of the recommendations, submit to the legislative body both the fact-finding report and recommendations and his own recommendations for settling the dispute. The employee organization also is authorized to submit its recommendations.

The legislative body is then directed to "forthwith conduct a public hearing at which the parties shall be required to explain their positions with respect to the report of the fact-finding board." These provisions led to the following comments by one respondent:

"These considerations lead me to conclude that the public's right to know about contracts with public employee groups arises at either of two points: when the contract has been negotiated *and executed,* or when agreement has not been possible and a public hearing is to be held on the fact-finder's report, and public opinion is to play its part in the legislative decision." The respondent added: "This conclusion is consistent with the rights and responsibilities that are a part of our representative system of government."

5. After agreement has been reached, but prior to employee ratification.

This question brought forth a two-part response. Assuming that negotiations have proceeded with no third-party assistance, there was agreement that public disclosure should await ratification by the parties. Full public disclosure should take place, employer associations felt, when ratification is accomplished so that the public may know what its elected representatives are doing and how public funds are being used.

If there has been fact-finding assistance, then the answers to Question 4 pertain — there should be disclosure simultaneously or shortly after the publication of the fact-finder's report and recommendations.

6. After agreement has been reached, but prior to the enactment of legislation required to implement the agreement.

At this point there was some disagreement. All agreed that there would be disclosure, but one respondent had a reservation:

"To reveal all of the details of an agreement and heed public reaction is tantamount to allowing the public to veto the agreement, or, in fact, to be a party to the negotiations. In a representative form of government ... the responsibility rests with the elected official to perform his duty ... and a remedy for the voter who does not approve of his representative's actions is in the ballot box."

This particular respondent felt that the above quote pertained in a situation where the parties had arrived at an agreement without third-party assistance and where the legislature, of course, has not been required to make a determination but to implement an agreement bilaterally negotiated.

The final, but unnumbered question, was:

*Should such disclosure as you consider to be appropriate be mandated by statute?*

Significantly, none of the respondents felt that disclosure, in the sense of full publication of the text of the contract, should be mandated prior to legislative implementation. Some felt that this was not necessary at all. Others felt that the full text of the agreement should be published in an official newspaper after ratification and after implementation but within a specified period. An alternative would be to print the agreement and to make it available to all interested parties including employees, residents, etc. It was pointed out that to require publication of the full text of an agreement in an official newspaper would be to impose a substantial financial burden upon an employer, particularly if there were several units.

*Public Employee Organizations.* The views of parent labor organizations representing public employees also were solicited. The views of locals were solicited by questionnaire and are discussed in a later section of this report.

The views of the leadership of parent organizations representing public employees can best be summarized by the following comment:

"I have no quarrel with full disclosure after the contract has been agreed upon or certainly disclosure to the legislative body as legislation is needed. . . . Only after a contract is consummated and ratified would I give it full public disclosure. Labor relations, like international relations, is much too sensitive and difficult a process without putting it in the glare of public emotion. The public has a right to know — after it's negotiated. The . . . legislature should be kept fully informed in terms of the process of negotiations, the goals of negotiations. . . ."

Public employee union leadership was in general agreement that there should be no disclosure until:

1. Agreement has been reached and ratified; or
2. The matter is before the legislative body.

### Panel Member Responses

Because of a wide variation in a number of impasses coming to the Public Employment Relations Board at various times of the year — half of the total impasses brought to the Board come in the second calendar quarter — and because PERB staff members do not engage in fact-finding the Board makes extensive use of panel mediators and fact-finders. These panel members are drawn from a variety of sources and have varying backgrounds and experience. The reactions of a sample of the members of the panel were sought to the same questions submitted to representatives of employer and employee organizations.

One panel respondent summarized the comments of most panel members who were queried.

"1. No disclosure should be required or even encouraged during the stages of negotiations, mediation or fact-finding. Such disclosure would not only inhibit the making of offers and counterproposals *between* the parties, but might also cause serious problems of internal communications within the ranks of the bargainers. Just as one example, when I entered the XYZ school district negotiations last May, the parties had wasted ten entire bargaining sessions engaging in mutual recriminations about releases of information to the press. The minutes of these sessions reflect the progressive animosities which developed over the winter — feelings which had hardened to such an extent that absolutely no discussion had taken place on substantive issues. I was able to get the dispute settled by mediation only after both parties had agreed that no one (including the mediator) would talk to the press until settlement had been achieved, or until the mediator released the parties from their pledge of silence both to the press *and* to their constituents.

"2. After a fact-finding report has been issued and following the expiration of the five-day negotiating period the Law already mandates the release of the report. I see nothing harmful in disclosure of the report at this point.

"3. Once agreement has been reached, the parties themselves should agree on the ground rules for disclosure of the terms to their constituents. Otherwise, the agreement may blow up or be rejected because of mistrust, misunderstandings, or mutual recriminations.

"4. After an agreement has been ratified and signed, I have no objection to its terms being disclosed before implementing legislation is enacted. In fact, such disclosure would seem to be in the public interest.

"5. I am opposed to any form of disclosure being mandated by law. [It] could more appropriately be handled by administrative rule making."

Disagreement with the positions articulated above centered on two factors:

1. The nature of the fact-finding process; and
2. The problem of disclosure itself.

Those panelists who had different views were, nevertheless, in agreement that there should be no disclosure at least until the beginning of fact-finding.

Some of the panelists felt that certain advantages might flow from public fact-finding proceedings, and perhaps more formalized ones. One advocate of public fact-finding hearings, operating on the assumption that only organized public groups would participate, summarized his position this way:

"1. The immediate advantage, it seems to me, would result from allowing parent groups in teacher disputes and general taxpayer groups involving other classes of public employees to get at first hand all the facts relating to the dispute. . . .

"2. Participation by the public in the fact-finding proceeding may alert the disputants to adopt a reasonable and rational approach to the ultimate solution of the dispute.

"3. Since participation should assume a real recognition of the opinions and judgments of the participants, the third parties (taxpayer groups, et al.) will bring to the proceedings evidence of the public interest and thus may affect the positions of the disputants. . . .

"4. Psychologically, public participation may result in public acceptance of the findings and recommendations even when they may be at variance of the opinions of the public participants. The right to participate in itself is a form of due process which in time makes adverse decisions palatable and acceptable. . . .

"5. Exposure of the fact-finding proceedings to the glare of interested public groups may result in a reduction of the many peripheral issues commonly raised by the disputants under existing procedures. . . ."

The problem of *how* to disclose bothered some panelists. One put it this way:

"As you well know, there are at least two ways to multiplying and adding the same set of figures — employer's way and union's way — and at least one more way of doing it objectively . . . it may seem possible to avoid all this by merely listing tersely the items in the memorandum of agreement or list of demands without costing or explanation. But what will it mean to the public? Very little. . . .

"I see one possible avenue in the direction of involving the taxpayers. That is, in enlarging the concept of the 'legislative body' as responsive to the community as a whole. Provide that no settlement may be finalized until there is a public hearing on it by the legislative body — similar to the 'show cause' hearing on the fact-finder's report, but for both instances with mandated advance notice to the public — at least 25 days. That is, no settlement may be final until it has been 'shown' to the public and an opportunity given to them to react to it."

Another panelist, accepting the concept that there should be no disclosure until the fact-finder has reported, commented as follows:

"After the fact-finder has issued his report and recommendations, the rules of the game change. The fact-finder is the voice of the public and his document, once issued, becomes public property. At the same time, however, I am fully aware that a fact-finder's report is subject to modifications and exchanges by the parties and they should be given the opportunity to make these changes within a reasonable time after the report is issued, and a period of five days appears reasonable.

"The activities of the parties starting with the sixth day after the issuance of a fact-finder's report should be given the full public exposure and the element of distortion by the media is substantially reduced because the fact-finder's document contains in written form . . . all the ingredients of the dispute and thus it is relatively easier for the media to give accurate, objective information when this document is available as a foundation.

"As a statutory provision for disclosure, I would advise amendment of the existing language on legislative hearing which would require same to be held within a precise and exact time insofar as the public employer is concerned. In order to put an end point to delay by design, I would further recommend that the results of the legislative hearing must be publicly communicated by a time certain after the issuance of the fact-finder's report and failure to so communicate would constitute acceptance of the report as final and binding, that this is also true as to the public employee organization where the employee organization does assert a definitive position within a time certain, and I think 20 days would be ample for the parties. The public employee organization would be deemed to have accepted the report as a final and binding document in the case of failure to declare within the specified time. . . ."

Thus the position of the panelists can be summed up by saying that they were unanimous in holding that there should be no disclosure until the beginning of fact-finding. A few thought that public participation in the fact-finding process might be helpful, but the vast majority did not. All of the panelists appeared to be in agreement with the present provision of the Taylor Law which requires disclosure of the fact-finding report and recommendations five days after receipt by the parties.

There was disagreement, and fairly wide disagreement, among the panelists as to whether some form of disclosure should be mandated by law. Many felt that if such action was required it could be done by administrative rule. They felt that this procedure would allow for some experimentation and less rigidity if whatever was proposed did not work.

Those panelists who felt that some form of disclosure should be mandated after issuance of the fact-finding report coupled such proposals with proposed modifications of the impasse procedure.

## "Expert" Respondents

A variety of labor relations "experts" also were canvassed. These included members of the Taylor Committee, heads of public sector labor relations agencies in other states, academic experts, and distinguished practitioners.

In those states which have "anti-secrecy" statutes, the mediation process is either exempt from such laws or the process has escaped being affected by such laws. In Michigan, a school board which insisted that the press be present during negotiations was held to be guilty of bad faith bargaining. In Wisconsin the Supreme Court held, contrary to the ruling of the Labor Relations agency, that a school board did not interfere with the rights of an employee who was a member of a minority organization by denying that individual the opportunity to speak at a public hearing conducted by the school board with reference to the negotiated agreement. All of the heads of the state labor relations agencies with public sector responsibilities canvassed were essentially in agreement. Their position can best be summarized by the following response:

"It has been our opinion that once the collective bargaining agreement has been tentatively approved by the negotiators for the public employer [and the] union, the details of the agreement should be made known. All three of the Commissioners — as well as our two staff men who do quite a bit of public speaking — have taken this position. We do so on the basis you state in your letter: that the agreements most often involve large sums of public funds and that the public is entitled to know."

Their only disagreement among administrators of state agencies is *when* there should be disclosure. Some feel that disclosure should occur at the tentative agreement stage while others contend that disclosure should not occur until after ratification.

Other experts and practitioners canvassed were similarly divided on this point. One stated:

". . . when agreement is reached by negotiators, there are often very delicate situations involved in achieving ratification, sometimes on both sides — by the union's general membership or by the legislative body involved. For this reason it is probably advisable to guard against premature release of the terms of the contract because of possible interference with the ratification. While I recognize the strength of the argument that the people who pay the bills should be entitled to know the cost of the agreement before it is finalized, I am experienced enough in the bargaining process to realize that such disclosure would make agreement more difficult to achieve. We must rely on the good faith of the municipal negotiators and the power of the public to change them by the process of recall or election, to assure the community that the agreement is a sound one.

"On the other hand, I do believe that a great deal more can be done to inform the public of the actual cost of finalized agreements — after ratification — so that they may be in a better position to judge the correctness of the agreement which has been acted upon. I refer to effective costing out of fringe benefits in general and pensions in particular. . . ."

Other groups of respondents were as concerned with the "how" of disclosure as with the "when" of disclosure. Among the academic-practitioner respondents concerned with this question, the following is a typical comment:

"The 'how' question is even more difficult. Even in the public sector, I have grave reservations about the ability of the general public to digest and appraise complicated issues. Simple publication of the terms usually is somewhat a waste of paper since few people will read a complete agreement. Moreover, even if they do, most people outside of the immediate scene cannot intelligently appraise the terms. Consequently well-written summaries that are interpretive are almost required. Who is to do this job? Good labor reporters are increasingly hard to find. Moreover, whoever prepares a summary can always be accused, sometimes rightly, of 'slanting the story.' I suspect that there is no perfect way of meeting these problems. The mediator, or the fact-finder, or P.R. personnel in the agency can be most helpful in the preparation of an accurate and understandable summary but some risks are involved. Probably the potential values are worth the risk."

### Responses of Parties

The comments from the parties generally opposed disclosure citing reasons as inhibiting the negotiations process, creating a fish bowl effect and polarizing the parties.

One employer replied:

"If agreements are made public before ratification, political pressures to turn down negotiated agreements will be brought against the legislative body with the only possible results being the rejection of negotiated agreements in greater numbers than have existed in the past and even greater distrust of the negotiating procedure on the part of employee organizations than at present."

The replies as to the actual amount of disclosure indicate that there was very little public disclosure. . . .

Most of the clients responding did not favor additional disclosure. Majorities ranging from 90 to 60 per cent were opposed to more disclosure. The highest vote for more disclosure was for releasing the fact-finding report to the public and the press at the same time it is released to the parties. Slightly under 40 per cent of the respondents favored this step.

There was slightly less support for public fact-finding hearings. The support for this viewpoint was strongest by employers. More than 44 per cent of them supported this idea. However, it seemed apparent that many of the replies favoring more disclosure were not advocating public policy but were advancing ideas that they thought would have aided their cause in recent negotiations.

In the instances in which there was public disclosure, the side making it often claimed that the "public" supported their side. It seems apparent that public disclosure is not being used as a means of informing the citizens but rather as a means of marshalling support for their respective position. There also were several comments that indicated that disclosure inhibited flexibility and compromise.

In terms of public impact, the comments varied from no impact to support of position by community (on both sides). There were several comments that positions as reported by media were distorted. However, in most cases the impact of the community toward reaching an agreement even after the fact-finder's report was published appeared to be slight. Those who commented on attendance at legislative hearings indicated that the public did not attend.

## NOTES

1. Despite the preference of most parties to negotiate in private, several states have enacted legislation which specifically requires that negotiations be conducted in public. For example, Section 11 of the Tennessee Education Professional Negotiations Act provides that "[a]ny negotiations under the provisions of this Act shall be meetings within the provisions of [the Tennessee Open Meetings Law]." TENN. CODE ANN. tit 49, § 11 (1978). The Florida Act provides that "collective bargaining negotiations between a chief executive officer or his representative and a bargaining agent shall not be exempt from [the Florida Sunshine Law]." However, Florida law does exempt "[a]ll discussions between the chief executive officer of the public employer or his representative and the legislative body or the public employer relative to collective bargaining. . . ." FLA. STAT. ANN. § 447.605 (1978).

2. The Texas bargaining law covering firefighters and police officers provides that "[a]ll deliberations pertaining to collective bargaining between an association and a public employer or any deliberation by a quorum of members of an association authorized to bargain collectively or by a member of a public employer authorized to bargaining collectively shall be open to the public and in compliance with the Acts of the State of Texas." TEX. REV. CIV. STAT. ANN. Article 6252-17a, § 1 (Supp. 1978). In Enterprise Co. v. City of Beaumont, —S.W.2d— (Tex. Ct. Civ. App. 1978), the court noted that "[t]he legislature has determined that the public's right to know what is going on in the negotiation sessions between its representatives and those representing its firefighters is entitled to statutory protection," even though "[i]t may very well be that such statutorily protected right may inhibit or prevent successful negotiations." The court, however, relying on another section of the Act which permitted a mediator to hold separate conferences with the parties, held that while the public "is entitled to be present and observe the *joint* conferences," it "has no right to see or observe the proceedings in the *separate* conferences with the mediator." *See also* Southwestern Oregon Publishing Co. v. Southwestern Oregon Community College Dist., 28 Or. App. 383, 559 P.2d 1289 (1977) (Oregon Public Meeting Law did not apply to labor negotiations conducted on behalf of a community college by a retained labor negotiator).

3. In the past couple of years several states have enacted legislation which seeks to balance the public's right to know what's happening in negotiations with the parties' normal preference to negotiate in private. For example, a 1977 amendment to the Wisconsin Municipal Employment Relations Act provides that the meetings that are held by the parties "for the purpose of presenting initial bargaining proposals, along with supporting rationale, shall be open to the public." WIS. STAT., Ch. 111,

§ 111.70(4)(cm)(2). Another example is the following public notice provision in the California Educational Employment Relations Act:

(a) All initial proposals of exclusive representatives and of public school employers, which relate to matters within the scope of representation, shall be presented at a public meeting of the public school employer and thereafter shall be public records.

(b) Meeting and negotiating shall not take place on any proposal until a reasonable time has elapsed after the submission of the proposal to enable the public to become informed and the public has the opportunity to express itself regarding the proposal at a meeting of the public school employer.

(c) After the public has had the opportunity to express itself, the public school employer shall, at a meeting which is open to the public, adopt its initial proposal.

(d) New subjects of meeting and negotiating arising after the presentation of initial proposals shall be made public within 24 hours. If a vote is taken on such subject by the public school employer, the vote thereon by each member voting shall also be made public within 24 hours.

(e) The board may adopt regulations for the purpose of implementing this section, which are consistent with the intent of the section; namely that the public be informed of the issues that are being negotiated upon and have full opportunity to express their views on the issues to the public school employer, and to know of the positions of their elected representatives.

Cal. Gov't Code § 3547.

## TALBOT v. CONCORD UNION SCHOOL DISTRICT

New Hampshire Supreme Court
323 A.2d 912, 87 L.R.R.M. 3159 (1974)

KENISON, Chief Justice: — The principal question raised by these proceedings is whether the defendant is required under the Right to Know Law (RSA ch. 91-A (Supp. 1973)) to open to the public, including the press, its collective bargaining sessions with the Concord Education Association concerning teacher salary scales, fringe benefits and other related matters. The plaintiffs brought a petition for an injunction pursuant to RSA 91-A:7 (Supp. 1973) to enjoin the defendant from excluding them from such collective bargaining sessions. After an evidentiary hearing, the Trial Court (Keller, C.J.) denied the plaintiffs' request for a temporary injunction on the grounds that such a remedy would disrupt negotiations and delay the adoption of the school budget. The parties subsequently agreed that the hearing for the temporary injunction should be treated as if it had been a hearing for a permanent injunction. The trial court reserved and transferred the plaintiffs' exception to its denial of the petition.

The basic facts of this case are not in dispute. The defendant school district is a corporation organized by special act of the legislature and is empowered by law to conduct the public schools within the geographic boundaries of the district, which includes a major portion of the City of Concord. Laws 1961, ch. 355, as amended Laws 1967, ch. 560 and Laws 1971, ch. 262. All powers of the district are vested in a board of education composed of nine members. The Concord Education Association is a local teachers' organization which is recognized by the board as the bargaining representative of the teachers in the district. The parties entered into a "negotiations contract" which establishes in pertinent part procedures governing negotiations between the parties concerning "salaries and other matters." It provides that the parties shall meet on the written request of either of them at a mutually convenient time to exchange "facts, opinions, proposals and counter-proposals . . . freely and in good faith during the meeting or meetings (and between meetings, if advisable) in an effort to reach mutual understanding and agreement." In practice, the negotiations between the parties are conducted in an informal manner by committees appointed by each of them. These committees have no authority to bind the parties to the terms of any collective bargaining agreement, but must return to their principals for approval of their recommendations. Although the bargaining sessions between the committees have been traditionally closed to the public, the recommendations of the committees are received and voted upon by the board in an open meeting.

The present action arose from the board's refusal to permit the plaintiff Roger G. Talbot, a reporter for the Concord Monitor, to attend one or more of the bargaining committees' sessions. The parties have agreed that none of the exceptions to the Right to Know Law (RSA 91-A:3 (Supp. 1973)) are applicable to these facts, and the narrow issue presented by this case is whether the bargaining sessions of the committees are within the purview of the act.

The parties have drawn this court's attention to two legislative policies which bear on this issue. The first policy is that of the Right to Know Law which is to protect the democratic process by making public the decisions and considerations on which government action is based. Carter v. Nashua, 113 N.H. 407, 416, 308 A.2d 847, 853 (1973). The second is that of the collective bargaining statute (RSA 31:3) which recognizes the right of public employees to negotiate the terms of their contractual relationship with the government by using the well-established techniques of private sector bargaining. Timberlane Regional School Dist. v. Timberlane Regional Educ. Ass'n, 114 N.H. ——, ——, 317 A.2d 555, 557, 87 LRRM 2015 (1973); Tremblay v. Berlin Police Union, 108 N.H. 416, 237 A.2d 668, 68 LRRM 2070 (1966). See also RSA ch. 98-C (Supp. 1973). The plaintiffs urge that the former policy must take precedence over the latter because the broad language used in RSA 91-A:2 (Supp. 1973) requires that all public proceedings of any school district board or subcommittee thereof must be open to the public. The defendant contends in response that the unlimited extension of the former policy would consume the latter because the collective bargaining process cannot operate effectively if exposed to the public eye.

There is nothing in the legislative history of the Right to Know Law to indicate that the legislature specifically considered the impact of its provisions on public sector bargaining. However, it is improbable that the legislature intended the law to apply in such a fashion as to destroy the very process it was attempting to open to the public. See Annot., 38 A.L.R.3d 1070 § 6 (b) (1971). There is substantial authority in support of the defendant's position that the delicate mechanisms of collective bargaining would be thrown awry if viewed prematurely by the public. Bassett v. Braddock, 262 So.2d 425, 80 LRRM 2955 (Fla. 1972); R. Smith, H. Edwards & R. Clark, Jr., Labor Relations Law in the Public Sector 569-594 (1974); Edwards, The Emerging Duty to Bargain in the Public Sector, 71 Mich. L. Rev. 885, 901-02 (1973); Wickham, Let the Sun Shine In! Open-Meeting Legislation Can Be Our Key to Closed Doors in State and Local Government, 68 Nw. U. L. Rev. 480, 491-92 (1973); see R. Smith, L. Merrifield & D. Rothschild, Collective Bargaining and Labor Arbitration 36-44 (1970). In fact, a number of State labor boards have gone so far as to hold that a party's insistence on bargaining in public constituted a refusal to negotiate in good faith, reasoning that bargaining in the public arena "would tend to prolong negotiations and damage the procedure of compromise inherent in collective bargaining." Menominee Bd. of Educ., MERC Lab. Op. 383, 386 (Mich. 1968); see Mayor Samuel E. Zoll and the City of Salem, MLRC Case No. MUP-309 (Mass. 1972); Bethlehem Area School Directors, Penn. Lab. Rel. Bd. Case No. PERA-C-2861-C, Gov't Employ Rel. Rep't No. 505, E-1

(1973). See also CAL. GOVT. CODE § 54957.6 (West 1974) (Authorizing school boards to deny public access to "consultations and discussions" with public employee representatives concerning salaries and other matters); Grodin, Public Employee Bargaining in California: The Meyers-Milias-Brown Act in the Court, 23 Hast. L. J. 719, 752 (1972); cf. Minn. Stat. Ann. ch. 179, § 179.69 (1971) (Permitting public access to all negotiating sessions *unless* otherwise provided by the director of mediation services).

The record is replete with evidence indicating that the presence of the public and the press at negotiating sessions would inhibit the free exchange of views and freeze negotiators into fixed positions from which they could not recede without loss of face. Moreover, in the opinion of one witness, the opening of such sessions to the public could result in the employment of professional negotiators, thus removing the local representatives from the bargaining process. See Mont. Rev. Code Ann. § 75-6127 (1971) (opening *professional* negotiating sessions but closing preliminary deliberations of school board).

We agree with the Florida Supreme Court "that meaningful collective bargaining in the circumstances here would be destroyed if full publicity were accorded at each step of the negotiations" (Bassett v. Braddock, 262 So.2d 425, 426, 80 LRRM 2955, 2956 (Fla. 1972)) and hold that the negotiation sessions between the school board and union committees are not within the ambit of the Right to Know Law. However, in so ruling, we would emphasize that these sessions serve only to produce recommendations which are submitted to the board for final approval. The board's approval must be given in an open meeting in accordance with RSA 91-A:3 (Supp. 1973), thus protecting the public's right to know what contractual terms have been agreed upon by the negotiators.

Plaintiffs' exception overruled.

All concurred.

## NOTES

1. *See also* Burlington Community School Dist. v. PERB, 96 L.R.R.M. 2571 (Ia. Dist. Ct. 1977) (unfair labor practice for employer to insist that negotiation sessions be conducted in public; negotiation sessions must be closed if the parties reach impasse on question).

2. In Chiglione v. School Committee of Southbridge, 1977-78 PBC ¶ 36,446 (Mass. Sup. Jud. Ct. 1978), the court held that it was permissible for a school board to meet in closed session to discuss a grievance since the Massachusetts Open Meeting Law permits closed sessions to conduct collective bargaining and since collective bargaining includes resolving grievances under a collective bargaining agreement.

3. In sharp contrast to the decision in the principal case, the North Dakota Supreme Court in Dickinson Education Ass'n v. Dickinson Public School Dist. No. 1, 252 N.W.2d 205, 95 L.R.R.M. 2744 (N.D. S. Ct. 1977), held that the North Dakota constitutional and statutory provisions concerning open meetings were violated when the school board and members of the board's bargaining team consulted in private to discuss and adopt bargaining positions. The court stated:

We find that our constitutional and statutory open meeting provisions require that all school board meetings at which teacher contract offers and school board offers and counter offers are considered shall be open to the public. We further find that our constitutional and statutory open meeting provisions require that all school board-teacher contract negotiating sessions, regardless of negotiating committee composition, shall be open to the public.

*Accord,* Littleton Education Ass'n v. Arapahoe County School Dist., 553 P.2d 793 (Colo. S. Ct. 1976).

4. In Cohalan v. Board of Education of Bayport-Blue Point School District, 1977-78 PBC ¶ 36,389 (N.Y. S. Ct. 1978), the court held that a taxpayer was not entitled to the proposals and demands made by the parties when they were engaged in mediation and prior to the time that the taxpayers voted on the school budget.

5. *See generally* Note, *Public Sector Collective Bargaining and Sunshine Laws — Needless Conflict,* 18 WM. & MARY L. REV. 159 (1976).

# Chapter 5

# UNION SECURITY IN PUBLIC EMPLOYMENT

## A. INTRODUCTION

There are six basic types of union security provisions — closed shop, union shop, maintenance of membership, agency shop, fair share, and dues checkoff. The general characteristics of each of these forms of union security are as follows:

1. *Closed Shop.* A closed shop provision requires that an employee as a condition of employment must become a member of the union prior to being employed and must remain a member. The closed shop was lawful under the National Labor Relations Act as originally enacted in 1935, but since 1947 has been prohibited under the Taft-Hartley Amendments. For all intents and purposes the closed shop is illegal in both the public and private sectors.

2. *Union Shop.* A union shop clause requires that an employee as a condition of employment become a member of the union within a stipulated period, usually 30 days, after being hired or after the effective date of the collective bargaining agreement, whichever is later. The NLRA specifically provides that private sector employers and unions may negotiate union shop agreements, except where such agreements are prohibited by state right-to-work laws. Sixty-two per cent of the collective bargaining agreements negotiated in the private sector include union shop clauses. BNA, COLLECTIVE BARGAINING NEGOTIATIONS AND CONTRACTS 87:1. In the public sector five states [1] have legislatively authorized the negotiation of union shop clauses for some or all categories of public employees.

3. *Maintenance of Membership.* A maintenance of membership clause requires that once an employee becomes a member of a union he/she must continue to be a member as a condition of employment. There is no requirement, however, that an employee initially become a member. Maintenance of membership agreements are permitted under the NLRA, although they are prohibited in those states with right-to-work laws. Only two states — California (teachers and state employees) and Pennsylvania — specifically permit public employers and unions to negotiate maintenance of membership clauses. Presumably, however, maintenance of membership clauses would also be permissible in states that permit the negotiation of union shop clauses.

4. *Agency Shop.* An agency shop clause requires that an employee as a condition of employment pay an amount equal to the periodic union dues uniformly required as a condition of acquiring or retaining membership. The agency shop is legal under the NLRA, but is prohibited by most state right-to-work laws. The negotiation of agency shop clauses is specifically permitted by law in at least six states [2] and the District of Columbia.

---

[1] Alaska, Kentucky (fire fighters, but only applicable to cities over 300,000 or cities petitioning for coverage), Maine (university employees), Vermont (municipal employees), and Washington (employees in higher education).

[2] Connecticut (state employees), Michigan, Montana, Rhode Island (teachers and state employees), Vermont (municipal employees), and Washington (teachers).

5. *Fair Share.* A fair share agreement is a variation of the agency shop which requires the employee as a condition of employment pay a proportionate share of the cost of collective bargaining activities but not the cost of other union activities. At least seven states [3] authorize fair share agreements.

In sharp contrast to the statutory provisions which permit the parties to voluntarily agree upon a fair share agreement, the Hawaii public sector law requires an employer, wholly independent of negotiations, to deduct from the pay of all employees in the appropriate unit service fees and remit same to the exclusive representative "upon receiving from an exclusive representative a written statement which specifies an amount of reasonable service fees necessary to defray the costs for its services rendered in negotiating and administering an agreement and computed on a pro rata basis among all employees within its appropriate bargaining unit. . . ." HAWAII REV. STAT. tit. 7, § 89-4 (Supp. 1971). Similarly, the Minnesota law provides that "the employer upon notification by the exclusive representative . . . shall be obligated to check off" from non-members "a fair share fee for services rendered by the exclusive representative." MINN. STAT. ANN. § 179.65(2) (Supp. 1973).

6. *Dues Checkoff.* Although not technically considered as such, the dues checkoff is, as a practical matter, a form of union security and will be so considered for the purposes of this chapter. A dues checkoff clause typically provides that upon receipt of a written authorization from an employee the employer will deduct the periodic union dues from the employee's pay and remit same directly to the union. Most of the comprehensive public sector collective bargaining laws specifically permit the checkoff of union dues. In addition, several states that have not enacted public sector bargaining laws have specific statutory provisions that permit the checkoff of union dues.

*Effect of Right to Work Laws.* Twenty states have adopted constitutional or statutory provisions prohibiting the negotiation of union security clauses.[4] While these enactments were intended primarily for the private sector, they have been interpreted to prohibit the negotiation of union shop, agency shop, or fair share agreements in the public sector. For example, in Florida Education Association v. PERC, 346 So.2d 551, 94 L.R.R.M. 2607 (Fla. Dist. Ct. App. 1977), an employee organization petitioned the Florida Commission to adopt a rule which would require that non-members in a certified bargaining unit pay the exclusive bargaining representative "a pro rata share of the specific expenses incurred for services rendered by the representative in relationship to negotiations and administration of grievance procedures." In upholding the Commission's decision that it did not have the authority to adopt such a rule, the court held that the proposed rule was repugnant to the right to work provisions of the Florida Constitution "because it would require non-union employees to purchase a right which the Constitution gives them." *Accord,* Levasseur v. Wheeldon, 79 S.D. 442, 112 N.W.2d 894 (1964) ("A municipality cannot by legislative action or otherwise require union membership as a prerequisite to employment").

---

[3] California (educational and state employees), Hawaii, Massachusetts, Minnesota, North Dakota, New York, and Oregon.

[4] Alabama, Arizona, Arkansas, Georgia, Iowa, Kansas, Louisiana, Mississippi, Nebraska, Nevada, North Carolina, North Dakota, South Carolina, South Dakota, Tennessee, Texas, Utah, Virginia, and Wyoming.

## B. GENERAL POLICY CONSIDERATIONS

**NEW YORK STATE COMMISSION ON THE QUALITY, COST, AND FINANCING OF ELEMENTARY AND SECONDARY EDUCATION, Vol. 3, Appendix 13C, pp. 10-16 (1972)**

The Commission has considered whether it ought to recommend to the Legislature that the Taylor Law be amended so as to authorize public employers and employee organizations to negotiate some form of organizational security provision. Since it is unlikely that the Legislature would consider authorizing the union shop because of the serious constitutional questions raised by compulsory membership, our discussion and tentative recommendations will concern only the agency shop.

There have been a number of cogent arguments advanced in support of legislative authorization of the agency shop. Foremost among them is the "free rider" argument: if it is public policy that public employees be granted collective bargaining rights, and that public employers be required to enter into collective agreements with organizations representing these employees, then it follows that those employees benefiting from this new arrangement have some obligation to lend financial support to the organization that wins these benefits. In short, the employee organization, through its authority to participate in the bilateral determination of economic benefits and other quasi policy issues, now serves a public purpose. To require employees to lend financial support to an employee organization is but the counterpart of requiring citizens to pay taxes to support local and state governments.

A second argument often advanced in support of legislative authorization of the agency shop is that those employers granting this provision find generally that their labor relations have become more stabilized. It is usually very difficult for rival organizations to unseat an incumbent organization when all employees in the bargaining unit are already paying dues. This means not only that the employer will be relatively free from the problems posed by frequent changes in bargaining agents, but also that there will be less pressure on the incumbent to outdo the "out" organization by becoming more strident in its pronouncements and more intransigent in its bargaining posture. By the same token, an agency shop allows the employee organization to become somewhat immune from the sometimes unreasonable demands of dissidents within the ranks; such dissidents lack the numerical strength to unseat current leadership, and there is no rival organization to which they can turn.

A third argument in support of legalizing agency shop arrangements is that they provide the employer with a certain amount of sorely needed bargaining leverage, yet at no cost to the taxpayer or to management prerogatives. If school management is determined to bargain hard on this issue — for example, if it refuses to grant the agency shop concession unless the employee organization agrees to remove some undesirable features from the existing contract — it is conceivable that certain gains, particularly in the area of administrative efficiency, will be achieved.

How persuasive are these arguments? To most teacher leaders, and probably to a majority of labor relations experts as well, they are quite persuasive. Yet there are counterarguments, and these too have cogency.

First, an agency shop provision would probably reduce by a significant degree whatever political leverage "satellite" personnel now enjoy within the employee organization. The language of criterion (c) of Section 207 of the Taylor Law, "the unit shall be compatible with the joint responsibilities of the public employer and public employees to serve the public," has generally been construed to mean that it is not in the public interest to fragment or "balkanize" bargaining units. Thus such satellite groups as counselors, nurse teachers, librarians and sometimes department chairmen and assistant principals are deemed to share a community of interest with teachers and are therefore included in the latter's bargaining units. To establish separate bargaining units for each of the above groups would not only invite whipsawing and leapfrogging tactics — to the detriment of both the employer and the public — but also require the employer to spend virtually all his time negotiating with each of the dozen or so bargaining agents representing these various groups.

Consequently, a number of nonteaching school employees are locked into the teacher unit. Relatively few in number, they lack political influence with the teacher organization leadership, which must direct most of its attention to winning benefits for the dominant political majority, the teachers. Thus satellite employees can only hope that when bargaining benefits are distributed the leadership will be generous. If such is not the case, under present circumstances they can threaten to withdraw membership. Thus the employee organization is instructed that even though satellite votes may not have much influence, there are other options open to them.

Under an agency shop arrangement it would not be possible to exercise this kind of leverage. Thus the complaints heard even now from satellite employees about the failure of the teacher organization to represent them fairly, will most assuredly be increased as teacher organizations become more politicized (majoritarian) and budget stringencies more acute.

As for the argument that the agency shop would engender greater stability in employer-employee relations, little can be said in opposition. Certainly the incumbent organization would become relatively immune from raids by rival organizations, just as the leadership of these organizations would enjoy greater insulation from the political machinations of dissident minorities within the ranks. But it can also be said that while stability is a laudable goal in labor relations, so too is freedom of choice. "Unions of their own choosing" was the slogan that accompanied the passage of the Wagner Act, and there is some merit in the argument that industrial democracy is better served if employee organizations are occasionally put to the political test by those whom they represent. This does not mean that the leadership is to be put to the test as there already exists adequate machinery to unseat unresponsive union leaders; it means that the organization itself ought to face the possibility of being voted out of office. Obviously, organizational security tends to reduce the chances of this happening. It is also arguable that a law that obliges an employee organization to win financial support by establishing a record as an effective and responsive bargaining agent, may prove in the long run to be more consistent with the public interest than a statutory provision that in many cases makes a dues collector out of the employer, willing as that employer may be.

The most troublesome feature of the agency shop, however, rests with its enforcement procedures. It was pointed out earlier that the enforcement technique most frequently applied is for the employer to agree to discharge any employee refusing to authorize deductions of the agency fee from his paycheck. . . . Under New York State's tenure law the only grounds for dismissal of a tenured teacher are "(a) insubordination, immoral character or conduct unbecoming a teacher; (b) inefficiency, incompetency, physical or mental disability or neglect of duty." It would be difficult, unless one put a strained interpretation on the term "insubordination," to so interpret any of the above grounds for dismissal to cover refusal to render funds to a private organization.

Surely the tenure law would have to be amended if the Legislature were to authorize the agency shop, particularly if the statute permitted enforcement procedures that included dismissal of noncomplying tenured teachers.

It is anyone's guess as to how many tenured teachers in the state would on grounds of principle refuse to sign an agency fee authorization card, thereby leaving no option to the employer but to initiate dismissal proceedings. Surely there would be several — probably not enough to cause irreparable damage to public education, but enough to give pause to those who value the rights of individuals at least as much as they value employee bargaining power and organizational security.

The question, then, is how to balance the advantages of some form of organizational security against the obvious disadvantages of forcing upon tenured teachers the option of signing an agency shop fee authorization card or face automatic dismissal. A legislative proposal of the New York State Teachers Association (NYSTA) would provide one answer, empowering employers to deduct agency shop fees without individual authorizations. Thus an employee who chose not to join the organization would have his fee deducted anyway, along with income tax and social security deductions, which are also obligatory.

While this arrangement would resolve the dilemma of forced dismissal of recalcitrant tenured teachers, it would also raise certain constitutional issues, particularly those rights that citizens enjoy under the Fourteenth Amendment. It could at least be argued that the state, acting through one of its agencies, the school boards, would be denying individuals their property (agency fees) without due process of law.

What the issue comes down to is whether there is sufficient merit in the agency shop provision for the Legislature to authorize it. While such authorization does not require the parties to incorporate the agency shop into the agreement, it is nevertheless implicit that this provision would not be contrary to the public interest as it is rare that legislatures deliberately act *against* the latter. A secondary consideration is whether the Legislature should allow for enforcement procedures including possible dismissal of tenured teachers refusing to authorize the agency fee deduction.

The arguments allowing for some form of organizational security are persuasive, although they become less so in the concept of statewide collective bargaining. While it is not known what the status of membership in local organizations now is, and while it is certainly not known what level of membership is required before an employee organization can represent it effectively, there is evidence that in a number of cases employee organizations need greater protection than now enjoyed if they are to carry out obligations under the law and at the same time be reasonably immune from those pressures that so frequently provoke irresponsible behavior. In one region, for example, NYSTA affiliates represent over 6,000 teachers, yet membership is slightly more than 3,000. Certainly it is difficult for these employee organizations to carry out their "public purpose" functions under such circumstances.

It does not follow, however, that enforcement by dismissal of those who refuse to comply with the agency shop agreement — or even the denial of options, as NYSTA has proposed — is consistent with public policy. What is needed is a mechanism that, without impeding opportunities to engage volunteer workers and in general attain more flexible staff arrangements, will also provide contractual protection for struggling organizations. In the context of local bargaining, we therefore propose legislative authorization that (1) would allow for contractual provisions requiring newly hired personnel to permit some form of fee deduction to support the collective bargaining activity, but that (2) would render those teachers already on the payroll immune from the provisions. Thus a new teacher would have the option of accepting or rejecting a position in New York State education where the payment of an agency fee was a condition of continuing employment, just as he might refuse employment because he did not like the pay, hours, or course load involved. However, this recommendation does not meet the objections raised by some satellite personnel that an agency shop clause would practically guarantee underrepresentation at the bargaining table. Conceivably, Section 209-a of the Taylor Law (improper practices) could be strengthened so as to provide a remedy for this problem. The proposal would seem, however, to provide a modicum of organizational security without undermining the spirit of the teacher tenure law.

## NOTE

Is there any relationship between the policy, espoused by many experts, of encouraging the establishment of broad bargaining units in the public sector and the negotiation of union security agreements? One commentator made the following observation:

> Even if a union succeeds in winning recognition in a large unit employees in that unit are generally not required to become members of the union. The relative lack of union security clauses in the collective bargaining agreements of the public service assures that, to a degree unparalleled in the private sector, dissident small-unit groups are able to maintain their separate identities and to prolong the battle for break-off from the larger group's exclusive bargaining agent. Rock, *The Appropriate Unit Question in the Public Service: The Problem of Proliferation,* 67 MICH. L. REV. 1001, 1005 (1969).

## GOTBAUM,* COLLECTIVE BARGAINING AND THE UNION LEADER, in PUBLIC WORKERS AND PUBLIC UNIONS 77, 84-85 (S. Zagoria ed. 1972) †

### The Less Union Security, the More Militant Leadership

In an open shop situation, the percentage of dues-paying members gives you an indication of the labor leader's militancy: the smaller the percentage of membership, the greater the militancy. In a newly organized situation or where organization hovers around the 50 percent area, the union leader knows that he must come up with something new and dramatic or at least look dramatic, in order to increase membership. Where organization approaches the 100 percent level, the union leader can afford the luxury of dealing with issues on their merits.

In one television discussion John DeLury was magnificently stylistic and involved himself in some beautiful rank and file prose. My wife, who watched the program, queried me as to whether this was going to bring the public over to his side. I submitted to her that it would be nice for him to bring the public over to his side, but it was much more important that in an open shop situation the New York City sanitationmen were 99 percent organized. Good public will is of little help to a leader whose union is poorly organized and whose opposition grows troublesome.

---

* Victor Gotbaum is the Executive Director of District Council 37 (New York City) of the American Federation of State, County and Municipal Employees, AFL-CIO.

† Copyright © 1972 by The American Assembly, Columbia University. Reproduced by permission of the publisher, Prentice-Hall, Inc.

In an open shop situation you do not want your contract just ratified: you want it *overwhelmingly* ratified. The opposition does not need a majority, all it needs is to keep the leadership off guard. If you lose a point at the bargaining table it is not considered by the opposition to be a part of normal bargaining. "You sold out" becomes the rallying cry for the opposition. In addition you never know how many members you are going to lose because you did not satisfy their specific desires. So you become an "irresponsible union boss" or a "pirate."

The fight for an agency shop in the public sector is almost ridiculous. Management's insistence on an open shop situation is the most counterproductive imaginable. It is to management's interest that the union be stable and representative of all the people in its unit. This would give the union leader maneuverability and flexibility. It would make him less demanding, less insecure, and less verbose. The agency shop is eminently fair; yet very few governments allow it. This makes little sense and is another example of public administration immaturity. It perhaps should be regarded in the same light as the public administrator who refuses to accept the role of management.

## ZWERDLING,* UNION SECURITY IN THE PUBLIC SECTOR, in LABOR RELATIONS IN THE PUBLIC SECTOR 156, 161-63) (A. Knapp ed. 1977) †

. . . .

Union organization and recognition often come hard, and once achieved are costly to maintain. Under the predominant type of state public employment collective bargaining legislation, the union that is the exclusive representative has a duty of fair representation with reference to *all* bargaining unit employees — union members and non-members alike. Proponents of service fee arrangements argue that if employees cannot be forced to join the union as a condition of continued employment, they should at least be required to share the costs of union representation — the costs of negotiating and administering the collective bargaining agreement which applies equally to them and from which they derive equal benefits.

Unions expend a large amount of financial and other resources in negotiating and administering collective bargaining agreements. Some of these expenses are borne by the respective local affiliates, but many services are provided by the locals' parent organizations. Examples of some of the more costly union functions include:

1) Payment of salaries and expenses for staff engaged in negotiation and administration of the contract;

2) Payment of general office and overhead expenses;

3) Maintenance of a research department which prepares local representatives for contract negotiations, prepares economic data, drafts contract language, and evaluates contract proposals;

4) Maintenance of a legal department or retained counsel which represents employees in arbitration, disciplinary proceedings, and negotiations; communicates significant legal developments in other parts of the country; and assists in significant legal cases;

---

* A.L. Zwerdling is General Counsel for the American Federation of State, County and Municipal Employees (AFSCME).

† Reprinted by permission of the American Bar Association and the Section of Labor Relations Law.

5) Provision of training in grievance handling — including arbitration and communication of local employee needs to their immediate employer or relevant government bodies and to their community;

6) Provision of information on activities of affiliates around the country, and their varying solutions to common problems;

7) Provision of assistance in federal and state legislative efforts with respect to public employees — including revenue sharing, civil rights, minimum wage laws, unemployment compensation, pension legislation, health insurance, public jobs programs, and occupational health and safety.

The requirement that all individuals who benefit from union activities contribute their fair share of the costs is but an application of the democratic concept. The service fee arrangement is plainly fair and equitable and consistent with the good labor relations policy as well as basic democratic values. It is analogous to all Americans being taxed for the costs of government expenditures and the benefits received therefrom.

## HAY,* UNION SECURITY AND FREEDOM OF ASSOCIATION, in LABOR RELATIONS IN THE PUBLIC SECTOR 145, 146-47 (A. Knapp ed. 1977) †

. . . .

... The paramount reason why public employers with whom I have dealt oppose union security is their unwillingness to discharge a good employee for a reason which has absolutely nothing to do with that employee's job performance. That is their compelling objection to union security.

Furthermore, many believe that voluntary as opposed to compulsory unionism limits a union's bargaining strength, and thus may well result in a more tolerable economic package than could otherwise be negotiated against a more cohesive labor organization — certainly a legitimate goal for the public employer. Furthermore, I believe that compulsory unionism increases rather than decreases the number and intensity of public employee strikes — again, a goal which public employers may legitimately seek to avoid.

Another very real concern expressed by many public employers is that increased membership and financial resources for public unions will enable them to make direct political or legislative intrusions into the public sector bargaining process. For example, strong public sector unions have already elected school board members whose first loyalty is to the union rather than to the school board, thereby undermining if not destroying the school board's ability to negotiate effectively.

Similarly, strong public sector unions may secure by political pressures on the legislature laws which distort the collective bargaining process, such as mandatory benefit levels or minimum pay increases or requirements now in existence in California that a school board's initial bargaining proposals must be announced and discussed in public meetings held prior to the first negotiating session — public meetings at which the union brings public and political pressure for a liberalization of the employer's position prior to the first negotiation.

In these and many other ways, strong public sector unions have been able to put themselves on both sides of the bargaining table, in pursuit of their own and their members' interests and to the detriment of the public employer and the public at large.

---

* Howard Hay is a California attorney who represents public employers.

† Reprinted by permission of the American Bar Association and the Section of Labor Relations Law.

So there are many very pragmatic reasons why a public employer, on behalf of itself and the society at large, may vigorously and legitimately oppose union security in the public sector. Furthermore, there is a serious question whether compulsory unionism has any advantage for the general public which outweighs its obvious disadvantages.

. . . .

## LARSON,* PUBLIC EMPLOYEES AND THEIR "RIGHT TO WORK" †

It is easy to figure out why union officials put compulsory membership at the top of their "want list" when negotiating with public agencies. There are more than twelve million public employees, including nearly three million Federal employees. If every public employee were under compulsion to pay union dues of $5 a month, the take would amount to $700 million a year — not counting millions in initiation fees!

The stakes are enormous and the union bosses are at work. As Jerry Wurf said, "Our potential is nothing less than fantastic . . . right now six out of every ten new jobs being created are jobs in government." He added that his union would have a million members now instead of just 400,000 if all his contracts called for compulsory unionism!

It is obvious to us that union officials, with the help of some politicians who receive campaign support from union treasuries, are making fantastic progress in a massive, coast-to-coast, community-by-community program aimed ultimately at locking every public employee into a contract forcing him to pay dues into a union treasury in order to keep his job.

To us the real threat in the compulsory unionization of government workers lies in the fact that it provides a thinly disguised pipeline diverting enforced salary deductions in the form of union dues to provide campaign funds for union-controlled politicians — politicians who as public officials are the government employee's bosses, and who are the very persons who forced him to pay the union in the first place.

The action of Mayor Lindsay is an excellent example of this problem and graphically illustrates why the AFL-CIO recently made an unprecedented decision at the national level to participate fully in campaigns for mayors and other local officials. In the past this has always been left to the local unions, some of which are effective and some of which are not. Our interpretation of this new emphasis is that it is part of an overall program aimed at obtaining union-controlled public officials at the local level who will — to put it bluntly — roll over and play dead whenever they are confronted by a union organizer representing a handful of militant employees.

The crux of the problem here is the inordinate influence of union political power on public officials charged with the responsibility of setting employee policies. In private industry, the interests of union officials are being served primarily on one side of the bargaining table. But in public employee bargaining we can see what amounts to an agent of union power representing both the employer and the organized employees. The solution, as we see it, is to make compulsory unionism illegal; to take the choice of membership or nonmembership in an employee union out of the hands of the politician and the union professionals, and keep it where it belongs — with the individual employee.

---

* Reed Larson is Executive Vice President of the National Right to Work Committee.

† Reprinted by permission of Mr. Reed Larson, The National Right to Work Committee, 1990 M Street, N.W., Washington, D.C., 20036.

It is the widespread practice of compulsory unionism in private industry that frees union officials from the normal responsibilities of operating a voluntary organization. It is compulsory unionism that releases a major percentage of union resources directly for political action rather than for selling and maintaining membership. According to union spokesmen, retention and expansion of compulsory membership is essential if they are to continue and expand the political activity which they consider necessary and desirable.

Union representative Walter H. Barnes, of the Teamsters Local 636 in New Jersey, let the cat out of the bag last fall after the New Jersey legislature, over the veto of Governor Richard Hughes, passed a Right to Work law covering the state's public employees. Barnes said, "Since we can't get the union shop I have orders from the President of our local to stop trying to organize the Department of Public Works in Englewood because it just isn't worthwhile."

The late President John F. Kennedy clearly recognized the danger involved in the forced unionization of public employees when he insisted that his 1962 Executive Order 10988, authorizing the unionization of Federal employees, also protect the right *not* to join. That order reads: "Employees of the Federal government shall have, and shall be protected in the exercise of the right, freely and without fear of penalty or reprisal, to form, join and assist any employee organization or to refrain from such activity." That part of the Kennedy Executive Order can properly be called the Federal employees' Right to Work law. And as long as it remains in existence compulsory unionism cannot exist for Federal employees.

President Kennedy's Secretary of Labor, Arthur Goldberg, in explaining the order in a speech to members of the American Federation of Government Employees AFL-CIO said,

> I know you will agree with me that the union shop and the closed shop are inappropriate to the Federal government. And because of this, there is a larger responsibility for enlightenment on the part of the government union. In your own organization you have to win acceptance by your own conduct, your own action, your own wisdom, your own responsibility and your own achievements. . . . So you have an opportunity to bring into your organization people who come in because they want to come in and who will participate, therefore, in the full activity of your organization.

. . . .

As a single-purpose organization the National Right to Work Committee is concerned only with compulsory versus voluntary unionism. We believe the drive for compulsory dues underlies most of the current turmoil in public employee-management relations. And we believe strongly that any meaningful labor legislation — for industrial as well as public employees — must have as its foundation the elimination of compulsory unionism. It is our firm belief that the record shows that voluntarism will go far to provide the checks and balances necessary to keeping union leadership responsive to the individual member.

## K. HANSLOWE, THE EMERGING LAW OF LABOR RELATIONS IN PUBLIC EMPLOYMENT 114-15 (1967) †

. . . [A] democratic political structure has limits as to the amount of organized

---

† Reprinted by permission of the New York State School of Industrial and Labor Relations, Cornell University.

group pressure it can tolerate. At some point the risk arises of a dangerous dilution of governmental authority by its being squeezed to death by conflicting power blocks. If that point is reached, foreign policy is made by defense industry, agricultural policy by farmers, and public personnel policy by employee organizations, and *not* by government representing the wishes of an electorate consisting of individual voters. If that point is reached, an orderly system of individual liberty under lawful rule would seem to be the victim. For surely it is difficult to conceive of a social order without a governmental repository of authority, which is authoritative for the very reason that it is representative and democratic.

To illustrate: Problems may arise, if public employee organizations begin to press, as they have already commenced to do, for union security arrangements of one sort or another, making financial support of the employee organization a condition of public employment. On the face of it, this sounds innocent enough, and legal objections of incompatibility with civil service concepts of merit employment are likely to be overridden. If an exclusive bargaining agent is empowered, and is therefore required, to represent all employees in the bargaining unit, it seems fair to require all those benefiting from such representation to contribute to its cost.

But the Supreme Court of the United States has decided, as to the private sector, that the contractual obligation (in the form of the union shop) to contribute to the costs of the representation may not lawfully include, as a condition of employment, coerced support of *political* activities of the organization to which an individual member objects. Support of *collective bargaining activity* is all that may be compelled. Yet, in the public sector, political activity is unavoidably part and parcel of the process of *bargaining with politicians.* Thus there arises the possibility of involuntary contributions to organizational support of politicians who, while ready to improve the working conditions of public employees, on other questions take positions of which such public employees disapprove. Unless careful protections are worked out, enabling individual public employees to "contract out" from compelled support of unwanted political parties, politicians, and public policies, the union shop in public employment has the potential of becoming a neat mutual back-scratching mechanism, whereby public employee representatives and politicians each reinforce the other's interests and domain, with the individual public employee and the individual citizen left to look on, while his employment conditions, and his tax rate, and public policies generally are being decided by entrenched and mutually supportive government officials and collective bargaining representatives over whom the public has diminishing control.

Such dangers are perhaps not immediate. The point needs, however, to be reiterated that there are limits on the amount of stress which a democratic governmental structure can tolerate from organized group pressure. At some point its fibre can be broken, and democratic rule under law be replaced by authoritarian rule by clique.

## NOTE

*See generally* K. Hanslowe, D. Dunn & J. Erstling, Union Security in Public Employment: Of Free Riding and Free Association, N.Y. St. Sch. Indus. & Lab. Rel., Inst. Pub. Employment, Monograph No. 8 (1978); Zwerdling, *Liberation of Public*

*Employees: Union Security in the Public Sector,* 17 B.C. Indus. & Com. L. Rev. 993 (1976); Najita, *The Mandatory Agency Shop in Hawaii's Public Sector,* 27 Indus. & Lab. Rel. Rev. 432 (1974); Blair, *"Union Security Agreements in Public Employment,"* 60 Cornell L. Rev. 183 (1975); Gromfine, *Union Security Clauses in Public Employment, N.Y.U. 22d Ann. Conf. on Labor, 285 (1970).*

# C. CONSTITUTIONAL CONSIDERATIONS

## CITY OF CHARLOTTE v. LOCAL 660, INT'L ASS'N OF FIREFIGHTERS

Supreme Court of the United States
426 U.S. 283, 96 S. Ct. 2036, 48 L. Ed. 2d 636 (1976)

Mr. Justice Marshall delivered the opinion of the Court.

The city of Charlotte, N. C., refuses to withhold from the paychecks of its firefighters' dues owing to their union, Local 660, International Association of Firefighters. We must decide whether this refusal violates the Equal Protection Clause of the Fourteenth Amendment.

I

Local 660 represents some 351 of the 543 uniformed members of the Charlotte Fire Department. Since 1969 the union and individual members have repeatedly requested the city to withhold dues owing to the union from the paychecks of those union members who agree to a check off. The city has refused each request. After the union learned that it could obtain a private group life insurance policy for its membership only if it had a dues checkoff agreement with the city, the union and its officers filed suit in federal court alleging, *inter alia,* that the city's refusal to withhold the dues of union members violated the Equal Protection Clause of the Fourteenth Amendment.[1] The complaint asserted that since the city withheld amounts from its employees' paychecks for payment to various other organizations, it could not arbitrarily refuse to withhold amounts for payment to the union.

On cross-motions for summary judgment, the District Court for the Western District of North Carolina ruled against the city. The Court determined that, although the city had no written guidelines, its "practice has been to allow check offs from employees' pay to organizations or programs as required by law or where the check off option is available to all employees within a single employee unit such as the Fire Department." 381 F. Supp. 500, 502 (1974). The Court further found that the city has "not allowed check off options serving only single employees or programs which are not available either to all City employees or to all employees engaged in a particular section of City employment." *Ibid.* Finding, however, that withholding union dues from the paychecks of union members would be no more difficult than processing any other deduction allowed by the city, the District Court concluded that the city had not offered a rational explanation for its refusal to withhold for the union. Accordingly, the District Court held that the city's refusal to withhold moneys when requested to do so by the respondents for the benefit of Local 660 "constitutes a violation of the

---

[1] Respondents brought suit under 42 U. S. C. § 1983, grounding jurisdiction in 28 U. S. C. §§ 1331 and 1343....

[respondents'] rights to equal protection of laws under the Fourteenth Amendment." *Id.*, at 502-503. The Court ordered that so long as the city continued "without clearly stated and fair standards to withhold moneys from the paychecks of City employees for other purposes," it was enjoined from refusing to withhold union dues from the paychecks of the respondents. *Id.*, at 503. The Court of Appeals for the Fourth Circuit affirmed, 518 F. 2d 83 (1975), and we granted certiorari. 423 U. S. 890 (1975). We reverse.

## II

Since it is not here asserted — and this Court would reject such a contention if it were made — that respondents' status as union members or their interest in obtaining a dues check off is such as to entitle them to special treatment under the Equal Protection Clause, the city's practice must meet only a relatively relaxed standard of reasonableness in order to survive constitutional scrutiny.

The city presents three justifications for its refusal to allow the dues checkoff requested by respondents. First, it argues, North Carolina law makes it illegal for the city to enter into a contract with a municipal union, N. C. Gen. Stat. 95-98, and an agreement with union members to provide a dues check off, with the union as a third-party beneficiary, would in effect be such a contract. See 40 N. C. Atty. Gen. Rep. 591 (1968-1970). Thus, compliance with the state law, and with the public policy it represents of discouraging dealing with municipal unions, is said to provide a sufficient basis for refusing respondents' request. Second, it claims, a dues check off is a proper subject of collective bargaining, which the city asserts Congress may shortly require of state and local governments. Under this theory, the desire to preserve the checkoff as a bargaining chip in any future collective-bargaining process is in itself an adequate basis for the refusal. Lastly, the city contends, allowing withholding only when it benefits all city or departmental employees is a legitimate method for avoiding the burden of withholding money for all persons or organizations that request a check off. Because we find that this explanation provides a sufficient justification for the challenged practice, we have no occasion to address the first two reasons proffered.

The city submitted affidavits to show that it would be unduly burdensome and expensive for it to withhold money for every organization or person that requested it. App. 17, 45, 55, and respondents did not contest this showing. As respondents concede, it was therefore reasonable, and permissible under the Equal Protection Clause, for the city to develop standards or restrictions to determine who would be eligible for withholding. Mathews v. Diaz, 426 U. S. 67, —, slip op., at 14-15 (1976). See Brief for Respondents 9. Within the limitations of the Equal Protection Clause, of course, the choice of those standards is for the city and not for the courts. Thus, our inquiry is not whether standards might be drawn that would include the union, but whether the standards that were drawn were reasonable ones with "some basis in practical experience." South Carolina v. Katzenbach, 383 U. S. 301, 331 (1966). Of course, the fact that the standards were drawn and applied in practice rather than pursuant to articulated guidelines is of no import for equal protection purposes.

The city allows withholding for taxes, retirement-insurance programs, savings programs, and certain charitable organizations. These categories, the District Court found, are those in which the checkoff option can, or must, be availed of by all city employees, or those in an entire department. Although the District Court found that this classification did not present a rational basis for rejecting respondents' requests, 381 F. Supp., at 502, we disagree. The city has determined that it will provide withholding only for programs of general interest in which all city or departmental employees can, without more, participate. Employees can participate in the union check off only if they join an outside organization — the union. Thus, Local 660 does not fit the category of groups for which the city will withhold. We cannot say that denying withholding to associational or special interest groups that claim only some departmental employees as members and that employees must first join before being eligible to participate in the check off marks an arbitrary line so devoid of reason as to violate the Equal Protection Clause. Rather, this division seems a reasonable method for providing the benefit of withholding to employees in their status as employees, while limiting the number of instances of withholding and the financial and administrative burdens attendant thereon.

Given the permissibility of creating standards and the reasonableness of the standards created, the District Court's conclusion that it would be no more difficult for the city to withhold dues for the union than to process other deductions is of no import. We may accept, *arguendo,* that the difficulty involved in processing any individual deduction is neither great nor different in kind from that involved in processing any other deduction. However, the city has not drawn its lines in order to exclude individual deductions, but in order to avoid the cumulative burden of processing deductions every time a request is made; and inherent in such a line-drawing process are difficult choices and "some harsh and apparently arbitrary consequences. . . ." Mathews v. Diaz, 426 U. S., at —, slip op., at15. See *id.,* at —, slip op., at 14-16; Dandridge v. Williams, 397 U. S. 471, 485 (1970). Cf. Schilb v. Kuebel, 404 U. S. 357, 364 (1972); Williamson v. Lee Optical, 348 U. S. 483, 489 (1955).

Respondents recognize the legitimacy of such a process and concede that the city "is free to develop fair and reasonable standards to meet any possible cost problem." Brief for Respondents, at 9. Respondents have wholly failed, however, to present any reasons why the present standards are not fair and reasonable — other than the fact that the standards exclude them. This fact, of course, is insufficient to transform the city policy into a constitutional violation. Since we find a reasonable basis for the challenged classification, the judgment of the Court of Appeals for the Fourth Circuit must be reversed, and the case remanded for further proceedings consistent with this opinion.

*It is so ordered.*

MR. JUSTICE STEWART concurs in the judgment upon the ground that the classification challenged in this case is not invidiously discriminatory and does not, therefore, violate the Equal Protection Clause of the Fourteenth Amendment.

## NOTES

1. Is it a violation of the Equal Protection Clause for a public employer to deny an employee organization the right to have its dues checked off if the public employer grants another employee organization this right? In Edwards v. Alhambra Elementary School Dist. No. 63, 488 P.2d 501 (Ariz. Ct. App. 1971), the court held that a school board's action in granting a dues checkoff to an employee organization representing teachers and denying the same right to an employee organization representing support staff was constitutional on the ground that it constituted a reasonable classification. The court noted that "the classification of teachers vis-a-vis non-teachers for purposes of employment and inducements for employment has long been recognized" and that "[o]ne

of the inducements which ... could be held out to teachers and withheld from non-teachers, is the privilege of payroll deductions."

2. In Local 995, IAFF v. City of Richmond, 415 F. Supp. 325 (E.D. Va. 1976), the court held a city did not infringe upon the First Amendment rights of union members in refusing to check off union dues. In rejecting the union's argument that without a dues checkoff it would be unable to adequately fund its operations, the court said the city's refusal did not "significantly impair the union's ability to organize and provide services for its members." The court further noted that "while the First Amendment protects the right of American citizens to freely associate, it was never intended to provide an affirmative factor in forcing the state to aid union organizational activities."

## BAUCH v. CITY OF NEW YORK

New York Court of Appeals
21 N.Y.2d 599, 237 N.E.2d 211, 289 N.Y.S.2d 951
*Cert. denied*, 393 U.S. 834 (1968)

FULD, Chief Judge.

This appeal, taken upon constitutional grounds, poses the question — of first impression in this court — whether the City of New York may grant a dues "check-off" privilege to a union representing a majority of the municipal employees in a city-wide bargaining unit and yet deny such privilege to a minority union.[1]

In 1956, the city's Board of Estimate adopted a resolution which granted the check-off privilege to all organizations of city employees whose members authorized the necessary payroll deductions. At that time, the city did not recognize any union as an agent for collective bargaining. Later, the city began to recognize unions as exclusive bargaining agents if they were chosen by a majority of the employees in an appropriate bargaining unit. Even then, however, the Board of Estimate resolution extending the check-off privilege to all unions alike was not changed and the city continued to give effect to its provisions.

In April, 1967, the city modified its union recognition policies by means of an executive order of the Mayor. The order provided (1) that appropriate bargaining units for municipal employees were to be established on a city-wide basis or, in some circumstances, on a departmental basis and (2) that the organization chosen by a majority of the employees in each such unit was to be recognized as the exclusive bargaining representative for all employees in the unit.

The Mayor proposes to round out this policy by means of a further executive order which will give the privilege of dues check-off solely to the exclusive bargaining agents and will withdraw it from all other unions. It is the declared opinion of the Mayor and the city's Director of Labor Relations that this plan for a restricted check-off policy, common in private industry, will afford the majority representatives a form of "union security," will increase their prestige and responsibility and will, in consequence, stabilize the collective bargaining process.

Local 832 (International Brotherhood of Teamsters, Chauffeurs, Warehousemen and Helpers of America) and District Council 37 (American Federation of State, County and Municipal Employees, AFL-CIO) are two unions which include persons employed by the city in nonsupervisory clerical titles.

---

[1] In labor relations parlance, the "check-off" is the practice whereby an employer deducts the amount of a union member's dues from his pay, usually on the employee's express authorization, and remits it directly to the union.

District Council 37 has been recognized by the city as the exclusive bargaining representative for such employees; under the proposed plan it will thus have the exclusive benefit of the dues check-off. Local 832, on the other hand, is a minority union and, accordingly, it will be deprived, under the proposed plan, of the check-off privilege it has enjoyed since 1956.[2] Strongly objecting, the latter organization, Local 832, has commenced this article 78 proceeding — through its president and several of its members on behalf of themselves and all others similarly situated — to require the city to continue the check-off of dues to it, and to enjoin the city from granting exclusive check-off privileges to District Council 37 or any other labor organization. The court at Special Term dismissed the petition and the Appellate Division unanimously affirmed the resulting order.

Under the 1963 New York City Charter (§ 8), the Mayor is authorized to "exercise all the powers vested in the city, except as otherwise provided by law." He is the successor to the residual powers originally possessed by the Board of Estimate under a similarly worded provision of the 1938 New York City Charter (§ 70) in effect in 1956, when that body adopted the "nondiscriminatory" check-off policy. (See, also, New York City Charter [1963], § 1142.) The city — and, thus, the Mayor on its behalf — is empowered to enter into contracts, to regulate the terms of employment and compensation of city employees and to determine the manner of transacting the city's business and affairs (General City Law, Consol. Laws, c. 21, § 20, subds. 1, 17, 19; § 23, subd. 1). The Charter also specifically authorizes the Mayor to supervise city offices and departments, fix salaries, adopt wage plans and prescribe rules governing working conditions (New York City Charter [1963], §§ 123, 124, 813 subd. i). His executive power and discretion thus amply extend to and encompass the proposed action here under review, and no further legislative sanction is required.

Contrary to the petitioners' contention, the Mayor's discretion to decide which employee organization should have check-off privileges is not curtailed by section 93-b of the General Municipal Law Consol. Laws, c. 24. That section provides, in its subdivision 1, that a municipality is "authorized" to deduct dues from its employees' pay.[4] It is unmistakably permissive, not obligatory. It does not control a municipality's selection of the unions, if any, to which it may grant the privilege of the check-off; and it certainly does not mandate the continuance of the check-off to minority unions. The only requirements which the section imposes are that, if a municipality does adopt the check-off for any union, (1) it must obtain an employee's written consent before deducting his dues; (2) it must allow the employee to withdraw that consent at any time; and (3) the procedure must be made available only to organizations of civil service employees. These conditions are met in the Mayor's proposed order.

---

[2] District Council 37 has majority representation status in city-wide units covering over 57,000 employees and in department-wide units covering some 1,300 more. In sharp contrast, Local 832, having an over-all membership in the neighborhood of 1,700 represents only about 1,000 nonsupervisory clerical workers.

[4] Subdivision 1 of section 93-b reads, in part, as follows: "The fiscal or disbursing officer of every municipal corporation . . . is hereby authorized to deduct from the . . . salary of any employee of such municipal corporation . . . such amount that such employee may specify in writing filed with such . . . officer for the payment of dues in a duly organized association or organization of civil service employees and to transmit the sum so deducted to the said . . . organization. Any such written authorization may be withdrawn by such employee or member at any time by filing written notice of such withdrawal with [such] officer."

That this State's legislative policy is not antagonistic to the check-off plan embodied in the proposed executive order is manifest also from the terms of the Public Employees' Fair Employment Act (Civil Service Law, Consol. Laws, c. 7, art. 14; L. 1967, ch. 392, known also as the Taylor Act). As the court noted in the course of its opinion at Special Term, that statute — which did not take effect until some months after it announced its decision — explicitly gives majority unions of public employees the right to have their members' check-off requests honored, and is silent concerning the right to such check-off on behalf of minority unions (Civil Service Law, § 208). Although our decision in this case will have prospective effect, we need not decide whether the Taylor Act is applicable; it is sufficient to observe that, if the act does apply, it can only reinforce the decision which we reached on the basis of the pre-existing law. In short, the Mayor's proposed policy is plainly consistent with the scheme set forth in the Taylor Act for according recognition, and a degree of union security, to bargaining agents for public employees; to mention but one provision, section 208 makes it mandatory upon a public employer to extend a "right" of membership dues deduction to a union "certified" or "recognized" pursuant to the statute. (See, also, Civil Service Law, §§ 204, 212.) Whatever discretion a public employer may have, under the act, to grant the check-off to a minority union not recognized as a bargaining agent — and that question is not before us — the employer is plainly under no obligation to do so.

Since we find no statutory obstacle in the way of the city's proposed check-off policy, we turn to a consideration of whether that policy would, as Local 832 urges, deprive it of due process or equal protection of the laws. We agree with the courts below that it would not. The requirements of due process are satisfied as long as the challenged measure is reasonably related to the attainment of a permissible objective. (See, e.g., Railway Employes' Dept. v. Hanson, 351 U.S. 225, 233-235, 76 S. Ct. 714, 719, 100 L. Ed. 1112; Virginian Ry. v. System Federation, 300 U.S. 515, 558-559, 57 S. Ct. 592, 605, 81 L. Ed. 789.) Similarly, the standards of equal protection are met if a classification, or a distinction among classes, has some reasonable basis. (See, e.g., Baxstrom v. Herold, 383 U.S. 107, 111, 86 S. Ct. 760, 762, 15 L. Ed. 2d 620; Morey v. Doud, 354 U.S. 457, 464-465, 77 S. Ct. 1344, 1349, 1 L. Ed. 2d 1485; Bucho Holding Co. v. State Rent Comm., 11 N.Y.2d 469, 477, 230 N.Y.S.2d 977, 983, 184 N.E.2d 569, 574.)

In the case before us, the existence of such a reasonable relationship and basis is apparent. The maintenance of stability in the relations between the city and employee organizations, as well as the avoidance of devastating work stoppages, are major responsibilities of the city administration. The Mayor seeks to further these objectives by introducing into city labor relations a practice which has become commonplace in private industry and in the labor policies of other governmental bodies. For example, the Federal Railway Labor Act specifically empowers the carrier and the exclusive bargaining agent to agree on an exclusive dues check-off (U.S. Code, tit. 45, § 152, subd. *Eleventh,* par. [b]); the practice is authorized for organizations of Federal civil service employees (Code of Fed. Reg., tit. 5, § 550.304, subd. [a], par. [5]; Executive Order 10988, §§ 5, 6, Jan. 17, 1962, 27 Federal Register 551); and it is also followed — according to the record before us — by the New York City Housing Authority and the New York City Transit Authority. The city program is in accord with national labor policy, which has been built on the premise that a majority organization is the most effective vehicle for improving wages, hours and working conditions. (See NLRB v. Allis-Chalmers Mfg. Co., 388 U.S. 175, 180, 87 S. Ct. 2001, 2006, 18 L. Ed. 2d 1123.) Be that as it may, we may not consider the merits or the ultimate wisdom of the policy (see Williamson v. Lee Opt. Co., 348 U.S. 483, 488, 75 S. Ct. 461, 464, 99 L. Ed. 563); it is enough, as already indicated, that a method of implementing union security, so widely utilized and so long tested as the one proposed by the Mayor, may not be said to lack a reasonable basis or to be unrelated to the city's legitimate purposes.

The petitioners also argue that the withdrawal of the dues check-off will weaken their minority union to the point of threatening its very existence. They will thus be deprived, they assert — pointing to such decisions as Bates v. City of Little Rock, 361 U.S. 516, 80 S. Ct. 412, 4 L. Ed. 2d 480, N.A.A.C.P. v. State of Alabama, 357 U.S. 449, 78 S. Ct. 1163, 2 L. Ed. 2d 1488 and Thomas v. Collins, 323 U.S. 516, 65 S. Ct. 315, 89 L. Ed. 430 [5] — of their right of freedom of association guaranteed by the First and Fourteenth Amendments of the Federal Constitution and by article I of the State Constitution. Their claim lacks substance. Nothing in the city's labor policy denies members of the petitioners' union the right to meet, to speak, to publish, to proselytize and to collect dues by the means employed by thousands of organizations of all kinds, that do not have the benefit of a dues check-off. Neither the First Amendment nor any other constitutional provision entitles them to the special aid of the city's collection and disbursing facilities.

The order appealed from should be affirmed, with costs.

BURKE, SCILEPPI, BERGAN, KEATING, BREITEL and JASEN, JJ., concur.

Order affirmed.

## NOTES

1. *Accord,* Sacramento County Employees Organization, Local 22 v. County of Sacramento, 28 Cal. App. 3d 424, 104 Cal. Rptr. 619 (1972). The Nevada Local Government Employee-Management Relations Board has held that the exclusive bargaining representative has the exclusive right to contract for the checkoff of union dues and that it is not a prohibited practice for an employer to refuse to grant a minority union the right to check off the dues of its members. Operating Engineers Local Union No. 3 v. City of Reno, Item #7 (1972); AFT Local 1800 v. Clark County School Dist., Item #2 (1970).

2. A number of state statutes provide that once an employee organization is certified or recognized as the exclusive bargaining representative, it has the exclusive right to have its dues deducted. For example, the California Education Employment Relations Act provides that once an employee organization has been recognized as the exclusive representative in an appropriate unit the deduction of membership dues as to any employee in that unit "shall not be permissible except to the exclusive representative." CAL. EDUC. CODE § 3543.1(d).

3. The Wisconsin Supreme Court in Board of School Directors of City of Milwaukee v. WERC, 42 Wis. 2d 637, 168 N.W.2d 92 (1969), held that granting a majority union an exclusive dues checkoff was a prohibited practice. The court approved the WERC's test that " '[t]hose rights or benefits which are granted exclusively to the majority representative, and thus denied its minority organizations, must in some rational manner be related to the functions of the majority organization in its representative capacity, and must not be granted to entrench such organization as the bargaining representative.' " The court, however, rejected the WERC's conclusion that granting an exclusive dues checkoff was permissible, stating:

---

[5] The petitioners' reliance on these decisions is misplaced. The cited cases involved attempts by states to hinder organizations by some affirmative prohibition upon, or intrusion into, their activities. There is not the slightest suggestion that a state or other body must provide services to an organization to help it maintain its competitive position with its rivals.

The WERC made no attempt to explain how the granting of exclusive checkoff was rationally related to the functioning of the majority organization *in its representative capacity;* nor can we see any relationship whatsoever. The sole and complete purpose of *exclusive* checkoff is self-perpetuation and entrenchment. While a majority representative may negotiate for checkoff, he is negotiating for all the employees, and, if checkoff is granted for any, it must be granted for all.

In 1971, the Wisconsin law was amended to provide that it is not a prohibited practice for an employer to enter into a fair-share agreement with a certified union. In Milwaukee Federation of Teachers Local 252 v. WERC, 98 L.R.R.M. 2870 (Wis. Sup. Ct. 1978), the Wisconsin Supreme Court reaffirmed its decision in *Board of School Directors* and held that it is a prohibited practice for a municipal employer to refuse to check off dues for a minority organization where such right is extended to the exclusive bargaining representative. The court stated:

> Although . . . both fair-share agreements and exclusionary checkoff privileges are union security devices, they differ . . . in function and effect. A legislative decision to permit the certified union to recoup some of its bargaining costs from non-union bargaining unit employees is perfectly compatible with this Court's holding that one union may not arrange a checkoff system to the exclusion of other unions. The first negates the possibility that there will be freeloaders who reap the benefits of collective bargaining without paying the costs; the latter tends to destroy competing unions or at least discourages membership in them. The legislature could very well permit the one without permitting the other.

The court also noted that "it is significant that the amendments to the statute do not expressly provide the certified union with a right to an exclusive checkoff arrangement."

## ABOOD v. DETROIT BOARD OF EDUCATION

Supreme Court of the United States
430 U.S. 209, 97 S. Ct. 1782, 52 L. Ed. 2d 261 (1977)

Mr. Justice Stewart delivered the opinion of the Court.

The State of Michigan has enacted legislation authorizing a system for union representation of local governmental employees. A union and a local government employer are specifically permitted to agree to an "agency shop" arrangement, whereby every employee represented by a union — even though not a union member — must pay to the union, as a condition of employment, a service fee equal in amount to union dues. The issue before us is whether this arrangement violates the constitutional rights of government employees who object to public sector unions as such or to various union activities financed by the compulsory service fees.

I

After a secret ballot election, the Detroit Federation of Teachers (the Union) was certified in 1967 pursuant to Michigan law as the exclusive representative of teachers employed by the Detroit Board of Education (the Board). The Union and the Board thereafter concluded a collective-bargaining agreement effective from July 1, 1969, to July 1, 1971. Among the agreement's provisions was an "agency shop" clause, requiring every teacher who had not become a Union member within 60 days of hire (or within 60 days of January 26, 1970, the effective date of the clause) to pay the Union a service charge equal to the regular dues required of Union members. A teacher who failed to meet this obligation was subject to discharge. Nothing in the agreement, however, required any teacher to join the Union, espouse the cause of unionism, or participate in any other way in union affairs.

On November 7, 1969 — more than two months before the agency-shop clause was to become effective — Christine Warczak and a number of other named teachers filed a class action in a state court, naming as defendants the Board, the Union, and several Union officials. Their complaint, as amended, alleged that they were unwilling or had refused to pay dues and that they opposed collective bargaining in the public sector. The amended complaint further alleged that the Union "carries on various social activities for the benefit of its members which are not available to non-members as a matter of right," and that the Union is engaged

> "in a number and variety of activities and programs which are economic, political, professional, scientific and religious in nature of which Plaintiffs do not approve, and in which they will have no voice, and which are not and will not be collective bargaining activities, i. e., the negotiation and administration of contracts with Defendant Board, and that a substantial part of the sums required to be paid under said Agency Shop Clause are used and will continue to be used for the support of such activities and programs, and not solely for the purpose of defraying the cost of Defendant Federation of its activities as bargaining agent for teachers employed by Defendant Board."

The complaint prayed that the agency-shop clause be declared invalid under state law and also under the United States Constitution as a deprivation of, *inter alia,* the plaintiffs' freedom of association protected by the First and Fourteenth Amendments, and for such further relief as might be deemed appropriate.

Upon the defendants' motion for summary judgment, the trial court dismissed the action for failure to state a claim upon which relief could be granted. 73 L.R.R.M. 2237 (Cir. Ct. Wayne County). The plaintiffs appealed, and while their appeal was pending the Michigan Supreme Court ruled in *Smigel v. Southgate Community School Dist.,* 388 Mich. 531, 202 N.W.2d 305, that state law prohibited an agency shop in the public sector. Accordingly, the judgment in the *Warczak* case was vacated and remanded to the trial court for further proceedings consistent with the *Smigel* decision.

Meanwhile, D. Louis Abood and other named teachers had filed a separate action in the same state trial court. The allegations in the complaint were virtually identical to those in *Warczak* and similar relief was requested. This second action was held in abeyance pending disposition of the *Warczak* appeal, and when that case was remanded the two cases were consolidated in the trial court for consideration of the defendants' renewed motion for summary judgment.

On November 5, 1973, that motion was granted. The trial court noted that following the *Smigel* decision, the Michigan Legislature had in 1973 amended its Public Employment Relations Act so as expressly to authorize an agency shop. 1973 Mich.Pub. Acts, No. 25, codified as Mich.Comp.Laws § 432.210 (1)(c).[7] This amendment was applied retroactively by the trial court to validate the

---

[7] That section provides in relevant part:

"[N]othing in this act or in any law of this state shall preclude a public employer from making an agreement with an exclusive bargaining representative as defined in section 11 to require as a condition of employment that all employees in the bargaining unit pay to the exclusive bargaining representative a service fee equivalent to the amount of dues uniformly required of members of the exclusive bargaining representative. . . ."

agency-shop clause predating 1973 as a matter of state law, and the court ruled further that such a clause does not violate the Federal Constitution.

The plaintiffs' appeals were consolidated by the Michigan Court of Appeals, which ruled that the trial court had erred in giving retroactive application to the 1973 legislative amendment. The appellate court proceeded, however, to consider the constitutionality of the agency-shop clause, and upheld its facial validity on the authority of this Court's decision in *Railway Employes' Department v. Hanson,* 351 U.S. 225, 76 S.Ct. 714, 100 L.Ed. 1112, which upheld the constitutionality under the First Amendment of a union-shop clause, authorized by the Railway Labor Act, requiring financial support of the exclusive bargaining representative by every member of the bargaining unit. *Id.,* at 238, 76 S.Ct., at 721. Noting, however, that Michigan law also permits union expenditures for legislative lobbying and in support of political candidates, the state appellate court identified an issue explicitly not considered in *Hanson* — the constitutionality of using compulsory service charges to further "political purposes" unrelated to collective bargaining. Although recognizing that such expenditures "could violate plaintiffs' First and Fourteenth Amendment rights," the court read this Court's more recent decisions to require that an employee who seeks to vindicate such rights must "make known to the union those causes and candidates to which he objects." Since the complaints had failed to allege that any such notification had been given, the court held that the plaintiffs were not entitled to restitution of any portion of the service charges. The trial court's error on the retroactivity question, however, led the appellate court to reverse and remand the case. 60 Mich.App. 92, 230 N.W.2d 322. After the Supreme Court of Michigan denied review, the plaintiffs appealed to this Court, 28 U.S.C. § 1257(2), and we noted probable jurisdiction, 425 U.S. 949, 96 S.Ct. 1723, 48 L.Ed.2d 192.

## II

### A

Consideration of the question whether an agency shop provision in a collective-bargaining agreement covering governmental employees is, as such, constitutionally valid must begin with two cases in this Court that on their face go far towards resolving the issue. The cases are *Railway Employes' Department v. Hanson, supra,* and *International Association of Machinists v. Street,* 367 U.S. 740, 81 S.Ct. 1784, 6 L.Ed.2d 1141.

In the *Hanson* case a group of railroad employees brought an action in a Nebraska court to enjoin enforcement of a union-shop agreement.[10] The

---

[10] Under a union-shop agreement, an employee must become a member of the union within a specified period of time after hire, and must as a member pay whatever union dues and fees are uniformly required. Under both the National Labor Relations Act and the Railway Labor Act, "[i]t is permissible to condition employment upon membership, but membership, insofar as it has significance to employment rights, may in turn be conditioned only upon payment of fees and dues." *NLRB v. General Motors Corp.,* 373 U.S. 734, 742, 83 S.Ct. 1453, 1459, 10 L.Ed.2d 670. See 29 U.S.C. § 158(a) (3); 45 U.S.C. § 152, Eleventh, quoted in n. 11, *infra.* Hence, although a union shop denies an employee the option of not formally becoming a union member, under federal law it is the "practical equivalent" of an agency shop. *NLRB v. General Motors, supra,* at 743, 83 S.Ct. at 1459. See also *Lathrop v. Donohue,* 367 U.S. 820, 828, 81 S.Ct. 1826, 1830, 6 L.Ed.2d 1191.    .

*Hanson* was concerned simply with the requirement of financial support for the union, and did not focus on the question whether the additional requirement of a union-shop arrangement that each employee formally join the union is constitutionally permissible. See *NLRB v. General Motors, supra,* challenged clause was authorized, and indeed shielded from any attempt by a State to prohibit it, by the Railway Labor Act, 45 U.S.C. § 152, Eleventh. The trial court granted the relief requested. The Nebraska Supreme Court upheld the injunction on the ground that employees who disagreed with the objectives promoted by union expenditures were deprived of the freedom of association protected by the First Amendment. This Court agreed that "justiciable questions under the First and Fifth Amendments were presented," 351 U.S., at 231, 76 S.Ct., at 718,[12] but reversed the judgment of the Nebraska Supreme Court on the merits. Acknowledging that "[m]uch might be said *pro* and *con*" about the union shop as a policy matter, the Court noted that it is Congress that is charged with identifying "[t]he ingredients of industrial peace and stabilized labor-management relations. . . ." 351 U.S., at 233-234, 76 S.Ct. at 719. Congress determined that it would promote peaceful labor relations to permit a union and an employer to conclude an agreement requiring employees who obtain the benefit of union representation to share its cost, and that legislative judgment was surely an allowable one. *Id.,* at 235, 76 S.Ct. at 719.

The record in *Hanson* contained no evidence that union dues were used to force ideological conformity or otherwise to impair the free expression of employees, and the Court noted that "[i]f 'assessments' are in fact imposed for purposes not germane to collective bargaining, a different problem would be presented." *Id.,* at 235, 76 S.Ct., at 720. (footnote omitted). But the Court squarely held that "the requirement for financial support of the collective-bargaining agency by all who receive the benefits of its work . . . does not violate . . . the First Amendmen[t]." *Id.,* at 238, 76 S.Ct., at 721.

The Court faced a similar question several years later in the *Street* case, which also involved a challenge to the constitutionality of a union shop authorized by the Railway Labor Act. In *Street,* however, the record contained findings that the union treasury to which all employees were required to contribute had been used "to finance the campaigns of candidates for federal and state offices whom [the plaintiffs] opposed, and to promote the propagation of political and economic doctrines, concepts and ideologies with which [they] disagreed." 367 U.S., at 744, 81 S.Ct., at 1787.

The Court recognized that these findings presented constitutional "questions of the utmost gravity" not decided in *Hanson, id.,* at 749, 81 S.Ct., at 1789, and therefore considered whether the Act could fairly be construed to avoid these constitutional issues. *Id.,* at 749-750, 81 S.Ct., at 1789-90.[13] The Court

---

373 U.S. at 744, 83 S.Ct. at 1460. ("Such a difference between the union and agency shop may be of great importance in some contexts . . . ."); cf. *Storer v. Brown,* 415 U.S. 724, 745-746, 94 S.Ct. 1274, 1286, 39 L.Ed.2d 714. As the agency shop before us does not impose that additional requirement, we have no occasion to address that question.

[12] Unlike § 14 (b) of the National Labor Relations Act, 29 U.S.C. § 164 (b), the Railway Labor Act pre-empts any attempt by a State to prohibit a union-shop agreement. Had it not been for that federal statute, the union-shop provision at issue in *Hanson* would have been invalidated under Nebraska law. The *Hanson* Court accordingly reasoned that government action was present: "the federal statute is the source of the power and authority by which any private rights are lost or sacrificed. . . . The enactment of the federal statute authorizing union ship agreements is the governmental action on which the Constitution operates . . . ." 351 U.S., at 232, 76 S.Ct. at 718. See also *ibid.,* n. 4. ("Once courts enforce the agreement the sanction of government is, of course, put behind them. See *Shelley v. Kraemer,* 334 U.S. 1, 68 S.Ct. 836, 92 L.Ed. 1161; *Hurd v. Hodge,* 334 U.S. 24, 63 S.Ct. 847, 92 L.Ed. 1187; *Barrows v. Jackson,* 346 U.S. 249, 73 S.Ct. 1031, 97 L.Ed. 1586.").

[13] In suggesting that *Street* "significantly undercut," and constituted a "rethinking" of, *Hanson, post,* at 1806, the concurring opinion loses sight of the fact that the record in *Street,* unlike that in *Hanson,* potentially presented constitutional questions arising from union expenditures for ideological purposes unrelated to collective bargaining.

concluded that the Act could be so construed, since only expenditures related to the union's functions in negotiating and administering the collective bargaining agreement and adjusting grievances and disputes fell within "the reasons . . . accepted by Congress why authority to make union-shop agreements was justified," *id.,* at 768, 81 S.Ct., at 1800. The Court rule [sic], therefore, that the use of compulsory union dues for political purposes violated the Act itself. Nonetheless, it found that an injunction against enforcement of the union-shop agreement as such was impermissible under *Hanson,* and remanded the case to the Supreme Court of Georgia so that a more limited remedy could be devised.

The holding in *Hanson,* as elaborated in *Street,* reflects familiar doctrines in the federal labor laws. The principle of exclusive union representation, which underlies the National Labor Relations Act as well as the Railway Labor Act, is a central element in the congressional structuring of industrial relations. . . . The designation of a single representative avoids the confusion that would result from attempting to enforce two or more agreements specifying different terms and conditions of employment. It prevents inter-union rivalries from creating dissension within the work force and eliminating the advantages to the employee of collectivization. It also frees the employer from the possibility of facing conflicting demands from different unions, and permits the employer and a single union to reach agreements and settlements that are not subject to attack from rival labor organizations. . . .

The designation of a union as exclusive representative carries with it great responsibilities. The tasks of negotiating and administering a collective-bargaining agreement and representing the interests of employees in settling disputes and processing grievances are continuing and difficult ones. They often entail expenditure of much time and money. See *Street, supra,* 367 U.S., at 760, 81 S.Ct., at 1795. The services of lawyers, expert negotiators, economists, and a research staff, as well as general administrative personnel, may be required. Moreover, in carrying out these duties, the union is obliged "fairly and equitably to represent all employees, . . . union and nonunion," within the relevant unit. *Id.,* at 761, 81 S.Ct., at 1796. A union-shop arrangement has been thought to distribute fairly the cost of these activities among those who benefit, and it counteracts the incentive that employees might otherwise have to become "free riders" — to refuse to contribute to the union while obtaining benefits of union representation that necessarily accrue to all employees.

To compel employees financially to support their collective bargaining representative has an impact upon their First Amendment interests. An employee may very well have ideological objections to a wide variety of activities undertaken by the union in its role as exclusive representative. His moral or religious views about the desirability of abortion may not square with the union's policy in negotiating a medical benefits plan. One individual might disagree with a union policy of negotiating limits on the right to strike, believing that to be the road to serfdom for the working class, while another might have economic or political objections to unionism itself. An employee might object to the union's wage policy because it violates guidelines designed to limit inflation, or might object to the union's seeking a clause in the collective-bargaining agreement proscribing racial discrimination. The examples could be multiplied. To be required to help finance the union as a collective-bargaining agent might well be thought, therefore, to interfere in some way with an employee's freedom to associate for the advancement of ideas, or to refrain from doing so, as he sees fit. But the judgment clearly made in *Hanson* and *Street* is that such interference as exists is constitutionally justified by the legislative assessment of the important contribution of the union shop to the system of labor relations established by Congress. "The furtherance of the common cause leaves some leeway for the leadership of the group. As long as they act to promote the cause which justified bringing the group together, the individual cannot withdraw his financial support merely because he disagrees with the group's strategy. If that were allowed, we would be reversing the *Hanson* case, *sub silentio.*" *International Association of Machinists v. Street, supra,* 367 U.S. at 778, 81 S.Ct. at 1805. (Douglas, J., concurring.)

### B

The National Labor Relations Act leaves regulation of the labor relations of state and local governments to the States. See 29 U.S.C. § 152 (2). Michigan has chosen to establish for local government units a regulatory scheme which, although not identical in every respect to the NLRA or RLA, is broadly modeled after federal law.... Under Michigan law employees of local government units enjoy rights parallel to those protected under federal legislation: the rights to self-organization and to bargain collectively, Mich.Comp.Laws §§ 423.209, 423.215; see 29 U.S.C. § 157; 45 U.S.C. § 152, Fourth; and the right to secret ballot representation elections, Mich.Comp.Laws § 423.212; see 29 U.S.C. § 159(e)(1); 45 U.S.C. § 152, Ninth.

Several aspects of Michigan law that mirror provisions of the Railway Labor Act are of particular importance here. A union that obtains the support of a majority of employees in the appropriate bargaining unit is designated the exclusive representative of those employees. Mich.Comp.Laws § 423.211. A union so designated is under a duty of fair representation to all employees in the unit, whether or not union members.... And in carrying out all of its various responsibilities, a recognized union may seek to have an agency-shop clause included in a collective-bargaining agreement. Mich.Comp.Laws § 423.210(1)(c). Indeed, the 1973 amendment to the Michigan Law was specifically designed to authorize agency shops in order that "employees in the bargaining unit ... share fairly in the financial support of their exclusive bargaining representative...." *Id.,* § 423.210 (2).

The governmental interests advanced by the agency shop provision in the Michigan statute are much the same as those promoted by similar provisions in federal labor law. The confusion and conflict that could arise if rival teachers' unions, holding quite different views as to the proper class hours, class sizes, holidays, tenure provisions, and grievance procedures, each sought to obtain the employer's agreement, are no different in kind from the evils that the exclusivity rule in the Railway Labor Act was designed to avoid.... The desirability of labor peace is no less important in the public sector, nor is the risk of "free riders" any smaller.

Our province is not to judge the wisdom of Michigan's decision to authorize the agency shop in public employment. Rather, it is to adjudicate the constitutionality of that decision. The same important government interests recognized in the *Hanson* and *Street* cases presumptively support the impingement upon associational freedom created by the agency shop here at issue. Thus, insofar as the service charge is used to finance expenditures by the union for the purposes of collective bargaining, contract administration, and grievance adjustment, those two decisions of this Court appear to require validation of the agency-shop agreement before us.

While recognizing the apparent precedential weight of the *Hanson* and *Street* cases, the appellants advance two reasons why those decisions should not control decision of the present case. First, the appellants note that it is *government* employment that is involved here, thus directly implicating constitutional guarantees, in contrast to the private employment that was the subject of the *Hanson* and *Street* decisions. Second, the appellants say that in the public sector collective bargaining itself is inherently "political," and that to require them to give financial support to it is to require the "ideological conformity" that the Court expressly found absent in the *Hanson* case. 351 U.S., at 238, 76 S.Ct., at 721. We find neither argument persuasive.

Because it is employment by the State that is here involved, the appellants suggest that this case is governed by a long line of decisions holding that public employment cannot be conditioned upon the surrender of First Amendment rights. But, while the actions of public employers surely constitute "state action," the union shop, as authorized by the Railway Labor Act, also was found to result from governmental action in *Hanson*. The plaintiffs' claims in *Hanson* failed, not because there was no governmental action, but because there was no First Amendment violation.[23] The appellants' reliance on the "unconstitutional conditions" doctrine is therefore misplaced.

The appellants' second argument is that in any event collective bargaining in the public sector is inherently "political" and thus requires a different result under the First and Fourteenth Amendments. This contention rests upon the important and often-noted differences in the nature of collective bargaining in the public and private sectors. A public employer, unlike his private counterpart, is not guided by the profit motive and constrained by the normal operation of the market. Municipal services are typically not priced, and where they are they tend to be regarded as in some sense "essential" and therefore are often priced inelastic. Although a public employer, like a private one, will wish to keep costs down, he lacks an important discipline against agreeing to increases in labor costs that in a market system would require price increases. A public sector union is correspondingly less concerned that high prices due to costly wage demands will decrease output and hence employment.

The government officials making decisions as the public "employer" are less likely to act as a cohesive unit than are managers in private industry, in part

---

[23] Nothing in our opinion embraces the "premise that public employers are under no greater constitutional constraints than their counterparts in the private sector," *post,* at 1804 (POWELL, J., concurring in the judgment), or indicates that private collective-bargaining agreements are, without more, subject to constitutional constraints, see *id.,* at 1808. We compare the union-shop agreement in this case to those executed under the Railway Labor Act simply because the existence of governmental action in both contexts requires analysis of the free expression question.

It is somewhat startling, particularly in view of the concession that *Hanson* was premised on a finding that governmental action was present, see *post,* at 1805 (POWELL, J., concurring in the judgment), to read in the concurring opinion that *Hanson* and *Street* "provide little or no guidance for the constitutional issues presented in this case," *post,* at 1809. *Hanson* nowhere suggested that the constitutional scrutiny of the union-shop agreement was watered down because the governmental action operated less directly than is true in a case such as the present one. Indeed, Mr. Justice Douglas, the author of *Hanson,* expressly repudiated that suggestion:

"Since neither Congress nor the state legislatures can abridge First Amendment rights, they cannot grant the power to private groups to abridge them. As I read the First Amendment, it forbids any abridgement by government whether directly or indirectly." *Street,* 367 U.S., at 777, 81 S.Ct., at 1804 (concurring opinion).

because different levels of public authority — department managers, budgetary officials, and legislative bodies — are involved, and in part because each official may respond to a distinctive political constituency. And the ease of negotiating a final agreement with the union may be severely limited by statutory restrictions, by the need for the approval of a higher executive authority or a legislative body, or by the commitment of budgetary decisions of critical importance to others.

Finally, decisionmaking by a public employer is above all a political process. The officials who represent the public employer are ultimately responsible to the electorate, which for this purpose can be viewed as comprising three overlapping classes of voters — taxpayers, users of particular government services, and government employees. Through exercise of their political influence as part of the electorate, the employees have the opportunity to affect the decisions of government representatives who sit on the other side of the bargaining table. Whether these representatives accede to a union's demands will depend upon a blend of political ingredients, including community sentiment about unionism generally and the involved union in particular, the degree of taxpayer resistance, and the views of voters as to the importance of the service involved and the relation between the demands and the quality of service. It is surely arguable, however, that permitting public employees to unionize and a union to bargain as their exclusive representative gives the employees more influence in the decisionmaking process than is possessed by employees similarly organized in the private sector.

The distinctive nature of public-sector bargaining has led to widespread discussion about the extent to which the law governing labor relations in the private sector provides an appropriate model. To take but one example, there has been considerable debate about the desirability of prohibiting public employee unions from striking, a step that the State of Michigan itself has taken, Mich.Comp.Laws § 423.202. But although Michigan has not adopted the federal model of labor relations in every respect, it has determined that labor stability will be served by a system of exclusive representation and the permissive use of an agency shop in public employment. As already stated, there can be no principled basis for according that decision less weight in the constitutional balance than was given in *Hanson* to the congressional judgment reflected in the Railway Labor Act. The only remaining constitutional inquiry evoked by the appellants' argument, therefore, is whether a public employee has a weightier First Amendment interest than a private employee in not being compelled to contribute to the costs of exclusive union representation. We think he does not.

Public employees are not basically different from private employees; on the whole, they have the same sort of skills, the same needs, and seek the same advantages. "The uniqueness of public employment is *not in the employees* nor in the work performed; the uniqueness is in the special character of the employer." Summers, Public Sector Bargaining: Problems of Governmental Decisionmaking, 44 Cinn.L.Rev. 669, 670 (1976) (emphasis added). The very real differences between exclusive agent collective bargaining in the public and private sectors are not such as to work any greater infringement upon the First Amendment interests of public employees. A public employee who believes that a union representing him is urging a course that is unwise as a matter of public policy is not barred from expressing his viewpoint. Besides voting in accordance with his convictions, every public employee is largely free to express his views, in public or private, orally or in writing. With some exceptions not pertinent here, public employees are free to participate in the full range of political activities open to other citizens. Indeed, just this Term we have held that the First and

Fourteenth Amendments protect the right of a public school teacher to oppose, at a public school board meeting, a position advanced by the teacher's union. *City of Madison Joint School District No. 8 v. Wisconsin Employment Relations Comm'n,* 429 U.S. 167, 97 S.Ct. 421, 50 L.Ed.2d 376 (1976). In so ruling we recognized that the principle of exclusivity cannot constitutionally be used to muzzle a public employee who, like any other citizen, might wish to express his view about governmental decisions concerning labor relations, *id.,* at 176, 97 S.Ct. at 426.

There can be no quarrel with the truism that because public employee unions attempt to influence governmental policymaking, their activities — and the views of members who disagree with them — may be properly termed political. But that characterization does not raise the ideas and beliefs of public employees onto a higher plane than the ideas and beliefs of private employees. It is no doubt true that a central purpose of the First Amendment "was to protect the free discussion of governmental affairs." *Post,* at 1811, citing *Buckley v. Valeo,* 424 U.S. 1, 14, 96 S.Ct. 612, 632, 46 L.Ed.2d 659, and *Mills v. Alabama,* 384 U.S. 214, 218, 86 S.Ct. 1434, 1436, 16 L.Ed.2d 484. But our cases have never suggested that expression about philosophical, social, artistic, economic, literary, or ethical matters — to take a nonexhaustive list of labels — is not entitled to full First Amendment protection. Union members in both the public and private sector may find that a variety of union activities conflict with their beliefs. . . . Nothing in the First Amendment or our cases discussing its meaning makes the question whether the adjective "political" can properly be attached to those beliefs the critical constitutional inquiry.

The differences between public and private sector collective bargaining simply do not translate into differences in First Amendment rights. Even those commentators most acutely aware of the distinctive nature of public-sector bargaining and most seriously concerned with its policy implications agree that "[t]he union security issue in the public sector . . . is fundamentally the same issue . . . as in the private sector. . . . No special dimension results from the fact that a union represents public rather than private employees." H. Wellington & R. Winter, The Unions and the Cities 95-96 (1971). We conclude that the Michigan Court of Appeals was correct in viewing this Court's decisions in *Hanson* and *Street* as controlling in the present case insofar as the service charges are applied to collective bargaining, contract administration, and grievance adjustment purposes.

## C

Because the Michigan Court of Appeals ruled that state law "sanctions the use of nonunion members' fees for purposes other than collective bargaining," 60 Mich.App., at 99, 230 N.W.2d, at 326, and because the complaints allege that such expenditures were made, this case presents constitutional issues not decided in *Hanson* or *Street.* Indeed, *Street* embraced an interpretation of the Railway Labor Act not without its difficulties, see 367 U.S., at 784-786, 81 S.Ct., at 1807-08. (Black, J., dissenting); *id.,* at 799-803, 81 S.Ct., at 1814-16. (Frankfurter, J., dissenting), precisely to avoid facing the constitutional issues presented by the use of union-shop dues for political and ideological purposes unrelated to collective bargaining, *id.,* at 749-750, 81 S.Ct., at 1789-90. Since the state court's construction of the Michigan statute is authoritative, however, we must confront those issues in this case.

Our decisions establish with unmistakable clarity that the freedom of an individual to associate for the purpose of advancing beliefs and ideas is protected by the First and Fourteenth Amendments. . . . Equally clear is the proposition that a government may not require an individual to relinquish rights guaranteed him by the First Amendment as a condition of public employment. *E. g., Elrod v. Burns, supra,* 427 U.S. at 357-360, 96 S.Ct. at 2681-2683 and cases cited; *Perry v. Sindermann,* 408 U.S. 593, 92 S.Ct. 2694, 33 L.Ed.2d 570; *Keyishian v. Board of Regents,* 385 U.S. 589, 87 S.Ct. 675, 17 L.Ed.2d 629. The appellants argue that they fall within the protection of these cases because they have been prohibited not from actively associating, but rather from refusing to associate. They specifically argue that they may constitutionally prevent the Union's spending a part of their required service fees to contribute to political candidates and to express political views unrelated to its duties as exclusive bargaining representative. We have concluded that this argument is a meritorious one.

One of the principles underlying the Court's decision in *Buckley v. Valeo,* 424 U.S. 1, 96 S.Ct. 612, 46 L.Ed.2d 659, was that contributing to an organization for the purpose of spreading a political message is protected by the First Amendment. Because "[m]aking a contribution . . . enables like-minded persons to pool their resources in furtherance of common political goals," *id.,* at 22, 96 S.Ct. at 636, the Court reasoned that limitations upon the freedom to contribute "implicate fundamental First Amendment interests," *id.,* at 23, 96 S.Ct. at 636.

The fact that the appellants are compelled to make, rather than prohibited from making, contributions for political purposes works no less an infringement of their constitutional rights. For at the heart of the First Amendment is the notion that an individual should be free to believe as he will, and that in a free society one's beliefs should be shaped by his mind and his conscience rather than coerced by the State. See *Elrod v. Burns, supra,* 427 U.S. at 356-357, 95 S.Ct. at 2681-82; *Stanley v. Georgia,* 394 U.S. 557, 565, 89 S.Ct. 1243, 1248, 22 L.Ed.2d 542; *Cantwell v. Connecticut,* 310 U.S. 296, 303-304, 60 S.Ct. 900, 903, 84 L.Ed. 1213. And the freedom of belief is no incidental or secondary aspect of the First Amendment's protections:

> "If there is any fixed star in our constitutional constellation, it is that no official, high or petty, can prescribe what shall be orthodox in politics, nationalism, religion, or other matters of opinion or force citizens to confess by word or act their faith therein." *West Virginia Board of Education v. Barnette,* 319 U.S. 624, 642, 63 S.Ct. 1178, 1187, 87 L.Ed. 1628.

These principles prohibit a State from compelling any individual to affirm his belief in God, *Torcaso v. Watkins,* 367 U.S. 488, 81 S.Ct. 1680, 6 L.Ed.2d 982, or to associate with a political party, *Elrod v. Burns, supra;* see *id.,* 427 U.S. at 363-364, n. 17, 95 S.Ct. at 2685, as a condition of retaining public employment. They are no less applicable to the case at bar, and they thus prohibit the appellees from requiring any of the appellants to contribute to the support of an ideological cause he may oppose as a condition of holding a job as a public school teacher.

We do not hold that a union cannot constitutionally spend funds for the expression of political views, on behalf of political candidates, or towards the advancement of other ideological causes not germane to its duties as collective bargaining representative.[32] Rather, the Constitution requires only that such

---

[32] To the extent that this activity involves support of political candidates, it must, of course, be conducted consistently with any applicable (and constitutional) system of election campaign regulation. See generally *Buckley v. Valeo, supra;* Developments in the Law — Election Law, 88 Harv.L.Rev. 1111, 1237-1271 (1975).

expenditures be financed from charges, dues, or assessments paid by employees who do not object to advancing those ideas and who are not coerced into doing so against their will by the threat of loss of governmental employment.

There will, of course, be difficult problems in drawing lines between collective bargaining activities, for which contributions may be compelled, and ideological activities unrelated to collective bargaining, for which such compulsion is prohibited.[33] The Court held in *Street,* as a matter of statutory construction, that a similar line must be drawn under the Railway Labor Act, but in the public sector the line may be somewhat hazier. The process of establishing a written collective-bargaining agreement prescribing the terms and conditions of public employment may require not merely concord at the bargaining table, but subsequent approval by other public authorities; related budgetary and appropriations decisions might be seen as an integral part of the bargaining process. We have no occasion in this case, however, to try to define such a dividing line. The case comes to us after a judgment on the pleadings, and there is no evidentiary record of any kind. The allegations in the complaint are general ones, see pp. 1787-1788, *supra,* and the parties have neither briefed nor argued the question of what specific union activities in the present context properly fall under the definition of collective bargaining. The lack of factual concreteness and adversary presentation to aid us in approaching the difficult line-drawing questions highlight the importance of avoiding unnecessary decision of constitutional questions. All that we decide is that the general allegations in the complaint, if proven, establish a cause of action under the First and Fourteenth Amendments.

### III

In determining what remedy will be appropriate if the appellants prove their allegations, the objective must be to devise a way of preventing compulsory subsidization of ideological activity by employees who object thereto without restricting the union's ability to require every employee to contribute to the cost of collective-bargaining activities.[35] This task is simplified by the guidance to be had from prior decisions. In *Street, supra,* the plaintiffs had proved at trial that expenditures were being made for political purposes of various kinds, and the Court found those expenditures illegal under the Railway Labor Act. See pp. 1791-1792, *supra.* Moreover, in that case each plaintiff had "made known to the union representing his craft or class his dissent from the use of his money for political causes which he opposes." 367 U.S., at 750, 81 S.Ct., at 1790; see *id.,* at 771, 81 S.Ct. at 1801. The Court found that "[i]n that circumstance, the respective unions were without power to use payments thereafter tendered by them for such political causes." *Ibid.* Since, however, *Hanson* had established that the union-shop agreement was not unlawful as such, the Court held that to enjoin its enforcement would "[sweep] too broadly." *Ibid.* The Court also found that an injunction prohibiting the union from expending dues for political purposes would be inappropriate, not only because of the basic policy reflected in the Norris-LaGuardia Act against enjoining labor unions, but also because those

---

[33] The appellants' complaints also alleged that the Union carries on various "social activities" which are not open to nonmembers. It is unclear to what extent such activities fall outside the Union's duties as exclusive representative or involve constitutionally protected rights of association. Without greater specificity in the description of such activities and the benefit of adversary argument, we leave those questions in the first instance to the Michigan courts.

[35] It is plainly not an adequate remedy to limit the use of the actual dollars collected from dissenting employees to collective-bargaining purposes. Such a limitation

union members who do wish part of their dues to be used for political purposes have a right to associate to that end "without being silenced by the dissenters." *Id.,* at 772-773, 81 S.Ct., at 1802.

After noting that "dissent is not to be presumed" and that only employees who have affirmatively made known to the union their opposition to political uses of their funds are entitled to relief, the Court sketched two possible remedies: first, "an injunction against expenditure for political causes opposed by each complaining employee of a sum, from those moneys to be spent by the union for political purposes, which is so much of the moneys exacted from him as is the proportion of the union's total expenditures made for such political activities to the union's total budget," and second, restitution of a fraction of union dues paid equal to the fraction of total union expenditures that were made for political purposes opposed by the employee. 367 U.S. at 774, 775, 81 S.Ct., at 1802-03.[38]

The Court again considered the remedial question in *Brotherhood of Railway & Steamship Clerks v. Allen,* 373 U.S. 113, 83 S.Ct. 1158, 10 L.Ed.2d 235. In that case employees who had refused to pay union shop dues obtained injunctive relief in state court against enforcement of the union shop agreement. The employees had not notified the Union prior to bringing the lawsuit of their opposition to political expenditures, and at trial, their testimony was principally that they opposed such expenditures, as a general matter. *Id.,* at 118-119, n. 5, 83 S.Ct., at 1161-62. The Court held that the employees had adequately established their cause of action by manifesting "opposition to *any* political expenditures by the union," *id.,* at 118, 83 S.Ct. at 1162 (emphasis in original), and that the requirement in *Street* that dissent be affirmatively indicated was satisfied by the allegations in the complaint that was filed, *id.,* at 118-119, and n. 6, 83 S.Ct., at 1161-62. The Court indicated again the appropriateness of the two remedies sketched in *Street;* reversed the judgment affirming issuance of the injunction; and remanded for determination of which expenditures were properly to be characterized as political and what percentage of total union expenditures they constituted.[40]

---

"is of bookkeeping significance only rather than a matter of real substance. It must be remembered that the service fee is admittedly the exact equal of membership initiation fees and monthly dues ... and that ... dues collected from members may be used for a 'variety of purposes, in addition to meeting the union's costs of collective bargaining.' Unions 'rather typically' use their membership dues 'to do those things which the members authorize the union to do in their interest and on their behalf.' If the union's total budget is divided between collective bargaining and institutional expenses and if nonmember payments, equal to those of a member, go entirely for collective bargaining costs, the nonmember will pay more of these expenses than his pro rata share. The member will pay less and to that extent a portion of his fees and dues is available to pay institutional expenses. The union's budget is balanced. By paying a larger share of collective bargaining costs the nonmember subsidizes the union's institutional activities." *Retail Clerks Local 1625 v. Schermerhorn,* 373 U.S. 746, 753-754, 83 S.Ct. 1461, 1465, 10 L.Ed.2d 678.

[38] In proposing a restitution remedy, the *Street* opinion made clear that "[t]here should be no necessity, however, for the employee to trace his money up to and including its expenditure; if the money goes into general funds and no separate accounts of receipts and expenditures of the funds of individual employees are maintained, the portion of his money the employee would be entitled to recover would be in the same proportion that the expenditures for political purposes which he had advised the union he disapproved bore to the total union budget." 367 U.S., at 775, 81 S.Ct. at 1803.

[40] The Court in *Allen* went on to elaborate:

"[s]ince the unions possess the facts and records from which the proportion of political to

The Court in *Allen* described a "practical decree" that could properly be entered, providing for (1) the refund of a portion of the exacted funds in the proportion that union political expenditures bear to total union expenditures, and (2) the reduction of future exactions by the same proportion. *Id.,* at 122, 83 S. Ct., at 1163. Recognizing the difficulties posed by judicial administration of such a remedy, the Court also suggested that it would be highly desirable for unions to adopt a "voluntary plan by which dissenters would be afforded an internal union remedy." *Ibid.* This last suggestion is particularly relevant to the case at bar, for the Union has adopted such a plan since the commencement of this litigation.[41]

Although *Street* and *Allen* were concerned with statutory rather than constitutional violations, that difference surely could not justify any lesser relief in this case. Judged by the standards of those cases, the Michigan Court of Appeals' ruling that the appellants were entitled to no relief at this juncture was unduly restrictive. For all the reasons outlined in *Street,* the court was correct in denying the broad injunctive relief requested. But in holding that as a prerequisite to any relief each appellant must indicate to the Union the *specific* expenditures to which he objects, the Court of Appeals ignored the clear holding of *Allen.* As in *Allen,* the employees here indicated in their pleadings that they opposed ideological expenditures of *any* sort that are unrelated to collective bargaining. To require greater specificity would confront an individual employee with the dilemma of relinquishing either his right to withhold his support of ideological causes to which he objects or his freedom to maintain his own beliefs without public disclosure. It would also place on each employee the considerable burden of monitoring all of the numerous and shifting expenditures made by the Union that are unrelated to its duties as exclusive bargaining representative.

The Court of Appeals thus erred in holding that the plaintiffs are entitled to no relief if they can prove the allegations contained in their complaints, and in depriving them of an opportunity to establish their right to appropriate relief, such, for example, as the kind of remedies described in *Street* and *Allen.* In view of the newly adopted union internal remedy, it may be appropriate under Michigan law, even if not strictly required by any doctrine of exhaustion of remedies, to defer further judicial proceedings pending the voluntary utilization by the parties of that internal remedy as a possible means of settling the dispute.[45]

---

total union expenditures can reasonably be calculated, basic considerations of fairness compel that they, not the individual employees, bear the burden of proving such proportion. Absolute precision in the calculation of such proportion is not, of course, to be expected or required; we are mindful of the difficult accounting problems that may arise. And no decree would be proper which appeared likely to infringe the unions' right to expend uniform exactions under the union-shop agreement in support of activities germane to collective bargaining and, as well, to expend nondissenters' such exactions in support of political activities." 373 U.S., at 122, 83 S.Ct., at 1163.

[41] Under the procedure adopted by the Union, as explained in the appellees' brief, a dissenting employee may protest at the beginning of each school year the expenditure of any part of his agency-shop fee for "activities or causes of a political nature or involving controversial issues of public importance only incidentally related to wages, hours, and conditions of employment." The employee is then entitled to a pro rata refund of his service charge in accordance with the calculation of the portion of total union expenses for the specified purposes. The calculation is made in the first instance by the Union, but is subject to review by an impartial board.

[45] We express no view as to the constitutional sufficiency of the internal remedy described by

The judgment is vacated, and the case is remanded for further proceedings not inconsistent with this opinion.

. . . .

[Concurring opinions of MR. JUSTICE REHNQUIST and MR. JUSTICE STEVENS are omitted.]

MR. JUSTICE POWELL, with whom THE CHIEF JUSTICE and MR. JUSTICE BLACKMUN join, concurring in the judgment.

The Court today holds that a State cannot constitutionally compel public employees to contribute to union political activities which they oppose. On this basis the Court concludes that "the general allegations in the complaint, if proven, establish a cause of action under the First and Fourteenth Amendments." *Ante,* at 1800. With this much of the Court's opinion I agree, and I therefore join the Court's judgment remanding this case for further proceedings.

But the Court's holding and judgment are but a small part of today's decision. Working from the novel premise that public employers are under no greater constitutional constraints than their counterparts in the private sector, the Court apparently rules that public employees can be compelled by the State to pay full union dues to a union with which they disagree, subject only to a possible rebate or deduction if they are willing to step forward, declare their opposition to the union, and initiate a proceeding to establish that some portion of their dues has been spent on "ideological activities unrelated to collective bargaining." *Ante,* at 1800. Such a sweeping limitation of First Amendment rights by the Court is not only unnecessary on this record; it is in my view unsupported by either precedent or reason.

. . . .

The ultimate objective of a union in the public sector, like that of a political party, is to influence public decisionmaking in accordance with the views and perceived interests of its membership. Whether a teachers' union is concerned with salaries and fringe benefits, teacher qualifications and in-service training, pupil-teacher ratios, length of the school day, student discipline, or the content of the high school curriculum, its objective is to bring school board policy and decisions into harmony with its own views. Similarly, to the extent that school board expenditures and policy are guided by decisions made by the municipal, state, and federal governments the union's objective is to obtain favorable decisions — and to place persons in positions of power who will be receptive to the union's viewpoint. In these respects, the public sector union is indistinguishable from the traditional political party in this country.

What distinguishes the public sector union from the political party — and the distinction is a limited one — is that most of its members are employees who share similar economic interests and who may have a common professional perspective on some issues of public policy. Public school teachers, for example, have a common interest in fair teachers' salaries and reasonable pupil-teacher ratios. This suggests the possibility of a limited range of probable agreement among the class of individuals that a public sector union is organized to represent. But I am unable to see why the likelihood of an area of consensus in the group should remove the protection of the First Amendment for the disagreements that

---

the appellees. If the appellants initially resort to that remedy and ultimately conclude that it is constitutionally deficient in some respect, they would of course be entitled to judicial consideration of the adequacy of the remedy.

inevitably will occur. Certainly, if individual teachers are ideologically opposed to public sector unionism itself, as are the appellants in this case, *ante,* at 1787-1788, one would think that compelling them to affiliate with the union by contributing to it infringes their First Amendment rights to the same degree as compelling them to contribute to a political party. Under the First Amendment, the protection of speech does not turn on the likelihood or frequency of its occurrence.

Nor is there any basis here for distinguishing "collective bargaining activities" from "political activities" so far as the interests protected by the First Amendment are concerned. Collective bargaining in the public sector is "political" in any meaningful sense of the word. This is most obvious when public sector bargaining extends — as it may in Michigan — to such matters of public policy as the educational philosophy that will inform the high school curriculum. But it is also true when public sector bargaining focuses on such "bread and butter" issues as wages, hours, vacations, and pensions. Decisions on such issues will have a direct impact on the level of public services, priorities within state and municipal budgets, creation of bonded indebtedness, and tax rates. The cost of public education is normally the largest element of a county or municipal budget. Decisions reached through collective bargaining in the schools will affect not only the teachers and the quality of education, but also the taxpayers and the beneficiaries of other important public services. Under our democratic system of government, decisions on these critical issues of public policy have been entrusted to elected officials who ultimately are responsible to the voters.

Disassociation with a public sector union and the expression of disagreement with its positions and objectives therefore lie at "the core of those activities protected by the First Amendment." . . .

. . . .

Before today it had been well established that when state law intrudes upon protected speech, the State itself must shoulder the burden of proving that its action is justified by overriding state interests. See *Elrod v. Burns, supra,* 427 U.S. at 363, 96 S. Ct. at 2685; *Healy v. James,* 408 U.S. 169, 184, 92 S. Ct. 2338, 2347, 33 L.Ed.2d 266 (1972); *Speiser v. Randall,* 357 U.S. 513, 525-526, 78 S. Ct. 1332, 1341-42, 2 L.Ed.2d 1460 (1958). The Court, for the first time in a First Amendment case, simply reverses this principle. Under today's decision, a nonunion employee who would vindicate his First Amendment rights apparently must initiate a proceeding to prove that the union has allocated some portion of its budget to "ideological activities unrelated to collective bargaining." *Ante,* at 1800-1803. I would adhere to established First Amendment principles and require the State to come forward and demonstrate, as to each union expenditure for which it would exact support from minority employees, that the compelled contribution is necessary to serve overriding governmental objectives. This placement of the burden of litigation, not the Court's, gives appropriate protection to First Amendment rights without sacrificing ends of government that may be deemed important.

# NOTES

1. *See generally* Levinson, *After Abood: Public Sector Union Security and the Protection of Individual Public Employee Rights,* 27 Am. U.L. Rev. 1 (1977); Mitchell, *Public Sector Union Security: The Impact of Abood,* 29 Lab. L.J. 697 (1978).

2. In Ball v. City of Detroit, 269 N.W.2d 607, 98 L.R.R.M. 3137 (Mich. Ct. App. 1978), the court, in a case involving a challenge to the agency shop fees required by a contract

between the City of Detroit and AFSCME, held that "[u]nder Abood the union is entitled only to that portion of the service fee used for collective bargaining, contract administration and grievance adjustment." The court stated "the use of the service fee to advance or promote 'religious' or 'economic' views would be no less an infringement on an objecting employee's First Amendment rights and the use of the fee to promote 'political' views." "Because the union is in possession of facts and records documenting union expenditures," the court said "basic fairness requires the union to carry the burden of proof to establish the cost of these legitimate uses of an objecting non-member service fee." Pending a judicial determination, the court held that the service fee for the objecting non-members should be placed in escrow since "fundamental First Amendment rights are at stake."

3. In Browne v. Milwaukee Board of School Directors, 98 L.R.R.M. 2574 (Wis. Sup. Ct.), *motion for rehearing denied,* 99 L.R.R.M. 2284 (Wis. Sup. Ct. 1978), the court upheld the constitutionality of fair-share agreements which would require non-members "to pay their proportionate share of the cost of the collective bargaining process and contract administration measured by the amount of dues uniformly required of all members." WIS. STATS. § 111.70(1)(h) (1975). After noting that "[t]he statute itself forbids use of fair-share funds for purposes unrelated to collective bargaining or contract administration," the court held that it was proper to transfer the case to the Wisconsin Employment Relations Commission to determine "what portion of the fair-share dues are being used for purposes unrelated to contract administration or collective bargaining, in contravention of the statute." The court noted that the use of fair-share funds for purposes unrelated to collective bargaining or contract administration interferes with, restrains, or coerces employees in the exercise of their rights guaranteed under the Wisconsin Act and therefore constitutes a prohibited practice. The court, however, denied plaintiff's motion to escrow all fair-share funds pending resolution of the factual question as to what portion of the fair-share dues were for purposes unrelated to collective bargaining or contract administration. The court observed that the Supreme Court's decisions in *Street* and *Allen* "stand for the proposition that employees who are compelled to pay union dues are still required to pay those dues pending a determination of what portion of those dues are being used for statutorily impermissible purposes."

4. In Jensen v. Yonamine, 437 F. Supp. 368 (D. Hawaii, 1977), a federal district court held that non-members stated a cause of action by alleging that the mandatory service fee required under the Hawaii law was being used by the bargaining representative for other than proper collective bargaining purposes to which they objected. The court held, however, that the abstention doctrine was applicable and that the Hawaii courts should be given the opportunity to determine whether the exclusive bargaining representative has "used monies from service fees for purposes other than the negotiation and administration of the collective bargaining agreement."

5. The collective bargaining ordinance for the District of Columbia permits the negotiation of a fair share agreement. DISTRICT PERSONNEL MANUAL, ch. 25, § A, Items 1(e) and 13. The ordinance provides that neither the employee organization nor the employer can take any action against an employee who refuses to pay the negotiated fair share fee. The ordinance provides, however, that the parties may agree that the employee organization may "refrain from representing any employee who declines to make such payments in any matters affecting such employee personally apart from other members of the unit. . . ." DISTRICT PERSONNEL MANUAL, ch. 25, § A, Item 13. Is this type of enforcement mechanism constitutional? Can an employee organization representing a public employee be absolved of its duty of fair representation if the employee decides not to contribute a fair share fee pursuant to a lawfully negotiated contractual provision?

6. The California Educational Employment Relations Act permits the negotiation of either a fair share agreement or a maintenance of membership clause. CAL. EDUC. CODE § 3540.1(i). The latter is defined as follows:

An arrangement pursuant to which a public school employee may decide whether or not to join an employee organization, but which requires him, as a condition of continued employment, if he does join, to maintain his membership in good standing for the duration of the written agreement. However, no such arrangement shall deprive the employee of the right to terminate his obligation to the employee organization within a period of 30 days following the expiration of the written agreement. . . . CAL. EDUC. CODE § 3540.1(i)(1). Is this maintenance of membership provision constitutional in light of the Supreme Court's decision in *Abood*? What difference, if any, does the "escape period" have on this determination?

7. The Massachusetts law permits the negotiation of the fair share or service fee which is "proportionately commensurate with the cost of collective bargaining and contract administration." MASS. GEN. LAWS ANN. ch. 150(e), § 12 (1976). Section 17.03(4) of the Rules and Regulations issued by the Massachusetts Labor Relations Commission provides that costs not related to collective bargaining and contract administration include the following:

(a) contributions to political parties or candidates for or holders of public office;

(b) contributions to charitable, religious, or political organizations or causes;

(c) fines, penalties, or damages arising from the unlawful activities of a bargaining agent or a bargaining agent's officers or agents or members;

(d) costs of social or recreational activities;

(e) costs of educational activities unrelated to collective bargaining and contract administration;

(f) costs of medical insurance, retirement benefits, or other benefit programs;

(g) costs incurred by the bargaining agent to organize employees who are not included in the bargaining unit;

(h) other costs unrelated to collective bargaining and contract administration.

In a state like Massachusetts which prohibits all public sector strikes but which permits fair share agreements, would it be permissible for the exclusive bargaining representative to include as part of its cost of representation any expenses related to an illegal strike, such as strike benefits, publicity expenses, litigation expenses, and the costs for picket signs, pamphlets and leaflets in support of such a strike?

## D. STATUTORY CONSIDERATIONS

### TOWN OF NORTH KINGSTOWN v. NORTH KINGSTOWN TEACHERS ASSOCIATION

Rhode Island Supreme Court
110 R.I. 698, 297 A.2d 342 (1972)

JOSLIN, J. This dispute arose under the School Teachers' Arbitration Act [G.L. 1956 (1968 Reenactment) ch. 9.3 of title 28]. A Superior Court justice certified it to this court for hearing and determination on an agreed statement of facts.

It appears that the School Committee of the Town of North Kingstown Teachers Association, bargaining agent for the certified teachers in that town's public school system, met for the purpose of determining what terms and conditions of employment for the school year 1971-72 should be included in a proposed collective bargaining agreement.

When an impasse in negotiations developed, the unresolved issues were submitted to arbitration pursuant to § 28-9.3-9. Included in the submission were association proposals for an agency shop, course reimbursement and longevity pay. Plaintiffs, being dissatisfied with the arbitrators' decision thereon, sought judicial review. Initially they filed a complaint in the Superior Court; they then moved that the case be certified to this court for hearing and determination on an agreed statement of facts. The case arrived here under a consent order which certifies three stated questions for our determination. . . .

We consider the case . . . as if it were properly certified on an agreed statement of facts. In that frame of reference, the issue is whether the arbitrators acted in excess of their jurisdiction with respect to three of the unresolved issues submitted to them.

The first of those issues relates to the arbitrators' authority to order execution of a collective bargaining agreement embodying a provision for what is known in the field of labor relations as an "agency shop." In general, such a provision requires a charge or fee to be paid to a certified labor organization by those employees who, although not members of that organization, are nonetheless part of the collective bargaining unit for which it, as bargaining agent, speaks. In this case, the arbitrators directed the parties "to write" language into their agreement which would give "full effect" to that portion of their award which states:

"... prior to the first payday in October, all teachers as a condition of employment would have to have paid to the Association dues or a sum equal to dues in the united profession. Such an arrangement does not require membership in the Association, it only requires that dues or an amount equal to dues be paid by all teachers in order to hold employment in the North Kingstown School System."

That directive's legality becomes suspect because of possible conflict between it and the right-to-work provision of the School Teachers' Arbitration Act (§ 28-9.3-7) which guarantees public school teachers the freedom "... to join *or to decline to join* any association or organization regardless of whether it has been certified as the exclusive representative of certified public school teachers." (emphasis added)

The plaintiffs argue that the two provisions are completely at odds. They rely upon the judgment of the Supreme Court that an agency shop conditions employment "upon the practical equivalent of union 'membership.' " [3] NLRB v. General Motors Corp., 373 U.S. 734, 743, 83 S. Ct. 1453, 1459, 10 L. Ed. 2d 670, 676 (1963). It is unthinkable to them that our Legislature would grant teachers freedom to choose whether or not to affiliate with a labor organization, and simultaneously compel those who opt against joining to pay that organization a "sum equal to [union] dues" in order to obtain or hold employment.

The defendant, on the other hand, sees nothing incongruous between the two. It argues that the legislators who enacted the School Teachers' Arbitration Act in 1966 must certainly have been aware that several states had by then enacted "right-to-work laws"; that while some of those laws were silent on whether nonunion members of a bargaining unit could be compelled to contribute to the union, most were restrictive and specifically prohibited the exaction of union dues or other fees from those nonmembers; and that the failure of our Legislature to pattern our act upon the more restrictive models clearly evidences its intention to allow, rather than to ban, the agency shop as a permissible form of union security arrangement.[4]

---

[3] In NLRB v. General Motors Corp., 373 U.S. 734, 83 S. Ct. 1453, 10 L. Ed. 2d 670 (1963), the Court held that the National Labor Relations Act does not prohibit inclusion of an agency shop clause in a collective bargaining agreement covering employment in a state having a right-to-work law. In the companion case of Retail Clerks, Local 1625, AFL-CIO v. Schermerhorn, 373 U.S. 746, 83 S. Ct. 1461, 10 L. Ed. 2d 678 (1963), it was held that the question of whether such an arrangement violated Florida law was for the Florida court to decide.

[4] Among the states then having constitutional or statutory right-to-work provisions specifically banning the agency shop were: Alabama, Arkansas, Georgia, Iowa, Louisiana, Mississippi, Nebraska, North Carolina, South Carolina, Tennessee, Utah, Virginia, and Wyoming. A typical provision was Ga. Code Anno. #54-903 (Rev. ed. 1961) which read as follows:

"No individual shall be required as a condition of employment, or of continuance of employment, to pay any fee, assessment, or other sum of money whatsoever, to a labor organization."

This approach finds support in Meade Elec. Co. v. Hagberg, 129 Ind. App. 631, 159 N.E.2d 408 (1959) where it was employed as a rationale for recognizing the legality of an agency shop. It is further aided by the rule of strict construction.[5] Application of that rule in this instance justifies the conclusion that the Legislature, by failing to abrogate, either specifically or by clear implication, the common law right of labor and management to include an agency shop clause in a collective bargaining agreement, is presumed not to have intended a change in that law. Hopfl, *The Agency Shop Question,* 49 Cornell L.Q. 478, 483 (1964).

Decisions elsewhere, however, reject these arguments and, in what apparently is the majority view, hold that a right-to-work law, even though lacking a specific prohibition against taxation of nonunion members, will not tolerate an agency shop. Higgins v. Cardinal Mfg. Co., 188 Kan. 11, 360 P.2d 456 (1961); Baldwin v. Arizona Flame Restaurant, Inc., 82 Ariz. 385, 313 P.2d 759 (1957); Schermerhorn v. Local 1625, Retail Clerks, AFL-CIO, 141 So. 2d 269 (Fla. 1962).

What underlies those decisions is the concept that legislation which ". . . clearly bestows on the workingman a right to join or not join a labor union, as he sees fit, without jeopardizing his job" must of necessity be repugnant to a contract stipulation which ". . . requires the nonunion employee to purchase from the labor union a right . . ." which the right-to-work law has given him. Schermerhorn v. Local 1625, Retail Clerks, AFL-CIO *supra* at 272-73. They rest also on the notion that "the real and rather well-hidden meaning" of a right-to-work law's ban on compulsory unionism includes by necessary implication a prohibition against any forced payment by a worker to a labor organization as the price for obtaining or holding employment. Higgins v. Cardinal Mfg. Co., *supra* at 23, 360 P.2d at 465.

The plaintiffs advance two further arguments in support of the position that it was illegal for the arbitrators to require an agency shop provision to be embodied in this agreement.

The first of those arguments declares that we must assume that the Legislature intended to ban the agency shop, inasmuch as a contrary assumption would subvert the purpose of the tenure laws which in G.L. 1956 (1969 Reenactment) § 16-13-3 make "good and just cause" the only ground for dismissing a tenured teacher.[6] The short answer is that the Legislature which established grounds for dismissal can also provide that noncompliance with an agency shop provision will constitute one of those grounds.

In their other and final argument, plaintiffs, in substance, observe that the School Teachers' Arbitration Act declares this state's public policy as affording public school teachers the rights to organize, to be represented, to negotiate professionally, and to bargain on a collective basis; that in similar declarations the Firefighters' and the Policemen's Arbitration Acts extend to firemen and policemen in § 28-9.1-2 and § 28-9.2-2, respectively, ". . . *all of the rights of labor* other than the right to strike, or engage in any work stoppage or slowdown." (emphasis added) The differences, plaintiffs say, are significant, and they argue that the more restrictive declaration of teachers' rights evidences a legislative intent to invalidate the agency shop as a union security arrangement.

---

[5] In this state we follow the rule that statutes in derogation of the common law should be strictly construed. Hodge v. Osteopathic Gen. Hosp., 107 R.I. 135, 144, 265 A.2d 733, 738-39 (1970); Pucci v. Algiere, 106 R.I. 411, 420-21, 261 A.2d 1, 7 (1970); Atlantic Ref. Co. v. Director of Pub. Works, 104 R.I. 436, 441, 244 A.2d 853, 856 (1968).

[6] The challenged portion of the award excepts "tenured teachers presently in the system" from the agency shop provision, and we are, therefore, not concerned with problems which might arise had they not been so excluded.

That argument, while perhaps ingenious, is nonetheless speculative for the differences on which they rely as a premise in nowise support their conclusion.

We have averted sufficiently to the arguments pro and con to make it apparent that for each which points to a possible legislative intention, there is a satisfactory counter pointing to an opposite intention. This is understandably so because nothing either in the language of the Act, or in the report of the legislative commission preceding its enactment, even hints at an attitudinal approach. Neither is there anything in the objectives which the Act was designed to serve or in the circumstances attendant upon its enactment from which a legislative intention can be ascertained. Instead, there is nothing but obscurity. It is as if there were a complete lack of awareness that there might someday be a proposal to include an agency shop provision in a labor agreement.

As we cannot extract meaning from an intention cloaked in obscurity, we must legislate "between gaps" and fill "the open spaces in the law." Cordozo, The Nature of the Judicial Process 113 (1921). We are guided in that task by "considerations . . . exactly of the same nature as those which ought to dominate legislative action itself, since it is a question in each case, of satisfying, as best may be, justice and social utility by an appropriate rule." Id. at 120. This, Judge Jerome Frank said, is "an activity which, no matter how one may label it, is in part legislative." Guiseppi v. Walling, 144 F.2d 608, 621 (2d Cir. 1944), aff'd sub nom. Gemsco, Inc. v. Walling, 324 U.S. 244, 65 S. Ct. 605, 89 L. Ed. 921 (1945).

In evaluating those considerations which in our judgment would be likely to prompt legislative action, foremost is the argument that a certified labor organization, as sole bargaining agent for all employees in the bargaining unit, is bound by law to negotiate for both unions and nonunion members; that the negotiations are costly; that it would be manifestly inequitable to permit those who see fit not to join the union to benefit from its services without at the same time requiring them to bear a fair and just share of the financial burdens; and that no member of a bargaining unit, be he a joiner or a nonjoiner, should expect or be allowed a "free-ride."

Because this argument is persuasive on the general question of the legitimacy of the agency shop does not mean that it is similarly convincing with respect to the validity of a provision calling for nonunion members to pay more than a just portion of the costs of the benefits conferred upon them. To accept such a provision as valid would, in effect, sanction an inverse "free-rider" situation in which the union member, rather than the nonjoiner, would be the "free-rider."

Accordingly, our approval is expressly limited to that kind of agency shop provision which neither requires a nonjoiner to share in expenditures for benefits he is not entitled to receive, nor exacts from him more than a proportionate share of the costs of securing the benefits conferred upon all members of the bargaining unit. An agency shop provision thus limited has been recognized both judicially [8] and at the bargaining table.[9]

---

[8] In Navy v. City of Detroit, Wayne County No. 123-642, 60 CCH Lab. Cas. 66,958 (Mich. Cir., April 23, 1969) the court said:

"It could be that thorough consideration might be given to the specific amount of contribution required under the agency shop provisions so that a non-union member would be making his fair contributions, only to the actual cost of the bargaining and the contract administration and not to the additional costs of other union expenses or activities which bear no relation to the services rendered and in which he plays no part or has no voice." Id. at 66,960.

[9] In New Jersey Turnpike Employees, Local 194, AFL-CIO v. New Jersey Turnpike Authority,

The accounting problems which may result from its use, although perhaps burdensome, should not be impossible. Hopfl, 49 Cornell L.Q., *supra* at 480. . . .

The papers in the case, with our decision endorsed thereon, are ordered sent back to the Superior Court for entry of judgment in accordance with said decision.

## NOTES

1. The court in *Town of North Kingstown* cited New Jersey Turnpike Employees, Local 194 v. New Jersey Turnpike Authority, 117 N.J. Super. 349, 284 A.2d 566 (1971), *aff'd,* 64 N.J. 579, 319 A.2d 324 (1974), to demonstrate that agency shop clauses limited to paying an amount equal to the pro rata cost of representing unit employees had been negotiated. The court neglected to note, however, that the New Jersey Superior Court held that such a limited agency shop clause was invalid ". . . in view of the legislative declaration of the right of public employees to refrain from union activity, even assisting a union, and in the absence of legislative authorization for an agency shop in public employment."

2. In Tremblay v. Berlin Police Union, 108 N.H. 416, 237 A.2d 668 (1968), a petition for declaratory judgment was filed to test the validity of a union shop clause contained in a municipal collective bargaining agreement which the court construed to impose "a financial obligation only." After noting that there was no New Hampshire law "which prohibits a union shop," and that "[t]he Legislature has declared as a matter of public policy that collective bargaining for municipal employees is a proper public purpose," the court held that the municipality had the necessary discretion to agree to the challenged clause. The court stated:

In the present case the police commissioners and the union have, in effect, declared in advance under the collective bargaining agreement that union security is a reasonable requirement with the efficient and orderly administration of the police department. . . . This is a decision they have the right to make. . . .

3. In states without laws authorizing public sector negotiations, it has generally been held that union security agreements are invalid. *See, e.g.,* Foltz v. City of Dayton, 27 Ohio App. 2d 35, 56 Ohio Op. 2d 213, 272 N.E.2d 169 (1970) (agency fee agreement "conflict[s] with the general laws of Ohio relating to civil service and is invalid"); Mo. Op. Att'y Gen. No. 473, 370 GERR B-8 (1970).

4. State statutory provisions which authorize the deduction of union dues upon the submission of written authorizations but which permit employees to revoke such authorizations at any time have been uniformly interpreted to prohibit union shop, agency shop, or fair share agreements in the absence of legislation specifically permitting these forms of union security. *See, e.g.,* Farrigan v. Helsby, 68 Misc. 2d 952, 327 N.Y.S.2d 909 (1971), *aff'd* 42 App. Div. 2d 2653, 346 N.Y.S.2d 39 (1973); Devita v. Scher, 52 Misc. 2d 138, 276 N.Y.S.2d 913 (Sup. Ct. Monroe Cty. 1966); Whipley v. Youngstown State Univ., 96 L.R.R.M. 3067 (Ohio Ct. C.P. 1977); Ill. Op. Att'y Gen. No. S-804 (1974).

In Beckman v. St. Louis County Board of Commissioners, 241 N.W.2d 302, 92 L.R.R.M. 2449 (Minn. Sup. Ct. 1976), the court held that an involuntary dues checkoff clause was invalid since the statutory provision which granted public employees the right to request a dues checkoff "carrie[d] with it by necessary implication the right to refuse such checkoff." In this case the court was interpreting the Minnesota law in effect prior to the 1973 amendments which authorized fair share deductions upon the request of the exclusive bargaining representative.

5. In Erdreich v. Bailey, 333 So.2d 810, 92 L.R.R.M. 3671 (Ala. Sup. Ct. 1976), the

---

117 N.J. Super. 349, 67 CCH Lab. Cas. 68,560 (1971) it is reported at 349-50, 67 CCH Lab. Cas. at 68,561 that the union proposal required ". . . monthly payment by non-members of the union of *their respective fair share of the cost* of collective negotiations, processing of grievances and other activities related to union representation, as a condition of employment." (emphasis added)

Alabama Supreme Court held that a public employer had the authority to deduct union dues from union members who voluntarily requested that their dues be deducted from their wages. The court reasoned that if employees have the right to present requests to a public employer concerning wages and conditions of employment, "it must necessarily follow that the employer has the legal authority to assent to such request." The court noted that the power of a public employer to decline a "request for a checkoff from wages can be meaningful only in the context of the comparable power of the [public employer] to assent."

## CITY OF HAYWARD v. SEIU

California Court of Appeals, First District
54 Cal. App. 3d 761, 126 Cal. Rptr. 710 (1976)

CHRISTIAN, Justice: — The City of Hayward and its city manager appeal from a judgment declaring that an "agency shop" agreement between the City and respondent United Public Employees, Local 390, is lawful.

Respondent (hereinafter "the Union") is a labor organization affiliated with the Service Employees International Union, AFL-CIO; certain employees of the City are members of the Union. On July 11, 1972, the Union and the City entered into a "Memorandum of Understanding," whereby the City recognized the Union as representing a majority of the employees in the City's Maintenance and Operations Unit.

The agreement covered wages, hours, and other terms and conditions of employment, about which there is no controversy. A dispute arose, however, over the validity of section 1.02 of the agreement, which provides that, although employees are not to be required to join the Union, all employees in the Maintenance and Operations Unit, including nonmembers of the Union,

"shall, as a condition of continued employment, pay to the union an amount of money equal to that paid by other employees in the appropriate unit who are members of the union, which shall be limited to an amount of money equal to the union's usual and customary initiation and monthly dues."

Except as may be authorized by statute, public employees have no right to bargain collectively with the employing agency. (Sacramento County Employees Organization, Local 22 etc. Union v. County of Sacramento (1972) 28 Cal.App.3d 424, 429, 81 LRRM 2841; City of San Diego v. American Federation of State etc. Employees (1970) 8 Cal.App.3d 308, 310, 74 LRRM 2407.) In 1961, California became one of the first states to create a right on the part of government employees to organize and to confer with management as to the terms and conditions of their employment. Another enactment, the Meyers-Milias-Brown Act (Gov. Code, §§ 3500-3510 [hereinafter "MMBA"]) has created certain additional rights of organization in employees of municipalities and local agencies, and authorized representatives of labor and management to enter into written agreements for presentation to the governing body. (Gov. Code, §§ 3505-3505.1.) [2]

The memorandum of understanding entered into by the parties was negotiated by means of procedures which conform to the MMBA. The sole question

---

[2] Unless otherwise indicated, all statutory references hereinafter are to the Government Code.

presented is whether the MMBA permits the creation of an agency shop in an agency of local government. An agency shop agreement is to be distinguished from a union shop agreement, which conditions the continuance of an employee's job on union membership; a union shop is prohibited by statute in public employment. (§ 3502.) In an agency shop, union membership is not a condition of employment, but all employees, including those who do not choose to join the union, must pay union dues. The MMBA does not explicitly refer to agency shop agreements; no reported decision has previously addressed the issue of the legality of this type of agreement.

Section 3502 provides: "Except as otherwise provided by the Legislature, public employees shall have the right to form, join, and participate in the activities of employee organizations of their own choosing for the purpose of representation on all matters of employer-employee relations. Public employees also shall have the right to refuse to join or participate in the activities of employee organizations *and shall have the right to represent themselves individually in their employment relations with the public agency.*" (Emphasis added.)

Section 3506 prohibits both public agencies and employee organizations from interfering with, intimidating, restraining, coercing or discriminating against public employees "because of their exercise of their rights under Section 3502." The freedom of choice provisions of each of these sections must be construed as prohibiting the extraction of union dues, or their equivalent, as a condition of continued employment. Otherwise the statutory right of employees to represent themselves would be defeated.

The trial judge did not address either of these sections; instead, he found that the agency shop provision was a "reasonable rule or regulation" adopted pursuant to the authority conferred by section 3507.

Section 3507 provides:

"A public agency may adopt reasonable rules and regulations after consultation in good faith with representatives of an employee organization or organizations for the administration of employer-employee relations under this chapter (commencing with Section 3500).

"Such rules and regulations may include provisions for (a) verifying that an organization does in fact represent employees of the public agency (b) verifying the official status of employee organization officers and representatives (c) recognition of employee organizations (d) exclusive recognition of employee organizations formally recognized pursuant to a vote of the employees of the agency or an appropriate unit thereof, subject to the right of an employee to represent himself as provided in Section 3502 (e) additional procedures for the resolutions of disputes involving wages, hours and other terms and conditions of employment (f) access of employee organization officers and representatives to work locations (g) use of official bulletin boards and other means of communication by employee organizations (h) furnishing nonconfidential information pertaining to employment relations to employee organizations (i) such other matters as are necessary to carry out the purposes of this chapter.

"Exclusive recognition of employee organizations formally recognized as majority representatives pursuant to a vote of the employees may be revoked by a majority vote of the employees only after a period of not less than 12 months following the date of such recognition.

"No public agency shall unreasonably withhold recognition of employee organizations."

The trial judge reasoned that the agency shop provision could be lawfully enacted under section 3507 because "(a) it obligates the Union to represent *all* employees, (b) it requires nonmembers to share the cost of the benefits which such representation is intended to provide, and (c) it clearly relates to the administration of employer-employee relationships." He recognized the inconsistency of the provision with the employees' statutorily guaranteed freedom of choice, but reasoned that the right of the individual should be subordinated to a policy in furtherance of collective bargaining "as a vehicle for improving employment relationships and avoiding the harsh consequences of labor disputes involving public services."

Courts must, if possible, harmonize statutes, reconcile seeming inconsistencies and construe them to give force and effect to all provisions thereof. . . . A court may not add to or detract from a statute or insert or delete words to accomplish a purpose that does not appear on its face or from its legislative history. . . .

The MMBA was enacted to promote "full communication between public employers and their employees by providing a reasonable method of resolving disputes regarding wages, hours, and other terms and conditions of employment. . . ." (§ 3500.) It was not intended to supersede existing systems for the administration of employer-employee relations in the public sector, but to strengthen such systems by improving communication. (Ibid.)

It is argued that an agency shop agreement is a reasonable method of resolving labor disputes and that, since it is not specifically prohibited, it should be held permissible under the MMBA. But that construction would render the provisions of sections 3502 and 3506 meaningless. Section 3502 implicitly recognizes that employees may choose to join or participate in different organizations. (See, e.g., Sacramento County Employees Organization, Local 22 etc. Union v. County of Sacramento, supra, 28 Cal.App.3d 424, 81 LRRM 2841.) It also confers upon each employee the right not to join or participate in the activities of any employee organization. Section 3506 not only prohibits management from interfering with an employee's section 3502 rights, but also imposes the same ban on employee organizations.

Without common law collective bargaining rights, public employees enjoy only those rights specifically granted by statute. Statutes governing the labor relations of other public employee groups indicate that when the Legislature has authorized union security devices, it has done so with explicit language. Certain public transit district employees have been granted extensive collective bargaining rights, including the right to contract for a closed or union shop. (See, e.g., Pub. Util. Code, §§ 25051-25057.) The labor relations of teachers and other school district employees have been governed by the Winton Act. (Ed. Code, §§ 13080-13090.) Sections 13082 and 13086 of that Act contain provisions paralleling sections 3502 and 3506 of the MMBA. The Winton Act has never been construed to authorize an agency shop. However, legislation recently enacted will repeal the Winton Act as of July 1, 1976, and add section 3540 et seq. to the Government Code. (Stats. 1975, ch. 961.)

Under the new law, school district employees still have the right to refuse to join or participate in the activities of employee organizations and the right to represent themselves in their employment relations with the school district *when no exclusive representative has been recognized.* (§ 3543.) When a majority organization is recognized as the exclusive representative pursuant to the prescribed procedures (§§ 3544-3544.9), employees may no longer represent themselves. (§ 3543.) The agency shop is explicitly authorized as an organizational security device (§ 3540.1, subd. (i)) subject to certain limitations.

(§§ 3546-3546.5.) Although the MMBA has been amended from time to time since its enactment, the Legislature has never modified the language of sections 3502 and 3506 nor added provisions limiting or enlarging the rights created therein.

Those rights cannot reasonably be reconciled with an agency shop provision. The forced payment of dues or their equivalent is, at the very least, "participation" in an employee organization. Practically, it would have the effect of inducing union membership on the part of unwilling employees. While increased participation and membership is a legitimate goal of labor organizations, coercion toward that end is forbidden by statute. Such union security devices as the agency shop must await authorization by the Legislature.

The courts of other states having similar statutes recognizing the right of a public employee not to join or participate in an employee organization have held the agency shop to be unlawful. (See Smigel v. Southgate Community School District (Mich. S. Ct. 1972), 388 Mich. 531, 202 N.W.2d 305, 81 LRRM 2944; New Jersey Turnpike Employees' Union, Local 194 v. New Jersey Turnpike Authority (N.J. Super. Ct. App. Div. 1973) 123 N.J. Super. 461, 303 A.2d 599, 83 LRRM 2250, aff'd (N.J. S.Ct. 1974), 64 N.J. 579, 319 A.2d 224, 86 LRRM 2842; Farrigan v. Helsby (S.Ct. 1971), 68 Misc.2d 952, 327 N.Y.S.2d 909, 68 LRRM 2360, aff'd (S.Ct. App. Div. 1973), 42 A.D. 2d 2653, 346 N.Y.S.2d 39, 83 LRRM 3052; Pennsylvania Labor Relations Board v. Zelem (1974), 329 A.2d 477, 88 LRRM 2524.) Apparently, only Rhode Island has held that there is a common law right to include an agency shop provision in a collective bargaining agreement. (Town of N. Kingstown v. North Kingstown Teach. Assn. (1972), 110 R.I. 698, 297 A.2d 342, 344-345, 82 LRRM 2010 [statute merely gave teachers the right "to join or to decline to join" any employee organization].)

This conclusion is further supported by a comparison with federal statutes. Recognizing that many state labor enactments have followed federal models, California courts have often looked to interpretations of federal labor legislation when construing similar state statutes. (E.g., Fire Fighters Union v. City of Vallejo (1974), 12 Cal.3d 608, 615-617, 87 LRRM 2453; Social Workers' Union, Local 535 v. Alameda County Welfare Dept. (1974) 11 Cal.3d 382, 391, 86 LRRM 2954; Englund v. Chavez (1972) 8 Cal.3d 572, 589-590, 80 LRRM 2653; Service Employees Internat. Union, Local No. 22 v. Roseville Community Hosp. (1972) 24 Cal.App.3d 400, 408-409, 80 LRRM 2098.) The National Labor Relations Act, 29 U.S.C. § 151 et seq. (hereinafter "NLRA"), contains provisions similar to sections 3502 and 3506 of the MMBA with one major difference. Section 7 of the federal act provides: "Employees shall have the right to self-organization, to form, join, or assist labor organizations, to bargain collectively through representatives of their own choosing, and to engage in other concerted activities for the purpose of collective bargaining or other mutual aid or protection, and shall have the right to refrain from any or all of such activities except to the extent that such right may be affected by an agreement requiring membership in a labor organization as a condition of employment as authorized in section 158(a)(3) of this title." (29 U.S.C. § 157.) Sections 8(a)(1) and 8(a)(3) make it unfair labor practices for an employer to threaten, restrain, or coerce employees in the exercise of their section 157 rights or to encourage or discourage union activity by discrimination in employment except for union shop agreements. (Id., §§ 158(a)(1), (a)(3).) The Supreme Court has held that, without the express provisos in section 7 and 8(a)(3), conditioning employment upon union membership would be an unfair labor practice. (Retail Clerks v. Schermerhorn (1963) 373 U.S. 746, 756, 53 LRRM 2318.) The court has further held that the agency shop is the practical equivalent of the union shop. (Id., 373 U.S. at p. 751; Labor Board v. General Motors (1963) 373 U.S. 734, 743, 53 LRRM 2313.)

The provisos permitting union security arrangements were enacted by Congress in 1935 and 1947. Sections 3502 and 3506 of the MMBA were not enacted until 1961, and major revisions were made in 1968. It is reasonable to infer that the California Legislature was aware of the analogous provisions of the NLRA, and the construction thereof, and chose not to permit the agency shop in public employment in California. (Cf. Fire Fighters Union v. City of Vallejo, supra, 12 Cal.3d 608 at pp. 615-617, 87 LRRM 2453.)

The judgment is reversed with directions to enter a new judgment declaring the agency shop provisions of the agreement to be unlawful.

## NOTE

*Accord,* Churchill v. School Admin. Dist. No. 49, 388 A.2d 186 (Me. Sup. Jud. Ct. 1977).

## KARCHMAR v. CITY OF WORCESTER

Supreme Judicial Court of Massachusetts
364 Mass. 124, 301 N.E.2d 570 (1973)

QUIRICO, Justice.

. . . .

At all times material to this case Local 495 has been the exclusive bargaining agent for five different collective bargaining units, each covering a different group of the employees of the city. There are about 1,600 employees in the five units combined, and all but 103 of them are protected by civil service status under G.L. c. 31. On and prior to December 27, 1971, the city and Local 495 had entered into three collective bargaining agreements which together covered the five bargaining units for a term to expire on July 7, 1973. Each of the contracts contained the following language (agency service fee provision): "Effective the ninetieth day following the beginning of employment or the sixtieth day following formal execution of this agreement, whichever is later, each employee of the bargaining unit who is not a member of the Union in good standing shall be required, as a condition of employment, to pay a monthly agency service fee during the life of this agreement to the Union in an amount equal to the monthly dues; provided however, that such fee shall not exceed $6.00 per month."

The basic controversy between the parties is whether the agency service fee provision has any application to those employees of the five bargaining units who enjoy civil service status. Local 495 contends that it applies to all employees of the bargaining units who do not belong to the union, regardless of whether they are included in civil service. The city contends that it applies only to those relatively few employees of the bargaining units who are not included in civil service. For the reasons discussed below, we hold that the position of Local 495 is the correct one.

The statutory labor relations law applicable to municipal employees in the Commonwealth is contained primarily in G.L. c. 149, § 178G through 178N, inserted by St. 1965, c. 763, § 2, and it was amended in a manner affecting this case by St. 1970, c. 463, § 1. Section 178H states in part that "[e]mployees shall have, and be protected in the exercise of, the right to self-organization, to form, join or assist any employee organization, to bargain collectively through representatives of their own choosing on questions of wages, hours and other conditions of employment and to engage in other concerted activities for the purpose of collective bargaining or other mutual aid or protection."

Section 178G, as originally enacted in 1965, defined the word "employee" as used in §§ 178H through 178N to mean "any employee of a municipal employer, *whether or not in the classified service of the municipal employer,* except elected officials, board and commission members, [police], and the executive officers of any municipal employer" (emphasis supplied). The definition continues the same except for the deletion therefrom of the word "police" by St. 1966, c. 156. The words "classified service" are not further defined in §§ 178H through 178N. However, the word "classified" is commonly used with reference to municipal civil service employees, particularly in G.L. c. 31, relating to civil service. The words "classified civil service," "classification," "classes," "classified," or "classified public service," appear in the following sections of c. 31: 1, 2A, 3, 4, 15, 15B, 22, 23, 33, 34, 38, 46H, and 49A. Section 1 thereof defines the words "civil service" to mean "classified civil service provided for by this chapter and the rules made thereunder." When enacting §§ 178G through 178N in 1965, the Legislature could easily have expressly excluded civil service employees from the definition of "employees," if it had so intended. It did not do so, but instead expressly negatived any such intention by its precise choice of words. We therefore conclude that in originally enacting §§ 178G through 178N the Legislature intended the word "employees" to include civil service employees.

Section 178H provides that the "employee organization recognized by a municipal employer or designated as the representative of the majority of the employees in an appropriate unit," which in this case means Local 495 as to each of the units involved, "shall be the exclusive bargaining agent for all employees of such unit, and shall act, negotiate agreements and bargain collectively for all employees in the unit, and shall be responsible for representing the interests of all such employees without discrimination and without regard to employee organization membership." Here again the Legislature used very clear language which permits no exception or exclusion of civil service employees from the operation and effect of this section. Local 495 is therefore the exclusive bargaining agent for all employees of each of the five units, whether members of the union or not, and whether in the civil service or not. . . .

As originally enacted, § 178L prohibited municipal employers from committing five types of acts commonly referred to as constituting unfair labor practices. By St. 1970, c. 463, § 1, the Legislature added at the end of the description of the five prohibited acts the following provision: "(6) nothing in this chapter shall prevent a municipal employer, which has duly accepted . . . [G.L. c. 180, § 17G], from requiring, as a condition of employment, during the life of a collective bargaining agreement so providing, the payment . . . of an agency service fee to the . . . exclusive bargaining agent for the unit in which such employee is employed; provided, however, that such agency service fee shall not be imposed unless the collective bargaining agreement requiring its payment as a condition of employment has been formally executed, pursuant to a vote of a majority of all employees in such bargaining unit present and voting. Such agency service fee shall be proportionately commensurate with the cost of collective bargaining and contract administration.

General Laws c. 180, § 17G, inserted by St. 1970, c. 463, § 2, provides in part as follows: "Deductions on payroll schedules may be made from the salary of any . . . municipal employee of any amount which such employee may specify in writing . . . for the payment of agency service fees to the employee organization which . . . [is] the exclusive bargaining agent for the appropriate unit in which such employee is employed. . . . Any such authorization may be withdrawn by the employee by giving . . . notice in writing of such withdrawal to the . . . [designated municipal officer], and by filing a copy thereof with the treasurer of the employee organization."

On September 29, 1970, the city accepted G.L. c. 180, § 17G, by the unanimous vote of its city council. Thereafter the city and Local 495 negotiated the three collective bargaining agreements covering all employees of the five bargaining units and containing the now disputed agency service fee provisions. The agreements were "formally executed, pursuant to a vote of a majority of all employees in [each] such bargaining unit present and voting." G.L. c. 149, § 178L, as amended. No question is raised about the legality of the negotiations, the votes of the employees authorizing the execution of the contracts, or the formal execution of the contracts.

Despite the 1970 statutory amendments (St. 1970, c. 463, §§ 1 and 2) expressly authorizing municipalities to enter into collective bargaining agreements containing provisions for the payment of agency service fees as a condition of employment and authorizing payroll deductions for payments of such fees on written request of employees, and despite the fact that the city and Local 495 have entered into three otherwise admittedly valid agreements containing agency service fee provisions, the city now contends that such provisions apply only to the 103 noncivil service employees out of the total of about 1,600 employees in the five units. Neither the collective bargaining agreements nor the applicable statutes contain any express language excluding civil service employees from the operation and effect of the agency service fee provision. The city asks us to read such an exclusion into the statute and agreements. It argues in support of this request (a) that the Legislature did not intend, either by the original statutes or by the 1970 amendments, to make civil service employees subject to discharge for nonpayment of an agency service fee, and (b) if it did so intend, the statutes thus construed would be unconstitutional. We reject both arguments.

Prior to May 28, 1970, the Legislature passed and sent to the Governor House Bill No. 4658 which would have inserted in the General Laws a requirement that all cities and towns, except Boston deduct an agency service fee from the salary of each of its employees if the collective bargaining agreement covering such employee provided for such a fee. However, the municipal collective bargaining statute (G.L. c. 149, §§ 178G through 178N) then in effect contained no specific authorization for the inclusion of an agency service fee provision in such agreements, and the bill as sent to the Governor did not correct that deficiency. On May 28, 1970, the Governor returned the bill to the Legislature without his signature and with an accompanying message (House Bill No. 5749). . . . The Governor indorsed the idea of permitting municipalities and their employees to negotiate and enter into collective bargaining agreements which include a provision requiring nonunion members to pay an agency service fee as a condition of employment, but he recommended that the following changes be made in the bill: (1) limit the proposed legislation to those cities or towns which vote to accept its provisions, (2) amend "the municipal collective bargaining law . . . to authorize specifically such an agency fee agreement," (3) give the employee "the option of requesting the treasurer to deduct the amount from his paycheck or of paying the fee in another manner of his choice," (4) provide "at least a thirty day grace period before an employee is liable for the payment of an agency service fee," and (5) permit the municipality to require proof that a union treasurer is properly bonded before paying him agency service fees deducted from the paychecks of employees. After receiving the Governor's message, the Legislature enacted St. 1970, c. 463, incorporating therein all of the Governor's suggestions.

The history, as recited above, of the statutes authorizing municipal collective bargaining agreements which contain provisions for the payment of agency service fees as a condition of employment is itself sufficient to refute the city's argument that the Legislature did not intend to impose such an obligation on civil service employees. The language used by the Governor in his message to the Legislature, and used by the Legislature in enacting the statutes, indicates a clear intent that collective bargaining agreements should cover all employees in the appropriate unit, and that all such employees should make a contribution to the expense of negotiating, administering and enforcing the agreements for the benefit of the employees collectively, the contribution of the union members to be included in their payment of union dues, and that of nonunion members to be by way of agency service fees.

The city argues that the statement in G. L. c. 149, § 178N, to the effect that "[n]othing in . . . [§§ 178F to 178M], inclusive, shall diminish the authority and power of the civil service commission," requires us to hold that civil service employees are not subject to collective bargaining agreement provisions for payment of an agency service fee to a union as a condition of their employment. We disagree.

By enacting the detailed provisions of G.L. c. 31, relating to civil service employees, the Legislature did not thereby exhaust its entire power with reference to such employees. It still had and has the power to prescribe, add to, or otherwise amend the rules of eligibility for appointment, and the conditions of, or grounds for, suspension or removal from all public employment. Nichols v. Commissioner of Pub. Welfare, 311 Mass. 125, 130-131, 40 N.E.2d 275. It may exercise that power either by attending [sic] G.L. c. 31, or by inserting appropriate provisions in other chapters of the General Laws. Reynolds v. Commissioner of Commerce & Dev., 350 Mass. 193, 194-195, 214 N.E.2d 69. It did just that when it enacted St. 1970, c. 463, § 1, amending G.L. c. 149, § 178L, to authorize contracts requiring payment of agency service fees as a condition of public employment. This amendment, even if it be treated as giving rise to a "just cause" for disciplinary action against a civil service employee under G.L. c. 31, § 43, as amended, did not "diminish the authority and power of the civil service commission" within the meaning of G.L. c. 149, § 178N. . . .

The city argues further that, because G.L. c. 180, § 17G, inserted by St. 1970, c. 463, § 2, gives municipal employees the option whether they shall give their employer written authority to deduct the applicable agency service fee from their paychecks and pay it over to the union, they therefore have the option to elect whether they shall become subject to the obligation to pay the fee. We reject that argument. If a municipality accepts § 17G and thereafter concludes a collective bargaining agreement with the employees' union as prescribed by G.L. c. 149, § 178L, as amended, all nonunion members of the particular bargaining unit are liable to the union for the agency service fee provided in that agreement. They may pay it by authorizing payroll deductions or in some other manner of their choice, but they cannot avoid liability by merely withholding authority for the employer to deduct it from their paychecks. Their only choice is how they pay it, but, however they choose to do so, they must pay it as a condition of their employment.

. . . .

## NOTES

1. Similarly, in Association of Capitol Powerhouse Engineers v. State of Washington, 96 L.R.R.M. 3004 (Wash. Sup. Ct. 1977), the court held that a negotiated agency shop clause authorized by statute did not contravene the rights of several state employees under the state civil service law. The court noted that the employees' civil service rights were derived from the civil service law of which the 1973 amendments authorizing the negotiation of "an agency shop are a part," and, as a result, "[t]hese rights are subject to the 1973 amendments, not violated by them."

2. In Dauphin County Technical School Educ. Ass'n v. Dauphin County Area Vocational-Technical School Bd., 357 A.2d 721, 92 L.R.R.M. 3129 (Pa. Commw. Ct. 1976), aff'd on other grounds, 99 L.R.R.M. 3275 (Pa. Sup. Ct. 1978), the court was faced with the question of whether a teacher who did not maintain membership in an employee organization in accordance with a maintenance membership clause could be terminated when the applicable provisions of the school code did not specify failure to maintain membership as a cause for termination. After noting that Section 703 of the Public Employees Relations Act provides that no provision in a collective bargaining agreement shall be implemented "if the implementation of that provision would be in violation of, or inconsistent with, or in conflict with any statute or statutes enacted by the General Assembly of the Commonwealth of Pennsylvania," the court held that the maintenance of membership provision was inconsistent with the provision of the school code which specified valid causes for termination "insofar as the remedy for non-compliance with the [maintenance of membership] provision is the termination of the services of the professional employee involved." While the court noted that the Pennsylvania act permits the parties to negotiate a maintenance of membership clause, the court noted that this "is not the case, however, where such provision is violative of an existing statute." Relying on Dauphin, the court in PLRB v. Union Town Area School Dist., 94 L.R.R.M. 2266 (Pa. Commw. Ct. 1977), set aside a decision of the Pennsylvania PLRB holding that a school board committed an unfair labor practice when it failed to comply with an arbitration award ordering the board to terminate two teachers for failure to maintain membership in an employee organization. In a related case, Langley v. Union Town Area School Dist., 367 A.2d 736, 94 L.R.R.M. 2278 (Pa. Commw. Ct. 1977), the court held that the Secretary of Education should determine in the first instance "whether, as a matter of law, the failure to pay valid association dues pursuant to a valid maintenance-of-membership clause can constitute a 'persistent and wilful violation of the school laws.' " The court noted that "[t]here is little doubt that [this] issue will ultimately and shortly be decided by the courts," but "that the orderly functioning of the administrative process demands that the Secretary first be allowed to address himself directly to the issues involved."

3. In Jackson v. Swartz Creek Community Schools, 749 GERR 15 (Mich. Tenure Comm'n, Feb. 9, 1978), the Michigan Tenure Commission in a 3-2 decision held that a school board's dismissal of a teacher for non-payment of agency shop fees which were required as a condition of employment in a collective bargaining agreement did not constitute cause for dismissal under the state's tenure act. The majority rejected the argument that the Michigan Statute which specifically permits the negotiation of an agency shop clause amended or impliedly repealed the tenure act. After noting that "it is a generalized rule of statutory construction and law that where two statutes address an issue, the statute of more specific application is controlling," the majority held "that non-payment of 'agency shop' fees or dues does not meet the standards of reasonable and just cause for discharge within the meaning of the Tenure Act." The two dissenting members asserted that "the Legislature was clearly providing that public employers may make it a condition of continued employment for an employee to pay an agency shop fee." The dissenters further stated that the tenure act "must be read in light of the Public Employment Relations Act. . . ." Compare this decision with the Michigan Supreme Court's decision in Civil Service Comm'n v. Wayne County Bd. of Supervisors at p. 351 supra.

4. The Oregon law provides for the negotiation of a fair share agreement, provided "[s]uch agreement shall reflect the opinion of a majority of the employes in the bargaining unit." ORS 243.650(10). In Oregon City Fed'n of Teachers v. PERB, 543 P.2d 297, 91

L.R.R.M. 2801 (Ore. Ct. App. 1975), the court rejected the contention that "the opinion of a majority" could only be ascertained by a formal vote. The court held "that the selection of a fair-share ratification procedure is for the exclusive bargaining agent and need only be some procedure which reasonably reflects the opinion of the majority of the bargaining unit members." The court did hold, however, that the procedure utilized to ascertain whether a majority agrees with a fair share agreement "must be submitted to the members of the bargaining unit separately," *i.e.,* a fair share agreement could not be submitted as part of an overall ratification vote.

# Chapter 6

# UNION COLLECTIVE ACTION—THE RIGHT TO STRIKE AND PICKET IN THE PUBLIC SECTOR

Like their private sector counterparts, labor union adherents in the public sector have established labor organizations which are not mere fraternal societies or innocuous professional associations. Many public sector unions have become militant groups formed for the primary purpose of advancing the perceived economic interests of their members, and they have not been content to rely exclusively upon the art of persuasion when endeavoring to extract bargaining concessions from public employers. Although concerted activity, in the form of the strike or the picket line, has usually been legally proscribed, public sector unions have frequently resorted to "economic action" to gain leverage at the negotiating table.

This chapter deals with this troublesome phase of public sector labor relations. In a sense, the construction of the chapter may be unrealistic, because union collective action is treated as a problem separate and distinct from the issue of impasse resolution. It is surely legitimate to contend that the crucial question is not whether strikes should be prohibited in public sector labor relations, but whether the bargaining process itself and dispute resolution procedures can be made so effective that the need for work stoppages will be obviated. However, given our present state of knowledge, it is unlikely that we can devise a system that would totally supplant the need (or desire) for work stoppages. This chapter deals with some of the considerations surrounding the difficult strike issue which, combined with the various impasse resolution devices discussed in the next

Table 1. Work Stoppages in Government, 1958-75 [1]
(Workers involved and days idle in thousands)

| Year | Total | | | Federal Government | | | State Government | | | Local Government | | |
|---|---|---|---|---|---|---|---|---|---|---|---|---|
| | Number | | | Number | | | Number | | | Number | | |
| | Stop-pages | Workers Involved | Days Idle | Stop-pages | Workers Involved | Days Idle | Stop-pages | Workers Involved | Days Idle | Stop-pages | Workers Involved | Days Idle |
| 1958 | 15 | 1.7 | 7.5 | — | — | — | 1 | 0.03 | 0.06 | 14 | 1.7 | 7.4 |
| 1959 | 25 | 2.0 | 10.5 | — | — | — | 4 | 0.4 | 1.6 | 21 | 1.6 | 57.2 |
| 1960 | 36 | 28.6 | 58.4 | — | — | — | 3 | 1.0 | 1.2 | 33 | 27.6 | 67.7 |
| 1961 | 28 | 6.6 | 15.3 | — | — | — | — | — | — | 28 | 6.6 | 15.3 |
| 1962 | 28 | 31.1 | 79.1 | 5 | 4.2 | 33.8 | 2 | 1.7 | 2.3 | 21 | 25.3 | 43.1 |
| 1963 | 29 | 4.8 | 15.4 | — | — | — | 2 | 0.3 | 2.2 | 27 | 4.6 | 67.7 |
| 1964 | 41 | 22.7 | 70.8 | — | — | — | 4 | 0.3 | 3.2 | 37 | 22.5 | 57.7 |
| 1965 | 42 | 11.9 | 146.0 | — | — | — | — | — | 1.3 [2] | 42 | 11.9 | 145.0 |
| 1966 | 142 | 105.0 | 455.0 | — | — | — | 9 | 3.1 | 6.0 | 133 | 102.0 | 449.0 |
| 1967 | 181 | 132.0 | 1,250.0 | — | — | — | 12 | 4.7 | 16.3 | 169 | 127.0 | 1,230.0 |
| 1968 | 254 | 201.8 | 2,545.2 | 3 | 1.7 | 9.6 | 16 | 9.3 | 42.8 | 235 | 190.0 | 2,492.8 |
| 1969 | 411 | 160.0 | 745.7 | 2 | 0.6 | 1.1 | 37 | 20.5 | 152.4 | 372 | 139.0 | 592.2 |
| 1970 | 412 | 333.5 | 2,023.2 | 3 | 155.8 | 648.3 | 23 | 8.8 | 44.6 | 386 | 168.9 | 1,330.5 |
| 1971 | 329 | 152.6 | 901.4 | 2 | 1.0 | 8.1 | 23 | 14.5 | 81.8 | 304 | 137.1 | 811.6 |
| 1972 | 375 | 142.1 | 1,257.3 | — | — | — | 40 | 27.4 | 273.7 | 335 | 114.7 | 983.5 |
| 1973 | 387 | 196.4 | 2,303.9 | 1 | 0.5 | 4.6 | 29 | 12.3 | 133.0 | 357 | 183.7 | 2,166.3 |
| 1974 | 384 | 160.7 | 1,404.2 | 2 | 0.5 | 1.4 | 34 | 24.7 | 86.4 | 348 | 135.4 | 1,316.3 |
| 1975 | 478 | 318.5 | 2,204.4 | — | — | — | 32 | 66.6 | 300.5 | 446 | 252.0 | 1,903.9 |

1. Includes stoppages lasting a full day or shift, or longer, and involving 6 workers or more.
2. Idleness in 1965 resulted from 2 stoppages that began in 1964.

chapter, may offer some suggestions as to how to achieve stable and harmonious labor relations in the public sector.

## A. THE NATURE OF THE PROBLEM

Statistics gathered by the Department of Labor, Bureau of Labor Statistics, illustrate the meteoric rise of the public sector strike from near oblivion in 1958 to substantial proportions by the 1970's.

### Table 2. Work Stoppages in Government
### by Major Issue, 1958-1975
### (Number involved and days idle in thousands)

| Year | General Wage Changes and Supplementary Benefits | | | Union Organizzation and Security | | | Job Security | | |
|------|------------|----------|-------|------------|----------|-------|------------|----------|-------|
|      | Stoppages | No. Involved | Days Idle | Stoppages | No. Involved | Days Idle | Stoppages | No. Involved | Days Idle |
| 1958 | 8 | 1.1 | 4.8 | 2 | 0.3 | 2.0 | – | – | – |
| 1959 | 7 | 1.0 | 2.6 | 9 | 0.8 | 4.6 | – | – | – |
| 1960 | 19 | 16.6 | 40.8 | 8 | 6.2 | 9.6 | – | – | – |
| 1961 | 22 | 6.0 | 13.6 | 1 | 0.02 | 0.02 | – | – | – |
| 1962 | 10 | 25.5 | 40.3 | 5 | 0.4 | 0.8 | 2 | 0.03 | 0.2 |
| 1963 | 15 | 1.7 | 8.4 | 5 | 2.8 | 6.1 | 2 | 0.09 | 0.2 |
| 1964 | 26 | 9.6 | 37.3 | 8 | 2.6 | 7.7 | – | – | – |
| 1965 | 25 | 9.8 | 128.0 | 12 | 0.9 | 11.5 | 1 | 0.08 | 0.08 |
| 1966 | 78 | 58.2 | 355.0 | 36 | 11.6 | 45.6 | 2 | 0.2 | 1.7 |
| 1967 | 128 | 118.0 | 1,040.0 | 29 | 6.7 | 99.3 | 2 | 0.7 | 1.4 |
| 1968 | 146 | 110.3 | 759.2 | 60 | 33.6 | 90.1 | 2 | 0.09 | 0.2 |
| 1969 | 259 | 3.9 | 492.1 | 63 | 14.4 | 145.0 | 7 | 1.4 | 3.3 |
| 1970 | 230 | 128.9 | 853.0 | 59 | 22.9 | 411.5 | 9 | 2.3 | 6.1 |
| 1971 | 193 | 95.1 | 631.2 | 43 | 5.6 | 47.7 | 13 | 1.8 | 8.9 |
| 1972 | 226 | 110.1 | 1,084.7 | 47 | 8.0 | 96.9 | 15 | 3.8 | 18.0 |
| 1973 | 239 | 159.6 | 2,007.8 | 42 | 10.7 | 123.7 | 26 | 13.1 | 91.9 |
| 1974 | 260 | 132.5 | 1,210.5 | 41 | 5.8 | 56.1 | 25 | 10.2 | 92.2 |
| 1975 | 316 | 145.3 | 1,255.2 | 25 | 8.2 | 82.6 | 54 | 90.3 | 449.2 |

Moreover, the increase of strike activity in the public sector vis-a-vis the total economy increased markedly during the same period. Although the percentage of the entire employed work force involved in strikes did not increase substantially from 1958 through 1975, the percentage participating in governmental stoppages rose dramatically from 0.022 in 1958 to 2.2 by 1975.

Many theories have been propounded to explain the cause of strikes in the public sector. Some have attributed this phenomenon to the increased militancy of public sector unions which, for the first time, possess sufficient power to use effectively the traditional methods of economic coercion. Others cite a shift in emphasis in public employment from the traditional concerns over job security to the more difficult issues of wages and conditions of employment. Indeed, statistical evidence seems to support the latter theory, since most of the increase in work stoppages in the public sector between 1958 and 1975 has been caused by disputes over wages and supplementary benefits rather than other items.

| Year | Administration Matters | | | Internunion and Intraunion Matters | | | Other Working Conditions | | |
|---|---|---|---|---|---|---|---|---|---|
| | Stop-pages | No. In-volved | Days Idle | Stop-pages | No. In-volved | Days Idle | Stop-pages | No. In-volved | Days Idle |
| 1958 | — | — | — | — | — | — | 5 | 0.3 | 0.7 |
| 1959 | — | — | — | 2 | 0.04 | 0.2 | 8 | 0.4 | 4.1 |
| 1960 | — | — | — | 1 | 0.01 | 0.01 | 8 | 5.8 | 8.0 |
| 1961 | — | — | — | 1 | 0.01 | 0.02 | 4 | 0.6 | 1.6 |
| 1962 | 8 | 2.4 | 6.1 | 3 | 2.9 | 31.7 | — | — | — |
| 1963 | 5 | 0.2 | 0.3 | 1 | 0.03 | 0.1 | 1 | 0.1 | 0.4 |
| 1964 | 7 | 10.6 | 25.9 | — | — | — | — | — | — |
| 1965 | 1 | 0.01 | 0.05 | 2 | 1.0 | 6.2 | — | — | — |
| 1966 | 21 | 33.3 | 46.5 | 5 | 1.8 | 5.8 | — | — | — |
| 1967 | 19 | 2.7 | 5.6 | 1 | 0.1 | 0.4 | 2 | 4.0 | 99.9 |
| 1968 | 33 | 53.2 | 1,684.2 | 5 | 2.7 | 4.9 | 5 | 1.7 | 6.2 |
| 1969 | 38 | 19.2 | 33.5 | 3 | 0.7 | 7.5 | 6 | 1.0 | 16.5 |
| 1970 | 71 | 11.2 | 32.4 | 3 | 0.9 | 1.8 | 10 | 3.4 | 35.0 |
| 1971 | 49 | 19.3 | 69.9 | — | — | — | 9 | 1.1 | 5.2 |
| 1972 | 61 | 7.9 | 24.6 | 3 | 0.1 | 0.3 | 6 | 5.6 | 10.4 |
| 1973 | 52 | 8.2 | 37.8 | 4 | 0.9 | 7.5 | 7 | 1.0 | 6.9 |
| 1974 | 33 | 8.1 | 22.7 | — | — | — | 3 | 0.4 | 10.2 |
| 1975 | 47 | 68.7 | 399.2 | 9 | 2.2 | 3.2 | 10 | 2.2 | 10.1 |

Regardless of the causes underlying these strikes, it is noteworthy that they have persisted during a period when, for the most part, work stoppages by public employees have been illegal. Thus, whatever may be said about the causes of public employee strikes, it is apparent that the present methods of dealing with them have not proved adequate to prevent them.

On the basis of these statistics, an ostrich-like approach to the problem is not indicated. If, as in the usual view, public sector strikes are inimical to the public interest and should be eliminated or kept to a minimum, action either in terms of eliminating their causes or in deterring them, or both, is needed. Alternatively, it is arguable that not all public sector work stoppages seriously damage the public interest and that public policy, therefore, should not reflect an absolute condemnation of strike action, but rather, as in the private sector, should accept such service disruptions except where a substantial public interest (such as health or safety) is involved. In facing the problem of strike activity, this over-all evaluation must surely constitute a threshold consideration.

## NOTES

1. Comprehensive statistical analyses of the problem are contained in Hall, *Work Stoppages in Government,* 91 MONTHLY LAB. REV. 53 (July, 1968); Torrence, *City Public Employee Work Stoppages: A Time-Line Analysis for Educational Purposes,* 27 LAB. L.J. 177 (1976); White, *Work Stoppages of Government Employees,* 92 MONTHLY LAB. REV. 29 (Dec., 1969); Young & Brewer, *Strikes by State and Local Government Employees,* 9 IND. REL. 356 (1970); and U.S. DEPT. OF LABOR, BUREAU OF LABOR STATISTICS, WORK STOPPAGES IN GOVERNMENT, 1975, *reprinted in* 71 GERR RF 1011.

2. Some commentators have suggested that strikes in the public sector may be reduced by extending private sector recognition and grievance procedures to the public sector. *See, e.g.,* Clark, *Public Employee Strikes: Some Proposed Solutions,* 23 LAB. L.J. 111 (1972); Zack, *Why Public Employees Strike,* 23 ARB. J. 69, 82-83 (1968). Available statistics indicate that the incidence of recognition and grievance strikes has been markedly reduced in those states providing for union recognition and unfair labor practice regulation. *See* Burton & Krider, *The Role and Consequence of Strikes by Public Employees,* 79 YALE L.J. 418, 439 (1970). *But see* PUB. SERV. RESEARCH COUNCIL, PUBLIC SECTOR BARGAINING AND STRIKES (1978), *summarized in* GERR No. 759, 25, wherein a positive statistical correlation between increased strike activity and the recent enactment of state public employee relations statutes is demonstrated.

# B. CONSTITUTIONAL CONSIDERATIONS

# 1. PRIVATE SECTOR PRECEDENTS

## UAW-AFL LOCAL 232 v. WISCONSIN EMPLOYMENT RELATIONS BOARD

United States Supreme Court
336 U.S. 245, 69 S. Ct. 516, 93 L. Ed. 651 (1949)

MR. JUSTICE JACKSON delivered the opinion of the Court . . . .

Briggs & Stratton Corporation operates two manufacturing plants in the State of Wisconsin engaging approximately 2,000 employees. These are represented by the International Union, Automobile Workers of America, A. F. of L., Local No. 232, as collective bargaining agent, it having been duly certified as such by the National Labor Relations Board in proceedings under the National Labor Relations Act. Under such certification, the Union had negotiated collective bargaining agreements, the last of which expired on July 1, 1944. Negotiation of a new one reached a deadlock and bargaining sessions continued for some time without success.

On November 3, 1945, its leaders submitted to the Union membership a plan for a new method of putting pressure upon the employer. The stratagem consisted of calling repeated special meetings of the Union during working hours at any time the Union saw fit, which the employees would leave work to attend. It was an essential part of the plan that this should be without warning to the employer or notice as to when or whether the employees would return. The device was adopted and the first surprise cessation of work was called on November 6, 1945; thereafter, and until March 22, 1946, such action was repeated on twenty-six occasions. The employer was not informed during this period of any specific demands which these tactics were designed to enforce nor what concessions it could make to avoid them.

This procedure was publicly described by the Union leaders as a new technique for bringing pressure upon the employer. It was, and is, candidly admitted that these tactics were intended to and did interfere with production and put strong economic pressure on the employer, who was disabled thereby from making any dependable production plans or delivery commitments. And it was said that "this can't be said for the strike. After the initial surprise of the walkout, the company knows what it has to do and plans accordingly." It was commended as a procedure which would avoid hardships that a strike imposes on employees and was considered "a better weapon than a strike."

The employer did not resort to any private disciplinary measures such as discharge of the employees; instead, it sought a much less drastic remedy by plea to the appropriate public authority under Wisconsin law to investigate and adjudge the Union's conduct under the law of the State. After the prescribed procedures, the Board ordered the Union to cease and desist from "(a) engaging in any concerted efforts to interfere with production by arbitrarily calling union meetings and inducing work stoppages during regularly scheduled working hours; or engaging in any other concerted effort to interfere with production of the complainant except by leaving the premises in an orderly manner for the purpose of going on strike."

Two court proceedings resulted from the Board's order: one by the Board to obtain enforcement and the other by the Union to obtain review. They are here considered, as they were below, together.

The Supreme Court of Wisconsin sustained the Board's order but significantly limited the effect of its otherwise general prohibitions. It held that what the order does, and all that it does, is to forbid individual defendants and members of the Union from engaging in concerted effort to interfere with production by doing the acts instantly involved. . . .

Our only question is, therefore, whether it is beyond the power of the State to prohibit the particular course of conduct described.

The Union contends that the statute as thus applied violates the Thirteenth Amendment in that it imposes a form of compulsory service or involuntary servitude. However, nothing in the statute or the order makes it a crime to abandon work individually (compare Pollock v. Williams, 322 U.S. 4) or collectively. Nor does either undertake to prohibit or restrict any employee from leaving the service of the employer, either for reason or without reason, either with or without notice. The facts afford no foundation for the contention that any action of the State has the purpose or effect of imposing any form of involuntary servitude.

It is further contended that the statute as applied invades rights of free speech and public assemblage guaranteed by the Fourteenth Amendment. We recently considered a similar contention in connection with other state action concerning labor relations. Lincoln Federal Labor Union v. Northwestern Iron & Metal Co., and Whitaker v. North Carolina, 335 U.S. 525, and American Federation of Labor v. American Sash & Door Co., 335 U.S. 538. For reasons there stated, these contentions are without merit.

No serious question is presented by the Commerce Clause of the Constitution standing alone. It never has been thought to prevent the state legislatures from limiting "individual and group rights of aggression and defense" or from substituting "processes of justice for the more primitive method of trial by combat." . . .

But it is claimed that the congressional labor legislation confers upon or recognizes and declares in unions and employees certain rights, privileges or immunities in connection with strikes and concerted activities, and that these are denied by the State's prohibition as laid down in this case. It is elementary that what Congress constitutionally has given, the state may not constitutionally take away. Hill v. Florida, 325 U.S. 538.

The argument is that two provisions, found in §§ 7 and 13 of the National Labor Relations Act, not relevantly changed by the Labor Management Relations Act of 1947, grant to the Union and its members the right to put pressure upon the employer by the recurrent and unannounced stoppage of work. Both Acts provide that "Employees shall have the right to self-organization, to form, join, or assist labor organizations, to bargain collectively through representatives of their own choosing, and to engage in concerted activities, for the purpose of collective bargaining or other mutual aid or protection." [12] Because the acts forbidden by the Wisconsin judgment are concerted activities and had a purpose to assist labor organizations in collective bargaining, it is said to follow that they are federally authorized and thereby immunized from state control. . . .

[The Court found that, since the Union activity was not protected by Section 7 of the NLRA, no exclusion of state authority to regulate the conduct was intended.]

Reliance also is placed upon § 13 of the National Labor Relations Act, which provided, "Nothing in this Act shall be construed so as to interfere with or impede or diminish in any way the right to strike." . . . The 1947 Amendment carries the same provision but that Act includes a definition. Section 501 (2) says that when used in the Act "The term 'strike' includes any strike or other concerted stoppage of work by employees (including a stoppage by reason of the expiration of a collective-bargaining agreement) and any concerted slow-down or other concerted interruption of operations by employees." . . .

This provision, as carried over into the Labor Management Relations Act, does not purport to create, establish or define the right to strike. On its face it is narrower in scope than § 7 — the latter would be of little significance if "strike" is a broader term than "concerted activity." Unless we read into § 13 words which Congress omitted and a sense which Congress showed no intention of including, all that this provision does is to declare a rule of interpretation for the Act itself which would prevent any use of what originally was a novel piece of legislation to qualify or impede whatever right to strike exists under other laws. It did not purport to modify the body of law as to the legality of strikes as it then existed. This Court less than a decade earlier had stated that law to be that the state constitutionally could prohibit strikes and make a violation criminal. It had unanimously adopted the language of Mr. Justice Brandeis that "Neither the common law, nor the Fourteenth Amendment, confers the absolute right to strike." Dorchy v. Kansas, 272 U.S. 306, 311. Dissenting views most favorable to labor in other cases had conceded the right of the state legislature to mark the limits of tolerable industrial conflict in the public interest. Duplex Co. v. Deering, 254 U.S. 443, 488. This Court has adhered to that view. Thornhill v.

---

[12] § 7 of National Labor Relations Act, 49 Stat. 449, 452. The Labor Management Relations Act of 1947 added a proviso that employees also have the right to refrain from any or all activities mentioned in this section, except to the extent that the right to refrain might conflict with an agreement requiring membership in a union as a condition of employment as authorized by the Act. 61 Stat. 140.

Alabama, 310 U.S. 88, 103. The right to strike, because of its more serious impact upon the public interest, is more vulnerable to regulation than the right to organize and select representatives for lawful purposes of collective bargaining which this Court has characterized as a "fundamental right" and which, as the Court has pointed out, was recognized as such in its decisions long before it was given protection by the National Labor Relations Act. . . .

That Congress has concurred in the view that neither § 7 nor § 13 confers absolute right to engage in every kind of strike or other concerted activity does not rest upon mere inference; indeed the record indicates that, had the courts not made these interpretations, the Congress would have gone as far or farther in the direction of limiting the right to strike. . . .

If we were to read § 13 as we are urged to do, to make the strike an absolute right and the definition to extend the right to all other variations of the strike, the effect would be to legalize beyond the power of any state or federal authorities to control not only the intermittent stoppages such as we have here but also the slowdown and perhaps the sit-down strike as well. Cf. Allen-Bradley Local v. Wisconsin Employment Relations Board, 315 U.S. 740, 751. And this is not all; the management also would be disabled from any kind of self-help to cope with these coercive tactics of the union except to submit to its undeclared demands. To dismiss or discipline employees for exercising a right given them under the Act or to interfere with them or the union in pursuing it is made an unfair labor practice and if the rights here asserted are rights conferred by the Labor Management Relations Act, it is hard to see how the management can take any steps to resist or combat them without incurring the sanctions of the Act. It is certain that such a result would be inconsistent with the whole purpose disclosed by the Labor Management Relations Act amendments to the National Labor Relations Act. Nor do we think such is the result of any fair interpretation of the text of the Act.

We think that this recurrent or intermittent unannounced stoppage of work to win unstated ends was neither forbidden by federal statute nor was it legalized and approved thereby. Such being the case, the state police power was not superseded by congressional Act over a subject normally within its exclusive power and reachable by federal regulation only because of its effects on that interstate commerce which Congress may regulate. . . .

The judgments are affirmed.

[The dissenting opinions of Douglas, J., with whom Black and Rutledge, JJ., concurred, and of Murphy, J., with whom Rutledge, J., concurred, are omitted.]

## NOTES

1. The portion of the decision sustaining the authority of the WERB to regulate the unprotected activity in issue was overruled in Machinists, Lodge 76 v. WERB, 427 U.S. 132, 96 S. Ct. 2548, 49 L. Ed.2d 396 (1976), wherein the Court indicated that where Congress must have intended to leave such unprotected yet unprohibited conduct

unregulated, subject only to the economic power available to the private disputants themselves, state jurisdiction is pre-empted.

2. As the principal case illustrates, the right to strike in the private sector is not now and has never been an absolute right. Although most work stoppages are protected by the NLRA, there are numerous instances where strikes are either unprotected or legally forbidden:

(a) Use of violence — see NLRB v. Fansteel Metallurgical Corp., 306 U.S. 240, 59 S. Ct. 490, 83 L. Ed. 627 (1939); NLRB v. Thayer Co., 213 F.2d 748 (1st Cir. 1954), cert. denied, 348 U.S. 883 (1954).

(b) Unlawful means — see NLRB v. Fansteel Metallurgical Corp., 306 U.S. 240, 59 S. Ct. 490, 83 L. Ed. 627 (1939) and Apex Hosiery Co. v. Leader, 310 U.S. 469, 60 S. Ct. 982, 84 L. Ed. 1311 (1940) (sit-down strikes); C.G. Conn. Ltd. v. NLRB, 108 F.2d 390 (7th Cir. 1939); Valley City Furniture Co., 110 N.L.R.B. 1589, enf'd, 230 F.2d 947 (6th Cir. 1956) (partial strike or slowdown); Allen Bradley Co. v. IBEW Local 3, 325 U.S. 797, 65 S. Ct. 1533, 89 L. Ed. 1939 (1945); United Mine Workers v. Pennington, 381 U.S. 657, 85 S. Ct. 1585, 14 L. Ed. 2d 626 (1965) (combination with business to violate antitrust laws); Carnegie-Illinois Steel Co. v. United Steelworkers, 353 Pa. 420, 45 A.2d 857 (1946) (mass picketing).

(c) Strikes in pursuit of unlawful objectives — see, e.g., NLRB v. IBEW Local 1212, 364 U.S. 573, 81 S. Ct. 330, 5 L. Ed. 2d 302 (1961) ("jurisdictional strike" in violation of Section 8 (b) (4) (D) of the NLRA); Brooks v. NLRB, 348 U.S. 96, 75 S. Ct. 176, 99 L. Ed. 125 (1954) (strike by uncertified union to gain recognition during period when another union has been certified).

3. In the private sector, strikes in violation of a contractual no-strike commitment constitute unprotected activity. See, e.g., NLRB v. Sands Mfg. Co., 306 U.S. 332, 59 S. Ct. 508, 83 L. Ed. 682 (1939). A union breach of a contractual no-strike pledge may be remedied by a damage action under Section 301 of the Labor Management Relations Act. See Atkinson v. Sinclair Ref. Co., 370 U.S. 238, 82 S. Ct. 1318, 8 L. Ed.2d 462 (1962). Furthermore, in the private sector it is now clear that a federal or state court may issue an injunction to halt a strike over a grievable or arbitrable matter where "a collective bargaining contract contains a mandatory grievance adjustment or arbitration procedure." Boys Markets, Inc. v. Retail Clerks Local 770, 398 U.S. 235, 90 S.Ct. 1583, 26 L.Ed.2d 199 (1970). But cf. Buffalo Forge Co. v. Steelworkers, 428 U.S. 397, 96 S. Ct. 3141, 49 L. Ed.2d 1022 (1976), where the Court held that the Norris-LaGuardia Act precludes a federal court from enjoining a sympathy strike supporting a work dispute involving a different bargaining unit.

4. Peaceful picketing in furtherance of a labor objective may raise special constitutional questions. In Thornhill v. Alabama, 310 U.S. 88, 60 S. Ct. 296, 84 L. Ed. 460 (1940), the Supreme Court equated peaceful picketing with freedom of speech and accorded it protection against abridgement under the First and Fourteenth Amendments, subject to the same legislative restrictions as other forms of speech. However, the expansive pronouncements of Thornhill were modified and limited by a later series of cases in which the Court held that picketing, because it involved not only communication of ideas but also elements of patrolling and signaling, was not immune from all state regulation. Since union picketers are not only exercising their right of speech, but also are engaging in an exercise of economic power, the Court held that when such activity is "counter to valid state policy in a domain open to state regulation," it can be restricted, even though it arises in the course of a labor controversy. See, e.g., Teamsters v. Vogt, Inc., 354 U.S. 284, 77 S. Ct. 1166, 1 L. Ed.2d 1347 (1957); Giboney v. Empire Storage Co., 336 U.S. 490, 69 S. Ct. 684, 93 L. Ed. 834 (1949).

5. In Hudgens v. NLRB, 424 U.S. 507, 96 S. Ct. 1029, 47 L. Ed.2d 128 (1976), the Supreme Court held that even though private shopping centers are open to the general public and frequently perform functions similar to traditional community business blocks,

persons desiring to engage in peaceful labor picketing on the private premises do not enjoy constitutional protection vis-a-vis the owners of such plazas. However, if such individuals have no alternative communication channels available through which they can reach their intended audience, they may receive protection from employer interference under the NLRA. *See* NLRB v. Babcock & Wilcox Co., 351 U.S. 105, 76 S. Ct. 679, 100 L. Ed. 975 (1956). *But cf.* Sears, Roebuck and Co. v. San Diego Dist. Council of Carpenters, 436 U.S. 180, 98 S. Ct. 1745, 56 L. Ed.2d 209 (1978), where the Court recognized the general authority of states to apply their trespass laws to peaceful labor pickets who trespass upon private retail premises.

6. Given the rationale of the *UAW-AFL Local 232* case and the rather extensive limitations on the right to strike in the private sector noted above, can you draft a comprehensive definition of the right to strike as it presently exists in the private sector? It is crucial to understand the precise parameters of this right in order to evaluate the argument that denying public employees the right to strike constitutes a violation of the Fourteenth Amendment's equal protection clause.

# 2. THE CONSTITUTIONAL ISSUES IN THE PUBLIC SECTOR

## UNITED FEDERATION OF POSTAL CLERKS v. BLOUNT

### 325 F. Supp. 879 (D.D.C.), *aff'd,* 404 U.S. 802 (1971)

PER CURIAM: This action was brought by the United Federation of Postal Clerks (hereafter sometimes referred to as "Clerks"), an unincorporated public employee labor organization which consists primarily of employees of the Post Office Department, and which is the exclusive bargaining representative of approximately 305,000 members of the clerk craft employed by defendant. Defendant Blount is the Postmaster General of the United States. The Clerks seek declaratory and injunctive relief invalidating portions of 5 U.S.C. § 7311, 18 U.S.C. § 1918, an affidavit required by 5 U.S.C. § 3333 to implement the above statutes, and Executive Order 11491, C.F.R., Chap. II, p. 191. A three-judge court was convened pursuant to 28 U.S.C. § 2282 and § 2284 to consider this issue.

### *The Statutes Involved*

5 U.S.C. § 7311 (3) prohibits an individual from accepting or holding a position in the federal government or in the District of Columbia if he

"(3) participates in a strike ... against the Government of the United States or the government of the District of Columbia. . . ."

Paragraph C of the appointment affidavit required by 5 U.S.C. § 3333, which all federal employees are required to execute under oath, states (POD Form 61):

"I am not participating in any strike against the Government of the United States or any agency thereof, and I will not so participate while an employee of the Government of the United States or any agency thereof."

18 U.S.C. § 1918, in making a violation of 5 U.S.C. § 7311 a crime, provides:

"Whoever violates the provision of section 7311 of title 5 that an individual may not accept or hold a position in the Government of the United States or the government of the District of Columbia if he . . .

"(3) participates in a strike, or asserts the right to strike, against the Government of the United States or the District of Columbia . . .

"shall be fined not more than $1,000 or imprisoned not more than one year and a day, or both."

Section 2(e) (2) of Executive Order 11491 exempts from the definition of a labor organization any group which:

"asserts the right to strike against the Government of the United States or any agency thereof, or to assist or participate in such a strike, or imposes a duty or obligation to conduct, assist or participate in such a strike. . . ."

Section 19(b) (4) of the same Executive Order makes it an unfair labor practice for a labor organization to:

"call or engage in a strike, work stoppage, or slowdown; picket an agency in a labor-management dispute; or condone any such activity by failing to take affirmative action to prevent or stop it; . . . ."

## Plaintiff's Contentions

Plaintiff contends that the right to strike is a fundamental right protected by the Constitution, and that the absolute prohibition of such activity by 5 U.S.C. § 7311 (3) and the other provisions set out above thus constitutes an infringement of the employees' First Amendment rights of association and free speech and operates to deny them equal protection of the law. Plaintiff also argues that the language to "strike" and "participates in a strike" is vague and overbroad and therefore violative of both the First Amendment and the due process clause of the Fifth Amendment. For the purposes of this opinion, we will direct our attention to the attack on the constitutionality of 5 U.S.C. § 7311 (3), the key provision being challenged. To the extent that the present wording of 18 U.S.C. § 1918(3) and Executive Order 11491 does not reflect the actions of two statutory courts in Stewart v. Washington, 301 F. Supp. 610 (D.C.D.C. 1969) and N.A.L.C. v. Blount, 305 F. Supp. 546 (D.C.D.C. 1969), said wording, insofar as it inhibits the *assertion* of the right to strike, is overbroad because it attempts to reach activities protected by the First Amendment and is therefore invalid. With this *caveat,* our treatment of the issue raised by plaintiffs with respect to the constitutionality of 5 U.S.C. § 7311(3) will also apply to 18 U.S.C. § 1918, the penal provision, and to Form 61, the affidavit required by 5 U.S.C. § 3333. For the reasons set forth below, we deny plaintiff's request for declaratory and injunctive relief and grant defendant's motion to dismiss.

## I. Public Employees Have No Constitutional Right to Strike.

At common law no employee, whether public or private, had a constitutional right to strike in concert with his fellow workers. Indeed, such collective action on the part of employees was often held to be a conspiracy. When the right of private employees to strike finally received full protection, it was by statute, Section 7 of the National Labor Relations Act, which "took this conspiracy weapon away from the employer in employment relations which affect interstate commerce" and guaranteed to employees in the private sector the right to engage in concerted activities for the purpose of collective bargaining. See discussion in International Union, U.A.W.A., A.F. of L. Local 232 v. Wisconsin Employment Relations Board, 336 U.S. 245, 257-259, 69 S. Ct. 516, 93 L. Ed. 651 (1948). It seems clear that public employees stand on no stronger footing in this regard than private employees and that in the absence of a statute, they too do not possess the right to strike. The Supreme Court has spoken approvingly of such a restriction, see Amell v. United States, 384 U.S. 158, 161, 86 S. Ct. 1384, 16 L. Ed. 2d 445 (1965), and at least one federal district court has invoked the provisions of a predecessor statute, 5 U.S.C. § 118p-r, to enjoin a strike by government employees. Tennessee Valley Authority v. Local Union No. 110 of Sheet Metal Workers, 233 F. Supp. 997 (D.C.W.D. Ky. 1962). Likewise, scores of state cases have held that state employees do not have a right to engage in concerted work stoppages, in the absence of legislative authorization. . . . It is fair to conclude that, irrespective of the reasons given, there is a unanimity of opinion in the part of courts and legislatures that government employees do not have the right to strike. See Moberly, The Strike and Its Alternative in Public Employment, University of Wisconsin Law Review (1966) pp. 549-550, 554.

Congress has consistently treated public employees as being in a different category than private employees. The National Labor Relations Act of 1937 and the Labor Management Relations Act of 1947, (Taft-Hartley) both defined "employer" as not including any governmental or political subdivisions, and thereby indirectly withheld the protections of § 7 from governmental employees. Congress originally enacted the no-strike provision separately from other restrictions on employee activity, i.e., such as those struck down in Stewart v. Washington and N.A.L.C. v. Blount, *supra,* by attaching riders to appropriations bills which prohibited strikes by government employees. See for example the Third Urgent Deficiency Appropriation Act of 1946, which provided that no part of the appropriation could be used to pay the salary of anyone who engaged in a strike against the Government. Section 305 of the Taft-Hartley Act made it unlawful for a federal employee to participate in a strike, providing immediate discharge and forfeiture of civil service status for infractions. Section 305 was repealed in 1955 by Public Law 330, and reenacted in 5 U.S.C. § 118p-r, the predecessor to the present statute.

Given the fact that there is no constitutional right to strike, it is not irrational or arbitrary for the Government to condition employment on a promise not to withhold labor collectively, and to prohibit strikes by those in public employment, whether because of the prerogatives of the sovereign, some sense of higher obligation associated with public service, to assure the continuing functioning of the Government without interruption, to protect public health and safety or for other reasons. Although plaintiff argues that the provisions in question are unconstitutionally broad in covering all Government employees regardless of the type or importance of the work they do, we hold that it makes no difference whether the jobs performed by certain public employees are regarded as "essential" or "non-essential," or whether similar jobs are performed by workers in private industry who do have the right to strike protected by statute. Nor is it relevant that some positions in private industry are arguably more affected with a public interest than are some positions in the Government service. While the Fifth Amendment contains no Equal Protection Clause similar to the one found in the Fourteenth Amendment, concepts of Equal Protection do inhere in Fifth Amendment Principles of Due Process. Bolling v. Sharpe, 347 U.S. 497, 74 S. Ct. 693, 98 L. Ed. 884 (1954). The Equal Protection Clause, however, does not forbid all discrimination. Where fundamental rights are not involved, a particular classification does not violate the Equal Protection Clause if it is not "arbitrary" or "irrational," i.e., "if any state of facts reasonably may be conceived to justify it." McGowan v. Maryland, 366 U.S. 420, 426, 81 S. Ct. 1101, 1105, 6 L. Ed. 2d 393 (1961). Compare Kramer v. Union Free School District, 395 U.S. 621, 627-628, 89 S. Ct. 1886, 23 L. Ed. 2d 583 (1969). Since the right to strike cannot be considered a "fundamental" right, it is the test enunciated in *McGowan* which must be employed in this case. Thus, there is latitude for distinctions rooted in reason and practice, especially where the difficulty of drafting a no-strike statute which distinguishes among types and classes of employees is obvious.

Furthermore, it should be pointed out that the fact that public employees may not strike does not interfere with their rights which are fundamental and constitutionally protected. The right to organize collectively and to select representatives for the purposes of engaging in collective bargaining is such a fundamental right. . . . But, as the Supreme Court noted in International Union, *etc.,* Local 232 v. Wisconsin Employment Relations Board, *supra,* "The right to strike, because of its more serious impact upon the public interest, is more vulnerable to regulation than the right to organize and select representatives for lawful purposes of collective bargaining which this Court has characterized as a 'fundamental right' and which, as the Court has pointed out, was recognized as such in its decisions long before it was given protection by the National Labor Relations Act." 336 U.S. at 259, 69 S. Ct. at 524.

Executive Order 11491 recognizes the right of federal employees to join labor organizations for the purpose of dealing with grievances, but that Order clearly and expressly defines strikes, work stoppages and slow-downs as unfair labor practices. As discussed above, that Order is the culmination of a long-standing policy. There certainly is no compelling reason to imply the existence of the right to strike from the right to associate and bargain collectively. In the private sphere, the strike is used to equalize bargaining power, but this has universally been held not to be appropriate when its object and purpose can only be to influence the essentially political decisions of Government in the allocation of its resources. Congress has an obligation to ensure that the machinery of the Federal Government continues to function at all times without interference. Prohibition of strikes by its employees is a reasonable implementation of that obligation.

## II. The Provisions are Neither Unconstitutionally Vague nor Overbroad.

Plaintiff contends that the word "strike" and the phrase "participates in a strike" used in the statute are so vague that "men of common intelligence must necessarily guess at [their] meaning and differ as to [their] application," Connally v. General Construction Co., 269 U.S. 385, 391, 46 S. Ct. 126, 127, 70 L. Ed. 322 (1926), and are therefore violative of the due process clause of the Fifth

Amendment. Plaintiff also contends that the provisions are overly broad. While there is no sharp distinction between vagueness and overbreadth, an overly broad statute reaches not only conduct which the Government may properly prohibit but also conduct which is beyond the reach of governmental regulation. A vague statute is merely imprecise in indicating which of several types of conduct which could be restricted has in fact been prohibited.

These concepts of "striking" and "participating in a strike" occupy central positions in our labor statutes and accompanying caselaw, and have been construed and interpreted many times by numerous state and federal courts. "Strike" is defined in § 501 (2) of the Taft-Hartley Act to include "any strike or other concerted stoppage of work by employees ... and any concerted slowdown or other concerted interruption of operations by employees." On its face this is a straightforward definition. It is difficult to understand how a word used and defined so often could be sufficiently ambiguous as to be constitutionally suspect. "Strike" is a term of such common usage and acceptance that "men of common intelligence" need not guess at its meaning. Connally v. General Construction Co., *supra,* at 391, 46 S. Ct. at 127.

Plaintiff complains that the precise parameters of "participation" are so unclear that employees may fail to exercise other, protected First Amendment rights for fear of overstepping the line; and that in any event, "participates" is too broad to withstand judicial scrutiny. Plaintiff urges that Congress is required to more specifically define exactly what activities are to be caught up in the net of illegality.

The Government, however, represented at oral argument that it interprets "participate" to mean "striking," the essence of which is an actual refusal in concert with others to provide services to one's employer. We adopt this construction of the phrase, which will exclude the First Amendment problems raised by the plaintiff in that it removes from the strict reach of these statutes and other provisions such conduct as speech, union membership, fund-raising, organization, distribution of literature and informational picketing, even though those activities may take place in concert during a strike by others. We stress that it is only an actual refusal by particular employees to provide services that is forbidden by 5 U.S.C. § 7311(3) and penalized by 18 U.S.C. § 1918. However, these statutes, as all criminal statutes, must be read in conjunction with 18 U.S.C. §§ 2 (aiding and abetting) and 371 (conspiracy). We express no views as to the extent of their application to cases that might arise thereunder as it is practically impossible to fashion a meaningful declaratory judgment in such a broad area.

This case does not involve a situation where we are concerned with a prior construction by a state supreme court, but rather one in which we are faced with the interpretation to be given a federal statute in the first instance by a federal court. Under such circumstances federal courts have broad latitude, the language of the statute permitting, to construe a statute in such terms as will save it from the infirmities of vagueness and overbreadth. Kent v. Dulles, 357 U.S. 116, 78 S. Ct. 1113, 2 L. Ed. 2d 1204 (1958). This principle of interpretation is equally true of cases which involve rights under the First Amendment. United States v. C.I.O., 335 U.S. 106, 120-122, 68 S. Ct. 1349, 92 L. Ed. 1849 (1948); Chaplinsky v. New Hampshire, 315 U.S. 568, 573-574, 62 S. Ct. 766, 86 L. Ed. 1031 (1942); see also Williams v. District of Columbia, 136 U.S. App. D.C. 56, 419 F.2d 638 (en banc, 1969). Such construction of the word "strike" and the phrase "participates in a strike" achieves the objective of Congress and, in defining the type of conduct which is beyond the reach of the statute, saves it from the risk of vagueness and overbreadth.

Accordingly, we hold that the provisions of the statute, the appointment affidavit and the Executive Order, as construed above, do not violate any constitutional rights of those employees who are members of plaintiff's union. The Government's motion to dismiss the complaint is granted. Order to be presented.

J. SKELLY WRIGHT, Circuit Judge (concurring):

I concur in Part II of the majority's opinion and in the result. My following comments are addressed to the main issue raised in Part I of the opinion — the validity of the flat ban on federal employees' strikes under the Fifth Amendment of the Constitution. This question is, in my view, a very difficult one, and I cannot concur fully in the majority's handling of it.

It is by no means clear to me that the right to strike is not fundamental. The right to strike seems intimately related to the right to form labor organizations, a right which the majority recognizes as fundamental and which, more importantly, is generally thought to be constitutionally protected under the First Amendment — even for public employees. See Melton v. City of Atlanta, 324 F. Supp. 315 (N.D. Ga. 1971); Atkins v. City of Charlotte, 296 F. Supp. 1068 (W.D.N.C. 1969). If the inherent purpose of a labor organization is to bring the workers' interests to bear on management, the right to strike is, historically and practically, an important means of effectuating that purpose. A union that never strikes, or which can make no credible threat to strike, may wither away in ineffectiveness. That fact is not irrelevant to the constitutional calculations. Indeed, in several decisions, the Supreme Court has held that the First Amendment right of association is at least concerned with essential organizational activities which give the particular association life and promote its fundamental purposes. See Williams v. Rhodes, 393 U.S. 23, 89 S. Ct. 5, 21 L. Ed. 2d 24 (1968); United Mine Workers, etc. v. Illinois State Bar Assn., 389 U.S. 217, 88 S. Ct. 353, 19 L. Ed. 2d 426 (1967). I do not suggest that the right to strike is co-equal with the right to form labor organizations. Nor do I equate striking with the organizational activities protected in *Williams* (access to the ballot) or *United Mine Workers* (group legal representation). But I do believe that the right to strike is, at least, within constitutional concern and should not be discriminatorily abridged without substantial or "compelling" justification.

Hence the real question here, as I see it, is to determine whether there is such justification for denying federal employees a right which is granted to other employees of private business. Plaintiff's arguments that not all federal services are "essential" and that some privately provided services are no less "essential" casts doubt on the validity of the flat ban on federal employees' strikes. In our mixed economic system of governmental and private enterprise, the line separating governmental from private functions may depend more on the accidents of history than on substantial differences in kind.

Nevertheless, I feel that I must concur in the result reached by the majority in Part I of its opinion. As the majority indicates, the asserted right of public employees to strike has often been litigated and, so far as I know, never recognized as a matter of law. The present state of the relevant jurisprudence offers almost no support for the proposition that the government lacks a "compelling" interest in prohibiting such strikes. No doubt, the line between "essential" and "non-essential" functions is very, very difficult to draw. For that reason, it may well be best to accept the demarcations resulting from the development of our political economy. If the right of public employees to strike — with all its political and social ramifications — is to be recognized and protected by the judiciary, it should be done by the Supreme Court which has the power to reject established jurisprudence and the authority to enforce such a sweeping rule.

## NOTES

1. Prohibitions against public employee strikes have been challenged on almost every conceivable basis. To date nearly every court ruling on this question has held that these prohibitions do not violate the Constitution. The case law includes:

(a) *First Amendment Challenges:* Abbott v. Myers, 20 Ohio App. 2d 65, 49 Ohio Op. 2d 85, 251 N.E.2d 869 (1969); Board of Educ. Community School Dist. No. 2 v. Redding, 32 Ill. 2d 567, 207 N.E.2d 427 (1965); City of Wauwatosa v. King, 49 Wis. 2d 398, 182 N.W.2d 530 (1971); Jefferson County Teachers Ass'n v. Board of Educ. of Jefferson County, 463 S.W.2d 627 (Ky. 1970), *cert. denied,* 404 U.S. 865 (1971); Board of Educ. of Kankakee School Dist. No. 111 v. Kankakee Fed'n of Teachers Local 886, 46 Ill. 2d 439, 264 N.E.2d 18 (1970), *cert. denied,* 403 U.S. 904 (1971); State v. Heath, 177 N.W.2d 751 (N.D. 1970); Regents of Univ. of Wisconsin v. Teaching Assistants' Ass'n, 74 L.R.R.M. 2049 (Wis. Cir. Ct. 1970); Rogoff v. Anderson, 34 App. Div. 2d 154, 310 N.Y.S.2d 174 (1970); Holland School Dist. v. Holland Educ. Ass'n, 380 Mich. 314, 157 N.W.2d 206 (1968); City of Pawtucket v. Pawtucket Teachers Alliance Local 930, 87 R.I. 364, 141 A.2d 621 (1958).

(b) *Thirteenth Amendment Challenges:* City of Evanston v. Buick, 421 F.2d 595 (7th Cir. 1970); *In re* Block, 50 N.J. 494, 236 A.2d 592 (1967); Pinellas County Classroom Teachers Ass'n, Inc. v. Board of Public Instruction of Pinellas County, 214 So. 2d 34 (Fla. 1968); Holland School Dist. v. Holland Educ. Ass'n, *supra.*

(c) *Fourteenth Amendment Challenges:* Abbott v. Myers, *supra;* City of New York v. DeLury, 23 N.Y.2d 175, 162 Misc. 2d 901, 243 N.E.2d 128, 295 N.Y.S.2d 901 (1968), *appeal dismissed,* 394 U.S. 455 (1969); Head v. Special School Dist. No. 1, 288 Minn. 496, 182 N.W.2d 887, *cert. denied,* 404 U.S. 886 (1970); *In re* Block, *supra;* Jefferson County Teachers Ass'n v. Board of Educ. of Jefferson County, *supra;* Holland School Dist. v. Holland Educ. Ass'n, *supra.*

(d) *Bill of Attainder Challenges:* Abbott v. Myers, *supra;* DiMaggio v. Brown, 19 N.Y.2d 283, 225 N.E.2d 871, 279 N.Y.S.2d 161 (1967).

2. The relevant case law to date also appears to support the proposition that strikes by public employees engaged in propriety as well as governmental functions are illegal: Delaware River & Bay Authority v. International Organization of Masters, Mates & Pilots, 45 N.J. 138, 211 A.2d 789 (1965); Port of Seattle v. ILWU, 52 Wash. 2d 317, 324 P.2d 1099 (1958); City of Alcoa v. IBEW Local 760, 203 Tenn. 12, 308 S.W.2d 476 (1957); City of Los Angeles v. Los Angeles Bldg. Constr. Trades Council, 94 Cal. App. 2d 36, 210 P.2d 305 (1949).

3. Judge Wright in *Blount* claims that "the relevant jurisprudence offers almost no support for the proposition that the government lacks a 'compelling' interest in prohibiting such strikes." What reasons cited by the majority in *Blount* seem most compelling? The court seems to reject out of hand the argument that it is irrational to totally prohibit strikes of municipal librarians, for example, while allowing strikes of telephone workers. Why?

## C. THEORETICAL CONSIDERATIONS RELATING TO THE RIGHT TO STRIKE

In dealing with theoretical considerations in this area, it might be well to question the assumption that strikes are not a fundamental and necessary part of the American collective bargaining system. Can a labor relations system work in the absence of some compulsion on both parties? If not, are there alternative devices to introduce compulsion into the system which are as effective as the strike yet not so disruptive?

## WELLINGTON & WINTER, STRUCTURING COLLECTIVE BARGAINING IN PUBLIC EMPLOYMENT, 79 Yale L.J. 805, 822 (1970) †

### A. The Role of the Strike

We have argued that distortion of the political process is the major, long-run social cost of strikes in public employment. The distortion results from unions obtaining too much power, relative to other interest groups, in decisions affecting the level of taxes and the allocation of tax dollars. This distortion may, therefore, result in a redistribution of income by government, one in which union members are subsidized at the expense of other interest groups. And, where non-monetary issues, such as the decentralization of the governance of schools or the creation of a civilian board to review police conduct, are resolved through bargaining in which the strike or threat thereof is used, the distortion of the political process is no less apparent.

It has been earnestly argued, however, that if public employee unions are successfully denied the strike, they will have too little relative power. To unpack the claims in this argument is crucially important. In the private sector collective bargaining depends upon the strike threat and the occasional strike. It is how deals are made, how collective bargaining works, why employers agree to terms and conditions of employment better than they originally offered. Intuition suggests that what is true of the private sector also is true of the public. Without the strike threat and the strike, the public employer will be intransigent; and this intransigence will, in effect, deprive employees of the very benefits unionization was intended to bring to them. Collective bargaining, the argument goes, will be merely a facade for "collective begging."

Initially, it must be noted that even in the absence of unionism and bargaining the market imposes substantial limitations on the ability of public employers to "take advantage" of their employees. Because they must compete with private employers, and other units of government as well, to hire workers, public employers cannot permit their wages and conditions of employment to be relatively poorer than those offered in the private sector and still get the needed workers. And, as we noted in the *Limits* article,[1] the fact that most public employees work in areas in which there are numerous alternative employment opportunities reduces the likelihood that many public employers are monopsonists. Even if they are, moreover, the lack of a profit motive reduces the likelihood that government's monopsony power, if it exists, will be exercised.

Much of the argument about the role of the strike is, in any event, overstated. First, is exaggerates the power of the strike weapon in the private sector. As we argued in the *Limits* article, the power of private sector unions to gain comparative advantages, while real, is inherently limited by what we there called the employment-benefit tradeoff.

---

† Reprinted by permission of The Yale Law Journal Company and Fred B. Rothman & Company.

[1] Wellington & Winter, *The Limits of Collective Bargaining in Public Employment*, 78 YALE L.J. 1107 (1969). [Ed.]

Second, the very unionization of public employees creates a powerful interest group, at least in large urban centers, that seems able to compete very well with other groups in the political decision-making process. Indeed, collective bargaining (the strike apart) is a method of channeling and underscoring the demands of public employees that is not systematically available to other groups. Public employee unions frequently serve as lobbying agents wielding political power quite disproportionate to the size of their membership. The failure of the Hartford firefighters, mentioned earlier, to seek formal status as a bargaining agent demonstrates how much punch such organizations can wield. And where a strong local labor council exists, association with it can significantly increase the power of public employee unions. This is some assurance, therefore, that public employees, even if prohibited from striking, will not be at a comparative disadvantage in bargaining with their employers.

Thus, on the merits, when one takes the trouble to unpack its claims, the argument for the strike in public employment is hardly inexorable.

## BURTON & KRIDER, THE ROLE AND CONSEQUENCES OF STRIKES BY PUBLIC EMPLOYEES, 79 Yale L.J. 418, 424-32 (1970) †

Wellington and Winter's discussion [*The Limits of Collective Bargaining in Public Employment,* 78 YALE L. J. 1107 (1969)] of the cost of substituting collective for individual bargaining in the public sector includes a chain of causation which runs from (1) an allegation that market restraints are weak in the public sector, largely because the services are essential; to (2) an assertion that the public puts pressure on civic officials to arrive at a quick settlement; to (3) a statement that other pressure groups have no weapons comparable to a strike; to (4) a conclusion that the strike thus imposes a high cost since the political process is distorted.

Let us discuss these steps in order:

(1) *Market Restraints:* A key argument in the case for the inappropriateness of public sector strikes is that economic constraints are not present to any meaningful degree in the public sector. This argument is not entirely convincing. First, wages lost due to strikes are as important to public employees as they are to employees in the private sector. Second, the public's concern over increasing tax rates may prevent the decision-making process from being dominated by political instead of economic considerations. The development of multilateral bargaining in the public sector is an example of how the concern over taxes may result in a close substitute for market constraints. In San Francisco, for example, the Chamber of Commerce has participated in negotiations between the city and public employee unions and has had some success in limiting the economic gains of the unions. A third and related economic constraint arises for such services as water, sewage, and, in some instances, sanitation, where explicit prices are charged. Even if representatives of groups other than employees and the employer do not enter the bargaining process, both union and local government are aware of the economic implications of bargaining which leads to higher prices which are clearly visible to the public. A fourth economic constraint on employees exists in those services where subcontracting to the private sector is a realistic alternative. Warren, Michigan, resolved a bargaining impasse with an American Federation of State, County and Municipal Employees (AFSCME) local by subcontracting its entire sanitation service; Santa Monica, California, ended a

† Reprinted by permission of The Yale Law Journal Company and Fred B. Rothman & Company.

strike of city employees by threatening to subcontract its sanitation operations. If the subcontracting option is preserved, wages in the public sector need not exceed the rate at which subcontracting becomes a realistic alternative.

An aspect of the lack-of-market-restraints argument is that public services are essential. Even at the analytical level, Wellington and Winter's case for essentiality is not convincing. They argue:

"The Services performed by a private transit authority are neither less nor more essential to the public than those that would be performed if the transit authority were owned by a municipality. A railroad or a dock strike may be much more damaging to a community than 'job action' by teachers. This is not to say that government services are not essential. They are both because they may seriously injure a city's economy and occasionally the physical welfare of its citizens."

This is a troublesome passage. It ends with the implicit conclusion that all government services are essential. This conclusion is important in Wellington and Winter's analysis because it is a step in their demonstration that strikes are inappropriate in all governmental services. But the beginning of the passage, with its example of "job action" by teachers, suggests that essentiality is not an *inherent* characteristic of government services but depends on the specific service being evaluated. Furthermore the transit authority example suggests that many services are interchangeable between the public and private sectors. The view that various government services are not of equal essentiality and that there is considerable overlap between the kinds of services provided in the public and private sectors is reinforced by our field work and strike data from the Bureau of Labor Statistics. Examples include:

1. Where sanitation services are provided by a municipality, such as Cleveland, sanitationmen are prohibited from striking. Yet, sanitationmen in Philadelphia, Portland, and San Francisco are presumably free to strike since they are employed by private contractors rather than by the cities.

2. There were 25 local government strikes by the Teamsters in 1965-68, most involving truck drivers and all presumably illegal. Yet the Teamsters' strike involving fuel oil truck drivers in New York City last winter was legal even though the interruption of fuel oil service was believed to have caused the death of several people.

(2) *Public Pressure:* The second argument in the Wellington and Winter analysis is that public pressure on city officials forces them to make quick settlements. The validity of this argument depends on whether the service is essential. Using as a criterion whether the service is essential in the short run, we believe a priori that services can be divided into three categories: (1) essential services — police and fire — where strikes immediately endanger public health and safety; (2) intermediate services — sanitation, hospitals, transit, water, and sewage — where strikes of a few days might be tolerated; (3) nonessential services — streets, parks, education, housing, welfare and general administration — where strikes of indefinite duration could be tolerated. These categories are not exact since essentiality depends on the size of the city. Sanitation strikes will be critical in large cities such as New York but will not cause much inconvenience in smaller cities where there are meaningful alternatives to governmental operation of sanitation services.

Statistics on the duration of strikes which occurred in the public sector between 1965 and 1968 provide evidence not only that public services are of unequal essentiality, but also that the a priori categories which we have used have some validity.... [S]trikes in the essential services (police and fire) had an average duration of 4.7 days, while both the intermediate and the nonessential services had an average duration of approximately 10.5 days. It is true that the duration of strikes in the intermediate and nonessential services is only half the average duration of strikes in the private sector during these years. However, this comparison is somewhat misleading since all of the public sector strikes were illegal, and many were ended by injunction, while presumably a vast majority of the private sector strikes did not suffer from these constraints. It would appear that with the exception of police and fire protection, public officials are, to some degree, able to accept long strikes. The ability of governments to so choose indicates that political pressures generated by strikes are not so strong as to undesirably distort the entire decision-making process of government. City officials in Kalamazoo, Michigan, were able to accept a forty-eight day strike by sanitationmen and laborers; Sacramento County, California, survived an eighty-seven day strike by welfare workers. A three month strike of hospital workers has occurred in Cuyahoga County (Cleveland), Ohio.

(3) *The Strike as a Unique Weapon:* The third objection to the strike is that it provides workers with a weapon unavailable to the employing agency or to other pressure groups. Thus, unions have a superior arsenal. The Taylor Committee Report opposes strikes for this reason, among others, arguing that "there can scarcely be a countervailing lockout." Conceptually, we see no reason why lockouts are less feasible in the public than in the private sector. Legally, public sector lockouts are now forbidden, but so are strikes; presumably both could be legalized. Actually, public sector lockouts have occurred. The Social Service Employees Union (SSEU) of New York City sponsored a "work-in" in 1967 during which all of the caseworkers went to their office but refused to work. Instead, union-sponsored lectures were given by representatives of organizations such as CORE, and symposia were held on the problems of welfare workers and clients. The work-in lasted for one week, after which the City locked out the caseworkers.

A similar assertion is made by Wellington and Winter, who claim that no pressure group other than unions has a weapon comparable to the strike. But this argument raises a number of questions. Is the distinctive characteristic of an inappropriate method of influencing decisions by public officials that it is economic as opposed to political? If this is so, then presumably the threat of the New York Stock Exchange to move to New Jersey unless New York City taxes on stock transfers were lowered and similar devices should be outlawed along with the strike.

(4) *Distortion of the Political Process:* The ultimate concern of both the Taylor Committee and Wellington and Winter is that "a strike of government employees . . . introduces an alien force in the legislative process." It is "alien" because, in the words of the Taylor Committee Report:

"Careful thought about the matter shows conclusively, we believe, that while the right to strike normally performs a useful function in the private enterprise sector (where relative economic power is the final determinant in the making of private agreements), it is not compatible with the orderly functioning of our democratic form of representative government (in which relative political power is the final determinant)."

The essence of this analysis appears to be that certain means used to influence the decision-making process in the public sector — those which are political —

are legitimate, while others — those which are economic — are not. For several reasons, we believe that such distinctions among means are tenuous.

First, any scheme which differentiates economic power from political power faces a perplexing definitional task. . . . The former concept would seem to be encompassed by the latter. The degree of overlap is problematical since there can be economic aspects to many forms of persuasion and pressure. It may be possible to provide an operational distinction between economic power and political power, but we do not believe that those who would rely on this distinction have fulfilled their task.

Second, even assuming it is possible to operationally distinguish economic power and political power, a rationale for utilizing the distinction must be provided. Such a rationale would have to distinguish between the categories either on the basis of characteristics inherent in them as a means of action or on the basis of the ends to which the means are directed. Surely an analysis of ends does not provide a meaningful distinction. The objectives of groups using economic pressure are of the same character as those of groups using political pressure — both seek to influence executive and legislative determinations such as the allocation of funds and the tax rate. If it is impossible effectively to distinguish economic from political pressure groups in terms of their ends, and it is desirable to free the political process from the influence of all pressure groups, then effective lobbying and petitioning should be as illegal as strikes.

If the normative distinction between economic and political power is based, not on the ends desired, but on the nature of the means, our skepticism remains undiminished. Are all forms of political pressure legitimate? Then consider the range of political activity observed in the public sector. Is lobbying by public sector unions to be approved? Presumably it is. What then of participation in partisan political activity? On city time? Should we question the use of campaign contributions or kickbacks from public employees to public officials as a means of influencing public sector decisions? These questions suggest that political pressures, as opposed to economic pressures, cannot *as a class* be considered more desirable.

Our antagonism toward a distinction based on means does not rest solely on a condemnation of political pressures which violate statutory provisions. We believe that perfectly legal forms of political pressure have no automatic superiority over economic pressure. In this regard, the evidence from our field work is particularly enlightening. First, we have found that the availability of political power varies among groups of employees within a given city. Most public administrators have respect for groups which can deliver votes at strategic times. Because of their links to private sector unions, craft unions are invariably in a better position to play this political role than a union confined to the public sector, such as AFSCME. In Chicago, Cleveland and San Francisco, the public sector craft unions are closely allied with the building trades council and play a key role in labor relations with the city. Prior to the passage of state collective bargaining laws such unions also played the key role in Detroit and New York City. . . .

Second, the range of issues pursued by unions relying on political power tends to be narrow. The unions which prosper by eschewing economic power and exercising political power are often found in cities, such as Chicago, with a flourishing patronage system. These unions gain much of their political power by cooperating with the political administration. This source of political power would vanish if the unions were assiduously to pursue a goal of providing job security for their members since this goal would undermine the patronage system. In Rochester, for example, a union made no effort to protect one of its members who was fired for political reasons. For the union to have opposed the city administration at that time on an issue of job security would substantially have reduced the union's influence on other issues. In Chicago, where public sector strikes are rare (except for education) but political considerations are not, the unions have made little effort to establish a grievance procedure to protect their members from arbitrary treatment.

Third, a labor relations system built on political power tends to be unstable since some groups of employees, often a substantial number, are invariably left out of the system. They receive no representation either through patronage or through the union. In Memphis, the craft unions had for many years enjoyed a "working relationship" with the city which assured the payment of the rates that prevailed in the private sector and some control over jobs. The sanitation laborers, however, were not part of the system and were able to obtain effective representation only after a violent confrontation with the city in 1968. Having been denied representation through the political process, they had no choice but to accept a subordinate position in the city or to initiate a strike to change the system. Racial barriers were an important factor in the isolation of the Memphis sanitation laborers. Similar distinctions in racial balance among functions and occupations appear in most of the cities we visited.

## C. Conclusions in Regard to Strikes and the Political Process

Wellington and Winter and the Taylor Committee reject the use of the Strike Model in the public sector. They have endorsed the No-Strike Model in order "to ensure the survival of the 'normal' American political process." Our field work suggests that unions which have actually helped their members either have made the strike threat a viable weapon despite its illegality or have intertwined themselves closely with their nominal employer through patronage-political support arrangements. If this assessment is correct, choice of the No-Strike Model is likely to lead to patterns of decision making which will subvert, if not the "normal" American political process, at least the political process which the Taylor Committee and Wellington and Winter meant to embrace. We would not argue that the misuse of political power will be eliminated by legalizing the strike; on balance, however, we believe that, in regard to most governmental functions, the Strike Model has more virtues than the No-Strike Model.

## NOTES

1. The literature on the theoretical aspects of the strike ban is voluminous with the following articles being perhaps the most comprehensive on the point: Anderson, *Strikes and Impasse Resolution in Public Employment,* 67 Mich. L. Rev. 943 (1969); Bilik, *Toward Public Sector Equality: Extending the Strike Privilege,* 21 Lab. L.J. 338 (1970); Comment, *Collective Bargaining for Public Employees and the Prevention of Strikes in the Public Sector,* 68 Mich. L. Rev. 260 (1969); Edwards, *The Developing Labor Relations Law in the Public Sector,* 10 Duquesne L. Rev. 357 (1972); Kheel, *Resolving Deadlocks Without Banning Strikes,* 92 Monthly Lab. Rev. 62 (July 1969) and *Strikes and Public Employment,* 67 Mich. L. Rev. 931 (1969); Note, *The Strike and Its Alternatives in Public Employment,* 1966 Wis. L. Rev. 549; Smith, *State and Local Advisory Reports on Public Employment Labor Legislation: A Comparative Analysis,* 67 Mich. L. Rev. 891 (1968);

Taylor, *Public Employment: Strikes or Procedures,* 20 IND. & LAB. REL. REV. 617 (1967); WELLINGTON & WINTER, THE UNIONS AND THE CITIES (Brookings Institution, 1971).

2. Should different treatment be accorded to public employees working in small versus large municipalities? It has been argued that strikes by public employees in smaller towns and cities may be tolerable, especially in non-essential services, but that in a city like New York any strike by public sector employees, because of its political and economic consequences, is too severe to be tolerated; therefore, it is claimed that the strike proscription in the largest cities must of necessity be absolute. Do you agree? Does it make sense to distinguish between large and small communities? Would such a distinction survive constitutional challenge?

3. A very important (and sometimes neglected) factor in the theoretical considerations is that any calculation of the legitimacy of public sector strikes on the basis of "essentiality" may be likely to have considerable spill-over effects in the private sector. Arvid Anderson, Chairman of the New York City Office of Collective Bargaining, raised this point in Anderson, *Strikes and Impasse Resolution in Public Employment,* 67 MICH. L. REV. 943, 950-51 (1969):

> For one thing, the ultimate resolution of public policy toward the strike issue is likely to affect the private as well as the public sector because it is difficult to distinguish between essential public and private services. Resolution of this problem is in turn complicated by the fact that federal law protects the right to strike in private employment, while public employment disputes are a matter for state regulation. The impact of certain critical disputes in the private sector has recently raised the question whether the NLRA machinery is adequate to deal with local emergencies. For example, during the strike against Consolidated Edison Company in the New York City area, the New York City Corporation Counsel considered whether the emergency procedures of the Taft-Hartley Act could be applied. A strike by fuel oil drivers resulted in the declaration by the Emergency Control Board of the City of New York that the city was in a state of imminent peril. The strike, which occurred during the midst of a flu epidemic, brought severe hardships to apartment dwellers, home owners, and hospital patients. Thus, any test which purports to relate the right to strike to the essentiality of the service involved cannot operate to prohibit strikes in the public sector alone; the private sector also provides countless vital services affecting the health and safety of the public.

*See generally* Howlett, *The Right to Strike in the Public Sector,* 53 CHI. B. REC. 108 (1971). Some commentators have noted that the utility of the strike in the private sector is increasingly being questioned. *See, e.g.,* Clark, *Public Employee Strikes: Some Proposed Solutions,* 23 LAB. L.J. 111 (1972). If public sector employees are given the right to strike, will this result in the extension of a right to the public sector which may be of doubtful value in the private sector?

## D. THE DEFINITION OF STRIKES AND OTHER COLLECTIVE ACTION SUBJECT TO REGULATION

UNITED FEDERATION OF POSTAL CLERKS V. BLOUNT, 325 F. Supp. 879, 884 (D.D.C.), *aff'd,* 404 U.S. 802 (1971). In response to plaintiff's claim that the federal statutory proscriptions against striking and participating in a strike were unconstitutionally vague, the court noted that:

> These concepts of "striking" and "participating in a strike" occupy central positions in our labor statutes and accompanying case law, and have been construed and interpreted many times by numerous state and federal courts. "Strike" is defined in § 501(d) of the Taft-Hartley Act to include "any concerted stoppage of work by employees ... and any concerted slow-down or other concerted interruption of operations by employees." On its face this is a straightforward definition. It is difficult to understand how a word used

and defined so often could be sufficiently ambiguous as to be constitutionally suspect. "Strike is a term of such common usage and acceptance that 'men of common intelligence' need not guess of its meaning." . . . The Government . . . interprets "participate" to mean "striking," the essence of which is an actual refusal in concert with others to provide services to one's employer. We adopt this construction of the phrase. . . .

## IN RE FORESTVILLE TRANSPORTATION ASSOCIATION
### 4 PERB ¶ 8020 (1971)

Before: I. Markowitz, Hearing Officer, New York State Public Employment Relations Board. . . .

On or about September 25, 1969, the respondent herein entered into an agreement with the Forestville Central School Board of Education. While this agreement is unusually short (1 page), it, in fact, pertains to terms and conditions of employment and was intended by the signatories to be a collective agreement. It was signed by the President of the Board of Education and by Phyllis Swanson who was denominated "President, Bus Drivers' Association." (sic) The agreement ran from July 1, 1969 through June 30, 1970.

During the term of the agreement, the bus drivers became dissatisfied with the maintenance of discipline among the students they were carrying to and from school. As a result of this dissatisfaction, on April 16, 1970, Phyllis Swanson wrote to the Board of Education requesting a meeting with the Board on Monday, April 20th, at 8:30 a.m. The letter was delivered to Dr. Thomas Marshall, supervising principal of the school district. On April 17, Dr. Marshall informed Mrs. Swanson that the Board could not meet at the requested time, but that a meeting could take place on April 22, at 8:00 p.m.

On Monday, April 20, twelve of the district's sixteen bus drivers called in sick. The absence continued through April 24 with the number dropping from 12 to 11 on this date.

On April 21, the school district caused a temporary restraining order to be served on the bus drivers. On the following evening three of the drivers met with three Board members at which time the drivers indicated that a return to work could be effected by the dropping of further injunctive proceedings and the resolution of the disciplinary problems. On April 24, eleven drivers tendered their resignations.

An accord was reached whereby the resignations would not be acted upon and the drivers would return to work Monday morning, April 27, 1970. The return to work accordingly took place.

Unlike most strikes in both the public and private sectors of our economy, the action herein took place not during contract negotiations, but well after the collective agreement had been executed. While such an action is by no means unique, and if proven to be a strike, no less illegal, the defenses of the respondent make this case somewhat extraordinary.

. . . The respondent asserts that it did not "cause, instigate, encourage, conduct, or engage in a strike." Such a denial suggests two questions. First, was the action complained of a strike, and second, what was the connection of the association with the action?

As to the first question, the respondent claims that the incidents occurring between April 20 and April 24 did not constitute a strike, but were in fact absences due to illness. This mass sickness, it is argued, was occasioned by both disciplinary problems and the emotional strain caused by Dr. Marshall's alleged refusal to deal with these problems. The absences are further justified by the respondent by reference to the *Manual of Instructions of School Bus Drivers* prepared by the New York State Education Department. This manual states at p. 29 "A school bus driver must never drive a school bus when he is ill, emotionally upset or fatigued." Thus it is argued that since an individual driver suffering from emotional upset has a responsibility to call in sick, 12 drivers acting in this manner cannot be considered to be conducting a strike. It is further contended that only an individual driver is capable of determining his emotional fitness for driving, the implication being that if a driver says he is emotionally upset, there is no way to show that he was not.

Under the Taylor Law, a strike is defined to include a "concerted stoppage of work or slowdown by public employees." (CSL § 201.10) It is well established that a mass sick call may not be used as a subterfuge for an illegal strike within this definition. In the Matter of the City School District of the City of Elmira 3 PERB 8122 (8124) the hearing officer stated:

"Certainly the subterfuge for an illegal strike by resort to the use of mass illness and the like is not a new phenomenon in labor relations. It has been uniformly held that such employee practices are deemed a strike or concerted stoppage of work." (See also the matter of Mahopac Civil Service Employees Association 3 PERB 8130.)

What must now be determined is whether or not the instant sick call constituted a concerted work stoppage or was in actuality the mere coincidence of a large number of employees becoming "emotionally upset" at the same time and for the same duration. In this connection, the testimony has indicated that normal absenteeism due to sickness was no more than two drivers per day. This alone raises serious doubt as to the probability that 12 employees could, independently of each other, get sick or upset at the same time. Additionally, the fact that all employees apparently "recovered" at the same moment increases this doubt.

The testimony of the drivers themselves does little to strengthen their case. By and large those who testified stated that they were upset either because of the summons served upon them or because of specific disciplinary incidents occurring on their respective busses. While it is conceivable that the service of process in conjunction with other difficulties could upset an employee, it is difficult to imagine that all employees would be equally upset and would remain so upset for exactly the same length of time. It is even more difficult to conceive that disciplinary problems were such that employees having them could report for work for several days after the problem occurred, and *then* become so upset that they could not report for work on the very day when a majority of other employees also became emotionally upset.

The sum and substance of respondent's argument is that the Drivers' Manual be interpreted to mean that any time an emotionally upsetting problem occurs in labor relations, drivers (or anyone else dealing with the health or safety of children) be permitted to strike. Thus, not only might a subpoena trigger an emotional upset but a low salary package might as well. This clearly is not the intent of the Taylor Law, nor is it the intent of any instructional or safety manual which the State might issue. The right to strike has been denied the public employee by the legislature and only the legislature may now grant that right. Thus, the Safety Manual notwithstanding, the mass sickness constituted a strike within the definition of the Taylor Law.

We now come to the question of whether or not the respondent caused, instigated, encouraged, condoned or engaged in the strike. To make this determination the Taylor Law sets up two specific guidelines (CSL § 210.3(e)). The first of these is whether the employee organization called the strike or tried to prevent it. The second is whether the employee organization made or was making good faith efforts to terminate the strike.

As has been indicated, the testimony shows that the employee organization has an unusually informal structure, and is not often looked to for guidance by the employees. This, of course, makes it somewhat difficult to determine what the respondent effectively did or did not do during the time of the strike.

On the other hand, its responsibilities during a strike are somewhat easier to ascertain. Thus, it has been held that even where there is no strike vote and the consensus to strike is obtained informally

"Where the officers and a majority of the membership of an employee organization engaged in a strike, the employee organization is responsible for such strike. 'As long as the union functions as a union, the union is responsible for the mass action of its members. This means when the members go out and act in a concerted fashion and do an illegal act, the union is responsible.' " In the Matter of School Bus Drivers' Association, Elmira City School District 3 PERB 8149 (8152).

Here, as we have indicated, the respondent did, in fact, function as a union, complete with officers and a negotiating team. At least 12 of the 16 drivers employed by the district participated in the strike. Most importantly, the officers of the respondent, as well as the members of its negotiating team did not attempt to prevent the strike, but instead actually participated in it. Lastly, it was only after the strike was a week old that a good faith effort by the respondent was made to terminate it. In short, it is clear that the respondent made no effort at any time between April 20 and April 24 to bring the employees back to work. At best it did nothing; at worst, it caused the strike to continue by the participation of its officers and negotiating team.

. . . The actions of the respondent from April 20 through April 24, 1970 constituted a strike in defiance of the "no-strike" provision of CSL § 210.1.

## NOTES

1. In City of Dover v. International Ass'n of Firefighters, Local 1312, 322 A.2d 918, 87 L.R.R.M. 3083 (N.H. 1974), it was held that the refusal of firefighters to respond to bell alarms and mutual aid calls during off-duty hours, in order to enhance their position during the negotiation of a new bargaining agreement, constituted a concerted "slowdown" which could properly be enjoined. The Court noted that "it is unlikely that any situation would arise wherein a court would permit firemen to curtail essential services without being enjoined." A similar conclusion was reached in Kiernan v. Bronstein, 342 N.Y.S.2d 977, 83 L.R.R.M. 3095 (N.Y. Sup. Ct. 1973), where the Court sustained penalties of fines and probation imposed upon police officers who were absent from work on the date when an unlawful strike occurred. The New York Taylor Law provides that "an employee who is absent from work without permission, or who abstains wholly or in part from the full performance of his duties . . . on the date or dates when a strike occurs, shall be presumed to have engaged in such strike . . ." The Court ruled that this provision did not violate due process because there was "no difficulty in overcoming the presumption and burden of proof by affidavit, ranging from death in the family to donating blood." For other cases which have considered the definitional problems relating to public sector

strikes, *see* Board of Educ., Borough of Union Beach v. New Jersey Educ. Ass'n., 53 N.J. 29, 247 A.2d 867 (1968); Board of Educ. of New York City v. Shanker, 283 N.Y.S.2d 548, *aff'd.,* 286 N.Y.S.2d 453 (N.Y. Sup. Ct., App. Div. 1967); Holland School Dist. v. Holland Educ. Ass'n., 380 Mich. 314, 157 N.W.2d 206 (1968). In all three cases, the strike prohibition was held to cover the disputed activities. Even more interesting problems arise when police officers, instead of walking off the job, perform their work so strictly as to cause great public annoyance. Should such assiduity be classified as a "strike?" *See generally* Comment, *Collective Bargaining for Public Employees and the Prevention of Strikes in the Public Sector,* 68 MICH. L.REV. 260, 263-65 (1969); Kheel, *Strikes and Public Employment,* 67 MICH. L.REV. 931, 935 (1969); Wortman, *Collective Bargaining Tactics in Federal Civil Service,* 15 LAB. L.J. 482 (1964).

2. In Area Board of Vocational, Technical and Adult Educ., Dist. No. 4 v. Wisconsin Dept. of Industry, Labor and Human Relations, 1977-78 PBC ¶36,013 (Wis. Cir. Ct. 1977), a governmental lockout of employees who were statutorily precluded from striking was found unlawful since "[t]he economic facts of life make it clear that striking and locking out are two sides of the same coin."

## BOARD OF EDUCATION OF COMMUNITY UNIT SCHOOL DISTRICT NO. 2 v. REDDING

Supreme Court of Illinois
32 Ill. 2d 567, 207 N.E.2d 427 (1965)

DAILY, Justice.

This action in chancery was brought in the circuit court of Bond County by plaintiff, the Board of Education of Community Unit School District No. 2 of said county, to enjoin defendants from conducting a strike against the board and from picketing its schools in support of such strike. The named defendants were a national union, its local counterpart, officials of the local, and thirteen members of the union who had been custodial employees of the board. After a hearing, the trial court denied injunctive relief and dismissed the complaint. Plaintiff has appealed directly to this court since questions arising under the State and Federal constitutions are involved. More specifically, it is the contention of plaintiff that the strike and picketing interfere with the constitutional duty of our General Assembly to "provide a thorough and efficient system of free schools," (const. of 1870, art. VIII, sec. 1, S.H.A.,) whereas defendants assert the picketing complained of is a valid exercise of free speech under the State and Federal constitutions.

Although the legal issues presented are narrow and well defined, we believe a consideration of those issues requires a statement in some detail of the facts surrounding the controversy. The plaintiff, duly and lawfully organized under the laws of Illinois, operates seven attendance centers, consisting of three grade schools, a junior high school and a senior high school in Greenville, and grade schools in Pocahontas and Sorento. It has approximately 2500 students enrolled at the seven centers, and employs 153 teachers and other personnel. Prior to September 2, 1964, its custodial force consisted of 13 employees, all of whom are defendants in this suit. The latter employees had joined or became affiliated with a local and national "Teamsters, Chauffeurs and Helpers" union and, on August 3, 1964, union officers presented to the plaintiff-board a proposed collective bargaining agreement on behalf of the thirteen employees. Plaintiff refused to sign the agreement for various reasons, the validity or propriety of which form no part of the issues in this proceeding.

On September 2, 1964, a regularly scheduled school day, the thirteen custodial employees did not report for work, but, with the help and financial support of the union, set up picket lines at each of the seven attendance centers. These lines have been maintained at all times pertinent to the case, and it appears that the picketing has been peaceful. In addition, there is no showing in the record that any of the defendants coerced or advised any persons not to cross the picket lines. The pickets carried and paraded with signs, the exact wording of which does not appear in the record; however, as recalled by witnesses, the placards stated in substance that members of "Teamsters Local No. 525" were "on strike" against "Bond County Unit District No. 2."

During the next eight days, except for nonschool days, normal school operations were disrupted as follows: (1) attendance figures were abnormally low, a circumstance which could indirectly affect State aid plaintiff would get on the basis of daily attendance averages; (2) milk and bread deliveries, as well as the deliveries of surplus foods, were not made to the school cafeterias when deliverymen would not cross the picket lines; (3) schools were not cleaned and no personnel were available for such cleaning; (4) the employees of a roofing contractor refused to cross the picket line to complete repairs on a leak in a school roof; (5) the transportation of pupils to schools was affected; and (6) the board closed the schools completely from September 8 through 10.

The complaint for injunctive relief was filed September 8 and, on such date, it appears that local union officials dispatched a telegram to plaintiff stating that the striking employees would "maintain essential sanitary services" upon request, but no such request was made. . . .

Between September 11 and 24 the picketing continued and the schools operated, but with the following deviations from normal: (1) cleaning was done by volunteers and temporary replacements but the cleanliness of the buildings was below standard; (2) no personnel were available to fire furnaces or operate hot water systems; (3) physical education classes had to be curtailed in the junior high school due to lack of hot water; (4) it became necessary to buy a new type water heater for one of the cafeterias in order for dishes to be washed; and (5) principals and other supervisory personnel were forced to perform many duties aside from their regular educational duties. As we interpret the record, union officials advised deliverymen they could cross the picket line if they chose and the delivery of milk and bread was resumed. Some drivers delivering other supplies, however, chose to honor the picket lines, and school personnel used their own cars to go to warehouses for essential supplies. The employees of the roofing contractor continued their refusal to cross the line and, during and after rains, the leak in the roof became worse and plaster fell from the ceiling. Vandalism occurred in one of the schools over a weekend, but there is no showing that it occurred at a time when the regular custodial personnel would have been present.

The trial court refused to enjoin either the strike or the picketing, and its order dismissing the complaint found that plaintiff had failed to show irreparable injury, that the picketing was peaceful and a valid exercise of the constitutional rights of free speech, and that there was no danger of interference with the operations of the schools. . . .

The scope of our review is limited to a consideration of whether such employees may strike against their school board employer, and whether they may picket to support their strike. . . .

[The court went on at length to find that the lower court erred by refusing to enjoin an unlawful strike].

Turning to the matter of picketing, which the trial court also refused to restrain, it is the position of defendants, and was apparently that of the trial court, that the right of working men to communicate their complaints by peaceful picketing is completely inviolable. That is to say, defendants insist that picketing is a form of free speech and when done in a peaceful and truthful manner may not otherwise be regulated or enjoined. However, the premise that peaceful picketing is immune from all regulation and control is a false one. While picketing has an ingredient of communication, the cases make it clear that it cannot be dogmatically equated with constitutionally protected freedom of speech, and that picketing is more than free speech because picket lines are designed to exert, and do exert, influences which produce actions and consequences different from other modes of communication. Indeed, these by-products of picketing which go beyond free speech are self-evident in this case. It is now well established that the latter aspects of picketing may be subject to restrictive regulations. (Bakery & Pastry Drivers and Helpers Local 802 of Intern. Brotherhood of Teamsters v. Wohl, 315 U.S. 769, 62 S. Ct. 816, 86 L. Ed. 1178,) and while the specific situation must control decision, it is more than clear that a State may, without abridging the right of free speech, restrain picketing where such curtailment is necessary to protect the public interest and property rights and where the picketing is for a purpose unlawful under State laws or policies, whether such policies have been expressed by the judicial organ or the legislature of the State. (Hughes v. Superior Court of State of California, etc., 339 U.S. 460, 70 S. Ct. 718, 94 L. Ed. 985; International Brotherhood of Teamsters Local 695, etc. v. Vogt, Inc., 354 U.S. 284, 77 S. Ct. 1166, 1 L. Ed. 2d 1347; Building Service Employees International Union, Local 262 v. Gazzam, 339 U.S. 532, 70 S. Ct. 784, 94 L. Ed. 1045.)

As stated by the late Mr. Justice Frankfurter in the Hughes case: "It has been amply recognized that picketing, not being the equivalent of speech as a matter of fact, is not its inevitable legal equivalent. Picketing is not beyond the control of a State if the manner in which picketing is conducted or the purpose which it seeks to effectuate gives ground for its disallowance. . . . 'A state is not required to tolerate in all places and all circumstances even peaceful picketing by an individual.' " 339 U.S. at 465-466, 70 S. Ct. at 721, 722, 94 L. Ed. at 992.

The picketing here, though peaceful, was for the purpose of fostering and supporting an unlawful strike against a governmental employer and, being for an unlawful purpose, should have been enjoined for this reason alone. Apart from this, however, the effect of the influences exerted by the picketing was to impede and obstruct a vital and important governmental function — the proper and efficient education of our children — making its curtailment necessary to protect the patently overriding public interest.

Reversed and remanded, with directions.

## NOTES

1. Most state courts have followed the view of *Redding* when determining the legality of peaceful public sector picketing conducted in conjunction with an unlawful work stoppage. *See, e.g.,* City of Minot v. Teamsters, Local 74, 142 N.W.2d 612 (N.D. 1966); State v. Heath, 177 N.W.2d 751 (N.D. 1970); City and County of San Francisco v. Evankovich, 69 Cal.App.3d 41, 137 Cal.Rptr. 883 (1977); Trustees of Calif. State Colleges v. Local 1352, San Francisco State College Fed'n of Teachers, 13 Cal.App.3d 863, 92 Cal.Rptr. 134 (1970). Although the *Redding* Court seemed to rely heavily upon the fact that the picketing involved tended to disrupt the orderly functioning of the school, picketing that occurs away from the site of the dispute may also be enjoined. *See* City of Wauwatosa v. King, 49 Wis.2d 398, 182 N.W.2d 530 (1971); Petrucci v. Hogan, 27 N.Y.S.2d 718 (Sup. Ct. 1941). *But see* Board of Educ., Union Free School Dist. No. 3,

Town of Brookhaven v. NEA, 30 N.Y.2d 938 (1972), where the New York Court of Appeals denied injunctive relief to prevent the teachers' association from distributing statements urging teachers not to work for the school district, since the record did not demonstrate that the school district's operations were so disrupted that the right of free expression could be judicially curtailed.

2. Peaceful picketing not related to or in furtherance of an illegal strike was permitted in Regents of Univ. of Wisconsin v. Teaching Assistants Ass'n., 74 L.R.R.M. 2049 (Wis. Cir. Ct. 1970), and in Board of Educ. of Danville Community Consol. School Dist. v. Education Ass'n., 376 N.E.2d 430, 1977-78 PBC ¶36,313 (Ill. App. Ct. 1978). *See also* School Board of Escambia County v. PERC, 350 So.2d 819 (Fla. Dist. Ct. App. 1977), wherein an unfair labor practice finding was sustained regarding an employer's photographic surveillance of peaceful picketing that was not connected with any work stoppage. In Tassin v. Local 832, Nat'l. Union of Police Officers, 311 So.2d 591 (1975), the Louisiana Court of Appeals held that the aldermen of Westwego, Louisiana, were not entitled to an injunction restraining picketing by police in front of the aldermen's private businesses, since the aldermen (who, with the mayor, embodied the city government) had no government-provided offices at which they might otherwise be effectively petitioned. The police began picketing after the union was formed, with signs describing the mayor and aldermen as unfair for refusing to recognize the union. To enjoin the pickets, said the court, would constitute a denial of the First Amendment freedom "peaceably to assemble, and to petition the government for redress of grievances." *See generally* Staudohar, *Rights and Limitations of Picketing by Public Employees,* 25 LAB. L.J. 632 (1974).

3. Section 19(b)(4) of E.O. 11491 specifically proscribed the picketing of "an agency in a labor-management dispute." In NTEU v. Fasser, 428 F.Supp. 295 (D.D.C. 1976), Judge Gesell indicated that to the extent Section 19(b)(4) prohibited all labor picketing by federal workers, including peaceful, informational, and non-disruptive picketing, it contravened the First Amendment free speech guarantee. *See* Note, *First Amendment Challenges by Federal Employees to the Broad Labor Picketing Proscription of Executive Order 11491,* 69 MICH. L. REV. 957 (1971). The prohibition contained in Section 7116(b)(7) of the Civil Service Reform Act of 1978 appears to satisfy Judge Gesell's concern, since it applies only "if such picketing interferes with an agency's operation," and language in Section 7116(b) expressly exempts non-interfering, peaceful picketing.

4. If you were requested to draft a statutory provision prohibiting all labor picketing by public employees that may constitutionally be proscribed, what language would you utilize?

# E. THE STRIKE PROSCRIPTION

## 1. AT COMMON LAW

ANDERSON FEDERATION OF TEACHERS, LOCAL 519 v. SCHOOL CITY OF ANDERSON, 252 Ind. 558, 251 N.E.2d 15 (1969), *cert. denied,* 399 U.S. 928 (1970). In upholding a trial court restraining order against a teachers' strike and a finding that the union was in contempt of court for violating the restraining order, the Indiana Supreme Court noted that:

> . . . [B]oth the federal and state jurisdictions and men both liberal and conservative in their political philosophies have uniformly recognized that to allow a strike by public employees is not merely a matter of choice of political philosophies, but is a thing which cannot and must not be permitted if the orderly function of our society is to be preserved. This is not a matter for debate in the political arena for it appears fundamental, as stated by Governor Dewey, public strikes would lead to anarchy, and, as stated by President Roosevelt, the public strike "is unthinkable and intolerable". . . .

The majority opinion cited a long list of state court opinions to support the proposition "that strikes by public employees are or should be prohibited and that injunctions should be granted to halt or prevent them." Chief Justice DeBruler, in a lengthy dissent, argued that "the majority opinion offers absolutely no justification for its holding that every strike by any public employees, including teachers is illegal, and therefore, enjoinable regardless of how peaceful and non-disruptive the strike is. . . ." Chief Justice DeBruler also argued extensively that since Indiana had an anti-injunction statute, the trial court should be reversed because it did not follow the procedures required by that statute and, therefore, it had no jurisdiction to issue a temporary restraining order or injunction without notice or hearing in a matter involving a labor dispute. On this point, the majority had ruled that Indiana's "Little Norris-LaGuardia Act" was not applicable to disputes concerning public employees.

## NOTE

Despite the impassioned exhortations of Chief Justice DeBruler, it is well established that at common law public employee strikes are illegal. In addition to the extensive list of cases cited in the majority opinion, see Board of Educ. of Kankakee School Dist. No. 111 v. Kankakee Fed'n of Teachers Local 886, 46 Ill. 2d 439, 264 N.E.2d 18 (1970), *cert. denied*, 403 U.S. 904 (1971); City of Evanston v. Buick, 421 F.2d 595 (7th Cir. 1970); City of San Diego v. AFSCME Local 127, 87 Cal. 258, 8 Cal. App. 3d 308 (1970); Delaware River Bay Authority v. International Organization of Masters, Pilots, and Mates, 45 N.J. 138, 211 A.2d 789 (1965); Kirker v. Moore, 308 F. Supp. 615 (1970), *aff'd*, 436 F.2d 423 (4th Cir.), *cert. denied*, 404 U.S. 824 (1971); State v. Heath, 177 N.W.2d 751 (N.D. 1970); Trustees of California State Colleges v. Local 1352, San Francisco State College Fed'n of Teachers, 13 Cal. App. 3d 863, 92 Cal. Rptr. 134 (1970).

## SCHOOL COMMITTEE OF THE TOWN OF WESTERLY v. WESTERLY TEACHERS ASSOCIATION

Supreme Court of Rhode Island
299 A.2d 441, 82 L.R.R.M. 2567 (1973)

KELLEHER, J. Last September when the public school bells rang to announce the beginning of a new school year, there was one group whose response was something less than unanimous. It was the schoolteachers. In several communities they appeared at the schoolhouse doors not to teach but to picket. A phrase was heard which until recently was usually uttered by those engaged in the private sector of employment. It was "no contract, no work." . . .

September 5, 1972 was teachers' orientation day. A substantial number of the teachers failed to attend the scheduled meetings. The next day was the first day of school. The students appeared but, once again, the teachers were conspicuous by their absence from the classrooms. At 10 a.m., the committee closed the schools and shortly thereafter a complaint was submitted to a justice of the Superior Court. He then issued an ex parte temporary restraining order which enjoined the strike and ordered the teachers to return to work. On September 7, 1972, the association sought from us certiorari and a stay of the Superior Court's order. We issued the writ but denied the request for a stay. Thereafter, the strike ended and school began in Westerly.

Our issuance of the writ has been motivated by the fact that within recent times, each and every time the public schools of our state have resumed operations after summer vacation, teachers in many of the public school systems have refused to return to their classrooms claiming that they have a right to strike. We have agreed to review the issuance of the Superior Court's restraining order because it is intertwined with an issue of substantial public interest which is capable of repetition yet evading review. . . .

In doing so we are reassessing a position first taken in City of Pawtucket v. Pawtucket Teachers' Alliance, 87 R.I. 364, 141 A.2d 624 (1958), and reaffirmed just about six years ago in Pawtucket School Committee v. Pawtucket Teachers' Alliance, 101 R.I. 243, 221 A.2d 806 (1966). The holding first expressed in 1958 states that striking by public schoolteachers is illegal and subject to being enjoined. We see no reason why this principle should be modified.

There is no constitutionally protected fundamental right to strike. In 1926, Mr. Justice Brandeis wrote that neither the common law nor the Fourteenth Amendment conferred the absolute right to strike. Dorchy v. Kansas, 272 U.S. 306, 47 S. Ct. 86, 71 L. Ed. 248 (1926). It was pointed out in United Federation of Postal Clerks v. Blount, 325 F. Supp. 879 (D.D.C. 1971), aff'd, 404 U.S. 802, 92 S. Ct. 80, 30 L. Ed. 2d 38 (1971), that at common law no employee whether private or public had a constitutional right to strike in concert with fellow workers because such an association was often regarded as an illegal conspiracy which was punishable under the criminal law. The conspiracy weapon was removed and the private employees' right to strike became fully protected with the passage of sec. 7 of the National Labor Relations Act, 49 Stat. 449 (1935) . . . . In the years that have ensued since the first Pawtucket schoolteachers' case, there has not been any instance where any court has held that public employees have a constitutional right to strike.

The diffusion of knowledge through the use of the public school system so that the advantages and opportunities afforded by education will be made available to the people is the constitutional responsibility of the state Article XII, sec. 1 of the Rhode Island constitution. This responsibility is carried on at the local level by the school committee as an agent of the state.

The state has a compelling interest that one of its most precious assets — its youth — have the opportunity to drink at the font of knowledge so that they may be nurtured and developed into the responsible citizens of tomorrow. No one has the right to turn off the fountain's spigot and keep it in a closed position. Likewise, the equal protection afforded by the Fourteenth Amendment does not guarantee perfect equality. There is a difference between a private employee and a public employee, such as a teacher who plays such an important part in enabling the state to discharge its constitutional responsibility.

The need of preventing governmental paralysis justifies the "no strike" distinction we have drawn between the public employee and his counterpart who works for the private sector within our labor force.

A thorough compilation of cases covering all facets of a public employee's right to strike can be found in Annot., 37 A.L.R.3d 1147 (1971). A study of this annotation makes it perfectly clear that a judicial or legislative interdiction against strikes by public employees does not constitute involuntary servitude or an unwarranted impingement on one's constitutional rights be they of free speech, assembly, due process or equal protection.

The teachers argue, however, that in the time that has elapsed since the first Pawtucket schoolteachers' case, the United States Supreme Court has treated public employees in such a way as to afford them rights previously denied them. They point to the holdings in Keyishian v. Board of Regents, 385 U.S. 589, 87 S. Ct. 675, 17 L. Ed. 2d 629 (1967) and Garrity v. New Jersey, 385 U.S. 493, 87 S. Ct. 616, 17 L. Ed. 2d 562 (1967).

In *Keyishian,* the Supreme Court described the classroom as the "marketplace of ideas" and invalidated the New York teachers' oath and loyalty law on the basis that their vagueness and ambiguity posed an unconstitutional threat to the teachers' right of free speech. The *Garrity* case dealt with a criminal conviction based upon evidence given by some defendants after they had been told that if they exercised their right against self-incrimination during an investigation of their conduct as policemen, they might be discharged. These cases are of no assistance to the teachers because here there is no effort being made to inhibit the give-and-take that goes on in the classroom between teacher and pupil nor are we concerned with any violation of the Fifth Amendment right.

Having failed in their efforts to persuade us that the right to strike has been elevated to constitutional status, the teachers point to various actions taken by the General Assembly and take the position that they have an implied right to strike. They embark on this effort by first pointing out that the General Assembly in its several enactments according collective bargaining rights to various groups of public employees has specifically stated that they shall not have the right to strike and then stress the absence of any such language as it concerns the teaching profession. The teachers look upon the legislative silence as implicit permission to go on strike. We disagree. . . .

While [the statute] fails to contain an express prohibition against a strike, it certainly does not give the public schoolteachers the right to strike. On such a vital issue, we will not attribute to the General Assembly an intent to depart from the common law unless such an intent is expressly and unmistakably declared. . . . If the Legislature wishes to give the public school pedagogues the right to strike, it must say so in clear and unmistakable language. Accordingly, we find no legislation implicitly granting such a right to the teachers of this state.

The sentiments we have just expressed relative to the implicit right to strike apply equally as well to the teachers' contention that their dispute with the school committee was subject to the anti-injunction provisions of § 28-10-2. In the first Pawtucket schoolteachers' case we rejected this argument. The only additional comment that might be made is that if striking public employees are to be given the advantages of the anti-injunction statute, such action will have to result from legislative action rather than judicial construction.

The teachers' inability to enjoy the benefits of the legislation which severely limits the Superior Court's jurisdiction to enjoin a labor dispute does not mean that every time there is a concerted work stoppage by public employees, it shall be subject to an automatic restraining order. Rule 65(b) of Super. R. Civ. P. specifically states that no temporary restraining order shall be granted without notice to the adverse party unless it clearly appears from specific facts by affidavit or verified complaint that irreparable harm will result before notice can be served and a hearing held.

We must concede that the mere failure of a public school system to begin its school year on the appointed day cannot be classified as a catastrophic event. We are also aware that there has been no public furor when schools are closed because of inclement weather, or on the day a presidential candidate comes to town, or when the basketball team wins the championship. The law requires that the schools be in session for 180 days a year. General Laws 1956 (1969 Reenactment) § 16-2-2. There is a flexibility in the calendaring of the school year that not only permits the makeup of days which might have been missed for one reason or another but may also negate the necessity of the immediate injunction which could conceivably subject some individuals to the court's plenary power of contempt.

It is true that the issuance of an interlocutory injunction lies within the sound discretion of the trial justice. The temporary restraining order was entered in the case at bar upon the verified complaint of the chairman of the school committee in which it is averred that schools had not opened as scheduled and that irreparable harm would be sustained by the students, parents and citizens of Westerly. We think that in the light of what we have just said such a declaration will no longer justify ex parte relief. . . .

Ex parte relief in instances such as teachers-school committee disputes can make the judiciary an unwitting third party at the bargaining table and potential coercive force in the collective bargaining processes. We embrace the position taken in School District v. Holland Education Ass'n, 380 Mich. 314, 157 N.W.2d 206 (1968), where it was held that the trial court, before giving affirmative relief, should normally conduct a hearing where it would review what has gone on between the disputants and then determine whether injunction should issue and if so, on what terms and for what period of time.

In conclusion, we would emphasize that the solution to the complex problem involving public schools, teachers and collective bargaining rests within the capable hands of the members of our Legislature. They will not want for proposed answers. During its January, 1969 session, the General Assembly created a "Commission to Study the Ways and Means of Avoiding and Resolving Impasses Which Arise During Contract Negotiations Between School Teachers' Organizations and School Committees." The Commission's report was published on March 2, 1970. A majority of the commission recommended compulsory and binding arbitration on all matters. Another commissioner asked for a qualified right to strike while two others declared that "teachers have an ethical, moral and professional right to withhold their services." One commission member took a neutral position by endorsing neither the Majority Report nor any of the Minority Reports. The diverse opinions expressed within the commission are ample proof that the policy to be followed is the one which must be laid out by the members of the Senate and House of Representatives.

The petition for certiorari is granted; the temporary restraining order is quashed pro forma and the papers in the case are returned to the Superior Court.

. . . .

Mr. Chief Justice Roberts, dissenting. . . .

The right to strike was never explicitly granted to any employees, public or private. The labor union and the strike arose out of economic struggle and not by the action of any legislature. Chief Justice Taft recognized the right of employees to strike long before the National Labor Relations Act (NLRA), 29 U.S.C.A. § 141 et seq., was passed. He described the development of the strike as follows:

> "Is interference of a labor organization by persuasion and appeal to induce a strike against low wages under such circumstances without lawful excuse and malicious? We think not. Labor unions are recognized by the Clayton Act as legal when instituted for mutual help and lawfully carrying out their legitimate objects. They have long been thus recognized by the courts. They were organized out of the necessities of the situation. A single employee was helpless in dealing with an employer. He was dependent ordinarily on his daily wage for the maintenance of himself and family. If the employer refused to pay him the wages that he thought fair, he was nevertheless unable to leave the employ and to resist arbitrary and unfair treatment. Union was essential to give laborers opportunity to deal on equality with their employer. They

united to exert influence upon him and to leave him in a body in order by this inconvenience to induce him to make better terms with them. They were withholding their labor of economic value to make him pay what they thought it was worth. The right to combine for such a lawful purpose has in many years not been denied by any court. The strike became a lawful instrument in a lawful economic struggle or competition between employer and employees as to the share or division between them of the joint product of labor and capital." American Steel Foundries v. Tri-City Central Trades Council, 257 U.S. 184, 208-09, 42 S. Ct. 72, 78, 66 L. Ed. 189, 199-200 (1921).

Nowhere in the NLRA or other labor legislation does Congress expressly grant to employees the right to strike. Rather, in my opinion, this legislation was enacted for the protection of a right already possessed. Such protection was necessary to curb the repressive attitude of many state courts toward labor organizations and their activities. . . .

Having concluded that the right to strike accrues to labor not by legislative grant, but by the irresistible thrust of socio-economic forces, I turn to the question of whether the right to strike is within the protection of the constitutional guarantees. The Supreme Court has long recognized that the right of labor to organize and to bargain collectively is a fundamental right with constitutional protection. NLRB v. Jones & Laughlin Steel Corp., 301 U.S. 1, 33-34, 57 S. Ct. 615, 622-23, 81 L. Ed. 893, 909 (1937). Obviously, the right to strike is essential to the viability of a labor union, and a union which can make no credible threat of strike cannot survive the pressures in the present day industrial world. If the right to strike is fundamental to the existence of a labor union, that right must be subsumed in the right to organize and bargain collectively. Bayonne Textile Corp. v. American Federation of Silk Workers, 116 N.J. Eq. 146, 152-53, 172 A. 551, 554-55 (1934).

I am persuaded that if the right to organize and to bargain collectively is constitutionally protected, then the right to strike, that is, for persons similarly situated to act in concert to promote and protect their economic welfare, must be an integral part of the collective bargaining process.

That being so, it follows that it must be within the protection of the constitutional guarantees of the First Amendment. The collective bargaining process, if it does not include a constitutionally protected right to strike, would be little more than an exercise in sterile ritualism.

I find further support for the proposition of the right of employees to strike in the First and Fifth Amendments to the Constitution of the United States. The First Amendment's protection of freedom of speech and freedom of association have been extended to union organizational activities. Thomas v. Collins, 323 U.S. 516, 532, 65 S. Ct. 315, 323-24, 89 L. Ed. 430, 441 (1945): Hague v. CIO, 307 U.S. 496, 59 S. Ct. 954, 83 L. Ed. 1423 (1939). Moreover, the right to select bargaining representatives has been declared to be a property interest protected by the Clayton Act. Texas & N.O.R.R. v. Brotherhood of Ry. & S.S. Clerks, 281 U.S. 548, 571, 50 S. Ct. 427, 434, 74 L. Ed. 1034, 1046-47 (1930). Such property interest would also be protected by the due process clause of the Fifth Amendment. In view of the fact that the protection of the First and Fifth Amendments is not alien to labor activity, I would conclude that the penumbra of those amendments protects individual workers while acting in concert to further their economic goals. Such activity by necessity includes the right to strike. . . .

I subscribe, then, to the proposition that the right to strike is fundamental and is an integral part of the collective bargaining process. I further hold that the right to strike as an inherent component of the collective bargaining process is constitutionally protected for the benefit of those employed in the public sector as well as those employed in the private sector. I recognize, however, that the state may, by a valid exercise of the police power, proscribe an exercise of the right to strike with respect to those employed in areas of the public service where to permit its exercise would be to make probable an adverse effect on the public health, safety, or welfare.

## NOTE

In Local 1494, IAFF v. City of Coeur d'Alene, 586 P.2d 1346, 1977-78 PBC ¶36,427 (1978), the Idaho Supreme Court was asked to decide whether firefighters were permitted to strike following the expiration of their collective bargaining contract. The applicable statute provides:

*Strikes prohibited during contract* — Upon consummation and during the term of the written contract or agreement, no firefighter shall strike or recognize a picket line of any labor organization while in performance of his official duties. [IDAHO CODE §44-1811]

The Court majority concluded that by negative implication the specific language of the strike proscription removed work stoppages following the termination of the applicable labor agreement from the legal prohibition. It went on to consider whether the firefighters' limited right to strike includes, as one of its elements, the right not to be discharged in the event such a stoppage occurs. Since there was no legislative indication that such strikers were to be accorded the same protections as are accorded their private sector counterparts under the N.L.R.A., the majority concluded that they are not automatically immune from disciplinary sanctions. However, it did decide that where a work stoppage has been precipitated by the public employer's refusal to bargain in good faith over the terms of a new contract, no good cause for termination would exist under the applicable civil service regulations. *But cf.* Oneida School Dist. v. Educ. Ass'n., 567 P.2d 830, 95 L.R.R.M. 3244 (1977), wherein the Idaho Supreme Court indicated that the absence of a provision in the state education labor relations statute expressly proscribing work stoppages by such personnel did not inferentially provide them with a right to strike.

## 2. STATUTORY PROSCRIPTION: THE QUESTION OF AP-PROPRIATE PENALTIES

The common-law prohibition against public sector strikes has one feature which makes it noteworthy, i.e., its simplicity. In essence the common-law strike proscription has usually been understood to mean that all strikes by all public employees are always illegal. Under this common-law rule, little attention has been paid to issues of enforcement schemes, sanctions, or mitigating circumstances which arguably tend to shift the onus of proving a strike unjustified to a public employer. Rather, at common law, public employers have relied upon the power of the judiciary to enjoin illegal strikes and to enforce civil and criminal contempts against those who fail to obey injunctions.

A large number of states have adopted the common-law strike proscription model in state statutes covering public employees. Perhaps typical of the ratification of the common-law approach is the strike proscription contained in the Connecticut collective bargaining statute: CONN. STAT. ANN. tit. 7, Sec. 7 —

Nothing in this act shall constitute a grant of the right to strike to employees of any municipal employer and such strikes are prohibited.

While this approach is superficially appealing, it has one great drawback, namely, it has not worked. The great increase in public sector strikes occurred in a period when a majority of the states relied upon the common-law approach to the problem. Partly for this reason, some states have used somewhat more inventive approaches in dealing with the strike prohibition. Alternatives to the traditional strike proscription which show some ingenuity may be seen in the Pennsylvania, New York and Hawaii state statutes covering public employees which are reprinted in the *Statutory Appendix.*

An interesting study in contrasting theories concerning the problem of enforcement of a statutory ban is found in the statements submitted by the governors' advisory committees in Michigan and New York in 1967 and 1969, respectively.

## REPORT TO GOVERNOR ROMNEY BY THE MICHIGAN ADVISORY COMMITTEE ON PUBLIC EMPLOYEE RELATIONS*

... The question has been raised whether the basic "no-strike" policy expressed in the present law should be revised so as to recognize the right to strike either generally (i.e., without any specific prohibition) or at least in non-critical situations. On this issue there appear to be (or to be developing) highly polarized positions between public employers and most organizations representing public employees. The former insist that the "no-strike" prohibition represents sound public policy, and that it must be applied uniformly and be supported by adequate sanctions. The organizations, for the most part, disagree, although we find a general consensus among them that police officers and firemen should not strike. "Neutral" opinion is divided, although predominantly, so far as our inquiries indicate, accepting the view that for a variety of reasons the strike is inappropriate in public employment. However, there appears to be wide disagreement on the kinds of sanctions which should or can, with effectiveness, be used.

We think the ultimate disposition of the strike issue is far from clear. Experience in the United States and in other countries over the next several years will clarify the underlying considerations and increase the experience necessary for sound evaluation.

We think, however, that existing Michigan policy with respect to the strike issue — which is reflective of state and federal policy generally — should be continued, at least pending further experience. Consistently therewith, certain changes should be made in the law which, on the one hand, will fairly and appropriately implement that policy, and, on the other hand, will clarify it in the important matter of the distinction between group or concerted action and individual employee action.

The legislature, in enacting the amendments of 1965, continued to make strikes by public employees illegal. Controversy exists as to whether it intended to restrict available sanctions to discipline or discharge action taken by the employer. We think in any event that there should, in addition, be available in appropriate circumstances the remedy of the injunction. We reject, however, the views, variously expressed, that criminal penalties should be applied; that strikers should automatically forfeit all job rights and be denied the opportunity for re-employment; that injunctions should always be sought and, whenever sought, should always be issued, regardless of circumstances, upon a finding that a strike

---

*The members of the Advisory Committee included Gabriel N. Alexander, Edward L. Cushman, Ronald W. Haughton, Charles C. Killingsworth and Russell A. Smith, Chairman.

has occurred or is threatened; that an injunction, once issued, should be supported by a fixed scale of fines for violation of the court's order, which may not be "forgiven"; and that other sanctions, such as loss of representation rights, should be used. In our opinion these provisions could be unduly punitive, or impractical, or damaging to the collective bargaining process.

We think that, where strikes are undertaken *before* the required statutory bargaining and other dispute settlement procedures are fully exhausted (and, in the case of police and firefighters, at any time), injunctive relief should be mandatory when requested. In all other cases, the courts should be authorized to exercise their traditional right to make the injunctive remedy available if warranted in terms of the total equities in the particular case (including, of course, as a primary consideration, the impact of a strike on the public) and should retain their traditional right to adapt sanctions imposed for violation of injunctions to the particular situation.

The court, under this approach, would be expected to inquire into all the circumstances pertinent in the case, including any claim made by the defendants that the employer has failed to meet some statutory obligation. This approach assumes that not all strikes will be enjoined, or at least enjoined forthwith, but by the same token it seems to us to be inconceivable that a strike which involved serious damage to the public interest will not be enjoined. It has been argued that the circuit courts should be removed from responsibility in the area of injunctive relief since they are subject to varying "political" pressures and are too close to the scene of the dispute. To the contrary, we believe the very facts that courts are in the locale of the dispute, bear a direct and immediate responsibility for total law enforcement, and are part of the "political" process in the broadest sense, mean that the responsibility for administering the statutory no-strike policy should rest with them whenever this legal remedy is sought. . . .

## NEW YORK GOVERNOR'S COMMITTEE ON PUBLIC EMPLOYEE RELATIONS (1969 Taylor Committee Report)

. . . Our emphasis has been, and continues to be, the development of procedures for the resolution of impasses which will assure equitable treatment for public employees and which will constitute an effective substitute for the strike. Notwithstanding the development of these procedures, there is an evident need for effective deterrents against illegal strikes. In our 1968 Interim Report we stated:

> In face of the safeguards set up in the Taylor Law for the employees, it seems indisputable that the interest of the public as a whole deserves at least the kind of protection reserved in the law as the ultimate method of concluding the most obstinate dispute.

> It is safe to say that however carefully the law may undertake to see that public employees are treated fairly and equitably, there will be those who, through impatience or in a desire to achieve more than is fair and equitable, will thoughtlessly advocate and support the use of the strike weapon. Aside from the harm this will inflict on the public and on the labor movement itself, it will promote lawlessness and disrespect for the law and the courts, which can lead to serious consequences. The fact of the matter is that Federal laws prohibiting strikes by public employees have been observed far more scrupulously, and court injunctions against strikes have been given a far higher level of respect and compliance.

It is primarily because we believe that interruption of services will not assure equity for all public employees and the public that we recommended in our 1966 Report that penalties be stipulated. Our hope was that they would serve as additional deterrents to those leaders who believe they are justified in using muscle they uniquely possess, rather than persuasion and orderliness, in advancing the cause of those they represent. The strongest deterrent should, of course, be the realization that justice can be obtained through the techniques set up in the legislation, without use of the public-punishing strike.

### a. *Union Deterrents*

### 1. *Deterrents Related to Contempt Proceedings*

At present, the Taylor Law provides that where an employee organization has violated an order of the Court enjoining an illegal public employees' strike, the Court's discretion to levy fines for such criminal contempt is substantially limited. Section 751(2) of the Judiciary Law, as amended by the Taylor Law, limits such fine to one week's dues collections of the respondent organization or $10,000, whichever is less, or a minimum fine of $1,000, for each day that the contempt persists.

In our judgment this is an inequitable limitation and does not serve as an effective deterrent. Some large employee organizations are not deterred from asserting the right to strike because the penalties impose no real economic burden upon them. Less affluent unions may find the provision to be an effective deterrent.

We believe that limits now imposed upon the discretion of the Court in the assessment of fines for criminal contempt of its orders are unwise. We would therefore recommend that such limits as to fines for employee organizations be removed.[2]

There seems to be considerable merit, however, in the mandatory and permissive guidelines in the present Taylor Law setting forth the criteria to be applied by the court in the assessment of fines. The provisions in the present law permitting deferral of payment of the fine until the appeal is finally determined

---

[2] Our 1968 Interim Report states in part:

We also thought, and recommended, that full discretion in the enforcement of its decrees restraining illegal strikes should be returned to the court. We are of the opinion that the court would be in the best position to determine the appropriate steps to compel compliance with its orders. In the Taylor Law, however, there is a stipulated maximum fine against a defiant labor organization of the lesser of $10,000 per day or one week's dues. To one union this may be very severe; to another it may be brushed off. Indeed, one union advocating the use of the strike publicly announced that it could purchase immunity from violation of the court's injunction for a price of 25 cents per member per day.

We would prefer to leave the appropriate penalties to the court's discretion. Respect for law and the courts should not be sold off at bargain rates. We proposed that there be no limit placed on the criminal contempt fines which the court might impose on a non-complying labor organization in order to assure compliance. We have no special comment to make about the permissible punishment that may be inflicted by the courts on individuals who refuse to comply, for if the shield is taken away from the labor organizations, we believe the likelihood is that there will be less non-compliance. In any event we did not suggest any change in the level of punishment that has been customarily imposed by the courts on individuals found to be in criminal contempt. The penalty of imprisonment for individual criminal contempt did not originate in the Taylor Law nor was it discussed in our 1966 Report.

and the granting a preference in appellate review of contempt convictions seem to be salutary.

We feel impelled to comment upon the imprisonment of union officials, and others, in consequence of the violation by them of an injunction against an illegal strike. From the standpoint of sound government-employee relations alone we are convinced that the possibility of such imprisonment is not an effective deterrent against engaging in illegal strikes. We have never recommended it. Nor is it a part of the Taylor Law. Indeed, achievement of the objectives of the Taylor Law could very well be enhanced if an imposition of this penalty was not a possibility. On the other hand, whether or not such a penalty is deemed by the courts to be essential for the preservation of the judicial process, upon which all of us depend for the protection of our basic rights, is a question which goes beyond the matter of government-employee relations with which we are here particularly concerned. This is a matter, therefore, for courts to determine.

## 2. *Deterrents Related to Administrative Proceedings*

The Taylor Law presently limits the authority of the State Board to suspend the right of check-off of an employee organization found to have been responsible for an illegal strike. There is a similar restriction upon the contempt power of the courts, pursuant to Section 751 (2) of the Judiciary Law involving a union in an exempted municipality under Section 212 of the Taylor Law. In each case, the maximum period of suspension is 18 months.

Our belief is that an uncertainty of the extent of this sanction would operate as a more effective deterrent. The limitations which now appear in Section 210(3) of the Taylor Law and Section 751(2) of the Judiciary Law restrict the effectiveness of this approach. We believe, therefore, that the deterrent as limited by the Taylor Law is not completely effective.

We recommend, accordingly, that an illegal strike should subject the responsible employee organization to a loss of the right or privilege of check-off. An employee organization having been denied this right should be accorded an opportunity to petition the State Board or the court and the suspension should be lifted only after the organization has proved that it has conformed to the law prohibiting strikes and has affirmed its readiness, willingness, and ability to conform to such law. In the ordinary case the organization could not be accorded the opportunity to prove its bona fides until there had passed without incident at least one full contract term next succeeding the term in which the strike occurred. The suspension of check-off by the State Board or the court, therefore, would be open-ended, subject to resumption upon convincing proof of the organization's record and its readiness to conform to the law.

## b. *Individual Deterrents*

Section 210 of the Taylor Law presently provides that a public employee who violates the prohibition against strikes *shall* be subject to certain disciplinary penalties provided by Civil Service Law for misconduct in accordance with procedures established by that law. Notwithstanding the fact that the language is mandatory rather than permissive, it appears that proceedings for individual misconduct under Section 75 of the Civil Service Law have not been undertaken to the extent necessary to serve as an effective deterrent to the participation in an illegal strike. This sanction remains within the control of the public employer. It has often become a negotiable matter in reaching a strike settlement. Where it has not been expressly waived by the public employer as a condition of restoring public services, public employers reportedly have been reluctant to impose these sanctions after a strike. It's easier that way.

In full recognition of these pragmatic considerations, we nonetheless believe that public employers have a responsibility to enforce the law. We believe it would be helpful if the officers or bodies having the power and responsibility to discipline public employees involved in a strike were required to submit to the chief executive officer of the government involved a written report dealing with the carrying out of their responsibilities to enforce disciplinary penalties upon individuals who engage in an illegal strike. Such a report should be submitted within one month after the termination of a strike, should be made public and should provide the following information: (i) the circumstances surrounding the commencement of the strike, (ii) the efforts used to terminate the strike, (iii) the names of those employees whom the officer or body had reason to believe were responsible for causing, instigating or encouraging the strike as well as findings as to their varying degrees of responsibility, and (iv) related to the varying degrees of individual responsibility, the sanctions imposed against such individual employees by such officer or body under the provisions of Section 75 of the Civil Service Law.

## NOTES

1. Controversy over the Taylor Act and its predecessor, the Condon-Wadlin Act of 1948, has been high-spirited and, at times, acrimonious. Some of the more temperate and helpful comments include Gould, *The New York Taylor Law: A Preliminary Assessment,* 18 LAB. L.J. 323 (1967); Montana, *Striking Teachers, Welfare, Transit and Sanitation Workers,* 19 LAB. L.J. 273 (1968); Rains, *New York Public Employee Relations Laws,* 20 LAB. L.J. 264 (1969); Waldman, *Damage Actions and Other Remedies in the Public Employee Strike,* in PROCEEDINGS OF THE TWENTIETH NEW YORK UNIVERSITY CONFERENCE ON LABOR 259 (1968); Wolk, *Public Employee Strikes — A Survey of the Condon-Wadlin Acts,* 13 N.Y.L. FORUM 69 (1967); and Raskin, *Politics Up-Ends the Bargaining Table,* in PUBLIC WORKERS AND PUBLIC UNIONS 122 (S. Zagoria ed. 1972), which provides an interesting analysis of the political machinations of New York City during the first five years of the Taylor Act.

2. A survey of some of the more inventive state legislation banning strikes shows a wide variety of sanctions being used. Some of the more stringent state laws include Georgia (GA. CODE ANN. ch. 89-13, §§ 1301-1303, covering state employees providing for five years probation for employees coupled with no pay increase for three years); Nevada (NEV. REV. STAT. ch. 288, §§ 288.230 — .260, covering state and local employees, providing for injunctions, a maximum fine of $50,000 per day against the union, a maximum fine of $1,000 per day against union officials coupled with an indeterminate prison sentence, and dismissal or suspension of the union rank and file); and South Dakota (S.D. COMP. LAWS ch. 3-18, §§ 3-18-9 — 3-18-14, covering state and local employees, providing for injunctive relief and misdemeanors for inciting or encouraging strikes punishable by a fine up to $50,000 for the union and up to $1,000 or one year in prison for the employees).

3. The penalty provisions of the Taylor Act survived constitutional challenge in Kiernan v. Lindsay, 334 F.Supp. 588 (S.D.N.Y. 1971), aff'd., 405 U.S. 1000 (1972), and Lawson v. Board of Educ. of Vestal Central School Dist. No. 1, 315 N.Y.S.2d 877, 35 App.Div.2d 878 (1970). *See also* Pruzan v. Board of Educ. of New York City, 25 Misc.2d 945, 209 N.Y.S.2d 966 (Sup. Ct. 1960), upholding the constitutionality of the Condon-Wadlin Act's penalty provision.

4. For a construction of what constitutes mitigating circumstances under New York's Taylor Act, *see* Associated Teachers of Huntington, Inc., 1 PERB ¶399.84 (1968); *compare* Troy Firemen's Ass'n., 2 PERB ¶3077 (1969), *with* Island Free Teachers, 2 PERB ¶3068 (1969). *See also* City of New York v. Social Service Employees' Union, 48 Misc.2d 820, 266 N.Y.S.2d 277 (1965), *aff'd.*, 271 N.Y.S.2d 585, 25 App.Div.2d 953 (1966); City of New York v. DeLury, 75 L.R.R.M. 2275 (N.Y. Sup. Ct. 1970).

5. Some statutes provide that reemployment of strikers is forbidden for a certain period following a strike. Should such provisions be subject to waiver at the discretion of the employer? *Compare* City of Detroit v. Division 26, A.A.S.S.R. & M.C.E., 332 Mich. 237, 51 N.W.2d 228 (1952), *with* East Bay Municipal Employees, Local 390 v. County of Alameda, 83 Cal.Rptr. 503, 3 Cal.App.3d 578 (1970) (agreement to reinstate strikers is binding regardless of contention that illegality of the strike served to negate consideration for the promise) and Durkin v. Board of Commissioners, 48 Wis.2d 112, 180 N.W.2d 1 (1970). Should the answer to this question also govern agreements to pay strikers for time missed while they were on strike? *See* Head v. Special School Dist. No. 1, 288 Minn. 496, 182 N.W.2d 887 (1970), *cert. denied,* 404 U.S. 886 (1971). Should a city be allowed to make special overtime payments to non-striking supervisory employees for emergency work performed during a work stoppage? *See* Mone v. Pezzano, 77 L.R.R.M. 2605 (N.Y. Sup. Ct. 1971).

6. Should an illegal strike constitute a defense to an employer's alleged violation of its statutory duty to bargain? *See* Saginaw Township Board of Educ., 1970 MERC Lab. Op. 127.

7. Union decertification prescribed by statute is a device which has been used by some states to enforce anti-strike provisions of their laws. Maryland Ann. Code, Art. 77, § 160 (1) provides in part:

"(1) *Strikes prohibited; penalties for violation of section.* — Employee organizations shall be prohibited from calling or directing a strike. If an employee organization designated as exclusive representative shall violate the provisions hereof, its designation as exclusive representative shall be revoked by the public school employer, and said employee organization and any other employee organization which violates any of the provisions hereof, shall be ineligible to be designated as exclusive representative for a period of two (2) years thereafter. . . ."

The 1973-1974 school year in Baltimore City had begun without a contract for the employment of teachers, and the Public School Teachers' Ass'n (PSTA) was certified in the fall of 1973 as the exclusive representative of teachers in the Baltimore City Public Schools. Contract negotiations broke down in February, 1974, when some teachers went on strike. In March, a settlement agreement was reached between the union and the school board which contained a nonreprisal clause covering teachers, city employees, and employee organizations involved in the strike. Upon appeal by the rival United Teachers' Guild, the State Board of Education held that the provisions of § 160(1) were mandatory, not subject to waiver by the parties, and decertified the PSTA (GERR No. 619, B-11, F-1). If you were a governmental negotiator, would you view such a result as beneficial or detrimental to the bargaining process?

8. Some state public sector labor relations statutes permit local jurisdictions to establish "mini"-public sector labor laws that are "substantially equivalent" to the state enactments. If a local jurisdiction's ordinance were to provide for the discretionary suspension of a striking union's dues checkoff privilege while the state law mandates automatic revocation of that right, would this difference in treatment constitute a denial of equal protection? *See* Buffalo Teachers Federation v. Helsby, 435 F.Supp. 1098 (S.D.N.Y. 1977). *But cf.* Civil Service Employees v. Helsby, 439 F.Supp. 1272 (S.D.N.Y. 1977).

9. Federal employees are prohibited from striking under 5 U.S.C. § 7311, which precludes the employment of any person who has engaged in a work stoppage against the federal government. Individuals violating § 7311 may additionally be fined and/or imprisoned pursuant to 18 U.S.C. § 1918. A strike authorized or supported by a labor organization constitutes an unfair labor practice under 5 U.S.C. § 7116(b)(7), which was added by the Civil Service Reform Act of 1978. A guilty union may forfeit its recognition

rights pursuant to 5 U.S.C. § 7120(f), with participating workers losing their "employee" status under § 7103(a)(2)(B)(5).

# F. ENFORCEMENT DEVICES

# 1. INJUNCTION

## HOLLAND SCHOOL DISTRICT v. HOLLAND EDUCATION ASSOCIATION

Michigan Supreme Court
380 Mich. 314, 157 N.W.2d 206 (1968)

O'HARA, Justice: — Leave to appeal was granted in this case to review an order of the Court of Appeals. The order denied a stay of proceedings previously granted and denied the prayer of the appellants to dissolve a temporary injunction. The order remanded the cause to the circuit court for hearing on the merits.

This is a chancery case. The constitutional provision (Const. 1963, art. 6, § 5) abolishes the distinctions between law and equity *proceedings.* It did not abolish the historic difference between law and equity. We note this because it is as a Court of Equity we sit in the case at bar. In this, as in all other cases clearly in equity, we hear appeals *de novo.* The reason for this restatement of principle will appear decisionally later in our opinion.

In 1947, the legislature enacted what is generally referred to as the Hutchinson Act. CL 1948, § 423.201 et seq., as amended by PA 1965, No. 379 (Stat. Ann. 1960 Rev. and Stat. Ann. 1968 Cum. Supp. § 17.455[1] et seq.).

We herewith set forth the title to the act as amended by PA 1965, No. 379:

"An act to prohibit strikes by certain public employees; to provide review from disciplinary action with respect thereto; to provide for the mediation of grievances and the holding of elections; to declare and protect the rights and privileges of public employees; and to prescribe means of enforcement and penalties for the violation of the provisions of this act."

Its first section, as amended by PA 1965, No. 379, defines a strike:

"As used in this act the word 'strike' shall mean the concerted failure to report for duty, the wilful absence from one's position, the stoppage of work, or the abstinence in whole or in part from the full, faithful and proper performance of the duties of employment, for the purpose of inducing, influencing or coercing a change in the conditions, or compensation, or the rights, privileges or obligations of employment."

The second section specifies the employees affected:

"No person holding a position by appointment or employment in the government of the state of Michigan, or in the government of any 1 or more of the political subdivisions thereof, or in the public school service, or in any public or special district, or in the service of any authority, commission, or board, or in any other branch of the public service, hereinafter called a 'public employee,' shall strike."

In the late summer of 1967 the teachers in the School District for the City of Holland, Ottawa and Allegan Counties, acting through their duly certified collective bargaining agency, did not resume their teaching duties on the day set by the board of education. If they were employees within the meaning of the statute they were on strike as that term is defined in the statute.

The school district sought an injunction restraining the teachers from withholding their services. A hearing was held and the trial chancellor issued a temporary injunction. The Court of Appeals denied continuation of a stay order previously granted and the prayer to dissolve the injunction. We likewise denied a stay order and declined to dissolve the injunction but granted leave to appeal. The case is before us in that posture. Regretably, we have a meager record, the pleadings, transcribed colloquies between court and counsel, and oral argument. To the extent possible, in order that our decision be precedentially meaningful, we will discuss those basic issues which relate to the legal concepts which we consider must govern, and will not limit ourselves to the narrow question of the propriety of the issuance of the temporary injunction. . . .

It is argued that if the act be constitutional, as we have here held, it is inapplicable to appellants for 2 reasons: first, because appellants are not "employees" within the meaning of the act, and second, that as to teachers, injunctive relief may not be granted because an alternative exclusive remedy is to be found in the act.

We consider the first. The principal thrust of this argument is that, because no contracts of employment were in force between appellants and appellee school district at the time the injunction issued, the involved teachers cannot be employees as a matter of law. It is contended that the school code, specifically CLS 1961, § 240.569, as amended by PA 1965, No. 14 (Stat. Ann. 1968 Rev. § 15.3569), mandates such conclusion. Appellants refer to this argument as the "keystone issue." . . .

In finality, we have come to the conclusion that Garden City School District v. Labor Mediation Board, 358 Mich. 258, of necessity must control. In that case the positions of the parties herein were reversed. In Garden City, the school board sought injunctive restraint against the State labor mediation board in its attempted mediation between teachers and the board. The school board challenged that jurisdiction, in part, on the ground that the school code required written contracts, and that the mediation board had no jurisdiction over the terms thereof. This Court said (pp. 262, 263):

> "Public school teachers are certainly persons 'holding a position by appointment or employment . . . in the public school service.'
>
> "Appellant school board contends, however, that the provisions of the school code of 1955 (CLS 1956, § 340.569 [Stat. Ann. 1959 Rev. § 15.3659]), by providing that teachers shall be hired by written contract, denies jurisdiction to the labor mediation board for mediation as to any terms which might be included in such contracts.
>
> "The written contract provision was first adopted in 1927, and the legislature was certainly familiar with its requirements when it adopted PA 1947, No. 336, which we have quoted. We read these 2 acts together as allowing mediation of salary disputes *in advance* of the determination of the salary provisions of individual teacher contracts." (Emphasis supplied.)

Since this Court concluded that there is jurisdiction to mediate grievances *"in advance* of the determination of salary provisions," it follows that such jurisdiction would necessarily attach in advance of the *executing* of the written contracts themselves, which are required in the case of teachers, by the School Code.

If teachers as we have held *are* subject to the provision of the Hutchinson Act dealing with the mediation of grievances *in advance* of signing written contracts, we can hardly hold with consistency that they *are not* subject to the no-strike provision of the same act for the same reason. We are constrained to hold that appellants were "employees" within the terms of the act.

We next turn to the exclusivity of remedy argument. It is based on § 6 of the act, which provides:

> "Notwithstanding the provisions of any other law, any person holding such a position who, by concerted action with others, and without the lawful approval of his superior, wilfully absents himself from his position, or abstains in whole or in part from the full, faithful and proper performance of his duties for the purpose of inducing, influencing or coercing a change in the conditions or compensation, or the rights, privileges or obligations of employment shall be deemed to be on strike but the person, upon request, shall be entitled to a determination as to whether he did violate the provisions of this act. The request shall be filed in writing, with the officer or body having power to remove or discipline such employee, within 10 days after regular compensation of such employee has ceased or other discipline has been imposed. In the event of such request the officer or body shall within 10 days commence a proceeding for the determination of whether the provisions of this act have been violated by the public employee, in accordance with the law and regulations appropriate to a proceeding to remove the public employee. The proceedings shall be undertaken without unnecessary delay. The decision of the proceeding shall be made within 10 days. If the employee involved is held to have violated this law and his employment terminated or other discipline imposed, he shall have the right of review to the circuit court having jurisdiction of the parties, within 30 days from such decision, for determination whether such decision is supported by competent, material and substantial evidence on the whole record."

In this regard we find ourselves in harmony with the holding of the Court of Appeals:

> "The claim of the defendants that § 6 of the public employees relations act is the only remedy available to the school board cannot be accepted by this Court. Its provisions for discipline of striking public employees and review procedure for them cannot be interpreted to imply removing the historic power of courts to enjoin strikes by public employees. See 31 ALR 2d 1142 and the cases cited therein."

Additionally, we deem it necessary to observe that the whole section deals with after-the-fact remedies by the employee. The withholding of services and the cessation of compensation for services has had to have taken place before the section can operate. It must be said that appellants' position is eminently, indeed inexorably logical in this regard. The section cannot operate within a situation where injunctive restraint of the withholding of such service has already been granted. We would find ourselves in a complete logical self-contradiction if we were to hold as we have here that courts retain their jurisdiction to issue a restraining order against withholding of services by public employees, and at the same time hold § 6 to be an exclusive remedy. The section seems to us to support the conclusion that the legislature intended that injunctive relief could be granted, but that courts are not required to grant it in every case involving a strike by public employees. To attempt to compel legislatively, a court of equity in every instance of a public employee strike to enjoin it would be to destroy the independence of the judicial branch of government.

Having held that the Hutchinson Act is without constitutional infirmity, that appellants are public employees and as such subject to its no-strike provisions, and that the courts have jurisdiction to restrain prohibited strikes by public employees, but are not required to do so in every case, we turn to the question of whether in the case at bar the chancellor had before him that quantum of proof or uncontradicted allegations of fact which would justify the issuance of an injunction in a labor dispute case.

We here hold it is insufficient merely to show that a concert of prohibited action by public employees has taken place and that *ipso facto* such a showing justifies injunctive relief. We so hold because it is basically contrary to public policy in this State to issue injunctions in labor disputes absent a showing of violence, irreparable injury, or a breach of the peace. For a recent discussion of this question, see Cross Company v. UAW Local No. 155 (AFL-CIO), 371 Mich. 184. . . . We further so hold because such an interpretation of the act would as before noted raise a serious constitutional question. . . .

We recognize that great discretion is allowed the trial chancellor in the granting or withholding of injunctive relief. We do not, in ordinary circumstances, substitute our judgment for his. We hold here, however, that there was a lack of proof which would support the issuance of a temporary injunction.

The order of the Court of Appeals, affirming the circuit court is reversed. Hearing the matter as we do *de novo,* we dissolve the temporary injunction hereinbefore issued, and remand to the circuit court for further proceedings. We suggest that such proceedings inquire into whether, as charged by the defendants, the plaintiff school district has refused to bargain in good faith, whether an injunction should issue at all, and if so, on what terms and for what period in light of the whole record to be adduced. No costs, a public question.

BLACK and ADAMS, JJ., concurred with O'HARA, J.

SOURIS, Justice concurring: — I agree that the temporary injunction should be vacated, but for reasons other than those stated by my Brethren.

It is my judgment that the individual defendants had not become employees of the plaintiff school district when the complaint was filed. None had entered into the contracts of employment with the school district our Legislature saw fit to require "be in writing and signed by a majority of the board in behalf of the district, or by the president and secretary, or by the superintendent of schools when so directed at a meeting of the board." Section 569, school code of 1955, as amended (CLS 1961, § 340.569, as amended by PA 1965, No. 14 [Stat. Ann. 1968 Rev. § 15.3569]). Absent such written contracts of employment, the teachers were not yet employees of the school district subject to the "no-strike" provisions of the Hutchinson Act. The act's definition of "strike" clearly supports my conclusion that the individual defendants, not yet employees of the school district, did not "strike" in violation of the act. Until written contracts of employment were executed, they were under no obligation to report for duty; they could not absent themselves from their positions, for they had none; they could not stop work, for they had not begun yet to work nor had they agreed even to work; and, finally, they could not abstain from performing the duties of employment for any purpose, for they had not assumed yet any such duties. . . .

No employment relationship yet having arisen between the individual defendants and the plaintiff school district when this action was filed, it follows that the injunctive order enjoining defendants from concerted abstention from

employment violated the involuntary servitude provisions of the Thirteenth
Amendment of the United States Constitution and Article I, section 9 of our state
Constitution.

I note my agreement with the latter part of Mr. Justice O'Hara's opinion
regarding the judicial inadequacy of the record to support the injunction issued.
In other words, even were these defendants employees, I would agree with Justice
O'Hara that the chancellor, on the record then before him, should not have
granted injunctive relief.

The injunction should be vacated. Defendants should be allowed to tax their
costs.

KAVANAGH, C.J., concurred with SOURIS, J.

BRENNAN, Justice (dissenting): — The tests for granting an injunction *pendente
lite* are different than the criterion used in granting permanent injunctive relief.
We said in the case of Niedzialek v. Barbers Union, 331 Mich. 296, at page 300,
28 LRRM 2626:

> "Under the record before us, it appears beyond cavil that when trial on
> the merits is had the issue will be: Should the picketing by defendants be
> permitted or should it be enjoined? The final result will depend upon the
> proof produced at the hearing bearing upon the issue of whether the
> picketing was pertinent to a lawful labor objective. And the issue may also
> be presented as to whether or not the picketing was peaceful or otherwise.
> Neither of these issues can be decided until there is a hearing on the merits.
> It is also clear, at least reasonably certain, that if in the instant case the
> picketing is continued in the interim until a hearing on the merits plaintiff
> will suffer irreparable injury. The contrary cannot be persuasively urged; nor
> can it reasonably be inferred from the record that enjoining picketing in the
> interim would result in any permanent or irreparable injury to defendants,
> even if the ultimate determination should be that the picketing was lawful.
> It is the settled policy of this Court under such circumstances to grant to a
> litigant who is threatened with irreparable injury temporary injunctive relief
> and thereby preserve the original status quo."

The function of an injunction *pendente lite* is to prevent irreparable harm
which would result from natural delay in reaching a trial on the merits. It may
be argued that in this case the status quo was summer vacation and that the
temporary injunction permitted a change in the status quo by permitting schools
to open at the usual time. But the maintenance of actual status quo is not the
only function of an injunction *pendente lite*. The court can consider whether
under all the facts and circumstances of the case the issuance of the temporary
injunction will maintain the parties in that status which is least likely to do
irreparable injury to the party who ultimately prevails.

In this case, the plaintiff school board will be entitled to a permanent injunction
unless at the trial on the merits the circuit judge should conclude that by reason
of its failure or refusal to do equity to the school teachers, it has forfeited its claim
to equitable relief. Such a judgment cannot be made by the circuit judge until
he has heard testimony on the extent of the bargaining and on the position taken
by both sides at the bargaining table. If at the hearing on the merits it should
appear that the school board's treatment of the teachers has been and is equitable

and reasonable, a permanent injunction will issue and the teachers will have no basis for complaint concerning the temporary injunction.

If, on the other hand, it should appear at the trial on the merits that the school board has not offered to do equity and has not taken a reasonable position at the bargaining table, then a permanent injunction will be denied and the temporary injunction will be dissolved. Under such circumstances the temporary injunction will merely have delayed the strike until the justice of the teachers' cause and the necessity for their strike will have been vindicated in a court of equity. Such delay is a benefit, not an injury, to the teachers.

The temporary injunction should be affirmed and the case remanded to the circuit court for a full evidentiary hearing on the question of whether a final injunction should issue. It is further directed that the court proceed with dispatch so that a decision on a final injunction can be made before the end of the present school year.

## NOTES

1. In Timberlane Regional School Dist. v. Timberlane Regional Educ. Ass'n, 317 A.2d 555, 87 L.R.R.M. 2015 (N.H. 1974), it was held that although the common law of the state made strikes by public employees illegal, the New Hampshire courts should apply equitable principles to determine whether an injunction should lie against such a strike in the absence of any directive from the legislature. The New Hampshire Supreme Court indicated that the trial courts should consider among other factors whether the public health, safety, and welfare would be substantially harmed if the strike were allowed to continue. *Accord,* Oneida School Dist. v. Oneida Educ. Ass'n, 567 P.2d 830, 95 L.R.R.M. 3244 (Idaho 1977).

In Joint School Dist. of Wisconsin Rapids v. Educ. Ass'n., 70 Wis.2d 292, 234 N.W.2d 289 (1975), the Wisconsin Supreme Court held that courts should not enjoin unlawful work stoppages by public employees merely because they are illegal, but should determine in each case whether irreparable harm would result if the particular strike were not enjoined. Nonetheless, the Court affirmed the lower court's issuance of an injunction against a teachers' strike and specifically approved its reliance upon criteria that would appear to indicate that a petitioning school district's burden may not be too substantial.

The primary issue in this case is whether the facts and circumstances warranted a finding of irreparable harm. In ordering the temporary injunction, the trial court concluded that irreparable harm was shown by the following factors: (1) The illegal nature of the strike; (2) inability of the board to operate the school system and thereby meet its statutory duties and responsibilities to the taxpayers in the school district; (3) inability of the students to obtain the benefits of a tax-supported educational process; (4) possible loss of state aids; (5) inability of parents to comply with statutory responsibility to educate their children; and (6) cancellation of athletic events and other school activities.

2. The majority of courts have followed the more traditional view that injunctive relief against unlawful work stoppages is available to governmental employers without a showing of irreparable harm or clean hands. *See, e.g.,* Board of Educ. of Community Unit School Dist. No. 2 v. Redding, 32 Ill.2d 567, 207 N.E.2d 427 (1965); Board of Educ., Borough of Union Beach v. New Jersey Educ. Ass'n., 53 N.J. 29, 247 A.2d 867 (1968). However, since temporary injunctive orders are generally considered to be extraordinary remedies, some courts have ruled that they should be issued ". . . only in cases of great emergency and gravity." *See, e.g.,* City of Rockford v. Firefighters, Local 413, 98 Ill.App.2d 36, 240 N.E.2d 705 (1968). *See also* School Committee, Town of Westerly v. Teachers Ass'n., 299 A.2d 441, 82 L.R.R.M. 2567 (R.I. 1973).

3. In Teaneck v. Firemen's Mut. Benefit Ass'n, Local 42, 1977-78 PBC ¶ 36,258 (N.J. Super. Ct., App. Div. 1978), however, it was decided that a Chancery Court did not have

the authority to condition the issuance of a strike injunction upon the participation of the petitioning public employer in court ordered mediation and negotiation sessions. "[I]n the absence of the most compelling circumstances wholly excusing the grant of an injunction, it is incumbent upon the trial court to prohibit unqualifiedly the illegal activity. For a trial court to do less would be for it to condone illegality and to trade one right for two wrongs." While the Chancery Court may impose appropriate affirmative obligations upon the petitioning public employer in such situations, any breach of such obligations must be remedied through means not affecting the continuation of the order enjoining the unlawful work stoppage.

4. Does a court possess jurisdiction to entertain a complaint in equity to enjoin a strike which is threatened but which has not yet commenced? *See* Commonwealth of Pennsylvania v. Ryan, 327 A.2d 47, 88 L.R.R.M. 2638 (Pa. 1974).

5. In Timberlane Regional School Dist. v. Crompton, 319 A.2d 632, 88 L.R.R.M. 3095 (N.H. 1974), the court ruled that a school district must furnish a teachers' union with the names and addresses of substitute teachers employed during a teachers' strike so that the union can contact the substitute teachers, examine their credentials, and determine whether there have been any statutory violations relating to the hiring of professional strikebreakers.

## 2. THE EFFECT OF ANTI-INJUNCTION STATUTES

In JOINT SCHOOL DIST. OF WISCONSIN RAPIDS V. EDUCATION ASS'N., 70 Wis.2d 292, 234 N.W.2d 289 (1974), the Wisconsin Supreme Court considered the applicability of the Wisconsin anti-injunction statute to public sector labor disputes.

While this court has not previously considered this issue, nearly all courts which have, have concluded that the provisions of state Little Norris-LaGuardia Acts are inapplicable to suits brought by states or their political subdivisions against governmental employees. These decisions follow the rationale of the Supreme Court in [United States v.] United Mine Workers (1947), 330 U.S. 258, 67 S.Ct. 677, 91 L.Ed. 884. In that case, which involved the federal Norris-LaGuardia Act, the court held that a labor dispute under 29 U.S.C.A., p. 53, sec. 113(a) must involve persons who have a certain status or relationship to other persons, and persons does not include the federal government. State courts have held that state copies of the federal act do not apply to public employees in the absence of an express statutory provision that they should so apply.

### NOTES

1. State court decisions regarding this issue have generally followed the *United Mine Workers'* reasoning and concluded that state anti-injunction statutes do not apply to governmental labor disputes. *See, e.g.,* Oneida School Dist. v. Oneida Educ. Ass'n., 567 P.2d 830, 95 L.R.R.M. 3244 (Idaho 1977); City of Minot v. Teamsters, Local 74, 142 N.W.2d 612, 62 L.R.R.M. 2283 (N.D. 1966); City of Pawtucket v. Pawtucket Teachers Alliance, Local 930, 87 R.I. 364, 141 A.2d 624 (1958); Delaware River and Bay Authority v. Int'l. Organization of Masters, Mates & Pilots, 45 N.J. 138, 211 A.2d 789 (1965); Hansen v. Commonwealth, 344 Mass. 214, 181 N.E.2d 843 (1962); Port of Seattle v. ILWU, 52 Wash.2d 317, 324 P.2d 1099 (1958); Rankin v. Shanker, 23 N.Y.2d 111, 242 N.E.2d 802 (1968), *appeal dismissed,* 396 U.S. 120 (1969); City of Los Angeles v. Los Angeles Building and Trades Council, 94 Cal.App.2d 36, 210 P.2d 305 (1949); Anderson Federation of Teachers, Local 519 v. School City of Anderson, 252 Ind. 558, 251 N.E.2d 15 (1969), *cert. denied,* 399 U.S. 928 (1970).

2. Although the Illinois Supreme Court initially ruled in County of Peoria v. Benedict, 47 Ill.2d 166, 265 N.E.2d 141 (1970), *cert. denied,* 402 U.S. 929 (1971), that the Illinois

anti-injunction act did apply to public sector labor disputes, it has since accepted the general view that such enactments are inapplicable to such disputes. *See* City of Pana v. Crowe, 57 Ill.2d 547, 316 N.E.2d 513 (1974). A similar judicial reversal occurred in Minnesota. *Compare* Board of Educ. v. Public School Employees Union, 233 Minn. 141, 45 N.W.2d 797 (1951), *with* Minneapolis Federation of Teachers v. Obermeyer, 275 Minn. 347, 147 N.W.2d 358 (1966).

## 3. CONTEMPT PROCEEDINGS

### STATE OF WISCONSIN v. KING

Wisconsin Supreme Court
82 Wis.2d 124, 262 N.W.2d 80 (1978)

BEILFUSS, Chief Justice: These two cases arise from a labor dispute between the Wisconsin State Employees Union, Council 24, representing the state employees, and the State of Wisconsin. The orders appealed from in both cases deal with contempt of court proceedings for the alleged violations of temporary injunctions which required the employees at two state mental health centers to refrain from picketing and to return to work.

The parties in both cases are the State of Wisconsin, the Union, and certain named officers and employees. The issues in both cases are basically the same and for that reason these issues will be decided in one opinion. . . .

Judge BARDWELL, a circuit judge for Dane county, presided over the Central Center case, and Judge PFIFFNER, the circuit judge for Chippewa county, presided over the Northern Center case. Central Center is located in Dane county and Northern Center in Chippewa county. Both institutions are state owned and operated by the State for the care, consultation, training and education for developmentally disabled persons.

Because of an unresolved labor dispute between the State and the Wisconsin State Employees Union, a statewide strike of state employees represented by the Union was called in the summer of 1977.

In both cases, during the strike, the State of Wisconsin commenced civil actions against the Wisconsin State Employees Union and some of its officers and agents. The State sought an injunction restraining the defendants from engaging in or encouraging others to engage in the strike at the two centers. These actions were commenced by the Attorney General at the request of the secretary of the Department of Administration and the Acting Governor.

On July 11, 1977, a temporary injunction was issued in the Central Center action enjoining the defendants from engaging in or encouraging others to engage in the strike. On July 8, 1977, a like temporary injunction was issued in the Northern Center case.

The employees in both cases ignored the temporary injunction and continued to strike in defiance of the injunction.

The strike was settled on July 17, 1977, and the employees returned to work forthwith. On July 20, 1977 the Attorney General received instructions from the secretary of the Department of Administration to compromise and discontinue all pending litigation pursuant to a non-recrimination clause agreed to by the Union and the State.

However, earlier in the day, on July 20th, the Attorney General had filed petitions for orders to show cause why the Union and designated employees should not be found in contempt of court for violating the temporary injunction. . . .

In Central Center the Attorney General filed a notice to dismiss. At the July 28th hearing Judge BARDWELL denied the motion and issued another order to show cause directing the Union to appear on September 12, 1977, in the contempt proceeding. On August 3d the trial court denied a motion by Thomas King, executive director of the Union, to dismiss the action and all proceedings.

The Attorney General was ordered to serve as special counsel for the September 12th hearing. King's subsequent motion to stay was denied. This court granted a temporary stay on August 31, 1977, and on September 8, 1977 King appealed from the various orders of the trial courts.

The proceedings in the Northern Center case were quite similar, but different in some important aspects. The Attorney General and the Union made motions to dismiss — both motions were denied. Judge PFIFFNER announced the contempt hearing would be held and decided to hear the alleged contempt of one of the employees, Norma Chance. Counsel for the Union moved for substitution of judge, which was denied. Judge PFIFFNER then proceeded to hear the matter. He called and examined witnesses and found Norma Chance in contempt of court for her violation of the temporary injunction. A fine of $10 per day for six days was imposed. Judge PFIFFNER then ordered the Attorney General to represent the court as special counsel in contempt proceedings against other named individuals.

There is no real challenge to the validity of the orders granting the temporary injunctions. The legislature has said it is an unfair labor practice for state employees to strike, — further, the only employees enjoined were those engaged in what may be regarded as essential services for the mentally disadvantaged at Central Center and Northern Center.

The Union and Norma Chance have appealed from the various orders.

The major issue is whether the court can conduct a civil contempt proceeding after the principal action has been settled.

In general there are two categories of contempt: civil and criminal.[2] In some instances the same conduct can constitute civil or criminal contempt. Several general rules have become well accepted. Usually a contempt action which seeks to vindicate the authority and dignity of the court is a criminal contempt, while a contempt which seeks to enforce a private right of one of the parties in an action is a civil contempt. This distinction is often expressed in the results which flow from the particular finding of contempt. If the order is coercive or remedial, the contempt is civil. If the order is purely punitive, the contempt is criminal.

When invoked to enforce a right of a party the contempt power manifests itself in fines or imprisonment (usually of an indeterminate duration), which can be purged if the party found in contempt obeys the order which led to the contempt. For example, if a party desires information and another party refuses to give it in spite of a court order commanding that he do so, that party may be held in civil contempt.[5]

---

[2] There are also direct contempts occurring in the presence of or having an effect upon court proceedings, and indirect contempts occurring outside the presence of the court, but these are not involved here.

[5] Note however that in refusing to obey an order for the benefit of a party the contemnor also challenges the authority of the court. Thus an element of criminal contempt is evident in some civil contempts.

The fact that civil contempts are remedial or coercive, *i. e.,* designed to force one party to accede to another's demand, is demonstrated by the statutory requirement that the sentences be purgable. Civil contempt looks to the present and future and the civil contemnor holds the key to his jail confinement by compliance with the order. On the other hand, the criminal contemnor is brought to account for a completed past action, his sentences are not purgable and are determinate. Criminal contempt is punitive. It is not intended to force the contemnor to do anything for the benefit of another party.

The distinction between the two forms of contempt is important because most of the constitutionally required bill of rights procedures and due process protections apply only to criminal contempt. With the major exception of contempt committed in the physical presence of the trial court (direct contempt), a criminal contemnor is entitled to, *inter alia,* an unbiased judge, *In re Murchison,* 349 U.S. 133, 137, 75 S.Ct. 623, 99 L.Ed. 942 (1955), *Mayberry v. Pennsylvania,* 400 U.S. 455, 91 S.Ct. 499, 27 L.Ed.2d 532 (1971); a presumption of innocence until found guilty beyond a reasonable doubt, a right against self-incrimination, *State ex rel. Rodd v. Verage,* 177 Wis. 295, 317, 187 N.W. 830 (1922), *Gompers v. Bucks Stove & Range Co.,* 221 U.S. 418, 444, 31 S.Ct. 492, 55 L.Ed. 797 (1911); notice of the charges, the right to call witnesses, time to prepare a defense, *Cooke v. United States,* 267 U.S. 517, 537, 45 S.Ct. 390, 69 L.Ed. 767 (1925); and a right to a jury trial if the sentence is for more than six months, *Cheff v. Schnackenberg,* 384 U.S. 373, 86 S.Ct. 1523, 16 L.Ed.2d 629 (1966), *Bloom v. Illinois,* 391 U.S. 194, 210, 88 S.Ct. 1477, 20 L.Ed.2d 522 (1968).

The courts have evidently declined to extend these rights to the civil contemnor, not because he may not serve sentences as long or even longer than those served by a criminal contemnor but on the theory that these rights are unnecessary because he holds the key to his confinement.

In these cases both the parties and both the trial courts agree that the procedures utilized were for civil contempt. In the cases at hand the acts complained of could have been the basis for criminal contempt. Although everyone concerned proclaims this to be a civil contempt, all the indicia of contempt point toward criminal contempt. These cases would have presented no foreseeable problems if they had been brought as criminal contempt.

On July 17, 1977, the strike by the Wisconsin State Employees Union against the State was settled. On July 20, 1977, the Attorney General petitioned the circuit courts for Dane and Chippewa counties to find the Union in contempt. Therefore at the time the contempt proceeding was commenced it was impossible to use it as a tool to enforce the injunction. If the strike had still been ongoing the contempt power could have been used for a coercive or remedial end, namely to get the workers at the Central and Northern Centers back on their jobs. However, by July 20th the strike had been settled, the workers were back on their jobs, and coercive or remedial action could serve no purpose at that time. The only purpose for a contempt action brought at the time the contempt was sought in these cases was punishment to vindicate the authority of the court.

In *Gompers v. Bucks Stove & Range Co.,* 221 U.S. 418, 31 S.Ct. 492, 55 L.Ed. 797 (1911), the United States Supreme Court held that settlement of the underlying controversy required dismissal of civil contempt grounded in that controversy. Thus, under this rule, civil contempt begun before or, as here, after the settlement of the underlying dispute, is moot because it cannot achieve a coercive or remedial effect.

The State argues that *Gompers* may be distinguished. It cites the following language from *Gompers:*

"When the main case was settled, every proceeding which was dependent upon it, or a part of it, was also necessarily settled — of course without prejudice to the power and right of the court to punish for contempt by proper proceedings." 221 U.S. at 451, 31 S.Ct. at 502.

The State contends that this contempt proceeding is in fact the "proper proceeding" referred to in *Gompers;* that it is a separate and independent proceeding prosecuted by the court on its own motion. The State, however, neglects to include the next sentence from *Gompers,* which provides:

"If this had been a separate and independent proceeding at law for criminal contempt, to vindicate the authority of the court . . . it could not, in any way, have been affected by any settlement which the parties to the equity cause made in their private litigation." 221 U.S. at 451, 31 S.Ct. at 502.

The separate proceeding referred to in *Gompers* is one in criminal contempt, not civil contempt as a supplementary proceeding in a civil action.

The State's next response goes to the heart of the issue — Wisconsin has explicitly rejected the *Gompers* holding. *Wisconsin E. R. Board v. Allis-Chalmers Workers' Union,* 249 Wis. 590, 599, 25 N.W.2d 425 (1946); *State ex rel. Rodd v. Verage,* 177 Wis. 295, 312-13, 187 N.W. 830 (1922). In doing so Wisconsin has created a unique third category of contempt — civil contempt with punitive sanctions.

In the *Rodd Case* the contemnor in a civil contempt was given a four month sentence with no opportunity to purge. In spite of the fact that the contemnor did not hold the keys to the jail as is normally required in civil contempt, the court held that the result was permissible in a civil contempt proceeding:

"So we arrive at the conclusion that where a court in order to protect private rights issues its order restraining the commission of certain acts, and it subsequently is made to appear to the court that one has committed the acts prohibited under circumstances which indicate a purpose on his part to disregard the order of the court and to continue in the performance of the acts prohibited, and that such continued conduct will injuriously affect the rights of a party to the action, the court may, as a remedial measure civil in character and for the purpose of preventing further injury to a suitor, imprison the contemnor; and especially is that so when the court is moved to action on the application of the aggrieved party. The dominant character of the imprisonment is remedial and coercive, although a punitive effect may also result." 177 Wis. at 314, 187 N.W. at 838.

On its language alone the *Rodd Case* is distinguishable because there is at least a colorable claim in it that the imprisonment is remedial and coercive in that there was a likelihood of continued violation of the court's order. But in these cases the orders — the injunctions — have become ineffectual because the parties have settled. Any sentence here, purgable or not, cannot be remedial because there is no threat nor possibility of continued violation. Any sentence here can only be punitive.

However, language in other cases dealing with this third category of contempt indicates that this court has permitted the imposition of punitive sanctions in civil contempt which have no remedial or coercive attributes. *Emerson v. Huss,* 127 Wis. 215, 106 N.W. 518 (1906); *Wisconsin E. R. Board v. Mews,* 29 Wis.2d 44, 138 N.W.2d 147 (1965).

If we adhere to the continued existence of this third category then the circuit courts should be affirmed. On the other hand, if the court accepts the Union's position and eliminates this category, then the State may still proceed in contempt but must do so in a new, criminal proceeding. We conclude that the latter course is preferable.

In support of this position is the fact that the legislature no longer recognizes punitive sanctions for civil contempt. Sec. 295.02(5), Stats. (1975), effective June 14, 1976, provides that no person shall be fined or imprisoned for civil contempt except as specified in subs. (1) and (2) which concern remedial and coercive measures and do not mention punitive actions.

The courts of this state and those of many other jurisdictions have long held that they possess an inherent contempt power over their branch of the government to maintain decorum and see that their orders are carried out. *State ex rel. Rodd v. Verage,* 177 Wis. 295, 305-06, 187 N.W. 830 (1922); *In re Hon. Chas. E. Kading,* 70 Wis.2d 508, 543b, 235 N.W.2d 409, 238 N.W.2d 63, 239 N.W.2d 297 (1975); *Ferris v. State ex rel. Maass,* 75 Wis.2d 542, 546, 249 N.W.2d 789 (1977); *Anderson v. Dunn,* 19 U.S. (6 Wheat.) 204, 226-27, 5 L.Ed. 242 (1821); *Doyle v. London Guarantee Co.,* 204 U.S. 599, 607, 27 S.Ct. 313, 51 L.Ed. 641 (1907).

However, this court has just as consistently held that this power is subject to reasonable legislative regulation:

"Doubtless, this power may be regulated, and the manner of its exercise prescribed, by statute, but certainly it cannot be entirely taken away, nor can its efficiency be so impaired or abridged as to leave the court without power to compel the due respect and obedience which is essential to preserve its character as a judicial tribunal." *State ex rel. Attorney General v. Circuit Court for Eau Claire County,* 97 Wis. 1, 8, 72 N.W. 193, 194 (1897). *See also, Upper Lakes Shipping v. Seafarers I. Union,* 22 Wis.2d 7, 17, 125 N.W.2d 324 (1963).

The Union cites the following language from a recent case in support of its claim that punitive sanctions are no longer allowed:

"While this court has reserved its traditional inherent powers in this area. . . . The differences between civil and criminal contempt are and have been statutorily defined." *Ferris v. State ex rel. Maass, supra,* 75 Wis.2d at 546, 249 N.W.2d at 791.

This language falls far short of indicating any abdication of the court's inherent powers. We believe the legislative prohibition of punitive civil contempt is a reasonable regulation and should be followed.

Punitive sanctions in civil contempt are contrary to the well recognized opposite natures of civil and criminal contempt. As this court recently stated: "Imprisonment under civil contempt . . . is coercive, whereas imprisonment for criminal contempt is punitive." *Ferris, supra,* 75 Wis.2d at 545, 249 N.W.2d at 791. We now conclude those cases which hold that courts in civil contempt may impose purely punitive sanctions are anomalies and should no longer be considered authority.

This holding will produce uniformity in the Wisconsin decisions which have seen the court declare in the *Rodd Case* that civil contempt may be punitive, while three years later the same court stated:

"While the proceeding is denominated a civil contempt and the procedure is that prescribed by ch. 295, nevertheless it was in the nature of a proceeding for criminal contempt. . . . The real character of the proceeding is to be determined by the relief sought. The relief sought here was not to enforce a private right but to punish the contemnor for a past offense." *Wetzler v. Glassner,* 185 Wis. 593, 595-96, 201 N.W. 740, 741 (1925).

Another reason for supporting this distinction is as noted above — criminal contemnors have the benefit of a multitude of constitutional procedural rights. The reason that civil contemnors do not possess the same rights is that they hold the keys to their own jails. A civil contemnor in Wisconsin who is fined or imprisoned for purely punitive reasons and does not have the ability to purge probably can make a good case for reversal on the grounds that he is entitled to the constitutional safeguards of the criminal contempt procedure.

The ultimate question in this case is whether the authority and dignity of the circuit courts for Dane and Chippewa counties can be vindicated if the concept of civil contempt with purely punitive sanctions is rejected. Sec. 295.02(6), Stats., declares that:

"Nothing in this section may prohibit the court from imposing punishment of fine or imprisonment for criminal contempt under ss. 256.03 to 256.07."

Although the procedure required in criminal contempt is much more cumbersome, costly and time-consuming, it is not the policy of the law to choose expediency over due process when it should be afforded.

We conclude in the cases before us that the remedy of civil contempt expired when the actions were settled and the parties moved to dismiss the actions. It follows therefore that the civil contempt proceedings in both cases must be dismissed.

Because we have concluded the civil contempt proceedings must be dismissed, the other issues raised in these appeals are not considered.

Orders reversed and remanded for proceedings not inconsistent with the opinion. No costs to be taxed.

## SCHOOL COMMITTEE OF NEW BEDFORD v. DLOUHY

Massachusetts Supreme Judicial Court
360 Mass. 109, 271 N.E.2d 655 (1971)

Quirico, Justice: These are two bills in equity entered in the Superior Court on September 16, 1968, and September 3, 1969, respectively. The plaintiffs in each bill are (a) the school committee of New Bedford (school committee) and (b) the city of New Bedford (city). The defendants in each bill are (a) certain named persons who are made defendants individually and in their representative capacities as officers and members of an unincorporated association (Association) which is the collective bargaining agent for all of the schoolteachers employed by the city, (b) all the members of the Association, and (c) Frederick J. Lambert who is described as the Director of Field Services of the Massachusetts Teachers Association of which the Association in New Bedford is an affiliate.

The plaintiffs seek by each bill to restrain and enjoin the defendants other than Lambert from engaging in a work stoppage or withholding of their services from the city, or engaging in or inducing or encouraging the withholding of services by the teachers of the city's school department. They also seek by each bill to restrain and enjoin the defendant Lambert from inducing or encouraging a work stoppage or withholding of services by these teachers. In each case the court granted such relief in the following stages: by a restraining order, by a preliminary injunction, and by a final decree. The final decree in the 1969 case further held forty-eight defendants, including Lambert, in civil contempt of court and imposed compensatory fines on them, and also held Lambert in criminal contempt of court and imposed a fine on him therefor. The cases are before us on the defendants' appeals from the final decrees in both cases.

1. *Appeal from Final Decree in 1968 Case.* The final decree in the 1968 case permanently enjoined the defendants other than Lambert "from engaging in a work stoppage or withholding of services . . . or inducing or encouraging the withholding of services by the teachers of the New Bedford School Department," and it permanently enjoined Lambert "from inducing or encouraging a work stoppage or withholding of services by teachers employed by the City of New Bedford." The decree states that "all parties by counsel in open court" consented to its entry. "The decree appearing to be made by consent, the appeal cannot be sustained." Winchester v. Winchester, 121 Mass. 127, 128. See Evans v. Hamlin, 164 Mass. 239, 240; New York Cent. & Hudson River R.R. v. T. Stuart & Son Co., 260 Mass. 242, 248; Fishman v. Alberts, 321 Mass. 280, 281-282. The final decree in the 1968 case, having been entered by consent of all of the parties, must stand.

2. *Appeal from Final Decree in 1969 Case — Permanent Injunction.* Paragraphs numbered 1 and 2 of the final decree in the 1969 case permanently enjoin the defendants in that case in substantially the same language used in the final decree entered in the 1968 case discussed above. There is a difference in the names of the persons, other than Lambert, who are enjoined, but that difference does not affect our decision. . . . What we have said above with reference to the final decree in the 1968 case applies equally to them.

3. *Appeal from Final Decree in 1969 Case — Adjudication of Civil Contempt.* On September 3, 1969, a judge of the Superior Court issued a restraining order against the defendants in the 1969 case, using therein the same language which he later incorporated in the first two numbered paragraphs of the final decree discussed above. On September 4, 1969, the plaintiffs filed a petition alleging that the defendant Lambert and 183 named teachers who were members of the New Bedford Educators' Association had violated the restraining order and asked that Lambert and such teachers be adjudged in contempt for such violation. When this petition was reached for hearing, counsel for the defendants stated to the court: "[M]y clients are all now, each and individually, every one of them, prepared and ready to plead guilty to what they understand is a charge of civil contempt." Thereupon the judge stated: "[T]he clerk will call the name of each person who has been cited for contempt. The clerk will inquire after the name has been called: Do you admit the allegation of contempt, or do you deny it? If you admit it, then I want each defendant as their name is called, to say, 'I admit.' If you deny it, then as your name is called, you say, 'I deny.' " The clerk then called the names of Lambert and of forty-seven other persons who were defendants in the petition for contempt. As each name was called, the person whose name was called replied, "I admit" or "I admit it."

. . . By reason of their admission of guilt of civil contempt, such defendants cannot now require us to decide the many legal and constitutional, but nonjurisdictional, questions which they raised before the trial judge prior to admitting their guilt. . . .

4. *Appeal from Final Decree in 1969 Case: Amounts of Fines Imposed for Civil Contempt.* As a part of the final decree which adjudged certain defendants guilty of civil contempt, the court also imposed a fine of $50,000 on them and the defendant Lambert. As to each of these fines the decree stated that it was "to compensate the . . . [city] for damages as a result of said civil contempt." It also

provided that the payment of $50,000 to the city "by one or all of said respondents on the civil contempts shall constitute full compliance with said orders for payment for civil contempts."

After such defendants admitted their guilt of civil contempt and before fixing the amount of the fines therefor, the judge held a hearing to receive evidence on the amount of damages which their contempt had caused to the city. The superintendent of schools testified that despite the work stoppage, many principals, directors, teachers, substitute teachers and cafeteria workers reported for work at schools which had to be closed and those persons had to be paid, that school buses were operated to the schools which had to be closed, that there were charges for utilities serving the schools on the days they had to be closed, and that the days of school thus lost would have to be made up later at which time the same expenditures would be required. He estimated that the total expense to the city for these categories would be about $79,172 [4] and that there were some variables and additional items of expense to the city which he could not compute at that time but which he thought would bring the total expense to the city to $100,000. He believed the latter figure to be a "fair figure" and a "conservative figure."

After hearing the evidence and statements by counsel the judge reviewed the background of the controversy and then stated: "It is my judgment that the responsibility for the situation that arose must be shared equally by the . . . [plaintiffs] as well as by the . . . [defendants]. . . . I find on the evidence that the loss to the . . . [city] is $100,000." He then imposed the fines of $50,000. The judge's finding that the loss to the city was $100,000 was supported by the testimony of the superintendent of schools who was the only witness on that subject.

"In cases of civil contempt such as the one before us, a fine may be assessed for the benefit of a party who has suffered injury because of the contempt. As are damages in tort, the fine is designed to compensate the injured party for actual losses sustained by reason of the contumacious conduct of the defendant, i.e., for the pecuniary injury caused by the act of disobedience." Lyon v. Bloomfield, 355 Mass. 738, 744; Root v. MacDonald, 260 Mass. 344, 361-365. The fine in such a case may also be designed to reimburse the plaintiff for counsel fees and other expenses incurred in enforcing his rights. Grunberg v. Louison, 343 Mass. 729, 736; Parker v. United States, 126 F.2d 370, 379-380 (1st Cir.). . . .

5. *Appeal from Final Decree in 1969 Case: Adjudication that Lambert is Guilty of Criminal Contempt.* After the judge heard the evidence from the superintendent of schools on the damages sustained by the city, and before he announced his decision thereon, he asked counsel for the plaintiffs what the evidence he "would have presented to the Court in the event of a trial . . . [would disclose] as to the leader in this strike, the guiding influence." Counsel answered in part that "the officers of the Association and Mr. Lambert would have been shown to have influenced the events of the last few days." The judge asked counsel for the defendants for some background information on Lambert and it was given to him. Without further hearing or evidence the judge then announced his finding that "Lambert was the director of the conduct of the other defendants and all the members of the New Bedford Educators Association . . .

---

[4] In arriving at this figure the superintendent said he was including payments of $60 a day to forty principals for eight days each and he computed this item at $11,200. The correct computation should be $19,200. With this correction, the categories of damages to which he testified included the following: $64,000 paid to teachers, $960 for school buses, $19,200 paid to principals, and $4,992 paid to cafeteria workers. These items alone amount to a total of $89,152 instead of the $79,172 stated by the witness.

[and] that his directing provided irresponsible leadership." He also stated: "I find Frederick J. Lambert guilty of criminal and civil contempt. On the criminal contempt, I impose a . . . fine of $5,000." This finding and fine were incorporated in the final decree, in addition to the findings and fines on civil contempt.

The defendant Lambert's admission of guilt was limited to civil contempt. He was never asked specifically whether he admitted guilt of criminal contempt, and he never specifically admitted such guilt. He was never put to trial on the question of criminal contempt, and no evidence was presented against him on that charge. The burden of proving that charge was on the plaintiffs, and it was not incumbent on Lambert to disprove it. This was not a case of a contempt which had occurred or been committed in the presence of the judge. It was a contempt sometimes referred to or described as an "indirect or constructive" contempt to distinguish it from a "direct" contempt committed in the presence of a judge who may act thereon summarily. Berlandi v. Commonwealth, 314 Mass. 424, 445-446.

"The punishment of . . . [criminal contempt] is solely for the vindication of public authority and the majesty of the law. In general, the proceedings leading up to the punishment should be in accordance with the principles which govern the practice in criminal cases. In a broad sense, the prosecution of such an offender is a criminal case, and the sentence to punishment is a judgment." Hurley v. Commonwealth, 188 Mass. 443, 445. Woodbury v. Commonwealth, 295 Mass. 316, 323. Dolan v. Commonwealth, 304 Mass. 325, 327. In such a prosecution, "the accused should be advised of the charges and have a reasonable opportunity to meet them by way of defense or explanation." Cooke v. United States, 267 U.S. 517, 537; Garabedian v. Commonwealth, 336 Mass. 119, 124-125.

The proceedings which concluded with the finding that Lambert was guilty of criminal contempt and the imposition of a fine of $5,000 on him did not comply with the basic requirements applicable to such cases. That adjudication therefore cannot stand.

In summary, (a) the final decree in the 1968 case is affirmed with costs of appeal to the plaintiffs, and (b) the final decree in the 1969 case is modified by striking therefrom so much of paragraph numbered 3 as holds the defendant Lambert guilty of criminal contempt and by striking therefrom paragraph numbered 4 imposing a fine of $5,000 on him for criminal contempt; as thus modified that final decree is affirmed.

So ordered.

## NOTES

1. In City of Wilmington v. General Teamsters, Local 326, 321 A.2d 123, 86 L.R.R.M. 2959 (Del. 1974), the Court considered the nature of contempt proceedings which followed defiance by city dockworkers of a court-ordered injunction. Concluding that the contempt in the case consisted of a combination of civil and criminal elements, the Court held that where the criminal elements predominated, they would control procedure on review, so that the city had no appeal from findings of not guilty with respect to the criminal contempt portion of the case. However, this did not preclude city appeal from the civil aspects of the proceeding. On this issue, the Court found the union responsible for the action of its members who had engaged in the unlawful strike, rejecting the union leadership's argument that it had "lost control" of the membership and should thus not be found responsible. Regarding the latter issue, see also Labor Relations Comm. v. Boston Teachers Union, Local 66, 371 N.E.2d 761, 97 L.R.R.M. 2507 (Mass. 1977), wherein the Court sustained civil contempt citations against union officers who failed to affirmatively endeavor to prevent an enjoined work stoppage.

2. In Board of Junior College Dist. No. 508 v. Cook County College Teachers Union, Local 1600, 126 Ill.App.2d 418, 262 N.E.2d 125 (1970), *cert. denied,* 402 U.S. 998 (1971), the court rejected a joint request made by the employer and the union during criminal contempt proceedings to dismiss the temporary injunction, stating: "Under no theory can a party that obtains an injunction bind the issuing court with condonation of contemptuous or illegal acts of those who violate the lower court's order. To give effect to such a theory would usurp the highest function of our courts."

3. Perhaps the most frequently litigated issue pertaining to the contempt process concerns the right of the charged party to a jury trial. It is established that in the case of purely civil contempt, the right to trial by jury is not constitutionally mandated and arises, if at all, statutorily. Shillitani v. United States, 384 U.S. 364, 86 S.Ct. 1531, 16 L.Ed.2d 622 (1966). As was noted in the *King* decision, a jury right attaches to indirect criminal contempt proceedings that are deemed "serious." Bloom v. Illinois, 391 U.S. 194, 88 S.Ct. 1477, 20 L.Ed.2d 522 (1968). The seriousness of the offense is usually determined by the penalty actually imposed (due to the plenary power of the court to administer criminal contempt sanctions), and a jury trial is not required for contempts not involving at least six months of incarceration. Cheff v. Schnackenberg, 384 U.S. 373, 86 S.Ct. 1523, 16 L.Ed.2d 629 (1966). Where lesser penalties are imposed and there is no statute providing a jury right, most courts have held that a jury trial is not required in criminal contempt cases. *See, e.g., In re* Block, 50 N.J. 494, 236 A.2d 589 (1967); City of New York v. DeLury, 23 N.Y.2d 175, 243 N.E.2d 128 (1968), *appeal dismissed,* 394 U.S. 455 (1969); and State v. Heath, 177 N.W.2d 751, 75 L.R.R.M. 2204 (N.D. 1970). It is interesting to note in this context that Sections 11 and 12 of the Norris-LaGuardia Act, 29 U.S.C. §§ 111 & 112, providing for a jury trial plus a change of presiding judge in any indirect contempt proceeding arising from the failure to obey an injunction issued by a federal court in a labor dispute, were repealed in 1948.

4. Since a contempt proceeding depends substantially upon the discretion of the presiding judge, the trial record is generally scrutinized on appeal to insure against judicial bias. *See In re* Murchison, 349 U.S. 133, 75 S.Ct. 623, 99 L.Ed. 942 (1955). *See also* Board of Educ. v. Morton Council West Suburban Teachers, Local 571, 50 Ill.2d 258, 278 N.E.2d 769 (1972), wherein the Court reversed criminal contempt convictions arising from the violation of an injunction restraining an illegal teachers' strike, where a request for a change of venue, based solely upon allegations of prejudice on the part of the trial judge, had been improperly denied.

5. Punishment for criminal contempt is usually permitted only for the wilful violation of an injunctive order. *See, e.g., In re* Jersey City Educ. Ass'n, 115 N.J. Super. 42, 278 A.2d 206 (App. Div.), *cert. denied,* 404 U.S. 948 (1971). However, knowledge of an injunction may be implied due to news media coverage. *Id.*

6. Penalties imposed for contempt are subject to appellate review, but it has been held that the imposition of greater sanctions by a reviewing court, without adequate reasons being adduced, constitutes reversible error. *See* Dade County Classroom Teachers v. Rubin, 258 So.2d 275 (Fla. Dist. Ct. App. 1972), *citing* North Carolina v. Pearce, 395 U.S. 711, 89 S.Ct. 2072, 23 L.Ed.2d 656 (1969).

7. A contempt proceeding generally may not be used as a vehicle for contesting the validity of the underlying injunction. *See, e.g.,* County of Peoria v. Benedict, 47 Ill.2d 166, 265 N.E.2d 141 (1970), *cert. denied,* 402 U.S. 929 (1971); Dade County Classroom Teachers Ass'n v. Rubin, 238 So.2d 284 (Fla. 1970), *cert. denied,* 400 U.S. 1009 (1971).

# 4. DISMISSALS, FINES, DAMAGES AND TAXPAYER SUITS

## HORTONVILLE JOINT SCHOOL DIST. NO. 1 v. HORTONVILLE EDUC. ASS'N

United States Supreme Court
426 U.S. 482, 96 S. Ct. 2308, 49 L. Ed. 2d 1 (1976)

MR. CHIEF JUSTICE BURGER delivered the opinion of the Court.
We granted certiorari in this case to determine whether school board members,

vested by state law with the power to employ and dismiss teachers, could, consistent with the Due Process Clause of the Fourteenth Amendment, dismiss teachers engaged in a strike prohibited by state law.

## I

The petitioners are a Wisconsin school district, the seven members of its school board, and three administrative employees of the district. Respondents are teachers suing on behalf of all teachers in the district and the Hortonville Education Association (HEA), the collective-bargaining agent for the district's teachers.

During the 1972-1973 school year Hortonville teachers worked under a master collective-bargaining agreement; negotiations were conducted for renewal of the contract, but no agreement was reached for the 1973-1974 school year. The teachers continued to work while negotiations proceeded during the year without reaching agreement. On March 18, 1974, the members of the teachers' union went on strike, in direct violation of Wisconsin law. On March 20, the district superintendent sent all teachers a letter inviting them to return to work; a few did so. On March 23, he sent another letter, asking the 86 teachers still on strike to return, and reminding them that strikes by public employees were illegal; none of these teachers returned to work. After conducting classes with substitute teachers on March 26 and 27, the Board decided to conduct disciplinary hearings for each of the teachers on strike. Individual notices were sent to each teacher setting hearings for April 1, 2, and 3.

On April 1, most of the striking teachers appeared before the Board with counsel. Their attorney indicated that the teachers did not want individual hearings, but preferred to be treated as a group. Although counsel agreed that the teachers were on strike, he raised several procedural objections to the hearings. He also argued that the Board was not sufficiently impartial to exercise discipline over the striking teachers and that the Due Process Clause of the Fourteenth Amendment required an independent, unbiased decisionmaker. An offer of proof was tendered to demonstrate that the strike had been provoked by the Board's failure to meet teachers' demands, and petitioner's counsel asked to cross-examine Board members individually. The Board rejected the request, but permitted counsel to make the offer of proof, aimed at showing that the Board's contract offers were unsatisfactory, that the Board used coercive and illegal bargaining tactics, and that teachers in the district had been locked out by the Board.

On April 2, the Board voted to terminate the employment of striking teachers, and advised them by letter to that effect. However, the same letter invited all teachers on strike to reapply for teaching positions. One teacher accepted the invitation and returned to work; the Board hired replacements to fill the remaining positions.

Respondents then filed suit against petitioners in state court, alleging, among other things, that the notice and hearing provided them by the Board were inadequate to comply with due process requirements. The trial court granted the Board's motion for summary judgment on the due process claim. . . .

On appeal, the Wisconsin Supreme Court reversed. Hortonville Education Ass'n v. Hortonville Joint School District No. 1, 66 Wis. 2d 469, 225 N. W. 2d

658 (1975). On the single issue now presented it held that the Due Process Clause of the Fourteenth Amendment to the Federal Constitution required that the teachers' conduct and the Board's response be evaluated by an impartial decisionmaker other than the Board. The rationale of the Wisconsin Supreme Court appears to be that although the teachers had admitted being on strike, and although the strike violated Wisconsin law, the Board had available other remedies than dismissal, including an injunction prohibiting the strike, a call for mediation, or continued bargaining. Relying on our holding in Morrissey v. Brewer, 408 U. S. 471 (1972), the Wisconsin court then held "it would seem essential, even in cases of undisputed or stipulated facts, that an impartial decision maker be charged with the responsibility of determining what action shall be taken on the basis of those facts." 66 Wis. 2d, at 493. . . .

Since it concluded that state law provided no adequate remedy, the Wisconsin Supreme Court fashioned one it thought necessary to comply with federal due process principles. To leave with the Board "[a]s much control as possible . . . to set policy and manage the school," the court held that the Board should after notice and hearing make the decision to fire in the first instance. A teacher dissatisfied with the Board's decision could petition any court of record in the county for a *de novo* hearing on *all* issues; the trial court would "resolve any factual disputes and provide the reasonable disposition." 66 Wis. 2d, at 498. The Wisconsin Supreme Court recognized that this remedy was "not ideal because a court may be required to make public policy decisions that are better left to a legislative or administrative body." *Ibid.* But it would suffice "until such time and only until such time as the legislature provides a means to establish a forum that will meet the requirements of due process." . . .

## II

. . . .

The sole issue in this case is whether the Due Process Clause of the Fourteenth Amendment prohibits this school board from making the decision to dismiss teachers admittedly engaged in a strike and persistently refusing to return to their duties. The Wisconsin Supreme Court held that state law prohibited the strike and that termination of the striking teachers' employment was within the Board's statutory authority. 66 Wis. 2d, at 479-481. . . .

## A

Respondents argue, and the Wisconsin Supreme Court held, that the choice presented for the Board's decision is analogous to that involved in revocation of parole in Morrissey v. Brewer, 408 U. S. 471 (1972), that the decision could be made only by an impartial decisionmaker, and that the Board was not impartial. In *Morrissey* the Court considered a challenge to state procedures employed in revoking the parole of state prisoners. There we noted that the parole revocation decision involved two steps: first an inquiry whether the parolee had in fact violated the conditions of his parole; second, determining whether violations found were serious enough to justify revocation of parole and the consequent deprivation of the parolee's conditional liberty. Nothing in this case is analogous to the first step in *Morrissey,* since the teachers admitted to being on strike. But respondents argue that the School Board's decision in this case is, for constitutional purposes, the same as the second aspect of the decision to revoke parole. The Board cannot make a "reasonable" decision on this issue, the Wisconsin Supreme Court held and respondents argue, because its members are biased in some fashion that the due process guarantees of the Fourteenth Amendment prohibit.[3]

*Morrissey* arose in a materially different context. We recognized there that a parole violation could occur at a place distant from where the parole revocation decision would finally be made; we also recognized the risk of factual error, such as misidentification. To minimize this risk, we held "due process requires that after the arrest [for parole violation], the determination that reasonable ground exists for revocation of parole should be made by someone not directly involved in the case." 408 U.S., at 485. But this holding must be read against our earlier discussion in *Morrissey* of the parole officer's role as counselor and confidant to the parolee; it is this same officer who, on the basis of preliminary information, decides to arrest the parolee. A school board is not to be equated with the parole officer as an arresting officer; the school board is more like the parole board, for it has ultimate plenary authority to make its decisions derived from the state legislature. General language about due process in a holding concerning revocation of parole is not a reliable basis for dealing with the school board's power as an employer to dismiss teachers for cause. We must focus more clearly on first, the nature of the bias respondents attribute to the Board, and second, the nature of the interests at stake in this case.

## B

Respondents' argument rests in part on doctrines that have no application to this case. They seem to argue the Board members had some personal or official stake in the decision whether the teachers should be dismissed, comparable to the stake the Court saw in Tumey v. Ohio, 273 U. S. 510 (1927), or Ward v. Village of Monroeville, 409 U. S. 57 (1972); see also Gibson v. Berryhill, 411 U. S. 564 (1973), and that the Board has manifested some personal bitterness toward the teachers, aroused by teacher criticism of the Board during the strike, *see, e.g.,* Taylor v. Hayes, 418 U. S. 488 (1974); Mayberry v. Pennsylvania, 400 U. S. 455 (1971). Even assuming those cases state the governing standards when the decisionmaker is a public employer dealing with employees, the teachers did not

---

[3] Respondents argue that the requirement that the Board's decision be "reasonable" is in fact a requirement of state law. From that premise and from the premise that the "reasonableness" determination requires an evaluation of the Board's negotiating stance, they argue that nothing but decision and review de novo by an "uninvolved" party will secure their right to a "reasonable" decision. See Withrow v. Larkin, 421 U. S. 35, n. 25, at 58-59 (1975). It is clear, however, that the Wisconsin Supreme Court held that the Board's decision must be "reasonable," not by virtue of state law, but because of its reading of the Due Process Clause of the Fourteenth Amendment. First, the Wisconsin court relied largely upon cases interpreting the Federal Constitution in this aspect of its holding. See 66 Wis. 2d, at 493. Second, the only state case the Wisconsin Supreme Court cited for more than a general statement of federal requirements was Durkin v. Board of Police & Fire Commissioners, 48 Wis. 2d 112, 180 N. W. 2d 1 (1970). There the Wisconsin Supreme Court interpreted a state statute that gave firemen and policemen the right to appeal a decision of the Board of Police and Fire Commissioners to a state court; the statute expressly provided that the court was to determine whether "upon the evidence the order of the Board was reasonable." 180 N. W. 2d, at 3. See Wis. Stat. Ann. § 62.13(5)(i). There is no comparable statutory provision giving teachers the right to review by this standard. Finally, to impose a "reasonableness" requirement, or any other test that looks to evaluation by another entity, makes semantic sense only where review is contemplated by the statute. Review, and the standard for review, are concepts that go hand in hand. The Wisconsin Supreme Court concluded both that review of the Board's decision was necessary and that a "reasonableness" standard was appropriate as a result of its reading of the Due Process Clause of the Fourteenth Amendment.

show, and the Wisconsin courts did not find, that the Board members had the kind of personal or financial stake in the decision that might create a conflict of interest, and there is nothing in the record to support charges of personal animosity. . . .

The only other factor suggested to support the claim of bias is that the School Board was involved in the negotiations that preceded and precipitated the striking teachers' discharge. Participation in those negotiations was a statutory duty of the Board. The Wisconsin Supreme Court held that this involvement, without more, disqualified the Board from deciding whether the teachers should be dismissed. . . . Mere familiarity with the facts of a case gained by an agency in the performance of its statutory role does not, however, disqualify a decisionmaker. Withrow v. Larkin, 421 U. S. 35, 47 (1975); Federal Trade Comm'n v. Cement Institute, 333 U. S. 683, 700-703 (1948). Nor is a decisionmaker disqualified simply because he has taken a position, even in public, on a policy issue related to the dispute, in the absence of a showing that he is not "capable of judging a particular controversy fairly on the basis of its own circumstances." United States v. Morgan, 313 U. S. 409, 421 (1941); see also *FTC v. Cement Institute, supra,* 701.

Respondents' claim and the Wisconsin Supreme Court's holding reduce to the argument that the Board was biased because it negotiated with the teachers on behalf of the school district without reaching agreement and learned about the reasons for the strike in the course of negotiating. From those premises the Wisconsin court concluded that the Board lost its statutory power to determine that the strike and persistent refusal to terminate it amounted to conduct serious enough to warrant discharge of the strikers. Wisconsin statutes vest in the Board the power to discharge its employees, a power of every employer, whether it has negotiated with the employees before discharge or not. The Fourteenth Amendment permits a court to strip the Board of the otherwise unremarkable power the Wisconsin Legislature has given it only if the Board's prior involvement in negotiating with the teachers means that it cannot act consistent with due process.

### C

Due process, as this Court has repeatedly held, is a term that "negates any concept of inflexible procedures universally applicable to every imaginable situation." Cafeteria Workers v. McElroy, 367 U. S. 886, 895 (1961). Determining what process is due in a given setting requires the Court to take into account the individual's stake in the decision at issue as well as the State's interest in a particular procedure for making it. See Mathews v. Eldridge, 424 U. S. 319 (1976); Arnett v. Kennedy, 416 U. S. 134, 168 (1974) (POWELL, J., concurring); *id.,* at 188 (WHITE, J., concurring and dissenting); Goldberg v. Kelly, 397 U. S. 254, 263-266 (1970). Our assessment of the interests of the parties in this case leads to the conclusion that this is a very different case from *Morrissey v. Brewer, supra,* and that the Board's prior role as negotiator does not disqualify it to decide that the public interest in maintaining uninterrupted classroom work required that teachers striking in violation of state law be discharged.

The teachers' interest in these proceedings is, of course, self-evident. They wished to avoid termination of their employment, obviously an important interest, but one that must be examined in light of several factors. Since the teachers admitted that they were engaged in a work stoppage, there was no possibility of an erroneous factual determination on this critical threshold issue.

Moreover, what the teachers claim as a property right was the expectation that the jobs they had left to go and remain on strike in violation of law would remain open to them. The Wisconsin court accepted at least the essence of that claim in defining the property right under state law, and we do not quarrel with its conclusion. But even if the property interest claimed here is to be compared with the liberty interest at stake in *Morrissey,* we note that both "the risk of an erroneous deprivation" and "the degree of potential deprivation" differ in a qualitative sense and in degree from those in *Morrissey.* Mathews v. Eldridge, *supra,* 424 U. S. 319, at 335, 341.

The governmental interests at stake in this case also differ significantly from the interests at stake in *Morrissey.* The Board's decision whether to dismiss striking teachers involves broad considerations, and does not in the main turn on the Board's view of the "seriousness" of the teachers' conduct or the factors they urge mitigated their violation of state law. It was not an adjudicative decision, for the Board had an obligation to make a decision based on its own answer to an important question of policy: what choice among the alternative responses to the teachers' strike will best serve the interests of the school system, the interests of the parents and children who depend on the system, and the interests of the citizens whose taxes support it? The Board's decision was only incidentally a disciplinary decision; it had significant governmental and public policy dimensions as well. See Summers, Public Employee Bargaining: A Political Perspective, 83 Yale L. J. 1156 (1974).

State law vests the governmental, or policymaking, function exclusively in the School Board and the State has two interests in keeping it there. First, the Board is the body with overall responsibility for the governance of the school district; it must cope with the myriad day-to-day problems of a modern public school system including the severe consequences of a teachers' strike; by virtue of electing them the constituents have declared the Board members qualified to deal with these problems, and they are accountable to the voters for the manner in which they perform. Second, the state legislature has given to the Board the power to employ and dismiss teachers, as a part of the balance it has struck in the area of municipal labor relations; altering those statutory powers as a matter of federal due process clearly changes that balance. Permitting the Board to make the decision at issue here preserves its control over school district affairs, leaves the balance of power in labor relations where the state legislature struck it, and assures that the decision whether to dismiss the teachers will be made by the body responsible for that decision under state law.

### III

Respondents have failed to demonstrate that the decision to terminate their employment was infected by the sort of bias that we have held to disqualify other decisionmakers as a matter of federal due process. A showing that the Board was "involved" in the events preceding this decision, in light of the important interest in leaving with the Board the power given by the state legislature, is not enough to overcome the presumption of honesty and integrity in policymakers with decisionmaking power. Cf. Withrow v. Larkin, 421 U. S. 35, 47 (1975). Accordingly, we hold that the Due Process Clause of the Fourteenth Amendment did not guarantee respondents that the decision to terminate their employment would be made or reviewed by a body other than the School Board. . . .

MR. JUSTICE STEWART, with whom MR. JUSTICE BRENNAN and MR. JUSTICE MARSHALL join, dissenting.

The issue in this case is whether the discharge of the respondent teachers by the petitioner school board violated the Due Process Clause of the Fourteenth Amendment because the board members were not impartial decisionmakers. It is now well established that "a biased decisionmaker [is] constitutionally unacceptable [and] 'our system of law has always endeavored to prevent even the probability of unfairness.'" Withrow v. Larkin, 421 U. S. 35, 47, quoting *In re* Murchison, 349 U. S. 133, 136....

The Court acknowledges, as it must, that it is "bound to accept the interpretation of Wisconsin law by the highest court of the State." *Ante,* at 6. Yet it then proceeds to reverse that court by assuming, as the petitioners urge, that under Wisconsin law the determination to discharge the striking teachers only "involved the [Board's] exercise of its discretion as to what should be done to carry out the duties that law placed on the Board." *Ibid.* It dismisses the respondents' version of Wisconsin law in a footnote. *Ante,* at pp. 7-8, n. 3.

But the fact is that the Wisconsin Supreme Court has not clearly delineated the state law criterion that governs the discharge of striking teachers, and this Court is wholly without power to resolve that issue of state law. I would therefore remand this case to the Wisconsin Supreme Court for it to determine whether, on the one hand, the school board is charged with considering the reasonableness of the strike in light of its own actions, or is, on the other, wholly free, as the Court today assumes, to exercise its discretion in deciding whether to discharge the teachers....

"[U]nder a realistic appraisal of psychological tendencies and human weaknesses," *Withrow v. Larkin, supra,* at 47, I believe that there is a constitutionally unacceptable danger of bias where school board members are required to assess the reasonableness of their own actions during heated contract negotiations that have culminated in a teachers' strike. If, therefore, the respondents' interpretation of the state law is correct, then I would agree with the Wisconsin Supreme Court that "the board was not an impartial decisionmaker in a constitutional sense and that the [teachers] were denied due process of law." 66 Wis. 2d 469, 494, 225 N. W. 2d 658, 671.

For the reasons stated, I would vacate the judgment before us and remand this case to the Supreme Court of Wisconsin....

## NOTES

1. The issue in Rockwell v. Crestwood School Dist. Bd. of Educ., 393 Mich. 616, 227 N.W.2d 736 (1975), *appeal dismissed,* 427 U.S. 901 (1976), was whether striking school teachers could be disciplined without a prior hearing. Section 6 of Michigan Public Employment Relations Act (PERA) provided for a post-discipline hearing at the employee's request, while the Teachers' Tenure Act provided for a pre-discharge hearing for teachers on continuing tenure. The court applied the PERA, rather than the Teachers' Tenure Act, on the grounds that the latter was designed to cover neither labor disputes nor concerted action by a group of individuals, as was the PERA. Addressing the constitutionality under the Due Process Clause of such discipline, the court relied on Arnett v. Kennedy, 416 U.S. 134, 94 S. Ct. 1633, 40 L.Ed.2d 15 (1974), *reh. denied and remanded,* 416 U.S. 977 (1974) in rejecting the teachers' arguments for a pre-disciplinary hearing, but it emphasized heavily the necessity of personal notice of the impending disciplinary action before the action was taken.

The union, the Crestwood Educ. Ass'n, had filed unfair labor practice charges with the MERC against the School Board prior to the discharge of the teachers. Relative to this issue, the court said:

The action of the Crestwood school board in discharging teachers for striking in violation of the provisions of the PERA prior to the hiring of replacements was not violative of that act. It does not necessarily follow, however, that these teachers may not be entitled to reinstatement should MERC determine that the school board engaged in an unfair labor practice. . . .

If MERC should determine that the employing school district committed an unfair labor practice, MERC *may*, despite the illegality of the teachers' strike, order reinstatement. . . . [Emphasis in the original.]

If the MERC finds that an unfair labor practice or other misconduct was committed by both sides, it should balance the competing equities to reach a result best effectuating the goals of the act.

In Garavalia v. City of Stillwater, 283 Minn. 354, 168 N.W.2d 336 (1969), several firefighters were dissatisfied with the extended time being taken by the city to consider the recommendations of a fact-finder concerning their wages and working conditions. They decided to walk off their jobs, although they informed the fire chief of their willingness to respond to siren calls. The city responded by terminating their employment. After the city refused to rehire them, the unemployed firefighters sought a declaratory judgment establishing their continued employment status.

The trial court found that the two plaintiffs who were not veterans of the armed services were discharged for proper cause under sections 179.51 and 179.54 of the Public Employees Labor Relations Act. Section 179.51 prohibits strikes by public employees and section 179.54 provides that one who violates the anti-strike provision is deemed to have abandoned his employment. However, the trial court also found that the four plaintiffs who were service veterans were denied the right to a hearing guaranteed by the Minnesota Veterans Preference Act. The Minnesota Supreme Court reversed the trial court with respect to this latter holding and remanded the case for dismissal. Following is an excerpt of the court's opinion:

The record here presents the issue of whether the requirement of § 197.46, commonly known as the Veterans Preference Act, that an honorably discharged veteran shall not be removed from a position of public employment without a hearing, upon due notice, upon stated charges in writing, applies to a veteran who was engaged in a strike or walkout in violation of § 179.51 and under § 179.54 would otherwise thereby have abandoned and terminated his appointment or employment. We think the court improperly found that the veteran-plaintiffs were discharged, when in fact they abandoned and terminated their own employment by their own acts. Therefore, the requirement of § 197.46 of hearing before *removal* has no application in this situation since that act controls the city's power to terminate the veteran's employment, and in this case the veteran-plaintiffs' employment was terminated by their own act and by operation of law. The trial court found as a fact that "the coordinated action of the plaintiffs constituted a strike or walk out in violation of M.S.A. 179.51 and 179.54." In the face of that finding, the court proceeded as if these statutes stated that such actions were proper grounds for discharge of the employees by the city and as if the city had availed itself of this ground and discharged the veteran-plaintiffs, even though the court in reference to plaintiffs Garavalia and Schrode found that "by their action they abandoned their employment with the City of Stillwater." The same is true of the other plaintiffs. Minn. St. 179.54 clearly provides that "any public employee who violates the provisions of sections 179.51 to 179.58 shall thereby abandon and terminate his appointment or employment. . . ." Under the terms of the statute, no authority to discharge is given the city if a violation occurs. The statute, instead of establishing grounds for discharge of municipal employees by the city, imposes restrictions upon the city's rights to contract with its employees. The contracts of all public employers with their employees are subject to these restrictions. See, City of Detroit v. Division 26 of Amalgamated Ass'n, 332 Mich. 237, 51 N.W.(2d) 228.

It is thus clear that when any municipal employee violates the provisions of §§ 179.51 to 179.58, his employment with the city is automatically terminated without any action by or on behalf of the city. Furthermore, the city under the terms of § 179.54 has no alternative except to consider such employment terminated, as is further illustrated by § 179.55 which places restrictions upon the right of a public employer to reemploy an employee who has violated §§ 179.51 to 179.58. Thus, the specific intent which plaintiffs may have entertained in this case becomes immaterial since the only material fact is that they violated the statute, which caused the termination of their employment to arise by operation of law due to their own conduct. The requirement of the Veterans Preference Act that there must be a hearing before removal of an employee entitled to the protection of that act has no application in this situation, since that statute controls the city's power to terminate the veteran's employment and, as stated, in this case the veteran-plaintiffs' employment was terminated by operation of law because of their own acts. . . .

2. In National Educ. Ass'n v. Lee County Board of Public Instruction, 260 So.2d 206, 80 L.R.R.M. 2368 (1972), the Florida Supreme Court considered the re-employment rights of teachers who had engaged in various work stoppages during 1968. Although the applicable Florida statute specifically precluded the re-employment for one year of any teachers who left their positions without school board approval, the Court sustained the right of the state superintendent to circumvent this provision, with respect to those who had merely walked off their jobs, by authorizing the local school boards to grant them emergency, retroactive leaves covering the respective periods they were away from work. This procedure was not available, however, for other teachers who had effectively resigned before leaving their positions. As to them, the Court affirmed the power of school boards to condition their re-employment upon the payment of $100 sums as the equivalent of "liquidated damages" covering the losses caused by their disingenuous resignations.

Following the Florida Supreme Court decision, the teachers who were each required to tender $100 to have their resignations revoked had their situation considered by the Fifth Circuit Court of Appeals. In National Educ. Ass'n v. Lee County Board of Public Instruction, 467 F.2d 447 (5th Cir. 1972), the court ruled:

Essentially the teachers' theory is that the forced exaction of a $100 payment from each of them in exchange for their returning to work with their pre-resignation status intact amounted to a fine or penalty for a legislatively undefined wrong, violative of their right to procedural due process because they were afforded no hearing or other opportunity to protest the payments or to contest their legality. . . .

Concededly it is now established to a point beyond all dispute that "public employment, including academic employment, may [not] be conditioned upon the surrender of constitutional rights which could not be abridged by direct governmental action." Keyishian v. Board of Regents, 1967, 385 U.S. 589. . . .

However, none of these cases have any application here unless the teachers were in fact compelled to forego the exercise of a Federal constitutional right in return for re-employment. The critical flaw in their argument is the uncritical (and, on this record, insupportable) assumption that the $100 payments constituted a *deprivation* of property without due process of law within the prohibition of the Fourteenth Amendment. The agreement clearly provided that the teachers would receive a benefit to which concededly they were not otherwise entitled — re-employment with full tenure rights and other accompanying privileges which they had enjoyed before their resignations — in return for a payment of $100. In substance, they were offered an opportunity to surrender one "property right" in order to acquire another "property right" that was plainly of greater value to them. Such a mutually advantageous exchange cannot be characterized as a *deprivation* of property, regardless of whether the teachers' payments are pejoratively denominated as "fines" and regardless of whether the subjective intention of the Board members who voted for it was to "punish" alleged past misconduct. . . . [W]e may concede that the teachers here were involuntarily subjected to choosing between paying consideration for an employment benefit of at least equivalent value and foregoing employment altogether. The choice between these options was admittedly coerced. But regardless of whether it was accepted or rejected the Board's offer did not entail a deprivation of property. Accordingly, the payment of the $100 could not have involved the surrender of the right to protection of that property guaranteed by the due process clause of the Fourteenth Amendment.

Obviously the teachers would be in an entirely different position if they were somehow able to establish that they were legally entitled to tenure without payment of $100 and were therefore unilaterally deprived of that money without due process. Instead they are forced to concede that they had effectively resigned their positions and that the Board was not even legally obligated to rehire them at all. In such circumstances their claim fares no better than that of a teacher who, having neither de facto tenure nor an objective expectancy of re-employment, is discharged for unspecified reasons without notice or a hearing.

3. Section 210 of the Taylor Law authorizes a public employer who determines that an employee has engaged in a strike to place the employee on probation for one year and to deduct from his pay twice his daily rate of pay for each day the worker was on strike. In Sanford v. Rockefeller, 35 N.Y.2d 547, 324 N.E.2d 113 (1974), the New York Court of Appeals, relying upon Arnett v. Kennedy, 416 U.S. 134, 94 S.Ct. 1633, 40 L.Ed.2d 15 (1974), and Mitchell v. W. T. Grant Co., 416 U.S. 600, 94 S.Ct. 1895, 40 L.Ed.2d 406 (1974), found no due process violation regarding this penalty procedure, even though the affected worker could not obtain a hearing on his objections to the employer's determination until after the imposition of the statutory sanctions. In Phillips v. New York City Health Corp., 44 N.Y.2d 807, 377 N.E.2d 742 (1978), the Court held that the Taylor Law strike penalty consists of twice each violator's gross wage, rather than net, after-taxes compensation. Furthermore, the court in Mineola School Dist. v. Teachers Ass'n, 97 L.R.R.M. 2144 (N.Y. Sup. Ct., Spec. term 1977), permitted the school district to include daily pay earned by employees for extracurricular activities when computing their strike assessments.

In Tucker v. Commissioner, 69 T.C. No. 54, GERR No. 748, 28 (U.S. Tax Ct. 1978), the Tax Court ruled that amounts withheld from a public employee's wages as a penalty for illegal strike activity constitutes taxable income and may not be deducted as an employee business expense since I.R.C. § 162 (f) expressly precludes the deduction of "any fine or similar penalty paid to a government for the violation of any law."

## CASO v. GOTBAUM

New York Supreme Court
67 Misc.2d 205, 323 N.Y.S.2d 742 (1971),
*reversed on other grounds,*
38 App.Div.2d 955, 331 N.Y.S.2d 507 (1972)

HARNETT, J.: Surrounded by walls of precedent, and moated by centuries of channelized thinking, the law can easily suppress newness and find itself critically apart from the social amalgam which is its very reason for existence. And, the risk of analyzing fine points in isolation is the loss of total fairness and justice in the sense it is understood by the society to be served. Such are the dangers in the case at hand.

The dispute here arises as a result of work stoppages affecting sewage treatment and garbage disposal in New York City instigated during June 1971. Nassau County, as well as the County Executive of Nassau County, and the Supervisors of the Towns of North Hempstead and Oyster Bay, in their individual and official capacities, sued the Executive Director of District Council 37, American Federation of State, County and Municipal Employees and the President of Local 237, International Brotherhood of Teamsters in their individual and representative capacities. The public officials (including Nassau County) charged the union leaders with conspiring and causing unlawful acts of work stoppage and coercion at City pollution control plants, pumping stations and yards, which resulted in contaminating the waters of Long Island Sound off the North Shore of the two involved towns. In their main complaint, the public officials ask for a permanent injunction against the union officials repeating their conduct, compensatory damages of $1,000,000 and punitive damages of $5,000,000. While this main action is pending, the public officials, by motion, have asked this court for a preliminary injunction against the union officials, and also to be permitted to examine these officials right away in preparation for an injunction hearing.

The union leaders have so far responded by moving to dismiss the complaint, essentially on the grounds that the complained of conduct is over, that the public officials have no right to be suing them, and that no damage has been demonstrated. . . .

For purposes of those motions then, the union leaders seek to win on the following necessary assumptions:

1. They conspired with others, used intimidation, and with malice, caused raw sewage to be poured into tidal waters;

2. They did this to pressure the New York State Legislature, and to injure those using the waters or living in proximity to them;

3. The waters were polluted and the ecological balances harmed as a result of their deliberate acts;

4. At least the expense of testing and patrolling the waters was occasioned to the County and Towns.

While these may not be the ultimate facts proven at the trial, the union officials claim on their motions to dismiss that they should win as a matter of law even if those are the facts. The Court disagrees.

The union leaders, in a well-reasoned attack, would pick their way through to success on a series of ripostes to arguments thrust forth by the public officials. They essentially argue four legal grounds:

1. The Taylor Law, dealing with strikes by municipal employees;

2. Public Health Law, sec. 1150;

3. Navigation Law, sec. 33; and

4. The Common Law.

Each of these will be dealt with separately.


### 1. *Taylor Law*

The complaint alleges that the public officials have instituted this action "as taxpayers pursuant to Civil Service Law, sec. 210, subd. 4 and pursuant to the other applicable statutes pertaining hereto." Despite the claim of legal grounds under the Taylor Law (Civil Service Law, sec. 200 *et seq.*), which is reiterated by the public officials in an affidavit submitted in support of this motion, the public officials concede, at page 17 of their reply memorandum, that:

> "they have no standing to sue under the Taylor Act for the simple reason that Nassau County, not being the employer of the striking unions' New York City employees, is not a proper party."

This admission is in accord with the provisions of the Taylor Law which provide a remedy against unlawful strikes of public employees only to the "government involved." Civil Service Law, sec. 211. Moreover, New York City, the involved employer, did sue.

## 2. *Public Health Law, section 1150*

Public Health Law, section 1150(l) says:

> "No person, corporation or municipality, shall place or cause to be placed or discharged or cause to be discharged into any of the waters of the State, in quantities injurious to the public health, any sewage, garbage, offal or any decomposable or putrescible matter of any kind or the effluent from any sewage disposal plant . . . or any refuse or waste matter . . . from any sewer or drainage system. . . ."

The statute is enforceable by the Board of Health and the State Commissioner of Health. The public officials assert that those bodies are not intended to be the sole enforcers, but even that argument must fail, for the right to maintain civil actions for violations is expressly limited to cities and villages. Public Health Law, sec. 1157.

## 3. *Navigation Law, section 33*

In Navigation Law, section 33, the State had decreed that:

> "[n]o person shall drain, deposit or cast any . . . offal, excrement, garbage or other putrid or offensive matter into the navigable waters of the states, except as the same may be authorized by the state department of health. Every person violating the provisions of this section shall upon conviction by any court of competent jurisdiction be guilty of a misdemeanor. . . ."

The statute vests enforcement rights in the District Attorney of the county where the offense was committed or exists. Clearly, this statute is penal in nature. The public officials argue, however, that it also confers a civil right of action.

The violation of a penal statute may, under certain circumstances, give rise to civil liability. This occurs where the penal statute was enacted for the benefit and protection of a particular class, where the plaintiff in the civil action is a member of the protected class, and where the harm which was done is that which the statute was intended to prevent (see Brody v. Save Way Northern Boulevard, Inc., 37 Misc. 2d 240, revd. 19 A.D. 2d 714, revd. 14 N.Y.2d 576; Murzer v. Braisdell, 183 Misc. 773, aff'd 269 App. Div. 970).

Under the law, the operation of such a rule must be misty. Can one distinguish penal statutes of "particular benefit" from those for the benefit of the public at large? Should such a concept exist? Is the whole approach anything different than seeking to find in the books an existing base for a legal duty, even in a penal statute? If so, is not the true problem of the case the one of duty under the circumstances, and this finally brings us to the crux of the motions to dismiss.

## 4. *The Common Law*

The public officials have argued they have legal rights under the common law, and could win in the main action apart from such statutory specifics as the Labor, Public Health and Navigation Laws. The Court here agrees with the public officials, although without embracing all their reasoning or articulation.

### C. *Responsibility for Wilful Wrong to the Environment*

### 1. *A Legal Need*

The law obviously cannot provide a civil remedy for every personal conflict in the world. Flamm v. Van Neirop, 56 Misc. 2d 1059. However, there are instances where substantial damage can be done to the public interest which do not fall within the usual categories of causes of action, and yet, redress should be provided for such demonstrated wrong. Battalla v. State, 10 N.Y.2d 237; Calloway v. Munzer, 57 Misc. 2d 163. As the Court of Appeals has noted:

> "a cause of action arises where that is done which should not be done." Gonzalez v. Industrial Bank (of Cuba), 12 N.Y.2d 33, 38.

See also, Merchants Mutual Ins. Co. v. Jackson Trucking Co., 21 Misc. 2d 1005.

The courts should not dismiss or reject claims merely because the claim is novel or a similar claim has not previously been asserted. Bolivar v. Monnat, 232 App. Div. 33. This rule should be particularly applicable where, as here, a substantial public right is involved.

The communications media daily remind us of the current ecological crisis which threatens the quality of our daily life. Paralleling those problems in importance to the continuation of orderly and healthy society is the need for obedience to lawful mandates. The facts as conceded in this motion present an unusual combination of the two, a blend resulting from the disregard of these union officials for the lawful processes, thereby affecting the health and welfare of people living on or near the water of Long Island Sound, those utilizing those waters for recreation, and marine life. It is an inadequate remedy to enjoin such behavior after it has occurred, for the damage to the environment is then already done. Organizations, whether unions or corporations, public or private, should not be permitted to escape the penalties of the acts which they wilfully perform to the detriment of the public or its physical setting.

Plainly, the legitimate interests of millions of people lie behind the institution of this suit by public officials elected by and representing those people. While courts have traditionally been reluctant to permit municipalities to take action on behalf of their residents in the absence of statutory authority, those cases generally deal with private rights. Marcus v. Village of Mamaroneck, 283 N.Y. 325; Buckley v. Baldwin, 230 App. Div. 245; Wollitzer v. Nat. Title Guaranty Co., 148 Misc. 529, affd. 241 App. Div. 757. Here, the public officials are acting in protection of public rights and public health. See, Nassau County Government Law, section 901; Public Health Law, section 347; People ex rel. Bennett v. Laman, 277 N.Y. 368.

### 2. *A New Rule of Law*

The Court does not rest this decision on any enunciated interpretation of the Public Health Law or the County Charter. Nor does the Court rest its decision on a policy interpolation from section 33 of the Navigation Law, even though that might be appropriate here. Nor does the Court seek to squeeze a prior case or judicial statement into some conformable pattern to lend authority.

Instead, the Court will simply state as its basis a new rule that persons maliciously polluting or contaminating the environment may be enjoined by the chief executive officer of a county or town whose residents are adversely affected by the offensive conduct, or by private citizens reasonably affected. Offensive effect may include economic loss, health hazard, whether immediate or reasonably threatening, recreational or aesthetic impairment, or destruction of wildlife. In addition to injunctive sanction, an offending polluter can be answerable in such compensatory damage as may be proven by or on behalf of an injured party, and made to pay punitive damages for deliberate or contemptuous disregard of the environmental rights of others.

### a. *Standing to Sue*

The Court cannot be persuaded by the mechanical application of the "standing to sue" to deny the rights of the public officials to bring this action.

Typically, it is stated a party cannot sue unless he is "aggrieved" or has an "interest," usually a financial one. These are historical notions of property law, and have no application to the articulation of public rights. In the growth of consumerism, and emerging public participation in legal processes, the elected executive of a municipality is the major unifying thread of the whole spectrum of his community. Moreover, he controls the extended resources necessary to do legal battle on behalf of the public interest, whether the opposition be giant business, giant labor or giant government. It is necessary that he be able to sue to protect the environment.

### b. *Wrong and Recompense*

Under the facts conceded for the purposes of this motion, New York City sewage plants discharge over 580,000,000 gallons of sewage each day into the Upper East River. The prevailing tides and mixtures carry the receiving waters to Long Island Sound including the tributory bays along the North Shore of Nassau County. The work stoppage here involved resulted in discharge of substantial untreated raw sewage into the river and thence to the Long Island Sound and the North Shore bays. The bacteria count tripled, and in some places increased much more. Algae disturbances resulted. The waters themselves developed a brown scum appearance. The fortuity of absence of normal rainfall permitted the Nassau County bay beaches to remain open, although the beaches on Manhasset Bay were placed on an alert.

The entire area is heavily residential with countless numbers of people involved in diverse residential, recreational and commercial respects.

Further, under the assumed facts, the polluting conduct was deliberate and wilful, motivated by a desire to pressure the State Legislature. There was no cloak of legality for the offensive conduct.

The preliminary injunction issued by the New York County Supreme Court is not a permanent one. Moreover, the record is replete with socially hostile statements supposedly made by the defendants, and disputes as to their context. It is not clear that the union leaders will, in fact, in 1972 get what they want. Accordingly, it is for the trial court to weigh the facts and reach a decision with respect to future jeopardy and a possible permanent injunction. There are at least damages for testing and patrolling the area of conceivable effect. And, finally, the sanction of punitive damage must overhang those who would for their own ends wound the public interest in its environment.

Under all these assumed circumstances, how could a court in this society conclude legal redress is unavailable? Could it turn its back on an admitted wrong, perpetrated on such a large scale, protested by the very elected representatives the system projects? Should it?

The conscience of our community is saturated with environmental awareness, and those deliberately contaminating the environment as an illegal tactic are conspicuously wrongdoers. For the law to ignore this would be to forfeit all credibility. Just as new torts have emerged with new technology, new torts must emerge with changing population pressures and acknowledged social responsibilities.

If the rule of this case is not the law, it should be. And if not now, when?

### 3. *Directions to File Answer*

Since the union officials' motions to dismiss are denied, they will be given ten days to file their answers to the complaint, and the matter will thereafter proceed according to law. CPLR 3211(f).

Short form order signed.

## NOTES

1. Although the principal decision was reversed on appeal because of a technical pleading deficiency, the fundamental rationale of that case was subsequently accepted by the Appellate Division in Caso v. Dist. Council 37, AFSCME, 43 App.Div.2d 159, 350 N.Y.S.2d 173 (1973). In rejecting the purely pecuniary interest test, the New York courts seem to be following the lead of cases such as Scenic Hudson Preservation Conf. v. FPC, 354 F.2d 608 (2d Cir. 1965), *cert. denied,* 384 U.S. 941 (1966). Concerning the liberalization of standing requirements generally in public actions, *see* L. Jaffe, JUDICIAL CONTROL OF ADMINISTRATIVE ACTION 459-545 (1965).

Even though the New York courts have applied liberal standing rules to this area, note that they have found no third party right to sue for strike damages under the Taylor Law. *See* Jamur Productions Corp. v. Quill, 51 Misc.2d 501, 273 N.Y.S.2d 348 (Sup. Ct. 1966). *See generally* Note, *Private Damage Actions Against Public Sector Unions for Illegal Strikes,* 91 HARV. L. REV. 1309 (1978), wherein three independent theories for providing damage relief to private parties injured by unlawful public employee work stoppages are explored: (1) Right of action emanating from statutory strike proscription; (2) Right of public as third party beneficiaries to recover for breach of contractual no-strike obligation; and (3) Cause of action based upon contention that illegal strike constitutes public nuisance. *See also* Waldman, *Damage Actions and Other Remedies in the Public Employee Strike,* 20TH ANN. N.Y.U. CONF. ON LABOR LAW 259 (T. Christensen ed. 1968).

2. In Lamphere Schools v. Federation of Teachers, 252 N.W.2d 818, 95 L.R.R.M. 2279 (1977), the Michigan Supreme Court utilized alternative theories to support its determination that a school district could not prosecute a tort action against a union for damages caused by a strike conducted in violation of state law.

> ... The PERA was intended to occupy the public employee labor relations field completely; no viable distinction exists between the constituent public employees and their unions in this context. Therefore, along with the equitable relief of injunction, the § 6 remedies of the PERA are presently the exclusive remedies available to plaintiff School District in the case at bar when confronted by an illegal, though peaceful, strike by the teachers, even if such strike was precipitated by defendant Federations.
>
> . . . .
>
> If this Court permitted plaintiff School District to pursue any of the three civil tort actions pled (causing teachers to breach a duty, tortious interference with existing individual contractual relationships, civil conspiracy), such a result would necessarily circumvent the authority of MERC to determine charges of unfair labor practices. This becomes apparent since the defendant Federations, as representatives of the teachers, would inevitably defend proposed civil actions by alleging unfair labor practices. Then

the determination of whether or not an unfair labor practice occurred would inexorably fall to the forum in which the tort action was brought — the circuit court.

....

Plaintiff School District correctly relies on the *Detroit* case [Detroit v. Division 26 of Amalgamated Ass'n of Street, Electric Railway & Motor Coach Employees of America, 332 Mich. 237 (1952)] for the proposition that strikes by public employees are unlawful at common law. However, that case falls far short of creating the classic "duty", "breach of duty", therefore, "monetary damages" triad of traditional tort law. The *Detroit* case stands for the limited proposition that strikes by public employees are against public policy *and are therefore subject to injunction.* There is no precedent establishing a common-law tort duty owned by the Federation or its teachers to the School Board regarding peaceful strike activities.

....

Furthermore, the ultimate legislative goal is to achieve a prompt, fair resolution of disputes while avoiding the disruption of the educational process. To recognize alternative tort remedies would result in a substantial negative impact upon such purposes. It would encourage future school board inaction. Eventual settlements could be prolonged pending the resolution of multiple tort claims and counterclaims. The inevitable result would be to create labor law logjams in our courts and, at the same time, to exacerbate labor-management disputes.

A California Court of Appeal, however, rejected at least part of the *Lamphere* court's reasoning when in Pasadena Unified School Dist. v. Pasadena Fed'n of Teachers, 72 Cal. App. 3d 100, *as modified on denial of rehearing,* 72 Cal. App. 3d 763d (1977), *appeal denied* (Cal. Sup. Ct. min. order 11/25/77), 96 L.R.R.M. 2363, it held that damages could be obtained against a labor organization which had precipitated an improper teacher work stoppage.

Labor unions are privileged to induce breach of contract or to interfere with contractual relationships by engaging in lawful concerted activity. Such privilege, however, does not protect the union when either the object or the means of the concerted action is unlawful.

... [T]he Legislature has consistently withheld from teachers the right to strike. The obligation not to interrupt or deny services on the basis of a strike is, therefore, a term of plaintiff's contract with each of its teachers. Consequently, the allegation of the complaint that the defendants "advised and induced" plaintiff's employees to "hold a work stoppage and strike" sufficiently alleges a breach of the employment contract.

Moreover, liability can be imposed on defendants upon a theory wholly independent of tortious inducement to breach the teachers' contract with plaintiff. The conduct of an unlawful strike is itself a tort for which damages may be recovered.

The *Pasadena* court did not have to decide if the strike conduct in issue was within the exclusive jurisdiction of the Educational Employment Relations Board, since the jurisdiction of that recently-created agency did not become operative until after the Pasadena work stoppage. Thus the court left "for future adjudication the question whether illegal strikes by educational employees after the effective date of [the EERB enabling legislation] are 'unfair practices' within the exclusive jurisdiction of the board."

3. Taxpayer suits under statutory provisions prohibiting strikes usually have taken the form of mandamus actions or suits to prevent waste of public treasury moneys. Suits to specifically enforce the penalty provisions of the state no-strike law were upheld in *In re* Weinstein, 267 N.Y.S.2d 111, 61 L.R.R.M. 2323 (N.Y. Sup. Ct. 1966), and Head v. Special School Dist. No.1, 288 Minn. 496, 182 N.W.2d 887 (1970) (joint suit by Attorney General and private individuals). *See also* City of Cincinnati v. Cincinnati Dist. Council 51, AFSCME, 35 Ohio St.2d 197, 299 N.E.2d 686 (1973), *cert. denied,* 415 U.S. 994 (1974). However, it has been held that where strike penalties are discretionary, rather than mandatory, no such private remedy is available. Markowski v. Backstrom, 39 Ohio Op.2d 247, 226 N.E.2d 825 (C.P. Lucas Co. 1967). Similarly, overtime payments to non-strikers is a proper municipal function which may not be enjoined. Mone v. Pezzano, 77 L.R.R.M.

2605 (N.Y. Sup. Ct. 1971). On the question of individual actions for injunctive relief, *see* Dade County Classroom Teachers Ass'n v. Rubin, 238 So.2d 284 (Fla. 1970), *cert. denied*, 400 U.S. 1009 (1971). *Compare* Durkin v. Board of Police & Fire Comm'rs, 48 Wis.2d 112, 180 N.W.2d 1 (1970) (city elector could sue director of firefighters' union which had struck, notwithstanding amnesty agreement between city and strikers), *with* Shanks v. Donovan, 32 App.Div.2d 1037, 303 N.Y.S.2d 783 (1969), and Shanks v. Procaccino, 70 L.R.R.M. 2741 (N.Y. Sup. Ct. 1968), *aff'd*, 306 N.Y.S.2d 416 (App. Div. 1969). *See also* Fire Fighters v. Board of Supervisors, 75 Cal.App.3d 807, 97 L.R.R.M. 2265 (1977).

4. In Allen v. Maurer, 6 Ill.App.3d 633, 286 N.E.2d 135 (1972), the court rejected the "public trust" concept in a taxpayer action to enjoin a teachers' union from engaging in an unlawful strike. The opinion held, in part:

> Here, the issue is whether or not taxpayers who have children in the public schools can maintain an action for injunctive relief grounded upon the duty of the State to maintain a free, efficient and high quality system of public education. We are not faced with an alleged misuse of public funds or conveyance of public property. We are concerned with the constitutionally mandated duty of the State to maintain a public school system. Can taxpayer-parents sue to enjoin a teachers strike in order to secure the performance of that constitutional duty under the facts presented by this record? We hold that they cannot.
>
> The Illinois Constitution S.H.A., provides that "a fundamental goal of the People of the State is the educational development of all persons to the limits of their capacities" and that "the State shall provide for an efficient system of high quality public educational institutions and services." Ill. Const., Art. X, Sec. 1. Hence, the State has a constitutional duty to provide and the public has a right to receive an efficient, high quality educational system. This duty is discharged by the State through local boards of education who are primarily responsible for fulfilling this constitutional mandate.
>
> The parties to this appeal have not cited, nor has our research disclosed, any precedent which would confer standing upon individual taxpayer-parents under the situation presented by the facts of this case. We hold that in the circumstances present here, the authority to seek an injunction rests in the State and its official representative, the Board of Education, the members of which are elected by the people to implement the command of the constitution. Any other decision would have the effect of usurping the Board of Education's control of the local educational system.

# G. THE LIMITED RIGHT TO STRIKE IN THE PUBLIC SECTOR

### EDWARDS, THE DEVELOPING LABOR RELATIONS LAW IN THE PUBLIC SECTOR, 10 Duquesne L. Rev. 357, 376-78 (1972) †

The last group of states — those with a legislatively granted limited right to strike — is certainly the most daring of the four. The problem in granting such a limited right to strike, in general, has been to define precisely the tolerable degree of pressure which the government and the public can withstand. Almost invariably, this is done by attempting to draw a line between essential services (wherein a strike is impermissible) and non-essential services where a strike may be tolerated. However, in most laws this line is very imprecisely delineated — usually by a formula based on some variant of "the public health, safety, or welfare" standard. Such a definition, while admirably flexible, may not be a sufficiently precise formulation to give meaningful guidance.

Another problem with the essential/non-essential calculus is that, in general, it fails to take into account the temporal dimension. A strike, for example, in a

---

† Reprinted by permission of the Duquesne Law Review.

highly automated industry, such as the telephone system, may be tolerable for a time. As it endures and the machines begin to break down, it may become intolerable. Other problems of a practical nature — such as who is to make the decision as to essentiality, when this decision is to be made, and whether the strike ban should be mandatory or imposed at the employer's option — are also involved in any partial strike programs.

While the difficulties are legion, there are four states — Hawaii, Pennsylvania, Montana, and Vermont — which have given public employees a limited right to strike. Of the four states, the most limited right is found in Montana, where a nurses law permits strikes, provided that another health care facility within a radius of 150 miles has not simultaneously been shut down. Of more general applicability is the Vermont Act covering municipal employees, which provides that "no public employee may strike or recognize a picket line of a labor organization while performing his official duties, if the strike or recognition of a picket line will endanger the health, safety or welfare of the public." Vermont totally prohibits strikes by "state employees," but it appears to insulate teachers' strikes from injunctive orders in the absence of a showing of a "clear and present danger to a sound program of school education."

Neither of these states have shown the creativity of Hawaii and Pennsylvania in responding to the problem. The Hawaii law, covering all public employees, conditions the right to strike upon:

(1) Good faith compliance with statutory impasse procedures;
(2) Passage of sixty days after findings and recommendations of a fact-finding board are made public; and
(3) The giving of 10 days' notice of desire to strike PERB and employer.

And while all categories of public employees are covered by the act, the Hawaii law also provides:

When the strike occurring, or is about to occur, endangers the public health or safety, the public employer concerned may petition the board to make an investigation. If the board finds that there is imminent a present danger to the health and safety of the public, the board shall set requirements that must be complied with to avoid or remove any such imminent or present danger.

Pennsylvania has adopted a slightly different approach. First, the law prohibits strikes by guards at mental hospitals or prisons or personnel necessary to functioning of the courts. (Police/Fire workers are covered by a separate compulsory arbitration statute.) For all other personnel, strikes are permitted if:

(a) Mediation and fact-finding procedures "have been completely utilized and exhausted"; and
(b) "[U]nless or until such a strike creates a clear and present danger or threat to the health, safety, or welfare of the public."

The basic difference between the Hawaii and Pennsylvania approaches is that when a strike endangers the public health, safety, or welfare, Hawaii's law allows the PERB to make adjustments as it sees fit to eliminate the dangerous aspects of the strike (such as requiring essential employees to work), while Pennsylvania presumably would ban the strike in toto. In the first court decision on record, Pennsylvania's judiciary has indicated the unsoundness of leaving the decision as to the tolerable limits of public employee strikes entirely to the courts. In *SEPTA v. Transport Workers of Philadelphia*,[3] the question of whether a strike

---

[3] 77 L.R.R.M. 2489 (1971). *But see* Hazelton Area School Dist. v. Education Ass'n, 2 CCH State Lab. Cases ¶ 52,684 (Pa. Comm. Pleas 1971).

of municipal transportation workers was prohibited by the threat to public welfare was answered affirmatively. The court based its holding on some rather tenuous findings that the strike caused increased traffic congestion. The court said that congestion was more than mere inconvenience since it caused a distinct threat to the safety and welfare of those travelling by car as well as pedestrians. It also increased the risk of crime and fire, prevented the aged from obtaining required medical assistance, and markedly interfered with the operation of job training programs, the school system, and the economic welfare in general. Under the rationale of the court in *SEPTA,* few if any public sector strikes will be held to be protected under the new state law. . . .

## ARMSTRONG EDUCATION ASSOCIATION v. ARMSTRONG SCHOOL DISTRICT

Commonwealth Court of Pennsylvania
291 A.2d 120 (1972)

BLATT, Judge: This is an appeal from an Order of the Court of Common Pleas of Armstrong County enjoining the appellant, the Armstrong Education Association ("Association"), from continuing to engage in a strike against the appellee, the Armstrong School District ("District"). The District has approximately 12,000 students, and it employs approximately 550 teachers, for whom the Association is the certified bargaining agent. Since December, 1970, the District and the Association have been engaged in negotiations in an effort to arrive at a collective bargaining agreement for the 1971-1972 school year.

In their negotiations, the parties followed the procedures outlined in the Public Employe Relations Act, Act of July 23, 1970, P.L. —, No. 195, 43 P.S. § 1101.101, et seq. (hereinafter "Act No. 195"), but they reached an impasse. In an effort to resolve this impasse, Association members began a strike against the District on April 27, 1971, and, in response to a complaint in equity filed on behalf of the District, the Court of Common Pleas of Armstrong County enjoined the strike on May 11, 1971, and ordered the teachers back to work. The teachers obeyed this Order and returned to work, finishing out the school year of 1970-1971.

Although negotiations continued, no agreement was reached and the teachers went out on strike again on August 30, 1971, just as the 1971-1972 school year was about to begin. Another complaint in equity was filed on behalf of the District, contending that the strike created "a clear and present danger or threat to the health, safety or welfare of the public," thus bringing the matter within the provisions of Section 1003 of Act No. 195, 43 P.S. § 1101.1003, and making it ripe for injunctive relief. Hearings were held by the Court of Common Pleas on September 1 and September 14, 1971, and the testimony at these hearings was substantially as follows:

The District Superintendent testified that the District was required to supply 180 instructional days prior to June 30, 1972 or be in danger of losing state subsidies, and that, with the school year scheduled to end on June 2, 1972, there might not be enough days remaining before June 30 to make up the time lost because of the strike.

The Assistant Superintendent testified that the strike had caused the cancellation of all extracurricular activities and varsity sports, and that, if permitted to continue, it would interfere with arrangements for "inservice days," which the District considered valuable for the teachers.

The testimony of the District Supervisor of Child Services was to the effect that a continuation of the strike would cause difficulties in obtaining qualified school bus drivers, and would bring about other problems concerning pupil transportation.

The Superintendent of Public Affairs testified that the strike had caused an interruption in his routine office procedures and that the negotiations had consumed so much of his time that a considerable backlog in his work was resulting.

The President of the School Board testified to several instances in which she and other Directors had been harassed by picketing and other disturbances at their homes and by the receipt of numerous unpleasant phone calls. She also testified as to the disorderly atmosphere in which a recent School Board meeting had been conducted, and as to the need for sheriff's deputies to be called in to keep order at the meeting. She at no time stated, however, that the matters complained of had been caused by Association members; in a few instances, she specifically denied that any teachers had been involved.

Following the September 1 hearing, the Court denied the request for an injunction on the ground that it was premature, but, following the September 14 hearing, the Court issued the requested injunction, finding that a clear and present danger or threat to the health, safety or welfare of the public existed. Such a finding was based on the strained atmosphere in the community as evidenced by the harassment of School Board Directors and of the Judge, and on the fact that 12 days of school, which would have to be made up, had already been lost. The teachers were ordered back to work as of September 15, 1971. It is from this injunction that the Association has appealed.

In reviewing the lower court's action in issuing an injunction, our scope of review, as with other types of equity matters, is limited. " '(W)e will look only to see if there were any apparently reasonable grounds for the action of the court below, and we will not further consider the merits of the case or pass upon the reasons for or against such action, unless it is plain that no such grounds existed or that the rules of law relied on are palpably wrong or clearly inapplicable: . . . .' "

It was long the law in almost all jurisdictions that strikes by public employees were illegal, and Pennsylvania was no exception to this rule. The last decade, however, has brought a tremendous increase in the unionization of public employees and a corresponding increase in illegal strikes by these employees, who claim to have found their remedies under the law inadequate. The leaders in this new militancy, perhaps with good reason, have often been school teachers.

In order to deal with the problem of public employee labor relations, the legislature in 1970 enacted Act No. 195.

This Act explicitly recognized the right of public employees to organize and to bargain collectively, and it also established specific procedures for collective bargaining which were intended to lessen the possibility of the development of an impasse. The Act provided, however, that if all the procedures have been complied with, and yet an impasse has developed, the right of the employees to strike must be recognized. The public employer is then given the right to seek equitable relief, including injunctions, in the court of common pleas of the jurisdiction where the strike occurs. Section 1003 of Act No. 195 provides, however, that an injunction may not issue unless ". . . the court finds that the strike creates a clear and present danger or threat to the health, safety or welfare of the public."

The determination of what is a "clear and present" danger under Act No. 195 presents some problems. The phrase has almost invariably been used heretofore in cases involving government interference with First Amendment rights. See, Dennis v. United States, 341 U.S. 494, 71 S. Ct. 857, 95 L. Ed. 1137 (1951); Terminiello v. City of Chicago, 337 U.S. 1, 69 S. Ct. 894, 93 L. Ed. 1131 (1949); Schenk v. United States, 249 U.S. 47, 39 S. Ct. 247, 63 L. Ed. 470 (1919). A definition of the term, however, which seems to be applicable here was stated in Communist Party of the United States v. Subversive Activities Control Board, 223 F.2d 531 (D.C. Cir. 1954), reversed on other grounds, 351 U.S. 115, 76 S. Ct. 663, 100 L. Ed. 1003 (1956), as follows:

> "The 'clear' in that epigram is not limited to a threat indubitably etched in every microscopic detail. It includes that which is not speculative but real, not imagined but actual. The 'present' in the epigram is not restricted to the climactically imminent. It includes that which exists as contrasted with that which does not yet exist and that which has ceased to exist." 223 F.2d at 544.

In this light, the determination of whether or not a strike presents a clear and present danger to the health, safety or welfare of the public must, therefore, require the court to find that the danger or threat is real or actual and that a strong likelihood exists that it will occur. Additionally, it seems to us that the "danger" or "threat" concerned must not be one which is normally incident to a strike by public employees. By enacting Act No. 195 which authorizes such strikes, the legislature may be understood to have indicated its willingness to accept certain inconveniences, for such are inevitable, but it obviously intended to draw the line at those which pose a danger to the public health, safety or welfare.[3]

The reasons indicated by the court for granting the injunction here fall generally into three categories: a) the disruption of routine procedures; b) the harassment of School Board Directors; and c) the danger of losing state subsidies because of the inability of the District to provide the full schedule of 180 instructional days.

The disruption and the harassment were certainly "clear and present," but they did not constitute a "danger" or "threat" as envisaged by Act No. 195. On the other hand, the loss of school subsidies was a "danger," but it was not, at least not yet, "clear and present."

The disruption of routine administrative procedures, the cancellation of extracurricular activities and sports and other such difficulties are most certainly inconvenient for the public, and especially for students and their parents. But these problems are inherent in the very nature of any strike by school teachers.

---

[3] "A strike by teachers . . . might be tolerated for an extended period of time before it could be demonstrated that continuation of the strike would constitute a similar threat [of danger to the public]. Teachers are customarily absent from their classrooms during weekends and holidays. Perhaps more significant is the fact that teacher services can be suspended for three months during the summer without any apparent adverse effect on the public welfare. The contrast between employment which normally involves such interruptions in service, and the necessity of continuous service by policemen, dramatizes the reason that the tolerance level for work stoppages differs so markedly.

"Although it has been suggested that a teacher strike might never create an immediate threat to public welfare, a court could conceivably find such a threat where a teacher strike continued for so long that make-up classes would not be feasible before a new school term would begin, or perhaps when the remaining vacation time for make-up classes becomes very short." Note, *Striking a Balance in Bargaining with Public School Teachers,* 56 Iowa L. Rev. 598, 610-611 (1971).

If we were to say that such inconveniences, which necessarily accompany any strike by school teachers from its very inception, are proper grounds for enjoining such a strike, we would in fact be nullifying the right to strike granted to school teachers by the legislature in Act No. 195.

A more serious problem is raised by the community unrest and the harassment of public officials which have apparently occurred in reaction to the strike. The testimony gives no indication as to who has been involved in these incidents, although it was made clear as to some situations that the Association's members were *not* so involved. We deplore such activities and sympathize with the lower court's wish to bring them to an end. Enjoining the strike, however, was not a proper method of accomplishing this purpose. In this situation it does not seem to be the strike which was the "danger" to the public, but the reaction to it by persons unknown. We cannot find that Section 1003 of Act No. 195 was intended to permit striking employees to be penalized by having their strike enjoined because a number of citizens oppose their stand and choose to show this by disrupting the community. There are other laws available to deal with such disorders.

The danger that the District will lose state subsidies because of a strike would be proper grounds for enjoining the strike if such danger were "clear and present." And, although it is not certain that subsidies will in fact have to be withheld because of the strike, it is a possibility which cannot be ignored. If the strike lasted so long, therefore, that any continuation would make it unlikely that enough days would be available to make up the 180 required, the teachers could be properly enjoined from continuing it. At the time of the last hearing, however, the strike had lasted only 12 days, and the District had 20 days available in June plus 19 holiday dates which could be used to make up time lost. The possibility that the strike would extend longer than the make-up time available did not yet exist. If a strike is to be enjoined on the basis that insufficient make-up time actually will exist, the strike must at the very least have reached the point where its continuation would make it either clearly impossible or extremely difficult for the District to make up enough instructional days to meet the subsidy requirement within the time available. This strike was far from that point when the Court below enjoined it. The fact that students and teachers might have to remain in school later in June than originally planned may be unfortunate, of course, but again it is merely an inconvenience inherent in the right of school teachers to strike, a right now guaranteed them by the law.

We must hold that at the time this injunction was issued, there were no reasonable grounds on which the lower court could find that the strike by the Association was a "clear and present danger or threat to the health, safety or welfare of the public." This is not to say, of course, that public employees may strike with impunity and ignore the public interest, nor that such inconveniences as those noted herein as incidental to a strike might not conceivably accumulate to such an extent, be continued so long or be aggravated by some unexpected development, so that the public health, safety and welfare would in fact then be endangered.

We must hold, however, that the proper purpose of an injunction under Act No. 195 is to avert present danger, not to prevent danger which may never occur at all or which can only occur, if it does occur, at some future time before which the grievances concerned can reasonably be expected to be settled.

For the reasons stated, the order of the lower court is reversed and the injunction is hereby dissolved.

## NOTES

1. Although Alaska and Oregon continue to prohibit strikes by essential government personnel, they now recognize a limited strike right for those public employees whose cessation of work would not cause serious consequences. *See generally* Comment, *Applying Private Sector Law to the Public Sector Strike in Oregon,* 56 ORE. L. REV. 251 (1977). Effective January 1, 1978, Wisconsin provided municipal employees (other than police and fire personnel) and teachers with a three-year experimental limited right-to-strike. If mediation is unable to resolve a bargaining impasse and *both* parties reject the binding arbitration option, work stoppages are permitted. *See* GERR No. 738, 12.

2. In State Dep't of Pub. Highways v. Pub. Employees' Craft Council of Montana, 529 P.2d 785 (1974), the Montana Supreme Court addressed the existence of the right to strike by public employees covered by Montana's Public Employees' Collective Bargaining Act, which provides:

> Public employees shall have and shall be protected in the exercise of, the right of self-organization, to form, join or assist any labor organization, to bargain collectively through representatives of their own choosing on questions of wages, hours, fringe benefits, and other conditions of employment and to engage in other *concerted activities* for the purpose of collective bargaining or other mutual aid or protection, free from interference, restraint or coercion. (Emphasis added.)

Noting the similarity between the Montana statute and the LMRA on the right of organization, the Court held that:

> After forty years of construction by federal and state courts, "concerted activities" indisputably has become a labor law term, a technical phrase which has "acquired a peculiar and appropriate meaning in law." That meaning includes strikes.

The Court but'ressed its decision by a comparison with two other classes of Montana public employees — nurses and teachers — who have specific restrictions or bans on their right to strike. Since the collective bargaining act at issue nowhere prohibited strikes by employees, the Court concluded that the legislature intended to confer the right to strike on employees covered by the act.

In Los Angeles Metropolitan Transit Authority v. Brotherhood of Railroad Trainmen, 54 Cal.2d 684, 355 P.2d 905 (1960), the California Supreme Court held that the statute creating the Los Angeles Metropolitan Transit Authority gave employees the right to strike by providing that they should have the right to bargain collectively and to engage in "other concerted activities for the purpose of collective bargaining or other mutual aid or protection." *See also* Local 266, IBEW v. Salt River Project, Agricultural Improvement & Power Dist., 78 Ariz. 30, 275 P.2d 393 (1954), where the Court sustained the right of public employees to strike in support of a demand for collective bargaining where their employer was engaged in proprietary and not governmental functions.

3. The Minnesota Public Employment Relations Act generally proscribes public sector work stoppages. However, nonessential government workers are provided with a defense against the statute's strike sanctions where their employer either refuses to submit to binding impasse arbitration or fails to comply with the provisions of a valid interest arbitration award. If one group of nonessential employees may strike with impunity where their public employer has rejected the interest arbitration option, should nonessential personnel in other bargaining units be able to engage in a sympathy stoppage in support of the initial strikers without being liable for strike penalties? *See* Teamsters, Local 120 v. City of St. Paul, 270 N.W.2d 877, 1977-78 PBC ¶ 36,397 (Minn. 1978).

New York's Taylor Law also has a provision ameliorating strike penalties in appropriate cases. Section 210-3(f) instructs PERB, when determining a strike sanction, to "consider all the relevant facts and circumstances, including but not limited to: (i) the extent of any wilful defiance . . . (ii) the impact of the strike on the public health, safety, and welfare of the community and (iii) the financial resources of the employee organization; and the board may consider (i) the refusal of the employee organization or the appropriate public employer . . . to submit [the dispute] to the mediation and fact-finding procedures . . . and (ii) whether, if so alleged by the employee organization, the appropriate public employer . . . engaged in such acts of extreme provocation as to detract from the responsibility of the employee organization for the strike." *See In re* Massapequa Local 1442, AFT, 4 PERB ¶8000 (1970) (giving definition to the statutory defense of "extreme provocation").

4. In Pennsylvania Labor Bd. v. New Castle Area School Dist., PLRB Case No. PERA-C-4217-W, GERR No. 567, B-2 (1974), the PLRB held that a lockout of local government employees for the purpose of enhancing the public employer's economic position at the bargaining table was lawful. The PLRB indicated, however, that if the lockout had been intended to undermine the union, it would have been impermissible. The PLRB's decision parallels in large part the Supreme Court's reasoning in American Shipbuilding Co. v. NLRB, 380 U.S. 300, 855 S. Ct. 955, 13 L. Ed. 2d 855 (1965).

5. Could a legislative enactment providing school teachers with a right to strike be challenged on the ground that it impermissibly interferes with the right to a public education which is guaranteed to children under the state constitution? *See* Butler Area School Dist. v. Butler Educ. Ass'n, 97 L.R.R.M. 2925 (Pa. Comm. Pl. Ct.), *dec. vacated as improvident,* 391 A.2d 1295, 100 L.R.R.M. 2185 (Pa. 1978).

6. Under the Canadian Public Service Staff Relations Act, CAN. REV. STAT. c. 72 (1967), covering federal employees, the exclusive bargaining agent is required, at the inception of the bargaining relationship, to decide which of two paths the relationship will follow: (1) Binding arbitration (with no right to strike) or; (2) Conciliation with the right to strike. If the latter alternative is chosen, certain employees whose jobs "consist in whole or in part of duties, the performance of which at any given time or after any specified period of time is or will be necessary in the interest of the safety or security of the public" are forbidden to strike. These employees are chosen, within twenty days of the decision on the conciliation alternative, by the employer, whose decision becomes final if no objection to it is filed. In the event of such an objection, the Public Service Staff Relations Board (PSSRB) established by law, holds a hearing to decide the matter. The PSSRB also provides accurate wage cost data to facilitate the fact finding for negotiation purposes. *See generally* Arthurs, *Collective Bargaining in the Public Service of Canada: Bold Experiment or Act of Folly?,* 67 MICH. L. REV. 971 (1969).

## BERNSTEIN, ALTERNATIVES TO THE STRIKE IN PUBLIC LABOR RELATIONS, 85 Harv. L. Rev. 459, 469-75 (1971) †

. . . It is reasonably clear that in public employment, the strike ban does not work; yet in most jurisdictions legalization of the strike is not a real possibility. And, I submit, the strike as it is known in the private sector would not function in the same way in the public sector and does not fit the peculiarities of public collective bargaining — diffuse responsibility and the consequent need for longer periods of time to reach settlements than in the private sector. Compulsory arbitration has serious drawbacks, not the least of which are its unacceptability to large segments of public management and unions and the likely instability of its results.

Therefore I suggest [4] that we explore the possibilities of two other

---

† Reprinted by permission of The Harvard Law Review Association and Professor Merton C. Bernstein, Washington University School of Law.

[4] I want to emphasize that the proposed procedures should be part of a comprehensive public labor relations scheme which provides protection of employees against reprisal for collective activity, procedures for ascertaining appropriate bargaining units, elections to determine employee preferences, recognition and mandatory bargaining, sanctions against improper union activity, mediation procedures for bargaining disputes, and factfinding with recommendations in the case of bargaining deadlock. Such procedures are necessary conditions to the proper functioning of the nonstoppage and graduated strikes. Happily, it is also the case that these procedures will work more effectively if the pressure devices I propose are available.

arrangements which have never been considered in the public sector [5] but which, I suggest, fit the needs of *all* the parties more adequately than either present practices or the currently proposed alternatives.

It will help to give a rough sketch of the functioning of these two arrangements before I go into them in detail. In a nonstoppage strike, operations would continue as usual, but both the employees and the employer would pay to a special fund an amount equal to a specified percentage of total cash wages. Thus, while both parties would be under pressure to settle, there would be no disruption of service. In a graduated strike, employees would stop working during portions of their usual workweek and would suffer comparable reductions of wages. Here, there would be pressure not only on employees and employer but also on the community; however, the decrease in public service would not be as sudden or complete as in the conventional strike. I believe that these two new types of strike substitutes would work best in tandem.

## A. *The Nonstoppage Strike*

Under my proposal, a public employee union would be free to declare a nonstoppage strike after all other bargaining procedures failed to produce a settlement. Employees would be obliged to continue to work full time but would forego a portion of their take-home pay. I suggest that, initially, ten percent would suffice. This money would be paid by the public employer directly into a special fund (more fully discussed below). In addition to paying the equivalent of regular wages, the employer would also put into the fund an extra amount equal to what the employees have given up; this latter sum would constitute a loss to the employer. The union would have the option periodically to increase the amount of the foregone wages and employer payment, perhaps by increments of ten percent every two weeks. The public employer would have the option to require the union to switch to a graduated strike. If the employer did this, the employees would continue to lose the same rate of pay, but the employer would forego services rather than pay out additional funds.

I believe that exercise of the option to initiate the nonstoppage strike and increase the percentage can be limited to the union. The union has little other leverage, since the conventional strike would still be prohibited. Also, were the public employer able to initiate a procedure under which employees would work without pay, questions of involuntary servitude might arise. In any event, the employer would still have the strategic bargaining advantage of instituting, after a deadlock in negotiations, certain changes in pay or other terms of employment which have been offered to the union and rejected.

---

[5] Several proposals for "nonstoppage" or "statutory" (because imposed by statute) strikes were made for the private sector starting in the late 1940's. They were, in chronological order, Marceau & Musgrave, *Strikes in Essential Industries: A Way Out*, 27 Harv. Bus. Rev. 287 (1949); Goble, *The Non-Stoppage Strike*, 2 Lab. L.J. 105 (1951); N. Chamberlain & J. Schilling, Social Responsibility and Strikes 279-86 (1952); Gregory, *Injunctions, Seizure and Compulsory Arbitration*, 26 Temp. L.Q. 397, 402 (1953). The major variations are summarized and assessed in McCalmont, *The Semi-Strike*, 15 Ind. & Lab. Rel. Rev. 191 (1962); Marshall & Marshall, *Nonstoppage Strike Proposals — A Critique*, 7 Lab. L.J. 299 (1956).

All of these proposals envisioned that employees continue at work and that the employer lose some income; and most involved a reduction of pay between declaration of the nonstoppage and settlement. All were limited to the private sector. The proposal I make here is the first to suggest application to the public sector and differs in several respects from each of the earlier versions.

The graduated strike is, to the best of my knowledge, original with me.

The nonstoppage strike would accommodate the peculiarities of public labor relations. It would attract the attention of and put pressure on both the public officials who deal directly with the union involved and other members of the executive branch whose own budgets might be affected, the local legislature, and state officials. And while a stoppage strike would not precipitate a crisis, its pressure would be steady and increasable. Thus, it may provide the necessary incentive for the various bodies of government to act, while allowing them the time they need to do so effectively. Moreover, it does not disturb consideration of the merits of the dispute with the hysteria and histrionics now typical of illegal strikes.

While nonstoppage strikes would create additional expense for public employers — many of whom are hard pressed as it is — they should also put an end to the present practice of paying the employees at overtime rates when a strike ends to reduce the backlog of work accumulated during the strike. Also, hopefully, the expense should be only temporary, and, as will be explained below, the money will not go to waste. In any event, the price does not seem too high to pay for a substantially improved process of bargaining.

Nonstoppage strikes offer significant advantages to employees, perhaps even more than would legalization of conventional strikes. In the first place, their rate of loss of pay would be lower at any given time than if there were an all-out strike. For employees with mortgage and other installment obligations to meet, this continuity of income is highly desirable. And, to the extent that the nonstoppage strike encourages more responsive bargaining without any stoppages, the total loss of pay may be less. In addition, in a full-scale strike, especially one of long duration, the employer is not liable for fringe benefit payments. Thus, life insurance policies may lapse or require payment by employees at a time when their income is interrupted, and group medical care insurance may have to be kept in force at the higher-cost individual rates. In a nonstoppage strike these benefits should continue.

Second, in actual strikes employees run the risk of losing their jobs. A common sanction in illegal strikes is to fire strikers. In the private strike, too, replacement of economic strikers has long been permitted, and while I have seen no data on public employer activity of this sort, I think it highly probable that permanent, nondiscriminatory replacement of strikers will become a feature of the legal public employee strike. In nonstoppage strikes, of course, jobs would be secure. Moreover, the absence of even temporary replacements would eliminate a traditionally potent source of violence, which everyone has a stake in averting.

Third, long-run employee and union interests are best served by a method that is legal and discomfits the community as little as possible. As union leadership knows from its post-World War II experience, unpopular strikes lead to distasteful legislation. And, by the same token, strikers, even if they feel their conduct justified, often must incur the disapproval of friends, neighbors, and others in the community. A peaceful method of pursuing demands seems clearly preferable.

The public employer would need some means of assuring union and employee compliance with the ground rules. Obviously, working full time for less than full pay might encourage some employees to slow down or "call in sick" — a favored device in strike-ban jurisdictions. Two procedures would minimize violations. First, the unions must see that it is to their advantage to persuade members that it is to *their* advantage to abide by the rules. That is, all must be made aware that the "struck" employer is indeed under strike-like pressure. Second, the statute should provide for an expedited (and I mean quick) unfair labor practice procedure to hear and determine charges of slowdown or improper absence. However, these areas are so sensitive and have such a potential for emotional overreaction that employer discipline of employees should be limited to those cases where impartial hearing officers make a finding that the improper action has taken place.

One serious problem with the nonstoppage strike is finding a suitable use for the special fund to which the public employer and employees have contributed. In order to insure that the loss will actually discipline the parties' conduct in bargaining, the fund would have to be placed effectively beyond their recapture.[6] I recommend that the fund be put at the disposal of a tripartite Public Purposes Committee in which respected community figures outnumber the total number of union and government members. This committee would be charged with the task of applying the money to publicly desirable, preferably short term projects that are not currently in the public budget — creation of scholarships or construction of public recreation facilities, for example. Certainly public employees would get little direct advantage from such a use of the money. Moreover, since these projects would not be currently funded, the committee's action would not discharge any of the government's present obligations; and since such contributions would occur irregularly, the government could not count on being relieved of any future burdens. Consequently, given public officialdom's abhorrence of losing control over money, this use of the funds should also provide an incentive for public employers to bargain.

Finally, I would like to dispel what may perhaps be a lingering doubt about nonstoppage strikes. Although they were initially proposed for use in the private sector more than two decades ago, they have had little acceptance by private parties. There are a number of reasons for this. First, although strikes have been the subject of some academic disapproval and periodic editorial dismay, they remain an acceptable device in the private sector. There has been, therefore, little real pressure for a substitute. Second, for a nonstoppage strike in the private sector to be as effective as the conventional strike, the contributions of the employer to the fund must be geared to the amount of profits it is spared from losing. Because of the obvious difficulty of calculating this figure, achieving a formula for employer contribution which is satisfactory to both parties could easily be more formidable an obstacle than resolving their basic economic differences. Third, any statutory imposition of a nonstoppage plan would, while solving in a crude way the complexities of computing the formula, raise the claim by employers of deprivation of property without due process and the analogous employee claim of involuntary servitude.

Clearly the first reason does not apply in the public sector, for strikes are not currently acceptable. Nor does the second carry much weight. There is no need in the public sector to base a formula on profits because there are no profits; what should be required by the employees is that there be sufficient pressure on the public employer, and I believe my proposal provides that. The third, too, is inapplicable. Government may of course impose conditions on itself; and since it is constitutional totally to deprive public employees of the right to strike, it should be permissible to provide them with a halfway measure, especially when it is the union which voluntarily initiates its use. In short, no significant barriers to adoption of nonstoppage strikes exist in the public sector.

---

[6] It might, however, be worthwhile to experiment with partial recapture as an incentive to rapid settlement. Thus, the amounts lost by the parties in the week in which they reach a settlement might be returned to them.

## B. *The Graduated Strike*

A nonstoppage strike may be insufficient to induce responsive bargaining. More direct pressure may be required, and the graduated strike would provide it.

In a graduated strike the union would call work to a halt in stages. During the first week or two of the strike the employees would not work for half a day; during the next period, if the union so chose, they would not work for one full day per week; and so on, until they reached some floor short of total stoppage. Employees' take-home pay would be cut proportionately.

The effect of a graduated strike would be to give the public a taste of reduced service without the shock of immediate and total deprivation. This would start in motion the political machinery I described earlier, but would not overload it. Citizens would make complaints about their inconvenience known to their elected representatives. Local officials, both executive and legislative, would thus be under pressure to *do* something, but would nevertheless be able to consult with each other and with the officials at higher levels of government. They would therefore be able to negotiate with the union in a reasonably coordinated and authoritative manner. Free of resentment and of posturing over illegality, the complicated political process of sorting out preferences between higher costs and fewer services and among competing demands could then work itself out.

To insure that employees really suffer proportionate loss of wages would require, first, that they be unable, after the strike, to reduce backlogs at overtime rates. This could probably be accomplished simply by a limitation on overtime pay for some period following the strike. It does not seem necessary to do more: to the extent the employees ultimately recoup their lost wages, the public will have the lost service restored; and in any case it is unlikely that either side's losses will ever be totally recovered. Second, it would be necessary that the shutdown not exceed the announced level. While enforcement of this requirement would not be easy, it would probably be satisfactory for an impartial body with an expedited hearing procedure to determine the actual extent of the employee stoppage and to mete out appropriate penalties, including reduction of wages. In addition, there would be another strong inducement to proper observance of the ground rules: union and employee recognition that they have an effective, fair, and acceptable weapon to encourage good faith bargaining.

As I stated before, I think that the graduated strike and nonstoppage strike would work best in tandem. Because a nonstoppage strike would cause the public less disruption, we should perhaps require that unions try it for at least four weeks; they would then have the option of instituting a graduated strike. However, since both types of strikes are certain to put pressure on the public employer, I think we should give the employer some limited options. If it feels itself financially hard pressed, it can select the graduated strike, which would result in no additional expense. If it believed that the service performed by the employees was so essential to the public that cessation could not be tolerated — for example, fire and police protection — it should have the opportunity to persuade an impartial, preferably expert, tribunal that the services are in reality so indispensable. If successful, it could limit the union to the ever-more-expensive nonstoppage strike.

## V. Conclusion

A blanket ban on strikes by public employees does not work. Illegal strikes are bad for labor relations and even worse for the rule of law. However, conventional strikes, if legalized, would be ill adapted to the complex procedures of public labor relations. Yet the public must accord its employees reasonable procedures that produce responsible bargaining. Under my proposals, bargaining could perform its salutary function, but without the disruption caused by the conventional strike and in ways adapted to the peculiarities of the public's needs and the government's intricate procedures for allocating resources.

Our federal system is complex and often awkward, but it enables us to experiment with various means of regulating public labor-management relations so that neither the public nor public employees are victimized. We should test the nonstoppage strike, the graduated strike, and indeed any other promising arrangement as we grope in this old field mined with so many new problems.

## NOTE

*See generally Exploring Alternatives to the Strike,* 96 Monthly Lab. Rev. 33-66 (Sept., 1973).

# SETTLEMENT OF COLLECTIVE BARGAINING IMPASSES

## A. INTRODUCTION

### 1. IMPASSE DISPUTES

Three kinds of impasse disputes arise in the course of labor-management relations in the public and private sectors. These are customarily referred to as "representational," "grievance" (or "rights"), and "collective bargaining" (or "interest") disputes, respectively. "Representational" disputes concern efforts by one or more labor organizations to obtain bargaining rights. These types of disputes constitute the subject matter of Chapter Three. "Grievance" ("rights") disputes arise subsequent to the negotiation of a collective bargaining agreement and ordinarily concern the interpretation or administration of the agreement. These controversies are generally resolved in accordance with contractually negotiated grievance procedures, which are discussed in Chapter Eight.

"Interest" disputes arise during the parties' attempt to negotiate the terms of a bargaining agreement. This chapter is devoted to a consideration of the various methods or procedures which have been employed or advocated for use in the public sector to resolve these types of bargaining disputes. With respect to the problem of the settlement of public sector bargaining impasses, the Taylor Report [1] warned:

> The design of dispute settlement procedures must constantly avoid at least two serious pitfalls. The first is that impasse procedures often tend to be overused; they may become too accessible and as a consequence, the responsibility and problem-solving virtues of constructive negotiations are lost. Dispute settlement procedures can become habitforming, and then negotiations become only a ritual. The second pitfall is that a standardized dispute settlement procedure is not ideally suited to all parties and to all disputes. Procedures work best which have been mutually designed, are mutually administered, and have been mutually shaped to the particular problem at hand.

## 2. A SURVEY OF IMPASSE PROCEDURES AND THEIR RATIONALE

### D. BOK AND J. DUNLOP, LABOR AND THE AMERICAN COMMUNITY 333-34, 337-38 (1970)†

Once a negotiating relationship has been established, the concern shifts to the resolution of disputes over the terms of employment. The settlement of these disputes calls for the design of procedures to govern collective negotiation and to provide effective alternatives to conflict. In the first instance, it is probably wise to ask the parties involved to design their own machinery. Employee

---

[1] Governor's Committee on Public Employee Relations, Final Report to Governor Nelson Rockefeller, State of New York, March 31, 1966, p. 33.

† Reprinted by permission of Simon & Schuster, Inc.

organizations differ widely in their objectives and methods: Governmental units are of varying size and confront diverse budgetary restraints and procedures. The scope of civil-service regulations and collective negotiations are far from uniform, and great differences appear in the nature of government operations and the authority of government negotiators. The influence of employee organizations and the labor movement in the community also varies sharply. It stands to reason, therefore, that no one procedure, imposed legislatively, will suit all the situations to which it would apply.

There are already a variety of procedures available in the public sector, and inventiveness in this field is at an early stage. The parties may develop some variant of the prevailing-wage approach and identify the procedures and the comparable sectors to be used in making these determinations. They may establish various study committees to operate during the term of the agreement, particularly on difficult prospective issues, with resort to fact finding and recommendations before a body of their own design and choice. They may design a system of public hearings with settlement through normal political processes. As George Meany has observed, "Perhaps the best answer in this field is some system of voluntary arbitration."

In the absence of procedures agreed to by the parties to resolve disputes over provisions of an agreement, or in the event that such machinery fails, the government involved in the dispute has an obligation to provide a general procedure. There is wide agreement that provision should be made for mediation between the employee organization and the governmental unit if the parties fail to resolve the dispute by direct negotiations. But what should happen in the event that the dispute remains unresolved and the parties have reached a serious impasse?

There are three groups of major contending views on impasse procedures: 1) Government employees should be allowed to strike except when the public health or safety is in jeopardy. 2) If the impasse cannot otherwise be settled, no strike of public employees is permissible and the dispute should be resolved by compulsory arbitration binding on both the governmental employer and the employee organization. 3) Recommendations should be made by a fact-finding body, and in the event further mediation around these recommendations does not resolve the dispute, the appropriate legislative body should review the dispute and enact a statute prescribing the terms and conditions of employment. The recommendations of the fact finders should have presumptive validity, but should not be binding on the legislature. . . .

The third alternative impasse procedure is fact finding with final resolution to be made, if necessary, by the legislative body. This procedure provides a role for both expert opinion of neutrals and for legislative judgment on questions beyond the province of the labor-management specialist.

Where it works well, fact finding can be a useful and even a powerful device. It seems to focus public opinion and to economize on the legislators' time, while providing them with the guidance they need. Fact finding is also a flexible procedure; it provides maximum opportunity for mediation, before, during, and after recommendations made privately or publicly. The exposure to hard facts also helps to deflate extreme positions; it allows neutrals to develop and "try on for size" possible accommodations, while permitting the parties to modify a recommendation to their mutual advantage. The uncertainty of the ultimate legislative action may stimulate a settlement, and the parties can preserve the opportunity for reaching such an agreement even after recommendations have been made.

In some instances, of course, the legislative body will unwisely reject the recommendations of a fact-finding board. Thus, critics may argue that the procedure is inherently unfair, since the employer — that is, the government — has the ultimate power to decide, even unfairly, in its own case. But what is the alternative? Some observers will suggest that the union be allowed to strike whenever the government refuses to accept the recommendations of the fact-finding body. But fact finders can make egregious errors, and surely they are not qualified to weigh the added labor costs of a settlement against tax increases and competing public programs and expenditures. Decisions of this kind may be more appropriately resolved by political processes and elected officials than by strikes or labor arbitrators. If so, the union is not without recourse, for it can bring political pressure to bear through its constituents and lobbyists. In this respect, the union occupies a very different position vis-a-vis the government than it would vis-a-vis a private employer with final power to fix the terms of employment. It is true that the union may have very little political influence and some legislative bodies may disregard its pleas for this reason. But similar drawbacks will exist in any system; if strikes were allowed, for example, many public employees would also have too little power to protect their legitimate interests. As a result, considering all the interests at stake, the wisest course may lie in letting the legislative body decide on the recommendations of a neutral panel. If the legislature disregards the recommendations too freely and too unfairly, strikes are likely to occur, regardless of the law, to bring home the interests of the employees. Short of this, the strike seems an inappropriate way to resolve the impasse.

**HILDEBRAND, THE RESOLUTION OF IMPASSES, in THE ARBITRATOR, THE NLRB, AND THE COURTS, PROCEEDINGS OF THE TWENTIETH ANNUAL MEETING OF THE NATIONAL ACADEMY OF ARBITRATORS 289-92 (D. Jones ed. 1967)†**

[The author first discusses impasse procedures used in the private sector and rejects as unworkable a full assimilation of those procedures to the public sector. After deciding that the public sector provides very special and necessary services, as a monopoly enterprise, which demands continuity of operations, the author continues:]

If these judgments are correct, then the government sector is indeed a special case. Accordingly, the critical task becomes that of designing a set of procedures that will accomplish three major objectives. The first one is to develop as fully as possible a role for collective bargaining as a method for achieving accommodation and mutual consent. The second is to protect the integrity of the bargaining process by insuring the independence of public management so that the process will not become transformed into a type of machine politics, hence political bargaining. Political bargaining is not collective bargaining. Whatever may be its own rationale, it carries real dangers to collective bargaining in the public service, and it cannot be defended by arguments in behalf of collective bargaining as such. If we seek the latter, we must insure the independence of public managements, and we must make it possible for such managements to sign binding agreements.

Third, the basic procedure must recognize the need to preserve continuity of operations, but, more than this, it should restrain reliance upon coercion as much

---

† Reprinted by permission of The Bureau of National Affairs, Inc.

as possible, so that bargained settlements can become the rule rather than the exception.

The first objective can be served best by provision for an independent public agency to deal with questions of representation and unfair labor practices. In addition, the enabling statute should provide the parties with incentive to devise their own procedures for resolving impasses, failing which one will be mandated by law.

## Treatment of Impasses

The second objective is self-evident, and needs no elaboration. The third refers to the treatment of impasses, about which the rest of my paper will be concerned.

Because the budget-making activities of public bodies are controlled by the calendar, the timing of negotiations becomes critical. They must begin early enough to permit the incorporation of settlements in the budget, and the negotiating period must allow for the possibility of intervention if voluntary agreement cannot be reached. Clearly, too, the whole process must provide sufficient opportunity for legislative consideration, open hearings, and clearance with civil service officials.

Because timing is so important, the procedure should make mediation available whenever serious conflict develops, at the option of either side or of the top public official within the jurisdiction. Obviously, too, this official must be kept continuously informed regarding the progress of negotiations. Furthermore, in my judgment it may well be desirable to provide for preventive mediation at the initiative of the independent agency charged with dealing with representation issues and unfair practices.

But suppose mediation fails. Then what? Here two alternative remedies are possible — compulsory arbitration and fact-finding without compulsory arbitration at its terminus. Recourse to either assumes, of course, that the parties have not built in their own procedure for resolving impasses, a procedure that in turn must be compatible with the fundamental policy laid down by statute.

To my mind, there are two basic weaknesses in the method of compulsory arbitration for dealing with disputes in the public service. One is that the certainty that it can be invoked constitutes an open invitation to extremist strategies. Ask for all you can, because you stand a chance of getting part of it. The insidious consequence is that this will vitiate the very process of collective bargaining. The pressures will then be shifted to what in fact is a juridical mechanism. What begins as collective bargaining ends in something quite different.[2] In the second place, compulsory arbitration amounts to a delegation of the responsibilities of public management and of the lawmakers to outsiders. In my view, this is incompatible with the basic principles of representative government. In fact, it can become a most convenient way to duck hard issues by passing them on to a board that is only temporarily in office and that is not responsible to the electorate. The result is likely to be labor policies that are unsound, because they will be more responsive to power relations than to the equitable accommodation of all interests — those of taxpayers, the citizens who use the service, management, and the whole body of public employees viewed collectively.

## The Fact-Finding Approach

The second technique for dealing with impasses is that of fact-finding,

---

[2] This danger might be reduced if the arbitration proceeding were made very costly to the parties, and its availability were made uncertain by provision of a choice-of-weapons approach.

following, of course, negotiations and mediation. In my view, and for the reasons just stated, this method should be an open-ended one. That is, if it issues in ultimate failure, compulsory arbitration should not be available at its terminus. I shall submit my reasons for leaving the process open-ended for subsequent consideration.

As I see the matter, fact-finding begins when mediation fails. I favor an all-public tripartite board for this purpose, to increase the likelihood of unanimity. Recourse to such a board should be at the initiative of either party or of the top public official, after the mediation period has run out. Precise time limits are required for hearing the dispute and rendering a report. It also seems to me desirable to provide that the recommendations of the board first should be submitted privately to the parties, coupled with a final mediatory effort by the board itself. If this step proves unsuccessful, the recommendations then should be made public, in hopes of building up public opinion in their behalf. If acceptance still cannot be gained, there may be some merit in having the chief executive assemble a carefully selected private committee to attempt quietly to persuade the intractable side to settle on the basis of these recommendations.

There is much to be said for the fact-finding approach. It is a logical extension of the process of collective bargaining because it continuously keeps open the possibility of voluntary settlement. I know of no other method that would serve this end as well. Moreover, it leaves the ultimate responsibility of the lawmakers intact, and, even more, it can produce a set of guidelines to a fair resolution of the dispute at their hands. In turn, this latter feature reduces the disabilities of attempting to legislate in a context of crisis, by men mostly lacking in the necessary expertise.

## B. AARON, L. BAILER & H. BLOCK, AN EMPLOYEE RELATIONS ORDINANCE FOR LOS ANGELES COUNTY, REPORT AND RECOMMENDATION OF CONSULTANTS' COMMITTEE 31-34 (July 25, 1968)

We have previously adverted to the rising incidence of strikes by public employees. We believe that such strikes are and should be unlawful, but to say so is merely to add a dimension to the problem and does not contribute to its solution. The only meaningful way to deal with strikes in the public sector is to devise settlement procedures which the parties will be willing to substitute for trial by economic combat. We offer no magic formula, no foolproof panacea; but we believe that our recommendations, if adopted, would substantially reduce the need for or the likelihood of strikes by County employees.

We assume that potential strike situations typically have their origin in disputes over proposed new wages, hours, and terms and conditions of employment. Disputes over existing terms and conditions involve rights, as opposed to interests; these disputes are classified as grievances and can be handled in accordance with established grievance procedures. In negotiating over new terms and conditions, however, the County and a certified employee organization may reach an impasse. We recommend that in such a case either party be permitted to invoke the assistance of the Commission [independently staffed, governmentally paid Employer-Employee Commission]. In order to prevent premature involvement of the Commission in the merits of the dispute, we also recommend that either party be permitted to raise the factual issue, to be decided by the Commission, whether an impasse has actually been reached. If that issue were raised and the Commission found that an impasse had not yet been reached, the parties would be obliged to continue their negotiations.

In the case of a genuine impasse, however, the Commission would itself be free to attempt to mediate a settlement of the dispute. Failing in that effort, it would ascertain whether the parties were willing, voluntarily, to submit the dispute to arbitration. If mediation failed and the parties would not mutually agree to arbitrate, the Commission would be empowered under the recommended ordinance to call in one or more neutral outsiders to assist in finding a solution to the dispute. Depending upon the requests of the parties and its own estimate of the situation, the Commission would ask the neutrals to undertake further mediation, or fact-finding with or without recommendations. Failure of any party to cooperate fully with the Commission or its agents at any stage of this procedure would constitute an unfair employee relations practice. The costs, if any, of such proceeding would be borne equally by the parties to the dispute.

Mediation reports would be filed with the Commission and would be kept confidential. Fact-finding reports would be filed with the Commission and transmitted by it to the parties within five calendar days after receipt. Release of the fact-finding report and recommendations, if any, in a given case, would be within the discretion of the Commission.

Release of a fact-finding report would exhaust the legal authority and responsibility of the Commission under the recommended ordinance in a given case. This would not preclude either party, however, from urging the Board of Supervisors to summon the disputants to a hearing to show cause why the recommendations of fact-finders had not been accepted.

## KHEEL, STRIKES AND PUBLIC EMPLOYMENT, 67 Mich. L. Rev. 931, 940-41 (1969)†

[After concluding that most compulsory arbitration procedures are unsatisfactory, because of issue framing difficulties and the lack of binding effect on the legislature, Mr. Kheel states:]

The simple lesson is that compulsory arbitration for all disputes and all issues is neither legally sound nor practically feasible. It would be a great mistake to adopt this procedure as the usual method prescribed in advance for all disputes in the expectation that it would signal an end to labor strife in public employment.

I believe, rather, that we should acknowledge the failure of unilateral determination, and turn instead to true collective bargaining, even though this must include the possibility of a strike. We would then clearly understand that we must seek to improve the bargaining process and the skill of the negotiators to prevent strikes. For in the end, the solution to the wide range of labor problems involving the many aspects of a dynamic and complicated human relationship must depend on the human factor. The most elaborate machinery is no better than the people who man it. It cannot function automatically. With skillful and responsible negotiators, no machinery, no outsiders, and no fixed rules are needed to settle disputes. For too long our attention has been directed to the mechanics and penalties rather than to the participants and the process. It is now time to change that, to seek to prevent strikes by encouraging collective bargaining to the fullest extent possible.

For the few strikes that might jeopardize public health or safety, I would favor legislation authorizing the governor of a state to seek an injunction for a specified period through procedures similar to those for emergency disputes under the

---

† Reprinted by permission of The Michigan Law Review.

Taft-Hartley Act. During the cooling-off period, the parties could continue their search for the basis of accommodation to end the dispute. If these procedures prove unavailing, then the legislature could consider means, but not the specific terms, of settlement, including the possibility of submitting the remaining issues to arbitration within specified bounds. In a particular situation, with issues sharply limited and defined through bargaining, arbitration imposed as a last resort by the legislature can effectively protect the public interest without making a sham of the bargaining process. Our primary reliance would then be placed, as I believe it must if we are to prevent strikes, on joint determination by parties in a true bargaining atmosphere.

I suggest, in short, that there is no workable substitute for collective bargaining — even in government — and that our best chance to prevent strikes against the public interest lies in improving the practice of bargaining. In an environment conducive to real bargaining, strikes will be fewer and shorter than in a system where employees are in effect invited to defy the law in order to make real the promise of joint determination. In a real bargaining environment, the employee representatives, I am convinced, can more effectively meet their dual responsibility to negotiate and to lead. Only if leaders do both can there be constructive labor relationships in place of the chaos resulting when agreements reached in negotiations are rejected by angry rank and file or defied by subterfuge forms of strikes such as working to the rule.

## NOTES

1. The preceding excerpts emphasize the need for impasse settlement procedures to provide a substitute for strike action. Is the theory, then, that such procedures will or must involve pressure tactics roughly the equivalent of those which would be generated by a strike or lockout? Alternatively, is the theory that settlement procedures properly designed and skillfully used can or should obviate the need for resort to or availability of the strike or lockout? Given that impasse resolution procedures in the public sector are usually mediation and fact-finding with recommendations, or, in some instances binding arbitration, does the question whether specific procedures are appropriate depend upon which of the suggested underlying theories is sound? Are such theories relevant to the determination of mediation and fact-finding methodology (e.g., with respect to the role of the mediator, and the question whether fact-finding recommendations are to be made public)? See Anderson, *Strikes and Impasse Resolution in Public Employment,* 67 Mich. L. Rev. 943, 947-48 (1969) (contending that strikes are not essential to effective dispute settlement given skilled bargainers and sound impasse resolution procedures); R. Doherty & W. Oberer, Teachers, School Boards and Collective Bargaining: A Changing of the Guard 96-113 (1967) (favoring binding arbitration to replace the need for strikes); and Taylor, *Using Factfinding and Recommendation in Impasses,* 92 Monthly Lab. Rev. 63 (July, 1969) (suggesting that the strike must be replaced by other equally effective processes for inducing equitable settlements).

2. If regardless of the *de jure* prohibition of strikes, strikes in fact occur to the point that there is really a *de facto* recognition of them as a part of the collective bargaining process, is it not obvious that an evaluation of existing or proposed dispute settlement procedures poses different theoretical and analytical considerations than if it were assumed that strikes are not only illegal, but because illegal will not occur? Does the situation then become roughly comparable to that obtaining in the private sector? If so, is Hildebrand wrong in rejecting the private sector "model?" To put the matter in different terms, is there any justification for structuring dispute settlement procedures as typically now done, mandating mediation and, in addition, fact-finding (or arbitration) for all disputes? For discussions of these questions and alternatives to the no strike ban, see: Garber, *Compulsory Arbitration in the Public Sector: A Proposed Alternative,* 26 Arb. J. 226 (1971) (proposing "final last offer arbitration," but permitting the arbitrator to

choose the more reasonable solution offered by the parties on each disputed issue); Bernstein, *Alternatives to the Strike in Public Labor Relations*, 85 HARV. L. REV. 459, 470-75 (1971) (finding strikes inevitable and proposing the use of the graduated strike and the nonstoppage strike, as necessary to give employees sufficient bargaining strength, while not totally disrupting society); Clark, *Public Employee Strikes: Some Proposed Solutions*, 23 LAB. L.J. 111 (1972) (questioning whether any categories of public employees should have the right to strike); Note, *The Strike and Its Alternatives in Public Employment*, 1966 WIS. L. REV. 549, 554-59 (reasons for denying right to strike). For a criticism of even a partial right to strike, see Foegan, *The Partial Strike: A Solution in Public Employment?*, 30 PUB. PER. REV. 83 (1969).

3. Should impasse resolution procedures in the public sector be designed to assure "equitable" settlements irrespective of the relative bargaining strength or weakness of the particular group of employees or the public employer; or, alternatively, should impasse procedures be primarily designed to induce settlements and avoid strikes? The 1966 report by the Michigan Advisory Committee on Public Employee Relations suggested that:

> We think the primary objectives of the law should be to maximize the opportunities for equitable settlement of employee relations disputes in the public sector while rejecting, at this juncture, both resort to the strike and (except in the case of police and firefighters) compulsory third party determination of unresolved new contract issues.

*Report to Governor George Romney by the Advisory Committee on Public Employee Relations* (1966), reprinted in COLLECTIVE BARGAINING IN THE PUBLIC SERVICE 100, 104 (D. Kruger and C. Schmidt eds. 1969).

For two different proposals of procedures which might increase chances of equitable solutions, see Lev, *Strikes by Government Employees: Problems and Solutions*, 57 A.B.A.J. 771 (1971) (suggesting the creation of a Federal Public Employee Mediation Board with mediators designated to issue awards in public sector impasse disputes and, in addition, federal contributions to assist local legislatures to meet monetary terms of awards); and Cole, *Devising Alternatives to the Right to Strike*, 92 MONTHLY LAB. REV. 60 (July 1969) (suggesting a public employment advisory council, which could recommend an appropriate level of increased labor costs to be absorbed by each governmental unit in each fiscal year). *See also Exploring Alternatives to the Strike*, 96 MONTHLY LAB. REV. 33-66 (Sept. 1973).

# B. EXISTING LEGISLATIVE APPROACHES

# 1. FEDERAL LEVEL

## CIVIL SERVICE REFORM ACT OF 1978 [3]

Sec. 7114(c)(1). An agreement between any agency and an exclusive representative shall be subject to approval by the head of the agency.

(2) The head of the agency shall approve the agreement within 30 days from the date the agreement is executed if the agreement is in accordance with the provisions of this chapter and any other applicable law, rule, or regulation (unless the agency has granted an exception to the provision).

(3) If the head of the agency does not approve or disapprove the agreement within the 30-day period, the agreement shall take effect and shall be binding on the agency and the exclusive representative subject to the provisions of this chapter and any other applicable law, rule, or regulation.

---

[3] The full text of Title VII of the Civil Service Reform Act of 1978 which pertains to federal sector labor-management relations is reprinted in the *Statutory Appendix.*

(4) A local agreement subject to a national or other controlling agreement at a higher level shall be approved under the procedures of the controlling agreement or, if none, under regulations prescribed by the agency.

**Sec. 7119. Negotiation impasses; Federal Service Impasses Panel.** — (a) The Federal Mediation and Conciliation Service shall provide services and assistance to agencies and exclusive representatives in the resolution of negotiation impasses. The Service shall determine under what circumstances and in what manner it shall provide services and assistance.

(b) If voluntary arrangements, including the services of the Federal Mediation and Conciliation Service or any other third-party mediation, fail to resolve a negotiation impasse —

(1) either party may request the Federal Service Impasses Panel to consider the matter, or

(2) the parties may agree to adopt a procedure for binding arbitration of the negotiation impasse, but only if the procedure is approved by the Panel.

(c)(1). . . . . .

(5)(A) The Panel or its designee shall promptly investigate any impasse presented to it under subsection (b) of this section. The Panel shall consider the impasse and shall either — (i) recommend to the parties procedures for the resolution of the impasse; or (ii) assist the parties in resolving the impasse through whatever methods and procedures, including factfinding and recommendations, it may consider appropriate to accomplish the purpose of this section. (B) If the parties do not arrive at a settlement after assistance by the Panel under subparagraph (A) of this paragraph, the Panel may — (i) hold hearings; (ii) administer oaths, take the testimony or deposition of any person under oath, and issue subpoenas as provided in section 7132 of this title; and (iii) take whatever action is necessary and not inconsistent with this chapter to resolve the impasse. (C) Notice of any final action of the Panel under this section shall be promptly served upon the parties, and the action shall be binding on such parties during the term of the agreement, unless the parties agree otherwise.

## NOTES

1. The two bodies involved with federal labor-management relations which have primary responsibility for assisting parties with contract negotiations are the Federal Mediation and Conciliation Service (FMCS) and the Federal Service Impasses Panel (FSIP). The FSIP consists of seven members appointed by the President for five year terms. A similar impasse resolution procedure existed under Executive Order 11491, which regulated federal labor-management relations before the enactment of the Civil Service Reform Act of 1978. Case experience under E.O. 11491 indicated that the FSIP will generally not intervene in a bargaining dispute unless the services of the FMCS have been utilized.

One of five determinations can be made by the FSIP: (1) that it has no jurisdiction; (2) that negotiations should be resumed; (3) that negotiations should be resumed with more mediation; (4) that other voluntary arrangements such as arbitration should be utilized; or (5) that advisory or binding fact-finding be conducted. When binding recommendations are made by the FSIP, the parties must either accept them or negotiate their own settlement of the disputed issues.

2. The major criticism of the impasse resolution procedures which existed under E.O. 11491 concerned their alleged inability to cope with emergency situations. Since Section 7119 of the Civil Service Reform Act has adopted the same basic procedures which were previously used, this problem may continue. Some experts have contended that conditioning FSIP intervention upon the request of a party, and thereafter FSIP discretion,

reduces the effectiveness of the impasse resolution procedures. However, others have argued that flexibility and uncertainty should be part of any impasse resolution scheme. In this regard, compare the impasse resolution procedures under the Civil Service Reform Act with the more rigid formula adopted under the Postal Reorganization Act, which is reprinted in the *Statutory Appendix. See generally* Willoughby, *The FMCS and Dispute Mediation in the Federal Government,* 92 MONTHLY LAB. REV. 27 (May, 1969); Hampton, *The Framework of E.O. 11491, Labor-Management Relations in the Federal Service,* 17 FED. B. NEWS 70 (1970); and Note, *Federal Services Impasses Panel: Procedural Flexibility and Uncertainty,* 9 HARV. J. LEGIS. 694 (1972).

3. The substantial differences between the Postal Reorganization Act impasse procedures and those prescribed in the Civil Service Reform Act may be more attributable to historical development than to any inherent differences regarding the negotiation problems likely to arise under the two schemes. The postal strike of 1970 provided the impetus for special legislation which was designed to prevent further strikes and, presumably, to eliminate the need for strikes by providing specific procedures to produce contract settlements. The various steps in the postal impasse procedures, which include binding arbitration, are mandatory. However, it is not clear that the procedures will adequately cope with a work stoppage if one were to occur. What fail-safe mechanisms can be incorporated in a statutory impasse procedure to deal with unlawful strikes? *See* Kennedy, *The Postal Reorganization Act of 1970: Heading Off Future Postal Strikes?,* 59 GEO. L.J. 305 (1970). *See also* Cohn, *Labor Features of the Postal Reorganization Act,* 22 LAB. L.J. 44 (1971).

## 2. STATE AND LOCAL LEVELS

### a. A Survey of Legislation

**DISPUTE SETTLEMENT IN THE PUBLIC SECTOR: THE STATE-OF-THE-ART, REPORT TO DEPARTMENT OF LABOR, DIVISION OF PUBLIC EMPLOYMENT RELATIONS SERVICES 8-15 (T. Gilroy & A. Sinicropi eds. 1971 — updated to 1978)†**

By August of 1978, at least thirty-seven states had enacted legislation dealing with interest dispute procedures in public employment. These states were: Alaska, California, Connecticut, Delaware, Florida, Georgia, Hawaii, Idaho, Illinois, Indiana, Iowa, Kansas, Kentucky, Maine, Maryland, Massachusetts, Michigan, Minnesota, Montana, Nebraska, Nevada, New Hampshire, New Jersey, New Mexico, New York, North Dakota, Oklahoma, Oregon, Pennsylvania, Rhode Island, South Dakota, Tennessee, Texas, Vermont, Washington, Wisconsin, and Wyoming.

Public employee statutes in the above states range in employee coverage from one specific occupational group, such as teachers or firefighters, to statutes with comprehensive coverage of most public employees in the state. Moreover, a number of states have separate statutes for different types of employees, such as state and municipal employees, teachers, and police and fire personnel.

In addition to variations in coverage, state legislation presents a diversified pattern of impasse procedures such as voluntary systems devised by the parties, mediation, factfinding, arbitration, and "show cause" hearings. Individual statutes often call for one or a combination of the above mentioned procedures. It should be noted that most of the state legislation which includes interest dispute procedures has been passed since 1967. . . .

The following is a summary of the pattern of impasse procedures in state law.

---

† Updated to 1978 by the editors of this casebook.

*Mediation*

At least thirty-five states provide in some way for mediation of negotiation disputes. These states are: Alaska, California, Connecticut, Delaware, Florida, Georgia, Hawaii, Idaho, Illinois, Indiana, Iowa, Kansas, Kentucky, Maine, Maryland, Massachusetts, Michigan, Minnesota, Montana, Nebraska, Nevada, New Hampshire, New Jersey, New Mexico, New York, North Dakota, Oregon, Pennsylvania, Rhode Island, South Dakota, Tennessee, Texas, Vermont, Washington, and Wisconsin.

The provisions for mediation differ among and within states with respect to how the procedure is initiated, who provides the service, the use of one mediator or a panel, the relationship of mediation to other impasse procedures, and provisions for payment of costs.

In most states, mediation can be requested by either party. However, under statutes in a few states (e.g., California, North Dakota), both parties must request the service. In some states, such as Kansas and New York, the Public Employment Relations Board will intervene either by request or on its own initiative.

The agencies providing the mediation services vary among states and in some cases within a state for different groups of employees. Some states, such as New Jersey, provide mediation services through a public employment relations board or commission. Other states use an agency previously established to handle private sector disputes. . . .

While most states provide for a single mediator, several states provide for a panel. Frequently, a tripartite panel is utilized in which each party selects one member of the panel, with the partisan members agreeing on a third panel member. . . .

With respect to the costs of mediation, in the private sector the costs are generally borne by the mediation agency. However, in the public sector, there is often an implication or requirement that the parties pay part of the mediation costs.

*Factfinding*

Unlike the private sector, where factfinding is limited primarily to so-called national emergency disputes, the public sector relies more heavily on this technique in negotiation impasse resolution. At least thirty-two states authorize the use of factfinding. These states are: California, Connecticut, Delaware, Florida, Hawaii, Idaho, Illinois, Indiana, Iowa, Kansas, Kentucky, Maine, Maryland, Massachusetts, Michigan, Montana, Nebraska, Nevada, New Hampshire, New Jersey, New Mexico, New York, North Dakota, Oklahoma, Oregon, Pennsylvania, Rhode Island, South Dakota, Tennessee, Vermont, Washington, and Wisconsin.

The normal procedure is that factfinding may be initiated by either party, a tripartite or neutral panel is utilized, and recommendations for settlement are made by that panel. These recommendations are either made public following the decision, or delayed pending further negotiation based on those recommendations. . . .

In most states, factfinders are not specifically authorized to attempt to mediate the dispute. However, a few states (e.g., Connecticut) make specific provisions for factfinders to attempt mediation.

Several states detail criteria for use in making factfinding reports. . . . For example, Florida requires a factfinder to consider: (1) the salaries paid for comparable jobs by local private employers; (2) the salaries paid public employees by public employers of comparable size within the state; (3) the interest and welfare of the public; and (4) the peculiarities of employment as compared with other occupations.

## Arbitration

Twenty-seven states have legislation authorizing voluntary or compulsory arbitration for the resolution of some or all outstanding issues in certain public sector disputes. These states are: Alaska, Connecticut, Delaware, Hawaii, Illinois, Indiana, Iowa, Maine, Massachusetts, Michigan, Minnesota, Montana, Nebraska, Nevada, New Hampshire, New Jersey, New Mexico, New York, Oklahoma, Oregon, Pennsylvania, Rhode Island, Texas, Vermont, Washington, Wisconsin, and Wyoming.

In some of the states the decisions are only advisory, in others they are binding, and in a few states the nature of the decision is left to the agreement of the parties. Several states provide for more than one type of arbitration decision under different statutes or in the same law. . . .

Some arbitration statutes cover only "essential" employees, while other laws provide more inclusive coverage. In some jurisdictions arbitration awards for certain workers (e.g., police and fire personnel) are binding, while those pertaining to other employees are merely advisory.

In states which provide for compulsory arbitration, the dispute is referred to an arbitration board rather than an individual arbitrator. Kansas and New York provide for hearings by the legislative body which may take such action as it deems to be in the public interest, including the interest of the involved public employees. In Nebraska, the dispute is resolved by the State Court of Industrial Relations.

Most of the states authorizing arbitration either impose no limit on the issues which may be resolved through this device or are silent on the matter. In Delaware, a limit is specified, while in Louisiana, one is implied. On the other hand, the Maine statute does not appear to limit the scope of arbitration when its use is voluntary, but does provide that determinations shall be advisory concerning salaries, pensions, and insurance, and binding regarding other issues, when compulsory arbitration is utilized. In Rhode Island, which authorizes compulsory arbitration, there is no limit with respect to issues in the case of police and firefighters, whereas arbitration determinations for municipal employees and teachers are binding except on matters involving the expenditure of money.

In some states, specific criteria for arbitration awards have been established. . . . The Michigan statute includes such criteria as the authority of the employer, the financial ability of the employer, the interests of the public, consumer prices, and comparable wages.

Some statutes, notably those in Michigan and Wyoming, specifically provide for appeal of arbitration awards. Michigan permits appeals if the order is unsupported by competent, material, and substantial evidence on the whole record. Wyoming permits appeals to vacate an award for such reasons as corruption, fraud, or partiality, or if the arbitrators exceed their authority. A court may modify or correct an award when there is miscalculation or mistakes, the arbitrators decided an issue not submitted to them, or the award is imperfect in form. . . .

*County and Municipal*

While these jurisdictions are in many cases covered by the state legislation previously referred to, in many other instances their labor relations activities take place within the framework of local resolutions or ordinances. In some cases, negotiations take place without any clear legislated guidelines. This is particularly true of larger cities in states without public employment statutes and also in local school districts. . . .

Local ordinances vary widely with respect to both employees covered and impasse resolution procedures adopted, with their variations being similar to those noted previously regarding the different state enactments.

## NOTE

See Armbrust, *Impasse Resolution Procedures in Public Employment Negotiations,* 8 URB. LAWYER 449 (1976). *See also* IMPASSE AND GRIEVANCE RESOLUTION (H. Kershen ed. 1977).

## b. Some Specific Models

**WISCONSIN MUNICIPAL EMPLOYMENT LAW — WIS. STAT. ANN. § 111.70(4) (c).** *See Statutory Appendix.*

## NOTE

There are three statutes covering three separate categories of public employees in Wisconsin: State, municipal, and municipal police and firefighters. The Wisconsin Employment Relations Commission supervises impasse procedures under all three statutes.

There are two separate statutory impasse procedures for police and firefighters disputes. One covers police and firefighters in cities with populations of 2,500 to 500,000 and provides for compulsory arbitration of interest disputes at the request of either party. WIS. STAT. ANN. ch. 247, § 111.77. (The statute specifies "final offer" arbitration, unless the parties jointly elect otherwise.) The other covers only the Milwaukee police force and it, too, provides for compulsory arbitration of interest disputes. However, the statute covering Milwaukee police does not adopt the "final offer" approach. WIS. STAT. ANN. § 111.70 (4)-(jm) 1-13.

---

**PENNSYLVANIA PUBLIC EMPLOYEE RELATIONS ACT — PA. STAT. ANN. tit. 43, ch. 19, §§ 1101.801-1101.807, 1101.1002-1101.1003.** *See Statutory Appendix.*

## NOTE

Pennsylvania requires binding arbitration of disputes involving prison and mental hospital guards and court personnel if an impasse is reached. *See Statutory Appendix,* PA. STAT. ANN. § 1101.805. A different statute, PA. STAT. ANN. §§ 217.1-217.10, provides for compulsory arbitration to resolve disputes involving police and firefighters. All other public employees may strike after statutory dispute resolution procedures have been exhausted, unless or until the strike endangers the public health, safety, or welfare.

## IOWA PUBLIC EMPLOYMENT RELATIONS ACT — IOWA CODE ANN. §§ 20.19-20.22. *See Statutory Appendix.*

### NOTE

The Iowa Act, which covers most governmental employees in the state, directs an arbitrator to render a decision on an issue-by-issue basis, selecting from the last offers of the parties or from the recommendations contained in the prior fact-finder report. *See* GERR No. 757, 31-40. *See generally* Gallagher, *Interest Arbitration Under the Iowa Public Employment Relations Act,* 33 ARB. J. 30 (1978).

---

## HAWAII PUBLIC EMPLOYMENT RELATIONS ACT — HAWAII REV. STAT. §§ 89-11, 89-12. *See Statutory Appendix.*

### NOTE

In allowing strike action after resort to the prescribed impasse procedures, Hawaii's statute departs sharply from the norm. Yet it encompasses features of other states in providing for mediation and fact-finding, and it also includes a detailed procedure for voluntary binding arbitration. Is the right to strike sufficiently restricted to minimize probable resort to strike action? *See* Pendleton, *Collective Bargaining in the Public Sector,* REPORT OF THE INDUSTRIAL RELATIONS CENTER, UNIV. OF HAWAII (May, 1971).

---

## NEW YORK EMPLOYEES' FAIR EMPLOYMENT ACT (TAYLOR LAW) — § 209 OF THE TAYLOR LAW. *See Statutory Appendix.*

### NOTE

Some have criticized the New York approach since it places the task of ultimate dispute resolution in the legislative body after fact-finding. The suggestion is that this may decrease serious bargaining efforts in the expectation that more favorable treatment will come from the legislature. Are there countervailing arguments? Statistics released by the New York PERB indicate that most disputes in which mediation or fact-finding are used are resolved short of legislative action.

For general discussions of the Taylor Act, *see* Anderson, MacDonald & O'Reilly, *Impasse Resolution in Public Sector Collective Bargaining — An Examination of Compulsory Interest Arbitration in New York,* 51 ST. JOHN'S L. REV. 453, 457-481 (1977); Doering, *Impasse Issues in Teacher Disputes Submitted to Fact Finding in New York,* 27 ARB. J. 1 (1972); Sabghii, *The Taylor Act: A Brief Look After Three Years,* 1970 SUPPLEMENT TO REPORT OF TASK FORCE ON STATE AND LOCAL GOVERNMENT LABOR RELATIONS (Chi.: Pub. Personnel Ass'n. 1971); Drotning & Lipsky, *The Outcome of Impasse Procedures in New York Schools Under the Taylor Law,* 26 ARB. J. 87 (1971); Yaffe & Goldblatt, *Factfinding in Public Employment Disputes in New York State: More Promise Than Illusion,* ILR Paperback No. 10 (1971).

NEW YORK CITY COLLECTIVE BARGAINING LAW — §§ 1173-5.0a, 1173-7.0 IN ADMINISTRATIVE CODE, CH. 54, LOCAL LAW 53-1967, AS AMENDED BY LOCAL LAWS 1 & 2 of 1972. *See Statutory Appendix.*

### NOTES

1. The New York City scheme evolved during the period when the Taylor Act was being developed. The Office of Collective Bargaining (OCB), which commenced operations on January 2, 1968, was the result of a 1967 agreement between the City and most of the municipal unions with which it bargained. *See generally* Raskin, *Politics Up Ends the Bargaining Table,* in PUBLIC WORKERS AND PUBLIC UNIONS 122 (S. Zagoria ed. 1972); Anderson, *Strikes and Impasse Resolution in Public Employment,* 67 MICH. L. REV. 943 (1969); Gotbaum, *Finality in Collective Bargaining Disputes: The New York Experience,* 21 CATHOLIC U. L.REV. 589 (1972); Schilian, *The Taylor Law, The O.C.B. and the Public Employee,* 35 BROOKLYN L.REV. 214 (1969).

2. It was hoped by City officials and union leaders that the ordinance and OCB structure would prevent strikes. Strikes were not specifically prohibited, but the strike proscription and sanctions of the Taylor Act remained applicable. There have been some problems, especially in the bargaining dispute settlement area. The 1968 sanitation worker strike, followed by police sick-ins and a large backlog of unresolved cases placed the OCB under stress. The ordinance was finally amended in 1972 to empower the OCB Board of Collective Bargaining to appoint Impasse Panels to resolve bargaining disputes. An Impasse Panel is authorized to take whatever action it considers necessary to end a dispute, including mediation or final and binding settlement recommendations. *See* § 1173-7.0c of the New York City ordinance. *See also* GERR No. 435, B-10.

## C. MEDIATION AND FACT-FINDING

## 1. UNDERLYING PRINCIPLES AND THEORIES

**PICKETS AT CITY HALL, REPORT AND RECOMMENDATIONS OF THE TWENTIETH CENTURY FUND TASK FORCE ON LABOR DISPUTES IN PUBLIC EMPLOYMENT 21-24 (1970)†**

*Mediation*

The function of mediation, as it works for an agreement that the negotiators could not find themselves, is to maintain communication between the parties, who may believe they have said everything they have to say and done everything they are able to do; to inject a neutral presence into what, because of the impasse, has become an adversary situation; to strip away the nonessential matters and frame the core issues in dispute; and to propose suggestions for settlement.

Mediation works best when it is jointly sought by the disagreeing parties. Each is acknowledging that outside help may be useful, a posture that launches the mediation effort under the most favorable auspices. But if one, or both, of the parties refuse to invite mediation, it should be initiated anyway, preferably by the labor agency we recommend be established.

Mediation has no power to compel. It is fruitful only through logic and persuasion. The parties may freely accept or reject a mediator's suggestions if he chooses to make them; they abdicate none of their sovereignty. Mediation has,

---

† Copyright © 1970 by The Twentieth Century Fund, New York. Reprinted by permission.

nevertheless, been the most effective process for the resolution of labor disputes. Only if it is employed to its limit and fails should other processes be invoked.

The quality of the mediator, his experience and skills, may mean the difference between success and failure. The parties must believe that he has no bias against them. He must have a broad knowledge of labor relations, knowing all of the formulas that have been used to settle issues such as the one he confronts, and he must be able to articulate them. He should be inventive in producing new formulas if the situation requires. Above all he must be patient and persevering in his effort to bring the alienated parties into agreement, meanwhile keeping their confidence.

A cadre of professional mediators with experience in the private sector is attached to the Federal Conciliation and Mediation Service, to various state agencies and to some local governments. In some disputes nonprofessionals who seem to have the necessary qualities are enlisted as mediators. In communities which do not have mediation resources, access to an established mediation service should be established, or such a service of their own should be created. It will have a central role in labor relations policy.

But while much private sector mediation expertness is readily transferable to use in public employment disputes, working with government as a party in negotiations and with a union proscribed from striking requires special techniques that must, in many instances, still be acquired. One example of a problem a mediator is likely to face in the public sector is the question of who, on behalf of the employer, can make and effectuate a final decision on disputed issues. Those who represent government in the negotiations may not have such authority. The mediator may have to work to persuade them, then seek and find the true locus of authority — governor, mayor, legislature, council or board — and persuade still further. In any agency, department or subdivision of government, that locus can vary. As the mediator in the private sector must operate with an awareness that the position taken by union representatives in the negotiations is influenced by whether or not they think their membership will ratify any agreement reached, the public sector mediator must be aware that not only is this same factor present but there is also the need for ratification on the employer side at a higher authority level than is often represented in the negotiations.

### Fact-Finding

If mediation should fail to achieve agreement in a dispute, there should follow, as a link in a chain, the process of fact-finding. It will be best initiated through appointive action by the independent agency, the establishment of which we have recommended. If such an agency does not exist, it should be initiated by a high level public official who has had no involvement in the dispute.

Fact-finding has been most effective in both the private and public sector where it has been conducted by an individual or by a panel (usually three in number) qualified as impartial, judicious-minded experts in labor relations whose standing and character attest to their competence and lack of bias. Such men start their work with the advantage of being acceptable to the parties in dispute.

The degree of formality in fact-finding proceedings is usually determined by the fact-finders themselves, depending on what manner appears most promising. In any event, full opportunity will be provided for both the disputing parties to make their case. This may include the testimony of witnesses, the submission of documents and statistics, the presentation of briefs, arguments and rebuttals. The fact-finders may want information beyond that presented and may undertake their own research and call witnesses on their own motion. Their first objective is to establish the true facts which, in the normal dispute, are inevitably in controversy.

Once the sifting and winnowing have disclosed the true facts to the panel's satisfaction — as opposed to what the parties may have alleged during negotiations — the fact-finders will frequently essay a mediatory role. They will try to disabuse one or the other or both parties of false notions or assertions and try to get the parties themselves to agree on settlement terms. In many instances the fact-finding process has succeeded at this point in bringing the disputants into agreement and this has completed its work.

Should the dispute still persist after such an effort, it is incumbent upon the panel to exercise its own judgment as to what the settlement terms should be.

A multiplicity of considerations are to be taken into account and weighed as the fact-finders formulate their conclusions. If disputes involve labor costs, as most do, the panel will have heard or studied cost of living figures, rates paid by other employers for comparable work, the historical trend of wage adjustments for the instant employees, non-wage benefit levels and, among much other data, the employer's ability or inability to meet union demands.

Virtually all of the matters that come under the fact-finders' scrutiny in a private industry dispute will be within the purview of a panel sitting on a government employee case. But if labor costs are involved, the fact-finders in public employment will most likely have to be concerned with another factor indigenous to public employment: where and how the incidence of increased labor costs will fall. Will it require the imposition of new or higher taxes? Will it have to be paid by curtailing some public service not involved in the case before the panel? Will an upward wage adjustment deprive some other group of public employees who are bound under the same limited budget appropriation of a deserved increase?

Fair-minded and conscientious men, assuming the responsibility of making a judgment on behalf of the whole community, which includes employees, government-as-employer and the public at large, will ponder these implications. For their conclusions to be as fair as humanly possible to all interests concerned, they will have to find some balance between the competing needs and equities.

When it has formulated the terms it will endorse, the panel may decide it will be most effective by not immediately making them public but communicating them privately to the parties. When this technique is followed, a revival of direct negotiations often occurs. The disputants learn the fact-finders' conclusions and have some sense of the public pressure they will be under to accept them when the conclusions of the impartial body that has made a careful study of the issues become widely known.

In this advanced stage of resumed negotiations, focused on the fact-finders' decision, concessions by one or the other or both sides may be offered and agreement may be reached. Or willingly or reluctantly, they may submit to the panel's terms as being the best possible way out of their dispute.

If, however, the time allotted for such further negotiations does not bring results, the fact-finders must make their conclusions public and hope that public opinion will make the unwilling party or parties accept them.

**SIMKIN, FACT-FINDING: ITS VALUES AND LIMITATIONS, in ARBITRATION AND THE EXPANDING ROLE OF NEUTRALS, PROCEEDINGS OF THE TWENTY-THIRD ANNUAL MEETING OF THE NATIONAL ACADEMY OF ARBITRATORS 165-72 (G. Somers ed. 1970)†**

The principal theme of this paper is that the words — fact-finding — should

---

† Reprinted by permission of The Bureau of National Affairs, Inc.

be substantially eliminated from the labor relations vocabulary or, more accurately, that they should be relegated to more limited usefulness. This has happened already in the private sector. Some day — but not soon — I predict it will also occur in the public sector.

The words fact-finding — conjure up notions of preciseness, of objectivity, of virtue. They even have a godlike quality. Who can disagree with facts? In contrast, the word — mediation — that I do espouse, tends to have an aura of compromise, of slipperiness, of connivance and of furtiveness. Since these are frequent impressions, why prefer the vulgar to the sublime?

There is a problem of semantics. Close examination of the actual functioning of Fact-Finding Boards and of mediators or of Mediation Boards shows that the labels are quite secondary. The abilities and proclivities of the individuals named to those Boards and — more important — the reactions of the parties to the process determine what really happens. Fact-finders do or do not mediate. Some fact-finders who mediate find no facts. Persons appointed as mediators frequently do not mediate in any meaningful way but may announce some real or alleged facts and conclusions. . . .

### Fact-Finding Without Recommendations

The basic notion about this type of fact-finding is that somebody does not know the real facts and that establishment and proclamation of the facts will somehow assist in settlement.

Who is that somebody who is ignorant of the facts? Is it the parties — the general public — or the public opinion makers?

Experienced negotiators will seldom be surprised or influenced very much by the results of such fact-finding.

In a limited number of situations, publications of unpleasant facts may bring pressure on the negotiators by their constituencies. Facts that are damaging to a union, published during a long strike, may result in diminished strike morale and more willingness of employees to compromise. Or, publicized facts detrimental to a company position may bring pressure on the company negotiators from the Board of Directors. However, these results are infrequent for a simple reason. Most labor disputes are so complicated that a mere portrayal of facts does not provide a "handle" for action or even suggest clear directional signals towards a likely settlement area.

Publication of facts will be of some minor interest to the general public but will not usually provide an adequate basis for translation into an informed opinion about the total dispute.

The opinion makers (columnists, editorial writers, etc.) may welcome such a report. They will make fewer goofs of factual content and have a new reason for writing something. But the facts will seldom change any preconceived ideas they may have already expressed.

On a few occasions, fact-finders not empowered to make recommendations on the issues have indulged in assessing blame on one of the parties. This device seldom accomplishes anything. It is much more likely to exacerbate the dispute.

In short, fact-finding without recommendations is likely to be an exercise in futility.

These observations may require modification in some current public employee disputes. Bargainers in the public sector sometimes lack some of the sophistication that is more typical in the private sector. Moreover, since the taxpayers are the employers, however far removed from the bargaining table, their appraisal of facts can assume more significance than is the case in a private dispute.

There is a potential and sometimes utilized variety of this general type of fact-finding that is seldom discussed. It is the use of impartial technicians — long in advance of negotiations — to work with the parties to develop pertinent background facts on such issues as pensions and insurance.

## Fact-Finding with Recommendations

When fact-finders are given the responsibility to make specific recommendations on the issues in dispute, the process becomes very familiar to an arbitrator. . . . It is arbitration with two major points to distinguish it from grievance arbitration. (1) Recommendations are not final and binding decisions. Either or both parties can reject. (2) The recommendations do not develop out of a contractual framework. They are legislative value judgments. Recommendations are not facts, nor are they based exclusively or even primarily on facts.

Many of you will disagree honestly with the last statement. One concept of this type of fact-finding is that the recommendations flow almost automatically out of the facts. In my considered opinion, this notion has little or no validity. . . .

In arms length fact-finding, where is the fact-finder to find a basis for his value judgments? In the last analysis, all he can do is to exercise his best intellectual powers and search his own soul. He has no adequate opportunity to gauge acceptability by the parties. No hearings can ever meet that need adequately.

This is especially true because the parties have known that recommendations will be forthcoming. During the interval between the appointment of the fact-finder and the issuance of his report, any bargaining that may have occurred is almost certain to stop. All efforts of the parties have been directed to getting the best possible set of recommendations. Nor is it an adequate refuge to conclude — as is sometimes the case — that the exposure of the parties to the fact-finder so frightens them that they will reach agreement to avoid recommendations.

We come now to the receipt of the recommendations. Either or both parties can say: "No." If that is not the situation, it is de facto arbitration and should be so labeled. If a "No" is voiced, the dispute has not been settled. The fact-finder has been rebuffed and usually he has no place to go. If he reacts defensively as he is likely to do, the dispute may be exacerbated. What has been a two-way dispute up to that point may become a three-way controversy. . . .

Where fact-finding has been successful, I would suggest — but cannot prove — that the fact-finder has mediated — deliberately, instructively or surreptitiously. When fact-finding without mediation has succeeded in the public sector, I would suspect that it is a transitory phenomenon. Until recently and even now in some jurisdictions, public employees have been so far behind that fact-finders have a broad target range. I would predict that the range will narrow in the years immediately ahead of us.

What do I mean by mediation? Time does not permit analysis of the remarkably wide spectrum of mediation activity — things that a mediator can do — or not do. At one end, the spectrum begins by a decision not to intervene at all — to provide no third party assistance. At the other end of the band, the mediator can issue public recommendations. A major principle is to maximize bargaining and minimize the role of the mediator — to exercise enough patience to let bargaining work. But the mediator must also be able and willing to "grasp the nettle" — to recognize when patience is not a virtue and to act accordingly. Most mediation decisions are decisions as to strategy and timing — not decisions on the specific issues.

In the hands of a skilled mediator, facts are potent tools. It is seldom that publication of facts is either necessary or desirable. But they can be most useful in hard-hitting deflation of extreme positions. This is accomplished in separate head-to-head conferences or meetings, absent the embarrassment of the other side's presence and certainly not in the press. Public reference to the facts, if required at all, comes after a settlement to help save face.

The mediator has unusual opportunities to explore a wide variety of solutions — to "try them on for size." Thus, he acquires a strong intuitive sense, if not the certainty, of the vital element of acceptability.

Package recommendations are a last resort device, to be utilized only if all else fails and maybe not issued even then. The mediator is never committed to the use of that device and he will steadfastly refuse to take such action unless he is convinced or has a strong hunch that it may be productive.

## 2. PROBLEM AREAS — MEDIATION

### W. SIMKIN, MEDIATION AND THE DYNAMICS OF COLLECTIVE BARGAINING 350-51 (1971)†

#### Separate Mediation Agency?

At the state level, it has been noted that PERB and OCB in New York and PERC in New Jersey have been established separate and apart from the mediation agencies for private disputes. In most other states, public disputes are handled by the same agency that mediates private disputes. In the Federal Government, consideration was given to establishment of a separate federal disputes mediation agency, but Executive Order 11491 reflects a decision to assign this work to the agency that handles private disputes (the FMCS). What are the pros and cons of these two courses of action?

There are major advantages to the single-agency approach. Economy of operation is one that is almost self-evident. Even the largest mediation agencies are small. Administrative costs of two separate agencies would be greater, and a single agency is likely to attract more competent leadership than two smaller ones. Moreover, mediators usually function best when they are stationed near the source of a dispute, and a larger agency can maintain offices in more cities. There is more flexibility of case assignment in each area and to adjacent areas if there is more than one mediator at a regular station.

It might be argued that the differences between public sector and private sector mediation demand specialization and therefore separate agencies. Granted that differences exist, the similarities are even more pronounced. Required mediation skills are essentially the same. It is much easier and quicker to acquaint a skilled mediator with the peculiar features of public disputes than to make a competent mediator out of an individual who happens to have knowledge of the special

---

† Reprinted by permission of The Bureau of National Affairs, Inc.

features of government employment but lacks mediation experience. A larger agency can do a much better job than a small one in training new mediators and in the continuous process of keeping experienced mediators up to date on changes in collective bargaining practices.

It might also be argued that mediators who work in the private sector will seek to transplant unwanted private practices and contract clauses into government agency contracts. Admittedly this is a danger. However, it is equally clear that there are some advantages to cross-fertilization. Moreover, the dangers will not be eliminated by having two separate mediation staffs. The unions (and agency management less frequently) will attempt to inject private sector experience in any case whenever it is to their advantage. The mediator who knows both the advantages and disadvantages of private sector practice is best able to know whether it should be transplanted, modified, or disregarded in a public sector dispute.

On balance, the advantages of a single agency for mediation of public and private disputes are overwhelming — if the agency restricts itself primarily to mediation.

## NOTES

1. For a different view, *see* Zack, *Improving Mediation and Fact Finding in the Public Sector*, 21 LAB. L.J. 264 (1970).

2. Should there be separate mediation agencies to deal with local, state, and federal public employment disputes, respectively? The FMCS avoids involvement in local and state public sector bargaining disputes except where no other mediation assistance is available and FMCS mediation aid has been specifically requested. *See generally* Fishgold, *Dispute Resolution in the Public Sector: The Role of FMCS*, 27 LAB. L. J. 731 (1976).

3. In *Collective Bargaining in State and Local Government*, FINAL REPORT OF THE GREAT LAKES ASSEMBLY, East Lansing, Michigan (1973), the following recommendations were made by the seventy-five participants representing public employers, public employee unions, impartials, academicians and government officials:

Public sector collective bargaining is relatively new. Therefore, the availability and use of skilled mediators provided by a state agency is even more important than in the private sector. Mediation should be available at the request of either party or at the initiation of the administrative agency. In situations in which mediation has not succeeded in resolving disputes, fact-finding procedures should be available, upon the request of either party. Care should be taken to keep fact-finding from becoming a routine procedure and to insure that it is utilized only after *bona fide* collective bargaining assisted by mediation has failed to resolve the dispute. Otherwise, fact-finding could become automatic and impede the collective bargaining process.

*Compare* Redenius, *Public Employees: A Survey of Some Critical Problems on the Frontier of Collective Bargaining*, 27 LAB. L. J. 588, 591-99 (1976), wherein it is suggested that resort to third-party intervention with respect to public sector bargaining disputes will decrease as the parties gain experience and recognize that voluntary collective bargaining is the preferred method for obtaining satisfactory agreements.

4. Some commentators have argued that the availability of fact-finding impairs the effectiveness of mediation and impedes the bargaining process. *See, e.g.,* Zack, *Impasses, Strikes, and Resolutions,* in PUBLIC WORKERS AND PUBLIC UNIONS 101 (S. Zagoria ed. 1972). For other views, see A. Anderson, *The Use of Fact-Finding in Dispute Settlement,* and Saxton, *The Employers View,* in ARBITRATION AND SOCIAL CHANGE, PROCEEDINGS OF THE TWENTY-SECOND ANNUAL MEETING OF THE NATIONAL ACADEMY OF ARBITRATORS 107, 127 (G. Somers ed. 1970).

5. Compare the various methods for initiating mediation and fact-finding under the public sector enactments set forth in the *Statutory Appendix*. Which dispute resolution

sequence is most likely to achieve the best results? Should mediation be an absolute prerequisite to fact-finding?

# 3. PROBLEM AREAS — FACT-FINDING

## a. Make-up of the Panel

### REPORT TO GOVERNOR GEORGE ROMNEY BY THE MICHIGAN ADVISORY COMMITTEE ON PUBLIC EMPLOYEE RELATIONS (1966)

The "fact-finding" function (which should include the making of recommendations) should be carried out through the instrumentality of a Public Employment Relations Panel, the members of which should be appointed by the Governor to serve for terms of two years. There should be twelve members of the Panel, one of whom should be designated as Chairman. The members of the Panel should be persons of recognized stature, competence, and fairness. The Governor should be authorized to enlarge the membership of the Panel, ad hoc, to the extent necessary. The Panel, for its initial two years of operation, should be attached to the executive offices of the Governor. Members of the Panel should serve as needed and be reimbursed for their expenses and compensated on a per diem basis. An Executive Secretary should be provided to assist in coordinating the operations of the Panel.

Upon the certification of the SLMB [State Labor Mediation Board] of an unsettled dispute to the Panel, the Chairman (or, in his absence a Vice-Chairman designated by him) should assign the matter to one or more members of the Panel to carry out the functions of the Panel. . . .

Several reasons support the establishment of the suggested Panel procedure, as distinguished from retaining the fact-finding function in the SLMB or its designees, or providing for the appointment of fact finders on a case by case basis by the Governor. The designation of a Panel by the Governor would enhance the prestige and increase the effectiveness of the fact finders. Advance designation of the members of the Panel, to serve for a stipulated period of time, would accomplish the desirable objective of reducing involvement and pressures upon the Governor in particular disputes. Moreover, it could reasonably be expected that establishment of the Panel would help assure the availability of competent persons to serve the fact-finding function, build up a body of experience which would be useful in view of the comparatively unique aspects of public employee relations, and tend toward some consistency of approach. . . .

### NOTES

1. Are these recommendations sound? What alternative methods of fact-finder selection are discernible from the acts contained in the *Statutory Appendix*? Should the parties be permitted to influence the selection process?

Under the New York City OCB procedures, the OCB submits a list of seven names from its register of Impasse Panel members, and each party informs the Director of its preferences, which are respected to the extent there is agreement. *See* New York City Collective Bargaining Law, § 1173-7.0c, set forth in the *Statutory Appendix*.

2. Is access to fact-finding without an evaluation of prior negotiation efforts undesirable? The Wisconsin and Connecticut statutes provide for a review of prior negotiations to determine whether a genuine impasse has been reached. If there should be such review, should it be by the fact-finder or by the agency administering the basic collective bargaining law? *See* McKelvey, *Fact-Finding in Public Employment Disputes: Promise or Illusion?*, 22 IND. & LAB. REL. REV. 528, 535 (1969), suggesting that in those

two states fact-finding has not been as addictive as in New York where the statute does not provide for such review. *But see* Yaffe and Goldblatt, *Factfinding in Public Employment in New York State: More Promise Than Illusion,* ILR Paperback No. 10, 25 (1971).

## b. Functions of the Fact-Finder

### DOERING, IMPASSE ISSUES IN TEACHER DISPUTES SUBMITTED TO FACT FINDING IN NEW YORK, 27 Arb. J. 1, 12-16 (March 1972)†

What . . . are the criteria upon which fact finders base their recommendations? There seem to be two major considerations involved, and one or both may be operative in any one situation. The standards of "acceptability" (what the parties will agree to) and of "equity" (the requirements of the fact finder's notions of fairness and good labor relations) appear to be determinative.

The weighting of these criteria will depend to some extent upon the fact finder's view of his own role: whether he sees his primary function as making proposals which will produce a settlement, or as a neutral third party whose major role is to make public the facts of the dispute and try to suggest an "equitable" (not merely "acceptable") resolution of issues. Actually both of these functions are part of the fact finder's role, and they need not necessarily be conflicting. If, however, they are not entirely compatible, the fact finder must choose which criterion to modify in light of the other.

*Acceptability*

"Acceptability" as an abstract criterion by which to decide the issues in dispute is fairly self evident — "to the lion shall go the lion's share." It means convincing the parties that the recommendations represent the best bargain they could have gotten based upon the power balance between them in free collective bargaining if stoppages were not illegal.

While the concept of "acceptability" is easily defined in the abstract, specific definition of the "acceptable" solution for any set of circumstances is often difficult. The neutral party must get the sense of the situation from the parties themselves and from that try to gauge the area of possible settlement. In addition to correctly judging what the area of settlement is, he must convince the parties that his interpretation is accurate and that the recommendations based upon it represent the best they will be able to get.

Sometimes the problem of persuasion becomes part of the criterion itself. A recalcitrant individual on one of the negotiating teams may have to be taken into consideration in defining the area of settlement, and the criterion of "acceptability" may end up relating as much to personalities and emotions around the bargaining table as to the facts in the case. The situation is peculiar to public sector bargaining. In a private sector strike situation, the personalities and rhetoric of the negotiators soon give way to a test of economic strength. In public employment, impasse procedures are designed to avoid such tests, and it is more difficult to call a bluff. Personalities and emotions creep into the process and cannot be ignored if settlement is the object. Another factor which may make the neutral person's job more difficult is the fact that in the public sector there are politics on both sides of the table. Management as well as union spokesmen are elected officials.

---

† Reprinted by permission of The American Arbitration Association, Inc.

Although some pressure can be brought to bear through publication of the fact finder's report, research indicated that attempts to arouse public interest have had only minimal effects on the actual settlement of the dispute. Thus the fact finder looking for a settlement is pretty well limited to the facts, both economic and political, and the personalities at the table.

## Equity

In addition to his appraisal of acceptability, the fact finder usually arrives at some notion of the "equity" involved before making his recommendations. The term equity here denotes considerations by the neutral party which are not influenced by the power balance between the parties, but by the arguments put forward and such abstract standards of justice as the fact finder may have.

From the presentations made by the parties the fact finder usually obtains several indications as to the equity of their proposals. Perhaps the most useful of these indicators are past practice within the district, and present practice in other neighboring and/or similar districts, with emphasis usually on the latter. Past practice within the district, except where a district has been a leader in a certain field, is usually de-emphasized because it is no longer current. Furthermore, the practices may be in dispute. Comparison with similar and neighboring districts has the advantage of being both an outside standard and a current one.

Through comparisons with neighboring and similar districts the fact finder can ascertain the level of settlements (or at least the relative positions of the parties if bargaining is incomplete) in other districts faced with the same geography, similar tax problems and the same increases in the cost of living. From this the fact finder gains an idea of the "going rate" and also of the competitive recruiting salaries. If neighboring districts are dissimilar in terms of size or tax-base, the fact finder may modify or weight the criterion of comparability accordingly.

In addition to comparability, past practice, and other arguments presented by the parties, the fact finder himself has professional standards from his training and experience in labor relations which may influence his findings. Certain issues may be handled from the point of view of good labor relations rather than on a basis of comparability, past practice, or even acceptability.

## The Weighting of the Criteria

Acceptability and equity are most likely to conflict when acceptability is less dependent on economics, and more a matter of personalities or politics. If agreement is to be achieved, such needs and individuals must be accommodated, sometimes at the expense of equity. Where acceptability is measured in economic terms it usually produces contracts similar to those negotiated in comparable districts if only because those districts also had to find acceptable solutions.

In mediation, which precedes fact finding, settlements (if they are achieved) are achieved on the basis of acceptability. If the mediator is successful in convincing the parties of his impression of the "acceptable" solution, there is no need to go on to fact finding. The disputes most likely to be carried further are those in which acceptability depends upon the personalities at the bargaining table, or on political rather than economic factors; in these disputes there is the greatest conflict between acceptability and equity and one party will undoubtedly feel aggrieved. One or both of the parties may opt for fact finding in hopes of finding someone with a different appraisal of acceptability, or someone who will modify what has already been identified as the "acceptable solution" in light of some higher equity. That is, teachers sometimes feel that if a position is morally right and equitable it should prevail even if the power balance in the community would not support such a position. They occasionally go to fact finding in the hope that the fact finder will lend his support to their position.

Fact finding gives the parties a second neutral interpretation of the "acceptable solution" and often an opinion of the equity as well. Having thus identified acceptability and equity as the major criteria, and having suggested that acceptability may be the more important since fact finding is a dispute settlement procedure, it would be interesting to know with what accuracy fact finders judge the area of settlement. If fact finders cannot be reasonably sure of correctly assessing acceptability, it would suggest that they ought not to place inordinate weight on this criterion, or that they should at least give equity the benefit of the doubt in situations where they perceive a conflict between the two criteria.

## GOULD, PUBLIC EMPLOYMENT: MEDIATION, FACT-FINDING AND ARBITRATION, 55 Am. Bar Ass'n J. 835, 837-38 (1969)†

Is the fact finder's position ... that of a judge or arbitrator, who makes a determination predicated upon purely objective criteria? Or is he more akin to the mediator, whose function is to be acceptable to the parties so that he may bring them together on an amicable basis? It is easy to see that the weight given to either of these functions may depend on the statutory timetable or lack of one.

Chairman Robert Howlett of the Michigan Labor Mediation Board has recently expressed his board's hostility toward mediation efforts by fact finders....

In my judgment, the fact-finding process necessarily partakes of both the mediatory and judicial disciplines. While the process is a fluid one about which the drawing of hard and fast lines is still an audacious act, I am convinced that Chairman Howlett's analogy to "in chambers" settlements is a good one. For it seems difficult for the fact finder to introduce himself as a mediator, gain the parties' confidence and trust and then — having failed to bring them together without recommendations — to put on his judicial robes and hear formal testimony on the issues in dispute. The parties are bound to feel confused and betrayed by this role switching, which can result in a "judge's" reliance on information obtained through informal and frank off-the-record mediation sessions.

On the other hand, the skillful fact finder may be able to find a stage of the proceeding when, in his opinion, a settlement is near and when it is therefore propitious to adjourn the hearing for a limited period of time. Sometimes the opportunity is presented through the appearance of misunderstandings by one side of the other's position. An attempt to obtain clarification concerning the differences between the parties may give the fact finder the chance to don his mediator's hat. But, at this "in chambers" stage — as distinguished from the beginning of the hearing — the parties should have acquired some measure of respect for and confidence in the fact finder. If not, his request to adjourn for clarification or for anything else will be met with a refusal or lack of enthusiasm.

However, even when the fact finder is proceeding down the "in chambers" route, the parties are very often inclined to hold back, anticipating the possible resumption of formal hearings. The fact finder must convince the parties that he will keep the two procedures separate in his own mind. It is an understatement to note that this is not always the easiest feat to carry off.

---

† Reprinted by permission of the American Bar Association.

**HOWLETT, COMMENT, in ARBITRATION AND THE EXPANDING ROLE OF NEUTRALS, PROCEEDINGS OF THE TWENTY-THIRD ANNUAL MEETING OF THE NATIONAL ACADEMY OF ARBITRATORS 175, 179-80 (G. Somers ed. 1970)†**

We are convinced, however, that if there has been effective mediation, the role of the fact-finder is primarily judicial. If the mediator has performed his role with excellence, a second mediator is generally not helpful. In our 1970 fact-finders' education seminar, two lawyers representing the Michigan Education Association and the Michigan Federation of Teachers, a lawyer representing school districts, and the executive secretary of the Michigan Association of School Boards were in accord that the role of a fact-finder should be judicial and not mediatory. As one lawyer said: "Fact-finding should not be super mediation. If it is used by the fact-finder to club a settlement, the value of the process will be destroyed."

After our initial wandering in the wilderness, we announced that we will not appoint fact-finders until the mediator assigned to the negotiations certifies that mediation has been exhausted and that every effort has been made to narrow the issues to those two or three key items which may make the difference between settlement and failure. Failure may result in a strike. The "strike" is a factor in settlement, as public employees retain the power to strike, even though they do not have that privilege. We do not authorize a fact-finder to return to the dispute after the issuance of his report. We require that our mediators re-enter each case after the fact-finding report if the report is not accepted immediately. Reports have been instrumental in mediated settlements, even though the fact-finder's report was not, per se, accepted.

The debate over whether to combine mediation and fact-finding appears to arise principally from those jurisdictions that do not have an established, competent mediation staff, as we do have in Michigan. I can understand a combination of mediation and fact-finding in those states that use ad hoc mediation and ad hoc fact-finding, with the same person performing both services. In Michigan, ad hoc mediation is seldom needed.

Nor have we found that our fact-finders react defensively if employer and union do not accept their recommendations. Perhaps this is because our fact-finders do not return to the bargaining scene, but are succeeded by a mediator. My knowledge of the ability and balance of our fact-finders, however, leads me to conclude that even though these men should engage in post-fact-finding mediation, few of them would react defensively or be unduly concerned at the failure of employer and union to accept their recommendations. Possibly Michigan fact-finders are more thick-skinned than fact-finders in other states, but I doubt it. Contacts with my "opposite numbers" in other states lead me to conclude that they, too, have able fact-finders who perform a significant role in resolving impasses and who are neither prima donnas nor live in a world of fantasy in which they believe that their dictates will, ipso facto, be accepted.

Bill Simkin opines that the fact-finder "has no adequate opportunity to gauge acceptability by the parties." Our experience denies the validity of this criticism *if the fact-finder is competent.* He has greater flexibility than the arbitrator, for he may meet with the parties separately because — in spite of our jaundiced view of mediation by fact-finders — fact-finders do engage in the "search for a solution." A fact-finder, unlike an arbitrator, may discuss the case with each party

---

† Reprinted by permission of The Bureau of National Affairs, Inc.

separately. The arbitrator, who renders a "legal" and binding solution, may not "trim." The fact-finder may, because his primary task is to find *an* equitable — not necessarily *the most* equitable — settlement.

### NOTES

1. *See also* Anderson, *Strikes and Impasse Resolution,* 67 MICH. L. REV. 943, 964-66 (1969); Armbrust, *Impasse Resolution Procedures in Public Employment Negotiations,* 8 URB. LAWYER 449, 451-56 (1976); Zack, *Impasses, Strikes and Resolutions,* in PUBLIC WORKERS AND PUBLIC UNIONS 101, 114 (S. Zagoria ed. 1972).

2. Should the parties be required to submit a jointly agreed upon statement of the issues to the fact-finder? Should the fact-finder commence the hearing as if nothing had transpired previously or should the last offers of the parties be regarded as their respective minimum positions?

3. A party's failure to comply in good faith with applicable fact-finding procedures may constitute an unfair labor practice. *See* Sanford Teachers Ass'n v. Sanford School Comm., Me.L.R.B., Case No. 77-36, 1977-78 PEB ¶ 40,216 (1977); In re Eastern Iowa Community College, Iowa P.E.R.B., Case No. 973, 1977-78 PEB ¶ 40,016 (1977). *See also* Ass'n of Classroom Teachers of Oklahoma City v. Independent School Dist. No. 89, 540 P.2d 1171 (1975), wherein the Oklahoma Supreme Court found it improper for a party to refuse to agree upon the impartial third member of a fact-finding panel. Finding the statutorily prescribed selection procedure to be mandatory, and not merely permissive, the Court ordered the school district to cooperate with the teachers' association in selecting the third panel member through the strike-off method.

## c. Procedure and Practice

The states are laboratories for experimentation with the fact-finding process. Variations exist as to a variety of incidentals of procedure including (1) who may invoke the process (whether a party or only the public labor relations law administrative agency), (2) how the tribunal is chosen, (3) who pays for its services, (4) time limitations on its functioning, (5) whether its procedures are to be public or private, (6) how "evidence" is to be presented, (7) which party is required to proceed first at the hearing, (8) what is the "burden of proof," if any, and where does it rest, (9) whether an official record of the "hearing" is to be taken, and, if so, who pays for it, (10) whether the tribunal is restricted to that record as the basis for its conclusions of fact, and (11) whether the tribunal's report and recommendations are to be made public. Differences in approach also exist, as must be apparent at this point, with respect to the question whether there is a "next step" (beyond additional bargaining) after the tribunal issues its report.

## 4. APPRAISAL OF EXPERIENCE

**DISPUTE SETTLEMENT IN THE PUBLIC SECTOR: THE STATE-OF-THE-ART, REPORT SUBMITTED TO THE U.S. DEP'T OF LABOR, DIVISION OF PUBLIC EMPLOYEE LABOR RELATIONS 59-60 (T. Gilroy & A. Sinicropi eds. 1971)**

The effectiveness of factfinding is very difficult to measure. As stated earlier, the process is fluid, often drifting from "mediation" to "arbitration." Also, factfinding usually is saddled with the tougher cases which mediation did not resolve. Moreover, some factfinding is merely reporting without recommendations and factfinding without recommendations is said to be about "as useful as a martini without gin."

Taking note of the misunderstanding and apprehensions concerning factfinding it is not surprising to learn that there has been no accurate manner to standardize the process for review and analysis. McKelvey summarized the assessments made through 1968 and the criteria used to make those appraisals, but she cautioned that such limited findings may only be "illusions." Nevertheless, some data on factfinding have become available and are worthy of note.

The figures most often cited as the percentage of cases going to factfinding that are resolved is ninety percent. It is estimated that sixty to seventy percent of the cases going to factfinding are recorded as having the factfinder's recommendations serve as a basis for settling the dispute. However, at the present time there is no way to determine how close to the recommendations the settlement comes. Stern cites an example of a case considered settled on the basis of a factfinder's recommendations where the actual agreement gave the union only one-third of what the factfinder had recommended.

The use of mediation techniques in factfinding further clouds any accurate assessment of the factfinding process. New York and New Jersey encourage factfinders to mediate and both states report that between twenty-five and thirty percent of all cases going to factfinding are resolved through mediation efforts. Yaffe and Goldblatt report that nearly eighty percent of factfinders in New York engage in mediation. The same study shows that where the factfinder engaged in mediation and where recommendations were subsequently issued, seventy-four percent of such recommendations served as a basis for settlement as against fifty-eight percent of the recommendations for cases where the factfinder did not engage in mediation. Gould points out that the participants themselves prefer the factfinder to act as a mediator and indicates that this most often does occur, even in Michigan where the policy is to separate the roles of the mediator and the factfinder.

Those who support factfinding do so with reservations. Zack states while factfinding works, it offers the risk of "perpetually extending procedures`... so that good faith bargaining occurs (only) at the last stages, if at all." McKelvey fears that "factfinding may become, as it has under the Railway Labor Act, an addictive habit, the first and not the final step in collective negotiations." Davey and Simkin reluctantly accept it, claiming it to be the least desirable (most undesirable, excluding the strike) method of settling negotiation impasses.

On the positive side, most of the above writers and several others applaud the record of factfinding, particularly as it continues to offer a means in resolving disputes short of the strike and as it educates and assists in the maturation of the parties. However, all of the observations and comments are offered without sufficient evidence....

The concluding note of the Yaffe and Goldblatt study perhaps best describes the status of factfinding: "Accordingly, the New York state experience seems to support the conclusion that factfinding offers more promise than illusion as a mechanism to facilitate the resolution of interest disputes in public sector negotiations."

## NOTE

See generally Wolkinson & Stieber, *Michigan Fact-finding Experience in Public Sector Disputes*, 31 ARB. J. 225 (1976); Wheeler, *Is Compromise the Rule in Fire Fighter Arbitration?*, 29 ARB. J. 176 (1974); Stern, *The Wisconsin Public Employee Factfinding*

*Procedure,* 20 Ind. & Lab. Rel. Rev. 3 (1966); Zack, *Improving Mediation and Fact-Finding in the Public Sector,* 21 Lab. L. J. 264 (1970); Zack, *Impasses, Strikes and Resolutions,* in Public Workers and Public Unions 111 (S. Zagoria ed. 1972); Anderson, *The Use of Fact-Finding in Dispute Settlement,* in Arbitration and Social Change, Proceedings of the Twenty-Second Annual Meeting of the National Academy of Arbitrators 107 (G. Somers ed. 1970); McKelvey, *Fact Finding in Public Employment Disputes: Promise or Illusion?,* 22 Ind. & Lab. Rel. Rev. 528 (1969); Yaffe & Goldblatt, *Factfinding in Public Employment in New York State: More Promise Than Illusion,* ILR Paperback No. 10 (1971); Doering, *Impasse Issues in Teacher Disputes Submitted to Fact Finding in New York,* 27 Arb. J. 1 (1972); Drotning & Lipsky, *The Outcome of Impasse Procedures in New York Schools Under the Taylor Law,* 26 Arb. J. 87 (1971); Gould, *Public Employment: Mediation, Fact-Finding and Arbitration,* 55 A.B.A.J. 835 (1969).

## D. THE PROBLEM OF "FINALITY"

## 1. ALTERNATIVE PROCEDURES FOLLOWING MEDIATION AND FACT-FINDING

The question of "finality" poses the following difficult issue: What mechanisms should be used to resolve interest disputes in the public sector in the event that negotiation, mediation, and fact-finding have failed to produce a settlement? In the private sector, if an impasse is reached, the union has two basic options: (1) accept the employer's last offer and settle; or (2) strike in an effort to gain leverage at the bargaining table.

Since strikes by most public employees are statutorily proscribed, the weapon of economic coercion is presumably removed as a bargaining stratagem. In the public sector, therefore, the issue arises as to whether there are any legitimate and viable substitutes for the strike weapon which can produce settlements of interest disputes on terms which are reasonable and are not necessarily limited to the public employer's last offer. In an effort to deal with this problem, numerous municipal, state, and federal jurisdictions have adopted a variety of legislative schemes aimed at achieving finality in the resolution of public sector bargaining disputes.[4] The most popular among these legislative schemes may be summarized as follows:

(1) *Fact-Finding Recommendations Backed by Show Cause Procedures* — This approach addresses the problem of how to make fact-finding with recommendations work well in providing a final solution to bargaining impasses. In a typical situation, only one party will accept the fact-finder's recommendations. The other party, for a number of reasons, rejects them in whole or in part. In the event this occurs, some have suggested that the rejecting party be required, in a quasi-judicial proceeding, to justify its failure to accept the terms of the proposed settlement.[5]

(2) *Legislative Determination* — Under this approach, the failure of either party to accept a fact-finder's recommendations, in whole or in part, leads to hearings before the governing legislative body which, after receiving input from all of the interested parties, decides the terms of the final settlement. This scheme

---

[4] For an excellent general summary of the various legislative schemes, see *Dispute Settlement in The Public Sector: The State-of-the-Art,* Report Submitted to the U.S. Dep't of Labor, Div. of Public Empl. Lab. Rel. 29-46 (T. Gilroy & A. Sinicropi eds. 1971).

[5] *See* Davey, *Dispute Settlement in Public Employment,* in Dispute Settlement in the Public Sector 12, 21 (T. Gilroy ed. 1972).

is typified by Section 209.3(e) of the New York Taylor Act, which is set forth in the *Statutory Appendix*.

(3) *Executive Declaration of Finality* — Nevada provides that prior to the submission of an interest dispute to fact-finding, either party may request that the governor exercise his emergency powers and declare that the recommendations shall be binding. Fact-finding then proceeds as usual, observing the criteria set out in the statute. *See* 9 NEV. REV. STAT. § 288.200. A somewhat different approach is taken under the New York City law, which makes the recommendations of an Impasse Panel final and binding as accepted or modified by the Board of Collective Bargaining. The details of the New York City scheme are set forth in the *Statutory Appendix* in § 1173-7.0c of the New York City Collective Bargaining Law.

(4) *Limited Right to Strike* — Several states, including Hawaii and Pennsylvania, have sought to resolve the finality problem by granting a limited right to strike to certain categories of public employees. The limited right to strike is discussed in Part G of Chapter Six.

(5) *"Advisory" Arbitration* — Several states have made "advisory" (i.e., non-binding) arbitration an alternative or a sequel to fact-finding. The Maine law provides for both binding and advisory arbitration, depending upon the issues involved. Arbitration may be requested by either party, with a tripartite panel made up of one member selected by each side and a neutral third member selected by the other two members or by the American Arbitration Association. The recommendations of the arbitration panel are advisory with respect to salaries, pensions, and insurance. *See* ME. REV. STAT. ANN. tit. 26, § 965(4).

Rhode Island statutes covering municipal employees and teachers also provide for voluntary arbitration, which is merely advisory with respect to matters involving the expenditure of money. *See* R.I. GEN. LAWS ANN. §§ 28-9.4-10 to 15 and §§ 28-9.3-9 to 14. Conversely, the Rhode Island laws covering police and fire personnel make compulsory arbitration mandatory and binding as to all issues. *See* R.I. GEN. LAWS ANN. §§ 28-9.2-7 to 11 and §§ 28-9.1-7 to 11.

The Pennsylvania law covering guards at prisons and mental hospitals and court personnel provides that all bargaining impasses "shall be submitted to a panel of arbitrators whose decision shall be final and binding . . . with the proviso that the decisions of the arbitrators which would require legislative enactment to be effective shall be considered advisory only." *See* PA. STAT. ANN. § 1101.805, set forth in the *Statutory Appendix*. A separate statutory provision requires binding arbitration, at the request of either party, covering all bargaining issues in dispute regarding police and fire personnel. PA. STAT. ANN. tit. 43, §§ 217.4-.8. It is also noteworthy that the Pennsylvania Public Employee Relations Act provides for "voluntary binding arbitration" of public employee interest disputes which are not otherwise covered by the compulsory arbitration provisions of Pennsylvania law. *See* PA. STAT. ANN. § 1101.804. Voluntary binding arbitration arises only pursuant to an agreement by the parties and, if it is utilized, "the decisions of the arbitrator which . . . require legislative enactment to be effective shall be considered advisory only."

In Oklahoma, either party may request advisory arbitration to resolve a police or firefighter bargaining dispute. However, if the award is accepted by the municipality involved, it becomes binding. *See* OKLA. SESS. LAWS, ch. 14, §§ 7-11.

Some commentators believe that advisory arbitration is more likely to encourage antecedent negotiations than is binding arbitration, since a party may think it has a good chance of receiving more favorable treatment through binding arbitration than through negotiations, whereas advisory arbitration is less stultifying of the bargaining process because the award can be rejected. For good discussions of the use of advisory arbitration in the telegraph and wire service industries, *see* Bryan, *Avoiding Confrontation by Advisory Arbitration,* and Groner, *Why Advisory Arbitration of New Contracts?* in Arbitration and the Expanding Role of Neutrals, Proceedings of the Twenty-Third Annual Meeting, Nat'l Academy of Arb. 55 (G. Somers ed. 1970). Is there any meaningful difference between advisory arbitration and fact-finding with recommendations?

(6) *Voluntary, Binding Arbitration* — At least eighteen states (Connecticut, Delaware, Hawaii, Illinois, Indiana, Iowa, Maine, Massachusetts, Minnesota, Montana, Nevada, New Jersey, New York, Oregon, Pennsylvania, Rhode Island, Texas, and Vermont) permit voluntary, binding arbitration of interest disputes involving some categories of public sector employees. The Postal Reorganization Act of 1970, which is set forth in the *Statutory Appendix,* provides for voluntary, binding arbitration, but also for compulsory arbitration if a voluntary arrangement is not reached. The Canadian Public Service Staff Relations Act gives unions at the federal level a choice, to be exercised in advance of bargaining, between the right to strike and the submission of disputes to binding arbitration. However, if the strike alternative is elected, essential employees may not strike. *See generally* Arthurs, *Collective Bargaining in the Public Service of Canada: Bold Experiment or Act of Folly?*, 67 Mich. L. Rev. 971 (1969).

## 2. COMPULSORY BINDING ARBITRATION

### a. Commentary

### H. WELLINGTON & R. WINTER, THE UNIONS AND THE CITIES 178-80 (1971)†

Compulsory and binding arbitration seeks to prevent strikes in two ways, neither of which is completely successful. First, it attempts to enforce a settlement by application of legal sanctions. Ordinarily this will be enough for all but the aberrational case. And the occasional strikes that still occur sometimes may be prevented if the law responds with very harsh penalties. Such penalties, however, often do not have the support of the community and may stir a feeling of revulsion. In those circumstances they are unlikely to be effective and, in any event, workers willing to accept such penalties can still make a strike effective. Legal sanctions, therefore, do not provide total protection.

Compulsory and binding arbitration, however, seeks to prevent strikes in a second way. Because the strike in private employment is viewed by many as a fundamental right located well within the foothills of the Constitution, there is in some places a corresponding sense that laws against strikes in the public sector are unfair. This attitude — which survives in a fierce state of tension with counter attitudes — emboldens public employees to break the law. A procedure that offers public employees a seemingly fair alternative to the strike, however, may change the community's sense of the propriety of the strike and may in the long run influence the attitude of public employees. They may in time reach that desirable state of accepting an award that they find less than totally fair. This is the goal of compulsory arbitration, and is what differentiates it from nonfinality procedures. No moral imperative, above and beyond the preexisting moral imperative of not breaking the no-strike law, is generated by nonfinality procedures such as fact-finding with recommendations. They are advisory only. An aim of arbitration binding on both parties is to generate just such an imperative. Again, however, total success cannot be expected.

The second factor limiting the effectiveness of arbitration is that it deters collective bargaining. The point is simple enough. Either the public employer or the union will reckon that an arbitration award will be more advantageous than a negotiated settlement. That party will then employ tactics to ensure arbitration by bargaining without a sincere desire to reach agreement.

It is almost impossible wholly to solve this problem; but the route to partial and perhaps satisfactory resolution is to fashion a procedure sufficiently diverse and uncertain as to make a negotiated settlement more attractive to the parties than arbitration.

The composition of an arbitration panel can importantly influence its award. Honest men acting disinterestedly often see things differently. The behaviorists are surely right in thinking that results are influenced by the perspectives of decision makers. Thus, to the extent that the composition of an arbitration panel is unknown beforehand and is outside the control of the parties, some uncertainty will exist. On the other hand, the parties are more likely to have confidence in an award rendered by arbitrators they have chosen. This tension can be eased by allowing each party to select one member of a three-man panel.

## G. TAYLOR, IMPASSE PROCEDURES — THE FINALITY QUESTION, GOVERNOR'S CONFERENCE ON PUBLIC EMPLOYMENT RELATIONS 5-6 (New York City, October 15, 1968)

There is considerable wishful thinking that the involvement of the legislative and executive branches of government can be minimized — or even avoided altogether — by having a board of impartial labor relations experts make a final and binding decision to resolve an impasse. While recognizing the apparent simplicity of compulsory arbitration, one should not be unaware of the consequences of the broad delegation of governmental authority which is entailed. An arbitration board would become a powerful arm of government acting without the checks and balances upon which we depend in the fashioning of our laws. Some additional difficult questions have to be faced. Is it sound and wise to consider the claims of one particular group of employees for their share of limited public funds in isolation from the claims of other employees? Or, to do so without regard to the leap-frogging effect upon the total wage bill of a decision made in narrow context? What effect would all this have upon the allocations of limited resources for other sorely needed services to the public? And, if a legislative body cannot or will not do what it takes to carry out an award by the impartial arbitrators, is it intended that a court will compel them to do so? Bringing such questions into the appraisal of compulsory arbitration transforms an apparently easy answer into a very doubtful one.

## A. ANDERSON, COMPULSORY ARBITRATION IN PUBLIC SECTOR DISPUTE SETTLEMENT — AN AFFIRMATIVE VIEW, in DISPUTE SETTLEMENT IN THE PUBLIC SECTOR 2-3 (T. Gilroy ed. 1972)†

[I]mpasse panel procedures may prove to be an interim step on the road to a system which features binding arbitration of contract terms in the public sector. In some cases, the parties have taken the additional step of agreeing to be bound

---

† Reprinted by permission of the Center for Labor and Management, College of Business Administration, University of Iowa.

by the recommendations of the impasse panel. In other instances, the parties have, in effect, requested the arbitrator to confirm their bargain by taking the responsibility of making an award confirming the agreement of the parties. There has also been an increase in the use of voluntary arbitration of contract terms in the public sector. Such arbitration is authorized by the Taylor Law.

President George Meany of the AFL-CIO, while expressing strong reservations about the use of arbitration in the private sector for resolving bargaining impasses, has suggested the use of binding arbitration in some circumstances in the public sector. The procedure for binding arbitration of contract terms under the new Postal Corporation Act was endorsed by the AFL-CIO. Mr. Meany, in supporting the Postal Corporation Act, stated that any procedure which preserves workers' rights without strikes is acceptable. Labor leaders who endorse the right to strike in public employment have at times qualified such advocacy by supporting binding arbitration of disputes for employees engaged in essential services such as law enforcement and fire fighting. In addition to the new laws and changed attitudes, the number of cases already submitted to arbitration in police and fire disputes in Pennsylvania and Michigan make an examination of compulsory arbitration procedures worthwhile.

The traditional attitudes of labor relations experts toward the binding arbitration process is that it's bad because it won't work and because it will destroy free collective bargaining. Arbitration of contract terms in public employment has been considered to be illegal in some jurisdictions because the process results in the unconstitutional delegation of responsibility to a third party, who is a private person of legislative and executive authority, to fix the terms and conditions of employment and the resulting budget changes and tax rates. Furthermore, it is charged that arbitration will not work because it will not prevent strikes or bring about settlements and will destroy the free collective bargaining process and the willingness of the parties to solve their own disputes. It is argued that compulsory arbitration will result in the piling up of all kinds of disputes to be submitted for resolution to a third party who neither understands the problems nor has a continuing responsibility for the results of the settlement. . . .

The adoption of compulsory and binding arbitration statutes in such jurisdictions as Michigan, Pennsylvania, Rhode Island, Maine and Wyoming for police and fire disputes is based on the premise that since the right to strike is legally.denied and cannot be realistically conferred on employees engaged in vital services, then a substitute bargaining balancer, the right to invoke binding arbitration by a neutral third party, is an effective and equitable substitute as a dispute settlement procedure. Arbitration transfers some of the powers of decision making about contract terms from the economic and political power of the parties involved to neutral arbitrators. Therefore, I don't accept the premise that the right to strike is the *sine qua non* to make the bargaining process work in the public sector. I think arbitration can work and has worked effectively for public employees as a substitute for the strike weapon.

## NOTES

1. Is it undemocratic for an individual who is not accountable to the electorate to make quasi-legislative budgetary determinations that may significantly affect the fiscal policies of a governmental entity? *See* Grodin, *Political Aspects of Public Sector Interest Arbitration*, 64 CAL. L. REV. 678 (1976); Bornstein, *Interest Arbitration in Public Employment: An Arbitrator Views the Process*, 29 LAB. L. J. 77 (1978); Barr, *The Public*

*Arbitration Panel as an Administrative Agency: Can Compulsory Interest Arbitration Be
an Acceptable Dispute Resolution Method in the Public Sector?*, 39 ALBANY L. REV. 377
(1975).

2. Does compulsory interest arbitration insulate elected officials from the difficult
political pressures they would encounter if they had to make the final decisions regarding
the employment conditions of their public employees? Does this fact actually inure to the
benefit of the public by minimizing the impact of special interest groups over this
important area?

## b. Legality

### DIVISION 540, AMALGAMATED TRANSIT UNION v.
### MERCER COUNTY IMPROVEMENT AUTHORITY

New Jersey Supreme Court
386 A.2d 1290, 98 L.R.R.M. 2526 (1978)

SULLIVAN, J.: This is a labor dispute in the public sector. The Mercer County
Improvement Authority (Mercer Metro Division) is the operator of a public
transportation facility in Mercer County. Division 540, Amalgamated Transit
Union, AFL-CIO, an unincorporated association, plaintiff herein, represents the
drivers, garage personnel and clerical workers of Mercer Metro.

During the spring of 1975 plaintiff and defendant met to negotiate the terms
and conditions of a collective bargaining agreement to replace an existing
agreement between the parties which was due to expire on March 31, 1975. Upon
failure to reach agreement, primarily over the issue of wages including a cost of
living allocation, plaintiff-union demanded that the dispute be submitted to
binding arbitration in accordance with *N.J.S.A.* 40:37A-96. When defendant
refused, the union filed the present suit which, *inter alia,* sought to compel
defendant to comply with the statutory provision which requires defendant to
offer to submit the dispute to binding arbitration. Defendant, on its part,
challenged the constitutionality of such provision.

The Superior Court, Chancery Division, upheld the constitutionality of
*N.J.S.A.* 40:37A-96 and entered final judgment ordering the defendant to submit
the labor dispute between it and plaintiff to final and binding arbitration pursuant
to the statute. On appeal by defendant, the Appellate Division affirmed the
Chancery Division ruling. Certification was granted by this Court on defendant's
petition, solely on the issue of the constitutionality of *N.J.S.A.* 40:37A-96.71 *N.J.*
518 (1976). We affirm.

. . . .

Capitol Transit, Inc. was a privately owned transportation facility operating bus
lines in Mercer County. In the 1960s, it began to sustain increasingly heavy
financial losses. During this period Mercer County tried to sustain the operation
by providing subsidies, but by 1968 Capitol Transit's condition had worsened
to a point where it faced bankruptcy and gave notice that it intended to cease
operations.

At this point the New Jersey Legislature, by *L.* 1968, *c.* 66, adopted
amendments to *N.J.S.A.* 40:37A-44 *et seq.* so as to permit a county improvement
authority to acquire a privately owned transportation system and operate the
same as a public transportation facility. Defendant Improvement Authority
thereupon purchased the assets of Capitol Transit and took over its operations
through its Mercer Metro Division.

The principal financing for this acquisition came from a federal grant made
under the Urban Mass Transporation Act of 1964, 49 *U.S.C.* § 1601 *et seq.*

However, federal assistance under this act is conditioned on fair and equitable arrangements being made to protect the interests of employees affected by such assistance. . . .

The New Jersey Legislature in empowering a county improvement authority to acquire a private transportation system and operate it, has specified protective conditions and benefits for the employees of a transportation system so acquired and operated. *N.J.S.A.* 40:37A-94 and -95. These include continuation of employment rights, privileges and benefits.

Another section, *N.J.S.A.* 40:37A-96 calls for arbitration of labor disputes as follows:

> In the case of any labor dispute between a county improvement authority operating a public transportation facility and its employees where collective bargaining does not result in agreement, irrespective of whether such dispute relates to the making or maintaining of collective bargaining agreements, the terms to be included in such agreements, the interpretation or application of such agreements, the adjustment of any grievance or any difference or any question that may arise between the authority and the labor organization representing its employees concerning wages, salaries, hours, working conditions or benefits including health and welfare, sick leave, insurance or pension or retirement provisions, the authority shall offer to submit such dispute to final and binding arbitration by a single arbitrator or by a tripartite board of arbitrators. Upon acceptance by the labor organization of such arbitration proposal, . . . [an arbitrator is then selected or tripartite board of arbitrators appointed in accordance with specified procedures]. The arbitration proceeding shall take place in the manner provided by the rules of the New Jersey State Board of Mediation applicable to arbitration of labor disputes and the decision of the arbitrator or board of arbitrators shall be final and binding upon the parties.

The foregoing section provides for arbitration of labor disputes involving the terms in collective bargaining agreements (interest arbitration). It is also to be noted that the requirement to submit to arbitration is imposed only on the Authority.

Other provisions of the statute emphasize the uniqueness of the authority's relationship with its transportation system employees. A county improvement authority is a public body corporate and politic. *N.J.S.A.* 40:37A-46. Nevertheless, if it operates a public transporation facility its employees in that facility have the right to "bargain collectively" through their union as to terms and conditions of employment. *N.J.S.A.* 40:37A-92. The Authority has the power to enter into a closed shop agreement with the union and to have a check-off system for the payment of union dues and assessments. *N.J.S.A.* 40:37A-97. As heretofore noted, the Authority is subject to compulsory and binding arbitration of labor disputes that arise between it and its transportation facility employees where collective bargaining does not result in agreement. *N.J.S.A.* 40:37A-96. The constitutionality of this latter provision is the issue in this case.

There can be no doubt but that under the provisions of the Urban Mass Transportation Act of 1965 and the implementing statutory provisions of *L.* 1968, *c.* 66 enacted by our Legislature, employees of a transportation facility taken over by a county improvement authority and operated by it, have some rights which are consistent with private employment. However, in the overall picture, they must be considered as public employees in the sense that they are employed by a public body corporate and politic. Counsel for plaintiff-union in his supplemental brief filed with this Court concedes that as employees of such a public body, they do not presently have the right to strike, a right they formerly enjoyed as employees of Capitol Transport.

We find the provisions for compulsory and binding arbitration contained in *N.J.S.A.* 40:37A-96 to be constitutional. The proliferation of labor disputes in the public sector and the resultant disruption of essential public services has caused many state legislatures to try to formulate new approaches to the resolution of these disputes. In the past, in New Jersey, statutory provisions for binding arbitration of labor disputes in the public area merely authorized the parties to enter into an agreement to submit the labor dispute to binding arbitration. *N.J.S.A.* 34:13A-5.3. However, this required mutual agreement and often did not provide resolution of the problem.

The concept of compulsory and binding arbitration of labor negotiation as well as grievance disputes in the public sector has been coming more and more into favor. See McAvoy, "Binding Arbitration of Contractual Terms: A New Approach to the Resolution of Disputes in the Public Sector," 72 *Colum. L. Rev.* 1192 (1972). The New Jersey Legislature has not only adopted this procedure in the statutory section under consideration, but also has recently imposed compulsory arbitration for resolution of such disputes between municipal bodies and their police and firemen, *N.J.S.A.* 34:13A-14 to 21.

The principal objection made to compulsory and binding arbitration of labor negotiation disputes in the public sector is that it constitutes an unlawful delegation of public authority and responsibility to a private person or persons. However, most of the cases that have dealt with the question have sustained the concept as an innovative way to avoid the morass of deadlocked labor disputes in the public sector. Nevertheless, in doing so, there must be excluded from the arbitration process matters involving governmental policy determinations which involve an exercise of delegated police power.

Some of the cases reason that there is no improper delegation involved as the arbitrator is deemed a public official when performing functions which are public in nature. *Town of Arlington v. Board of Concil.& Arbit.,* — Mass. —, 352 N.E.2d, 914, 93 L.R.R.M. 2494 (Sup. Jud. Ct. 1976); *City of Warwick v. Warwick Regular Firemen's Assn.,* 106 *R.I.* 109, 256 A. 2d 206, 71 L.R.R.M. 3192 (Sup. Ct. 1969). Others hold that legislative delegation is not illegal as long as adequate standards and safeguards are provided. *City of Amsterdam v. Helsby,* 37 *N.Y.* 2d 19, 332 N.E. 2d 290, 89 L.R.R.M. 2871 (Ct. App. 1975). Still other decisions hold that statutory provisions for compulsory arbitration of labor disputes in the public sector do not really entail the delegation of a governmental function at all, but rather in the exercise of that function, merely utilize a well-established procedure for the resolution of deadlocked labor disputes. *State* v. *City of Laramie,* 437 P. 2d 295, 68 L.R.R.M. 2038 (Wyo. Sup. Ct. 1968). See generally Annotation, "Validity and construction of statutes or ordinances providing for arbitration of labor disputes involving public employees," 68 *A.L.R.* 3d 885 (1976). Some authorities are critical of the standards rule as applied to delegation of power. They suggest that procedural safeguards and judicial review are more important than a requirement of standards. See 1 *Davis, Administrative Law Treatise,* § 2.15 at 148-151 (1958).

There are decisions to the contrary, such as *Greeley Police Union* v. *City Council of Greeley,* 553 P.2d 790 (Colo. Sup. Ct. 1976); *Dearborn Firefighters, Local 412* v. *City of Dearborn,* 394 *Mich.* 229, 231 *N.W.* 2d 226, 90 L.R.R.M. 2002 (Sup. Ct. 1975); *City of Sioux Falls* v. *Sioux Fall Firefighters,* 234 *N.W.* 2d

35, 90 L.R.R.M. 2945 (S.D. Sup. Ct. 1975). However, most of them have been decided on the basis of specific constitutional provisions or statutory language.

In the instant case, defendant, citing *Van Riper* v. *Traffic Tel. Workers Fed. of N.J.,* 2 *N.J.* 335 (1949), suggests that the arbitration clause under consideration is invalid because it lacks standards to govern the arbitrator in the exercise of the power delegated to him. *Van Riper* was decided almost thirty years ago.[3] In the interim, the widening use of arbitration in labor disputes, particularly in the public sector, has resulted in the development of standards and criteria which are inherent in the present-day process.

Thus, the arbitrator must act within the scope of the authority delegated to him. He must consider the public interest and the impact of his decision on the public welfare. He must act fairly and reasonably to the end that labor peace between the public employer and its employees will be stabilized and promoted. He must make findings which are adequate, and sufficient to support the award. *N.J.S.A.* 40:37A-96 should be construed as incorporating these inherent standards and criteria in its provisions for compulsory arbitration. See *Avant* v. *Clifford,* 67 *N.J.* 496, 549-554 (1976).

In addition to these implied standards, these are explicit standards set forth in the statute. *N.J.S.A.* 40:37A-92 confines the scope of the collective bargaining to wages, hours, working conditions and welfare, pension and retirement provisions. As heretofore noted, *N.J.S.A.* 40:37A-94 and -95 specify protective conditions and benefits such as continuation of employment rights, privileges and benefits. Under *N.J.S.A.* 40:37A-96 the procedural rules and practices of the State Board of Mediation, promulgated pursuant to *N.J.S.A.* 34:13A-11, govern the arbitration. *See N.J.A.C.* 12:105-5.1 to -5.12 and *N.J.A.C.* 12:105-6.1 to -6.6, which establish procedures governing stenographic recording of hearings, representation, evidence, briefs and the form of award. The method of selection of the arbitrator or arbitrators is also provided for in *N.J.S.A.* 40:37A-96.

Although *N.J.S.A.* 40:37A-96 has no express requirement for judicial review of the arbitrator's award, we conclude that such review must be available if the statutory provision is to be sustained. The statute subjects the development Authority to compulsory and binding arbitration. Because it is compulsory, principles of fairness, perhaps even due process, require that judicial review be available to ensure that the award is not arbitrary or capricious and that the arbitrator has not abused the power and authority delegated to him.

Also, because the arbitration process is imposed by law, the judicial oversight available should be more extensive than the limited judicial review had under *N.J.S.A.* 2A:24-8 to parties who voluntarily agree to submit their dispute to binding arbitration. See *Daly* v. *Komline-Sanderson Engineering Corp.,* 40 N.J. 175, 178 (1963). We conclude that when, as here, the arbitration process is compulsory,[4] the judicial review should extend to consideration of whether the award is supported by substantial credible evidence present in the record. This

---

[3] The original statute declared invalid for lack of standards in *Van Riper,* was amended by *L.* 1949, c. 308 so as to include specific standards. See *N.J.S.A.* 34:13B-27(b). As amended, the statute was upheld in *N.J. Bell Tel. Co.* v. *Communications Workers, etc.,* 5 *N.J.* 354 (1950).

[4] Although the arbitration process herein is compulsory only as to defendant-Authority, the union and the Authority should stand on equal terms insofar as the right to judicial review and scope thereof are concerned.

is the test normally applied to the review of administrative agency decisions and is particularly appropriate here. See *City of Amsterdam v. Helsby, supra, 37 N.Y. 2d* at 38-41, 332 *N.E. 2d* at 300-302 (Fuchsberg, J., concurring).

We find no merit in defendant-Authority's equal protection argument. Even assuming its standing to raise an equal protection issue, it is clear that the unique status of employees of a transportation facility taken over and operated by a County Improvement Authority serves as a rational basis for the statutory classification made and the imposition of unilateral compulsory arbitration.

In short, we uphold *N.J.S.A.* 40:37A-96 as a constitutional expression of legislative policy. We find therein, and in its companion statutory sections, standards, express and implied, to guide the arbitrator in the exercise of his authority. Adequate procedural safeguards have been established. We also conclude that the arbitrator's decision is subject to judicial review, the scope of such review being the same as that normally had in appeals from decisions of administrative agencies. Affirmed.

# NOTES

1. State courts have increasingly been called upon to determine the legality of compulsory and binding interest arbitration laws. Several courts, as noted in the principal case, have found such arbitration provisions to be constitutional where legislatively defined or judicially recognized safeguards and standards were present to adequately guide the arbitrators when they reached their decisions. *See, e.g.,* City of Richfield v. Firefighters Local 1215, —— N.W.2d ——, 1979-80 PBC ¶ 36,501 (Minn. 1979); Arlington v. Board of Conciliation & Arbitration, 352 N.E.2d 914, 93 L.R.R.M. 2494 (Mass. 1976); Spokane v. Spokane Police Guild, 553 P.2d 1316, 93 L.R.R.M. 2373 (Wash. 1976); City of Amsterdam v. Helsby, 37 N.Y.2d 19, 332 N.E.2d 290, 89 L.R.R.M. 2871 (1975); City of Biddeford v. Biddeford Teachers Ass'n, 304 A.2d 387, 83 L.R.R.M. 2098 (Me. 1973). However, other courts have struck down such interest arbitration provisions as constituting unconstitutional delegations of legislative authority. *See, e.g.,* Salt Lake City v. International Ass'n of Firefighters, 563 P.2d 786, 95 L.R.R.M. 2383 (Utah 1977); City of Aurora v. Aurora Firefighters' Protective Ass'n, 556 P.2d 1356, 96 L.R.R.M. 2252 (Colo. 1977); Greeley Police Union v. City Council, 553 P.2d 790, 93 L.R.R.M. 2382 (Colo. 1976); City of Sioux Falls v. Sioux Falls Firefighters' Local 814, 234 N.W.2d 35, 90 L.R.R.M. 2945 (S. D. 1975). In Dearborn Firefighters' Union Local 412 v. City of Dearborn, 324 Mich. 229, 231 N.W.2d 226, 90 L.R.R.M. 2002 (1975), the court divided equally on the issue, affirming a lower court ruling that the Michigan compulsory arbitration law was constitutional. Nevertheless, a majority of the court concluded that the legislation's delegation to an arbitration panel selected only by the parties, instead of through the statutory alternative of appointment by the chairman of the state mediation board, was unconstitutional.

2. In Firefighters Union, Local 1186 v. City of Vallejo, 12 Cal.3d 608, 87 L.R.R.M. 2453 (1974), the California Supreme Court sustained the constitutionality of a city charter provision that prescribed compulsory arbitration in the event of a bargaining impasse regarding wages, hours, or working conditions. However, where such a dispute resolution procedure was merely established through the parties' negotiated memorandum of understanding instead of in a charter provision, a California Court of Appeal found it to constitute an impermissible delegation of legislative authority, since it was not effectuated through the constitutionally recognized charter amendment process. Firefighters v. San Francisco, 68 Cal. App. 3d 896, 95 L.R.R.M. 2835, *petition for hearing denied,* 95 L.R.R.M. 3069 (Cal. Sup. Ct. 1977). In Bagley v. City of Manhattan Beach, 18 Cal. 3d 22, 553 P.2d 1140, 93 L.R.R.M. 2435 (1976), a city council refused to place a charter amendment initiative seeking compulsory interest arbitration on the election ballot. The court declined to issue a mandamus compelling such action on the ground that the applicable state enabling statute specifically directed the city council to determine the

employment conditions of its employees, thus precluding the delegation of that responsibility by city charter amendment initiative to other parties.

3. *See generally* Note, *Binding Interest Arbitration in the Public Sector: Is It Constitutional?*, 18 WM & MARY L. REV. 787 (1977); Staudohar, *Constitutionality of Compulsory Arbitration Statutes in Public Employment,* 27 LAB. L.J. 670 (1976); Weisberger, *Constitutionality of Compulsory Public Sector Interest Arbitration Legislation: A 1976 Perspective* in LABOR RELATIONS LAW IN THE PUBLIC SECTOR 35 (A. Knapp ed. 1977). *See also* Petro, *Sovereignty and Compulsory Public Sector Bargaining,* 10 WAKE FOREST L.REV. 25, 103-112 (1974).

## c. A Survey of Legislation: Practice and Procedure

### McAVOY, BINDING ARBITRATION OF CONTRACT TERMS: A NEW APPROACH TO THE RESOLUTION OF DISPUTES IN THE PUBLIC SECTOR, 72 Colum. L. Rev. 1192-1205 (1972)†

In an effort to avoid the work stoppages that may follow deadlocked negotiations, ... [many states] have instituted binding arbitration of contract terms in the public sector.[6] Though the earliest statutes covering public employees were passed in 1947, the majority of them have been enacted since 1968. ...

The essential characteristics of binding arbitration are submission of unresolved issues to a panel and a decision by the panel that is final and binding on both parties. The term does not include "one-sided" arbitration, where the award is binding on the employees only if accepted by the employer, who has the option to reject it. The statutes, which may provide for awards containing both binding and advisory provisions, fall generally into three categories: those that mandate arbitration; those that permit one party to mandate arbitration; and those that allow the parties to agree to arbitration. ...

I. *Statutory Provisions*

A. *Employees Covered*

The present pattern of coverage of arbitration statutes seems to reflect a degree of uncertainty as to the wisdom or desirability of such measures. The applicability of the few state statutes that mandate arbitration if agreement is not reached within a stated time period is usually limited to firefighters or police.[7] Both the number and scope of the statutes increase as the parties are granted a voice in the implementation of the arbitration procedure. [Some of the statutes

---

† Reprinted by permission of Columbia Law Review.

6 [As of 1978, the states authorizing compulsory ("c") or voluntary ("v") interest arbitration for at least some categories of public employees were: Alaska (c); Connecticut (c & v); Delaware (v); Hawaii (v); Illinois (v); Indiana (v); Iowa (c); Maine (c & v); Massachusetts (c & v); Michigan (c); Minnesota (c & v); Montana (v); Nebraska (c); Nevada (c & v); New Hampshire (v); New Jersey (c & v); New Mexico (v); New York (v); Oklahoma (c); Oregon (c & v); Pennsylvania (c & v); Rhode Island (c & v); Texas (v); Vermont (v); Washington (c); Wisconsin (c & v); and Wyoming (c).

[Binding interest arbitration for federal workers may only be used when authorized by the Federal Service Impasses Panel under the Civil Service Reform Act of 1978. Under the Postal Reorganization Act, binding arbitration of contract terms covering the Postal Service is required if no agreement is reached within a specified period following the commencement of negotiations. A tripartite panel is used, unless the parties agree upon some other procedure. Eds.]

7 [Alaska (police, fire, correctional, and hospital personnel); Connecticut (municipal workers); Nevada (firefighters); New Jersey (police and firefighters); Rhode Island (police, firefighters, and state workers); Washington (police and firefighters); and Wyoming (firefighters). Eds.]

in the ten] states that require arbitration when requested by one party cover, in addition to firemen and police, hospital and public transportation workers, Port Authority employees, and others.[8] The largest category of statutes, which covers "public employees generally," applies only when both parties agree to the arbitration procedure.[9] ...

## B. *Timing of Award*

Submission to arbitration deprives the public employer of the power to determine the proportion of its budget it will allocate for employee salaries. As a result, reallocation of previously budgeted funds may be required to satisfy the terms of an award. Many statutes, including the majority of those authorizing arbitration upon agreement of both parties, do not attempt to deal with the problem; however, eleven statutes seek to require completion of arbitration prior to the last date on which money can be appropriated for the new fiscal year. The manifest purpose of these provisions is to afford the employer the opportunity to tailor its budget requests with a view to the allocations required by all awards effective for the new fiscal year.

Most statutes that look to completion of arbitration prior to a budget appropriation date provide a detailed timetable, specifying dates for the commencement of bargaining, submission to arbitration, selection of arbitrators, holding of hearings, and issuance of the award. Although most statutes mandating arbitration contain such a schedule, only Minnesota's statute expressly requires the issuance of an award before a date related to appropriations.

As an alternative solution, South Dakota and Michigan minimize the disruptive effect of an arbitration award on the employer's budget by providing that the effective date of any determination on wages shall be the beginning of the next fiscal year. Nevada's law requires that in a regular legislative year the arbitration hearing be stayed up to ten days following the adjournment of the legislature *sine die*. Thus the arbitrator can be aware of legislative appropriations before making a determination that must be based on a current ability to pay.

## C. *Composition of the Panel*

Although most statutes authorizing arbitration upon the agreement of both parties permit an ad hoc determination of the size of the panel, the great majority of arbitration laws provide for a tripartite panel composed of one member selected by each party plus a chairman chosen by the two appointees. This type of panel carries the collective bargaining process over into arbitration, since the first two appointees are likely to maintain a partisan stance. In justification of such an approach, it is argued that the labor and employer members will be more familiar with the issues and their sponsors' positions and thus able to help the neutral arbitrator avoid any serious error that might result in an award competely unacceptable to one side. In contrast, statutes in Minnesota and Denver remove collective bargaining procedures from the arbitration process by providing that

---

[8] [Iowa (all public employees); Maine (state employees); Michigan (police and firefighters); Minnesota (most public employees); Nebraska (all public employees); Oklahoma (police and firefighters); Oregon (police, fire, and institutional personnel); Pennsylvania (police and firefighters); Rhode Island (municipal employees and teachers); and Wisconsin (police and firefighters). Eds.]

[9] [See "voluntary" statutes set forth in note 6, *supra*. Eds.]

the parties select the entire tripartite panel from a list of seven names submitted by an independent, neutral board.

## D. *Dissenting Opinions*

Most statutes providing for tripartite panels permit a decision by majority vote, thus creating the possibility of a dissent, either in whole or in part, by one of the arbitrators. Undoubtedly, in jurisdictions that require each party to appoint an arbitrator, the dissenter will most probably be a partisan, rather than the neutral chairman. Present experience is inadequate to indicate what effect such dissents will have on the use of arbitration procedures. A dissenting opinion by the employee-arbitrator may cause the union membership to reject the settlement, while an employer might seek repeal of the arbitration statute following too many dissents by its panel member. Tripartite panels are in fact not mandated in New York City because of apprehension concerning the dissents in other jurisdictions. On the other hand, after a dissent, a party may pursue collective bargaining more aggressively in an attempt to avoid arbitration. Such a result might lead to smoother negotiation of subsequent contracts.

## E. *Residency Requirement*

The majority of statutes have no residency requirement for panel members, although a few impose such a requirement on a judge-appointed chairman of a tripartite panel selected when the two other members, who normally select a chairman, are unable to agree. Only Minnesota's law directs that the names of the arbitrators submitted to the parties contain "whenever possible . . . names of persons from the geographical area in which the public employer is located."

When a city must lay off employees and reduce city services to comply with a binding arbitration award, a likely result is public resentment against an "outside" arbitrator who need not live with the consequences of his award. In 1970, the Mayor of Detroit blamed an award covering policemen for the necessity to reduce city services, to lay off at least 542 city employees, and to increase working hours from 35 to 40 a week. Amidst the ensuing turmoil, the Mayor announced that he was looking for alternative procedures to propose to the state legislature. One of the proposals he considered was to replace the "out-of-town arbitrator" with a permanent umpire who would be familiar with the problems of the city and the unions.

## F. *Criteria for Award*

Most statutes mandating arbitration establish some criteria for the arbitrators to follow in making their award. . . . [Some provide only general standards, instructing the arbitration panel to consider such factors as the types of employment involved, the public interest, and the relative equities of the parties.] The Rhode Island Policemen's Arbitration Act typifies the use of longer and more specific criteria:

The factors, among others, to be given weight by the arbitrators in arriving at a decision shall include:

(a) Comparison of wage rates or hourly conditions of employment of the police department in question with prevailing wage rates or hourly conditions of employment of skilled employees of the building trades and industry in the local operating area involved.

(b) Comparison of wage rates or hourly conditions of employment of the police department in question with wage rates or hourly conditions of employment of police departments in cities or towns of comparable size.

(c) Interest and welfare of the public.

(d) Comparison of peculiarities of employment in regard to other trades or professions, specifically:

(1) Hazards of employment

(2) Physical qualifications

(3) Educational qualifications

(4) Mental qualifications

(5) Job training and skills.

In contrast to the statutes mandating arbitration, there are no criteria in seven of the eleven statutes that require arbitration upon the request of one party, and there are no criteria in most of the statutes that authorize arbitration upon the consent of both parties.

Among the statutes with standards, few attempt to deal with the complex question of the employer's ability to pay, which may be computed by reference to either revenues presently available or the community's capacity to tax and its utilization of its fiscal resources as compared to other communities. As public employers increasingly claim inability to provide higher compensation and to cover the costs of non-salary demands, arbitrators, in the absence of specific guidelines, will probably tend to base awards on the jurisdiction's potential ability to increase its revenues.

Nevada's statute provides the clearest standard concerning an employer's ability to pay. The arbitrators must first determine that there is

a current financial ability to grant monetary benefits based on all existing available revenues as established by the local government employer, and with due regard for the obligation of the local government employer to provide facilities and services. . . .

Once that finding has been made, "normal criteria for interest disputes" may be employed. Such a formulation avoids the possibility of an award that would necessitate increased taxes, employee lay-offs or reduced municipal services.

When a statute does not prescribe rules for decision, arbitrators will presumably apply "general standards." In these circumstances, articulation of the rationale underlying the award is important to forestall a charge of arbitrariness by a disgruntled party. Similarly, decisions that demonstrably correspond to prevailing wages, terms, and conditions of employment in comparable jurisdictions will be more readily accepted by the parties.

## G. *Terms of an Award*

All but four jurisdictions permit arbitrators wide latitude in the selection of settlement terms. Minnesota, Wisconsin, Michigan, and Eugene, Oregon, however, limit awards to either of the parties' final offers. The Michigan statute provides for a choice on each economic issue, while the others mandate a selection of a "package" deal. The primary effect of these provisions is to encourage reasonable bargaining positions at the negotiation stage, since an unreasonable offer will probably lead to adoption of the other party's position in the arbitration award.

The Michigan approach, termed "last offer" arbitration, is favored by at least one commentator who would allow the arbitrator to

> make a choice between the final offers of the parties on an issue-by-issue basis. In this way, the arbitrator would have the prerogative of considering each issue on its merits and of accepting the "most reasonable" offer.

It would thus not be necessary to choose between two packages, each possibly containing some unreasonable demands, and intransigence would never be rewarded.

Despite the seeming superiority of "last offer" arbitration, Professor Carl Stevens advocates the "one-or-the-other" method used by Minnesota, Wisconsin and Eugene. If arbitrators are forced to choose between two "objectionable and arbitrary" offers, he argues, they can remand the case to the parties requesting more reasonable packages. Remand, however, may exacerbate rather than ease a tense situation involving two determined parties. Furthermore, the Michigan statute demonstrates that a provision for remand can be used in conjunction with "last offer" arbitration as well. Finally, the public interest requires the elimination of as many irrational items in an award as possible, a goal best achieved under the Michigan approach. . . .

## H. *Limitations on an Award*

Although it seems clear that an arbitrator cannot require either party to act illegally or beyond its authority, a few statutes contain provisions explicitly dealing with the possibility of a conflict between an arbitrator's award and existing law. The Vallejo law seeks to avoid any conflict *ab initio* by defining the efficacy of an award by reference to "applicable law." An after-the-fact approach is taken by provisions in Vermont and Minnesota that void portions of an award found to contravene pre-existing statutes. In contrast to these absolute provisions, the New York City ordinance and a Pennsylvania statute adopt a median course. When a term of an award would require enabling legislation, New York City stays its effect "until the appropriate legislative body enacts such [a] law," while Pennsylvania considers the term "advisory only." In such a case the employer's obligation is probably limited to sponsoring and supporting the necessary legislation.

A unique provision of the Pennsylvania statute covering firemen and police attempts to guarantee the binding effect of any award:

> Such determination shall constitute a mandate to the head of the political subdivision which is the employer, or to the appropriate officer of the Commonwealth, if the Commonwealth is the employer, with respect to matters which can be remedied by administrative action, and to the lawmaking body of such political subdivision or of the Commonwealth with respect to matters which require legislative action, to take the action necessary to carry out the determination of the board of arbitration.

Despite the vigor of this language, the Pennsylvania Supreme Court has limited its scope by ruling that in the case of direct conflict, existing laws need not be altered, and the offending terms of the award are therefore void. [City of Washington v. Police Dep't, 436 Pa. 168, 179, 259 A.2d 437, 443 (1969).]

Five statutes limit an arbitration panel's power to affect a jurisdiction's taxing or budgeting operations by rendering advisory terms relating to monetary expenditures. Practical assessment of the significance of these provisions is difficult. A public employer may feel great pressure to accept what is technically a recommendation when it is part of an award containing other binding terms. The pressure will be expecially intense if the award fails to distinguish nonbinding from binding provisions and thus raises the expectation of employees that the employer must accept the entire package. In addition arbitrators may well make less costly determinations knowing their decisions are only advisory. Such a result is probably intended by the statutes, which implicitly warn the parties that excessively costly terms may be rejected.

## I. *Judicial Review*

The majority of statutes are silent on the question of appeal from an award, and while no reported decisions have considered the issue as to them, the absence of a specific provision usually will not preclude judicial review on grounds such as fraud, lack of impartiality or wrongful assumption of power by the panel. Ten statutes, however, do explicitly provide for a right to appeal to the courts. South Dakota allows the broadest "appeal de novo"; Michigan permits review on the grounds, *inter alia,* that "the order is unsupported by competent, material and substantial evidence on the whole record." Other laws authorize review of questions of law, and, more narrowly, allegations of fraud, misconduct, and wrongful assumption of power. Consistent with the legislative intent that awards covering firemen and police be absolutely binding, a Pennsylvania statute denies any right to appeal from an award. The Pennsylvania Supreme Court, however, has held that this provision allows review to determine if the panel has exceeded its authority.

## J. *Expenses*

Since a right to arbitrate at the expense of the other party may lead to obstinacy at the bargaining table, who must compensate the arbitrators is a question of some importance. Most statutes require the parties to share the costs of arbitration. The majority of the laws authorizing arbitration by mutual consent are silent on the question, in keeping with the statutory purpose of permitting, but not requiring, the parties to work out their own arrangements.

## NOTES

1. The Pennsylvania, Michigan, and Wisconsin compulsory interest arbitration statutes are representative of the variations indigenous to such enactments. Pennsylvania allows the arbitration panel to make its own determination with respect to the different issues without being bound by the positions of the parties. In Michigan, the panel must select from the parties' respective positions on an issue-by-issue basis, while in Wisconsin, the more reasonable total package must be chosen. For excellent evaluations of the procedures and experiences under these three schemes, *see* J. STERN, C. REHMUS, J. LOEWENBERG, H. KASPER & B. DENNIS, FINAL-OFFER ARBITRATION (1975). Concerning the Massachusetts experience, *see* Lipsky & Barocci, *Public Employees in Massachusetts and*

*Final-Offer Arbitration,* 101 MONTHLY LAB. REV. 34 (April, 1978). Regarding the application of compulsory arbitration to disputes involving protective employees, *see* Loewenberg, *Compulsory Arbitration for Police and Fire Fighters in Pennsylvania in 1968,* 23 IND. & LAB. REL. REV. 367 (1969) (containing excellent statistical breakdowns by size of cities, location, salary, and the experience of the negotiators); Anderson, *A Survey of Statutes with Compulsory Arbitration Provisions for Fire and Police* in ARBITRATION OF POLICE AND FIREFIGHTERS DISPUTES, PROCEEDINGS OF A CONFERENCE ON ARBITRATION OF NEW CONTRACT TERMS FOR THE PROTECTIVE SERVICES, AM. ARB. ASS'N., New York (March 9, 1971) (discussing the various state approaches and evaluating their effectiveness). *See also* Newman, *Interest Arbitration — Practice and Procedures* in LABOR RELATIONS LAW IN THE PUBLIC SECTOR 44 (A. Knapp ed. 1977); Zack, *Final Offer Selection — Panacea or Pandora's Box?,* 19 N.Y.L.F. 567 (1974); Clark, *Public Employee Strikes: Some Proposed Solutions,* 23 LAB. L. J. 111 68 Lab.Arb. 454 (Witney, Arb. 1977); City of Rialto, 67 Lab.Arb. 654 (Gentile, Arb. 1976); SECTOR 25 (T. Gilroy ed. 1972); Garber, *Compulsory Arbitration in the Public Sector: A Proposed Alternative,* 26 ARB. J. 226 (1971); Stevens, *The Management of Labor Disputes in the Public Sector,* 51 ORE. L. REV. 191 (1971).

2. If a public employer improperly refuses to submit unresolved issues to binding arbitration after a bargaining impasse has been reached, this could constitute an unfair labor practice. *See* St. Paul Professional Employees Ass'n v. City of St. Paul, 226 N.W.2d 311, 88 L.R.R.M. 2861 (Minn. 1975).

3. In Milwaukee Deputy Sheriffs Ass'n. v. Milwaukee County, 221 N.W.2d 673, 88 L.R.R.M. 2169 (Wis. 1974), a case involving "final offer" arbitration, the Court held that an arbitrator could not adopt a final offer that was never discussed by the parties during their collective negotiations.

4. Where a statute provides for an "issue-by-issue" arbitral determination based upon the final offers of the parties, how should the term "issue" be defined? If the parties have disagreed about four separate aspects of the grievance procedure, should this be considered a dispute over a single issue, or should each point of contention be regarded as a separate impasse item? *See* West Des Moines Educ. Ass'n. v. PERB, 266 N.W.2d 118, 1977-78 PBC ¶ 36,284 (Iowa 1978).

5. The Canadian Public Service Staff Relations Act permits the use of binding interest arbitration in lieu of a strike option. Regarding the strengths and weaknesses of the Canadian approach, *see* Arthurs, *Collective Bargaining in the Public Service Act of Canada: Bold Experiment or Act of Folly?,* 67 MICH. L. REV. 971 (1969); Crispo, *Dispute Settlement in the Canadian Public Service* in PROCEEDINGS OF THE INT'L. SYMPOSIUM ON PUBLIC EMPLOYMENT LABOR RELATIONS 89 (1971). *See also* Arthurs, *The Arbitral Process* in PROCEEDINGS OF THE INT'L. SYMPOSIUM ON PUBLIC EMPLOYMENT LABOR RELATIONS 134 (1971).

6. Assume that you have been asked to draft a compulsory interest arbitration statute for your state. Should you allow the arbitration panel to use its own discretion in fashioning the final result, or would a "final offer" limitation, either on an issue-by-issue or total package basis, be preferable? If some "final offer" restriction is adopted, should you follow the approach of the Iowa scheme (*see* § 20.22 in *Statutory Appendix*) and permit the arbitral panel to reject the positions of the parties in favor of the recommendations contained in the prior fact-finding report? What criteria would you provide to guide the panel when it makes its determination? Should you provide specifically for judicial review of arbitral awards and, if so, what standards of review should be applicable?

## d. Enforcement of Decisional Standards

## CITY OF BOSTON and INT'L. ASS'N OF FIREFIGHTERS, LOCAL 718

Compulsory Arbitration Arising Pursuant to Mass. Firemen
and Policemen Binding Arbitration Act 70
Lab. Arb. 154 (1977).

ROBERT M. O'BRIEN, Chairman:

[The initial portion of the opinion, which recounts the developmental stages of the bargaining dispute in issue, has been omitted.]

In Chapter 1078, Section 4, of the Acts of 1973, the Massachusetts Legislature enumerated the factors that must be considered by an Arbitration Panel in arriving at its Award in each case. Those factors consist of the following:

1. The financial ability of the municipality to meet costs.

2. The interests and welfare of the public.

3. The hazards of employment, physical, education, and mental qualifications, job training and skills involved.

4. A comparison of wages, hours and conditions of employment of the employees involved in the arbitration proceedings with the wages, hours and conditions of employment of other employees performing similar services and with other employees generally in public and private employment in comparable communities.

5. The decisions and recommendations of the fact finder.

6. The average consumer prices for goods and services, commonly known as the cost of living.

7. The overall compensation presently received by the employees, including direct wages and fringe benefits.

8. Changes in any of the foregoing circumstances during the pendency of the arbitration proceedings.

9. Such other factors, not confined to the foregoing, which are normally or traditionally taken into consideration in the determination of wages, hours, and conditions of employment through voluntary collective bargaining, mediation, fact-finding, arbitration or otherwise between the parties, in the public service or in private employment.

10. The stipulation of the parties.

This Arbitration Panel has carefully studied the evidence and arguments proffered by both parties in the light of the aforementioned statutory criteria. Upon full consideration of the entire record before us, and giving weight to each of the statutory factors, this Arbitration Panel hereby selects the final offer submitted by the Association, a copy of which is attached to this Award.

In the light of the fact that this arbitration proceeding consumed nine (9) full days of hearings during which time the parties introduced over three hundred (300) exhibits, it would serve no useful purpose for us to restate in any great detail the evidence submitted to this Arbitration Panel. However, the Panel, speaking, of course, through the Chairman, deems it appropriate to briefly advert to the evidence that the Panel accorded significant probative weight in reaching the decision herein. It should be noted, parenthetically, that the views expressed herein represent those of the Chairman, and do not necessarily reflect those of the other members of the Panel.

*Ability To Pay*

In reaching its decision, one of the factors that must be considered by the Panel is "the financial ability of the municipality to meet costs", euphemistically referred to as "ability to pay". The Chairman has carefully considered the extensive oral and documentary evidence proffered by the City which purportedly evidenced their inability to accord Firefighters the salary increase sought by them for Fiscal Year 1977. Based thereon, the Panel cannot concur with Fact Finder Nadworny that the City's financial condition is resilient and healthy. Nor, however, do we entirely agree with the opinions expressed by Professor Raymond Torto, Special Assistant to the Mayor for Tax Policies, and James Young, Deputy Mayor for fiscal affairs, that the City lacks the ability to accord any salary increases at this time.

It is readily apparent to the undersigned that Boston's current fiscal problem is caused by a proliferation of costs and spending, coupled with inadequate sources of revenue to meet these burgeoning expenditures. Massachusetts law prohibits the City from levying any form of tax other than a tax on real and personal property. As a result of this legal impediment, for Fiscal Year 1977 (FY 1977), the period involved herein, approximately 65-70% of the City's revenue was derived from the tax levy on property compared to an average of 41.3% for the nation's forty-nine largest cities. Moreover, the effective tax rate for FY 1977 on property was 9.7%, and as high as 12% on industrial property, the highest effective property tax rate for the thirty largest cities in the nation. (The effective tax rate is the total tax levy divided by the full value of all taxable property). It should be noted that Mr. Torto considers the 9.7% a conservative figure. He further opined that it was twice as high as it should be. Further, Boston's $123.92 full value tax rate is unquestionably the highest in Massachusetts. And while Boston must rely on the property tax as its sole means of raising revenue, it is paradoxical that approximately 58% of the total assessed valuation in the City is exempt from taxation. Professor Torto testified that Boston has sought payment from many of these tax exempt institutions in lieu of taxes. However, so far the total amount of payments in lieu of taxes has only been 5% of what would have been received were the property taxable. He estimated that Boston's tax rate is affected by this tax exempt property in the amount of $198.92. There are additional factors which support the City's contention relative to their inability to pay. For example, based on a study by Terry Nichols Clark of the University of Chicago, Boston ranked second to New York in the overall fiscal strain index, which index is a composite of twenty-nine indicators. And of the four principal indicators of fiscal strain, Boston ranked tenth among fifty-four cities in long term per capita debt; fifth highest in short term per capita debt; third highest in per capita expenditures for nine common city functions; and second in the ratio of revenues to sales value of taxable property. We also consider it significant that in January, 1976, Moody's Investor's Service lowered its rating on Boston general obligation bonds from A to Baa, and Standard and Poor's lowered its rating from A to A- in September, 1976. These lower ratings, of course, are indicative of the level of investor confidence in the City's bonds.

An additional factor that must be considered when ascertaining whether Boston has the ability to pay the wage increase sought by the Union is the current status of the pension liability of the City. The unfunded pension liability of the City is approximately $1,113,000,000. However, approximately one-third of this liability relates to teacher retirement benefits which are reimbursed by the Commonwealth of Massachusetts. Mr. Young stated that the City's pension costs increase 15% yearly. Also significant is the unemployment rate in Boston which as of May, 1977 was 7.056%. And while the unemployment rate is down from the January, 1975 rate of 9.1%, nevertheless, it is still excessively high, and has been consistently higher than communities in the Boston SMSA. Further, in Boston, approximately 14% of the residents receive some form of welfare payments compared to a nationwide city average of 8%.

It should further be observed that Boston's 1974 per capita income of $4157 ranks 25th of the 30 local communities relied on by the City for comparative purposes, and twenty-ninth of the thirty-four largest cities in the nation. And of this per capita income, it is estimated that 11% is expended on property taxes. The City submits that the present salary level of Boston Firefighters, however, places them seventh in the local universe of thirty jurisdictions, and seventh in the national universe consisting of the nation's thirty-four largest cities. (These figures include the night shift differential which all employees in the bargaining unit receive). The City's conclusion is that The Boston Firefighter is appreciably better off than the average Boston resident.

Although the foregoing data certainly illustrates a grim fiscal posture for the City, there is also evidence in the record that Boston's future financial prospects may be improving. While this Panel is not unmindful of the fact that the instant Opinion concerns a collective bargaining agreement effective July 1, 1976 through June 30, 1977, however, inasmuch as the revenue needed to fund any wage increase to be accorded Firefighters for FY 1977 must be raised in FY 1978 and will impact on the FY 1979 tax rate, we deem it appropriate to consider the current and prospective financial condition of the City. It is noteworthy that the City was able to hold the nominal tax rate at $252.90 for FY 1978 after the $56.20 increase in FY 1977. (It should be observed, however, that Deputy Mayor Young had advised the Mayor to increase the tax rate by $6.00). Further, the deficit for FY 1977 was $65 Million, down $17 Million from the FY 1976 deficit of $82 Million. And while we agree with the City that this deficit should be eradicated, the data reveals that the prospects of eliminating the deficit have improved somewhat. Additionally, the latest interest rate on general obligation bonds sold by the City was 6.449%, as opposed to the 9.2% rate on similar bonds sold in February, 1977. And while Mr. Young states that this rate is still 1% higher than the average interest rate on most city bonds, nonetheless the downward trend evidences increased investor confidence in the City's bonds, and arguably an improvement in its fiscal condition.

This Panel must also take note of the fact that the City reduced its overall level of personnel by 900 employees during FY 1977 an indication that the City has initiated a program of strict management controls. Of even greater significance, in our opinion, is the fact that the City has proposed a fiscal legislative package, which if approved by the Massachusetts Legislature, will accord the City new additional sources of revenue, and thus relieve to some extent Boston's excessive reliance on the property tax. Although these new revenue sources have heretofore yielded only $700,000 to the City, Mr. Torto testified that the Mayor will resubmit the legislative package to the Legislature for consideration in Calendar Year 1978.

The projected budget estimates for FY 1978, if accurate, lend further support to our contention that Boston's fiscal condition is indeed improving. For example, it is projected that the Commonwealth's reimbursements to the City will increase by $17 Million over the FY 1977 State aid, and that the amount of Federal financial assistance will remain approximately the same as the FY 1977 level. Moreover, the City estimates that FY 1978 expenditures will increase $19.3 Million while nonproperty tax revenue will increase $30.4 Million. If the foregoing figures stand the test of time, then the City projects a surplus of $17 Million for FY 1978. When one considers that the City had a surplus of $24.8 Million for FY 1977, which surplus was used to reduce Boston's cumulative operating deficit, the financial climate of Boston, while not healthy and resilient, is indeed not as bleak as it had been only one year ago.

This Panel further deems it noteworthy that the City has decided to reinstitute C. 121A projects. While such projects yield the City somewhat less than it would receive were those projects subject to the property tax, nonetheless they are a significant source of revenue for the City. For example, C. 121A distributions from the Commonwealth are estimated to be $7.2 Million for FY 1978, an increase of $846,700 over FY 1977 distributions. And the revenue received by the City from C. 121A projects has increased $5 Million since 1970.

Several conclusions can be discerned from the foregoing data. For instance, while it is true that the nominal tax rate increased by 28% in FY 1977, it is also true that there had been no increase in the rate since 1972. Further, although Boston has experienced a deficit for each of the three fiscal years prior to 1977, there is evidence that it has now begun to reverse this trend. Additionally, although Boston is forced to place an inordinate reliance on the property tax as a source of revenue, a tax which by its very nature is regressive, inelastic and disfunctional, nevertheless the City has initiated steps to lessen this excessive reliance on the property tax. Moreover, it should be noted that the ability of the municipality to pay is only one factor, albeit a significant one, that must be considered by this Panel in arriving at its decision.

Using the City's personnel figures of 1976 uniformed employees plus 71 fire alarm division employees in the bargaining units involved herein, the cost of the Association's proposal is approximately $1,250,000 for FY 1977. Inasmuch as every $1 Million in expenditures causes approximately a $.63 increase in the Boston tax rate the cost of the instant Award is an additional $.78 on the tax rate. It is our considered opinion that such an increase certainly lies within the City's ability to pay.

### The interests and welfare of the public

It is the opinion of this Arbitration Panel that the aforementioned statutory criterion perforce involves a balance between the public's concern over the increased tax burden attendant any incremental change in wages and fringe benefits, and their interest in a well-trained, efficient and motivated fire suppression force. As noted heretofore, the financial cost of this Award lies within the City's financial ability to pay. The effect on Boston's tax rate is approximately $.78, certainly not an onerous increase. And while the cost of fire protection in Boston is admittedly high, so too is the workload of the Boston Fire Department personnel. Although the actual number of fire incidents to which personnel responded decreased during 1977, Boston consistently ranks first among the nation's largest cities in the number of incidents per 1,000 population; total alarms; total fires; total structural fires; and total alarms per square mile. Moreover, the Department's suppression force has decreased over the past several years, thus increasing the workload of individual Firefighters. On balance, we find that the interest and welfare of the public is best served by adoption of the Association's proposal.

### The hazards of employment, physical, education, and mental qualifications, job training and skills involved

It is universally accepted that Firefighting is a hazardous profession. Indeed the U.S. Department of Labor has declared it to be the most hazardous profession in the United States. This is especially true in a municipality such as Boston where not only the residents must be served but also the large influx of daily workers estimated between 250,000 and 300,000. The high population density of Boston; the age and physical characteristics of the City; the traffic congestion; the nature and composition of Boston's dwellings, all combine to make firefighting in the City a formidable undertaking. Moreover, no citation of authority is needed to support the well documented conclusion that the incidents of deaths; occupational injuries; heart and lung diseases; and other disabilities attendant the firefighting profession are among the highest of any occupation in the country. The dangers inherent in this profession are so generally understood that no elaboration is deemed necessary.

Regardless of the statistical variations from year to year, it is patently clear that the frequency of fires in Boston is well above the national average. Thus, while the number of incidents to which personnel responded decreased 9% between 1976 and 1977, the frequency of fires and responses to alarms is still excessively high for a municipality the size of Boston. Moreover, the evidence reveals that the number of multiple alarms have, in fact, increased during this period, and in Deputy Chief Stapleton's opinion, the aforementioned decrease in the number of incidents was due to a decrease in the number of false alarms. And in any event, Deputy Stapleton testified that the firefighters' workload did not diminish between 1976 and 1977 despite the decrease in the number of incidents.

This Panel further deems it significant that while the number of incidents has decreased in 1976, the number of job related injuries has increased. There were 308 more job related injuries in 1976 than 1975 and this trend has continued during the first six months of 1977. While the injury rate per incident was .037 in 1975 it rose to .046 during 1976 and .051 for the first half of 1977. Moreover, injuries sustained by Boston Firefighters increased from 1,631 in 1972 to 2,352 in 1975, over a 40% increment.

We also take note of the fact that the manpower level in the Department has not expanded commensurately with the increase in the workload. Deputy Chief Stapleton stated that prior to 1977 16 Companies had a complement of one Officer and four Firefighters while now only four Companies have such a complement. Additionally, the normal Company complement is now one Officer and three Firefighters, a decrease from the one and five complement prevalent in the 1950's. It is significant that during FY 1977, the fire suppression force decreased by 76 employees.

Also affecting the work of Firefighters is the increase in the incidents of harrassment [sic] by the public. Although the Boston Police Department had previously assigned so-called P cars to accompany fire vehicles, this practice is no longer in effect.

It is noteworthy that the level of training and education by members of the bargaining unit has increased. For example, currently over 400 employees, 20% of the fire suppression force, have qualified as Emergency Medical Technicians although the Department has not required them to do so. And the entire complement of the suppression force has completed the first responder course. Moreover, 162 employees have Fire Science credits, 56 of which have earned an Associate Degree despite the fact that the City has no educational incentive plan for Firefighters.

The conclusion to be drawn from the foregoing is that firefighting is an extremely hazardous profession requiring those engaged therein to be skilled, trained, and qualified to adequately perform the technical duties thereof. The evidence clearly supports the proposition that Firefighters in Boston have the requisite skill, training and qualifications to meet the challenge. The Award of this Panel is clearly supported by this statutory factor.

*A comparison of wages, hours and conditions of employment of the employees involved in the arbitration proceeding with the wages, hours and conditions of employment of other employees performing similar services and with other employees generally in public and private employment in comparable communities*

Although time constraints preclude this Panel from addressing this statutory factor in any great detail, we do wish to make several observations respecting the subject of comparability. The City has proffered evidence comparing Boston Firefighters with other City of Boston employees; with private sector employees; with Firefighters in large New England cities and with Firefighters in the 34 largest cities in the United States. For their part, the Association has compared Boston Firefighters with their counterparts in principal cities in Standard Metropolitan Statistical areas (SMSAs) with populations of 2,000,000 or more; with cities with populations between 500,000 and 1,000,000; and with Massachusetts communities with populations in excess of 50,000 and located within ten (10) miles of Boston. As is readily apparent from the foregoing, the parties are not in accord on the universe of communities, either local or national, that should be used for comparative purposes. And the Panel will not endeavor to render judgment on what indeed are the proper comparable universes. However, the Chairman has carefully studied the documentary and testimonial evidence submitted by the parties relative to this statutory factor. While that evidence is not unequivocal, nonetheless when considered in its entirety we believe that it supports the Association's position in this proceeding.

Although the City asserts that no other City employees have received a wage increase for FY 1977 as of this date, it should be noted that several bargaining units of City employees, including the Boston Police Patrolmen's Association and the Boston Police Superior Officers Federation, have not yet settled their contracts for FY 1977. (We are not unmindful of the fact that Fact Finder Levine has recommended no salary increase for Patrolmen for FY 1977).

Respecting employees in the private sector, the Bureau of Labor Statistics' national survey of private sector settlements evidences that 1976 settlements for those employers with 1000 workers or more averaged 8.3% while similar settlements for the first six months of 1977 averaged 8.0%. Moreover, as far as can be discerned, the private sector settlements in the Boston area are analogous to those nationwide. Additionally, white collar salaries increased an average of 6.86 between March, 1976 and March, 1977 according to the Bureau of Labor Statistics.

Comparing the January 1, 1977 maximum Boston Firefighter salary of $14,908 with the salaries of Firefighters in the City's national universe, the salary increase advanced Boston's relative rank from 21st to 16th of the 34 cities included therein. Boston's position moved from 9th to 3rd of the 32 communities used by the City in their local universe. Including night shift differential and 10 years longevity payments then the salary adjustment places Boston second of those 32 communities. It should be noted, however, that the City's local and national universe both reflect extensive 1975 and 1976 salary rates while Boston's salary increase will not take effect until January 1, 1977.

Comparing Boston's maximum Firefighter salary of $15,206 (including the night shift differential) with the Association's national universe, Boston ranks 8th of 13 cities, $969 below the average. Comparing maximum salary with the 13 communities in the Association's local universe, the facts evidence that Boston moves from 5th to 3rd, $625 above the average. If the City's Offer had been adopted by this Panel, however, Boston would rank 8th among the 13 communities, $346 below the average. Moreover, Firefighters in a majority of those 13 communities received a salary increase greater than Boston's 3.5% for FY 1977.

While the matter of comparability cannot be measured with any mathematical certainty, nonetheless on balance this Panel believes that this statutory factor lends somewhat more support to the Association's Last, Best Offer than to the City's Offer.

*The decisions and recommendations of the fact finder*

It is readily apparent to this Panel that the Report of Fact Finder Milton J. Nadworny issued May 4, 1977, comports more with the Association's Final Offer than with the City's Final Offer. The City has taken vigorous exception to the conclusions reached by the Fact Finder. They assert that in the light of the Fact Finder's Reports in disputes between the City and the Boston Police Patrolmen's Association and the Boston Teachers Union, it is obvious that Fact Finder Nadworny's Report is patently erroneous. The Chairman has carefully studied the Fact Finder's Report, and he does not consider it as egregious as the City avers. The Fact Finder considered the same statutory factors that must be considered by this Panel. However, he did not have before him all the financial data relative to FY 1977 and this forced him to make certain assumptions. While Professor Nadworny was not certain whether the tax levy in Boston increased in FY 1977, this Panel wishes to note that we are well aware that the tax levy increased by over $90 Million in FY 1977 resulting in a $56.20 increase in the nominal tax rate in Boston. Yet, as stated heretofore, it is our opinion that the City has the ability to meet the cost of the Association's Last, Best Offer.

The Fact Finder recommended a 9% salary increase effective January 1, 1977. The Association has moved from this recommendation to a 7% salary increase also effective January 1, 1977. Moreover, their proposal for an annual clothing allowance of $200; their proposal relative to the health insurance carrier; their proposal for incorporation of specialist categories into the contract; their proposal relative to temporary service in a higher rank; and their proposal concerning Article XVII, Section 9 all parallel the recommendations of the Fact Finder.

The applicable statute compels this Panel to give consideration to the decisions and recommendations of the fact finder and this we have done. We would hasten to add, however, that the Report of the Fact Finder is merely one factor that was accorded weight by this Panel.

*The average consumer prices for goods and services, commonly known as the cost of living*

When giving weight to the statutory factor of cost of living it is always a vexing problem for the Panel to determine during, what period of time any increase in the cost of living should be measured. For example, since 1967, the Boston Consumer Price Index (CPI) has increased 85%. Yet, during this same period, Firefighters' salaries (including night shift differential and ten-year longevity pay) have increased 102.7% on an annual basis and 133.5% on an hourly basis. Thus, if the period from 1967 is the relevant period, then it is obvious that Firefighters' salaries have increased at a rate in excess of the increase in the cost of living as measured by the Boston CPI. Using the period March, 1973 to January 1, 1977, however, we observe that while the Boston CPI increased 36.4%, Firefighters' salaries have increased only 15.9%, 20.5% less than the increase in the Boston CPI. Or if we consider the period July 1, 1975, when Firefighters were last accorded a salary increase, to January 1, 1977, we see that the Boston CPI has increased by 10.1%.

The foregoing facts evidence that while the Firefighters' salaries have more than offset the increase in the cost of living since 1967, their salaries have lagged behind the increase in the cost of living over the past several years. And the

Association's Offer of a 7% increase effective January 1, 1977 will still not totally recoup this erosion in the Firefighters' purchasing power over the past several years. Nor will the 3.5% effective salary increase for FY 1977 completely offset the 5.2% increase in the Boston CPI for this same period of time. Moreover, the Bureau of Labor Statistics has estimated that the Boston intermediate family budget increased 7.2% between August, 1975 and August, 1976, placing the budget at $19,384, the highest in the continental United States.

If the Panel had accepted the City's Last, Best Offer (assuming for the sake of argument that the $300 bonus represented a salary adjustment), members of bargaining unit A would have received approximately a 2% salary increase while those in unit B would have been accorded an average salary increase of 1.5%. It is thus patently obvious that the City's Offer would only slightly allow Firefighters to offset the recent increase in the cost of living.

*The overall compensation presently received by the employees, including direct wages and fringe benefits*

Without elaborating thereon, this Panel wishes to observe that in rendering the instant Award, we have considered the total compensation of $16,551 which will be accorded Firefighters subsequent to FY 1977. The $16,551 is a composite of wages, holidays, longevity payments and night shift differential. We have also considered the fringe benefits enjoyed by Firefighters including, but not limited to, vacations; clothing allowance; sick leave; medical insurance; and personal leave. As noted heretofore, the level of compensation and fringe benefits of Firefighters in Boston is compatible with that accorded Firefighters in comparable communities. Further, they are justified by the training, skills and qualifications attributable to Boston Firefighters.

*Changes in any of the foregoing circumstances during the pendency of the arbitration proceedings*

The City asserts that two important changes have taken place during the pendency of this proceeding. First, the largest City bargaining units in the City have settled contracts for FY 1977, and those settlements provide for no wage increase in FY 1977. Secondly, two other fact finding reports have been issued which address the question of the City's ability to pay. It should be noted that both these subjects have been addressed by the Panel elsewhere in this Award. However, we wish to briefly observe that neither of the other two uniformed bargaining units in the City, viz. the Boston Police Patrolmen's Association and the Boston Police Superior Officers Federation, has settled contracts for FY 1977.

This Panel must concede, however, that we have carefully studied Fact Finder Levine's Report respecting the Boston Police Patrolmen's Association, and we are unable to reconcile his conclusions relative to the City's ability to pay with those of Fact Finder Nadworny's. Yet, Mr. Levine's findings are certainly not dispositive of the dispute presently before this Panel. They are simply one element that should be considered by this Panel. It should also be noted that in his Report in the Boston Teachers Union case, Fact Finder Edwards recommended a 3% salary increase to be effective midpoint in the 1976-77 school year. The cost of this recommendation to the City of Boston would have been $1.3 Million which, of course, is comparable to the cost of the Association's Last, Best Offer.

Accordingly, the Panel opines that while we have considered the City's assertions relative to this statutory factor, nonetheless we are not persuaded that the City's Last, Best Offer is more reasonable. All the statutory criteria must be accorded weight in reaching a decision. Inasmuch as the statute does not state what weight must be ascribed to each factor, we must presume that the

Legislature has left that determination to each Arbitration Panel. It is our opinion that the weight of the evidence, when measured in the light of the statutory criteria, compels the conclusion that the Association's Last, Best Offer should be adopted by this Panel.

. . . .

## NOTES

1. Probably the most perplexing consideration raised in most interest arbitration proceedings concerns the financial capacity of the public employer in question. In a 1970 compulsory arbitration decision involving the City of Detroit and the Detroit Fire Fighters Ass'n., Panel Chairman Harry H. Platt stated:

The City strongly urges us to take into account its precarious financial condition and to find that it lacks the "ability to pay" any salary increase in excess of 6%. Indeed, we do find that the City's financial adversity will unquestionably require it to continue to operate on a deficit financing basis. Yet we are mindful that an efficient fire department which pays fair compensation and provides adequate benefits to its employees is essential to the public welfare. Unquestionably, fire fighting services, like other essential public safety services, are becoming more expensive. So are the personal and family needs of the fire fighters. If, as we believe it to be the case, the general public and the taxpayers wish to continue to have a modern, efficient fire fighting service in the City of Detroit they must be willing to bear the increased cost.

We are fully aware that many employers cite unsatisfactory circumstances when supporting a claim of inability to meet employee demands. We are equally mindful that virtually all of these employers somehow find some source of necessary funds after the demands are met.

In the case at hand we are also aware, as the Association has pointed out, that year-end deficits and revenue gaps have been a "normal" way of life in Detroit for many years. We also understand that the increase in the real estate tax rate, the enactment of the excise tax on utilities, and the Urban Assistance Grant, all of which occurred after the original salary offer was made, have alleviated the fiscal problems somewhat. We do not, in other words, accept the stated inability of the City to meet fire fighter demands as a reason in and of itself for rejecting those demands. Nor would the provisions of the Act permit us to do so.

But we do not believe the City's financial condition can be ignored or that it is a wholly irrelevant consideration in determining pay levels which are above the level of substandard or minimum pay. Indeed, we must, as a practical matter and in prudence and good conscience, try to balance the needs of fire fighters for a pay increase and the City's ability and the taxpayers' willingness to meet the cost. . . .

City witnesses testified that the current financial condition has prevented the filling of many budget positions, including those in essential service areas. Subsequent published figures update this testimony and disclose that there were in mid-November some 2,365 unfilled positions on the City's tax supported payroll. This figure, we believe, is directly translatable into discontinued and reduced municipal services to the citizens of Detroit.

Even more indicative of the validity of the City's claim is the information which it has presented relative to layoffs. There is evidence that some 539 City employees have been laid off from their jobs in recent months solely for budgetary reasons and that the City has not as yet been able to recall most of them or to place them in other positions.

Perhaps most important, evidence was offered that the layoff of some 329 City employees was announced on July 2, 1970, in an effort to reduce costs and that an additional 214 employees were similarly dropped from the payroll following an announcement on July 30. . . .

The implication of this testimony was that the cost of meeting fire fighter demands was translatable in terms of additional layoffs and reductions in municipal services. . . .

As a Board, we must therefore face the likelihood that increased costs ensuing from our decision, quite apart from the merits of the fire fighters' demands, would probably produce still further impacts on the City's ability to carry out its obligations to the people of Detroit.

Accordingly, we have strived to temper our decision in keeping with our perception of the City's fiscal facts of life. Our conclusion is that while the financial condition in which the City finds itself does not warrant a denial of a fair and equitable pay increase for fire fighters in the current fiscal year, a postponement of the effective date of part of our pay award, which will lessen the cost impact of a full application of the parity principle, is appropriate. Our pay award is therefore as follows:

Pay parity between the police and fire service has been an established City policy for more than 63 years and, no sufficient showing having been made to justify a disruption of that parity relationship, it shall be continued. . . .

In the 1971-72 compulsory arbitration involving the City of Detroit and the Detroit Police Officers Ass'n., the Panel was similarly confronted with an assertion that the City was "sinking into a financial quagmire." In evaluating the evidence regarding the City's ability to pay, Panel Chairman Gabriel N. Alexander observed:

The evidence establishes that the City has been unable to extricate itself from a steadily increasing year to year deficit for several years, and that it is powerless to do anything by way of increasing revenues without additional legislation from other governments, state or federal. I am convinced to a depressing certainty that the City cannot survive as an independent unit of government as that concept was understood, say, a decade ago.

DPOA argues, and I agree, that the "financial ability" criterion set forth in Section 9(c) is not controlling. If it were, I might well conclude that there should be no salary increases, or even (considering what has happened on some occasions in private employment) that salaries should be reduced. But this is beside the point. The city acknowledges that some increase is appropriate. The statute commands us to take into account other criteria, in addition to financial ability, and what I have asserted as the ruling is a reflection of the amalgam of all the considerations pro and con which bear upon the ultimate point in issue. As DPOA points out, Detroit cannot buy coal for its generating plants or salt for its streets for less than the "going rate" because it is impoverished. Why then should it be able to "buy" the labor of its policemen for less than the "going rate" because it is impoverished? Of course the answer lies in the statute which defines the "going rate" (in statutory words "just and reasonable") as that rate which shall be fixed by the Panel after taking into account, among other things, the "financial ability of the unit of government to meet those costs."

Are you satisfied with the manner in which these arbitration decisions have treated the fiscal problems of Boston and Detroit? Could you articulate a preferable approach?

2. How much financial destitution must be documented by a municipality before it significantly influences an arbitration decision? *See* Sioux County and AFSCME, Local 1774, 68 Lab.Arb. 1258, 1262 (Gruenberg, Arb. 1978), wherein the arbitrator stated: "While both the County and the fact finder made much of [the ability to pay] factor, the arbitrator is of the opinion that changing priorities in the public sector facilitate payment of reasonable wage increases to employees. Unless the fiscal situation of the public employer is verging on bankruptcy, ability to pay is a flexible standard."

3. For some excellent discussions of the problem of ability to pay, *see generally* Zack, *Ability to Pay in Public Sector Bargaining,* in PROCEEDINGS OF NEW YORK UNIVERSITY TWENTY-THIRD ANNUAL CONFERENCE ON LABOR (Christenson ed. 1970); Ross, *The Arbitration of Public Employee Wage Disputes,* 23 IND. & LAB. REL. REV. 3 (1969); Block, *Criteria in Public Sector Interest Disputes,* in ARBITRATION AND THE PUBLIC INTEREST, PROCEEDINGS OF THE TWENTY-FOURTH ANNUAL MEETING OF THE NATIONAL ACADEMY OF ARBITRATORS 171 (G. Somers ed. 1971).

4. On the question of the competence of arbitrators to deal with issues arising pursuant to a government employer's claim of "inability to pay," see Smith, *Comment,* in

Arbitration and the Public Interest, Proceedings of the Twenty-Fourth Annual Meeting of the National Academy of Arbitrators 180, 184-87 (G. Somers ed. 1971). Professor Smith argues that "inability to pay" is not a difficult issue in a case where the employer is "utterly without financial resources to fund *any* increase in labor costs"; however, he makes the following additional observations with respect to the problem:

[T]hese simplistic remarks dodge a whole series of problems for the neutral ranging from the factual to the basic questions of principle. I suggest that among the very serious questions are several that are not within the realm of expertise of labor dispute arbitrators on the basis solely of their private sector experience. The initial question is in a sense factual only. It is: What is the public body's actual fiscal position in terms of its ability to absorb *any* increased operating costs? Any sound analysis of this matter often requires an exhaustive and knowledgeable inquiry into budget allocations, revenue sources, transferability of appropriations, borrowing capability, and the like. The second question is whether, if the public body's ability to absorb increased operating costs is limited (which is probably the typical situation), the neutral should attempt to determine the gross amount of increased labor costs, if any, which the public body can finance. This in itself may turn out to be a fairly complicated problem. But, assuming this gross amount can be determined, the next and crucial question is whether the neutral should assume that this fund is all that can be provided, by way of increases, for any and all groups of employees — given the repercussionary effects of an increase awarded to the group before him — or should act on the basis that this fund can be enlarged by the public body by reductions in force or rearrangements of priorities. Obviously related is the question whether the neutral should attempt to determine the impact his award will have in terms of affecting the economic demands of other groups of employees and their ultimate settlement. Bear in mind, of course, that it is assumed that these other groups of employees, and their bargaining representatives, if any, are not parties to his proceeding or represented in it.

Now I submit that inquiries of these kinds pose problems which are so serious and difficult as to make the criterion ability to pay or, more realistically, alleged inability to pay, one which, if deemed to be relevant or required by law to be taken into consideration, is likely to be taken less seriously than others, such as comparison data. One of Howard Block's observations is that he "is inclined to agree with those who insist that when a neutral rules out inability to pay as a valid defense, he should also assume some responsibility for finding the funds to implement his award," although he also adds, apparently as a proviso, "if the parties have authorized him to do so." I interpret this remark as implying that Howard not only regards ability to pay as a proper criterion for consideration, where advanced by a party, but further as stating that the neutral does, indeed, have the full responsibility, somehow, of dealing with the series of problems which, I have suggested, then must be addressed. But I doubt very much that he can or should attempt any assignment of that magnitude except perhaps in a situation where all parties concerned, including other unions, have deliberately vested in him what would be tantamount to the full authority of the public body with respect to its budget, allocations, and priorities.

What, then, is the likely result where ability to pay is accepted by the neutral, or by law forced upon him, as a factor to be taken into account? Only a searching analysis of arbitral decisions would provide anything like an accurate answer. I have knowledge of some, however, including several in which I have participated. My impression is that a number of arbitrators, absent any statutory compulsion to take fiscal matters into account, tend to regard them as substantially irrelevant. But my impression, further, is that where, as under the Michigan police and firefighter compulsory arbitration law, this is one of the several factors specified for consideration as applicable, there has been a more or less valiant effort to analyze the public body's fiscal position, and, upon finding a very tight situation, to make an award on economic issues which would be somewhat less, or stated as being somewhat less, than otherwise would have been considered justified, but yet not to let the fiscal factor predominate.

## INTERNATIONAL ASSOCIATION OF FIRE FIGHTERS, LOCAL 1285, LAS VEGAS, NEVADA and CITY OF LAS VEGAS (1972)

HOWARD S. BLOCK, Fact-Finder:

[The parties came to impasse in negotiations over a number of "economic" issues, including wages. NEV. REV. STAT. § 288.200-7 empowers the Governor to make the anticipated findings and recommendations of the factfinder binding at the request of either party. The Fire Fighters invoked this provision and, after a hearing, Governor O'Callaghan ordered that the factfinder's recommendations be final and binding as to six issues, including wages. Subsequent to the hearing, the parties jointly selected Howard S. Block to serve as Factfinder (from a list submitted by the American Arbitration Association). The decision was as follows with respect to "binding monetary issues":] . . .

### 1. *Binding Monetary Issues*

(a) *Salary Grade Adjustments* — The parties are ordered to negotiate the issue of Salary Grade Adjustments for the classifications of Alarm Operator and Hydrant Repairman. The Factfinder reserves jurisdiction to determine this issue if the parties are unable to resolve it within thirty days from the date of this Report.

(b) As to all other monetary issues, the Factfinder rules that the City does not have the financial ability to pay the additional wages and benefits proposed by the Fire Fighters. . . .

For the current (1972-73) fiscal year, the City offered an across-the-board wage increase of 5% to all employees which, when added to the reclassification study increase, amounts to a total wage advance averaging 6.6% for Fire Fighters. This does not include instep and longevity increases already built into the salary schedule, and a number of minor fringe benefit items, which together add 4.39% to the average income of City employees. According to the Fire Fighters, this 4.39% is significantly less in the Fire Department.

The City's 1972-73 wage proposal was accepted by the City Employees Association. It was rejected by the Police Protective Association and the resulting impasse was submitted to Factfinder Joseph F. Gentile who submitted a comprehensive report on May 5, 1972 (City Exhibit 1) which concluded that the City did not have the financial ability to grant additional monetary benefits. Chronologically, that brings us down to the instant case to which we now turn.

### *Preliminary Determination Pursuant to NRS 288.200-8(a)*

For a Factfinder, the crux of the Nevada Statute is found in NRS 288.200-8(a) which delineates the criteria he must apply in arriving at his decision. Because of its importance in this proceeding, that statutory language is set forth below:

"8. Any factfinder, whether acting in a recommendatory or binding capacity, shall base his recommendations or award on the following criteria:

"(a) *A preliminary determination shall be made as to the financial ability* of the local government employer based on all existing available revenues as established by the local government employer, and with due regard for the obligation of the local government employer to provide facilities and services guaranteeing the health, welfare and safety of the people residing within the political subdivision.

"(b) Once the factfinder has determined in accordance with paragraph (a) that there is a current financial ability to grant monetary benefits, he shall use normal criteria for interest disputes regarding the terms and provisions to be included in an agreement in assessing the reasonableness of the position of each party as to each issue in dispute.

"The factfinder's report shall contain the facts upon which he based his recommendations or award." [Emphasis added.]

It is clear from the foregoing provision that the Legislature has established a two-step procedure, with the first step being a preliminary determination of financial ability. What is not at all clear is the test to be applied in making this "preliminary determination," and the parties are in sharp disagreement on this point. Thus, the "preliminary determination" question poses two issues for the Factfinder: (1) the meaning that can reasonably be ascribed to this statutory requirement and (2) how that meaning should be applied to the instant case.

The City's position on the first issue was summarized by Counsel as follows:

". . . if the Board of City Commissioners with reference to the budget have made the allocations reasonably, that the Factfinder cannot tamper with them. In essence, turning the coin around, it is the City's position that the Factfinder has to be able to say that as a matter of law the Commission's allocations were unreasonable."

In other words, the City maintains that its budgetary allocations are conclusive upon all parties unless it can be determined that some of its allocations are unreasonable. The Factfinder cannot accept this interpretation for the following two principal reasons: (1) it is readily apparent to the most casual observer that, over at least the past several years, financial constraints upon local government in Nevada, and elsewhere across the United States, make it impossible to satisfy all of the requirements that would fall within the broad classification of a "reasonable allocation." Therefore, if a Union's right to negotiate matters within the scope of representation were limited to funds "unreasonably allocated," it would make the negotiating process a meaningless ritual; and (2) if the Legislature intended the budgetary allocations of local government to be conclusive, it could have easily said so. There is simply no justification for "reading-in" such an interpretation which, in practical effect, would restore employer-employee relations to where they were before the Dodge Act was passed.

In the Factfinder's opinion, if the criteria imposed by NRS 288.200-8(a) are to be reconciled, in any meaningful way, with the duty to negotiate over wages, hours and conditions of employment as prescribed by NRS 288.150, then, once the City has determined the sums that are necessary ". . . to provide facilities and service guaranteeing the health, welfare and safety of the people residing within [the City limits] . . ." [NRS 288.200-8(a)], it must then establish priorities in its allocation of remaining funds as between all claimants — e.g. capital expenditures, employee requests, taxpayer proposals, and all of the other competing claims upon the limited funds available. The ranking of these priorities may be reviewed by a Factfinder as to its reasonableness. Indeed, this is ordinarily the principal function of the interest dispute factfinder in the public sector where, as here, there are insufficient funds to meet all legitimate demands. Were the Factfinder barred from reviewing the order of priorities, as the City has argued, then this entire factfinding procedure would serve little, if any, purpose. The Factfinder rules, therefore, that a review of City established priorities is proper under the statutory language.

We turn now to the principal and remaining question bearing on the "preliminary determination" issue — whether the City's priorities should be revised in order to meet the Union's demands. Or, stating the question in statutory terms, whether the City has the financial ability to pay such demands. The parties focused their attention on this key issue because the answer to it determines, in large measure, the extent to which the Union's demands can be satisfied, if at all.

Both the Fire Fighters and the City offered an analysis of budget expenditures and revenues through expert testimony. In addition, each submitted comprehensive exhibits into evidence which compared the City's salaries and benefits with Fire Fighters in other public jurisdictions of Nevada, California and elsewhere in the United States. All of these data were then summarized and ably argued by Counsel for each side in his closing argument. The exigencies of time make it impractical for the Factfinder to review all of the arguments advanced or even most of them. However, on the basis of a careful scrutiny of the entire record of this proceeding, the Factfinder concludes that he would not be justified in altering the priorities established by the Board of City Commissioners. He has reached this conclusion for the following principal reasons:

1. The Fire Fighters salary schedule compares favorably with those of other Nevada jurisdictions. On the basis of the record before him, the Factfinder cannot agree with the Union's argument that the proper comparison is with the salary schedule of the City of Los Angeles. In support of this contention, the Union relied upon the following two principal arguments: (a) this was the recommendation of Factfinder Johns in his 1971 Report and (b) the Los Angeles rates were the guideline for voter approval, in 1968, of the $144 increase for Fire Fighters.

As to the first point, it must be noted that Professor Johns' recommendation was not adopted by the Board of City Commissioners; furthermore, this Factfinder would hesitate to adopt the conclusions of a prior Factfinder without examining the evidence upon which his conclusions were based — evidence which is not before him. With regard to the second argument advanced by the Union, it does appear from Fire Fighters Exhibit 41 that the 1968 $144 increase was based upon a comparison with Los Angeles rates, although that explanation did not appear on the ballot (City Exhibit 51). Whatever may have been the motivation in basing the 1968 increase on Los Angeles rates, the record since then negates any intent to use Los Angeles as a guideline. For this Factfinder to conclude that the Los Angeles and Las Vegas Fire Fighter salary schedules should be linked together permanently, it would take far more persuasive evidence than is present in this record.

2. The 6.6% increase offered by the City (5% general increase and 1.6% reclassification) approximates the change in the cost of living since the last general increase and, in addition, is comparable to the increases granted other public employees in Clark County.

3. The Fire Fighters cannot be viewed in isolation from other City employees. While the relationship of their salaries and benefits to other employees in the City cannot be decisive, it is, nevertheless, a factor entitled to considerable weight. The evidence reveals that Policemen (450 unit employees) and Fire Fighters (250 unit employees), and to a lesser extent

members of the City Employees Association (700 unit employees) have been granted similar increases in prior years. For this Factfinder to depart from the established past practice in granting such general increases, it would require clear and convincing proof — a level of proof that cannot be discerned in the record of this proceeding.

4. An analysis of the fund allocations in the 1972-73 budget, taken together with the respectable relationship between income and expenditures in prior years, is convincing to the Factfinder that current budget projections are realistic. Any significant revision or reduction in the expenditures as allocated by the City in the current budget could seriously impair its ability to furnish essential facilities and services.

The finding on this crucial point of ability to pay disposes of all monetary issues save one — Salary Grade Adjustments. For the reasons set forth below in the discussion of this item, the Factfinder has remanded it back to the parties for negotiation. The sum required to meet the Union's demand on this issue is not significant, and is well within the City's ability to pay. Following consideration of Salary Grade Adjustments, the Factfinder will then take up the nonmonetary issues, namely, Benefits, Duration, Savings Clause, Civil Service Rules, and Sick Leave.

## NOTES

1. Did Fact-Finder Block assume more responsibility than the statute really authorized? Does his interpretation result in a usurpation of legislative authority? Did he avoid this legal question by refusing to alter the City's priorities? If this statutory analysis is valid, will it encourage Las Vegas public employees to try to negotiate together as one group?

2. For two of the earliest reported decisions involving the "final offer" approach, see City of Indianapolis, 58 Lab. Arb. 1302 (Witney & Dworkin, Arbs. 1972); City of Eugene, GERR No. 451, B-1, E-1 (Hanlon, Arb. 1972). For more recent interest arbitration awards, see Sioux County, 68 Lab.Arb. 1258 (Gruenberg, Arb. 1977); City of Burlington, Iowa, 68 Lab.Arb. 454 (Witney, Arb. 1977); City of Rialto, 67 Lab. Arb. 654 (Gentile, Arb. 1976); Door County, Wisconsin, 62 Lab.Arb. 869 (Rauch, Arb. 1974).

## CASO v. COFFEY

New York Court of Appeals
41 N.Y.2d, 153, 359 N.E.2d 683 (1976)

FUCHSBERG, J.: In these two cases we confront directly the question of the manner and scope of judicial review of awards made by public arbitration panels acting pursuant to subdivision 4 of section 209 of the Civil Service Law in their determination of disputes arising from failures of local governments and their employees to reach collective bargaining agreements.

The County of Nassau and its police and the City of Albany and its firefighters, after exhausting all intermediate steps in negotiating new contracts, submitted their controversies to binding, compulsory arbitration pursuant to the mandate of the Taylor Law (Civil Service Law, § 209, subd. 4). Each arbitration panel reached a determination and made an award which reflected in part the requests of the government and in part those of the employees.

In the first case, the Appellate Division dismissed an article 78 proceeding [10] (with a request for relief in the alternative under article 75) brought by Ralph Caso, the County Executive of Nassau County, against the Nassau County Public

[10] [Pertaining to review of administrative action. Eds.]

Relations Board to review and annul a panel's award of a wage increase to the police and granted the cross motion of the board to confirm the award, holding that article 78 is the proper procedural vehicle for its review and that on such review the appropriate standard is whether the award is supported by substantial evidence (CPLR 7803, subd. 4). The county had joined the collective bargaining agent for the police, Nassau County Patrolmen's Benevolent Association, as a respondent.

In the second case, a proceeding pursuant to CPLR article 75 (CPLR 7510) [11] brought by the Albany Permanent Professional Firefighters Association to confirm a panel's award was consolidated by the Appellate Division with an article 78 proceeding brought by the city against both the Albany Public Employment Relations Board (PERB) and the members of the arbitration panel to annul that award. The firefighters were intervenors in the latter proceeding. The Appellate Division unanimously affirmed judgments of the Supreme Court which confirmed the award in the firefighters' proceeding and dismissed the city's article 78 proceeding, holding that article 75 was the proper procedural vehicle, but "broadened in scope" by our decision in *Mount St. Mary's Hosp. v. Catherwood,* 26 N.Y.2d 493, 311 N.Y.S.2d 863, 260 N.E.2d 508 to make applicable on review the test as to whether the determination "was arbitrary or capricious". (51 A.D.2d 386, 390, 381 N.Y.S.2d 699, 702.)

Preliminarily, we note that subdivision 4 of section 209 of the Taylor Law, applicable when local governments and their police or firefighters cannot reach agreement on a new contract, does not specify either the procedure or the standard by which the arbitrations it mandates are to be tested. Indeed, it does not expressly provide for any review. But such legislative silence does not mean that the actions of the arbitrators are therefore unreviewable (see *Matter of Guardian Life Ins. Co. v. Bohlinger,* 308 N.Y. 174, 183, 124 N.E.2d 110, 113). At least since our decision in *Mount St. Mary's Hosp. v. Catherwood (supra),* a case that arose under a different statute, it has been clear that, in New York, when arbitration has been made compulsory rather than consensual, availability of review sufficient to meet due process standards is required (*Mount St. Mary's Hosp. v. Catherwood, supra,* 26 N.Y.2d pp. 501, 508, 311 N.Y.S.2d pp. 868, 874, 260 N.E.2d pp. 511, 516).

We therefore focus first on the proper procedural path for review of compulsory Taylor Law arbitrations, a question which, though it has previously invited judicial concern (see *City of Amsterdam v. Helsby,* 37 N.Y.2d 19, 38-41, 371 N.Y.S.2d 404, 417-420, 332 N.E.2d 290, 300-302; *Matter of Buffalo Police Benevolent Assn. v. City of Buffalo,* 81 Misc.2d 172, 364 N.Y.S.2d 362), is met head on by us for the first time today. We now decide that the appropriate vehicle for review is article 75.

A number of considerations dictate that view. Section 209, in denominating "arbitration" as the final step in resolving these disputes, makes unqualified use of that word; article 75 is our only statutory vehicle for the enforcement of arbitration. It is structured to provide the procedural and practical guidance most useful to both courts and parties in obtaining review in an orderly fashion (see, e. g., CPLR 7511). Perhaps most importantly, it is not the PERB or the arbitration panel but the local governments and their employees who are the real parties in interest; it is under article 75 procedure, and not under that provided by article

---

[11] [Pertaining to review of arbitration awards. Eds.]

78, that both parties in interest will be brought face to face with one another as advocates of their respective positions. In contrast, the PERB, which itself possesses no power to review the arbitration award, after having completed its role in facilitating the mediational and negotiational steps the statute requires of the parties preceding arbitration (Civil Service Law, § 209, subd. 4, pars. [a], [b]), and after setting up the arbitration itself (§ 209, subd. 4, par. [c], cls. [i], [ii]), plays no part in the actual conduct or decision-making of the arbitration panel and, as a consequence, will not be possessed of the knowledge relevant to facilitate review. There is no logical reason to call upon the PERB to defend a decision which, for all that appears, may be different from the one it would itself have reached.

For its part, the arbitration panel, as pointed out in the Albany case by Mr. Justice Larkin at the Appellate Division, Third Department, is an *ad hoc* body composed of three citizens (§ 209, subd. 4, par. [c], cl. [ii]); by the time of review, it will already have made its views available to the court in its decision and on the record in the case. It is called into existence only to decide the dispute before it. It represents neither of the parties. Moreover, a requirement that those who serve on such panels be prepared to defend their awards in court, perhaps even at their own expense, could only work to discourage qualified and competent persons from serving as arbitrators and, perhaps, even to frustrate the flexible design of the arbitral process itself.

We turn next to the question of whether the arbitration awards made under subdivision 4 of section 209 are to be treated as quasi-judicial or as quasi-legislative for purposes of review.

In that connection, we note first that, though the statute itself pointedly directs the attention of the panel to such vital factors as the comparability of the benefits received by the employees before it with those of similar employees in public and private employment in comparable communities, the financial ability of the public employer to pay, and the public interest (§ 209, subd. 4, par. [c], cl. [v], subcls. a-d), it mandates that they be taken into "consideration" only "so far as it deems them applicable" (§ 209, subd. 4, par. [c], cl. [v]). Similarly, the precatory language that the "panel shall make a just and reasonable determination of the matters in dispute", an injunction expressly intended for the panel and not reviewing courts, bespeaks a like elasticity. (§ 209, subd. 4, par. [c], cl. [v].) The latitude with which these phrases are to be applied is suggested also by the fact that the essential function of these compulsory arbitration panels is to "write collective bargaining agreements for the parties" (*Mount St. Mary's Hosp. v. Catherwood,* 26 N.Y.2d 493, 503, 311 N.Y.S.2d 863, 870, 260 N.E.2d 508, 513, *supra*). It follows that such awards, on judicial review, are to be measured according to whether they are rational or arbitrary and capricious in accordance with the principles articulated in *Mount St. Mary's Hosp. v. Catherwood (supra)* (see CPLR 7803, subd. 3, for parallel language).

Of course, the presence of evidence pertaining to any or all of the specific criteria which are to be "considered" is a factor to be taken into account when determining whether the award itself is founded on a rational basis (see *Matter of Pell v. Board of Educ.,* 34 N.Y.2d 222, 356 N.Y.S.2d 833, 313 N.E.2d 321; *Matter of Graziani v. Rohan,* 10 A.D.2d 154, 198 N.Y.S.2d 383, affd. 8 N.Y.2d 967, 204 N.Y.S.2d 346, 169 N.E.2d 8). An award may be found on review to be rational if any basis for such a conclusion is apparent to the court (*Matter of Pell v. Board of Educ., supra;* see *Matter of Campo Corp. v. Feinberg,* 279 App. Div. 302, 110 N.Y.S.2d 250, affd. 303 N.Y. 995, 106 N.E.2d 70). And it need only appear from the decision of the arbitrators that the criteria specified in the statute were "considered" in good faith and that the resulting award has a "plausible basis" (*Matter of Caruci v. Dulan*, 41 Misc.2d 859, 862, 246 N.Y.S.2d 727, 730, revd. on other grounds 24 A.D.2d 529, 261 N.Y.S.2d 677). Though the presence of evidence which could have met a substantial evidence test may serve to meet the test of rationality, the substantial evidence test as such is not the criterion here (*Mount St. Mary's Hosp. v. Catherwood, supra,* 26 N.Y.2d 493, p. 508, 311 N.Y.S.2d p. 874, 260 N.E.2d p. 516).

In point of fact, in each of the cases before us, the records and the opinions of the arbitrators indicate that the panels gave careful consideration to the criteria enumerated by subdivision 4 of section 209 and were alert to the ravages which rising inflation and economic stress are now visiting on local governments and their employees alike. In the Albany case, voluminous and detailed exhibits and its Mayor's vigorous amplification of the city's written and detailed presentation of its tax resource limitations and over-all costs were presented; in juxtaposition the firefighters presented their own economic and comparative scale proof in great detail. The panel there, obviously selective in its award, while allowing a wage increase equal to that earlier recommended by the impartial fact finder, rejected the firefighters' economic benefit demands relating, among other things, to pension, longevity, vacation, overtime, personal leave and release time. In the *Caso* case, Mr. Justice Hopkins, writing for the Appellate Division, Second Department, went so far as to describe the extended evidence presented there as "monumental" and specifically found that "serious and close attention was devoted to all of the matters mandated for consideration by the statute". (53 A.D.2d 373, 379, 385 N.Y.S.2d 593, 597.)

Nevertheless, we comment on two subsidiary issues raised by the parties. First is the county's contention, in the *Caso* case, that the burden of proof to show that it has the ability to pay the award should be placed upon the employees under a kind of presumption that the county's best offer during bargaining prior to arbitration represented its good faith statement of the most it could afford. But our statutes and case law indicate plainly that the burden to show invalidity of any arbitral award is upon the party who brings a proceeding to set it aside (see *Korein v. Rabin,* 29 A.D.2d 351, 287 N.Y.S.2d 975; *Matter of Brill [Muller Bros.],* 40 Misc.2d 683, 243 N.Y.S.2d 905, revd. on other grounds 17 A.D.2d 804, 232 N.Y.S.2d 806, affd. 13 N.Y.2d 776, 242 N.Y.S.2d 69, 192 N.E.2d 34, cert. den. 376 U.S. 927, 84 S.Ct. 693, 11 L.Ed.2d 623; see, generally, 16 Williston, Contracts [3d ed.], § 1923A, p. 650) and, for that matter, in a proceeding brought to review a quasi-legislative determination made by an agency, the burden again is on the party who challenges to show that the determination lacks rational basis (see *Matter of Pell v. Board of Educ.,* 34 N.Y.2d 222, 356 N.Y.S.2d 833, 313 N.E.2d 321, *supra; Matter of Mallen v. Morton,* 199 Misc. 805, 99 N.Y.S.2d 521; 1 N.Y.Jur., Administrative Law, § 182, and cases cited therein).

The second subsidiary issue was raised by the City of Albany. It contends that, as no "record" of the proceedings before the arbitration panel was made, proper review cannot be had here. It is undisputed that neither party in the Albany case made advance written request for a reporter for the purpose of making a verbatim transcript (see PERB's rules, 4 NYCRR 205.7[d]), not even when the chairman of the panel made particular inquiry of both sides at the outset of the hearings.

Finally, the fact that the *Caso* proceeding was brought solely under article 78 and was adjudicated on review by the Appellate Division under the substantial evidence test is no bar to our upholding that court's confirmation of the arbitral award in this instance. Although in a proceeding brought in form under article 78 the governmental or administrative agency rather than the employees or their collective bargaining agent would be expected to be the respondent, here the collective bargaining agent was joined and has submitted a brief on this appeal in which it is made clear that confirmation is exactly what the employees seek; thus, they are not prejudiced by an affirmance. Moreover, the opinion in the Appellate Division, in detailing its reasons for confirming the award, more than adequately shows that the panel had a rational basis for the result it reached.

Accordingly, the determination of the Appellate Division in each case should be affirmed.

## NOTES

1. In City of Buffalo v. Rinaldo, 41 N.Y.2d 764, 364 N.E.2d 817, 95 L.R.R.M. 2776 (1977), the New York Court of Appeals recognized that while the financial ability of the public employer to pay the increases requested is one of the relevant criteria for consideration by the arbitrator, it is not necessarily the dispositive factor. So long as there is support for the award based upon the statutorily prescribed criteria, it is entitled to enforcement. But cf. Nebraska City Educ. Ass'n. v. School Dist., 267 N.W.2d 530, 98 L.R.R.M. 3228 (Neb. 1978), wherein the Court found that the employer's ability to finance the requested wage increases was not a relevant factor, since it was not one of the criteria specified in the statute to guide the Court of Industrial Relations when it resolved impasse disputes. Compare Firefighters, Local 644 v. City of Lincoln, 198 Neb. 174, 252 N.W.2d 607, 2 PBC ¶ 20,431 (1977), wherein the court refused to enforce part of an interest arbitration award since it failed to adequately consider the economic dissimilarities that existed between Lincoln and the cities utilized for comparison purposes.

2. The Comptroller General has sustained an arbitrator's interest decision ordering the implementation of new contract wage rates retroactive to the date impasse was acknowledged, stating a general rule that if there is no preliminary agreement setting the effective date and the issue of wages is submitted to arbitration, the effective date may be no earlier than the date impasse was reached, if that can be determined, or the date arbitration was requested. CG Ruling, Case No. B-180080.07, April, 1976, GERR No. 656, A-1. In late 1977, Michigan amended its police-firefighter interest arbitration statute to similarly permit the award of retroactive pay increases. See GERR No. 743, 25.

3. In Town of Tiverton v. Police Lodge 23, 372 A.2d 1273, 95 L.R.R.M. 2993 (R.I. 1977), the court held that an interest arbitration decision that directed the implementation of a pension plan after the one-year period covered by the award was unenforceable. Cf. Marlborough Firefighters, Local 1714 v. City of Marlborough, 378 N.E.2d 437, 1977-78 PBC ¶ 36,342 (Mass. 1978), wherein the Court vacated an improper provision contained in an interest arbitration award, while affirming the remaining portions of the award.

4. In Superintending School Comm. of the Town of Winslow v. Winslow Educ. Ass'n, 363 A.2d 229, 93 L.R.R.M. 2398 (1976), the court held that a school committee could not be compelled through interest arbitration to broaden the teachers' rights clause of a contract by imposing a "just cause" requirement on the employer's disciplinary actions. Deciding whether a matter is subject to interest arbitration involves a two-step inquiry: (1) is the matter within the statutorily-defined scope of bargaining, and, if so, (2) is it limited by any other existing statutory enactments. The court focused on the conflict between interest arbitration and other laws governing the rights and duties of school committees. Since pre-existing education laws provided school committees with exclusive authority over dismissals and the non-renewal of teacher contracts, the Court concluded, without deciding whether the issue would otherwise constitute a mandatory bargaining subject, that this power could not be diminished by an interest arbitration award. Compare Boston School Committee v. Teachers Local 66, 363 N.E.2d 485, 95 L.R.R.M. 2855 (Mass. 1977), wherein the court held that where no statutory provision expressly or impliedly restricted the scope of interest arbitration and the parties had contractually agreed to submit bargaining impasses to binding arbitration, permissive as well as mandatory topics may be presented for arbitral resolution. Would the latter approach allow a party to obtain

through interest arbitration a benefit or privilege that it could not insist upon at the bargaining table?

5. In Bethlehem Steel Corp. v. Fennie, 383 N.Y.S.2d 948, 92 L.R.R.M. 3470 (Sup. Ct. Erie Co. 1976), *affirmed*, 391 N.Y.S.2d 227, 95 L.R.R.M. 2099 (Sup. Ct., App. Div. 1977), a 2-1 interest arbitration decision was vacated for impropriety where the majority consisted of the union and police department representatives and it was clear that the employer representative, who was then the city safety commissioner, had shifted his loyalty prior to the award from the police department to the union, following a recent mayoral election, since he would no longer be retained as safety commissioner but would instead be returning to his former position as police captain.

6. In Local 66, Boston Teachers Union v. School Comm. of Boston, 363 N.E.2d 492, 95 L.R.R.M. 3126 (Mass. 1977), the court ruled that where an employer failed to comply with the terms of a bargaining agreement obtained through an interest arbitration award that had been judicially enforced, the proper recourse was through the contractual grievance-arbitration procedure and not through a civil contempt proceeding, since the judicial enforcement of the interest arbitration award could not be viewed as having incorporated the provisions of the sustained agreement into the injunctive order of the enforcing court.

# Chapter 8

# ENFORCEMENT OF THE COLLECTIVE BARGAINING AGREEMENT

## A. PRIVATE SECTOR CONCEPTS CONCERNING THE LEGAL STATUS OF THE COLLECTIVE AGREEMENT

### The Legal Status of the Collective Agreement [1]

Early court decisions advanced at least three separate theories, along with variants, to explain the legal nature and effect of the collective agreement.

1. The labor agreement establishes local customs or usages, which are then incorporated into the individual employee's contract of hire. This seems to have been the orthodox view of the American courts, at least prior to the era of the labor relations acts.[2] Under the original form of this theory, the collective agreement itself was not regarded as a contract. It had legal effect only as its terms were absorbed into individual employment contracts. Somewhat similar is the traditional English concept that collective agreements are merely "gentlemen's agreements" or moral obligations not enforceable by the courts. Some American scholars also have voiced an occasional plea that court litigation over collective agreements should be rejected as detrimental to the parties' continuing relationship.[3] Nevertheless, judicial enforcement at the behest of either employers or unions became generally accepted in this country well before the passage of the LMRA in 1947, and was confirmed by that act. To account for the recognition eventually granted to both the union and individuals as possessors of enforceable rights under labor agreements, a refinement of the custom and usage theory posits the existence of two bilateral contracts. One contract consists "partly of promises running to the benefit of the union as an organization . . . and partly of provisions relating to wages, hours and job security which the employer promises to incorporate in a second bilateral contract — the contract of hire between the employer and the individual employees."[4]

2. The collective agreement is a contract that is negotiated by the union as the agent for the employees, who become the principals on the agreement. This so-called agency theory was adopted by a few courts which could not rationalize the enforceability of an instrument executed by an unincorporated association lacking juristic personality. Suits between individual employees and employers were maintainable, however, on the theory the union had merely served as the employees' agent in negotiations.

3. The collective agreement is a third party beneficiary contract, with the employer and union the mutual promisors and promisees, and with the employees the beneficiaries. Despite arguable shortcomings (is the employer to be left without recourse against the employee beneficiary, who has made no promises?), the third party beneficiary theory became rather widely accepted as

---

[1] From R. SMITH, L. MERRIFIELD, AND T. ST. ANTOINE, LABOR RELATIONS LAW: CASES AND MATERIALS (5TH ED., 1974).

[2] *See* Rice, *Collective Labor Agreements in American Law,* 44 HARV. L. REV. 572, 582 (1931).

[3] *See* Shulman, *Reason, Contract, and Law in Labor Relations,* 68 HARV. L. REV. 999 (1955).

[4] Cox, *The Legal Nature of Collective Bargaining Agreements,* 57 MICH. L. REV. 1, 20 (1958); *see* Association of Westinghouse Salaried Employees v. Westinghouse Elec. Corp., 210 F.2d 623 (3rd Cir. 1954), *aff'd,* 348 U.S. 437 (1955).

the best explanation of the collective agreement in terms of traditional common-law concepts.[5]

Today, collective-bargaining agreements in industries affecting commerce are enforced as a matter of federal law under § 301 of the LMRA. This means that the Supreme Court's views on the nature of the labor contract are now of primary concern. Two characteristics of the Court's thinking stand out. First, the Court is eclectic in its approach to common-law doctrines; it refuses to confine itself to any single theory, but draws upon whatever elements may be helpful in a variety of theories. Second, the Court has increasingly emphasized what may be described as the "constitutional" or "governmental" quality of the labor agreement. Thus, the collective agreement has been described as "not an ordinary contract" but rather a "generalized code" for "a system of industrial self-government." [6] In analogizing the plant or industrial community to a political society, it might be said the collective agreement serves as a sort of basic legislation or constitution, and the grievance and arbitration procedure for the resolution of day-to-day disputes arising under the agreement constitutes a sort of judicial system.[7]

The Supreme Court's eclectic approach to the nature of the labor contract is reflected in the following well-known comments by Mr. Justice Jackson in J.I. Case Co. v. NLRB, 321 U.S. 332, 334-35 (1944):

> Contract in labor law is a term the implications of which must be determined from the connection in which it appears. Collective bargaining between employer and the representatives of a unit, usually a union, results in an accord as to terms which will govern hiring and work and pay in that unit. The result is not, however, a contract of employment except in rare cases; no one has a job by reason of it and no obligation to any individual ordinarily comes into existence from it alone. The negotiations between union and management result in what often has been called a trade agreement, rather than in a contract of employment. Without pushing the analogy too far, the agreement may be likened to the tariffs established by a carrier, to standard provisions prescribed by supervising authorities for insurance policies, or to utility schedules of rates and rules for service, which do not of themselves establish any relationships but which do govern the terms of the shipper or insurer or customer relationship whenever and with whomever it may be established. Indeed, in some European countries, contrary to American practice, the terms of a collectively negotiated trade agreement are submitted to a government department and, if approved, become a governmental regulation ruling employment in the unit.
>
> After the collective trade agreement is made, the individuals who shall benefit by it are identified by individual hirings. The employer, except as restricted by the collective agreement itself and except that he must engage in no unfair labor practice or discrimination, is free to select those he will employ or discharge. But the terms of the employment already have been traded out. There is little left to individual agreement except the act of hiring. This hiring may be by writing or by word of mouth or may be implied from

---

[5] See C. Gregory, Labor and the Law 447 (2d rev. ed. 1961).

[6] See John Wiley & Sons, Inc. v. Livingston, 376 U.S. 543, 550 (1964); United Steelworkers v. Warrior & Gulf Nav. Co., 363 U.S. 574, 578-80 (1960); Aeronautical Ind. Dist., Lodge 72 v. Campbell, 337 U.S. 521, 528 (1949).

[7] For elaboration, see Chamberlain, *Collective Bargaining and the Concept of Contract*, 48 Colum. L. Rev. 829 (1948); Cox, *The Legal Nature of Collective Bargaining Agreements*, 57 Mich. L. Rev. 1, 25-36 (1958).

conduct. In the sense of contracts of hiring, individual contracts between the employer and employee are not forbidden, but indeed are necessitated by the collective bargaining procedure.

But, however engaged, an employee becomes entitled by virtue of the Labor Relations Act somewhat as a third party beneficiary to all benefits of the collective trade agreement, even if on his own he would yield to less favorable terms. The individual hiring contract is subsidiary to the terms of the trade agreement and may not waive any of its benefits, any more than a shipper can contract away the benefit of filed tariffs, the insurer the benefit of standard provisions, or the utility customer the benefit of legally established rates.

## NOTE

Much has been written on the legal nature of the collective agreement, with most commentators noting its unique characteristics and the difficulties and dangers of adopting traditional doctrines developed in other fields of contract law. *See* Burstein, *Enforcement of Collective Agreements by the Courts*, in N.Y.U. Sixth Annual Conference on Labor 31 (1953); Chamberlain, *Collective Bargaining and the Concept of Contract*, 48 Colum. L. Rev. 829 (1948); Cox, *Rights Under a Labor Agreement*, 69 Harv. L. Rev. 601 (1956); Cox, *The Legal Nature of Collective Bargaining Agreements*, 57 Mich. L. Rev. 1 (1958); Feller, *A General Theory of the Collective Bargaining Agreement*, 61 Calif. L. Rev. 663 (1973); Gregory, *The Law of the Collective Agreement*, 57 Mich. L. Rev. 635 (1959); Gregory, *The Collective Bargaining Agreement: Its Nature and Scope*, 1949 Wash. U.L.Q. 3; Rice, *Collective Labor Agreements in American Law*, 44 Harv. L. Rev. 572 (1931); Shulman, *Reason, Contract, and Law in Labor Relations*, 68 Harv. L. Rev. 999 (1955); Warns, *The Nature of the Collective Bargaining Agreement*, 3 U. Miami L.Q. 235 (1949); Witmer, *Collective Labor Agreements in the Courts*, 48 Yale L.J. 195 (1938).

# B. THE LEGALITY AND ENFORCEABILITY OF THE COLLECTIVE BARGAINING AGREEMENT

# 1. THE AUTHORITY OF GOVERNMENT EMPLOYERS TO EXECUTE COLLECTIVE BARGAINING AGREEMENTS

## DAYTON TEACHERS ASSOCIATION v. BOARD OF EDUCATION

Ohio Supreme Court
41 Ohio St.2d 127, 323 N.E.2d 714 (1975)

Brown, Justice: Appellant, Dayton Classroom Teachers Association (D.C.T.A.), a labor organization, is the collective bargaining representative for all "professional staff members" employed by appellee Dayton Board of Education (board).

Appellant, the board, and appellee Superintendent of the Dayton Public Schools (superintendent), have, since 1967, engaged in collective negotiations, and have published their agreements as "Master Agreements." The latest Master Agreement (hereinafter the agreement) covered the period July 24, 1972, to March 3, 1974, and from year to year thereafter unless modified by the parties.

The agreement contains provisions which relate to the following matters: teaching environment, salaries, payroll deductions, leaves of absence, promotions, teacher enforcement of discipline, teacher evaluation, transfers, paydays and academic freedom.

In addition, the agreement contains a four-step procedure for the resolution of grievances. For grievances which cannot be resolved by the parties, the agreement provides for binding grievance arbitration. However, at that stage "the arbitrator shall have no power to alter, add to, or subtract from the terms of * * * [the] agreement or to change official board policies."

The present controversy arose when members of the D.C.T.A. filed grievances concerning allegedly inadequate parking facilities, allegedly unsuitable working conditions, the board's alleged failure to comply with the agreement's job posting provisions, and the board's alleged wrongful failure to place a substitute teacher on regular salary.

At the outset, the board took the position that such "grievances" were not proper grievances, and therefore refused to allow the matter to go to arbitration.

The D.C.T.A. then instituted an action in the Court of Common Pleas of Montgomery County, requesting that the board be enjoined to honor the agreement's grievance procedure and to proceed to arbitration.

The Court of Common Pleas entered summary judgment for the board, after finding that neither the board nor the superintendent "can delegate the responsibility of operating" the Dayton schools, that the agreement "is an attempt on the part of" the D.C.T.A., the board and the superintendent to "delegate this authority contrary to" law, and that the agreement is, therefore, unlawful and unenforceable.

Upon appeal, the Court of Appeals modified the judgment of the trial court, by holding that the agreement was valid in principle, but affirmed the judgment to the extent that the agreement's arbitration clause unlawfully delegated the board's responsibilities and was, therefore, invalid.

The cause is now before this court pursuant to the allowance of D.C.T.A. motion to certify the record.

Labor relations law in the public sector lacks uniformity from state to state. For instance, that of Hawaii is regulated by an extremely comprehensive statutory scheme. Public labor relations Acts are present in an overwhelming majority of states, but Ohio has none. Some commentators argue that such Acts are an anathema to democratic government, whereas others believe that the adoption of such Acts only serves to deter public-sector collective bargaining which flourishes in the absence of such legislation.

I. This case presents two questions: (1) Whether a board of education may validly enter into a collective bargaining agreement and (2) whether a binding grievance arbitration clause in such agreement is valid and enforceable.

The board argues that the agreement is "extra-legal," an "understanding" rather than a contract, and, that even if it were a contract, it would be unlawful, constituting an improper delegation of the board's power. Another implicit defect is that a binding contract would restrain the board from changing its policy at will.

II. The board's basic reason for failing to enter into arbitration is its belief that it lacks capacity to enter into, and become bound by, the agreement herein.

A board's contractual capacity, or power, is described in paragraph one of the syllabus of Schwing v. McClure (1929), 120 Ohio St. 335, as follows:

"Members of a board of education of a school district are public officers, whose duties are prescribed by law. Their contractual powers are defined by the statutory limitations existing thereon, and they have no power except such as is expressly given, or such as is necessarily implied from the powers that are expressly given."

In addition, it has been recognized that "* * * [i]n democratic political systems dealings between public employers and public employee organizations — whether they are called negotiations or discussions — must necessarily be limited by legislatively determined policies and goals."

Thus, the question becomes whether a board's attempt to bind itself to a written collective bargaining agreement exceeds statutory limitations placed upon its contractual power.

R.C. 3313.47 grants to a board of education the management and control of all public schools within its district. R.C. 3313.17 provides: "The board of education of each school district shall be a body politic and corporate, and, as such, *capable of * * * contracting and being contracted with * * *.*" (Emphasis ours.) The latter section is slightly modified by R.C. 3313.33, which provides that "[n]o contract shall be binding upon any board unless it is made or authorized at a regular or special meeting of such board."

R.C. 3319.08 requires boards of education to "enter into *written contracts* for the employment and reemployment of all teachers." (Emphasis ours.)

Finally, a board of education is required to "make such rules and regulations as are necessary for its government and the government of its employees * * *." R.C. 3313.20.

From the foregoing, we conclude that a board of education has been granted broad discretionary powers in its dual role of manager of schools and employer of teachers.

Our research discloses that agreements entered into by boards of education are generally invalidated by courts upon unlawful-delegation grounds only when the board seeks to absolve itself of the duties acquired thereunder.

On the other hand, where a school board has benefited from an agreement and seeks to have it upheld, the courts generally apply normal principles of contract law to test the contract's validity and binding effect.

In one such case, this court held that a board of education is vested with discretionary authority to authorize one of its schools to join a private association wherein member schools were bound to "* * * abide by and conform to the constitution and rules, bylaws, interpretations and decisions of the association." State, ex rel. Ohio H.S. Athletic Assn. v. Judges of the Court of Common Pleas (1963), 173 Ohio St. 239, 241.

In principle, we cannot distinguish that case from the one here under consideration. The issues presented in both cases are whether a school board may authorize entry into a pact, and whether decisions made by tribunals that administer the pact are binding on entities of the board of education. In Athletic Assn. this court answered both questions in the affirmative.

Accordingly, we hold that a board of education is vested with discretionary authority to negotiate and to enter into a collective bargaining agreement with its employees.

III. Much of what has been said in part II concerning the validity of the agreement herein applies as well to the binding grievance arbitration clause.

"It is the policy of the law to favor and encourage arbitration and every reasonable intendment will be indulged to give effect to such proceedings and to favor the regularity and integrity of the arbitrator's acts. * * *"

Arbitration is favored because its purpose is "to avoid needless and expensive litigation." Springfield v. Walker (1885), 42 Ohio St. 543, 546.

We also recognize that the availability of arbitration may contribute to more harmonious relations between a school board and its employees [14] and that

---

[14] "* * * Labor difficulties like strikes, walkouts, slowdowns, etc., have been avoided or lessened because of the availability of arbitration. The public interest is best served in education, as well as

factor fosters the public policy of keeping the schools open. Although teacher strikes are illegal in practically every state, during the period July 1960 through June 1971, teacher strikes numbered 631 nationwide and 72 in Ohio, resulting in lost time of 5,955,689 and 51,434 man-days, respectively.

Against that backdrop, and finding no statutory promotion against the subject arbitration clause, we reject appellees' contention that such clause is invalid and unenforceable.

We find that the following discussion of the Wisconsin Supreme Court applies with equal force to the case before us:

"The city has contended that to require the city to submit to binding arbitration is an unlawful infringement upon the legislative power of the city council and a violation of its home-rule powers. Yet in all of its arguments the city is talking about arbitration in the collective-bargaining context — arbitration to set the terms of a collective-bargaining agreement. Such is not this case, which involves arbitration to resolve a grievance arising under an existing agreement to which the city is a party. * * *" Local 1226 v. Rhinelander (1967), 35 Wisc. 2d 209, 220, 151 N. W. 2d 30, 65 LRRM 2793. See, also, State ex rel. Fire Fighters Local No. 946, I.A.F.F. v. Laramie (Wyo., 1968), 437 P.2d 295, 68 LRRM 2038; Harney v. Russo (1969), 435 Pa. 183, 255 A.2d 560, 71 LRRM 2817; Warwick v. Warwick Regular Firemen's Assn. (1969), 106 R. I. 109, 256 A.2d 206, 71 LRRM 3192.

IV. Neither reason nor authority prohibits a board of education from manifesting its policy decisions in written form and calling the writing an agreement or contract. It can not be seriously argued that entering into such agreement is a departure from, or surrender of, independent exercise of a board's policy-making power.[20]

Accordingly, it is the judgment of this court that the agreement herein is a valid and enforceable contract, and that the board is obligated to arbitrate any grievance arising thereunder where the grievance involves the application or interpretation of a valid contractual term and the arbitrator is specifically prohibited from making any decision which is inconsistent with the terms of the agreement or contrary to law.

Therefore, we affirm that part of the judgment of the Court of Appeals which holds the agreement valid, but we reverse that part of the judgment which holds

---

other activities, if a means is found to resolve differences within the framework and language of a labor contract." Local 953 v. School Dist. (Mich. Cir. Ct. 1967), 66 LRRM 2419, 2421.

[20] The agreement herein, by its own terms, is board policy. Agreement, Article V of Appendix B, at page 79, reads:

"When a substantive agreement is reached, it shall then be made in writing and submitted for ratification to the * * * [D.C.T.A.] and then to the board of education. When approved by both parties, it shall be signed by their respective presidents and shall be entered into the official minutes of the board of education. Thereupon, *the agreement shall constitute a revision of school policies.* Provisions of the substantive agreement shall be reflected in the individual contract or statement of conditions of service as submitted to employees." (Emphasis ours.)

Also, we agree with the New York Court of Appeals, that the absence of such contract-making power must be proved by the board:

"* * * It is hardly necessary to say that, if the board asserts a lack of power to agree to any particular term or condition of employment, it has the burden of demonstrating the existence of a specific statutory provision which circumscribes the exercise of such power * * *." Board of Edn. of Union Free School Dist. No. 3 of Town of Huntington v. Associated Teachers of Huntington (1972), 30 N.Y.2d 122, 130, 282 N.E.2d 109, 79 LRRM 2881, 2885.

the binding grievance arbitration clause invalid, and we remand the cause to the Court of Common Pleas for proceedings consistent with this opinion.

Judgment affirmed in part and reversed in part.

## NOTES

1. A result consistent with that achieved in the principal case was obtained in Peters v. Bd. of Educ., 506 S.W.2d 429, 87 L.R.R.M. 2092 (Mo. 1974). However, in Commonwealth of Virginia v. County Bd. of Arlington County, 217 Va. 558, 232 S.E.2d 30 (1977), the Virginia Supreme Court reached a contrary conclusion when it held that agreements negotiated by school districts with teacher unions are invalid on the ground that such public entities possess no express statutory authority to enter into collective bargaining contracts. *See also* School Bd., City of Richmond v. Parham, 243 S.E.2d 468, 1977-78 PBC ¶36,269 (1978), wherein the Virginia Supreme Court negated a grievance-arbitration procedure contained in a negotiated agreement on the same ground. If a public employer possesses the usual authority to enter into such contractual arrangements as are reasonably necessary for it to function, should agreements made with labor organizations be treated differently from other contractual undertakings? Given the fact that a governmental entity can enter into individual employment contracts with its employees, should the Virginia Supreme Court have sustained the terms of the applicable bargaining agreements by recognizing that their terms were implicitly incorporated into each employee's enforceable employment contract?

2. Generally the authority to bargain collectively is given to the public employer by state statute or local ordinance. But this power may not be sufficient to validate a particular bargaining agreement. Before the court can decide whether it will enforce an agreement, a number of preliminary questions must be answered: (a) Does the statute apply to the parties to the contract? Some statutes apply only to certain specific groups of public employees, such as fire fighters, police, or teachers. (b) Do any explicit constitutional or statutory provisions preclude the parties from negotiating a contract covering certain subjects? (c) Are there any constitutional or statutory provisions which would implicitly prevent the parties from concluding an agreement covering particular areas?

The absence of conflicting state law or policy was found to be an important factor in the decision of the New Hampshire Supreme Court when it upheld the validity of a contested union security provision in Tremblay v. Berlin Police Union, 108 N.H. 416, 237 A.2d 668 (1968). There the Court stated:

> It is argued that this union shop clause of the collective bargaining agreement is invalid as an unlawful delegation of municipal power and is "ultra vires and void." There is no law which prohibits a union shop in this state. . . . The Legislature has declared as a matter of public policy that collective bargaining for municipal employees is a proper public purpose. In making this declaration it has not excluded police departments (as some statutes do) or other public employees in equally essential positions. . . . Opinions may differ as to the desirability of collective bargaining for public employees but that discretionary decision has been lodged in the municipalities.

*Accord,* Bd. of Educ. of Union Free School Dist. No. 3 v. Associated Teachers of Huntington, 30 N.Y.2d 122, 282 N.E.2d 109 (1972). *See also* Libertyville Educ. Ass'n. v. Bd. of Educ., 371 N.E.2d 676, 97 L.R.R.M. 2718 (Ill. App. Ct. 1977), wherein the court even sustained the right of a school board to negotiate a five-year bargaining agreement that would be binding upon subsequently elected school boards. *But see* Zderick v. Silver Bow County, 154 Mont. 118, 460 P.2d 749 (1969), where the Montana Supreme Court disallowed a claim by an employee against the county for accumulated sick leave, since it found that the state legislature had made piecemeal grants of authority to political subdivisions in a number of fringe benefit areas but had not acted with respect to accumulated sick leave.

3. The idea that the legislature is *delegating power* to the government employer to enter into enforceable contracts with public employee unions is a constant feature of cases

dealing with the enforcement of collective bargaining agreements in the public sector. Even if the power is not held to be inherently nondelegable, there are still two crucial questions the court must answer: (1) Did the legislature intend to delegate the power to contract with unions? (2) If the legislature did so intend, did it provide adequate standards for the exercise of that power? Regarding this overall area, it is important to distinguish a power that cannot be delegated from an ineffective delegation of power. For a case involving ineffective delegation, *see* Ohio Civil Service Employees Ass'n. v. Div. 11, Ohio Dep't. of Highways, 79 L.R.R.M. 2559 (Ohio Ct. of Apps. 1971).

4. Although a public employer may be required to negotiate with respect to a particular subject, the resulting agreement on that topic may not be enforceable against the employer until the appropriate legislative body has approved the agreement. This is particularly true where fiscal matters are concerned, since the general rule is that the parties to an agreement cannot bind a legislative body to make an appropriation of public funds in order to pay for agreed upon increases in wages or fringe benefits. *But see* Wheatley v. City of Covington, 79 L.R.R.M. 2614 (Ky. Cir. Ct. 1972).

The New York Taylor Act, N.Y. CIVIL SERVICE LAW § 204a(1), requires the following clause to be included in negotiated employment contracts:

> It is agreed . . . that any provision of this agreement requiring legislative action to permit its implementation by amendment of law or by providing the additional funds therefor, shall not become effective until the appropriate legislative body has given approval.

The Connecticut Municipal Employee Relations Act, CONN. GEN. STAT. ANN. tit. 7, §§ 7-467 to 7-475, likewise reserves final judgment for the legislature at the same time that it alleviates the problem of conflict with existing legislation:

> Any agreement reached by the negotiators shall be reduced to writing. . . . [A] request for funds necessary to implement such written agreement and for approval of any provisions of the agreement which are in conflict with any charter, special act, ordinance, rule or regulation adopted by the municipal employer or its agents, such as a personnel board or civil service commission, or any general statute directly regulating the hours of work of policemen or firemen . . . shall be submitted by the bargaining representative of the municipality within fourteen days . . . to the legislative body which may approve or reject such request as a whole by a majority vote . . .; but, if rejected, the matter shall be returned to the parties for further bargaining. [*Id.* at § 7-474(b)]

However, the Connecticut statute provides further that:

> Notwithstanding any provision of any general statute, charter, special act or ordinance to the contrary, the budget-appropriating authority of any municipal employer shall appropriate whatever funds are required to comply with a collective bargaining agreement, provided the request . . . [for funds] has been approved by the legislative body. . . . [*Id.* at § 7-474 (c)]

5. In some states, a public employer is statutorily obligated to request the legislative body to appropriate the funds necessary to finance a negotiated agreement. Is there any way to guarantee that the employer will present the strongest possible case in support of its legislative request?

6. Once a bargaining agreement has been properly approved by the parties, a public employer's unilateral decision to modify or negate its terms may subject it to liability. For example, in Firefighters, Local 8 v. Great Falls, 568 P.2d 541, 96 L.R.R.M. 2581 (1977), the Montana Supreme Court ruled that where a city council resolution providing for longevity pay had been incorporated in a bargaining agreement, the subsequent repeal of that resolution constituted an unconstitutional impairment of that contractual obligation. Furthermore, in Barclay v. City of Spokane, 521 P.2d 930, 88 L.R.R.M. 2207 (1974), the Washington Supreme Court held that police officers who retired, resigned, or were discharged prior to the date on which a retroactive wage increase was executed were entitled to the increase from its effective date to the dates of their respective

terminations, since they were employed by the department on the effective date of the negotiated increase. *See* Barbee v. City of Omaha, 260 N.W.2d 493, 97 L.R.R.M. 2658 (Neb. 1977); City Employees Ass'n. v. City of Glendale, 15 Cal.3d 328, 540 P.2d 609 (1975), *cert. denied,* 424 U.S. 943 (1976). However, if a public employer agrees to a contractual limitation which conflicts with its express statutory authority, it may be allowed to ignore the contractual restriction. *See, e.g.,* Great Neck Bd. of Educ. v. Areman, 41 N.Y.2d 527, 362 N.E.2d 943 (1977).

# 2. WHAT CONSTITUTES AN ENFORCEABLE CONTRACT?

## PATROLMEN'S BENEVOLENT ASSOCIATION v. CITY OF NEW YORK

Court of Appeals of New York
27 N.Y.2d 410, 267 N.E.2d 259 (1971)

BERGAN, Judge.

The action is to enforce a purported collective bargaining agreement between the Patrolmen's Benevolent Association and the City of New York for the period October 1, 1968 to December 31, 1970. The complaint alleges the agreement was made January 28, 1969 between the association and the city and that among its provisions was the establishment of a ratio of 3 to 3.5 between patrolmen's and sergeants' salaries to be maintained during the term of contract; that sergeants' salaries were increased by the city December 18, 1969 and that accordingly patrolmen are entitled to an increase conformably to the ratio.

The action is described in the moving affidavit for summary judgment by plaintiff Edward J. Kiernan, president of the association, as "a simple action for the breach of the salary provisions of a collective bargaining agreement." Plaintiffs have had summary judgment at Special Term, which has been affirmed by a divided court at the Appellate Division.

The issue on appeal as it reaches this court is whether the existence of a purported integrated agreement is left so uncertain in the record as to require a trial; or whether it appears so clearly that plaintiffs are entitled to summary judgment on the papers without trial.

There is a threshold difficulty as to summary judgment in the form the plaintiffs have chosen to plead the contract terms and to formulate their motion for judgment. A party seeking judgment on the basis of a writing must show the writing he relies on is the writing agreed to. But the text of agreement pleaded in the complaint and recited in the moving Kiernan affidavit is the text of a descriptive circular sent by the association to its members February 3, 1969 to be voted on.

The text of this circular is not shown to have been accepted by the city; and the initialed agreement relied on by plaintiffs in this court as showing there had been a written contract was expressed in a different text. In an action based, as this one is, on a specific writing, summary judgment ought not be granted on showing a different writing, even though the two texts have similarity, without appropriate amendment of pleading and proof to conform the basis for relief claimed to the actual writing relied upon.

There is a more fundamental obstacle to summary judgment here. Not any of the papers or writings in the record, signed or unsigned, show a complete collective bargaining agreement between the association and the city embracing all the terms and conditions which had been canvassed by negotiators.

There is a writing initialed on January 29 by a representative of the association and of the city which shows an accord on some terms, including the ratio with sergeants' salaries, but both in what it says and what it covers it is not a complete or independent collective bargaining agreement. This is the specific instrument which plaintiffs in this court say is an independently enforceable agreement on which they are entitled to summary judgment.

The affidavit of Herbert L. Haber, Director of Labor Relations of the city, who handled the negotiations with the association and who initialed the January 29 accord, filed in opposition to plaintiffs' motion for summary judgment, states not only that there was "no written collective bargaining agreement" between the association and the city as of May 7, 1970, but that for the preceding year "the parties [including the association and city] have been attempting to set forth the terms of the entire agreement in a formal written collective bargaining contract."

He swore further that in the fall of 1969 the association had submitted "a proposed draft of a written contract." On the motion for summary judgment these statements must be accepted as true and they require a trial on the issue whether it was the intention of the parties to integrate their preliminary understandings and accords reached in the course of negotiation into a formal and final writing covering the full contractual relation.

The issue, then, is whether it was the intention of the parties that the accord as to part of the subjects of negotiation should become an independent agreement; or whether it was intended, as the Haber affidavit indicates, there should be further and ultimate formalization in writing. The Restatement notes that "An agreement is integrated" when the parties adopt a writing or writings "as the final and complete expression of the agreement" (Restatement, Contracts, § 228). The draft of Restatement, Second (§ 235, subd. [3]) broadens this somewhat but is in the same sense. On the showing made on this record the question whether there has been integration here is a question of fact.

The decisional law in New York is consistent with this. In Scheck v. Francis, 26 N.Y.2d 466, 311 N.Y.S.2d 841, Chief Judge Fuld wrote for the court that "if parties to an agreement do not intend it to be binding upon them until it is reduced to writing and signed by both of them, they are not bound and may not be held liable until it has been written out and signed." . . .

Corbin regards this kind of situation as typically presenting a question of fact, i.e., where the parties have "the understanding during this process [settling some details] that the agreement is to be embodied in a formal written document." (1 Corbin, Contracts, pp. 97, 98.)

If there are conditions which are regarded as important still left for adjustment it may be held that there has been no enforceable agreement. In Arliss v. Herbert Brenon Film Corp., 230 N.Y. 390, 130 N.E. 587, Judge Hogan, writing for the court, was of opinion that the evidence disclosed an intention that a contract should not be deemed to have been made "until such conditions should be mutually agreed upon and embodied in a written contract." . . .

In support of the Haber affidavit stating that it was the intention of the parties to formalize their understanding in a complete contract is the text of the written accord of January 29 itself. Its fragmentary internal structure strongly suggests other things were necessary to full integration of the agreement of the parties.

This instrument describes itself as a "Modification of 'Proposed Collective Bargaining Agreement'" between the association and the city. The proposed agreement to which this refers is the text of a draft distributed to the association members November 21, 1968. This proposed agreement had been previously rejected by the members of the association.

It seems obvious that this modification of a proposed agreement is not itself a complete agreement and the change in details all hang on some final formalization. Some of them, e.g., that referring to the time of work of the 5% night shift, is unintelligible without being filled in by some other interpretive writing.

The court inquired of the city on the argument about its custom followed in executing complete collective bargaining agreements, formalizing all terms. There has been filed with the court the texts of some 28 complete collective bargaining agreements executed between 1966 and 1969.

The city on January 4, 1971, in lieu of a sur-rebuttal brief, filed with the court the constitution and by-laws of plaintiff association which require that collective bargaining agreements with the city shall be reduced to writing. Plaintiffs reply under the same date that this is what was done here; but, of course, the question remains whether it was intended by the parties in this negotiation that there should be a further rounded agreement.

Plaintiffs argue also in support of summary judgment that the city had recognized "the agreement" by paying the salaries which had been fixed in the accord of January 29, 1969. The city did pay those salaries retroactively to October 1, 1968 under the authority of an order made by the Mayor March 28, 1969, but it expressly provided that positions covered by it "shall not be eligible for any further salary or fringe benefit increases prior to January 1, 1971," the end of the contract period.

This would seem to negate a contemporaneous intention by the city to have the tie-in with sergeants' salaries effect an increase before the end of the contract period and would bear on one of the issues to be tried out in the action.

The evident fact seems to be that this was a piecemeal negotiation and settlement in writing of contract terms. That, however, does not make the terms binding if there were any condition to their being binding dependent upon a more formal writing or upon agreement on other material terms. Whether there were such conditions is shown by the papers to be a sharply controverted issue, and, hence, one not determinable on summary judgment.

Nor does the issue of fact dissolve into one determinable as a matter of law because there was part performance of the written piecemeal agreement. That would occur, despite the conditions if they existed, if the parties were satisfied that any future agreement must and would contain the elements performed, namely, the salary increase.

The important and only issue in this case is whether the piecemeal agreement, and such agreement there certainly was, for a ratio between sergeants and patrolmen, was conditional, either on a full collective agreement signifying total agreement of all issues in dispute, or on a formal written collective agreement signifying not only full agreement on all terms but documentation removing risks of dispute as to terms. That issue is, on the present record of affidavits, and concededly incomplete and unapproved drafts and counter-drafts, an issue of fact.

The counterclaim of the city was properly dismissed.

The order should be modified by reversing so much thereof as grants summary judgment to plaintiffs on the complaint and otherwise affirmed, without costs.

FULD, Chief Judge (dissenting).

Contrary to intimations in the city's argument, no one could seriously urge a court to announce an inflexible rule that a collective bargaining agreement must be embodied in a formal written document and that neither party is bound by its terms until each has signed and executed it. Having in mind the manner in which collective bargaining has been carried on between public employers and their employees, such a principle would be completely unworkable. In any event, though, absent such an inexorable rule, we see no escape from the conclusion, reached by the courts below, that no issue of fact exists as to the city's acquiescence in the terms of the parity provision — which is the heart of this controversy — or as to the intent of the parties that there be a binding collective bargaining agreement even though not reduced to a formal written contract. Accordingly, we would affirm the order granting summary judgment to the plaintiffs for the reasons set forth in the memorandum decision of the Appellate Division and the opinion of the court at Special Term.

BREITEL, JASEN and GIBSON, JJ., concur with BERGAN, J.

FULD, C.J., dissents and votes to affirm in a separate opinion in which Burke and SCILEPPI, JJ., concur.

Ordered accordingly.

# NOTES

1. The progression of the *Patrolmen's Benevolent Ass'n* case through the New York State court system provides an interesting study of the difficulties encountered by an employer who fails to coordinate commitments to various groups of employees. The heart of the problem was the City's very real fear that if a contract were found to exist between the PBA and the city, it would set in motion an unending cycle of wage demands. The City had entered into three wage ratio commitments: a 3.0-3.5 PBA-police sergeants' wage ratio agreement, a 3.0-3.8 firemen's-fire officers' wage ratio agreement, and an agreement to maintain wage parity between police sergeants and fire lieutenants. If the PBA agreement were honored, one or the other of the other two ratios would always be out of balance. One raise would always trigger a demand for another. Before the New York County Supreme Court, the city argued that the contract was void because of impossibility of performance. Patrolmen's Benevolent Ass'n v. City of New York, 75 L.R.R.M. 2293 (N.Y. Sup. Ct. 1970). The court found no merit to this argument, holding that the city had voluntarily entered into the contracts; the difficulty was of the city's own making and therefore the impossibility of performance doctrine did not apply. The Appellate Division affirmed the Supreme Court's summary judgment finding that a valid contract existed. Patrolmen's Benevolent Ass'n. v. City of New York, 35 App.Div.2d 697, 314 N.Y.S.2d 762 (1970).

Following the Court of Appeals' remand, the Supreme Court again held, this time after trial, that the PBA and the City had reached a mutually enforceable agreement. Patrolmen's Benevolent Ass'n. v. City of New York, 76 L.R.R.M. 3087 (1971). *See also* Patrolmen's Benevolent Ass'n. v. City of New York, 78 L.R.R.M. 2747 (N.Y. Sup. Ct. 1971).

2. In State *ex rel.* Bain v. Clallam County Bd. of County Comm'rs, 77 Wash. 2d 542, 463 P.2d 617 (1970), mandamus was sought to require the county commissioners to adopt and perform an oral collective bargaining agreement calling for a pay increase for employees of the City of Port Angeles. The Washington Supreme Court found the agreement to be too vague and uncertain to be susceptible to a decree of specific enforcement. The court also held that the state collective bargaining statute requires agreements to be in writing, suggesting the following policy reason for its decision:

> Obviously, the legislature in authorizing and in empowering the county commissioners to enter into *written* agreements did so to avoid the very thing that happened here: conducting county business privately — as in the Elks' Club — from which the public could be excluded, possibly binding the county and its treasury to contractual obligations established only by parol evidence, and leaving the county dependent on the memory and recollection of the negotiators.

3. Where a statute provided that a negotiated agreement would become binding if not rejected within thirty days at a regular or special town meeting and a proposed contract was not rescinded until about forty days after its negotiation, the agreement was

determined to be binding upon the town. Educ. Ass'n v. Town of Madison, 384 A.2d 361, 97 L.R.R.M. 2631 (Conn. 1978).

4. In Police Protective Ass'n v. City of Casper, 575 P.2d 1146, 98 L.R.R.M. 2113 (1978), a collective bargaining agreement that contained no provision for its termination but continued "until altered or modified," was found by the Wyoming Supreme Court to constitute a perpetual contract that was considered unenforceable.

# C.  THE  ENFORCEMENT  OF  THE  COLLECTIVE AGREEMENT THROUGH THE GRIEVANCE PROCEDURE AND ARBITRATION

## PICKETS AT CITY HALL: REPORT AND RECOMMENDATIONS OF THE TWENTIETH CENTURY FUND TASK FORCE ON LABOR DISPUTES IN PUBLIC EMPLOYMENT 17-18 (1970) †

In any agreement negotiated, the public employer and the union should be strongly encouraged to provide a system for the presentation and disposition of grievances as they may be alleged by employees. One of the most positive values to be found in a union-employer relationship is that it establishes a formal process through which complaints that might otherwise be unknown and unattended by management are brought into the light.

No matter how detailed the agreement between union and management may be, it cannot take into account all of the problems that will arise during its term. Nor can it anticipate what differences there may be over interpreting provisions in the agreement and their application. Hence the grievance procedure is a safety valve. Rather than let a difference that arises while the agreement is in force develop into a deadlock which might disrupt the work place or lead to a strike, formal grievance machinery should be established. As it functions, the individual employee has assurance that he will not suffer from management arbitrariness while the union has assurance that it will be heard and management has assurance that employee claims will not be supported by coercive pressures.

The lack of formal grievance machinery has led to public employee disputes, as employees have no alternative method of pressing a claim against unfair treatment, real or imagined. Established grievance procedures, leading ultimately to arbitration, have proved essential in achieving peaceful resolution of disputes in the private sector. Such procedures are equally essential for public employment.

Giving an outsider (the arbitrator) power to render a binding decision on a grievance involving internal organizational or operational matters may appear to be a momentous step for the responsible administrator of a government agency. His protection is that despite any ruling by an arbitrator, he cannot be required to do something beyond his legal authority or contrary to law. Against this hazard he will be protected by the courts. If his interpretation or application of the terms of an agreement seem wrong to his employees, with no opportunity to appeal they cannot escape a frustration that can seriously damage employee relations.

Unless specifically proscribed by law from agreeing to binding arbitration — and where such laws exist they should be repealed — a government agency should accept the arbitration of grievance matters in its own protection against

---

† Copyright © 1970 by The Twentieth Century Fund, New York. Reprinted by permission.

unresolved and potentially explosive disputes. In jurisdictions where binding arbitration remains impermissible, the arbitrator's award should be taken as advisory and, if necessary, referred for implementation to the body or official with authority to order it.

# 1. THE GRIEVANCE PROCEDURE

One of the most significant accomplishments of labor law in the private sector has been the development of a system of industrial jurisprudence, a system whereby the parties themselves establish the machinery for the resolution of day-to-day disputes over the interpretation and application of the collective bargaining agreement. Almost all of these disputes are settled by means of this machinery; few disputes get as far even as the last step in the process, which is usually some form of arbitration.

> The essence of a grievance procedure is to provide a means by which an employee, without jeopardizing his job, can express a complaint about his work or working conditions and obtain a fair hearing through progressively higher levels of management. Under collective bargaining, four important and related features have been added to this concept. First, the collective bargaining contract, while it drastically limits the area of legitimate complaints by establishing the basic conditions of employment and rules for day-to-day administration deemed to be fair by mutual agreement, at the same time may create a source of grievances and disagreements through ambiguities of language and omissions, as do changing circumstances and violations. Second, the union is recognized and accepted as the spokesman for the aggrieved worker, and an inability to agree on a resolution of the issue becomes a dispute between union and management. Third, because an unresolved grievance becomes a union-management dispute, a way ultimately must be found to reach settlements short of a strike or lockout or substitutes for such actions. Final and binding arbitration is the principal means to this end. Fourth, the process of adjusting grievances and grievance disputes is itself defined in the agreement, and, along with other aspects of collective bargaining, tends to become increasingly formal.[8]

Private sector grievance procedures typically consist of a series of steps, with the employee-grievant and the management seeking to resolve the dispute at successively higher levels. The employee normally takes his grievance first to his foreman or to his union steward. If the union steward is consulted first, he will present the grievance on behalf of the employee to the foreman. Normally, the employee is entitled to union representation at each step. If no resolution is achieved, the matter may be taken to a higher company official, often the foreman's immediate superior; this is the second step. If no solution is found here, the matter may then go to a still higher company official or to a hearing before a union shop committee and certain company officials who have been designated to meet regularly with this committee. If the grievance is denied at this level, but the union continues to deem it meritorious, it may go to a conference of regional union officials and high company officers. Failure to settle the grievance at this step may result in a union demand that the matter be arbitrated. The number of steps in the procedure will of course vary from contract

    [8] U.S. Bureau of Labor Statistics Bull. No. 1425-1, Major Collective Bargaining Agreements: Grievance Procedures 1 (1964).

to contract, and the nature of the proceedings at each step may differ, but the pattern is fairly well established in the private sector.

Public sector grievance procedures in the past have generally not followed the private sector pattern. There are two major reasons for this.[9] First, the sovereignty doctrine led many public employers to conclude that they were powerless to negotiate any kind of procedure which would result in the sharing of decision-making authority or its transfer to any third party. Second, a negotiated grievance procedure was thought to be superfluous; often, a grievance procedure already existed in the form of a civil service appeals system.

There are major differences, however, between civil service appeals procedures in the public sector and a private sector model grievance procedure.[10] A civil service procedure is normally established unilaterally by the public employer or through the legislative process, though employee organizations are generally consulted. In contrast, a negotiated grievance procedure is by definition established bilaterally through collective bargaining; it exists by virtue of the effort and approval of both parties. Processing a grievance is usually an individual matter in a civil service procedure, though the individual is generally allowed union representation at some stage of the proceedings; in a negotiated procedure, however, it is a union matter, the union taking up the cudgel for the employee and determining how far and how fast to process the grievance dispute. A civil service procedure is an "appeals" procedure; the employee is seen as appealing to higher authority from the decision of a public official. A negotiated grievance procedure, however, is less an appeal than a continuation of the collective bargaining process, a method by which the rights and responsibilities of the parties are continually clarified in the developing "common law of the shop."

Further distinctions between civil service appeal procedures and grievance procedures are detailed in Massey, *Employee Grievance Procedures*, in DEVELOPMENTS IN PUBLIC EMPLOYEE RELATIONS 64-65 (1965):

> [A] civil service commission is not like an arbitrator. An arbitrator, hopefully at least, is a disinterested party. On the other hand, when a commission is hearing an appeal, it is passing on the application by an operating agency of regulations issued by the commission pursuant to law. It is enforcing its own regulations.
>
> Also, a civil service commission is not an integral part of management, as is the personnel department of a private business. While many commissions have taken a positive role in personnel administration and have become to a degree an arm of management, they are not in a position to be an integral part of management. They have a legal existence independent of management. Moreover, historically, they were established as the protector of job applicants and employees against political favoritism by management, and they are now regarded by employees as the protector of a number of employee rights. Incidentally, some unions of government employees seem to consider it an advantage to apply more-or-less continuous pressure on the commissions. Of course, some other organizations with a considerable

---

[9] Ullman & Begin, *The Structure and Scope of Appeals Procedures for Public Employees*, 23 IND. & LAB. REL. REV. 323 (1970).

[10] Amundson, *Negotiated Grievance Procedures in California Public Employment: Controversy and Confusion*, 6 CAL. PUB. EMPL. REL. 2 (August 1970).

population of government employees as members — veterans' organizations, for example — do the same. Thus, civil service commissioners are likely to have a dual loyalty — to management, on the one hand, and to employees, on the other. This arrangement has endured for many years and may have its advantages. It is, however, a different arrangement than is found in private business.

Conceptually, there is also a great difference in the subject matter covered by the two types of procedures. A grievance procedure, as a matter of contract, may cover such subjects as wages, fringe benefits, working conditions, and other matters not normally covered by civil service appeals procedures. The scope of a civil service appeals procedure, on the other hand, depends on the applicable statute or city ordinance; typically, civil service laws deal almost exclusively with the manner of appointment, promotions, discharges and changes of status of employees. Civil service regulations in these areas have historically been considered non-negotiable.

As a practical matter, however, there is often a considerable overlap of grievance and appeals procedures. Indeed, employees sometimes may have a choice of procedures, or the procedure may be mandated by the type of incident that has occurred. An "adverse action," for example — an official reprimand, suspension or discharge — may require an appeal to the civil service commission or supervisory political body rather than a grievance within the management structure.

In the last few years there has been increasing reliance on the private sector model in the formulation of public sector grievance procedures.[11] In part, this is due to the trend away from viewing the doctrine of sovereignty as a complete bar to the adoption and enforcement of public sector collective bargaining agreements containing grievance procedures, even those which culminate in binding arbitration.[12] In part, too, it is due to the recognition that negotiated grievance procedures are capable of coexisting with or supplanting civil service appeals procedures.

Whatever the motivating factors, one recent study shows negotiated grievance procedures to be on the increase.[13] In the federal service, it was found that about 38 percent of the employees were covered by collective bargaining agreements, approximately half of which contained negotiated procedures. Among state and local government employees, 21 percent were covered by collective agreements; 90 percent of these agreements contained negotiated procedures.

---

[11] Begin, *The Private Grievance Model in the Public Sector*, 10 IND. REL. 21 (1971); Lewin, *Collective Bargaining Impacts on Personnel Administration in the American Public Sector*, 27 LAB. L.J. 426 (1976).

[12] *See, e.g.,* Tremblay v. Berlin Police Union, 108 N.H. 416, 237 A.2d 668 (1968); Bd. of Educ. of Union Free School Dist. No. 3 v. Associated Teachers of Huntington, 30 N.Y.2d 122, 282 N.E.2d 109 (1972). *See also* Note, *Legality and Propriety of Agreements to Arbitrate Major and Minor Disputes in Public Employment*, 54 CORNELL L. REV. 129 (1968).

[13] Ullman & Begin, *The Structure and Scope of Appeals Procedures for Public Employees*, 23 IND. & LAB. REL. REV. 323 (1970). *See, e.g.,* FLA. STAT. § 447.401 (Supp. 1978), which requires public sector bargaining agreements to contain grievance machinery culminating in binding arbitration. *See also* Township of West Windsor v. PERC, —— N.J. ——, 393 A.2d 255 (1978), wherein the Court indicated that while the public sector statute requires parties to provide grievance procedures covering all employment disputes, it does not obligate them to provide for arbitration of all such matters.

In the private sector, 32 percent of employees are under collective agreements,[14] almost all of which have negotiated grievance procedures and 94 percent of which culminate in binding arbitration.[15] Fifty-three percent of state and local government contracts also provide for binding arbitration; [16] binding arbitration is yet rare in federal labor agreements, though 40 percent of them do provide for advisory arbitration.[17] The National Postal Agreement of 1971 does provide for binding arbitration, but the U.S. Postal Service Corporation is not a typical federal agency; by virtue of the passage of the Postal Reorganization Act,[18] it is now under the jurisdiction of the National Labor Relations Board.

## REPORT OF THE COMMITTEE ON THE LAW OF FEDERAL GOVERNMENT EMPLOYEE RELATIONS, SECTION OF LABOR RELATIONS LAW, AMERICAN BAR ASSOCIATION 1972 COMMITTEE REPORTS 144-46 (1972) †

The Federal Labor Relations Council, charged with the responsibility of overseeing the Federal service labor relations program, is not only charged with a decision-making role, . . . but is responsible for recommending to the President changes in the program.

In accordance with this responsibility, the Council conducted public hearings in October 1970 to review the program. After a substantial delay, the Council made recommendations to the President in June 1971. . . .

The Council's recommendation [in the area of grievances and arbitration] were accepted by the President, who issued Executive Order 11616 on August 26, 1971, amending Executive Order 11491. The . . . major changes are as follows:

The Council was concerned with the right of employees to select a representative other than the exclusive representative to process grievances arising under the negotiated grievance procedure. It felt that permitting employees to select a rival union to process employee grievances which were related to the negotiated agreement was undesirable. Accordingly, the Order was amended to provide that only a representative approved by the exclusive bargaining agent which negotiated the agreement could represent employees in processing grievances under the agreement.

Employees or groups of employees were, however, given the right to present their own grievances without the intervention of the exclusive representative. The rights of the exclusive representative to administer the agreement were protected by a proviso that if the employee presents his own grievance the exclusive union representative shall be given an opportunity to be present at the adjustment and the adjustment of the grievance shall not be inconsistent with the terms of the agreement.

---

[14] Ullman & Begin, note 13 *supra,* at 327.

[15] U.S. BUREAU OF LABOR STATISTICS, BULL. NO. 1425-6, MAJOR COLLECTIVE BARGAINING AGREEMENTS: ARBITRATION PROCEDURES 5 (1966).

[16] Ullman & Begin, note 13 *supra,* at 329.

[17] *Id.* A major reason for the restricted use of binding arbitration in the federal service has been that § 8(b) of Executive Order 10988 provided for advisory arbitration only. In 1969, Executive Order 11491 eliminated this restriction, opening the door for the first time to negotiated grievance procedures containing binding arbitration provisions.

[18] 39 U.S.C.A. § 101 *et seq.* (Supp. 1972).

† Reprinted by permission of the American Bar Association.

The Council found that the existing mix of employee "grievances" and union "disputes" involving agency regulations, application of laws, or agency policy, all considered under a negotiated grievance procedure, created a situation under which employees were faced with complicated choices in seeking relief. In order to correct this problem, the Order was amended to confine the negotiated grievance procedure to grievances, whether employee or union instigated, concerning the interpretation or application of the terms of the agreement and not other matters.

The Council noted that a grievance procedure limited to the interpretation or application of the agreement would not only simplify grievance processing, but "in addition, an incentive will be created for unions to negotiate substantive agreements within the full scope of negotiations authorized by the Order." The extent to which this goal has been achieved is unknown at this time. Whether unions are seeking or will seek more substantive agreements and thereby broaden the scope of the agreement in order to provide wider latitude to process grievances remains to be seen.

The Council's recommendations, which were adopted by the President, further clarified the situation by permitting all other grievances, *i.e.,* those not involving the interpretation or application of the terms of the agreement, to be processed through any other avenue available to the employees. In the case of grievances not cognizable under the agreement, the employees could select any representative they desired to represent them. The prior practice of excluding matters covered by statutory appeals procedures was retained.

In order to enhance further the role of the exclusive representative, the amendments eliminated the requirement that the employee agree to arbitration. Furthermore, the employer was also given the right to invoke arbitration.

Finding the need for a procedure to resolve questions as to what is grievable or arbitrable, the Council recommended that such disagreements be resolved by the Assistant Secretary of Labor. In the private sector, those issues are customarily disposed of by arbitration or in the courts. The Council stated that the machinery created by the amendments to handle these disagreements "is appropriate in order to insure consistent application of the recommended revisions with respect to negotiated grievance procedures." It should be noted that the courts have indicated that they do not have jurisdiction over matters arising under the Executive Order or agreements which result from the Executive Order. Bronx-Manhattan Postal Union v. Gronouski, 350 F.2d 451.

Subsequent to the amendments of Executive Order 11491, the Federal Labor Relations Council, on March 22, 1972, issued an Information Bulletin to clarify certain provisions of the amended order as they related to the grievance procedure.

Inasmuch as the Council found that a substantial number of agreements executed under the Order did not contain any type of grievance procedure, it resolved this problem by mandating that all negotiated agreements entered into, renewed or extended, after the effective date of the amendments, November 24, 1971, must contain a grievance procedure. The grievance procedure could contain binding arbitration and the sharing of the cost of arbitration was made negotiable.

## NOTES

1. Though a method for handling grievances is a nearly universal feature of collective bargaining agreements in both the public and private sectors, not all contracts define "grievance" in the same way. Some contracts, in fact, detail the procedure without defining the term at all. The language outlining the scope of the grievance procedure may be very broad, or it may detail the matters which are subject to the procedure in very specific terms. Other provisions generally exclude certain subjects from the grievance procedure as matters of management prerogative.

2. The scope of the grievance procedure should not be confused with the scope of arbitration. The two are often not coextensive. Some disputes may be grievable even though they concern matters which the parties have not agreed to submit to arbitration. In most cases, however, at least in the private sector, the scope of the grievance procedure and the scope of arbitration coincide.[19]

# 2. NEGOTIATING THE GRIEVANCE PROCEDURE

In the private sector, the most important element in negotiating a grievance procedure is the intent of the parties as to what should and what should not be a grievable dispute. In the public sector, other factors are also important. Principal among those other factors is the intent of the legislature. Did the state legislature or city council, in enacting a public employee bargaining law, intend that the area in question be subject to the grievance procedure, or did they intend that it be left to the unbridled discretion of the public employer? Also relevant is the effect of past or existing civil service systems. In addition to the procedures they establish, civil service appeals procedures also create customs and attitudes as to the proper way to do things. How are the procedures and their attendant customs to be accommodated?

In negotiating a grievance procedure, the following questions are likely to be of concern to the parties:

1. Is the procedure to culminate in final and binding arbitration?

2. How extensively is the employee organization to be involved in the procedure? Are stewards or other union representatives to be present from the initial stages of the grievance? Will the individual employee or the organization have the final say as to whether the grievance is processed through the succeeding stages of the procedure, settled, or dropped? Unions typically want control of the procedure to insure uniformity in its operation and to facilitate the development of informal channels of communication, customs, practices and settlement mechanisms. On the other hand, the individual in civil service systems has always been responsible for processing his own appeals, with union advice but not control; the practice is not easily supplanted.

3. What are the time limits to be for filing and processing grievances? Should time limits begin to run from the time of a grievable occurrence or from the time the employee realizes he has a grievance?

4. Should the union have the right to file general "policy" grievances or should it be restricted to filing specific grievances on behalf of designated employee grievants?

5. What should be considered a grievable dispute? What type of complaints is the grievance procedure designed to handle? Generally, employee organizations seek to broaden the scope of the procedure to include as many specific subjects as possible and to open the door to new grievable matters by

---

[19] U.S. BUREAU OF LABOR STATISTICS BULL. NO. 1425-6, MAJOR COLLECTIVE BARGAINING AGREEMENTS: ARBITRATION PROCEDURES 6, 8 (1966).

adding "past practices" and other open-ended clauses. Management, just as in the private sector, seeks to reserve as much as possible to its own discretion by the insertion of a broad "management rights" clause. Of course, the scope is often circumscribed by the legislature.

## NOTES

1. The scope of a grievance procedure and the obligation of workers to resort to that mechanism before seeking external assistance regarding a particular employment problem may occasionally arise with respect to government personnel. In Trepedino v. Dumpson, 24 N.Y.2d 705, 249 N.E.2d 751 (1969), the New York Court of Appeals negated disciplinary action which had been taken against Department of Welfare employees on account of their having written to the U.S. Department of Health, Education, and Welfare to complain about problems existing in their office. After finding that the workers' communication to H.E.W. was generally protected by free speech principles, the Court had to resolve the contention that the employees were nonetheless deserving of punishment for having not first attempted to alleviate their complaints through the provided grievance machinery.

There can be no doubt that it is highly disruptive and not conducive to maintaining the morale of an office or the efficiency of its workers if employees were to be permitted to go outside their organization initially to register complaints concerning its operations. If, therefore, a designated grievance procedure has been prescribed, it is desirable, nay necessary, that the employees pursue and exhaust such procedure....

The communication to the Director of the Federal Bureau in Washington was ill-considered, apparently written by the petitioners out of pique because they believed they were being saddled with an unduly heavy and burdensome case load. However, be that as it may, the record in the present case demonstrates that the subject matter of the letter, critical though it may have been of the Welfare Department's operations, could not be appropriately raised or dealt with through its grievance machinery. The procedure established by the Commissioner . . . simply establishes machinery in the Department for dealing with the *individual* problems of employees. The plan of this so-called "grievance procedure" is not unlike those found in private collective bargaining agreements which are neither designed nor intended to deal with such broad issues as those raised in the petitioners' letter to the Federal Bureau in Washington.

*Accord,* Bd. of Educ., Union Free School Dist. No. 27 v. West Hempstead Chapter, New York State Teachers Ass'n., 311 N.Y.S.2d 708 (Sup. Ct. 1970).

If public employees seek outside relief from employment complaints which could possibly be resolved through their grievance procedure, should they be subject to discipline if they fail to seek redress initially through that internal mechanism?

2. Where the applicable labor relations statute provides that the labor organization selected by the majority of employees in an appropriate bargaining unit shall constitute the workers' exclusive representative, it is generally recognized that an aggrieved employee may not be represented by a rival minority union. *See, e.g.,* Diablo Valley Fed'n of Teachers and Mount Diablo Unified School Dist., Cal.PERB Case No. SF-CE-88, 1977-78 PEB ¶40,452 (1977); Bayonne Bd. of Educ. and Bayonne Fed'n of Teachers, N.J. PERC, Case No. 78-60, GERR No. 765, 11 (1978). *See generally* R. GORMAN, BASIC TEXT ON LABOR LAW 394-95 (1976). However, in the absence of such statutory recognition of the "exclusivity" principle, a bargaining agent may not always be permitted to act as the sole bargaining representative for nonconsenting employees. *See* Dade County Classroom Teachers Ass'n v. Ryan, 225 So.2d 903, 71 L.R.R.M. 2958 (Fla. 1969).

3. Should an employer be permitted to insist that all grievances be initiated only by individual employees, or should a representative labor organization possess the inherent right to file grievances on behalf of unit workers? *See* Red Bank Regional Educ. Ass'n v. High School Bd. of Educ., — N.J. —, 393 A.2d 267 (1978). Why would a union desire the right to institute grievances where no individual has done so?

4. For an early in-depth study of public employee grievance procedures, *see* Berger, *Grievance Process in the Philadelphia Public Service,* 13 IND. & LAB. REL. REV. 568 (1960). Later studies may be found in Ullman & Begin, *The Structure and Scope of Appeals Procedures for Public Employees,* 23 IND. & LAB. REL. REV. 323 (1970), and Begin, *The Private Grievance Model in the Public Sector,* 10 IND. REL. 21 (1971). *See generally* M. BOWERS, CONTRACT ADMINISTRATION IN THE PUBLIC SECTOR (1976); U.S. BUREAU OF LABOR STATISTICS, BULL. No. 1661, NEGOTIATION IMPASSE, GRIEVANCE, AND ARBITRATION IN FEDERAL AGREEMENTS (1970); KORETZ, *Labor Relations Law,* 22 SYRACUSE L. REV. 133, 136-39 (1971); Wolf, *Grievance Procedures for School Employees* in EMPLOYER-EMPLOYEE RELATIONS IN THE PUBLIC SCHOOLS 133 (R. Doherty ed. 1967).

# 3. GRIEVANCE ARBITRATION

Almost universally in the private sector and increasingly in the public sector,[20] negotiated grievance procedures are capped by an arbitration provision. Grievance arbitration involves the adjudication of disputes which the parties have been unable to settle among themselves by a neutral third-party or panel. The neutral may be a single arbitrator or a multi-member (either tripartite or all-neutral) panel; an arbitrator or panel may be *ad hoc* (temporary, invited by the parties to hear one or a series of cases) or permanent (as an umpire who is hired to hear all disputes between the parties). The arbitrator's decision may be final and binding on the parties or advisory only.

In the private sector, grievance arbitration performs a number of very important functions.[21] First, it provides a relatively speedy and inexpensive means of settling disputes. Secondly, it gives the employee the security of knowing that the ultimate recourse for the resolution of any grievance he may have lies with a neutral and not with his employer. Thirdly, it helps conserve judicial resources by providing a means to settle most disputes without court action. Fourthly, and most importantly, it serves national labor policy as a mechanism for the maintenance of industrial peace, providing an alternative to the strike in the resolution of day-to-day disputes.

Arbitration of grievances is a method of industrial self-regulation, a private rather than a governmental proceeding. Yet, private sector arbitration enjoys the sanction and support of law. Section 203(d) of the Labor Management Relations Act of 1947 [22] states: "Final adjustment by a method agreed upon by the parties is hereby declared to be the desirable method for settlement of grievance disputes arising over the application or interpretation of an existing collective-bargaining agreement. . . ." In the 1957 case of *Textile Workers Union v. Lincoln Mills,*[23] the Supreme Court held that arbitration agreements were specifically enforceable in the federal courts under § 301(a) of the LMRA; [24] and in the 1960 *Steelworkers' Trilogy* [25] cases, the Court determined that arbitration agreements

---

[20] Howlett, *Arbitration in the Public Sector,* PROCEEDINGS OF THE SOUTHWESTERN LEGAL FOUNDATION 15TH ANNUAL INSTITUTE ON LABOR LAW 262 (1969).

[21] *See generally* D. ROTHSCHILD, L. MERRIFIELD & H. EDWARDS, COLLECTIVE BARGAINING AND LABOR ARBITRATION (1979).

[22] 29 U.S.C. § 173 (d).

[23] 353 U.S. 448 (1957).

[24] 29 U.S.C. § 185 (a).

[25] United Steelworkers v. American Mfg. Co., 363 U.S. 564, 80 S. Ct. 1343, 4 L. Ed. 2d 1403 (1960); United Steelworkers v. Warrior & Gulf Nav. Co., 363 U.S. 574, 80 S. Ct. 1347, 4 L. Ed. 2d 1409 (1960); United Steelworkers v. Enterprise Wheel Car Corp., 363 U.S. 593, 80 S. Ct. 1358, 4 L. Ed. 2d 1424 (1960).

and awards should be reviewable by the courts only according to a very narrowly prescribed standard, thus discouraging both refusals to arbitrate and appeals from arbitration awards.

The reasons for enforcing arbitration agreements and awards in the private sector are frequently applicable in the public sector too. Some objection has been voiced against the legality of grievance arbitration on the ground that it is in derogation of the power of legislatures to determine public policy.[26] However, the judicially created principle that an agreement to arbitrate constitutes an unlawful delegation of governmental authority has begun to lose much of its force, and some courts have recently indicated an inclination to follow the enforcement rules developed in *Lincoln Mills* and the *Steelworkers' Trilogy* when dealing with public sector grievance arbitration. Nonetheless, other courts have continued to demonstrate either a reluctance to adopt entirely the private sector precedents or an outright hostility toward doctrines they believe are inapposite with respect to public sector grievance disputes.

There are two quite different types of labor arbitration: grievance arbitration, or "arbitration of rights," and impasse arbitration, or "arbitration of interests." In dealing with public sector labor relations, it is particularly important to be aware of the differences between the two. In the private sector, impasse arbitration is seldom used; references to "arbitration" almost always mean grievance arbitration. But in the public sector, where strikes by public employees are usually illegal, impasse arbitration is important and occasionally mandated by statute. Grievance arbitration involves the determination of rights under an *existing* contract by an arbitrator acting in a judicial capacity. Impasse arbitration, on the other hand, is utilized when the parties are unable to agree to the provisions of a labor contract at the bargaining table; it is a substitute for the economic weaponry of strikes and lockouts in the determination of what the contract rights of the parties *shall be.* The impasse arbitrator is a combination policy-maker, administrator, and chancellor at equity; in contrast to the grievance arbitrator, he is a formulator, rather than a follower of the parties' contract.

## ROCKLAND PROFESSIONAL FIRE FIGHTERS ASSOCIATION v. CITY OF ROCKLAND

Supreme Judicial Court of Maine
261 A.2d 418 (1970)

WEATHERBEE, Justice.

In 1957 our Legislature enacted "An Act Relating to Arbitration Pursuant to Collective Bargaining Contracts." This legislation as amended is now 26 M.R.S.A. § 951, et seq. Section 951 reads:

"A written provision in any collective bargaining contract to settle by arbitration a controversy thereafter arising out of such contract or out of the refusal to perform the whole or any part thereof, or an agreement in writing to submit to arbitration an existing controversy arising out of such a contract, or such refusal, herein designated in this subchapter as 'a written submission

---

[26] *See, e.g.,* Fellows v. LaTronica, 151 Colo. 300, 377 P.2d 547 (1962).

agreement,' shall be valid, irrevocable and enforceable, save upon such grounds, independent of the provisions for arbitration, as exist at law or in equity for the revocation of any contract."

Section 954 provides for the appointment of arbitrators by the Court in the event that the collective bargaining contract fails to establish a method for their appointment or if the method so provided is ignored by one party. Section 956 details methods for obtaining testimony of witnesses at the arbitration hearing, and for the fees of witnesses. Section 957 provides for the enforcement by the Superior Court of the award of arbitration upon application of a party that judgment shall be entered for the party. Section 958 enumerates grounds which would justify vacating an award.

In 1965 the Legislature enacted a statute which is referred to as the Fire Fighters Arbitration Law which is now 26 M.R.S.A. § 980, et seq. In doing so the Legislature declared it to be the public policy of the State that this particular class of municipal employees in their position of high responsibility should be given the right to organize and bargain collectively with the municipalities in arriving at a contract of employment.

Section 981 reads:

"The protection of the public health, safety and welfare demands that the permanent uniformed members of any paid fire department in any municipality not be accorded the right to strike or engage in any work stoppage or slowdown. This necessary prohibition does not, however, require the denial to such municipal employees of other recognized rights of labor such as the right to organize, to be represented by a labor organization of their choice, and the right to bargain collectively concerning wages, rates of pay and other terms and conditions of employment."

Following the broad statement of policy of section 981 the Fire Fighters Arbitration Law proceeds to empower the fire fighters to compel the municipality to meet with the fire fighters' bargaining agent to bargain collectively in the formation of a written contract of employment. Section 986 provides that if the parties cannot reach a contract the unresolved issues shall be submitted to arbitration at the option of the association. Section 987 sets out the method of selecting the arbitrators. Section 988 describes the rules under which hearings shall be conducted and specifies that a less-than-unanimous decision of the arbitrators shall not be binding on either party.

Section 991 includes the words:

"Any collective bargaining agreement negotiated under this chapter shall specifically provide that the fire fighters who are subject to its terms shall have no right to engage in any work stoppage, slowdown or strike, the consideration for such provision being the right to a resolution of disputed questions." . . .

Under the authority of the Fire Fighters Arbitration Law the firemen of Rockland organized and entered into a contract of employment for the calendar year of 1967. . . .

[The contract established a grievance procedure] consisting of four steps, the third of which provided for a hearing before an Appeal Grievance Board. . . .

The contract then provided that:

"Arbitration shall be in accordance with Title 26, Sect. 987 of the Maine Revised Statutes Annotated."

... [H]owever, section 987 only sets up machinery for the organization and operation of an arbitration board for the purpose of resolving disputes concerning the negotiation of a labor contract and makes no provision for arbitration of disputes arising later under the contract.

On April 27, 1967 Walter R. Dyer, a Rockland fireman, was suspended for six days allegedly for insubordinate conduct. Dyer and the Plaintiff exhausted the grievance processes provided in the contract and the matter went on to arbitration. The parties followed the provisions of section 987 in selecting the members of the arbitration board but on June 12, before the Board could hear the matter, Dyer was discharged for a similar reason.

Plaintiff and Defendant then combined the two grievances and submitted to the arbitration board the single issue of whether the discharge of Dyer was for sufficient cause. After hearing, a majority of the board returned an award which read:

> "1. There was not sufficient cause for the discharge of Walter R. Dyer on June 12, 1967.
> 2. If Dyer resigns from office in Local 1584 of the International Association of Firefighters, the City of Rockland shall offer him reinstatement to his former position without back pay."

Dyer did resign from office in the union but the city refused to reinstate him. Plaintiff then brought an application for judgment upon the arbitration award in the Superior Court in Knox County. Defendant moved to dismiss the application for judgment on the grounds that:

1) The award was not unanimous and therefore was invalid.
2) The board abused its discretion and exceeded the powers given it in going beyond the single question submitted to them.
3) The city has the right to discharge any employee when, in his best judgment, the City Manager considers that the city's interest requires it.

The matter was heard before a Justice of the Superior Court who granted Defendant's motion to dismiss the application for judgment on the award. The ruling of the Justice was based on his conclusion that

> "... [T]he Legislature intended that whatever benefits it was conferring upon the Fire Fighters, the right to organize, bargain collectively, arbitrate and all other rights being granted, were to be viewed entirely in the light of the language of the Fire Fighters Arbitration Law...."

As the Fire Fighters Arbitration Law provided only for arbitration of disputes surrounding the *making* of a contract, the Justice held the Fire Fighters had been given no right to arbitration of disputes arising *subsequent* to the contract and therefore had no right to enforcement of an award....

We find that the Fire Fighters Arbitration Law, in spite of the scope suggested by its title, provides for arbitration only as to the negotiation of a labor contract. The parties here did negotiate a contract as the Fire Fighters Arbitration Law empowered them to do. The contract bound the parties to submit unresolved grievances to arbitration at the option of the union. The Legislature intended the Fire Fighters to have all the rights of labor organizations except those specifically withheld and in section 951, years earlier, the Legislature had given all labor organizations the right to provide in their contracts for arbitration of grievances arising out of such contracts. The fire fighters' authority to agree with the city to submit their unresolved grievances to arbitration is found in section 951. The provision in Plaintiff and Defendant's contract that arbitration of their labor grievances should be in accordance with section 987 appears to us to be best explained by the fact that the 1957 general statute authorizing arbitration makes no provision for the method in which the arbitrators shall be chosen (except that if the contract fails to provide a method or if a party refuses to proceed under the method agreed upon, resort may be had to the Court for appointment of the arbitrator). It leaves the parties to state in their contracts the method they prefer for selecting arbitrators.

We view the reference to section 987 as the parties' agreement that the arbitrators should be chosen by the method provided in section 987. . . .

Applying the *in pari materia* rule of construction and reading in connection with the Fire Fighters Arbitration Law the 1957 general arbitration statute having the same general purpose, it appears clear that the grant to the fire fighters of "all of the rights of labor other than the right to strike, or engage in any work stoppage or slowdown" found in section 981 included the right to submit grievances to binding arbitration. We hold that the Plaintiff was entitled to submit to arbitration grievances arising under the labor contract and was not limited to the specific issue of formation of a contract.

The Justice in the Superior Court did not reach the issues concerning the validity of the award itself. . . . They remain to be determined in the Superior Court. . . .

## NOTES

1. It has frequently been held that state statutes pertaining to employer-employee relations "must be construed to apply only to private industry, at least until such time as the legislature shows a definite intent to include political subdivisions." Wichita Public Schools Employees Union, Local 513 v. Smith, 194 Kan. 2, 397 P.2d 357 (1964). *See also* Miami Water Works Local 654 v. City of Miami, 157 Fla. 445, 26 So. 2d 194 (1946). The 1957 grievance arbitration statute in the principal case was not made specifically applicable to the public sector. How, then, did the Supreme Court of Maine determine that this statute was applicable to the collective bargaining agreement between the city and the firemen's union? Did the Court rule in effect that the Fire Fighters Arbitration Law was itself sufficient to compel the enforcement of the arbitration award?

2. *In pari materia* means, generally, "on the same subject." Statutes *in pari materia,* according to the rules of statutory construction, are intended by the legislature to be part of a single legislative scheme and are intended to be construed together. Do you think that the Maine legislature intended that the 1957 arbitration law and the Fire Fighters Arbitration Act were to be construed together? Are they part of a "single legislative scheme" or were they enacted to serve altogether different functions?

3. The principal case was cited as authority and a nearly identical result was reached in Providence Teachers Union Local 958 v. School Committee of Providence, 108 R.I. 444, 276 A.2d 762 (1971). Look again at the language of section 981 of the Maine Fire Fighters Arbitration Law, reprinted in the principal case. The court in *Providence Teachers* found that the presence of similar language in the Rhode Island law demonstrated that the state legislature intended public sector unions to have the same rights as other labor organizations, except for those rights specifically withheld. Does the right to bargain collectively necessarily imply the right to enter into contracts providing for the binding arbitration of grievances?

4. Concerning the general subject of grievance arbitration, *see* D. ROTHSCHILD, L. MERRIFIELD & H. EDWARDS, COLLECTIVE BARGAINING AND LABOR ARBITRATION (1979); F. ELKOURI & E. ELKOURI, HOW ARBITRATION WORKS (1973); R. FLEMING, THE LABOR ARBITRATION PROCESS (1965). Regarding grievance arbitration in the public sector, *see*

Frazier, *Labor Arbitration in the Federal Service,* 45 GEO. WASH. L. REV. 712 (1977); Rock, *The Role of the Neutral in Grievance Arbitration in Public Employment* in COLLECTIVE BARGAINING IN GOVERNMENT 141 (J. Loewenberg & M. Moskow eds. 1972); U.S. BUREAU OF LABOR STATISTICS, BULL. NO. 1661, NEGOTIATION IMPASSE, GRIEVANCE, AND ARBITRATION IN FEDERAL AGREEMENTS (1970); Note, *Legality and Propriety of Agreements to Arbitrate Major and Minor Disputes in Public Employment,* 54 CORNELL L. REV. 129 (1968); Krislov & Schmulowitz, *Grievance Arbitration in State and Local Government Units,* 18 ARB. J. 171 (1963); Killingsworth, *Grievance Adjudication in Public Employment,* 13 ARB. J. 3 (1958). *See also* Granof & Moe, *Grievance Arbitration in the U.S. Postal Service: The Postal Service View,* 29 ARB. J. 1 (1974); Cohen, *Grievance Arbitration in the United States Postal Service,* 28 ARB. J. 258 (1973).

# 4. GRIEVANCE AND ARBITRATION AT THE FEDERAL LEVEL: THE ROLE OF THE COMPTROLLER GENERAL

## KAGEL, GRIEVANCE ARBITRATION IN THE FEDERAL SERVICE: HOW FINAL AND BINDING?, 51 Ore. L. Rev. 134, 146-49 (1971)†

As head of the General Accounting Office, the Comptroller General is charged with assuring that public funds are disbursed in accordance with law. By express statute, his office is independent of the executive branch.[27] He is empowered to issue decisions on legal questions asked by agency disbursing officers as well as to audit their accounts. A finding by advance decision that expenditures are lawful is binding on the heads of executive departments and agencies [28] as well as on the Government Accounting Office.[29]

The Comptroller General's advance decisions may be sought whenever a disbursing officer or agency head [30] believes that an advance opinion will shield him from later liability for illegally disbursing government funds, and since such advance permission can be obtained, his decision will presumably be sought before nonroutine government expenditures are made. . . . In 1845 in *United States v. Ames,*[31] the court held that a government officer has no power to bind the United States to an arbitration clause unless authorized by statute. The Comptroller General has consistently rendered decisions which follow *Ames.*[32] . . . The Comptroller General's view of arbitration has adversely affected federal service labor arbitrations. One advisory arbitration decision [33] held that a schedule change by an agency violated its collective bargaining agreement. The decision recommended that employees be compensated for any losses incurred as a result of the violation. The agency then sought a determination by the

---

† Reprinted by permission. Copyright © 1971 by The University of Oregon.

[27] 31 U.S.C. § 41 (1970).

[28] 31 U.S.C. § 44 (1970).

[29] 31 U.S.C. § 74 (1970). *See generally* Comment, *The Control Powers of the Comptroller General,* 56 COLO. L. REV. 1199 (1956).

[30] 31 U.S.C. § 74 (1970).

[31] 24 Fed. Cas. 784, No. 14,411 (C.C. Mass. 1845).

[32] *See generally,* Katzman, *Arbitration in Government Contracts: The Ghost at the Banquet,* 24 ARB. J. 133 (1969); Mosk, *Arbitration in Government,* in ARBITRATION AND PUBLIC POLICY 168 (Proceedings of the Fourteenth Annual Meeting, Nat'l Acad. of Arbitrators, BNA ed. 1961).

[33] Dec. Comptroller Gen. E-163422, Apr. 8, 1971, Current Gov't Emp. Rel. Rep. No. 401, at E-1 (May 17, 1971). This is not an isolated case. *See also* Current Gov't Emp. Rel. Rep. No. 408, at A-10 (July 5, 1971) citing from Dec. Comp. Gen. E-172671 (June 14, 1971), holding to the same effect.

Comptroller General with respect to whether it could comply with the advisory decision. Although the schedule change was a violation of the bargaining agreement, the Comptroller General, relying in part on Executive Order 10,988, § 12 (b) which spells out broad management rights that cannot be bargained away by an agency, held that the agency acted within its right to "maintain the efficiency of government operations." He reasoned that since schedule changes were authorized by regulation, the bargaining agreement therefore authorized changes and the agency acted in accordance with its rights. "[I]t does not appear that the . . . work week . . . established in accordance with . . . regulations . . . would be subject to arbitration." [34] The award, therefore, could not be paid by the agency. . . . Under Executive Orders 10,988 and 11,491, there have been and will be arbitration cases recommending or ordering back pay or other economic relief to employees because of agency agreement violations. Unlike Executive Order 10,988, however, the situation concerning nonadvisory arbitration under Executive Order 11,491 could be interpreted differently by the Comptroller General. Under § 13 (b) of Executive Order 11,491, as amended, agencies can file exceptions to the award with the Federal Labor Relations Council. That section was designed to police arbitration decisions and especially to determine whether decisions comply with applicable law and regulations. Section 13 (b) will, to some extent, provide the same review as the Comptroller General's and should therefore "police" the legality of the award for the Comptroller General. Deference by him to the Federal Labor Relations Council's decision would then be in order.

Other considerations, however, militate against a conclusion that this approach will be adopted. Apparently, an agency or federal officer cannot be precluded by the terms of an Executive Order from appealing to the Comptroller General for his decision with respect to whether payment of any funds required by an arbitration award is proper. In addition, appeal may not be taken to the Council because of failure to comply with requisite time limits. In the cases cited, the Comptroller General, in addition to interpreting the Executive Order, has directly involved himself in the determination of the merits of those cases.

Accordingly, the choice of seeking a Comptroller General's decision gives agencies a second avenue of appeal, one that is possibly more responsive to the agency's view than the arbitrator's decision or the limited appeal to the Federal Labor Relations Council. An appeal to the Comptroller General, in view of the attitude shown to date with respect to arbitration, is apparently a dependable method to overturn virtually all arbitration decisions where monetary relief is granted. The dilemma for the agency is that even if it wanted to comply with such an arbitration decision in good faith, the disbursing agency could find himself in a position where his disbursement would later be disallowed if no advance opinion was sought.

In all future cases in which an agency seeks a determination from the Comptroller General whether to abide by an arbitration award, it is conceivable that payment of otherwise valid awards will be disallowed. The Comptroller General could use § 12 (b) of Executive Order 11,491 to preclude arbitration for most fact situations. Section 12 (b) is broad in scope and could be used to justify any decision the Comptroller General wishes to make.

The Comptroller General's decisions thus pose a difficult obstacle if arbitration is to be an effective process in federal labor relations.

---

[34] Dec. Comptroller Gen. B-163422 (Apr. 8, 1971).

## NOTES

1. The management prerogatives previously defined in section 12(b) of Executive Orders 10988 and 11491 are now codified in Section 7106 of the Civil Service Reform Act of 1978.

**Sec. 7106. Management rights.** — (a) subject to subsection (b) of this section, nothing in this chapter shall affect the authority of any management official of any agency —

(1) to determine the mission, budget, organization, number of employees, and internal security practices of the agency; and

(2) in accordance with applicable laws — (A) to hire, assign, direct, layoff, and retain employees in the agency, or to suspend, remove, reduce in grade or pay, or take other disciplinary action against such employees; (B) to assign work, to make determinations with respect to contracting out, and to determine the personnel by which agency operations shall be conducted; (C) with respect to filling positions, to make selections for appointments from — (i) among properly ranked and certified candidates for promotion; or (ii) any other appropriate source; and (D) to take whatever actions may be necessary to carry out the agency mission during emergencies.

(b) Nothing in this section shall preclude any agency and any labor organization from negotiating—

(1) at the election of the agency, on the numbers, types, and grades of employees or positions assigned to any organizational subdivision, work project, or tour of duty, or on the technology, methods, and means of performing work;

(2) procedures which management officials of the agency will observe in exercising any authority under this section; or

(3) appropriate arrangements for employees adversely affected by the exercise of any authority under this section by such management officials.

Section 7122 of the Civil Service Reform Act provides that either party to a collective bargaining agreement containing a grievance-arbitration procedure may file an exception to an arbitrator's award with the Federal Labor Relations Authority if it believes that the decision is contrary to some law or regulation or is invalid for reasons similar to those applied by federal courts to assess the propriety of private sector grievance arbitration awards. Since one of the principal functions of the Authority is to review such arbitration awards, it is possible, as suggested by Kagel, that the Comptroller General may adopt a policy of deference with respect to decisions of the Authority. However, nothing in the law appears to require this.

2. In Dec. Comptroller Gen. B-175867, GERR No. 460, A-9 (1972), the Comptroller General ruled that there was no authority in federal personnel law which would allow the payment of overtime pay to a Hill Air Force Base employee, who was denied the opportunity to put in eight hours of overtime work in violation of the labor agreement between the Utah base and a union local, despite a favorable ruling on the grievance which the employee later filed.

The applicable clause in the agreement between Hill AFB and American Federation of Government Employees Local 1592, while stating that the administration of overtime is solely a function of management, also provided that "first consideration" for overtime shall be given employees currently assigned to the job in question, and that "second consideration" shall go to those qualified to do the job in the area or function in which overtime work is required. The grievant claimed that the contract had been violated when another man, who was entitled only to "second consideration," worked the overtime instead of the grievant, who had "first consideration" rights. Following a hearing, the Secretary of the Air Force agreed that the contract had indeed been violated, and proposed the payment of the eight hours' overtime as a remedy. Before doing so, however, the agency sought clearance from the Comptroller General. In denying the claim for back pay, the Comptroller General ruled that, "although there appears to have been a violation of . . . the union-management agreement . . . it is our opinion that there is no authority for the payment of overtime compensation in the instant case since no actual work has been performed by the employee."

*See also* Dec. Comptroller Gen. B-190494, GERR No. 760, 4 (1978), wherein an arbitration award was reversed by the Comptroller General, who ruled that time spent by employees on Sunday to travel to a government-sponsored training program which commenced early Monday morning was not compensable.

3. *See generally* U.S.C.S.C./O.L.M.R., Grievance Arbitration in the Federal Service: Principles, Practices and Precedents (1977). *See also* Note, *Arbitration Awards in Federal Sector Public Employment: The Compelling Need Standard of Appellate Review,* 1977 B.Y.U. L. Rev. 429.

4. Section 702 of the Civil Service Reform Act of 1978 *(see Statutory Appendix)* has amended 5 U.S.C. § 5596(b) (1) to provide in relevant part:

> An employee of an agency who, on the basis of a timely appeal or an administrative determination (including a decision relating to an unfair labor practice or a grievance) is found by appropriate authority under applicable law, rule, regulation, or collective bargaining agreement, to have been affected by an unjustified or unwarranted personnel action which has resulted in the withdrawal or reduction of all or part of the pay, allowances, or differentials of the employee — (A) is entitled, on correction of the personnel action, to receive for the period for which the personnel action was in effect — (i) an amount equal to all or any part of the pay, allowances, or differentials, as applicable which the employee normally would have earned or received during the period if the personnel action had not occurred, less any amounts earned by the employee through other employment during that period; . . .

Does this statutory modification restrict the right of the Comptroller General to review arbitration awards which mandate the payment of money to aggrieved employees?

# D. ENFORCEMENT OF VOLUNTARY ARBITRATION AGREEMENTS

## 1. THE PRIVATE SECTOR PRECEDENTS: LINCOLN MILLS AND THE "TRILOGY"

### H. WELLINGTON, LABOR AND THE LEGAL PROCESS 97-100 (1968)†

When Congress enacted the Taft-Hartley Act, it was not centrally concerned with the question of judicial enforcement of the collective agreement. Congressional tolerance for strikes and other types of labor disputes, however, was low, and the strike during contract time was one of the many sorts of union activity that came in for censure. Some thought was given to making any such strike an unfair labor practice; but this was not done. Procedures were erected limiting the union's freedom to strike, and the strike in breach of the collective agreement was itself "left to the usual processes of law" — whatever they might be. The procedural difficulties involved in suing a union because it was an unincorporated association, however, did engage the attention of Congress, and unions were made suable as entities. The legislative process in the end produced a seemingly innocuous section providing in part that: "Suits for violation of contracts between an employer and a labor organization representing employees in an industry affecting commerce . . . may be brought in any district court of the United States having jurisdiction of the parties, without respect to the amount in controversy or without regard to the citizenship of the parties." But this section — 301 of the Labor Management Relations Act — has proved to be far reaching

---

† Reprinted by permission of The Yale University Press.

in its impact. Indeed, the reach given to it by the Supreme Court of the United States is well beyond any that Congress could have foreseen. The law of the collective agreement has been turned around. Today it is one of the most rapidly developing segments of American jurisprudence.

*Textile Workers v. Lincoln Mills* [35] is the case that began this quiet revolution. It was decided by the Supreme Court in 1957, and it grew out of the effort of a union to compel an employer to submit grievances to arbitration. The union brought suit in a federal district court under section 301. It asserted that the employer had promised in the collective agreement to arbitrate grievances which arose during contract time; that he had broken this promise, and that, therefore, the court should order specific performance of the promise to arbitrate. The employer in turn raised some interesting defenses going to the question of whether the court had the power to grant equitable relief in these circumstances.

The first of these defenses relied on the Norris-LaGuardia Act's prohibition against federal courts issuing injunctions in labor disputes. But while an order compelling specific performance is quite properly thought of as a mandatory injunction, it is not the type of injunction which is a central concern of the Norris-LaGuardia Act, and the Supreme Court ultimately had little difficulty in concluding that the anti-injunction statute did not apply in a suit for specific performance of an arbitration promise.[36]

Much less easily resolved, however, was another of the employer's contentions. At common law in most states the promise to arbitrate was not enforceable by an order of specific performance.[37] This was so whether the promise was contained in a commercial contract or in a collective agreement. Theoretically one might recover damages for breach of this promise, but practically one could never show damages. This state rule was also the federal rule.[38] Some states,[39] and the federal government,[40] had legislation which, for some types of contracts at least, changed the common law rule. But the law of the relevant state apparently could not help the union in *Lincoln Mills,* and there was serious doubt whether the United States Arbitration Act applied to arbitration promises in collective bargaining agreements.[41]

Moreover, it was unclear which body of law governed a suit brought under section 301. The statute appeared to be no more than a grant of jurisdiction to the federal courts. It said nothing about the substantive rights of the parties. The early law — what there was of it — on the subject of rights under the collective agreement was, as noted, of state, not federal, origin. Nor was it clear whether the law governing the availability of the equitable remedy of specific performance was the law of the forum or the law which created the cause of action.

---

[35] 353 U.S. 448 (1957).

[36] 353 U.S. at 457-59. . . .

[37] *See, e.g.,* Rowe v. Williams, 97 Mass. 163 (1867). *Cf.* Cogswell v. Cogswell, 70 Wash. 178, 126 P. 431 (1912).

[38] *See* Red Cross Line v. Atlantic Fruit Co., 264 U.S. 109, 120-22 (1924).

[39] The statutes are collected in 4 BNA LABOR RELATIONS REPORTER.

[40] 9 U.S.C. §§ 1-14 (1964).

[41] *Compare* United Furniture Workers v. Colonial Hardwood Flooring Co., 168 F.2d 33 (4th Cir. 1948), *with* Mercury Oil Refining Co. v. Oil Workers Int'l Union, 187 F.2d 980 (10th Cir. 1951) *and* Tenney Engineering Inc. v. United Elec. Workers, 207 F.2d 450 (3rd Cir. 1953).

All of these problems were serious. They had split the lower courts for ten years; they had worried the commentators and disturbed the private orders. All of these serious problems were solved by the Supreme Court in the *Lincoln Mills* case by judicial fiat. No serious attempt was made by that Court to bridge with reasoned elaboration the gap between question and conclusion. The majority opinion is simply an *ipse dixit.*

The Court held that section 301 was a charter to the courts to develop a federal "common law" of the collective bargaining agreement, and that section 301 itself empowered the courts to grant specific performance of the promise to arbitrate.

## R. SMITH & D. JONES, THE SUPREME COURT AND LABOR DISPUTE ARBITRATION: THE EMERGING FEDERAL LAW, 63 Mich. L. Rev. 751, 755-60 (1965)†

The so-called "Trilogy" of 1960 consisted of three cases in which, in each instance, the union involved was the United Steelworkers of America. The cases have been stated, dissected, and critically examined to the point that we now have a wealth of literature concerning them. A brief review of the issues presented and the decisions is, nevertheless, desirable as part of our background recital.

In *Warrior & Gulf,*[42] the grievances brought by the Union protested the contracting out of certain maintenance work clearly encompassed by the bargaining unit. There was a layoff situation at the time the grievances were filed which, in part, was due to the contracting out of such work. The labor agreement was silent on the subject of contracting out; however, it undoubtedly contained recognition, wage, and seniority provisions. The agreement also contained a no-strike provision. Excluded from the arbitration process were matters that were "strictly a function of management," but otherwise the arbitration clause was unusually broad. It stated:

> "Should differences arise between the Company and the Union or its members . . . as to the meaning and application of the provisions of this Agreement, or should any local trouble of any kind arise, there shall be no suspension of work on account of such differences, but an earnest effort shall be made to settle such differences in the following manner [referring to the grievance and arbitration procedure]."

In a suit by the Union under section 301 to compel arbitration, the district court granted the Company's motion to dismiss, holding that the agreement did not confide in an arbitrator the right to review the defendant's business judgment in contracting out work and that contracting out was strictly a function of management within the meaning of the exclusionary language of the arbitration clause. The court of appeals affirmed, but the Supreme Court reversed and the Company was forced to arbitrate.

In *American Manufacturing,*[43] the question was whether the Company was required to submit to arbitration a grievance based on its refusal to reinstate an employee who had suffered an industrial injury. In a consent decree settlement of a workmen's compensation claim, the employee had been awarded a lump-sum payment plus costs on the basis that he had incurred a permanent partial disability of twenty-five per cent. His subsequent demand for reinstatement was predicated

---

† Reprinted by permission of The Michigan Law Review.

[42] United Steelworkers v. Warrior & Gulf Nav. Co., 363 U.S. 574 (1960).

[43] United Steelworkers v. American Mfg. Co., 363 U.S. 564 (1960).

on a statement by his physician (who had supported the earlier claim of permanent partial disability) that the employee "is now able to return to his former duties without danger to himself or to others." Contractually, the demand was based on a provision in the seniority article of the labor agreement which recognized "the principle of seniority as a factor in the selection of employees for promotion, transfer, layoff, re-employment, and filling of vacancies, where ability and efficiency are equal." The arbitration clause was standard in that it permitted arbitration of "any disputes, misunderstandings, differences or grievances arising between the parties as to the meaning, interpretation and application of the provisions of this agreement." The district court and court of appeals refused to require the Company to arbitrate, although they disagreed on the basis of decision. The district court used an estoppel theory; the court of appeals held that estoppel did not go to the question of arbitrability, but it examined the cited seniority provisions and concluded that the grievance was "a frivolous, patently baseless one" and hence not within the arbitration clause. Again, the Supreme Court reversed and ordered arbitration.

In *Enterprise*,[44] the grievance sought the reinstatement of certain employees who had been discharged because they had left their jobs in protest against the discharge of a fellow employee. The Company refused to arbitrate the grievance, but was ordered to do so by a federal district court. The arbitrator's decision reduced the penalty of discharge to a ten-day disciplinary layoff and ordered the grievants reinstated with back pay adjusted for the ten-day penalty. The decision was handed down five days after the labor agreement had expired, and the Company refused to comply with the award on the ground, *inter alia,* that the arbitrator lacked the authority either to order back pay for any period subsequent to the expiration date of the labor agreement or to order reinstatement. The district court directed the Company to comply with the award, but the court of appeals reversed on the ground urged by the Company. The Supreme Court, however, once more upheld the authority of the arbitrator.

Seven Justices concurred in these decisions. Mr. Justice Whitaker dissented, and Mr. Justice Black did not participate. The principal opinion for the majority was written by Mr. Justice Douglas. Mr. Justice Frankfurter did not join in this opinion, but concurred in the results in each case. Justices Brennan and Harlan, while joining the Douglas opinion in each case, also added "a word" in *Warrior & Gulf* and *American Manufacturing.*

The decisions have been viewed as indicating a strong federal policy favoring the arbitration process as a means of resolving disputes concerning the interpretation or application of collective bargaining agreements and as restricting the role of the courts in this area. This interpretation, we think, is correct, although it derives its principal support from the content of the opinions, especially the opinion by Mr. Justice Douglas, rather than from the specific dispositions of the issues presented. . . .

Considering at this point only the 1960 decisions, the following propositions seem to have been declared as a matter of federal substantive law with respect to labor agreements subject to enforcement under section 301 of the Labor Management Relations Act of 1947:

(1) The existence of a valid agreement to arbitrate, and the arbitrability of a specific grievance sought to be arbitrated under such an agreement, are questions for the courts ultimately to decide (if such an issue is presented for

---

44 United Steelworkers v. Enterprise Wheel & Car Corp., 363 U.S. 593 (1960).

judicial determination) unless the parties have expressly given an arbitrator the authority to make a binding determination of such matters.

(2) A court should hold a grievance non-arbitrable under a valid agreement to use arbitration as the terminal point in the grievance procedure only if the parties have clearly indicated their intention to exclude the subject matter of the grievance from the arbitration process, either by expressly so stating in the arbitration clause or by otherwise clearly and unambiguously indicating such intention.

(3) Evidence of intention to exclude a claim from the arbitration process should not be found in a determination that the labor agreement could not properly be interpreted in such manner as to sustain the grievance on its merits, for this is a task assigned by the parties to the arbitrator, not the courts.

(4) An award should not be set aside as beyond the authority conferred upon the arbitrator, either because of claimed error in interpretation of the agreement or because of alleged lack of authority to provide a particular remedy, where the arbitral decision was or, if silent, might have been the result of the arbitrator's interpretation of the agreement; if, however, it was based not on the contract but on an obligation found to have been imposed by law, the award should be set aside unless the parties have expressly authorized the arbitrator to dispose of this as well as any contract issue.[45]

## 2. COMPELLING ARBITRATION

### A.F.S.C.M.E., LOCAL 1226, RHINELANDER CITY EMPLOYEES v. CITY OF RHINELANDER

Supreme Court of Wisconsin
35 Wis. 2d 209, 151 N.W.2d 30 (1967)

HANLEY, Justice.

On December 10, 1964, the plaintiff, Frances Bischoff, was discharged from her job as an administrative assistant in the water department of the city by order of the city mayor. At that time Mrs. Bischoff was a member of the union. The local union was the exclusive bargaining agent for city employees in several city departments, including the water department. The city and the union had a written collective bargaining agreement which in Article X provided [for a grievance procedure concluding in binding arbitration]. . . .

---

[45] *See also Report of Special Warrior & Gulf Committee,* in 1963 PROCEEDINGS OF THE ABA SECTION OF LABOR RELATIONS LAW 196-97, in which the following six general propositions with respect to arbitration under collective bargaining agreements were said to have been established by the Trilogy: "(1) Arbitration is a matter of contract, not of law; parties are required to arbitrate only if, and to the extent that, they have agreed to do so. (2) The question of arbitrability under a collective bargaining agreement is a question for the courts, not for the arbitrator, unless the parties specifically provide otherwise in their agreement. (3) Since arbitration under a collective bargaining agreement is an alternative to strike, rather than to litigation, as in commercial arbitration, the traditional judicial reluctance toward compelling parties to arbitrate is not applicable to labor arbitration. (4) When the parties have provided for arbitration of all disputes as to the application or interpretation of a collective bargaining agreement, the courts should order arbitration of any grievance which claims that management has violated the provisions of the agreement, irrespective of the courts' views as to the merits of the claim. (5) When the parties have coupled with a provision for arbitration of all disputes a clause specifically excepting certain matters from arbitration, the courts should order arbitration of a claim that the employer has violated the agreement unless it may be said with positive assurance that the subject matter falls within the exception clause. (6) An arbitral award should be enforced (absent fraud or similar vitiating circumstance) unless it is clear that the arbitrator has based that award upon matters outside the contract he is charged with interpreting and applying."

Mrs. Bischoff felt that by her discharge her rights and privileges under the collective bargaining agreement had been violated, and submitted the problem to the union grievance committee. The union determined that a grievance existed and processed Mrs. Bischoff's grievance through the first four steps of the Article X proceeding without solution satisfactory to both sides. Thereupon the union chose its member of the arbitration panel as provided in Article X of the collective bargaining agreement. The city refused to choose its member of the arbitration board and refused to follow the procedures set out in the agreement for choosing the third member chairman of the arbitration board.

Mrs. Bischoff and the union commenced this action for specific performance of the arbitration clause of the agreement for Mrs. Bischoff's grievance on her discharge. The city demurred upon the ground that the plaintiffs' complaint failed to state facts sufficient to constitute a cause of action. The trial court sustained the demurrer, basically upon the ground that the city had no statutory authority to enter into a binding arbitration agreement, and that therefore no cause of action will lie to specifically enforce such an agreement. From the judgment sustaining the demurrer, the plaintiffs appeal. . . .

The following issues are presented on this appeal:

1. Is the arbitration clause contained in the collective bargaining agreement binding on the city?

2. If the clause is binding, is it specifically enforceable in the courts?

3. Is the question of whether Mrs. Bischoff was discharged for just cause an arbitrable issue under the agreement?

### 1. Binding effect of the agreement to arbitration.

At the conclusion of the agreement, prior to the signatures of the officials of the city and the union, is the following provision:

"This Agreement shall be binding upon both the Employer and the Union."

The initial question is whether that part of the "agreement," Article X, which provides an arbitration procedure as a final step in the processing of grievances is binding upon the city.

We think it is binding. By sec. 111.70 (4) (i), Stats., the legislature has decreed that written collective bargaining agreements between municipal employers and labor organizations "shall be binding" if they contain express language to that effect. Here we have such an agreement which contains such express language. Thus the contract comes exactly within the provision of the statute and is binding.

### 2. Specific enforceability of the agreement to arbitrate grievances.

In the leading case on the point of enforceability, Local 1111 of United Electrical, Radio & Machine Workers of America v. Allen-Bradley Co. (1951), 259 Wis. 609, 49 N.W.2d 720, this court held that a collective bargaining contract containing provisions for the arbitration of grievances was legal and in full force in Wisconsin, but that without some statutory basis the courts have no power to order an employer to perform its agreement to arbitrate. The basis of the court's opinion was that courts may specifically enforce agreements to arbitrate differences arising under an existing contract only under sec. 298.01, Stats. Since sec. 298.01 specifically does not apply to contracts between employers and employees, except as provided in sec. 111.10, Stats., the court reasoned that the union was not entitled to a judgment requiring the employer to arbitrate.

It should be noted that in Local 1111, etc. v. Allen-Bradley, supra, the court was divided. Mr. Justice CURRIE, joined by Mr. Justice BROADFOOT, dissented on the grounds that Wisconsin courts are not so impotent as to be unable to enforce valid and lawful agreements and that the declaratory judgment statute under which the action was brought authorized the court to grant supplementary relief when necessary and proper.

Mr. Justice CURRIE in his dissenting opinion, at page 618, 49 N.W.2d at page 725, stated:

"I cannot subscribe to the theory that the common law is an inflexible instrument which does not permit growth and adjustment to meet the social needs of the times. This court in the past has repudiated this very theory. Mr. Justice Nelson in his opinion in Schwanke v. Garlt, 219 Wis. 367, 371, 263 N.W. 176, 178, declared:

" 'While we are at all times bound to uphold the Constitution of this state and to give due effect to its paramount provisions, we may not ignore the fact "that the common law is susceptible of growth and adaptation to new circumstances and situations, and that the courts have power to declare and effectuate what is the present rule in respect of a given subject without regard to the old rule.... The common law is not immutable, but flexible, and upon its own principles adapts itself to varying conditions." Dimick v. Schiedt, 293 U.S. 474, 55 S. Ct. 296, 301, 79 L. Ed. 603. To the same effect is Funk v. United States, 290 U.S. 371, 54 S. Ct. 212, 78 L. Ed. 369.' "

We believe the rule that the enforcement of an arbitration provision in a collective bargaining agreement is not enforceable at common law should be repudiated.

The very purpose of grievance arbitration is to prevent individual problems from blossoming into labor disputes which cause strikes and lockouts and which require collective bargaining to restore peace and tranquility.

We now adopt the view expressed by Mr. Justice CURRIE in his dissent in *Local 1111,* supra, and conclude that it is illogical to hold in this case that the arbitration provisions are valid but the court is powerless to enforce them by compelling the city to arbitrate Mrs. Bischoff's grievance, especially in the light of the legislative enactment in sec. 111.70(4) (i), Stats., that "... Such agreements shall be binding. . . ."

The city and the trial court in its decision contend that the legislative history of sec. 111.70(4), Stats., demonstrates that the legislature rejected the use of grievance arbitration as a means of settling disagreements which arise under collective bargaining agreements with municipal employees. Actually, if the legislative history demonstrates anything, it is that the legislature rejected the idea of extending the jurisdiction to the Wisconsin Employment Relations Board to handle or enforce arbitration agreements in municipal employment relations. . . .

### 3. Arbitrability of the discharge.

The city contends that even if Article X of the collective bargaining agreement is binding upon the city, Mrs. Bischoff's discharge is not a grievance subject to arbitration under the terms of that article. The trial court did not consider this question, but the parties have argued it and it is a question of law which the court will consider in order to avoid additional appeals.

According to Article X of the agreement, the following matters are subject to the grievance procedure:

> ". . . differences [which may] arise between the Employer and the Union as to the meaning and application of the provisions of this agreement or as to any question relating to wages, hours, and conditions of employment. . . ."

Article IV of the agreement provides the following with respect to probationary employment:

> "Section 1. New employees without prior service shall be employed on a six (6) months probationary basis, and during said period may be discharged for cause without recourse through the Union."

Mrs. Bischoff was apparently a permanent employee who claims that this section of the agreement, at least by implication, protects her from discharge without cause, and that she was discharged without cause. It would thus seem that Mrs. Bischoff's grievance, processed by the union, can fairly be said to be a difference "as to the meaning and application of the provisions" of the agreement, if not a "question relating to wages, hours, and conditions of employment." Moreover, Mrs. Bischoff felt that her rights and privileges under the agreement were violated by her discharge. The question of her discharge would seem to be arbitrable under sec. 2 of Article X, which in part provides:

> "Should an employee feel that his rights and privileges under this Agreement have been violated he shall first submit the problem to the Union Grievance Committee. If it is determined after investigation by the Union that a grievance does exist it shall be processed in the manner described below: . . . ."

### 4. Arbitration is not an unlawful infringement on the legislative power of the city.

The city has contended that to require the city to submit to binding arbitration is an unlawful infringement upon the legislative power of the city council and a violation of its home rule powers. Yet in all of its arguments the city is talking about arbitration in the collective bargaining context — arbitration to set the terms of a collective bargaining agreement. Such is not this case, which involves arbitration to resolve a grievance arising under an existing agreement to which the city is a party. The legislature has passed statutes doubtless of statewide concern, which provide that the city's agreement to arbitrate grievances is binding on the city.

We conclude that the arbitration clause contained in the collective bargaining agreement is binding upon the city and is specifically enforceable in the courts and that Mrs. Bischoff's discharge is an arbitrable issue under the agreement.

Judgment reversed and cause remanded for further proceedings in conformity with the opinion.

## BOARD OF EDUCATION OF THE TOWNSHIP OF ROCKAWAY v.
## ROCKAWAY TOWNSHIP EDUCATION ASSOCIATION

New Jersey Superior Court
81 L.R.R.M. 2462 (1972)

STAMLER, Judge: — Plaintiff is The Board of Education of the Township of Rockaway in Morris County. Defendants are Rockaway Township Education Association (hereinafter RTEA) and Joseph Youngman, a teacher in the employ of the Board. The Board asks that defendants be enjoined from proceeding before the American Arbitration Association on the question of interference with the "academic freedom" of the teacher in violation of a contract between the Board and RTEA. . . .

On June 23, 1971, the Board and RTEA entered into a contract which provided for the terms and conditions of employment of teachers in the Rockaway Township School District. In February 1972, Youngman, a teacher of Humanities, was directed by the Superintendent of the school district not to conduct in his 7th grade class a previously announced "debate" on the subject of abortion. The 7th grade class is composed of eleven and twelve year old children. . . .

Defendants contend that the preclusion decision of the Superintendent and its affirmance by the Board was a denial of "academic freedom" to defendants and a violation of Article XXVII, Paragraph C of the collective bargaining contract between the parties.

Paragraph C reads as follows:

"The Board and the Association agree that academic freedom is essential to the fulfillment of the purposes of the Rockaway Township School District. Free discussion of controversial issues is the heart of the democratic process. Through the study of such issues, political, economic or social, youth develops those abilities needed for functional citizenship in our democracy. *Whenever appropriate for the maturation level of the group,* controversial issues may be studied in an unprejudiced and dispassionate manner. It shall be the duty of the teacher to foster the study of an issue and not to teach a particular viewpoint in regard to it." (Emphasis supplied.)

Defendants demanded of the Board that the issue of the alleged violation of Article XXVII, Par. C as well as the issue of academic freedom of a member of the teaching staff be processed as a "grievance" before the American Arbitration Association as provided in the contract. Notice of its intention to proceed before the Arbitration Association was given to the Board. The Board filed its complaint seeking an injunction, asserting that the appropriate forum is a proceeding before the Commissioner of Education. . . .

Article III, Paragraph A (1) of the contract defines "grievance" as:

"The term 'grievance' means a complaint by an employee of the Association that, as to him, there has been a personal loss or injury because of an administrative decision affecting said employee, or an unjust application, interpretation or violation of a policy, or agreement. The term 'grievance' and the procedure relative thereto shall not apply to a complaint of a non-tenure teacher which arises by reason of his not being re-employed after only two years on probation."

It is clear that both the Board and RTEA agreed that "academic freedom" is essential to the fulfillment of the purposes of the School District. The heart of the problem is the fourth sentence in the quoted section of Article XXVII (C):

> "Whenever appropriate for the maturation level of the group, controversial issues may be studied in an unprejudiced and dispassionate manner." . . .

To determine "maturation level" requires expertise in education. One proposition upon which the authors of the articles cited above agree: a trial court is not so qualified.

This then places the obligation on either the teacher or the Board or both. When disagreement arises, shall it be settled before a panel selected from the American Arbitration Association or before the Commissioner of Education with review by the State Board of Education and thereafter the Appellate Courts?

The New Jersey Employer-Employee Relations Act, P.L., 1968, Ch. 303, requires a public employer, including a board of education, to negotiate with the majority representative of an appropriate unit of its employees concerning the terms and conditions of employment. Specifically to be negotiated is a grievance procedure. N.J.S.A. 34:13A-53. In N.J.S.A. 34:13A-10 the following appears:

> "Nothing in this act shall be construed to annul or modify, or to preclude the renewal or continuation of any agreement heretofore entered into between any public employer and any employee organization, *nor shall any provision hereof annul or modify any statute or statutes of the state.*" (Emphasis added.)

It cannot be argued, therefore, that Title 18 "Education" insofar as it is concerned with relationship between Boards, teachers *and* pupils has been superseded. Even were this language eliminated from Chapter 303, our Supreme Court has held that the general rule of statutory construction, in the absence of clear legislative direction to the contrary, requires a determination that a later statute will not be deemed to repeal or modify an earlier one, but all existing statutes pertaining to the same subject matter "are to be construed together as a unitary and harmonious whole, in order that each may be fully effective." Clifton v. Passaic County Board of Taxation, 28 N.J. 411, 421 (1958). Thus, the provisions of both Title 18A and Chapter 303 must be read together so that both are harmonized and each is given its appropriate role.

The selection of courses to be presented to students and the subjects to be presented or discussed cannot be a "term or condition of employment." Defendants argue "there can be no doubt that the methods of selecting courses and even more clearly, the procedures and methods by which these courses are to be presented, may be negotiated at least in broad terms." This proposition is untenable.

The Board is responsible for the production of a "thorough and efficient" school system (N.J. Constitution, Art. 8 Sec. 4 P.1) and particularly the statutory obligation to provide "courses of study suited to the ages and attainments of all pupils." N.J.S. 18A:33-1. The Board has a continuing obligation placed upon it by the Legislature to adopt and alter courses of study. . . .

In Porcelli v. Titus, 108 N.J. Super. 301, 2 FEP Cases 344 (App. Div. 1970), cert. denied, 55 N.J. 310 (1970), the following appears at p. 312, 2 FEP Cases at 348:

" 'The public schools were not created, nor are they supported for the benefit of the teachers therein, . . . but for the benefit of the pupils, and the resulting benefit to their parents and the community at large.' "

The courts have recognized that public employees cannot make contracts with public agencies that are contrary to the dictates of the Legislature. Lullo v. International Association of Fire Fighters, 55 N.J. 409, 73 LRRM 2680 (1970). Nor can public agencies such as a board of education "abdicate or bargain away their continuing legislative or executive obligations or discretion." Lullo, supra, 440, 73 LRRM at 2693.

It is concluded therefore that if the contract is read to delegate to a teacher or to a teacher's union the subject of courses of study, the contract in that respect is *ultra vires* and unenforceable. It must follow therefore that the American Arbitration Association cannot be the subdelegee of the Board and of the teachers. Additionally, it is to be noted that the American Arbitration Association may be well qualified to "arbitrate" compensation, hours of work, sick leave, fringe-benefits and the like, but they and their panels possess no expertise in arbitrating the maturation level of a 7th grade student in the elementary schools of Rockaway Township.

However, defendants who were dissatisfied with the action of the Superintendent and the Board are not without a remedy. N.J.S. 18A:6-9 provides that the Commissioner of Education "shall have jurisdiction to hear and determine, without cost to the parties, all controversies and disputes arising under the school laws. . . ." On subsequent appeal, our appellate courts will have the benefit of the special experience of the administrative agencies operating in the vital area of education, especially of the young. . . .

## BOARD OF EDUCATION OF CENTRAL SCHOOL DISTRICT NO. 1, TOWN OF CLARKSTOWN v. CRACOVIA

New York Supreme Court, Appellate Division
36 App. Div. 2d 851, 321 N.Y.S.2d 496 (1971)

In a proceeding to stay arbitration which had been demanded by respondent Clarkstown Teachers' Association, petitioner appeals from an order of the Supreme Court, Rockland County, entered August 20, 1970, which denied the application, granted respondents' cross motion to compel arbitration, directed petitioner to proceed to arbitration and enjoined petitioner from commencing or prosecuting any action with respect to the dispute ordered to be arbitrated.

Order affirmed, with $10 costs and disbursements.

In September, 1969 petitioner entered into a collective bargaining agreement with respondent Clarkstown Teachers' Association effective July 1, 1969 to June 30, 1970. Paragraph (a) of Article XVI of the agreement contained a provision relative to class size which read as follows:

"Maximum Class Sizes — Facilities permitting, for the maximum teacher effectiveness and pupil involvement class sizes will be no larger than (25) twenty-five on the elementary and (27) twenty-seven on the secondary levels."

The agreement also included an extensive grievance procedure in Article XXIII, which contained four separate stages. The fourth and final stage was the arbitration stage which in part stated:

"The decision of the arbitrator shall be final and binding only with respect to grievances concerning the interpretation or application of the specific terms of this Agreement; provided that binding arbitration shall not be had for any grievance concerning provisions of this contract that involve the Board's discretion or right to set policy. In grievances other than those covered in the above sentence, while the decision shall be advisory, each side will have a moral obligation to seriously consider the recommendation."

On January 20, 1970, the Teachers' Association duly served a notice of intention to arbitrate an alleged grievance relating to "Maximum Class Sizes" which remained unresolved after completion of the first three stages of the grievance procedure.

In its petition in this stay proceeding petitioner contended that the provisions of the agreement excerpted above bound it to so-called "advisory arbitration" and not "binding arbitration." Its position is that article 75 of the CPLR does not empower a court to direct parties to arbitrate a dispute which results in an award which can only be advisory in nature. The Teachers' Association cross-moved to compel arbitration.

In our opinion, it is no longer necessary, as it was under section 1448 of the Civil Practice Act, that a contractual dispute be of a justiciable nature before arbitration will be ordered. Such limitation has been expressly removed by the Legislature in its enactment of CPLR 7501 which reads:

"A written agreement to submit any controversy . . . is enforceable without regard to the justiciable character of the controversy."

We can see no compelling reason why article 75 of the CPLR should not be applicable to "advisory arbitration" if that is what the parties intended. Arbitration is a creature of contract and its scope can be very broad or very narrow, depending on the provisions of the contract. At bar, the parties have agreed to submit their disputes to arbitration although additionally agreeing to limit the impact of the arbitrator's award to that of merely an advisory nature in some instances.

We do not now decide whether the posed grievances are subject to an arbitration decision which is binding.

## NOTES

1. If the courts can enforce an agreement to arbitrate, even though the subject matter of the dispute is not justiciable, as in the *Cracovia* case, can the courts enforce the resulting award? *See* Johnson v. Village of Plymouth, 288 Minn. 300, 180 N.W.2d 184 (1970); Schwartz v. North Salem Bd. of Educ., 65 Misc. 2d 472, 318 N.Y.S.2d 774 (Sup. Ct. 1971).

2. *See generally* Note, *Legality and Propriety of Agreements to Arbitrate Major and Minor Disputes in Public Employment,* 54 CORNELL L. REV. 129 (1968); Killingsworth, *Grievance Adjudication in Public Employment,* 13 ARB. J. 3 (1958); Howlett, *Arbitration in the Public Sector,* PROCEEDINGS OF THE SOUTHWESTERN LEGAL FOUNDATION 15TH ANNUAL INSTITUTE ON LABOR LAW 231 (1969).

# 3. DECIDING QUESTIONS OF ARBITRABILITY

## POLICEMEN'S AND FIREMEN'S RETIREMENT BOARD v. SULLIVAN

Connecticut Supreme Court
173 Conn. 1, 376 A.2d 399 (1977)

LONGO, Justice:

Since these cases arise from the same factual situation and since they have been treated as companion cases throughout the course of their development we shall treat them in a single opinion. In the first case the plaintiffs, the Policemen's and Firemen's Retirement Board of the city of New Haven and the city of New Haven, sought an injunction, which was granted by the Superior Court (*Mulvey, J.*), restraining and prohibiting the defendants from initiating or proceeding with arbitration. In the second case, the plaintiffs, New Haven Police Union Local 530 et al., sought an order, which was denied, directing the defendant to proceed with arbitration. The union appealed from both judgments, along with Donald R. Sullivan and James Jackson who appealed with it from the former judgment.

The parties filed a stipulation of facts applicable to both cases from which the following summary may be drawn: Donald R. Sullivan and James Jackson are city of New Haven police officers who suffered injuries in the course of their employment whereupon they applied for disability retirement and were rejected by the Policemen's and Firemen's Retirement Board. Instead, they were offered less strenuous duty, which they refused. The New Haven Police Union Local 530, of which Sullivan and Jackson were members, initiated a grievance pursuant to the procedure provided in an agreement between the city of New Haven and the New Haven Police Union Local 530 and Council 15, AFSCME, AFL-CIO, hereinafter referred to as the agreement, and claimed that the dispute should go to arbitration under the terms of the agreement. The Policemen's and Firemen's Retirement Board of the city of New Haven and the city of New Haven instituted an action in Superior Court seeking an injunction restraining Officers Sullivan and Jackson, the union and the Connecticut Board of Mediation and Arbitration from proceeding with arbitration. The union, on the same date, filed an action to compel the city to proceed with arbitration. The issues posed by these appeals are whether the court erred in ruling that the union was not entitled to an order directing the city to proceed with arbitration and in ruling that the union et al. were enjoined from seeking arbitration.

The first question requiring resolution is whether the issue of the arbitrability of the grievance is a question for the court or for the arbitrator to decide. The determination of this issue requires a preliminary examination of the agreement and the grievance procedure provided therein. The grievance procedure established by article 3 of the agreement consists of a four-step process, the last step of which provides: "If the complainant and his representative, if represented, are not satisfied with the decision rendered, he or his representative may submit the grievance to the Connecticut State Board of Mediation and Arbitration, and the decision rendered by the arbitrator(s) shall be final and binding upon both parties." In order to invoke article 3, the claimant must have a grievance, which is defined by article 3(b) as follows: "A grievance for the purpose of this procedure shall be considered to be an employee or Union complaint concerned with: (1) Discharge, suspension or other disciplinary action. (2) Charge of favoritism or discrimination. (3) Interpretation and application of rules and regulations and policies of the Police Department. (4) *Matters relating to the interpretation and application of the Articles and Sections of this Agreement.*" (Emphasis supplied.) The union et al. seek to reach arbitration through the application of part 4 of article 3(b). They contend that the dispute involves the interpretation or application of the agreement since it involves a determination of the applicability and interpretation of article 15 of the agreement. Article 15 states: "Section 1. Police Pension Plan # 1, and all amendments thereto, shall continue to be the Police Pension for all members of the Department employed prior to December 31, 1957. Section 2. Police Pension Plan # 2, and all amendments thereto, shall continue to be the Police Pension for all members of the Department employed on or after January 1, 1958." If article 15 were intended by the parties to the agreement to incorporate the provisions of the pension plans in the agreement, then it would appear that the determination of the pension claims of Sullivan and Jackson would be matters relating to the interpretation and application of the articles and sections of the agreement. This final issue, however, need not be reached if we decide that the question of arbitrability is enough to send the dispute to arbitration.

The agreement sets forth the boundaries of the disputes the parties have agreed to submit to arbitration in article 3, step 4(e), which states in part: "The arbitrator(s) jurisdiction to make an award shall be limited by the submission and confined to the interpretation and/or application of the provisions of this Agreement." It is clear that by using the broad language of this provision the parties intended to allow submission of legal, as well as factual, questions to the arbitrators. The authority to allow arbitrators to resolve legal questions is clearly established in our law. *United Electrical Radio & Machine Workers v. Union Mfg. Co.,* 145 Conn. 285, 141 A.2d 479; *Colt's Industrial Union v. Colt's Mfg. Co.,* 137 Conn. 305, 77 A.2d 301. Granting the arbitrator's authority to resolve legal questions, however, does not automatically require that the issue of arbitrability go to arbitration. As we stated in the leading case of *Connecticut Union of Telephone Workers v. Southern New England Telephone Co.,* 148 Conn. 192, 197, 169 A.2d 646: "Whether the parties have agreed to submit to arbitration not only the merits of the dispute but the very question of arbitrability, as well, depends upon the intention manifested in the agreement they have made. No one is under a duty to submit any question to arbitration except to the extent that he has signified his willingness." We stated further (p. 198, 169 A.2d p.649): "Whether a dispute is an arbitrable one is a legal question for the court rather than for arbitrators, in the absence of a provision in the agreement giving arbitrators such jurisdiction. The parties may manifest such a purpose by an express provision or by the use of broad terms." Such broad terms were found to exist in a case where the contract called for the submission to arbitration of " '[a]ny dispute that cannot be adjudicated between the Employer and Union' "; *International Brotherhood v. Trudon & Platt Motor Lines, Inc.,* 146 Conn. 17, 20, 147 A.2d 484, 487; and where arbitration was required of "[a]ll questions in dispute and all claims arising out of said contract"; *Liggett v. Torrington Building Co.,* 114 Conn. 425, 430, 158 A. 917, 918. Shortly after we decided *Connecticut Union of Telephone Workers v. Southern New England Telephone Co.,* supra, we decided *International Union v. General Electric Co.,* 148 Conn. 693, 174 A.2d 298, in which we applied the controlling federal law as declared in *United Steelworkers of America v. American Mfg. Co.,* 363 U.S. 564, 80 S.Ct. 1343, 4 L.Ed.2d 1403, and *United Steelworkers of America v. Warrior & Gulf Navigation Co.,* 363 U.S. 574, 80 S.Ct. 1347, 4 L.Ed.2d 1409, to a dispute involving interstate commerce. We quoted from *Warrior,* supra, 582,

80 S.Ct. 1347, the rule that "the judicial inquiry [as to the scope of an arbitration clause in a labor management contract] . . . must be strictly confined to the question whether the reluctant party did agree to arbitrate the grievance . . .. An order to arbitrate the particular grievance should not be denied unless it may be said with positive assurance that the arbitration clause is not susceptible of an interpretation that covers the asserted dispute. Doubts should be resolved in favor of coverage." *International Union v. General Electric Co.,* supra, 148 Conn. 700-701, 174 A.2d 302. Though it was our duty in that case, and in *Hudson Wire Co. v. Winsted Brass Workers Union,* 150 Conn. 546, 191 A.2d 557, to apply the federal rule; *Textile Workers Union v. Lincoln Mills,* 353 U.S. 448, 456, 77 S.Ct. 912, 1 L.Ed.2d 972; this court has subsequently indicated its approval of application of the *Warrior* rule to situations in which Connecticut law applied. In the recent case of *Board of Police Commissioners v. Maher,* 171 Conn. 613, 621, 370 A.2d 1076, 1080, in ruling that the board of mediation and arbitration was authorized by the agreement presently under consideration to arbitrate a grievance concerning disciplinary action against a New Haven police officer, this court stated: "[T]he trial court correctly concluded that the bargaining agreement conferred on the defendant board the authority to arbitrate disciplinary grievances. *International Brotherhood v. Trudon & Platt Motor Lines, Inc.,* 146 Conn. 17, 21, 147 A.2d 484; *Pratt, Read & Co. v. United Furniture Workers,* 136 Conn. 205, 209, 70 A.2d 120. This is especially true since any '[d]oubts [concerning arbitrability] should be resolved in favor of coverage.' *United Steelworkers of America v. Warrior & Gulf Navigation Co.,* 363 U.S. 574, 583, 80 S.Ct. 1347, 1353, 4 L.Ed.2d 1409; *International Union v. General Electric Co.,* 148 Conn. 693, 701, 702, 174 A.2d 298." Despite our acceptance of the federal rule favoring arbitration, we are unpersuaded that the language of this agreement requires that we send the question of the arbitrability of the dispute to arbitration. The question of arbitrability is not one which requires a court to interject its presence into the merits of a labor dispute. Rather, the question of arbitrability is purely a question of contract interpretation in which courts have expertise and an historically established role to play. Indeed, in discussing the leading federal case of *United Steelworkers of America v. Warrior & Gulf Navigation Co.,* supra, the United States Supreme Court stated that pursuant to a grievance procedure submitting to arbitration "all disputes between the parties 'as to the meaning, interpretation and application of the provisions of this agreement' "; *United Steelworkers of America v. American Mfg. Co.,* supra, 363 U.S. 565, 80 S.Ct. 1345; the question of arbitrability should be resolved by the court. The court stated in *Warrior,* supra, 583 n. 7: "It is clear that under both the agreement in this case and that involved in [*United Steelworkers of America v.*] *American Manufacturing Co.* [363 U.S. 564, 80 S.Ct. 1343, 4 L.Ed.2d 1403], the question of arbitrability is for the courts to decide. Cf. Cox, Reflections Upon Labor Arbitration, 72 Harv.L.Rev. 1482, 1508-1509. Where the assertion by the claimant is that the parties excluded from court determination not merely the decision of the merits of the grievance but also the question of its arbitrability, vesting power to make both decisions in the arbitrator, the claimant must bear the burden of a clear demonstration of that purpose." We can find no such clear demonstration in the present case where the arbitrator's power is "limited by the submission and confined to the interpretation and/or application of the provisions of this Agreement."

Having determined that the court was correct in ruling that it had the authority to decide whether the dispute should go to arbitration, we must now turn to the issue whether it properly decided that issue against sending the dispute to arbitration. By requesting the lower court to issue an injunction restraining the union et al. from proceeding with arbitration, the plaintiffs were, in effect, asking the court to interpret the substantive provisions of the agreement. As the court stated in *United Steelworkers of America v. Warrior & Gulf Navigation Co.,* supra, 363 U.S. 585, 80 S.Ct. 1354: "[T]he court should view with suspicion an attempt to persuade it to become entangled in the construction of the substantive provisions of a labor agreement." We are also mindful of the court's distinction in *Warrior,* supra, 578, 80 S.Ct. 1351, between arbitration of commercial and labor disputes. The court stated: "In the commercial case, arbitration is the substitute for litigation. Here arbitration is the substitute for industrial strife. Since arbitration of labor disputes has quite different functions from arbitration under an ordinary commercial agreement, the hostility evinced by courts toward arbitration of commercial agreements has no place here. For arbitration of labor disputes under collective bargaining agreements is part and parcel of the collective bargaining process itself." This court must, therefore, look carefully at any order which seeks to interject a judicial body into the functioning of the collective bargaining process. As we stated in *Waterbury Board of Education v. Waterbury Teachers Assn.,* 168 Conn. 54, 64, 357 A.2d 466, 471: "Arbitration is a creature of contract. *Connecticut Union of Telephone Workers v. Southern New England Telephone Co.,* 148 Conn. 192, 197, 169 A.2d 646. The continued autonomy of that process can be maintained only with a minimum of judicial intrusion."

Under the grievance procedure established by the agreement "[m]atters relating to the interpretation and application of the Articles and Sections of this Agreement" are considered grievances subject to arbitration under step four of the grievance procedure. Since there is no claim that the parties have not complied with the procedural requirements of the grievance procedure, the only question confronting us is whether there is doubt that the dispute should not go to arbitration. If there is any doubt, the issue must be resolved in favor of arbitration. *Board of Police Commissioners v. Maher,* supra.

We conclude that the trial court did not err in deciding that the parties did not intend that disputes involving disability retirement should be the subject of arbitration under the procedure established by article 3 of the agreement. Those seeking arbitration argue that the parties to the agreement, by agreeing to article 15 of the agreement, intended to incorporate the provisions of the two police pension plans mentioned therein into the agreement. We do not agree. Article 15 merely states which pension plans shall apply to which employees and states nothing about the provisions of either. Further, the pension plans were not established by the agreement, but were created by Special Act. The police officers, Sullivan and Jackson, fall into the category of employees covered by Special Acts 1957, No. 531, entitled "An Act Establishing a Pension Fund for New Haven Policemen and Firemen Employed after December 31, 1957." Section 2 of No. 531 of the 1957 Special Acts states, in part: "The management and administration of the pension plan are hereby vested in a pension board, which shall consist of seven members." The pension board is a distinct entity which was not made a party to the agreement and could not, therefore, have agreed to grant its powers to an arbitrator, who derives his powers from the agreement. Further, the provisions of article 15 of the agreement may be compared to those of article 17, § 1, of the agreement by which "[t]he City agrees to continue to provide for the member and his enrolled dependents, at no cost to the employee, the Blue Cross Semi-Private Room Plan with the Maternity Care Rider, Major Medical insurance coverage and the CMS Community Plan." Clearly, the parties, by agreeing to article 17, did not intend to allow the submission to arbitration of claims by covered employees which had been disallowed by Blue Cross, CMS or the major medical carrier. The pension plans are not incorporated by reference nor are they set forth verbatim in the agreement. It is, therefore, impossible to say that the substantive provisions of the pension plans were made part of the agreement or that the parties signified their willingness to submit pension disputes to arbitration. As stated before: "No one is under a duty to submit any question to arbitration except to the extent that he has signified his willingness." *Connecticut Union of Telephone Workers v. Southern New England Telephone Co.*, supra, 148 Conn. 197, 169 A.2d 649. Therefore, since the city did not signify its willingness to submit such disputes to arbitration, the court properly denied the application of Local 530 and Council 15 for an order directing the city to proceed with arbitration.

. . . .

[The final portion of the opinion sustained the lower court's order enjoining the parties from proceeding with arbitration of the dispute.]

LOISELLE, Justice (dissenting):

These consolidated appeals present two questions. The first is: Does the contract at issue here assign to the arbitrators the duty of *deciding* which disputes are arbitrable, or is that decision one for the courts? I agree with the majority opinion that this contract does not assign that duty to the arbitrators. The arbitration clause requires arbitration of "[m]atters relating to the interpretation and application of the Articles and Sections of this Agreement." I understand that we have decided to follow the United States Supreme Court in arbitration matters. The language of this arbitration clause tracks that of a contract which the United States Supreme Court held left the *decision* as to which disputes are arbitrable to the courts. The language in that contract required arbitration of all disputes " 'as to the meaning, interpretation and application of the provisions of this agreement.' " *United Steelworkers of America v. American Mfg. Co.*, 363 U.S. 564, 565, 80 S.Ct. 1343, 1345, 4 L.Ed.2d 1403.

Once the decision as to which disputes are arbitrable has been determined to be one for the court to make, the second question arises: Is *this* dispute arbitrable? It is in answering this question that I disagree with the majority. If we follow the United States Supreme Court, and apply the same test it applied in *United Steelworkers of America v. American Mfg. Co.*, supra, this dispute is arbitrable.

*United Steelworkers of America v. American Mfg. Co.*, supra, involved a grievance which the Court of Appeals had determined to be frivolous and patently baseless, thus not subject to arbitration. The Supreme Court reversed, holding that even frivolous, baseless claims must go to arbitration if "the party seeking arbitration is making a claim which on its face is governed by the contract." Id., 568, 80 S.Ct. 1346. The Court explained: "The courts . . . have no business weighing the merits of the grievance, considering whether there is equity in a particular claim, or determining whether there is particular language in the written instrument which will support the claim. . . . The processing of even frivolous claims may have therapeutic values of which those who are not a part of the plant environment may be quite unaware." Ibid. I submit that the majority opinion weighs the merits and looks for language in the written instrument to support the claim.

The grievance in this case is a claim by the union that the "contract provided for a review of the orders and decision of the Policemen's and Firemen's Retirement Board." The majority tests the arbitrability of the dispute by asking whether the agreement incorporated the provisions of the police pension plans, or whether the parties signified their willingness to submit *pension disputes* to arbitration. I think those are the wrong yardsticks. The contract clearly indicates the willingness of the parties to submit to arbitration disputes concerning the application and interpretation of the contract, and one party has asserted that the contract should be interpreted to provide for review of the decision of the pension board. This is a dispute concerning interpretation of the contract, and it must go to arbitration.

Applying the test of *United Steelworkers of America v. American Mfg. Co.,* supra, "whether the party seeking arbitration is making a claim which on its face is governed by the contract," it is clear that this claim, that the contract provides for review, is determined *by the contract.* The fact that examination of the contract shows that no review is provided for does not make the dispute less arbitrable, but more arbitrable. This is a claim not governed by statute, by general contract law or, indeed, by any authority other than the contract itself. Only by looking *to the contract* may its validity or lack of validity be seen.

. . . .

## ACTING SUPERINTENDENT v. UNITED LIVERPOOL FACULTY ASSOCIATION

Court of Appeals of New York
42 N.Y.2d 509, 369 N.E.2d 746 (1977)

JONES, Judge:

We hold that in arbitrations which proceed under the authority of the Taylor Law, the scope of the particular arbitration clause, and thus whether the question sought to be submitted to arbitration is within or without the ambit of that clause, is to be determined by the courts. In making such determinations the courts are to be guided by the principle that the agreement to arbitrate must be express, direct and unequivocal as to the issues or disputes to be submitted to arbitration; anything less will lead to a denial of arbitration.

In this case Liverpool Central School District and the United Liverpool Faculty Association entered into a collective bargaining agreement which provided a grievance procedure, the fourth and final step of which called for submission of an unresolved grievance to arbitration. Tracking the provisions of subdivision 4 of section 682 of the General Municipal Law, the school district and the faculty association defined a grievance as follows: "*Grievance* shall mean any claimed violation, misinterpretation, or inequitable application of the existing laws, rules, procedures, regulations, administrative orders or work rules of the District, which relates to or involves Teachers' health or safety, physical facilities, materials or equipment furnished to teachers or supervision of Teachers; provided, however, that such term shall not include any matter involving a Teacher's rate of compensation, retirement benefits, disciplinary proceeding or any matter which is otherwise reviewable pursuant to law or any rule or regulation having the force and effect of law."

In November, 1974, Mrs. Lorraine Gargiul, an elementary school teacher, was obliged to take sick leave due to illness. In February, 1975 she notified the school district that she would be able to return to her teaching duties the following month. On February 26 she was advised that pursuant to the provisions of section 913 of the Education Law she would be required to submit to a complete medical examination by the school district physician, Dr. Paul Day, before being permitted to return to the classroom. The teacher took the position that she would participate only in an examination by a female physician. Following further correspondence of similar tenor, on March 17, 1975 the board of education passed a resolution directing her to be examined by Dr. Day before returning to her teaching responsibilities, if, after reviewing her health history, he determined that such examination was necessary. On the same day, based on the teacher's refusal to be examined by Dr. Day, she was placed on leave of absence without pay until the matter was resolved.

On April 10, 1975 the faculty association instituted grievance procedures on behalf of Mrs. Gargiul. When the issue was not resolved, the faculty association demanded arbitration in accordance with the provisions of the collective bargaining agreement. The school district promptly applied for a stay of arbitration which was granted at Special Term. The Appellate Division reversed. We now reverse the determination of that court and reinstate the disposition of Special Term.

It will be useful to place this case, and indeed all arbitration under the Taylor Law, in a broader context. Generally speaking, as the law of arbitration between private parties has developed and progressed, a difference in perspective and approach has evolved between arbitration in commercial matters and arbitration in labor relations. In the former it is the rule that the parties will not be held to have chosen arbitration as the forum for the resolution of their disputes in the absence of an express, unequivocal agreement to that effect; absent such an explicit commitment neither party may be compelled to arbitrate (*Gangel v. DeGroot,* 41 N.Y.2d 840, 841, 393 N.Y.S.2d 698, 699, 362 N.E.2d 249, 250; *Matter of Riverdale Fabrics Corp. [Tillinghast-Stiles Co.],* 306 N.Y. 288, 289, 292, 118 N.E.2d 104, 105, 106). In the field of labor relations, by contrast, the general rule is the converse. Because of the recognition that arbitration has been demonstrated to be a salutary method of resolving labor disputes, because of the public policy (principally expressed in the Federal cases) which favors arbitration as a means of resolving such disputes, and because of the associated available inference that the parties to a collective bargaining agreement probably intended to resolve their differences by arbitration, the courts have held that controversies arising between the parties to such an agreement fall within the scope of the arbitration clause unless the parties have employed language which clearly manifests an intent to exclude a particular subject matter (*Matter of Howard & Co. v. Daley,* 27 N.Y.2d 285, 289-290, 317 N.Y.S.2d 326, 329-331, 265 N.E.2d 747, 749-751; *Matter of Long Is. Lbr. Co. [Martin],* 15 N.Y.2d 380, 385, 259 N.Y.S.2d 142, 146, 207 N.E.2d 190, 193).[1]

Arbitration agreements that derive their vitality from the Taylor Law (Civil Service Law, art. 14) are sufficiently different that they cannot properly be categorized under either of these headings. Initially we observe that our court has never held that boards of education, unless authorized by specific legislation, are free to delegate to arbitrators the resolution of issues for which the boards have official responsibility. The enactment of the Taylor Law, establishing authority for the use of voluntary arbitration, confirmed rather than vitiated the principle of the nondelegable responsibility of elected representatives in the

---

[1] In our view the not infrequent reference to a "presumption of arbitrability", while understandable, does not advance analysis and indeed in some instances serves rather to obfuscate. In the field of labor relations, however, experience has demonstrated that an inference may usually be drawn that the signatories to a collective bargaining agreement between private parties intended to submit their differences to arbitration.

public sector. Hence, we approach consideration of the scope of arbitration clauses in public employment from this perspective.

When challenge is raised to the submission to arbitration of a dispute between employer and employee in the public sector the threshold consideration by the courts as to whether there is a valid agreement to arbitrate (CPLR 7503, subd. [a]) must proceed in sequence on two levels. Initially it must be determined whether arbitration claims with respect to the particular subject matter are authorized by the terms of the Taylor Law. The permissible scope of arbitration under that law is variously limited (*Matter of Susquehanna Val. Cent. School Dist. at Conklin [Susquehanna Val. Teacher's Assn.], 37* N.Y.2d 614, 616-617, 376 N.Y.S.2d 427, 428-430, 339 N.E.2d 132, 133-134; *Syracuse Teachers Assn. v. Board of Educ.,* 35 N.Y.2d 743, 744, 361 N.Y.S.2d 912, 320 N.E.2d 646; *Board of Educ. v. Associated Teachers of Huntington,* 30 N.Y.2d 122, 130, 331 N.Y.S.2d 17, 23, 282 N.E.2d 109, 113). If, of course, the subject matter of the dispute between the parties falls outside the permissible scope of the Taylor Law, there is no occasion further to consider the language or the reach of the particular arbitration clause (*Matter of Candor Cent. School Dist. [Candor Teachers Assn.],* 42 N.Y.2d 266, 397 N.Y.S.2d 737, 366 N.E.2d 826; *Matter of Cohoes City School Dist. v. Cohoes Teachers Assn.,* 40 N.Y.2d 774, 390 N.Y.S.2d 53, 358 N.E.2d 878).

If it is concluded, however, that reference to arbitration is authorized under the Taylor Law, inquiry then turns at a second level to a determination of whether such authority was in fact exercised and whether the parties did agree by the terms of their particular arbitration clause to refer their differences in this specific area to arbitration. In the field of public employment, as distinguished from labor relations in the private sector, the public policy favoring arbitration — of recent origin — does not yet carry the same historical or general acceptance, nor, as evidenced in part by some of the litigation in our court, has there so far been a similar demonstration of the efficacy of arbitration as a means for resolving controversies in governmental employment. Accordingly, it cannot be inferred as a practical matter that the parties to collective bargaining agreements in the public sector always intend to adopt the broadest permissible arbitration clauses. Indeed, inasmuch as the responsibilities of the elected representatives of the tax-paying public are overarching and fundamentally nondelegable, it must be taken, in the absence of clear, unequivocal agreement to the contrary, that the board of education did *not* intend to refer differences which might arise to the arbitration forum. Such reference is not to be based on implication.

We turn then to the appeal now before us to make the necessary judicial determinations both with respect to Taylor Law authorization and as to the scope of this arbitration clause, i.e., whether Mrs. Gargiul's present complaint falls within the contract definition of grievance. We have no difficulty at the first level in concluding that there is nothing in statute, decisional law or public policy which would preclude the board of education, acting in behalf of the district, and the association, should they agree to do so, from referring disputes of the present nature to arbitration.

At the second level, we address the particular language employed by the parties for the articulation of their agreement to arbitrate. Surely their definition of grievances does not approach the breadth of provisions which in other contexts are referred to as "broad arbitration clauses". This clause is explicitly a limited one. Indeed in form it expresses two separate agreements. First, the parties agree that certain disputes ("claimed violation, misinterpretation or inequitable application of existing laws, rules, procedure, regulations, administrative orders or work rules of the District which relate to or involve Teachers' health or safety, physical facilities, materials or equipment furnished to teachers or supervision of Teachers") shall be submitted to arbitration. In the same paragraph they then agree that other disputes shall not be referred to arbitration ("any matter involving a Teacher's rate of compensation, retirement benefits, disciplinary proceeding").[2] Thus, the question is not to determine the outer boundaries of a single definition; the problem is rather to determine into which of two different classifications the present dispute falls, or more precisely in this instance, how it shall be treated when it may reasonably be included within both groups.

As is evident from the arguments pressed by the parties, as well as from the decisions in the courts below, the present controversy could be classified both in surface description and substantive context in either category. On the one hand, although contending principally that the issue of arbitrability is for the arbitrator and not for the courts, the faculty association has labeled the board's action a claimed violation or inequitable application of existing laws and rules relating to the teacher's health, thus in the included category. On the other hand, the school district classifies the dispute as a matter involving disciplinary proceedings, in the excluded category. The labels attached by the parties, each evidently for its own advantage, can never be determinative. A very reasonable assertion can be made that this particular controversy falls within both the included and the excluded categories.

In this circumstance, we cannot conclude that the present dispute falls clearly and unequivocally within the class of claims agreed to be referred to arbitration. Accordingly, the application of the school district for a stay of arbitration was properly granted.

For the reasons stated, the order of the Appellate Division should be reversed, without costs, and the order of Supreme Court, Onondaga County, reinstated. [The concurring opinion of Gabrielli, J., is omitted.]

## NOTES

1. Courts appear to be more willing to declare a dispute non-arbitrable in the public sector than in the private sector. This phenomenon has probably resulted because governmental employers are generally considered to retain broader discretion and "management rights" to control the employment relationship than are their private sector counterparts. In addition, collective agreements in the public sector are likely to exclude in specific terms more subjects from arbitration, and statutes and public policy considerations often reserve other areas for final decision by management alone. *See generally* Toole, *Judicial Activism in Public Sector Grievance Arbitration: A Study of Recent Developments,* 33 ARB. J. 6 (1978).

2. In Kaleva-Norman-Dickson School Dist. v. Teachers Ass'n, 227 N.W.2d 500, 89 L.R.R.M. 2078 (1975), the Michigan Supreme Court adopted the private sector presumption of arbitrability in holding that even though a school board in a negotiated agreement had reserved to itself without limitation all statutory powers vested in it, including the right to hire all employees and to determine the conditions of their continued employment or their dismissal, where the contract required the arbitration of claims concerning the violation or misinterpretation of any provision and provided that no teacher could be reduced in rank or compensation without just cause, a probationary teacher's claim that the nonrenewal of her contract violated the agreement was subject to arbitration. The Pennsylvania Supreme Court has similarly ruled that just cause for the

---

[2] No claim is made that the present dispute falls within the very broad category of "any matter which is otherwise reviewable pursuant to law".

dismissal of a non-tenured teacher is arbitrable and that such a contractual provision does not constitute an impermissible delegation of school board authority to the arbitrator. Philadelphia Bd. of Educ. v. Teachers Local 3, 346 A.2d 35, 90 L.R.R.M. 2879 (1975). Other courts, however, have determined that since decisions regarding the retention or nonrenewal of non-tenured teachers fall within the exclusive competence of school boards, public policy considerations dictate that disagreements concerning such judgments are not subject to grievance arbitration. *See, e.g.,* Moravek v. Davenport Community School Dist., 262 N.W.2d 797, 1977-78 PBC ¶ 36,182 (Iowa 1978); Chassie v. School Dist., 356 A.2d 708, 92 L.R.R.M. 3359 (Me. 1976). *See also* Wibaux Educ. Ass'n v. Wibaux High School, 573 P.2d 1162, 97 L.R.R.M. 2592 (1978), wherein the Montana Supreme Court indicated that while decisions regarding the continuation of probationary teachers would not themselves be arbitrable, a claim that a school district failed to comply properly with contractually specified evaluation or hearing procedures would be subject to arbitration.

Should disputes pertaining to the modification of a teacher's extra-curricular activities be subject to arbitration? *See* Napoleon Bd. of Educ. v. Anderson, 240 N.W.2d 262, 92 L.R.R.M. 2681 (Mich. Ct. App. 1976); Port Washington Union Free School Dist. v. Teachers Ass'n, 45 N.Y.2d 411, 380 N.E.2d 280 (1978).

3. In Bd. of Police Commissioners of New Haven v. White, 171 Conn. 553, 370 A.2d 1070 (1976), and Bd. of Police Commissioners of New Haven v. Maher, 171 Conn. 613, 370 A.2d 1076 (1976), the Connecticut Supreme Court held that police officers discharged for misconduct were entitled to invoke the grievance-arbitration procedures contained in the applicable bargaining agreement between the City and the Connecticut Council of Police Unions. The court indicated that the employer's "positive duty" to bargain about discipline and discharge matters altered the managerial right of the Board of Police Commissioners to suspend and terminate employees. In *White,* the Court found no serious conflict between charter provisions giving the employer disciplinary authority and a contract providing for the arbitration of discharge grievances. The Court also noted that the General Statutes provide that collective bargaining agreements shall supersede charters when there is a conflict. In *Maher,* the Court ruled that while the state mediation board lacked the automatic jurisdiction to hear grievance arbitrations, it could do so when so authorized in a contract. However, its arbitration authority would be "strictly limited by the contract." *But cf.* AFSME Council 23, Local 1905 v. Recorder's Court Judges, 248 N.W.2d 220, 94 L.R.R.M 2392 (1976), wherein the Michigan Supreme Court held that Recorder's Court judges who complied with the probation officer removal statute were not required to arbitrate an officer's discharge grievance under the grievance-arbitration procedures of the applicable bargaining agreement, since such specific statutory procedures controlled exclusively, despite any conflict with P.E.R.A. obligations.

4. When a permissive subject for bargaining is included in a negotiated agreement that contains a broad grievance-arbitration provision, the representative labor organization may be able to obtain arbitration of disputes pertaining to that non-mandatory topic. *See, e.g.,* Minneapolis Teachers Fed'n v. School Dist., 258 N.W.2d 802, 96 L.R.R.M. 2706 (Minn. 1977) (teacher transfers); Susquehanna Valley Central School Dist. v. Teachers Ass'n, 37 N.Y.2d 614, 339 N.E.2d 132 (1975) (staff reduction). However, other courts have indicated that contractual disputes relating to such non-mandatory items are not arbitrable, particularly where matters of basic government policy are involved. *See, e.g.,* Ridgefield Park Educ. Ass'n v. Bd. of Educ., 393 A.2d 278, 98 L.R.R.M. 3285 (N.J. 1978); Dunellen Bd. of Educ. v. Educ. Ass'n, 64 N.J. 17, 311 A.2d 737 (1973). *See also* School Committee of Portland v. Teachers Ass'n, 338 A.2d 155, 90 L.R.R.M. 2597 (1975), where the Maine Supreme Judicial Court set aside an arbitrator's award concerning a permissive issue, since the contractual language covering class size provided "Nothing in this Article shall be construed to be a contractual obligation on the part of the Committee" and "This Article shall not be subject to the grievance procedure contained therein."

5. Because of a financial crisis, the New York legislature passed a special law in 1971 prohibiting the granting of sabbatical leaves to public employees. In Central School Dist. No. 2 v. Ramapo Central School Dist. No. 2 Teachers Ass'n, 67 Misc.2d 317, 324 N.Y.S.2d 260 (Sup. Ct. 1971), *aff'd.,* 40 App.Div.2d 861, 388 N.Y.S.2d 399 (1972), the questions presented to the Rockland County Supreme Court were whether certain teachers had

enforceable contractual rights to sabbatical leave before the new law took effect and whether the court or the grievance arbitrator should decide the issue. The court granted the petition to stay arbitration, concluding:

> The Court fully subscribes to the line of cases which encourage the arbitration of disputes arising under collective bargaining agreements. However, where a major public policy is involved, as expressed in section 82, the Court is of the opinion that the public interest requires that issues of law and of fact as to the application of such legislation should be resolved by a Court rather than an arbitrator.

*Cf.* Southbridge School Committee v. Brown, 377 N.E.2d 935, 98 L.R.R.M. 3178 (Mass. 1978), where the Court indicated that while a school committee's contractually recognized discretionary authority over sabbatical leaves was not itself subject to arbitration, a claim that the denial of a particular sabbatical request violated a provision prohibiting the "inequitable or unfair application" of any contract term was arbitrable.

6. In the private sector, issues concerning "procedural arbitrability" are generally held to be matters to be decided by the arbitrator, not the court. In John Wiley & Sons v. Livingston, 376 U.S. 543, 557-58, 84 S.Ct. 909, 11 L.Ed.2d 898 (1964), it was held that:

> Once it is determined . . . that the parties are obligated to submit the subject matter of a dispute to arbitration, "procedural" questions which grow out of the dispute and bear on its final disposition should be left to the arbitrator. Even under a contrary rule, a court could deny arbitration only if it could confidently be said not only that a claim was strictly "procedural," and therefore within the purview of the court, but also that it should operate to bar arbitration altogether, and not merely limit or qualify an arbitral award. In view of the policies favoring arbitration and the parties' adoption of arbitration as a preferred means of settling disputes, such cases are likely to be rare indeed. In all other cases, those in which arbitration goes forward, the arbitrator would ordinarily remain free to reconsider the ground covered by the Court insofar as it bore on the merits of the dispute, using the flexible approaches familiar to arbitration. Reservation of "procedural" issues for the courts would thus not only create the difficult task of separating related issues, but would also produce frequent duplication of effort.

In essence, the basis of the *Wiley* decision on this issue was that the "procedural disagreements," to use the Court's term, constitute aspects of the merits of the dispute and that such matters should usually be decided by arbitrators, not courts. Such arbitral deference regarding procedural arbitrability issues is generally followed in the public sector too. *See, e.g.,* West Fargo School Dist. v. Educ. Ass'n, 259 N.W.2d 612, 97 L.R.R.M. 2361 (N. Dak. 1977); Duquesne School Dist. v. Educ. Ass'n, 380 A.2d 353, 97 L.R.R.M. 2011 (Pa. 1977).

7. In Director of the Div. of Employee Relations v. Labor Relations Commission, 346 N.E.2d 852, 2 PBC ¶ 20,392 (1976), the Massachusetts Supreme Judicial Court ruled that the Labor Relations Commission erred in ordering a public employer and a union to submit a dispute concerning a "hiring freeze" to arbitration where neither the employer nor the union had sought arbitration under their bargaining agreement, since without a request from the parties, the Commission had no authority to compel arbitration under the state labor relations statute.

8. Should a grievance arising *after* the expiration date of the relevant agreement be arbitrable? *Compare* I.R.S. Brookhaven Center, A/SLMR No. 859 (6/29/77), GERR No. 722, 7 (arbitrable), *with* City of White Plains v. Professional Fire Fighters Ass'n, 95 L.R.R.M. 3150 (N.Y. Sup. Ct. 1977), and PLRB v. Williamsport Area School Dist., 370 A.2d 1241, 94 L.R.R.M. 3130 (Pa. Commonwealth Ct. 1977) (not arbitrable). *See also* Nolde Bros. v. Local 358, Bakery & Confectionery Workers Union, 430 U.S. 243, 97 S.Ct. 1067, 51 L.Ed.2d 300 (1977), wherein the Supreme Court held arbitrable a private sector severance pay dispute that did not arise until after the expiration of the controlling contract. Can a stronger argument be made to support post-expiration arbitrability in the public sector, since most governmental employees, unlike their private sector counterparts, cannot strike to enhance their claims even after the bargaining agreement has expired?

# 4. JUDICIAL REVIEW OF ARBITRATION AWARDS

## LEECHBURG AREA SCHOOL DISTRICT v. LEECHBURG EDUCATION ASSOCIATION

Pennsylvania Supreme Court
380 A.2d 1203, 97 L.R.R.M. 2133 (1977)

MANDERINO, Justice:

The issue in this appeal is whether the Commonwealth Court erred in reversing an arbitrator's award in a dispute submitted to binding arbitration pursuant to a collective bargaining agreement.

The appellant, Leechburg Education Association (Association) is the exclusive bargaining agent for the professional employees of the Leechburg Area School District, and was duly selected under the provisions of the Public Employe Relations Act of 1970 (PERA), Act of July 23, 1970, P.L. 563 No. 195, art. I, § 101 *et seq.,* 43 P.S. §§ 1101.101-1101.2301 (Supp.1977-1978). The appellee, Leechburg Area School District (District) is a public employer in the Commonwealth of Pennsylvania.

The facts are not in dispute. Clara Battist and Margaret Smith were hired as teachers by the District for the 1974-75 school year. They agreed to accept the salaries which were offered by the District.

A grievance was later filed by the Association contending that the District violated the collective bargaining agreement in effect between the District and the Association in that the two teachers hired were not being paid the salary to which they were entitled. The dispute was submitted to binding arbitration according to the collective bargaining agreement in effect between the parties.

The arbitrator ruled in favor of the Association. An appeal was then taken to the Commonwealth Court by the District. The Commonwealth Court reversed the arbitrator's award. *Leechburg Area School District v. Leechburg Education Association,* 24 Pa.Cmwlth 256, 355 A.2d 608 (1976). The Association's petition for allowance of appeal was granted by this Court, and this appeal followed. We vacate the order of the Commonwealth Court and affirm the arbitrator's award.

The scope of the court's review of a binding arbitration award under PERA is limited by the Act of April 25, 1927, P.L. 381 No. 248. *Community College of Beaver v. Community College of Beaver County, Society of the Faculty (PSEA/NEA),* 473 Pa. 576, 375 A.2d 1267 (1977).

Section 10 of the Act of 1927 outlines four situations in which a court may *vacate* an arbitration award. Section 11 of the Act of 1927 outlines four other situations in which a court may *modify or correct* an award. If a party seeks to vacate an award, it must allege one of the four conditions contained in section 10. If a party seeks to modify or correct an arbitration award, it must allege one of the conditions specified in section 11.

The appellee District in this case sought to vacate the arbitrator's award. It was therefore bound to seek judicial review under one of the four categories specified in section 10 of the Act.

The four situations covered in section 10 are:

"(a) Where the award was procured by corruption, fraud, or undue means.

(b) Where there was evident partiality or corruption on the part of the arbitrators, or any of them.

(c) Where the arbitrators were guilty of misconduct in refusing to postpone the hearing upon sufficient cause shown, or in refusing to hear evidence pertinent and material to the controversy, or any other misbehavior by which the rights of any party have been prejudiced.

(d) Where the arbitrators exceeded their powers or so imperfectly executed them that a final and definite award upon the subject matter submitted was not made."

The first issue raised by the District before the Commonwealth Court was a claim that the arbitrator had not properly interpreted the collective bargaining agreement between the parties. That contention is not one cognizable under section 10 as a basis for vacating an arbitrator's award.

The first category requires a claim that the award "was procured by corruption, fraud, or undue means." Appellee has never raised any such issue. The second category permits judicial review to determine whether there was "evident partiality or corruption on the part of the arbitrators." Appellee never raised that issue. The third category permits judicial review if it is claimed that there was "misconduct" in certain respects or "misbehavior" prejudicing rights. Appellee never raised that issue. The fourth category allows judicial review if the arbitrators "exceeded their powers or so imperfectly executed them that a final and definite award . . . was not made." It is only this fourth category under which appellee's claims could conceivably fall.

Appellee, however, does not claim that the arbitrator "exceeded his powers." If we allowed a claim of improper interpretation of an agreement to fall under the category of "exceeded powers," binding arbitration would be a useless procedure. The determination of whether an arbitrator "exceeded proper powers" depends upon whether the arbitrator decided a dispute over which he had no jurisdiction, or granted an award which is prohibited by law.

The claim that a court should interpret an agreement differently than did the arbitrator would convert binding arbitration into "unbinding" arbitration. If binding arbitration has any meaning, the arbitrator must be considered the court of last resort except in the very limited categories specified in the Act of 1927. Where an arbitrator has jurisdiction, and where the arbitrator's award is not contrary to any legislative enactment, and where the arbitrator is not attacked as being corrupt, partial, or having engaged in misconduct or misbehavior, the award must stand.

For these reasons, we have not considered the provisions of the collective bargaining agreement before us. We have no jurisdiction to determine the question of whether the arbitrator mistakenly interpreted the agreement.

Appellee raises other issues which are properly reviewable under the Act of 1927. Appellee contends that the arbitrator's award is illegal because it is in direct conflict with Section 706 of PERA, 43 P.S. § 1101.706. Section 706 states:

"Nothing contained in this act shall impair the employer's right to hire employes or to discharge employes for just cause consistent with existing legislation."

Appellee appears to be arguing that this statute gives the District the exclusive right to "hire employees" on whatever salary terms the District and the individual employee agree to. Section 706, however, must be read in the context of other sections of PERA. PERA provides for the recognition of exclusive collective bargaining representatives. In this case, the Association is the exclusive bargaining agent for the teachers in the Leechburg Area School District.

Accepting appellee's argument would destroy the authority of the Association as exclusive bargaining representative. Were appellee's view to prevail, a school district could effectively emasculate any salary scales contained in collective bargaining agreements by entering into individual agreements with each teacher. This is exactly the evil intended to be eliminated by the recognition of exclusive bargaining agents, agents who act for all employees the moment they are hired. As the United States Supreme Court recognized over thirty years ago, to allow individual contracts to interfere with the functioning of the collective bargaining agreement would reduce laws providing for collective bargaining to a futility. *J. I. Case Co. v. NLRB,* 321 U.S. 332, 337, 64 S.Ct. 576, 580, 88 L.Ed. 762, 767-68 (1944).

Appellee also points to section 1142 of the Public School Code of 1949, Act of May 10, 1949, P.L. 30, as amended, 24 P.S. § 1-101, *et seq.* Section 1142 in relevant part states:

> "all school districts . . . shall pay all regular and temporary teachers . . . the minimum salaries and increments for the school year 1968-69 and each school year thereafter, as provided in the following tabulation in accordance with the column in which the professional employe is grouped and the step which the professional employe has attained by years of experience *within the school district* . . . When a school district, *by agreement,* places a professional employe on a step in the salary scale, each step thereafter shall constitute one year of service. . . ." (Emphasis added.)

According to the appellee, section 1142 authorizes a school district to agree with an individual teacher as to a salary scale and ignore the collective bargaining agreement. We reject such an interpretation. If the word "agreement" in section 1142 was interpreted to be an agreement with an individual teacher rather than the collective bargaining agreement, section 1142 would completely emasculate PERA's recognition of exclusive bargaining representatives.

A collective bargaining agreement would eventually become ineffective if a district could, over a period of years, hire new teachers, without adhering to the wage salary scale in the collective bargaining agreement. After a period of time, the same evils would be present which brought about the need for PERA. Employees in a given district could all be paid wage levels totally unrelated to their background, qualifications, or experience, but related only to the particular personal or financial pressures of the employee or the employer at the time of hiring.

As in this case, the two teachers desiring employment were willing to accept a lower wage rather than lose the employment. After such teachers become a part of the system, the discrepancies in salary between them and others similarly situated over a period of time is a cause for unrest.

We have examined section 10 of the Arbitration Act of 1927, and not section 11, because the appellee is asking that an arbitrator's award be *vacated.* We note, however, that the issue raised by the appellee would not be cognizable under section 11 either. The first part of section 11 requires some miscalculation. None has been alleged in this case. The second part of section 11 deals with the situation where the arbitrators have decided a matter not submitted to them. No such claim is made in this case. The third part of section 11 deals with the claim that the award is imperfect in form. No such claim has been made in this case. The fourth part of section 11 involves a claim that "the award is against the law." As indicated earlier, however, we are unable to conclude that the arbitrator's award in this case was prohibited by any legislative enactment.

Accordingly, the order of the Commonwealth Court is vacated and the award of the arbitrator is affirmed.

ROBERTS, Justice, concurring:

I agree with the majority that the award of the arbitrator should be affirmed. I do not believe, however, that the Arbitration Act of 1927, Act of April 25, 1927, P.L. 381, §§ 1 et seq., 5 P.S. §§ 161-181 (1963), is controlling.

The Legislature, in enacting the Public Employee Relations Act of 1970, P.L. 563, §§ 101 et seq., 43 P.S. §§ 1101.101 — 1101.2301 (Supp.1977) [Act 195], established a self-contained system for the resolution of disputes in the public sector through arbitration. Act 195 contemplates an arbitration scheme which is different from the Arbitration Act of 1927: Act 195 prescribes its own method for the selection of arbitrators which is different from the Arbitration Act of 1927; Act 195 allows the parties to bargain over the procedures to be followed while the Arbitration Act of 1927 specifies those procedures. These differences convince me that the Legislature did not intend the Arbitration Act of 1927 to apply.[*]

While I do not believe that the Arbitration Act of 1927 applies, I agree with the conclusion of the majority in *Community College of Beaver v. Community College of Beaver County, Society of the Faculty (PSEA/NEA)*, 473 Pa. 576, 375 A.2d 1267 (1977), that the award of the arbitrator is to be affirmed if it "draws its essence from the collective bargaining agreement." *Community College of Beaver v. Community College of Beaver County, Society of Faculty (PSEA/NEA)*, supra at —, 375 A.2d at 1272, quoting *United Steelworkers v. Enterprise Wheel and Car Corp.*, 363 U.S. 593, 597, 80 S.Ct. 1358, 1361, 4 L.Ed.2d 1424 (1960).

I believe that the Commonwealth Court incorrectly decided the question whether the award of the arbitrator here drew its essence from the agreement. "It is the arbitrator's construction which was bargained for and so far as the arbitrator's decision concerns construction of the contract, the courts have no business overruling him because their interpretation of the contract is different from his." *United Steelworkers v. Enterprise Wheel and Car Corp.*, 363 U.S. at 599, 80 S. Ct. at 1362. Accordingly, I concur in the result.

[The concurring opinion of Pomeroy, J., is omitted.]

## NOTES

1. In the private sector, the Supreme Court has made it clear that "the courts . . . have no business weighing the merits of the grievance, considering whether there is equity in a particular claim, or determining whether there is particular language in the written instrument which will support the claim." United Steelworkers of America v. American Mfg. Co., 363 U.S. 564, 568, 80 S.Ct. 1343, 4 L.Ed.2d 1403 (1960). "[T]he judicial inquiry . . . must be strictly confined to the question of whether the [parties] did agree to arbitrate the grievance or did agree to give the arbitrator power to make the award he made." United Steelworkers of America v. Warrior & Gulf Navigation Co., 363 U.S. 574, 582, 80 S.Ct. 1347, 4 L.Ed.2d 1409 (1960). Although an arbitrator's "award is legitimate only so long as it draws its essence from the collective bargaining agreement, . . . a mere ambiguity in the opinion accompanying an award, which permits the inference that the arbitrator may have exceeded his authority, is not a reason for refusing to enforce the award." United

[*] The arbitration scheme set forth in Act 195 is similar to the one found in the Act of June 24, 1968, P.L. 237, §§ 1 et seq., P.S. 43 §§ 217.1 — 217.10 (Supp.1977) [Act 111]. We considered this arbitration scheme in *City of Washington v. Police Department*, 436 Pa. 168, 259 A.2d 437 (1969), and concluded that the court reviewing the award of the arbitrator should ask whether the arbitrator acted in excess of his power as authorized by the collective bargaining agreement.

Steelworkers of America v. Enterprise Wheel & Car Co., 363 U.S. 593, 597-98, 80 S.Ct. 1358, 4 L.Ed.2d 1424 (1960).

2. Courts reviewing public sector grievance arbitration awards have generally followed the private sector practice of according substantial deference to the arbitrators' grievance resolutions, with awards being denied affirmance only where the arbitrators have clearly exceeded their contractual authority or issued decisions directly contravening law or public policy. *See, e.g.,* Minnesota v. Berthiaume, 259 N.W.2d 104, 96 L.R.R.M. 3240 (Minn. 1977) (also placing burden of proof on party challenging award); Int'l Brotherhood of Firemen v. School Dist. of Philadelphia, 350 A.2d 804, 91 L.R.R.M. 2710 (Pa. 1976). Doubts regarding the propriety of an award are usually resolved in favor of enforcement. *See, e.g.,* Community College of Beaver County v. Community College Society of Faculty, 375 A.2d 1267, 96 L.R.R.M. 2375 (Pa. 1977); Darien Educ. Ass'n v. Bd. of Educ., 374 A.2d 1081, 94 L.R.R.M. 2895 (Conn. 1977). Nevertheless, if an arbitrator exercises jurisdiction over an issue that is expressly excluded from the coverage of the grievance-arbitration procedures (School Committee of Portland v. Teachers Ass'n, 338 A.2d 155, 90 L.R.R.M. 2597 (Me. 1975)) or issues an award that is contrary to law (Machinists, Lodge 2424 v. United States, 96 L.R.R.M. 2720 (U.S. Ct. of Claims 1977)), enforcement will be denied. *See also* Bd. of Trustees, Community College Dist. No. 508 v. Cook County Teachers, Local 1600, — N.E.2d —, 1979-80 PBC ¶36,497 (Ill. 1979), wherein the Court vacated an arbitration award which had the effect of providing teachers who had engaged in an illegal work stoppage with extra work assignment preference over teachers who had not participated in the strike, since such a result was found to contravene public policy.

Section 7122 of the Civil Service Reform Act of 1978 defines the limited grounds upon which a party may challenge a federal grievance arbitration award. The Federal Labor Relations Authority may only sustain a party's objection to an award where either the decision is contrary to some law, rule, or regulation, or is otherwise invalid for reasons similar to those utilized by federal courts to evaluate the propriety of private sector grievance arbitration awards. The private sector grounds for challenging an award include assertions that the arbitrator exceeded his authority, that the award does not draw its essence from the bargaining agreement, that the award is incomplete, ambiguous, or contradictory, that the award is based upon a "nonfact," that the arbitrator was biased or partial, or that the arbitrator refused to hear pertinent and material evidence. *See* GERR No. 665, A-2. *See generally* Kagel, *Grievance Arbitration in the Federal Service: How Final and Binding?*, 51 ORE. L. REV. 134 (1971).

3. In Holodnak v. Avco Corp., 514 F.2d 285 (2d Cir.), *cert. denied,* 423 U.S. 892 (1975), a private sector arbitration award was set aside because the "conduct of the arbitrator demonstrated evident partiality." In reaching this result, the Court noted that the arbitrator "seemed principally concerned with [the grievant's] political views, and [he] labored to convince [the grievant] that the union's representation in the past had been effective." The Court also noted that the arbitrator had written an "unreasoned decision" which was "cryptically stated" and not supported by the evidence. *But cf.* Lodge 1296, UAFF v. City of Kennewick, 542 P.2d 1252, 92 L.R.R.M. 2118 (1976), wherein the Washington Supreme Court reversed a lower court decision that had set aside an arbitration award where the arbitration panel chairman had consumed several drinks with a union official and the trial court had found this to constitute a violation of the "appearance of fairness" rule. The Supreme Court held that the only relevant statute in Washington was the collective bargaining law for local government employees which provides for review of such awards solely upon a question of arbitrary and capricious decision making. Since the trial court had found no such circumstances, the panel's award was sustained. *See also* City of Hartford v. Police Officers, Local 308, 370 A.2d 996, 93 L.R.R.M. 2321 (Conn. 1976), where the Court found no partiality where the arbitrator indicated that he would automatically reinstate a dismissed employee if the employer did not respond to subpoenas issued by the grievant's attorney and would dismiss the hearing if it was not conducted expeditiously.

4. Courts have not always agreed upon the authority arbitrators possess to review disciplinary decisions of public employers. In Gresham School Dist. v. ERB, 570 P.2d 682, 97 L.R.R.M. 2143 (Ore. Ct. App. 1977), the court upheld an arbitrator's award that

reinstated a probationary teacher, thereby affording her tenure, where she had been terminated in reprisal for having previously utilized the grievance procedure. Other arbitral decisions ordering the re-employment of improperly terminated employees have been similarly sustained. *See, e.g.,* Minnesota v. Berthiaume, 259 N.W.2d 104, 96 L.R.R.M. 3240 (Minn. 1977); Middlesex County Commissioners v. AFSCME, 362 N.E.2d 523, 95 L.R.R.M. 2864 (Mass. 1977) (requiring employer to follow "progressive discipline" concept). *See also* Binghamton Civil Service Forum v. Binghamton, 44 N.Y.2d 23, 374 N.E.2d 380 (1978), where the Court sustained an arbitration award reducing the penalty imposed upon a worker who accepted bribes from dismissal to a six-month suspension, since the Court did not believe that the public policy of the state automatically required the discharge of any employee who accepted a bribe. *But cf.* Fairchild v. West Rutland School Dist., 376 A.2d 28, 95 L.R.R.M. 3006 (1977), wherein the Vermont Supreme Court vacated an award that reversed the school district's decision not to renew a teacher's contract, since neither the individual teaching agreement nor the negotiated contract contained any provision regarding the renewal of teaching contracts.

Other courts have indicated that while any contractual provision restricting the unfettered right of public employers to terminate probationary personnel would conflict with public policy and thus be unenforceable, they would enforce arbitration awards ordering the reinstatement of discharged workers where necessary to allow employers to provide the grievants with their procedural right under their contract to a proper evaluation or a fair hearing before dismissal. *See, e.g.,* School Committee v. Korbut, 369 N.E.2d 1148, 97 L.R.R.M. 2447 (Mass. 1977); Candor School Dist. v. Teachers Ass'n, 42 N.Y.2d 266, 366 N.E.2d 826 (1977); Cohoes City School Dist. v. Teachers Ass'n, 40 N.Y.2d 774, 358 N.E.2d 878 (1976). *See also* Bd. of Directors of Maine School Dist. No. 75 v. Merrymeeting Educators Ass'n, 354 A.2d 169, 92 L.R.R.M. 2268 (Me. 1976), wherein the Court upheld an arbitrator's decision to reinstate a nonprobationary teacher where the school principal had failed to provide the teacher with the assistance that had been recommended by her evaluators and the superintendent. In deciding that the arbitrator had not exceeded his authority under the contract, the Court implied a reciprocal obligation on the part of school administrators to correct deficiencies in teacher performance, if possible, before resorting to discharge.

5. The authority of arbitrators to review sabbatical leave decisions of school districts has also presented courts with some problems. In Rochester City School Dist. v. Teachers Ass'n, 41 N.Y.2d 578, 362 N.E.2d 977 (1977), the Court held that while the granting of sabbatical leaves is a matter of discretion for the school board, it is subject to interpretation by an arbitrator once the board has agreed to include the issue in a bargaining agreement. Although contractual surrender of the exclusive authority over the granting of sabbatical leaves may be "inconvenient" to the employer, the Court found that the board members chose to negotiate the matter and agreed to exercise their discretion in a certain manner. The Court thus upheld the arbitration award which granted sabbatical leaves to a specific number of Rochester teachers pursuant to the applicable contract provision. *Accord,* Bridgeport Bd. of Educ. v. Educ. Ass'n., 377 A.2d 323, 96 L.R.R.M. 2567 (Conn. 1977). *See also* Associated Teachers of Huntington v. Bd. of Educ., 33 N.Y.2d 229, 306 N.E.2d 791 (1973), where an arbitral award finding that teachers had an enforceable right to sabbatical leaves under a bargaining agreement was confirmed, nothwithstanding a state statute declaring a statewide moratorium on such leaves. *But see* South Stickney Bd. of Educ. v. Murphy, 372 N.E.2d 899, 97 L.R.R.M. 2441 (Ill. Ct. App. 1978), wherein it was determined that a school board's authority over sabbatical leaves is non-delegable, thus rendering unenforceable a contractual provision restricting that prerogative. An arbitral award applying that provision was therefore denied enforcement.

6. There is reason to believe that some courts will be more active in reviewing the merits of public sector arbitration awards that require the granting of economic benefits than they will be with respect to non-monetary awards. In the private sector, there is usually no question regarding the power of an arbitrator to order back pay or other "make whole" relief in appropriate cases; nor is there any question concerning the authority of an employer to comply with such an award. In the public sector, however, public policy considerations may raise special problems with respect to the enforcement of such "make

whole" remedies. For example, in Boston Teachers Union v. School Committee of Boston, 350 N.E.2d 707, 93 L.R.R.M. 2205 (1976), the Massachusetts Supreme Judicial Court held that an arbitrator exceeded his authority when he directed the school board to pay $52,000 to a teachers union scholarship fund as damages that allegedly resulted when the board violated its bargaining agreement with the teachers union by refusing to hire substitute teachers to replace regular teachers during absences. It was determined that an arbitrator could not require a city to pay funds for purposes for which municipal funds could not properly be expended. *But cf.* Waterbury Bd. of Educ. v. Teachers Ass'n, 384 A.2d 350, 97 L.R.R.M. 2401 (Conn. 1977), and Wayne County Bd. of Commissioners v. Nat'l Union of Police Officers, 254 N.W.2d 896, 95 L.R.R.M. 3396 (Mich. Ct. App. 1977), where the courts sustained monetary awards contained in arbitral decisions. *See also* Antonopoulou v. Beame, 67 Misc.2d 851, 325 N.Y.S.2d 12 (Sup. Ct. 1971), *aff'd,* 332 N.Y.S.2d 464 (Sup. Ct., App. Div. 1972), *rev'd,* 32 N.Y.2d 126, 296 N.E.2d 247 (1973).

7. Where the parties have included nothing in their bargaining agreement concerning past practices which have been observed and an arbitration award orders the continuation of such established practices on the ground they have been implicitly incorporated in the contract, the award may be denied enforcement as being beyond the authority of the arbitrator to merely apply and interpret the actual terms of the agreement. *See* County of Allegheny v. County Prison Employees Independent Union, 381 A.2d 849, 96 L.R.R.M. 3396 (Pa. 1977); Milwaukee Professional Firefighters, Local 215 v. Milwaukee, 253 N.W.2d 481, 95 L.R.R.M. 2684 (Wis. 1977).

8. Where parties to a negotiated agreement expressly authorize the arbitrator to make a final and binding resolution of arbitrability questions, reviewing courts will generally defer to the arbitrator's decision regarding that issue. However, if the clause does not indicate the parties' intent that the arbiter's resolution will be final, or the contractual arbitration provision is narrowly drawn, reviewing courts will frequently not feel bound by the arbitrator's determination. *See* Joint School Dist. No. 10 of Jefferson v. Educ. Ass'n, 253 N.W.2d 536, 95 L.R.R.M. 3117 (Wis. 1977); Glendale Policemen's Ass'n, v. Glendale, 264 N.W.2d 594, 1977-78 PBC ¶36,246 (Wis. 1978).

# E. INDIVIDUAL RIGHTS UNDER THE COLLECTIVE BARGAINING AGREEMENT

## 1. INTRODUCTION

### H. WELLINGTON & R. WINTER, THE UNIONS AND THE CITIES 162-64 (1971)†

The interest of the individual employee is generally well served in the grievance procedure by his representative, the union. Typically, it is the union that brings the grievance and pursues it through the several steps spelled out in the contract, and, if necessary, on to arbitration. But, as we have learned from experience in the private sector, it would be a terrible mistake to assume that congruity of interests between union and individual always exists. Divergence is possible because of a reasonable disagreement as to what the contract provides, because the interests of the individual and those of a majority of employees do not coincide, because the individual is a political rival of the union president, because he is black and a majority of the union is white, because he is disliked, against union policy, unwilling to do what he is told to do, and so forth. And divergence of interests may occur at any stage of the grievance procedure. The union may decline to process a grievance at all, take it through some steps and drop it, or refuse to go to arbitration.

---

While potential conflict between individual and union exists at the precontract negotiation stage as well, it is most troublesome during contract administration. This may be because at that stage the employee is viewed as having rights that grow out of an existing agreement, rather than amorphous and hard-to-define interests in a yet to be achieved contractual settlement.

Be that as it may, the private sector has developed a bewilderingly complicated and relatively unsatisfactory body of law to deal with the problem. The law is complicated largely because of the complexities in the underlying problem. On the one hand, if collective bargaining is to be an orderly, efficient process that brings stability to labor relations, it is desirable to place the employer in a position where he is able to work out binding settlements with the union, and the union alone. On the other hand, the individual needs protection from the union that fails adequately to represent his interests.

One approach to the problem is to give the individual employee a cause of action against the union if it fails to represent him fairly; but to give him no redress against the employer. Indeed, the duty of fair representation exists in the private sector under federal law. It has, however, been much hedged about. The other approach is to give the employee a direct and individual right in the collective agreement, recognize the fact that this right may undercut efficiency and stability, but recognize also that the effect of this can be grossly overestimated and that institutions have ways of adapting themselves. Federal law recognizes individual rights in the contract. It also hedges them about.

Whatever one's position as to what the law should be in the private sector, it seems clear that in municipal collective bargaining the individual should have access, as an individual, to the grievance procedure, arbitration, and the courts. Without collective bargaining, there is no comparable right in private employment. In public employment such a right generally does obtain and is administered by civil service commissions. While it has been argued that these commissions have no legitimate role in the resolution of grievances where collective bargaining is established, the protection afforded the individual under civil service should not be lost with their demise. Such protection may be retained by giving the employee generous individual rights in the collective agreement.

Of course, the union's interests must be protected. It should be able to argue for its interpretation of the contract at each level of the grievance procedure, in arbitration, and before the court. Nor, where its antagonistic position is reasonable, should it have to bear the costs of the individual's case. But these are minor and easily resolved difficulties when compared to some of the . . . problems that must be faced when techniques of contract administration are transplanted from the private to the public sector.

## 2. EXHAUSTION OF CONTRACTUAL REMEDIES AS PREREQUISITE TO JUDICIAL ENFORCEMENT ACTION BY INDIVIDUAL EMPLOYEES

### MORTON v. SUPERIOR COURT, FRESNO COUNTY

California Court of Appeals
9 Cal. App. 3d 977, 88 Cal. Rptr. 533 (1970)

GARGANO, Justice: The City of Fresno and its Chief of Police, H.R. Morton, have applied for a writ of prohibition to prevent further proceedings in the lawsuit now pending in the Superior Court of Fresno County, in which real parties in interest, hereafter referred to as real parties, seek a writ of mandate and declaratory relief. Petitioners contend that the superior court lacks jurisdiction because real parties did not exhaust their administrative remedy before filing the action. Petitioners allege that real parties are city employees with a labor grievance, and that they by-passed the grievance procedure adopted by the city manager to resolve such grievances. . . .

It is undisputed that the action which petitioners seek to enjoin is primarily concerned with a labor dispute between real parties and the City of Fresno; real parties are police officers employed by the city, and they brought the action on behalf of themselves and all members of the Fresno Police Relief Association to secure a judicial declaration that the time consumed by policemen in putting on and taking off their uniforms and during lunch periods is compensable overtime. It is also undisputed that real parties intentionally by-passed the city's grievance procedure. Real parties contend that their controversy with the city does not come within the scope of that procedure and that in any event, the exhaustion doctrine does not apply to this case. Because it is settled that the exhaustion of an administrative remedy, where one is available, is a condition precedent to obtaining judicial relief, and that "a court violating the rule acts in excess of jurisdiction" . . . we shall consider petitioners' application for a writ of prohibition on the merits. . . . If there was any question about the applicability of the grievance procedure, it was incumbent upon real parties to present the question to the city manager so that he could decide the issue in the first instance. It lies within the power of the administrative agency (in this case the city manager) to determine, in the first instance and before judicial relief may be obtained, whether a given controversy falls within its granted jurisdiction. . . .

Real parties apparently believe that because an employee is not required to file a written grievance, he may resort to the judicial process without first submitting to the grievance procedure. The basic purpose for the exhaustion doctrine is to lighten the burden of overworked courts in cases where administrative remedies are available and are as likely as the judicial remedy to provide the wanted relief. It is the rule that if an administrative remedy is available, it must be exhausted even though the administrative remedy is couched in permissive language. . . .

Understandably, a city employee is not required to file a grievance if he does not wish to do so, but he must first pursue this administrative remedy before resorting to the judicial process.

The city's grievance procedure is somewhat cumbersome, and in some cases partially regressive; for example, real parties' request for overtime credit was refused by the chief of police, and under the grievance procedure they were required to backtrack and file a grievance with their immediate supervisor who is a subordinate to the chief. Nevertheless, the procedure provides for a thorough review of an employee's grievance by a representative committee, and then for an appeal to the city manager who must make a decision. Had the present controversy been presented to the city manager, and had he decided that real parties were entitled to overtime credit under the city charter or municipal ordinance for time consumed in putting on and taking off their uniforms and during lunch periods, he could have enforced this interpretation of the law by ordering the chief of police to approve the overtime. . . .

We turn to real parties' contention that they were not required to exhaust their administrative remedy in this case, first because their lawsuit is a class action, and second, because the action is primarily concerned with questions of law.

We do not believe that a city employee may dispense with the city's grievance procedure merely because his grievance affects more than one employee or member of a class. If we were to permit a city employee, on important policy questions which vitally affect the city, to by-pass the very office charged with the duty of managing the city's affairs solely because his grievance affects more than one employee, we would foist upon the judicial branch the arduous task of solving governmental policy questions without giving the responsible governmental branch the opportunity to solve its own problems at the administrative level.

We conclude that because real parties have failed to demonstrate that the city grievance procedure was inadequate to protect the members of the class they allegedly represent, they cannot prevail on this point. If real parties had filed a grievance, and if the city manager had ruled in their favor, the ruling would have applied to all police officers similarly affected. By the same token, if the city manager's decision had been adverse to real parties, it would have had the finality necessary to enable them to bring a class action. . . .

There is authority for the rule that the exhaustion doctrine is inapplicable when constitutional or jurisdictional issues or questions of law are raised. However, the decisions are by no means uniform, and this view is not followed in California. In United States v. Superior Court, 19 Cal. 2d 189, the California Supreme Court held that the exhaustion doctrine not only applies to orders which are erroneous but also to those assailed as nullities because illegally adopted. In Security First Nat. Bank v. County of Los Angeles, 35 Cal. 2d 319, 217 P.2d 946, our Supreme Court held that resort to the administrative remedy was required even though the statute sought to be applied and enforced by the administrative agency was challenged upon constitutional grounds. It stands to reason that the exhaustion doctrine is applicable in a case such as this, which not only raises mixed questions of law and fact but also involves fundamental policy questions which should be resolved on the local level if at all possible.

The writ is granted.

Stone, P.J., concurred.

### NOTES

1. The exhaustion doctrine has generally been applied in situations where individual employees seek judicial enforcement of rights allegedly existing under collective bargaining agreements without first seeking redress of their claims through contractually established grievance procedures. Thus, in the private sector, the Supreme Court has ruled that an individual worker may not sue his employer directly for an alleged breach of contract without first processing his claim through the contractual grievance procedure. Republic Steel Corp. v. Maddox, 379 U.S. 650, 85 S.Ct. 614, 13 L.Ed.2d 580 (1965). As indicated by the principal case, this exhaustion requirement is similarly followed in the public sector. See Coffee v. Bd. of Educ. of New York City, 65 Misc.2d 931, 319 N.Y.S.2d 249 (Sup. Ct. 1971); Clampitt v. Bd. of Educ., Warren Consolidated Schools, 68 L.R.R.M. 2996 (Mich. Cir. Ct. 1968); Central School Dist. v. Litz, 60 Misc.2d 1009, 304 N.Y.S.2d 372 (Sup. Ct. 1969), aff'd., 34 App.Div.2d 1092, 314 N.Y.S.2d 176 (1970).

The Supreme Court has recognized that the failure to exhaust contractual procedures will be excused if the representative union has breached its duty of fair representation by wrongfully refusing to process the individual employee's claim under the grievance or arbitration machinery. Vaca v. Sipes, 386 U.S. 171, 87 S.Ct. 903, 17 L.Ed.2d 842 (1967). Other defenses against a failure to exhaust contractual procedures include the repudiation of the bargaining agreement by the employer or a demonstration that pursuit of the grievance procedure would almost inevitably have been futile. See Glover v. St. Louis-San Francisco Ry., 393 U.S. 324, 89 S.Ct. 548, 21 L.Ed.2d 519 (1969); Ricciotti v. Warwick School Committee, 319 F.Supp. 1006 (D.R.I. 1970); In re Tischler v. Bd. of Educ.,

Monroe-Woodbury Central School Dist. No. 1, 37 App.Div.2d 261, 323 N.Y.S.2d 508 (1971).

2. In Browne v. Milwaukee Bd. of School Directors, 230 N.W.2d 704, 90 L.R.R.M. 2412 (1975), nonunion municipal employees challenging the constitutionality of the provision in the Wisconsin Municipal Employment Relations Act authorizing the negotiation of "fair share" union security agreements were not required by the Wisconsin Supreme Court to exhaust contractual remedies or internal union procedures before seeking judicial relief. The Court held that plaintiffs need not pursue contractual remedies, since their action was to overturn part of the same agreement and there was no procedure under the contract which would permit them to challenge directly the constitutionality of the statutory provision in issue. Furthermore, any requirement that they exhaust internal union procedures would have been equally futile, since the union could not have corrected the allegedly unconstitutional legislation. The plaintiffs were not quarreling with what the union had done in acting pursuant to the statute, but rather sought to overturn the enactment itself. *Accord,* Zylstra v. Pira, 539 P.2d 823, 90 L.R.R.M. 2832 (Wash. 1975).

3. Parallel procedures were allowed to go forward concurrently by the New York Court of Appeals in City School Dist. of Poughkeepsie v. Teachers Ass'n., 35 N.Y.2d 599, 324 N.E.2d 144 (1974). One appeal was to the Commissioner of Education by a teacher who challenged the school district's refusal to appoint her to a specified position, while the union simultaneously initiated the contractual grievance-arbitration machinery on her behalf. The bargaining agreement recognized both procedures, but did not provide for exclusivity regarding the matter of promotions, and certain aspects of each procedure were available to the teacher or the union, but not to both. More significantly, however, the two remedial avenues, which had been commenced on the same date, had been pursued so diligently that the Court felt that neither could be said to have been waived, nor could priority be assigned to one. To avoid such duplicative proceedings in the future, the Court suggested that the parties negotiate an amendment to their agreement.

4. In Antinore v. New York, 49 App.Div.2d 6, 371 N.Y.S.2d 213 (1975), *aff'd.,* 40 N.Y.2d 921 (1976), the court considered the validity of a contract provision that mandated binding arbitration of disciplinary matters involving civil service employees, and it held that § 76 of the Civil Service Law, as amended in 1972, lawfully provided for the substitution of the statutory appeal procedures by grievance machinery negotiated by employers and labor organizations. Plaintiff, a child care worker at a State Training School who was being terminated for disciplinary reasons, contended that his restriction to the contractual grievance-arbitration procedures deprived him of due process and equal protection. The court ruled that the plaintiff waived the due process and equal protection rights in question by his membership in an association that voluntarily agreed to a contract dispensing with such rights.

> [D]ue process requirements — and we think equal protection as well — are not relevant when they have been waived by the party seeking to assert them, as by voluntarily entering into an agreement for the resolution of disputes in a manner which dispenses with one or more of the rights constitutionally guaranteed. "Parties in voluntary agreement are not limited, except for rare matters contrary to public policy, from agreeing to anything they wish" (Mount St. Mary's Hosp. v. Catherwood, [26 N.Y.2d 493], p. 507). As the justice at Special Term recognized, constitutional rights can be waived in most situations (Gardner v. Broderick, 392 U.S. 273; Matter of Lee v. County Court of Erie County, 27 N.Y.2d 432, *cert. denied,* 404 U.S. 823), and we believe that in the case before us they have been waived.
>
> Unlike Special Term, we do not view the collective bargaining agreement entered into by the State with the authorized, designated representative of its employees as an instrument instinct with compulsion by virtue of its nascence from the Public Employees' Fair Employment Act's recognition of public employee bargaining agencies in exchange for the employees' loss of the right to strike (Civil Service Law § 200 et seq.). To the contrary, the very circumstance identified by the court below as indicative of the nonconsensual nature of the agreement in question — the almost singular and total power of CSEA to bargain for public employees — lends support to a contrary conclusion, i.e., that the agreement represents a reciprocal negotiation between forces

with strengths on both sides, reflecting the reconciled interests of employer and employees, voluntarily entered into, CSEA, as designated bargaining agent for a group of public employees in which plaintiff was included, was agent for plaintiff, such that its assent to the agreement was plaintiff's assent. "... [T]he union represents all the employees as to all covered matters ..." (Chupka v. Lorenz-Schneider Co., 12 N.Y.2d 1, 6). The fact that this plaintiff did not himself approve the agreement negotiated by his representative and now disclaims satisfaction with one aspect of the agreement makes it no less binding upon him. Labor relations involving any sizeable group cannot be expected to proceed only with the consent of each member of the group. Orderly process requires that agreements be made and complied with even in the face of minority dissent or disapproval. Plaintiff, as employee, has the benefits of the contract; he must accept also what he may regard as the disadvantages, for in the bargaining process it may well be that the latter were assumed in exchange for the conferral of the former. If plaintiff or others in his unit are dissatisfied with their agent's product, there are means available to effect a change in representation and certification (4 NYCRR Part 201). Meantime, he can no more claim exemption from the negotiated agreement than may a citizen, with impunity, withhold compliance with a statute because he disfavored his legislator's affirmative vote on the enactment.

5. If public employees bring suit under 42 U.S.C. §§ 1983 and 1985 challenging employment practices which they claim are impermissibly infringing their federal rights, should they be required to exhaust available contractual grievance procedures before being permitted to prosecute their judicial action? *See* Steele v. Haley, 335 F.Supp. 659 (D. Mass.), *aff'd.,* 451 F.2d 1105 (1st Cir. 1971). Should your answer be influenced by the fact that most federal courts do not require the exhaustion of state *administrative* procedures in non-employment contexts as a prerequisite to judicial relief under §§ 1983 and 1985? *See* Burnett v. Short, 441 F.2d 405 (5th Cir. 1971); Whitner v. Davis, 410 F.2d 24 (9th Cir. 1969). *See also* Wilwording v. Swenson, 404 U.S. 249, 92 S.Ct. 407, 30 L.Ed.2d 418 (1971); King v. Smith, 392 U.S. 309, 88 S.Ct. 2128, 20 L.Ed.2d 1118 (1968); Damico v. California, 389 U.S. 416, 88 S.Ct. 526, 19 L.Ed.2d 647 (1967). *But see* Eisen v. Eastman, 421 F.2d 560 (2d Cir. 1969), *cert. denied,* 400 U.S. 841 (1970).

# 3. THE UNION'S DUTY OF FAIR REPRESENTATION

## KAUFMAN v. GOLDBERG

New York Supreme Court, Special Term, Kings County
64 Misc. 2d, 524, 315 N.Y.S.2d 35 (1970)

LIEBOWITZ, Justice.

[Petitioner Kaufman, an employee of the New York City Department of Social Services, complained that he had been punitively transferred and demoted from Resource Consultant to Caseworker, with a loss of seniority. In accordance with procedures established in a collective bargaining agreement between the City and the Social Service Employees Union, Local 371, the petitioner filed a grievance alleging violation of the agreement on the part of the Department of Social Services. The grievance was denied at Steps I, II, and III of the grievance procedure. Kaufman claimed he then requested that the union take the grievance to Step IV by demanding arbitration, but that the request was refused because of Kaufman's non-membership in the union. The petitioner then brought this action against the Commissioner of the Department of Social Services, the Director of the Office of Labor Relations, and the City Civil Service Commission, seeking an order to vacate the determinations which denied the grievance at each step of the procedure and to direct the Civil Service Commission to reinstate his seniority and restore his title of Resource Consultant. After determining that the petitioner had failed to establish any contractual violation on the part of the Department of Social Services, the court went on to discuss whether Kaufman had in fact demanded arbitration and whether the union had wrongfully refused to proceed to arbitration on his behalf.]

If petitioner had established that his "transfer" was in violation of the contract, there would remain the issue as to whether petitioner could resort to direct action in face of the Step IV provision for arbitration which, pursuant to the contract, could be prosecuted only by the Union, and whether there was truth in his statement that his request for arbitration was rejected by the Union because of his non-membership.

The law is well established that by union membership an employee indicates he "has entrusted his rights to his union representative" and ordinarily has no individual right to demand or control the arbitration procedures (Parker v. Borock, 5 N.Y.2d 156, 182 N.Y.S.2d 577, 156 N.E.2d 297; Matter of Soto [Goldman], 7 N.Y.2d 397, 198 N.Y.S.2d 282, 165 N.E.2d 855; Chupka v. Lorenz-Schneider, 12 N.Y.2d 1, 233 N.E.2d 929, 186 N.E.2d 191). There is however, a line of cases in other jurisdictions which imposes on a union the duty of fair representation to its members and that the violation of that duty permits the employee to proceed directly against the employer. The authorities are exhaustively researched and discussed in Jenkins v. Schluderberg-T, etc., Co., 217 Md. 556, 144 A.2d 88 (see 45 Corn. L.Q. 25). In *Jenkins,* the court held that where the union acted in an arbitrary and discriminatory manner in failing to proceed on behalf of the employee against the employer, the employee may proceed directly. The court quoted (at pp. 564-565, 144 A.2d at p. 93) from the article by Professor Cox in 69 Harvard Law Review 601, 652:

> " 'While the rule which bars an individual employee from bringing an action on the contract when the union is unwilling to take the case to arbitration is sound if the union has made an adjustment or is satisfied that the grievance lacks merit, nevertheless it would work injustice in situations where the union is unwilling to press the claim because of indifference or reluctance to suffer the expense. Both factors come into play under open-shop contracts when a grievance having no precedent value is filed by a nonmember, whose failure to pay dues means that he contributes nothing to the cost of acting as his representative. One solution would be to open arbitration proceedings to individual grievants. Another alternative is to allow the employees to bring suit against the employer and union as codefendants upon analogy to the bill in equity which the beneficiary of a trust may maintain against the trustee who fails to press a claim against a third person. The suit would fail on the merits if it appeared that the collective bargaining representative had dropped the grievance for *lack of merit or had negotiated a reasonable adjustment.*' "

The court also quoted (p. 565, 144 P.2d p. 93) from Professor Cox's article, "Individual Enforcement of Collective Bargaining Agreements," (8 Lab. L.J. 850, 858), which is most pertinent to a situation where the employee is a non-member of the union, as follows:

> " 'In my opinion the presumption should be against individual enforcement of a collective bargaining agreement *unless the union has unfairly refused* to act. . . . The bargaining representative would be guilty of a breach of duty if it refused to press a justifiable grievance either because of laziness, prejudice or *unwillingness to expend* money *on behalf of employees who were not*

*members of the union.* Individual enforcement would then become appropriate. . . .' (Emphasis added.)"

The broad authority of the union as exclusive bargaining agent, even where it springs from statute, in the negotiation and administration of a collective bargaining agreement, is accompanied by the responsibility of fair representation (Humphrey v. Moore, 375 U.S. 335, 342, 84 S. Ct. 363, 11 L. Ed. 2d 370; Vaca v. Sipes, 386 U.S. 171, 177, 87 S. Ct. 903, 17 L. Ed. 2d 842). In *Vaca,* the court, in firm dictum, stated (pp. 184-186, 87 S. Ct. p. 914):

"However, if the wrongfully discharged employee himself resorts to the courts before the grievance procedures have been fully exhausted, the employer may well defend on the ground that the exclusive remedies provided by such a contract have not been exhausted. Since the employee's claim is based upon breach of the collective bargaining agreement, he is bound by terms of that agreement which govern the manner in which contractual rights may be enforced. For this reason, it is settled that the employee must at least attempt to exhaust exclusive grievance and arbitration procedures established by the bargaining agreement. Republic Steel Corp. v. Maddox, 379 U.S. 650, 85 S. Ct. 614, 13 L. Ed. 2d 580. However, because these contractual remedies have been devised and are often controlled by the union and the employer, they may well prove unsatisfactory or unworkable for the individual grievant. The problem then is to determine under what circumstances the individual employee may obtain judicial review of his breach-of-contract claim despite his failure to secure relief through the contractual remedial procedures.

. . . .

"We think that another situation when the employee may seek judicial enforcement of his contractual rights arises if, as is true here, the union has sole power under the contract to invoke the higher stages of the grievance procedure, *and* if, as is alleged here, the employee-plaintiff has been prevented from exhausting his contractual remedies by the union's *wrongful* refusal to process the grievance. It is true that the employer in such a situation may have done nothing to prevent exhaustion of the exclusive contractual remedies to which he agreed in the collective bargaining agreement. But the employer has committed a wrongful discharge in breach of that agreement, a breach which could be remedied through the grievance process to the employee-plaintiff's benefit were it not for the union's breach of its statutory duty of fair representation to the employee. To leave the employee remediless in such circumstances would, in our opinion, be a great injustice. We cannot believe that Congress, in conferring upon employers and unions the power to establish exclusive grievance procedures, intended to confer upon unions such unlimited discretion to deprive injured employees of all remedies for breach of contract. Nor do we think that Congress intended to shield employers from the natural consequences of their breaches of bargaining agreements by wrongful union conduct in the enforcement of such agreements. Cf. Richardson v. Texas & N.O.R. Co., 242 F.2d 230, 235-236 (C.A. 5th Cir.).

For these reasons, we think the wrongfully discharged employee may bring an action against his employer in the face of a defense based upon the failure to exhaust contractual remedies, provided the employee can prove that the union as bargaining agent breached its duty of fair representation in its handling of the employee's grievance. . . ."

(*See,* also, Thomas P. Lewis, "Fair Representation in Grievance Administration: Vaca v. Sipes" in the Supreme Court Review [1967], p. 81; see, also, dictum in Belinski v. Delco Appliance Corporation, 23 A.D.2d 805, 258 N.Y.S.2d 61, lv. to app. den. 16 N.Y.2d 482, 261 N.Y.S.2d 1026, 209 N.E.2d 563, citing Humphrey v. Moore, 375 U.S. 335, 84 S. Ct. 363, 11 L. Ed. 2d 370).

The authority of the Social Service Employees Union in the case at bar arises from statute (N.Y.C. Collective Bargaining Law, Administrative Code, Chap. 54; Local Law 53-1967; and implemented by the Mayor's Executive Order No. 52). The Union by its contract undertook to represent *all* Caseworkers as their "sole and exclusive" agent (Art. I). As such it was under a duty to entertain and consider petitioner's alleged grievance on the merits so as to determine whether to prosecute it to arbitration if, in fact, a demand had been made upon it for such relief. The court determines, however, that the Union did not violate this duty since it finds as a fact that petitioner at no time made a request of the Union to demand arbitration of his alleged grievances. Under the circumstances, it may not be said that petitioner has fully exhausted his contractual grievance procedures, since, as expressed in Vaca v. Sipes (*supra,* citing Republic Steel Corp. v. Maddox, 379 U.S. 650, 85 S. Ct. 614, 13 L. Ed. 2d 580), the employee must at least *attempt* to exhaust exclusive grievance and arbitration procedures established by the bargaining agent as a condition precedent to proceeding against the employer. (See, also, Bilinski v. Delco Appliance Division, General Motors Corporation, 23 A.D.2d 805, 258 N.Y.S.2d 61, lv. to app. den. 16 N.Y.2d 482, 261 N.Y.S.2d 1026, 209 N.E.2d 563, *supra,* but cf. Pattenge v. Wagner Iron Works, 275 Wis. 495, 82 N.W.2d 172).

Assuming, therefore, that the petitioner was transferred in violation of the collective bargaining agreement (which the court found earlier not to be the case), it is, nonetheless, clear that the petitioner would not be entitled to relief, even under the theory of "Jenkins," "Vaca" and allied cases, because petitioner failed to first exhaust his contractual remedies.

Accordingly, judgment is directed dismissing the petition on the merits.

## BELANGER v. MATTESON

Rhode Island Supreme Court
346 A.2d 124 (1975), *cert. denied,* 424 U.S. 968 (1976)

KELLEHER, Justice: — This is an appeal from a Superior Court judgment vacating an arbitration award which had been granted under the terms of a collective bargaining agreement between the Warwick Teachers' Union Local 915, AFT, AFL-CIO (Union) and the Warwick School Committee (School Committee).

The Union is the exclusive bargaining agent of all the teachers employed by the School Committee.... The controversy in this case concerns, in part, the provisions of the contract which was in force from February 1, 1972 to January 31, 1973.

On June 22, 1972, the School Committee posted a notice of a vacancy for the position of Business Department Head at Warwick Veterans' Memorial High School. The vacancy was a "promotional position" within the terms of the contract, and the notice was posted in compliance with its terms. Four teachers applied for the position, including plaintiff and one of the named defendants, Arthur B. Matteson. The candidates were interviewed, and their credentials reviewed by a committee of school administrators.... This committee unanimously recommended the appointment of Belanger to the vacant position.

Its recommendation was in turn reviewed by the superintendent, who concurred in its decision. Finally, the matter was put before the School Committee who voted to appoint Belanger to the post.

Upon learning that he had been unsuccessful in his bid for the promotion, Matteson met with Mr. Venditto, the Assistant Superintendent in Charge of Personnel to discuss his dissatisfaction. This was his right under art. V, sec. 4(d) of the agreement. He did not obtain satisfaction from this discussion, and thereafter wrote to his union representative and requested the Union to invoke on his behalf the grievance procedures provided in the collective bargaining agreement. The core of Matteson's grievance rested with his belief that the School Committee had violated the agreement by appointing Belanger. Article V, sec. 4(b) provides that, "[c]andidates shall be recommended on the basis of qualifications for the position. Where qualifications are considered equal, seniority in the Warwick School System shall prevail." It is undisputed that Matteson has more seniority than Belanger. Throughout this controversy, Matteson and the Union have insisted that since Matteson was at least as equally qualified for the position as Belanger, the appointment should have been given to the senior person.

The School Committee appointed Belanger on August 1, 1972. On August 7, 1972, the Union filed a written notice of Matteson's grievance with the Assistant Superintendent in Charge of Personnel. The Assistant Superintendent met with Matteson and a union representative in early September. On October 11, 1972, he sent Matteson a letter notifying him that his decision was to retain Belanger in the post of department head. The Union followed the grievance procedures set forth in the agreement. It first placed Matteson's cause before the Superintendent and then went before the School Committee. Matteson, having had no success at the administrative level, requested the Union to take his complaint to arbitration. The Union met in executive committee and voted to initiate the arbitration.

A hearing was held on April 6, 1973, before three arbitrators . . .

The issue submitted to the arbitrators by both sides was: "Has the Committee violated Article V, Section 4(b) of the collective bargaining agreement by not appointing Mr. Arthur Matteson as Business Department Head at Veterans' Memorial High School? If so, what shall the remedy be?"

. . . . On August 16, 1973 the arbitrators rendered a decision. They ruled that Matteson was entitled to the appointment as head of the Business Department.

After a full year on the job, Belanger found himself deprived of his promotion and back in the classroom. He wrote to his principal and the Union and requested that a grievance be filed on his behalf as he wished to challenge this demotion.

The Union president responded that, although the Union would be happy to file a grievance for him alleging that the School Committee had not adequately represented or protected his interest in his former position as department head, it would not ask for his reinstatement in that position because: "We [the Union] cannot, at this time, however, ask for a remedy which in effect would reverse a decision which was a result of a grievance filed by the Union. This would be illogical and inconsistent with our role as bargaining agent and our obligation under the contract. We have, after all, agreed to make binding arbitration the final step in our grievance procedure."

Thereafter, Belanger instituted this ligitation in the Superior Court. He named as defendants Matteson, the Union, the arbitrators, and the School Committee and asked the court to overturn the arbitrators' decision and reinstate him. His suit was based on 2 grounds: (1) that the arbitrators exceeded their jurisdiction, and (2) that the Union breached its duty to fairly represent his interests when it decided to pursue Matteson's grievance.

The trial justice found that there existed a duty of fair representation which the Union had breached, and that the award was in excess of the arbitrators' power and thus void. He vacated the award, and reinstated Belanger. Matteson and the Union appealed. We will first consider the duty of fair representation facet of this appeal. . . . The question of the duty owed by a union to its members is one of first impression in this court. It has, however, been extensively litigated in other jurisdictions, most notably in the federal courts, in cases arising under the National Labor Relations Act, 29 U.S.C.A. § 151 et seq. (1973), the Labor Management Relations Act, 1947, 29 U.S.C.A. § 141 et seq. (1973), and the Railway Act, 45 U.S.C.A. § 151 et seq. (1972).

The first of what has become a long line of cases was Steele v. Louisville & Nashville R. R., 323 U.S. 192, 65 S.Ct. 226, 89 L.Ed. 173, 15 LRRM 708 (1944). There, the Court held that the Railway Labor Act, in providing that an organization chosen by the majority of employees would be the exclusive representative of all the employees within its class, mandated a concomitant duty "to act for and not against those whom it represents," and "to exercise fairly the power conferred upon it in behalf of all those for whom it acts . . . ." [Citing cases.]

By taking away the right of individual employees to further their interests individually or to organize into numerous small units to deal with their employer, Congress has given a union power and control over the working lives of each of its members. A corollary of such power is the duty to act for the benefit of its members.

Our Legislature has created a structure of labor regulations which parallels in many significant respects the federal scheme. Our focus here is G.L. 1956 (1968 Reenactment) § 28-9.3-1 et seq., entitled Arbitration of School Teacher Disputes. . . ." Section 28-9.3-3 mandates that the school committee recognize the labor organization chosen by the teachers to be their "sole and exclusive" bargaining agent. Thus, a labor organization representing teachers of this state has the same broad authority in the negotiation, administration, and enforcement of the collective bargaining agreement as does a union regulated by federal law. We find ourselves in agreement with the persuasive logic of the Steele opinion and its progeny, and, therefore hereby recognize, as implicit in our Act, a statutory duty on the part of an exclusive bargaining agent to fairly and adequately represent the interests of all of those for whom it negotiates and contracts, not only those who are members, but all those who are part of the bargaining unit.

The union and its bargaining unit are necessarily composed of many individuals with diverse views and oft-times conflicting employment demands. The whole purpose behind the creation of the union is, however, to present a solid, unified front to the employer. "In unity there is strength," went the old organizing slogan, and it was the truth. In dealing with the employer, the union gains its negotiating power from the fact that it speaks with one voice for all the employees.

That we find a duty on the part of the union does not, however, solve the controversy before us. We must define the parameters of the duty, and then apply it to the facts as found by the Superior Court. . . .

In the negotiation process, we hold that a union must make an honest effort to serve the interest of all of its members, without hostility to any, and its power must be exercised in complete good faith and with honesty of purpose. Ford Motor Co. v. Huffman, supra.

Where the union and the employer have provided by contract for the internal settlement of disputes by means of grievance and arbitration procedures, and where these settlement procedures can be initiated and continued solely by the union, the union is likewise subject to a duty of fair representation in its handling of employee grievances. As in contract negotiations, the union as it deals with grievances must often take a position which is detrimental to some employees as it is helpful to others. The duty upon the Union here is to "... in good faith and in a nonarbitrary manner, make decisions as to the merits of particular grievances," Vaca v. Sipes, 386 U.S. 171, 194, 87 S.Ct. 903, 919, 17 L.Ed.2d 842, 860, 64 LRRM 2369, 2378 (1967), and, if it decides to pursue a grievance, it must not do so in a perfunctory manner.

Applying these standards of conduct to the facts of this case, we are faced with a clear breach by the Union of the duty it owed to Belanger. The testimony was undisputed, and the trial justice found that throughout the grievance procedure, the Union and its representatives acted without ever contacting Belanger or considering his qualifications for the position; the Union aligned itself with Matteson in seeking Belanger's removal; and at the arbitration hearing the union representatives attempted to demonstrate that Matteson, rather than Belanger, was entitled to the position. . . .

We have said a union may, and often must, take sides. But we wish to make it clear that it must act, when it does, in a nonarbitrary, nonperfunctory manner. Here the Union chose sides totally on the fortuitous circumstances of who the School Committee did not hire. It is true, in a very simplistic sense, that Matteson, being the only member of the bargaining unit with "a grievance," is therefore the only individual in need of Union support. But one would require blinders to accept this view. It should have been apparent to the Union that Matteson's grievance, although theoretically against the School Committee, was in reality against Belanger. Any action the Union took on Matteson's behalf threatened Belanger's job.

The Union had as much of an obligation to support Belanger as it had to support Matteson until such time as it had examined the qualifications of both candidates, and it believed that the seniority clause would control the selection process.

This was clearly a situation that was akin to the situations found in Humphrey, Huffman, and Vaca where a union faced with conflicting loyalties must make a choice as to which member it will support. To enforce a requirement of neutrality on the union in cases such as this would not, in our opinion, further the purposes of the statute which was designed to strengthen the power of teachers in controlling their employment situation by allowing them all to speak through a single, but strong voice. Neutrality could only weaken the power of employees to deal with their employer. Even if in any particular grievance procedure neutrality would not be harmful, the [cumulative] effect of such a stance taken over a period of time would undermine the position of the union as employee advocate in its dealings with the employer.

Also, by remaining neutral, the union would lose the ability to control the scope and focus of the arguments made on behalf of the employees. Professor Cox has argued that the settlement of an individual employee grievance involves more than the individual because precedent is established which will control the course of future employer-employee relations. This distinguished educator also points out that any time the parties do battle over their contract, they are also engaging in a process of negotiation over its terms.

The Union must choose its side in a nonarbitrary manner, based on its good-faith judgment as to the merits of the conflicting claims. In the present case the Union never offered Belanger an opportunity to present his case to them. It never recognized its duty to independently determine whether Matteson or Belanger was entitled to the job. It seems to us that the only fair procedure in this type of a conflict is for the Union, at the earliest stages of the grievance procedure, to investigate the case for both sides, to give both contestants an opportunity to be heard, and to submit their qualifications to the Union. We are not mandating a full-blown hearing, replete with strict rules of procedure and adversary proceedings. If the Union investigates in an informal manner, this would be sufficient so long as its procedure affords the two employees the ability to place all the relevant information before the Union. See Bures v. Houston Symphony Soc'y, 503 F.2d 842, 87 LRRM 3124 (5th Cir. 1974); Waiters' Union, Local 781 v. Hotel Ass'n, 162 U.S.App.D.C. 265, 498 F.2d 998, 86 LRRM 2001 (1974).

For a union to make a decision affecting its members without investigating the underlying factual situation is a clear breach of the duty of fair representation. De Arroyo v. Sindicato De Trabajadores Packinghouse, AFL-CIO, 425 F.2d 281, 74 LRRM 2028 (1st Cir. 1970). In an examination of the union's conduct in its discharge of its duty to the members of the bargaining unit, there are three possible foci for our analysis; the union's motives, its decision making procedures, and the reasons for its acting as it did. A court's investigation into the first two questions is proper and necessary. We will, however, be more careful in any review of the merits of the Union's decision. An inquiry into the merits would open the way for our substituting our judgment for that of the Union, and that is not our role. It will be enough protection for an employee represented by a union if we inquire into motives and ensure that the union has fairly considered both sides before taking a stand.

[The balance of the court's opinion limits the scope of the proper remedy for the breach of the duty of fair representation under the facts of this case, and holds that the panel of arbitrators did not exceed its authority in its decision to replace Belanger with Matteson.]

## NOTES

1. In Lowe v. Hotel & Restaurant Employees Union, Local 705, 389 Mich. 123, 205 N.W.2d 167 (1973), the Michigan Supreme Court sustained a jury verdict in favor of an employee against his union representatives for a breach of the duty of fair representation. The employee had been discharged from his job and the union refused to process his grievance to arbitration under the collective bargaining agreement. In rejecting defendants' argument that the suit should have been dismissed because the employee failed to exhaust his internal union remedies, the Michigan court set forth the following general principles with respect to duty of fair representation:

In the case before us, plaintiff's complaint alleges a duty of representation and a breach of that duty. It does not allege the conclusion that the defendant union's action was arbitrary and the product of bad faith, but it does allege facts from which such conclusions could be drawn.

The trial judge instructed the jury in these words:

"In other words, it is a question of pure reasonableness in the assessment of the action of the Union. Did they do what any prudent outfit would do in the circumstances that faced them? Did they make an honest effort to find out who was right and who was wrong, and did they let the blame fall right where it should; or did they take an arbitrary position, and not do what they should have done on behalf of this man?''

Defendants did not object to the charge. Under the charge as given, the jury was properly advised that the plaintiff should recover only if they found the union's refusal to take plaintiff's grievance to arbitration was arbitrary and not a fair, reasonable and honest judgment on their part.

If that standard is less exacting than has appeared in other cases, it reflects a belief that a union owes a greater duty to its members than merely to refrain from persecuting them.

Every man's employment is of utmost importance to him. It occupies his time, his talents, and his thoughts. It controls his economic destiny. It is the means by which he feeds his family and provides for their security. It bears upon his personal well-being, his mental and physical health.

In days gone by, a man's occupation literally gave him his name. Even today, continuous and secure employment contributes to a sense of identity for most people.

It is no solace to a man fired from his job that his union acted without spite, animosity, ill will, and hostility toward him. If he has been wrongfully discharged by his employer, in violation of his contract of employment, a collective bargaining agreement made for his benefit and protection, it is unthinkable that he should be denied relief — denied justice — by the courts.

But it is argued that precedential authority places the worker in a cross fire between two rules of law.

He cannot bring an action against his employer because the grievance procedure established by the collective bargaining agreement must be exhausted as a condition precedent to such action. Leadon v. Detroit Lumber Co., 340 Mich. 74 (1954); Cortez v. Ford Motor Co., 349 Mich. 108 (1957); and Spencer v. Wall Wire Products Co., 357 Mich. 296 (1959). And he cannot exhaust his contract remedy because the final stages of the grievance machinery can only be activated by the union. . . .

This, of course, is the precise dilemma propounded so eloquently by Mr. Justice Black in his ringing dissent in Vaca v. Sipes:

"Today the Court holds that an employee with a meritorious claim has no absolute right to have it either litigated or arbitrated."

Indeed, the rule in Vaca, as observed by Mr. Justice Black, gives the employee either two remedies or none. Absent union bad faith, he can recover against neither the union nor the company. Given union bad faith, he has an action against both. . . .

In this case . . . there is no basis to conclude that the trial court thought, or led the jury to believe, that the question of whether or not Lowe had been wrongfully discharged was dispositive of the issue of the union's liability. . . .

In summary, we hold that the testimony adduced at the trial of this cause and the evidence presented to the jury, taken in the light most favorable to the plaintiff, was sufficient for the jury to have concluded that the plaintiff was wrongfully discharged by his employer and that the defendant union violated its obligation toward him to afford him fair representation by making no effort whatsoever to settle his grievance, by ignoring his grievance, by processing it in a perfunctory manner, and that the plaintiff was not required, either as a matter of fact or law, to make a formal appeal to the international president or the international executive board as a condition precedent to this action against the employer and the union.

2. Compare the *Belanger* case with Matter of Brighton Transportation Ass'n., N.Y. PERB Case No. U-2543, 1977-78 PEB ¶40,129 (1977), wherein the PERB found that a union's decision not to take a member's grievance to arbitration was made too casually, without sufficient opportunity having been given to the member to persuade the union to proceed further, since he had not been provided with a chance to respond to the presentation of the employer. Nonetheless, because the evidence failed to indicate that the union's conduct was improperly motivated or so irresponsible as to constitute a breach of its duty of fair representation, the worker's unfair representation charge was dismissed. *But cf.* Ruzicka v. General Motors Corp., 523 F.2d 306 (6th Cir. 1975), *reh'g denied,* 528 F.2d 912 (1976), wherein the Court held that bad faith is not an essential element of an

unfair representation claim, indicating that it is enough if the union arbitrarily ignores an employee's grievance and merely allows it to expire out of negligent and perfunctory handling.

3. In McGrail v. Detroit Fed'n. of Teachers, 82 L.R.R.M. 2623 (Mich. Cir. Ct. 1973), substitute teachers sued the union which represented them and regular teachers for allegedly breaching its duty of fair representation for failing to obtain a pay increase for them during the 1967-68 year when raises were procured for regular personnel. The court quoted from Ford Motor Co. v. Huffman, 345 U.S. 330, 73 S.Ct. 681, 97 L.Ed. 1048 (1953), and then proceeded to reject the plaintiffs' contention:

> "The mere existence of . . . differences does not make them invalid. The complete satisfaction of all who are represented is hardly to be expected. A wide range of reasonableness must be allowed a statutory bargaining representative in serving the unit it represents subject always to complete good faith and honesty of purpose in the exercise of its discretion.
>
> *"Compromises on a temporary basis, with a view to long range advantages are natural incidents of negotiation. Differences in wages, hours and conditions of employment reflect countless variables."* (Emphasis added)
>
> . . . . . .
>
> In the present case before the court the plaintiff has simply alleged a breach of a duty to fair representation and bases this solely on the fact that the classes he represents did not receive a raise during a certain period covered under a contract. This in itself does not constitute arbitrary or discriminatory action, bad faith or fraud. At most, the facts plaintiff shows amount to a temporary compromise for the benefit of all, which the union is entitled to make.

What if substitutes were denied such increases for three consecutive years while regular teachers were obtaining annual raises?

4. The California Supreme Court has ruled that a public employee has a statutory right to have a union representative accompany him to a meeting with his employer when the worker reasonably anticipates that such a meeting may involve his union activities and disciplinary sanctions may be invoked against him because of those activities. Social Workers Union v. Alameda County Welfare Dept., 11 Cal.3d 382, 521 P.2d 453 (1974). Furthermore, in Malone v. United States Postal Service, 526 F.2d 1099 (6th Cir. 1975), the court held that an employee who chose to appeal his discharge through the contractual grievance-arbitration procedures, rather than through a Civil Service Commission procedure available to him as a preference-eligible veteran, was provided with the "fair hearing" guaranteed by the Postal Reorganization Act, and that since he opted for grievance-arbitration, he was required to be represented by an official of his exclusive bargaining agent instead of his own attorney. What fair representation standard should be applied to a union representative in such situations?

5. Should an arbitration award denying a grievance be set aside on the basis of meritorious charges by the affected grievant that the union failed to represent him adequately at the hearing? Compare De Losa v. Transport Workers Union, 73 L.R.R.M. 2620 (N.Y. Sup. Ct. 1970), with Hines v. Anchor Motor Freight, Inc., 424 U.S. 554, 96 S.Ct. 1048, 47 L.Ed.2d 231 (1976).

6. Individuals who believe that their union has not fairly represented them may not always be able to obtain judicial relief. A Wisconsin Circuit Court has held that the WERC has exclusive jurisdiction over claims that a union has breached its duty of fair representation. Bodensack v. AFSCME, Local 587, 81 L.R.R.M. 2639 (1972). Although in Kuhn v. Letter Carriers, 570 F.2d 757 (1978), the Eighth Circuit Court ruled that a federal district court lacked subject matter jurisdiction under 28 U.S.C. § 1331, which provides district courts with jurisdiction over actions arising under the "Constitution, laws, or treaties of" the United States, of a federal worker's claim that a union representing him under Executive Order 11491 had breached its duty of fair representation, since Executive Orders are not "laws" of the United States within the meaning of § 1331, the fact that the duty of fair representation for federal workers is now codified in the Civil Service Reform Act of 1978 would appear to negate the impact of this holding.

7. In the private sector, allegations of a breach of the duty of fair representation may appear in two different contexts: as a defense to the charge of failure to exhaust contract remedies in a breach of contract suit against the employer, Vaca v. Sipes, 386 U.S. 171, 87 S. Ct. 903, 17 L. Ed. 2d 842 (1967), or as the basis for a direct action against the union itself, Syres v. Oil Workers Local 23, 223 F.2d 739 (5th Cir.), *rev'd per curiam,* 350 U.S. 892 (1955). *Also see generally,* Steele v. Louisville & Nashville R.R., 323 U.S. 192, 65 S. Ct. 226, 89 L. Ed. 173 (1944); Brotherhood of Ry. Trainmen v. Howard, 343 U.S. 768, 72 S. Ct. 1022, 96 L. Ed. 1283 (1952); Ford Motor Co. v. Huffman, 345 U.S. 330, 73 S. Ct. 681, 97 L. Ed. 1048 (1953); Conley v. Gibson, 355 U.S. 41, 78 S. Ct. 99, 2 L. Ed. 2d 80 (1957); Humphrey v. Moore, 375 U.S. 335, 84 S. Ct. 363, 11 L. Ed. 2d 370 (1964).

The burden of proving a breach of the duty of fair representation is not one which is easily carried. "A breach of the statutory duty of fair representation occurs only when a union's conduct toward a member of the collective bargaining unit is arbitrary, discriminatory, or in bad faith." Vaca v. Sipes, *supra,* 386 U.S. at 189-90.

Consider the duty of fair representation in light of the principle of majority rule. Should the burden of proof in a breach of fair representation case be so stringent? Evaluate the following arguments:

*For a lighter burden of proof:* By establishing itself as exclusive representative (where this is permitted by law in the public sector) a union acquires great power to affect the wages and working conditions of the employees in the unit. The union's responsibility to members of the collective bargaining unit should be commensurate with its power. A lighter burden of proof would enable the courts to better protect the interests of members of minority racial and ethnic groups, minority-union and non-union members of this unit, and others who might be subject to union discrimination. In addition, the unions themselves would be helped; they would be forced to remain constantly aware of their obligation to represent *all* the employees in the unit.

*For the continuation of a heavy burden of proof:* Private dispute settlement in employment relationships can operate efficiently only if union officials remain relatively free to compromise grievance claims and even to refuse to press unmeritorious grievances. If burden of proof standards were lowered, union officials would feel more pressure to avoid charges of unfair representation by taking each claim to the final stage of the grievance procedure. Early settlement would be discouraged; frivolous claims would be encouraged. In addition, judges would be more inclined to evaluate the merits of arbitration cases, thus hampering the efficacy of the arbitration process. The individual employee has other ways of vindicating his rights through the courts (as by Title VII or § 1983 suits) which do not involve harm to private dispute settlement mechanisms. There is no reason, therefore, to change the rule that a union is presumed to be acting in the best interest of the employees in the unit and will not be found guilty of unfair representation in the absence of clear proof of willful misconduct.

8. Most collective bargaining agreements specify that the right to invoke the grievance-arbitration machinery is a union prerogative. *Cf.* Black-Clawson Co. v. IAM, Lodge 355, 313 F.2d 179 (2d Cir. 1962). Should an individual employee have the right to have his grievance arbitrated, even if the union does not concur? If yes, should the grievant be required to reimburse the employer for its expenses if the grievance is denied? Should the union have to reimburse the grievant for his expenses if he prevails before the arbitrator?

9. *See* Note, *Public Sector Grievance Procedures, Due Process, and the Duty of Fair Representation,* 89 HARV. L. REV. 752 (1976). *See generally* Aaron, *Some Aspects of the Union's Duty of Fair Representation,* 22 OHIO ST. L.J. 39 (1961); Clark, *The Duty of Fair Representation: A Theoretical Structure,* 51 TEXAS L. REV. 1119 (1973); Cox, *The Duty of Fair Representation,* 2 VILL. L. REV. 151 (1957); Gould, *Labor Arbitration of Grievances Involving Racial Discrimination,* 118 PA. L. REV. 40 (1969); Wellington, *Union Democracy and Fair Representation: Federal Responsibility in a Federal System,* 67 YALE L.J. 1327 (1958); Note, *Union Discretion and the Abridgement of Employee Rights,* 51 ORE. L. REV. 248 (1971).

# F. LEGALLY IMPOSED FINANCIAL LIMITATIONS ON PUBLIC EMPLOYERS

## NORTON TEACHERS ASSOCIATION v. TOWN OF NORTON

Massachusetts Supreme Judicial Court
361 Mass. 150, 279 N.E.2d 659 (1972)

REARDON, Justice: This is a bill brought under G.L. c. 231A, in which the Norton Teachers Association and the Norton School Committee seek a determination of the validity of certain provisions of a collective bargaining contract entitling teachers to a salary increase in 1969. The plaintiffs seek also an order requiring the town of Norton and Edward S. Smith, Jr., its treasurer, to make payments in accordance with the provisions of the agreement. The defendants appeal from a final decree ordering them to pay the sums due under the agreement for 1969.

The trial judge made certain findings, rulings, and an order, which he adopted as a report of material facts. We summarize those facts, together with others we find for ourselves.

On September 3, 1968, the plaintiffs entered into a collective bargaining agreement pursuant to G.L. c. 149, §§ 178G-178N. The agreement, which covered the period between September 2, 1968, and August 31, 1970, provided for a higher salary schedule than one previously in effect.[1] The contract contained provisions for renegotiation on compensation. The 1968 appropriation of the school committee was insufficient to cover the increased salaries for the period September 2, 1968, to December 31, 1968. For that period the teachers were thus paid at a rate lower than that called for by the September 3 agreement.

On March 4, 1969, the annual town meeting voted down the following item in the warrant requested by the school committee: "To see if the Town will vote to raise sufficient money for teachers' salary and interest from September 1, 1968, to December 31, 1968, or take any action relative thereto." At that same meeting $1,287,462 was appropriated for the schools for 1969. It was a blanket appropriation and not detailed item by item.

On March 26, 1969, the collective bargaining agreement was amended for the second time. The amendment revised the salary schedule in the following way: (a) salaries for the period September 3-December 31, 1968, were reduced to correspond with the amounts actually paid; (b) salaries for January 1, 1969-March 9, 1969, were left at the levels originally provided for by the September 3, 1968, agreement; (c) salaries for March 10, 1969, to June 30, 1969, were higher than provided for in the September 3, 1968, agreement. The preamble to the amendment suggests the purpose of placing the teachers and other professional employees covered by the agreement in the financial position which would have been theirs had the school committee been able to meet its salary obligations under the original agreement from September 2 to December 31, 1968, or had the town voted in favor of the warrant item requested by the committee. The total appropriation for the 1969 school budget was sufficient to cover the higher salaries provided for in the amendment. The trial judge found that "the School

---

[1] On December 9, 1968, the contract was first amended to provide for an even higher salary schedule effective September 2, 1969. This amendment is not in issue.

Committee at all times was acting in good faith in an effort to meet its obligations under said contract of September 3, 1968 . . . and without any intent or purpose to evade the provisions of G.L. c. 44, § 31."

We face another in a long line of cases where the powers and duties of the school committee under G.L. c. 71 are challenged as being in conflict with certain provisions of the Municipal Finance Act, G.L. c. 44. See Casey v. Everett, 330 Mass. 220, 222, and cases cited.

The defendants base their argument on two sections of G.L. c. 44. Section 31, as amended by St. 1955, c. 259, provides, in pertinent part, that "[n]o department financed by municipal revenue . . . shall incur a liability in excess of the appropriation made for the use of such department. . . ." (It is uncontested that the 1968 school appropriation was insufficient to pay the salaries of the professional employees as agreed upon by the school committee and the teachers association for the period September 2, 1968, to December 31, 1968.)

Section 64, inserted by St. 1941, c. 179, provides: "Any town having unpaid bills of previous years which may be legally unenforceable due to the insufficiency of an appropriation in the year in which such bills were incurred, may, at an annual meeting by a four-fifths vote, or at a special meeting by a nine-tenths vote, of the voters present and voting at a meeting duly called, appropriate money to pay such bills. . . ." As noted above, the annual town meeting on March 4, 1969, rejected the school committee's request under this section to pay the teachers' salary increase for the period September 1, 1968 to December 31, 1968.

The defendants argue that the school committee, in the face of the town's rejection of its request, should not be allowed to achieve the same result indirectly by an increase in the 1969 salary level sufficient to compensate teachers for what they lost in 1968. It is further argued that the school committee in 1968 was prohibited from entering into a contract increasing salaries in excess of the amount appropriated because of G.L. c. 44, § 31. Picking up the increase in the form of a higher 1969 salary schedule, according to the defendants, constitutes a mere gratuity and an invalid action. The defendants further argue that this was, in substance, the payment of a bill for salaries incurred in a prior year without compliance with G.L. c. 44, § 64.

We held in Callahan v. Woburn, 306 Mass. 265, that the school committee could bind the city by contracts of employment with teachers in excess of appropriations available at the time the contracts were made. Before us is a case distinguishable from the Callahan case since in this instance there was no discrepancy between the amount appropriated by the town for the schools for 1968 and the amount requested by the school committee. Yet as indicated in the preamble to the March 26 amendment, the higher salaries were provided for by this amendment in recognition that the teachers were required to accept lower salaries in the latter part of 1968 than they contracted for.

It does not follow necessarily that the increases for 1969 were gifts of what could not have legally been paid to the teachers in 1968. It is significant that only those teachers who actually worked in 1969 received the increase. This situation is to be contrasted with Whittaker v. Salem, 216 Mass. 483, 485. There a school committee's grant to a principal of a year's leave of absence at one half his regular salary was held invalid as a "pure gratuity." This was held notwithstanding that the principal in question had overworked during the previous year and endangered his health. On the other hand, in Averell v. Newburyport, 241 Mass. 333, 335, we said in upholding the school committee provision for paid sick leave, "Although the rule increasing the possible length of absence without loss of pay was adopted after the salaries for the year had been fixed by vote of the committee, that is not decisive against the plaintiff. *In principle it stands on the same footing as an increase of salary during the period of a contract. It was not a mere gratuity. It may have been regarded as an additional incentive to superior work"* (emphasis supplied). See Attorney Gen. v. Woburn, 317 Mass. 465, 467; Fitchburg Teachers Assn. v. School Comm. of Fitchburg, — Mass. —, —, 77 LRRM 3132. We think the statement in the Averell case is sound.

We are further supported in our determination by the unwavering line of cases enforcing, when possible, "the supremacy of the school committee's authority in matters pertaining to the management of the public schools." Casey v. Everett, 330 Mass. 220, 222, and cases cited. In particular, we have often held that the school committee has complete power to fix the compensation of teachers. See Leonard v. School Comm. of Springfield, 241 Mass. 325, 329-330; Watt v. Chelmsford, 323 Mass. 697, 700; Lynch v. Fall River, 336 Mass. 558, 559; Collins v. Boston, 338 Mass. 704, 707. The only question is the sufficiency of funds available to the school committee. Fitchburg Teachers Assn. v. School Comm. of Fitchburg, — Mass. —, —, 77 LRRM 3132. Here it was uncontested that the total appropriation for the 1969 school budget was sufficient to cover the increases due under the amendment.

The problem of Callahan v. Woburn, 306 Mass. 265, came here in part because the contracts with the teachers did not run from year to year concurrently with the town's successive fiscal years. We held in the Callahan case, at page 268, that such contracts were nonetheless proper.

Furthermore, it cannot be denied that if the original agreement of September 3, 1968, had contained those salary schedules as finally provided for by the March 26, 1969, amendment (i.e., with the increases not coming into effect until 1969), there would be no question as to its validity. The impact on the town would have been the same. All circumstances considered, the agreement with the March 26 amendment is valid and enforceable. There was no error.

Decree affirmed.

## BOARD OF EDUCATION, YONKERS CITY SCHOOL DISTRICT v. YONKERS FEDERATION OF TEACHERS

New York Court of Appeals
40 N.Y.2d 268, 353 N.E.2d 569 (1976)

BREITEL, Chief Judge: — This appeal, in arbitration, involves a so-called "job security" clause in a collective agreement between a public employer and public employees. The Yonkers City Board of Education, because of the City's severe financial stringency, terminated the services of some teachers covered by the "job security" clause. The Yonkers City School District is not "independent" but receives its funds from the City of Yonkers.

The teachers' union demanded arbitration under the collective agreement and the board brought this proceeding to stay arbitration (CPLR art. 75). Supreme Court granted the stay and declared the job security provision invalid as contrary to public policy. The Appellate Division affirmed and the teachers' union appeals.

The issue is whether a public employer is free to bargain voluntarily about job security and also free, under the collective agreement's provisions, to submit to arbitration disputes about job security.

There should be a reversal. A provision in a collective agreement guaranteeing public employees job security for a reasonable period of time is not prohibited by any statute or controlling decisional law and is not contrary to public policy.

Hence, the board of education was free to bargain voluntarily about job security and was also, therefore, free to agree to arbitration of prospective disputes about job security.

In November, 1974, the board of education and the teachers' union entered into a collective agreement covering the period from July 1, 1974, to June 30, 1977. Paragraph A of Article VIII of the agreement provides: "During the life of this contract no person in this bargaining unit shall be terminated due to budgetary reasons or abolition of programs as provided for under the Tenure Law." Article XIII contains relatively broad grievance and arbitration clauses (§ A, subd 2; § C, subd 3, par a).

In October, 1975, faced with sharp cuts in its budget made by the City of Yonkers, the board of education decided to lay off approximately 50 of its employees, including a number of teachers. The teachers' union filed a grievance with the Acting Superintendent, which was denied, and then demanded arbitration. On October 28, 1975, the board brought this proceeding for a stay of arbitration.

On November 11, 1975, the Legislature passed, and the Governor approved, the New York State Financial Emergency Act for the City of Yonkers (L. 1975, ch. 871). The financial condition of the city was declared to be a "disaster" (id., § 1). The city was directed to develop an 18-month plan to balance the municipal budget by July 1, 1977 and to repay its creditors (§ 8, subd 1). In developing the plan the City was required to seek a stabilization of its work force and, to the extent that a reduction in the work force was necessary, attrition was to be the primary means to accomplish the reduction (§ 8, subd 2). The statute further provides that "[n]othing in this act shall be construed to impair the right of employees to organize or to bargain collectively" (§ 3, subd 3). The Emergency Financial Control Board was created and empowered to oversee the city's efforts and to approve the financial plan (§ 8, subd 3).

After the passage of the Financial Emergency Act and Supreme Court's subsequent decision denying the stay of arbitration, further layoffs occurred.

The teachers' union contends that neither statute nor controlling decisional law, nor public policy, prohibited the board from voluntarily negotiating, before the onset of the legislatively declared emergency, about job security and agreeing to submit to arbitration disputes about job security.

Section 200 of the Civil Service Law provides:

"The legislature of the state of New York declares that it is the public policy of the state and the purpose of this act to promote harmonious and cooperative relationships between government and its employees and to protect the public by assuring, at all times, the orderly and uninterrupted operations and functions of government. These policies are best effectuated by (a) granting to public employees the right of organization and representation, (b) requiring the state, local governments and other political subdivisions to negotiate with, and enter into written agreements with employee organizations representing public employees which have been certified or recognized, (c) encouraging such public employer and such employee organizations to agree upon procedures for resolving disputes . . ."

It has been held that, as a matter of public policy, an authorized procedure for resolving labor disputes is arbitration (Board of Educ. v. Bellmore, 39 N.Y.2d 167, 171, 92 LRRM 2244; Matter of Associated Teachers of Huntington v. Board of Educ., 33 N.Y.2d 229, 236, 85 LRRM 2795).

Under Article 14 of the Civil Service Law (Taylor Law), public employers are required to negotiate collectively with public employee organizations in determining the "terms and conditions of employment" (Civil Service Law, § 204, subd 2). But this is not the limit of the public employer's power. To effectuate the public policy favoring negotiation as the means of insuring "harmonious and cooperative relationships between government and its employees," a public employer possesses broad power voluntarily to negotiate all matters in controversy, whether or not they involve "terms and conditions of employment" subject to mandatory bargaining, and to agree to submit such controversies to arbitration (see Matter of Board of Education v. Associated Teachers of Huntington, 30 N.Y.2d 122, 130, 79 LRRM 2881, 2884).

The public employer's power to bargain collectively, while broad, is not unlimited. Although a public employer is free to negotiate any matter in controversy, whether or not it involves a term or condition of employment subject to mandatory bargaining, it may do so only in the absence of "plain and clear" prohibitions in statute or controlling decisional law, or restrictive public policy (see Matter of Susquehanna Valley School Dist. at Conklin [Susquehanna Valley Teachers' Assn.], 37 N.Y.2d 614, 616-618, 90 LRRM 3046; Syracuse Teachers' Assn. v. Board of Educ., 35 N.Y.2d 743, 744, 88 LRRM 2112; Matter of Board of Educ. v. Associated Teachers of Huntington, 30 N.Y.2d 122, 130, 79 LRRM 2881, 2884, supra).

The controversy in the Susquehanna case (supra) involved teacher staff size. The school district in a collective agreement had agreed to a stabilization of staff size, thus providing staff members with "job security" for the duration of the contract. In its 1973-1974 school budget, however, the school district abolished a number of staff positions. The teachers sought arbitration. On appeal, this court found no statute or controlling decisional law, nor any restrictive public policy, limiting the board of education's freedom to contract about staff size. Thus, the court held that the board was free to agree to submit to arbitration disputes about staff size.

The Susquehar.na case (supra) is dispositive of the instant case. There is no statute or controlling decisional law or other source of public policy prohibiting a public employer from voluntarily agreeing to submit controversies over staff size or "job security" to arbitration (see Matter of Brookhaven Comsewogue Union Free School Dist. [Port Jefferson Sta. Teachers' Assn.], — Misc.2d —, 91 LRRM 2824, N.Y.L.J., Jan. 9, 1976, at p. 11, col. 2).

Matter of Lippmann v. Delaney (48 A.D.2d 913, 90 LRRM 2186), decided by a divided court and relied upon by the board of education, was incorrectly decided (see, also, Matter of Carmel Cent. School Dist. [Carmel Teachers' Assn.], 76 Misc. 2d 63, 66-67). In the Lippmann case (supra), it was held that, since the public employer has the statutory power to abolish positions in good faith, it does not surrender that power in a collective bargaining agreement unless the abolition of a position constitutes a term or condition of employment and thus is subject to mandatory collective bargaining. Relying upon past determinations by the Public Employment Relations Board, the court concluded that abolition of a position was not a term or condition of employment and thus was not a proper subject of a collective bargaining agreement.

In the Lippmann case (supra), Mr. Justice Hopkins, joined by Mr. Justice Brennan, dissented. The dissenters correctly perceived the distinction between terms or conditions of employment which are subject to mandatory collective bargaining under the Taylor Law, and matters in controversy which, although not subject to mandatory bargaining, may voluntarily be included within a collective agreement by a public employer (see Matter of Susquehanna Valley School Dist. at Conklin [Susquehanna Valley Teachers' Assn.], 37 N.Y.2d 614,

616, 90 LRRM 3046, supra, for an elaboration of the distinction). As to such matters in controversy, the dissenters noted that the scope of the public employer's power to include them within a collective agreement is limited by plain and clear prohibitions in statute or decisional law (48 A.D.2d at p. 915). Thus, Mr. Justice Hopkins stated (p. 916, 90 LRRM p. 2188):

"The enlightened attitude of the [public employer] in making an agreement to protect its long-term employees who might be adversely affected by a reorganization should not be equated with a refusal of a municipality to negotiate terms freezing positions or salaries."

The board also contends that the Financial Emergency Act evinces a legislative determination of public policy that job abolition must be permitted in this case. In fact, quite the contrary is true.

The act evidences no policy favoring abrogation of collective agreements and abolition of teacher positions. As noted earlier, the act provides that it should not be construed to impair the right of employees to bargain collectively and specifies that primary recourse must be had to attrition to effect any reduction in the work force. Indeed, the overriding purpose of the act was to protect those who had entered into agreements with the city and to insure that these agreements would be kept not only by bondholders and noteholders, but all others who had engaged in contractual arrangements with the city.

A job security provision insures that, at least for the duration of the agreement, the employee need not fear being put out of a job. Such absence of fear may be critical to the maintenance and efficiency of public employment, just as the fear of inability to meet its debts may destroy the credit of the municipality. A job security clause is useless if the public employer is free to disregard it when it is first needed.

This is not to say, however, that all job security clauses are valid and enforceable or that they are valid and enforceable under all circumstances. Notably, the job security clause involved in this case and the staff size clause in the Susquehanna case (supra) were of relatively brief duration, three years and two years, respectively. Nor were the clauses negotiated in a time of financial emergency between parties of unequal bargaining power. Most important, the job security clause in the instant case is explicit in its protection of the teachers from abolition of their positions due to budgetary stringencies (compare the clauses involved in this case and in Matter of Burke v. Bowen, — N.Y.2d —, 92 LRRM 3331, decided herewith, with the clause involved in Yonkers School Crossing Guard Union v. City of Yonkers, — N.Y.2d —, 92 LRRM 3333, decided herewith).

Of course, collective bargaining agreements, and particularly job security clauses, do not derive from a "higher law" giving them a status denied to other public and contractual arrangements. To paraphrase language in another context, a collective bargaining agreement may not become a "suicide pact," as has been said of the Constitution. Ultimately, the saving of a municipality from bankruptcy is equally important to its employees as it is to its banking creditors, or to its citizenry. In bankruptcy all obligations may suffer impairment or dissolution, job security clauses included. But the collective agreement in question, negotiated before a legislatively declared emergency, short-term in length, and indistinguishable from the city's other contractual obligations which remain enforceable, is not yet vulnerable to attack as in violation of public policy.

Consequently, in this arbitration proceeding, the court has no power to pass upon the merits of the dispute (CPLR 7501). The merits are for the arbitrators to decide. It is also for the arbitrators to fashion the remedy appropriate to the circumstances, if it is determined that the agreement has been breached. In this context, of course, the financial condition of the city and its ability to fund the teaching positions are relevant and may be considered. But since there is no statute or controlling decisional law, or public policy prohibiting a public employer from voluntarily agreeing to a job security clause, the clause was valid and the parties should proceed to arbitration.

On this analysis, it is unnecessary, if it is at all relevant, to reach the constitutional question of whether the employer's action constituted an impairment of the contract between the parties.

Accordingly, the order of the Appellate Division should be reversed, with costs, the application for a stay of arbitration denied, and the cross-motion to compel arbitration granted.

## NOTES

1. In Providence Teachers Union, Local 953 v. McGovern, 319 A.2d 358, 86 L.R.R.M. 2899 (R.I. 1974), it was decided that money due to retired teachers under the terms of an arbitration award interpreting the severance pay provisions of a bargaining agreement constituted a debt of the city which had to be satisfied by the city treasurer. In reaching this result, the Court indicated that a provision in the city charter requiring the approval of the city controller before a purchase order could be issued or a contract executed was not applicable to collective bargaining agreements. See Mendes v. City of Taunton, 366 Mass. 109, 315 N.E.2d 865 (1974). See also Providence Teachers Union, Local 958 v. School Committee of Providence, 276 A.2d 762, 77 L.R.R.M. 2530 (R.I. 1971) (alleged unavailability of appropriated funds not defense to enforcement of arbitration award); Dist. Council 33, AFSCME v. Philadephia, 81 L.R.R.M. 2539 (Pa. C.P., Phila. County 1971) (exhaustion of municipal funds does not relieve city of obligations under bargaining agreement).

2. In Newark Teachers Ass'n v. Bd. of Educ., 57 N.J. 100, 270 A.2d 14 (1970), defendant Board of Education adopted a salary schedule calling for teacher pay increases. However, the Teachers Association was informed that the schedule would not go into effect until the City appropriated the funds necessary to implement it. Had it been applicable to the current (1969-70) school year, the adopted salary schedule would have provided for salary increases in excess of the budget. In an action to compel the Board of Education to effectuate the salary increases immediately, the New Jersey Supreme Court affirmed the lower court's finding that state law did not require a school board's resolution to be given immediate effect.

3. In sharp contrast to the *Yonkers School District* decision, the court held in Clifton Teachers Ass'n v. Bd. of Educ., 346 A.2d 107, 90 L.R.R.M. 3085 (N.J. Super. Ct., App. Div. 1975), that the school board could condition salary increases upon satisfactory service, even though the negotiated agreement between the board and its teachers contained a salary guide providing for annual increments. According to the court, the power to withhold salary increases is non-negotiable and part of a school board's "inherent right" to pass upon the quality of teacher performance.

4. In Patrolmen's Benevolent Ass'n v. City of New York, 41 N.Y.2d 205, 359 N.E.2d 1338 (1976), the Court indicated that outstanding judgment debts will generally be enforced against a government entity. It thus ordered the enforcement of a judgment which had confirmed an interest arbitration award granting New York police officers a salary increase effective July 1, 1975, notwithstanding the intervening enactment of a wage freeze. The wage freeze was held to apply only to bargaining agreements, without suspending the enforcement of judgments such as the one the police union had obtained against New York when it refused to implement the recommendations of the impasse panel. The same Court subsequently ruled that the prospective application of the wage freeze to previously negotiated agreements did not constitute an unconstitutional impairment of contract rights, since it was "reasonable and necessary to serve an important public purpose." Subway-Surface Supervisors Ass'n v. New York City Transit Authority, 44 N.Y.2d 101, 375 N.E.2d 384 (1978). But see Sonoma County Organization of Public Employees v. County of Sonoma, — Cal.3d —, — P.2d — (1979), wherein the California Supreme Court invalidated the portion of a post-Proposition 13 funding enactment which

precluded local governments from honoring wage increase provisions contained in previously negotiated agreements, on the ground that, unlike the circumstances underlying the statute sustained in the *Subway-Surface* decision, the California financial situation was not sufficiently precarious to warrant such a direct infringement of contract rights.

5. Where unilateral changes have been made by a public employer because of financial considerations, most of the resulting union complaints have been processed as refusal to bargain charges (*see* Ch. 4, §§ C and D, *supra*). When at the expiration of the then-current bargaining agreement the City of New York proposed an $87 million budget reduction program at City University of New York (CUNY) which would mean more and larger classes for instructors with less research and leave time, the court permitted the instructors' union to sue, stating that the City's "unfortunate financial situation" did not give it the right unilaterally to change the working conditions of the teachers employed at CUNY. The Taylor Law, it continued, "allows no violation of law or breach of contracts." However, the court did not find the situation to warrant the injunctive relief sought by the CUNY staff. Professional Staff Congress v. Bd. of Higher Educ., City of New York, 373 N.Y.S.2d 453, 90 L.R.R.M. 3042 (Sup. Ct. 1975). In a similar case, the Maine Supreme Court issued a preliminary injunction preventing the School Committee of Kittery from reducing pay increases negotiated by the Kittery Teachers Association. Justice Wernick found that the School Committee violated the Municipal Employees Relations Law in attempting to eliminate the salary increases after the town Council deleted $55,000 from the school budget with the recommendation that $20,000 of the reduction come from the teacher salary item. In response to the School Committee's claim that it was merely following the mandate of the town council, Justice Wernick ruled that the council lacked the authority to restrict the use of funds allocated to the School Committee to particular items. GERR No. 418, B-12 (1971). *See also* City of Boston v. Massachusetts Bay Transp. Author., 370 N.E.2d 1359, 97 L.R.R.M. 2584 (Mass. 1977), where the Court held that while the Advisory Board of MBTA had the power to reduce the wage item of the MBTA budget, it lacked the authority to direct MBTA to cease paying cost-of-living increases specified in its negotiated contracts.

6. Public employers have had some success in effectuating staff reductions to save money as a management prerogative, although courts have carefully scrutinized contract language for any employment guarantees and have usually given effect to employment security provisions which have been negotiated by employers and unions. *See, e.g.,* Burke v. Bowen, 40 N.Y.2d 264, 353 N.E.2d 567 (1976). Courts have also sustained arbitration awards enforcing such contractual provisions. *See, e.g.,* Matter of Yonkers Fed'n of Teachers v. Bd. of Educ., 44 N.Y.2d 752, 376 N.E.2d 1326 (1978). However, where a bargaining agreement containing a job security provision expires, previously laid off employees who may still be entitled to damages for breach of the prior contract may lose their right to reinstatement. *See* Schwab v. Bowen, 41 N.Y.2d 907, 363 N.E.2d 341 (1977).

7. What recourse does a municipality have if it lacks sufficient financial resources to satisfy its obligations under collective bargaining agreements? *See* Note, *Executory Labor Contracts and Municipal Bankruptcy,* 85 YALE L.J. 957 (1976).

# G. BREACH OF CONTRACT AS AN UNFAIR LABOR PRACTICE

## 1. CONTRACT DISPUTES BEFORE A STATE AGENCY

### BOARD OF EDUCATION, UNION FREE SCHOOL DISTRICT NO. 3, TOWN OF HEMPSTEAD, NASSAU COUNTY and EAST MEADOW TEACHERS ASSOCIATION

New York Public Employment Relations Board
4 PERB ¶ 4-4018 (1971)

The East Meadow Teachers Association (EMTA) filed an improper practice charge against the Board of Education, Union Free School District No. 3, Town of Hempstead, Nassau County (respondent).

The charge alleged a violation of § 209-a.1 (d) [1] of the Public Employees' Fair Employment Act (Act) in that the respondent unilaterally changed the terms and conditions relating to sabbatical leaves by requiring all applicants for such leaves to agree to return to the employment of respondent for a period of two years following the termination of the sabbatical leave.

EMTA and respondent entered into a written agreement in July, 1969 setting forth the terms and conditions of employment for teaching personnel. The agreement became effective on September 1, 1969, and terminated on August 31, 1970.

The agreement provided in ¶ 5.1:

"Sabbatical Leave — The existing practices, policies and procedures respecting sabbatical leaves to teaching personnel are confirmed and shall remain in effect except that (a) a teacher eligible for sabbatical may select a half-year sabbatical at full pay for full-time study or its equivalent upon approval of the Superintendent of Schools, either in the United States or abroad and (b) in selecting among applicants for sabbatical leave, length of service in the District shall be one of the prime considerations."

In April, 1970 the respondent changed its policy relating to sabbatical leave to require, as a condition to the granting thereof, an agreement to work for respondent for a two-year period following the leave. It is conceded that in effecting this change respondent did not negotiate with EMTA.

The hearing officer concluded that procedures and policies relating to sabbatical leave are a mandatory subject of collective negotiations and that there is an obligation on the part of the respondent to negotiate with EMTA "prior to implementing a change in its sabbatical leave policy."

The hearing officer, after giving consideration to several affirmative defenses asserted by respondent and finding them lacking in merit, thereupon found that respondent violated § 209-a.1 (d) of the Act.

Respondent has excepted to the decision and recommended order of the hearing officer.

The arguments in defense of the position of respondent may be summarized as (1) Sabbatical Leave is not a term or condition of employment under the Act; (2) The conduct of respondent alleged as the basis of the charge herein would constitute a breach of the agreement between the parties and, therefore, the grievance procedure set forth in the contract is the sole remedy available to EMTA; (3) The question has become moot in that in the subsequent agreement between the parties there is a contractual provision covering sabbatical leave, the point at issue. . . .

First, we agree with the hearing officer that the issue of sabbatical leave is a term and condition of employment and thus is a proper subject of collective negotiations. The provisions of § 1709, subdivision 16 of the Education Law does not negate this conclusion.

Therefore, either party has the duty to negotiate concerning this subject if requested by the other. This duty to negotiate, of course, does not compel one party to agree to the proposal of the other. Rather, this duty requires each party to negotiate in good faith on all mandatory subjects of negotiations.

As to respondent's second contention that the respondent's conduct herein should be relegated to the grievance procedure agreed upon by the parties in their negotiated agreement, the hearing officer reasoned that the "claim here does not relate to the interpretation of any clause of the collective agreement." The hearing officer concluded that, "this dispute is not one of contract

---

[1] "to refuse to negotiate in good faith with the duly recognized or certified representatives of its public employees."

interpretation but of statutory obligation" and, therefore, EMTA could properly invoke the improper practice section of the Act, rather than the grievance procedures in the negotiated agreement.

This issue raised by respondent is one of first impression before this Board and raises some basic questions. The first question is: Does this Board have general jurisdiction to police and enforce negotiated agreements between public employers and employee organizations within this state?

We conclude that it does not. The legislature of this state has not dealt explicitly with this problem, as have the legislatures of Wisconsin,[2] or Hawaii,[3] in making the breach of a collective bargaining agreement an unfair labor practice. While the legislature of this state has stated that, in the administration of improper practices, decisions in the private sector shall not be binding or controlling precedent [4] nevertheless such statutory mandate does not by its terms preclude this Board from considering the vast reservoir of experience in the private sector.

In decisions construing the National Labor Relations Act, it appears to be well-settled that the National Labor Relations Board does not have general jurisdiction over alleged violations of collective bargaining agreements.[5] In reaching this conclusion, the Supreme Court relied upon the legislative history of the enactment of the Taft-Hartley Act [6] and concluded that Congress "deliberately chose to leave the enforcement of collective agreements to the usual processes of law." [7]

There is no such legislative history as to the Act herein. Nevertheless, we find the conclusion reached by the Supreme Court in the private sector to be a salutary approach, particularly since the legislature of this state did not provide that a breach of a negotiated agreement would constitute an improper practice. However, this is not dispositive of the issue raised by respondent, for all that has been concluded so far is that a breach of contract is not *per se* an improper labor practice.

A second question arises whether conduct which constitutes a breach of contract may also constitute an improper practice. This question requires an affirmative answer in the light of facts of this case.

Respondent herein agreed, in the negotiated agreement, to maintain existing policies, practices and procedures relating to sabbatical leave. Respondent unilaterally changed such practices, policies and procedures without negotiating such change with the representative of its employees. This constitutes a violation of § 209-a.1 (d) of the Act in that it violates respondent's obligation "to negotiate in good faith" with such representative.

The fact that respondent, in effecting such change, contends that it acted in the public interest, does not cure the violation herein. The Act mandates that a public employer negotiate terms and conditions of employment with the certified or recognized representative of its employees. This obviously precludes the unilateral imposition of terms and conditions of employment.

We do not reach the question here of whether, in such circumstances, this Board should defer to the grievance and arbitration procedures in an agreement because the subject contract does not provide for binding arbitration.

The third defense, to wit, the allegation that the question has become moot,

---

[2] State Employment Labor Relations Act, § 111.84(I)(e).

[3] State of Hawaii, Act 171, L. 1970, § 13(a)(8).

[4] CSL § 209-a.8.

[5] NLRB v. C & C Plywood Corp., 385 U.S. 421; NLRB v. M & M Oldsmobile Inc., 377 F.2d 712.

[6] NLRB v. C & C Plywood Corp., supra, footnote 5.

[7] Charles Dowd Box Co. v. Courtney, 368 U.S. 518.

is not a defense at all; rather, its relevance in this case is only to the nature of the remedial order to be issued by this Board. . . .

## NOTE

If a party refuses to comply with its contractual obligation to participate in the selection of a grievance arbitrator, it may be found guilty of an unfair refusal to bargain, since the administration of a collective agreement is generally considered to constitute part of the bargaining process. *See* Blackhawk School Dist., Pa.LRB Case No. PERA-C-10, 466-W, 1977-78 PEB ¶ 40,390 (1977). However, where a party simply declines to honor an adverse arbitration award, the prevailing party may be required to seek judicial enforcement, with no redress being available through unfair labor practice proceedings. *See* West Bloomfield Bd. of Educ., Mich.BER Case No. C76 E-148, 1977-78 PEB ¶ 40,033 (1977). Is this distinction logical?

# 2. DEFERENCE TO ARBITRATION

## NEW YORK CITY TRANSIT AUTHORITY and TRANSPORT WORKERS OF AMERICA LOCAL 100

New York Public Employment Relations Board
4 PERB ¶ 4504 (1971)

J. Axelrod, Hearing Officer — On April 13, 1970, pursuant to Part 204 of the Rules of Procedure (herein referred to as the Rules) of the New York State Public Employment Relations Board (herein referred to as the Board), Harry Bordansky (herein referred to as the charging party) filed a charge [2] against the New York City Transit Authority (herein referred to as respondent Transit Authority) and the Transport Workers Union of America, AFL-CIO and Local 100, Transport Workers Union of America, AFL-CIO (herein referred to as respondent TWU), alleging that they had violated § 209-a.1(a) [3] and § 209-a.2(a) [4] respectively, of the Public Employees' Fair Act (herein referred to as the Act) by discriminating against the charging party in the assignment of overtime work because of his non-union status. The charging party also alleged that a grievance on this issue which he had filed under the contractual grievance procedure established by the respondents was then stalled at Step 4 because of respondent Transit Authority's failure to file a timely determination.

Thereafter, each respondent filed an answer denying the material allegations of the charge and also raising certain affirmative defenses, including, on the part of respondent Transit Authority, the charging party's alleged failure to exhaust his administrative remedies.

At a pre-hearing conference conducted by me on May 11, 1970, the parties agreed by stipulation to adjourn a hearing on the charge, *sine die,* "pending the charging party's exhaustion of his remedies under the contractual grievance procedure" which included binding arbitration. On August 4, the designated impartial arbitrator, Theodore Kheel, issued an award dismissing the grievance as without merit.

A formal hearing was then held before me on October 13. At the hearing, respondent Transit Authority sought dismissal of the charge without a hearing

---

[2] Mr. Bordansky filed the charge on behalf of himself and several other employees.

[3] This section makes it an improper practice for an employer "deliberately . . . to interfere with, restrain or coerce public employees in the exercise of their rights guaranteed in section two hundred two for the purpose of depriving them of such rights. . . ."

[4] This section makes it an improper practice for an employee organization "deliberately . . . to interfere with, restrain or coerce public employees in the exercise of the rights granted in section two hundred two, or to cause, or attempt to cause, a public employer to do so. . . ."

on the merits, on the ground that the issues raised in the charge had already been resolved by the arbitral award to which PERB should defer in furtherance of the recognized public policy of encouraging voluntary dispute settlement procedures. Respondent Transit Authority pointed out, in support of its contention, that the U.S. Supreme Court had long recognized the efficacy of arbitration as a stabilizing force in labor relations and had approved the National Labor Relations Board's policy [5] of accepting an arbitral determination as dispositive of an unfair labor practice case where the same issue was being litigated, the proceedings were fair and regular, and the award did not conflict with the precepts or provisions of the National Labor Relations Act.[6] Following litigation of the circumstances of the arbitral award in the instant case, I granted the respondent Transit Authority's motion to dismiss the charge, and said I would explain my ruling in a decision.

### Facts

Respondent TWU has for many years been the recognized negotiating representative of, *inter alia,* hourly paid operating and maintenance employees of the respondent Transit Authority, including the charging party. At all times pertinent herein, the charging party was not a member of respondent TWU.

Article VIII of the collective agreement between respondents establishes a five-step grievance procedure and then provides for arbitration before a designated impartial arbitrator, whose determination "... shall be final and binding on both parties." Any individual employee may invoke the grievance machinery on his own behalf.[7]

In mid March, 1970, the charging party filed a grievance at Step 2 of the contractual grievance procedure alleging that he had been discriminatorily by-passed in the assignment of overtime on March 16 because of his non-union status.[8] Unsatisfied with the determination at Step 2, the charging party processed the grievance to Step 3, and then Step 4. While the Step 4 determination was not forthcoming following the expiration of the contractual deadline, the charging party filed the instant charge on April 13.

As of May 11, the date of the pre-hearing conference in the instant case, the grievance had been processed through a Step 5 hearing and, as noted above, the parties agreed to adjourn further proceedings herein until the contractual grievance arbitration machinery had been exhausted.

Thereafter, following the issuance of a Step 5 determination dismissing his grievance, the charging party submitted the matter to arbitration. ...

At the arbitration, in accordance with a long standing custom of the parties, the arbitrator took notes in lieu of a formal transcript.[9] The charging party admittedly was afforded unlimited opportunity to present all information and documents he wished in support of his grievance. Respondent Transit Authority

---

[5] See, e.g., Spielberg Manufacturing Co., 112 NLRB 1080 (1955).

[6] Carey v. Westinghouse Electric Corp., 375 U.S. 261, 55 LRRM 2042 (1964).

[7] Under certain circumstances TWU, although not representing a grieving employee, must be notified of and be allowed to participate in each step of the procedure.

[8] The subject of overtime assignment is covered in a written schedule of working conditions and is clearly grievable.

[9] Mr. Kheel, the designated impartial arbitrator, was out of the country on the assigned day for the arbitration hearing. The parties agreed to have Mr. Messina, an associate of Mr. Kheel, sit as the arbitrator, with the understanding that Mr. Kheel would render the decision based upon Mr. Messina's notes.

also presented evidence but respondent TWU, although represented, did not present independent evidence.

The arbitrator, Mr. Kheel, in his decision and award, framed the grievance as follows:

> "Harry Bordansky, a Bus Maintainer B, who is not a member of the Union, claims that the Authority discriminated against non-Union men in his shop in the assignment of overtime during the pick year ending in May 1970. Mr. Bordansky alleges that the average of overtime hours awarded to non-Union men was less than average for Union men and there were specific occasions when the Authority exhibited distinct favoritism to Union men over non-Union men in the assignment of overtime."

The arbitrator evaluated the overtime assignments on one such "specific" occasion, March 16, and found no evidence to support Mr. Bordansky's claim. . . .

## Discussion

Preliminarily, it will be useful to isolate the precise matter at issue in this proceeding. The Board's authority to hear and determine an improper practice charge in the face of an outstanding arbitral determination resolving the same point alleged in the charge *is not* at issue. The Legislature has entrusted the Board, under § 205.5(d) of the Act, with the task of "establishing procedures for the prevention of improper employer and employee organization practices as provided in section two hundred nine-a of this article" except for cases involving parties under the jurisdiction of the New York City Office of Collective Bargaining. The commission of improper employer and employee organization practices threatens the established public policy of maintaining "harmonious and cooperative relationships between government and its employees." Such practices thus are public wrongs with ramifications for the public interest far beyond their effects on the parties immediately concerned. Clearly, then, the Legislature could not have intended that the determination in a private forum of a matter alleged to be an improper practice would oust the Board of its statutory jurisdiction over the matter. But, while the Board may consider the matter *de novo* under such circumstances, it is not bound to do so if it is satisfied that the public interest will be otherwise served. This brings me to the only question which *is* at issue in this proceeding, namely, the effect the Board should give to an existing arbitral award resolving the same matters raised by an improper practice charge.

Consideration of the role of arbitration in labor relations is a necessary predicate to any discussion of the issue at bar. The United States Supreme Court has for many years held that national labor policy in the private sector accords arbitration a position of primacy as a medium for settling labor disputes and preserving industrial stability. . . .

The importance to public sector labor relations of voluntary dispute settlement procedures, including arbitration, was recognized in the 1966 "Report of the Governor's Committee on Public Employee Relations" (Taylor Committee), a document widely regarded as the most complete source of legislative history of the ensuing Taylor Act. . . .

The Legislature took to heart the Committee's advice to encourage private dispute settlement procedures. Section 200 of the Act, entitled "Statement of Policy," declares:

". . . it is the public policy of the State and the purpose of this Act to promote harmonious and cooperative relationships between government and its employees and to protect the public by assuring, at all times, the orderly and uninterrupted operations and functions of government. These policies are best effectuated by . . . (c) encouraging . . . public employers and . . . employee organizations to agree upon procedures for resolving disputes. . . ."

It follows that every effort must be made to insure the integrity of those private arrangements which the parties have devised for conclusively resolving disputes. Where an alleged improper practice has been litigated in a forum designated by the parties for the final and binding resolution of disputes, this objective can best be accomplished if the resulting private determination is given conclusive effect in the improper practice proceeding. However, to satisfy the public interest, which is always at stake in an improper practice proceeding but rarely involved in a private proceeding, the Board should defer to the arbitration award only under the following circumstances:

1. the same issue raised in the improper practice charge was aired and determined in the arbitration proceeding;

2. the arbitration proceeding was conducted with fairness and regularity of procedure;

3. the resulting award is final and binding on the parties; and

4. the award does not contravene the Act or offend public policy.

By deferring to an award meeting these standards, the Board will be able to implement its statutory mandate to redress improper practices while carrying out the statutory objective of encouraging private dispute settlement procedures.

I now turn to an application of these policy considerations to the case at bar. At the hearing in the instant case, the charging party contended that the award should be disregarded because no stenographic record was kept during the arbitration hearing, and the award did not answer every question raised by the charging party during the arbitration. Contrary to the charging party's assertion, neither of these facts impugns the fairness or the regularity of the arbitration proceeding nor the integrity of the award. As to the former point, it is an accepted custom in many arbitration proceedings to dispense with a formal transcript and to have the matter decided upon the exhibits and the arbitrator's notes. Regarding the issue about the completeness of the award, the arbitrator conclusively disposed of the grievance for clearly stated reasons. There is no requirement that an arbitral (or for that matter, a judicial) determination provide specific answers to each argument made during the course of a proceeding and any such expectation would be manifestly unreasonable.

As previously noted, the charging party invoked the contractual grievance machinery, even prior to filing the instant charge. The issue submitted to arbitration was identical to that raised in the charge. At the arbitration proceeding, the charging party had every opportunity to air his grievance and present evidence. The arbitrator, after evaluating the competing contentions in his binding award dismissed the grievance as unsubstantiated by the evidence. Finally, the award does not offend the policies of the Act. Accordingly, I find that the four criteria set forth *supra* have been satisfied and this Board therefore should decline to exercise jurisdiction.

In view of the above findings of fact and conclusions of law, I therefore recommend that the charge be dismissed in its entirety.

[The decision of the Hearing Officer was adopted and affirmed by the New York Public Employment Relations Board in New York City Transit Authority, 4 PERB ¶ 4-3031 (1971).]

## CITY OF WILMINGTON v. WILMINGTON FIREFIGHTERS, LOCAL 1590

Delaware Supreme Court
385 A.2d 720 (1978)

DUFFY, Justice:

This appeal involves a controversy between the City of Wilmington and a union representing Wilmington firemen over the proper forum for resolving the union's complaint that the City, by amending a medical plan covering its firefighters, violated both a State statute and the contract between the parties.

I

The facts are these:

The City (defendant) made a collective bargaining agreement with Wilmington Firefighters Local 1590, International Association of Firefighters (plaintiff) governing wages and other terms of employment. The official personnel rules and regulations of the Wilmington Bureau of Fire were incorporated in the contract. Thereafter, the City abolished the position of Fire Physician and adopted a revised medical plan for its firemen. The Association then filed an action in the Court of Chancery alleging that the City had, by so doing, violated 19 *Del.C.* ch. 13 and the collective bargaining agreement. The Union sought injunctive relief which would eliminate the alleged violations.

The City moved to dismiss the complaint on jurisdictional grounds, arguing that the collective bargaining agreement, which created a grievance and arbitration procedure for resolving disputes, was the Union's exclusive remedy. The parties agreed to a stay until the Court decided a then pending action brought by Wilmington policemen against the City and involving the same issues. *Fraternal Order of Police, Lodge No. 1 v. City of Wilmington,* Del.Ch., C.A. No. 4783. The latter case was decided by an unpublished opinion, dated December 23, 1975, in which the then Chancellor stayed the action on condition that the City agree to certain modifications in the grievance procedure established by the contract between the City and the Union.[2] Relying on the stipulation of the parties and the principle of *stare decisis,* the Court, in this case, denied the City's motion to dismiss and imposed the same conditions as those fixed in *Fraternal Order of Police, Lodge No. 1.* The City filed this appeal. We reverse.

II

The ultimate question before us concerns the action which should be taken by a Delaware Court when it is asked to award relief on grounds that allegedly violate both a State statute and a labor relations contract in which the parties established a binding and final settlement procedure for disputes.

In considering the question and in formulating an opinion, we emphasize that the alleged violation concerns a refusal-to-bargain. That is important in limiting the impact of this ruling on judicial determinations of future labor disputes in which public employees are involved.

The Union argues that the Court should proceed to determine the merits of the case, that the arbitration clause in a labor agreement is an optional remedy

---

[2] The Court's order included the following conditions: (1) that the grievance procedure begin with a written complaint which must be discussed with the Director of Personnel and the Commissioner of Public Safety; (2) that the City must supply at its expense the means of securing a verbatim record in any Grievance Appeal Board proceeding; (3) that depositions can be taken by plaintiff of persons noticed (not exceeding 3) between the filing of the complaint and the discussion required by (1), supra.

for breach of contract and, in any event, that the procedure adopted by the Trial Court is reasonable and should be approved.

The City, on the other hand, contends that the Court of Chancery should have abstained from exercising its jurisdiction until contract arbitration had been completed and that the Court erred by imposing terms which amount to an amendment of the contract without the City's consent.

The statutory sections allegedly violated by the City, 19 *Del.C.* ch. 13, concern a public employer's duty to engage in collective bargaining with an exclusive bargaining representative.[3] And the contract provisions allegedly violated are the Bureau of Fire rules and regulations incorporated into the collective bargaining agreement. As we have noted, the violations are said to result from the City's independent or unilateral abolition of the Fire Physician position and implementation of a revised medical plan. The charge is that such actions constitute a refusal-to-bargain, and interference, restraint and coercion of protected labor rights, and a violation of contractually agreed-upon medical programs.

## III

The appropriate point of entry for a Delaware Court into this kind of controversy is an issue of first impression. In beginning our review, we assume that the City's actions constitute both a statutory and a contractual violation. This kind of controversy has been litigated elsewhere and so we look for guidance to the procedure adopted in the Federal forums and by the Courts and administrative tribunals in other States for dealing with such situations.

First, as to Federal precedent: Section 10 of the National Labor Relations Act (Act), 29 *U.S.C.* § 151, et seq., authorizes the National Labor Relations Board (NLRB) to adjudicate statutory violations constituting unfair labor practices arising under the Act. However, the existence of a claimed contract violation and the availability of a contract remedy — arbitration, for example — does not divest the NLRB of jurisdiction to adjudicate an alleged statutory violation for the same conduct. *NLRB v. Acme Industrial Co.,* 385 U.S. 432, 87 S.Ct. 565, 17 L.Ed.2d 495 (1967). NLRB jurisdiction continues but, if the labor dispute involves both allegations (that is, statutory as well as contract violations) and if it is at a pre-arbitral stage, the NLRB will defer to the contractually agreed-upon arbitration procedures when the issue is a refusal-to-bargain. *Collyer Insulated Wire,* 192 NLRB 837, 77 LRRM 1931 (1971).

Speaking of the NLRB policy with approval, the United States Supreme Court in *William E. Arnold Co. v. Carpenters District Council,* 417 U.S. 12, 94 S.Ct. 2069, 40 L.Ed.2d 620 (1974), said this:

"... Board policy is to refrain from exercising jurisdiction in respect of disputed conduct arguably both an unfair labor practice and a contract violation when, as in this case, the parties have voluntarily established by contract a binding settlement procedure. *See, e.g., The Associated Press,* 199 N.L.R.B. 1110 (1972); Eastman Broadcasting Co., 199 N.L.R.B. 434 (1972); *Laborers Local 423,* 199 N.L.R.B. 450 (1972); *Collyer Insulated Wire,* 192 N.L.R.B. 837 (1971). The Board said in *Collyer,* 'an industrial relations dispute

---

[3] 19 Del.C. ch. 13, which became effective on June 15, 1965, confers rights on public employees, including the right to organize, § 1302; to be free from restraint, coercion or discrimination in the free exercise of any rights under chapter 13, § 1303; to have bargaining units established and exclusive bargaining representatives elected, §§ 1304 — 1306; and the right to bargain collectively with the public employer, § 1309.

may involve conduct which, at least arguably, may contravene both the collective agreement and our statute. When the parties have contractually committed themselves to mutually agreeable procedures for resolving their disputes during the period of the contract, we are of the view that those procedures should be afforded full opportunity to function.... We believe it to be consistent with the fundamental objectives of Federal law to require the parties ... to honor their contractual obligations rather than, by casting [their] dispute in statutory terms, to ignore their agreed-upon procedures.' *Id.,* at 842-843. The Board's position harmonizes with Congress' articulated concern that, '[f]inal adjustment by a method agreed upon by the parties is ... the desirable method for settlement of grievance disputes arising over the application or interpretation of an existing collective-bargaining agreement ...' § 203(d) of the LMRA, 29 U.S.C. § 173(d)."

94 *S.Ct.* at 2072.

When the NLRB does defer, it retains jurisdiction to consider an application for additional relief on a showing that either: (1) the dispute has not been resolved or submitted to arbitration with reasonable promptness, or (2) the arbitration procedures have been unfair or have rendered a result repugnant to the Act. *Collyer Insulated Wire,* supra.

The Federal Courts of Appeal have consistently upheld the *Collyer* deferral policy. See, e.g., *Local Union No. 2188, Int. Bro. of Elec. Wkrs. v. NLRB,* 161 U.S.App.D.C. 168, 494 F.2d 1087 (1974), *cert. denied,* 419 U.S. 835, 95 S.Ct 61, 42 L.Ed.2d 61 (1974); *Provision House Workers Union Local 274 v. NLRB,* 9 Cir., 493 F.2d 1249 (1974), *cert. denied,* 419 U.S. 828, 95 S.Ct. 47, 42 L.Ed.2d 52 (1974); *Nabisco, Inc. v. NLRB,* 2 Cir., 479 F.2d 770 (1973). And, as we have indicated, the United States Supreme Court noted its approval by saying that the pre-arbitral deferral policy "harmonizes" with a Legislative preference for voluntary settlement procedures in labor disputes. *William E. Arnold Co. v. Carpenters District Council,* supra.

A number of State labor commissions, including those in Massachusetts, Michigan, New Jersey and New York, have adopted deferral doctrines in public employee refusal-to-bargain situations. 1 *Pub.Empl.Barg.* (CCH) ¶ 5015. For example, the Michigan Employment Relations Commission has expressly approved and cited the *Collyer* deferral doctrine. Deferral has been held appropriate in Michigan public employee cases where there is a contractual provision for arbitration and the dispute can arguably be resolved under the contract language; and allegations of unilateral changes in terms and conditions of employment in violation of Michigan's Public Employment Relations Act have frequently prompted deferral to arbitration. See 1 *Pub.Empl.Barg.* (CCH) Michigan ¶ 5015 and cases cited therein.

We conclude from this brief review that a deferral policy is widely followed and has much to commend it in practice.

## IV

Returning now to the present dispute, when it was placed before the Court of Chancery, that Court had several options available. We know, of course, what the Court did. But, it could have taken jurisdiction and adjudicated the dispute. Or, it could have dismissed the action as premature and left the parties to pursue their contract remedies. Or, the Court could have followed the *Collyer* practice by taking jurisdiction and then staying the action until after the parties had followed the contract procedure.

We conclude that the *Collyer* deferral to arbitration is a sound and sensible policy for Delaware to follow. Other States, many of them with large populations and complex governments have followed the Federal lead. And there is similarity between the Federal Labor Act and 19 *Del.C.* ch. 13, as expressly noted by Judge Stapleton in *Cofrancesco v. City of Wilmington,* D.Del., 419 F.Supp. 109 (1976):

"Delaware law extends to State, county and municipal employees many of the same rights to . . . bargain collectively that the [federal labor law] affords to employees in the private sector. 19 *Del.C.* § 1301, et seq. In cases where the problems raised under Delaware's labor law are similar to those that arise under the [federal law], Delaware could be expected to consider and, in all likelihood, follow federal law."

*Id.,* at 111.

And our holding is supported by the long-accepted view that a settlement in a labor dispute is often best achieved through use of the parties' voluntary agreement to arbitrate. *United Steelwkrs. of Amer. v. American Mfg. Co.,* 363 U.S. 564, 80 S.Ct. 1343, 4 L.Ed.2d 1403 (1960); *United Steelwkrs. of Am. v. Warrior & Gulf N. Co.,* 363 U.S. 574, 80 S.Ct. 1347, 4 L.Ed.2d 1409 (1960); *United Steelwkrs. of A. v. Enterprise W. & Co. Corp.,* 363 U.S. 593, 80 S.Ct. 1358, 4 L.Ed.2d 1424 (1960) — *Steelworkers Trilogy.* For that reason, the arbitral process is sometimes viewed as superior to the judicial process because of an arbitrator's greater knowledge and experience regarding the parties, and because he has been selected by them. Along the same line, we note that Title 19 of the Delaware Code indicates a strong State policy favoring voluntary mediation as a means to promote industrial peace in Delaware. See 19 *Del.C.* §§ 110, 111(a), 1310. And pre-arbitral deferral will "require the parties here to honor their contractual obligations rather than, by casting this dispute in statutory terms, to ignore their agreed-upon procedures." *Collyer Insulated Wire,* supra. Finally, in this case, the parties' own agreement reveals a preference for the grievance-arbitration procedure by stating in Article III-A, Section 1:

"The grievance procedures set forth in this section are established in order to provide adequate opportunity for members of the Department of Public Safety to bring forth their views relating to any unfair or improper aspect of their employment situation and to seek correction thereof."

It follows that the Court of Chancery was correct in accepting jurisdiction while ordering the parties to arbitrate, but that the Court erred in requiring modifications to the contractually agreed-upon grievance procedures. Undoubtedly the Court wanted to be helpful but, under the circumstances, that constituted unwarranted judicial meddling in the parties' contractual relations. See *John Wiley & Sons, Inc. v. Livingston,* 376 U.S. 543, 84 S.Ct. 909, 912, 913, 11 L.Ed.2d 898 (1964); and compare *Safe Harbor Fishing Club v. Safety Harbor Realty Co.,* 34 Del.Ch. 28, 107 A.2d 635 (1953). The case should have been stayed and the parties directed to proceed under the contract. And jurisdiction should have been retained by the Court to consider any application for relief on the ground that the dispute is not being resolved by arbitration with reasonable promptness, or that the arbitral process had been unfair, or that it resulted in an award repugnant to 19 *Del.C.* ch. 13, or that it failed to resolve the statutory claim. But, otherwise the Court should not have encumbered the agreement which the parties had made with its own notion of what was fair.

. . .

In adopting a pre-arbitral deferral policy, we emphasize that while the parties are a public employer and public employees, the present dispute is grounded in a nonpublic interest, private sector-type issue which arises in a refusal-to-bargain context. The case involves only that kind of controversy and our ruling and comments are limited to it. In other words, nothing said herein applies to an action which affects the public interest — a strike by public employees, for example. In that kind of situation the issues are different and so is the Court's responsibility. Nor are we here concerned with a post-arbitral dispute between the parties.

. . .

Reversed and remanded for further proceedings consistent herewith.

## NOTES

1. Suppose that in a previous grievance-arbitration proceeding the unfair labor practice issue that has now been presented to a labor relations board for resolution could have been litigated as part of the basic arbitration case, but the grieving party elected not to have that specific question determined by the arbitrator. If the prior arbitral proceeding was fair and regular, should the board accept the arbitration decision as conclusive regarding the unlitigated issue, to encourage the complete resolution of such related matters before a single forum? See Electronic Reproduction Service Corp., 213 N.L.R.B. 758, 87 L.R.R.M. 1211 (1974).

2. In Appleton Professional Policemen's Ass'n. v. City of Appleton, WERC Case No. 20446 MP-615, 1977-78 PEB ¶40,143 (1978), the Wisconsin Employment Relations Commission declined to defer to arbitration an unfair labor practice charge that involved the interpretation of contractual provisions, since both parties had submitted to WERC's jurisdiction, with neither requesting deferral to arbitration.

3. When an unfair labor practice issue that could be resolved through the grievance-arbitration process is initially presented to a labor relations board for determination and the board is deciding whether to defer the matter to arbitration, should a distinction be made between refusal to bargain charges that directly affect the status of the representative labor organization, with deferral of such cases being appropriate, and those charges pertaining to the restraint or coercion of individual employees, where it might be preferable to have the board itself hear the case to best insure the full protection of individual rights? Cf. General American Transp. Corp., 228 N.L.R.B. 808, 94 L.R.R.M. 1483 (1977).

4. See generally Cowden, Deferral to Arbitration by the Pennsylvania Labor Relations Board, 80 DICK. L. REV. 666 (1976).

## H. TAXPAYER SUITS AS AN ENFORCEMENT MECHANISM

In private sector collective bargaining, members of the public are remote third parties to the process, involved to the extent that they are consumers and stockholders, yet not really participants. In the public sector, members of the public are afforded many more opportunities to participate at key points in the bargaining process — at school board and city council meetings, in the legislature where legislative approval of collective bargaining agreements is required, and even in millage elections where the fate of negotiated increases in employee benefits may be decided. In part, public participation in public sector bargaining is attributable to the close relationship between the bargaining and political processes; public participation is invited as a matter of democratic privilege. In part, too, participation is enhanced by the essential nature of many public employee services. Yet another factor is the popular perception of a much more direct financial link between the citizen as taxpayer and the wages of public servants than is the case between the citizen as stockholder or consumer and the wages of the private sector employee.

Most states now permit taxpayer suits challenging the constitutionality of legislation or charging administrative agencies with abuse of discretion, provided that the taxpayer can show a sufficient financial stake in the outcome. *See* Jaffe, *Standing to Secure Judicial Review: Public Actions*, 74 HARV. L. REV. 1265, 1276-81 (1961); Comment, *Taxpayers' Suits: A Survey and Summary*, 69 YALE L.J. 895 (1960). In some states the taxpayer is regarded as a private attorney general seeking to vindicate the public interest. *See* the concurring opinion of Justice Douglas in Flast v. Cohen, 392 U.S. 83, 108, notes 2-5 (1968). This concept is applicable to the collective bargaining process in the public sector in those cases in which the interests of the public employer and the public unions seem to be arrayed against the interests of the taxpayer. This is especially true where a taxpayer suit may be the only means of invoking the provisions of a punitive law, as the following cases illustrate.

## LEGMAN v. SCHOOL DISTRICT OF CITY OF SCRANTON

Pennsylvania Supreme Court, Eastern District
432 Pa. 342, 247 A.2d 566 (1968)

ROBERTS, Justice: — Appellee instituted this action in equity to enjoin the school district from paying increased salaries to certain teachers in the Scranton school system who allegedly went on strike in December 1967. The gravamen of his complaint is that such action by the school board (which has already progressed to the point of approving this raise in the 1968 budget) would violate the Strike by Public Employees Act, Act of June 30, 1947, P.L. 1883, § 1 et seq., 43 P.S. § 215.1 et seq. This statute provides that whenever a "public employee" goes "on strike" such employee may return to his previous employment only on the condition that his compensation remain the same as before the walkout for a period of three years. Appellants (a group which now includes as intervening parties the two teachers' unions) filed preliminary objections to the complaint. It is from the dismissal of these objections that appellants lodge this appeal.

Their first contention is that equity has no jurisdiction to hear this case. The argument is based on the proposition that the Strike by Public Employees Act contains the exclusive means for determining whether a violation of the act has occurred. The section relied upon provides:

"Notwithstanding the provisions of any other law, any person holding such a position who, without the lawful approval of his superior, fails to report for duty or otherwise absents himself from his position or abstains, in whole or in part, from the full, faithful and proper performance of his position shall be deemed on strike: Provided, That such person, upon request, shall be entitled to establish that he did not violate the provisions of this act. Such request must be filed in writing within ten days after regular compensation of such employee has ceased. In the case of a public employee who is entitled by law to a hearing upon dismissal or removal, such written request shall be filed with the officer or body having power to remove such employee, and such officer or body shall within ten days conduct a hearing to determine whether the provisions of this act have been violated by such public employee in the manner provided by law, appropriate to a proceeding to dismiss or remove such public employee."

We agree that this part of the statute clearly provides the *sole* procedure by which it may be determined whether a school employee violated the act. But this conclusion is not dispositive of the issue before this Court. Here we have a taxpayer of the school district complaining that the school board is about to make illegal payments. He seeks to guarantee by restraining the school board that no such payments are made. Thus it is a controversy between the taxpayer and the school board. This type of litigation clearly does not come within the language of section 5 of the Strike by Public Employees Act which directs: "That such person, [public employee allegedly on strike] upon request, shall be entitled to establish that he did not violate the provisions of the act." The section five procedure only comes into play *once* the school board has determined that one or more of its employees has been "on strike" and decides that such striking employee or employees are not entitled to increased compensation because of the penalty provision of section 4 of the act.

What the taxpayer in the instant action seeks is to restrain illegal payments by the school board; if successful in obtaining the injunction, the school board will be required to make the initial determination whether or not any of its employees were on strike. Once it decides which, if any, of the teachers were on strike and refuses to pay the increased compensation to those employees because of the section 4 penalty, *then* section 5 becomes operative. This latter section will provide a procedure by which teachers who have been adjudged "on strike" and who wish to appeal such determination may have their grievances adjudicated.

But section 5 may never come into play if the school board decided that it would be appropriate to disregard the penalties imposed by section 4. Thus some procedure is required to compel the school board to give effect to the act. Certainly the Strike by Public Employees Act provides no such procedure, let alone the exclusive procedure as alleged by appellants. However, for this purpose an action in equity is perfectly suitable. Equity can mold a decree which precludes the school district from ignoring the act. In fact, equity can be said to supply the *only* adequate and complete remedy available to appellee in this case. See Schrader v. Heath, 408 Pa. 79, 182 A.2d 696 (1962). Moreover, when the sustaining of preliminary objections will result in a denial of claim, or a dismissal of suit, preliminary objections should be sustained only in cases which are clear and free from doubt. Conrad v. Pittsburgh, 421 Pa. 492, 218 A.2d 906 (1966); Baker v. Brennan, 419 Pa. 222, 213 A.2d 362 (1965); Schrader v. Heath, supra. . . .

The order of the court below dismissing the preliminary objections is affirmed. Each party to pay own costs.

COHEN, Justice (dissenting): — I cannot agree with the majority because plaintiff-appellee has failed to state a cause of action. The only allegation of impropriety on the part of the school board is that in its budget the board provided for salary increases. Such allegation should not elicit the courts' intrusion into the local affairs of a school board as a "super board" or as a policeman. Members of the school board know that any illegal act will expose them to surcharge. We cannot restrain anticipated illegalities or improprieties on the mere allegation that a budget provides the funds for such anticipated improprieties. I would reverse the lower court and dismiss the complaint.

## DURKIN v. BOARD OF POLICE AND FIRE COMMISSIONERS
## FOR THE CITY OF MADISON

Wisconsin Supreme Court
48 Wis. 112, 180 N.W.2d 1 (1970)

The Board of Police and Fire Commissioners for the City of Madison, Wisconsin, appellant, entered an order determining that Edward D. Durkin, respondent, had violated sec. 111.70 (4) (1), Stats., SLL 60:244, and certain rules of the fire department of the city of Madison, and thereupon suspended the respondent from the fire department. Respondent petitioned the circuit court for Dane County for review. The trial court entered judgment reversing the order of the Board and the Board has appealed from the judgment of the circuit court.

This action was commenced before the Board of Police and Fire Commissioners for the City of Madison, Wisconsin, upon a complaint of an elector of the city of Madison against Edward D. Durkin, a captain of the fire department for the city of Madison and president of the City Fire Fighters Union Local No. 311.

On March 27, 28 and 29, 1969, there occurred a strike by the firemen for the city of Madison. During this period negotiations were conducted between the city of Madison (City) and the Fire Fighters Union Local No. 311 (Union), which resulted in the signing of an agreement by the City and the Union and an end to the strike. The agreement included a clause whereby the Union and members of the fire department were granted amnesty for their activity in connection with the strike.

Following the settlement, an investigation of the strike was conducted by the appellant, but no charges were filed against any member of the fire department. Thereafter, on June 27, 1969, an elector of the city of Madison, filed a complaint with the appellant charging respondent with having counseled, abetted and led a strike by the Union, and with having participated in that strike by absenting himself from duty during his assigned hours. The complaint alleged that respondent was guilty of violating sec. 111.70 (4) (1), Stats., which prohibits strikes by municipal employees, and of "contumacious conduct endangering the public safety." A hearing on the complaint pursuant to sec. 62.13 (5), was requested.

A hearing on the complaint was conducted by appellant, and on August 24, 1969, an order was entered finding that respondent had participated in the strike and was guilty of violating sec. 111.70 (4) (1), Stats., "contumacious conduct endangering the public safety," and of violating Rules 34, 89 and 100 of the Rules of the Fire Department of Madison, Wisconsin. Respondent was suspended from the fire department for a period of one hundred eighty days.

On petition of the respondent, the order was reviewed by the circuit court for Dane County. The court entered judgment reversing appellant's order on a finding that the order was affected by an error of law in that appellant did not consider itself bound by the terms of an amnesty clause in the collective bargaining agreement signed by the City and the Union. The circuit court held that the amnesty clause prevented appellant from suspending respondent and, therefore, ordered the respondent reinstated, with back pay. . . .

The collective bargaining agreement between the City and the Union included a clause by which the City agreed to dismiss all legal proceedings commenced by it and pending against the Union and its members, to waive all other causes of action arising out of the negotiations or the strike, and to refrain from directly or indirectly commencing an action that would in any way discipline any employee for participation in the strike.

The narrow issue presented by this case is whether the amnesty clause above referred to and contained in the collective bargaining agreement abrogates the statutory right of an elector to file a complaint with the appellant contained in sec. 62.13 (5) (b), Stats. We are of the opinion that it does not.

The first paragraph of the agreement specifically refers to proceedings commenced by the City and to causes of action by the City. The filing of a complaint by an elector with the Board constitutes neither.

The second paragraph of the agreement recites, "Consistent with appropriate Wisconsin statutes, it is the express policy of the City that *it* will not directly or indirectly commence an action that will in any way discipline. . . ." (Emphasis added.)

It is the contention of the appellant that the processing of the elector's complaint by the appellant constitutes the City indirectly commencing an action to discipline the respondent. However, the elector has a statutory right to file charges and if the city council could somehow foreclose the right of the Board to process charges filed by the elector, it follows that the lawful right of an elector to file charges as provided in sec. 62.13 (5) (b), Stats., would be rendered meaningless. The Board is required to process charges filed with it by an elector in accordance with the statutes of the State of Wisconsin and such rules and regulations as it may adopt which are not inconsistent therewith. The ultimate disposition by the Board of the charges so filed by an elector will be considered later in this opinion.

We find no authority which is particularly helpful on this issue and have considered all authorities advanced by both parties. Among other authorities, our attention has been directed to Muskego-Norway C.S.J. S.D. No. 9 v. W.E.R.B. (1967), 35 Wis. 2d 540, 151 N.W.2d 617, and Joint School Dist. No. 8 v. W.E.R.B. (1967), 37 Wis. 2d 483, 155 N.W.2d 78. Respondent advances an argument on the same principle as that adopted in Joint School Dist. No. 8 v. W.E.R.B., supra, that since sec. 111.70, Stats., was enacted subsequent to sec. 62.13 (5), the latter must yield to sec. 111.70 (4) (i), SLL 60:244, and thus a city may agree to a provision granting amnesty when entering into a binding, collective bargaining agreement pursuant to sec. 111.70 (4) (i) even though it would defeat the lawful right of an elector to file charges. The argument, however, assumes that sec. 111.70 (4) (i), does authorize a municipality to agree to an amnesty clause in a collective bargaining agreement which would abrogate the right of an elector to file charges. We find no authority to support such a position. . . .

We conclude that the case must be remanded to the Board for further proceedings for the reason that the respondent was not afforded due process.

Respondent had notice of and an opportunity to defend against charges that he was guilty of violating sec. 111.70 (4) (1), Stats., and of "contumacious conduct endangering the public safety." The charges filed by the elector against the respondent did not allege that he had violated any rules of the fire department. It appears the respondent had no notice of these alleged rule violations until it was pronounced by the Board that he had so violated the three rules in its written decision filed after the hearing. Due process of law requires that an individual have notice of and an opportunity to defend against charges proffered against him. In General Electric Co. v. Wisconsin E. R. Board (1958), 3 Wis. 2d 227, 241, 88 N.W.2d 691, 700, 42 LRRM 2187, 2192, this court held:

> "The principle of fair play is an important factor in a consideration of due process of law. Parties in a legal proceeding have a right to be apprised of the

issues involved, and to be heard on such issues. A finding or order made in a proceeding in which there has not been a 'full hearing' is a denial of due process and is void. . . ."

No court of review has the means of determining whether the Board would have imposed the same penalty had it found the respondent in violation of only two of the violations charged in the complaint.

On this appeal, the respondent contends that based upon the evidence before it, the order of the Board was arbitrary and discriminatory and also unreasonable. However, this issue was not passed upon by the circuit court; and also in view of our remand to the Board for further proceedings because of the lack of due process, it is not properly raised in this court. Nevertheless, we would observe that the Board does have the authority to dismiss the complaint after it has been processed if, in its judgment it should determine such was a proper disposition of the charges filed by the elector. Also, should the Board decide further proceedings are necessary, on the basis of the record now before us, various factors should be taken into consideration by the Board in its ultimate decision. Among these are: (1) The amnesty clause in the agreement which unequivocally sets forth the position of the city council in its relation with the Union and its members; (2) the decision of the Board, as such, and its individual members, not to file charges against any fireman; and (3) the fact that the Board had knowledge of the fact that over 270 firemen participated in the strike and that no charges were filed against anyone except the respondent.

We reach our conclusions as to the disposition of this case upon different grounds than those considered by the circuit court. However, the effect of our decision is that the judgment of the circuit court which reverses the order of the Board of Police and Fire Commissioners is affirmed. That part of the judgment ordering the Madison fire department to forthwith reinstate the respondent, and that he be paid as though he had been in continuous service, is reversed, and the cause is remanded to the Board of Police and Fire Commissioners for further proceedings consistent with this opinion.

*By the Court* — Affirmed in part; reversed in part.

## NOTES

1. The final result of the *Legman* case was a victory for the teachers and the school board. In Legman v. School Dist. of City of Scranton, 438 Pa. 157, 263 A.2d 370 (1970), the Pennsylvania Supreme Court held that, regardless of the legality of the initial action under the Pennsylvania Public Employees Anti-Strike Act of 1947, the school board's action in raising the salaries of teachers who had participated in the strike was ratified by the legislature by the passage of an amendment to the 1968 School Code, 43 PA. STAT. ANN. §§ 215.1 to 215.5. In 1970, the Public Employees Anti-Strike Act was repealed in large part by the Public Employees Relations Act, 43 PA. STAT. ANN. §§ 1101.101 *et seq.,* § 1101.2201 (Supp. 1978).

2. An important consideration raised in *Legman* and *Durkin* types of cases concerns the question of whether a statute designed to punish striking public employees is self-executing. If the statute is not self-executing, and the public employer chooses not to invoke the statutory provisions, does a subsequent invocation of the statute by a taxpayer violate the strikers' right to due process? *Compare* the principal cases *with* Goldberg v. City of Cincinnati, 26 Ohio St. 228, 271 N.E.2d 284 (1971).

3. Is a taxpayer required to accept a public employer's findings of fact with respect to a possible violation of the law? In Head v. Special School Dist. No. 1, 80 L.R.R.M. 2459 (Minn. Dist. Ct. 1971), the court held that taxpayers seeking to enjoin a school board from making illegal payments to teachers who had struck were entitled to an order requiring

the teachers to give depositions regarding their conduct during the strike. The taxpayers were entitled to determine for themselves whether the board had acted arbitrarily in deciding that the teachers, who had not worked during the period of the work stoppage, had nonetheless not been on strike. *See also* Head v. Special School Dist. No. 1, 288 Minn. 496, 182 N.W.2d 887 (1970), *cert. denied,* 404 U.S. 886 (1971), which recognized the right of taxpayers to join with the State Attorney General to challenge a strike settlement agreement between a school board and a teachers' association.

4. Other courts have been less willing to allow taxpayer intervention in the employer-employee relationship. For example, in Wilson v. Evans, 70 L.R.R.M. 2094 (N.Y. Sup. Ct. 1968), an action was brought by parents and taxpayers seeking an injunction to prevent a school custodian from interfering with academic instruction by failing to provide custodial services. The court held that it was without jurisdiction to intervene in a purely administrative matter between a civil service employee and his employer. If the actions of the custodian constituted a strike, the court said, school officials had the power to deal with the situation under the applicable state law. In San Francisco v. Cooper, 13 Cal.3d 898, 534 P.2d 403 (1975), the California Supreme Court similarly ruled that a city ordinance and a school board resolution granting salary increases to public employees could not be invalidated on the ground that they were enacted as a result of an illegal public employees strike. The Court rejected a taxpayer's argument that the duly enacted provisions were invalid because they had been adopted "as a result of" and "under the coercion of" an illegal strike. The Court concluded that since California has no constitutional, statutory, or charter provisions prohibiting a city or school board from enacting legislation as a result of an illegal strike, the Court had no authority to nullify the ordinance or resolution merely because individual legislators may have been subjected to improper influences.

5. In Parents Union for Public Schools in Philadelphia v. Bd. of Educ., 389 A.2d 577, 1977-78 PBC ¶36,396 (1978), the Pennsylvania Supreme Court held that interested taxpayers and students could sue directly in court, without first seeking relief before the PERB, where they were endeavoring to enjoin the school district from complying with contractual provisions which allegedly contravened state policy by impermissibly transferring control over educational policy from the school board to the representative labor union.

# Chapter 9

# THE POLITICAL AND CIVIL RIGHTS OF PUBLIC EMPLOYEES

No study of labor relations law in the public sector would be complete without some analysis of the political and civil rights of public employees. The line that divides the "public" and the "private" employment sectors is frequently obscure. Nevertheless, partly because of certain overriding constitutional principles, the history of regulation of employment relations in the public sector in the United States has posed many special problems which have not been seen in the private sector. As Robert M. O'Neil so aptly noted in his book, *The Price of Dependency: Civil Liberties In The Welfare State,* 61-62 (1970):

> Much of what government can do *for* its own work force, it can also require private employers to do for their workers. The harder question remains, and will be the crux of this chapter: What can government do *to* its employees — what conditions and restrictions can it impose upon them — which it could not do to employees of private firms?

On the one hand, history has demonstrated that public employees in the United States may be made subject to rigid conditions of employment. The most familiar general restrictions on public employment relate to political activities and associations. However, several other types of employment restrictions have also proven to be controversial in the public service; among these have been included loyalty oaths, bans on partisan political activities, reprisals for criticizing government officials or policies, and employment disabilities created by criminal records, personal appearance, sexual activity, private associations and deviant conduct.

On the other hand, although it is clear that the public employee may be burdened by special job conditions and restrictions, it is likewise clear that, as a public servant, the government worker cannot be saddled with unconstitutional conditions or restrictions of employment. Public workers, therefore, enjoy certain constitutional protections, privileges and rights which provide a framework for the regulation of employment relations in the government service. For example, constitutional issues concerning the freedom of association and expression, the privilege against self incrimination, due process as a protection against dismissal, and protections against race, sex, national origin and religious discrimination, have an important and direct bearing on employment relations law in the public sector.

Since these constitutional issues and related statutory applications are matters transcending labor relations law and collective bargaining in the public sector, they cannot be ignored. With this in mind, the following materials are presented to help the student of labor relations law in the public sector to comprehend some of the important legal principles, both constitutional and statutory, which affect the political and civil rights of public employees.

McAULIFFE v. MAYOR OF NEW BEDFORD, 155 Mass. 216, 29 N.E. 517 (1892). In a decision written by Justice Oliver Wendell Holmes, the Massachusetts court upheld a city rule which prohibited policemen from joining labor unions. In reaching this conclusion, the court rendered its now famous dictum that:

The petitioner may have a constitutional right to talk politics, but he has no constitutional right to be a policeman. There are few employments for hire in which the servant does not agree to suspend his constitutional right of free speech, as well as of idleness, by the implied terms of his contract. The servant cannot complain, as he takes the employment on the terms which are offered him.

## O'NEIL, THE PRIVATE LIVES OF PUBLIC EMPLOYEES, 51 Ore. L. Rev. 70, 82-83 (1971) †

The public employee's legal status is vastly better today than at the time when Justice Holmes remarked that Officer McAuliffe might "have a constitutional right to talk politics, but . . . no right to be a policeman." [1] If it is true that the Supreme Court has never squarely relieved the government worker of Holmes' dilemma, one who enters the public service may still (save in California [2] and Oregon[3]) be compelled to steer clear of partisan politics.[4] But that is one of the few lacunae remaining from a time when public employment and other government benefits were classed as "privileges which could be conditioned, denied, or terminated as agency heads or legislators saw fit."

All that has changed. The principal catalyst for reform has been the recent development of the doctrine of unconstitutional conditions, applied with particular force to government employment.[5] Courts have consistently repudiated the notion that because government was under no legal obligation to offer employment to any person, it might therefore withhold such employment on arbitrary or discriminatory grounds or encumber public service with onerous and instrusive conditions. In a host of recent decisions, the Supreme Court has cautioned that "public employment . . . may [not] be conditioned upon the surrender of constitutional rights which could not be abridged by direct government action." [6]

## A. RESTRICTIONS AND PRIVILEGES OF PUBLIC EMPLOYMENT

## 1. LOYALTY OATHS

GARNER v. BOARD OF PUBLIC WORKS OF LOS ANGELES, 341 U.S. 716, 71 S. Ct. 909, 95 L. Ed. 1317 (1951). Held valid a municipal ordinance which required

---

† Reprinted by permission. Copyright © by The University of Oregon.

[1] McAuliffe v. New Bedford, 155 Mass. 216, 220, 29 N.E. 517 (1892).

[2] Bagley v. Washington Township Hosp. Dist., 65 Cal. 2d 499, 421 P.2d 409, 55 Cal. Rptr. 401 (1966); Fort v. Civil Serv. Comm'n, 61 Cal. 2d 331, 392 P.2d 385, 38 Cal. Rptr. 625 (1964).

[3] Minielly v. State, 242 Ore. 490, 411 P.2d 69 (1966).

[4] United Public Workers v. Mitchell, 330 U.S. 75 (1947). Despite a constant barrage from scholars and critics and growing pressures for reform within the civil service, the Hatch Act survives. *See, e.g.,* Esman, *The Hatch Act: A Reappraisal,* 60 YALE L.J. 986 (1951); Nelson, *Public Employees and the Right to Engage in Political Activity,* 9 VAND. L. REV. 27 (1955); Rose, *A Critical Look at the Hatch Act,* 75 HARV. L. REV. 510 (1962); Note, *The Public Employee and Political Activity,* 3 SUFFOLK L. REV. 380 (1969).

[5] *See* especially the works of the two most thoughtful commentators on this development, Linde, *Justice Douglas on Liberty in the Welfare State: Constitutional Rights in the Public Sector,* 40 WASH. L. REV. 10 (1965); and Van Alstyne, *The Constitutional Rights of Public Employees: A Comment on the Inappropriate Uses of an Old Analogy,* 16 U.C.L.A.L. REV. 751 (1969). For more specialized comments on a particular application of the doctrine, see O'Neil, *Public Employment, Antiwar Protest and Preinduction Review,* 17 U.C.L.A.L. REV. 1028 (1970).

[6] Keyishian v. Board of Regents, 385 U.S. 589, 605-06, 87 S. Ct. 675, 17 L. Ed. 2d 629 (1967).

municipal employees, as a condition of employment, to sign an affidavit disclosing whether they were or ever had been a member of the Communist Party and to take an oath declaring that for five years prior to the effective date of the ordinance they did not advocate the overthrow of government by force or belong to any organization that advocated such doctrine. In upholding both the oath and affidavit portions of the ordinance, the Court ruled that it was not invalid as a bill of attainder and held further that "we are unable to conclude that punishment is imposed by a general regulation which merely provides standards of qualification and eligibility for employment." 341 U.S. at 722.

BAGGETT V. BULLITT, 377 U.S. 360, 84 S. Ct. 1316, 12 L. Ed. 2d 377 (1960). Held unconstitutional two loyalty oaths required by the State of Washington: a "positive loyalty oath" imposed on teachers, making them subscribe that they "will by precept and example promote respect for the flag and [federal and state] institutions, reverence for law and order and undivided allegiance to the [federal] government;" and a "negative disclaimer" imposed on all state employees, requiring them to disclaim being a "subversive person" or members of a "subversive organization." "Subversive person" was defined pursuant to state law to mean "any person who commits, attempts to commit, or aids in the commission, or advocates, abets, advises or teaches by any means any person to commit, attempt to commit, or aids in the commission of any act intended to overthrow, destroy or alter [or 'to assist' in same] the constitutional form of . . . government . . . or with knowledge that the organization is [subversive] . . . becomes or remains a member of a subversive organization. . . ." "Subversive organization" was defined in similar terms under the state law and the Communist Party was declared subversive. The Court held, per Justice White writing for the majority, that "Persons required to swear they understand this oath may quite reasonably conclude that any person who aids the Communist Party or teaches or advises known members of the Party is a subversive person because such teaching or advice may now or at some future date aid the activities of the Party. Teaching and advising are clearly acts, and one cannot confidently assert that his counsel, aid, influence or support which adds to the resources, rights and knowledge of the Communist Party or its members does not aid the Party in its activities, activities which the statute tells us are all in furtherance of the stated purpose of overthrowing the Government by revolution, force, or violence."

The Court also indicated that the Washington statute was unconstitutionally vague.

"A person is subversive not only if he himself commits the specified acts but if he abets or advises another in aiding a third person to commit an act which will assist yet a fourth person in the overthrow or alteration of constitutional government. The Washington Supreme Court has said that knowledge is to be read into every provision and we accept this construction. . . . But what is it that the Washington Professor must 'know'? Must he know that his aid or teaching will be used by another and that the person aided has the requisite guilty intent or is it sufficient that he knows that his aid or teaching would or might be useful to others in the commission of acts intended to overthrow the Government? Is it subversive activity, for example, to attend and participate in international conventions of mathematicians and exchange views with scholars from Communist countries? . . .

"The Washington oath goes beyond overthrow or alteration by force or violence. It extends to alteration by 'revolution' which, unless wholly redundant and its ordinary meaning distorted, includes any rapid or fundamental change. Would, therefore, any organization or any person supporting, advocating or teaching peaceful but far-reaching constitutional amendments be engaged in subvervise [*sic*] activity?"

Finally, the Court ruled that the "positive loyalty oath" offended "due process because of vagueness." On this last point, the Court noted that: "The range of activities which are or might be deemed inconsistent with the required promise is very wide indeed.... The uncertain meanings of the oaths require the oathtaker — teachers and public servants — to 'steer far wider of the unlawful zone' ... than if the boundaries of the forbidden areas were clearly marked. Those with a conscientious regard for what they solemnly swear or affirm, sensitive to the perils posed by the oath's indefinite language, avoid the risk of loss of employment, and perhaps profession, only by restricting their conduct to that which is unquestionably safe. Free speech may not be so inhibited."

ELFBRANDT V. RUSSELL, 384 U.S. 11, 86 S. Ct. 1238, 16 L. Ed. 2d 321 (1966). The Court invalidated an Arizona law which required an oath from state employees. The oath was the conventional one whereby the employee swore or affirmed that he would support the United States Constitution and the constitution and laws of the State of Arizona. However, the state legislature had put a gloss on the oath by subjecting to a prosecution for perjury and for discharge from public office anyone who took the oath and who "knowingly and willfully becomes or remains a member of the Communist Party of the United States ..." or any other organization having for one of its purposes the overthrow of the government of Arizona. Petitioner, a public school teacher and a member of the Quaker faith, claimed that good conscience prevented her from taking the oath because she did not know what the oath meant and she had been unable to get a hearing at which the scope and definition of the oath could be determined. Petitioner thus brought a suit for declaratory relief. The Court held that the oath, as it had been construed by the state legislature, violated petitioner's right to freedom of association. The Court noted in particular that the oath was overly broad because it applied to mere membership in the Communist Party, or to any subversive organization, without requiring "the specific intent" to further the illegal aims of the organization. Consequently, the oath was read to be founded on the impermissible doctrine of "guilt by association." The Court cited *Baggett* and held that a statute touching rights protected by the First Amendment must be narrowly drawn, to define and punish specific conduct as constituting a clear and present danger to a substantial interest of the state. Mr. Justice White, along with Justices Clark, Harlan and Stewart, dissented. The dissenting opinion cited earlier Court opinions which had indicated that a state is permitted to require its public employees, as a condition of employment, to abstain from knowing membership in organizations advocating the violent overthrow of government and that the state is constitutionally free to inquire into such associations and to discharge those public employees who decline to affirm or deny them.

KEYISHIAN V. BOARD OF REGENTS, 385 U.S. 589, 87 S. Ct. 675, 17 L. Ed. 2d 629 (1967). The Court held unconstitutionally vague certain provisions of New York law which provided that "the utterance of any treasonable or seditious word or words or the doing of any treasonable or seditious acts" were grounds for removal and that any person who "by word of mouth or writing willfully and deliberately advocates, advises or teaches the doctrine" of forceful overthrow of government was barred or disqualified from employment. Stating that academic freedom is a special concern of the First Amendment, the Court emphasized that " '[P]recision of regulation must be the touchstone in an area so closely touching our most precious freedoms' NAACP v. Button, 371 U.S. 415, 438;" and that New York's intricate and uncertain plan could not meet the necessary standard of specificity.

In addition, the Court held that provisions of New York law which made Communist Party membership, without more, evidence of prima facie disqualification were unconstitutional. The Court stated the governing standard to be "legislation which sanctions membership unaccompanied by specific intent to further the unlawful goals of the organization or which is not active membership violates constitutional limitations," and held that the New York provisions constituted an overbroad limitation on freedom of association.

## NOTE

For an excellent analysis of the evolution of the law in this area, see Israel, *Elfbrandt v. Russell — The Demise of the Oath?*, 1966 SUP. CT. REV. 193. *See also* Leahy, *Loyalty and the First Amendment — A Concept Emerges*, 43 N.D.L. REV. 53 (1966); Comment, 77 YALE L. J. 739 (1968).

## CONNELL v. HIGGINBOTHAM

Supreme Court of the United States
403 U.S. 207, 91 S. Ct. 1772, 29 L. Ed. 2d 418 (1971)

PER CURIAM.

This is an appeal from an action ... challenging the constitutionality of ... various loyalty oaths upon which appellant's employment as a school teacher was conditioned.

The three-judge U.S. District Court declared three of the five clauses contained in the oaths to be unconstitutional,* and enjoined the State from conditioning employment on the taking of an oath including the language declared unconstitutional. The appeal is from that portion of the District Court decision, 305 F. Supp. 445, which upheld the remaining two clauses in the oath: I do hereby solemnly swear or affirm (1) "that I will support the Constitution of the United States and of the State of Florida"; and (2) "that I do not believe in the overthrow of the Government of the United States or of the State of Florida by force or violence." ... Appellant was dismissed from her teaching position on March 18, 1969, for refusing to sign the loyalty oath required of all Florida public employees, Fla. Stat. § 876.05.

The first section of the oath upheld by the District Court, requiring all applicants to pledge to support the Constitution of the United States and of the State of Florida, demands no more of Florida public employees than is required of all state and federal officers. U.S. Const., Art. VI, cl. 3. The validity of this section of the oath would appear settled. ... The second portion of the oath, approved by the District Court, falls within the ambit of decisions of this Court

---

* The clauses declared unconstitutional by the court below required the employee to swear: (a) "that I am not a member of the Communist Party"; (b) "that I have not and will not lend my aid, support, advice, counsel or influence to the Communist Party"; and (c) "that I am not a member of any organization or party which believes in or teaches, directly or indirectly, the overthrow of the Government of the United States or of Florida by force or violence."

proscribing summary dismissal from public employment without hearing or inquiry required by due process. Slochower v. Board of Education, 350 U.S. 551, 76 S. Ct. 637, 100 L. Ed. 692 (1956). . . .

MR. JUSTICE MARSHALL, with whom MR. JUSTICE DOUGLAS and MR. JUSTICE BRENNAN join, concurring in the result.

I agree that Florida may require state employees to affirm that they "will support the Constitution of the United States and of the State of Florida." Such a forward-looking, promissory oath of constitutional support does not in my view offend the First Amendment's command that the grant or denial of governmental benefits cannot be made to turn on the political viewpoints or affiliations of a would-be beneficiary. I also agree that Florida may not base its employment decisions, as to state teachers or any other hiring category, on an applicant's willingness *vel non* to affirm "that I do not believe in the overthrow of the Government of the United States or of the State of Florida by force or violence."

However, in striking down the latter oath, the Court has left the clear implication that its objection runs, not against Florida's determination to exclude those who "believe in the overthrow," but only against the State's decision to regard unwillingness to take the oath as conclusive, irrebuttable proof of the proscribed belief. Due process may rightly be invoked to condemn Florida's mechanistic approach to the question of proof. But in my view it simply does not matter what kind of evidence a State can muster to show that a job applicant "believe[s] in the overthrow." For state action injurious to an individual cannot be justified on account of the nature of the individual's beliefs, whether he "believe[s] in the overthrow" or has any other sort of belief. "If there is any fixed star in our constitutional constellation, it is that no official, high or petty, can prescribe what shall be orthodox in politics, nationalism, religion, or other matters of opinion. . . ." West Virginia State Board of Education v. Barnette, 319 U.S. 624, 642, 63 S. Ct. 1178, 1187, 87 L. Ed. 1628 (1943).

I would strike down Florida's "overthrow" oath plainly and simply on the ground that belief as such cannot be the predicate of governmental action.

## COLE v. RICHARDSON

Supreme Court of the United States
405 U.S. 676, 92 S. Ct. 1332, 31 L. Ed. 2d 593 (1972)

MR. CHIEF JUSTICE BURGER delivered the opinion of the Court.

In this appeal we review the decision of the three-judge District Court holding a Massachusetts loyalty oath unconstitutional, 300 F. Supp. 1321. . . .

[Appellee], Mrs. Richardson, was asked to subscribe to the oath required of all public employees in Massachusetts. The oath is as follows:

"I do solemnly swear (or affirm) that I will uphold and defend the Constitution of the United States of America and the Constitution of the Commonwealth of Massachusetts and that I will oppose the overthrow of the government of the United States of America or of this Commonwealth by force, violence or by any illegal or unconstitutional method." . . .

[Appellee was advised that she could not continue as an employee of the Boston State Hospital unless she subscribed to the oath. When she refused to comply, her employment was terminated.] . . .

A three-judge District Court held the oath statute unconstitutional and enjoined the appellant from applying the statute to prohibit Mrs. Richardson from working for Boston State Hospital. The District Court found the attack on the "uphold and defend" clause, the first part of the oath, foreclosed by Knight v. Board of Regents, 269 F. Supp. 339 (S.D.N.Y. 1967), affirmed, 390 U.S. 36, 88 S. Ct. 816, 19 L. Ed. 2d 812 (1968). But it found that the "oppose and overthrow" clause was "fatally vague and unspecific," and therefore a violation of First Amendment rights. The court granted the requested injunction but denied the claim for damages. . . .

We conclude that the Massachusetts oath is constitutionally permissible. . . .

A review of the oath cases in this Court will put the instant oath into context. We have made clear that neither federal nor state governments may condition employment on taking oaths which impinge rights guaranteed by the First and Fourteenth Amendments respectively, as for example those relating to political beliefs. . . . Nor may employment be conditioned on an oath that one has not engaged, or will not engage, in protected speech activities such as the following: criticizing institutions of government; discussing political doctrine that approves the overthrow of certain forms of government; and supporting candidates for political office. Keyishian v. Board of Regents, 385 U.S. 589, 87 S. Ct. 675, 17 L. Ed. 2d 629 (1967); Baggett v. Bullitt, 377 U.S. 360, 84 S. Ct. 1316, 12 L. Ed. 2d 377 (1964); Cramp v. Board of Public Instruction, 368 U.S. 278, 82 S. Ct. 275, 7 L. Ed. 2d 285 (1961). Employment may not be conditioned on an oath denying past, or abjuring future, associational activities within constitutional protection; such protected activities include membership in organizations having illegal purposes unless one knows of the purpose and shares a specific intent to promote the illegal purpose. Whitehill v. Elkins, 389 U.S. 54, 88 S. Ct. 184, 19 L. Ed. 2d 228 (1967); Keyishian v. Board of Regents, *supra;* Elfbrandt v. Russell, 384 U.S. 11, 86 S. Ct. 1238, 16 L. Ed. 2d 321 (1966); Wieman v. Updegraff, 344 U.S. 183, 73 S. Ct. 215, 97 L. Ed. 216 (1952). . . . And, finally, an oath may not be so vague that " 'men of common intelligence must necessarily guess at its meaning and differ as to its application, [because such an oath] violates the first essential of due process of law.' " Cramp v. Board of Public Instruction, 368 U.S., at 287, 82 S. Ct. at 280. . . .

An underlying, seldom articulated concern running throughout these cases is that the oaths under consideration often required individuals to reach back into their pasts to recall minor, sometimes innocent, activities. They put the government into "the censorial business of investigating, scrutinizing, interpreting, and then penalizing or approving the political viewpoint" and past activities of individuals. Law Students Civil Rights Research Council v. Wadmond, 401 U.S., at 192, 91 S. Ct. at 740 (Marshall, J., concurring).

Several cases recently decided by the Court stand out among our oath cases because they have upheld the constitutionality of oaths, addressed to the future, promising constitutional support in broad terms. These cases have begun with a recognition that the Constitution itself prescribes comparable oaths in two articles. Article II, § 1, cl. 7, provides that the President shall swear that he will "faithfully execute the office . . . and will to the best of my ability preserve, protect and defend the Constitution of the United States." Article VI, cl. 3, provides that all state and federal officers shall be bound by an oath "to support this Constitution." . . .

Bond v. Floyd, 385 U.S. 116, 87 S. Ct. 339, 17 L. Ed. 2d 235 (1966), involved Georgia's statutory requirement that state legislators swear to "support the Constitution of this State and of the United States," a paraphrase of the constitutionally required oath. The Court there implicitly concluded that the First Amendment did not undercut the validity of the constitutional oath provisions. Although in theory the First Amendment might have invalidated those provisions, approval of the amendment by the same individuals who had included the oaths in the Constitution suggested strongly that they were consistent. The Court's recognition of this consistency did not involve a departure from its many decisions striking down oaths which infringed First and Fourteenth Amendment rights. The Court read the Georgia oath as calling simply for an acknowledgment of a willingness to abide by "constitutional processes of government." 385 U.S., at 135, 87 S. Ct. 339, 349, 17 L. Ed. 2d 235. . . .

Although disagreeing on other points, in *Wadmond, supra,* all members of the Court agreed on this point. Mr. Justice Marshall noted there, while dissenting as to other points,

"The oath of constitutional support requires an individual assuming public responsibilities to affirm . . . that he will endeavor to perform his public duties lawfully." 401 U.S., at 192, 91 S. Ct. at 740.

The Court has further made clear that an oath need not parrot the exact language of the constitutional oaths to be constitutionally proper. Thus in Ohlson v. Phillips, 397 U.S. 317, 90 S. Ct. 1124, 25 L. Ed. 2d 337 (1970), we sustained the constitutionality of a state requirement that teachers swear to "uphold" the Constitution. . . . The District Court in the instant case properly recognized that the first clause of the Massachusetts oath, in which the individual swears to "uphold and defend" the constitutions of the United States and the Commonwealth, is indistinguishable from the oaths this Court has recently approved. Yet the District Court applied a highly literalistic approach to the second clause to strike it down. We view the second clause of the oath as essentially the same as the first.

The second clause of the oath contains a promise to "oppose the overthrow of the government of the United States of America or of this Commonwealth by force, violence or by any illegal or unconstitutional method." The District Court sought to give a dictionary meaning to this language and found "oppose" to raise the specter of vague, undefinable responsibilities actively to combat a potential overthrow of the government. That reading of the oath understandably troubled the court because of what it saw as vagueness in terms of what threats would constitute sufficient danger of overthrow to require the oath-giver to actively oppose overthrow, and exactly what actions he would have to take in that respect. . . . We have rejected such rigidly literal notions and recognized that the purpose leading legislatures to enact such oaths, just as the purpose leading the Framers of our Constitution to include the two explicit constitutional oaths, was not to create specific responsibilities but to assure that those in positions of public trust were willing to commit themselves to live by the constitutional processes of our system as Mr. Justice Marshall suggested in *Wadmond,* 401 U.S., at 192, 91 S. Ct. 720. Here the second clause does not require specific action in some hypothetical or actual situation. Plainly "force, violence or . . . any illegal or unconstitutional method" modifies "overthrow" and does not commit the oath taker to meet force with force. Just as the connotatively active word "support" has been interpreted to mean simply a commitment to abide by our constitutional system, the second clause of this oath is merely oriented to the negative implication of this notion; it is a commitment not to use illegal and constitutionally unprotected force to change the constitutional system. The second clause does not expand the obligation of the first; it simply makes clear the application of the first clause to a particular issue. Such repitition, whether for emphasis or cadence, seems to be wont with authors of oaths. That the second clause may be redundant is no ground to strike it down; we are not charged with correcting grammar but with enforcing a constitution.

The purpose of the oath is clear on its face. We cannot presume that the Massachusetts legislature intended by its use of such general terms as "uphold," "defend," and "oppose" to impose obligations of specific, positive action on oath takers. Any such construction would raise serious questions whether the oath was so vague as to amount to a denial of due process. . . . Nor is the oath as interpreted void for vagueness. . . . It is punishable only by a prosecution for perjury and, since perjury is a knowing and willful falsehood, the constitutional vice of punishment without fair warning cannot occur here. Nor here is there any problem of the punishment inflicted by mere prosecution. See Cramp v. Board of Public Instruction, 368 U.S., at 284, 82 S. Ct. at 279, 7 L. Ed. 2d 285. There has been no prosecution under this statute since its 1948 enactment, and there is no indication that prosecutions have been planned or begun. The oath "triggered no serious possibility of prosecution" by the Commonwealth. Were we confronted with a record of actual prosecutions or harassment through threatened prosecutions, we might be faced with a different question. . . .

Appellee mounts an additional attack on the Massachusetts oath program in that it does not provide for a hearing prior to the determination not to hire the individual based on the refusal to subscribe to the oath. All of the cases in this Court which require a hearing before discharge for failure to take an oath involved impermissible oaths. In Slochower v. Board of Education, 350 U.S. 551, 76 S. Ct. 637, 100 L. Ed. 692 (1956) (not an oath case), the State sought to dismiss a professor for claiming the Fifth Amendment privilege in a United States Senate committee hearing; the Court held the State's action invalid because the exercise of the privilege was a constitutional right from which the State could not draw any rational inference of disloyalty. Appellee relies on Nostrand v. Little, 362 U.S. 474, 80 S. Ct. 840, 4 L. Ed. 2d 892 (1960), and Connell v. Higginbotham, 403 U.S. 207, 91 S. Ct. 1772, 29 L. Ed. 2d 418 (1971), but in those cases the Court held only that the mere refusal to take the particular oath was not a constitutionally permissible basis for termination. In the circumstances of those cases only by holding a hearing, showing evidence of disloyalty, and allowing the employee an opportunity to respond might the State develop a permissible basis for concluding that the employee was to be discharged.

Since there is no constitutionally protected right to overthrow a government by force, violence, or illegal or unconstitutional means, no constitutional right is infringed by an oath to abide by the constitutional system in the future. Therefore there is no requirement that one who refuses to take the Massachusetts oath be granted a hearing for the determination of some other fact before being discharged.

The judgment of the District Court is reversed and the case is remanded for further proceedings consistent with this opinion.

[The dissenting opinions of Justice Douglas and Justice Marshall have been omitted.]

## NOTES

1. Does the majority opinion in *Cole* reflect a somewhat strained effort to save the challenged oath from constitutional infirmity? Is the rationale in *Cole* consistent with the approach taken in United States v. Robel, 389 U.S. 258, 88 S. Ct. 419, 19 L. Ed. 2d 508 (1967)? In *Robel*, section 5 (a) (1) (D) of the Subversive Activities Control Act of 1950 — which imposed criminal sanctions on any member of a Communist action group who

engaged in employment in a defense facility — was declared to be unconstitutional for want of clarity and precision. In *Robel,* the Court refused to save the challenged statute from constitutional infirmity by limiting its application to active members of Communist action organizations who had the specific intent of furthering the unlawful goals of the organizations.

2. For some useful comments on the general subject of loyalty oaths and related topics, see Bruff, *Unconstitutional Conditions upon Public Employment: New Departures in the Protection of First Amendment Rights,* 21 HASTINGS L.J. 129 (1969); Leahy, *The Public Employee and the First Amendment — Must He Sacrifice His Civil Rights To Be a Civil Servant,* 4 CALIF. W.L. REV. 1 (1968); Van Alstyne, *The Constitutional Rights of Public Employees: A Comment on the Inappropriate Use of an Old Analogy,* 16 U.C.L.A.L. REV. 751 (1969); Israel, *Elfbrandt v. Russell — The Demise of the Oath?,* 1966 SUP. CT. REV. 193; Van Alstyne, *The Demise of the Right — Privilege Distinction in Constitutional Law,* 81 HARV. L. REV. 1439 (1968).

# 2. PRIVILEGE AGAINST SELF INCRIMINATION AND THE DUTY OF DISCLOSURE

## GARRITY v. NEW JERSEY

Supreme Court of the United States
385 U.S. 493, 87 S. Ct. 616, 17 L. Ed. 2d 562 (1967)

MR. JUSTICE DOUGLAS delivered the opinion of the Court.

Appellants were police officers in certain New Jersey boroughs. The Supreme Court of New Jersey ordered [an investigation of] alleged fixing of traffic tickets.

Before being questioned, each appellant was warned (1) that anything he said might be used against him in any state criminal proceeding; (2) that he had the privilege to refuse to answer if the disclosure would tend to incriminate him; but (3) that if he refused to answer he would be subject to removal from office.

Appellants answered the questions. No immunity was granted. . . . Over their objections, some of the answers given were used in subsequent prosecutions for conspiracy to obstruct the administration of the traffic laws. Appellants were convicted and their convictions were sustained over their protests that their statements were coerced, by reason of the fact that, if they refused to answer, they could lose their positions with the police department. . . .

We postponed the question of jurisdiction to a hearing on the merits. 383 U.S. 941. The statute whose validity was sought to be "drawn in question," 28 U.S.C. § 1257 (2), was the forfeiture statute.[3] But the New Jersey Supreme Court refused to reach that question (44 N.J., at 223, 207 A.2d, at 697), deeming the voluntariness of the statements as the only issue presented. *Id.,* at 220-222, 207

---

[3] "Any person holding or who has held any elective or appointive public office, position or employment (whether state, county or municipal), who refuses to testify upon matters relating to the office, position or employment in any criminal proceeding wherein he is a defendant or is called as a witness on behalf of the prosecution, upon the ground that his answer may tend to incriminate him or compel him to be a witness against himself or refuses to waive immunity when called by a grand jury to testify thereon or who willfully refuses or fails to appear before any court, commission or body of this state which has the right to inquire under oath upon matters relating to the office, position or employment of such person or who, having been sworn, refuses to testify or to answer any material question upon the ground that his answer may tend to incriminate him or compel him to be a witness against himself, shall, if holding elective or public office, position or employment, be removed therefrom or shall thereby forfeit his office, position or employment and any vested or future right of tenure or pension granted to him by any law of this state provided the inquiry relates to a matter which occurred or arose within the preceding five years. Any person so forfeiting his office, position or employment shall not thereafter be eligible for election or appointment to any public office, position or employment in this state." N.J. Rev. Stat. § 2A:81-17.1 (Supp. 1965).

A.2d, at 695-696. The statute is therefore too tangentially involved to satisfy 28 U.S.C. § 1257 (2), for the only bearing it had was whether, valid or not, the fear of being discharged under it for refusal to answer on the one hand and the fear of self-incrimination on the other was "a choice between the rock and the whirlpool" which made the statements products of coercion in violation of the Fourteenth Amendment. We therefore dismiss the appeal, treat the papers as a petition for certiorari (28 U.S.C. § 2103), grant the petition and proceed to the merits.

We agree with the New Jersey Supreme Court that the forfeiture-of-office statute is relevant here only for the bearing it has on the voluntary character of the statements used to convict petitioners in their criminal prosecutions. . . .

The choice given petitioners was either to forfeit their jobs or to incriminate themselves. The option to lose their means of livelihood or to pay the penalty of self-incrimination is the antithesis of free choice to speak out or to remain silent. That practice, like interrogation practices we reviewed in Miranda v. Arizona, 384 U.S. 436, 464-465, is "likely to exert such pressure upon an individual as to disable him from making a free and rational choice." We think the statements were infected by the coercion inherent in this scheme of questioning and cannot be sustained as voluntary under our prior decisions. . . .

In these cases . . . though petitioners succumbed to compulsion, they preserved their objections, raising them at the earliest possible point. . . . The cases are therefore quite different from the situation where one who is anxious to make a clean breast of the whole affair volunteers the information.

Mr. Justice Holmes in McAuliffe v. New Bedford, 155 Mass. 216, 29 N.E. 517, stated a dictum on which New Jersey heavily relies:

> "The petitioner may have a constitutional right to talk politics, but he has no constitutional right to be a policeman. There are few employments for hire in which the servant does not agree to suspend his constitutional right of free speech, as well as of idleness, by the implied terms of his contract. The servant cannot complain, as he takes the employment on the terms which are offered him. On the same principle, the city may impose any reasonable condition upon holding offices within its control." *Id.*, at 220, 29 N.E., at 517-518.

The question in this case, however, is not cognizable in those terms. Our question is whether a State, contrary to the requirement of the Fourteenth Amendment, can use the threat of discharge to secure incriminatory evidence against an employee.

We held in Slochower v. Board of Education, 350 U.S. 551, that a public school teacher could not be discharged merely because he had invoked the Fifth Amendment privilege against self-incrimination when questioned by a congressional committee:

> "The privilege against self-incrimination would be reduced to a hollow mockery if its exercise could be taken as equivalent either to a confession of guilt or a conclusive presumption of perjury. . . . The privilege serves to protect the innocent who otherwise might be ensnared by ambiguous circumstances." *Id.*, at 557-558.

We conclude that policemen, like teachers and lawyers, are not relegated to a watered-down version of constitutional rights. . . .

Reversed.

MR. JUSTICE HARLAN, whom MR. JUSTICE CLARK and MR. JUSTICE STEWART join, dissenting. . . .

The majority is apparently engaged in the delicate task of riding two unruly horses at once: it is presumably arguing simultaneously that the statements were involuntary as a matter of fact, in the same fashion that the statements in Chambers v. Florida, 309 U.S. 227, and Haynes v. Washington, 373 U.S. 503, were thought to be involuntary, and that the statements were inadmissible as a matter of law, on the premise that they were products of an impermissible condition imposed on the constitutional privilege. These are very different contentions and require separate replies, but in my opinion both contentions are plainly mistaken, for reasons that follow. . . .

As interrogation commenced, each of the petitioners was sworn, carefully informed that he need not give any information, reminded that any information given might be used in a subsequent criminal prosecution, and warned that as a police officer he was subject to a proceeding to discharge him if he failed to provide information relevant to his public responsibilities. . . .

All of the petitioners testified at trial, and gave evidence essentially consistent with the statements taken from them. . . .

The issue remaining is whether the statements were inadmissible because they were "involuntary as a matter of law," in that they were given after a warning that New Jersey policemen may be discharged for failure to provide information pertinent to their public responsibilities. What is really involved on this score, however, is not in truth a question of "voluntariness" at all, but rather whether the condition imposed by the State on the exercise of the privilege against self-incrimination, namely dismissal from office, in this instance serves in itself to render the statements inadmissible. Absent evidence of involuntariness in fact, the admissibility of these statements thus hinges on the validity of the consequence which the State acknowledged might have resulted if the statements had not been given. If the consequence is constitutionally permissible, there can surely be no objection if the State cautions the witness that it may follow if he remains silent. If both the consequence and the warning are constitutionally permissible, a witness is obliged, in order to prevent the use of his statements against him in a criminal prosecution, to prove under the standards established since Brown v. Mississippi, 297 U.S. 278, that as a matter of fact the statements were involuntarily made. The central issues here are therefore identical to those presented in *Spevack v. Klein:* whether consequences may properly be permitted to result to a claimant after his invocation of the constitutional privilege, and if so, whether the consequence in question is permissible. For reasons which I have stated in *Spevack v. Klein,* in my view nothing in the logic or purposes of the privilege demands that all consequences which may result from a witness' silence be forbidden merely because that silence is privileged. The validity of a consequence depends both upon the hazards, if any, it presents to the integrity of the privilege and upon the urgency of the public interests it is designed to protect.

It can hardly be denied that New Jersey is permitted by the Constitution to establish reasonable qualifications and standards of conduct for its public employees. Nor can it be said that it is arbitrary or unreasonable for New Jersey to insist that its employees furnish the appropriate authorities with information pertinent to their employment. Cf. Beilan v. Board of Education, 357 U.S. 399; Slochower v. Board of Education, 350 U.S. 551. Finally, it is surely plain that New Jersey may in particular require its employees to assist in the prevention and detection of unlawful activities by officers of the state government. The urgency of these requirements is the more obvious here, where the conduct in question is that of officials directly entrusted with the administration of justice. . . .

## NOTES

1. In Spevack v. Klein, 385 U.S. 511, 87 S. Ct. 625, 17 L. Ed. 2d 574 (1967), the companion case to *Garrity,* the Court held an attorney's refusal to testify at a judicial investigation of his alleged professional misconduct and refusal to produce certain financial records on the ground that to do so might tend to incriminate him, an impermissible basis for his disbarment. After reaffirming the idea that the Fifth Amendment's privilege against self-incrimination was made applicable to the states by the Fourteenth Amendment, the Court stated that "[t]he threat of disbarment and the loss of professional standing, professional reputation, and of livelihood are powerful forms of compulsion to make a lawyer relinquish the privilege" and furthermore that "the imposition of any sanction which makes assertion of the Fifth Amendment privilege 'costly' " was, in this context, the imposition of a penalty. The Court pointed out that the Self-Incrimination Clause "extends its protection to lawyers as to other individuals and that it should not be watered down by imposing the dishonor of disbarment and the deprivation of a livelihood as a price for asserting it," and also that "[l]ike the school teacher in *Slochower* . . . and the policeman in *Garrity* . . . lawyers also enjoy first-class citizenship."

Justice Harlan argued, in dissent, that "so long as state authorities do not derive any imputation of guilt from a claim of the privilege, they may in the cause of a bona fide assessment of an employee's fitness for public employment require that the employee disclose information reasonably related to his fitness, and may order his discharge if he declines." According to the dissenters, "petitioner was not denied his privilege against self-incrimination, nor was he penalized for its use; he was denied his authority to practice law . . . by reason of his failure to satisfy valid obligations imposed by the State as a condition of that authority." In a separate dissenting opinion Mr. Justice White stated that the Court's holding would "seem justifiable only on the ground that it is an essential measure to protect against self-incrimination — to prevent what may well be a successful attempt to elicit incriminating admissions" but that since *Garrity* "excludes such statements . . . from a criminal proceeding . . . [there is] little legal or practical basis . . . for preventing the discharge of a public employee or the disbarment of a lawyer who refuses to talk about the performance of his public duty." In a separate concurring opinion, Justice Fortas suggested that "a public employee who is asked questions specifically, directly, and narrowly relating to the performance of his official duties" could be terminated for declining to answer. But Justice Fortas expressed the view that "a lawyer is not an employee of the State. He does not have the responsibility of an employee to account to the State for his actions. . . . The special responsibilities that he assumes as licensee of the State and officer of the court do not carry with them a diminution, however limited, of his Fifth Amendment rights."

2. The companion cases Gardner v. Broderick, 392 U.S. 273, 88 S. Ct. 1913, 20 L. Ed. 2d 1082 (1968) and Uniformed Sanitation Men Ass'n, Inc. v. Commissioner of Sanitation of the City of New York, 392 U.S. 280 (1968) involved the validity of the terminations of public employees who refused to waive immunity from prosecution or testify at grand jury hearings concerning alleged bribery and corruption. The Court, in striking down the employee dismissals as unconstitutional, stressed the fact that in neither case were the dismissals based on the employees' refusal to answer pertinent questions about their official duties, but instead were for their refusal to waive their constitutionally protected privilege against self-incrimination. The Court, per Justice Fortas, concluded that "if New York had demanded that petitioners answer questions specifically, directly and narrowly relating to the performance of their official duties in pain of dismissal from public employment without requiring relinquishment of the benefits of the constitutional privilege, and if they had refused to do so, this case would be entirely different," but that in the instant case they had instead been presented with a choice between waiving their constitutional rights or losing their jobs. All of the employees had been terminated in

accordance with a New York City Charter provision which required the discharge of public servants who invoked the privilege against self-incrimination during authorized investigations of public employees' conduct or who refused to waive immunity against prosecution prompted by their testimony.

3. Broadly applying the standard set out in *Uniformed Sanitation Men Ass'n.* that the privilege against self-incrimination is not infringed if an employee is discharged for failure to answer questions "specifically, directly and narrowly" related to the job, the First Circuit upheld a Boston Police Department requirement that police officers submit copies of their state and federal income tax forms along with other financial information, including a list of significant assets of all household members. The court found that the questions about the officers' personal finances were sufficiently closely related to their jobs because "[e]ven a hint of police corruption endangers respect for the law." O'Brien v. DiGrazia, 544 F.2d 543 (1st Cir. 1976).

4. In a subsequent case, Lefkowitz v. Turley, 414 U.S. 70, 94 S. Ct. 316, 38 L. Ed. 2d 274 (1973), the Court extended the privilege against self-incrimination to government contractors, declaring unconstitutional a provision of New York law which permitted cancellation of existing contracts and disqualification from future contracts if the contractor refused to waive the privilege if called upon to testify concerning his or her state contracts. In clarifying its actions in past cases, the Court stated:

> We should make clear, however, what we have said before. Although due regard for the Fifth Amendment forbids the State to compel incriminating answers from its employees and contractors that may be used against them in criminal proceedings, the Constitution permits that very testimony to be compelled if neither it nor its fruits are available for such use. Kastigar v. United States, *supra.* Furthermore, the accommodation between the interest of the State and the Fifth Amendment requires that the State have means at its disposal to secure testimony if immunity is supplied and testimony is still refused. This is recognized by the power of the courts to compel testimony, after a grant of immunity, by use of civil contempt and coerced imprisonment. Shillitani v. United States, 384 U.S. 364, 86 S. Ct. 1531, 16 L.Ed.2d 622 (1966). Also, given adequate immunity, the State may plainly insist that employees either answer questions under oath about the performance of their job or suffer the loss of employment. By like token, the State may insist that the architects involved in this case either respond to relevant inquiries about the performance of their contracts or suffer cancellation of current relationships and disqualification from contracting with public agencies for an appropriate time in the future. But the State may not insist that appellees waive their Fifth Amendment privilege against self-incrimination and consent to the use of the fruits of the interrogation in any later proceedings brought against them. Rather, the State must recognize what our cases hold: that answers elicited upon the threat of the loss of employment are compelled and inadmissible in evidence. Hence, if answers are to be required in such circumstances States must offer to the witness whatever immunity is required to supplant the privilege and may not insist that the employee or contractor waive such immunity.

414 U.S. 84-85.

See also, Lefkowitz v. Cunningham, 431 U.S. 801 (1977) (New York statute unconstitutional where it required termination of office of political party official who refused to answer potentially incriminating questions at grand jury investigation of the conduct of his office.)

5. The earlier decision of Slochower v. Board of Higher Educ. of New York City, 350 U.S. 551, 76 S. Ct. 637, 100 L. Ed. 692 (1956), held invalid the summary dismissal of a teacher pursuant to a section of the Charter of the City of New York which provided for dismissal of any city employee who invoked the privilege against self-incrimination and thereby refused to answer questions of a legislative committee. The Appellant, a teacher in a college maintained by the city, had been summarily discharged from his position when he refused to answer certain questions asked by a Senate Sub-Committee regarding his alleged membership in the Communist Party some eleven years prior to the hearing. He had stated, however, that he was not currently a member of the Communist Party and would answer all questions relating to the eleven-year period subsequent to his alleged

membership. In upholding appellant's dismissal the State's highest court construed the charter section as providing that "the assertion of the privilege against self-incrimination is equivalent to a resignation" thereby attempting to avert conflict with the state law which allowed for discharge of a person in appellant's position "only for cause, and after notice, hearing, and appeal." The Supreme Court, in overturning the dismissal, stated that "[t]he privilege against self-incrimination would be reduced to a hollow mockery if its exercise could be taken as equivalent either to a confession of guilt or a presumption of perjury." Since no inference of guilt was permissible from appellant's assertion of privilege the Court held the dismissal arbitrary, and therefore a denial of Fourteenth Amendment due process of law.

6. In Baxter v. Palmigiano, 96 S. Ct. 1551 (1976), the Supreme Court sustained the action of prison officials who told a prisoner charged with inciting a prison disturbance that he had the right to remain silent at his disciplinary hearing, but warned him that such silence would be held against him. The Court noted that, under Rhode Island law, silence alone would be insufficient support for an adverse decision, and that the respondent's silence was given no greater evidentiary value than was appropriate under the circumstances. In cases of prison disciplinary hearings, the Court adopted a position consistent with the rule in civil, rather than criminal, cases that the Fifth Amendment does not preclude an unfavorable inference against parties who refuse to testify when evidence is offered against them.

# 3. FREEDOM OF ASSOCIATION

## SHELTON v. TUCKER

Supreme Court of the United States
364 U.S. 479, 81 S. Ct. 247, 5 L. Ed. 2d 231 (1960)

MR. JUSTICE STEWART delivered the opinion of the Court.

An Arkansas statute compels every teacher, as a condition of employment in a state-supported school or college, to file annually an affidavit listing without limitation every organization to which he has belonged or regularly contributed within the preceding five years. At issue in these two cases is the validity of that statute under the Fourteenth Amendment to the Constitution. . . .

The provisions of the Act are summarized in the opinion of the District Court as follows:

"Act 10 provides in substance that no person shall be employed or elected to employment as a superintendent, principal or teacher in any public school in Arkansas, or as an instructor, professor or teacher in any public institution of higher learning in that State until such person shall have submitted to the appropriate hiring authority an affidavit listing all organizations to which he at the time belongs and to which he has belonged during the past five years, and also listing all organizations to which he at the time is paying regular dues or is making regular contributions, or to which within the past five years he has paid such dues or made such contributions. The Act further provides, among other things, that any contract entered into with any person who has not filed the prescribed affidavit shall be void; that no public moneys shall be paid to such person as compensation for his services; and that any such funds so paid may be recovered back either from the person receiving such funds or from the board of trustees or other governing body making the payment. The filing of a false affidavit is denounced as perjury, punishable by a fine of not less than five hundred nor more than one thousand dollars, and, in addition, the person filing the false affidavit is to lose his teaching license." 174 F. Supp. 353-354. . . .

The plaintiffs in the Federal District Court (appellants here) were B.T. Shelton, a teacher employed in the Little Rock Public School System, suing for himself and others similarly situated, together with the Arkansas Teachers Association and its Executive Secretary, suing for the benefit of members of the Association. Shelton had been employed in the Little Rock Special School District for twenty-five years. In the spring of 1959 he was notified that, before he could be employed for the 1959-1960 school year, he must file the affidavit required by Act 10, listing all his organizational connections over the previous five years. He declined to file the affidavit, and his contract for the ensuing school year was not renewed. At the trial the evidence showed that he was not a member of the Communist Party or of any organization advocating the overthrow of the Government by force, and that he was a member of the National Association for the Advancement of Colored People. The court upheld Act 10, finding the information it required was "relevant," and relying on several decisions of this Court, particularly Garner v. Board of Public Works of Los Angeles, 341 U.S. 716; Adler v. Board of Education, 342 U.S. 485; Beilan v. Board of Education, 357 U.S. 399; and Lerner v. Casey, 357 U.S. 468.

The plaintiffs in the state court proceedings (petitioners here) were Max Carr, an associate professor at the University of Arkansas, and Ernest T. Gephardt, a teacher at Central High School in Little Rock, each suing for himself and others similarly situated. Each refused to execute and file the affidavit required by Act 10. . . .

Both were advised that their failure to comply with the requirements of Act 10 would make impossible their re-employment as teachers for the following school year. The Supreme Court of Arkansas upheld the constitutionality of Act 10, on its face and as applied to the petitioners. 231 Ark. 641, 331 S.W.2d 701.

I.

It is urged here, as it was unsuccessfully urged throughout the proceedings in both the federal and state courts, that Act 10 deprives teachers in Arkansas of their rights to personal, associational, and academic liberty, protected by the Due Process Clause of the Fourteenth Amendment from invasion by state action. In considering this contention, we deal with two basic postulates.

*First.* There can be no doubt of the right of a State to investigate the competence and fitness of those whom it hires to teach in its schools, as this Court before now has had occasion to recognize. . . .

This controversy is thus not of a pattern with such cases as N.A.A.C.P. v. Alabama, 357 U.S. 449, and Bates v. Little Rock, 361 U.S. 516. In those cases the Court held that there was no substantially relevant correlation between the governmental interest asserted and the State's effort to compel disclosure of the membership lists involved. Here, by contrast, there can be no question of the relevance of a State's inquiry into the fitness and competence of its teachers.

*Second.* It is not disputed that to compel a teacher to disclose his every associational tie is to impair that teacher's right of free association, a right closely allied to freedom of speech and a right which, like free speech, lies at the foundation of a free society. DeJonge v. Oregon, 299 U.S. 353, 364; Bates v. Little Rock, *supra,* at 522-523. Such interference with personal freedom is conspicuously accented when the teacher serves at the absolute will of those to whom the disclosure must be made — those who any year can terminate the teacher's employment without bringing charges, without notice, without a hearing, without affording an opportunity to explain.

The statute does not provide that the information it requires be kept confidential. Each school board is left free to deal with the information as it wishes. The record contains evidence to indicate that fear of public disclosure is neither theoretical nor groundless. Even if there were no disclosure to the general public, the pressure upon a teacher to avoid any ties which might displease those who control his professional destiny would be constant and heavy. Public exposure, bringing with it the possibility of public pressures upon school boards to discharge teachers who belong to unpopular or minority organizations, would simply operate to widen and aggravate the impairment of constitutional liberty. . . .

## II.

The question to be decided here is not whether the State of Arkansas can ask certain of its teachers about all their organizational relationships. It is not whether the State can ask all of its teachers about certain of their associational ties. It is not whether teachers can be asked how many organizations they belong to, or how much time they spend in organizational activity. The question is whether the State can ask every one of its teachers to disclose every single organization with which he has been associated over a five-year period. The scope of the inquiry required by Act 10 is completely unlimited. The statute requires a teacher to reveal the church to which he belongs, or to which he has given financial support. It requires him to disclose his political party, and every political organization to which he may have contributed over a five-year period. It requires him to list, without number, every conceivable kind of associational tie — social, professional, political, avocational, or religious. Many such relationships could have no possible bearing upon the teacher's occupational competence or fitness.

In a series of decisions this Court has held that, even though the governmental purpose be legitimate and substantial, that purpose cannot be pursued by means that broadly stifle fundamental personal liberties when the end can be more narrowly achieved. The breadth of legislative abridgment must be viewed in the light of less drastic means for achieving the same basic purpose. . . .

The unlimited and indiscriminate sweep of the statute now before us brings it within the ban of our prior cases. The statute's comprehensive interference with associational freedom goes far beyond what might be justified in the exercise of the State's legitimate inquiry into the fitness and competency of its teachers. The judgments in both cases must be reversed.

*It is so ordered.*

Mr. Justice Frankfurter, dissenting.

As one who has strong views against crude intrusions by the state into the atmosphere of creative freedom in which alone the spirit and mind of a teacher can fruitfully function, I may find displeasure with the Arkansas legislation now under review. But in maintaining the distinction between private views and constitutional restrictions, I am constrained to find that it does not exceed the permissible range of state action limited by the Fourteenth Amendment. By way of emphasis I therefore add a few words to the dissent of Mr. Justice Harlan, in which I concur. . . .

Where state assertions of authority are attacked as impermissibly restrictive upon thought, expression, or association, the existence *vel non* of other possible less restrictive means of achieving the object which the State seeks is, of course, a constitutionally relevant consideration. This is not because some novel, particular rule of law obtains in cases of this kind. Whenever the reasonableness and fairness of a measure are at issue — as they are in every case in which this Court must apply the standards of reason and fairness, with the appropriate scope to be given those concepts, in enforcing the Due Process Clause of the Fourteenth Amendment as a limitation upon state action — the availability or unavailability of alternative methods of proceeding is germane. Thus, a State may not prohibit the distribution of literature on its cities' streets as a means of preventing littering, when the same end might be achieved with only slightly greater inconvenience by applying the sanctions of the penal law not to the pamphleteer who distributes the paper but to the recipient who crumples it and throws it away. Hague v. C.I.O., 307 U.S. 496; Schneider v. State, 308 U.S. 147; Jamison v. Texas, 318 U.S. 413. . . . But the consideration of feasible alternative modes of regulation in these cases did not imply that the Court might substitute its own choice among alternatives for that of a state legislature, or that the States were to be restricted to the "narrowest" workable means of accomplishing an end. . . .

In the present case the Court strikes down an Arkansas statute requiring that teachers disclose to school officials all of their organizational relationships, on the ground that "Many such relationships could have no possible bearing upon the teacher's occupational competence or fitness." Granted that a given teacher's membership in the First Street Congregation is, standing alone, of little relevance to what may rightly be expected of a teacher, is that membership equally irrelevant when it is discovered that the teacher is in fact a member of the First Street Congregation *and* the Second Street Congregation *and* the Third Street Congregation *and* the 4-H Club *and* the 3-H Club *and* half a dozen other groups? Presumably, a teacher may have so many divers associations, so many divers commitments, that they consume his time and energy and interest at the expense of his work or even of his professional dedication. Unlike wholly individual interests, organizational connections — because they involve obligations undertaken with relation to other persons — may become inescapably demanding and distracting. Surely, a school board is entitled to inquire whether any of its teachers has placed himself, or is placing himself, in a condition where his work may suffer. . . .

If I dissent from the Court's disposition in these cases, it is not that I put a low value on academic freedom. See Wieman v. Updegraff, 344 U.S. 183, 194 (concurring opinion); Sweezy v. New Hampshire, 354 U.S. 234, 255 (concurring opinion). It is because that very freedom, in its most creative reaches, is dependent in no small part upon the careful and discriminating selection of teachers. This process of selection is an intricate affair, a matter of fine judgment, and if it is to be informed, it must be based upon a comprehensive range of information. I am unable to say, on the face of this statute, that Arkansas could not reasonably find that the information which the statute requires — and which may not be otherwise acquired than by asking the question which it asks — is germane to that selection. Nor, on this record, can I attribute to the State a purpose to employ the enactment as a device for the accomplishment of what is constitutionally forbidden. Of course, if the information gathered by the required affidavits is used to further a scheme of terminating the employment of teachers solely because of their membership in unpopular organizations, that use will run afoul of the Fourteenth Amendment. It will be time enough, if such use is made, to hold the application of the statute unconstitutional. . . .

I am authorized to say that MR. JUSTICE CLARK, MR. JUSTICE HARLAN and MR. JUSTICE WHITTAKER agree with this opinion.

MR. JUSTICE HARLAN, whom MR. JUSTICE FRANKFURTER, MR. JUSTICE CLARK and MR. JUSTICE WHITTAKER join, dissenting. . . .

The legal framework in which the issue must be judged is clear. The rights of free speech and association embodied in the "liberty" assured against state action by the Fourteenth Amendment (see DeJonge v. Oregon, 299 U.S. 353, 364; Gitlow v. New York, 268 U.S. 652, 672, dissenting opinion of Holmes, J.) are not absolute. Near v. Minnesota, 283 U.S. 697, 708; Whitney v. California, 274 U.S. 357, 373 (concurring opinion of Brandeis, J.). Where official action is claimed to invade these rights, the controlling inquiry is whether such action is justifiable on the basis of a superior governmental interest to which such individual rights must yield. When the action complained of pertains to the realm of investigation, our inquiry has a double aspect: first, whether the investigation relates to a legitimate governmental purpose; second, whether, judged in the light of that purpose, the questioned action has substantial relevance thereto. See Barenblatt v. United States, 360 U.S. 109; Uphaus v. Wyman, 360 U.S. 72.

In the two cases at hand, I think both factors are satisfied. It is surely indisputable that a State has the right to choose its teachers on the basis of fitness. And I think it equally clear, as the Court appears to recognize, that information about a teacher's associations may be useful to school authorities in determining the moral, professional, and social qualifications of the teacher, as well as in determining the type of service for which he will be best suited in the educational system. . . .

Despite these considerations this statute is stricken down because, in the Court's view, it is too broad, because it asks more than may be necessary to effectuate the State's legitimate interest. Such a statute, it is said, cannot justify the inhibition on freedom of association which so blanket an inquiry may entail. Cf. N.A.A.C.P. v. Alabama, *supra;* Bates v. Little Rock, *supra.*

I am unable to subscribe to this view because I believe it impossible to determine *a priori* the place where the line should be drawn between what would be permissible inquiry and overbroad inquiry in a situation like this. Certainly the Court does not point that place out. There can be little doubt that much of the associational information called for by the statute will be of little or no use whatever to the school authorities, but I do not understand how those authorities can be expected to fix in advance the terms of their inquiry so that it will yield only relevant information. . . .

## NOTES

1. Is Justice Frankfurter's dissenting opinion persuasive? Is it not possible for a school board to judge a teacher's performance without knowing of his outside associations?

2. How should the Arkansas statute have been drafted so as to avoid constitutional infirmity? In a situation like the one posed in the *Shelton* case, is it possible to determine where the line should be drawn between what would be permissible inquiry and overbroad inquiry?

3. In a case involving a private employer engaged in defense work, the Court held unconstitutional the section of the Subversive Activities Control Act, enacted under the war power, which prohibited any employment of members of a Communist-action organization in any defense facility. The Court stated that the statute lacked the precision required when an important governmental objective impinges on a First Amendment freedom because it barred employment both for association which could be proscribed and for association which could not be proscribed under the First Amendment. United States v. Robel, 389 U.S. 258, 88 S. Ct. 419, 19 L. Ed. 2d 508 (1967). See also, Schneider v. Smith, 390 U.S. 17, 88 S. Ct. 682, 19 L. Ed. 2d 799 (1968) (regulations promulgated

to prohibit subversive activity cannot be used to withhold seaman's license to serve on merchant ships when the withholding is based on beliefs, reading habits, or social, educational or political associations of the applicant). In both cases, the Court indicated that subversive actions must be distinguished from passive membership.

4. Norbeck v. Davenport Community School District, 545 F.2d 63 (8th Cir., 1976), *cert. denied*, 97 S. Ct. 2179 (1977), held that a high school principal had no constitutional right to negotiate on behalf of a teachers' union that represented teachers whom the principal supervised. The Davenport school board did not violate the school principal's First Amendment rights when it refused to renew the principal's contract because the board's interest in efficient school administration outweighed any right the principal might have had to associate freely with the teachers' union.

# 4. FREEDOM OF EXPRESSION

## PICKERING v. BOARD OF EDUCATION

Supreme Court of the United States
391 U.S. 563, 88 S. Ct. 1731, 20 L. Ed. 2d 811 (1968)

MR. JUSTICE MARSHALL delivered the opinion of the Court.

Appellant Marvin L. Pickering, a teacher in Township High School District 205, Will County, Illinois, was dismissed from his position by the appellee Board of Education for sending a letter to a local newspaper in connection with a recently proposed tax increase that was critical of the way in which the Board and the district superintendent of schools had handled past proposals to raise new revenue for the schools. Appellant's dismissal resulted from a determination by the Board, after a full hearing, that the publication of the letter was "detrimental to the efficient operation and administration of the schools of the district" and hence, under the relevant Illinois statute, Ill. Rev. Stat., c. 122, § 10-22.4 (1963), that "interests of the school require[d] [his dismissal]." . . . At the hearing the Board charged that numerous statements in the letter were false and that the publication of the statements unjustifiably impugned the "motives, honesty, integrity, truthfulness, responsibility and competence" of both the Board and the school administration. The Board also charged that the false statements damaged the professional reputations of its members and of the school administrators, would be disruptive of faculty discipline, and would tend to foment "controversy, conflict and dissension" among teachers, administrators, the Board of Education, and the residents of the district. . . .

The Illinois courts reviewed the proceedings solely to determine whether the Board's findings were supported by substantial evidence and whether, on the facts as found, the Board could reasonably conclude that appellant's publication of the letter was "detrimental to the best interests of the schools." Pickering's claim that his letter was protected by the First Amendment was rejected on the ground that his acceptance of a teaching position in the public schools obliged him to refrain from making statements about the operation of the schools "which in the absence of such position he would have an undoubted right to engage in."
. . .

To the extent that the Illinois Supreme Court's opinion may be read to suggest that teachers may constitutionally be compelled to relinquish the First Amendment rights they would otherwise enjoy as citizens to comment on matters of public interest in connection with the operation of the public schools in which they work, it proceeds on a premise that has been unequivocally rejected in numerous prior decisions of this Court. . . . At the same time it cannot be gainsaid that the State has interests as an employer in regulating the speech of its employees that differ significantly from those it possesses in connection with regulation of the speech of the citizenry in general. The problem in any case is to arrive at a balance between the interests of the teacher, as a citizen, in commenting upon matters of public concern and the interest of the State, as an employer, in promoting the efficiency of the public services it performs through its employees. . . .

Because of the enormous variety of fact situations in which critical statements by teachers and other public employees may be thought by their superiors, against whom the statements are directed, to furnish grounds for dismissal, we do not deem it either appropriate or feasible to attempt to lay down a general standard against which all such statements may be judged. However, in the course of evaluating the conflicting claims of First Amendment protection and the need for orderly school administration in the context of this case, we shall indicate some of the general lines along which an analysis of the controlling interests should run.

An examination of the statements in appellant's letter objected to by the Board reveals that they, like the letter as a whole, consist essentially of criticism of the Board's allocation of school funds between educational and athletic programs, and of both the Board's and the superintendent's methods of informing, or preventing the informing of, the district's taxpayers of the real reasons why additional tax revenues were being sought for the schools. The statements are in no way directed towards any person with whom appellant would normally be in contact in the course of his daily work as a teacher. Thus no question of maintaining either discipline by immediate superiors or harmony among coworkers is presented here. Appellant's employment relationships with the Board and, to a somewhat lesser extent, with the superintendent are not the kind of close working relationships for which it can persuasively be claimed that personal loyalty and confidence are necessary to their proper functioning. Accordingly, to the extent that the Board's position here can be taken to suggest that even comments on matters of public concern that are substantially correct . . . may furnish grounds for dismissal if they are sufficiently critical in tone, we unequivocally reject it.

We next consider the statements in appellant's letter which we agree to be false. The Board's original charges included allegations that the publication of the letter damaged the professional reputations of the Board and the superintendent and would foment controversy and conflict among the Board, teachers, administrators, and the residents of the district. However, no evidence to support these allegations was introduced at the hearing. So far as the record reveals, Pickering's letter was greeted by everyone but its main target, the Board, with massive apathy and total disbelief. The Board must, therefore, have decided, perhaps by analogy with the law of libel, that the statements were *per se* harmful to the operation of the schools.

However, the only way in which the Board could conclude, absent any evidence of the actual effect of the letter, that the statements contained therein were *per se* detrimental to the interest of the schools was to equate the Board members' own interests with that of the schools. Certainly an accusation that too much money is being spent on athletics by the administrators of the school system . . . cannot reasonably be regarded as *per se* detrimental to the district's schools. Such an accusation reflects rather a difference of opinion between Pickering and the Board as to the preferable manner of operating the school system, a difference of opinion that clearly concerns an issue of general public interest. . . .

More importantly, the question whether a school system requires additional funds is a matter of legitimate public concern on which the judgment of the school administration, including the School Board, cannot, in a society that leaves such questions to popular vote, be taken as conclusive. On such a question free and open debate is vital to informed decision-making by the electorate. Teachers are, as a class, the members of a community most likely to have informed and definite opinions as to how funds allotted to the operation of the schools should be spent. Accordingly, it is essential that they be able to speak out freely on such questions without fear of retaliatory dismissal.

In addition, the amounts expended on athletics which Pickering reported erroneously were matters of public record on which his position as a teacher in the district did not qualify him to speak with any greater authority than any other taxpayer. The Board could easily have rebutted appellant's errors by publishing the accurate figures itself, either via a letter to the same newspaper or otherwise. We are thus not presented with a situation in which a teacher has carelessly made false statements about matters so closely related to the day-to-day operations of the schools that any harmful impact on the public would be difficult to counter because of the teacher's presumed greater access to the real facts. Accordingly, we have no occasion to consider at this time whether under such circumstances a school board could reasonably require that a teacher make substantial efforts to verify the accuracy of his charges before publishing them.[4]

What we do have before us is a case in which a teacher has made erroneous public statements upon issues then currently the subject of public attention, which are critical of his ultimate employer but which are neither shown nor can be presumed to have in any way either impeded the teacher's proper performance of his daily duties in the classroom [5] or to have interfered with the regular operation of the schools generally. In these circumstances we conclude that the interest of the school administration in limiting teachers' opportunities to contribute to public debate is not significantly greater than its interest in limiting a similar contribution by any member of the general public.

The public interest in having free and unhindered debate on matters of public importance — the core value of the Free Speech Clause of the First Amendment — is so great that it has been held that a State cannot authorize the recovery of damages by a public official for defamatory statements directed at him except when such statements are shown to have been made either with knowledge of their falsity or with reckless disregard for their truth or falsity. New York Times Co. v. Sullivan, 376 U.S. 254 (1964); St. Amant v. Thompson, 390 U.S. 727 (1968). Compare Linn v. United Plant Guard Workers, 383 U.S. 53 (1966). The same test has been applied to suits for invasion of privacy based on false statements where a "matter of public interest" is involved. Time, Inc. v. Hill, 385 U.S. 374 (1967). It is therefore perfectly clear that, were appellant a member of the general public, the State's power to afford the appellee Board of Education

[4] There is likewise no occasion furnished by this case for consideration of the extent to which teachers can be required by narrowly drawn grievance procedures to submit complaints about the operation of the schools to their superiors for action thereon prior to bringing the complaints before the public.

[5] We also note that this case does not present a situation in which a teacher's public statements are so without foundation as to call into question his fitness to perform his duties in the classroom. In such a case, of course, the statements would merely be evidence of the teacher's general competence, or lack thereof, and not an independent basis for dismissal.

or its members any legal right to sue him for writing the letter at issue here would be limited by the requirement that the letter be judged by the standard laid down in *New York Times.*

This Court has also indicated, in more general terms, that statements by public officials on matters of public concern must be accorded First Amendment protection despite the fact that the statements are directed at their nominal superiors. Garrison v. Louisiana, 379 U.S. 64 (1964); Wood v. Georgia, 370 U.S. 375 (1962). In *Garrison,* the *New York Times* test was specifically applied to a case involving a criminal defamation conviction stemming from statements made by a district attorney about the judges before whom he regularly appeared.

While criminal sanctions and damage awards have a somewhat different impact on the exercise of the right to freedom of speech from dismissal from employment, it is apparent that the threat of dismissal from public employment is nonetheless a potent means of inhibiting speech. We have already noted our disinclination to make an across-the-board equation of dismissal from public employment for remarks critical of superiors with awarding damages in a libel suit by a public official for similar criticism. However, in a case such as the present one, in which the fact of employment is only tangentially and insubstantially involved in the subject matter of the public communication made by a teacher, we conclude that it is necessary to regard the teacher as the member of the general public he seeks to be.

In sum, we hold that, in a case such as this, absent proof of false statements knowingly or recklessly made by him, a teacher's exercise of his right to speak on issues of public importance may not furnish the basis for his dismissal from public employment. Since no such showing has been made in this case regarding appellant's letter ... his dismissal for writing it cannot be upheld and the judgment of the Illinois Supreme Court must, accordingly, be reversed and the case remanded for further proceedings not inconsistent with this opinion.

*It is so ordered.*

MR. JUSTICE WHITE, concurring in part and dissenting in part. . . .

The core of today's decision is the holding that Pickering's discharge must be tested by the standard of New York Times Co. v. Sullivan, 376 U.S. 254 (1964). To this extent I am in agreement. . . .

The Court devotes several pages to re-examining the facts in order to reject the determination below that Pickering's statements harmed the school system, *ante,* at 570-573, when the question of harm is clearly irrelevant given the Court's determination that Pickering's statements were neither knowingly nor recklessly false and its ruling that in such circumstances a teacher may not be fired even if the statements are injurious.

. . . Deliberate or reckless falsehoods serve no First Amendment ends and deserve no protection under that Amendment. The Court unequivocally recognized this in *Garrison,* where after reargument the Court said that "the knowingly false statement and the false statement made with reckless disregard of the truth, do not enjoy constitutional protection." 379 U.S., at 75. The Court today neither explains nor justifies its withdrawal from the firm stand taken in *Garrison.* As I see it, a teacher may be fired without violation of the First Amendment for knowingly or recklessly making false statements regardless of their harmful impact on the schools. As the Court holds, however, in the absence of special circumstances he may not be fired if his statements were true or only negligently false, even if there is some harm to the school system. I therefore see no basis or necessity for the Court's foray into fact-finding with respect to whether the record supports a finding as to injury. If Pickering's false statements were either knowingly or recklessly made, injury to the school system becomes irrelevant, and the First Amendment would not prevent his discharge. For the State to be constitutionally precluded from terminating his employment, reliance on some other constitutional provision would be required. . . .

## NOTES

1. In Watts v. Seward, 454 P.2d 732 (Alas.), *cert. denied,* 397 U.S. 921 (1969), it was held that teachers could properly be dismissed for circulating an open letter and making other statements (some of which were found to be false) criticizing the school superintendent who had a close relationship with teachers and students. The court distinguished *Pickering* by finding that the conduct was detrimental to discipline and harmony within the school system, that the teachers' criticism did not relate to the expenditure of school funds, but rather, to day-to-day operations of the school, and that available grievance procedures had not been followed.

2. A California appellate court in Norton v. City of Santa Ana, 15 Cal. App. 3d 419, 93 Cal. Rptr. 37 (1971), used the so-called *"Bagley* formula" to weigh the interests of the governmental agency against the constitutional interests of a policeman, who had been discharged for bringing a lawsuit against the police chief. In sustaining the dismissal, the court ruled that:

When such a conflict does arise, the governmental agency seeking to impose restrictions on the exercise of an employee's constitutional rights must demonstrate that: (1) the governmental restraint rationally relates to the enhancement of the public service; (2) the benefits that the public gains by the restraint outweigh the resulting impairment of the constitutional right; and (3) no alternatives less subversive to the constitutional right are available. (Bagley v. Washington Township Hosp. Dist., 65 Cal. 2d 499, 501-502, 55 Cal. Rptr. 401, 421 P.2d 409.) In other words, a public employee may speak freely so long as he does not impair the administration of the public service in which he is engaged. (Belshaw v. City of Berkeley, 246 Cal. App. 2d 493, 497, 54 Cal. Rptr. 727.) Similarly, a public employee may engage in political activity providing it does not affect the administrative functioning or public integrity of the governmental agency. 93 Cal. Rptr. at 41.

Is the *"Bagley* formula" significantly different from the tests set forth in *Pickering?*

3. The Courts have applied the *Pickering* tests and requirements in various areas and circumstances of public employment. In Tinker v. Des Moines Community School Dist., 393 U.S. 503, 509, 89 S. Ct. 733, 21 L. Ed. 2d 731 (1969), the Court held that the problem presented by public school children wearing black armbands (during school hours, on school property and in violation of a school regulation) as a symbolic act to publicize their objections to the hostilities in Vietnam, did not involve aggressive, disruptive action or even group demonstration. Rather, the conduct was viewed as involving direct, primary First Amendment rights akin to "pure speech." The Court stated:

In order for the State . . . to justify prohibition of a particular expression of opinion, it must be able to show that its action was caused by something more than a mere desire to avoid the discomfort and unpleasantness that always accompany an unpopular viewpoint. Certainly where there is no finding and no showing that engaging in the forbidden conduct would "materially and substantially interfere with the requirements of appropriate discipline in the operation of the school" the prohibition cannot be sustained.

*See also,* Healy v. James, 408 U.S. 169, 92 S. Ct. 2338, 33 L. Ed. 2d 266 (1972) (refusal of state college to recognize Students for a Democractic Society without a showing of disruptiveness held unconstitutional abridgement of right to free association and speech).

4. In Swaaley v. United States, 376 F.2d 857 (Ct. Cl. 1967), Swaaley, a naval shipyard worker, wrote the Secretary of the Navy a petition for redress of grievances which included charges that some of his superior officials were guilty of favoritism in the matter of promotions. He was discharged. The Court held that the defamatory statements were not

shown to have been wilfully false or made with reckless disregard for truth or falsity and that Swaaley's discharge was improper. A similar ruling was made by the same Court in Burkett v. United States, 402 F.2d 1002 (Ct. Cl. 1968). *See also* Murray v. Vaughn, 300 F. Supp. 688, 703-05 (D.R.I. 1969), which involved a Peace Corps volunteer, and Puentes v. Board of Educ. of Union Free School Dist. No. 21, 24 N.Y.2d 996, 250 N.E.2d 232, 302 N.Y.S.2d 824 (Ct. App. 1969), in which a teacher (a union official) wrote letters to teachers and administrators within the school district criticizing the failure of the school administration to renew the employment of a probationary teacher and was suspended without pay. The Court of Appeals of New York cited *Pickering* and said:

> There is no suggestion in the record that petitioner's indiscretions led to any deleterious effects within the school system and it is unlikely that they should have. Indiscreet bombast in an argumentative letter, to the limited extent present here, is insufficient to sanction disciplinary action. . . .

Concededly, petitioner's direct teaching and in-class performance were correct and not affected by the writing or sending of the letter. 250 N.E.2d at 233.

*See also* the prior case of Trepedino v. Dumpson, 24 N.Y.2d 705, 249 N.E.2d 751 (1969) (involving social workers). For other applications of the *Pickering* principle, see Muller v. Conlisk, 429 F.2d 901 (7th Cir. 1970); McGee v. Richmond Unified School Dist., 306 F. Supp. 1052 (N.D. Cal. 1969); Meehan v. Macy, 425 F.2d 469 (D.C. Cir. 1968), *aff'd after rehearing en banc,* 425 F.2d 472 (D.C. Cir. 1969).

5. In Sprague v. Fitzpatrick, 516 F.2d 560 (1976), *cert. denied,* 97 S. Ct. 2619 (1977), the Third Circuit Court of Appeals ruled that an assistant district attorney who served as the Philadelphia district attorney's deputy in administrative and policy-making matters and was discharged for publicly disputing his superior's integrity with respect to handling of criminal matters is not entitled to First Amendment protection for speech that seriously undermined his employment relationship with his superior and aroused public controversy.

In a similar case, the Ninth Circuit distinguished *Pickering* and held that the suspension of a police lieutenant did not violate his constitutional right where he had criticized his superior officer to his subordinates. The court held that the comments were made as an officer of the department, not as a member of the general public, and that questions of harmony and discipline were raised by the incident. Kannisto v. City and County of San Francisco, 541 F.2d 841 (9th Cir. 1976).

6. In Byrd v. Gain, 558 F.2d 553 (9th Cir. 1977), *cert. denied,* 98 S. Ct. 1282 (1978), the court denied relief to two police officers who had received written reprimands following their issuance of a press release criticizing the police department's stop-and-frisk procedure because of its disparate effect on Black male citizens. The court distinguished *Pickering* and related cases, stating that "substantial differences between the public interest in education and the public interest in safety and order justify a difference in the standards by which the respective institutions may protect themselves from attempted destruction by their employees." See also, Hanneman v. Breier, Chief of Police, Minneapolis, Minnesota, 528 F.2d 750 (7th Cir. 1976); Gasparinetti v. Kerr, 568 F.2d 311 (3rd Cir. 1977), *cert. denied,* 98 S. Ct. 2232 (1978).

## JAMES v. BOARD OF EDUCATION

United States Court of Appeals, Second Circuit
461 F.2d 566 (1972), *cert. denied,* 409 U.S. 1042 (1972), *rehearing denied,* 410 U.S. 947 (1973)

IRVING R. KAUFMAN, Circuit Judge:

[T]he issue in this case is whether, in assuming the role of judge and disciplinarian, a Board of Education may forbid a teacher to express a political opinion, however benign or noncoercive the manner of expression. We are asked to decide whether a Board of Education, without transgressing the first amendment, may discharge an 11th grade English teacher who did no more than wear a black armband in class in symbolic protest against the Vietnam War, although it is agreed that the armband did not disrupt classroom activities, and as far as we know did not have any influence on any students and did not engender protest from any student, teacher or parent. We hold that the Board may not take such action. . . .

James appealed his dismissal to the New York State Commissioner of Education, Ewald B. Nyquist, asserting that his dismissal infringed upon his first amendment rights and deprived him of due process of law. The "hearing" before the Commissioner, as we were informed at the argument of this appeal, was no more than an informal roundtable discussion between the Commissioner, the parties and their attorneys. No transcript of the proceedings was made. On September 23, 1970, Commissioner Nyquist filed his decision. Although he recognized that a board of education does not have unfettered discretion to dismiss a probationary teacher, he concluded that James had violated "sound educational principles" and that his actions "were not constitutionally protected." In addition, he reaffirmed the Board of Education's absolute right to dismiss a probationary teacher without affording the teacher a hearing or explaining the basis of the discharge.

Thereupon, James instituted this action in the Western District of New York. . . . Judge Burke denied James's motion for summary judgment and granted the defendants' motion for summary judgment, summarily dismissing the complaint on the merits, seemingly on two grounds: first, that the issues raised by the complaint were *res judicata,* and second that none of James's federally protected rights was violated. . . .

At the outset we are presented with the contention that the claims asserted below are *res judicata.* We consider this to be wholly without merit. Appellees argue that James, at his own choosing, was given the full opportunity to litigate his claims before the Commissioner of Education, a "judicial officer" of the State, and therefore that James should be bound by the Commissioner's decision. Judge Burke buttressed their position with a pointed reference to James's failure to appeal the Commissioner's decision to the New York courts.

It is no longer open to dispute that a plaintiff with a claim for relief under the Civil Rights Act, 42 U.S.C. § 1983, is not required to exhaust state judicial remedies. It is still the law in this Circuit, however, that a Civil Rights plaintiff must exhaust state administrative remedies. It hardly can be suggested that a plaintiff having followed the course laid out by *Eisen,* was to be barred henceforth from pressing his claim to final judicial review or to be deprived of his opportunity to litigate his constitutional claims in the judicial forum of his choice. To adopt the full implication of appellees' argument would be to effect a judicial repeal of 42 U.S.C. § 1983 and strike down the Supreme Court's decision in Monroe v. Pape, *supra.* James would be placed in the paradoxical position of being barred from the federal courts if he had not exhausted administrative remedies and barred if he had.

We come now to the crucial issue we must decide—did the Board of Education infringe James's first amendment right to freedom of speech?

Any meaningful discussion of a teacher's first amendment right to wear a black armband in a classroom as a symbolic protest against this nation's involvement in the Vietnam War must begin with a close examination of the case which dealt with this question as it applied to a student. Tinker v. Des Moines Independent

Community School District [393 U.S. 503 (1969)]. Mary Beth Tinker, a junior high school student, her older brother and his friend, both high school students, were suspended from school for wearing black armbands in school to publicize their opposition to the war in Vietnam. Noting that neither students nor teachers "shed their constitutional rights to freedom of speech or expression at the schoolhouse gate," 393 U.S. at 506, 89 S. Ct. at 736, the Supreme Court held that a school cannot bar or penalize students' exercise of primary first amendment rights akin to "pure speech" without "a showing that the students' activities would materially and substantially disrupt the work and discipline of the school." *Id.* at 513, 89 S. Ct. at 740.

With respect to both teacher and student, the responsibility of school authorities to maintain order and discipline in the schools remains the same. The ultimate goal of school officials is to insure that the discipline necessary to the proper functioning of the school is maintained among both teachers and students. Any limitation on the exercise of constitutional rights can be justified only by a conclusion, based upon reasonable inferences flowing from concrete facts and not abstractions, that the interests of discipline or sound education are materially and substantially jeopardized, whether the danger stems initially from the conduct of students or teachers. Although it is not unreasonable to assume that the views of a teacher occupying a position of authority may carry more influence with a student than would those of students *inter sese,* that assumption merely weighs upon the inferences which may be drawn. It does not relieve the school of the necessity to show a reasonable basis for its regulatory policies. . . .

"The problem in any case is to arrive at a balance between the interests of the teacher, as a citizen, in commenting upon matters of public concern and the interest of the State, as an employer, in promoting the efficiency of the public services it performs through its employees." Pickering v. Board of Education, 391 U.S. 563, 568, 88 S. Ct. 1731, 1734, 20 L. Ed. 2d 811 (1968).

It is to be noted that in this case, the Board of Education has made no showing whatsoever at any stage of the proceedings that Charles James, by wearing a black armband, threatened to disrupt classroom activities or created any disruption in the school. . . .

Appellees urge us not to conclude that schools must wait until disruption is on the doorstep before they may take protective action. We do not suggest this course, but if anything is clear from the tortuous development of the first amendment right, freedom of expression demands breathing room. To preserve the "marketplace of ideas" so essential to our system of democracy, we must be willing to assume the risk of argument and lawful disagreement. . . . This is entirely different, however, from saying that the school must await open rebellion, violence or extensive disruption before it acts. . . .

That does not end our inquiry, however. The interest of the state in promoting the efficient operation of its schools extends beyond merely securing an orderly classroom. . . . Accordingly, courts consistently have affirmed that curriculum controls belong to the political process and local school authorities. "Courts do not and cannot intervene in the resolution of conflicts which arise in the daily operation of school systems and which do not directly and sharply implicate constitutional values." Epperson v. Arkansas, 393 U.S. 97, 104, 89 S. Ct. 266, 270, 21 L. Ed. 2d 228 (1968).[16]

---

[16] Even in this area there are constitutional limitations. In *Epperson,* for example, the Court held that a state could not prevent a high school biology teacher from teaching students about Darwin's theory of evolution because the regulation would be an establishment of religion in violation of the

Appellees argue that this broad power extends to controlling a teacher's speech in public schools, that "assumptions of the 'free marketplace of ideas' on which freedom of speech rests do not apply to school-aged children, especially in the classroom where the word of the teacher may carry great authority." Note, Developments in the Law-Academic Freedom, 81 Harv. L. Rev. at 1053. Certainly there must be some restraints because the students are a "captive" group. But to state the proposition without qualification is to uncover its fallacy. More than a decade of Supreme Court precedent leaves no doubt that we cannot countenance school authorities arbitrarily censoring a teacher's speech merely because they do not agree with the teacher's political philosophies or leanings. This is particularly so when that speech does not interfere in any way with the teacher's obligations to teach, is not coercive and does not arbitrarily inculcate doctrinaire views in the minds of the students. . . .

Although sound discussions of ideas are the beams and buttresses of the first amendment, teachers cannot be allowed to patrol the precincts of radical thought with the unrelenting goal of indoctrination, a goal compatible with totalitarianism and not democracy. When a teacher is only content if he persuades his students that his values and only his values ought to be their values, then it is not unreasonable to expect the state to protect impressionable children from such dogmatism. But, just as clearly, those charged with overseeing the day-to-day interchange between teacher and student must exercise that degree of restraint necessary to protect first amendment rights. The question we must ask in every first amendment case is whether the regulatory policy is drawn as narrowly as possible to achieve the social interests that justify it, or whether it exceeds permissible bounds by unduly restricting protected speech to an extent "greater than is essential to the furtherance of" those interests. . . .

Several factors present here compel the conclusion that the Board of Education arbitrarily and unjustifiably discharged James for wearing the black armband. Clearly, there was no attempt by James to proselytize his students. It does not appear from the record that any student believed the armband to be anything more than a benign symbolic expression of the teacher's personal views. Moreover, we cannot ignore the fact that James was teaching 11th grade (high school) English. His students were approximately 16 or 17 years of age, thus more mature than those junior high school students in *Tinker.* . . .

Finally, James was first removed from class while he was teaching poetry. There is no suggestion whatsover that his armband interfered with his teaching functions, or, for that matter, that his teaching ever had been deficient in any respect.

We emphasize that we do not question the broad discretion of local school authorities in setting classroom standards, nor do we question their expertise in evaluating the effects of classroom conduct in light of the special characteristics of the school environment. The federal courts, however, cannot allow unfettered discretion to violate fundamental constitutional rights. . . .

It is characteristic of resolutions of first amendment cases, where the price of freedom of expression is so high and the horizons of conflict between countervailing interests seemingly infinite, that they do not yield simplistic formulas or handy scales for weighing competing values. "The best one can hope for is to discern lines of analysis and advance formulations sufficient to bridge past decisions with new facts. One must be satisfied with such present solutions

---

first amendment. Nor can a state prevent the teaching of modern foreign languages under the guise of promoting "civic development." Meyer v. Nebraska, 262 U.S. 390, 43 S. Ct. 625, 67 L. Ed. 1042 (1923).

and cannot expect a clear view of the terrain beyond the periphery of the immediate case." Eisner v. Stamford Board of Education, 440 F.2d 803, 804 n.1 (2d Cir. 1971).

It is appropriate, however, lest our decision today (which is based on the total absence of any facts justifying the Board of Education's actions) be misunderstood, that we disclaim any intent to condone partisan political activities in the public schools which reasonably may be expected to interfere with the educational process.

Accordingly, we conclude that the district court erred. The judgment of the district court is reversed and the case remanded for proceedings not inconsistent with this opinion.

## NOTES

1. Should *Pickering* have been distinguished in the *James* decision because the first amendment rights in *Pickering* were exercised outside of the classroom? *See* Goldwasser v. Brown, 417 F.2d 1169 (D. C. Cir.), *cert. denied,* 397 U.S. 922 (1969) (*Pickering* test applies to teacher's classroom speech at Air Force language school).

2. In Hanover v. Northrup, 325 F. Supp. 170 (D. Conn. 1970), it was held that it was a violation of first amendment rights to dismiss a junior high school teacher who refused to lead her class in the Salute to the Flag because she believed the phrase "with liberty and justice for all" was an untrue statement. Does the decision in *Hanover* comport with the principles outlined in *James?*

3. *See generally* Kaufman, I., *The Medium, the Message and the First Amendment,* 45 N.Y.U.L. REV. 761 (1970).

## MT. HEALTHY CITY SCHOOL DISTRICT
## BOARD OF EDUCATION v. DOYLE

Supreme Court of the United States
429 U.S. 274 (1977)

MR. JUSTICE REHNQUIST delivered the opinion of the Court.

Respondent Doyle sued petitioner Mt. Healthy Board of Education in the United States District Court for the Southern District of Ohio. Doyle claimed that the Board's refusal to renew his contract in 1971 violated his rights under the First and Fourteenth Amendments to the United States Constitution. After a bench trial the District Court held that Doyle was entitled to reinstatement with backpay. The Court of Appeals for the Sixth Circuit affirmed the judgment, 529 F.2d 524, and we granted the Board's petition for certiorari, 425 U. S. 933, to consider an admixture of jurisdictional and constitutional claims. . . .

The District Court found it unnecessary to decide whether the Board was entitled to immunity from suit in the federal courts under the Eleventh Amendment, because it decided that any such immunity had been waived by Ohio statute and decisional law. In view of the treatment of waiver by a State of its Eleventh Amendment immunity from suit in *Ford Motor Co.* v. *Dept. of Treasury,* 323 U. S. 459, 464-466 (1945), we are less sure than was the District Court that Ohio had consented to suit against entities such as the Board in the federal courts. We prefer to address instead the question of whether such an entity had any Eleventh Amendment immunity in the first place, since if we conclude that it had none it will be unnecessary to reach the question of waiver.

The bar of the Eleventh Amendment to suit in federal courts extends to States and state officials in appropriate circumstances, *Edelman v. Jordan,* 415 U.S. 651 (1974); *Ford Motor Co. v. Dept. of Treasury, supra,* but does not extend to counties and similar municipal corporations. See *Lincoln County v. Luning,* 133 U. S. 529, 530 (1890); *Moor v. County of Alameda,* 411 U.S. 693, 717-721 (1973). The issue here thus turns on whether the Mt. Healthy Board of Education is to be treated as an arm of the State partaking of the State's Eleventh Amendment immunity, or is instead to be treated as a municipal corporation or other political subdivision to which the Eleventh Amendment does not extend. The answer depends, at least in part, upon the nature of the entity created by state law. Under Ohio law the "State" does not include "political subdivisions," and "political subdivisions" do include local school districts. Ohio Rev. Code Ann. § 2743.01 (Page Supp. 1975). Petitioner is but one of many local school boards within the State of Ohio. It is subject to some guidance from the State Board of Education, Ohio Rev. Code Ann. § 3301.07 (Page 1972 and Supp. 1975), and receives a significant amount of money from the State. Ohio Rev. Code Ann. § 3317 (Page 1972 and Supp. 1975). But local school boards have extensive powers to issue bonds, Ohio Rev. Code Ann. § 133.27 (Page 1969), and to levy taxes within certain restrictions of state law. Ohio Rev. Code Ann. §§ 5705.02, 5705.03, 5705.192, 5705.194 (Page 1973 and Supp. 1975). On balance, the record before us indicates that a local school board such as petitioner is more like a county or city than it is like an arm of the State. We therefore hold that it was not entitled to assert any Eleventh Amendment immunity from suit in the federal courts.

Having concluded that respondent's complaint sufficiently pleaded jurisdiction under 28 U. S. C. § 1331, that the Board has failed to preserve the issue whether that complaint stated a claim upon which relief could be granted against the Board, and that the Board is not immune from suit under the Eleventh Amendment, we now proceed to consider the merits of respondent's claim under the First and Fourteenth Amendments.

Doyle was first employed by the Board in 1966. He worked under one-year contracts for the first three years, and under a two-year contract from 1969 to 1971. In 1969 he was elected president of the Teachers' Association, in which position he worked to expand the subjects of direct negotiation between the Association and the Board of Education. During Doyle's one-year term as president of the Association, and during the succeeding year when he served on its executive committee, there was apparently some tension in relations between the Board and the Association.

Beginning early in 1970, Doyle was involved in several incidents not directly connected with his role in the Teachers' Association. In one instance, he engaged in an argument with another teacher which culminated in the other teacher's slapping him. Doyle subsequently refused to accept an apology and insisted upon some punishment for the other teacher. His persistence in the matter resulted in the suspension of both teachers for one day, which was followed by a walkout by a number of other teachers, which in turn resulted in the lifting of the suspensions.

On other occasions, Doyle got into an argument with employees of the school cafeteria over the amount of spaghetti which had been served him; referred to students, in connection with a disciplinary complaint, as "sons of bitches"; and made an obscene gesture to two girls in connection with their failure to obey commands made in his capacity as cafeteria supervisor. Chronologically the last in the series of incidents which respondent was involved in during his employment by the Board was a telephone call by him to a local radio station.

It was the Board's consideration of this incident which the court below found to be a violation of the First and Fourteenth Amendments.

In February 1971, the principal circulated to various teachers a memorandum relating to teacher dress and appearance, which was apparently prompted by the view of some in the administration that there was a relationship between teacher appearance and public support for bond issues. Doyle's response to the receipt of the memorandum—on a subject which he apparently understood was to be settled by joint teacher-administration action—was to convey the substance of the memorandum to a disc jockey at WSAI, a Cincinnati radio station, who promptly announced the adoption of the dress code as a news item. Doyle subsequently apologized to the principal, conceding that he should have made some prior communication of his criticism to the school administration.

Approximately one month later the superintendent made his customary annual recommendations to the Board as to the rehiring of nontenured teachers. He recommended that Doyle not be rehired. The same recommendation was made with respect to nine other teachers in the district, and in all instances, including Doyle's, the recommendation was adopted by the Board. Shortly after being notified of this decision, respondent requested a statement of reasons for the Board's actions. He received a statement citing "a notable lack of tact in handling professional matters which leaves much doubt as to your sincerity in establishing good school relationships." That general statement was followed by references to the radio station incident and to the obscene-gesture incident.[1]

The District Court found that all of these incidents had in fact occurred. It concluded that respondent Doyle's telephone call to the radio station was "clearly protected by the First Amendment," and that because it had played a "substantial part" in the decision of the Board not to renew Doyle's employment, he was entitled to reinstatement with backpay. Pet. for Cert., App. 12a-13a. The District Court did not expressly state what test it was applying in determining that the incident in question involved conduct protected by the First Amendment, but simply held that the communication to the radio station was such conduct. The Court of Appeals affirmed in a brief *per curiam* opinion. 529 F. 2d 524.

Doyle's claims under the First and Fourteenth Amendments are not defeated by the fact that he did not have tenure. Even though he could have been discharged for no reason whatever, and had no constitutional right to a hearing prior to the decision not to rehire him, *Board of Regents* v. *Roth,* 408 U. S. 564 (1972), he may nonetheless establish a claim to reinstatement if the decision not to rehire him was made by reason of his exercise of constitutionally protected First Amendment freedoms. *Perry* v. *Sindermann,* 408 U. S. 593 (1972).

That question of whether speech of a government employee is constitutionally protected expression necessarily entails striking "a balance between the interests of the teacher, as a citizen, in commenting upon matters of public concern and

---

[1] "I. You have shown a notable lack of tact in handling professional matters which leaves much doubt as to your sincerity in establishing good school relationships.

"A. You assumed the responsibility to notify W.S.A.I. Radio Station in regards to the suggestion of the Board of Education that teachers establish an appropriate dress code for professional people. This raised much concern not only within this community, but also in neighboring communities.

"B. You used obscene gestures to correct students in a situation in the cafeteria causing considerable concern among those students present.

> "Sincerely yours,
> "Rex Ralph
> "Superintendent"

the interest of the State, as an employer, in promoting the efficiency of the public services it performs through its employees." *Pickering* v. *Board of Education,* 391 U. S. 563, 568 (1968). There is no suggestion by the Board that Doyle violated any established policy, or that its reaction to his communication to the radio station was anything more than an *ad hoc* response to Doyle's action in making the memorandum public. We therefore accept the District Court's finding that the communication was protected by the First and Fourteenth Amendments. We are not, however, entirely in agreement with that court's manner of reasoning from this finding to the conclusion that Doyle is entitled to reinstatement with backpay.

The District Court made the following "conclusions" on this aspect of the case:

"1) If a non-permissible reason, e.g., exercise of First Amendment rights, played a substantial part in the decision not to renew — even in the face of other permissible grounds—the decision may not stand (citations omitted).

"2) A non-permissible reason did play a substantial part. That is clear from the letter of the Superintendent immediately following the Board's decision, which stated two reasons—the one, the conversation with the radio station clearly protected by the First Amendment. A court may not engage in any limitation of First Amendment rights based on 'tact'—that is not to say that the 'tactfulness' is irrelevant to other issues in this case." Pet. for Cert., App. 12a-13a.

At the same time, though, it stated that

"[i]n fact, as this Court sees it and finds, both the Board and the Superintendent were faced with a situation in which there did exist in fact reason . . . independent of any First Amendment rights or exercise thereof, to not extend tenure." *Id.,* at 12a.

Since respondent Doyle had no tenure, and there was therefore not even a state-law requirement of "cause" or "reason" before a decision could be made not to renew his employment, it is not clear what the District Court meant by this latter statement. Clearly the Board legally *could* have dismissed respondent had the radio station incident never come to its attention. One plausible meaning of the court's statement is that the Board and the Superintendent not only could, but in fact *would* have reached that decision had not the constitutionally protected incident of the telephone call to the radio station occurred. We are thus brought to the issue whether, even if that were the case, the fact that the protected conduct played a "substantial part" in the actual decision not to renew would necessarily amount to a constitutional violation justifying remedial action. We think that it would not.

A rule of causation which focuses solely on whether protected conduct played a part, "substantial" or otherwise, in a decision not to rehire, could place an employee in a better position as a result of the exercise of constitutionally protected conduct than he would have occupied had he done nothing. The difficulty with the rule enunciated by the District Court is that it would require reinstatement in cases where a dramatic and perhaps abrasive incident is inevitably on the minds of those responsible for the decision to rehire, and does indeed play a part in that decision — even if the same decision would have been reached had the incident not occurred. The constitutional principle at stake is sufficiently vindicated if such an employee is placed in no worse a position than if he had not engaged in the conduct. A borderline or marginal candidate should not have the employment question resolved against him because of constitutionally protected conduct. But that same candidate ought not to be able, by engaging in such conduct, to prevent his employer from assessing his performance record and reaching a decision not to rehire on the basis of that record, simply because the protected conduct makes the employer more certain of the correctness of its decision.

This is especially true where, as the District Court observed was the case here, the current decision to rehire will accord "tenure." The long-term consequences of an award of tenure are of great moment both to the employee and to the employer. They are too significant for us to hold that the Board in this case would be precluded, because it considered constitutionally protected conduct in deciding not to rehire Doyle, from attempting to prove to a trier of fact that quite apart from such conduct Doyle's record was such that he would not have been rehired in any event.

In other areas of constitutional law, this Court has found it necessary to formulate a test of causation which distinguishes between a result caused by a constitutional violation and one not so caused. We think those are instructive in formulating the test to be applied here.

In *Lyons* v. *Oklahoma,* 322 U. S. 596 (1944), the Court held that even though the first confession given by a defendant had been involuntary, the Fourteenth Amendment did not prevent the State from using a second confession obtained 12 hours later if the coercion surrounding the first confession had been sufficiently dissipated as to make the second confession voluntary. In *Wong Sun* v. *United States,* 371 U. S. 471, 491 (1963), the Court was willing to assume that a defendant's arrest had been unlawful, but held that "the connection between the arrest and the statement [given several days later] had 'become so attenuated as to dissipate the taint.' *Nardone* v. *United States,* 308 U. S. 338, 341." *Parker* v. *North Carolina,* 397 U. S. 790, 796 (1970), held that even though a confession be assumed to have been involuntary in the constitutional sense of the word, a guilty plea entered over a month later met the test for the voluntariness of such a plea. The Court in *Parker* relied on the same quoted language from *Nardone, supra,* as did the Court in *Wong Sun, supra.* While the type of causation on which the taint cases turn may differ somewhat from that which we apply here, those cases do suggest that the proper test to apply in the present context is one which likewise protects against the invasion of constitutional rights without commanding undesirable consequences not necessary to the assurance of those rights.

Initially, in this case, the burden was properly placed upon respondent to show that his conduct was constitutionally protected, and that this conduct was a "substantial factor" — or, to put it in other words, that it was a "motivating factor" [2] in the Board's decision not to rehire him. Respondent having carried that burden, however, the District Court should have gone on to determine whether the Board had shown by a preponderance of the evidence that it would have reached the same decision as to respondent's reemployment even in the absence of the protected conduct.

We cannot tell from the District Court opinion and conclusions, nor from the opinion of the Court of Appeals affirming the judgment of the District Court, what conclusion those courts would have reached had they applied this test. The judgment of the Court of Appeals is therefore vacated, and the case remanded for further proceedings consistent with this opinion.

*So ordered.*

---

[2] See *Village of Arlington Heights v. Metropolitan Housing Development Corp., ante,* at 270-271, n. 21.

## NOTES

1. Without the causation requirement set out by the Court in *Mt. Healthy,* what could be the effect on employment decisions concerning a reinstated teacher in succeeding years if the same decision-maker were involved? Could a successful suit by a teacher terminated in part for exercise of protected First Amendment rights result in disparate treatment between that teacher and others who had not exercised their First Amendment rights when rehiring decisions were made?

2. The Court's opinion in *Mt. Healthy* does not consider the possible chilling effect that a public employer's action might have on other employees. Should it matter that other employees might be inhibited in exercising their First Amendment rights in the future? How can this danger be mitigated?

## GIVHAN v. WESTERN LINE CONSOLIDATED SCHOOL DISTRICT

United States Supreme Court
99 S.Ct. 693 (1979)

MR. JUSTICE REHNQUIST delivered the opinion of the Court.

Petitioner Bessie Givhan was dismissed from her employment as a junior high English teacher at the end of the 1970-1971 school year.[1] At the time of petitioner's termination, respondent Western Line Consolidated School District was the subject of a desegregation order entered by the United States District Court for the Northern District of Mississippi. Petitioner filed a complaint in intervention in the desegregation action, seeking reinstatement on the dual grounds that nonrenewal of her contract violated the rule laid down by the Court of Appeals for the Fifth Circuit in *Singleton v. Jackson Municipal Separate School District,* 419 F.2d 1211 (C.A.5 1969), rev'd and remanded *sub nom. Carter v. West Feliciana Parish School Board,* 396 U.S. 290, 90 S.Ct. 608, 24 L.Ed.2d 477 (1970), on remand, 425 F.2d 1211 (C.A.5 1970), and infringed her right of free speech secured by the First and Fourteenth Amendments of the United States Constitution. In an effort to show that its decision was justified, respondent school district introduced evidence of, among other things [2] a series of private encounters between petitioner and the school principal in which petitioner allegedly made "petty and unreasonable demands" in a manner variously described by the principal as "insulting," "hostile," "loud," and "arrogant."

---

[1] In a letter to petitioner dated July 23, 1971, District Superintendent C. L. Morris gave the following reasons for the decision not to renew her contract:

"(1)[A] flat refusal to administer standardized National tests to the pupils in your charge; (2) an announced intention not to cooperate with the administration of the Glen Allan Attendance Center; (3) and an antagonistic and hostile attitude to the administration of the Glen Allan Attendance Center demonstrated throughout the school year."

[2] In addition to the reasons set out in the District Superintendent's termination letter to petitioner, n. 1, *ante,* the school district advanced several other justifications for its decision not to rehire petitioner. The Court of Appeals dealt with these allegations in a footnote.

"Appellants also sought to establish these other bases for the decision not to rehire: (1) that Givhan 'downgraded' the papers of white students; (2) that she was one of a number of teachers who walked out of a meeting about desegregation in the fall of 1969 and attempted to disrupt it by blowing automobile horns outside the gymnasium; (3) that the school district had received a threat by Givhan and other teachers not to return to work when schools reopened on a unitary basis in February, 1970; and (4) that Givhan had protected a student during a weapons shakedown at Riverside in March, 1970, by concealing a student's knife until completion of a search. The evidence on the first three of these points was inconclusive and the district judge did not clearly err in rejecting or ignoring it. Givhan admitted the fourth incident, but the district judge properly rejected that as a justification for her not being rehired, as there was no evidence that [the principal] relied on it in making his recommendation." 555 F.2d, at 1313, n. 7.

After a two-day bench trial, the District Court held that petitioner's termination had violated the First Amendment. Finding that petitioner had made "demands" on but two occasions and that those demands "were neither 'petty' nor 'unreasonable,' insomuch as all of the complaints in question involved employment policies and practices at [the] school which [petitioner] conceived to be racially discriminatory in purpose or effect," the District Court concluded that "the primary reason for the school district's failure to renew [petitioner's] contract was her criticism of the policies and practices of the school district, especially the school to which she was assigned to teach." Pet. for Cert. 35A. Accordingly, the District Court held that the dismissal violated petitioner's First Amendment rights, as enunicated in *Perry v. Sindermann,* 408 U.S. 593, 92 S.Ct. 2694, 33 L.Ed.2d 570 (1972), and *Pickering v. Board of Education,* 391 U.S. 563, 88 S.Ct. 1731, 20 L.Ed.2d 811 (1968), and ordered her reinstatement.

The Court of Appeals for the Fifth Circuit reversed. Although it found the District Court's findings not clearly erroneous, the Court of Appeals concluded that because petitioner had privately expressed her complaints and opinions to the principal, her expression was not protected under the First Amendment. Support for this proposition was thought to be derived from *Pickering, supra, Perry, supra,* and *Mt. Healthy City School District v. Doyle,* 429 U.S. 274, 97 S.Ct. 568, 50 L.Ed.2d 471 (1977), which were found to contain "[t]he strong implication . . . that private expression by a public employee is not constitutionally protected." 555 F.2d 1309, 1318 (C.A.5 1977). The Court of Appeals also concluded that there is no constitutional right to "press even 'good' ideas on an unwilling recipient," saying that to afford public employees the right to such private expression "would in effect force school principals to be ombudsmen, for damnable as well as laudable expressions." *Id.,* at 1319. We are unable to agree that private expression of one's views is beyond constitutional protection, and therefore reverse the Court of Appeals' judgment and remand the case so that it may consider the contentions of the parties freed from this erroneous view of the First Amendment.

This Court's decisions in *Pickering, Perry,* and *Mt. Healthy* do not support the conclusion that a public employee forfeits his protection against governmental abridgment of freedom of speech if he decides to express his views privately rather than publicly. While those cases each arose in the context of a public employee's public expression, the rule to be derived from them is not dependent on that largely coincidental fact.

In *Pickering* a teacher was discharged for publicly criticizing, in a letter published in a local newspaper, the school board's handling of prior bond issue proposals and its subsequent allocation of financial resources between the schools' educational and athletic programs. Noting that the free speech rights of pubic employees are not absolute, the Court held that in determining whether a government employee's speech is constitutionally protected, "the interests of the [employee], as a citizen, in commenting upon matters of public concern" must be balanced against "the interest of the State, as an employer, in promoting the efficiency of the public services it performs through its employees." *Pickering v. Board of Education, supra,* 391 U.S., at 568, 88 S.Ct., at 1734. The Court concluded that under the circumstances of that case "the interest of the school administration in limiting teachers' opportunities to contribute to public debate [was] not significantly greater than its interest in limiting a similar contribution by any member of the general public." *Id.,* at 573, 88 S.Ct., at 1737. Here the opinion of the Court of Appeals may be read to turn in part on its view that the working relationship between principal and teacher is significantly different from the relationship between the parties in *Pickering,* as is evidenced by its reference to its own opinion in *Abbott v. Thetford,* 534 F.2d 1101 (C.A.5 1976) (en banc), cert. denied, 430 U.S. 954, 97 S.Ct. 1598, 51 L.Ed.2d 804 (1977). But we do not feel confident that the Court of Appeals' decision would have been placed on that ground notwithstanding its view that the First Amendment does not require the same sort of *Pickering* balancing for the private expression of a public employee as it does for public express.[4]

*Perry* and *Mt. Healthy* arose out of similar disputes between teachers and their public employers. As we have noted, however, the fact that each of these cases involved public expression by the employee was not critical to the decision. Nor is the Court of Appeals' view supported by the "captive audience" rationale. Having opened his office door to petitioner, the principal was hardly in a position to argue that he was the "*unwilling* recipient" of her views.

The First Amendment forbids abridgment of the "freedom of speech." Neither the Amendment itself nor our decisions indicate that this freedom is lost to the public employee who arranges to communicate privately with his employer rather than to spread his views before the public. We decline to adopt such a view of the First Amendment. . . .

The Court of Appeals in the instant case rejected respondents' *Mt. Healthy* claim that the decision to terminate petitioner would have been made even if her encounters with the principal had never occurred:

> "The [trial] court did not make an express finding as to whether the same decision would have been made, but on this record the [respondents] do not, and seriously cannot, argue that the same decision would have been made without regard to the 'demands.' Appellants seem to argue that the preponderance of the evidence shows that the same decision would have been justified, but that is not the same as proving that the same decision would have been made. . . . Therefore [repondents] failed to make a successful 'same decision anyway' defense." 555 F.2d, at 1315.

Since this case was tried before *Mt. Healthy* was decided, it is not surprising that respondents did not attempt to prove in the District Court that the decision not to rehire petitioner would have been made even absent consideration of her "demands." Thus, the case came to the Court of Appeals in very much the same posture as *Mt. Healthy* was presented in this Court. And while the District Court found that petitioner's "criticism" was the "primary" reason for the school district's failure to rehire her, it did not find that she would have been rehired *but for* her criticism. Respondents' *Mt. Healthy* claim called for a factual determination which could not, on this record be resolved by the Court of Appeals.[5]

---

[4] Although the First Amendment's protection of government employees extends to private as well as public expression, striking the *Pickering* balance in each context may involve different considerations. When a teacher speaks publicly, it is generally the *content* of his statements that must be assessed to determine whether they "in any way either impeded the teacher's proper performance of his daily duties in the classroom or . . . interfered with the regular operation of the schools generally." *Pickering v. Board of Education, supra,* 391 U.S., at 572-573, 88 S.Ct., at 1737. Private expression, however, may in some situations bring additional factors to the *Pickering* calculus. When a government employee personally confronts his immediate superior, the employing agency's institutional efficiency may be threatened not only by the content of the employee's message, but also by the manner, time, and place in which it is delivered.

[5] We cannot agree with the Court of Appeals that the record in this case does not admit of the argument that petitioner would have been terminated regardless of her "demands." Even absent

Accordingly, the judgment of the Court of Appeals is vacated and the case remanded for further proceedings consistent with this opinion.

*So ordered.*

# 5. REGULATION OF THE PRIVATE LIVES OF PUBLIC EMPLOYEES

## McCONNELL v. ANDERSON

United States Court of Appeals, Eighth Circuit
451 F.2d 193 (1971)
*cert. denied,* 405 U.S. 1046 (1972)

STEPHENSON, Circuit Judge.

This case has its origin in a July 9, 1970 resolution of the University of Minnesota Board of Regents not to approve the application of James Michael McConnell to head, at the rank of Instructor, the cataloging division of the University's St. Paul campus library on the ground that his "personal conduct, as represented in the public and University news media, is not consistent with the best interest of the University." McConnell's complaint alleged that he was offered the division head appointment in April 1970; that he accepted the offer in May 1970, but that the offer was withdrawn, pursuant to the foregoing resolution, after he and another male publicly applied for a marriage license at the Hennepin County, Minnesota Clerk's office. . . . In addition to the allegations above, his complaint asserted that he was a homosexual and that the Board's resolution not to approve his employment application was premised on the fact of his homosexuality and upon his desire, as exemplified by the marriage license incident, specifically to publicly profess his "earnest" belief that homosexuals are entitled to privileges equal to those afforded heterosexuals. . . .

Federal jurisdiction was claimed, *inter alia,* under 42 U.S.C.A. § 1983 and 28 U.S.C.A. § 1343 (3). Judge Neville, after conducting an oral hearing at which evidence was taken, entered judgment for McConnell and enjoined the Board from refusing to employ him "solely because, and on the grounds that he is a homosexual." . . .

Judge Neville stayed the judgment and suspended the injunction pending disposition of this appeal. We must reverse. . . .

McConnell apparently is well-educated and otherwise able, possessing both an academic degree and a master's degree; that he formerly was employed as Acquisitions Librarian at Park College in Missouri; that he is a member of the organization known as FREE (Fight Repression of Erotic Expression); that on May 18, 1970, McConnell and a friend referred to in the record as "Jack Baker" encountered Dr. Hopp and informed him of their intention to obtain a license to marry; that during this conversation Dr. Hopp expressed concern that such an occurrence might well jeopardize favorable consideration of McConnell's employment application; that about three hours later on the same day, McConnell and Jack Baker appeared at the Hennepin County Clerk's office and

---

consideration of petitioner s private encounters with the principal, a decision to terminate based on the reasons detailed at nn. 1 and 2, *ante* would hardly strike us as surprising. Additionally, in his letter to petitioner setting forth the reasons for her termination, District Superintendent Morris makes no mention of petitioner's "demands" and "criticism." See n. 1, *ante.*

made formal application for the license; that this event received the attention of the local news and television media; that the Board's Faculty, Staff and Student Affairs Committee, on June 24, 1970, convened to initially consider the matter of McConnell's proposed appointment and voted that it be not approved; that McConnell promptly was so advised and given notice that he could request a hearing at the Committee's next scheduled meeting on July 9; that McConnell requested a hearing; that he and his counsel appeared at the meeting and were furnished copies of the resolution in its proposed form; that McConnell and his counsel took advantage of this opportunity to present information they deemed supportive of his application, and that at the conclusion of the presentation on McConnell's behalf, the Committee adopted the resolution. It perhaps is well at this point to note that McConnell makes no claim that the Board denied him procedural due process.

The Board's primary demand for reversal is based upon a most fundamental contention. It is the Board's claim that Judge Neville, in issuing the injunction, exceeded his proper function and authority by superimposing his own situational judgment upon legitimate Board action supported by substantial and material factual data. . . .

We focus our initial attention upon our standard of review of the Board's action. The Minnesota Supreme Court has had no less than five occasions to determine and review the proper role and function of the Board of Regents in the management, control and administration of the University of Minnesota. From these decisions we think it can be said generally that, insofar as Minnesota's highest court is concerned, the Board is vested with plenary and exclusive authority to govern, control and oversee the administration of the University and that the role of Minnesota courts in reviewing Board action is limited to determining whether the Board has kept within the scope of its constitutional powers. . . .

[T]he discretion of the Board necessarily is broad and subject only to such judicial review as normally is available to litigants allegedly aggrieved by administrative action generally. We think the attitude and approach to the Board's role by Minnesota's court is sound and instructive and we adopt it as our own.

Without question, then, the Board is on relevant and sound ground in asserting that the decision embodied in its resolution cannot be overturned in the absence of a clear and affirmative showing that it was premised upon arbitrary or capricious conduct. That a court is, in reviewing a determination of an administrative body, limited to deciding whether the administrative action was arbitrary, unreasonable or capricious long has been settled. . . .

It is McConnell's position that the Board's decision not to approve his employment application reflects "a clear example of the unreasoning prejudice and revulsion some people feel when confronted by a homosexual." That being so, he argues that the Board's action was arbitrary and capricious and thus violative of his constitutional rights. We do not agree.

It is our conclusion that the Board possessed ample specific factual information on the basis of which it reasonably could conclude that the appointment would not be consistent with the best interests of the University. . . .

[I]t is at once apparent that this is not a case involving mere homosexual propensities on the part of a prospective employee. Neither is it a case in which an applicant is excluded from employment because of a desire clandestinely to pursue homosexual conduct. It is, instead, a case in which something more than remunerative employment is sought; a case in which the applicant seeks employment on his own terms; a case in which the prospective employee demands, as shown both by the allegations of the complaint and by the marriage license incident as well, the right to pursue an activist role in *implementing* his unconventional ideas concerning the societal status to be accorded homosexuals and, thereby, to foist tacit approval of this socially repugnant concept upon his employer, who is, in this instance, an institution of higher learning.[7] We know of no constitutional fiat or binding principle of decisional law which requires an employer to accede to such extravagant demands. We are therefore unable fairly to categorize the Board's action here as arbitrary, unreasonable or capricious. . . .

Reversed, with directions to dissolve the injunction and to dismiss the action on the merits.

## NORTON v. MACY

United States Court of Appeals, District of Columbia Circuit
417 F.2d 1161 (1969)

BAZELON, Chief Judge:

Appellant, a former GS-14 budget analyst in the National Aeronautics and Space Administration (NASA), seeks review of his discharge for "immoral conduct" and for possessing personality traits which render him "unsuitable for further Government employment." As a veterans preference eligible, he could be dismissed only for "such cause as will promote the efficiency of the service." Since the record before us does not suggest any reasonable connection between the evidence against him and the efficiency of the service, we conclude that he was unlawfully discharged.

Appellant's dismissal grew out of his arrest for a traffic violation. In the early morning of October 22, 1963, he was driving his car in the vicinity of Lafayette Square. He pulled over to the curb, picked up one Madison Monroe Procter, drove him once around the Square, and dropped him off at the starting point. The two men then drove off in separate cars. Two Morals Squad officers, having observed this sequence of events, gave chase, traveling at speeds of up to 45 miles per hour. In the parking lot of appellant's Southwest Washington apartment building, Procter told the police that appellant had felt his leg during their brief circuit of Lafayette Square and had then invited him to appellant's apartment for a drink. The officers arrested both men and took them "to the Morals Office to issue a traffic violation notice."

Pending issuance of the traffic summons, the police interrogated appellant and Procter for two hours concerning their activities that evening and their sexual histories. Meanwhile, pursuant to an arrangement, the head of the Morals Squad telephoned NASA Security Chief Fugler, who arrived on the scene at 3:00 a.m. in time to hear the last of the interrogation. . . . Throughout, appellant steadfastly denied that he had made a homosexual advance to Procter. . . .

---

[7] Compare Pickering v. Board of Education, 391 U.S. 563, 568-575, 88 S. Ct. 1731, 20 L. Ed. 2d 811 (1968). In the District Court McConnell apparently argued that he has the right to apply for a marriage license and that such is "symbolic speech" within the protection of the Free Speech and Due Process clauses of the First and Fourteenth Amendments. See McConnell v. Anderson, p. 815 of 316 F. Supp. He relies largely on Tinker v. Des Moines Ind. School Dist., 393 U.S. 503, 89 S. Ct. 733, 21 L. Ed. 2d 731 (1969), a case from this circuit. Although this contention is not pressed here, we feel constrained to observe that we do not believe that *Tinker*, when read in light of its distinctive facts, can afford McConnell any comfort in this regard.

[However, during a later] interrogation, appellant allegedly conceded that he had engaged in mutual masturbation with other males in high school and college, that he sometimes experienced homosexual desires while drinking, that on rare occasions he had undergone a temporary blackout after drinking, and that on two such occasions he suspected he might have engaged in some sort of homosexual activity. . . .

NASA concluded that appellant did in fact make a homosexual advance on October 22, and that this act amounted to "immoral, indecent, and disgraceful conduct." It also determined that . . . appellant possesses "traits of character and personality which render [him] . . . unsuitable for further Government employment." A Civil Service Appeals Examiner and the Board of Appeals and Review upheld these conclusions. In appellant's action for reinstatement, the District Court granted appellee's motion for summary judgment.

Congress has provided that protected civil servants shall not be dismissed except "for such cause as will promote the efficiency of the service." The Civil Service Commission's regulations provide that an appointee may be removed, *inter alia,* for "infamous . . . , immoral, or notoriously disgraceful conduct" and for "any . . . other disqualification which makes the individual unfit for the service." We think — and appellant does not strenuously deny — that the evidence was sufficient to sustain the charge that, consciously or not, he made a homosexual advance to Procter. Accordingly, the question presented is whether such an advance, or appellant's personality traits as disclosed by the record, are "such cause" for removal as the statute requires.

The Fifth Circuit Court of Appeals recently refused to consider a substantive attack on a dismissal for private homosexual conduct, apparently believing that it had no authority to review on the merits a Civil Service determination of unfitness.[5] The courts have, it is true, consistently recognized that the Commission enjoys a wide discretion in determining what reasons may justify removal of a federal employee; but it is also clear that this discretion is not unlimited. The Government's obligation to accord due process sets at least minimal substantive limits on its prerogative to dismiss its employees: it forbids all dismissals which are arbitrary and capricious. These constitutional limits may be greater where, as here, the dismissal imposes a "badge of infamy," disqualifying the victim from any further Federal employment, damaging his prospects for private employ, and fixing upon him the stigma of an official defamation of character. The Due Process Clause may also cut deeper into the Government's discretion where a dismissal involves an intrusion upon that ill-defined area of privacy which is increasingly if indistinctly recognized as a foundation of several specific constitutional protections. Whatever their precise scope, these due process limitations apply even to those whose employment status is unprotected by statute. And statutes such as the Veterans' Preference Act were plainly designed to confer some additional job security not enjoyed by unprotected federal employees. . . .

---

[5] Anonymous v. Macy, 398 F.2d 317 (5th Cir. 1968). The Court said only:

Counsel for appellant . . . argue at great length, and with considerable ability, that homosexual acts constitute private acts upon the part of such employees, that they do not affect the efficiency of the service, and should not be the basis of discharge. That contention is not accepted by this Court. See Hargett v. Summerfield, 100 U.S. App. D.C. 85, 243 F.2d 29 (1957).

398 F.2d at 318. Although Hargett v. Summerfield eschews any absolute bar to judicial review of a discharge on the merits, it contains language which approaches such a bar. Thus, it is not altogether clear whether the Fifth Circuit thought it had no authority to consider the arguments presented or whether it thought only that the particular matters raised fell within the area of agency discretion.

Accordingly, this court has previously examined the merits of a dismissal involving a statutorily protected employee charged with off-duty homosexual conduct. In other cases, we have recognized that, besides complying with statutory procedural requirements, the employer agency must demonstrate some "rational basis" for its conclusion that a discharge "will promote the efficiency of the service." ...

Preliminarily, we must reject appellee's contention that once the label "immoral" is plausibly attached to an employee's off-duty conduct, our inquiry into the presence of adequate rational cause for removal is at an end. A pronouncement of "immorality" tends to discourage careful analysis because it unavoidably connotes a violation of divine, Olympian, or otherwise universal standards of rectitude. However, the Civil Service Commission has neither the expertise nor the requisite anointment to make or enforce absolute moral judgments, and we do not understand that it purports to do so. Its jurisdiction is at least confined to the things which are Caesar's, and its avowed standard of "immorality" is no more than "the prevailing mores of our society." ...

We are not prepared to say that the Commission could not reasonably find appellant's homosexual advance to be "immoral," "indecent," or "notoriously disgraceful" under dominant conventional norms. But the notion that it could be an appropriate function of the federal bureaucracy to enforce the majority's conventional codes of conduct in the private lives of its employees is at war with elementary concepts of liberty, privacy, and diversity. And whatever we may think of the Government's qualifications to act *in loco parentis* in this way, the statute precludes it from discharging protected employees except for a reason related to the efficiency of the service. Accordingly, a finding that an employee has done something immoral or indecent could support a dismissal without further inquiry only if all immoral or indecent acts of an employee have some ascertainable deleterious effect on the efficiency of the service. The NASA official who fired him, Mr. Garbarini, testified that appellant was a "competent employee" doing "very good" work. ...

Appellant's duties apparently did not bring him into contact with the public, and his fellow employees were unaware of his "immorality." Nonetheless, Garbarini's advisers told him that dismissal for any homosexual conduct was a "*custom* within the agency," and he decided to follow the custom because continued employment of appellant might "turn out to be embarrassing to the agency" in that "if an incident like this occurred again, it could become a public scandal on the agency."

Thus, appellee is now obliged to rely solely on this possibility of embarrassment to the agency to justify appellant's dismissal. The assertion of such a nebulous "cause" poses perplexing problems for a review proceeding which must accord broad discretion to the Commission. We do not doubt that NASA blushes whenever one of its own is caught *in flagrante delictu;* but if the possibility of such transitory institutional discomfiture must be uncritically accepted as a cause for discharge which will "promote the efficiency of the service," we might as well abandon all pretense that the statute provides any substantive security for its supposed beneficiaries. A claim of possible embarrassment might, of course, be a vague way of referring to some specific potential interference with an agency's performance; but it might also be a smokescreen hiding personal antipathies or moral judgments which are excluded by statute as grounds for dismissal. A reviewing court must at least be able to discern some reasonably foreseeable, specific connection between an employee's potentially embarrassing conduct and the efficiency of the service. Once the connection is established, then it is for the agency and the Commission to decide whether it outweighs the loss to the service of a particular competent employee.

In the instant case appellee has shown us no such specific connection. Indeed, on the record appellant is at most an extermely infrequent offender, who neither openly flaunts nor carelessly displays his unorthodox sexual conduct in public. Thus, even the potential for the embarrassment the agency fears is minimal. We think the unparticularized and unsubstantiated conclusion that such possible embarrassment threatens the quality of the agency's performance is an arbitrary ground for dismissal. . . .

Lest there be any doubt, we emphasize that we do not hold that homosexual conduct may never be cause for dismissal of a protected federal employee. Nor do we even conclude that potential embarrassment from an employee's private conduct may in no circumstances affect the efficiency of the service. What we do say is that, if the statute is to have any force, an agency cannot support a dismissal as promoting the efficiency of the service merely by turning its head and crying "shame."

Since we conclude that appellant's discharge cannot be sustained on the grounds relied on by the Commission, the judgment of the District Court must be

Reversed.

TAMM, Circuit Judge (dissenting): . . .

This court plainly held in the case of Hargett v. Summerfield, 100 U.S. App. D.C. 85, 88, 243 F.2d 29, 32 (1957), that "employee removal and discipline are almost entirely matters of executive agency discretion," and "that, so long as there [is] substantial compliance with applicable procedures ... the administrative determination [is] not reviewable as to the wisdom or good judgment of the department . . . exercising [its] discretion." (Citations omitted.) I have felt constrained to follow this view time and again, *see, e.g.,* dissenting opinion in Meehan v. Macy, U.S. App. D.C. (No. 20.812, decided May 12, 1969) (*en banc*), although in so doing I remain a *vox clamantis in deserto.* . . . Homosexuals, sadly enough, do not leave their emotions at Lafayette Square and regardless of their spiritual destinies they still present targets for public reproach and private extortion. I believe this record supports the finding that this individual presents more than a potential risk in this regard and that his termination will serve the efficiency of the service. Despite the billows of puffery that continue to float out of recent opinions on this subject, I believe that the theory that homosexual conduct is not in any way related to the efficiency and effectiveness of governmental business is not an evil theory — just a very unrealistic one.

## NOTES

1. In contrast to the decision in Norton v. Macy, the court in *McConnell* appears wholly insensitive to homosexuality, describing it as a "socially repugnant concept." However, is it clear that the D.C. Circuit would have decided *McConnell* differently than the 8th Circuit if it had heard and decided the case? The D.C. Circuit in *Norton* suggests that, pursuant to the Veterans' Preference Act, the government employer must show "some reasonably foreseeable, specific connection between an employee's potentially embarrassing conduct and the efficiency of the service." What is the standard of review expressed in *McConnell* and where does the burden of proof lie?

2. The Ninth Circuit upheld the termination of a probationary clerk-typist at the Equal Employment Opportunity Commission who was openly homosexual and active in working

for homosexual rights, in the course of which he had received considerable publicity. The discharge was based on the employee's " 'openly and publicly flaunting his homosexual way of life and indicating further continuance of such activities' while identifying himself as a member of a federal agency," ostensibly resulting in lowered public confidence in the agency's ability to perform its function. The court distinguished other homosexual termination cases in which violations of the First and Fourteenth Amendments had been found on the ground that Singer, unlike the homosexual employees in other cases, had openly and publicly flaunted or advocated homosexual conduct. Singer v. United States Civil Service Commission, 530 F.2d 247 (9th Cir. 1976), *vacated and remanded,* 429 U.S. 1034 (1977) ("for reconsideration in light of the position now asserted by the Solicitor General in his memorandum on behalf of the United States Civil Service Commission"). Although *Singer* at least implies that some cases have held that homosexuality itself involves a form of free expression, no case can be found to support such a view.

3. One case distinguished in *Singer* was Acanfora v. Board of Education of Montgomery County, 491 F.2d 498 (4th Cir. 1974), in which a teacher was removed from the classroom and given administrative duties after school officials learned that he was a homosexual. After his transfer, Acanfora granted several interviews with the media in which he discussed the difficulties experienced by homosexuals. The Court found no evidence that Acanfora's statements had caused or were likely to cause disruption of the school or to affect his performance as a teacher, and held that his *statements* were protected by the First Amendment. Because he withheld information concerning his membership in a campus homosexual organization on his application for the teaching position, however, the court held that he could not "invoke the process of the court to obtain a ruling on an issue [the constitutionality of the school's refusal to employ homosexual teachers] that he practiced deception to avoid."

4. In Burton v. Cascade School Dist. Union High School No. 5, 512 F.2d 850 (9th Cir. 1975), a non-tenured teacher dismissed for active homosexual activity brought suit seeking damages and reinstatement. She was awarded damages and attorney's fees and appealed for reinstatement. The Fifth Circuit held that the lower court's refusal to order reinstatement was not an abuse of discretion where the damages awarded equalled the balance of her yearly salary plus one-half her teaching salary for the following year.

5. In Morrison v. State Bd. of Educ., 1 Cal. 3d 214, 82 Cal. Rptr. 175, 461 P.2d 375 (1969), the California Supreme Court held that a school teacher could not be dismissed for a single homosexual act. The court noted, in dictum, that a broad prohibition against "immoral acts" would raise serious constitutional questions. In this regard, the court observed that "school officials concerned with enforcing such broad prohibitions might be inclined to probe into the private life of each and every teacher, no matter how exemplary his classroom conduct. Such prying might all too readily lead school officials to search for 'telltale signs' of immorality in violation of the teacher's constitutional rights."

6. The court in *Morrison* suggests that an individual cannot be removed from the teaching profession in the absence of a showing that his retention in the public service poses a significant danger of harm to either students, school employees, or others who might be affected by his actions as a teacher. Other courts have subscribed to this view in cases involving hair style, private correspondence, and heterosexual relations. *See, e.g.,* Mindel v. United States Civil Serv. Comm'n, 312 F. Supp. 485 (N.D. Cal. 1970); Forstner v. City and County of San Francisco, 243 Cal. App. 2d 625, 52 Cal. Rptr. 621 (1966); Jarvella v. Willoughby-Eastlake City School Dist. Bd. of Educ., 12 Ohio Misc. 288, 41 Ohio Op. 2d 423, 233 N.E.2d 143 (C.P. Lake County 1967). *Compare* the holding in *Morrison* *with* Board of Trustees v. Stubblefield, 16 Cal. App. 3d 820, 94 Cal. Rptr. 318 (1971) (extra-marital involvement with student).

## CARTER v. UNITED STATES

United States Court of Appeals, District of Columbia Circuit
407 F.2d 1238 (1968)

LEVENTHAL, Circuit Judge:

Appellant Carter brought an action asserting that his discharge from Government service deprived him of statutory and constitutional rights. He appeals to this court on the ground that the District Court erred when it granted judgment in favor of the Government without a trial.

The facts shown on the record before us are these. Carter was hired by the Federal Bureau of Investigation (FBI) in 1960 as a clerk in its identification division. His employment with the Bureau was interrupted by his enlistment in the Air Force. After completing his military service in 1965 he was reinstated at his old job. In August 1965, the FBI received an anonymous letter complaining that Carter was "sleeping with young girls and carrying on." When questioned about the matter by his supervisor, Carter admitted that a female friend had twice stayed overnight at his apartment. He admitted that they slept together, although not nude, in the same bed, but insisted that they did not have sexual relations. He told his supervisor that the lady had been visiting Washington from out of town for a period of three days, that they had been going together for several years, and that he was seriously considering marriage. On one occasion she had visited at his home in Kentucky and stayed with his brother and sister-in-law. . . .

Carter was dismissed by the FBI for "conduct unbecoming an employee of this Bureau." . . . Carter sued for reinstatement and backpay, and served interrogatories. Without answering, the Government pressed a motion for summary judgment, which the District Court granted, holding that appellant was not entitled to a trial.

We affirm the District Court's ruling that Carter had no statutory rights to employment under the Civil Service laws or the Veterans Preference Act. However we cannot agree with the District Court's conclusion that Carter was not entitled to a trial to determine whether the discharge violated Section 9 (c) of the Universal Military Training and Service Act, 50 U.S.C. App. § 459 (c) (1964). We do not rule on appellant's claim of unconstitutional arbitrariness.[4]

Because of the exemption of the FBI from the civil service laws, the Bureau is generally free to discharge its employees for any reasons it chooses, subject only to constitutional limitations. Obviously, however, that discretion is subject to any specific limitations that Congress has chosen to impose. This much is conceded by appellee. Thus, like any other employer, the FBI is subject to the provisions of § 9 (c) of the Universal Military Training and Service Act by which Congress granted special rights and protections to the returning veteran: the right to reinstatement in the civilian job he held prior to military service; the right to be free in the first year after resumption of civilian life from discharge for other than "cause."

The law giving a returning veteran a right to be free of discharge except for "cause" puts on the employer the burden of coming forward with a cause sufficient to justify the discharge. . . .

The FBI asserts that it had "cause" to dismiss Carter. Essentially the contention is that any FBI employee would be fired for this conduct, and the application of

---

[4] It seems plain to us that no discharge could be for "cause" within the meaning of § 9 (c) if it were so arbitrary and unreasonable as to violate due process. We therefore need not reach constitutional questions in this case.

a general FBI personnel policy which does not discriminate against veterans must be upheld unless so arbitrary as to violate due process.

A private employer may have the right, in the absence of statute or contract to the contrary, to fire an employee for personal reasons, unrelated to job function, that appeal to the employer, the color of hair, a dislike of men who smoke, or have a tattoo, etc. That does not mean that the employer can fire a returning veteran for the same reason as constituting "cause." . . .

The "cause" provision was inserted by Congress to provide the reemployed veteran with a protection of reasonableness similar to that enjoyed by a union member protected by provisions in a collective bargaining agreement limiting discharge to cause. The ultimate criterion, whether the employer acted reasonably, is the one generally applied where an employment contract is terminated by an employer because of employee misconduct, and that standard is appropriate under this Federal statute. Kemp v. John Chattillon & Sons, 169 F.2d 203 (3rd Cir. 1948). We think a discharge may be upheld as one for "cause" only if it meets two criteria of reasonableness: one, that it is reasonable to discharge employees because of certain conduct, and the other, that the employee had fair notice, express or fairly implied, that such conduct would be ground for discharge. . . .

The District Judge granted summary judgment on the ground that regardless of whether Carter's action was moral or immoral, he had been indiscreet in carrying on his relationship. The Government's brief also treats the nexus of the case as including: "that appellant's sexual misadventures had become sufficiently public knowledge to cause an anonymous complaint to the FBI" (p. 15).

That theory is not maintainable on the present record so as to support summary judgment without a trial. The only conduct before us on this record was limited to two occasions, and in Carter's own apartment. There is no suggestion here that Carter was notoriously promiscuous, consorted with prostitutes or anything of that sort. Certainly Carter's admitted conduct cannot be equated with that generally "loose" conduct likely to become a matter of public notoriety. The only basis for inferences as to the extent to which Carter's conduct was known outside the circle of his roommates — also employed by the FBI — is an anonymous letter. The letter does not indicate how the writer came to know of Carter's acts. . . .

The FBI may well have made an informed appraisal, or investigation, that permitted it to ascertain that Carter so conducted himself as to turn a private relationship into a public affront. But that is a question of fact and Carter is entitled to a trial of that fact.

We turn to the issue whether "cause" for discharge was established as a matter of law by Carter's admitted overnight "necking" and "petting" with his young lady in his apartment on two occasions. . . .

Appellant's counsel point out that Carter did nothing more than the "bundling" condoned in Puritan New England. As for more modern precedent, the law is clear that an unmarried man does not have an "immoral" character for purposes of exclusion from citizenship even if he goes beyond necking and engages in heterosexual relations. Judge Learned Hand pointed out, "we have answered in the negative the question whether an unmarried man must live completely celibate, or forfeit his claim to a 'good moral character.'" Schmidt v. United States, 177 F.2d 450, 452 (2d Cir. 1949).

The Government's motion put before the court, as an exhibit, the Handbook for FBI Employees, distributed to all FBI employees. We consider whether that Handbook shows that Carter was put on notice that his admitted conduct was prohibited. The Handbook is a description of the FBI and its work, as well as a "guide" to "help you refrain from doing anything which would in any way detract from the Bureau's reputation or embarrass it in any manner." The sole relevant passage is one stating — "personal misbehavior of Bureau employees reflecting unfavorably upon them or the Bureau, and neglect of duty cannot be tolerated."

The Government invokes the standard of the lady from Dubuque and argues that as the FBI relies on the cooperation of the citizenry it is reasonable to compel moral standards for all employees — clerks as well as agents — that would satisfy that most upright lady. Pretermitting the issue whether the standard of the lady from Dubuque would have been reasonable if announced, there is a threshold problem, whether the employees have adequate notice of such a standard. The FBI employees are expressly told in the Handbook that legal gambling is permitted, as is off-duty use of intoxicants, yet these sit poorly with many upright citizens. We do not think a court can deny an employee a trial of the issue on the ground that this Handbook clearly puts FBI employees on notice that they must meet not only the general standards of their own community, but also the special standards of the lady from Dubuque. . . .

The question is whether the limitation on private life now asserted to apply to all FBI employees is something the average FBI clerical employee should and does know as contemplated by "ordinarily expected standards of personal conduct." We cannot say that the answer is so clear that Carter is not even entitled to a trial. . . .

The order of the District Court is vacated and the case remanded for further proceedings.

So ordered.

DANAHER, Circuit Judge (dissenting): . . .

This court on many occasions has recognized the principle that the power to remove inferior Government employees is an incident of the power to appoint them, following the statement in Myers v. United States, 272 U.S. 52, 161, 47 S. Ct. 21, 71 L. Ed. 160 (1925). Put another way the interest of a Government employee in retaining his job can be summarily denied. "It has become a settled principle that government employment, in the absence of legislation, can be revoked at the will of the appointing officer." Cafeteria and Restaurant Workers, etc. v. McElroy, 367 U.S. 886, 896, 81 S. Ct. 1743, 1749, 6 L. Ed. 2d 1230 (1961); Vitarelli v. Seaton, 359 U.S. 535, 539, 79 S. Ct. 968, 3 L. Ed. 2d 1012 (1959). No matter who has stated the law, no one has said it better than Mr. Justice Reed speaking for the Court of Claims in Batchelor v. United States, 169 Ct. Cl. 180, 183, cert. denied, 382 U.S. 870, 86 S. Ct. 147, 15 L. Ed. 2d 109 (1965), where we read:

"The Supreme Court in Keim v. United States, 177 U.S. 290 (1900), considered the question of whether or not the courts may supervise the acts of an executive department head in discharging an employee. The Court's decision in that case clearly placed the removal of executive department employees within the ambit of executive discretion, and ruled that until Congress, by 'special and direct legislation makes provisions to the contrary,' the courts cannot review the soundness or propriety of the exercise of the department head's discretion. This case stands as a solid milestone in a long line of unbroken authorities holding that where there are no established procedures or statutes to be followed, removal of an employee is solely within the discretion of agency officials and accordingly may be effected without giving reason. See Cafeteria Workers v. McElroy, 367 U.S. 886, 896-97 (1961) and cases cited therein.". . .

It has been suggested that the Handbook for FBI Employees is not sufficiently specific in pointing out that the Bureau cannot tolerate personal misbehavior of its employees "reflecting unfavorably upon them or the Bureau." It is true that the Handbook does not say that an FBI employee may not use profane and obscene language in denouncing his superiors in the presence of others. A fingerprint clerk is not enjoined against mocking or vilifying a police officer who brings in a "lifted" fingerprint for classification in furtherance of cooperation with the Bureau. Myriad examples of unspecified misbehavior will suggest themselves. Something is lacking, it is argued, in that the Handbook did not particularize with respect to any such illustration, or by way of denouncing the very conduct under discussion here, admitted by Carter who "told exactly what happened." If an employee of the Bureau did not know that he was expected to comply satisfactorily with "ordinarily accepted standards of personal conduct," I would suppose he did not belong in the Bureau in the first place. Were I required to do so, I would rule that the Director had ample cause for dismissing Carter. . . .

## ANDREWS v. DREW MUNICIPAL SCHOOL DISTRICT

United States Court of Appeals, Fifth Circuit
507 F.2d 611 (1975),
*cert. dismissed*, 44 USLW 4627 (1976)

SIMPSON, Circuit Judge:

This suit attacking the validity of the Drew Municipal School District's rule against employing parents of illegitimate children was initiated by two such parents, both mothers, against whom the rule militated. Named as defendants were the Drew Municipal School District (the District), George Ferris Pettey, its Superintendent, and the individual members of the District's Board of Trustees (the Board).

The complaint sought declaratory and injunctive relief to "redress the deprivation of rights and privileges and immunities of the plaintiffs guaranteed by the (sic) 42 U.S.C. 1981, 1983 et seq., Title VI of the Civil Rights Act of 1964, 42 U.S.C. Section 2000d et seq., the Fifth and Fourteenth Amendments to the United States Constitution. Plaintiffs further asked for declaratory relief under 28 U.S.C. Sections 2201, 2202." Jurisdiction was invoked under Title 28 U.S.C. Section 1343.

Following a series of hearings the district court decided the case on the merits, holding that the rule violated both the Equal Protection Clause and the Due Process Clause of the Fourteenth Amendment. . . . We affirm for reasons stated below.

In the Spring of 1972, Superintendent Pettey learned that there were some teacher aides presently employed in the District who were parents of illegitimate children. Disturbed by this knowledge, Pettey immediately implemented an unwritten edict to the effect that parenthood of an illegitimate child would automatically disqualify an individual, whether incumbent or applicant, from employment with the school system.[2] . . .

---

[2] Pettey in testimony indicated confusion as to the expanse of the policy he had promulgated. He was positive that the rule should apply to all instructional personnel. Upon questioning, he expanded the list to include not only teachers and teacher aides, but also secretaries, librarians, dieticians, cafeteria operators, nurses, social workers, school principals, school volunteers and even PTA presidents. Although he was not positive, he did not think the rule should apply to bus drivers, janitors or maids.

Mrs. Fred McCorkle is one of the administrators responsible for implementing the unwed parent policy. As Coordinator of Elementary Instruction for the school district, she is in charge of the teacher aide program and recommends to Pettey who shall be hired to fill teacher aide vacancies. . . .

Both plaintiffs-appellees, Lestine Rogers and Katie Mae Andrews, were victims of the unwed parent policy. Lestine Rogers was hired as a teacher aide in the Fall preceding the initiation of the rule, although her application stated that she was single and had a child. After the Pettey policy rule was announced, Mrs. McCorkle informed Ms. Rogers that because she was the parent of an illegitimate child, she would not be re-hired for the following year. Katie Mae Andrews, on the other hand, knew about the Pettey rule prior to applying for a teacher aide position. Although she too was the mother of an illegitimate child, she did not so indicate on her application. Mrs. McCorkle learned of Ms. Andrews' illegitimate child in the course of her investigation of the application. . . .

From the beginning, unwed mothers only, not unwed fathers, were adversely affected by the rule. This factor coupled with the conclusion that the policy, by its nature, could only be applied against females, led the district court to hold alternatively that "assuming a rational relation does exist between the Drew policy and legitimate educational objectives, the rule creates an inherently suspect classification based on sex, i.e. single women, which cannot survive strict scrutiny mandated by the Fourteenth Amendment." 371 F.Supp. at 35. The district court's primary holding was that the rule "has no rational relation to the objectives ostensibly sought to be achieved by the school officials and is fraught with invidious discrimination; thus it is constitutionally defective under the traditional, and most lenient, standard of equal protection and violative of due process as well." Ibid. at 31. Thus this appeal concerns a policy or rule that has not only been held to violate equal protection for alternative reasons, but has also been held to violate due process. On the basis relied upon by the district court of traditional notions of equal protection, because the policy created an irrational classification, we affirm.[5]

"Traditional" equal protection analysis requires that legislative classifications must be sustained as long as the classification itself is rationally related to a legitimate governmental interest. . . .

. . . To find the governmental objective ostensibly served by the rule, we turn to the testimony of Superintendent Pettey, the rule's originator and explicator. Pettey's avowed objective was to create a scholastic environment which was conducive to the moral development as well as the intellectual development of the students. Certainly this objective is not without legitimacy. . . .

Schools have the right, if not the duty, to create a properly moral scholastic environment. See Beilan v. Board of Education, 1958, 357 U.S. 399, 78 S.Ct. 1317, 2 L.Ed.2d 1414. But the issue is not simply whether the objective itself is legitimate, but rather whether the Pettey rule "advances that objective in a manner consistent with the Equal Protection Clause," Reed v. Reed, 1971, 404 U.S. 71, 76, 92 S.Ct. 251, 254, 30 L.Ed.2d 225. We hold that it does not.

The District offers three possible rationales through which it asserts that its rule under attack furthers the creation of a properly moral scholastic environment: (1) unwed parenthood is prima facie proof of immorality; (2) unwed parents are improper communal role models, after whom students may pattern

---

[5] Because we affirm upon traditional equal protection grounds, we do not consider the district court's alternative finding of a sex based classification or its legal conclusion that such classifications are inherently suspect.

their lives; (3) employment of an unwed parent in a scholastic environment materially contributes to the problem of school-girl pregnancies.

The first of these postulates violates not only the Equal Protection Clause, but the Due Process Clause as well. The law is clear that due process interdicts the adoption by a state of an irrebuttable presumption, as to which the presumed fact does not necessarily follow from the proven fact. See Cleveland Board of Education v. LaFleur, 1974, 414 U.S. 632, 94 S.Ct. 791, 39 L.Ed.2d 52; Vlandis v. Kline, 1973, 412 U.S. 441, 93 S.Ct. 2230, 37 L.Ed.2d 63; Stanley v. Illinois, 1972, 405 U.S. 645, 92 S.Ct. 1208, 31 L.Ed.2d 551. Thus, unless the presumed fact here, present immorality, necessarily follows from the proven fact, unwed parenthood, the conclusiveness inherent in the Pettey rule must be held to violate due process. We agree with the district court that the one does not necessarily follow the other:

> By the rule, a parent, whether male or female, who has had such a child, would be forever precluded from employment. Thus no consideration would be given to the subsequent marriage of the parent or to the length of time elapsed since the illegitimate birth, or to a person's reputation for good character in the community. A person could live an impeccable life, yet be barred as unfit for employment for an event, whether the result of indiscretion or not, occurring at any time in the past. But human experience refutes the dogmatic attitude inherent in such a policy against unwed parents. Can it be said that an engaged woman, who has premarital sex, becomes pregnant, and whose fiance dies or is killed prior to their marriage, is morally depraved for bearing the posthumous child? The rule allows no compassion for the person who has been unwittingly subjected to sexual relations through force, deceptive design or while under the influence of drugs or alcohol, yet chooses to have the child rather than to abort it. The rules makes no distinction between the sexual neophyte and the libertine. In short, the rule leaves no consideration for the multitudinous circumstances under which illegitimate childbirth may occur and which may have little, if any, bearing on the parent's present moral worth. A past biological event like childbirth out of wedlock, even if relevant to the issue, may not be controlling; and that it may be considered more conventional or circumspect for the infant to be surrendered to others for upbringing rather than be reared by the natural parent is hardly determinative of the matter. Furthermore, the policy, if based on moral judgment, has inherent if unintended defects or shortcomings. While obviously aimed at discouraging prematerial (sic) sex relations, the policy's effect is apt to encourage abortion, which is itself staunchly opposed by some on ethical or moral grounds. It totally ignores, as a disqualification, the occurrence of extra-marital sex activity, though thought of by many as a more serious basis for moral culpability. Indeed, the superintendent's fiat, altogether unsupported by sociological data, equates the single fact of illegitimate birth with irredeemable moral disease. Such a presumption is not only patently absurd, it is mischievous and prejudicial, requiring those who administer the policy to "investigate" the parental status of school employees and prospective applicants. Where no stigma may have existed before, such inquisitions by overzealous officialdom can rapidly create it. 371 F.Supp. at 33-34 (footnotes deleted).

The school district urges a second rationale for its rule based upon the holding in McConnell v. Anderson, 8 Cir. 1971, 451 F.2d 193:

"What the school board looks at is whether, moral considerations aside, proper educational growth can be furthered and respect for marriage ingrained by employing unwed parents. The question then becomes whether the open and notorious existence of the status as an unwed parent would injure the affected students." Reply Brief of Defendants/Appellants, p. 5. . . .

We do not consider *McConnell* supportive of the District's position. The record before us contains no evidence of proselytizing of pupils by the plaintiffs and reveals instead that each plaintiff, along with her illegitimate offspring, is living under the same roof as her parents, brothers and sisters. It would be a wise child indeed who could infer knowledge of either plaintiff's unwed parent status based on the manner of plaintiffs' existence. . . .

The third rationale proffered by the school district in hopes of salvaging the Pettey rule, that the presence of unwed parents in a scholastic environment materially contributes to school-girl pregnancies is without support, other than speculation and assertions of opinion, in the record before us.

Because we hold that the Board rule under attack violated traditional concepts of equal protection, we find it unnecessary to discuss numerous other issues urged on appeal by appellees or in their behalf by *amici curiae*; for example, whether the rule creates a suspect classification based upon race or sex, or whether it infringes upon some constitutionally protected interest such as the right to privacy or the right to procreation. . . .

## NOTES

1. To what extent should the "right of privacy" protect public employees against arbitrary employment regulations? *Cf.* Griswold v. Connecticut, 381 U.S. 479 (1965) (invalidating Connecticut's ban against giving information about contraception or using birth control devices); Stanley v. Georgia, 394 U.S. 557 (1969) (holding that the private and personal use and viewing of obscene materials may not be made a crime).

2. In O'Neil, *The Private Lives of Public Employees,* 51 Ore. L. Rev. 70, 105-106 (1971), the author suggests that the courts must evaluate the following factors in weighing the substantiality of governmental interests against infringement of personal freedoms in cases involving the regulation of the private lives of public employees: What is the effect, if any, upon the individual's job performance? What is the effect, if any, upon the efficiency of the agency? What is the effect, if any, on the image of and public confidence in the agency? O'Neil concludes that "judgments about governmental interests cannot be made in the abstract . . . [and that] the following factors . . . have been deemed pertinent by courts in passing upon recent public employment dismissals: (a) How sensitive is the position held or sought? . . . (b) Have other members of the agency or institution been involved? . . . (c) Was the behavior recent and is it recurrent? . . . (d) What is the probability of repetition? . . . (e) How does the transgression relate to the employee's entire record? . . . What is the status of the behavior outside the public service? . . . How clear and specific is the standard of conduct? . . . What less onerous alternatives are available to the agency? . . . What procedures are provided within the agency?"

## MURRAY v. JAMISON

### 333 F. Supp. 1379 (W.D.N.C. 1971)

McMillan, D. J.: The plaintiff was discharged from employment as a switchboard operator or dispatcher by the Building Inspection Department of the City of Charlotte immediately after his supervisors discovered that he was the Grand Dragon of the Ku Klux Klan of North Carolina. Under the circumstances this discharge was unlawful under the First and Fourteenth Amendments to the United States Constitution, and the defendants will be directed to take appropriate remedial action. . . .

The Ku Klux Klan is known and shown by this record to be a segregationist "white supremacy" organization. Its bloody history is well known. Its oath of allegiance requires secrecy; its history is totally repugnant to all who favor constitutional government or who believe that all persons are entitled to due process and to equal protection of laws.

Klansmen, like Negroes, are people. They are entitled to associate together and to speak their minds. They are not by virtue of Klan membership disqualified from holding public employment any more than is a Presbyterian or a Black Panther or a member of the United Daughters of the Confederacy or of the Daughters of the American Revolution or the American Legion or the NAACP.

If membership in the Klan does prevent adequate performance of public duty it may be cause for discharge or discipline. The objectives of employment are usually fairly well defined, and they do not ordinarily include using the employer's time or the position of the job to further private pursuits. However, in the absence of a showing that Klansmanship has produced or is genuinely likely to produce a lower quality of performance of the employee's duties, the constitutional rights of free speech and free association and the interests of society in the encouragement of free thought and debate prevent public authorities from discharging public employees merely because of views and associations not approved of by the temporary bearer of the supervisory duty. Constitution of the United States, First and Fourteenth Amendments; Wieman v. Updegraff, 344 U.S. 183 (1952); Battle v. Mulholland, 439 F.2d 321 (5th Cir. 1971).

Plaintiff was wrongfully discharged.

## KELLEY v. JOHNSON

United States Supreme Court
425 U.S. 238 (1976)

MR. JUSTICE REHNQUIST delivered the opinion of the Court.

The District Court for the Eastern District of New York originally dismissed respondent's complaint seeking declaratory and injunctive relief against a regulation promulgated by petitioner limiting the length of a policeman's hair. On respondent's appeal to the Court of Appeals for the Second Circuit, that judgment was reversed, and on remand the District Court took testimony and thereafter granted the relief sought by respondent. The Court of Appeals affirmed, and we granted certiorari, 421 U.S. 987 (1975), to consider the constitutional doctrine embodied in the rulings of the Court of Appeals. We reverse.

I

In 1971 respondent's predecessor, individually and as president of the Suffolk County Patrolmen's Benevolent Association, brought this action under the Civil Rights Act of 1871, 42 U.S.C. § 1983, against petitioner's predecessor, the Commissioner of the Suffolk County Police Department. The Commissioner had promulgated Order No. 71-1, which established hair grooming standards applicable to male members of the police force.[1] . . . The regulation was attacked as violative of respondent patrolman's right of free expression under the First Amendment and his guarantees of due process and equal protection under the Fourteenth Amendment, in that it was "not based upon the generally accepted standard of grooming in the community" and placed "an undue restriction" upon his activities therein.

The Court of Appeals held that cases characterizing the uniform civilian services as "para-military," and sustaining hair regulations on that basis, were not soundly grounded historically. It said the fact that a police force is organized "with a centralized administration and a disciplined rank and file for efficient conduct of its affairs" did not foreclose respondent's claim, but instead bore only upon "the existence of a legitimate state interest to be reasonably advanced by the regulation." Dwen v. Barry, 483 F.2d 1126, 1128-1129 (1973). The Court of Appeals went on to decide that "choice of personal appearance is an ingredient of an individual's personal liberty" and is protected by the Fourteenth Amendment. It further held that the police department had "failed to make the slightest showing of the relationship between its regulation and the legitimate interest it sought to promote." Id., at 1130-1131. On the basis of this reasoning it concluded that neither dismissal nor summary judgment in the District Court was appropriate, since the department "has the burden of establishing a genuine public need for the regulation." Id., at 1131.

Thereafter the District Court, under the compulsion of the remand from the Court of Appeals, took testimony on the question of whether or not there was a "genuine public need." The sole witness was the Deputy Commissioner of the Suffolk County Police Department, petitioner's subordinate, who testified as to the police department's concern for the safety of the patrolmen, and the need for some standards of uniformity in appearance. The District Court held that "no proof" was offered to support any claim of the need for the protection of the police officer, and that while "proper grooming" is an ingredient of a good police department's "esprit de corps," petitioner's standards did not establish a public need because they ultimately reduced to "[u]niformity for uniformity's sake." The District Court granted the relief prayed for by respondent, and on petitioner's appeal that judgment was affirmed without opinion by the Court of Appeals.

## II

Section I of the Fourteenth Amendment to the United States Constitution provides in pertinent part:

"[No State] shall . . . deprive any person of life, liberty, or property, without due process of law."

This section affords not only a procedural guarantee against the deprivation of "liberty," but likewise protects substantive aspects of liberty against unconstitutional restriction by the State. Board of Regents v. Roth, 408 U.S. 564,

---

[1] "2/75.1 HAIR: Hair shall be neat, clean, trimmed, and present a groomed appearance. Hair will not touch the ears or the collar except the closely cut hair on the back of the neck. Hair in front will be groomed so that it does not fall below the band of properly worn headgear. In no case will the bulk or length of the hair interfere with the proper wear of any authorized headgear. The acceptability of a member's hair style will be based upon the criteria in this paragraph and not upon the style in which he chooses to wear his hair."

572 (1972); Griswold v. Connecticut, 381 U.S. 479, 502 (1965) (WHITE, J., concurring).

The "liberty" interest claimed by respondent here, of course, is distinguishable from those protected by the Court in Roe v. Wade, 410 U.S. 113 (1973); Eisenstadt v. Baird, 405 U.S. 438 (1972); Stanley v. Illinois, 405 U.S. 645 (1972); *Griswold v. Connecticut, supra;* and Meyer v. Nebraska, 262 U.S. 390 (1923). Each of those cases involved a substantial claim of infringement on the individual's freedom of choice with respect to certain basic matters of procreation, marriage, and family life. But whether the citizenry at large has some sort of "liberty" interest within the Fourteenth Amendment in matters of personal appearance is a question on which this Court's cases offer little, if any, guidance. We can, nevertheless, assume an affirmative answer for purposes of deciding this case, because we find that assumption insufficient to carry the day for respondent's claim.

Respondent has sought the protection of the Fourteenth Amendment not as a member of the citizenry at large, but on the contrary as an employee of the police force of Suffolk County, a subdivision of the State of New York. While the Court of Appeals made passing reference to this distinction, it was thereafter apparently ignored. We think, however, it is highly significant. In Pickering v. Board of Education, 391 U.S. 563, 568 (1968), after noting that state employment may not be conditioned on the relinquishment of First Amendment rights, the Court stated that "[a]t the same time it cannot be gainsaid that the State has interests as an employer in regulating the speech of its employees that differ significantly from those it possesses in connection with regulation of the speech of the citizenry in general." More recently, we have sustained comprehensive and substantial restrictions upon activities of both federal and state employees lying at the core of the First Amendment. Civil Serv. Comm'n v. Letter Carriers, 413 U.S. 548 (1973); Broadrick v. Oklahoma, 413 U.S. 601 (1973). If such state regulations may survive challenges based on the explicit language of the First Amendment, there is surely even more room for restrictive regulations of state employees where the claim implicates only the more general contours of the substantive liberty interest protected by the Fourteenth Amendment.

The hair length regulation here touches respondent as an employee of the county and, more particularly, as a policeman. Respondent's employer has, in accordance with its well-established duty to keep the peace, placed myriad demands upon the members of the police force, duties which have no counterpart with respect to the public at large. Respondent must wear a standard uniform, specific in each detail. When in uniform he must salute the flag. He cannot take an active role in local political affairs by way of being a party delegate or contributing or soliciting political contributions. He cannot smoke in public. All of these and other regulations of the Suffolk County Police Department infringe on respondent's freedom of choice in personal matters, and it was apparently in view of the Court of Appeals that the burden is on the State to prove a "genuine public need" for each and every one of these regulations.

. . . .

The promotion of safety of persons and property is unquestionably at the core of the State's police power, and virtually all state and local governments employ a uniformed police force to aid in the accomplishment of that purpose. Choice of organization, dress, and equipment for law enforcement personnel is a decision entitled to the same sort of presumption of legislative validity as are state choices designed to promote other aims within the cognizance of the State's police power. Day-Brite Lighting, Inc. v. Missouri, 342 U.S. 421, 423 (1952);

Prince v. Massachusetts, 321 U.S. 158, 168-170 (1944); Olsen v. Nebraska, 313 U.S. 236, 246-247 (1941). Having recognized in other contexts the wide latitude accorded the Government in the "dispatch of its own internal affairs," Cafeteria Workers v. McElroy, 367 U.S. 886, 896 (1961), we think Suffolk County's police regulations involved here are entitled to similar weight. Thus the question is not, as the Court of Appeals conceived it to be, whether the State can "establish" a "genuine public need" for the specific regulation. It is whether respondent can demonstrate that there is no rational connection between the regulation, based as it is on respondent's method of organizing its police force, and the promotion of safety of persons and property. United Public Workers v. Mitchell, 330 U.S. 75, 100-101 (1947); Jacobson v. Massachusetts, 197 U.S. 11, 30-31, 35-37 (1905).

We think the answer here is so clear that the District Court was quite right in the first instance to have dismissed respondent's complaint. Neither this Court, the Court of Appeals, or the District Court is in a position to weigh the policy arguments in favor of and against a rule regulating hair styles as a part of regulations governing a uniformed civilian service. The constitutional issue to be decided by these courts is whether petitioner's determination that such regulations should be enacted is so irrational that it may be branded "arbitrary," and therefore a deprivation of respondent's "liberty" interest in freedom to choose his own hair style. Williamson v. Lee Optical Co., 348 U.S. 483, 487-488 (1955). The overwhelming majority of state and local police of the present day are uniformed. This fact itself testifies to the recognition by those who direct those operations, and by the people of the States and localities who directly or indirectly choose such persons, that similarity in appearance of police officers is desirable. This choice may be based on a desire to make police officers readily recognizable to the members of the public, or a desire for the *esprit de corps* which such similarity is felt to inculcate within the police force itself. Either one is a sufficiently rational justification for regulations so as to defeat respondent's claim based on the liberty guaranty of the Fourteenth Amendment.

The regulation challenged here did not violate any right guaranteed respondent by the Fourteenth Amendment to the United States Constitution, and the Court of Appeals was therefore wrong in reversing the District Court's original judgment dismissing the action. The judgment of the Court of Appeals is

*Reversed.*

## NOTES

1. A board of education dress code requiring male teachers to wear neckties was held to be unconstitutional in that it interfered with a teacher's constitutional rights without significantly furthering the board's stated objectives. The plaintiff teacher claimed that somewhat less formal dress would help him achieve a better rapport with the students and thus enhance his teaching ability. The court held that there was a liberty interest involved in personal dress, an issue not decided in *Kelley,* and that a First Amendment academic freedom concern was raised by the teacher's contention that his teaching was impeded by the dress code. The board's countervailing interests in establishing a professional image for teachers, promoting good grooming in students, and maintaining decorum in the classroom were insufficient to outweigh the intrusion on both First and Fourteenth Amendment rights. East Hartford Education Association v. Board of Education, 562 F.2d 838 (2nd Cir. 1977).

2. In Keckeisen v. Independent School District No. 612, 509 F.2d 1062 (8th Cir. 1975), *cert. denied,* 423 U.S. 833 (1975), a Minnesota public school board policy prohibiting employment of a husband and wife in an administrator/teacher relationship "where a

conflict of interest could arise" was held not to be an unconstitutional violation of the right to marry.

3. In a case challenging the Illinois Supreme Court rule that official court reporters abstain from private reporting activities, the Seventh Circuit, citing *Kelley v. Johnson,* held that the regulation did not violate the Fourteenth Amendment. The court reporters had failed to meet the burden of demonstrating that "there is no rational connection between the regulation and the state purpose it promotes, based as it is upon the state's need for the expeditious handling of their work and the avoidance of any conflict of interest which may arise from their outside commercial activities." Youker v. Gulley, 536 F.2d 184 (7th Cir. 1976).

4. Some municipalities require that public employees reside within city limits while employed by the city. Challenges to such regulations as violative of the individual employee's right to travel have not been sustained. In McCarthy v. Philadelphia Civil Service Commission, 424 U.S. 645 (1976), an employee of the Philadelphia Fire Department pursuant to a municipal regulation was terminated because he moved his permanent residence from Philadelphia to New Jersey. The Supreme Court, in a per curiam decision, upheld the regulation, stating that under the circumstances of this case, the regulation was valid as to both initial hiring and the duration of employment.

5. The criminal conviction for possession of marijuana of a 53 year old worker with 17 years combined military and civilian service was held to be insufficient cause for terminating his employment in Young v. Hampton, 568 F.2d 1253 (7th Cir. 1977). Citing *Norton,* the court held that since the government had produced no evidence that the efficiency of the service would be promoted in any way by the discharge, and the evidence submitted by the appellant indicated that there would be no impairment of efficiency, the conviction alone was insufficient to justify termination. For other cases involving termination for criminal activity, distinguished on various grounds by the court in *Young,* see Taffel v. Hampton, 463 F.2d 251 (5th Cir. 1972); Dew v. Halaby, 317 F.2d 582 (D.C. Cir. 1963), *cert. dismissed,* 379 U.S. 951, 85 S.Ct. 452, 13 L. Ed. 2d 550 (1964); Embrey v. Hampton, 470 F.2d 146 (4th Cir. 1972); Wathen v. United States, 527 F.2d 1191 (Ct. Cl. 1975), *cert. denied,* 429 U.S. 821, 97 S.Ct. 69, 50 L. Ed. 2d 82 (1976); Giles v. United States, 553 F.2d 647 (Ct. Cl. 1977); Gueory v. Hampton, 510 F.2d 1222 (D.C. Cir. 1974).

6. A regulation of the New York City Transit Authority which excluded all persons from employment if they were participating in or had successfully concluded a methadone maintenance program was challenged under § 1983 and held to be an unconstitutional violation of the equal protection and due process clauses of the Fourteenth Amendment. The Second Circuit stated that the District Court's conclusion that the rule has no rational relationship to the performance of the jobs affected was firmly supported by the Supreme Court decision in *Sugarman v. Dougall,* 413 U.S. 634 (1973). The Supreme Court has granted certiorari to decide, inter alia, if the denial of employment to former heroin addicts participating in methadone programs is unconstitutional under the Fourteenth Amendment. Beazer v. New York City Transit Authority, 558 F.2d 97 (2d Cir. 1977), *cert. granted,* 46 USLW 3787 (June 27, 1978).

# B. PROCEDURAL DUE PROCESS AS A PROTECTION AGAINST DISMISSAL FROM PUBLIC EMPLOYMENT

## BOARD OF REGENTS v. ROTH

Supreme Court of the United States
408 U.S. 564, 92 S. Ct. 2701, 33 L. Ed. 2d 548 (1972)

MR. JUSTICE STEWART delivered the opinion of the Court.

In 1968 the respondent, David Roth was hired for his first teaching job as assistant professor of political science at Wisconsin State University-Oshkosh. He was hired for a fixed term of one academic year. The notice of his faculty appointment specified that his employment would begin on September 1, 1968, and would end on June 30, 1969. The respondent completed that term. But he was informed that he would not be rehired for the next academic year.

The respondent had no tenure rights to continued employment. Under Wisconsin statutory law a state university teacher can acquire tenure as a "permanent" employee only after four years of year-to-year employment. Having acquired tenure, a teacher is entitled to continued employment "during efficiency and good behavior." A relatively new teacher without tenure, however, is under Wisconsin law entitled to nothing beyond his one-year appointment. There are no statutory or administrative standards defining eligibility for re-employment. State law thus clearly leaves the decision whether to rehire a nontenured teacher for another year to the unfettered discretion of University officials. . . . Rules promulgated by the Board of Regents provide that a nontenured teacher "dismissed" before the end of the year may have some opportunity for review of the "dismissal." But the Rules provide no real protection for a nontenured teacher who simply is not re-employed for the next year. He must be informed by February first "concerning retention or non-retention for the ensuing year." But "no reason for non-retention need be given. No review or appeal is provided in such case."

In conformance with these Rules, the President of Wisconsin State University-Oshkosh informed the respondent before February 1, 1969, that he would not be rehired for the 1969-1970 academic year. He gave the respondent no reason for the decision and no opportunity to challenge it at any sort of hearing.

The respondent then brought this action in a federal district court alleging that the decision not to rehire him for the next year infringed his Fourteenth Amendment rights. He attacked the decision both in substance and procedure. First, he alleged that the true reason for the decision was to punish him for certain statements critical of the University administration, and that it therefore violated his right to freedom of speech.[5] Second, he alleged that the failure of University officials to give him notice of any reason for nonretention and an opportunity for a hearing violated his right to procedural due process of law.

The District Court granted summary judgment for the respondent on the procedural issue, ordering the University officials to provide him with reasons and a hearing. 310 F. Supp. 972. The Court of Appeals, with one judge dissenting, affirmed this partial summary judgment. 446 F.2d 806. We granted certiorari. 404 U.S. 909, 92 S. Ct. 227, 30 L. Ed. 2d 181. The only question presented to us at this stage in the case is whether the respondent had a constitutional right to a statement of reasons and a hearing on the University's decision not to rehire him for another year.[6] We hold that he did not.

---

[5] While the respondent alleged that he was not rehired because of his exercise of free speech, the petitioners insisted that the non-retention decision was based on other, constitutionally valid grounds. The District Court came to no conclusion whatever regarding the true reason for the University President's decision. . . .

[6] The courts that have to decide whether a nontenured public employee has a right to a statement of reasons or a hearing upon nonrenewal of his contract have come to varying conclusions. Some have held that neither procedural safeguard is required. *E.g.*, Orr v. Trinter, 444 F.2d 128 (CA6); Jones v. Hopper, 410 F.2d 1323 (CA10); Freeman v. Gould Special School District, 405 F.2d 1153 (CA8). At least one court has held that there is a right to a statement of reasons but not a hearing. Drown v. Portsmouth School District, 435 F.2d 1182 (CA1). And another has held that both requirements depend on whether the employee has an "expectancy" of continued employment. Ferguson v. Thomas, 430 F.2d 852, 856 (CA5).

The requirements of procedural due process apply only to the deprivation of interests encompassed within the Fourteenth Amendment's protection of liberty and property. When protected interests are implicated the right to some kind of prior hearing is paramount.[7] But the range of interests protected by procedural due process is not infinite. . . .

Undeniably, the respondent's re-employment prospects were of major concern to him — concern that we surely cannot say was insignificant. And a weighing process has long been a part of any determination of the *form* of hearing required in particular situations by procedural due process. But, to determine whether due process requirements apply in the first place, we must look not to the "weight" but to the *nature* of the interest at stake. See Morrissey v. Brewer, 405 U.S. —, —, 92 S. Ct. 2593, 32 L. Ed. 2d —. We must look to see if the interest is within the Fourteenth Amendment's protection of liberty and property.

"Liberty" and "property" are broad and majestic terms. They are among the "[g]reat [constitutional] concepts . . . purposely left to gather meaning from experience. . . . [T]hey relate to the whole domain of social and economic fact, and the statesmen who founded this Nation knew too well that only a stagnant society remains unchanged." National Mutual Ins. Co. v. Tidewater Transfer Co., 337 U.S. 582, 646, 69 S. Ct. 1173, 1195, 93 L. Ed. 1556 (Frankfurter, J., dissenting). For that reason the Court has fully and finally rejected the wooden distinction between "rights" and "privileges" that once seemed to govern the applicability of procedural due process rights.[9] The Court has also made clear that the property interests protected by procedural due process extend well beyond actual ownership of real estate, chattels, or money.[10] By the same token, the Court has required due process protection for deprivations of liberty beyond the sort of formal constraints imposed by the criminal process.

Yet, while the Court has eschewed rigid or formalistic limitations on the protection of procedural due process, it has at the same time observed certain boundaries. For the words "liberty" and "property" in the Due Process Clause of the Fourteenth Amendment must be given some meaning. . . .

The State, in declining to rehire the respondent, did not make any charge against him that might seriously damage his standing and associations in his community. It did not base the nonrenewal of his contract on a charge, for example, that he had been guilty of dishonesty, or immorality. Had it done so, this would be a different case. For "[w]here a person's good name, reputation, honor, or integrity is at stake because of what the government is doing to him, notice and an opportunity to be heard are essential." . . .

---

[7] Before a person is deprived of a protected interest, he must be afforded opportunity for some kind of a hearing, "except for extraordinary situations where some valid governmental interest is at stake that justifies postponing the hearing until after the event." . . .

[9] In a leading case decided many years ago, the Court of Appeals for the District of Columbia Circuit held that public employment in general was a "privilege," not a "right," and that procedural due process guarantees therefore were inapplicable. Bailey v. Richardson, 86 U.S. App. D.C. 248, 182 F.2d 46, aff'd by an equally divided Court, 341 U.S. 918, 71 S. Ct. 669, 95 L. Ed. 1352. The basis of this holding has been thoroughly undermined in the ensuing years. For, as Mr. Justice Blackmun wrote for the Court only last year, "this Court now has rejected the concept that constitutional rights turn upon whether a governmental benefit is characterized as a 'right' or as a 'privilege.' " Graham v. Richardson, 403 U.S. 365, 374, 91 S. Ct. 1848, 1853, 29 L. Ed. 2d 534.

[10] *See, e.g.,* Connell v. Higginbotham, 403 U.S. 207, 208, 91 S. Ct. 1772, 1773, 29 L. Ed. 2d 418; Bell v. Burson, 402 U.S. 535, 91 S. Ct. 1586, 29 L. Ed. 2d 90; Goldberg v. Kelly, 397 U.S. 254, 90 S. Ct. 1011, 25 L. Ed. 2d 287.

In such a case, due process would accord an opportunity to refute the charge before University officials. In the present case, however, there is no suggestion whatever that the respondent's interest in his "good name, reputation, honor or integrity" is at stake.

Similarly, there is no suggestion that the State, in declining to re-employ the respondent, imposed on him a stigma or other disability that foreclosed his freedom to take advantage of other employment opportunities. The State, for example, did not invoke any regulations to bar the respondent from all other public employment in State universities. Had it done so, this, again, would be a different case. . . .

To be sure, the respondent has alleged that the nonrenewal of his contract was based on his exercise of his right to freedom of speech. But this allegation is not now before us. The District Court stated proceedings on this issue, and the respondent has yet to prove that the decision not to rehire him was, in fact, based on his free speech activities.[14]

Hence, on the record before us, all that clearly appears is that the respondent was not rehired for one year at one University. It stretches the concept too far to suggest that a person is deprived of "liberty" when he simply is not rehired in one job but remains as free as before to seek another. Cafeteria Workers v. McElroy, 367 U.S. at 895-896, 81 S. Ct. at 1748-1749, 6 L. Ed. 2d 1230.

The Fourteenth Amendment's procedural protection of property is a safeguard of the security of interests that a person has already acquired in specific benefits. These interests — property interests — may take many forms.

Thus the Court has held that a person receiving welfare benefits under statutory and administrative standards defining eligibility for them has an interest in continued receipt of those benefits that is safeguarded by procedural due process. Goldberg v. Kelly, 397 U.S. 254, 90 S. Ct. 1011, 25 L. Ed. 2d 287. Similarly, in the area of public employment, the Court has held that a public college professor dismissed from an office held under tenure provisions, Slochower v. Board of Education, 350 U.S. 551, 76 S. Ct. 637, 100 L. Ed. 692, and college professors and staff members dismissed during the terms of their contracts, Wieman v. Updegraff, 344 U.S. 183, 73 S. Ct. 215, 97 L. Ed. 216, have interests in continued employment that are safeguarded by due process. Only last year, the Court held that this principle "proscribing summary dismissal from public employment without hearing or inquiry required by due process" also applied to a teacher recently hired without tenure or a formal contract, but nonetheless with a clearly implied promise of continued employment. Connell v. Higginbotham, 403 U.S. 207, 208, 91 S. Ct. 1772, 1773, 29 L. Ed. 2d 418.

---

[14] See n. 5, *infra*. The Court of Appeals, nonetheless, argued that opportunity for a hearing and a statement of reasons were required here "as a *prophylactic* against non-retention decisions improperly motivated by exercise of protected rights." 446 F.2d, at 810 (emphasis supplied). While the Court of Appeals recognized the lack of a finding that the respondent's nonretention was based on exercise of the right of free speech, it felt that the respondent's interest in liberty was sufficiently implicated here because the decision not to rehire him was made "with a background of controversy and unwelcome expressions of opinion." *Ibid.*

When a State would directly impinge upon interests in free speech or free press, this Court has on occasion held that opportunity for a fair adversary hearing must precede the action, whether or not the speech or press interest is clearly protected under substantive First Amendment standards. . . .

In the respondent's case, however, the State has not directly impinged upon interests in free speech or free press in any way comparable to a seizure of books or an injunction against meetings. Whatever may be a teacher's rights of free speech, the interest in holding a teaching job at a state university, *simpliciter,* is not itself a free speech interest.

Certain attributes of "property" interests protected by procedural due process emerge from these decisions. To have a property interest in a benefit, a person clearly must have more than an abstract need or desire for it. He must have more than a unilateral expectation of it. He must, instead, have a legitimate claim of entitlement to it. It is a purpose of the ancient institution of property to protect those claims upon which people rely in their daily lives, reliance that must not be arbitrarily undermined. It is a purpose of the constitutional right to a hearing to provide an opportunity for a person to vindicate those claims.

Property interests, of course, are not created by the Constitution. Rather they are created and their dimensions are defined by existing rules or understandings that stem from an independent source such as state law — rules or understandings that secure certain benefits and that support claims of entitlement to those benefits. Thus the welfare recipients in Goldberg v. Kelly, *supra*, had a claim of entitlement to welfare payments that was grounded in the statute defining eligibility for them. The recipients had not yet shown that they were, in fact, within the statutory terms of eligibility. But we held that they had a right to a hearing at which they might attempt to do so.

Just as the welfare recipients' "property" interest in welfare payments was created and defined by statutory terms, so the respondent's "property" interest in employment at the Wisconsin State University-Oshkosh was created and defined by the terms of his appointment. Those terms secured his interest in employment up to June 30, 1969. But the important fact in this case is that they specifically provided that the respondent's employment was to terminate on June 30. They did not provide for contract renewal absent "sufficient cause." Indeed, they made no provision for renewal whatsoever.

Thus the terms of the respondent's appointment secured absolutely no interest in re-employment for the next year. They supported absolutely no possible claim of entitlement to re-employment. Nor, significantly, was there any state statute or University rule or policy that secured his interest in re-employment or that created any legitimate claim to it.[16] In these circumstances, the respondent surely had an abstract concern in being rehired, but he did not have a *property* interest sufficient to require the University authorities to give him a hearing when they declined to renew his contract of employment. . . .

We must conclude that the summary judgment for the respondent should not have been granted, since the respondent has not shown that he was deprived of liberty or property protected by the Fourteenth Amendment. The judgment of the Court of Appeals, accordingly, is reversed and the case is remanded for further proceedings consistent with this opinion. It is so ordered. Reversed and remanded.

Mr. Justice Douglas, dissenting. . . .

Though Roth was rated by the faculty as an excellent teacher, he had publicly criticized the administration for suspending an entire group of 94 Black students without determining individual guilt. He also criticized the university's regime as being authoritarian and autocratic. He used his classroom to discuss what was being done about the Black episode; and one day, instead of meeting his class, he went to the meeting of the Board of Regents. . . .

---

[16] To be sure, the respondent does suggest that most teachers hired on a year-to-year basis by the Wisconsin State University-Oshkosh are, in fact, rehired. But the District Court has not found that there is anything approaching a "common law" of re-employment, see Perry v. Sindermann, 405 U.S. — at —, 92 S. Ct. 2694, at —, 32 L. Ed. 2d —, so strong as to require University officials to give the respondent a statement of reasons and a hearing on their decision not to rehire him.

Professor Will Herberg of Drew University. in wrting of "academic freedom" recently said:

> ". . . it is sometimes conceived as a basic constitutional right guaranteed and protected under the First Amendment.
>
> "But, of course, this is not the case. Whereas a man's right to speak out on this or that may be guaranteed and protected, he can have no imaginable human or constitutional right to remain a member of a university faculty. Clearly, the right to academic freedom is an acquired one, yet an acquired right of such value to society that in the minds of many it has verged upon the constitutional." Washington Evening Star, Jan. 23, 1972.

There may not be a constitutional right to continued employment if private schools and colleges are involved. But Prof. Herberg's view is not correct when public schools move against faculty members. For the First Amendment, applicable to the States by reason of the Fourteenth Amendment, protects the individual against state action when it comes to freedom of speech and of press and the related freedoms guaranteed by the First Amendment; and the Fourteenth [Amendment] protects "liberty" and "property" as stated by the Court in *Sindermann.*

No more direct assault on academic freedom can be imagined than for the school authorities to be allowed to discharge a teacher because of his or her philosophical, political, or ideological beliefs. . . .

When a violation of First Amendment rights is alleged, the reasons for dismissal or for nonrenewal of an employment contract must be examined to see if the reasons given are only a cloak for activity or attitudes protected by the Constitution. A statutory analogy is present under the National Labor Relations Act, 29 U.S.C. § 151 et seq. While discharges of employees for "cause" are permissible (Fibreboard Paper Products Corp. v. National Labor Relations Board, 379 U.S. 203, 217, 85 S. Ct. 398, 406, 13 L. Ed. 2d 233), discharges because of an employee's union activities is banned by § 8(a) (3), 29 U.S.C. § 158(c) (3). So the search is to ascertain whether the stated ground was the real one or only a pretext. See J.P. Stevens & Co. v. National Labor Relations Board, 380 F.2d 292, 300 (2nd Cir.). . . .

There is sometimes a conflict between a claim for First Amendment protection and the need for orderly administration of the school system, as we noted in Pickering v. Board of Education, 391 U.S. 563, 569, 88 S. Ct. 1731, 1735, 20 L. Ed. 2d 811. That is one reason why summary judgments in this class of cases are seldom appropriate. Another reason is that careful factfinding is often necessary to know whether the given reason for nonrenewal of a teacher's contract is the real reason or a feigned one. . . . In Wieman v. Updegraff, 344 U.S. 183, 73 S. Ct. 215, 97 L. Ed. 216, we held that an applicant could not be denied the opportunity for public employment because he had exercised his First Amendment rights. And in Speiser v. Randall, 357 U.S. 513, 78 S. Ct. 1332, 2 L. Ed. 2d 1460, we held that a denial of a tax exemption unless one gave up his First Amendment rights was an abridgement of Fourteenth Amendment rights.

As we held in Speiser v. Randall, *supra,* when a State proposes to deny a privilege to one who it alleges has engaged in unprotected speech, Due Process requires that the State bear the burden of proving that the speech was not protected. "The 'protection of the individual against arbitrary action' . . . [is] the very essence of due process." Slochower v. Board of Higher Education, 350 U.S. 551, 559, 76 S. Ct. 637, 641, 100 L. Ed. 692 (1956), but where the State is allowed to act secretly behind closed doors and without any notice to those who are affected by its actions, there is no check against the possibility of such "arbitrary action." . . .

Mr. JUSTICE MARSHALL, dissenting. . . .

I would go further than the Court does in defining the terms "liberty" and "property."

The prior decisions of this Court, discussed at length in the opinion of the Court, established a principle that is as obvious as it is compelling — *i.e.,* federal and state governments and governmental agencies are restrained by the Constitution from acting arbitrarily with respect to employment opportunities that they either offer or control. Hence, it is now firmly established that whether or not a private employer is free to act capriciously or unreasonably with respect to employment practices, at least absent statutory or contractual controls, a government employer is different. The government may only act fairly and reasonably.

This Court has long maintained that "the right to work for a living in the common occupations of the community is of the very essence of the personal freedom and opportunity that it was the purpose of the [Fourteenth] Amendment to secure." Truax v. Raich, 239 U.S. 33, 41, 36 S. Ct. 7, 10, 60 L. Ed. 131 (1915) (Hughes, J.). See also Meyer v. Nebraska, 262 U.S. 390, 399, 43 S. Ct. 625, 626, 67 L. Ed. 1042 (1923). . . .

In my view, every citizen who applies for a government job is entitled to it unless the government can establish some reason for denying the employment. This is the "property" right that I believe is protected by the Fourteenth Amendment and that cannot be denied "without due process of law." And it is also liberty — liberty to work — which is the "very essence of the personal freedom and opportunity" secured by the Fourteenth Amendment.

This Court has often had occasion to note that the denial of public employment is a serious blow to any citizen. See, *e.g.,* Joint Anti-Fascist Refugee Committee v. McGrath, 341 U.S. 123, 185, 71 S. Ct. 624, 655, 95 L. Ed. 817 (1951) (Jackson, J., concurring); United States v. Lovett, 328 U.S. 303, 316-317, 66 S. Ct. 1073, 1079, 90 L. Ed. 1252 (1946). Thus, when an application for public employment is denied or the contract of a government employee is not renewed, the government must say why, for it is only when the reasons underlying government action are known that citizens feel secure and protected against arbitrary government action.

Employment is one of the greatest, if not the greatest, benefits that governments offer in modern-day life. When something as valuable as the opportunity to work is at stake, the government may not reward some citizens and not others without demonstrating that its actions are fair and equitable. And it is procedural due process that is our fundamental guarantee to fairness, our protection against arbitrary, capricious, and unreasonable government action.

We have often noted that procedural due process means many different things in the numerous contexts in which it applies. See, *e.g.,* Goldberg v. Kelly, 397 U.S. 254, 262, 90 S. Ct. 1011, 1017, 25 L. Ed. 2d 287 (1970); Bell v. Burson, 402 U.S. 535, 91 S. Ct. 1586, 29 L. Ed. 2d 90 (1971). Prior decisions have held that an applicant for admission to practice as an attorney before the United States Board of Tax Appeals may not be rejected without a statement of reasons and a chance for a hearing on disputed issues of fact; [4] that a tenured teacher could not be summarily dismissed without notice of the reasons and a hearing; [5] that

---

[4] Goldsmith v. United States Board of Tax Appeals, 270 U.S. 117, 46 S. Ct. 215, 70 L. Ed. 494 (1926).

[5] Slochower v. Board of Higher Education, 350 U.S. 551, 76 S. Ct. 637, 100 L. Ed. 692 (1956).

an applicant for admission to a state bar could not be denied the opportunity to practice law without notice of the reasons for the rejection of his application and a hearing; [6] and even that a substitute teacher who had been employed only two months could not be dismissed merely because she refused to take a loyalty oath without an inquiry into the specific facts of her case and a hearing on those in dispute.[7] I would follow these cases and hold that respondent was denied due process when his contract was not renewed and he was not informed of the reasons and given an opportunity to respond.

It may be argued that to provide procedural due process to all public employees or prospective employees would place an intolerable burden on the machinery of government. Cf. Goldberg v. Kelly, *supra.* The short answer to that argument is that it is not burdensome to give reasons when reasons exist. Whenever an application for employment is denied, an employee is discharged, or a decision not to rehire an employee is made, there should be some reason for the decision. It can scarcely be argued that government would be crippled by a requirement that the reason be communicated to the person most directly affected by the government's action.

Where there are numerous applicants for jobs, it is likely that few will choose to demand reasons for not being hired. But, if the demand for reasons is exceptionally great, summary procedures can be devised that would provide fair and adequate information to all persons. As long as the government has a good reason for its actions it need not fear disclosure. It is only where the government acts improperly that procedural due process is truly burdensome. And that is precisely when it is most necessary. . . .

Moreover, proper procedures will surely eliminate some of the arbitrariness that results not from malice, but from innocent error. . . . When the government knows it may have to justify its decisions with sound reasons, its conduct is likely to be more cautious, careful, and correct. . . .

Mr. CHIEF JUSTICE BURGER, concurring.

I concur in the Court's judgments and opinions in *Perry* and *Roth,* but there is one central point in both decisions that I would like to underscore since it may have been obscured in the comprehensive discussion of the cases. That point is that the relationship between a state institution and one of its teachers is essentially a matter of state concern and state law. The Court holds today only that a state-employed teacher who has a right to re-employment under state law, arising from either an express or implied contract, has, in turn, a right guaranteed by the Fourteenth Amendment to some form of prior administrative or academic hearing on the cause for nonrenewal of his contract. Thus whether a particular teacher in a particular context has any right to such administrative hearing hinges on a question of state law. . . .

## PERRY v. SINDERMANN

Supreme Court of the United States
408 U.S. 593, 92 S. Ct. 2694, 33 L. Ed. 2d 570 (1972)

MR. JUSTICE STEWART delivered the opinion of the Court.

From 1959 to 1969 the respondent, Robert Sindermann, was a teacher in the state college system of the State of Texas. After teaching for two years at the University of Texas and for four years at San Antonio Junior College, he became

---

[6] Willner v. Committee on Character, 373 U.S. 96, 83 S. Ct. 1175, 10 L. Ed. 2d 224 (1963).
[7] Connell v. Higginbotham, 403 U.S. 207, 91 S. Ct. 1772, 29 L. Ed. 2d 418 (1972).

a professor of Government and Social Science at Odessa Junior College in 1965. He was employed at the college for four successive years, under a series of one-year contracts. He was successful enough to be appointed, for a time, the cochairman of his department.

During the 1968-1969 academic year, however, controversy arose between the respondent and the college administration. The respondent was elected president of the Texas Junior College Teachers Association. In this capacity, he left his teaching duties on several occasions to testify before committees of the Texas Legislature, and he became involved in public disagreements with the policies of the college's Board of Regents. In particular, he aligned himself with a group advocating the elevation of the college to four-year status — a change opposed by the Regents. And, on one occasion, a newspaper advertisement appeared over his name that was highly critical of the Regents.

Finally, in May 1969, the respondent's one-year employment contract terminated and the Board of Regents voted not to offer him a new contract for the next academic year. The Regents issued a press release setting forth allegations of the respondent's insubordination.[1] But they provided him no official statement of the reasons for the nonrenewal of his contract. And they allowed him no opportunity for a hearing to challenge the basis of the nonrenewal. . . .

The Court of Appeals reversed the judgment of the District Court. Sindermann v. Perry, 430 F.2d 939. First, it held that, despite the respondent's lack of tenure, the nonrenewal of his contract would violate the Fourteenth Amendment if it in fact was based on his protected free speech. Since the actual reason for the Regents' decision was "in total dispute" in the pleadings the court remanded the case for a full hearing on this contested issue of fact. *Id.* at 942-943. Second, the Court of Appeals held that, despite the respondent's lack of tenure, the failure to allow him an opportunity for a hearing would violate the constitutional guarantee of procedural due process if the respondent could show that he had an "expectancy" of re-employment. It, therefore, ordered that this issue of fact also be aired upon remand. . . .

The first question presented is whether the respondent's lack of a contractual or tenure right to re-employment, taken alone, defeats his claim that the nonrenewal of his contract violated the First and Fourteenth Amendments. We hold that it does not.

For at least a quarter century, this Court has made clear that even though a person has no "right" to a valuable governmental benefit and even though the government may deny him the benefit for any number of reasons, there are some reasons upon which the government may not act. It may not deny a benefit to a person on a basis that infringes his constitutionally protected interests — especially, his interest in freedom of speech. For if the government could deny a benefit to a person because of his constitutionally protected speech or associations, his exercise of those freedoms would in effect be penalized and inhibited. This would allow the government to "produce a result which [it] could not command directly." Speiser v. Randall, 357 U.S. 513, 526, 78 S. Ct. 1332, 1342, 2 L. Ed. 2d 1460. Such interference with constitutional rights is impermissible. . . . We have applied the principle regardless of the public

---

[1] The press release stated, for example, that the respondent had defied his superiors by attending legislative committee meetings when college officials had specifically refused to permit him to leave his classes for that purpose.

employee's contractual or other claim to a job. Compare Pickering v. Board of Education, *supra*, with Shelton v. Tucker, *supra*.

Thus the respondent's lack of a contractual or tenure "right" to re-employment for the 1969-1970 academic year is immaterial to his free speech claim. Indeed, twice before, this Court has specifically held that the nonrenewal of a nontenured public school teacher's one-year contract may not be predicated on his exercise of First and Fourteenth Amendment rights. Shelton v. Tucker, *supra;* Keyishian v. Board of Regents, *supra.* We reaffirm those holdings here.

In this case, of course, the respondent has yet to show that the decision not to renew his contract was, in fact, made in retaliation for his exercise of the constitutional right of free speech. The District Court foreclosed any opportunity to make this showing when it granted summary judgment. Hence, we cannot now hold that the Board of Regents' action was invalid.

But we agree with the Court of Appeals that there is a genuine dispute as to "whether the college refused to renew the teaching contract on an impermissible basis — as a reprisal for the exercise of constitutionally protected rights." 430 F.2d, at 943. The respondent has alleged that his nonretention was based on his testimony before legislative committees and his other public statements critical of the Regents' policies. And he has alleged that this public criticism was within the First and Fourteenth Amendment's protection of freedom of speech. Plainly, these allegations present a *bona fide* constitutional claim. For this Court has held that a teacher's public criticism of his superiors on matters of public concern may be constitutionally protected and may, therefore, be an impermissible basis for termination of his employment. Pickering v. Board of Education, *supra.*

For this reason we hold that the grant of summary judgment against the respondent, without full exploration of this issue, was improper.

The respondent's lack of formal contractual or tenure security in continued employment at Odessa Junior College, though irrelevant to his free speech claim, is highly relevant to his procedural due process claim. But it may not be entirely dispositive.

We have held today in Board of Regents v. Roth, *supra*, that the Constitution does not require opportunity for a hearing before the nonrenewal of a nontenured teacher's contract, unless he can show that the decision not to rehire him somehow deprived him of an interest in "liberty" or that he had a "property" interest in continued employment, despite the lack of tenure or a formal contract. In *Roth* the teacher had not made a showing on either point to justify summary judgment in his favor.

Similarly, the respondent here has yet to show that he has been deprived of an interest that could invoke procedural due process protection. As in *Roth,* the mere showing that he was not rehired in one particular job, without more, did not amount to a showing of a loss of liberty.[5] Nor did it amount to a showing of a loss of property.

But the respondent's allegations — which we must construe most favorably to the respondent at this stage of the litigation — do raise a genuine issue as to his interest in continued employment at Odessa Junior College. He alleged that this interest, though not secured by a formal contractual tenure provision, was

---

[5] The Court of Appeals suggested that the respondent might have a due process right to some kind of hearing simply if he *asserts* to college officials that their decision was based on his constitutionally protected conduct. 430 F.2d at 944. We have rejected this approach in Board of Regents v. Roth, *supra*, 408 U.S. at — n.14, 92 S. Ct., at 2708 n.14.

secured by a no less binding understanding fostered by the college administration. In particular, the respondent alleged that the college had a *de facto* tenure program, and that he had tenure under that program. He claimed that he and others legitimately relied upon an unusual provision that had been in the college's official Faculty Guide for many years:

> "*Teacher Tenure:* Odessa College has no tenure system. The Administration of the College wishes the faculty member to feel that he has a permanent tenure as long as his teaching services are satisfactory and as long as he displays a cooperative attitude toward his co-workers and his superiors, and as long as he is happy in his work."

Moreover, the respondent claimed legitimate reliance upon guidelines promulgated by the Coordinating Board of the Texas College and University System that provided that a person, like himself, who had been employed as a teacher in the state college and university system for seven years or more has some form of job tenure. Thus the respondent offered to prove that a teacher, with his long period of service, at this particular State College had no less a "property" interest in continued employment than a formally tenured teacher at other colleges, and had no less a procedural due process right to a statement of reasons and a hearing before college officials upon their decision not to retain him.

We have made clear in *Roth* . . . that "property" interests subject to procedural due process protection are not limited by a few rigid, technical forms. Rather, "property" denotes a broad range of interests that are secured by "existing rules or understandings." . . . A person's interest in a benefit is a "property" interest for due process purposes if there are such rules or mutually explicit understandings that support his claim of entitlement to the benefit and that he may invoke at a hearing.

A written contract with an explicit tenure provision clearly is evidence of a formal understanding that supports a teacher's claim of entitlement to continued employment unless sufficient "cause" is shown. Yet absence of such an explicit contractual provision may not always foreclose the possibility that a teacher has a "property" interest in re-employment. For example, the law of contracts in most, if not all, jurisdictions long has employed a process by which agreements, though not formalized in writing, may be "implied." 3 Corbin on Contracts, §§ 561-672A. Explicit contractual provisions may be supplemented by other agreements implied from "the promisor's words and conduct in the light of the surrounding circumstances." *Id.*, at § 562. And, "[t]he meaning of [the promisor's] words and acts is found by relating them to the usage of the past." *Ibid.*

A teacher, like the respondent, who has held his position for a number of years, might be able to show from the circumstances of this service — and from other relevant facts — that he has a legitimate claim of entitlement to job tenure. Just as this Court has found there to be a "common law of a particular industry or of a particular plant" that may supplement a collective-bargaining agreement, United Steelworkers v. Warrior & Gulf Nav. Co., 363 U.S. 574, 579, 80 S. Ct. 1347, 1351, 4 L. Ed. 2d 1409, so there may be an unwritten "common law" in a particular university that certain employees shall have the equivalent of tenure. This is particularly likely in a college or university, like Odessa Junior College, that has no explicit tenure system even for senior members of its faculty, but that nonetheless may have created such a system in practice. See Byse & Joughin, Tenure in American Higher Education 17-28.

In this case, the respondent has alleged the existence of rules and understandings, promulgated and fostered by state officials, that may justify his legitimate claim of er titlement to continued employment absent "sufficient cause." We disagree with the Court of Appeals insofar as it held that a mere subjective "expectancy" is protected by procedural due process, but we agree that the respondent must be given an opportunity to prove the legitimacy of his claim of such entitlement in light of "the policies and practices of the institution." 430 F.2d, at 942. Proof of such a property interest would not, of course, entitle him to reinstatement. But such proof would obligate college officials to grant a hearing at his request, where he could be informed of the grounds for his nonretention and challenge their sufficiency.

Therefore, while we do not wholly agree with the opinion of the Court of Appeals, its judgment remanding this case to the District Court is affirmed.

Affirmed.

## ARNETT v. KENNEDY

Supreme Court of the United States
94 S. Ct. 1633 (1974)

On appeal from the United States District Court for the Northern District of Illinois.

Mr. Justice Rehnquist announced the judgment of the Court in an opinion in which The Chief Justice and Mr. Justice Stewart join.

Prior to the events leading to his discharge, appellee Wayne Kennedy was a nonprobationary federal employee in the competitive Civil Service. He was a field representative in the Chicago Regional Office of the Office of Economic Opportunity (OEO). In March 1972, he was removed from the federal service pursuant to the provisions of the Lloyd-LaFollette Act, 5 U.S.C. § 7501, after Wendell Verduin, the Regional Director of the OEO, upheld written administrative charges made in the form of a "notification of proposed adverse action" against appellee. The charges listed five events occurring in November and December 1971; the most serious of the charges was that appellee "without any proof whatsoever and in reckless disregard of the actual facts" known to him or reasonably discoverable by him had publicly stated that Verduin and his administrative assistant had attempted to bribe a representative of a community action organization with whom the OEO had dealings. The alleged bribe consisted of an offer of a $100,000 grant of OEO funds if the representative would sign a statement against appellee and another OEO employee.

Appellee was advised of his right under regulations promulgated by the Civil Service Commission and the OEO to reply to the charges orally and in writing, and to submit affidavits to Verduin. He was also advised that the material on which the notice was based was available for his inspection in the Regional Office, and that a copy of the material was attached to the notice of proposed adverse action.

Appellee did not respond to the substance of the charges against him, but instead asserted that the charges were unlawful because he had a right to a trial-type hearing before an impartial hearing officer before he could be removed from his employment, and because statements made by him were protected by the First Amendment to the United States Constitution. On March 20, 1972, Verduin notified appellee in writing that he would be removed from his position at the close of business on March 27, 1972. Appellee was also notified of his right to appeal Verduin's decision either to the Office of Economic Opportunity or to the Civil Service Commission.

Appellee then instituted this suit in the United States District Court for the Northern District of Illinois on behalf of himself and others similarly situated, seeking both injunctive and declaratory relief. In his amended complaint, appellee contended that the standards and procedures established by and under the Lloyd-LaFollette Act for the removal of nonprobationary employees from the federal service unwarrantedly interfere with those employees' freedom of expression and deny them procedural due process of law. The three-judge District Court, convened pursuant to 28 U.S.C. §§ 2282 and 2284, granted summary judgment for appellee. The court held that the discharge procedures authorized by the Act and attendant Civil Service Commission and OEO regulations denied appellee due process of law because they failed to provide for a trial-type hearing before an impartial agency official prior to removal; the court also held the Act and implementing regulations unconstitutionally vague because they failed to furnish sufficiently precise guidelines as to what kind of speech may be made the basis of a removal action. The court ordered that appellee be reinstated in his former position with backpay, and that he be accorded a hearing prior to removal in any future removal proceedings. Appellants were also enjoined from further enforcement of the Lloyd-LaFollette Act, and implementing rules, as "construed to regulate the speech of competitive service employees."

## I

The numerous affidavits submitted to the District Court by both parties not unexpectedly portray two widely differing versions of the facts which gave rise to this lawsuit. Since the District Court granted summary judgment to appellee, it was required to resolve all genuine disputes as to any material facts in favor of appellant, and we therefore take as true for purposes of this opinion the material particulars of appellee's conduct which were set forth in the notification of proposed adverse action dated February 18, 1972. The District Court's holding necessarily embodies the legal conclusions that even though all of these factual statements were true, the procedure which the Government proposed to follow in this case was constitutionally insufficient to accomplish appellee's discharge, and the standard by which his conduct was to be judged in the course of those procedures infringed his right of free speech protected by the First Amendment.

The statutory provisions which the District Court held invalid are found in 5 U.S.C. § 7501. Subsection (a) of that section provides that "[a]n individual in the competitive service may be removed or suspended without pay only for such cause as will promote the efficiency of the service."

Subsection (b) establishes the administrative procedures by which an employee's rights under subsection (a) are to be determined, providing:

"(b) An individual in the competitive service whose removal or suspension without pay is sought is entitled to reasons in writing and to —

"(1) notice of the action sought and of any charges preferred against him;

"(2) a copy of the charges;

"(3) a reasonable time for filing a written answer to the charges, with affidavits; and

"(4) a written decision on the answer at the earliest practicable date.

"Examination of witnesses, trial, or hearing is not required but may be provided in the discretion of the individual directing the removal or suspension without pay. Copies of the charges, the notice of hearing, the answer, the reasons for and the order of removal or suspension without pay, and also the reasons for reduction in grade or pay, shall be made a part of the records of the employing agency, and, on request, shall be furnished to the individual affected and to the Civil Service Commission."

This codification of the Lloyd-LaFollette Act is now supplemented by the regulations of the Civil Service Commission, and, with respect to OEO, by the regulations and instructions of that agency. Both the Commission and OEO have by regulation given further specific content to the general removal standard in subsection (a) of the Act. The regulations of the Commission and OEO, in nearly identical language, require that employees "avoid any action . . . which might result in, or create the appearance of . . . [a]ffecting adversely the confidence of the public in the integrity of (OEO and) the Government," and that employees not "engage in criminal, infamous, dishonest, immoral, or notoriously disgraceful or other conduct prejudicial to the Government." OEO further provides by regulation that its Office of General Counsel is available to supply counseling on the interpretation of the laws and regulations relevant to the conduct of OEO employees.

Both the Commission and OEO also follow regulations enlarging the procedural protections accorded by the Act itself. The Commission's regulations provide, inter alia, that the employing agency must give 30 days' advance written notice to the employee prior to removal, and make available to him the material on which the notice is based. They also provide that the employee shall have an opportunity to appear before the official vested with authority to make the removal decision in order to answer the charges against him, that the employee must receive notice of an adverse decision on or before its effective date, and that the employee may appeal from an adverse decision. This appeal may be either to a reviewing authority within the employing agency, or directly to the Commission, and the employee is entitled to an evidentiary trial-type hearing at the appeal stage of the proceeding. The only trial-type hearing available within the OEO is, by virtue of its regulations and practice, typically held after actual removal; but if the employee is reinstated on appeal, he receives full back pay.

We must first decide whether these procedures established for the purpose of determining whether there is "cause" under the Lloyd-LaFollette Act for the dismissal of a federal employee comport with procedural due process, and then decide whether that standard of "cause" for federal employee dismissals was within the constitutional power of Congress to adopt.

[The Court here discusses the establishment and history of the federal Civil Service.]

That Act, as now codified, 5 U.S.C. § 7501 (1970), together with the administrative regulations issued by the Civil Service Commission and the OEO, provided the statutory and administrative framework which the Government contends controlled the proceedings against appellee. The District Court, in its ruling on appellee's procedural contentions, in effect held that the Fifth Amendment to the United States Constitution prohibited Congress, in the Lloyd-LaFollette Act, from granting protection against removal without cause and at the same time — indeed, in the same sentence — specifying that the determination of cause should be without the full panoply of rights which attend a trial-type adversary hearing. We do not believe that the Constitution so limits Congress in the manner in which benefits may be extended to federal employees.

Appellee recognizes that our recent decisions in Board of Regents of State Colleges v. Roth, 408 U.S. 564, 92 S. Ct. 2701, 33 L. Ed. 2d 548 (1972), and Perry

v. Sindermann, 408 U.S. 593, 92 S. Ct. 2694, 33 L. Ed. 2d 570 (1972), are those most closely in point with respect to the procedural rights constitutionally guaranteed public employees in connection with their dismissal from employment. Appellee contends that he had a property interest or an expectancy of employment which could not be divested without first affording him a full adversary hearing. . . .

Here appellee did have a statutory expectancy that he not be removed other than for "such cause as will promote the efficiency of the service." But the very section of the statute which granted him that right, a right which had previously existed only by virtue of administrative regulation, expressly provided also for the procedure by which "cause" was to be determined, and expressly omitted the procedural guarantees which appellee insists are mandated by the Constitution. Only by bifurcating the very sentence of the Act of Congress which conferred upon appellee the right not to be removed save for cause could it be said that he had an expectancy of that substantive right without the procedural limitations which Congress attached to it. In the area of federal regulation of government employees, where in the absence of statutory limitation the governmental employer has had virtually uncontrolled latitude in decisions as to hiring and firing. Cafeteria and Restaurant Workers v. McElroy, 367 U.S. 886, 896-897, 81 S. Ct. 1743, 1749-1750, 6 L. Ed. 2d 1230, we do not believe that a statutory enactment such as the Lloyd-LaFollette Act may be parsed as discretely as appellee urges. Congress was obviously intent on according a measure of statutory job security to governmental employees which they had not previously enjoyed, but was likewise intent on excluding more elaborate procedural requirements which it felt would make the operation of the new scheme unnecessarily burdensome in practice. Where the focus of legislation was this strongly on the procedural mechanism for enforcing the substantive right which was simultaneously conferred, we decline to conclude that the substantive right may be viewed wholly apart from the procedure provided for its enforcement. The employee's statutorily defined right is not a guarantee against removal without cause in the abstract, but such a guarantee as enforced by the procedures which Congress has designated for the determination of cause. . . .

"It is an elementary rule of constitutional law that one may not 'retain the benefits of an Act while attacking the constitutionality of one of its important conditions.' United States v. San Francisco, 310 U.S. 16, 29 [60 S. Ct. 749, 84 L. Ed. 1050]. As formulated by Mr. Justice Brandeis, concurring in Ashwander v. Tennessee Valley Authority, 297 U.S. 288, 348 [56 S. Ct. 466, 80 L. Ed. 688], 'The Court will not pass upon the constitutionally of a statute at the instance of one who has availed himself of its benefits.' " Id., p. 255, 67 S. Ct., p. 1557.

This doctrine has unquestionably been applied unevenly in the past, and observed as often as not in the breach. We believe that at the very least it gives added weight to our conclusion that where the grant of a substantive right is inextricably intertwined with the limitations on the procedures which are to be employed in determining that right, a litigant in the position of appellee must take the bitter with the sweet.

To conclude otherwise would require us to hold that although Congress chose to enact what was essentially a legislative compromise, and with unmistakable clarity granted governmental employees security against being dismissed without "cause," but refused to accord them a full adversary hearing for the determination of "cause," it was constitutionally disabled from making such a choice. We would be holding that federal employees had been granted, as a result of the enactment of the Lloyd-LaFollette Act, not merely that which Congress had given them in the first part of a sentence, but that which Congress had expressly withheld from them in the latter part of the same sentence. Neither the language of the Due Process Clause of the Fifth Amendment nor our cases construing it require any such hobbling restrictions on legislative authority in this area.

Appellees urge that the judgment of the District Court must be sustained on the authority of cases such as Goldberg v. Kelly, 397 U.S. 254, 90 S. Ct. 1011, 25 L. Ed. 2d 287; Fuentes v. Shevin, 407 U.S. 67, 92 S. Ct. 1983, 32 L. Ed. 2d 556; Bell v. Burson, 402 U.S. 535, 91 S. Ct. 1586, 29 L. Ed. 2d 90, and Sniadach v. Family Finance Corp., 395 U.S. 337, 89 S. Ct. 1820, 23 L. Ed. 2d 349. Goldberg held that welfare recipients are entitled under the Due Process Clause of the Fifth and Fourteenth Amendments to an adversary hearing before their benefits are terminated. Fuentes v. Shevin held that a hearing was generally required before one could have his property seized under a writ of replevin. In Bell v. Burson the Court held that due process required a procedure for determining whether there was a reasonable possibility of a judgment against a driver as a result of an accident before his license and vehicle registration could be suspended for failure to post security under Georgia's uninsured motorist statute. And in Sniadach v. Family Finance Corp. a Wisconsin statute providing for prejudgment garnishment without notice to the debtor or prior hearing was struck down as violative of the principles of due process. These cases deal with areas of the law dissimilar to one another and dissimilar to the area of governmental employer-employee relationships with which we deal here. The types of "liberty" and "property" protected by the Due Process Clause vary widely, and what may be required under that clause in dealing with one set of interests which it protects may not be required in dealing with another set of interests.

"The very nature of due process negates any concept of inflexible procedures universally applicable to every imaginable situation." Cafeteria and Restaurant Workers v. McElroy, 367 U.S. 886, 895, 81 S. Ct. 1743, 1748, 6 L. Ed. 2d 1230.

Here the property interest which appellee had in his employment was itself conditioned by the procedural limitations which had accompanied the grant of that interest. The Government might, then, under our holdings deal with government employees in Roth, *supra,* and Perry, *supra,* constitutionally deal with appellee's claims as it proposed to do here.[21]

[21] Our Brother White would hold that Verduin himself might not make the initial decision as to removal on behalf of the agency, because he was the victim of the alleged libel which was one of the bases for appellee's removal. Because of our holding with respect to appellee's property-type expectations under Roth and Sindermann, we do not reach this question in its constitutional dimension. But since our Brother White suggests that he reaches that conclusion as a matter of statutory construction, albeit because of constitutional emanations, we state our reasons for disagreeing with his conclusion. We, of course, find no constitutional overtones lurking in the statutory issue, because of our holding as to the nature of appellee's property interest in his employment. The reference in the Lloyd-LaFollette Act itself to the discretion "of the officer making the removal" suggests rather strongly that he is likewise the officer who will have brought the charges, and there is no indication that during the 60 years' practice under the Act it has ever been administratively construed to require the initial hearing on the discharge to be before any official other than the one making the charges. And while our Brother White's statement of his conclusion suggests that it may be limited to facts similar to those presented here, post, p. 1666, we doubt that in practice it could be so confined. The decision of an employee's supervisor to dismiss an employee "for such cause as will promote the efficiency of the service" will all but invariably involve a somewhat subjective judgment on the part of the supervisor that the employee's performance is not up to snuff. Employer-employee disputes of this sort can scarcely avoid involving clashes of personalities, and while a charge that an employee has libeled a supervisor may generate a maximum of personal involvement on the part of the latter, a statement of more typical charges will necessarily engender some degree of personal involvement on the part of the supervisor.

Additional difficulties in applying our Brother White's standard would surely be found if the official

Appellee also contends in this Court that because of the nature of the charges on which his dismissal was based, he was in effect accused of dishonesty, and that therefore a hearing was required before he could be deprived of this element of his "liberty" protected by the Fifth Amendment against deprivation without due process. In Board of Regents v. Roth, 408 U.S., at 573, 92 S. Ct., at 2707, we said:

"The State, in declining to rehire the respondent, did not make any charge against him that might seriously damage his standing and associations in his community. It did not base the nonrenewal of his contract on a charge, for example, that he had been guilty of dishonesty, or immorality. . . . In such a case, due process would accord an opportunity to refute the charge before University officials."

The liberty here implicated by petitioner's action is not the elemental freedom from external restraint such as was involved in Morrissey v. Brewer, 408 U.S. 471, 92 S. Ct. 2593, 33 L. Ed. 2d 484, but is instead a subspecies of the right of the individual "to enjoy those privileges long recognized . . . as essential to the orderly pursuit of happiness by free men." Meyer v. Nebraska, 262 U.S. 390, 399, 43 S. Ct. 625, 627, 67 L. Ed. 1042. But that liberty is not offended by dismissal from employment itself, but instead by dismissal based upon an unsupported charge which could wrongfully injure the reputation of an employee. Since the purpose of the hearing in such a case is to provide the person "an opportunity to clear his name," a hearing afforded by administrative appeal procedures after the actual dismissal is a sufficient compliance with the requirements of the Due Process Clause. Here appellee chose not to rely on his administrative appeal, which if his factual contentions are correct might well have vindicated his reputation and removed any wrongful stigma from his reputation.

Appellee urges that the delays in processing agency and Civil Service Commission appeals, amounting to more than three months in over 50% of agency appeals, mean that the available administrative appeals do not suffice to protect his liberty interest recognized in Roth. During the pendency of his administrative appeals, appellee asserts, a discharged employee suffers from both the stigma and the consequent disadvantage in obtaining a comparable job that result from dismissal for cause from government employment. We assume that some delay attends vindication of an employee's reputation throughout the hearing procedures provided on appeal, and conclude that at least the delays cited here do not entail any separate deprivation of a liberty interest recognized in Roth.

### III

Appellee also contends that the provisions of 5 U.S.C. § 7501 (a), authorizing removal or suspension without pay "for such cause as will promote the efficiency of the service," are vague and overbroad. The District Court accepted this contention: "Because employees faced with the standard of 'such cause as will promote the efficiency of the service' can only guess as to what utterances may cost them their jobs, there can be little question that they will be deterred from exercising their First Amendment rights to the fullest extent."

---

bringing the charges were himself the head of a department or an agency, for in that event none of his subordinates could be assumed to have a reasonable degree of detached neutrality, and the initial hearing would presumably have to be conducted by someone wholly outside of the department or agency. We do not believe that Congress, clearly indicating as it did in the Lloyd-LaFollette Act its preference for relatively simple procedures, contemplated or required the complexities which would be injected into the Act by our Brother White.

A certain anomaly attends appellee's substantive constitutional attack on the Lloyd-LaFollette Act just as it does his attack on its procedural provisions. Prior to the enactment of this language in 1912, there was no such statutory inhibition on the authority of the Government to discharge a federal employee, and an employee could be discharged with or without cause for conduct which was not protected under the First Amendment. Yet under the District Court's holding, a federal employee after the enactment of the Lloyd-LaFollette Act may not even be discharged for conduct which constitutes "cause" for discharge and which is not protected by the First Amendment, because the guarantee of job security which Congress chose to accord employees is "vague" and "overbroad."

We hold the standard of "cause" set forth in the Lloyd-LaFollette Act as a limitation on the Government's authority to discharge federal employees is constitutionally sufficient against the charges both of overbreadth and of vagueness. In Civil Service Commission v. National Association of Letter Carriers, 413 U.S. 548, 578-579, 93 S. Ct. 2880, 2897, 37 L. Ed. 2d 796, we said:

"[T]here are limitations in the English language with respect to being both specific and manageably brief, and it seems to us that although the prohibitions may not satisfy those intent on finding fault at any cost, they are set out in terms that the ordinary person exercising ordinary common sense can sufficiently understand and comply with, without sacrifice to the public interest. '[T]he general class of offense to which . . . [the provisions are] directed is plainly within [their] terms . . . [and they] will not be struck down as vague, even though marginal cases could be put where doubts might arise.' United States v. Hariss, 347 U.S. 612, 618 [74 S. Ct. 808, 812, 98 L. Ed. 989] (1954)."

Congress sought to lay down to an admittedly general standard, not for the purpose of defining criminal conduct, but in order to give myriad different federal employees performing widely disparate tasks a common standard of job protection. We do not believe that Congress was confined to the choice of enacting a detailed code of employee conduct, or else granting no job protection at all. As we said in Colten v. Kentucky, 407 U.S. 104, 92 S. Ct. 1953, 32 L. Ed. 2d 584:

"The root of the vagueness doctrine is a rough idea of fairness. It is not a principle designed to convert into a constitutional dilemma the practical difficulties in drawing criminal statutes both general enough to take into account a variety of human conduct and sufficiently specific to provide fair warning that certain kinds of conduct are prohibited." 407 U.S., at 110, 92 S. Ct., at 1957.

Here the language "such cause as will promote the efficiency of the service" was not written upon a clean slate in 1912, and it does not appear on a clean slate now. The Civil Service Commission has indicated that what might be said to be longstanding principles of employer-employee relationships, like those developed in the private sector, should be followed in interpreting the language used by Congress. Moreover, OEO has provided by regulation that its Office of General Counsel is available to counsel employees who seek advice on the interpretation of the Act and its regulations. We found the similar procedure offered by the Civil Service Commission important in rejecting the respondents' vagueness contentions in Civil Service Commission v. National Association of Letter Carriers, 413 U.S. 548, 580, 93 S. Ct. 2880, 2897, 37 L. Ed. 2d 796.

The phrase "such cause as will promote the efficiency of the service" as a standard of employee job protection is without doubt intended to authorize dismissal for speech as well as other conduct. Pickering v. Board of Education, 391 U.S. 563, 568, 88 S. Ct. 1731, 1734, 20 L. Ed. 2d 811, makes it clear that in certain situations the discharge of a government employee may be based on his speech without offending guarantees of the First Amendment. . . .

Because of the infinite variety of factual situations in which public statements by government employees might reasonably justify dismissal for "cause," we conclude that the Act describes, as explicitly as is required, the employee conduct which is grounds for removal. The essential fairness of this broad and general removal standard, and the impracticability of greater specificity, were recognized by Judge Leventhal writing for a panel of the United States Court of Appeals for the District of Columbia Circuit in Meehan v. Macy, 129 U.S. App. D.C. 217, 392 F.2d 822, 835, modified, 138 U.S. App. D.C. 38, 425 F.2d 469, affirmed en banc, 138 U.S. App. D.C. 41, 425 F.2d 472. . . .

Since Congress when it enacted the Lloyd-LaFollette Act did so with the intention of conferring job protection rights on federal employees which they had not previously had, it obviously did not intend to authorize discharge under the Act's removal standard for speech which is constitutionally protected. The Act proscribes only that public speech which improperly damages and impairs the reputation and efficiency of the employing agency, and it thus imposes no greater controls on the behavior of federal employees than are necessary for the protection of the Government as an employer. Indeed the Act is not directed at speech as such, but at employee behavior, including speech, which is detrimental to the efficiency of the employing agency. We hold that the language "such cause as will promote the efficiency of the service" in the Act excludes constitutionally protected speech, and that the statute is therefore not overbroad. Colten v. Kentucky, 407 U.S. 104, 111, 92 S. Vt. 1953, 1957, 32 L. Ed. 2d 584. We have observed previously that the Court has a duty to construe a federal statute to avoid constitutional questions where such a construction is reasonably possible. United States v. 12 200-ft. Reels of Film, 413 U.S. 123, 130 n.7, 93 S. Ct. 2665, 2670, 37 L. Ed. 2d 500; United States v. Thirty-seven Photographs, 402 U.S. 363, 368-369, 91 S. Ct. 1400, 1404-1405, 28 L. Ed. 2d 822.

We have no hesitation in saying, as did the District Court, that on the facts alleged in the administrative charges against appellee, the appropriate tribunal would infringe no constitutional right of appellee in concluding that there was "cause" for his discharge. Pickering v. Board of Education, 391 U.S. 563, 569, 88 S. Ct. 1731, 1735, 20 L. Ed. 2d 811. Nor have we any doubt that satisfactory proof of these allegations could constitute "such cause as will promote the efficiency of the service" within the terms of 5 U.S.C. § 7501 (a). Appellee's contention then boils down to the assertion that although no constitutionally protected conduct of his own was the basis for his discharge on the Government's version of the facts, the statutory language in question must be declared inoperative, and a set of more particularized regulations substituted for it, because the generality of its language might result in marginal situations in which other persons seeking to engage in constitutionally protected conduct would be deterred from doing so. But we have held that Congress in establishing a standard of "cause" for discharge did not intend to include within that term any constitutionally protected conduct. We think that our statement in Colten v. Kentucky, supra, is a complete answer to appellee's contention: "As we understand this case, appellant's own conduct was not immune under First Amendment and neither is his conviction vulnerable on the ground that the statute threatens constitutionally protected conduct of others." 407 U.S. 104, 111, 92 S. Ct. 1953, 1958.

In sum, we hold that the Lloyd-LaFollette Act, in at once conferring upon nonprobationary federal employees the right not to be discharged except for "cause" and prescribing the procedural means by which that right was to be protected, did not create an expectancy of job retention in those employees requiring procedural protection under the Due Process Clause beyond that afforded here by the statute and related agency regulations. We also conclude that the post termination hearing procedures provided by the Civil Service Commission and OEO adequately protect those federal employees' liberty interest, recognized in Roth, *supra,* in not being wrongfully stigmatized by untrue and unsupported administrative charges. Finally, we hold that the standard of employment protection imposed by Congress in the Lloyd-LaFollette Act, is not impermissibly vague or overbroad in its regulation of the speech of federal employees and therefore unconstitutional on its face. Accordingly, we reverse the decision of the District Court on both grounds on which it granted summary judgment and remand for further proceedings not inconsistent with this opinion.

Reversed.

MR. JUSTICE POWELL, with whom MR. JUSTICE BLACKMUN joins, concurring in part and concurring in the result in part.

For the reasons stated by MR. JUSTICE Rehnquist, I agree that the provisions of 5 U.S.C. § 7501 (a) are neither unconstitutionally vague nor overbroad. I also agree that appellee's discharge did not contravene the Fifth Amendment guarantee of procedural due process. Because I reach that conclusion on the basis of different reasoning, I state my views separately.


I


The applicability of the constitutional guarantee of procedural due process depends in the first instance on the presence of a legitimate "property" or "liberty" interest within the meaning of the Fifth or Fourteenth Amendment. Governmental deprivation of such an interest must be accompanied by minimum procedural safeguards, including some form of notice and a hearing. The Court's decisions in Board of Regents of State Colleges v. Roth, 408 U.S. 564, 92 S. Ct. 2701, 33 L. Ed. 2d 548 (1972), and Perry v. Sindermann, 408 U.S. 593, 92 S. Ct. 2694, 33 L. Ed. 2d 570 (1972), provide the proper framework for analysis of whether appellee's [employment] constituted a "property" interest under the Fifth Amendment. In Roth, the Court ... recognized that the "wooden distinction" between "rights" and "privileges" was not determinative of the applicability of procedural due process and that a property interest may be created by statute as well as by contract. Id., at 571, 92 S. Ct., at 2706. In particular, the Court stated that a person may have a protected property interest in public employment if contractual or statutory provisions guarantee continued employment absent "sufficient cause" for discharge. Id., at 576-578, 92 S. Ct., at 2708-2710.

In Sindermann, the Court again emphasized that a person may have a protected property interest in continued public employment. There, a state college teacher alleged that the college had established a de facto system of tenure and that he had obtained tenure under that system. The Court stated that proof of these allegations would establish the teacher's legitimate claim of entitlement to continued employment absent "sufficient cause" for discharge. In these circumstances, the teacher would have a property interest safeguarded by due process and deprivation of that interest would have to be accompanied by some form of notice and a hearing.

Application of these precedents to the instant case makes plain that appellee is entitled to invoke the constitutional guarantee of procedural due process.

Appellee was a nonprobationary federal employee, and as such he could be discharged only "for cause." 5 U.S.C. § 7501. The federal statute guaranteeing appellee continued employment absent "cause" for discharge conferred on him a legitimate claim of entitlement which constituted a "property" interest under the Fifth Amendment. Thus termination of his employment requires notice and a hearing.

The plurality opinion evidently reasons that the nature of appellee's interest in continued federal employment is necessarily defined and limited by the statutory procedures for discharge and that the constitutional guarantee of procedural due process accords to appellee no procedural protections against arbitrary or erroneous discharge other than those expressly provided in the statute. The plurality would thus conclude that the statute governing federal employment determines not only the nature of appellee's property interest, but also the extent of the procedural protections to which he may lay claim. It seems to me that this approach is incompatible with the principles laid down in Roth and Sindermann. Indeed, it would lead directly to the conclusion that whatever the nature of an individual's statutorily-created property interest, deprivation of that interest could be accomplished without notice or a hearing at any time. This view misconceives the origin of the right to procedural due process. That right is conferred not by legislative grace but by constitutional guarantee. While the legislature may elect not to confer a property interest in federal employment,[2] it may not constitutionally authorize the deprivation of such an interest, once conferred, without appropriate procedural safeguards. As our cases have consistently recognized, the adequacy of statutory procedures for deprivation of a statutorily created property interest must be analyzed in constitutional terms. Goldberg v. Kelly, 397 U.S. 254, 90 S. Ct. 1011, 25 L. Ed. 2d 287 (1970); [3] Bell v. Burson, 402 U.S. 535, 91 S. Ct. 1586, 29 L. Ed. 2d 90 (1971); Board of Regents of State Colleges v. Roth, supra; Perry v. Sindermann, supra.

## II

Having determined that the constitutional guarantee of procedural due process applies to appellee's discharge from public employment, the question arises whether an evidentiary hearing, including the right to present favorable witnesses and to confront and examine adverse witnesses, must be accorded *before* removal. The resolution of this issue depends on a balancing process in which the Government's interest in expeditious removal of an unsatisfactory employee is weighed against the interest of the affected employee in continued public employment. Goldberg v. Kelly, 397 U.S. 254, 263-266, 90 S. Ct. 1011, 1018-1020, 25 L. Ed. 2d 287 (1970). As the Court stated in Cafeteria and Restaurant Workers Union Local 473, AFL-CIO v. McElroy, 367 U.S. 886, 895, 81 S. Ct. 1743, 1748, 6 L. Ed. 2d 1230 (1961), "consideration of what procedures due process may require under any given set of circumstances must begin with

---

[2] No property interest would be conferred, for example, where the applicable statutory or contractual terms, either expressly or by implication, did not provide for continued employment absent "cause." See Board of Regents of State Colleges v. Roth, 408 U.S. 564, 578, 92 S. Ct. 2701, 2709-2710, 33 L. Ed. 2d 548 (1972).

[3] In Kelly, for example, the statutes and regulations defined both eligibility for welfare benefits and the procedures for termination of those benefits. The Court held that such benefits constituted a statutory entitlement for persons qualified to receive them and that the constitutional guarantee of procedural due process applied to termination of benefits. 397 U.S., at 261-263, 90 S. Ct., at 1016-1018.

a determination of the precise nature of the government function involved as well as of the private interest that has been affected by governmental action."

In the present case, the Government's interest, and hence the public's interest, is the maintenance of employee efficiency and discipline. Such factors are essential if the Government is to perform its responsibilities effectively and economically. To this end, the Government, as an employer, must have wide discretion and control over the management of its personnel and internal affairs. This includes the prerogative to remove employees whose conduct hinders efficient operation and to do so with dispatch. Prolonged retention of a disruptive or otherwise unsatisfactory employee can adversely affect discipline and morale in the work place, foster disharmony, and ultimately impair the efficiency of an office or agency. Moreover, a requirement of a prior evidentiary hearing would impose additional administrative costs, create delay, and deter warranted discharges. Thus, the Government's interest in being able to act expeditiously to remove an unsatisfactory employee is substantial.[4]

Appellee's countervailing interest is the continuation of his public employment pending an evidentiary hearing. Since appellee would be reinstated and awarded backpay if he prevails on the merits of his claim, appellee's actual injury would consist of a temporary interruption of his income during the interim. To be sure, even a temporary interruption of income could constitute a serious loss in many instances. But the possible deprivation is considerably less severe than that involved in Kelly, for example, where termination of welfare benefits to the recipient would have occurred in the face of "brutal need." 397 U.S., at 261, 90 S. Ct., at 1017. Indeed, as the Court stated in that case, "the crucial factor in this context — *a factor not present in the case of . . . the discharged government employee . . .* — is that termination of aid pending resolution of a controversy over eligibility may deprive an eligible recipient of *the very means by which to live while he waits."* Id., at 264, 90 S. Ct., at 1018 (italics added). By contrast, a public employee may well have independent resources to overcome any temporary hardship, and he may be able to secure a job in the private sector. Alternatively, he will be eligible for welfare benefits.

Appellee also argues that the absence of a prior evidentiary hearing increases the possibility of wrongful removal and that delay in conducting a post-termination evidentiary hearing further aggravates his loss. The present statute and regulations, however, already respond to these concerns. The affected employee is provided with 30 days advance written notice of the reasons for his proposed discharge and the materials on which the notice is based. He is accorded the right to respond to the charges both orally and in writing,

---

[4] My Brother Marshall rejects the Government's interest in efficiency as insignificant, citing Goldberg v. Kelly, 397 U.S. 254, 266, 90 S. Ct. 1011, 1019-1020, 25 L. Ed. 2d 287 (1970), and Fuentes v. Shevin, 407 U.S. 67, 90-91, n.22, 92 S. Ct. 1983, 1999, 32 L. Ed. 2d 556 (1972). He also notes that nine federal agencies presently accord prior evidentiary hearings. Post, at 1679.

Neither Goldberg nor Fuentes involved the Government's substantial interest in maintaining the efficiency and discipline of its own employees. Moreover, the fact that some federal agencies may have decided to hold prior evidentiary hearings cannot mean that such a procedure is constitutionally mandated. The Federal Government's general practice to the contrary argues that efficiency is in fact thought to be adversely affected by prior evidentiary hearings.

Nor do I agree with my Brother White's argument that suspension with pay would obviate any problem posed by prolonged retention of a disruptive or unsatisfactory employee. Aside from the additional financial burden which would be imposed on the Government, this procedure would undoubtedly inhibit warranted discharges and weaken significantly the deterrent effect of immediate removal. In addition, it would create a strong incentive for the suspended employee to attempt to delay final resolution of the issues surrounding his discharge.

including the submission of affidavits. Upon request, he is entitled to an opportunity to appear personally before the official having the authority to make or recommend the final decision. Although an evidentiary hearing is not held, the employee may make any representations he believes relevant to his case. After removal, the employee receives a full evidentiary hearing, and is awarded back-pay if reinstated. *See* 5 CFR §§ 752.262, 771.208, and 772.305; 5 U.S.C. § 5596. These procedures minimize the risk of error in the initial removal decision and provide for compensation for the affected employee should that decision eventually prove wrongful.[5]

On balance, I would conclude that a prior evidentiary hearing is not required and that the present statute and regulations comport with due process by providing a reasonable accommodation of the competing interests.[6]

Mr. Justice White, concurring in part and dissenting in part.

. . .

## I

In my view, three issues must be addressed in this case. First, does the Due Process Clause require that there be a full trial-type hearing *at some time* when a Federal Government employee in the competitive service is terminated? Secondly, if such be the case, must this hearing be held *prior* to the discharge of the employee, and, if so, was the process afforded in this case adequate? Third, and as an entirely separate matter, are the Lloyd-LaFollette Act and its attendant regulations void for vagueness or overbreadth? I join in the Court's opinion as to the third issue.

## II

I differ basically with the Court's view that "where the grant of a substantive right is inextricably interwined with the limitations on the procedures which are to be employed in determining that right, a litigant in the position of appellee must take the bitter with the sweet," and that "the property interest which appellee had in his employment was itself conditioned by the procedural limitations which had accompanied the grant of that interest." Ante, p. —. The rationale of this position quickly leads to the conclusion that even though the statute requires cause for discharge, the requisites of due process could equally

---

[5] My Brother White argues that affirmance is required because the supervisory official who would have conducted the pre-removal hearing was the "object of slander that was the basis for the employee's proposed discharge." Post, at 1666. He would conclude that this violated the statutory requirement of an "impartial decisionmaker." I find no such requirement anywhere in the statute or the regulations. Nor do I believe that due process so mandates at the pre-removal stage. In my view, the relevant fact is that an impartial decisionmaker is provided at the post-removal hearing where the employee's claims are finally resolved.

There are also significant practical considerations that argue against such a requirement. In most cases, the employee's supervisor is the official best informed about the "cause" for termination. If disqualification is required on the ground that the responsible supervisor could not be wholly impartial, the removal procedure would become increasingly complex. In effect, a "mini-trial" would be necessary to educate the impartial decisionmaker as to the basis for termination.

[6] Appellee also argues the failure to provide a prior evidentiary hearing deprived him of his "liberty" interest in violation of the Fifth Amendment. For the reasons stated above, I find that the present statute comports with due process even with respect to appellee's liberty interest.

have been satisfied had the law dispensed with any hearing at all. Whether pre- or post-termination.

The past cases of this Court uniformly indicate that some kind of hearing is required at some time before a person is finally deprived of his property interests.[7] . . .

This basic principle has unwaveringly been applied when private property has been taken by the State. . . .

This principle has also been applied in situations where the State has licensed certain activities. . . .

Similar principles prevail when the State affords its process and mechanism of dispute settlement, its law enforcement officers and its courts, in aiding one person to take property from another. . . .

Since there is a need for some kind of hearing before a person is finally deprived of his property, the argument in the instant case, and that adopted in the Court's opinion, is that there is something different about a final taking from an individual of property rights which have their origin in the public rather than the private sector of the economy, and, as applied here, that there is no need for any hearing at any time when the State discharges a person from his job, even though good cause for the discharge is required.

In cases involving employment by the State, the earliest cases of this Court have distinguished between two situations, where the entitlement to the job is conditioned "at pleasure" of the employer and where the job is to be held subject to certain requirements being met by the employee, as when discharge must be for "cause." The Court has stated "The inquiry is, therefore, whether there were any causes of removal prescribed by law. . . . If there were, then the rule would apply that where causes of removal are specified by Constitution or statute, as also where the term of office is for a fixed period, notice and hearing are essential. If there were not, the appointing power could remove at pleasure or for such cause as it deemed sufficient." Reagan v. United States, 182 U.S. 419, 425, 21 S. Ct. 842, 845, 45 L. Ed. 1162 (1901); Shurtleff v. United States, 189 U.S. 311, 314, 23 S. Ct. 535, 536, 47 L. Ed. 828 (1903). The Court has thus made clear that Congress may limit the total discretion of the Executive in firing an employee, by providing that termination be for cause, and only for cause, and, if it does so, notice and a hearing are "essential."

Where Executive discretion is not limited, there is no need for a hearing. . . .

The concern of the Court that fundamental fairness be observed when the State deals with its employees has not been limited to action which is discriminatory and infringes on constitutionally protected rights, as in Wieman v. Updegraff, 344 U.S. 183, 73 S. Ct. 215, 97 L. Ed. 216 (1952); Slochower v. Board of Education, 350 U.S. 551, 76 S. Ct. 637, 100 L. Ed. 692 (1956); Speiser v. Randall, 357 U.S. 513, 78 S. Ct. 1332, 2 L. Ed. 2d 1460 (1958); Sherbert v. Verner, 374 U.S. 398, 83 S. Ct. 1790, 10 L. Ed. 2d 965 (1963). See also Connell v. Higginbotham, 403 U.S. 207, 91 S. Ct. 1772, 29 L. Ed. 2d 418 (1971). It has been observed that "constitutional protection does extend to the public servant whose exclusion pursuant to a statute is *patently arbitrary* or discriminatory." (Emphasis added.) Wieman v. Updegraff, *supra,* 344 U.S., at 192, 73 S. Ct., at 219; Slochower v. Board of Education, *supra,* 350 U.S., at 556, 76 S. Ct., at 640. In Slochower, *supra,* New York law provided that a tenured employee taking the

---

[7] My views as to the requirements of due process where property interests are at stake does not deal with the entirely separate matter and requirements of due process when a person is deprived of liberty.

Fifth Amendment before a legislative committee inquiring into his official conduct could be fired. Quite apart from the Fifth Amendment "penalty" assessed by the State, the Court was concerned with the arbitrariness of drawing a conclusion, without a hearing, that any employee who took the Fifth Amendment was guilty or unfit for employment. The Court stated:

"This is not to say that Slochower has a constitutional right to be an associate professor of German at Brooklyn College. The State has broad powers in the selection and discharge of its employees, and it may be that proper inquiry would show Slochower's continued employment to be inconsistent with a real interest of the State. But there has been no such inquiry here." 350 U.S., at 559, 76 S. Ct., at 641.

The Court's decisions in the Board of Regents of State Colleges v. Roth, 408 U.S. 564, 92 S. Ct. 2701, 33 L. Ed. 2d 548 (1972), and Perry v. Sindermann, 408 U.S. 593, 92 S. Ct. 2694, 33 L. Ed. 2d 570 (1972), reiterate the notion that the Executive cannot be arbitrary in depriving a person of his job, when the legislature has provided that a person cannot be fired except for cause, and, if anything, extend the principles beyond the facts of this case. . . .

These cases only serve to emphasize that where there is a legitimate entitlement to a job, as when a person is given employment subject to his meeting certain specific conditions, due process requires, in order to insure against arbitrariness by the State in the administration of its law, that a person be given notice and a hearing before he is finally discharged. . . .

I conclude, therefore, that as a matter of due process, a hearing must be held at some time before a competitive civil service employee may be finally terminated for misconduct. Here, the Constitution and the Lloyd-LaFollette Act converge, because a full trial-type hearing is provided by statute before termination from the service becomes final, by way of appeal either through OEO or the Civil Service Commission, or both.

A different case might be put, of course, if the termination were for reasons of pure inefficiency, assuming such a general reason could be given, in which case it would be at least arguable that a hearing would serve no useful purpose and that judgments of this kind are best left to the discretion of administrative officials. This is not such a case, however, since Kennedy was terminated on specific charges of misconduct.

## III

The second question which must be addressed is whether a hearing of some sort must be held *before* any "taking" of the employee's property interest in his job occurs, even if a full hearing is available before that taking becomes final. I must resolve this question because in my view a full hearing must be afforded at some juncture and the claim is that it must occur prior to termination. If the right to any hearing itself is a pure matter of property definition, as the Court's opinion suggests, then that question need not be faced, for any kind of hearing, or no hearing at all, would suffice. As I have suggested, the State may not dispense with the minimum procedures defined by due process, but different considerations come into play when deciding whether a pretermination hearing is required and, if it is, what kind of hearing must be had.

In passing upon claims to a hearing before preliminary but nonfinal deprivations, the usual rule of this Court has been that a full hearing at some time suffices. . . .

In recent years, however, in a limited number of cases, the Court has held that a hearing must be furnished at the first stage of taking, even where a later hearing was provided. [Bell, Fuentes, Sniadach, and Goldberg cited.]

These conflicting lines of cases demonstrate [that in] assessing whether a prior hearing is required, the Court has looked to how the legitimate interests asserted by the party asserting the need for a hearing, and the party opposing it, would be furthered or hindered.

In many cases, where the claim to a pretermination hearing has been rejected, it appears that the legitimate interest of the party opposing the hearing might be defeated outright if such hearing were to be held. . . .

. . . In all such cases it is also significant that the party advancing the claim to a summary procedure stands ready to make whole the party who has been deprived of his property, if the initial taking proves to be wrongful, either by the credit of the public fisc or by posting a bond. . . .

However, other considerations have proved decisive, such as: the risk that the initial deprivation may be wrongful; the impact on the claimant to a hearing of not having the property while he waits for a full hearing; the interest of the party opposing the prior hearing and asserting the need for immediate possession in not alerting the current possessor to the lawsuit; and the risk of leaving the property in possession of the current possessor between the time notice is supplied and the time of the preliminary hearing. . . .

The last factor to be weighed in the balance is the danger to the party claiming possession occasioned by alerting the current possessor to the lawsuit, and then leaving the property in his hands pending the holding of the preliminary hearing. . . .

With the above principles in hand, is the tenured civil-service employee entitled to a pretermination hearing, such as that provided by the Lloyd-LaFollette Act?

There would be a problem of uncompensated loss to the Government, if the employee were to draw wages without working for the period between notice of a discharge and a preliminary hearing. Yet, if the charge against the employee did not indicate that the employee should be excluded from the workplace pending this hearing, some work could be exacted by the Government in exchange for its payment of salary. One must also consider another type of cost to the Government if preseparation hearings were provided — the necessity of keeping a person on the scene who might injure the public interest through poor service or might create an uproar at the work place. However, suspension with pay would obviate this problem.

On the employee's side of the ledger, there is the danger of mistaken termination. Discharge decisions, made ex parte, may be reversed after full hearing. One study reveals that in fiscal year 1970, in agencies where full pretermination hearings were routine, employees contesting removal were successful almost 20% of the time. R. Merrill, Procedures for Adverse Actions Against Federal Employees, 59 Va. L. Rev. 196, 204 n.35 (1973).

The impact on the employee of being without a job pending a full hearing is likely to be considerable because "[m]ore than 75 percent of actions contested within employing agencies require longer to decide than the 60 days prescribed by [Civil Service] Commission regulations. Over 50 percent take more than three months, and five percent are in process for longer than a year." Id., at 206. Of course, the discharged civil servant, deprived of his source of income, can seek employment in the private sector and so cut or minimize his losses, opportunities largely unavailable to the welfare recipient in Goldberg or the garnishee in Sniadach. Nonetheless, the employee may not be able to get a satisfactory position in the private sector, particularly a tenured one, and his marketability may be under a cloud due to the circumstances of his dismissal. See Lefkowitz v. Turley, 414 U.S. 70, 83, 94 S. Ct. 316, 325, 38 L. Ed. 2d 274 (1973). Cf. Board of Regents v. Roth, supra, 408 U.S., at 574 n.13, 92 S. Ct., at 2707. It should be stressed that if such employment is unavailable the Government may truly be pursuing a partially counter-productive policy by forcing the employee onto the welfare rolls.

Finally, by providing a pretermination hearing, the Government runs no risk through providing notice, since the employee cannot run away with his job, and can surely minimize its risk of uncompensated loss by eliminating the provision for personal appearances and setting early dates for filing written objections. Altogether different considerations, as to notice, might be applicable, if the employee would be likely to do damage to the Government if provided with such notice. See 5 CFR § 752.202 (c) (2) (1972), providing that an agency may dispense with the 30-day notice requirement "when there is reasonable cause to believe [an employee] is guilty of a crime for which a sentence of imprisonment can be imposed."

Perhaps partly on the basis of some of these constitutional considerations, Congress has provided for pretermination hearings. Certainly the debate on the Lloyd-LaFollette Act indicates that constitutional considerations were present in the minds of congressmen speaking in favor of the legislation. In any event, I conclude that the statute's provisions to the extent they require 30 days advance notice and a right to make a written presentation satisfy minimum constitutional requirements.

## IV

[MR. JUSTICE WHITE here states that since the supervisor who acted at the preliminary hearing was the person possibly defamed by the discharged employee, an impartial hearing official was required by due process. White concludes, however, that a full trial-type hearing was not necessary at the pretermination stage.]

In accord with these views, I would affirm the judgment of the three-judge court, ordering reinstatement and backpay, due to the failure to provide an impartial hearing officer at the pretermination hearing. I would reverse that part of the court's order enjoining the application of the statute on First Amendment vagueness and overbreadth grounds.

Mr. Justice DOUGLAS, dissenting.

The federal bureaucracy controls a vast conglomerate of people who walk more and more submissively to the dictates of their superiors. Our federal employees have lost many important political rights. . . .

There is more than employment and a job at issue in this case. The stake of the federal employee is not only in a livelihood but in his right to speak guaranteed by the First Amendment. He is charged with having stated that his superior and the superior's assistant had attempted to bribe a representative of a community action organization with whom the agency (OEO) had dealings. He is charged with having stated that those men offered a bribe of $100,000 in OEO funds to that organization if its representative would sign a statement against appellee and another OEO employee. This statement in my view was on a subject in the public domain. We all know merely by living in Washington, D.C., the storms that have swept through that agency and its branches. It has dealt with inflammatory problems in the solution of which inflammatory utterances are often made. I realize that it is the tradition of the Court to "balance" the right of free speech against other governmental interests and to sustain the First Amendment right only when the Court deems that in a given situation its importance outweighed competing interests. That was the approach in Pickering v. Board of Education, 391 U.S. 563, 88 S. Ct. 1731, 20 L. Ed. 2d 811, where the Court deemed what a teacher said against the school board was more important than the board's sensibilities. The Court, however, reserved decision where the comments of an employee involved "either discipline by immediate superiors or harmony among coworkers" id., at 570, 88 S. Ct. at 1735. That is one reason why Justice Black and I concurred in the result citing, inter alia, our opinion in Time Inc. v. Hill, 385 U.S. 374, 87 S. Ct. 534, 17 L. Ed. 2d 456. Justice Black said that the "balancing" or "weighing" doctrine "plainly encourages and actually invites judges to choose for themselves between conflicting values, even where, as in the First Amendment, the Founders made a choice of values, one of which is a free press. Though the Constitution requires that judges swear to obey and enforce it, it is not altogether strange that all judges are not always dead set against constitutional interpretations that expand their powers, and that when power is once claimed by some, others are loath to give it up." Id., 399-400, 87 S. Ct. 548.

The fact that appellee in the present case inveighed against his superior is irrelevant. The matter on which he spoke was in the public domain. His speaking may well have aroused such animosity in his superior as to disqualify him from being in charge of disciplinary proceedings; and conceivably it could cause disharmony among workers. And these consequences are quite antagonistic to the image which agencies have built. Their dominant characteristic is the application of Peter's Inversion. See: Peter and Hull, The Peter Principle (Bantam ed. 1970), pp. 24-26. In a few words Peter's Inversion marks the incompetent cadre's interest in his employee's *input*, not his *output.*

His *input* reflects his attitude toward the *cadre,* and toward his work. A pleasant manner, promotion of staff harmony, servility to the *cadre,* and promptness, civility, and submissiveness are what count. The result is a great levelling of employees. They hear the beat of only one drum and march to it. These days employers have psychological tests by which they can separate the ingenious, off-beat character who may make trouble from the more subservient type. It is, of course, none of a court's problem what the employment policies may be. But once an employee speaks out on a public issue and is punished for it, we have a justiciable issue. Appellee is in my view being penalized by the Federal Government for exercising his right to speak out. The excuse or pretense is an Act of Congress and an agency's regulations promulgated under it in the teeth of the First Amendment; "Congress shall make no law . . . abridging the freedom of speech or of the press. . . ." Losing one's job with the Federal Government because of one's discussion of an issue in the public domain is certainly an abridgement of speech.

MR. JUSTICE MARSHALL, with whom MR. JUSTICE DOUGLAS and MR. JUSTICE BRENNAN concur, dissenting.

[MR. JUSTICE MARSHALL first states that a government job is a type of property interest and not just a privilege. He concludes that a full evidentiary hearing was required *before* dismissal, because the repercussions of discharge were much more serious than the plurality opinion suggests and the government's interests in efficiency and harmony among workers were insufficient to diminish the employee's constitutional rights.]

Given the importance of the interest at stake, the discharged employee should be afforded an opportunity to test the strength of the evidence of his misconduct by confronting and cross-examining adverse witnesses and by presenting witnesses in his own behalf, whenever there are substantial disputes in testimonial evidence. See Morrissey v. Brewer, 408 U.S., at 487, 92 S. Ct., at 2603. A dismissal for cause often involves disputed questions of fact raised by accusations of misconduct. Mistakes of identity, distortions caused by the failure of information sources, faulty perceptions or cloudy memories as well as fabrications born of personal antagonisms are among the factors which may undermine the accuracy of the factual determinations upon which dismissals are based. The possibility of error is not significant. Almost a fourth of all appeals from adverse agency actions result in reversal.

In our system of justice, the right of confrontation provides the crucible for testing the truth of accusations such as those leveled by appellee's superior and strenuously denied by appellee. . . .

## II

The court below also held that the provision of the Lloyd-LaFollette Act which authorizes dismissal of tenured Government employees for "such cause as will promote the efficiency of the service" is unconstitutionally vague and overbroad. . . .

The "efficiency of the service" standard would appear to bring within its reach, as permissible grounds for dismissal, even truthful criticism of an agency that in any way tends to disrupt its operation. One can be sure, for example, that the criticism of the young man in Senator LaFollette's example disrupted the operation of the Chicago Post Office. It seems clear that the standard could be construed to punish such protected speech.

The majority purports to solve this potential overbreadth problem merely by announcing that the standard in the Act "excludes protected speech." Nonetheless, it leaves the statutory standard intact and offers no guidance other than this general observation as to what conduct is or is not punishable. The Court's answer is no answer at all. To accept this response is functionally to eliminate overbreadth from the First Amendment lexicon. No statute can reach and punish constitutionally protected speech. The majority has not given the statute a limiting construction but merely repeated the obvious.

The majority misunderstands the overbreadth principle which concerns the potential deterrent effect on constitutionally protected speech of a statute that is overbroad or vague on its face. The focus of the doctrine is not on the individual actor before the court but on others who may forego protected activity rather than run afoul of the statute's proscriptions. Hence, the Court has reversed convictions where the subject speech could have been punished under a more narrowly drawn statute because the statute as drawn purported to cover, and might deter others from engaging in, protected speech. The Court explained this vagueness-overbreadth relationship in Keyishian v. Board of Regents, 385 U.S. 589, 603-605, 87 S. Ct. 675, 684, 17 L. Ed. 2d 629 (1967). . . .

By the uncertainty of its scope, the standard here creates the very danger of a chilling effect that concerned the Court in Keyishian. Employees are likely to limit their behavior to that which is unquestionably safe, for "the threat of dismissal from public employment is . . . a potent means of inhibiting speech." Pickering, supra, 391 U.S., at 574, 88 S. Ct., at 1737. The dismissal standard hangs over their heads like a sword of Damocles, threatening them with dismissal for any speech that might impair the "efficiency of the service." That this Court will ultimately vindicate an employee if his speech is constitutionally protected is of little consequence — for the value of a sword of Damocles is that it hangs — not that it drops. For every employee who risks his job by testing the limits of the statute, many more will choose the cautious path and not speak at all. . . .

I respectfully dissent.

## BISHOP v. WOOD

United States Supreme Court
96 S. Ct. 2074 (1976)

MR. JUSTICE STEVENS delivered the opinion of the Court.

Acting on the recommendation of the Chief of Police, the City Manager of Marion, North Carolina, terminated petitioner's employment as a policeman without affording him a hearing to determine the sufficiency of the cause for his discharge. Petitioner brought suit contending that since a city ordinance classified him as a "permanent employee," he had a constitutional right to a pretermination hearing.[1] During pretrial discovery petitioner was advised that his dismissal was based on a failure to follow certain orders, poor attendance at police training classes, causing low morale, and conduct unsuited to an officer. Petitioner and several other police officers filed affidavits essentially denying the truth of these charges. The District Court granted defendants' motion for summary judgment. The Court of Appeals affirmed and we granted certiorari, 423 U. S. 890.

The questions for us to decide are (1) whether petitioner's employment status was a property interest protected by the Due Process Clause of the Fourteenth Amendment, and (2) assuming that the explanation for his discharge was false, whether that false explanation deprived him of an interest in liberty protected by that clause.

I

Petitioner was employed by the city of Marion as a probationary policeman on June 9, 1969. After six months he became a permanent employee. He was dismissed on March 31, 1972. He claims that he had either an express or an implied right to continued employment.

A city ordinance provides that a permanent employee may be discharged if he fails to perform work up to the standard of his classification, or if he is negligent, inefficient or unfit to perform his duties.[5] Petitioner first contends that even

---

[1] He relied on 42 U. S. C. § 1983, invoking federal jurisdiction under 28 U. S. C. § 1343 (3). He sought reinstatement and back pay. The defendants were the then city manager, chief of police, and the city of Marion. Since the city is not a "person" within the meaning of the statute, it was not a proper defendant. Monroe v. Pape, 365 U. S. 167, 187-192.

[5] Article II, § 6, of the Personnel Ordinance of the city of Marion, reads as follows:

"*Dismissal.* A permanent employee whose work is not satisfactory over a period of time shall be notified in what way his work is deficient and what he must do if his work is to be satisfactory. If a permanent employee fails to perform work up to the standard of the classification held, or continues to be negligent, inefficient, or unfit to perform his duties, he may be dismissed by the City Manager. Any discharged employee shall be given written notice of his discharge setting forth the effective date and reasons for his discharge if he shall request such a notice."

though the ordinance does not expressly so provide, it should be read to prohibit discharge for any other reason, and therefore to confer tenure on all permanent employees. In addition, he contends that his period of service, together with his "permanent" classification, gave him a sufficient expectancy of continued employment to constitute a protected property interest.

A property interest in employment can, of course, be created by ordinance, or by an implied contract. In either case, however, the sufficiency of the claim of entitlement must be decided by reference to state law. The North Carolina Supreme Court has held that an enforceable expectation of continued public employment in that State can exist only if the employer, by statute or contract, has actually granted some form of guarantee. Still v. Lance, 275 N. C. 254, 182 S. E. 2d 403 (1971). Whether such a guarantee has been given can be determined only by an examination of the particular statute or ordinance in question.

On its face the ordinance on which petitioner relies may fairly be read as conferring such a guarantee. However, such a reading is not the only possible interpretation; the ordinance may also be construed as granting no right to continued employment but merely conditioning an employee's removal on compliance with certain specified procedures.[8] We do not have any authoritative interpretation of this ordinance by a North Carolina state court. We do, however, have the opinion of the United States District Judge who, of course, sits in North Carolina and practiced law there for many years. Based on his understanding of state law, he concluded that petitioner "held his position at the will and pleasure of the city." [9] This construction of North Carolina law was upheld by the Court of Appeals for the Fourth Circuit, albeit by an equally divided Court. In comparable circumstances, the Court has accepted the interpretation of state law in which the District Court and the Court of Appeals have concurred even if an examination of the state law issue without such guidance might have justified a different conclusion.

In this case, as the District Court construed the ordinance, the City Manager's determination of the adequacy of the grounds for discharge is not subject to judicial review; the employee is merely given certain procedural rights which the District Court found not to have been violated in this case. The District Court's reading of the ordinance is tenable; it derives some support from a decision of the North Carolina Supreme Court, *Still v. Lance, supra;* and it was accepted by

---

[8] This is not the construction which six Members of this Court placed on the federal regulations involved in Arnett v. Kennedy, 416 U. S. 134. In that case the Court concluded that because the employee could only be discharged for cause, he had a property interest which was entitled to constitutional protection. In this case, a holding that as a matter of state law the employee "held his position at the will and pleasure of the city" necessarily establishes that he had no property interest. The Court's evaluation of the federal regulations involved in *Arnett* sheds no light on the problem presented by this case.

[9] "Under the law in North Carolina, nothing else appearing, a contract of employment which contains no provision for the duration or termination of employment is terminable at the will of either party irrespective of the quality of performance by the other party. By statute, G. S. 115-142 (b), a County Board of Education in North Carolina may terminate the employment of a teacher at the end of the school year without filing charges or giving its reasons for such termination, or granting the teacher an opportunity to be heard. Still v. Lance, 279 N. C. 254, 182 S. E. 2d 403 (1971).

"It is clear from Article II, Section 6, of the City's Personnel Ordinance, that the dismissal of an employee does not require a notice or hearing. Upon request of the discharged employee, he shall be given written notice of his discharge setting forth the effective date and the reasons for the discharge. It thus appears that both the city ordinance and the state law have been complied with.

"It further appears that the plaintiff held his position at the will and pleasure of the city."

the Court of Appeals for the Fourth Circuit. These reasons are sufficient to foreclose our independent examination of the state law issue.

Under that view of the law, petitioner's discharge did not deprive him of a property interest protected by the Fourteenth Amendment.

## II

Petitioner's claim that he has been deprived of liberty has two components. He contends that the reasons given for his discharge are so serious as to constitute a stigma that may severely damage his reputation in the community; in addition, he claims that those reasons were false.

In our appraisal of petitioner's claim we must accept his version of the facts since the District Court granted summary judgment against him. His evidence established that he was a competent police officer; that he was respected by his peers; that he made more arrests than any other officer on the force; that although he had been criticized for engaging in high speed pursuits, he had promptly complied with such criticism; and that he had a reasonable explanation for his imperfect attendance at police training sessions. We must therefore assume that his discharge was a mistake and based on incorrect information.

In Board of Regents v. Roth, 408 U. S. 564, we recognized that the nonretention of an untenured college teacher might make him somewhat less attractive to other employers, but nevertheless concluded that it would stretch the concept too far "to suggest that a person is deprived of 'liberty' when he simply is not retained in one position but remains as free as before to seek another." *Id.,* at 575. This same conclusion applies to the discharge of a public employee whose position is terminable at the will of the employer when there is no public disclosure of the reasons for the discharge.

In this case the asserted reasons for the City Manager's decision were communicated orally to the petitioner in private and also were stated in writing in answer to interrogatories after this litigation commenced. Since the former communication was not made public, it cannot properly form the basis for a claim that petitioner's interest in his "good name, reputation, honesty, or integrity" was thereby impaired. And since the latter communication was made in the course of a judicial proceeding which did not commence until after petitioner had suffered the injury for which he seeks redress, it surely cannot provide retroactive support for his claim. A contrary evaluation of either explanation would penalize forthright and truthful communication between employer and employee in the former instance, and between litigants in the latter.

Petitioner argues, however, that the reasons given for his discharge were false. Even so, the reasons stated to him in private had no different impact on his reputation than if they had been true. And the answers to his interrogatories, whether true or false, did not cause the discharge. The truth or falsity of the City Manager's statement determines whether or not his decision to discharge the petitioner was correct or prudent, but neither enhances nor diminishes petitioner's claim that his constitutionally protected interest in liberty has been impaired.[13] A contrary evaluation of his contention would enable every

---

[13] Indeed, the impact on petitioner's constitutionally protected interest in liberty is no greater even if we assume that the City Manager deliberately lied. Such fact might conceivably provide the basis for a state law claim, the validity of which would be entirely unaffected by our analysis of the federal constitutional question.

discharged employee to assert a constitutional claim merely by alleging that his former supervisor made a mistake.

The federal court is not the appropriate forum in which to review the multitude of personnel decisions that are made daily by public agencies.[14] We must accept the harsh fact that numerous individual mistakes are inevitable in the day-to-day administration of our affairs. The United States Constitution cannot feasibly be construed to require federal judicial review for every such error. In the absence of any claim that the public employer was motivated by a desire to curtail or to penalize the exercise of an employee's constitutionally protected rights, we must presume that official action was regular and, if erroneous, can best be corrected in other ways. The Due Process Clause of the Fourteenth Amendment is not a guarantee against incorrect or ill-advised personnel decisions.

The judgment is affirmed.

MR. JUSTICE BRENNAN, with whom MR. JUSTICE MARSHALL concurs, dissenting.

Petitioner was discharged as a policeman on the grounds of insubordination, "causing low morale," and "conduct unsuited to an officer." *Ante,* at 1. It is difficult to imagine a greater "badge of infamy" that could be imposed on one following petitioner's calling; in a profession in which prospective employees are invariably investigated, petitioner's job prospects will be severely constricted by the governmental action in this case. Although our case law would appear to require that petitioner thus be accorded an opportunity "to clear his name" of this calumny, see, *e.g.,* Board of Regents v. Roth, 408 U.S. 564, 573 and n. 12 (1972), Arnett v. Kennedy, 416 U.S. 134, 157 (1974) (opinion of REHNQUIST, J.), the Court condones this governmental action and holds that petitioner was deprived of no liberty interest thereby.

. . .

MR. JUSTICE WHITE, with whom MR. JUSTICE BRENNAN, MR. JUSTICE MARSHALL, and MR. JUSTICE BLACKMUN join, dissenting.

I dissent because the decision of the majority rests upon a proposition which was squarely addressed and in my view correctly rejected by six Members of this Court in Arnett v. Kennedy, 416 U. S. 134 (1974).

Petitioner Bishop was a permanent employee of the Police Department of the City of Marion, N. C. The city ordinance applicable to him provides:

. . .

"*Dismissal.* A permanent employee whose work is not satisfactory over a period of time shall be notified in what way his work is deficient and what he must do if his work is to be satisfactory. *If* a permanent employee fails to perform work up to the standard of the classification held, or continues to be negligent, inefficient, or unfit to perform his duties, he may be dismissed by the City Manager. Any discharged employee shall be given written notice of his

---

[14] The cumulative impression created by the three dissenting opinions is that this holding represents a significant retreat from settled practice in the federal courts. The fact of the matter, however, is that the instances in which the federal judiciary has required a state agency to reinstate a discharged employee for failure to provide a pretermination hearing are extremely rare. The reason is clear. For unless we were to adopt MR. JUSTICE BRENNAN's remarkably innovative suggestion that we develop a federal common law of property rights, or his equally far reaching view that almost every discharge implicates a constitutionally protected liberty interest, the ultimate control of state personnel relationships is, and will remain, with the States; they may grant or withhold tenure at their unfettered discretion. In this case, whether we accept or reject the construction of the ordinance adopted by the two lower courts, the power to change or clarify that ordinance will remain in the hands of the City Council of the city of Marion.

discharge setting forth the effective date and reasons for his discharge if he shall request such a notice." (Emphasis added.)

The second sentence of this ordinance plainly conditions petitioner's dismissal on cause — *i.e.,* failure to perform up to standard, negligence, inefficiency, or unfitness to perform the job. The District Court below did not otherwise construe this portion of the ordinance. In the only part of its opinion rejecting petitioner's claim that the ordinance gave him a property interest in his job, the District Court said, in an opinion predating this Court's decision in *Arnett v. Kennedy, supra,*

"It is clear from Article II, Section 6, of the City's Personnel Ordinance, that the dismissal of an employee does not require a notice or hearing. Upon request of the discharged employee, he shall be given written notice of his discharge setting forth the effective date and the reasons for the discharge. It thus appears that both the city ordinance and the state law have been complied with."

Thus in concluding that petitioner had no "property interest" in his job entitling him to a hearing on discharge and that he held his position "at the will and pleasure of the city," the District Court relied on the fact that the ordinance described its own *procedures* for determining cause which procedures did not include a hearing. The majority purports, at pp. 3-4, n. 8, to read the District Court's opinion as construing the ordinance not to condition dismissal on cause, and, if this is what the majority means, its reading of the District Court's opinion is clearly erroneous for the reasons just stated.[1] However, later in its opinion the majority appears to eschew this construction of the District Court's opinion and of the ordinance. In the concluding paragraph of its discussion of petitioner's property interest, the majority holds that since neither the ordinance nor state law provides for a hearing, or any kind of review of the City Manager's dismissal decision, petitioner had no enforceable property interest in his job. The majority concludes:

"In this case, as the District Court construed the ordinance, the City Manager's *determination of the adequacy of the grounds for discharge* is not subject to judicial review; the employee is merely given certain procedural rights which the District Court found not to have been violated in this case. The District Court's reading of the ordinance is tenable; . . ." (Emphasis added.)

The majority thus implicitly concedes that the ordinance supplies the "grounds" for discharge and that the City Manager must determine them to be "adequate" before he may fire an employee. The majority's holding that petitioner had no property interest in his job in spite of the unequivocal language in the city ordinance that he may be dismissed only for certain kinds of cause rests, then, on the fact that state law provides no *procedures* for assuring that the City Manager dismiss him only for cause. The right to his job apparently given by the

---

[1] The Court accepts the District Court's conclusion that the city employee holds his position at the will and pleasure of the city. If the Court believes that the District Court's conclusion did not rest on the procedural limitations in the ordinance, then the Court must construe the District Court's opinion — and the ordinance — as permitting, but not limiting, discharges to those based on the causes specified in the ordinance. In this view, discharges for other reasons or for no reason at all could be made. Termination of employment would in effect be within the complete discretion of the city; and for this reason the employee would have no property interest in his employment which would call for the protections of the Due Process Clause. As indicated in the text, I think this construction of the ordinance and of the District Court's opinion is in error.

first two sentences of the ordinance is thus redefined, according to the majority, by the procedures provided for in the third sentence and as redefined is infringed only if the procedures are not followed.

This is precisely the reasoning which was embraced by only three and expressly rejected by six Members of this Court in *Arnett v. Kennedy, supra.* . . .

## CODD v. VELGER

United States Supreme Court
429 U.S. 624 (1977)

PER CURIAM.

Respondent Velger's action shifted its focus, in a way not uncommon to lawsuits, from the time of the filing of his complaint in the United States District Court for the Southern District of New York to the decision by the Court of Appeals for the Second Circuit which we review here. His original complaint alleged that he had been wrongly dismissed without a hearing or a statement of reasons from his position as a patrolman with the New York City Police Department, and under 42 U.S.C. § 1983, sought reinstatement and damages for the resulting injury to his reputation and future employment prospects. After proceedings in which Judge Gurfein (then of the District Court) ruled that respondent had held a probationary position and therefore had no hearing right based on a property interest in his job, respondent filed an amended complaint. That complaint alleged more specifically than had the previous one that respondent was entitled to a hearing due to the stigmatizing effect of certain material placed by the City Police Department in his personnel file. He alleged that the derogatory material had brought about his subsequent dismissal from a position with the Penn-Central Railroad Police Department, and that it had also prevented him from finding other employment of a similar nature for which his scores on numerous examinations otherwise qualified him.[1]

The case came on for a bench trial before Judge Werker, who, in the words of his opinion on the merits, found "against plaintiff on all issues." He determined that the only issue which survived Judge Gurfein's ruling on the earlier motions was whether petitioners, in discharging respondent had "imposed a stigma on Mr. Velger that foreclosed his freedom to take advantage of other employment opportunities." After discussing the evidence bearing upon this issue, Judge Werker concluded that "[i]t is clear from the foregoing facts that plaintiff has not proved that he has been stigmatized by defendants."

Among the specific findings of fact made by the District Court was that an officer of the Penn-Central Railroad Police Department was shown the City Police Department file relating to respondent's employment, upon presentation of a form signed by respondent authorizing the release of personnel information. From an examination of the file, this officer "gleaned that plaintiff had been dismissed because while still a trainee he had put a revolver to his head in an

---

[1] Respondent's amended complaint did not seek a delayed *Roth* hearing to be conducted by his former employer at which he would have the opportunity to refute the charge in question. *Board of Regents v. Roth,* 408 U.S. 564, 573, 92 S.Ct. 2701, 2707, 33 L.Ed.2d 548. The relief he sought was premised on the assumption that the failure to accord such a hearing when it should have been accorded entitled him to obtain reinstatement and damages resulting from the denial of such hearing. We therefore have no occasion to consider the allocation of the burden of pleading and proof of the necessary issues as between the federal forum and the administrative hearing where such relief is sought.

apparent suicide attempt." The Penn-Central officer tried to verify this story, but petitioner's office refused to cooperate with him, advising him to proceed by letter. In rendering judgment against the respondent, the court also found that he had failed to establish "that information about his Police Department service was publicized or circulated by defendants in any way that might reach his prospective employers."

Respondent successfully appealed this decision to the Court of Appeals for the Second Circuit. That court held that the finding of no stigma was clearly erroneous. It reasoned that the information about the apparent suicide attempt was of a kind which would necessarily impair employment prospects for one seeking work as a police officer. It also decided that the mere act of making available personnel files with the employee's consent was enough to place responsibility for the stigma on the employer, since former employees had no practical alternative but to consent to the release of such information if they wished to be seriously considered for other employment.

We granted certiorari, — U.S. —, 96 S.Ct. 3188, 49 L.Ed.2d 1197 (1976), and the parties have urged us to consider whether the report in question was of a stigmatizing nature, and whether the circumstances of its apparent dissemination were such as to fall within the language of *Board of Regents v. Roth,* 408 U.S. 564, 573, 92 S.Ct. 2701, 2707, 33 L.Ed.2d 548 (1972) and *Bishop v. Wood,* 426 U.S. 341, 96 S.Ct. 2074, 48 L.Ed.2d 684 (1976). We find it unnecessary to reach these issues, however, because of respondent's failure to allege or prove one essential element of his case.

Assuming all of the other elements necessary to make out a claim of stigmatization under *Roth* and *Bishop,* the remedy mandated by the Due Process Clause of the Fourteenth Amendment is "an opportunity to refute the charge." 408 U.S., at 573, 92 S.Ct. at 2707. "The purpose of such notice and hearing is to provide the person an opportunity to clear his name," *id.,* n. 12. But if the hearing mandated by the Due Process Clause is to serve any useful purpose, there must be some factual dispute between an employer and a discharged employee which has some significant bearing on the employee's reputation. Nowhere in his pleadings or elsewhere has respondent affirmatively asserted that the report of the apparent suicide attempt was substantially false. Neither the District Court nor the Court of Appeals made any such finding. When we consider the nature of the interest sought to be protected, we believe the absence of any such allegation or finding is fatal to respondent's claim under the Due Process Clause that he should have been given a hearing.

Where the liberty interest involved is that of conditional freedom following parole, we have said that the hearing required by the Due Process Clause in order to revoke parole must address two separate considerations. The first is whether the parolee in fact committed the violation with which he is charged, and the second is whether if he did commit the act his parole should, under all the circumstances, therefore be revoked. *Morrissey v. Brewer,* 408 U.S. 471, 479-480, 92 S.Ct. 2593, 2599, 33 L.Ed.2d 484 (1972); *Gagnon v. Scarpelli,* 411 U.S. 778, 784, 93 S.Ct. 1756, 1760, 36 L.Ed.2d 656 (1973). The fact that there was no dispute with respect to the commission of the act would not necessarily obviate the need for a hearing on the issue of whether the commission of the act warranted the revocation of parole.

But the hearing required where a nontenured employee has been stigmatized in the course of a decision to terminate his employment is solely "to provide the person an opportunity to clear his name." If he does not challenge the substantial truth of the material in question, no hearing would afford a promise of achieving that result for him. For the contemplated hearing does not embrace any determination analogous to the "second step" of the parole revocation proceeding, which would in effect be a determination of whether or not, conceding that the report were true, the employee was properly refused re-employment. Since the District Court found that respondent had no Fourteenth Amendment property interest in continued employment,[2] the adequacy or even the existence of reasons for failing to rehire him presents no federal constitutional question. Only if the employer creates and disseminates a false and defamatory impression about the employee in connection with his termination is such a hearing required. *Roth, supra; Bishop, supra.*

Our decision here rests upon no overly technical application of the rules of pleading. Even conceding that the respondent's termination occurred solely because of the report of an apparent suicide attempt, a proposition which is certainly not crystal clear on this record, respondent has at no stage of this litigation affirmatively stated that the "attempt" did not take place as reported. The furthest he has gone is a suggestion by his counsel that "i[t] might have been all a mistake, [i]t could also have been a little horseplay." This is not enough to raise an issue about the substantial accuracy of the report. Respondent has therefore made out no claim under the Fourteenth Amendment that he was harmed by the denial of a hearing, even were we to accept in its entirety the determination by the Court of Appeals that the creation and disclosure of the file report otherwise amounted to stigmatization within the meaning of *Board of Regents v. Roth, supra.*

The judgment of the Court of Appeals is reversed with instructions to reinstate the judgment of the District Court.

Mr. Justice BLACKMUN, concurring.

I join the Court's *per curiam* opinion, but I emphasize that in this case there is no suggestion that the information in the file, if true, was not information of a kind that appropriately might be disclosed to prospective employers. We therefore are not presented with a question as to the limits, if any, on the disclosure of prejudicial, but irrelevant, accurate information.

Mr. Justice BRENNAN, with whom Mr. Justice MARSHALL joins, dissenting.

I dissent from today's holding substantially for the reasons expressed by my Brother STEVENS in Part I of his dissent, despite my belief that the Court's ruling is likely to be of little practical importance. . . .

I also agree with Part III of Mr. Justice STEVENS' dissenting opinion, and I would therefore remand this case to the Court of Appeals for further proceedings.

Mr. Justice STEWART, dissenting.

Although sharing generally the views expressed in the Court's opinion, I agree with Part III of Mr. Justice STEVENS' dissenting opinion, and I would for that reason remand this case to the Court of Appeals for further proceedings.

Mr. Justice STEVENS, dissenting.

---

[2] The Court of Appeals did not pass on this "property interest" question. Respondent has not urged it as an alternative basis for affirming the judgment of that court, and indeed has all but conceded in his brief that the District Court's interpretation of the relevant New York cases is correct in this respect. Brief of Respondent, at 14. The opinion of the District Court on this point reflects a proper understanding of *Roth, supra,* and of *Perry v. Sindermann,* 408 U.S. 593, 92 S.Ct. 2694, 33 L.Ed.2d 570, and we see no reason to disturb its application of those cases to particular facets of the New York law of entitlement to public job tenure. *Perry, supra,* at 602 n. 7, 92 S.Ct. at 2700 n. 7.

There are three aspects of the Court's disposition of this case with which I disagree. First, I am not persuaded that a person who claims to have been "stigmatized" by the State without being afforded due process need allege that the charge against him was false in order to state a cause of action under 42 U.S.C. § 1983. Second, in my opinion the Court should not assume that this respondent was stigmatized, because the District Court's contrary finding was not clearly erroneous. Third, I would remand the case to the Court of Appeals to consider the claim that respondent had a property interest in his job, since that court did not decide this issue.

I

The Court holds that respondent's failure to allege falsity negates his right to damages for the State's failure to give him a hearing. This holding does not appear to rest on the view that a discharged employee has no right to a hearing unless the charge against him is false. If it did, it would represent a radical departure from a principle basic to our legal system — the principle that the guilty as well as the innocent are entitled to a fair trial. It would also be a departure from *Board of Regents v. Roth,* 408 U.S. 564, 572-575, 92 S.Ct. 2701, 2707, 33 L.Ed.2d 548. In that case the Court concluded that a person is deprived of liberty when the State's refusal to rehire him destroys his "good name" in the community or forecloses him from practicing his profession. A hearing may establish that such a deprivation of liberty is warranted because the charges are correct. But *Bishop v. Wood,* 426 U.S. 341, 349, 96 S.Ct. 2074, 2080, 48 L.Ed.2d 684, makes it clear that the truth or falsity of the charge "neither enhances nor diminishes [the employee's] claim that his constitutionally protected interest in liberty has been impaired." If the charge, whether true or false, involves a deprivation of liberty, due process must accompany the deprivation. And normally, as *Roth* plainly states, the Constitution mandates "a full prior hearing." *Id.,* 408 U.S. at 574, 92 S.Ct. at 2707.[3]

This hearing must include consideration of whether the charge, if true, warrants discharge. The discharge itself is part of the deprivation of liberty against which the employee is entitled to defend. Release of unfavorable information can damage an employee's reputation and employment prospects, but far greater injury is caused by an official determination, based on such information, that the employee is unfit for public employment. Indeed the Court has held that an injury to reputation had not resulted in a deprivation of liberty *because* it was not associated with the termination of employment. *Paul v. Davis,* 424 U.S. 693, 709-710, 96 S.Ct. 1155, 47 L.Ed.2d 405. Since allowing the

---

[3] As I read Part II of *Roth* (408 U.S. 572-575, 92 S.Ct. 2706-2708) which discusses the kind of "liberty" that is protected by the Due Process Clause of the Fourteenth Amendment, there are two quite different interests which may be implicated when a nontenured employee is discharged. First, in the full paragraph in the middle of p. 573, 92 S.Ct. p. 2707, the Court considers the individual's interest in "good name, reputation, honor, or integrity." It is with respect to this reputational interest that the footnote on p. 573 indicates that a name-clearing hearing is constitutionally required. That footnote does not tell us whether that hearing must precede the injury to reputation, and surely does not imply that such a hearing is the only remedy available to an employee whose constitutional right to due process has been violated.

Second, in the ensuing paragraphs, the *Roth* opinion considers the individual interest in avoiding "a stigma or other disability" that forecloses employment opportunities. With respect to this interest, on p. 574 of 408 U.S., p. 2707, of 92 S.Ct. the Court rather clearly indicates that no such stigma may be imposed without a "full prior hearing."

employee to keep his job would eliminate (or at least lessen) the loss of liberty, due process requires that the hearing include the issue whether the facts warrant discharge.[4] In short, the purpose of the hearing, as is true of any other hearing which must precede a deprivation of liberty, is two-fold: first to establish the truth or falsity of the charge, and second, to provide a basis for deciding what action is warranted by the facts.[5] Even when it is perfectly clear that the charge is true, the Constitution requires that procedural safeguards be observed. Cf. *Groppi v. Leslie,* 404 U.S. 496, 503, 92 S.Ct. 582, 586, 30 L.Ed.2d 632. For these reasons, I disagree with the Court's assertion that the purpose of the hearing is "solely" to provide the person with an opportunity to clear his name.

Even, if I agreed with the Court that this was the sole purpose of the hearing, I could not agree with its holding that failure to demonstrate falsity is fatal to the employee's suit. Surely the burden should be on the State to show that failure to provide due process was harmless error because the charges were true. . . .

## II

Although the plaintiff does not have the burden of proving that he was discharged for a false reason, if he claims that the discharge deprived him of liberty, he does have the burden of proving that he was stigmatized. The District Court found that respondent did not meet that burden in this case. Under the proper standard of appellate review, I cannot say that finding was clearly erroneous, particularly when the record discloses that the respondent did not prove exactly what the unfavorable information in his file was, or exactly what information was disseminated to others.

. . .

I conclude that the Court of Appeals was incorrect in setting aside the District Court's findings of fact. Since those findings do not establish the existence of a stigma, the Court of Appeals erred in holding on this basis that a hearing was required.

## III

It is possible, however, that a hearing was required because the discharge deprived respondent of a property interest. The District Court rejected the claim

---

[4] Similarly, since disclosure of the charges is also part of the deprivation of liberty, *Bishop v. Wood,* 426 U.S. 341, 348, 96 S.Ct. 2074, 2079, 48 L.Ed.2d 684, the hearing could properly include the issue whether the charges should remain confidential, or whether the written record should at least be modified to reflect a less one-sided description of the events.

[5] At p. 884, *ante,* the Court states:

"Where the liberty interest involved is that of conditional freedom following parole, we have said that the hearing required by the Due Process Clause in order to revoke parole must address two separate considerations. The first is whether the parolee in fact committed the violation with which he is charged, and the second is whether if he did commit the act his parole should, under all the circumstances, therefore be revoked. *Morrissey v. Brewer,* 408 U.S. 471, 479-480, 92 S.Ct. 2593, 33 L.Ed.2d 484 (1972); *Gagnon v. Scarpelli,* 411 U.S. 778, 784, 93 S.Ct. 1756, 1760, 36 L.Ed.2d 656 (1973). The fact that there was no dispute with respect to the commission of the act would not necessarily obviate the need for a hearing on the issue of whether the commission of the act warranted the revocation of parole."

This reasoning is equally applicable to a decision to revoke a person's employment for a stigmatizing reason. The fact that there is no dispute with respect to the commission of the act involved does not necessarily obviate the need for a hearing on the issue of whether employment should be terminated.

that he had an entitlement to his job as a matter of state law, but the Court of Appeals found it unnecessary to reach this issue. I believe there is enough merit to the property claim to justify a remand to the Court of Appeals with directions to reconsider it.

In *Bishop v. Wood,* the plaintiff's job was "terminable at the will of either party irrespective of the quality of performance by the other party." 426 U.S. 341, 345 n. 9, 96 S.Ct. 2074, 2078, 48 L.Ed.2d 684 and accompanying text. There was no right to state judicial review. In this case, however, the state law may afford the employee some protection against arbitrary discharge. According to the state case cited by Judge Gurfein, App., at 37a, the police commissioner may terminate only "unsatisfactory employees," [13] and his determination is reviewable in the state courts on an "arbitrary and capricious" standard. *In re Going v. Kennedy,* 5 A.D.2d 173, 176-177, 170 N.Y.S.2d 234, 237-238 (1958), aff'd, 5 N.Y.2d 900, 183 N.Y.S.2d 81, 156 N.E.2d 711 (1959); see *In re Talamo v. Murphy,* 38 N.Y.2d 637, 382 N.Y.S.2d 3, 345 N.E.2d 546 (1976). Unlike *Bishop,* in which a hearing would have been pointless because nothing plaintiff could prove would entitle him to keep his job, in this case the plaintiff may have had a right to continued employment if he could rebut the charges against him.[15]

By directing the Court of Appeals to reinstate the District Court judgment, the Court summarily rejects this claim without the benefit of briefing or oral argument on the point. I would remand the case to the Court of Appeals for consideration of this claim.

## NOTES

1. In Lake Michigan College Fed'n of Teachers v. Lake Michigan Community College, 89 L.R.R.M. 2865 (1975), *cert. denied,* 96 S. Ct. 3189 (1976), the Sixth Circuit applied the standards of *Roth* and *Arnett* to find that Michigan college teachers who participated in an illegal strike had been properly discharged since neither that state's Public Employment Relations Act nor the collective bargaining agreement between the parties granted any property interest in continued employment to the teachers. The court also held that the teachers' Fourteenth Amendment liberty interests were not automatically implicated when they were accused of breaking the law absent a showing that (1) the allegations discredited the teachers' honesty, morality, and integrity; (2) their reputations were seriously damaged in the community; or (3) a definite range of opportunities was no longer open to them.

2. In Soni v. Board of Trustees of the Univ. of Tennessee, 513 F.2d 347 (6th Cir., 1975), *cert. denied,* 44 LW 3699, a nontenured university professor who had been terminated claimed a violation of his due process rights. The court there held that the existence of a formal tenure system would not automatically foreclose a determination that a nontenured professor has acquired a property interest in his employment. Where the university objectively acted toward the plaintiff in such a manner as to lead the professor

---

[13] In *Arnett v. Kennedy,* 416 U.S. 134, 94 S.Ct. 1633, 40 L.Ed.2d 15, the employee could be discharged only "for 'such cause as will promote the efficiency of [the] service,' " *id.,* at 151-152, 94 S.Ct. at 1643 (Opinion of Rehnquist, J.). Six Members of the Court were satisfied that that standard was sufficient to create an entitlement protected by the Due Process Clause. This respondent had a right to keep his job if he proved "satisfactory." I do not know whether the difference between Kennedy's entitlement and this respondent's is of constitutional dimensions, but the similarity to *Arnett* is sufficient to justify a remand.

[15] *Cf. Perry v. Sindermann,* 408 U.S. 593, 601, 92 S.Ct. 2694, 2699, 33 L.Ed.2d 570:
"A person's interest in a benefit is a 'property' interest for due process purposes if there are such rules or mutually explicit understandings that support his claim of entitlement to the benefit and that he may invoke at a hearing." Even if respondent's entitlement is a sufficient property interest to trigger due process, he is not necessarily entitled to an elaborate adversary hearing. "Once it is determined that due process applies, the question remains what process is due." *Morrissey v. Brewer,* 408 U.S. 471, 481, 92 S.Ct. 2593, 2600, 33 L.Ed.2d 484. But at *least* respondent would be entitled to notice of the charge against him and an opportunity to respond, if only in writing.

reasonably to believe his employment was relatively permanent, a lower court finding that he had acquired a property interest which could not be terminated without procedural due process was not clearly erroneous and would not be overturned. *Cf.* Cusumano v. Ratchford, 507 F.2d 980 (8th Cir., 1975), *cert. denied,* 96 S. Ct. 48 (1975), where professors hired under "term appointments" as opposed to continuous or tenured appointments were held to have acquired no tenure, de facto or otherwise, under the University of Missouri's academic tenure regulations and had no constitutional or contractual right to a statement of reasons for nonreappointment or a hearing.

3. In Hostrop v. Board of Junior College Dist. No. 515, 523 F.2d 569 (7th Cir., 1975), *cert. denied,* 96 S. Ct. 1748 (1976), termination of the president of a public junior college without notice and impartial hearing was held actionable despite the trial court finding that his conduct in withholding information from the board constituted just cause for dismissal. Damages, however, were limited to those which were attributable only to the failure to afford due process and not for the termination of employment itself. On a theory of recovery for tortious injury, such an award could include damages for constitutional deprivation, as well as mental distress, humiliation, and any other injury caused as a result of being deprived of federally protected rights, but not attorneys' fees.

4. Procedural due process requirements for dismissal of faculty members with *de facto* tenure were the subject of two Ninth Circuit cases. In Bignall v. No. Idaho College, 538 F.2d 243 (9th Cir. 1976), the court, discussing the nature of *de facto* tenure in a footnote, noted that holding that a faculty member has the expectancy of continuous employment does not necessarily indicate that she has rights identical to those with tenure granted under the tenure program, but may "merely signify that the holder of the expectancy cannot be summarily dismissed." In Decker v. No. Idaho College, 552 F.2d 872 (9th Cir. 1977), the court held that a faculty member with *de facto* tenure was entitled to a hearing before his dismissal and awarded him one year back pay because he had been deprived of this right. Because he had been dismissed for cause, however, the court did not order reinstatement.

5. In a memorandum decision, the Supreme Court vacated the finding of the Oregon Supreme Court that procedural due process required that a tenured corrections officer receive notice of the charges against him and have the opportunity to respond before dismissal. The Court remanded the case for consideration in light of Dixon v. Love, 431 U.S. 105, 97 S.Ct. 1723 (1977). A strong dissent by Justice Stevens, joined by Justices Brennan, Stewart and Marshall, noted that *Dixon,* a case involving the automatic suspension of a driver's license because of accumulated traffic convictions, was "wide of the mark." The dissent emphasized that in *Dixon* the Court held that "something less than an evidentiary hearing is sufficient prior to adverse administrative action," and that this was consonant with the holding of the Oregon Court that a pretermination hearing was not necessary, but that notice and the opportunity to respond were required. Oregon State Penitentiary v. Hammer, 98 S.Ct. 469 (1977).

6. For some interesting opinions about the nature of the "liberty" interest that will justify procedural due process, see the majority opinion by Justice Stevens and the dissenting opinion by Justice Rehnquist in Hampton v. Mow Sun Wong, 96 S. Ct. 1895 (1976). The Court in *Hampton,* with four Justices dissenting, declared unconstitutional a Civil Service Commission regulation which excluded all persons except American citizens and natives of Samoa from employment in most positions of federal service.

# C. REGULATION OF PARTISAN POLITICAL ACTIVITIES OF PUBLIC EMPLOYEES

## 1. THE HATCH ACT

### COMMENT, THE HATCH ACT — A CONSTITUTIONAL RESTRAINT OF FREEDOM?, 33 Albany L. Rev. 345-47 (1969) †

The Hatch Act was the product of two Congressional enactments [7] and was

---

† Reprinted by permission of the Albany Law Review.
[7] Act of Aug. 2, 1939, ch. 410, 53 Stat. 1147; Act of July 19, 1940, ch. 640, 54 Stat. 767.

intended to prevent what Congress deemed to be "pernicious political activities" [8] among certain federal,[9] state and local [10] employees. In the opinion of one author, the purpose of the act was to insure the political neutrality of federal and state bureaucracies because "political neutrality among career civil servants is a necessary corollary to efficient and responsible administration." [11] It has been claimed that the Hatch Act, by eliminating partisan political activity among federal employees, combats four evils: the act prevents the bureaucracy from becoming a united political power bloc; it prevents the party in power from using government workers to promote the continued dominance of the party; it prevents competition between the party and the department head for the employee's loyalty; and it prevents employee demoralization which results from promotions and rewards based on politics rather than merit.[12]

With regard to political activity, the act prohibits specified employees of the federal executive department from either affecting the result of an election or from actively participating in political management or political campaigns.[13] Generally, every employee in the executive branch of the federal government falls within the prohibition of the act. However, there are several notable exceptions. The prohibition against political management and political campaigns does not apply to any person employed as the head or assistant head of an executive department, or paid from the appropriations of the President's office, or appointed as a member of the executive department, by the President with the advice and consent of the Senate.[14] Likewise, not all political activities are prohibited. Section 7326 exempts nonpartisan political activities from the scope of the act.[15] Penalties for violations of the act range from thirty days suspension without pay to removal from office.[16]

---

[8] *Id.*

[9] 5 U.S.C. §§ 7321-7327 (Supp. III, 1968).

[10] 5 U.S.C. §§ 1501-1508 (Supp. III, 1968).

[11] Esman, *The Hatch Act — A Reappraisal,* 60 YALE L.J. 986, 995 (1951).

[12] *Id.* at 994-95.

[13] 5 U.S.C. § 7324 provides: "(a) An employee in an Executive agency or an individual employed by the government of the District of Columbia may not —

(1) use his official authority or influence for the purpose of interfering with or affecting the result of an election; or

(2) take an active part in political management or in political campaigns."

This language was adopted from Executive Order No. 642 (June 3, 1907). This order became a rule of the Civil Service Commission until 1939 when it was adopted as § 9(a), 53 Stat. 1147. *See also* 5 C.F.R. § 4.1 (1968).

[14] 5 U.S.C. § 7324 (d) (Supp. III, 1968): "Subsection (a)(2) of this section does not apply to —

(1) an employee paid from the appropriation for the office of the President;

(2) the head or the assistant head of an Executive department or military department;

(3) an employee appointed by the President, by and with the advice and consent of the Senate, who determines policies to be pursued by the United States in its relations with foreign powers or in the nationwide administration of Federal laws; . . . ."

[15] 5 U.S.C. § 7326 (Supp. III, 1968) provides: "Section 7324(a) (2) of this title does not prohibit political activity in connection with —

(1) an election and the preceding campaign if none of the candidates is to be nominated or elected at that election as representing a party any of whose candidates for presidential elector received votes in the last preceding election at which presidential electors were selected; or

(2) a question which is not specifically identified with a National or State political party or political party of a territory or possession of the United States.

For the purpose of this section, questions relating to constitutional amendments, referendums, approval of municipal ordinances, and others of a similar character, are deemed not specifically identified with a National or State political party or political party of a territory or possession of the United States."

[16] 5 U.S.C. § 7325 (Supp. III, 1968). The appropriate Civil Service Commission Regulations may be found in 5 C.F.R. §§ 733.101-733.808 (1968).

With respect to state and local government employees, the act seeks to regulate the political conduct of only those employees who work for state or local agencies and whose activities are "financed in whole or in part by loans or grants made by the United States or Federal agency." [17] Thus, for example, most employees of a state department of social welfare come within the act since this department probably receives federal funds under the categorical assistance programs of the Social Security Act.[18] One important exception to the act's restrictions involves those individuals "employed by an educational or research institution, establishment, agency or system which is supported in whole or in part by a State or political subdivision thereof." [19] Similar to the provisions for federal employees, various non-partisan activities of state and local government employees are exempt.[20] Employees who violate the act are liable for removal from office.[21] Additionally, should the state or local government either fail to remove the offending employee or reappoint the employee to another state agency, the Civil Service Commission may direct the appropriate federal agency to withhold from the state agency a sum equal to two years' salary of the employee charged with the violation.[22]

---

[17] 5 U.S.C. § 1502 (Supp. III, 1968) provides: "(a) A State or local officer or employee may not—
    (1) use his official authority or influence for the purpose of interfering with or affecting the result of an election or a nomination for office;
    (2) . . .
    (3) take an active part in political management or in political campaigns."
5 U.S.C. § 1501 (4) (Supp. III, 1968) defines a state or local officer or employee as "an individual employed by a State or local agency whose principal employment is in connection with an activity which is financed in whole or in part by loans or grants made by the United States or Federal Agency. . . ."

[18] E.G., Title IV (Aid to Dependent Children) 42 U.S.C. §§ 601-09 (1964); Title XIX (Medical Assistance) 42 U.S.C. §§ 1396-96d (Supp. I, 1965); Title I (Aid to the Aged) 42 U.S.C. §§ 301-06 (1964). The same applies to employees of state labor departments which receive grants under Title III (Unemployment Compensation) of the Social Security Act. 42 U.S.C. §§ 501-03 (1964).

[19] 5 U.S.C. § 1501(4)(B) (Supp. III, 1968). In addition, § 1502(c)(1) specifically exempts the governor and lieutenant governor from the provisions of § 1502(a)(3).

[20] 5 U.S.C. § 1503 (Supp. III, 1968) provides: "Section 1502(a)(3) of this title does not prohibit political activity in connection with —
    (1) an election and the preceding campaign if none of the candidates is to be nominated or elected at that election as representing a party any of whose candidates for presidential elector received votes in the last preceding election at which presidential electors were selected; or
    (2) a question which is not specifically identified with a National or State political party.
For the purpose of this section, questions relating to constitutional amendments, referendums, approval of municipal ordinances, and others of a similar character, are deemed not specifically identified with a National or State political party."

[21] 5 U.S.C. § 1505(2) (Supp. III, 1968).

[22] 5 U.S.C. § 1506 (Supp. III, 1968). For a more thorough analysis of the provisions of the Hatch Act, see Clark, Federal Regulation of Campaign Activities, 6 FED. B.J. 5 (1944); Friedman and Klinger, The Hatch Act: Regulation by Administrative Action of Political Activities of Governmental Employees, 7 FED. B.J. 5 (1945); Howard, Federal Restrictions upon Political Activity of Government Employees, 35 AM. POL. SCI. REV. 470 (1941). For a comprehensive list of those activities which are barred by the Hatch Act see Friedman and Klinger, supra, at 9-13.

# UNITED PUBLIC WORKERS OF AMERICA v. MITCHELL

Supreme Court of the United States

330 U.S. 75, 67 S. Ct. 556, 91 L. Ed. 754 (1947)

MR. JUSTICE REED delivered the opinion of the Court.

The Hatch Act, enacted in 1940, declares unlawful certain specified political activities of federal employees. Section 9 forbids officers and employees in the executive branch of the Federal Government, with exceptions, from taking "any active part in political management or in political campaigns." Section 15 declares that the activities theretofore determined by the United States Civil Service Commission to be prohibited to employees in the classified civil service of the United States by the Civil Service Rules shall be deemed to be prohibited to federal employees covered by the Hatch Act. These sections of the Act cover all federal officers and employees whether in the classified civil service or not and a penalty of dismissal from employment is imposed for violation. There is no designation of a single governmental agency for its enforcement. . . .

The present appellants sought an injunction before a statutory three-judge district court of the District of Columbia against appellees, members of the United States Civil Service Commission, to prohibit them from enforcing against appellants the provisions of the second sentence of § 9 (a) of the Hatch Act . . . [which] reads, "No officer or employee in the executive branch of the Federal Government . . . shall take any active part in political management or in political campaigns." . . .

None of the appellants, except George P. Poole, has violated the provisions of the Hatch Act. They wish to act contrary to its provisions and those of § 1 of the Civil Service Rules and desire a declaration of the legally permissible limits of regulation. Defendants moved to dismiss the complaint for lack of a justiciable case or controversy. The District Court determined that each of these individual appellants had an interest in their claimed privilege of engaging in political activities, sufficient to give them a right to maintain this suit. United Federal Workers of America (C.I.O.) v. Mitchell, 56 F. Supp. 621, 624. The District Court further determined that the questioned provision of the Hatch Act was valid and that the complaint therefore failed to state a cause of action. It accordingly dismissed the complaint and granted summary judgment to defendants. . . .

At the threshold of consideration, we are called upon to decide whether the complaint states a controversy cognizable in this Court. . . .

As is well known, the federal courts established pursuant to Article III of the Constitution do not render advisory opinions. For adjudication of constitutional issues, "concrete legal issues, presented in actual cases, not abstractions," are requisite. This is as true of declaratory judgments as any other field. These appellants seem clearly to seek advisory opinions upon broad claims of rights protected by the First, Fifth, Ninth and Tenth Amendments to the Constitution. As these appellants are classified employees, they have a right superior to the generality of citizens, compare Fairchild v. Hughes, 258 U.S. 126, but the facts of their personal interest in their civil rights, of the general threat of possible interference with those rights by the Civil Service Commission under its rules, if specified things are done by appellants, does not make a justiciable case or controversy. Appellants want to engage in "political management and political campaigns," to persuade others to follow appellants' views by discussion, speeches, articles and other acts reasonably designed to secure the selection of appellants' political choices. Such generality of objection is really an attack on the political expediency of the Hatch Act, not the presentation of legal issues. It is beyond the competence of courts to render such a decision.

The power of courts, and ultimately of this Court, to pass upon the constitutionality of acts of Congress arises only when the interests of litigants require the use of this judicial authority for their protection against actual interference. A hypothetical threat is not enough. We can only speculate as to the kinds of political activity the appellants desire to engage in or as to the contents of their proposed public statements or the circumstances of their publication. It would not accord with judicial responsibility to adjudge, in a matter involving constitutionality, between the freedom of the individual and the requirements of public order except when definite rights appear upon the one side and definite prejudicial interferences upon the other. . . . . We should not take judicial cognizance of the situation presented on the part of the appellants considered in this subdivision of the opinion. These reasons lead us to conclude that the determination of the trial court, that the individual appellants, other than Poole, could maintain this action, was erroneous.

The appellant Poole does present by the complaint and affidavit matters appropriate for judicial determination.[23] The affidavits filed by appellees confirm that Poole has been charged by the Commission with political activity and a proposed order for his removal from his position adopted subject to his right under Commission procedure to reply to the charges and to present further evidence in refutation.[24] We proceed to consider the controversy over constitutional power at issue between Poole and the Commission as defined by the charge and preliminary finding upon one side and the admissions of Poole's affidavit upon the other. Our determination is limited to those facts. This proceeding so limited meets the requirements of defined rights and a definite threat to interfere with a possessor of the menaced rights by a penalty for an act done in violation of the claimed restraint. . . .

---

[23] "I have for a long time been interested in political activities. Both before and since my employment in the United States Mint, I have taken an active part in political campaigns and political management. In the 28th Ward, 7th Division in the City of Philadelphia I am and have been a Ward Executive Committeeman. In that position I have on many occasions taken an active part in political management and political campaigns. I have visited the residents of my Ward and solicited them to support my party and its candidates; I have acted as a watcher at the polls; I have contributed money to help pay its expenses; I have circulated campaign literature, placed banners and posters in public places, distributed leaflets, assisted in organizing political rallies and assemblies, and have done any and all acts which were asked of me in my capacity as a Ward Executive Committeeman. I have engaged in these activities both before and after my employment in the United States Mint. I intend to continue to engage in these activities on my own time as a private citizen, openly, freely, and without concealment.

"However, I have been served with a proposed order of the United States Civil Service Commission, dated January 12, 1944, which advises me that because of the political activities mentioned above, and for no other reason, 'it is, . . ., the opinion of this Commission that George P. Poole, an employee of the United States Mint at Philadelphia, Pennsylvania, has been guilty of political activity in violation of Section 1, Civil Service Rule I' and that unless I can refute the charges that I have engaged in political activity, I will be dismissed from my position as a Roller in the United States Mint at Philadelphia, Pennsylvania."

[24] The tentative charge and finding reads:

I.

"It is charged: That . . .

"The said George P. Poole held the political party office of Democratic Ward Executive Committeeman in the City of Philadelphia, Pennsylvania.

"The said George P. Poole was politically active by aiding and assisting the Democratic Party in the capacity of worker at the polls on general election day, November 5, 1940, and assisted in the

This brings us to consider the narrow but important point involved in Poole's situation. Poole's stated offense is taking an "active part in political management or in political campaigns." He was a ward executive committeeman of a political party and was politically active on election day as a worker at the polls and a paymaster for the services of other party workers. The issue for decision and the only one we decide is whether such a breach of the Hatch Act and Rule 1 of the Commission can, without violating the Constitution, be made the basis for disciplinary action.

When the issue is thus narrowed, the interference with free expression is seen in better proportion as compared with the requirements of orderly management of administrative personnel. Only while the employee is politically active . . . must he withhold expression of opinion on public subjects. We assume that Mr. Poole would be expected to comment publicly as committeeman on political matters, so that indirectly there is an attenuated interference. We accept appellants' contention that the nature of political rights reserved to the people by the Ninth and Tenth Amendments are involved. The right claimed as inviolate may be stated as the right of a citizen to act as a party official or worker to further his own political views. Thus we have a measure of interference by the Hatch Act and the Rules with what otherwise would be the freedom of the civil servant under the First, Ninth and Tenth Amendments. And, if we look upon due process as a guarantee of freedom in those fields, there is a corresponding impairment of that right under the Fifth Amendment. Appellants' objections under the Amendments are basically the same.

We do not find persuasion in appellants' argument that such activities during free time are not subject to regulation even though admittedly political activities cannot be indulged in during working hours. The influence of political activity by government employees, if evil in its effects on the service, the employees or people dealing with them, is hardly less so because that activity takes place after hours. Of course, the question of the need for this regulation is for other branches of government rather than the courts. Our duty in this case ends if the Hatch Act provision under examination is constitutional.

Of course, it is accepted constitutional doctrine that these fundamental human rights are not absolutes. The requirements of residence and age must be met. The essential rights of the First Amendment in some instances are subject to the elemental need for order without which the guarantees of civil rights to others would be a mockery. The powers granted by the Constitution to the Federal Government are substracted from the totality of sovereignty originally in the states and the people. Therefore, when objection is made that the exercise of a federal power infringes upon rights reserved by the Ninth and Tenth Amendments, the inquiry must be directed toward the granted power under which the action of the Union was taken. If granted power is found, necessarily the objection of invasion of those rights, reserved by the Ninth and Tenth Amendments, must fail. Again this Court must balance the extent of the guarantees of freedom against a congressional enactment to protect a democratic society against the supposed evil of political partisanship by classified employees of government. . . .

---

distribution of funds in paying party workers for their services on general election day, November 5, 1940."

### III.

"The above described activity constitutes taking an active part in political management and in a political campaign in contravention of Section 1, Civil Service Rule I, and the regulations adopted by the Commissioners thereunder."

[T]he practice of excluding classified employees from party offices and personal political activity at the polls has been in effect for several decades. Some incidents similar to those that are under examination here have been before this Court and the prohibition against certain types of political activity by officeholders has been upheld. The leading case was decided in 1882. Ex parte Curtis, 106 U.S. 371. There a subordinate United States employee was indicted for violation of an act that forbade employees who were not appointed by the President and confirmed by the Senate from giving or receiving money for political purposes from or to other employees of the government on penalty of discharge and criminal punishment. Curtis urged that the statute was unconstitutional. This Court upheld the right of Congress to punish the infraction of this law. The decisive principle was the power of Congress, within reasonable limits, to regulate, so far as it might deem necessary, the political conduct of its employees. A list of prohibitions against acts by public officials that are permitted to other citizens was given. This Court said, p. 373:

> "The evident purpose of Congress in all this class of enactments has been to promote efficiency and integrity in the discharge of official duties, and to maintain proper discipline in the public service. Clearly such a purpose is within the just scope of legislative power, and it is not easy to see why the act now under consideration does not come fairly within the legitimate means to such an end."

The right to contribute money through fellow employees to advance the contributor's political theories was held not to be protected by any constitutional provision. It was held subject to regulation. . . . The conclusion of the Court, that there was no constitutional bar to regulation of such financial contributions of public servants as distinguished from the exercise of political privileges such as the ballot, has found acceptance in the subsequent practice of Congress and the growth of the principle of required political neutrality for classified public servants as a sound element for efficiency. The conviction that an actively partisan governmental personnel threatens good administration has deepened since Ex parte Curtis. Congress recognizes danger to the service in that political rather than official effort may earn advancement and to the public in that governmental favor may be channeled through political connections.

In United States v. Wurzbach, 280 U.S. 396, the doctrine of legislative power over actions of governmental officials was held valid when extended to members of Congress. The members of Congress were prohibited from receiving contributions for "any political purpose whatever" from any other federal employees. Private citizens were not affected. The argument of unconstitutionality because of interference with the political rights of a citizen by that time was dismissed in a sentence. Compare United States v. Thayer, 209 U.S. 39.

The provisions of § 9 of the Hatch Act and the Civil Service Rule 1 are not dissimilar in purpose from the statutes against political contributions of money. The prohibitions now under discussion are directed at political contributions of energy by government employees. These contributions, too, have a long background of disapproval. Congress and the President are responsible for an efficient public service. If, in their judgment, efficiency may be best obtained by prohibiting active participation by classified employees in politics as party officers or workers, we see no constitutional objection. . . . To declare that the present supposed evils of political activity are beyond the power of Congress to redress would leave the nation impotent to deal with what many sincere men believe is a material threat to the democratic system. Congress is not politically naive or regardless of public welfare or that of the employees. It leaves untouched full participation by employees in political decisions at the ballot box and forbids only the partisan activity of federal personnel deemed offensive to efficiency. With that limitation only, employees may make their contributions to public affairs or protect their own interests, as before the passage of the Act.

The argument that political neutrality is not indispensable to a merit system for federal employees may be accepted. But because it is not indispensable does not mean that it is not desirable or permissible. Modern American politics involves organized political parties. Many classifications of government employees have been accustomed to work in politics — national, state and local — as a matter of principle or to assure their tenure. Congress may reasonably desire to limit party activity of federal employees so as to avoid a tendency toward a one-party system. It may have considered that parties would be more truly devoted to the public welfare if public servants were not overactive politically. . . .

It is only partisan political activity that is interdicted. It is active participation in political management and political compaigns. Expressions, public or private, on public affairs, personalities and matters of public interest, not an objective of party action, are unrestricted by law so long as the government employee does not direct his activities toward party success.

It is urged, however, that Congress has gone further than necessary in prohibiting political activity to all types of classified employees. It is pointed out by appellants "that the impartiality of many of these is a matter of complete indifference to the effective performance" of their duties. Mr. Poole would appear to be a good illustration for appellants' argument. The complaint states that he is a roller in the mint. We take it this is a job calling for the qualities of a skilled mechanic and that it does not involve contact with the public. Nevertheless, if in free time he is engaged in political activity, Congress may have concluded that the activity may promote or retard his advancement or preferment with his superiors. Congress may have thought that government employees are handy elements for leaders in political policy to use in building a political machine. For regulation of employees it is not necessary that the act regulated be anything more than an act reasonably deemed by Congress to interfere with the efficiency of the public service. There are hundreds of thousands of United States employees with positions no more influential upon policy determination than that of Mr. Poole. Evidently what Congress feared was the cumulative effect on employee morale of political activity by all employees who could be induced to participate actively. It does not seem to us an unconstitutional basis for legislation. . . .

We have said that Congress may regulate the political conduct of government employees "within reasonable limits," even though the regulation trenches to some extent upon unfettered political action. The determination of the extent to which political activities of governmental employees shall be regulated lies primarily with Congress. Courts will interfere only when such regulation passes beyond the generally existing conception of governmental power. That conception develops from practice, history, and changing educational, social and economic conditions. The regulation of such activities as Poole carried on has the approval of long practice by the Commission, court decisions upon similar problems and a large body of informed public opinion. Congress and the administrative agencies have authority over the discipline and efficiency of the public service. When actions of civil servants in the judgment of Congress menace the integrity and the competency of the service, legislation to forestall such danger and adequate to maintain its usefulness is required. The Hatch Act is the answer of Congress to this need. We cannot say with such a background that these restrictions are unconstitutional. . . .

The judgment of the District Court is accordingly

*Affirmed.*

[The dissenting opinions of Justice Douglas and Justice Black, concurred in by Justice Rutledge, and the concurring opinion of Justice Frankfurter, are omitted.]

## NOTES

1. In Oklahoma v. United States Civil Serv. Comm'n, 330 U.S. 127 (1947), decided the same day as *Mitchell,* the Supreme Court upheld the constitutionality of those provisions of the Hatch Act which limited the right of certain state employees to participate in partisan politics. Oklahoma brought suit to review a determination of the Civil Service Commission that a member of the state's highway commission had, by acting as chairman of the Democratic State Central Committee, violated the Hatch Act. The Commission directed the state to remove this member.

The state contended that the Hatch Act was unconstitutional because it regulated the internal affairs of a state and intruded upon state sovereignty in violation of the Tenth Amendment. While concluding that the federal government could not directly regulate the political activities of state or local employees, the Court held that the federal government could do so indirectly by fixing the terms and conditions upon which federal moneys would be allotted to the states. The Court held that the Tenth Amendment did not deprive the federal government of its power to use any necessary and proper means in the exercise of a granted power to attain a permissible goal. The Court defined the permissible goal as "better public service" which was to be attained by "requiring those who administered funds for national needs to abstain from active political partisanship." 330 U.S. at 143.

2. The holding in *Mitchell* has been soundly criticized over the years. For example, in Hobbs v. Thompson, 448 F.2d 456, 457 (5th Cir. 1971), the court considered the constitutionality of a city ordinance which provided that no employee of the fire department

> . . . "shall take an active part in any primary or election, and all [such] employees are hereby prohibited from contributing any money to any candidate, soliciting votes or prominently identifying themselves in a political race with or against any candidate for office."

The court rejected the argument that the constitutionality of the ordinance should be determined by the *Mitchell* "rational basis" balancing test. Instead, the court ruled that the treatment in *Mitchell* of First Amendment rights was inconsistent with other First Amendment cases decided in the same time period as well as those decided subsequently and that the "privilege theory" of public employment, seemingly adopted by the Court in *Mitchell,* was no longer tenable. The court applied traditional overbreadth principles to the ordinance and held it to be "fatally overbroad and vague" because it "failed to focus narrowly upon a substantial state interest which might justify some proscription of the political activity of . . . firemen." 448 F.2d at 475.

3. For a good discussion of many of the court decisions since *Mitchell* dealing with state and federal legislation, see Shartis, *The Federal Hatch Act and Related State Court Trends — A Time for a Change?,* 1970 The Business Lawyer 1381. *See also* Esman, *The Hatch Act—A Reappraisal,* 60 Yale L.J. 986 (1951); Heady, *The Hatch Act Decisions,* 41 Am. Pol. Sci. Rev. 687 (1947); Mosher, *Government Employees Under the Hatch Act,* 22 N.Y.U.L.Q. Rev. 233 (1947); Note, *Political Sterilization of Government Employees,* 47 Colum. L. Rev. 295 (1947); Note, *Restrictions on the Civil Rights of Federal Employees,* 47 Colum. L. Rev. 1161 (1947); Note, *Constitutional Limitations on Political Discrimination in Public Employment,* 60 Harv. L. Rev. 779 (1947); Bruff,

*Unconstitutional Conditions upon Public Employment; New Departures in the Protection of First Amendment Rights,* 21 HASTINGS L.J. 129 (1969); Comment, *The Hatch Act — A Constitutional Restraint of Freedom?,* 33 ALBANY L. REV. 345 (1969); Note, *The Public Employee and Political Activity,* 3 SUFFOLK L. REV. 380 (1969); Buckley, *Political Rights of Government Employees,* 19 CLEV. ST. L. REV. 568 (1970); Leahy, *The Public Employee and the First Amendment — Must He Sacrifice His Civil Rights To Be a Civil Servant?,* 4 CALIF. W.L. REV. 1 (1968); Note, *The First Amendment and Public Employees — An Emerging Constitutional Right To Be a Policeman?,* 37 GEO. WASH. L. REV. 409 (1968); Van Alstyne, *The Constitutional Rights of Public Employees: A Comment on the Inappropriate Use of an Old Analogy,* 16 U.C.L.A.L. REV. 751 (1969).

4. A federal government Commission on Political Activity of Government Personnel concluded that the existing political restrictions imposed on public servants are far in excess of what appears to be needed. *See* Jones, Charles O., *Reevaluating the Hatch Act: A Report on the Commission on Political Activity of Government Personnel,* 29 PUBLIC ADMIN. REV. 249 (1969). The Commission indicated that there should become clear a relationship between the dangers feared and the corrective measures used to regulate political activities. For cases which have tended to adopt this view, see Fort v. Civil Serv. Comm'n, 61 Cal. 2d 331, 38 Cal. Reptr. 625, 392 P.2d 385 (1964); Bagley v. Washington Township Hosp. Dist., 65 Cal. 2d 449, 55 Cal. Rptr. 401, 421 P.2d 409 (1966); Minielly v. State, 242 Ore. 490, 411 P.2d 69 (1966); De Stefano v. Wilson, 96 N.J. Super. 592, 233 A.2d 682 (1967); Gray v. City of Toledo, 323 F. Supp. 1281 (N.D. Ohio 1971) (upholding a state statute restricting policeman's right to engage in political activity, but indicating that only partisan political action which directly and adversely affected the employee's ability to perform his job efficiently, could be constitutionally prohibited).

*See also* Huerta v. Flood, 103 Ariz. 608, 447 P.2d 866 (1968) and City of Miami v. Sterbenz, 203 So. 2d 4 (Fla. 1967) (both holding unconstitutional laws against solicitation for political contributions as too indefinite as to the acts which were illegal). *But see* State *ex rel.* Baldwin v. Strain, 152 Neb. 763, 42 N.W. 2d 796 (1950); Lecci v. Looney, 33 App. Div. 2d 916, 307 N.Y. S.2d 594, 595 (1970) (citing *Mitchell* and *McAuliffe,* the court held that the law prohibiting a policeman from being "a delegate or representative to, or tak[ing] active part in any movement for the nomination or election of candidates for political office or public office" is constitutional); Lecci v. Cahn, 37 App. Div. 2d 779, 325 N.Y.S.2d 400, *cert. denied,* 405 U.S. 1073 (1971) (holding constitutional a state law making contributions to or collections on behalf of political clubs by policemen, a misdemeanor); Fishkin v. United States Civil Serv. Comm'n, 309 F. Supp. 40 (N.D. Cal. 1969), *appeal dismissed,* 396 U.S. 278, *reh. den.,* 397 U.S. 958 (1970).

5. *Standing:* The courts have generally rejected the holding in *Mitchell* that a party must be charged with a violation of the act challenged in order to have standing. Most courts have held, as in Hobbs v. Thompson, *supra* note 2, that where the act challenged may have adverse effects on the parties challenging it, the parties have standing. In N.A.A.C.P. v. Button, 371 U.S. 415, 83 S. Ct. 328, 9 L. Ed. 2d 405 (1963), the Court stated, in this regard, that:

the instant decree may be invalid if it prohibits privileged exercises of First Amendment rights whether or not the record discloses that the petitioner has engaged in privileged conduct. For in appraising a statute's inhibitory effect upon such rights, this Court has not hesitated to take into account possible applications of the statute in other factual contexts besides that at bar. Thornhill v. Alabama, 310 U.S. 88, 97-98, 60 S. Ct. 736, 741-742, 84 L. Ed. 1093; Winters v. New York, supra, 333 U.S. at 518-520, 68 S. Ct. at 671-672. Cf. Staub v. City of Baxley, 355 U.S. 313, 78 S. Ct. 277, 2 L. Ed. 2d 302. [371 U.S. at 432.]

# UNITED STATES CIVIL SERVICE COMMISSION v. NATIONAL ASSOCIATION OF LETTER CARRIERS

Supreme Court of the United States
413 U.S. 548, 93 S. Ct. 2880, 37 L. Ed. 2d 796 (1973)

MR. JUSTICE WHITE delivered the opinion of the Court.

On December 11, 1972, we noted probable jurisdiction of this appeal, 409 U.S. 1058, based on a jurisdictional statement presenting the single question whether the prohibition in § 9 (a) of the Hatch Act, now codified in 5 U.S.C. § 7324 (a) (2), against federal employees taking "an active part in political management or in political campaigns," is unconstitutional on its face. Section 7324 (a) provides:

"An employee in an Executive agency or an individual employed by the government of the District of Columbia may not —

"(1) use his official authority or influence for the purpose of interfering with or affecting the result of an election; or

"(2) take an active part in political management or in political campaigns.

"For the purpose of this subsection, the phrase 'an active part in political management or in political campaigns' means those acts of political management or political campaigning which were prohibited on the part of employees in the competitive service before July 19, 1940, by determinations of the Civil Service Commission under the rules prescribed by the President."

A divided three-judge court sitting in the District of Columbia had held the section unconstitutional. 346 F. Supp. 578 (1972). We reverse the judgment of the District Court.

## I

The case began when the National Association of Letter Carriers, six individual federal employees and certain local Democratic and Republican political committees filed a complaint, asserting on behalf of themselves and all federal employees that 5 U.S.C. § 7324 (a) (2) was unconstitutional on its face and seeking an injunction against its enforcement.

Each of the plaintiffs alleged that the Civil Service Commission was enforcing, or threatening to enforce, the Hatch Act's prohibition against active participation in political management or political campaigns with respect to certain defined activity in which that plaintiff desired to engage. The Union, for example, stated among other things that its members desired to campaign for candidates for public office. The Democratic and Republican Committees complained of not being able to get federal employees to run for state and local offices. Plaintiff Hummel stated that he was aware of the provision of the Hatch Act and that the activities he desired to engage in would violate that Act as, for example, his participating as a delegate in a party convention or holding office in a political club.

A three-judge court was convened, and the case was tried on both stipulated evidence and oral testimony. The District Court then ruled that § 7324 (a) (2) was unconstitutional on its face and enjoined its enforcement. The court recognized the "well-established governmental interest in restricting political activities by federal employees which [had been] asserted long before enactment of the Hatch Act," 346 F. Supp., at 579, as well as the fact that the "appropriateness of this governmental objective was recognized by the Supreme

Court of the United States when it endorsed the objective of the Hatch Act. United Public Workers v. Mitchell, 330 U.S. 75 . . . (1947) . . . ." *Id.,* at 580. The District Court ruled, however, that *Mitchell* left open the constitutionality of the statutory definition of "political activity," *ibid.,* and proceeded to hold that definition to be both vague and overbroad, and therefore unconstitutional and unenforceable against the plaintiffs in any respect. The District Court also added, *id.,* at 585, that even if the Supreme Court in *Mitchell* could be said to have upheld the definitional section in its entirety, later decisions had so eroded the holding that it could no longer be considered binding on the District Court.

## II

As the District Court recognized, the constitutionality of the Hatch Act's ban on taking an active part in political management or political campaigns has been here before.

This very prohibition was attacked in the *Mitchell* case by a labor union and various federal employees as being violative of the First, Ninth, and Tenth Amendments and as contrary to the Fifth Amendment as being vague and indefinite, arbitrarily discriminatory, and a deprivation of liberty. . . . As to the plaintiff Poole, [in *Mitchell*] the court noted that "he was a ward executive committeeman of a political party and was politically active on election day as a worker at the polls and a paymaster for the services of other party workers." 330 U.S., at 94. Plainly, the Court thought, these activities fell within the prohibition of § 9 of the Hatch Act against taking an active part in political management or political campaigning; and "[t]hey [were] also covered by the prior determinations of the [Civil Service] Commission," *id.,* at 103 (footnote omitted), as incorporated by § 15 of the Hatch Act [4] the Court relying on a Civil Service Commission publication, Political Activity and Political Assessments, Form 1236, September 1939, for the latter conclusion. *Id.,* at 103, n. 38. Poole's complaint thus presented a case or controversy for decision, the question being solely whether the Hatch Act "without violating the Constitution, [could make this conduct] the basis for disciplinary action." 330 U.S. at 94. The court held that it could. . . .

We unhesitatingly reaffirm the *Mitchell* holding that Congress had, and has, the power to prevent Mr. Poole and others like him from holding a party office, working at the polls and acting as party paymaster for other party workers. An Act of Congress going no farther would in our view unquestionably be valid. So would it be if, in plain and understandable language, the statute forbade activities such as organizing a political party or club; actively participating in fund-raising activities for a partisan candidate or political party; becoming a partisan candidate for, or campaigning for, an elective public office; actively managing the campaign of a partisan candidate for public office; initiating or circulating a partisan nominating petition or soliciting votes for a partisan candidate for public office; or serving as a delegate, alternate or proxy to a political party convention. Our judgment is that neither the First Amendment nor any other provision of the

---

[4] Section 15 of the Hatch Act, now codified in 5 U.S.C. § 7324 (a) (2), see n. 1, *supra,* defined the prohibition against taking "an active part in political management or in political campaigns" as proscribing those activities that the Civil Service Commission had determined up to the time of the passage of the Hatch Act were prohibited for classified civil service employees. The role and scope of § 15 are discussed in the text, *infra.*

Constitution invalidates a law barring this kind of partisan political conduct by federal employees.

## A

Such decision on our part would no more than confirm the judgment of history, a judgment made by this country over the last century that it is in the best interest of the country, indeed essential, that federal service should depend upon meritorious performance rather than political service, and that the political influence of federal employees on others and on the electoral process should be limited. . . .

The original Civil Service rules were promulgated on May 7, 1883, by President Arthur. Civil Service Rule I repeated the language of the Act that no one in the executive service should use his official authority or influence to coerce any other person or to interfere with an election, but went no further in restricting the political activities of federal employees. 8 Richardson, Messages and Papers of the Presidents 161 (1899). Problems with political activity continued to arise. Twenty-fourth Annual Report of the Civil Service Commission, 7-9 (1908), and one form of remedial action was taken in 1907 when in accordance with Executive Order 642 issued by President Theodore Roosevelt, 1 Report of Commission on Political Activity, *supra,* at 9, § 1 of Rule I was amended to read as follows:

> "No person in the Executive civil service shall use his official authority or influence for the purpose of interfering with an election or affecting the results thereof. *Persons who, by the provisions of these rules are in the competitive classified service, while retaining the right to vote as they please and to express privately their opinions on all political subjects, shall take no active part in political management or in political campaigns."* Twenty-fourth Annual Report of the Civil Service Commission, *supra,* at 104 (emphasis added).

It was under this rule that the Commission thereafter exercised the authority it had to investigate, adjudicate, and recommend sanctions for federal employees thought to have violated the rule. See Howard, Federal Restrictions on the Political Activity of Government Employees, 35 Am. Pol. Sci. Rev. 470, 475 (1941). In the course of these adjudications, the Commission identified and developed a body of law with respect to the conduct of federal employees that was forbidden by the prohibition against taking an active part in political management or political campaigning. Adjudications under Civil Service Rule I spelled out the scope and meaning of the rule in the mode of the common law, 86 Cong. Rec. 2341-2342; and the rules fashioned in this manner were from time to time stated and restated by the Commission for the guidance of the federal establishment. Civil Service Form 1236 of September 1939, for example, purported to publish and restate the law of "Political Activity and Political Assessments" for federal office holders and employees.

Civil Service Rule I covered only the classified service. The experience of the intervening years, particularly that of the 1936 and 1938 political campaigns, convinced a majority in Congress that the prohibition against taking an active part in political management and political campaigns should be extended to the entire federal service. 84 Cong. Rec. 4304, 9595, 9604, and 9610. A bill introduced for this purpose, S. 1871, "to prevent pernicious political activities," easily passed the Senate, 84 Cong. Rec. 4191-4192; but both the constitutionality and the advisability of purporting to restrict the political activities of employees were heatedly debated in the House. *Id.,* at 9594-9639. The bill was enacted, however, 53 Stat. 1147. This was the so-called Hatch Act, named after the Senator who was its chief proponent. . . .

Section 9(a), which provided the prohibition against political activity now found in 5 U.S.C. § 7324 (a) (2), with which we are concerned in this case, essentially restated Civil Service Rule I, with an important exception. *Id.,* at 1148. It made it

> "unlawful for any person employed in the executive branch of the Federal Government, or any agency or department thereof, to use his official authority or influence for the purpose of interfering with an election or affecting the result thereof. No officer or employee of the executive branch of the Federal Government, or any agency or department thereof, shall take any part in political management or in political campaigns. All such persons shall retain the right to vote as they may choose and to express their opinions on all political subjects." . . .

Section 9 differed from Civil Service Rule I in important respects. It applied to all persons employed by the Federal Government, with limited exceptions; it made dismissal from office mandatory upon an adjudication of a violation; and, whereas Civil Service Rule I had stated that persons retained the right to express their private opinions on all political subjects, the statute omitted the word "private" and simply privileged all employees "to express their opinions on all political subjects."

On the day prior to signing the bill, President Roosevelt sent a message to Congress stating his conviction that the bill was constitutional and recommending that Congress at its next session consider extending the Act to state and local government employees. 84 Cong. Rec. 10745-10747 and 10875. This, Congress quickly proceeded to do. The Act of July 19, 1940, c. 640, 54 Stat. 767, in § 12(a), *ibid.,* amended the Hatch Act by extending its provisions to officers and employees of state and local agencies "whose principal employment is in connection with any activity which is financed in whole or in part by loans or grants made by the United States. . . ." The Civil Service Commission was empowered under § 12(b), *id.,* at 768, to investigate and adjudicate violations of the Act by state and local employees. Also relevant for present purposes, § 9(a) of the Hatch Act was amended so that all persons covered by the Act were free to "express their opinions on all political subjects *and candidates." Id.,* at 767 (emphasis added). Moreover, § 15, *id.,* at 771, defined § 9(a)'s prohibition against taking an active part in political management or in political campaigns as proscribing "the same activities on the part of such persons as the United States Civil Service Commission has heretofore determined are at the time this section takes effect prohibited on the part of employees in the classified Civil Service of the United States by the provisions of the civil service rules prohibiting such employees from taking any active part in political management or in political campaigns." . . .

In 1966, Congress determined to review the restrictions of the Hatch Act on the partisan political activities of public employees. For this purpose, the Commission on Political Activity of Government Personnel was created. 80 Stat. 868. The Commission reported in 1968, recommending some liberalization of the political activity restrictions on federal employees, but not abandoning the fundamental decision that partisan political activities by government employees must be limited in major respects. 1 Report of Commission on Political Activity of Government Personnel, *supra.* Since that time, various bills have been introduced in Congress, some following the Commission's recommendations and some proposing much more substantial revisions of the Hatch Act. In 1972, hearings were held on some proposed legislation; but no new legislation has resulted.

This account of the efforts by the Federal Government to limit partisan political activities by those covered by the Hatch Act should not obscure the equally relevant fact that all 50 States have restricted the political activities of their own employees.

## B

Until now, the judgment of Congress, the Executive and the country appears to have been that partisan political activities by federal employees must be limited if the Government is to operate effectively and fairly, elections are to play their proper part in representative government and employees themselves are to be sufficiently free from improper influences. *E.g.*, 84 Cong. Rec. 9598, 9603; 86 Cong. Rec. 2360, 2621, 2864, 9376. The restrictions so far imposed on federal employees are not aimed at particular parties, groups or points of view, but apply equally to all partisan activities of the type described. They discriminate against no racial, ethnic or religious minorities. Nor do they seek to control political opinions or beliefs, or to interfere with or influence anyone's vote at the polls.

But as the Court held in Pickering v. Board of Education, 391 U.S. 563, 568 (1968), the government has an interest in regulating the conduct and "the speech of its employees that differ[s] significantly from those it possesses in connection with regulation of the speech of the citizenry in general. The problem in any case is to arrive at a balance between the interest of the [employee], as a citizen, in commenting upon matters of public concern and the interest of the [government], as an employer, in promoting the efficiency of the public services it performs through its employees." Although Congress is free to strike a different balance than it has, if it so chooses, we think the balance it has so far struck is sustainable by the obviously important interests sought to be served by the limitations on partisan political activities now contained in the Hatch Act. . . .

## III

But however constitutional the proscription of identifiable partisan conduct in understandable language may be, the District Court's judgment was that § 7324 (a) (2) was both unconstitutionally vague and fatally overbroad. . . .

Section 7324 (a) (2) provides that an employee in an executive agency must not take "an active part in political management or in political campaigns" and goes on to say that this prohibition refers to "those acts of political management or political campaigning which were prohibited on the part of employees in the competitive service before July 19, 1940, by determinations of the Civil Service Commission under the rules prescribed by the President." Section 7324 (b) privileges an employee to vote as he chooses and to express his opinion on political subjects and candidates, and § 7324 (c) and (d), as well as § 7326, also limit the applicability of the section.[15] The principal issue with respect to this

---

[15] 5 U.S.C. § 7324 provides:

"(a) An employee in an Executive agency or an individual employed by the government of the District of Columbia may not —

"(l) use his official authority or influence for the purpose of interfering with or affecting the result of an election; or

"(2) take an active part in political management or in political campaigns.

"For the purpose of this subsection, the phrase 'an active part in political management or in political campaigns' means those acts of political management or political campaigning which were prohibited on the part of employees in the competitive service before July 19, 1940, by determinations of the Civil Service Commission under the rules prescribed by the President."

statutory scheme is what Congress intended when it purported to define "an active part in political management or in political campaigns," as meaning the prior interpretations by the Civil Service Commission under Civil Service Rule I which contained the identical prohibition.

Earlier in this opinion it was noted that this definition was contained in § 15 of the 1940 Act. As recommended by the Senate Committee, S. Rep. No. 1236, 76th Cong., 3d Sess., 2, 4, § 15 conferred broad rule-making authority on the Civil Service Commission to spell out the meaning of "an active part in political management and political campaigns." There were, in any event, strong objections to extending the Hatch Act to those state employees working in federally financed programs, e.g., 86 Cong. Rec. 2486, 2793-2794, 2801-2802, and to § 15, in particular, as being an unwise and invalid delegation of legislative power to the Commission. E.g., id., at 2352, 2426-2427, 2579, 2794, 2875. The matter was vigorously debated; and ultimately Senator Hatch, the principal proponent and manager of the bill, offered a substitute for § 15, id., at 2928 and 2937, limiting the reach of the prohibition to those same activities that the Commission "has heretofore determined are at the time of the passage of this Act prohibited on the part of employees" in the classified service by the similar provision in Civil Service Rule I. The matter was further debated, and the amendment carried. Id., at 2958-2959.

The District Court and appellees construe § 15, now part of § 7324 (a) (2), as incorporating each of the several thousand adjudications of the Civil Service Commission under Civil Service Rule I, many of which are said to be undiscoverable, inconsistent, or incapable of yielding any meaningful rules to govern present or future conduct. In any event, the District Court held the prohibition against taking an active part in political management and political campaigns to be itself an insufficient guide to employee behavior and thought the definitional addendum of § 15 only added additional confusion by referring the concerned employees to an impenetrable jungle of Commission proceedings, orders, and rulings. 346 F. Supp. 582-583, 585.

We take quite a different view of the statute. As we see it, our task is not to destroy the Act if we can, but to construe it, if consistent with the will of Congress, so as to comport with constitutional limitations. With this in mind and having examined with some care the proceedings surrounding the passage of the 1940 Act and adoption of the substitute for § 15, we think it appears plainly enough that Congress intended to deprive the Civil Service Commission of rule-making power in the sense of exercising a subordinate legislative role in fashioning a more expansive definition of the kind of conduct that would violate the prohibition against taking an active part in political management or political campaigns. But it is equally plain, we think, that Congress accepted the fact that the Commission had been performing its investigative and adjudicative role under Civil Service Rule I since 1907 and that the Commission had, on a case-by-case basis, fleshed out the meaning of Rule I and so developed a body of law with respect to what partisan conduct by federal employees was forbidden by the rule. 86 Cong. Rec. 2342, 2353. It is also apparent, in our view, that the rules that had evolved over the years from repeated adjudications were subject to sufficiently clear and summary statement for the guidance of the classified service. Many times during the debate on the floor of the Senate, Senator Hatch and others referred to a summary list of such prohibitions, e.g., id., at 2929, 2937-2938, 2942-2943, 2949, 2952-2953, the Senator's ultimate reference being to Civil Service Form No. 1236 of September 1939, the pertinent portion of which he placed in the Record, *id.,* at 2938-2940,[18] and which was the Commission's then current effort to restate the prevailing prohibitions of Civil Service Rule I, as spelled out in its adjudications to that date. It was this administrative restatement of Civil Service Rule I law, modified to the extent necessary to reflect the provisions of the 1939 and 1940 Acts themselves, that, in our view, Congress intended to serve as its definition of the general proscription against partisan activities. It was within the limits of these rules that the Civil Service Commission was to proceed to perform its role under the statute.

---

[18] See Appendix, *infra.* Senator Hatch did not have Form 1236 with him on the floor during debate on § 15 and provided the pertinent portion from the Form for insertion into the Congressional Record after debate had been completed on the section. 86 Cong. Rec. 2938, 2940. However, the Senator had provided the Senate with a card listing 18 rules which were described as the Civil Service Commission's construction of Civil Service Rule I, *id.,* at 2937-2938, 2943. The card, prepared by Senator Hatch with assistance from the Commission, was a summary of pertinent portions of Form 1236, *id.,* at 2937-2938, and was inserted into the Congressional Record, *id.,* at 2943. It provided:

"The pertinent language in section 9 is practically a duplication of the civil-service rule prohibiting activity of employees under the classified civil service.

"The section provides in substance, among other things, that no such officer or employee shall take any active part in political management or in political campaigns.

"The same language of the civil-service rule has been construed as follows:

"1. Rule prohibits participation not only in national politics but also in State, county, and municipal politics.

"2. Temporary employees, substitutes, and persons on furlough or leave of absence with or without pay are subject to the regulation.

"3. Whatever an official or employee may not do directly he may not do indirectly or through another.

"4. Candidacy for or service as delegate, alternate, or proxy in any political convention is prohibited.

"5. Service for or on any political committee is prohibited.

"6. Organizing or conducting political rallies or meetings or taking any part therein except as a spectator is prohibited.

"7. Employees may express their opinions on all subjects, but they may not make political speeches.

"8. Employees may vote as they please, but they must not solicit votes; mark ballots for others; help to get out votes; act as checkers, marker or challenger for any party or engage in other activity at the polls except the casting of his own ballot.

"9. An employee may not serve as election official unless his failure or refusal so to do would be a violation of State laws.

"10. It is political activity for an employee to publish or be connected editorially, managerially, or financially with any political newspaper. An employee may not write for publication or publish any letter or article signed or unsigned in favor of or against any political party, candidate, or faction.

"11. Betting or wagering upon the results of a primary or general election is political activity.

"12. Organization or leadership of political parades is prohibited but marching in such parades is not prohibited.

"13. Among other forms of political activity which are prohibited are distribution of campaign literature, assuming political leadership, and becoming prominently identified with political movements, parties, or factions or with the success or failure of supporting any candidate for public office.

"14. Candidacy for nomination or for the election to any National, State, county, or municipal office is within the prohibition.

"15. Attending conventions as spectators is permitted.

"16. An employee may attend a mass convention or caucus and cast his vote, but he may not pass this point.

"17. Membership in a political club is permitted, but employees may not be officers of the club nor act as such.

"18. Voluntary contributions to campaign committees and organizations are permitted. An employee may not solicit, collect, or receive contributions. Contributions by persons receiving remuneration from funds appropriated for relief purposes are not permitted."

Not only did Congress expect the Commission to continue its accustomed role with respect to federal employees, but also in § 12 (b) of the 1940 Act Congress expressly assigned the Commission the enforcement task with respect to state employees now covered by the Act. The Commission was to issue notice, hold hearings, adjudicate and enforce. This process, inevitably and predictably, would entail further development of the law within the bounds of, and necessarily no more severe than, the 1940 rules and would be productive of a more refined definition of what conduct would or would not violate the statutory prohibition of taking an active part in political management and political campaigns.

It is thus not surprising that there were later editions of Form 1236, or that in 1970 the Commission again purported to restate the law of forbidden political activity and, informed by years of intervening adjudications, again sought to define those acts which are forbidden and those which are permitted by the Hatch Act. These regulations, 5 CFR Part 733, are wholly legitimate descendants of the 1940 restatement adopted by Congress and were arrived at by a process that Congress necessarily anticipated would occur down through the years. We accept them as the current and, in most respects, the long-standing interpretations of the statute by the agency charged with its interpretation and enforcement. It is to these regulations purporting to construe § 7234 as actually applied in practice, as well as to the statute itself, with its various exclusions, that we address ourselves in rejecting the claim that the Act is unconstitutionally vague and overbroad.

Whatever might be a difficulty with a provision against "taking active part in political management or in political campaigns," the Act specifically provides that the employee retains the right to vote as he chooses and to express his opinion on political subjects and candidates. The Act exempts research and educational activities supported by the District of Columbia or by religious, philanthropic or cultural organizations, 5 U.S.C. § 7324 (c); and § 7326 exempts nonpartisan political activity: questions, that is, that are not identified with national or state political parties are not covered by the Act, including issues with respect to constitutional amendments, referendums, approval of municipal ordinances and the like. Moreover, the plain import of the 1940 amendment to the Hatch Act is that the proscription against taking an active part in the proscribed activities is not open-ended but is limited to those rules and proscriptions that had been developed under Civil Service Rule I up to the date of the passage of the 1940 Act. Those rules, as refined by further adjudications within the outer limits of the 1940 rules, were restated by the Commission in 1970 in the form of regulations specifying the conduct that would be prohibited or permitted by § 7324 and its companion sections.

We have set out these regulations in the margin.[21] We see nothing

---

[21] The pertinent regulations, appearing in 5 CFR Part 733, provide:

"PERMISSIBLE ACTIVITIES

"§ 733.111 Permissible activities.

"(a) All employees are free to engage in political activity to the widest extent consistent with the restrictions imposed by law and this subject. Each employee retains the right to —

"(1) Register and vote in any election;

"(2) Express his opinion as an individual privately and publicly on political subjects and candidates;

"(3) Display a political picture, sticker, badge, or button;

"(4) Participate in the nonpartisan activities of a civic, community, social, labor, or professional organization, or of a similar organization;

"(5) Be a member of a political party or other political organization and participate in its activities to the extent consistent with law;

impermissibly vague in 5 CFR § 733.122, which specifies in separate paragraphs the various activities deemed to be prohibited by § 7324 (a) (2). There might be quibbles about the meaning of taking an "active part in managing" or about "actively participating in fund-raising" or about the meaning of becoming a "partisan" candidate for office; but there are limitations in the English language with respect to being both specific and manageably brief, and it seems to us that although the prohibitions may not satisfy those intent on finding fault at any cost, they are set out in terms that the ordinary person exercising ordinary common sense can sufficiently understand and comply with, without sacrifice to the public interest. . . .

"(6) Attend a political convention, rally, fund-raising function, or other political gathering;

"(7) Sign a political petition as an individual;

"(8) Make a financial contribution to a political party or organization;

"(9) Take an active part, as an independent candidate, or in support of an independent candidate, in a partisan election covered by § 733.124;

"(10) Take an active part, as a candidate or in support of a candidate, in a nonpartisan election;

"(11) Be politically active in connection with a question which is not specifically identified with a political party, such as a constitutional amendment, referendum, approval of a municipal ordinance or any other question or issue of a similar character;

"(12) Serve as an election judge or clerk, or in a similar position to perform nonpartisan duties as prescribed by State or local law; and

"(13) Otherwise participate fully in public affairs, except as prohibited by law, in a manner which does not materially compromise his efficiency or integrity as an employee or the neutrality, efficiency, or integrity of his agency.

"(b) Paragraph (a) of this section does not authorize an employee to engage in political activity in violation of law, while on duty, or while in a uniform that identifies him as an employee. The head of an agency may prohibit or limit the participation of an employee or class of employees of his agency in an activity permitted by paragraph (a) of this section, if participation in the activity would interfere with the efficient performance of official duties, or create a conflict or apparent conflict of interests.

### "PROHIBITED ACTIVITIES

"§ 733.121 Use of official authority; prohibition.

"An employee may not use his official authority or influence for the purpose of interfering with or affecting the result of an election.

"§ 733.122 Political management and political campaiging; prohibitions.

"(a) An employee may not take an active part in political management or in a political campaign, except as permitted by this subpart.

"(b) Activities prohibited by paragraph (a) of this section include but are not limited to—

"(1) Serving as an officer of a political party, a member of a National, State, or local committee of a political party, an officer or member of a committee of a partisan political club, or being a candidate for any of these positions;

"(2) Organizing or reorganizing a political party organization or political club;

"(3) Directly or indirectly soliciting, receiving, collecting, handling, disbursing, or accounting for assessments, contributions, or other funds for a partisan political purpose;

"(4) Organizing, selling tickets to, promoting, or actively participating in a fund-raising activity of a partisan candidate, political party, or political club;

"(5) Taking an active part in managing the political campaign of a partisan candidate for public office or political party office;

"(6) Becoming a partisan candidate for, or campaigning for, an elective public office;

"(7) Soliciting votes in support of or in opposition to a partisan candidate for public office or political party office;

"(8) Acting as recorder, watcher, challenger, or similar officer at the polls on behalf of a political party or partisan candidate;

"(9) Driving voters to the polls on behalf of a political party or partisan candidate;

"(10) Endorsing or opposing a partisan candidate for public office or political party office in a political advertisement, a broadcast, campaign literature, or similar material;

"(11) Serving as a delegate, alternate, or proxy to a political party convention;

"(12) Addressing a convention, caucus, rally, or similar gathering of a political party in support of or in opposition to a partisan candidate for public office or political party office; and

"(13) Initiating or circulating a partisan nominating petition."

The Act permits the individual employee to "express his opinion on political subjects and candidates," 5 U.S.C. § 7324 (b); and the corresponding regulation, 5 CFR § 733.111 (a) (2), privileges the employee to "[e]xpress his opinion as an individual privately and publicly on political subjects and candidates." The section of the regulations which purports to state the partisan acts that are proscribed, *id.,* § 733.122, forbids in subparagraph (a) (10) the endorsement of "a partisan candidate for public office or political party office in a political advertisement, a broadcast, campaign literature or similar material," and in subparagraph (a) (12), prohibits "[a]ddressing a convention, caucus, rally or similar gathering of a political party in support of or in opposition to a partisan candidate for public office or political party office." Arguably, there are problems in meshing § 733.111 (a)(2) with §§ 733.122(a) (10) and (12), but we think the latter prohibitions sufficiently clearly carve out the prohibited political conduct from the expressive activity permitted by the prior section to survive any attack on the grounds of vagueness or in the name of any of those policies that doctrine may be deemed to further.

It is also important in this respect that the Commission has established a procedure by which an employee in doubt about the validity of a proposed course of conduct may seek and obtain advice from the Commission and thereby remove any doubt there may be as to the meaning of the law, at least insofar as the Commission itself is concerned.

Neither do we discern anything fatally overbroad about the statute when it is considered in connection with the Commission's construction of its terms represented by the 1970 regulations we now have before us. The major difficulties in this respect again relate to the prohibition in § 733.122 (a) (10) and (12) on endorsements in advertisements, broadcasts, and literature and on speaking at political party meetings in support of partisan candidates for public or party office. But these restrictions are clearly stated, they are political acts normally performed only in the context of partisan campaigns by one taking an active role in them, and they are sustainable for the same reasons that the other acts of political campaigning are constitutionally proscribable. They do not, therefore, render the remainder of the statute vulnerable by reason of overbreadth.

Even if the provisions forbidding partisan campaign endorsements and speech making were to be considered in some respects unconstitutionally overbroad, we would not invalidate the entire statute as the District Court did. The remainder of the statute, as we have said, covers a whole range of easily identifiable and constitutionally proscribable partisan conduct on the part of federal employees, and the extent to which pure expression is impermissibly threatened, if at all, by § 733.122 (a) (10) and (12), does not in our view make the statute substantially overbroad and so invalid on its face.

For the foregoing reasons, the judgment of the District Court is reversed.

## NOTES

1. In Broadrick v. Oklahoma, 413 U.S. 601, 93 S. Ct. 2908, 37 L. Ed. 2d 830 (1973), decided the same day as the principal case, the Supreme Court upheld the constitutionality of the Oklahoma state merit system act. The state statute prohibited any state classified employee from being "an officer or member" of a "partisan political club" or a candidate for "any paid public office." The law also forbade the solicitation of contributions "for any political organization, candidacy or other political purpose" and the taking part "in the management or affairs of any political party or in any political campaign." Appellants argued that the statute was unconstitutionally vague and that its prohibitions were too

broad in their sweep, failing to distinguish between conduct that may be proscribed and conduct that must be permitted. In rejecting these arguments, the Court ruled that:

> where conduct and not merely speech is involved, we believe that the overbreadth of a statute must not only be real, but substantial as well, judged in relation to the statute's plainly legitimate sweep. It is our view that § 818 is not substantially overbroad and that whatever overbreadth may exist should be cured through case-by-case analysis of the fact situations to which its sanctions, assertedly, may not be applied.

Unlike ordinary breach of the peace statutes or other broad regulatory acts, § 818 is directed, by its terms, at political expression which if engaged in by private persons would plainly be protected by the First and Fourteenth Amendments. But at the same time, § 818 is not a censorial statute, directed at particular groups or viewpoints. Cf. Keyishian v. Board of Regents, *supra.* The statute, rather, seeks to regulate political activity in an even-handed and neutral manner. . . .

Under the decision in *Letter Carriers,* there is no question that § 818 is valid at least insofar as it forbids classified employees from: soliciting contributions for partisan candidates, political parties, or other partisan political purposes; becoming members of national, state, or local committees of political parties, or officers or committee members in partisan political clubs, or candidates to any paid public office; taking part in the management or affairs of any political party's partisan political campaign; serving as delegates or alternates to caucuses or conventions of political parties; addressing or taking an active part in partisan political rallies or meetings; soliciting votes or assisting voters at the polls or helping in a partisan effort to get voters at the polls; participating in the distribution of partisan campaign literature; initiating or circulating partisan nominating petitions; or riding in caravans for any political party or partisan political candidate.

These proscriptions are taken directly from the contested paragraphs of § 818, the Rules of the State Personnel Board and its interpretive circular, and the authoritative opinions of the State Attorney General. . . .

Appellants further point to the Board's interpretive rules purporting to restrict such allegedly protected activities as the wearing of political buttons or the use of bumper stickers. It may be that such restrictions are impermissible and that § 818 may be susceptible of some other improper applications. But as presently construed, we do not believe that § 818 must be discarded *in toto* because some persons' arguably protected conduct may or may not be caught or chilled by the statute. Section 818 is not substantially overbroad and is not, therefore, unconstitutional on its face.

2. In 1974, following the *National Letter Carriers* and *Broadrick* decisions, Congress passed the Federal Election Campaign Act Amendments, 5 U.S.C. § 1502 (Supp. IV, 1974), which deleted the prohibition against state and local employees principally employed in federally funded activities taking "an active part in political management or in political campaigns," substituting a prohibition against being "a candidate for public office." The Amendments, however, did permit state and local government employees to be non-partisan candidates for public office. 5 U.S.C. § 1594 (Supp. IV, 1974).

3. The proposed Federal Employees Political Activities Act was passed by Congress in 1976, but vetoed by President Ford. The bill deleted the prohibition on voluntary political activities by federal employees, but provided safeguards against coercing federal employees to take part in political activities and against using a government position for political ends.

For an interesting historical and political analysis of legislation in this area, see Vaughn, *Restrictions on the Political Activities of Public Employees: The Hatch Act and Beyond,* 44 Geo. Wash. L. Rev. 516 (1976).

4. All 50 States have passed statutes modeled on the Hatch Act which limit the political activities of state employees. These statutes are listed in Broadrick v. Oklahoma, 413 U.S. 601, 604 n.2 (1973).

5. The dismissal of non-civil service employees of the Cook County Sheriff's Office, solely because they were not affiliated with the political party of the newly elected sheriff,

was held to be unconstitutional under the First and Fourteenth Amendments in Elrod v. Burns, 427 U.S. 347, 96 S.Ct. 2673, 49 L. Ed. 2d 547 (1976). Mr. Justice Brennan, joined by Justices White and Marshall, examined the history of patronage and its effect on freedom of belief and association. Noting that First Amendment freedoms are not absolute, they stated that any countervailing state interest must be "paramount, one of vital importance" and must be a *governmental* interest, not just that of partisan organizations. After examining the interests advanced to support patronage dismissals, Mr. Justice Brennan said:

> In summary, patronage dismissals severely restrict political belief and association. Though there is a vital need for government efficiency and effectiveness, such dismissals are on balance not the least restrictive means for fostering that end. There is also a need to insure that policies which the electorate has sanctioned are effectively implemented. That interest can be fully satisfied by limiting patronage dismissals to policymaking positions. Finally, patronage dismissals cannot be justified by their contribution to the proper functioning of our democratic process through their assistance to partisan politics since political parties are nurtured by other, less intrusive and equally effective methods. More fundamentally, however, any contribution of patronage dismissals to the democratic process does not suffice to override their severe encroachment on First Amendment freedoms. We hold, therefore, that the practice of patronage dismissals is unconstitutional under the First and Fourteenth Amendments, and that respondents thus stated a valid claim for relief.

427 U.S. at 372-373.

Justices Stewart and Blackmun concurred in the judgment that a nonpolicy-making, nonconfidential government employee cannot be dismissed from a job which he has successfully performed solely because of his political beliefs. Chief Justice Burger, and Justices Powell and Rehnquist dissented.

## 2. POLITICAL ACTIVITY BY UNIONS REPRESENTING EMPLOYEES IN THE PUBLIC SECTOR

### H. WELLINGTON AND R. WINTER, THE UNIONS AND THE CITIES 24-25, 28-31 (1971)†

Although the market does not discipline the union in the public sector to the extent that it does in the private, the municipal employment paradigm, nevertheless, would seem to be consistent with what Robert A. Dahl has called the "'normal' American political process," which is "one in which there is a high probability that an active and legitimate group in the population can make itself heard effectively at some crucial stage in the process of decision," for the union may be seen as little more than an "active and legitimate group in the population." With elections in the background to perform, as Mr. Dahl notes, "the critical role ... in maximizing political equality and popular sovereignty," all seems well, at least theoretically, with collective bargaining and public employment.

But there is trouble even in the house of theory if collective bargaining in the public sector means what it does in the private. The trouble is that if unions are able to withhold labor—to strike—as well as to employ the usual methods of political pressure, they may possess a disproportionate share of effective power in the process of decision. Collective bargaining would then be so effective a pressure as to skew the results of the "'normal' American political process."

† Copyright 1971 by The Brookings Institution, Washington, D.C. Reprinted by permission.

One should straightway make plain that the strike issue is not simply the importance of public services as contrasted with services or products produced in the private sector. This is only part of the issue, and in the past the partial truth has beclouded analysis. The services performed by a private transit authority are neither less nor more important to the public than those that would be performed if the transit authority were owned by a municipality. A railroad or a dock strike may be more damaging to a community than "job action" by police. This is not to say that governmental services are not important. They are, both because the demand for them is inelastic and because their disruption may seriously injure a city's economy and occasionally impair the physical welfare of its citizens. Nevertheless, the importance of governmental services is only a necessary part of, rather than a complete answer to, the question: Why be more concerned about strikes in public employment than in private?

The answer to the question is simply that, because strikes in public employment disrupt important services, a large part of a mayor's political constituency will, in many cases, press for a quick end to the strike with little concern for the cost of settlement. This is particularly so where the cost of settlement is borne by a different and larger political constituency, the citizens of the state or nation. Since interest groups other than public employees, with conflicting claims on municipal government, do not, as a general proposition, have anything approaching the effectiveness of the strike—or at least cannot maintain that relative degree of power over the long run—they may be put at a significant competitive disadvantage in the political process. . . .

The strike and its threat, moreover, exacerbate the problems associated with the scope of bargaining in public employment. This seems clear if one attends in slightly more detail to techniques of municipal decision making.

Few students of our cities would object to Herbert Kaufman's observation that:

> Decisions of the municipal government emanate from no single source, but from many centers; conflicts and clashes are referred to no single authority, but are settled at many levels and at many points in the system: no single group can guarantee the success of any proposal it supports, the defeat of every idea it objects to. Not even the central governmental organs of the city—the Mayor, the Board of Estimate, the Council—individually or in combination, even approach mastery in this sense.

> Each separate decision center consists of a cluster of interested contestants, with a "core group" in the middle, invested by the rules with the formal authority to legitimize decisions (that is to promulgate them in binding form) and a constellation of related "satellite groups" seeking to influence the authoritative issuances of the core group.

Nor would many disagree with Nelson W. Polsby when, in discussing community decision making that is concerned with an alternative to a "current state of affairs," he argues that the alternative "must be politically palatable and relatively easy to accomplish; otherwise great amounts of influence have to be brought to bear with great skill and efficiency in order to secure its adoption."

It seems probable that such potential subjects of bargaining as school decentralization and a civilian police review board are, where they do not exist, alternatives to the "current state of affairs," which are not "politically palatable and relatively easy to accomplish." If a teachers' union or a police union were to bargain with the municipal employer over these questions, and were able to use the strike to insist that the proposals not be adopted, how much "skill and efficiency" on the part of the proposals' advocates would be necessary to effect a change? And, to put the shoe on the other foot, if a teachers' union were to insist through collective bargaining (with the strike or its threat) upon major changes in school curriculum, would not that union have to be considerably less skillful and efficient in the normal political process than other advocates of community change? The point is that with respect to some subjects, collective bargaining may be too powerful a lever on municipal decision making, too effective a technique for changing or preventing the change of one small but important part of the "current state of affairs."

Unfortunately, in this area the problem is not merely the strike threat and the strike. In a system where impasse procedures involving third parties are established in order to reduce work stoppages—and this is common in those states that have passed public employment bargaining statutes—third party intervention must be partly responsive to union demands. If the scope of bargaining is open-ended, the neutral part, to be effective, will have to work out accommodations that inevitably advance some of the union's claims some of the time. And the neutral, with his eyes fixed on achieving a settlement, can hardly be concerned with balancing all the items on the community agenda or reflecting the interests of all relevant groups. . . .

Collective bargaining by public employees and the political process cannot be separated. The costs of such bargaining, therefore, cannot be fully measured without taking into account the impact on the allocation of political power in the typical municipality. If one assumes, as here, that municipal political processes should be structured to ensure "a high probability that an active and legitimate group in the population can make itself heard effectively at some crucial stage in the process of decision," then the issue is how powerful unions will be in the typical municipal political process if a full transplant of collective bargaining is carried out.

The conclusion is that such a transplant would, in many cases, institutionalize the power of public employee unions in a way that would leave competing groups in the political process at a permanent and substantial disadvantage. . . .

A teachers' strike may not endanger public health or welfare. It may, however, seriously inconvenience parents and other citizens who, as voters, have the power to punish one of the parties—and always the same party, the political leadership—to the dispute. How can anyone any longer doubt the vulnerability of a municipal employer to this sort of pressure? Was it simply a matter of indifference to Mayor Lindsay in September 1969 whether another teachers' strike occurred on the eve of a municipal election? Did the size and the speed of the settlement with the United Federation of Teachers (UFT) suggest nothing about one first-rate politician's estimate of his vulnerability? And are the chickens now coming home to roost because of extravagant concessions on pensions for employees of New York City the result only of mistaken actuarial calculations? Or do they reflect the irrelevance of long-run considerations to politicians vulnerable to the strike and compelled to think in terms of short-run political impact?

## RASKIN, POLITICS UP-ENDS THE BARGAINING TABLE, in PUBLIC WORKERS AND PUBLIC UNIONS 122, 142-43 (S. Zagoria ed. 1972)†

It is in this area of the scope of bargaining that bitter battles lie ahead for New

---

† A.H. Raskin, *Politics Up-Ends the Bargaining Table,* in PUBLIC WORKERS AND PUBLIC UNIONS (Sam Zagoria ed.). Copyright © 1972 by The American Assembly, Columbia University. Reprinted by permission of Prentice-Hall, Inc.

York City's ultra-political labor movement. Every union contract is a limit on management's freedom, and nowhere is that tug-of-war more difficult to resolve than in governmental service. Everything a teachers' union does affects the quality of education, and in New York the cross-over from straight bread-and-butter concerns to the nature of the educational system is profound. The United Federation of Teachers was not only dominant in the legislative hassle over school decentralization but it incorporated into its contracts a provision for double-manned "More Effective Schools" as the chief vehicle for educational reform. The extent to which such incursions into policy determination would be prohibited by the proposed curbs in Albany has already prompted the UFT to fuse its strength with that of other teacher groups all over the state to mount a militant counteroffensive next year.

Realistically, no legal walls are going to keep civil service unions from moving increasingly into the policy field. Private industry learned many years ago that unions are ingenious enough to find a hundred expedients for punching holes in "management's rights" clauses. Manpower is so much a bedrock of all municipal services that public unions will find ways to tie considerations of job security or working conditions into every policy issue they want to have a voice in.

## NOTES

1. Wellington and Winter argue that if traditional collective bargaining is transplanted in the public sector, "such a transplant would, in many cases, institutionalize the power of public employee unions in a way that would leave competing groups in the political process at a permanent and substantial disadvantage." Assuming that this view is correct, can the dangers and problems posed be effectively protected against by strict enforcement of the Hatch Act or comparable legislation? Does the Hatch Act purport to deal with the kind of problems posed by Wellington and Winter? *See generally* Love and Sulzner, *Political Implications of Public Employee Bargaining,* 11 IND. REL. 18 (Feb. 1972).

2. The Federal Election Campaign Act of 1976, 2 U.S.C. § 441b, prohibits contributions or expenditures by labor organizations "in connection with any election at which presidential and vice-presidential electors or a Senator or Representative in, or a Delegate or Resident Commissioner to, Congress are to be voted for, or in connection with any primary election or political convention or caucus held to select candidates for any of the foregoing offices." The Act permits communications by unions to their members on any subject and non-partisan get-out-the-vote drives aimed at members and their families. In addition, the Act allows the establishment and solicitation of contributions for special segregated funds to be used for political purposes by labor organizations. The Act prohibits reprisals for failure to contribute and restricts the manner in which solicitations may be carried out.

## 3. THE RIGHT TO PETITION

Section 7102 of the statute governing employee relations in the federal service provides that:

> The right of employees individually or collectively, to petition Congress, or a Member of Congress, or to furnish information to either House of Congress, or to a Committee or Member thereof, may not be interfered with or denied. [5 U.S.C. § 7102 (Supp. IV 1969)]

This section, which first appeared as part of the Lloyd-LaFollette Act of 1912 (37 Stat. 555), was specifically directed at the "gag rule" initiated by President Theodore Roosevelt in 1902. As first instituted, the "gag rule" absolutely prohibited employees of the executive department from petitioning Congress to remedy job grievances. (Exec. Order No. 163, Jan. 31, 1902, *reprinted in* 48 Cong. Rec. 5223 (1912)). Later, in 1909, President Taft issued a similar executive order. The Taft "gag rule" (Exec. Order 1142, Nov. 26, 1909, *reprinted in* 48 Cong. Rec. 4513 (1912)), broadly prohibited employee petitions seeking "congressional action of any kind," however, it did allow employees to present petitions with the "consent and knowledge" of their department heads.

The "gag rule" was severely criticized, especially by postal employees who comprised the largest block of civil servants affected by the rule and against whom the rule was strictly enforced. As a consequence, Congress passed section 6 of the 1912 Act, which read as follows:

The right of persons employed in the civil service of the United States, either individually or collectively, to petition Congress, or any Member thereof, or to furnish information to either House of Congress, or to any Committee or member thereof, shall not be denied or interfered with.

This section subsequently appeared as 5 U.S.C. § 652 (d) [62 Stat. 356 (1948)], which is the forerunner of the current provision in 5 U.S.C. § 7102. An excellent review of the legislative history of the act may be found in Comment, *Dismissals of Public Employees for Petitioning Congress: Administrative Discipline and 5 U.S.C. Section 652(d),* 74 YALE L.J. 1156, 1161 (1965), where it is reported that:

The dominant theme in the House and Senate debates seems to have been that the act was designed to insure that unjust treatment of government employees would promptly and effectively be brought to the attention of Congress. Many Congressmen felt that redress of job grievances could not be satisfactorily obtained by employee appeals to superiors; the gag rule "instead of promoting discipline and efficiency, produces the worst kind of tyranny" by department heads. . . .

It is apparent, then, that section 652 (d) was intended to encompass job grievance petitions. It also seems clear that Congress meant to prevent the *act* of petitioning from being used as grounds for discipline or dismissal. . . . [citations omitted]

*See also* Note, *The Right of Government Employees to Furnish Information to Congress: Statutory and Congressional Aspects,* 57 VA. L. REV. 885, 893-95 (1971),† which gives the following summary of the leading judicial opinions construing Section 7102:

The judicial history of section 7102 is confined to seven cases,[23] of which only two have examined the scope of the protection afforded petitions submitted to Congress. In *Steck v. Connally,*[24] Judge Holtzoff of the District Court for the District of Columbia ordered the reinstatement of a federal employee who had been dismissed on charges that he had circulated among his fellow employees a petition which he forwarded to a member of Congress.

---

† Reprinted by permission of the Virginia Law Review and Fred B. Rothman & Company.

[23] Of the five cases that did not examine the legislative history of section 7102 to determine its scope, four involved statements made either to both Congress and the public, or solely to the public: Meehan v. Macy, 392 F.2d 822 (D.C. Cir.), *modified,* 425 F.2d 469 (1968), *vacated,* 425 F.2d 472 (1969) (en banc, per curiam); Levine v. Farley, 107 F.2d 186 (D.C. Cir. 1939), *cert. denied,* 308 U.S. 622 (1940); Eustace v. Day, 198 F. Supp. 233 (D.D.C. 1961); Ruderer v. United States, 412 F.2d 1285 (Ct. Cl. 1969), *cert. denied,* 398 U.S. 914 (1970). In each of these cases, the court held that the right to petition Congress under section 7102 did not encompass the right to direct statements at the public to induce others to write to their Congressmen. In Swaaley v. United States, 376 F.2d 857 (Ct. Cl. 1967), the court cited section 7102 as analogous protection of the right of government employees to petition their department head.

[24] 199 F. Supp. 104 (D.D.C. 1961).

The Court explained that section 7102 guaranteed to all civil servants the right to furnish information to Congress "free from *any restriction* or interference on the part of their superior officers." It further found that a department head could not censor the contents of the petition or dismiss the petitioner even if the statements in the petition were untrue. In response to the argument that administrative efficiency, discipline, and morale required that the statute be narrowly construed, the court noted: "[t]o be sure an activity of this kind can adversely affect the morale of a Government department. It can be vexatious and annoying at times if the employee acts unreasonably, but the statute contains no limitation."

Despite this broad holding, in *Turner v. Kennedy,*[25] the District Court for the District of Columbia rendered summary judgment against an FBI agent who asked the court to overturn a Civil Service Commission's finding that letters he wrote to several members of Congress were false, irresponsible, and unjustified, and therefore demonstrated his unsuitability for continued employment in the FBI. The court did not discuss the scope of protection guaranteed by section 7102, and seemingly assumed that it did not protect the plaintiff's activities. In a four-line per curiam decision — which alluded neither to the statutory history nor to *Steck v. Connally* — the Court of Appeals affirmed.[26]

Circuit Judge Fahy dissented, relying on the broad language of section 7102 and citing *Steck* with approval. After examining the legislative history, he concluded that the tenor of the debate indicated Congressional intent "that full First Amendment rights were to be extended to a Civil Service employee by Section [7102]." Nevertheless, Judge Fahy went on to reason that "perhaps his right is conditioned to a degree by the circumstance that he is in government service." He therefore proposed to limit the protection of section 7102 in the same way that the Supreme Court, in *New York Times Co. v. Sullivan,*[27] had limited the right of freedom of the press. Adapting the *New York Times* rules to the *Turner* case, Fahy would have excluded from the protection of section 7102 all statements "made with actual malice, that is, with knowledge that they were false or with reckless disregard of whether [they were] false or not."[28] In a footnote he cautioned that he did not reach such questions as whether "the contents of a petition furnishing classified information or confidential information of a nature that is in the public interest not to disclose is privileged."

The significance of *Turner v. Kennedy* lies not so much in its holding as in the suggestion, implicit in the District Court's opinion and in the per curiam and dissenting opinions of the Court of Appeals, that section 7102 is susceptible of limitation despite its sweeping language and its legislative history. In the future courts confronted with the issue of the statute's scope of protection are faced with two alternatives. On the one hand, they may leave to the executive branch the decision whether the information in question is of "a nature that is in the public interest not to [be] disclosed" or constitutes

---

[25] Civil No. 3160-62 (D.D.C., Oct. 5, 1962), aff'd, 332 F.2d 304 (D.C. Cir.), *cert. denied,* 379 U.S. 901 (1964).

[26] 332 F.2d 304 (D.C. Cir. 1964).

[27] 376 U.S. 255 (1964).

[28] 332 F.2d at 307. Consequently, Judge Fahy would have remanded the case to the Civil Service Commission for a determination of whether the statements met the test he formulated. *Id.*

activity that "causes the agency immediate and substantial harm." [29] There is considerable precedent for this course. As early as 1840, the Supreme Court asserted that "interference of the courts with the performance of the ordinary duties of the executive departments of the government, would be productive of nothing but mischief." [30] The consequences of this abdication are twofold. First, the fate of the federal employee who furnished information to Congress would be placed in the hands of his department head or other superior officers — the precise situation Congress sought to change. Second, as the ultimate arbiter, the executive branch could effectively foreclose to Congress an important source of its information.

On the other hand, courts that seek to safeguard the civil servant's right to petition may adopt a strict standard in reviewing executive action. They would then face the difficult task of striking a balance among conflicting interests. In determining whether a civil servant has the right to furnish information to Congress, the courts would have to decide what information must not be disclosed in the public interest, and under what circumstances the agency's interest in discipline, morale, and efficiency overrides the right of the federal employee to consult his representatives. Clearly, these questions could be resolved more effectively if the legislative and executive branches could agree upon a precise statute that would balance their conflicting interests.

SWAALEY V. UNITED STATES, 376 F.2d 857, 862 (Ct. Cl. 1967), gives definition to the "right of petition" enjoyed by government employees under the First Amendment:

We think the freedom of the press to criticize and it may be, defame, public officials has no better support than the freedom of petition here involved. We agree with Judge Fahy's suggestion that the doctrine of New York Times Co. v. Sullivan, supra, applies to federal employee's petitions. See Turner v. Kennedy, 118 U.S. App. D.C. 104, 332 F.2d 304, 307 (1964), cert. denied, 379 U.S. 901, 85 S. Ct. 189, 13 L. Ed. 2d 175 (dissenting opinion).

. . . These suggestions, it is true, relate to petitions to Congress. But, it would seem that whatever rights a civil service employee has under the First Amendment include petitions to the head of his own department as well as those to Congress. Mr. Justice Story, in his Commentaries on the Constitution, Vol. II, Section 1895, at 645, note b (5th ed. 1891), said of the right to petition:

"The statements made in petitions addressed to the proper authority, in a matter within its jurisdiction, are so far privileged that the petitioner is not liable, either civilly or criminally, for making them, though they prove to be untrue and injurious, unless he has made them maliciously."

---

[29] The Civil Service Commission used the latter standard in *Turner*. In Meehan v. Macy, 392 F.2d 822, 830 (D.C. Cir. 1968), the Court of Appeals for the District of Columbia stated its standard of review:

[I]n general the courts defer to the agency as the appropriate judge of what is an appropriate cause for discharge as needed to promote efficiency of the service, provided its decision is not arbitrary or capricious.

*See also* De Fino v. McNamara, 287 F.2d 339 (D.C. Cir.), *cert. denied,* 366 U.S. 976 (1961) (agency is not required to consider the employee's entire performance record in applying its standard); Taylor v. Macy, 252 F. Supp. 1021 (S.D. Cal. 1966) (dismissal based on criminal convictions that had been expunged).

[30] Decatur v. Paulding, 39 U.S. (14 Pet.) 497, 516 (1840).

This statement was also quoted with approval in Turner v. Kennedy, supra, 332 F.2d at 307 (dissenting opinion). In Bridges v. State of California, 314 U.S. 252, 277, 62 S. Ct. 190, 86 L. Ed. 192 (1941), a telegram to the Secretary of Labor was held to be a First Amendment petition. . . .

Therefore, we hold that a petition by a federal employee to one above him in the executive hierarchy is covered by the First Amendment and if it includes defamation of any Federal official, protection is lost only under the circumstances in which a newspaper article would lose such protection if it defamed such official. "Criticism of . . . official conduct does not lose its constitutional protection merely because it is effective criticism and hence diminishes . . . official reputations. If neither factual error nor defamatory content suffices to remove the constitutional shield from criticism of official conduct, the combination of the two elements is no less inadequate." New York Times Co. v. Sullivan, supra, 376 U.S. at 273, 84 S. Ct. at 722.

## NOTES

1. Can it be argued that the *New York Times* doctrine should have full application to government employees who criticize superiors "through channels," as in *Swaaley, supra,* but that some lesser standard should apply in cases involving appeals to the public? *Compare* Los Angeles Teachers Union, Local 1021 v. Los Angeles City Bd. of Educ., 71 Cal. 2d 551, 78 Cal. Rptr. 723, 455 P.2d 827 (1969) and Hudson v. Gray, 285 Ala. 546, 234 So. 2d 564 (1970), *with* the holding in Meehan v. Macy, 425 F.2d 469 (D.C. Cir. 1968), *aff'd after rehearing en banc,* 425 F.2d 472 (D.C. Cir. 1969).

2. In T. EMERSON, THE SYSTEM OF FREEDOM OF EXPRESSION 590 (1970), the author argues that:

Restriction on the political conduct of government employees does not abridge their freedom of expression to the extent that it is indispensably required as part of the employment relation; that is to say, is essential to the government's power to carry out its functions through engaging the services of its citizens. Controls are permissible at the point where the expression can be shown to relate to job performance, either by way of indicating the employee's competence, interfering with his capacity to carry out orders, or impairing his relationship with the rest of the organization. Hence regulations concerned with the making of deliberately false statements that may reflect on competence, carrying on political activities during working hours, campaigning against or running for office against an immediate superior, would be justified. So also would controls aimed at eliminating a direct conflict of interest between an employee's political activity and his government position. In addition, needless to say, prohibition of political activities that are no expression at all, such as using official authority for partisan political coercion of subordinates, or refusal to comply with the merit system in promotion, would raise no First Amendment problems.

## 4. POLITICAL LOBBYING

Political lobbying is, to some extent, subsumed under the more general heading of the right to petition. Lobbying by public employees is frequently a supplement to or replacement for traditional collective bargaining. Many of the statutes and executive orders regulating collective bargaining in the public sector have narrowly limited the scope of bargaining; for example, section 11 (b) of Executive Order 11491 (see *Statutory Appendix*), specifically excludes from bargaining:

[M]atters with respect to the mission of the agency; its budget; its organization; the number of employees; and the number, types, and grades of positions of employees assigned to an organizational unit, work project, or tour of duty; the technology of performing its work; or its internal security practices.

Thus, unions representing employees in the federal service are frequently forced to make direct appeals to Congress to achieve bargaining goals.

Even when a public agency or department is authorized to negotiate and agree to certain substantive items, there may remain the requirement of legislative approval of some parts of the agreement. The New York Taylor Law, for example, includes the following requirement:

> Any written agreement between a public employer and an employee organization determining the terms and conditions of employment of public employees shall contain the following notice in type not smaller than the largest type used elsewhere in such agreement.
>
> "It is agreed by and between the parties that any provision of this agreement requiring legislative action to permit its implementation by amendment of law or by providing the additional funds therefor, shall not become effective until the appropriate legislative body has given approval." [NEW YORK CIVIL SERVICE LAW § 204-a (McKinney Supp. 1971)]

The Wisconsin State Employment Labor Relations Act, requires that agreements involving state employees must be sent to a joint legislative committee for approval once they have been approved by the union representative. A public hearing must then be held. If the committee approves the agreement, it introduces bills in both legislative houses to implement those portions of the agreement, such as wage adjustments, which require legislative approval. If the committee rejects the agreement, or if it approves but the legislature rejects the resultant bills, the agreement is sent back to the parties for further negotiation. WIS. STAT. ANN. §§ 111.80-111.97 (Wis. Leg. Serv. Supp. 1972).

Given these types of legislative enactments, it would appear that unions in the public sector must necessarily become involved in the "political process" in order to achieve legislative ratification of negotiated benefits.

For a series of articles discussing the lobbying problem, see Moskow, Loewenberg and Koziara, *Lobbying* 216, Nilan, *Union Lobbying at the Federal Level* 221, McLennan and Moskow, *Multilateral Bargaining in the Public Sector* 227, and Belasco, *Municipal Bargaining and Political Power* 235, in COLLECTIVE BARGAINING IN GOVERNMENT (Loewenberg & Moskow eds. 1972).

## NOTES

1. The need to gain legislative approval for negotiated agreements, suggests that the legislators should remain neutral arbiters. However, in New York, the Taylor Law does not prohibit a legislator from also acting as a negotiator, even if he is later to decide whether agreement should be approved. *See* County of Broome and Deputy Sheriff's Benevolent Ass'n of Broome County, 3 PERB ¶ 3103 (1970), where the Board, after concluding that it was statutorily permissible for legislators to act as negotiators, stated that,

> While we do conclude that the participation of the legislators herein does not constitute a violation of the duty to negotiate in good faith, we repeat the warning set forth in the *Vestal* decision that pragmatically it is most difficult for legislators to participate actively in the negotiations and then step back and act objectively as arbiters, the role which was envisioned for the legislature by the Taylor Law.

2. Can an argument be made that, because of the unique nature of collective bargaining in the public sector, all political activity which is not directly disruptive of departmental efficiency to a harmful degree should be permitted? Many of these problems may be partially alleviated by compulsory binding arbitration or mediation, which may reduce the need for political action by unions in the public sector.

# D. CONSTITUTIONAL PROTECTIONS AGAINST EMPLOYMENT DISCRIMINATION ON THE BASIS OF RACE, SEX, NATIONAL ORIGIN AND AGE

## 1. INTRODUCTION

Since the publication of the first edition of the casebook, there has been a literal explosion in the law dealing with equal employment opportunity, most notably under Title VII of the Civil Rights Act of 1964. As a consequence, the authors have decided that it is no longer possible to give adequate treatment to this subject in a book dealing with labor relations law in the public sector. Employment discrimination is now the subject of several entire books, *see, e.g.,* Smith, EMPLOYMENT DISCRIMINATION LAW (Bobbs-Merrill 1978), and it is plainly too broad a topic for coverage here. Therefore, employment discrimination materials here will be limited to those cases arising under the United States Constitution, *i.e.,* primarily under the Fifth and Fourteenth Amendments. There will be no coverage of cases arising under Title VII, the Equal Pay Act, Executive Order 11246, or other like enactments.

## 2. RACE DISCRIMINATION

### JOHNSON v. BRANCH

United States Court of Appeals, Fourth Circuit
364 F.2d 177 (1969)

J. SPENCER BELL, Circuit Judge:
This is an appeal from a judgment of the district court dismissing with prejudice the plaintiff's complaint seeking reversal of the action of her school committee which refused to renew her contract of employment as a teacher. She contends that the committee acted either in an arbitrary and capricious manner or acted to penalize her for exercising her constitutional rights. Jurisdiction is based upon Title 28 U.S.C. § 1343 (3), Title 42 U.S.C. §§ 1971, 1981, 1983 and 1985, and the First, Fifth, Thirteenth, Fourteenth and Fifteenth Amendments to the Constitution of the United States.

The record discloses, the defendants concede, and the court found that the plaintiff, a Negro, was a well qualified, conscientious, and competent teacher . . . for a period of nearly twelve years preceding the incidents involved here. In addition to her teaching duties she had done a great deal of "extracurricular" work for the school and for student activities which indicated her devotion to her professional task. During the year 1962-1963 the Principal graded her in all fields as excellent and above average, the two highest possible ratings used in the system of grading teachers by the Halifax school system. Her superintendent, a defendant, testified that she had been an above average teacher and was doing very satisfactory work.

Beginning in the month of April 1963, the town of Enfield became a focal point of civil rights activity which included a voter registration drive, the candidacy of a number of Negroes for public offices, a major federal voting suit, an attempt to use the public library by Negro high school students, and the picketing of places of public accommodation. . . .

The plaintiff was a participant in one of the demonstrations and in the voter registration and voting activity. Both her husband and her father were candidates for public office. Her uncle brought suit in the federal district court in an effort to secure the Negroes an adequate opportunity to register.

The civil rights movement in Enfield became increasingly active and controversial during the summer and fall of 1963 and continued into the winter of 1964. It had not terminated at the time that teaching contracts came up for renewal at the April 23, 1964, meeting of the District School Committee. In March, Mrs. Johnson received from her Principal, L.M. Williams, a letter dated March 10, 1964, listing seven infractions of the school rules which he asked her to correct. The plaintiff offered expert evidence to show, and the district court in its comments appeared to agree, that these infractions individually and collectively were not in themselves justification for failure to re-employ the plaintiff. None of them involved the quality of her classroom work. Instead they covered such matters as being 15 minutes late to supervise an evening athletic contest; arriving at the school building a few minutes after the prescribed sign-in-time but before any class was due to commence; failure to furnish a written explanation for not attending a P.T.A. meeting; failure to stand in the door of her classroom to supervise pupils as the classes changed, and failure to see that the cabinets in her home room were clean and free of fire hazard. To all of these, the plaintiff offered explanations, and early in April the plaintiff received a letter dated March 31, 1964, in which the Principal informed her that he had seen improvement "in the areas mentioned" in the letter of March 10th. The letter continued "I am recommending you for re-election for a teacher for the 1964-1965 school term on condition that you continue to show improvement. . . ." Prior to the meeting of the District School Board in April, Principal Williams did in fact sign the plaintiff's contract, thus complying with the state's legal requirement that he recommend her before the Committee could act on her contract. The record discloses that the former pleasant relationship between Mrs. Johnson and the Principal, Williams, became strained over the period of her civil rights activities. The plaintiff contends that Williams was opposed to such activity on the part of school teachers and exhibited his hostility by criticizing her. She concedes that she took offense at his actions. However, she insisted that at no time were their relations such that they interfered with her official duties, and Williams also conceded that he could not specify a single infringement of the rules after the warning of March 10th. In any event, his testimony confirmed his statement of March 31st that she had improved and that he had recommended extending her contract for another year.

The District Committee met on April 23, 1964, to consider renewal of teacher contracts. . . .

All the members of the school committee knew of the civil rights activity in general and of the participation of Mr. Johnson, the plaintiff's husband, therein, though they denied specific knowledge of the plaintiff's part or of her relationship as wife to the Mr. Johnson who was running for the State Senate from that district. At this meeting all the committee members (except the Chairman, Coppage, who had received copies) first became aware of the two letters to Mrs. Johnson. In their testimony before the court they all declared that their decision was based solely on the letters. Superintendent Overman testified that at the meeting Williams renewed his favorable recommendation of March 31st. None of the members was able to testify to any inquiry into further details made at the meeting. . . . [Also present at the meeting] . . . was a member of the County School Board who had previously told Mrs. Johnson's husband that a teacher would be fired for voting activity. The members voted 2 to 1 against renewing Mrs. Johnson's contract. There was no discussion of her conduct. The two members who voted against renewal conceded frankly that they were opposed to integration of the schools. On June 2nd, the Principal told Mrs. Johnson that her contract had not been renewed because of insubordination to him. The district court, after reviewing the record, found that ". . . there was good cause for not re-employing the plaintiff under the circumstances as established by the evidence" because of the "plaintiff's inability to perform those extracurricular duties required of her promptly and in a cooperative manner. . . ." We hold that the court committed clear error in this finding, but before discussing the facts we turn to the law of the case.

The law of North Carolina is clear on the procedure for hiring teachers. All contracts are for one year only, renewable at the discretion of the school authorities. A contract must be signed by the Principal as an indication of his recommendation and then transmitted to the District School Committee, whose business it is either to approve or disapprove in their discretion. (N.C.G.S. § 115-72). There is no vested right to public employment. No one questions the fact that the plaintiff had neither a contract nor a constitutional right to have her contract renewed, but these questions are not involved in this case. It is the plaintiff's contention that her contract was not renewed for reasons which were either capricious and arbitrary or in order to retaliate against her for exercising her constitutional right to protest racial discrimination. . . .

[I]n Franklin v. County School Board of Giles County, 360 F.2d 325 (4th Cir. 1966), this court ordered that Negro teachers whose contracts were not renewed because of their race be reinstated. There the Board contended that they had, in the act of failure to renew the contracts, compared the qualifications of the teachers with others in the system and found them inferior, but the record disclosed no objective evidence of such inferiority in the face of equal certification and experience. However wide the discretion of School Boards, it cannot be exercised so as to arbitrarily deprive persons of their constitutional rights. . . .

While there is some ambiguity in the court's findings and conclusions, we think it a fair summary to say that the court found that the plaintiff's civil rights activities consumed so much of her time and interest that they interfered with her "extracurricular" activities at the school; created some dissension between her and the Principal, and caused the Board's refusal to renew her contract. This independent finding of the court is irrelevant because it is not the reason advanced by the Board members for refusing to execute her contract. The statute gives discretion to the school board in deciding whether or not to continue the employment of a teacher. Discretion means the exercise of judgment, not bias or capriciousness. Thus it must be based upon fact and supported by reasoned analysis. In testing the decision of the school board the district court must consider only the facts and logic relied upon by the board itself. It is "a simple but fundamental rule of administrative law . . . that a reviewing court, in dealing with a determination or judgment which an administrative agency alone is authorized to make, must judge the propriety of such action solely by the grounds invoked by the agency. If those grounds are inadequate or improper, the court is powerless to affirm the administrative action by substituting what it considers to be a more adequate or proper basis. To do so would propel the court into the domain which Congress has set aside for the administrative agency." S.E.C.

v. Chenery Corp., 332 U.S. 194, 196, 67 S.Ct. 1575, 1577, 91 L. Ed. 1995 (1947). Similarly the district court may not usurp the discretionary power of the school board but must judge the constitutionality of its action on the basis of the facts which were before the Board and on its logic. The testimony of all the members of the Board was that they did not know of the plaintiff's civil rights activities, or at least the extent thereof, and that their action was based solely upon the letters of March 10th and March 31st. We accept the defendants' statements that they were not aware of the extent of the plaintiff's personal participation in this activity because the district court credited them. Thus the record offers no objectively substantiated facts known to the Board with regard to the plaintiff's civil rights activity which would justify the Board's action as found by the court.
. . .

That the plaintiff had her disagreements with her Principal is obvious from the record. In such periods of great emotional stress there is no more reason to expect the Negro community to be unanimous than to expect the white to be so. But that these disagreements had been satisfactorily settled by March 31st in such a manner as not to interfere with her school work was shown both by the Principal's letter of that date and by his testimony. He testified that the plaintiff had improved in her attitude toward him and that she had not violated any of the rules since the warning of March 10th. Furthermore, the members of the Board testified that they had not further questioned the Principal and that they acted solely on the strength of the letters and their personal opinions that the Principal did not want the plaintiff's contract renewed. Thus there is no support in the record for the court's finding that the extent of the plaintiff's activities interfered with her school work or that the Principal and the plaintiff had not reached a satisfactory understanding of their differences. We take it to be self-evident that the objections held either by the Board or the Principal to the plaintiff's exercise of her personal and associational liberty to express her feelings about segregation would not justify refusal to renew her contract so long as these activities did not interfere with her performance of her school work. We feel that the infractions enumerated in the March 10th letter were neither individually nor collectively such as to justify failure to renew the contract of a teacher with the plaintiff's record of twelve years. The district court did not seek to rely on these infractions to support the dismissal. These being the only basis for the school board's decision, we find that the action of the school board was arbitrary and capricious.

We, with the district court, accept the defendants' statements that they did not know of the extent of the plaintiff's activities for civil rights but they knew of her attitude towards the civil rights movement. She made no secret of it. The Principal forced her to cancel an invitation to a local civil rights leader to talk to the students in her lecture course, even though he was not to talk about civil rights (she acceded to this order). Mr. Copeland, the member who moved not to renew her contract, was a member of the Town Council which rejected an equal accommodations ordinance strenuously backed by both Mrs. Johnson and her husband several weeks before the April meeting. Three days before the meeting, Mr. Coppage pointed out the plaintiff's husband to his fellow board member Thorne at the polling place.

In this factual context we think the court committed error in separately weighing the facts with respect to the plaintiff's two contentions: first, that the Board either acted arbitrarily or capriciously, or second, that it acted to penalize her for her civil rights activity. In weighing the reason offered by the Board to support its contention that it did not act arbitrarily, we cannot ignore the highly charged emotional background of a small eastern North Carolina community in the throes of a civil rights campaign where more than 51% of the population was Negro and where the two members of the Board who voted against the plaintiff confessed to knowledge of her husband's activity and their opposition to school desegregation. To accept such an analysis we would have to pretend not to know as judges what we know as men. It is apparent on this record that absent the racial question, the issue would not have arisen. The only reasonable inference which may be drawn from the failure to renew Mrs. Johnson's contract in the face of her splendid record of twelve years on such trivial charges was the Board members' objections to her racial activity. We cannot weigh the separate contentions in airtight compartments.

For these reasons the order of the district court is reversed and the case remanded with instructions to enter an order directing the Board to renew her contract for the next school year (1966-1967) and to determine her damages.

Reversed and remanded.

[The dissenting opinion of ALBERT V. BRYAN, Circuit Judge, is omitted.]

## NOTES

1. Many of the cases of alleged discrimination in public education have arisen pursuant to court ordered shifts from segregated to unitary school systems in the South. In 1969, the Supreme Court rendered two important decisions in this area. In one, Alexander v. Holmes County Bd. of Educ., 396 U.S. 19, 90 S.Ct. 29, 24 L. Ed. 2d 19 (1969), the Court ruled that the aging order of Brown v. Board of Educ., 347 U.S. 483 (1954), was to take effect "immediately" and that school districts could no longer operate dual school systems based on race or color. In the second case, United States v. Montgomery County Bd. of Educ., 395 U.S. 225, 89 S.Ct. 1670, 23 L. Ed. 2d 263 (1969), the Court ruled that the legal requirement of desegregation included an obligation to integrate public school faculties. The Court in *Montgomery County* ordered the school board to move toward a goal whereby in each school the ratio of white to Negro faculty members was substantially the same throughout the school system.

2. Another important decision in this area is Singleton v. Jackson Municipal Separate School Dist., 419 F.2d 1211 (5th Cir. 1970), *cert. denied,* 396 U.S. 1032 (1970). The *Singleton* decision set forth standards to be followed in the event of personnel reductions occurring as a result of the transition to unitary school systems. In essence the court ordered that if, during the process of desegregation, staff reductions, resulting in dismissal or demotion of professional personnel, become necessary, the school district must proceed to select the staff members to be displaced on the basis of previously developed "non-racial objective criteria." The criteria must be made available for public inspection and must be retained by the school district. Additionally, the school district must also "record and preserve the evaluation of staff members under the criteria" and make the evaluation available to the displaced employee upon his request. The court in *Singleton* also made the significant ruling that, in the event of staff displacements—

"no staff vacancy may be filled through recruitment of a person of a race, color, or national origin different from that of the individual dismissed or demoted, until each displaced staff member who is qualified has had an opportunity to fill the vacancy and has failed to accept an offer to do so." 419 F.2d at 1218.

For more recent decisions following the mandate of *Singleton,* see Lee v. Macon County Bd. of Educ., 455 F.2d 978 (5th Cir. 1971) and Lee v. Macon County Bd. of Educ., 456 F.2d 1371 (5th Cir. 1972).

3. Minority teachers may properly be displaced pursuant to a transition from a segregated to a unitary school system, *see, e.g.,* Thomas v. Board of Educ. of the Plum Bayou Tucker School Dist., 457 F.2d 1268 (8th Cir. 1972), however, as the cases clearly recognize, unless objective standards are required, not only would the displaced minority staff remain displaced but, in all probability, the overwhelming numbers of minority

applicants for new employment would remain unhired. The applicable judicial precedents also make it clear that job criteria must bear some provable relationship to the position in question when the use of the criteria results in unfavorable differentials along racial lines. The problems encountered in this area are graphically illustrated by two 1971 Mississippi cases in which the school district imposed the requirement that both incumbent teachers and prospective applicants attain certain scores on the National Teachers Examinations (NTE) and the Graduate Record Examinations (GRE) in order to retain or obtain employment. Baker v. Columbus Municipal Separate School Dist., 329 F. Supp. 706 (N.D. Miss. 1971), aff'd, 462 F.2d 1112 (5th Cir. 1972); Armstead v. Starkville Municipal Separate School Dist., 325 F. Supp. 560 (N.D. Miss. 1971), modified, 461 F.2d 276 (5th Cir. 1972). In both situations the local boards were aware of the fact that a disproportionate number of Blacks, as compared with whites, had failed to achieve these scores and therefore the pool of eligible teachers would be virtually all white. The court in both cases ruled that the use of these criteria as conditions of employment was illegal because (1) the tests had a disproportionately adverse impact on Black versus white job candidates and (2) the tests were never clearly shown to measure or predict a person's ability to be a good teacher. The courts also found that the GRE and NTE were not designed to facilitate the selection or identification of effective teachers. Rather, it was found that the purpose of the GRE was to assist in the identification of candidates for graduate study; and the purpose of the NTE was to measure the academic achievement of seniors in teacher education programs. There was no evidence of positive correlation between scores on either examination and effective teaching skills and ability.

## WASHINGTON v. DAVIS

United States Supreme Court
96 S. Ct. 2040 (1976)

MR. JUSTICE WHITE delivered the opinion of the Court.

This case involves the validity of a qualifying test administered to applicants for positions as police officers in the District of Columbia Metropolitan Police Department. The test was sustained by the District Court but invalidated by the Court of Appeals. We are in agreement with the District Court and hence reverse the judgment of the Court of Appeals.

I

This action began on April 10, 1970, when two Negro police officers filed suit against the then Commissioner of the District of Columbia, the Chief of the District's Metropolitan Police Department and the Commissioners of the United States Civil Service Commission. An amended complaint, filed December 10, alleged that the promotion policies of the Department were racially discriminatory and sought a declaratory judgment and an injunction. The respondents Harley and Sellers were permitted to intervene, their amended complaint asserting that their applications to become officers in the Department had been rejected, and that the Department's recruiting procedures discriminated on the basis of race against black applicants by a series of practices including, but not limited to, a written personnel test which excluded a disproportionately high number of Negro applicants. These practices were asserted to violate respondents' rights "under the due process clause of the Fifth Amendment to the United States Constitution, under 42 U. S. C. § 1981 and under D. C. Code § 1-320."

According to the findings and conclusions of the District Court, to be accepted by the Department and to enter an intensive 17-week training program, the police recruit was required to satisfy certain physical and character standards, to be a high school graduate or its equivalent and to receive a grade of at least 40 on

"Test 21," which is "an examination that is used generally throughout the federal service," which "was developed by the Civil Service Commission not the Police Department" and which was "designed to test verbal ability, vocabulary, reading and comprehension." 348 F. Supp., at 16.

The validity of Test 21 was the sole issue before the court on the motions for summary judgment. The District Court noted that there was no claim of "an intentional discrimination or purposeful discriminatory actions" but only a claim that Test 21 bore no relationship to job performance and "has a highly discriminatory impact in screening out black candidates." 348 F. Supp., at 16. Petitioners' evidence, the District Court said, warranted three conclusions: "(a) The number of black police officers, while substantial, is not proportionate to the population mix of the city. (b) A higher percentage of blacks fail the Test than whites. (c) The Test has not been validated to establish its reliability for measuring subsequent job performance." *Ibid.* This showing was deemed sufficient to shift the burden of proof to the defendants in the action, petitioners here; but the court nevertheless concluded that on the undisputed facts, respondents were not entitled to relief. The District Court relied on several factors. Since August 1969, 44% of new police force recruits had been black; that figure also represented the proportion of blacks on the total force and was roughly equivalent to 20-29-year-old blacks in the 50-mile radius in which the recruiting efforts of the Police Department had been concentrated. It was undisputed that the Department had systematically and affirmatively sought to enroll black officers many of whom passed the test but failed to report for duty. The District Court rejected the assertion that Test 21 was culturally slanted to favor whites and was "satisfied that the undisputable facts prove the test to be reasonably and directly related to the requirements of the police recruit training program and that it is neither so designed nor operated to discriminate against otherwise qualified blacks." . . .

Having lost on both constitutional and statutory issues in the District Court, respondents brought the case to the Court of Appeals claiming that their summary judgment motion, which rested on purely constitutional grounds, should have been granted. The tendered constitutional issue was whether the use of Test 21 invidiously discriminated against Negroes and hence denied them due process of law contrary to the commands of the Fifth Amendment. The Court of Appeals, addressing that issue, announced that it would be guided by Griggs v. Duke Power Co., 401 U.S. 424 (1971), a case involving the interpretation and application of Title VII of the Civil Rights Act of 1964, and held that the statutory standards elucidated in that case were to govern the due process question tendered in this one. 168 U. S. App. D. C. 42, 512 F. 2d 956 (1975). The court went on to declare that lack of discriminatory intent in designing and administering Test 21 was irrelevant; the critical fact was rather that a far greater proportion of blacks — four times as many — failed the test than did whites. This disproportionate impact, standing alone and without regard to whether it indicated a discriminatory purpose, was held sufficient to establish a constitutional violation, absent proof by petitioners that the test was an adequate measure of job performance in addition to being an indicator of probable success in the training program, a burden which the court ruled petitioners had failed to discharge. That the Department had made substantial efforts to recruit blacks was held beside the point and the fact that the racial distribution of recent hirings and of the Department itself might be roughly equivalent to the racial makeup of the surrounding community, broadly conceived, was put aside as a "comparison [not] material to this appeal.". . .

## II

Because the Court of Appeals erroneously applied the legal standards applicable to Title VII cases in resolving the constitutional issue before it, we reverse its judgment in respondents' favor. Although the petition for certiorari did not present this ground for reversal, our Rule 40(1)(d)(2) provides that we "may notice a plain error not presented"; and this is an appropriate occasion to invoke the rule.

As the Court of Appeals understood Title VII,[10] employees or applicants proceeding under it need not concern themselves with the employer's possibly discriminatory purpose but instead may focus solely on the racially differential impact of the challenged hiring or promotion practices. This is not the constitutional rule. We have never held that the constitutional standard for adjudicating claims of invidious racial discrimination is identical to the standards applicable under Title VII, and we decline to do so today.

The central purpose of the Equal Protection Clause of the Fourteenth Amendment is the prevention of official conduct discriminating on the basis of race. It is also true that the Due Process Clause of the Fifth Amendment contains an equal protection component prohibiting the United States from invidiously discriminating between individuals or groups. Bolling v. Sharpe, 347 U.S. 497 (1954). But our cases have not embraced the proposition that a law or other official act, without regard to whether it reflects a racially discriminatory purpose, is unconstitutional solely because it has a racially disproportionate impact.

... Wright v. Rockefeller, 376 U.S. 52 (1964), upheld a New York congressional apportionment statute against claims that district lines had been racially gerrymandered. The challenged districts were made up predominantly of whites or of minority races, and their boundaries were irregularly drawn. The challengers did not prevail because they failed to prove that the New York legislature "was either motivated by racial considerations or in fact drew the districts on racial lines"; the plaintiffs had not shown that the statute "was the product of a state contrivance to segregate on the basis of race or place of origin." 376 U.S., at 56, 58. The dissenters were in agreement that the issue was whether the "boundaries . . . were purposefully drawn on racial lines." 376 U.S., at 67.

The school desegregation cases have also adhered to the basic equal protection principle that the invidious quality of a law claimed to be racially discriminatory must ultimately be traced to a racially discriminatory purpose. That there are both predominantly black and predominantly white schools in a community is not alone violative of the Equal Protection Clause. The essential element of *de jure* segregation is "a current condition of segregation resulting from intentional state action . . . the differentiating factor between *de jure* segregation and so-called *de facto* segregation . . . is *purpose* or *intent* to segregate." Keyes v. School District No. 1, 413 U.S. 189, 205, 208 (1973). See also *id.,* at 199, 211, 213. The Court has also recently rejected allegations of racial discrimination based solely on the statistically disproportionate racial impact of various provisions of the Social Security Act because "the acceptance of appellant's constitutional theory

---

[10] Although Title VII standards have dominated this case, the statute was not applicable to federal employees when the complaint was filed, and although the 1972 amendments extending the title to reach government employees were adopted prior to the District Court's judgment, the complaint was not amended to state a claim under that title, nor did the case thereafter proceed as a Title VII case. Respondents' motion for partial summary judgment, filed after the 1972 amendments, rested solely on constitutional grounds; and the Court of Appeals ruled that the motion should have been granted. . . .

would render suspect each difference in treatment among the grant classes, however lacking the racial motivation and however rational the treatment might be." Jefferson v. Hackney, 406 U.S. 535, 548 (1972).

This is not to say that the necessary discriminatory racial purpose must be express or appear on the face of the statute, or that a law's disproportionate impact is irrelevant in cases involving Constitution-based claims of racial discrimination. A statute, otherwise neutral on its face, must not be applied so as invidiously to discriminate on the basis of race. Yick Wo v. Hopkins, 118 U.S. 356 (1886). It is also clear from the cases dealing with racial discrimination in the selection of juries that the systematic exclusion of Negroes is itself such an "unequal application of the law . . . as to show intentional discrimination." *Akins v. Texas, supra,* at 404. Smith v. Texas, 311 U.S. 128 (1940); Pierre v. Louisiana, 306 U.S. 354 (1939); Neal v. Delaware, 103 U.S. 370 (1881). . . . With a prima facie case made out, "the burden of proof shifts to the State to rebut the presumption of unconstitutional action by showing that permissible racially neutral selection criteria and procedures have produced the monochromatic result." [citing cases.]

Necessarily, an invidious discriminatory purpose may often be inferred from the totality of the relevant facts, including the fact, if it is true, that the law bears more heavily on one race than another. It is also not infrequently true that the discriminatory impact — in the jury cases for example, the total or seriously disproportionate exclusion of Negroes from jury venires — may for all practical purposes demonstrate unconstitutionality because in various circumstances the discrimination is very difficult to explain on nonracial grounds. Nevertheless, we have not held that a law, neutral on its face and serving ends otherwise within the power of government to pursue, is invalid under the Equal Protection Clause simply because it may affect a greater proportion of one race than of another. Disproportionate impact is not irrelevant, but it is not the sole touchstone of an invidious racial discrimination forbidden by the Constitution. Standing alone, it does not trigger the rule. McLaughlin v. Florida, 379 U.S. 184 (1964), that racial classifications are to be subjected to the strictest scrutiny and are justifiable only by the weightiest of considerations.

[Here follows a discussion of Palmer v. Thompson, 403 U.S. 217 (1971) and Wright v. Council of the City of Emporia, 407 U.S. 451 (1972), which indicate that in certain circumstances racial impact of a law, rather than discriminatory purpose, may be the critical factor invalidating the law.]

Both before and after *Palmer v. Thompson,* however, various Courts of Appeals have held in several contexts, including public employment, that the substantially disproportionate racial impact of a statute or official practice standing alone and without regard to discriminatory purpose, suffices to prove racial discrimination violating the Equal Protection Clause absent some justification going substantially beyond what would be necessary to validate most other legislative classifications. The cases impressively demonstrate that there is another side to the issue: but, with all due respect, to the extent that those cases rested on or expressed the view that proof of discriminatory racial purpose is unnecessary in making out an equal protection violation, we are in disagreement.

As an initial matter, we have difficulty understanding how a law establishing a racially neutral qualification for employment is nevertheless racially discriminatory and denies "any person equal protection of the laws" simply because a greater proportion of Negroes fail to qualify than members of other racial or ethnic groups. Had respondents, along with all others who had failed Test 21, whether white or black, brought an action claiming that the test denied each of them equal protection of the laws as compared with those who had passed with high enough scores to qualify them as police recruits, it is most unlikely that their challenge would have been sustained. Test 21, which is administered generally to prospective government employees, concededly seeks to ascertain whether those who take it have acquired a particular level of verbal skill; and it is untenable that the Constitution prevents the government from seeking modestly to upgrade the communicative abilities of its employees rather than to be satisfied with some lower level of competence, particularly where the job requires special ability to communicate orally and in writing. Respondents, as Negroes, could no more successfully claim that the test denied them equal protection than could white applicants who also failed. The conclusion would not be different in the face of proof that more Negroes than whites had been disqualified by Test 21. That other Negroes also failed to score well would, alone, not demonstrate that respondents individually were being denied equal protection of the laws by the application of an otherwise valid qualifying test being administered to prospective police recruits.

Nor on the facts of the case before us would the disproportionate impact of Test 21 warrant the conclusion that it is a purposeful device to discriminate against Negroes and hence an infringement of the constitutional rights of respondents as well as other black applicants. As we have said, the test is neutral on its face and rationally may be said to serve a purpose the government is constitutionally empowered to pursue. Even agreeing with the District Court that the differential racial effect of Test 21 called for further inquiry, we think the District Court correctly held that the affirmative efforts of the Metropolitan Police Department to recruit black officers, the changing racial composition of the recruit classes and of the force in general, and the relationship of the test to the training program negated any inference that the Department discriminated on the basis of race or that "a police officer qualifies on the color of his skin rather than ability." 348 F. Supp., at 18.

Under Title VII, Congress provided that when hiring and promotion practices disqualifying substantially disproportionate numbers of blacks are challenged, discriminatory purpose need not be proved, and that it is an insufficient response to demonstrate some rational basis for the challenged practices. It is necessary, in addition, that they be "validated" in terms of job performance in any one of several ways, perhaps by ascertaining the minimum skill, ability or potential necessary for the position at issue and determining whether the qualifying tests are appropriate for the selection of qualified applicants for the job in question. However this process proceeds, it involves a more probing judicial review of, and less deference to, the seemingly reasonable acts of administrators and executives than is appropriate under the Constitution where special racial impact, without discriminatory purpose, is claimed. We are not disposed to adopt this more rigorous standard for the purposes of applying the Fifth and the Fourteenth Amendments in cases such as this.

A rule that a statute designed to serve neutral ends is nevertheless invalid, absent compelling justification, if in practice it benefits or burdens one race more than another would be far reaching and would raise serious questions about, and perhaps invalidate, a whole range of tax, welfare, public service, regulatory, and licensing statutes that may be more burdensome to the poor and to the average black than to the more affluent white.

Given that rule, such consequences would perhaps be likely to follow. However, in our view, extension of the rule beyond those areas where it is already applicable by reason of statute, such as in the field of public employment, should await legislative prescription.

### III

[Part III of the Court's opinion holds that statutory standards similar to those under Title VII were also satisfied in this case. The District Court's conclusion that Test 21 was directly related to the requirements of the police training program and that a positive relationship between the test and the program was sufficient to validate the test was fully supported by the record, so that no remand to establish further validation would be appropriate.]

The judgment of the Court of Appeals accordingly is reversed. *So ordered.*

MR. JUSTICE STEWART joins Parts I and II of the Court's opinion.

MR. JUSTICE BRENNAN, with whom MR. JUSTICE MARSHALL joins, dissenting. [Justice Brennan would affirm the Court of Appeals ruling on the basis that petitioners failed to prove Test 21 satisfies applicable statutory standards under either applicable Civil Service Commission rules or EEOC guidelines.]

MR. JUSTICE STEVENS, concurring.

While I agree with the Court's disposition of this case, I add these comments on the constitutional issue discussed in Part II and the statutory issue discussed in Part III of the Court's opinion.

The requirement of purposeful discrimination is a common thread running through the cases summarized in Part II. These cases include criminal convictions which were set aside because blacks were excluded from the grand jury, a reapportionment case in which political boundaries were obviously influenced to some extent by racial considerations, a school desegregation case, and a case involving the unequal administration of an ordinance purporting to prohibit the operation of laundries in frame buildings. Although it may be proper to use the same language to describe the constitutional claim in each of these contexts, the burden of proving a prima facie case may well involve differing evidentiary considerations. The extent of deference that one pays to the trial court's determination of the factual issue, and indeed, the extent to which one characterizes the intent issue as a question of fact or a question of law, will vary in different contexts.

Frequently the most probative evidence of intent will be objective evidence of what actually happened rather than evidence describing the subjective state of mind of the actor. For normally the actor is presumed to have intended the natural consequences of his deeds. This is particularly true in the case of governmental action which is frequently the product of compromise, of collective decisionmaking, and of mixed motivation. It is unrealistic, on the one hand, to require the victim of alleged discrimination to uncover the actual subjective intent of the decisionmaker or, conversely, to invalidate otherwise legitimate action simply because an improper motive affected the deliberation of a participant in the decisional process. A law conscripting clerics should not be invalidated because an atheist voted for it.

My point in making this observation is to suggest that the line between discriminatory purpose and discriminatory impact is not nearly as bright, and perhaps not quite as critical, as the reader of the Court's opinion might assume. I agree, of course, that a constitutional issue does not arise every time some disproportionate impact is shown. On the other hand, when the disproportion is as dramatic as in *Gomillion* or *Yick Wo*, it really does not matter whether the standard is phrased in terms of purpose or effect. Therefore, although I accept the statement of the general rule in the Court's opinion, I am not yet prepared to indicate how that standard should be applied in the many cases which have formulated the governing standard in different language.

My agreement with the conclusion reached in Part II of the Court's opinion rests on a ground narrower than the Court describes. I do not rely at all on the evidence of good-faith efforts to recruit black police officers. In my judgment, neither those efforts nor the subjective good faith of the District administration, would save Test 21 if it were otherwise invalid.

There are two reasons why I am convinced that the challenge to Test 21 is insufficient. First, the test serves the neutral and legitimate purpose of requiring all applicants to meet a uniform minimum standard of literacy. Reading ability is manifestly relevant to the police function, there is no evidence that the required passing grade was set at an arbitrarily high level, and there is sufficient disparity among high schools and high school graduates to justify the use of a separate uniform test. Second, the same test is used throughout the federal service. The applicants for employment in the District of Columbia Police Department represent such a small fraction of the total number of persons who have taken the test that their experience is of minimal probative value in assessing the neutrality of the test itself. That evidence, without more, is not sufficient to overcome the presumption that a test which is this widely used by the Federal Government is in fact neutral in its effect as well as its "purpose" as that term is used in constitutional adjudication.

My study of the statutory issue leads me to the same conclusion reached by the Court in Part III of its opinion. . . .

## NOTES

1. In Village of Arlington Heights v. Metropolitan Housing Development Corp., 429 U.S. 252 (1977), which involved the denial of a request for rezoning to accommodate low and middle income housing, the Supreme Court expanded upon their holding in *Washington v. Davis*. The Court in *Arlington Heights* defined the nature and degree of discriminatory "purpose" necessary to show a violation of the Equal Protection Clause, stating that:

*Davis* does require a plaintiff to prove that the challenged action rested solely on racially discriminatory purposes. Rarely can it be said that a legislature or administrative body operating under a broad mandate made a decision motivated by a single concern, or even that a particular purpose was the "dominant" or "primary" one. In fact, it is because legislators and administrators are properly concerned with balancing numerous competing considerations that courts refrain from reviewing the merits of their decisions, absent a showing of arbitrariness or irrationality. But racial discrimination is not just another competing consideration. When there is a proof that a discriminatory purpose has been a motivating factor in the decision, this judicial deference is no longer justified.

429 U.S. at 265-66.

2. A Black female medical technologist who had satisfactorily performed her job for years was demoted because she did not have a college degree, pursuant to a recently imposed prerequisite to taking a competitive examination for the position of medical technologist. The Second Circuit rejected the district court's finding of discrimination based on a statistical showing that a college degree requirement had a disparate effect on Blacks and on the failure of the employer to show job-relatedness. The circuit court, citing *Washington v. Davis,* said that the plaintiff failed to show any intentional discrimination on the part of the employer. The court also held that statistics relating to the general population rather than the employment practices of the particular defendant

were not enough to raise a presumption against the requirement of a college degree. Townsend v. Nassau County Medical Center, 558 F.2d 117 (2nd Cir. 1977), *cert. denied,* 98 S.Ct. 732 (1978).

3. In a summary disposition, the U.S. Supreme Court affirmed a lower court opinion upholding the use of standardized tests to hire teachers in South Carolina, despite the fact that the tests had a strong disparate effect on Black applicants. The tests were challenged under Title VII and the Constitution because they disqualified 83 percent of Black applicants, but only 17.5 percent of White applicants. The lower court had emphasized the requirement in *Washington v. Davis* that discriminatory intent be proved under the Fourteenth Amendment and said that state officials had no such intent. National Education Association v. State of South Carolina, 98 S.Ct. 756 (1978).

4. As in *Washington v. Davis,* many constitutional claims of employment discrimination have been brought against governmental bodies under the Civil Rights Act of 1871, 42 U.S.C. § 1983, which incorporates the Fourteenth Amendment Equal Protection Clause. Section 1983 reads as follows:

Every person who, under color of any statute, ordinance, regulation, custom, or usage, of any State or Territory, subjects, or causes to be subjected, any citizen of the United States or other person within the jurisdiction thereof to the deprivation of any rights, privileges, or immunities secured by the Constitution and laws, shall be liable to the party injured in an action at law, suit in equity, or other proper proceeding for redress.

5. In addition to Section 1983, large numbers of employment discrimination claims have been brought under Section 1981 of the Civil Rights Act of 1866 (42 U.S.C. § 1981). Section 1981 reads as follows:

All persons within the jurisdiction of the United States shall have the same right in every State and Territory to make and enforce contracts, to sue, be parties, give evidence, and to the full and equal benefit of all laws and proceedings for the security of persons and property as is enjoyed by white citizens, and shall be subject to like punishment, pains, penalties, taxes, licenses, and exactions of every kind, and to no other.

The Supreme Court, in the *Civil Rights Cases,* 109 U.S. 3 (1883), determined that the Civil Rights Act of 1866 was passed pursuant to the Thirteenth Amendment prohibition of slavery and that Congress ". . . undertook to wipe out these burdens and disabilities, the necessary incidents of slavery, constituting every race and color, and without regard to previous servitude, those fundamental rights which are the essence of civil freedom. . . ." Since the Thirteenth Amendment had no "state action" requirement, the Court suggested that, under the amendment, "legislation, so far as necessary and proper to eradicate all forms and incidents of slavery and involuntary servitude, may be direct and primary, operating upon the acts of individuals, whether sanctioned by State legislation or not. . . ." 109 U.S. at 22. In Jones v. Mayer Co., 392 U.S. 409, 422-37 (1968), the Supreme Court examined the legislative history of § 1981 and concluded that Congress had intended to reach purely private conduct.

The use of § 1981 in cases involving private employment discrimination was approved by the Supreme Court in Johnson v. Railway Express Agency, Inc., 421 U.S. 454 (1975).

In general, § 1981 has been utilized extensively only in racial discrimination cases. The Supreme Court added a new dimension to the law in McDonald v. Santa Fe Trail Transportation Co., 427 U.S. 273 (1976), when it found that "§ 1981 is applicable to racial discrimination in private employment against white persons." 427 U.S. at 287. It deduced from the legislative history that the law was intended to protect "all persons" from racial discrimination in the making and enforcement of contracts.

Courts have also held that § 1981, unlike Title VII, prohibits discrimination based on alienage. *See, e.g.,* Guerra v. Manchester Terminal Corp., 498 F.2d 641 (5th Cir. 1974) ("as the detailed study of the legislative history by the able district judge below demonstrates, subsequent congressional action explicitly broadened the language of the portion of the 1866 Act that has become § 1981 to include 'all persons' in order to bring aliens within its coverage." 498 F.2d at 653). Several courts have permitted an action to be brought under § 1981 on the basis of national origin where the plaintiff is

Spanish-surnamed, but have usually barred such actions where other national origins are involved. *See, e.g.,* Sabala v. Western Gillette, Inc., 516 F.2d 1251 (5th Cir. 1975) (protection extended to Mexican-Americans); Maldonado v. Broadcast Plaza, Inc., 10 FEP Cas. 839 (D. Conn. 1974) (protection extended to Puerto Ricans); Budinsky v. Corning Glass Works, 425 F.Supp. 786 (D. Pa. 1977) (protection denied to plaintiff of Slavic origin). Coverage of sex discrimination under § 1981, however, has been consistently rejected. *See, e.g.,* League of Academic Women v. Regents of University of California, 343 F.Supp. 636 (N.D. Cal. 1972); Braden v. University of Pittsburgh, 343 F.Supp. 836 (W.D. Pa. 1972), 477 F.2d 1 (3rd Cir. 1973) (remanding on other grounds).

Because the Civil Rights Act of 1866 contains no federal statute of limitations, the Supreme Court has held that federal district courts should apply the most appropriate state statute, except in those cases where its application would be inconsistent with the federal policy underlying § 1981. Johnson v. Railway Express Agency, 421 U.S. 454, 463-65 (1975). For a method of determining which state statute is most appropriate, *see* Shaw v. Garrison, 545 F.2d 980 (5th Cir. 1977). Does the absence of uniformity by the application of state law encourage "forum shopping" by plaintiffs bringing § 1981 actions?

5. The Ninth Circuit has held that a showing of discriminatory intent is unnecessary in an action brought under § 1981 where there is a strong showing of the disparate effect of an employer's hiring practices. The court stressed that *Washington v. Davis* was decided on the constitutional issue alone; the Supreme Court did not mention § 1981, nor did they cite cases construing it. In view of other overwhelming case law interpreting § 1981 to bar employment discrimination and applying Title VII principles to determine the existence of discrimination, the Ninth Circuit was unwilling to find a distinction between § 1981 and Title VII with regard to the treatment of disparate impact without an express statement by the Supreme Court. The Supreme Court has *granted certiorari* in the case to decide this issue and whether a racial quota hiring order issued by the district court can stand without a specific finding of discriminatory intent on the part of the employer. Davis v. County of Los Angeles, 566 F.2d 1334 (9th Cir. 1977), *cert. granted,* 46 U.S.L.W. 3775 (June 20, 1978).


## REGENTS OF THE UNIVERSITY OF CALIFORNIA v. BAKKE

98 S.Ct. 2733 (1978)

In this landmark decision, the Supreme Court upheld the constitutionality of certain "affirmative action" plans designed to remedy the effects of racial discrimination in university admissions. In *Bakke,* the Medical School of the University of California at Davis had two admissions programs for an entering class of 100 students — a regular admissions program and a special admissions program. A California trial court found that the special admissions program operated as a racial quota, because minority applicants in that program were rated only against one another, and 16 places in the class of 100 were reserved for them. The trial court concluded that the university could not take race into account in making admissions decisions and, therefore, the program was found to violate the Federal and State Constitutions and Title VI of the Civil Rights Act of 1964, 42 U.S.C. § 2000d. On review, the California Supreme Court ruled that the Davis special admissions program violated the Equal Protection Clause. Since Davis could not satisfy its burden of demonstrating that Bakke, absent the special program, would not have been admitted to medical school, the California Supreme Court ordered his admission to Davis.

In a five-four decision, the Supreme Court affirmed the judgment of the California Supreme Court insofar as it ordered Bakke's admission to Davis and invalidated the Davis special admissions program; however, the judgment of the

California Supreme Court was reversed insofar as it prohibited Davis from taking race into account as a factor in future admissions decisions.

Justice Powell, providing the swing vote and announcing the judgment of the Court, concluded that Title VI proscribed only those racial classifications that would violate the Equal Protection Clause if employed by a State or its agencies; racial and ethnic classifications of any sort are inherently suspect and call for the most exacting judicial scrutiny; and, while the goal of achieving a diverse student body is sufficiently compelling to justify consideration of race in admissions decisions under some circumstances, the Davis special admissions program, which foreclosed consideration to white applicants like Bakke, was unnecessary to the achievement of this compelling goal and therefore invalid under the Equal Protection Clause.

The decision of Justice Powell noted that prior cases in which racial preferences had been ordered or sanctioned to remedy the effects of employment discrimination could not be seen to justify the Davis affirmative action plan which established a fixed quota for minority admissions. However, Justice Powell did appear to cite with approval several of the prior employment cases upholding preferential remedies:

> For example, in *Franks v. Bowman Transportation Co.*, 424 U.S. 747 (1975), we approved a retroactive award of seniority to a class of Negro truck drivers who had been the victims of discrimination — not just by society at large, but by the respondent in that case. While this relief imposed some burdens on other employees, it was held necessary "to make [the victims] whole for injuries suffered on account of unlawful employment discrimination." . . . The courts of appeals have fashioned various types of racial preferences as remedies for constitutional or statutory violations resulting in identified, race-based injuries to individuals held entitled to the preference. *E.g., Bridgeport Guardians, Inc. v. Civil Service Commission*, 482 F.2d 1333 (2d Cir. 1973); *Carter v. Gallagher*, 452 F.2d 315, *modified on rehearing en banc*, 452 F.2d 327 (8th Cir. 1972). Such preferences also have been upheld where a legislative or administrative body charged with the responsibility made determinations of past discrimination by the industries affected, and fashioned remedies deemed appropriate to rectify the discrimination. *E.g., Contractors Association of Eastern Pennsylvania v. Secretary of Labor*, 442 F.2d 159 (3d Cir.), *cert. denied*, 404 U.S. 954 (1970). [40]

In the opinion of Justice Powell it is made clear that such remedies which fix preferences for an identifiable class must be done pursuant to specific judicial, legislative or administrative findings:

> The State certainly has a legitimate and substantial interest in ameliorating, or eliminating where feasible, the disabling effects of identified discrimination. . . . We have never approved a classification that aids persons perceived as members of relatively victimized groups at the expense of other innocent individuals in the absence of judicial, legislative, or administrative findings of constitutional or statutory violations. . . . After such findings have been made, the governmental interest in preferring members of the injured groups at the expense of others is substantial, since the legal rights of the

---

[40] Every decision upholding the requirement of preferential hiring under the authority of Executive Order 11246 has emphasized the existence of previous discrimination as a predicate for the imposition of a preferential remedy. *Contractors Association, supra; Southern Illinois Builders Assn. v. Ogilvie*, 471 F.2d 680 (7th Cir. 1972); . . .

victims must be vindicated. In such a case, the extent of the injury and the consequent remedy will have been judicially, legislatively, or administratively defined. Also, the remedial action usually remains subject to continuing oversight to assure that it will work the least harm possible to other innocent persons competing for the benefit. Without such findings of constitutional or statutory violations, it cannot be said that the government has any greater interest in helping one individual than in refraining from harming another. Thus, the government has no compelling justification for inflicting such harm.

Justice Powell did add, however, that at least in the academic context, universities may, in the name of academic freedom, "take race into account in achieving the educational diversity valued by the First Amendment." He stated that, "in such an admissions program, race or ethnic background may be deemed a 'plus' in a particular applicant's file, yet it does not insulate the individual from comparison with all other candidates for the available seats." Thus, according to Justice Powell, "the applicant who loses out on the last available seat to another candidate receiving a 'plus' on the basis of ethnic background will not have been foreclosed from all consideration for that seat simply because he was not the right color or had the wrong surname."

Justices Brennan, White, Marshall and Blackmun agreed with Justice Powell that affirmative action plans were permissible under the Fourteenth Amendment. However, these four Justices expressed the additional view that the Davis plan should have been upheld as lawful because it was designed to overcome the substantial, chronic minority underrepresentation in the medical profession. In differing with Justice Powell, Justices Brennan, White, Marshall and Blackmun expressed the view that Davis should have been allowed to voluntarily adopt an affirmative action plan including fixed racial preferences (without judicial, legislative or administrative findings) to overcome the effects of past racial discrimination.

Chief Justice Burger, Justices Stevens, Stewart and Rehnquist expressed the view that the Davis special admissions plan violated the statutory mandate of Title VI and, therefore, it was unnecessary to decide whether race can ever be a factor in an admissions policy.

## 3. SEX DISCRIMINATION

### CLEVELAND BD. OF EDUC. v. LAFLEUR

Supreme Court of the United States
94 S. Ct. 791 (1974)

MR. JUSTICE STEWART delivered the opinon of the Court.

The respondents in No. 72-777 and the petitioner in No. 72-1129 are female public school teachers. During the 1970-1971 school year, each informed her local school board that she was pregnant; each was compelled by a mandatory maternity leave rule to quit her job without pay several months before the expected birth of her child. These cases call upon us to decide the constitutionality of the school boards' rules.

I

Jo Carol LaFleur and Ann Elizabeth Nelson, the respondents in No. 72-777, are junior high school teachers employed by the Board of Education of Cleveland, Ohio. Pursuant to a rule first adopted in 1952, the school board requires every pregnant school teacher to take a maternity leave without pay, beginning five months before the expected birth of her child. Application for such leave must be made no later than two weeks prior to the date of departure. A teacher on maternity leave is not allowed to return to work until the beginning of the next regular school semester which follows the date when the child attains the age of three months. A doctor's certificate attesting to the health of the teacher is a prerequisite to return; an additional physical examination may be required. The teacher on maternity leave is not promised re-employment after the birth of the child; she is merely given priority in reassignment to a position for which she is qualified. Failure to comply with the mandatory maternity leave provisions is grounds for dismissal.

Neither Mrs. LaFleur nor Mrs. Nelson wished to take an unpaid maternity leave; each wanted to continue teaching until the end of the school year. Because of the mandatory maternity leave rule, however, each was required to leave her job in March of 1971. The two women then filed separate suits in the United States District Court for the Northern District of Ohio under 42 U.S.C. § 1983, challenging the constitutionality of the maternity leave rule. The District Court tried the cases together, and rejected the plaintiffs' arguments. 326 F.Supp. 1208. A divided panel of the United States Court of Appeals for the Sixth Circuit reversed, finding the Cleveland rules in violation of the Equal Protection Clause of the Fourteenth Amendment. 465 F.2d 1184.

The petitioner in No. 72-1129, Susan Cohen, was employed by the School Board of Chesterfield County, Virginia. That school board's maternity leave regulation requires that a pregnant teacher leave work at least four months prior to the expected birth of her child. Notice in writing must be given to the school board at least six months prior to the expected birth date. A teacher on maternity leave is declared re-eligible for employment when she submits written notice from a physician that she is physically fit for re-employment, and when she can give assurances that care of the child will cause minimal interferences with her job responsibilities. The teacher is guaranteed re-employment no later than the first day of the school year following the date upon which she is declared re-eligible.

Mrs. Cohen informed the Chesterfield County School Board in November 1970, that she was pregnant and expected the birth of her child about April 28, 1971. She initially requested that she be permitted to continue teaching until April 1, 1971. The school board rejected the request, as it did Mrs. Cohen's subsequent suggestion that she be allowed to teach until January 21, 1971, the end of the first school semester. Instead, she was required to leave her teaching job on December 18, 1970. She subsequently filed this suit under 42 U.S.C. § 1983 in the United States District Court for the Eastern District of Virginia. The District Court held that the school board regulation violates the Equal Protection Clause, and granted appropriate relief. 326 F.Supp. 1159. A divided panel of the Fourth Circuit affirmed, but, on rehearing *en banc,* the Court of Appeals upheld the constitutionality of the challenged regulation in a 4-3 decision. 474 F.2d 395.

We granted certiorari in both cases, 411 U.S. 947, 93 S.Ct. 1921, 36 L.Ed.2d 408, in order to resolve the conflict between the Courts of Appeals regarding the constitutionality of such mandatory maternity leave rules for public school teachers.[8]

---

[8] The practical impact of our decision in the present cases may have been somewhat lessened by several recent developments. At the time that the teachers in these cases were placed on maternity leave, Title VII of the Civil Rights Act of 1964, 42 U.S.C. § 2000e et seq., did not apply to state

## II

This court has long recognized that freedom of personal choice in matters of marriage and family life is one of the liberties protected by the Due Process Clause of the Fourteenth Amendment. . . .

As we noted in Eisenstadt v. Baird, 405 U.S. 438, 453, 92 S.Ct. 1029, 1038, 31 L.Ed.2d 349, there is a right "to be free from unwarranted governmental intrusion into matters so fundamentally affecting a person as the decision whether to bear or beget a child."

By acting to penalize the pregnant teacher for deciding to bear a child, overly restrictive maternity leave regulations can constitute a heavy burden on the exercise of these protected freedoms. Because public school maternity leave rules directly affect "one of the basic civil rights of man," Skinner v. Oklahoma, supra, 316 U.S., at 541, 62 S.Ct., at 1113, the Due Process Clause of the Fourteenth Amendment requires that such rules must not needlessly, arbitrarily, or capriciously impinge upon this vital area of a teacher's constitutional liberty. The question before us in these cases is whether the interests advanced in support of the rules of the Cleveland and Chesterfield County School Boards can justify the particular procedures they have adopted.

The school boards in these cases have offered two essentially overlapping explanations for their mandatory maternity leave rules. First, they contend that the firm cut-off dates are necessary to maintain continuity of classroom instruction, since advance knowledge of when a pregnant teacher must leave facilitates the finding and hiring of a qualified substitute. Secondly, the school boards seek to justify their maternity rules by arguing that at least some teachers become physically incapable of adequately performing certain of their duties during the latter part of pregnancy. By keeping the pregnant teacher out of the classroom during these final months, the maternity leave rules are said to protect the health of the teacher and her unborn child, while at the same time assuring that students have a physically capable instructor in the classroom at all times.[9]

---

agencies and educational institutions. 42 U.S.C. §§ 2000e-1 and 2000e(b) (1970). On March 27, 1972, however, the Equal Employment Act of 1972 amended Title VII to withdraw those exemptions. Pub.L. 92-261; 86 Stat. 103. Shortly thereafter, the Equal Employment Opportunity Commission promulgated guidelines providing that a mandatory leave or termination policy for pregnant women presumptively violates Title VII. 29 CFR § 1604.10, 37 Fed.Reg. 6837. While the statutory amendments and the administrative regulations are of course inapplicable to the cases now before us, they will affect like suits in the future.

In addition, a number of other federal agencies have promulgated regulations similar to those of the Equal Employment Opportunity Commission, forbidding discrimination against pregnant workers with regard to sick leave policies. See e.g., 5 CFR § 630.401(b) (Civil Service Commission); 41 CFR § 60-20.3(g) (Office of Federal Contract Compliance). See generally Koontz, Childbirth and Child Rearing Leave: Job-Related Benefits, 17 N.Y.L.F. 480, 487-490; comment, Love's Labors Lost: New Conceptions of Maternity Leaves, 7 Harv.Civ.Rights-Civ.Lib.L.Rev. 260, 280-281. We of course express no opinion as to the validity of any of these regulations.

[9] The records in these cases suggest that the maternity leave regulations may have originally been inspired by other, less weighty, considerations. For example, Dr. Mark C. Schinnerer, who served as Superintendent of Schools in Cleveland at the time the leave rule was adopted, testified in the District Court that the rule had been adopted in part to save pregnant teachers from embarrassment at the hands of giggling schoolchildren: the cut-off date at the end of the fourth month was chosen because this was when the teacher "began to show." Similarly, at least several members of the Chesterfield County School Board thought a mandatory leave rule was justified in order to insulate schoolchildren from the sight of conspicuously pregnant women. One member of the school board

It cannot be denied that continuity of instruction is a significant and legitimate educational goal. Regulations requiring pregnant teachers to provide early notice of their condition to school authorities undoubtedly facilitate administrative planning toward the important objective of continuity. But, as the Court of Appeals for the Second Circuit noted in Green v. Waterford Board of Education, 473 F.2d 629, 635:

> "Where a pregnant teacher provides the Board with a date certain for commencement of leave, however, that value [continuity] is preserved; an arbitrary leave date set at the end of the fifth month is no more calculated to facilitate a planned and orderly transition between the teacher and a substitute than is a date fixed closer to confinement. Indeed, the latter . . . would afford the Board more, not less, time to procure a satisfactory long-term substitute." (Footnote omitted.)

Thus, while the advance notice provisions in the Cleveland and Chesterfield County rules are wholly rational and may well be necessary to serve the objective of continuity of instruction, the absolute requirements of termination at the end of the fourth or fifth month of pregnancy are not. . . .

In fact, since the fifth or sixth months of pregnancy will obviously begin at different times in the school year for different teachers, the present Cleveland and Chesterfield County rules may serve to hinder attainment of the very continuity objectives that they are purportedly designed to promote. For example, the beginning of the fifth month of pregnancy for both Mrs. LaFleur and Mrs. Nelson occurred during March of 1971. Both were thus required to leave work with only a few months left in the school year, even though both were fully willing to serve through the end of the term. . . .

We thus conclude that the arbitrary cut-off dates embodied in the mandatory leave rules before us have no rational relationship to the valid state interest of preserving continuity of instruction. As long as the teacher is required to give substantial advance notice of her condition, the choice of firm dates later in pregnancy would serve the boards' objectives just as well, while imposing a far lesser burden on the women's exercise of constitutionally protected freedom.

The question remains as to whether the fifth and sixth month cut-off dates can be justified on the other ground advanced by the school boards — the necessity of keeping physically unfit teachers out of the classroom. There can be no doubt that such an objective is perfectly legitimate, both on educational and safety grounds. And, despite the plethora of conflicting medical testimony in these cases, we can assume *arguendo* that at least some teachers become physically disabled from effectively performing their duties during the latter stages of pregnancy.

The mandatory termination provisions of the Cleveland and Chesterfield County rules surely operate to insulate the classroom from the presence of potentially incapacitated pregnant teachers. But the question is whether the rules sweep too broadly. See Shelton v. Tucker, 364 U.S. 470, 81 S.Ct. 247, 5 L.Ed.2d 231. That question must be answered in the affirmative, for the provisions amount to a conclusive presumption that every pregnant teacher who reaches the fifth or sixth month of pregnancy is physically incapable of continuing. There is

---

thought that it was "not good for the school system" for students to view pregnant teachers, "because some of the kids say, my teacher swallowed a watermelon, things like that."

The school boards have not contended in this Court that these considerations can serve as a legitimate basis for a rule requiring pregnant women to leave work; we thus note the comments only to illustrate the possible role of outmoded taboos in the adoption of the rules. Cf. Green v. Waterford Board of Education, 473 F.2d 629, 635 (CA2) ("Whatever may have been the reaction in Queen Victoria's time, pregnancy is no longer a dirty word.").

no individualized determination by the teacher's doctor — or the school board's — as to any particular teacher's ability to continue at her job. The rules contain an irrebuttable presumption of physical incompetency, and that presumption applies even when the medical evidence as to an individual woman's physical status might be wholly to the contrary.

As the Court noted last Term in Vlandis v. Kline, 412 U.S. 441, 446, 93 S.Ct. 2230, 2233, 37 L.Ed.2d 63, "permanent irrebuttable presumptions have long been disfavored under the Due Process Clause of the Fifth and Fourteenth Amendments." In *Vlandis,* the Court declared unconstitutional, under the Due Process Clause, a Connecticut statute mandating an irrebuttable presumption of nonresidency for the purposes of qualifying for reduced tuition rates at a state university. We said in that case, 412 U.S., at 452, 93 S.Ct., at 2236:

> "[I]t is forbidden by the Due Process Clause to deny an individual the resident rates on the basis of a permanent and irrebuttable presumption of nonresidence, when that presumption is not necessarily or universally true in fact, and when the State has reasonable alternative means of making the crucial determination."

Similarly, in Stanley v. Illinois, 405 U.S. 645, 92 S.Ct. 1208, 31 L.Ed.2d 551, the Court held that an Illinois statute containing an irrebuttable presumption that unmarried fathers are incompetent to raise their children violated the Due Process Clause. . . .

These principles control our decision in the cases before us. While the medical experts in these cases differed on many points, they unanimously agreed on one — the ability of any particular pregnant woman to continue at work past any fixed time in her pregnancy is very much an individual matter. Even assuming *arguendo* that there are some women who would be physically unable to work past the particular cut-off dates embodied in the challenged rules, it is evident that there are large numbers of teachers who are fully capable of continuing work for longer than the Cleveland and Chesterfield County regulations will allow. Thus, the conclusive presumption embodied in these rules, like that in *Vlandis,* is neither "necessarily nor universally true," and is violative of the Due Process Clause. . . .

While it might be easier for the school boards to conclusively presume that all pregnant women are unfit to teach past the fourth or fifth month or even the first month of pregnancy, administrative convenience alone is insufficient to make valid what otherwise is a violation of due process of law.[13] The Fourteenth Amendment requires the school boards to employ alternative administrative means, which do not so broadly infringe upon basic constitutional liberty, in support of their legitimate goals.

We conclude, therefore, that neither the necessity for continuity of instruction nor the state interest in keeping physically unfit teachers out of the classroom can justify the sweeping mandatory leave regulations that the Cleveland and Chesterfield County School Boards have adopted. . . .

---

[13] This is not to say that the only means for providing appropriate protection for the rights of pregnant teachers is an individualized determination in each case and in every circumstance. We are not dealing in these cases with maternity leave regulations requiring a termination of employment at some firm date during the last few weeks of pregnancy. We therefore have no occasion to decide whether such regulations might be justified by considerations not presented in these records. . . .

## III

In addition to the mandatory termination provisions, both the Cleveland and Chesterfield County rules contain limitations upon a teacher's eligibility to return to work after giving birth. . . .

Under the Cleveland rule, . . . the school board requires the mother to wait until her child reaches the age of three months before the return rules begin to operate. The school boards have offered no reasonable justification for this supplemental limitation, and we can perceive none. To the extent that the three months provision reflects the school board's thinking that no mother is fit to return until that point in time, it suffers from the same constitutional deficiencies that plague the irrebuttable presumption in the termination rules.[15] The presumption, moreover, is patently unnecessary, since the requirement of a physician's certificate or a medical examination fully protects the school's interests in this regard. And finally, the three-month provision simply has nothing to do with continuity of instruction, since the precise point at which the child will reach the relevant age will obviously occur at a different point throughout the school year for each teacher.

Thus, we conclude that the Cleveland return rule, insofar as it embodies the three months age provision, is wholly arbitrary and irrational, and hence violates the Due Process Clause of the Fourteenth Amendment. . . .

We perceive no such constitutional infirmities in the Chesterfield County rule. In that school system, the teacher becomes eligible for reemployment upon submission of a medical certificate from her physician: return to work is guaranteed no later than the beginning of the next school year following the eligibility determination. The medical certificate is both a reasonable and narrow method of protecting the school board's interest in teacher fitness, while the possible deferring of return until the next school year serves the goal of preserving continuity of instruction. . . .

## IV

For the reasons stated, we hold that the mandatory termination provisions of the Cleveland and Chesterfield County maternity regulations violate the Due Process Clause of the Fourteenth Amendment, because of their use of unwarranted conclusive presumptions that seriously burden the exercise of protected constitutional liberty. For similar reasons, we hold the three months' provision of the Cleveland return rule unconstitutional. . . .

It is so ordered.

Judgment in No. 72-777 affirmed.

Judgment in No. 72-1129 reversed and case remanded. . . .

MR. JUSTICE POWELL (concurring in the result).

I concur in the Court's result, but I am unable to join its opinion. In my view these cases should not be decided on the ground that the mandatory maternity

---

[15] It is clear that the factual hypothesis of such a presumption — that no mother is physically fit to return to work until her child reaches the age of three months — is neither necessarily nor universally true. . . .

Of course, it may be that the Cleveland rule is based upon another theory — that new mothers are too busy with their children within the first three months to allow a return to work. Viewed in that light, the rule remains a conclusive presumption, whose underlying factual assumptions can hardly be said to be universally valid.

leave regulations impair any right to bear children or create an "irrebuttable presumption." It seems to me that equal protection analysis is the appropriate frame of reference.

These regulations undoubtedly add to the burdens of childbearing. But certainly not every government policy that burdens childbearing violates the Constitution. . . .

I am also troubled by the Court's return to the "irrebuttable presumption" line of analysis of Stanley v. Illinois, 405 U.S. 645, 92 S.Ct. 1208, 31 L.Ed.2d 551 (1972) (Powell, J., not participating), and Vlandis v. Kline, 412 U.S. 441, 93 S.Ct. 2230, 37 L.Ed.2d 63 (1973). Although I joined the opinion of the Court in *Vlandis* and continue fully to support the result reached there, the present cases have caused me to re-examine the "irrebuttable presumption" rationale. This has led me to the conclusion that the Court should approach that doctrine with extreme care. There is much to what MR. JUSTICE REHNQUIST says in his dissenting opinion, *post,* at 804, about the implications of the doctrine for the traditional legislative power to operate by classification. As a matter of logic, it is difficult to see the terminus of the road upon which the Court has embarked under the banner of "irrebuttable presumptions." If the Court nevertheless uses "irrebuttable presumption" reasoning selectively, the concept at root often will be something else masquerading as a due process doctrine. That something else, of course, is the Equal Protection Clause.

These cases present precisely the kind of problem susceptible to treatment by classification. Most school teachers are women, a certain percentage of them are pregnant at any given time, and pregnancy is a normal biological function possessing, in the great majority of cases, a fairly well defined term. The constitutional difficulty is not that the boards attempted to deal with this problem by classification. Rather, it is that the boards chose irrational classifications.

To be sure, the boards have a legitimate and important interest in fostering continuity of teaching. And, even a normal pregnancy may at some point jeopardize that interest. But the classifications chosen by these boards, so far as we have been shown, are either contraproductive or irrationally overinclusive even with regard to this significant, nonillusory goal. Accordingly, in my opinion these regulations are invalid under rational basis standards of equal protection review. . . . I believe the linkage between the boards' legitimate ends and their chosen means is too attenuated to support these portions of the regulations overturned by the Court. Thus, I concur in the Court's result. But I think it important to emphasize the degree of latitude the Court, as I read it, has left the boards for dealing with the real and recurrent problems presented by teacher pregnancies. Boards may demand in every case "substantial advance notice of [pregnancy] . . . ." *Ante,* at 798. Subject to certain restrictions, they may require all pregnant teachers to cease teaching "at some firm date during the last few weeks of pregnancy . . . ." *Id.,* at 799, n. 13. The Court further holds that boards may in all cases restrict reentry into teaching to the outset of the school term following delivery. *Id.,* at 800.

In my opinion, such class-wide rules for pregnant teachers are constitutional under traditional equal protection standards. . . .

But despite my reservations as to the rationale of the majority, I nevertheless conclude that in these cases the gap between the legitimate interests of the boards and the particular means chosen to attain them is too wide. A restructuring generally along the lines indicated in the Court's opinion seems unavoidable. Accordingly, I concur in its result.

[The dissenting opinion of JUSTICE REHNQUIST, with whom CHIEF JUSTICE BURGER joined, is omitted.]

## NOTES

1. The Supreme Court has adopted a standard for gender-based discrimination which falls at some point between "rational basis" and "strict scrutiny." A gender-based classification must serve important governmental objectives and be substantially related to the achievement of those objectives. In adopting this standard in Craig v. Boren, 429 U.S. 190, 97 S.Ct. 451, 50 L. Ed. 2d 397 (1976), the Court traced the recent development of equal protection in the area of sex discrimination:

> Analysis may appropriately begin with the reminder that *Reed v. Reed, supra,* emphasized that statutory classifications that distinguish between males and females are "subject to scrutiny under the Equal Protection Clause." 404 U.S., at 75, 92 S.Ct., at 253. To withstand constitutional challenge, previous cases establish that classifications by gender must serve important governmental objectives and must be substantially related to achievement of those objectives. Thus, in *Reed,* the objectives of "reducing the workload on probate courts," *id.,* at 76, 92 S.Ct., at 254, and "avoiding intra-family controversy," *id.,* at 77, 92 S.Ct., at 254, were deemed of insufficient importance to sustain use of an overt gender criterion in the appointment of intestate administrators. Decisions following *Reed* similarly have rejected administrative ease and convenience as sufficiently important objectives to justify gender-based classifications. See, *e. g., Stanley v. Illinois,* 405 U.S. 645, 656, 92 S. Ct. 1208, 1215, 31 L.Ed.2d 551 (1972); *Frontiero v. Richardson,* 411 U.S. 677, 690, 93 S.Ct. 1764, 1772, 36 L.Ed.2d 583 (1973); cf. *Schlesinger v. Ballard,* 419 U.S. 498, 506-507, 95 S.Ct. 572, 576-577, 42 L.Ed.2d 610 (1975). And only two Terms ago, *Stanton v. Stanton,* 421 U.S. 7, 95 S.Ct. 1373, 43 L.Ed.2d 688 (1975), expressly stating that *Reed v. Reed* was "controlling," *id.,* at 13, 95 S.Ct., at 1377, held that *Reed* required invalidation of a Utah differential age-of-majority statute, notwithstanding the statute's coincidence with and furtherance of the State's purpose of fostering "old notions" of role-typing and preparing boys for their expected performance in the economic and political worlds. *Id.,* at 14-15, 95 S.Ct., at 1378.[6]

> *Reed v. Reed* has also provided the underpinning for decisions that have invalidated statutes employing gender as an inaccurate proxy for other, more germane bases of classification. Hence, "archaic and overbroad" generalizations, *Schlesinger v. Ballard, supra,* 419 U.S., at 508, 95 S.Ct., at 577, concerning the financial position of service-women, *Frontiero v. Richardson, supra,* 411 U.S., at 689 n. 23, 93 S.Ct., at 1772, and working women, *Weinberger v. Wiesenfeld,* 420 U.S. 636, 643, 95 S.Ct. 1225, 1230, 43 L.Ed.2d 514 (1975), could not justify use of a gender line in determining eligibility for certain governmental entitlements. Similarly increasingly outdated misconceptions concerning the role of females in the home rather than in the "marketplace and world of ideas" were rejected as loose-fitting characterizations incapable of supporting state statutory schemes that were premised upon their accuracy. *Stanton v. Stanton, supra; Taylor v. Louisiana,* 419 U.S. 522, 535 n. 17, 95 S.Ct. 692, 700, 42 L.Ed.2d 690 (1975). In light of the weak congruence between gender and the characteristic or trait that gender purported to represent, it was necessary that the legislatures choose either to realign their substantive laws in a gender-neutral fashion, or to adopt procedures for identifying those instances where the sex-centered generalization actually comported to fact. See, *e. g., Stanley v. Illinois, supra,* 405 U.S., at 658, 92 S.Ct., at 1216; cf. *Cleveland Board of Educ. v. LaFleur,* 414 U.S. 632, 650, 94 S.Ct. 791, 801, 39 L.Ed.2d 52 (1974).

2. In Geduldig v. Aiello, 417 U.S. 484, 94 S.Ct. 2485, 41 L. Ed. 2d 256 (1974), the Court upheld the constitutionality of a California disability insurance program which excluded

---

[6] *Kahn v. Shevin,* 416 U.S. 351, 94 S.Ct. 1734, 40 L.Ed.2d 189 (1974) and *Schlesinger v. Ballard,* 419 U.S. 498, 95 S.Ct. 572, 42 L.E.2d 610 (1975), upholding the use of gender-based classifications, rested upon the Court's perception of the laudatory purposes of those laws as remedying disadvantageous conditions suffered by women in economic and military life. See 416 U.S., at 353-354, 94 S.Ct. at 1736-1737; 419 U.S., at 508, 95 S.Ct., at 577. Needless to say, in this case Oklahoma does not suggest that the age-sex differential was enacted to ensure the availability of 3.2% beer for women as compensation for previous deprivations.

coverage for pregnancy in order to maintain the self-supporting nature of the insurance program. The Court distinguished *Reed* and *Frontiero* in a footnote:
> The dissenting opinion to the contrary, this case is thus a far cry from cases like Reed v. Reed, 404 U.S. 71, 92 S.Ct. 251, 30 L. Ed. 2d 225 (1971), and Frontiero v. Richardson, 411 U.S. 677, 93 S.Ct. 1764, 36 L. Ed. 2d 583 (1973), involving discrimination based upon gender as such. The California insurance program does not exclude anyone from benefit eligibility because of gender but merely removes one physical condition — pregnancy — from the list of compensable disabilities. While it is true that only women can become pregnant it does not follow that every legislative classification concerning pregnancy is a sex-based classification like those considered in *Reed, supra,* and *Frontiero, supra.* Normal pregnancy is an objectively identifiable physical condition with unique characteristics. Absent a showing that distinctions involving pregnancy are mere pretexts designed to effect an invidious discrimination against the members of one sex or the other, lawmakers are constitutionally free to include or exclude pregnancy from the coverage of legislation such as this on any reasonable basis, just as with respect to any other physical condition.
>
> The lack of identity between the excluded disability and gender as such under this insurance program becomes clear upon the most cursory analysis. The program divides potential recipients into two groups — pregnant women and nonpregnant persons. While the first group is exclusively female, the second includes members of both sexes. The fiscal and actuarial benefits of the program thus accrue to members of both sexes.

3. In Davis v. Passman, 571 F.2d 793 (5th Cir. 1978), the Fifth Circuit *en banc* reversed a panel opinion which found unlawful discrimination under the Fifth Amendment and awarded damages to a woman administrative assistant who was fired by former Congressman Otto Passman because he wanted a man in the job. Using a two-step approach, the court first determined that a damage remedy could not be implied from existing statutes, and then determined that a damage remedy was not constitutionally compelled by the Due Process Clause of the Fifth Amendment, indicating that Congressional employees could seek equitable relief, such as reinstatement, if their employers were still in office.

# 4. AGE DISCRIMINATION

## MASSACHUSETTS BOARD OF RETIREMENT v. MURGIA

Supreme Court of the United States
427 U.S. 307 (1976)

PER CURIAM.

This case presents the question whether the provision of Mass.Gen.Laws Ann. c. 32, § 26(3)(a) (1969), that a uniformed state police officer "shall be retired ... upon his attaining age fifty," denies appellee police officer equal protection of the laws in violation of the Fourteenth Amendment.

Appellee Robert Murgia was an officer in the Uniformed Branch of the Massachusetts State Police. The Massachusetts Board of Retirement retired him upon his 50th birthday. Appellee brought this civil action in the United States District Court for the District of Massachusetts, alleging that the operation of § 26(3)(a) denied him equal protection of the laws and requesting the convening of a three-judge court under 28 U.S.C. §§ 2281, 2284. ...

The primary function of the Uniformed Branch of the Massachusetts State Police is to protect persons and property and maintain law and order. Specifically, uniformed officers participate in controlling prison and civil disorders, respond to emergencies and natural disasters, patrol highways in marked cruisers, investigate crime, apprehend criminal suspects, and provide backup support for local law enforcement personnel. As the District Court observed, "service in this branch is, or can be, arduous." 376 F.Supp., at 754. "[H]igh versatility is required, with few, if any, backwaters available for the partially superannuated." *Ibid.* Thus, "even [appellee's] experts concede that there is a general relationship between advancing age and decreasing physical ability to respond to the demands of the job." *Id.,* at 755.

These considerations prompt the requirement that uniformed state officers pass a comprehensive physical examination biennially until age 40. After that, until mandatory retirement at age 50, uniformed officers must pass annually a more rigorous examination, including an electrocardiogram and tests for gastro-intestinal bleeding. Appellee Murgia had passed such an examination four months before he was retired, and there is no dispute that, when he retired, his excellent physical and mental health still rendered him capable of performing the duties of a uniformed officer.

The record includes the testimony of three physicians: that of the State Police Surgeon, who testified to the physiological and psychological demands involved in the performance of uniformed police functions; that of an associate professor of medicine, who testified generally to the relationship between aging and the ability to perform under stress; and that of a surgeon, who also testified to aging and the ability safely to perform police functions. The testimony clearly established that the risk of physical failure, particularly in the cardiovascular system, increases with age, and that the number of individuals in a given age group incapable of performing stress functions increases with the age of the group. App. 77-78, 174-176. The testimony also recognized that particular individuals over 50 could be capable of safely performing the functions of uniformed officers. The associate professor of medicine, who was a witness for the appellee, further testified that evaluating the risk of cardiovascular failure in a given individual would require a number of detailed studies. *Id.,* at 77-78.

In assessing appellee's equal protection claim, the District Court found it unnecessary to apply a strict-scrutiny test, see *Shapiro v. Thompson,* 394 U.S. 618, 89 S.Ct. 1322, 22 L.Ed.2d 600 (1969), for it determined that the age classification established by the Massachusetts statutory scheme could not in any event withstand a test of rationality, see *Dandridge v. Williams,* 397 U.S. 471, 90 S.Ct. 1153, 25 L.Ed.2d 491 (1970). Since there had been no showing that reaching age 50 forecasts even "imminent change" in an officer's physical condition, the District Court held that compulsory retirement at age 50 was irrational under a scheme that assessed the capabilities of officers individually by means of comprehensive annual physical examinations. We agree that rationality is the proper standard by which to test whether compulsory retirement at age 50 violates equal protection. We disagree, however, with the District Court's determination that the age 50 classification is not rationally related to furthering a legitimate state interest.

I

We need state only briefly our reasons for agreeing that strict scrutiny is not the proper test for determining whether the mandatory retirement provision denies appellee equal protection. *San Antonio School District v. Rodriguez,* 411 U.S. 1, 16, 93 S.Ct. 1278, 1287, 36 L.Ed.2d 16 (1973), reaffirmed that equal protection analysis requires strict scrutiny of a legislative classification only when the classification impermissibly interferes with the exercise of a fundamental right [3] or operates to the peculiar disadvantage of a suspect class.[4] Mandatory retirement at age 50 under the Massachusetts statute involves neither situation.

This Court's decisions give no support to the proposition that a right of governmental employment *per se* is fundamental. See *San Antonio School District v. Rodriguez, supra; Lindsey v. Normet,* 405 U.S. 56, 73, 92 S.Ct. 862, 874, 31 L.Ed.2d 36 (1972); *Dandridge v. Williams, supra,* 397 U.S. at 485, 90 S.Ct. at 1162. Accordingly, we have expressly stated that a standard less than strict scrutiny "has consistently been applied to state legislation restricting the availability of employment opportunities." *Ibid.*

Nor does the class of uniformed state police officers over 50 constitute a suspect class for purposes of equal protection analysis. *Rodriguez, supra,* 411 U.S. at 28, 93 S.Ct. at 1294, observed that a suspect class is one "saddled with such disabilities, or subjected to such a history of purposeful unequal treatment, or relegated to such a position of political powerlessness as to command extraordinary protection from the majoritarian political process." While the treatment of the aged in this Nation has not been wholly free of discrimination, such persons, unlike, say, those who have been discriminated against on the basis of race or national origin, have not experienced a "history of purposeful unequal treatment" or been subjected to unique disabilities on the basis of stereotyped characteristics not truly indicative of their abilities. The class subject to the compulsory retirement feature of the Massachusetts statute consists of uniformed state police officers over the age of 50. It cannot be said to discriminate only against the elderly. Rather, it draws the line at a certain age in middle life. But even old age does not define a "discrete and insular" group, *United States v. Carolene Products Co.,* 304 U.S. 144, 152-153, n. 4, 58 S.Ct. 778, 783, 82 L.Ed. 1234 (1938), in need of "extraordinary protection from the majoritarian political process." Instead, it marks a stage that each of us will reach if we live out our normal span. Even if the statute could be said to impose a penalty upon a class defined as the aged, it would not impose a distinction sufficiently akin to those classifications that we have found suspect to call for strict judicial scrutiny.

Under the circumstances, it is unnecessary to subject the State's resolution of competing interests in this case to the degree of critical examination that our cases under the Equal Protection Clause recently have characterized as "strict judicial scrutiny."

## II

We turn then to examine this state classification under the rational-basis standard. This inquiry employs a relatively relaxed standard reflecting the Court's awareness that the drawing of lines that create distinctions is peculiarly a legislative task and an unavoidable one. Perfection in making the necessary

---

[3] *E.g., Roe v. Wade,* 410 U.S. 113, 93 S.Ct. 705, 35 L.Ed.2d 147 (1973) (right of a uniquely private nature); *Bullock v. Carter,* 405 U.S. 134, 92 S.Ct. 849, 31 L.Ed.2d 92 (1972) (right to vote); *Shapiro v. Thompson,* 394 U.S. 618, 89 S.Ct. 1322, 22 L.Ed.2d 600 (1969) (right of interstate travel); *Williams v. Rhodes,* 393 U.S. 23, 89 S.Ct. 5, 21 L.Ed.2d 24 (1968) (rights guaranteed by the First Amendment); *Skinner v. Oklahoma ex rel. Williamson,* 316 U.S. 535, 62 S.Ct. 1110, 86 L.Ed. 1655 (1942) (right to procreate).

[4] *E.g., Graham v. Richardson,* 403 U.S. 365, 91 S.Ct. 1848, 29 L.Ed.2d 534 (1971) (alienage); *McLaughlin v. Florida,* 379 U.S. 184, 85 S.Ct. 283, 13 L.Ed.2d 222 (1964) (race); *Oyama v. California,* 332 U.S. 633, 68 S.Ct. 269, 92 L.Ed. 249 (1948) (ancestry).

classifications is neither possible nor necessary. *Dandridge v. Williams, supra,* 397 U.S., at 485, 90 S.Ct., at 1162. Such action by a legislature is presumed to be valid.[5]

In this case, the Massachusetts statute clearly meets the requirements of the Equal Protection Clause, for the State's classification rationally furthers the purpose identified by the State: Through mandatory retirement at age 50, the legislature seeks to protect the public by assuring physical preparedness of its uniformed police. Since physical ability generally declines with age, mandatory retirement at 50 serves to remove from police service those whose fitness for uniformed work presumptively has diminished with age. This clearly is rationally related to the State's objective. There is no indication that § 26(3)(a) has the effect of excluding from service so few officers who are in fact unqualified as to render age 50 a criterion wholly unrelated to the objective of the statute.

That the State chooses not to determine fitness more precisely through individualized testing after age 50 is not to say that the objective of assuring physical fitness is not rationally furthered by a maximum-age limitation. It is only to say that with regard to the interest of all concerned, the State perhaps has not chosen the best means to accomplish this purpose. But where rationality is the test, a State "does not violate the Equal Protection Clause merely because the classifications made by its laws are imperfect." *Dandridge v. Williams,* 397 U.S., at 485, 90 S.Ct., at 1161.

We do not make light of the substantial economic and psychological effects premature and compulsory retirement can have on an individual; nor do we denigrate the ability of elderly citizens to continue to contribute to society. The problems of retirement have been well documented and are beyond serious dispute. But "[w]e do not decide today that the [Massachusetts statute] is wise, that it best fulfills the relevant social and economic objectives that [Massachusetts] might ideally espouse, or that a more just and humane system could not be devised." *Id.,* at 487, 90 S.Ct., at 1162. We decide only that the system enacted by the Massachusetts Legislature does not deny appellee equal protection of the laws.

*The judgment is reversed.*

Mr. Justice Stevens took no part in the consideration or decision of this case. [Mr. Justice Marshall dissented.]

## NOTES

1. In Bradley v. Vance, 436 F.Supp. 134 (D.D.C. 1977), *cert. granted,* 46 U.S.L.W. 3703 (May 16, 1978), the court held that the Foreign Service Retirement System, which requires personnel to retire at age 60, violated the equal protection guarantees under the Fifth Amendment. The court found that the system was "patently arbitrary and irrational" in view of the fact that the vast preponderance of government personnel working under similar conditions in foreign countries fell under the Civil Service system which did not require retirement until age 70.

2. The Federal Employees Early Retirement Act, which offers employees meeting the minimum age and length-of-service requirements the option of early retirement if their agency is undergoing a major reduction-in-force, was upheld by the U.S. Court of Appeals for the Fifth Circuit. The court held that the plan could withstand a Fourteenth Amendment challenge because it was rationally related to a legitimate governmental objective. Mason v. Lister, 562 F.2d 343 (5th Cir. 1977).

---

[5] See, e. g., *San Antonio School District v. Rodriguez,* 411 U.S. 1, 40-41, 93 S.Ct. 1278, 1300, 36 L.Ed.2d 16 (1973); *Madden v. Kentucky,* 309 U.S. 83, 88, 60 S.Ct. 406, 408, 84 L.Ed. 590 (1940); *Lindsley v. Natural Carbonic Gas Co.,* 220 U.S. 61, 78-79, 31 S.Ct. 337, 340, 55 L.Ed. 369 (1911).

# 5. ALIENS

## HAMPTON v. MOW SUN WONG

Supreme Court of the United States
426 U.S. 88 (1976)

MR. JUSTICE STEVENS delivered the opinion of the Court.

Five aliens, lawfully and permanently residing in the United States, brought this litigation to challenge the validity of a policy, adopted and enforced by the Civil Service Commission and certain other federal agencies, which excludes all persons except American citizens and natives of American Samoa from employment in most positions subject to their respective jurisdictions. . . .

I

Each of the five plaintiffs was denied federal employment solely because of his or her alienage. They were all Chinese residents of San Francisco and each was qualified for an available job.

After performing satisfactory work for the Post Office Department for 10 days, respondent Kae Cheong Lui was terminated because his personnel record disclosed that he was not a citizen. Respondents Mow Sun Wong and Siu Hung Mok also demonstrated their ability to perform on the job; they both participated in the California Supplemental Training and Education Program (STEP) and were assigned to federal agencies until the STEP program ended. As a noncitizen, Mow Sun Wong, who had been an electrical engineer in China, was ineligible for employment as a janitor for the General Services Administration. Siu Hung Mok, who had 18 years' experience as a businessman in China, could not retain his job as a file clerk with the Federal Records Center of GSA.

Respondent Francene Lum was not permitted to take an examination for a position as evaluator of educational programs in the Department of Health, Education, and Welfare. Her background included 15 years of teaching experience, a master's degree in education, and periods of graduate study at four universities. Anna Yu, the fifth plaintiff, who is not a respondent because she did not join in the appeal from the adverse decision of the District Court, sought a position as a clerk-typist, but could not take the typing test because she was not a citizen.

Two of the plaintiffs, Mow Sun Wong and Siu Hung Mok, had filed declarations of intent to become citizens; the other three had not. They were all lawfully admitted, Francene Lum in 1946, Anna Yu in 1965, Siu Hung Mok and Kae Cheong Lui in 1968, and Mow Sun Wong in 1969.

On December 22, 1970, they commenced this class action in the Northern District of California. As defendants they named the Chairman and the Commissioners of the Civil Service Commission and the heads of the three agencies which had denied them employment.

The complaint alleged that there are about four million aliens living in the United States; they face special problems in seeking employment because our culture, language, and system of government are foreign to them; about 300,000 federal jobs become available each year, but noncitizens are not permitted to compete for those jobs except in rare situations when citizens are not available or when a few positions exempted from the competitive civil service are being filled. Plaintiffs further alleged that the advantage given to citizens seeking federal civil service positions is arbitrary and violates the Due Process Clause of the Fifth Amendment to the United States Constitution and Executive Order No. 11,478, 3 CFR 803 (1966-1970 Comp.), which forbids discrimination in federal employment on the basis of "national origin." The complaint sought declaratory and injunctive relief. . . .

. . . The District Court held that the reference to "national origin" in the Executive Order prohibited discrimination among citizens rather than discrimination between citizens and noncitizens. The court also rejected an argument that the Civil Service Commission regulation was inconsistent with § 502 of the Public Works for Water Pollution Control, and Power Development and Atomic Energy Commission Appropriation Act, 1970, which permitted payment to classes of persons who are made ineligible by the Civil Service regulation. . . .

Finally, the District Court held that the Commission's discrimination against aliens was constitutional. The court noted that the federal power over aliens is "quite broad, almost plenary," and therefore the classification needed only a rational basis. . . .

Four of the plaintiffs appealed. During the period of over two years that the appeal was pending in the Ninth Circuit, we decided two cases that recognized the importance of protecting the employment opportunities of aliens. In *Sugarman v. Dougall,* 413 U.S. 634, 93 S.Ct. 2842, 37 L.Ed.2d 853, we held that a section of the New York Civil Service Law which provided that only United States citizens could hold permanent positions in the competitive class of the State's civil service violated the Equal Protection Clause of the Fourteenth Amendment; that Clause also provided the basis for our holding in *In re Griffiths,* 413 U.S. 717, 93 S.Ct. 2851, 37 L.Ed.2d 910 decided on the same day, that Connecticut's exclusion of aliens from the practice of law was unconstitutional.

In this case, the Court of Appeals recognized that neither *Sugarman* nor *Griffiths* was controlling because the Fourteenth Amendment's restrictions on state power are not directly applicable to the Federal Government and because Congress and the President have broad power over immigration and naturalization which the States do not possess. Nevertheless, those decisions provided the Court of Appeals with persuasive reasons for rejecting the bases asserted by the defendants in the District Court as justifications for the Civil Service Commission's policy of discriminating against noncitizens. For we specifically held that the State's legitimate interest in the undivided loyalty of the civil servant who participates directly in the formulation and execution of government policy, was inadequate to support a state restriction indiscriminately disqualifying the "sanitation man, class B," the typist, and the office worker, 413 U.S., at 641-643, 93 S.Ct., at 2847-2848, 37 L.Ed.2d, at 859-860, moreover, we expressly considered, and rejected, New York's contention that its special interest in the advancement and profit of its own citizens could justify confinement of the State's civil service to citizens of the United States, *id.,* at 643-645, 93 S.Ct., at 2848-2849, 37 L.Ed.2d, at 860-861.

The Court of Appeals reversed; it agreed with the District Court's analysis of the nonconstitutional issues, but held the regulation violative of the Due Process Clause of the Fifth Amendment. Although refusing to accept respondents' contention that the protection against federal discrimination provided by the Fifth Amendment is coextensive with that applicable to the States under the Equal Protection Clause of the Fourteenth Amendment, the court concluded that the Commission regulation which "sweeps indiscriminately excluding *all* aliens from *all* positions requiring the competitive Civil Service examination" could not be supported by justifications which related to only a small fraction of the positions covered by the rule. 500 F.2d 1031, 1037. Thus, the court accepted the argument that citizenship might properly be required in positions involving policymaking decisions, or in positions involving national security interests, but the court was unwilling to support an extraordinarily broad exclusion on such narrow shoulders. . . .

We granted certiorari to decide the following question presented by the petition:

"Whether a regulation of the United States Civil Service Commission that bars resident aliens from employment in the federal competitive civil service is constitutional."

We now address that question.

## II

Petitioners have chosen to argue on the merits a somewhat different question. In their brief, the petitioners rephrased the question presented as "[w]hether the Civil Service Commission's regulation . . . is within the constitutional powers of Congress and the President and hence not a constitutionally forbidden discrimination against aliens."

This phrasing of the question assumes that the Commission regulation is one that was mandated by the Congress, the President, or both. On this assumption, the petitioners advance alternative arguments to justify the discrimination as an exercise of the plenary federal power over immigration and naturalization. First, the petitioners argue that the equal protection aspect of the Due Process Clause of the Fifth Amendment is wholly inapplicable to the exercise of federal power over aliens, and therefore no justification for the rule is necessary. Alternatively, the petitioners argue that the Fifth Amendment imposes only a slight burden of justification on the Federal Government, and that such a burden is easily met by several factors not considered by the District Court or the Court of Appeals. Before addressing these arguments, we first discuss certain limitations which the Due Process Clause places on the power of the Federal Government to classify persons subject to its jurisdiction.

The federal sovereign, like the States, must govern impartially. The concept of equal justice under law is served by the Fifth Amendment's guarantee of due process, as well as by the Equal Protection Clause of the Fourteenth Amendment. Although both Amendments require the same type of analysis, see *Buckley v. Valeo,* 424 U.S. 1, 93, 96 S.Ct. 612, 670, 46 L.Ed.2d 659, 730 (1976), the Court of Appeals correctly stated that the two protections are not always coextensive. . . .

In this case we deal with a federal rule having nationwide impact. The petitioners correctly point out that the paramount federal power over immigration and naturalization forecloses a simple extension of the holding in *Sugarman* as decisive of this case. We agree with the petitioners' position that overriding national interests may provide a justification for a citizenship requirement in the federal service even though an identical requirement may not be enforced by a State.

We do not agree, however, with the petitioners' primary submission that the federal power over aliens is so plenary that any agent of the National Government may arbitrarily subject all resident aliens to different substantive rules from those applied to citizens. We recognize that the petitioners' argument draws support from both the federal and the political character of the power over immigration and naturalization. Nevertheless, countervailing considerations require rejection of the extreme position advanced by the petitioners.

The rule enforced by the Commission has its impact on an identifiable class of persons who, entirely apart from the rule itself, are already subject to disadvantages not shared by the remainder of the community. Aliens are not entitled to vote and, as alleged in the complaint, are often handicapped by a lack of familiarity with our language and customs. The added disadvantage resulting from the enforcement of the rule — ineligibility for employment in a major sector of the economy — is of sufficient significance to be characterized as a deprivation of an interest in liberty.[23] Indeed, we deal with a rule which deprives a discrete class of persons of an interest in liberty on a wholesale basis. By reason of the Fifth Amendment, such a deprivation must be accompanied by due process. It follows that some judicial scrutiny of the deprivation is mandated by the Constitution. . . .

When the Federal Government asserts an overriding national interest as justification for a discriminatory rule which would violate the Equal Protection Clause if adopted by a State, due process requires that there be a legitimate basis for presuming that the rule was actually intended to serve that interest. If the agency which promulgates the rule has direct responsibility for fostering or protecting that interest, it may reasonably be presumed that the asserted interest was the actual predicate for the rule. That presumption would, of course, be fortified by an appropriate statement of reasons identifying the relevant interest. Alternatively, if the rule were expressly mandated by the Congress or the President, we might presume that any interest which might rationally be served by the rule did in fact give rise to its adoption.

In this case the petitioners have identified several interests which the Congress or the President might deem sufficient to justify the exclusion of noncitizens from the federal service. They argue, for example, that the broad exclusion may facilitate the President's negotiation of treaties with foreign powers by enabling him to offer employment opportunities to citizens of a given foreign country in exchange for reciprocal concessions — an offer he could not make if those aliens were already eligible for federal jobs. Alternatively, the petitioners argue that reserving the federal service for citizens provides an appropriate incentive to aliens to qualify for naturalization and thereby to participate more effectively in our society. They also point out that the citizenship requirement has been imposed in the United States with substantial consistency for over 100 years and accords with international law and the practice of most foreign countries. Finally, they correctly state that the need for undivided loyalty in certain sensitive positions clearly justifies a citizenship requirement in at least some parts of the federal service, and that the broad exclusion serves the valid administrative purpose of avoiding the trouble and expense of classifying those positions which properly belong in executive or sensitive categories.

The difficulty with all these arguments except the last is that they do not identify any interest which can reasonably be assumed to have influenced the Civil Service Commission, the Postal Service, the General Services Administration, or the Department of Health, Education, and Welfare in the administration of their

---

[23] See *Board of Regents v. Roth,* 408 U.S. 564, 573-574, 92 S.Ct. 2701, 2707, 33 L.Ed.2d 548, 558-559, and cases cited. See also the statement for the Court by Mr. Justice Hughes in *Truax v. Raich, supra,* a case dealing with the employment opportunities of aliens:

"it requires no argument to show that the right to work for a living in the common occupations of the community is of the very essence of the personal freedom and opportunity that it was the purpose of the Amendment to secure. . . . If this could be refused solely upon the ground of race or nationality, the prohibition of the denial to any person of the equal protection of the laws would be a barren form of words." 239 U.S., at 41, 36 S.Ct., at 10, 60 L.Ed., at 135.

respective responsibilities or, specifically, in the decision to deny employment to the respondents in this litigation. . . .

## III

It is perfectly clear that neither the Congress nor the President has ever *required* the Civil Service Commission to adopt the citizenship requirement as a condition of eligibility for employment in the federal civil service. On the other hand, in view of the fact that the policy has been in effect since the Commission was created in 1883, it is fair to infer that both the Legislature and the Executive have been aware of the policy and have acquiesced in it. . . .

We have no doubt that the statutory directive which merely requires such regulations "as will best promote the efficiency of [the] Service," 5 U.S.C. § 3301(1), as well as the pertinent Executive Order, gives the Civil Service Commission the same discretion that the Postal Service has actually exercised; the Commission may either retain or modify the citizenship requirement without further authorization from Congress or the President.[46] We are therefore persuaded that our inquiry is whether the national interests which the Government identifies as justifications for the Commission rule are interests on which that agency may properly rely in making a decision implicating the constitutional and social values at stake in this litigation.

We think the petitioners accurately stated the question presented in their certiorari petition. The question is whether the regulation of the United States Civil Service Commission is valid. We proceed to a consideration of that question assuming, without deciding, that the Congress and the President have the constitutional power to impose the requirement that the Commission has adopted.

## IV

It is the business of the Civil Service Commission to adopt and enforce regulations which will best promote the efficiency of the federal civil service. That agency has no responsibility for foreign affairs, for treaty negotiations, for establishing immigration quotas or conditions of entry, or for naturalization policies. Indeed, it is not even within the responsibility of the Commission to be concerned with the economic consequences of permitting or prohibiting the participation by aliens in employment opportunities in different parts of the national market. On the contrary, the Commission performs a limited and specific function.

The only concern of the Civil Service Commission is the promotion of an efficient federal service. In general it is fair to assume that its goal would be best served by removing unnecessary restrictions on the eligibility of qualified applicants for employment. With only one exception, the interests which the petitioners have put forth as supporting the Commission regulation at issue in this case are not matters which are properly the business of the Commission. That

---

[46] Even if this conclusion were doubtful, in view of the consequences of the rule it would be appropriate to require a much more explicit directive from either Congress or the President before accepting the conclusion that the political branches of Government would consciously adopt a policy raising the constitutional questions presented by this rule. Cf. *Peters v. Hobby,* 349 U.S. 331, 345, 75 S.Ct. 790, 797, 99 L.Ed. 1129, 1140; *Ex parte Endo,* 323 U.S. 283, 299-300, 65 S.Ct. 208, 217, 89 L.Ed. 243, 254.

one exception is the administrative desirability of having one simple rule excluding all noncitizens when it is manifest that citizenship is an appropriate and legitimate requirement for some important and sensitive positions. Arguably, therefore, administrative convenience may provide a rational basis for the general rule.

For several reasons that justification is unacceptable in this case. The Civil Service Commission, like other administrative agencies, has an obligation to perform its responsibilities with some degree of expertise, and to make known the reasons for its important decisions. There is nothing in the record before us, or in matter of which we may properly take judicial notice, to indicate that the Commission actually made any considered evaluation of the relative desirability of a simple exclusionary rule on the one hand, or the value to the service of enlarging the pool of eligible employees on the other. Nor can we reasonably infer that the administrative burden of establishing the job classifications for which citizenship is an appropriate requirement would be a particularly onerous task for an expert in personnel matters; indeed, the Postal Service apparently encountered no particular difficulty in making such a classification. Of greater significance, however, is the quality of the interest at stake. Any fair balancing of the public interest in avoiding the wholesale deprivation of employment opportunities caused by the Commission's indiscriminate policy, as opposed to what may be nothing more than a hypothetical justification, requires rejection of the argument of administrative convenience in this case.[48]

In sum, assuming without deciding that the national interests identified by the petitioners would adequately support an explicit determination by Congress or the President to exclude all noncitizens from the federal service, we conclude that those interests cannot provide an acceptable rationalization for such a determination by the Civil Service Commission. The impact of the rule on the millions of lawfully admitted resident aliens is precisely the same as the aggregate impact of comparable state rules which were invalidated by our decision in *Sugarman.* By broadly denying this class substantial opportunities for employment, the Civil Service Commission rule deprives its members of an aspect of liberty. Since these residents were admitted as a result of decisions made by the Congress and the President, implemented by the Immigration and Naturalization Service acting under the Attorney General of the United States, due process requires that the decision to impose that deprivation of an important liberty be made either at a comparable level of government or, if it is to be permitted to be made by the Civil Service Commission, that it be justified by reasons which are properly the concern of that agency. We hold that § 338.101(a) of the Civil Service Commission Regulations has deprived these respondents of liberty without due process of law and is therefore invalid.

The judgment of the Court of Appeals is

*Affirmed.*

Mr. Justice Brennan, with whom Mr. Justice Marshall joins, concurring.

---

[48] We find no merit in the petitioners' argument that a more discriminating rule would inevitably breed litigation which in turn would enhance the administrative burden. For even though the argument of administrative convenience may not support a total exclusion, it would adequately support a rather broad classification of positions reflecting the considered judgment of an agency expert in personnel matters. For the classification itself would demonstrate that the Commission had at least considered the extent to which the imposition of the rule is consistent with its assigned mission.

I join the Court's opinion with the understanding that there are reserved the equal protection questions that would be raised by congressional or Presidential enactment of a bar on employment of aliens by the Federal Government.

MR. JUSTICE REHNQUIST, with whom THE CHIEF JUSTICE, MR. JUSTICE WHITE, and MR. JUSTICE BLACKMUN join, dissenting.

The Court's opinion enunciates a novel conception of the procedural due process guaranteed by the Fifth Amendment, and from this concept proceeds to evolve a doctrine of delegation of legislative authority which seems to me to be quite contrary to the doctrine established by a long and not hitherto questioned line of our decisions. Neither of the Court's innovations is completely without appeal in this particular case, but even if we were to treat the matter as an original question I think such appeal is outweighed by the potential mischief which the doctrine bids fair to make in other areas of the law.

I

At the outset it is important to recognize that the power of the federal courts is severely limited in the areas of immigration and regulation of aliens. . . .

It is also clear that the exclusive power of Congress to prescribe the terms and conditions of entry includes the power to regulate aliens in various ways once they are here. *E. g., Hines v. Davidowitz,* 312 U.S. 52, 69-70, 61 S.Ct. 399, 405, 85 L.Ed. 581, 588 (1941). Indeed the Court, by holding that the regulation in question would presumptively have been valid if "expressly mandated by the Congress," *ante,* at 1905, concedes the congressional power to exclude aliens from employment in the civil service altogether if it so desires or to limit their participation.

This broad congressional power is in some respects subject to procedural limitations imposed by the Due Process Clause of the Fifth Amendment. If an alien subject to deportation proceedings claims to be a citizen, he is entitled to a judicial determination of that claim. *Ng Fung Ho v. White,* 259 U.S. 276, 42 S.Ct. 492, 66 L.Ed. 938 (1922). If he lawfully obtains tenured Government employment, and is thereby protected against discharge except for cause, he is entitled to a hearing before being discharged. *Arnett v. Kennedy,* 416 U.S. 134, 94 S.Ct. 1633, 40 L.Ed.2d 15 (1974); *Perry v. Sindermann,* 408 U.S. 593, 92 S.Ct. 2694, 33 L.Ed.2d 570 (1972). But neither an alien nor a citizen has any protected liberty interests in obtaining federal employment. *Cafeteria Workers v. McElroy,* 367 U.S. 886, 896-899, 81 S.Ct. 1743, 1749-1750, 6 L.Ed.2d 1230, 1236-1238 (1961). Nor in the absence of some form of statutory tenure is a Government employee entitled to a hearing prior to discharge, for "government employment, in the absence of legislation, can be revoked at the will of the appointing officer." *Id.,* at 896, 81 S.Ct., at 1749, 6 L.Ed.2d, at 1237. See also *Vitarelli v. Seaton,* 359 U.S. 535, 79 S.Ct. 968, 3 L.Ed.2d 1012 (1959).

The Court, however, seems to overlook this limitation on judicial power in justifying judicial intervention by holding:

"The rule enforced by the Commission has its impact on an identifiable class of persons who, entirely apart from the rule itself, are already subject to disadvantages not shared by the remainder of the community." *Ante,* p. 1905.

This is a classic equal protection analysis such as formed the basis of the Court's holding in *Sugarman v. Dougall,* 413 U.S. 634, 641, 93 S.Ct. 2842, 2847, 37 L.Ed.2d 853, 859 (1973), that States could not bar aliens from the *state* civil service. *Sugarman* specifically did not decide whether similar restrictions by the

Federal Government would violate equal protection principles (as applied to the Federal Government by the Due Process Clause of the Fifth Amendment, *Bolling v. Sharpe,* 347 U.S. 497, 74 S.Ct. 693, 98 L.Ed. 884 (1954)).

However, while positing an equal protection problem, the Court does not rely on an equal protection analysis, conceding that "overriding national interests may provide a justification for a citizenship requirement in the federal service even though an identical requirement may not be enforced by a State." *Ante,* at 1904. Thus the Court seems to agree that the Equal Protection Clause does not provide a basis for invalidating this denial of *federal* civil service employment. The Court instead inexplicably melds together the concepts of equal protection and procedural and substantive due process to produce the following holding:

"The added disadvantage resulting from the enforcement of the rule — ineligibility for employment in a major sector of the economy — is of sufficient significance to be characterized as a deprivation of an interest in liberty. Indeed, we deal with a rule which deprives a discrete class of persons of an interest in liberty on a wholesale basis. By reason of the Fifth Amendment, such a deprivation must be accompanied by due process." *Ante,* at 1905.

The meaning of this statement in the Court's opinion is not immediately apparent. As already noted, there is no general "liberty" interest in either acquiring federal employment or, in the absence of a statutory tenure, in retaining it, so that the person who is denied employment or who is discharged may insist upon a due process hearing. *Truax v. Raich,* 239 U.S. 33, 41, 36 S.Ct. 7, 10, 60 L.Ed. 131, 135 (1915), is cited by the Court to support the proposition that there is a "liberty" interest at stake here. But to the extent that the holding of that case remains unmodified by *Cafeteria Workers, supra,* it deals with a *substantive* liberty interest which may not be arbitrarily denied by legislative enactment; that interest is closely akin to the interest of the aliens asserted in *Sugarman, supra,* and *In re Griffiths,* 413 U.S. 717, 93 S.Ct. 2851, 37 L.Ed.2d 910 (1973). Since the Court declines to pass upon the claim asserted by respondents based upon those cases, it is difficult to see how *Truax* is relevant to its analysis.

There is a liberty interest in obtaining public employment which is protected against procedural deprivation in certain circumstances, as the Court's citation to *Board of Regents v. Roth,* 408 U.S. 564, 573-574, 92 S.Ct. 2701, 2707, 33 L.Ed.2d 548, 558-559 (1972) *ante,* at 1905, n. 23, indicates. But the cases cited in that passage from *Roth,* cases such as *Schware v. Board of Bar Examiners,* 353 U.S. 232, 77 S.Ct. 752, 1 L.Ed.2d 796 (1957), and *Willner v. Committee on Character,* 373 U.S. 96, 83 S.Ct. 1175, 10 L.Ed.2d 224 (1963), are distinguishable from the present case in at least two respects. In the first place they were both efforts by States, not to deny *public* employment, but to go further and proscribe the right to practice one's chosen profession in the *private* sector of the economy. Even more importantly, the vice found in each of those cases was the failure of the State to grant a "full prior hearing," 408 U.S., at 574, 93 S.Ct., at 2707, 33 L.Ed.2d, at 559.

But in the case presently before the Court, there is simply no issue which would require a hearing in order to establish any matter of disputed fact. . . .

Yet the Court does not decide this issue, but proceeds instead to hold that procedural due process includes not only a shield against arbitrary action but a scalpel with which one may dissect the administrative organization of the Federal Government.

. . . .

...It is not necessary for the petitioners to demonstrate why they chose to exclude aliens from the civil service. To require them to do so is to subject the Government to the same type of equal protection analysis to which the States are subject under *Sugarman v. Dougall, supra,* 413 U.S. 634, 93 S.Ct. 2842, 37 L.Ed.2d 853, a result which the Court specifically abjures....

## II

The sole ground by which such procedures may properly be challenged is to argue that there was an improper delegation of authority, which has not previously been thought to depend upon the procedural requirements of the Due Process Clause.

The Court, while not shaping its argument in these terms seems to hold that the delegation here was faulty. Yet, it seems to me too clear to admit of argument that under the traditional standards governing the delegation of authority the Civil Service Commission was fully empowered to act in the manner in which it did in this case.

....

For this Court to hold *ante,* at 1910, that the agency chosen by Congress, through the President, to effectuate its policies, has "no responsibility" in that area is to interfere in an area in which the Court itself clearly has "no responsibility": the organization of the Executive Branch. Congress, through the President, obviously *gave* responsibility in this area to the Civil Service Commission. The wisdom of that delegation is not for us to evaluate....

## III

Since I do not believe that the Court is correct in concluding that the regulation promulgated by the Civil Service Commission is invalid because of any lack of authority in the Commission to promulgate the rule, I must address the question of whether "the national interests" identified by the petitioners would adequately support a "determination . . . to exclude all noncitizens from the federal service." *Ante,* at 1911. This question was saved in both *Sugarman v. Dougall,* 413 U.S. 634, 93 U.S. 2842, 37 L.Ed.2d 853 (1973), and in *In re Griffiths,* 413 U.S. 717, 93 S.Ct. 2851, 37 L.Ed.2d 910 (1973), and I agree with the Court that "the paramount federal power over immigration and naturalization forecloses a simple extension of the holding in *Sugarman* as decisive of this case." *Ante,* at 1904.

"For reasons long recognized as valid, the responsibility for regulating the relationship between the United States and our alien visitors has been committed to the political branches of the Federal Government." *Mathews v. Diaz,* 426 U.S. 67, 81, 96 S.Ct. 1883, 1892, 48 L.Ed.2d 478, 490 (1975).

"[A]ny policy toward aliens is vitally and intricately interwoven with contemporaneous policies in regard to the conduct of foreign relations, the war power, and the maintenance of a republican form of government. Such matters are so exclusively entrusted to the political branches of government as to be largely immune from judicial inquiry or interference." *Harisiades v. Shaughnessy,* 342 U.S. 580, at 588-589, 72 S.Ct. 512, at 519, 96 L.Ed. 586, at 598, quoted in *Mathews v. Diaz,* 426 U.S. 67, 81 n. 17, 96 S.Ct. 1883, 1892, 48 L.Ed.2d 478, 490.

See also *Kleindienst v. Mandel,* 408 U.S., at 765-767, 92 S.Ct., at 2582-2584, 33 L.Ed.2d, at 693-694; *Fong Yue Ting v. United States,* 149 U.S. 698, 711-713, 13 S.Ct. 1016, 1021-1022, 37 L.Ed. 905, 912-913 (1893).

I conclude therefore that Congress, in the exercise of its political judgment, could have excluded aliens from the civil service. The face that it chose, in a separate political decision, to allow the Civil Service Commission to make this determination does not render the governmental policy any less "political" and, consequently, does not render it any more subject to judicial scrutiny under the reasoning of *Diaz, supra,* 426 U.S. 67, 96 S.Ct. 1883, 48 L.Ed.2d 478. The regulations here, enforced without question for nearly a century, do not infringe upon any constitutional right of these respondents. I would therefore reverse the judgment of the Court of Appeals.

## FOLEY v. CONNELIE

Supreme Court of the United States
98 S.Ct. 1067 (1978)

MR. CHIEF JUSTICE BURGER delivered the opinion of the Court.

We noted probable jurisdiction in this case to consider whether a State may constitutionally limit the appointment of members of its police force to citizens of the United States. . . .

### I

The essential facts in this case are uncontroverted. New York Executive Law § 215(3) prohibits appellant and his class from becoming State Troopers. It is not disputed that the State has uniformly complied with this restriction since the statute was enacted in 1927. Under it, an alien who desires to compete for a position as a New York State Trooper must relinquish his foreign citizenship and become an American citizen. . . .

### II

Appellant claims that the relevant New York statute violates his rights under the Equal Protection Clause.

The decisions of this Court with regard to the rights of aliens living in our society have reflected fine, and often difficult questions of values. . . .

. . . Our cases generally reflect a close scrutiny of restraints imposed by States on aliens. But we have never suggested that such legislation is inherently invalid, nor have we held that all limitations on aliens are suspect. See *Sugarman v. Dougall,* 413 U.S. 634, 648, 93 S.Ct. 2842, 2850, 37 L.Ed.2d 853 (1973). Rather, beginning with a case which involved the denial of welfare assistance essential to life itself, the Court has treated certain restrictions on aliens with "heightened judicial solicitude," *Graham v. Richardson,* 403 U.S. 365, 372, 91 S.Ct. 1848, 1852, 29 L.Ed.2d 534 (1971), a treatment deemed necessary since aliens — pending their eligibility for citizenship — have no direct voice in the political processes. See *United States v. Carolene Products,* 304 U.S. 144, 152-153, 58 S.Ct. 778, 783-784, 82 L.Ed. 1234, n. 4 (1938).

Following *Graham,* a series of decisions has resulted requiring state action to meet close scrutiny to exclude aliens as a class from educational benefits, *Nyquist v. Mauclet,* 432 U.S. 1, 97 S.Ct. 2120, 53 L.Ed.2d 63 (1977); eligibility for a broad range of public employment, *Sugarman v. Dougall,* 413 U.S. 634, 93 S.Ct. 2842, 37 L.Ed.2d 853 (1973); or the practice of licensed professions, *Examining Board v. Flores de Otero,* 426 U.S. 572, 96 S.Ct. 2264, 49 L.Ed.2d 65 (1976); *In re Griffiths,* 413 U.S. 717, 93 S.Ct. 2851, 37 L.Ed.2d 910 (1973). These exclusions struck at the noncitizens' ability to exist in the community, a position seemingly inconsistent with the congressional determination to admit the alien to permanent residence. See *Graham, supra,* 403 U.S. at 377-378, 91 S.Ct. at 1854-1855; Barrett, Judicial Supervision of Legislative Classifications, 1976 B.Y.U.L.Rev. 89, 101 (1976).

It would be inappropriate, however, to require every statutory exclusion of aliens to clear the high hurdle of "strict scrutiny," because to do so would "obliterate all the distinctions between citizens and aliens, and thus depreciate the historic values of citizenship." . . .

. . . Accordingly, we have recognized "a State's historical power to exclude aliens from participation in its democratic political institutions," *Dougall, supra,* 413 U.S. at 648, 93 S.Ct. at 2850, as part of the sovereign's obligation "to preserve the basic conception of a political community." *Id.,* at 647, 93 S.Ct., at 2850.

The practical consequence of this theory is that "our scrutiny will not be so demanding where we deal with matters firmly within a State's constitutional prerogatives." *Dougall, supra,* at 648, 93 S.Ct. at 2850. The State need only justify its classification by a showing of some rational relationship between the interest sought to be protected and the limiting classification. . . .

The essence of our holdings to date is that although we extend to aliens the right to education and public welfare, along with the ability to earn a livelihood and engage in licensed professions, the right to govern is reserved to citizens.

## III

A discussion of the police function is essentially a description of one of the basic functions of government, especially in a complex modern society where police presence is pervasive. . . .

Clearly the exercise of police authority calls for a very high degree of judgment and discretion, the abuse or misuse of which can have serious impact on individuals. The office of a policeman is in no sense one of "the common occupations of the community" that the then Mr. Justice Hughes referred to in *Truax v. Raich,* 239 U.S. 33, 41, 36 S.Ct. 7, 10, 60 L.Ed. 131 (1915). A policeman vested with the plenary discretionary powers we have described is not to be equated with a private person engaged in routine public employment or other "common occupations of the community" who exercises no broad power over people generally. Indeed, the rationale for the qualified immunity historically granted to the police rests on the difficult and delicate judgments these officers must often make. See *Pierson v. Ray,* 386 U.S. 547, 555-557, 87 S.Ct. 1213, 1218-1219, 18 L.Ed.2d 288; cf. *Scheuer v. Rhodes,* 416 U.S. 232, 245-246, 94 S.Ct. 1683, 1691, 40 L.Ed.2d 90 (1974).

In short, it would be as anomalous to conclude that citizens may be subjected to the broad discretionary powers of noncitizen police officers as it would be to say that judicial officers and jurors with power to judge citizens can be aliens. It is not surprising, therefore, that most States expressly confine the employment of police officers to citizens, whom the State may reasonably presume to be more familiar with and sympathetic to American traditions. Police officers very clearly fall within the category of "important nonelective . . . officers who participate directly in the . . . *execution* . . . of broad public policy." *Dougall, supra,* 413 U.S. at 647, 93 S.Ct. at 2850 (emphasis added). In the enforcement and execution of the laws the police function is one where citizenship bears a rational relationship to the special demands of the particular position. A State may, therefore, consonant with the Constitution, confine the performance of this important public responsibility to citizens of the United States.

Accordingly, the judgment of the District Court is

*Affirmed.*

MR. JUSTICE STEWART, concurring.

The dissenting opinions convincingly demonstrate that it is difficult if not impossible to reconcile the Court's judgment in this case with the full sweep of the reasoning and authority of some of our past decisions. It is only because I have become increasingly doubtful about the validity of those decisions (in at least some of which I concurred) that I join the opinion of the Court in this case.

MR. JUSTICE MARSHALL, with whom MR. JUSTICE BRENNAN and MR. JUSTICE STEVENS joins, dissenting.

Almost a century ago, in the landmark case of *Yick Wo v. Hopkins,* 118 U.S. 356, 369, 6 S.Ct. 1064, 1070, 30 L.Ed. 220 (1886), this Court recognized that aliens are "persons" within the meaning of the Fourteenth Amendment. Eighty-five years later, in *Graham v. Richardson,* 403 U.S. 365, 91 S.Ct. 1848, 29 L.Ed.2d 534 (1971), the Court concluded that aliens constitute a " 'discrete and insular' minority," and that laws singling them out for unfavorable treatment "are therefore subject to strict judicial scrutiny." *Id.* at 372, 376, 91 S.Ct., at 1854. During the ensuing six Terms, we have invalidated state laws discriminating against aliens on four separate occasions, finding that such discrimination could not survive strict scrutiny. *Sugarman v. Dougall,* 413 U.S. 634, 93 S.Ct. 2842, 37 L.Ed.2d 853 (1973) (competitive civil service); *In re Griffiths,* 413 U.S. 717, 93 S.Ct. 2851, 37 L.Ed.2d 910 (1973) (attorneys); *Examining Board v. Flores de Otero,* 426 U.S. 572, 96 S.Ct. 2264, 49 L.Ed.2d 65 (1976) (civil engineers); *Nyquist v. Mauclet,* 432 U.S. 1, 97 S.Ct. 2120, 53 L.Ed.2d 63 (1977) (financial assistance for higher education).

Today the Court upholds a law excluding aliens from public employment as state troopers. It bases its decision largely on dictum from *Sugarman v. Dougall, supra,* to the effect that aliens may be barred from holding "state elective or important nonelective executive, legislative, and judicial positions," because persons in these positions "participate directly in the formulation, execution, or review of broad public policy." 413 U.S., at 647, 93 S.Ct., at 2850. I do not agree with the Court that state troopers perform functions placing them within this "narrow . . . exception," *Nyquist v. Mauclet, supra,* 432 U.S., at 11, 97 S.Ct., at 2126, to our usual rule that discrimination against aliens is presumptively unconstitutional. Accordingly I dissent.

. . . Although every state employee is charged with the "execution" of public policy, *Sugarman* unambiguously holds that a blanket exclusion of aliens from state jobs is unconstitutional.

Thus the phrase "execution of broad public policy" in *Sugarman* cannot be read to mean simply the carrying out of government programs, but rather must be interpreted to include responsibility for actually setting government policy pursuant to a delegation of substantial authority from the legislature. . . .

There is a vast difference between the formulation and execution of broad public policy and the application of that policy to specific factual settings. While the Court is correct that "the exercise of police authority calls for a very high degree of judgment and discretion," *ante,* at 1072, the judgments required are factual in nature; the policy judgments that govern an officer's conduct are contained in the federal and state Constitutions, statutes, and regulations. The officer responding to a particular situation is only applying the basic policy choices — which he has no role in shaping — to the facts as he perceives them. . . .

The Court places great reliance on the fact that policemen make arrests and perform searches, often "without prior judicial authority." *Ante,* at 1071-1072. I certainly agree that "[an] arrest is a serious matter," and that we should be concerned about all "intru[sions] on the privacy of the individual." *Ibid.* But these concerns do not in any way make it "anomalous" for citizens to be arrested and searched by "noncitizen police officers," *id.,* at 1072, at least not in New York State. By statute, New York authorizes "any person" to arrest another who has actually committed a felony or who has committed any other offense in the arresting person's presence. N.Y. Crim.Proc.Law § 140.30. Moreover, a person making an arrest pursuant to this statute is authorized to make a search incident to the arrest. While law enforcement is primarily the responsibility of state troopers, it is nevertheless difficult to understand how the Court can imply that the troopers' arrest and search authority justifies excluding aliens from the police force when the State has given all private persons, including aliens, such authority. . . .

MR. JUSTICE STEVENS, with whom MR. JUSTICE BRENNAN joins, dissenting.

A State should, of course, scrutinize closely the qualifications of those who perform professional services within its borders. Police officers, like lawyers, must be qualified in their field of expertise and must be trustworthy. Detailed review of each individual's application for employment is therefore appropriate. Conversely, a rule which disqualifies an entire class of persons from professional employment is doubly objectionable. It denies the State access to unique individual talent; it also denies opportunity to individuals on the basis of characteristics that the group is thought to possess.

The first objection poses a question of policy rather than constitutional law. The wisdom of a rule denying a law enforcement agency the services of Hercule Poirot or Sherlock Holmes is thus for New York, not this Court, to decide. But the second objection raises a question of a different kind and a satisfactory answer to this question is essential to the validity of the rule: What is the group characteristic that justifies the unfavorable treatment of an otherwise qualified individual simply because he is an alien?

No one suggests that aliens as a class lack the intelligence or the courage to serve the public as police officers. The disqualifying characteristic is apparently a foreign allegiance which raises a doubt concerning trustworthiness and loyalty so pervasive that a flat ban against the employment of any alien in any law enforcement position is thought to be justified. But if the integrity of all aliens is suspect, why may not a State deny aliens the right to practice law? . . .

. . . In *Elrod v. Burns,* 427 U.S. 347, 96 S.Ct. 2673, 49 L.Ed.2d 547, the Court held that most public employees are protected from discharge because of their political beliefs but recognized that an exception was required for policymaking officials. The exception identified in *Burns* was essentially the same as the category of "officers who participate in the formulation, execution or review of broad public policy" described in *Sugarman v. Dougall,* 413 U.S. 634, 647, 93

S.Ct. 2842, 2850, 37 L.Ed.2d 853. In both cases the special nature of the policymaking position was recognized as justifying a form of discriminatory treatment that could not be applied to regular employees.

The Court should draw the line between policymaking and nonpolicymaking positions in as consistent and intelligible a fashion as possible. As MR. JUSTICE MARSHALL points out, *ante,* at 1075, in the context of immunity from liability under 42 U.S.C. § 1983, the Court placed the police officer in a different category from the governor of Ohio. See *Scheuer v. Rhodes,* 416 U.S. 232, 245-247, 94 S.Ct. 1683, 1691-1692, 40 L.Ed.2d 90. And under *Elrod v. Burns, supra,* the Court would unquestionably condemn the dismissal of a citizen state trooper because his political affiliation differed from that of his superiors. Yet, inexplicably, every state trooper is transformed into a high ranking, policymaking official when the question presented is whether persons may be excluded from all positions in the police force simply because they are aliens.

Since the Court does not purport to disturb the teaching of *Sugarman,* this transformation must rest on the unarticulated premise that the police function is at "the heart of representative government" and therefore all persons employed by the institutions performing that function "participate directly in the formulation, execution, or review of broad public policy ...." *Sugarman v. Dougall,* 413 U.S., at 647, 93 S.Ct., at 2850. In my judgment, to state the premise is to refute it. Respect for the law enforcement profession and its essential function, like respect for the military, should not cause us to lose sight of the fact that in our representative democracy neither the constabulary nor the military is vested with broad policymaking responsibility. Instead, each implements the basic policies formulated directly or indirectly by the citizenry. Under the standards announced in *Sugarman,* therefore, a blanket exclusion of aliens from this particular governmental institution is especially inappropriate. . . .

In final analysis, therefore, our society is governed by its citizens. But it is a government of and for all persons subject to its jurisdiction, and the Constitution commands their equal treatment. Although a State may deny the alien the right to participate in the making of policy, it may not deny him equal access to employment opportunities without a good and relevant reason. *Sugarman* plainly teaches us that the burgeoning public employment market cannot be totally foreclosed to aliens. Since the police officer is not a policymaker in this country, the total exclusion of aliens from the police force must fall.

Even if the Court rejects this analysis, it should not uphold a statutory discrimination against aliens, as a class, without expressly identifying the group characteristic that justifies the discrimination. . . .

Because the Court's unique decision fails either to apply or to reject established rules of law, and for the reasons stated by MR. JUSTICE MARSHALL, I respectfully dissent.

## NOTE

The New York Education law, which provides that aliens may not teach in public schools unless they have applied for U.S. citizenship, was held to violate the rights of nonapplicant aliens to equal protection under the Fourteenth Amendment. The district court deciding the case applied a strict judicial scrutiny test in striking down the state requirement. Norwick v. Nyquist, 417 F.Supp. 913 (S.D.N.Y. 1976), *cert. granted,* 46 U.S.L.W. 3703 (May 16, 1978).

# 6. VETERANS' PREFERENCE

## FEENEY v. COMMONWEALTH OF MASSACHUSETTS

United States District Court
District of Massachusetts
F.Supp. , 17 FEP Cas. 659 (1978)

TAURO, District Judge: — By order of remand from the Supreme Court, we have been instructed to reconsider our decision in Anthony v. Commonwealth, 415 F.Supp. 485, 12 FEP Cases 915 (D. Mass. 1976), in light of the Court's subsequent decision in Washington v. Davis, 426 U.S. 229, 12 FEP Cases 1415 (1976). After further briefing and oral argument, we conclude that Davis does not require us to alter our original holding. To the contrary, we have determined that both Davis and the Court's later opinion in Village of Arlington Heights v. Metropolitan Housing Development Corp., 429 U.S. 252 (1977), support our conclusion that the challenged Massachusetts Veterans' Preference statute deprives women of equal protection of the laws and, therefore, is unconstitutional.

I

### The Anthony Decision

The broad issues in this case are treated extensively in our prior opinion. 415 F.Supp. 485, 12 FEP Cases 915. In order to put in context our reconsideration of Anthony, however, it is useful to outline briefly some of its major points.

The statutory scheme challenged in Anthony established a formula that permanently prevents a non-veteran from achieving a place on the civil service appointment list ahead of a veteran, regardless of comparative test scores. We pointed out that "(a)s a practical matter . . . the Veterans' Preference replaces testing as the criterion for determining which eligibles will be placed at the top of the list." 415 F.Supp. at 489, 12 FEP Cases at 916-917.

The selection formula, geared as it is to veteran status, is necessarily controlled by federal military proscriptions limiting the eligibility of women for participation in the military. Longstanding federal policy limited to 2% the number of women who could participate in the armed forces. Anthony v. Commonwealth, supra, at 489, 12 FEP Cases at 917. Traditionally, enlistment and appointment criteria have been more restrictive for women than for men. An inevitable consequence of this federal policy limiting women's participation in the military is that only 2% of Massachusetts veterans are women. Id. . . .

We recognized that the prime legislative motive of the challenged statute, that of rewarding public service in the military was worthy. . . .

We determined that the means chosen by the Massachusetts Legislature to reward veterans were not grounded "on a convincing factual rationale." Id. at 495, 12 FEP Cases at 922. We pointed out that the challenged statutory formula was not an effort by the state to set priorities for finite resources; that there were less drastic alternatives available to the state, such as a point system; and that any argument attempting to relate the challenged formula to job performance or qualification was "specious." Id. at 495-499, 12 FEP Cases at 922-925. We concluded that the formula relegated job-related criteria and professional qualifications to a secondary position. Id. at 497, 12 FEP Cases at 924.

Moreover, we emphasized that the challenged preference was absolute and permanent. No time limit was imposed or attempt made "to tailor its use to those who have shortly returned to civilian life." Id. at 499, 12 FEP Cases at 925. Such a broad-brush approach may be administratively convenient, but mere administrative convenience is not a legitimate basis for benefiting one identifiable class at the expense of another. Reed v. Reed, 404 U.S. 71 (1971).

Although the Veterans' Preference statute was not designed for the sole purpose of subordinating women, Anthony v. Commonwealth, supra, at 495, 12 FEP Cases at 922, its clear intent was to benefit veterans even at the expense of women. As we stated,

> (T)he formula's impact, triggered by decades of restrictive federal enlistment regulations, makes the operation of the Veterans' Preference in Massachusetts anything but an impartial, neutral policy of selection, with merely an incidental effect on the opportunities for women.

Id. at 495, 12 FEP Cases at 922.
Rather, we found the preference formula to be

> a deliberate, conscious attempt on the part of the state to aid one clearly identifiable group of its citizens, those who qualify as veterans, . . . at the absolute and permanent disadvantage of another clearly identifiable group, Massachusetts women.

Id. at 496, 12 FEP Cases at 923.
The consequences of adopting a permanent absolute preference formula tied to federal enlistment restrictions were more than predictable, they were inevitable.


## II

### The Impact of Davis on Anthony

At issue in Davis was a pre-employment literacy test used by the District of Columbia police department. The district court rejected plaintiffs' allegation that the test was "culturally slanted" to favor whites. It determined further that the test was "reasonably and directly" related to the requirements of the police recruit training program, although unrelated to actual job performance. 426 U.S. at 235, 12 FEP Cases at 1417. The D.C. Circuit reversed, holding irrelevant the failure of plaintiffs to allege and prove discriminatory intent in the exam's design and administrattion. It determined that the disproportionate percentage of blacks who had failed the exam sufficed to establish a constitutional violation. Id. at 236-37, 12 FEP Cases at 1418.

In reversing the court of appeals, the Supreme Court stated that claims of invidious discrimination under the fifth or fourteenth amendments require proof of a discriminatory purpose. A facially neutral statute may not be deemed vulnerable to equal protection challenge solely because it has a disproportionate impact. The Court emphasized that discriminatory intent need not be "express or appear on the face of the statute." 426 U.S. at 241, 12 FEP Cases at 1419, but that consideration must be given to the totality of the circumstances. Disproportionate impact is one such highly relevant circumstance we must consider.

. . . .

The district court in Davis determined that the challenged test was neutral on its face. Id. at 235, 12 FEP Cases at 1417. This determination apparently provided a basis for the Court's statement that,

> A rule that a statute designed to serve neutral ends is nevertheless invalid, absent compelling justification, if in practice it benefits or burdens one race

more than another would be far reaching and would raise serious questions about, and perhaps invalidate, a whole range of tax, welfare, public service, regulatory, and licensing statutes that may be more burdensome to the poor and to the average black than to the more affluent white.

Id. at 248, 12 FEP Cases at 1422. (Footnotes omitted.)

The factual underpinning in this case is entirely different. As we have already emphasized, the Veterans' Preference statute is "anything but an impartial, neutral policy of selection with merely an incidental effect on the opportunities for women." 415 F.Supp. at 495, 12 FEP Cases at 922. Here, plaintiff does not challenge the civil service written examination but, rather, the overriding ranking formula that mandates an absolute job preference to veterans over nonveterans, regardless of comparative test scores. This preference formula effectively "replaces testing as the criterion for determining which eligibles will be placed at the top of the list." Id. at 489, 12 FEP Cases at 917.

In analyzing the "totality of the relevant facts" so as to determine the legislative intent underlying the challenged statute, we must of necessity examine official acts or policies to determine whether they had the natural, foreseeable and inevitable effect of producing a discriminatory impact. . . .

The legislature was, at the least, chargeable with knowledge of the longstanding federal regulations limiting opportunities for women in the military, and the inevitable discriminatory consequences produced by their application to the challenged formula.

. . . .

We must also assume that the legislature was cognizant of the fact that the stringent entry criteria embodied in the federal military regulations bore "no demonstrable relation to an individual's fitness for civilian public service." Id. at 498-99, 12 FEP Cases at 925. We realize that a due process or equal protection claim is not to be judged by the standards applicable under Title VII. Washington v. Davis, supra, at 239, 12 FEP Cases at 1418. Our holding that the Massachusetts civil service selection process is unconstitutional is not based solely on the fact that it bears no relationship to job performance. But the fact that the criteria set forth in the challenged statutory formula fail to measure job performance is one additional circumstance bearing on the question of discriminatory intent.

Finally, the statistical evidence presented by plaintiff demonstrates a pattern of exclusion of women from the civil service. At the time the suit was filed, only 2% of Massachusetts veterans were women. Although 43% of the civil service appointees were women, a large percentage of them served in lower grade positions for which men traditionally did not apply. Of the women appointed over a ten year period, from July 1, 1963 through June 30, 1973, only 1.8% were veterans, while 54% of the men had veteran status. 415 F.Supp. at 488, 12 FEP Cases at 916.

The facts demonstrate that this absolute job preference formula had a devastating impact on the plaintiff's attempts to advance her position in the civil service. In 1971, she received the second highest test score for the position of Assistant Secretary to the Board of Dental Examiners, but was ranked sixth on the list of eligibles, behind five male veterans, four of whom had received lower scores. She was not certified and a male veteran with a lower examination score was appointed.

Two years later when she applied for another administrative post, plaintiff received the third highest mark on the exam, but only ranked fourteenth on the list, behind twelve male veterans, eleven of whom had lower test scores. Again, plaintiff was not certified for appointment. The third time she applied for an administrative position, plaintiff received a score that would have placed her within the top twenty places on the eligibles list. By operation of the formula, however, she was ranked 70th on the list, behind 50 male veterans with lower test scores. Id. at 497-498, 12 FEP Cases at 924.

These figures, and others cited in our earlier opinion, show a clear pattern of exclusion of women from competitive civil service positions. Unlike the defendants in Davis, the Commonwealth has not made any showing of affirmative efforts to recruit women, or of a recent rise in the percentage of women appointed to competitive civil service positions. In Davis the district court found that 44% of the new police recruits over the preceding three years had been black, a figure roughly approximating the proportion of blacks in the area. That court also found that the Department had "systematically and affirmatively sought to enroll black officers, many of whom passed the test but failed to report for duty." 426 U.S. at 236, 12 FEP Cases at 1417.

The situation here is in marked contrast. The Commonwealth's proffered 57-43 ratio of men to women is misleading. A large percentage of female appointees serve in lower grade permanent positions for which males traditionally have not applied. Some women received their appointments through a now defunct practice by which the appointing authorities would requisition only women applicants for certain jobs. 415 F.Supp. at 488, 12 FEP Cases at 916. While the officials in Davis sought "systematically" to recruit minorities who had passed the preemployment test, the defendants here have demonstrated no attempt to mitigate the permanent and absolute impact on women of a formula that systematically excludes them from desirable public service positions even though they have demonstrated their qualifications by passing a written exam.

The Commonwealth argues that,

> historical analysis makes it clear that the enactment of this legislation by the General Court was in no way motivated by a desire to discriminate against women. Rather, the legislative motivations for Massachusetts Veterans' Preference statutes were: (1) to reward those who have sacrificed in the service of their country; (2) to assist veterans in their readjustment to civilian life; and (3) to encourage patriotic service.

Brief for Defendants at 24, 25.

We disagree. It is clear that the Commonwealth's motive was to benefit its veterans. Equally clear, however, is that its intent was to achieve that purpose by subordinating employment opportunities of its women. The course of action chosen by the commonwealth had the inevitable consequence of discriminating against the women of this state. See Anthony v. Commonwealth, supra, at 496, 12 FEP Cases at 923. The fact that the Commonwealth had a salutary motive does not justify its intention to realize that end by disadvantaging its women.

> Davis does not require a plaintiff to prove that the challenged action rested solely on racially discriminatory purposes. Rarely can it be said that a legislature or administrative body operating under a broad mandate made a decision solely by a single concern, or even that a particular purpose was the "dominant" or "primary" one.

Village of Arlington Heights v. Metropolitan Development Housing Corp., supra, at 265. (Footnotes omitted.)

The fact that there are less drastic alternatives available to the state to achieve its purpose of aiding veterans, underscores our conclusion that the absolute and permanent preference adopted by the Commonwealth resulted from improper evaluation of competing considerations. By intentionally sacrificing the career opportunities of its women in order to benefit veterans, the Commonwealth made a constitutionally impermissible value judgment.

We reaffirm our holding that the Massachusetts Veterans' Preference Act denies equal protection under the law and, therefore, is unconstitutional. . . .

CAMPBELL, Circuit Judge (concurring): — This is not an easy case to deal with under Washington v. Davis, 426 U.S. 229, 12 FEP Cases 1415 (1977). On the one hand, there can be no question about the unequal impact of this law: practically speaking, it permanently shuts off whole areas of state employment to women. On the other hand, as Judge Murray points out in his dissent, a strong initial case can be made for the proposition that it is "neutral on its face," and not motivated in any ordinary sense by a discriminatory intent. Arguably, therefore, the challenged statute is the kind of law which, notwithstanding its widespread impact on women's employment opportunities, should be upheld as constitutional. The thrust of Washington v. Davis and related decisions such as Village of Arlington Heights v. Metropolitan Housing Corporation, 429 U.S. 252 (1977), is that we must accept that well-intentioned programs may have uneven side effects: society is too complicated for every discriminatory consequence to disqualify legitimate policies. Welfare programs, for example, foreseeably benefit minority groups disproportionately, just as tax deductions do whites. Examinations (as in Washington v. Davis) designed reasonably to weed out those unqualified for police work, may eliminate minority applicants more than others. Town and city planning laws, designed to improve community life, may because of separate economic factors, create barriers to minorities. Society would soon be in a state of paralysis if it could adopt only laws having strictly equal impact upon all groups and classes within it.

But while I fully recognize not only that Washington v. Davis is the law of the land but also that its principle reflects an essential limitation upon the sweep of the equal protection clause, I do not believe that the Massachusetts veterans preference law actually falls within its ambit. This, as Judge Tauro convincingly demonstrates, is not ordinary statute having merely an incidental unequal impact. It is a statute which goes a long way towards making upper level state employment a male preserve. Upon close inspection, the seeming "neutrality" of the veterans preference law, and even its seeming absence of intentional discrimination, are both open to serious question.

I turn first to the matter of its neutrality. While the dividing line between veterans and non-veterans is not the same as the dividing line between men and women, the ineluctable effect of this law is to confer an absolute priority upon a class that is 98% male in a sphere of employment where women, generally, should have the same access as men. What the law does, is to take a group which has, for unique reasons, been selected almost exclusively from the male population (military service being what it was and is), and grant it an absolute preference in an entirely different sphere of public employment where male preference is not only not the rule but is constitutionally impermissible. The law may be "facially neutral" in the limited sense that it is not based overtly on selection by sex, but since the preferred class is 98% male the effect is virtually the same as if it were.

. . . .

This same inevitability of exclusionary impact upon women also undermines the argument of no discriminatory intent. There is a difference between goals and intent. Conceding, as we all must, that the goal here was to benefit the veteran, there is no reason to absolve the legislature from awareness that the means chosen to achieve this goal would freeze women out of all those state jobs actively sought by men. To be sure, the legislature did not wish to harm women. But the cutting-off of women's opportunities was an inevitable concomitant of the chosen scheme — as inevitable as the proposition that if tails is up, heads must be down. Where a law's consequences are *that* inevitable, can they meaningfully be described as unintended? . . .

This is not to say that society may not bestow benefits upon veterans. But I think it may not construct a system of absolute preference which makes it virtually impossible for a woman, no matter how talented, to obtain a state job that is also of interest to males. Such a system is fundamentally different from the conferring upon veterans of financial benefits to which all taxpayers contribute, or from the giving to them of some degree of preference in government employment, as under a point system, as a *quid pro quo* for time lost in military service. The latter measures do not impose unfairly upon one segment of our society; the instant law, in contrast, forces women to pay a disproportionate share of the cost of benefiting veterans by sacrificing their own chance to be selected for state employment.

. . . .

MURRAY, Senior District Judge. (Dissenting): — Washington v. Davis, 426 U.S. 229, 239, 242, 12 FEP Cases 1475, 1418-1419, 1420 (1977) holds:

. . . [O]ur cases have not embraced the proposition that a law or other official act, without regard to whether it reflects a racially discriminatory purpose, is unconstitutional *solely* because it has a racially disproportionate impact. [Emphasis in original.] . . .

. . . [W]e have not held that a law, neutral on its face and serving ends otherwise within the power of government to pursue, is invalid under the Equal Protection Clause simply because it may affect a greater proportion of one race than of another.

The majority today determines that Washington v. Davis, supra, supports their previous holding that the Massachusetts Veterans' Preference statute, Mass. Gen. Laws ch. 31, § 23, deprives women of equal protection of the laws in violation of the Fourteenth Amendment in all areas of civil service employment in the Commonwealth. . . .

I

The Veterans' Preference statute is not on its face gender-based. Anthony v. Commonwealth of Massachusetts, 415 F. Supp. 485, 501, 12 FEP Cases 915, 927 (1976) (Campbell, C.J., concurring). Clearly the statutory "division between veterans and non-veterans is not drawn along sex lines and does not provide for dissimilar treatment for similarly situated men and women. On its face the statute is neutral . . .". Id. at 503, 12 FEP Cases at 929 (Murray, J., dissenting). Most persons favored by the statutory preference are males, although a substantial number of those not so favored are also males. Non-veteran women in larger numbers share with non-veteran men the disfavor of the statute, but a number of those aided by the statute indeed are women. The statute explicitly includes women in its requirement for service during time of war, but not combat duty. . . .

The attempted distinction between the test in Davis and the statute here is totally unconvincing: one is no more neutral than the other. In each case the classification is facially neutral, and in operation the effects are uneven; the only difference is that the statute here has a weightier impact on the relevant group,

and impact alone is not determinative, Washington v. Davis, supra, at 239, 12
FEP Cases at 1418-1419.

## II

The record before the court, to the extent that it provides direct and
circumstantial evidence of intent, does not show the operation of the statute and
its effect to be a clear pattern, unexplainable on grounds other than an intent
to limit the employment opportunities of women. This is so, whether the relevant
facts are viewed totally or separately. Conceding the factor of unequal impact and
that it was foreseeable, a showing of unconstitutional action has not been made.
Even in Davis the government officials there might well have foreseen that blacks
would not do as well on the test as whites. See Boston Chapter, N.A.A.C.P. v.
Beecher, 504 F.2d 1017, 1021, 8 FEP Cases 855 (1st Cir. 1974). Awareness on
the part of the legislature that disproportionate impact would follow is not
enough. Awareness, like foreseeability, is not proof of discriminatory intent, and
other evidence is required. The legislative history of the statute with its unequal
impact on women is clearly explainable as having the purpose of preferring
qualified veterans for consideration for civil service jobs.

. . . .

The statistical evidence presented by plaintiff provides no support for an
inference of a discriminatory purpose. This is an impact argument, and Arlington
Heights (and Davis) requires proof of intent as "a motivating factor". Plaintiff's
systematic exclusion argument analogizes the jury-selection cases, but those cases
do not apply in the context of this case. Arlington Heights pointed out that
"[b]ecause of the nature of the jury-selection task, however, we have permitted
a finding of constitutional violation even when the statistical pattern does not
approach the extremes of Yick Wo [v. Hopkins, 118 U.S. 356 (1886)] or
Gomillion [v. Lightfoot, 364 U.S. 339 (1960)] . . .". 429 U.S. at 266, n.13.
Whatever the exact focus of the Court in jury-selection cases, the Court makes
it clear that even in those cases impact alone is determinative only when it
emerges as "a clear pattern, unexplainable on grounds other than race",
Arlington Heights, supra at 266. The facts here do not fit into that mold: it is
undisputed that the preference here is based on a determination to help veteran
men and women and not non-veterans.

. . . .

## III

The principle applied in tort and criminal actions, that an actor is presumed
to intend the natural and foreseeable consequences of his deeds, must yield to
the entirely different considerations at work when a federal court is addressing
an equal protection challenge to state legislation. Principles of federalism involve
a "recognition of the value of state experimentation with a variety of means for
solving social and economic problems", Anthony, supra at 502, 12 FEP Cases
at 928 (Murray, J., dissenting), and considerations of federalism require that an
impermissible motive in enacting state legislation be not lightly inferred. . . .

## IV

Since Washington v. Davis, three veterans' preference provisions have been
subjected to equal protection challenge; all three have been upheld. Bannerman

v. Dept. of Youth Authority, 436 F.Supp. 1273, 17 FEP Cases — (N.D. Cal. 1977); Branch v. DuBois, 418 F.Supp. 1128, 13 FEP Cases 758 (N.D. Ill. 1976); Ballou v. State, Dept. of Civil Service, 372 A.2d 333, 17 FEP Cases — (N.J. App. Div. 1977), aff'd, 46 LW 2454, 17 FEP Cases at — (N.J. 1978). Three of the decisions distinguish Anthony v. Commonwealth, supra, as having been based on a stronger negative effect on women than those courts faced. The California court, however, states that the approach used in Anthony was "rejected in Washington v. Davis", Bannerman, 436 F.Supp. at 1280, 17 FEP Cases at —. Each court had little trouble in concluding that no intent to harm women was present, even in the "absolute" preference at issue in New Jersey. The Illinois court's language is representative.

> While those who never served in the armed forces, those who served at times not within the statutory periods and women who are not veterans suffer a disadvantage in hiring and promotion, this is an incidental result of a statute intended to reward veterans and not one intended to discriminate against men and women who are not veterans or those whose service was in times of limited military action.

Branch v. DuBois, 418 F.Supp. at 1133, 13 FEP Cases at 761.

The impact of the statute at issue here does not approach the extremes described in Arlington Heights, supra at 266, and plaintiff must prove intent by other evidence. This she has not done. The question: Would the veterans' preference statute have been enacted if women were represented in the armed services in such numbers that the preference would have no discriminatory effect? has not been addressed by plaintiff, and she has given the court absolutely no reason to answer this question in the negative. She has failed to make out a prima facie case of discriminatory intent. See Mt. Healthy City Board of Ed. v. Doyle, 429 U.S. 274, 287 (1977). In light of Washington v. Davis I would not hold, as the majority does, that the Massachusetts Veterans' Preference statute violates the Equal Protection Clause of the Fourteenth Amendment. I dissent.

## NOTE

The Massachusetts absolute veterans' preference scheme placed all veterans who passed an examination on the eligibility list ahead of all non-veterans, even though some of the non-veterans may have achieved much higher scores on the examination than any of the veterans. The court in *Feeney* indicated, however, that the case might have been decided differently if Massachusetts used a system giving a veteran a certain number of points to be added onto his (or in rare cases, her) examination score. Congress has approved a modified point system for veterans' preference and given certain other benefits (such as priority in the event of a reduction in work force) for veterans in federal jobs. Nevertheless, this modified system has also resulted in inequities for non-veterans. For example, according to figures issued in January, 1978 by Chairman A. Campbell of the federal Civil Service Commission, veterans comprised 50% of the federal service, although they were only 25% of the national labor force. Ninety-eight percent of the veterans in the federal service were reported to be white males. At the higher levels of government employment, veterans accounted for over 60% of those federal employees in grades 15 and over. Only 3% of the positions at the top of the civil service system were held by women and only 5% were held by minorities. Only 5.9% of the positions at grades 13, 14 and 15 were held by women and 5% by minorities. The domination of top positions by white male veterans was caused in part by the requirement that the federal employer select from the top three candidates. If one of the top three candidates is a veteran, the employer must show that this candidate is not qualified, not that the other candidates are more qualified. The Civil Service Commission has proposed, as part of a Civil Service Reform Bill, changes in this system which would alleviate some of these discriminatory effects and enhance the possibility that employment and advancement through the civil service system be based on merit. However, Congress has yet to adopt any such statutory revisions.

Is it enough to say that the problem of sex discrimination attributable to veterans' preference will be alleviated in time as more women join the armed forces?

# E. PUBLIC EMPLOYERS' IMMUNITY FROM SUIT

## MONELL v. DEPARTMENT OF SOCIAL SERVICES

Supreme Court of the United States
U.S.   , 17 FEP Cas. 873 (1978)

MR. JUSTICE BRENNAN delivered the opinion of the Court.

Petitioners, a class of female employees of the Department of Social Services and the Board of Education of the City of New York, commenced this action under 42 U.S.C. § 1983 in July 1971. The gravamen of the complaint was that the Board and the Department had as a matter of official policy compelled pregnant employees to take unpaid leaves of absence before such leaves were required for medical reasons. Cf. Cleveland Board of Education v. LaFleur, 414 U. S. 632, 6 FEP Cases 1253 (1974). The suit sought injunctive relief and back pay for periods of unlawful forced leave. Named as defendants in the action were the Department and its Commissioner, the Board and its Chancellor, and the city of New York and its Mayor. In each case, the individual defendants were sued solely in their official capacities.

On cross-motions for summary judgment, the District Court for the Southern District of New York held moot petitioners' claims for injunctive and declaratory relief since the city of New York and the Board, after the filing of the complaint, had changed their policies relating to maternity leaves so that no pregnant employee would have to take leave unless she was medically unable to continue to perform her job. 394 F.Supp. 853, 855, 10 FEP Cases 769, 770. No one now challenges this conclusion. The court did conclude, however, that the acts complained of were unconstitutional under LaFleur, supra. 394 F.Supp., at 855, 10 FEP Cases at 770. Nonetheless plaintiff's prayers for back pay were denied because any such damages would come ultimately from the City of New York and, therefore, to hold otherwise would be to "circumvent" the immunity conferred on municipalities by Monroe v. Pape, 365 U.S. 167 (1961). See 394 F.Supp., at 855, 10.FEP Cases, at 770-771.

On appeal, petitioners renewed their arguments that the Board of Education was not a "municipality" within the meaning of Monroe v. Pape, supra, and that, in any event, the District Court had erred in barring a damage award against the individual defendants. The Court of Appeals for the Second Circuit rejected both contentions.

. . . .

> We granted certiorari in this case, 429 U.S. 1071, 14 FEP Cases 417, to consider "Whether local governmental officials and/or local independent school boards are "persons" within the meaning of 42 U.S.C. § 1983 when equitable relief in the nature of back pay is sought against them in their official capacities?" Pet. for Cert. 8.

. . . .

... [W]e indicated in Mt. Healthy City Board of Ed. v. Doyle, 429 U.S. 274, 279 (1977), last Term that the question presented here was open and would be decided "another day." That other day has come and we now overrule Monroe v. Pape, supra, insofar as it holds that local governments are wholly immune from suit under § 1983.

I

In Monroe v. Pape, we held that "Congress did not undertake to bring municipal corporations within the ambit of [§ 1983]." 365 U.S., at 187. The sole basis for this conclusion was an inference drawn from Congress' rejection of the "Sherman amendment" to the bill which became Civil Rights Act of 1871, 17 Stat. 13 — the precursor of § 1983 — which would have held a municipal corporation liable for damage done to the person or property of its inhabitants by *private* persons "riotously and tumultuously assembled." Cong. Globe, 42d Cong., 1st Sess., 749 (1871) (hereinafter "Globe"). Although the Sherman amendment did not seek to amend § 1 of the Act, which is now § 1983, and although the nature of the obligation created by that amendment was vastly different from that created by § 1, the Court nonetheless concluded in Monroe that Congress must have meant to exclude municipal corporations from the coverage of § 1 because " 'the House [in voting against the Sherman amendment] had solemnly decided that in their judgment Congress had no constitutional power to impose any *obligation* upon county and town organizations, the mere instrumentality for the administration of state law.' " 365 U.S., at 190 (emphasis added), quoting Globe, at 804 (Rep. Poland). This statement, we thought, showed that Congress doubted its "constitutional power . . . to impose *civil liability* on municipalities," 365 U.S., at 190 (emphasis added), and that such doubt would have extended to any type of civil liability.

A fresh analysis of debate on the Civil Rights Act of 1871, and particularly of the case law which each side mustered in its support, shows, however, that Monroe incorrectly equated the "obligation" of which Representative Poland spoke with "civil liability." . . .

[Here the Court examines at length the legislative history and relevant caselaw surrounding Congress' rejection of the "Sherman Amendment."]

. . . .

C. Debate on § 1 of the Civil Rights Bill

From the foregoing discussion, it is readily apparent that nothing said in debate on the Sherman amendment would have prevented holding a municipality liable under § 1 of the Civil Rights Act for its own violations of the Fourteenth Amendment. The question remains, however, whether the general language describing those to be liable under § 1 — "any person" — covers more than natural persons. An examination of the debate on § 1 and application of appropriate rules of construction shows unequivocally that § 1 was intended to cover legal as well as natural persons.

Representative Shellabarger was the first to explain the function of § 1:

> "[Section 1] not only provides a civil remedy for persons whose former condition may have been that of slaves, but also to all people where, under color of State law, they or any of them may be deprived of rights to which they are entitled under the Constitution by reason and virtue of their national citizenship." Globe App., at 68.

By extending a remedy to all people, including whites, § 1 went beyond the mischief to which the remaining sections of the 1871 Act were addressed.

Representative Shellabarger also stated without reservation that the constitutionality of § 2 of the Civil Rights Act of 1866 controlled the constitutionality of § 1 of the 1871 Act, and that the former had been approved by "the supreme courts of at least three States of this Union" and by Mr. Justice Swayne, sitting on circuit, who had concluded "We have no doubt of the constitutionality of every provision of this act." Ibid. He then went on to describe how the courts would and should interpret § 1:

> "This act is remedial, and in aid of the preservation of human liberty and human rights. All statutes and constitutional provisions authorizing such statutes are liberally and beneficently construed. It would be most strange and, in civilized law, monstrous were this not the rule of interpretation. As has been again and again decided by your own Supreme Court of the United States, and everywhere else where there is wise judicial interpretation, the largest latitude consistent with the words employed is uniformly given in construing such statutes and constitutional provisions as are meant to protect and defend and give remedies for their wrongs to all the people . . . .
> Chief Justices Jay and also Story say:
> " 'Where a power is remedial in its nature there is much reason to contend that it ought to be construed liberally, and it is generally adopted in the interpretation of laws.' — 1 *Story on Constitution,* sec. 429." Globe App., at 68.

The sentiments expressed in Representative Shellabarger's opening speech were echoed by Senator Edmunds, the manager of H. R. 320 in the Senate:

> "The first section is one that I believe nobody objects to, as defining the rights secured by the Constitution of the United States when they are assailed by any State law or under color of any State law, and it is merely carrying out the principles of the civil rights bill [of 1866] which have since become a part of the Constitution." Globe, at 568.
> "[Section 1 is] so very simple and really reenacting the Constitution." Id., at 569.
> And he agreed that the bill "secure[ed] the rights of white men as much as of colored men." Id., at 696.

In both Houses, statements of the supporters of § 1 corroborated that Congress, in enacting § 1, intended to give a broad remedy for violations of federally protected civil rights. Moreover, since municipalities through their official acts, could equally with natural persons create the harms intended to be remedied by § 1, and, further, since Congress intended § 1 to be broadly construed, there is no reason to suppose that municipal corporations would have been excluded from the sweep of § 1. Cf., e.g., Ex parte Virginia, 100 U.S. 339, 346-347 (1880); Home Tel. & Tel. Co. v. Los Angeles, 227 U.S. 278, 286-287, 294-296 (1913). One need not rely on this inference alone, however, for the debates show that Members of Congress understood "persons" to include municipal corporations.

Representative Bingham, for example, in discussing § 1 of the bill, explained that he had drafted § 1 of the Fourteenth Amendment with the case of Barron v. Baltimore, 7 Pet. 243 (1834), especially in mind. "In [that] case the *city* had taken private property for public use, without compensation . . ., and there was no redress for the wrong . . . ." Globe App., at 84 (emphasis added). Bingham's further remarks clearly indicate his view that such takings by cities, as had occurred in Barron, would be redressable under § 1 of the bill. See id., at 85. More generally, and as Bingham's remarks confirm, § 1 of the bill would logically be the vehicle by which Congress provided redress for takings, since that section provided the only civil remedy for Fourteenth Amendment violations and that Amendment unequivocally prohibited uncompensated takings. Given this purpose, it beggars reason to suppose that Congress would have exempted municipalities from suit, insisting instead that compensation for a taking come from an officer in his individual capacity rather than from the government unit that had the benefit of the property taken.

In addition, by 1871, it was well understood that corporations should be treated as natural persons for virtually all purposes of constitutional and statutory analysis. . . .

That the "usual" meaning of the word person would extend to municipal corporations is also evidenced by an Act of Congress which had been passed only months before the Civil Rights Act was passed. This Act provided that

> "in all acts hereafter passed . . . the word 'person' may extend and be applied to bodies politic and corporate . . . unless the context shows that such words were intended to be used in a more limited sense[]." Act of Feb. 25, 1871, ch. 71, § 2, 16 Stat. 431.

Municipal corporations in 1871 were included within the phrase "bodies politic and corporate" and, accordingly, the "plain meaning" of § 1 is that local government bodies were to be included within the ambit of the persons who could be sued under § 1 of the Civil Rights Act.

. . . .

## II

Our analysis of the legislative history of the Civil Rights Act of 1871 compels the conclusion that Congress *did* intend municipalities and other local government units to be included among those persons to whom § 1983 applies.[54] Local governing bodies,[55] therefore, can be sued directly under § 1983 for monetary, declaratory, or injunctive relief where, as here, the action that is alleged to be unconstitutional implements or executes a policy statement, ordinance, regulation, or decision officially adopted and promulgated by that body's officers. Moreover, although the touchstone of the § 1983 action against a government body is an allegation that official policy is responsible for a deprivation of rights protected by the Constitution, local governments, like every other § 1983 "person," by the very terms of the statute, may be sued for constitutional deprivations visited pursuant to governmental "custom" even though such a custom has not received formal approval through the body's official decisionmaking channels. As Mr. Justice Harlan, writing for the Court,

---

[54] There is certainly no constitutional impediment to municipal liability. "The Tenth Amendment's reservation of nondelegated powers to the States is not implicated by a federal-court judgment enforcing the express prohibitions of unlawful state conduct enacted by the Fourteenth Amendment." Milliken v. Bradley, 433 U.S. 267, 291 (1977); see Ex parte Virginia, 100 U.S. 339, 347-348 (1880). For this reason, National League of Cities v. Usery, 426 U.S. 833, 22 WH Cases 1064 (1976), is irrelevant to our consideration of this case. Nor is there any basis for concluding that the Eleventh Amendment is a bar to municipal liability. See, e. g., Fitzpatrick v. Bitzer, 427 U.S. 445, 456, 12 FEP Cases 1586 (1976); Lincoln County v. Luning, 133 U.S. 529, 530 (1890). Our holding today is, of course, limited to local government units which are not considered part of the State for Eleventh Amendment purposes.

[55] Since official capacity suits generally represent only another way of pleading an action against an entity of which an officer is an agent — at least where Eleventh Amendment considerations do not control analysis — our holding today that local governments can be sued under § 1983 necessarily decides that local government officials sued in their official capacities are "persons" under § 1983 in those cases in which, as here, a local government would be suable in its own name.

said in Adickes v. S. H. Kress & Co., 398 U.S. 144, 167-168 (1970): "Congress included custom and usage [in § 1983] because of persistent and widespread discriminatory practices of State officials. . . . Although not authorized by written law such practices of state officials could well be so permanent and well settled as to constitute a 'custom or usage' with the force of law."

On the other hand, the language of § 1983, read against the background of the same legislative history, compels the conclusion that Congress did not intended muncipalities to be held liable unless action pursuant to official municipal policy of some nature caused a constitutional tort. In particular, we conclude that a municipality cannot be held liable *solely* because it employs a tortfeasor — or, in other words, a municipality cannot be held liable under § 1983 on a *respondeat superior* theory.

We begin with the langauge of § 1983 as passed:

> "*[A]ny person who,* under color of any law, statute, ordinance, regulation, custom, or usage of any State, *shall subject, or cause to be subjected,* any person . . . to the deprivation of any rights, privileges, or immunities secured by the Constitution of the United States, shall, any such law, statute, ordinance, regulation, custom, or usage of the State to the contrary notwithstanding, be liable to the party injured in any action at law, suit in equity, or other proper proceeding for redress. . . ." Globe App., at 335 (emphasis added).

The italicized language plainly imposes liability on a government that, under color of some official policy, "causes" an employee to violate another's constitutional rights. At the same time, that language cannot be easily read to impose liability vicariously on governing bodies solely on the basis of the existence of an employer-employee relationship with a tortfeasor. Indeed, the fact that Congress did specifically provide that *A*'s tort became *B*'s liability if *B* "caused" *A* to subject another to a tort suggests that Congress did not intend § 1983 liability to attach where such causation was absent. See Rizzo v. Goode, 423 U.S. 362, 370-371 (1976).

. . . .

We conclude, therefore, that a local government may not be sued for an injury inflicted solely by its employees or agents. Instead, it is when execution of a government's policy or custom, whether made by its lawmakers or by those whose edicts or acts may fairly be said to represent official policy, inflicts the injury that the government as an entity is responsible under § 1983. Since this case unquestionably involves official policy as the moving force of the constitutional violation found by the District Court, see pp. 1-2, and n. 2, supra, 17 FEP Cases, p. 874, we must reverse the judgment below. In so doing, we have no occasion to address, and do not address, what the full contours of municipal liability under § 1983 may be. We have attempted only to sketch so much of the § 1983 cause of action against a local government as is apparent from the history of the 1871 Act and our prior cases and we expressly leave further development of this action to another day.

## III

Although we have stated that *stare decisis* has more force in statutory analysis than in constitutional adjudication because, in the former situation, Congress can correct our mistakes through legislation, see, e. g., Edelman v. Jordan, 415 U.S.

651, 671, and n. 14 (1974), we have never applied *stare decisis* mechanically to prohibit overruling our earlier decisions determining the meaning of statutes. . . .

. . . .

First, Monroe v. Pape, supra, insofar as it completely immunizes municipalities from suit under § 1983, was a departure from prior practice.

. . . .

Moreover, the constitutional defect that led to the rejection of the Sherman amendment would not have distinguished between municipalities and school boards, each of which is an instrumentality of state administration. See pp. 14-22, supra, 17 FEP Cases, pp. 879-881. For this reason, our cases — decided both before and after Monroe, see n. 5, supra — holding school boards liable in § 1983 actions are inconsistent with Monroe, especially as Monroe's immunizing principle was extended to suits for injunctive relief in City of Kenosha v. Bruno, 412 U.S. 507 (1973).

. . . .

Thus, while we have reaffirmed Monroe without further examination on three occasions, it can scarcely be said that Monroe is so consistent with the warp and woof of civil rights law as to be beyond question.

. . . .

Second, the principle of blanket immunity established in Monroe cannot be cabined short of school boards. Yet such an extension would itself be inconsistent with recent expressions of congressional intent. In the wake of our decisions, Congress not only has shown no hostility to federal court decisions against school boards, but it has indeed rejected efforts to strip the federal courts of jurisdiction over school boards.

. . . .

Third, municipalities can assert no reliance claim which can support an absolute immunity. As Mr. Justice Frankfurter said in Monroe, "[t]his is not an area of commercial law in which, presumably, individuals may have arranged their affairs in reliance on the expected stability of decision." 365 U.S., at 221-222 (dissent). Indeed, municipalities simply cannot "arrange their affairs" on an assumption that they can violate constitutional rights indefinitely since injunctive suits against local officials under § 1983 would prohibit any such arrangement.

. . . .

Finally, even under the most stringent test for the propriety of overruling a statutory decision proposed by Mr. Justice Harlan in Monroe — "that it must appear beyond doubt from the legislative history of the 1871 statute that [Monroe] misapprehended the meaning of the [section]," Monroe v. Pape, supra, at 192 (concurring opinion) — the overruling of Monroe insofar as it holds that local governments are not "persons" who may be defendants in § 1983 suits is clearly proper. It is simply beyond doubt that, under the 1871 Congress' view of the law, were § 1983 liability unconstitutional as to local governments, it would have been equally unconstitutional as to state officers. Yet everyone — proponents and opponents alike — knew § 1983 would be applied to state officers and nonetheless stated that § 1983 was constitutional. See pp. 21-22, supra 17 FEP Cases, p. 881-882. And, moreover, there can be no doubt that § 1 of the Civil Rights Act was intended to provide a remedy, to be broadly construed, against all forms of official violation of federally protected rights. Therefore, absent a clear statement in the legislative history supporting the conclusion that § 1 was not to apply to the official acts of a municipal corporation — which simply is not present — there is no justification for excluding municipalities from the "persons" covered by § 1.

For the reasons stated above, therefore, we hold that *stare decisis* does not bar our overruling of Monroe insofar as it is inconsistent with Parts I and II of this opinion.

## IV

Since the question whether local government bodies should be afforded some form of official immunity was not presented as a question to be decided on this petition and was not briefed by the parties nor addressed by the courts below, we express no views on the scope of any municipal immunity beyond holding that municipal bodies sued under § 1983 cannot be entitled to an absolute immunity, lest our decision that such bodies are subject to suit under § 1983 "be drained of meaning," Scheuer v. Rhodes, 416 U.S. 232, 248 (1974). Cf. Bivens v. Six Unknown Federal Narcotics Agents, 403 U.S. 389, 397-398 (1971).

## V

For the reasons stated above, the judgment of the Court of Appeals is
*Reversed.*

MR. JUSTICE STEVENS, concurring in part.

Since Parts II and IV of the opinion of the Court are merely advisory and are not necessary to explain the Court's decision, I join only Parts I, III, and V.

MR. JUSTICE REHNQUIST, with whom THE CHIEF JUSTICE joins, dissenting.

Seventeen years ago, in Monroe v. Pape, 365 U.S. 167 (1961), this Court held that the 42d Congress did not intend to subject a municipal corporation to liability as a "person" within the meaning of 42 U.S.C. § 1983. Since then, the Congress has remained silent, but this Court has reaffirmed that holding on at least three separate occasions.

. . . .

Today, the Court abandons this long and consistent line of precedents, offering in justification only an elaborate canvass of the same legislative history which was before the Court in 1961. Because I cannot agree that this Court is "free to disregard these precedents," which have been "considered maturely and recently" by this Court, Runyon v. McCrary, 426 U.S. 160, 186 (1976) (POWELL, J., concurring), I am compelled to dissent.

. . . .

The decision in Monroe v. Pape, was the fountainhead of the torrent of civil rights litigation of the last 17 years. Using § 1983 as a vehicle, the courts have articulated new and previously unforeseeable interpretations of the Fourteenth Amendment. At the same time, the doctrine of municipal immunity enunciated in Monroe has protected municipalities and their limited treasuries from the consequences of their officials' failure to predict the course of this Court's constitutional jurisprudence. None of the Members of this Court can foresee the practical consequences of today's removal of that protection. Only the Congress, which has the benefit of the advice of every segment of this diverse Nation, is equipped to consider the results of such a drastic change in the law. It seems all but inevitable that it will find it necessary to do so after today's decision.

## PROCUNIER v. NAVARETTE

Supreme Court of the United States
98 S.Ct. 855 (1978)

MR. JUSTICE WHITE delivered the opinion of the Court.

Respondent Navarette, an inmate of Soledad Prison in California when the events revealed here occurred, filed his second amended complaint on January 19, 1974, charging six prison officials with various conduct allegedly violative of his constitutional rights and of 42 U.S.C. §§ 1983 and 1985. Three of the defendants were subordinate officials at Soledad; three were supervisory officials: the director of the State Department of Corrections and the warden and assistant warden of Soledad. The first three of nine claims for relief alleged wrongful interference with Navarette's outgoing mail. The first claim charged that the three subordinate officers, who were in charge of mail handling, had failed to mail various items of correspondence during the 15 months that respondent was incarcerated at Soledad, from September 1, 1971 to December 11, 1972. These items, described in 13 numbered paragraphs, included letters to legal assistance groups, law students, the news media and inmates in other state prisons, as well as personal friends. Some of these items had been returned to Navarette, some the defendants had refused to send by registered mail as Navarette had requested and, it was alleged, none of the items had ever reached the intended recipient. This "interference" or "confiscation" was asserted to have been in "knowing disregard" of the applicable statewide prisoner mail regulations and of Navarette's "constitutional rights," including his rights to free speech and due process as guaranteed by the First, Fifth, and Fourteenth Amendments to the United States Constitution. The three supervisory officers were alleged to have knowingly condoned this conduct and to have conspired with their subordinates for forbidden ends.

The second claim for relief alleged wrongful failure to mail the same items of correspondence and asserted that the "interference and confiscation" had been conducted with "bad faith disregard" for Navarette's rights. The third claim posed the same failures to mail but claimed that the "interference" or "confiscation" had occurred because the three subordinate officers had "negligently and inadvertently" misapplied the prison mail regulations and because the supervisory officers had "negligently" failed to provide sufficient training and direction to their subordinates, all assertedly in violation of Navarette's constitutional rights.

Petitioners moved for dismissal for failure to state a claim on which relief could be granted or alternatively for summary judgment. Affidavits in support of the motion and counter-affidavits opposing it were also before the District Court. By order and without opinion, the court then granted summary judgment for petitioners on the first three claims and dismissed the remaining claims for failure to state a federal claim.

The Court of Appeals reversed as to the first three claims. *Navarette v. Enomoto,* 536 F.2d 277 (CA9 1976). It held, first, that prisoners themselves are entitled to First and Fourteenth Amendment protection for their outgoing mail and that Navarette's allegations were sufficient to encompass proof that would entitle him to relief in damages. Second, the court ruled that summary judgment on the first two claims was improper because there were issues of fact to be tried, particularly with respect to the claim that "a reasonable and good faith belief of a state official that his or her conduct is lawful, even where in fact it is not, constitutes a complete defense to a § 1983 claim for damages." 536 F.2d, at 280. Third, the Court of Appeals held that Navarette's "allegations that state officers negligently deprived him of [his constitutional rights] state a § 1983 cause of action" and that summary judgment on the third purported claim was "improper because, as in the case of counts 1 and 2, viewing the evidence in the light most favorable to Navarette, we are unable to say appellees are entitled to prevail as a matter of law." 536 F.2d at 282 n. 6.

We granted certiorari, 429 U.S. 1060, 97 S.Ct. 783, 50 L.Ed.2d 776, and the question before us is whether the Court of Appeals correctly reversed the District Court's judgment with respect to Navarette's third claim for relief alleging negligent interference with a claimed constitutional right.

In support of their motion for summary judgment, petitioners argued that on the record before the Court they were immune from liability for damages under § 1983 and hence were entitled to judgment as a matter of law. The claim was not that they shared the absolute immunity accorded judges and prosecutors but they that were entitled to the qualified immunity accorded those officials involved in *Scheuer v. Rhodes,* 416 U.S. 232, 94 S.Ct. 1683, 40 L.Ed.2d 90 (1974), and *Wood v. Strickland,* 420 U.S. 308, 95 S.Ct. 992, 43 L.Ed.2d 214 (1975). The Court of Appeals appeared to agree that petitioners were entitled to the claimed degree of immunity but held that they were nevertheless not entitled to summary judgment because in the court's view there were issues of fact to be resolved and because when the facts were viewed most favorably to respondents, it could not be held that petitioners were entitled to judgment as a matter of law. Without disagreeing that petitioners enjoyed a qualified immunity from damages liability under § 1983, respondent defends the judgment of the Court of Appeals as a proper application of § 1983 and of the Court's cases construing it.

Although the Court has recognized that in enacting § 1983 Congress must have intended to expose state officials to damages liability in some circumstances, the section has been consistently construed as not intending wholesale revocation of the common-law immunity afforded government officials. Legislators, judges, and prosecutors have been held absolutely immune from liability for damages under § 1983. *Tenney v. Brandhove,* 341 U.S. 367, 71 S.Ct. 783, 95 L.Ed. 1019 (1951); *Pierson v. Ray,* 386 U.S. 547, 87 S.Ct. 1213, 18 L.Ed.2d 288 (1967); *Imbler v. Pachtman,* 424 U.S. 409, 96 S.Ct. 984, 47 L.Ed.2d 128 (1976). Only a qualified immunity from damages is available to a state governor, a president of a state university, and officers and members of a state national guard. *Scheuer v. Rhodes,* 416 U.S. 232, 94 S.Ct. 1683, 40 L.Ed.2d 90 (1974). The same is true of local school board members, *Wood v. Strickland,* 420 U.S. 308, 95 S.Ct. 992, 43 L.Ed.2d 214 (1975); of the superintendent of a state hospital, *O'Connor v. Donaldson,* 422 U.S. 563, 95 S.Ct. 2486, 45 L.Ed.2d 396 (1975); and of policemen, *Pierson v. Ray, supra;* see *Imbler v. Pachtman,* 424 U.S., at 418-419, 96 S.Ct., at 989.

We agree with petitioners that as prison officials and officers, they were not absolutely immune from liability in this § 1983 damages suit and could rely only on the qualified immunity described in *Scheuer v. Rhodes, supra,* and *Wood v. Strickland, supra. Scheuer* declared that:

"[I]n varying scope, a qualified immunity is available to officers of the executive branch of government, the variation being dependent upon the scope of discretion and responsibilities of the office and all the circumstances as they reasonably appeared at the time of the action on which liability is sought to be based. It is the existence of reasonable grounds for the belief formed at the time and in light of all the circumstances, coupled with good-faith belief, that affords a basis for qualified immunity of executive officers for acts performed in the course of official conduct." *Scheuer v. Rhodes, supra,* 416 U.S., at 247-248, 94 S.Ct., at 1692.

We further held in *Wood v. Strickland, supra,* that "if the work of the schools is to go forward," there must be a degree of immunity so that "public school officials understand that action taken in the good-faith fulfillment of their responsibilities and within the bounds of reason under all the circumstances will not be punished and that they need not exercise their discretion with undue timidity." 420 U.S., at 321, 95 S.Ct., at 1000. This degree of immunity would be unavailable, however, if the official "knew or reasonably should have known that the action he took within his sphere of official responsibility would violate the rights of the student affected, or if he took the action with the malicious intention to cause a deprivation of constitutional rights or other injury to the student." 420 U.S., at 322, 95 S.Ct., at 1001. The official cannot be expected to predict the future course of constitutional law, *id.; Pierson v. Ray,* 386 U.S., at 557, 87 S.Ct., at 1219, but he will not be shielded from liability if he acts "with such disregard of the [plaintiffs'] clearly established constitutional rights that his action cannot reasonably be characterized as being in good faith." 420 U.S., at 322, 95 S.Ct., at 1001.

Under the first part of the *Wood v. Strickland* rule, the immunity defense would be unavailing to petitioners if the constitutional right allegedly infringed by them was clearly established at the time of their challenged conduct, if they knew or should have known of that right and if they knew or should have known that their conduct violated the constitutional norm. Petitioners claim that in 1971 and 1972 when the conduct involved in this case took place there was no established First Amendment right protecting the mailing privileges of state prisoners and that hence there was no such federal right about which they should have known. We are in essential agreement with petitioners in this respect and also agree that they were entitled to judgment as a matter of law.

. . . .

Whether the state of the law is evaluated by reference to the opinions of this Court, of the Courts of Appeals, or of the local District Court, there was no "clearly established" First and Fourteenth Amendment right with respect to the correspondence of convicted prisoners in 1971-1972. As a matter of law, therefore, there was no basis for rejecting the immunity defense on the ground that petitioners knew or should have known that their alleged conduct violated a constitutional right. Because they could not reasonably have been expected to be aware of a constitutional right that had not yet been declared, petitioners did not act with such disregard for the established law that their conduct "cannot reasonably be characterized as in good faith." *Wood v. Strickland, supra,* 420 U.S., at 322, 95 S.Ct., at 1001.

Neither should petitioners' immunity defense be overruled under the second branch of the *Wood v. Strickland* standard, which would authorize liability where the official has acted with "malicious intention" to deprive the plaintiff of a constitutional right or to cause him "other injury." This part of the rule speaks of "intentional injury," comtemplating that the actor intends the consequences of his conduct. See Restatement (Second) of Torts, § 8A. The third claim for relief with which we are concerned here, however, charges negligent conduct, which normally implies that although the actor has subjected the plaintiff to unreasonable risk, he did not intend the harm or injury that in fact resulted. See *id.,* § 282 and comment d. Claims 1 and 2 of the complaint alleged intentional and bad-faith conduct disregard of Navarette's constitutional rights; but claim 3, as the court below understood it and as the parties have treated it, was limited to negligence. The prison officers were charged with negligent and inadvertent interference with the mail and the supervisory personnel with negligent failure to provide proper training. To the extent that a malicious intent to harm is a ground for denying immunity, that consideration is clearly not implicated by the negligence claim now before us.[14]

We accordingly conclude that the District Court was correct in entering summary judgment for petitioners on the third claim of relief and that the Court of Appeals erred in holding otherwise. The judgment of the Court of Appeals is

*Reversed.*

MR. CHIEF JUSTICE BURGER, dissenting.

I dissent because the Court's opinion departs from our practice of considering only the question upon which certiorari was granted or questions "fairly comprised therein." Supreme Court Rule 23.1(c). We agreed to consider only one question: "whether negligent failure to mail certain of a prisoner's outgoing letters states a cause of action under section 1983?" The Court decides a different question: whether the petitioners in this case are immune from § 1983 damages for the negligent conduct alleged in count three of Navarette's complaint. That question is not "comprised" within the question that we agreed to consider. . . .

MR. JUSTICE STEVENS, dissenting.

Today's decision, coupled with *O'Connor v. Donaldson,* 422 U.S. 563, 95 S.Ct. 2486, 45 L.Ed.2d 396, strongly implies that every defendant in a § 1983 action is entitled to assert a qualified immunity from damage liability. As the immunity doctrine developed, the Court was careful to limit its holdings to specific officials, and to insist that a considered inquiry into the common law was an essential precondition to the recognition of the proper immunity for any official. These limits have now been abandoned. In *Donaldson,* without explanation and without reference to the common law, the Court held that the standard for judging the immunity of the superintendent of a mental hospital is the same as the standard for school officials; today the Court purports to apply the same standard to the superintendent of a prison system and to various correction officers.

I have no quarrel with the extension of a qualified immunity defense to all state agents. A public servant who is conscientiously doing his job to the best of his ability should rarely, if ever, be exposed to the risk of damage liability. But when the Court makes the qualified immunity available to all potential defendants, it is especially important that the contours of this affirmative defense be explained with care and precision. Unfortunately, I believe today's opinion significantly changes the nature of the defense and overlooks the critical importance of carefully examining the factual basis for the defense in each case in which it is asserted.

. . . .

To establish their defense, all the defendants except Procunier have filed an affidavit stating that they made a good-faith effort to comply with prison mail regulations while handling Navarette's mail. But Navarette's affidavit challenges this assertion. According to Navarette, the prison warden took the position, despite contrary prison regulations, that officials had a right to confiscate any mail, "if we don't feel it is right or necessary." Record, at 78. Navarette also claims

---

[14] Because of the disposition of this case on immunity grounds, we do not address petitioners' other submissions: that § 1983 does not afford a remedy for negligent deprivation of constitutional rights and that state prisoners have no First and Fourteenth Amendment rights in their outgoing mail.

that his writing activities led authorities to punish him by taking away his job as a prison librarian and by seizing his mail.

With the record in this state, the defendants have not established good faith. [Discussion omitted]. . .

In sum, I am persuaded that the Court has acted unwisely in reaching out to decide the merits of an affirmative defense before any evidence has been heard and that the record as now developed does not completely foreclose the possibility that the plaintiff might be able to disprove a good-faith defense that has not yet even been pleaded properly.

Accordingly, I respectfully dissent from the decision to decide a question which is not properly presented and from the way the Court decides that question.

## BUTZ v. ECONOMOU

Supreme Court of the United States
98 S.Ct. 2894 (1978)

MR. JUSTICE WHITE delivered the opinion of the Court.

This case concerns the personal immunity of federal officials in the Executive Branch from claims for damages arising from their violations of citizens' constitutional rights. Respondent filed suit against a number of officials in the Department of Agriculture claiming that they had instituted an investigation and an administrative proceeding against him in retaliation for his criticism of that agency. The District Court dismissed the action on the ground that the individual defendants, as federal officials, were entitled to absolute immunity for all discretionary acts within the scope of their authority. The Court of Appeals reversed, holding that the defendants were entitled only to the qualified immunity available to their counterparts in state government. 535 F.2d 688. Because of the importance of immunity doctrine to both the vindication of constitutional guarantees and the effective functioning of government, we granted certiorari. — U.S. —.

I

Respondent controls Arthur N. Economou and Co., Inc., which was at one time registered with the Department of Agriculture as a commodity futures commission merchant. Most of respondent's factual allegations in this lawsuit focus on an earlier administrative proceeding in which the Department of Agriculture sought to revoke or suspend the company's registration. On February 19, 1970, following an audit, the Department of Agriculture issued an administrative complaint alleging that respondent, while a registered merchant, had willfully failed to maintain the minimum financial requirements prescribed by the Department. After another audit, an amended complaint was issued on June 22, 1970. A hearing was held before the Chief Hearing Examiner of the Department, who filed a recommendation sustaining the administrative complaint. The Judicial Officer of the Department, to whom the Secretary had delegated his decisional authority in enforcement proceedings, affirmed the Hearing Examiner's decision. On respondent's petition for review, the Court of Appeals for the Second Circuit vacated the order of the Judicial Officer. It reasoned that "the essential finding of willfulness . . . was made in a proceeding instituted without the customary warning letter, which the Judicial Officer conceded might well have resulted in prompt correction of the claimed insufficiencies." *Economou v. United States Department of Agriculture,* 494 F. 2d 519 (1974).

While the administrative complaint was pending before the Judicial Officer, respondent filed this lawsuit in federal district court. Respondent sought initially to enjoin the progress of the administrative proceeding, but he was unsuccessful in that regard. On March 31, 1975, respondent filed a second amended complaint seeking damages. Named as defendants were the individuals who had served as Secretary and Assistant Secretary of Agriculture during the relevant events; the Judicial Officer and Chief Hearing Examiner; several officials in the Commodity Exchange Authority; the Agriculture Department attorney who had prosecuted the enforcement proceeding; and several of the auditors who had investigated respondent or were witnesses against respondent.

The complaint stated that prior to the issuance of the administrative complaints respondent had been "sharply critical of the staff and operations of Defendants and carried on a vociferous campaign for the reform of Defendant Commodity Exchange Authority to obtain more effective regulation of commodity trading." App. 158. The complaint also stated that some time prior to the issuance of the February 19 complaint, respondent and his company had ceased to engage in activities regulated by the defendants. The complaint charged that each of the administrative complaints had been issued without the notice or warning required by law; that the defendants had furnished the complaints to interested persons and others without furnishing [respondent's] answers as well; and that following the issuance of the amended complaint, the defendants had issued a "deceptive" press release that "falsely indicated to the public that [respondent's] financial resources had deteriorated, when Defendants knew that their statement was untrue and so acknowledge[d] previously that said assertion was untrue." App.158.

The complaint then presented 10 "causes of action," some of which purported to state claims for damages under the United States Constitution. For example, the first cause of action alleged that respondent had been denied due process of law because the defendants had instituted unauthorized proceedings against him without proper notice and with the knowledge that respondent was no longer subject to their regulatory jurisdiction. The third cause of action stated that by means of such actions "the Defendants discouraged and chilled a campaign of criticism [respondent] directed against them, and thereby deprived the [respondent] of [his] rights to free expression guaranteed by the First Amendment of the United States Constitution."

. . . .

The single submission by the United States on behalf of petitioners is that all of the federal officials sued in this case are absolutely immune from any liability for damages even if in the course of enforcing the relevant statutes they infringed respondent's constitutional rights and even if the violation was knowing and deliberate. Although the position is earnestly and ably presented by the United States, we are quite sure that it is unsound and consequently reject it. . . .

[The Court here discusses relevant case law.]

None of these decisions with respect to state officials furnishes any support for the submission of the United States that federal officials are absolutely immune from liability for their constitutional transgressions. On the contrary, with impressive unanimity, the federal courts of appeals have concluded that federal officials should receive no greater degree of protection from *constitutional* claims than their counterparts in state government. Subsequent to *Scheuer,* the Court of Appeals for the Fourth Circuit concluded that: "Although *Scheuer* involved a suit against state executive officers, the court's discussion of the qualified nature of executive immunity would appear to be equally applicable to federal executive officers." *States Marine Lines v. Shultz,* 498 F.2d 1146, 1159 (1974). In the view of the Court of Appeals for the Second Circuit,

"it would be 'incongruous and confusing, to say the least' to develop different standards of immunity for state officials sued under § 1983 and federal officers sued on similar grounds under causes of action founded directly on the Constitution." *Economou v. U.S. Dept. of Agriculture, supra,* 535 F. 2d, at 688, quoting *Bivens v. Six Unknown Named Agents of the Federal Bureau of Narcotics,* 456 F.2d 1339, 1346-1347 (CA2 1972) (on remand).

The Court of Appeals for the Ninth Circuit has reasoned:

"[Defendants] offer no significant reason for distinguishing, as far as immunity doctrine is concerned, between litigation under § 1983 against state officers and actions against federal officers alleging violation of constitutional rights under the general federal question statute. In contrast, the practical advantage of having just *one* federal immunity doctrine for suits arising under federal law is self-evident. Further, the rights at stake in a suit brought directly under the Bill of Rights are no less worthy of full protection than the constitutional and statutory rights protected by § 1983." *Mark v. Groff,* 521 F. 2d 1376, 1380 (1975).

Other courts have reached similar conclusions. *E.g., Apton v. Wilson,* 165 U. S. App. D. C. 22, 506 F.2d 83 (1974); *Brubaker v. King,* 505 F.2d 534 (CA7 1974); see *Weir v. Muller,* 527 F.2d 872 (CA5 1977); *Paton v. La Prade,* 524 F.2d 862 (CA3 1975); *Jones v. United States,* 536 F.2d 269 (CA8 1976); *G. M. Leasing Corp. v. United States,* 560 F.2d 1011 (CA 10 1977).

We agree with the perception of these courts that, in the absence of congressional direction to the contrary, there is no basis for according to federal officials a higher degree of immunity from liability when sued for a constitutional infringement as authorized by *Bivens* than is accorded state officials when sued for the identical violation under § 1983. The constitutional injuries made actionable by § 1983 are of no greater magnitude than those for which federal officials may be responsible. The pressures and uncertainties facing decisionmakers in state government are little if at all different from those affecting federal officials. We see no sense in holding a state governor liable but immunizing the head of a federal department; in holding the administrator of a federal hospital immune where the superintendent of a state hospital would be liable; in protecting the warden of a federal prison where the warden of a state prison would be vulnerable; or in distinguishing between state and federal police participating in the same investigation. Surely, *federal* officials should enjoy no greater zone of protection when they violate *federal* constitutional rules than do *state* officers.

The Government argues that the cases involving state officials are distinguishable because they reflect the need to preserve the effectiveness of the right of action authorized by § 1983. But as we discuss more fully below, the cause of action recognized in *Bivens v. Six Unknown Named Agents of the Federal Bureau of Narcotics,* 403 U. S. 388 (1971), would similarly be "drained of meaning" if federal officials were entitled to absolute immunity for their constitutional transgressions. Cf. *Scheuer v. Rhodes, supra,* at 248.

Moreover, the Government's analysis would place undue emphasis on the congressional origins of the cause of action in determining the level of immunity. It has been observed more than once that the law of privilege as a defense to damage actions against officers of Government has "in large part been of judicial making." *Barr v. Matteo, supra,* at 569; *Doe v. McMillan,* 412 U. S. 306, 318 (1973). Section 1 of the Civil Rights Act of 1871 —the predecessor of § 1983— said nothing about immunity for state officials. It mandated that any person who under color of state law subjected another to the deprivation of his constitutional rights would be liable to the injured party in an action at law. This Court nevertheless ascertained and announced what it deemed to be the appropriate type of immunity from § 1983 liability in a variety of contexts. *Pierson v. Ray, supra; Imbler v. Pachtman, supra; Scheuer v. Rhodes, supra.* The federal courts are equally competent to determine the appropriate level of immunity where the suit is a direct claim under the Federal Constitution against a federal officer.

The presence or absence of congressional authorization for suits against federal officials is of course relevant to the question whether to infer a right of action for damages for a particular violation of the Constitution. In *Bivens,* the Court noted the "absence of affirmative action by Congress" and therefore looked for "special factors counselling hesitation." 403 U.S., at 396. Absent congressional authorization, a court may also be impelled to think more carefully about whether the type of injury sustained by the plaintiff is normally compensable in damages, 403 U.S., at 388, and whether the courts are qualified to handle the types of questions raised by the plaintiff's claim, see 403 U. S., at 409 (Harlan, J., concurring).

But once this analysis is completed, there is no reason to return again to the absence of congressional authorization in resolving the question of immunity. Having determined that the plaintiff is entitled to a remedy in damages for a constitutional violation, the court then must address how best to reconcile the plaintiff's right to compensation with the need to protect the decisionmaking processes of an executive department. Since our decision in *Scheuer* was intended to guide the federal courts in resolving this tension in the myriad factual situations in which it might arise, we see no reason why it should not supply the governing principles for resolving this delemma in the case of federal officials. The Court's opinion in *Scheuer* relied on precedents dealing with federal as well as state officials, analyzed the issue of executive immunity in terms of general policy considerations, and stated its conclusion, quoted *supra,* in the same universal terms. The analysis presented in that case cannot be limited to actions against state officials.

Accordingly, without congressional directions to the contrary, we deem it untenable to draw a distinction for purposes of immunity law between suits brought against state officials under § 1983 and suits brought directly under the Constitution against federal officials. The § 1983 action was provided to vindicate federal constitutional rights. That Congress decided, after the passage of the Fourteenth Amendment, to enact legislation specifically requiring state officials to respond in federal court for their failures to observe the constitutional limitations in their powers is hardly a reason for excusing their federal counterparts for the identical constitutional transgressions. To create a system in which the Bill of Rights monitors more closely the conduct of state officials than it does that of federal officials is to stand the constitutional design on its head.

## IV

As we have said, the decision in *Bivens, supra,* established that a citizen suffering a compensable injury to a constitutionally protected interest could invoke the general federal question jurisdiction of the district courts to obtain an award of monetary damages against the responsible federal official. As Mr. Justice Harlan, concurring, pointed out, the action for damages recognized in *Bivens* could be a vital means of providing redress for persons whose constitutional rights have been violated. The barrier of sovereign immunity is frequently impenetrable. Injunctive or declaratory relief is useless to a person who has already been injured. "For people in Bivens' shoes, it is damages or nothing." 403 U. S., at 410.

Our opinion in *Bivens* put aside the immunity question; but we could not have contemplated that immunity would be absolute. If, as the Government argues, all officials exercising discretion were exempt from personal liability, a suit under the Constitution could provide no redress to the injured citizen, nor would it in any degree deter federal officials from committing constitutional wrongs. Moreover, no compensation would be available from the Government, for the Tort Claims Act prohibits recovery for injuries stemming from discretionary acts, even when that discretion has been abused.

The extension of absolute immunity from damages liability to all federal executive officials would seriously erode the protection provided by basic constitutional guarantees. The broad authority possessed by these officials enables them to direct their subordinates to undertake a wide range of projects — including some which may infringe such important personal interests as liberty, property and free speech. It makes little sense to hold that a Government agent is liable for warrantless and forcible entry into a citizen's house in pursuit of evidence, but that an official of higher rank who actually orders such a burglary is immune simply because of his greater authority. Indeed, the greater power of such officials affords a greater potential for a regime of lawless conduct. Extensive Government operations offer opportunities for unconstitutional action on a massive scale. In situations of abuse, an action for damages against the responsible official can be an important means of vindicating constitutional guarantees.

Our system of jurisprudence rests on the assumption that all individuals, whatever their position in government, are subject to federal law: . . .

This is not to say that considerations of public policy fail to support a limited immunity for federal executive officials. We consider here, as we did in *Scheuer,* the need to protect officials who are required to exercise their discretion and the related public interest in encouraging the vigorous exercise of official authority. Yet *Scheuer* and other cases have recognize that it is not unfair to hold liable the official who knows or should know he is acting outside the law, and that insisting on an awareness of clearly established constitutional limits will not unduly interfere with the exercise of official judgment. We therefore hold that, in a suit for damages arising from unconstitutional action, federal executive officials exercising discretion are entitled only to the qualified immunity specified in *Scheuer,* subject to those exceptional situations where it is demonstrated that absolute immunity is essential for the conduct of the public business.

The *Scheuer* principle of only qualified immunity for constitutional violations is consistent with *Barr v. Matteo, supra, Spalding v. Vilas, supra,* and *Kendall v. Stokes, supra.* Federal officials will not be liable for mere mistakes in judgment, whether the mistake is one of fact or one of law. But we see no substantial basis for holding, as the United States would have us do, that executive officers generally may with impunity discharge their duties in a way that is known to them to violate the United States Constitution or in a manner that they should know transgresses a clearly established constitutional rule. The principle should prove as workable in suits against federal officials as it has in the context of suits against state officials. Insubstantial lawsuits can be quickly terminated by federal courts alert to the possibilities of artful pleading. Unless the complaint states a compensable claim for relief under the Federal Constitution, it should not survive a motion to dismiss. Moreover, the Court recognized in *Scheuer* that damage suits concerning constitutional violations need not proceed to trial, but can be terminated on a properly supported motion for summary judgment based on the defense of immunity. See 416 U. S., at 250. In responding to such a motion, plaintiffs may not play dog in the manger; and firm application of the Federal Rules of Civil Procedure will ensure that federal officials are not harassed by frivolous lawsuits.

## V

Although a qualified immunity from damages liability should be the general rule for executive officials charged with constitutional violations, our decisions recognize that there are some officials whose special functions required a full exemption from liability. *E. g., Bradley v. Fisher,* 13 Wall. (80 U. S.) 335 (1872); *Imbler v. Pachtman,* 424 U. S. 409 (1976). In each case, we have undertaken "a considered inquiry into the immunity historically accorded the relevant official at common law and the interests behind it." *Imbler v. Pachtman, supra,* at 421.

In *Bradley v. Fisher, supra,* the Court analyzed the need for absolute immunity to protect judges from lawsuits claiming that their decisions had been tainted by improper motives. The Court began by noting that the principle of immunity for acts done by judges "in the exercise of their judicial functions" had been "the settled doctrine of the English courts for many centuries, and has never been denied, . . . that we are aware of, in the courts of this country." *Id.,* at 347. The Court explained that the value of this rule was proved by experience. Judges were often called to decide "[c]ontroversies involving not merely great pecuniary interests, but the liberty and character of the parties, and consequently exciting the deepest feelings." *Id.,* at 348. Such adjudications invariably produced at least one losing party, who would "accept[] anything but the soundness of the decision in explanation of the action of the judge." *Ibid.* "Just in proportion to the strength of his convictions of the correctness of his own view of the case is he apt to complain of the judgment against him, and from complaints of the judgment to pass to the ascription of improper motives to the judge." *Ibid.* If a civil action could be maintained against a judge by virtue of an allegation of malice, judges would lose "that independence without which no judiciary could either be respectable or useful." *Id.,* at 247. Thus, judges were held to be immune from civil suit "for malice or corruption in their action whilst exercising their judicial functions within the general scope of their jurisdiction." *Id.,* at 354.

The principle of *Bradley* was extended to federal prosecutors through the summary affirmance in *Yaselli v. Goff,* 275 U. S. 503 (1927), aff'g mem., 12 F.2d 396 (CA2 1926) . . . .

We recently reaffirmed the holding of *Yaselli v. Goff* in *Imbler v. Pachtman,* 424 U. S. 409 (1976), a suit against a state prosecutor under § 1983. The Court's examination of the leading precedents led to the conclusion that "The common law immunity of a prosecutor is based upon the same considerations that underlie the common law immunities of judges and grand jurors acting within the scope of their duties."

. . . .

In light of these and other practical considerations, the Court held that the defendant in that case was entitled to absolute immunity with respect to his activities as an advocate, "activities [which] were intimately associated with the judicial phase of the criminal process, and thus were functions to which the reasons for absolute immunity apply with full force." *Id.,* at 430.

Despite these precedents, the Court of Appeals concluded that all of the defendants in this case — including the hearing examiner, Judicial Officer, and prosecuting attorney — were entitled to only a qualified immunity. The Court of Appeals reasoned that officials within the Executive Branch generally have more circumscribed discretion and pointed out that, unlike a judge, officials of the Executive Branch would face no conflict of interest if their legal representation was provided by the Executive Branch. The Court of Appeals recognized that "some of the Agriculture Department officials may be analogized to criminal prosecutors, in that they initiated the proceedings against [respondent], and presented evidence therein," 535 F. 2d, at 696 n. 8, but found that attorneys in administrative proceedings did not face the same "serious constraints of time and even information" which this Court has found to be present frequently in criminal cases. See *Imbler v. Pachtman, supra,* at 425.

We think that the Court of Appeals placed undue emphasis on the fact that the officials sued here are — from an administrative perspective — employees of the Executive Branch. Judges have absolute immunity not because of their particular location within the Government, but because of the special nature of their responsibilities. . . .

We think that adjudication within a federal administrative agency shares enough of the characteristics of the judicial process that those who participate in such adjudication should also be immune from suits for damages. The conflicts which federal hearing examiners seek to resolve are every bit as fractious as those which come to court. As the *Bradley* opinion points out, "When the controversy involves questions affecting large amounts of property or relates to a matter of general public concern, or touches the interests of numerous parties, the disappointment occasioned by an adverse decision often finds vent in imputations of [malice]." 13 Wall. (80 U. S.), at 348. Moreover, federal administrative law requires that agency adjudication contain many of the same safeguards as are available in the judicial process. The proceedings are adversarial in nature. See 5 U. S. C. § 555(b). They are conducted before a trier of fact insulated from political influence. See *id.,* at § 554(d). A party is entitled to present his case by oral or documentary evidence, *id.,* at § 556(d), and the transcript of testimony and exhibits together with the pleadings constitutes the exclusive record for decision. *Id.,* at § 556(e). The parties are entitled to know the findings and conclusions on all of the issues of fact, law or discretion presented on the record. *Id.,* at § 557(c).

There can be little doubt that the role of the modern federal hearing examiner or administrative law judge within this frame work is "functionally comparable" to that of a judge. His powers are often, if not generally, comparable to those of a trial judge: he may issue subpoenas, rule on proffers of evidence, regulate the course of the hearing, and make or recommend decisions. See *id.,* at § 556(c). More importantly, the process of agency adjudication is currently structured so as to assure that the hearing examiner exercises his independent judgment on the evidence before him, free from pressures by the parties or other officials within the agency.

. . . .

In light of these safeguards, we think that the risk of an unconstitutional act by one presiding at an agency hearing is clearly outweighed by the importance of preserving the independent judgment of these men and women. We therefore hold that persons subject to these restraints and performing adjudicatory functions within a federal agency are entitled to absolute immunity from damages liability for their judicial acts. Those who complain of error in such proceedings must seek agency or judicial review.

We also believe that agency officials performing certain functions analogous to those of a prosecutor should be able to claim absolute immunity with respect to such acts. The decision to initiate administrative proceedings against an individual or corporation is very much like the prosecutor's decision to initiate or move forward with a criminal prosecution. An agency official, like a prosecutor, may have broad discretion in deciding whether a proceeding should be brought and what sanctions should be sought. The Secretary of Agriculture, for example, may initiate proceedings whenever he has "reason to believe" that any person "is violating or has violated any of the provisions of this chapter or of the rules, regulations, or orders of the Secretary of Agriculture of the Commission." 7 U. S. C. § 9. A range of sanctions is open to him. *Ibid.*

We believe that agency officials must make the decision to move forward with an administrative proceeding free from intimidation or harassment. Because the legal remedies already available to the defendant in such a proceeding provide sufficient checks on agency zeal, we hold that those officials who are responsible for the decision to initiate or continue a proceeding subject to agency adjudication are entitled to absolute immunity from damages liability for their parts in that decision.

We turn finally to the role of an agency attorney in conducting a trial and presenting evidence on the record to the trier of fact. We can see no substantial difference between the function of the agency attorney in presenting evidence in an agency hearing and the function of the prosecutor who brings evidence before a court. In either case, the evidence will be subject to attack through cross-examination, rebuttal or reinterpretation by opposing counsel. Evidence which is false or unpersuasive should be rejected upon analysis by an impartial trier of fact. If agency attorneys were held personally liable in damages as guarantors of the quality of their evidence, they might hesitate to bring forward some witnesses or documents. "This is particularly so because it is very difficult, if not impossible for attorneys to be certain of the objective truth or falsity of the testimony which they present." *Imbler v. Pachtman, supra,* at 440 (WHITE, J., concurring in the judgment). Apart from the possible unfairness to agency personnel, the agency would often be denied relevant evidence. Cf. *Imbler v. Pachtman, supra,* at 426. Administrative agencies can act in the public interest only if they can adjudicate on the basis of a complete record. We therefore hold that an agency attorney who arranges for the presentation of evidence on the record in the course of an adjudication is absolutely immune from suits based on the introduction of such evidence.

VI

There remains the task of applying the foregoing principles to the claims against the particular petitioner-defendants involved in this case. Rather than attempt this here in the first instance, we vacate the judgment of the Court of Appeals and remand the case to that Court with instructions to remand the case to the District Court for further proceedings consistent with this opinion.

*So ordered.*

MR. JUSTICE REHNQUIST, with whom THE CHIEF JUSTICE, MR. JUSTICE STEWART, and MR. JUSTICE STEVENS join, concurring in part and dissenting in part.

I concur in that part of the Court's judgment which affords absolute immunity to those persons performing adjudicatory functions within a federal agency, *ante,* p. 35, those who are responsible for the decision to initiate or continue a proceeding subject to agency adjudication, *ante,* p. 37, and those agency personnel who present evidence on the record in the course of an adjudication, *ante,* p. 38. I cannot agree, however, with the Court's conclusion that in a suit for damages arising from allegedly unconstitutional action federal executive officials, regardless of their rank or the scope of their responsibilities, are entitled to only qualified immunity even when acting within the outer limits of their authority. The Court's protestations to the contrary notwithstanding, this decision seriously misconstrues our prior decisions, finds little support as a matter of logic or precedent, and perhaps most importantly, will, I fear, seriously "dampen the ardor of all but the most resolute, or the most irresponsible, in the unflinching discharge of their duties." *Gregoire v. Biddle,* 177 F.2d 579, 581 (CA2 1948) (Learned Hand, J.).

## NOTE

Where two students who were suspended from school without procedural due process brought an action against school officials under 42 U. S. C. § 1983, the Supreme Court has held that they are entitled to nominal damages without proof of actual injury. Recovery of compensatory damages, however, requires proof of actual injury. Carey v. Piphus, 98 S. Ct. 1042 (1978).

# Index

References are to page numbers.

## A

## B

## C

## U

## V

## W